THE PEOPLE OF THE VALLEY

VOLUME I
THE AWAKENING

BY FRANCES ELLEN CRARY

ASHBROOK PUBLISHING
10089 BARTHOLOMEW RD.
CHAGRIN FALLS, OHIO 44022

ISBN: 0-09629950-1-0 Volume I
ISBN: 0-09629950-3-7 Two Volume Set

Library of Congress Catalog Number: 91-073346

A publication of Ashbrook Publishing
10089 Bartholomew Rd.
Chagrin Falls, Ohio 44022

Printed in the United States of America

Copyright (c) 1992 by Frances E. Crary--All rights reserved.

This book is dedicated to the world of humanity which is very rapidly growing into a spiritual consciousness that brings its souls to an awaress of the eternality of the unity of all life. There is modest hope that the book may contribute to this great birthing of spiritual consciousness. It is a novel, a fantasy, but yet it deals with a reality that may well help to carry this human race out of their world of illusion.

I want to express my gratitude to Helen, Emily, Anne, Cheryl, Eunice and Elbert who actually read, advised, edited etc.; and to every other friend who has encouraged me, and to my daughter Jennifer, to Kit and Linda, Justin, Nathan and Linda K. who have taught me much about life.

> How can we lose our desparate clutch
> At ourselves as the central actors on Life's stage
> And welcome Life, Mother of all lives?
> How can we shake from our humanity
> Dark strains of fear,
> Where greed and lust are nourished
> And wake ourselves to Light?
> To breathing Love
> While Life transforms all Vision.
>
> Frances Ellen Crary

This is a story about possibility. It is a dream about what might be, of what is presently shaping itself, of the phoenix-like rising up of a new civilization out of the ashes of our old and sorry world. A new Earth and a new People whose eyes are opened and whose hearts have welcomed the inflow of Light and Love radiating through this universe. A new people accepting their own transcendent nature.

It is the story of humankind's waking from millinia of sleep and beginning finally to accept Vision, the nature of reality and the wonder of Life, and to do this through an Earth itself wakened to new dimensions of relationship. The recovery of humakind from the anguish and greed of historical civilization, from pain and hunger, from power misused by selfish leaders, could only happen through new vision. This new vision has filled the eyes and hearts of the People of the Valley. With struggle and steady realization, pain and joy, tearing old patterns from their minds and hearts, they lead us into possibility.

WEBS

Web of spiders!
Trap for the unwary fly, the burdened bee.
Carnal house of insects, wrestling with their shrouds.
And yet - webs hung in sunlight,
Glimmering wheels of light
Gleaming filiments of startling streanth
Tangled carelessly to dry whisps on the horn of a cow.

Webs of living!
Humankind caught in ancient patterns,
In rituals of assumption that the real is known.
What dark one sits upon the webbing of our life
And hears our desparate writhing and our pain,
Keeps us captive, blind in shrouds of fear

Web of Spirit!
A shimmering whorl of light, catching at mind,
Strung with beads of consciousness,
Bright in cosmic sun
That rises just behind our eyes,
Reflecting Being in those shimmering beads.

Seeing through, we know there cannot be
A path upon the web, but only through.
Seeing through, we long with Hearts of grief
For that which breaks one strand and let's us See.

Grown still in weary hopelessness we glimpse
Between our strands of darkness, beads of light
Unnamed, unknown, reflecting what is real!
On that reflection, catapulted through,
We see the real - are Joined - we know!
Mind soars, Heart Sings, Life IS.

Frances Ellen Crary

CHAPTER ONE

Reflections

At the north end of a great Valley, left undisturbed for a number of years, enough to rebuild itself, heal the wounds of civilization and call back to its revitalized land, creatures great and small, was a farm on which lived an extended family. Though nearly a mile out of town the farm people were citizens of Adwin. These were typical Valley citizens, people who had rebuilt their own world within Earth and knew her nourishment when they lived in harmony with her. The family consisted of nine who lived on the farm, six living in Adwin, and six living in Altos. Among those on the farm was Rose, mate to Ben, mother of Anna and Andrew, twins nearly sixteen years old. On a cold winter morning, lingering before going out to the main Hall for breakfast, Rose felt the pull toward reflection that characterized much of her life in these turbulent days. She leaned against the window frame, her hands pressing the smooth stone sill.

Rose always thought that the moment she passed from girl to woman was late until she began to notice the lives of others. Then she could see how some made that leap from childhood late and others early, some in swift moments of insight and others so slowly they hardly noticed. She saw how some did not make it at all or imperfectly and felt a nagging guilt. She was one of those women who thought she should do something to correct whatever she thought was wrong in the world.

Sitting in her cottage on this winter morning, she thought of the day that transition in awareness had occurred. But the memory brought with it old pain and she pressed it aside to go look out her windows. Her three room cottage was one of a group clustered on a broad hill top a mile from the small town of Adwin. They were arranged far enough from one another to ensure privacy, but close enough to feel they were a Family. In the center was the large Main Hall, where most meals were eaten, gatherings and social events took place. From her window she could see the bright winter green of fields below the hill and across the gardens, now snow covered, looking through the barren limbs of an oak and walnut growing between her cottage and the Hall deck, she could see lights warm and welcoming in the Hall. Beyond that deck and below, lay the winding paths through fruit and nut groves, various berry bushes, and perennial edible plants.

Those paths wound their way down to the Great Highway, the ancient roadway system, short thick grasses replaced the old hard macadam, clusters of fruit or nut trees punctuated the miles of Highway. Beyond the Highway, up another hill lay the three broad half mile knolls on which the town Adwin was built. From the air it could be seen that each knoll was crowned with three concentric rings of stone and plasteel, two and three stories each with blazing gardens between each circle, That was her town, the town she and her Family had been

THE PEOPLE OF THE VALLEY

helping to build for so many years. Between the knolls were saddles in which hundreds of cluster residences were built. These were well separated groups of three or four houses, backed up around a single utility core and each looking out over the open parkland. Trees and shrubs gave each cluster privacy. Along the River, around the bend from the fish packing barns and the docks, were curving towers of apartments. Spacious and also surrounded with gardens, fruit trees, berry vines and the ubiquitous flowering shrubs of Adwin, these buildings included the student quarters for exchange students.

To the east the land dropped down to the Farm fields, and then to the Green River that ran winding through the Great Valley. At this point, it touched the edge of the Farm land, curved in a sharp bend and ran along rock cliff faces. These cliffs were the eastern edge of Adwin. From Rose's cottage she could not see the cliffs that edged the River because between them grew dark forest. In this northern end of the Great Valley a mixed evergreen and deciduous forests ran in broad strips, broken often by patches of deep wild meadow, on each side of the Green River. To the east a pattern of meadow, farm land and forest alternated across the flat land and over the low hills then gradually became mostly forest in the high mountains. Running south in a broad meandering for hundreds of miles, the Green River passed cities and towns, curled around hills and received the water from smaller streams running down from the hills and lakes among those hills. To the east at the center of the Valley there was a hundred miles between the River and the dark, high mountains that lifted white peaks in the sky even in summer. North and south these mountains closed in so that the Valley had the shape of a vase.

Rose could see little to the north except the rolling hills that led into other dense high mountains out of which the great River was born. That was country little traveled by Valley people. The mountains closed in fifty miles north of Adwin and out of them the Green River was born. To the west, Farm gardens lay bleak and winter cold between Rose's cottage and the Hall. A few slim evergreen shrubs still held dollops of snow from the last storm.

She looked out, seeking that point far beyond vision, south of Santiago, The Great Valley's capital City, where her Mother and Father in law had lived. She could see the Green River beyond Adwin, looking thin and sparkling in the early morning sun. From this high hill top, she could make out tributaries coming into it, gleaming down from foothills, or through the wild meadows and Farm fields. She leaned pensively on one elbow, studying the scene. The fields around Adwin and the Farm were radiantly green, she loved that faint whisper of spring in the air, but she knew it would not last. Already the snow fell in the high hills to the east, and it was still dry enough to slide from birch and oak limbs and sustain a shadow wash on the evergreens.

It was cold out there. Late February could shift from white winter to bright spring in a matter of hours. They'd all appreciate a little spring weather now. It had been a cold winter, snow for days at a time. At least the Family members were all home. That was a blessing of winter. Children and adults alike studied and worked at home on bitter, windy days. Their Farm computer room had connecting links with the Learning Center Library and film rooms and Teachers were available by videophone for questions. Their lives had grown closer through the years. Why was it she felt a sense of despair today. Was it all because Benjamin was going away? Old memories seemed at the edge of consciousness, pressing, bringing feelings of loneliness, sorrow and uncertainty. With a sigh, she turned to them, remembering.

Always she had known that instant when the world had pressed itself upon her and made her 'adult'. It was fourteen years ago and the memory was sharp. She had been twenty one, and the twins were only two. Benjamin, her Mate, was twenty two. They had not felt young, but now, she thought they had been very young. Strong feelings of amazement and sadness, of acute loss came up through everything else. It was as if she relived that day. But there were also feelings of gladness and subtle pride. She smiled, sliding down into those memories, reliving. It had happened at the house of her father-in-law, John, there on the sloping hillside just south of Santiago,. She and Ben and their twins, Anna and Andrew, had come to celebrate John's sixty third birthday. She had not been to visit since his wife Margo died, and her grief was still fresh enough that when she walked through the old woman's garden she kept finding herself looking for the bent figure among the glowing blooms. each time she was brought up short by the acid pain of fact. Margo was no longer there! That was when the shift in perspective occurred, there in those gardens, planted to give pleasure to those who came to sit in the carefully arranged little nooks where chairs and table made them welcome. Rose had sat down on the sun warmed walnut bench, wet eyed, still listening, refusing to finally know that her friend and loved Mother would not come. Somehow, knowing Margo was gone, attending her memorial with the family, and comforting John when he came to them there, had not been enough. She had had to go to the house where Margo had lived, and created gardens, the house Margo had designed and helped to build, and find it empty of her, in order to finally know her absence.

Rose had lost her own mother, Ruth, when she was barely ten. Her parents had been victims of the terrible period following the destruction, the upheaval of economic and industrial reforms, and the surges of angry people through the whole world. The upheaval that split country after country apart and continued until the World Government was tentatively formed and brought some precise changes in the distribution of wealth and goods. It had begun with the world depression, that broke the economic stability of even the most powerful nations. People avoided having children,unsure whether they would have a world to grow up in. So later, Margo's generation had their babies at age forty or so. Humankind had not been the same since. The Earth had suffered, but not as much as the human race, for millions had died or been wounded.

But something else had happened that no one had understood, or even correctly valued at the time. A shift in perspective in human attitude toward their fellows. It was as though humanity lifted its head, looked at itself, and realized its kind was precious. No military commander could persuade troops to stand against their own countrymen. Justice became a world wide cry and nothing could stop the demand. There was no war between nations, each traditional government was having too many internal problems to look beyond itself.The few despots who attacked smaller countries, thinking to prosper from the misery and despair, were immediately surrounded by troops from a majority of the world governments with the demand that they retreat. The new time had come. Out of the simple need for survival, rulers had learned how to talk out differences. In the midst of a profound grief at itself, humankind began to discover a faint seam of hope in the human heart.

Rose knew that Benjamin's parents had been major figures in the making of changes. And her own parents had been resistance workers, taking people from place to place, providing hideouts for those who openly resisted oppressive governments, They had persistently been part of the activities that made them hated and feared by those power groups. They had been wounded, more than once, and their health suffered seriously. Her mother had grieved that she must leave her daughter and son.But she had asked John and Margo for their help. She feared Rose and Jerry would be orphaned and so they nearly were.

The great nations of the world had finally met and joined in building a world government that could bring an end to the military excesses of governments whose corruptions were endemic. Had that world Council not succeeded , the world as it had been would never have survived. Her parents had pushed the terrible years out of mind and tried to heal one another, love their children and mend their lives enough to begin again in the land that was grown wild even where cities had once been. Her father had left them first. Hurt in body and spirit, he struggled to keep the life in his thin, pain filled flesh, and failed. And his young wife, old beyond her years, had held on until the children were ten and twelve, but even then, Rose and her brother knew that she would follow him.

Margo and John were neighbors in the little village that was a gathering of those whose dreams of rebuilding a new land, a new life, brought them together. Clandor was the first real town of the Valley, people building into the forests, refusing to harm or cut the forests, finding ways to make a town, and later a city so much a part of the land it was invisible to any casual traveler. Margo had done much of the planning, had helped to work out the engineering for that first tree town. And Ruth had brought her children to them and asked that they be God-parents. Two years later, after Rose and Jerry had already formed a deep loving relationship with Margo and John, Ruth died. Ruth had watched the friendship grow between her children and these foster parents, grateful but jealous all at once. And yet, she knew that her body was barely able to keep itself going. And when she knew that the children felt truly at home with these good friends, she let herself relax, allowed herself release.

Ruth had managed to stand above the pain, enough to give them a legacy of her own bouancy of spirit, her fierce vision of a future where greatness could occur, a dream of a world where every human being would be called precious from birth itself. Ruth had talked of that, worked, even during those last years to set up the Valley convictions, to build the IDEA among her fellows. And she had given her children an ability to delight in everyday living, in the moment of perception of a leaf, a bird, a bit of sky through a window, a touch of a loved one, a single word spoken in love. She had taught them all, Margo and John had learned also, for their own home was taking its shape from these dreams.

Rose thought of those last years, remembering and letting tears slide unhindered down her face. And then she remembered again that day in the garden, searching for a Mother she knew could not be there. The second mother who had died from her. Margo had been a source of her heart's ease. It was nearly fourteen years ago, when she sat in the garden, watching wrens picking about under the sturdy Rose bushes, smiling to see one suddenly lift itself without visible preparation and soar through leaf and branch, touching neither and passing beyond them until it was a tiny dark star moving against the blue sky. It seemed like yesterday.

She had sat, watching that bird, and without warning, the flood of grief burst in her and she sobbed aloud. The unexpected spasm of giref seemed to dislodge something that had been caught within her. In that instant she reached the beginning of acceptance of her loss and was able to cry. Later, squaring her shoulders, she knew a firmer sense of herself. She had known then, without thinking or reasoning, that she was the woman now, that her childhood had ended. She must stand alone and be a source of strength, just as Margo had. She smiled now, remembering. It was like Margo to have given her that. She remembered looking around, seeing the garden, the color and the balance of the stone, plants and water as if for the first time. The very air seemed clearer. She had stood up, feeling taller, stronger, and yet, afraid of that very strength. Of what it would ask of her.

Then wiping the tears from her face, with the back of her hand as a child would, she understood something that she wanted for her life. Something her own, not yet complete, but which came from that seed of recognition. She had walked around the garden then seeing things anew. It was as though she had shed an old smaller skin and stepped out, still vulnerable, still tender with this birth of herself. When Benjamin came out to her there, he thought she glowed as from an inner light. He had said that, making her smile and kiss him. He had stopped, watching, knowing much. She knew he had witnessed much that she might not be able to tell.

They had stood together, feeling the fragrance around them. The warmth and color filled them. They looked at each other and Ben smiled as if acknowledging something himself. He had glanced up, struck as always by the visible magnificance of that city to the north of the gardens, rising above forest and field, standing like a massive giant vine on three 'root bases'. It soared high, sprouting 'branch', 'leaf', and 'fruit' in brilliant colors a thousand feet or more in the air. Santiago was the jewel city of the Valley. the brightest, most miraculous city. It had solved the problem of avoiding harm to the Earth by simply being built completely above it and of rising from untouched forest and meadow. Except for the three or four hundred acres of carefully managed farm fields that provided Santiago's staple foods, she was exactly as she had been then. As Rose and Benjamin gazed up through the clear sunmmer air at her, they thought of those thousands of people living in those great round 'fruits' that were homes, and working and doing business in the great broad trunks and branches. Broad 'leaves' created parkland in the air. On those broad 'leaves' were the market places where people walked to look, buy, or just to gather and talk and enjoy one another.And there were playgrounds for children and adults alike on the broad open sky plazas where hundreds of people could gather, meet, dance and celebrate Festival times. The city was a busy place, people moved so constantly through her inner veins and trunks and out on the leaf surfaces that there was never a time, day or night that the city was not streaming with people.

With a shrug, Ben had pulled his eyes away and met Rose's, "It's an awesome sight, Sweetheart. Every time I come here it amazes me. My Mother loved the fact that Santiago is visible from her garden, her two finest creations. She thought of it as "her' city, because in a way it was, she designed and helped plan it and supervised every hour of its building. And yet, even though every citizen of the Valley is proud of it, so far we've not built another like it.

Rose had shaken her head, "No, and we probably won't.People want to create their cities from their own dreams, and each must be different. Maybe after a long time, there will be another similar .I don't think Margo was sorry it wasn't copied."

Ben nodded, "She did accept that. And now, you must accept something too.No?" He touched her hands, saw the tears start again, drew her hands into his own. "This is a wonderful place for it to happen, this thing that you realize today." Will you tell me, my dearest?" He leaned to kiss her lips, letting one finger caress the soft skin of her neck.He was only a finger or two taller than she.His shoulders were wide and powerful, but his body slimmed to narrow muscled hips. He was smiling as he led her to the bench and she leaned close to him, her dark skin shining like amber in the sun, her long curling hair dark against her white blouse. She said, "Yes, I think I want to tell you. If I can"

She told him and he watched her, his fair hair touching against her dark head, his eyes intent on hers. Her firm mouth serious under a slight puzzled frown The sadness in her eyes seemed soft, distant, not harsh. he said, "Remembering makes you sad, doesn't it, Love?"

She nodded,"I know. I've changed, my memories are more than memory, it's reliving. But I've not ever finished the grief, I think." They walked slowly toward the house from which they could hear the sound of music, the happy sounds of a piano concerto by Mario Jones. Rose's mind identified it absently as they walked. John, playing to the garden where once his wife worked and listened and enjoyed with him. John, who would not play his own music now for it had been too intimately connected with her.They were glad to hear that he was playing at all. Rose slid her arm through Benjamin's to draw them close as they neared the house. Their eyes nearly at a level, met, and she spoke, "It's also pride that I feel, Love and - other things I haven't worked out yet. That's for later." She frowned again, and then with a sudden lift of her head, she laughed out right, shedding the melancholy as one might an unwanted sweater. She squeezed his arm. He felt again the power of her presence,the power of her whole being as if they surrounded each other at times like this. He basked in it. His true Mate. And he had known her as Mate before they were nineteen and had convinced his parents enough to get their willingness for their marriage so young. A true Mate was often not known until later and a number of love affairs gone.

John had nodded at them absently as he played. They stood listening to the music until he stopped. He sat with his hands on the keys. The children, Anna and Andrew, sitting on each side of him, simultaniously stood to wrap their arms around his neck in pleasure. He was visibly moved by their response. He grinned sheepishly out at Rose and Ben, tears in his eyes and he wrapped both arms around the two babies and drew them into his lap. He looked down at them,"Now, would YOU like to play some music." Benjamin was startled, it was not his usual habit with the children.

Anna looked seriously at the key board and nodded at her Grandfather, her large brown eyes thoughtful and Rose knew she understood what might be meant by such a committment. Andrew reached to wrap one small hand around John's chin and draw his face toward himself."Grandpa, I want to play now. I want to play the way you do." John shot a questioning look at Rose. It was not a two year old's statement. He was puzzled.

"Andy, you will learn all you want. I'll teach you. How would you like that?" John heard himself saying words he had thought he would never say. Making promises he could not have made yesterday. But Andrew, seriously and trustfully studied his face and nodded,"Yes, Grandpa,I'd like that." He set his tiny brown fingers on the keyboard, moving them to reach and then to everyone's surprise, played a lovely chord, clear and precise. Then, shifting his hands, he played another, complementing it. But this time John was convinced. It couldn't be an accident twice. He looked at the boy's parents in startled appeal, then smiling and knowing, he turned his full attention on Andrew.

The little boy's face was intent, purposeful and they heard a delicate melody played, built from those chords.John could barely conceal his excitement. Anna leaned against him hiding her own delighted smile in his collar. Andy continued, creating something that was far more than child's play. John felt something loosen within him, something that shifted the blocked flow of his life since Margo's death. He knew now there was a wonderful purpose for living. He trembled as he set the children down and he said hastily,"We'll make plans for you to learn, Son. Yes, and you too little Anna. Right away.!" His face was radiant and Rose and Benjamin were overjoyed.

Rose remembered now, tears coming again to her eyes at that great love of life that re- awakened in John. And it had been so!. Both the children had studied under their Grandfather until his death. Andrew was talented beyond his teacher, and required, before he was ten, a more skilled Master Teacher in the Music School at Santiago . Andrew began to compose for the Festivals by the time he was nine and already had a beginning career in Music, even though he studied physics and cabinet making and planned to combine the fields to create new musical instruments and to study the effects of sounds on living bodies and minds. He had no question about his life work.

In that long gone day, they had all gone to the table to serve the birthday cake and to plan and it had been a joyous time. As though one parent who still lived made up for those who were lost.

Rose wiped her eyes, the memories had been as real as this morning to her. Now those old ones were gone. The young had begun the creation of this Valley. Their children, born in most cases late in their lives, had had to learn and work with each other, read and remember and record their histories as swiftly as possible,for too many of the old had died. There were not enough alive to help their young with their experiences and tell of the lessons learned .

John had continued to live there, in the family home, alone. Except for when the children went to spend weeks with him. Sometimes they were able to bring him to Adwin to teach in the newly built Learning Center, to create songs for the Festivals and music for dances. Finally, just a year before his death, he had written one last symphony, 'Valley Measure'. It was Rose's favorite of all he had written. The Adwin Orchestra, young and just forming, had been the first group to play it and it had been recorded to be sent out to other towns. She and Ben and felt so proud then.

Rose and Benjamin had already settled at the Farm. The Farm Family had begun to come together. Paul and Jennifer first, and then Tom and Angy and Mary, his two wives. They each had children, all young. Most Adwin settlers did, and they learned to share their care so they could work.The work was hard but the building went on. She sighed, remembering," When you are that young, your energy seems never to end. I don't think I could do it today."

The Family had gradually increased and committed themselves.Paul and Jennifer had left them to live in Altos and build there, but had never ceased being part of the family. Silvia had arrived, a friend of Jerry's, Rose's brother, and then Jane had come. Jane, from the world of cities, they had not thought would find a vocation among them, but she had taken to farming like a duck to water. Steve, with his baby daughter Cassandra, had come to them at first out of lonliness and dispair, and had gradually found that this was his home too. And then Ned, arriving at the same time as Steve. Ned was a black, giant of a man now, but he had been a beanpole then, young and searching for a home. He was even taller now, but the shoulders that had been narrow, had needed only a few years to build out into a balance with his body.

Ned was a fine stone worker and sculpture and had organized the building of the Hall which was all of local stone. Silvia learned from him,and the two had been inseparable for a time, much to Jerry's consternation. They were so utterly different. She tiny, oriental, pale as he was dark, with startlingly blue black long shining hair. Yet they had taken to one another immediately. And Jerry had found himself jealous. His first really difficult 'balancing' training with the Master Teachers, had had to do with that jealousy. A jealousy complicated by his very real love for Ned himself. That had been going on for some years now.

The town of Adwin had been well under way when the farm was begun. The fields had fed the people while they built. Food plants designed by Altos Plant wizards had given endless variety in fewer acres than any one had dared hope for. The Adwin Master Farmer rotated crops, protected wild meadow and forest and learned from the plants how they could protect one another from disease and insects if they were planted as companions. Everyone worked to build the town, though several groups had founded their own Farm Families within a mile or two of the town limits. Town Council elected in the third year, limited Adwin to a total of eight thousand people. It had seemed too many at the time, because there were only twenty four hundred and fifty three living citizens then . But now, fifteen years later, they would soon reach that number.

Rose got up to look from the window toward the Hall. She went to her own auto-server to refill her cup with hot coffee. Cradling it in both hands, she watched the activity outside. Andrew, a tall lanky boy of sixteen now, ran along the path to catch his Uncle Jerry. Jerry stopped to greet him, their brown cheerful faces shining in the morning sun. Andrew had turned from both music and Physics to discover whether he might be limiting himself. It was the common practice of all young people to do this, and Andrew did that year of "survey" with eager interest, but he had come back to his original decision. Only in the study of history did he find a possible rival for his first two interests. He and Anna and a group of their friends had spent long days watching historical films, holograph enactments and reading until their eyes were blurred when they went home at night. They had been fascinated at first, and then gradually both had decided this must remain a hobby, not a vocation. The long debates, discussions of that period when the economic systems of the world had failed, the military powers had recognized they were obsolete, and world government was beginning to shape its self, had sharpened their understanding of their world, given them a keen interest in government itself.

Of the whole group, only one of Anna's friends, working with them, writing a commentary as she studied, decided to make that recreation of history a life work, combining it with her own interest in holographic re-enactments, which allowed her to use drama, play writing, and stage creation along with it. She had gone to study in Budapest, whose learning center housed a Master Teacher who had made the best of the ones they found in their own library.

Andrew spent his fourteenth year in Europe with musicians there, and had gone to other major cities in his own country during some month long study periods. Andrew's obvious talents in music had been the beginning of a new life for John. He had begun to form little study groups to talk of the past, the history of the Valley and drew Anna and Andrew into their work because he was such a grand story teller. He made those early years alive for them, better than film or

THE PEOPLE OF THE VALLEY

book.He became a resource creating re-enactments of those early years and even of the years before the devastations and changes. And so had shaped Anna's interest in the history of their world.

Many of the old ones didn't like to talk of the past. So many had been killed or died of disease or starvation during that time, so that the number of people able and willing to talk usefully of those years was not great, and the children knew it. Adwin knew it and brought John to their Learning Center whenever he would come. He liked to be in his own home. He liked to sit and watch the changing colors of the great City that had been Margo's finest creation. Watch the changing movements of people, crowds along the walkways, the vast spread of 'Leaf' parks and the twinkling of lights through the openings in the huge branches and trunks as freight cars or trolley systems moved through. She remembered Ben's asking him that day, how his mother had chosen that design, so utterly different from any city ever built.

John had hesitated,still reluctant to speak of Margo.Finally, with a sigh, he said, "It's no wonder you don't know, Son.There's been so much to do, during the years. So much we haven't said. We ought to have better records,you know. You young ones will have to do the history for us." He had heaved a sigh as if the thought saddened him." Son.I think, she - - we -- all of us were still hurting from the ache of destruction, the confusion and pain of those long decades . We didn't know the problems we'd have to meet. We'd probably never have tried otherwise. We didn't have a Valley Council, nor Learning Centers, nor were there more than a few Monitors serving the entire Valley communications system." He stopped, glanced at their surprised faces,"That's what they were at first, you know, a communication system. We didn't even know that they didn't have - or need- electronic or telephone equipment. It wasn't until the Council was formed years after, that we -- at least some of us, realized they were using mental Talents,-- and other Talents too actually --. By then, they were indispensible to us."

He laughed,then "I'm rambling, I'm afraid. However, when Margo first submitted her plans to the committee , I thought she'd never get it accepted."

He smiled, his eyes far distant now, remembering,"She wanted to build a City that didn't have to squat on the Earth, that didn't have to destroy living things in order just to exist, that would look out over very far distance, from every point of the city, a wonderful view would delight the eye. She thought people were inspired when they lived in inspiring surroundings. You know, the Valley Commitments were already created by then,were finally adopted.We were absolutely committed to the idea that no human being would ever again live in the poverty and squalor of uglyness that so many had had to live in in the past. If one lived in beauty, then somehow, all must live in beauty." He had stopped, his pipe needing attention, and Rose had asked what she had long wanted to ask. "John, that was an idea like the old communist systems. It didn't work for them, why did it work here?"

He laughed, and now they knew they had found an avenue to bring him from his dispair.A new brightness in his eyes, a great drawn breath, "Oh, my Dear, it was because for them it was an edict placed on the people from above, or it was an IDEA the idealistic dreamed of. With us, with our Valley people, it was a CHOICE, a decision from the heart.We had lost all heart for lies and chicanery.For one-up-man ship. We had ALL seen people starve. Something in us had changed! Something we couldn't have named. But people voted, CHOSE, with a fierce committment that no person would live less comfortably than another. It was a choice that rose from our own greater hearts and vision. I think the human race had grown a little somewhere along the way, some new Spirit had penetrated our greedy lustful hearts and lifted them into finer possibilities."

He looked at them sharply for a moment, and then asked,"You do know of the tale of the New People coming into this Valley,don't you? The first of us ever to enter here?

They looked at each other, puzzled, then Benjamin said, "Papa, I know we've heard of that terrible, wonderful day. tell us of it the way you know it."

For a moment John hesitated as if he was not sure he could tell again that very first story. Then he nodded curtly, "Perhaps I had better." He sighed, looked far into the hills, as if finding inspiration and began. "There were about four hundred and fifty people who gathered there to the south of the valley and chose to go north together into the land they believed was recovering from the destruction. They thought there were no other people living there."

"They had made the choice and had known from the heart they could never again live in a world of their fathers. They were weary to the heart of the greed and fear that had dominated that world. They vowed that destroying and killing in order to live or to have - was anathema - was intolerable to being human".

"They had felt that wind of Love roused in the new waking of Earth Herself. They had known the wisdom of new knowledge through their minds and they saw the world would not change until humankind lived that love and knowledge. They vowed they would live so. They looked on one another with eyes washed clean of old fears, of old hungers. They saw the absolute futility of acquisitiveness, the emptyness of it".

"They had seen death become a welcome release from the terrible cruelty that humans practiced upon humans in the name of freedom,justice and government. They vowed death was better than to live as such monsters. They had practiced such a life themselves and knew a small glimpse of what people were capable of, what love, selflessness, generosity of heart, and they vowed that would be the direction of their lives. Or else they would have no life. They knew that to 'fight'for such a life was a contradiction of its possibility".

"And so when they met the raggle taggle mob of those still living by the old ways, at the southern entrance to this Great Valley, they stopped. These old ones were still fighting one another, vicious and ruthless to gain power, each insisting he or she did this for the good of all. Even though they'd just seen a world destroyed for such selfish ends, they seemed to know no other way. They lived in fear." He drew a long trembling sigh, for this was the moment of great power in this story.

"The new People stopped there, before the old ones already shooting, already killing their people. They held out their hands, began to sing, four hundred and

THE PEOPLE OF THE VALLEY

more strong, their voices rose powerful into the land, called upon Earth Herself for help, upon the Spirit of the Love that lit their hearts. They gathered their own inner power and sent out that Love in one constant out-pouring. They stood, seeing their loved ones fall, refusing to fight."

"The mob hesitated, then began again to shoot, but among them many held their weapons, even as their leaders, desparate to keep total command,insisted they kill. The New People stood resolute that death was preferable to living as humankind had lived. Many fell and blood soaked again the Earth."

"Then, Earth Herself, wakened from long sleep by the resolution of her new People rumbled beneath them all, terrifying those people of the mob." John's voice became soft, and the story totally immersed them all.

"But now many of the mob stopped their firing, drew back, feeling the inflow of that genuine Love from these people brave beyond anything they had ever seen. A people resolute and with utterly peaceful faces.These of the mob saw the fallen, the pain of the wounded, the stillness of the dead, and stood finally aware of what monsters they were. Their own hearts were touched, tears filled their eyes, the best of what they were rose to push aside the worst."

"A few fired still when the leaders cried out, but these were broken of heart, empty of Soul and lost to Light. Yet the New People quietly began seeing to their wounded, and laying out their dead. They called their Healers who began healing without fear."

"The mob stood unable to run away, or fire or even to speak until those of the New People came among them. The Love that blazed through these New People was like a gift of water to the thirsty and unknowing, at first, they drank of it and it healed their own hearts, so that they finally could hope again. Even the leaders, violent in their private hells, found the tender Touch of Love stilling that violence. They saw into the peaceful faces and were ashamed but their shame did not anger them, rather it made them sad. They threw down their weapons and cried out for help. Those who resisted the power of that Love longest, could find none to follow them. Rather, their follows risked their lives to disarm even their leaders. More and more came before the New People to be taught."

"Then the new People drew all together and welcomed them among them to learn the Way. And that was the beginning of our Valley and the People of the Way." John stopped, but the others were spellbound. The old story never failed to fascinate.

After a few minutes, John looked at each of them, then noticed the children, so deeply intent. He knew with surprise that they understood well what he meant. "Do you see how we have changed? Look at the children!" He turned to them. "You two understand me, don't you? You know the difference already and you're only babies. " His voice broke, so deeply did that realization effect him." It's impossible to pretend we aren't a different people today. That's why it began to work because we ALL wanted it to". He thought a moment, his forehead wrinkled, "No,perhaps not all, but so many that the balance tipped to our direction. We CARED about our fellow men and women. Really cared and that made the difference. Someone once said that all people are selfish, the difference is in the size of the self. Well, the people of the Valley at least,(I don't know how this applies elsewhere in the world), were people with very large and inclusive 'selves'. Perhaps they had become so from those years of mutual suffering, or perhaps there has been an actual expansion of consciousness among us, among humankind itself.That is what some of my friends believe. I hope it is so.For then it would mean that this is permanent. That we are truly an evolved humanity with a greater consciousness, nearer to that called Soul Consciousness."

He was silent, then he went on,"Well, out of all that, Margo designed the city to resemble as nearly as she could, the great vines that grow in the central Valley stream beds. They bear all manner of fruits now, that the Altos Plant Wizards have developed them but at that time, they bore only small grapes, or round tart berries, good for pies and jelly. They are incredibly TOUGH, persistent, and fruitful which is the reason the plant people started working with them. She found such a vine growing out of our meadow. It had climbed an old dead tree and as the tree rotted it had become so thick and strong it could hold up its own upper vines. They reached out, seemed to catch at the sky itself, and bore round and oval shaped bright colored fruits. She thought, it took no space from any other plant, yet it bore food for many creatures. It was beautiful and perhaps it was more like a tree than a vine by then. At any rate, she and her engineer friends solved all the engineering problems and they designed it within months."

He laughed,"She covered so many sheets of paper,and her friends would come and they would litter the place, worse than when I am working on music. then,she submitted it.And to my complete surprise the plan was accepted." He turned then to them, grinning with pride and pleasure ." I think people were in the mood for something different, we'd already built Clandor, or rather the people of the South Valley had,and we central Valley people wanted something just as unusual as that forest city. So when she came flying in that day -- " his mouth was smiing but his eyes were soft with tears, "she just radiated, like a light blazed inside her.

Rose nodded, "You know, Papa, there was a little rivalry between Santiago and Clandor in those early days, wasn't there? Clandor built entirely inside the trees, or in those hill sized boulders that litter that country. The first time I walked there, it was very early morning and I couldn't believe that there were thirty thousand people living there. Yet,if you walk in the underground parks, and the hill top plazas, it's obvious in the middle of the day. It's like a festival,coming and going." She sat smiling, remembering too, and Anna crawled into her lap and suggled down, rapidly losing the battle to keep her eyes open.

John had watched her for a long moment, his head nodding slowly,"It's perhaps the best mark of us as a people, how we've changed, those two cities. We set a precedent and every town or city has followed, creating something new and designed to last. We've actually been able to keep our land, let it maintain its wild state, live with the animals without destroying their territory, and at the same time we have cities that the whole world envies. We have farms that produce enough for our people and use little land, and we keep up a good brisk trade with out Valley cities. We have civilizaton at its peak, for our time at least, and yet, we have a natural and lovely world. And that couldn't have happened before, all the centuries when we dreamed of it, the books written, philosophy built around the IDEA of it, and yet, the very naked greed of our selves made us unable to create what we longed for. We couldn't rise out of old rigid systems in which profit was the ONLY criteria for business. I envy you young ones, growing up in this world with a new kind of people, a new humanity. It is - literally, you know!"

He was silent and the two young people watched his face, full of memory,"You know, we came out of a world in which everything was seen as something to exploit. Not to do so meant you were a fool. So people were means to an end too. And Benjamin! Rose! That is not so today! That is not so! I live in a kind of profound Joy to know that. I don't think WE did it.I don't think we could have done it. I think it is a real, actual change in the very consciousness of humanity itself. We are not the same kind of people that our ancestors were. I think that you, your generation and even more the generation of these young ones, are an even greater kind of people. The quality of perception, the range of awareness among you, it is so much -- more, but even more important, it is COMMON! Everyone seems to have these attitudes, these perceptions."

Benjamin stood up, excited and with shining eyes, Andrew followed his fathers movement as if he understood. Ben said,"Dad, you've said something of this before but not so clearly. I think we need to hear that. To know that there is a difference, because lots of people worry that we can-- that we will revert to those old ways. I think enough time has passed now that we might know we will not."

Rose nodded,"There is something else too, Father, there's something I've felt in myself. Something that is like a seeking, a searching for what lies deeper in life --, maybe even in me!" She spoke softly, a sense of embarrassment making her hesitate , but he did not cut her off as she had feared, he nodded.

"I understand that, Dear. Margo said it was there in you, the deep search, the spark that she called a touch of Spirit Itself. She always thought you would some day find out what that was."

"And she never spoke of it to me!" Rose felt like crying, that someone so dear had known these inner urges, these longings that she felt and had not spoken of them with her. But she did not know how to tell him that.

But John was already thinking of those changes that for him had meant everything. "That was a kind of miracle, you know the way it happened. The reason people could create and follow as though it were simply right, those Convictions that are the corner stone of our Valley life,was because we are a different people. Humanity is not obsessed by the old need to control and possess. That was empty, ugly.In my childhood people talked a lot about it, but they didn't LIVE differently. But we did, we began it, and you carry it on. We have more, much more to think about, to strive for,today. I think that is the crucial part of it. We are alive, awake, and eager as a people."

" Margo and I, we used to talk of it, and we were afraid that it would die out, that it was only a result of the pain, the suffering, the recognitions we had to face of our cruelty and evil as a people during those terrible times. We could not pretend any more, we had to see what we did to one another, what we did to those outside our personal groups, whether it was family or nation or race. We could no longer pretend that there were not nations starving, wars kept going to feed our greed, fought even with young children as soldiers, forests cleared and its creatures including entire tribes of people, lost , just because we wanted to replace or manufacture throwaway goods that had so little value we bought them and forgot them. We had never acknowledged that that was literal murder."

"We had been caught in a denial so massive we didn't see it. Couldn't! To do so would have meant we had to see all the rest. But, slowly, people were beginning to admit what we were lying to ourselves and that admission came from those inner changes already occurring. We had to admit our absolute selfishness and greed and pure obsession with possessing things. Just things. It had become so bad that we would make and sell junk to one another, Anything to make profit and anything to have something we hadn't had before. No matter whether it had any value at all, or was beautiful or well made or whether our having it meant that some unfortunate people suffered. It was a time of terrible shame for us as a people."

He was silent, looking far into his memories. "The first step in the growth of the self is to recognize the self. Well, in those terrible years, we couldn't avoid recognizing, and what we saw sickened us. And maybe that was the first part of the changing, that we were able finally to see what we had become." He looked so sad, Rose wanted finally to change the subject, even though such a silloquy was rare from an old one.

Rose said, "I remember that you once told me that the creating of our Family groups was one of our best devices for learning. I never understood exactly what that meant."

He nodded, Because one of our first tasks was to learn to handle emotions. It became evident as our own recognitions, our admissions of our nature was clearer. We had to help each other, to meet needs, fears, angers, all the many powerful feelings that provided the energy for all our evil as well as for our good." He shook his head as if shaking off a memory. "Oh, my dears, the pain of it, the pain of it. You cannot imagine. To come face to face with the reality of what we were doing, HAD been doing as a people for centuries. Allowing even torture to occur among us, allowing nations and military groups to take and hurt fellow citizens for private ends . For power or for control. And the rest of us pretended we didn't know!"

" Actually we struggled to deny such things went on. Fought to deny it until we could no longer deny, because we are intelligent people and we could not simply refuse to believe exposed facts. And there were those who exposed the facts early enough that they were in danger of being killed, or imprisoned, but they did anyway. For so many years we kept little by little facing ourselves, facing what we were and when we finally realized, finally admitted AS A POEPLE, as humanity, we nearly became racially suicidal. There were hundreds who killed themselves in a self hate so pervasive that it could not be born. Because we finally saw ourselves. The Master teachers have always told us that this pattern is common for us as individuals. But never before had a PEOPLE become self aware! The path to self understanding goes through that dangerous country of self-exposure as well as that unbelievable country of Self discovery. They have said that if Self discovery can come soon enough, it brings humility and acceptance, but for many, it was not soon enough.!" Self discovery meant exposure of our basest nature, before we were able to know of our true nature clearly enough to realize we could rise out of that past."

There was silence between them, the garden seemed to them then to be a place of safety, of wonderful beauty and life. The air blew lightly across it, stirring the leaves on the shrubs and creating a mild swaying among the trees. They felt the beauty of the Earth here like a tonic. Rose said, "It is so absolutely beautiful, this Earth, Father. How could anyone think to harm it?"

He laughed shortly, adjusting his lap to make Andrew's sleeping body more comfortable for himself. "You can think that! You've been taught in Learning Centers that beauty is a right that every citizen knows he deserves. You have Learning Centers where people come during their entire lives to learn, all of us together. Monitors came to teach us. Then, Master Teachers took their places when they built the Stations." He frowned, then returned to his thoughts." You have all that! And you do not think as our people did. For you are taught with every day's breath to care for others, and to value yourself and other people. It is as natural as breathing is and so, it is part of our changed Valley, our changed people."

"So we learned together, it was ourselves who decided about the Learning Centers. My generation that decided! We knew that school should not be a place divided into a few years of early life, or for training in skills to earn money enough ot live on. We knew that learning had to be something available to us all and that we must learn together, old and young, every day of our lives." He stopped, and a subtle sorrow shadowed his face,"It was hard, daughter, it was hard for us. There were many times that we thought we were insane to try to reach toward that dream. But we learned to listen and to tolerate. Those were the two lessons the Monitors taught the Valley! The two most important skills. If they did not teach anything else, that would have sufficed perhaps."He repeated the words slowly,"To listen and to tolerate". Then he laughed, remembering." We weren't easy learners at first, either. Opinionated and stubborn, most of us. But something inside had changed, something pushed us to listen to them.We weren't so afraid for our survival any more. WHAT would survive, maybe. That's when we began the Valley system of Peer Support Groups where our differences could be worked out early enough so that they didn't grow. It's still functioning, that system, isn't it?"

Rose nodded, "It surely is,. One of the most important parts of our lives. The children already belong to one.They learn by the time they are three how to negotiate and how to listen." She laughed,"They don't do it very well, and they don't always try even, but they know how. And John, you're right, already they balance internally, emotionally better than we ever could at twice their age. They simply seem to be ABLE!"

John sighed and said,"It's like a lot of things, you take for granted, but we were just beginning to know, to think, to See. And we began learning to Meditate. Not just a few - but a lot of us. Now, nearly everyone practices that skill without second thought.And what'll it be with your children? They'll go on to something even greater. Perhaps to understand how to enter into contemplation! To discover from that -- that place, what we never could. They'll use those skills to meet new problems, to create, to imagine, and to simply explore and know themselves. Morning meditation in a Temple is a normal part of every morning for nearly everyone today. And it's a CHOICE! I doubt if there are many who miss many days, and even those who turn away for a time,tend to return to the practice,because it makes life better,it's as simple as that. No one has ever told anyone that they must. Never! And yet, even children naturally gravitate to the temples to sit in thoughtful, or self aware silence, or for some, complete inner silence, finding their own center before the day begins.I've heard them speak of it. They've found how valuable it is. And it took us, took my generation , years of irritable refusals before it was easy for us." He shook his head,"I think you have no idea how different you are from even your grandparents."

"It's true, Dad, we don't.And it's people like you who might help us learn. We've not had much of this, this remembering from you older folk."

"I can perhaps, do that!" He spoke as if the idea was completely new to him. And Rose always remembered that moment as a second turning point in his life .Then he had said,"You know, with everything -- the Monitors, with the dreams and the Convictions, with our horror of what we had been, I'm convinced it still couldn't have happened if there had not been something different, something awake and alive in our hearts, something that made us see and know possibilities previously invisible to us." He looked at each of them,"I think the important thing for you to remember is that a person today is a greater, more conscious being. That humankind has taken a step in evolution beyond anything we have ever been." He stopped, meeting their eyes,"That is MY Conviction." Then he frowned, and swiftly his face cleared and he laughed,"It's something I've thought much about here, alone, trying to heal. And I've wanted so much to tell you, but never could seem to begin! I bless this day, children, I do indeed!" He was silent again, looking down at the sleeping baby, his expression taut, and they knew he had not finished.Finally he spoke, his voice so soft they had to strain to hear."I believe, actually, I do, that Margo has been with me here ,helping me to realize -- all this. And that I must tell you.So in that sense, it's a message from your Mother." He looked up a small smile lighting his face.

Benjamin sighed, reached a hand to lay it on his father's arm, their eyes met. He said,"Thank you Dad!"

Rose said," John, I don't know how we can thank you. Do you know how precious this telling is? So much is unknown among us.There are only so many history films, and they do tell us a lot, but the theatre at the Learning Center where we produce the history films and the re-enactments, are also our training centers for new actors and dancers and singers. They must go by old tapes, films and books. A lot of it is guesswork. We need your help in making more personal, more immediate those tales". She looked away, breathing a long deep breath, "But perhaps especially what you just said, that there has been a changing, something in us has taken a leap, we've lifted ourselves higher or maybe more accuratly, we've expanded our consciousness! We don't know enough about that.If its true, we need to understand it."

John nodded,"It's not something that has been written about a lot. But for me it seemed that there was a -- a fresh breeze through our land, a new Light.It was followed by that capacity for seeing ourselves, for suspecting ourselves and for watching ourselves and our actions without justifying ourselves. We just watched honestly and that is when the dispair began for we saw what we were. The initial impetus, was from that new fire in our hearts. I think that we had always thought that human beings were so much superior to other animals.It was a shock to our pride to acknowledge our depth of evil and depravity. What we were capable of and what we actually were DOING.We were no longer able to justify ourselves, lie to ourselves."

Benjamin was frowning,"It's true, we're trained to watch ourselves. The teachers train us with guided daydreams, meditation disciplines, lifting of consciousness to break the hold of old patterns.They want to know our capacity to see beyond assumptions, to reason beyond assumption, habits, community ritual, and so on. Essentially, its a training in questioning one's own integrity, until that integrity is truly established." Does that sound right?" Benjamin's young face was intense, understanding what he had not.

John nodded, his face serious,"I'm glad for that. I hadn't known just how they practiced. But then even in our own time, we began to notice that we were obsessed with the need to survive, to destroy the other fellow because he might be a potential rival. And it was obvious when we really looked around that there is enough on this planet for everyone. Enough that no one need be without even the 'good life". Buckminster Fuller, a philosopher and writer of the last century told us that, and showed us that.But it was seventy five years after his death before anyone even took him seriously, at any level of power that is. And it was only because of the changes that they did then, I think.We had begun to notice, to pay attention, to ourselves and we saw that our lives had been based on fear. One kind or another. We talked about it at first, grieved , accused each other of it, and finally realized we had never trusted anyone, not even ourselves."

Rose said, "It's the noticing, the paying attention, that gives us insight, you know. The teachers tell us that even when we are very little."

John nodded vigorously, surprised and a little envious that it was not harder for them.He saw that envy , frowned and set it aside to be thought about later. With a wrench he said, "Then there was the recognition of -- of what Death is. That made a tremendous difference. To know that Death is not an ending of existence.Though it may be of this personality, but not of all we are, of all the memories, learnings, realizations, etc. that there is an on going Self who stores up these learnings and realizations and brings them back again to give another life a new impetus. A new opportunity built on the old one. We KNOW now that we are part of something greater. Can you imagine a whole people realizing so? What time would they have for making useless things, or for war?"

Benjamin nodded,It's still taking a lot of our energy to realize."

John shook his head, "There was change, as I've said. A new note in things.A kind of gentle humility among some world leaders. It was as though they finally realized seriously,"What does it benefit a nation to gain wealth, possessions, everything it wants, and have no love, no trust, no happy citizens, no integrity among its own people. The truth of emptyness had come home to us."

"Some nations, simply refused acknowledgement and struck out to try to avoid the facts, just as individuals do. Some accepted them all and fell in on themselves and were almost massochistic, so that there were mass suicides, some seemed to breath a long painful sigh and settle down to think and to rebuild. It was a terrible time. Most could not believe that we could be better. That we were more than we had ever known ourselves to be. It was that Vision, the new perception the DREAM, that began to give us hope that we could -- perhaps, we could be more than we had been."

"And so the World Charter was born. Finally after so much violence, so much loss and pain, the Charter came from the World Court and World government Council. And that Charter is a miracle itself, how it managed to be created, I don't know. I think it was -- there had to be Monitors serving on that council because you know they used to live among us, not in the Stations as they do now."

" But John, the Monitors are simply ordinary people who have -- who have realized more than most of us, you know. They would be the right ones to sit on such a Council."

He nodded,"I suppose so. But today, they won't, they insist it's up to us."The Valley itself gave that beginning Charter to the world.It was developed from our own Convictions. And we have felt -- I have felt such great pride. Do you suppose it is wrong to feel such pride in our own Valley?" There were tears in his eyes and he smiled such a gentle smile, like a child, trusting them. Ben smiled back,his own eyes wet.

He said, "Papa, it doesn't seem to me that pride is wrong, as long as it isn't twisted into reasons for acting against others, or standing apart from them."

John pointed a finger, crying out,"You see! You See! We wouldn't have known that , wouldn't have thought it. It's something you young ones would think of right away. You are a new people, Son. You trust! You Love! We couldn't! We longed to. We dreamed of it. But didn't even know it was possible! I think we didn't know what Love was at all. I think we thought it was something we FELT, something given to another, or received from someone. We thought it was part of sex, even. It was a terribly limited concept of Love and yet, for you, it is not any of those."

They sat in silence then, sipping their coffee, listening to the sounds of the afternoon. The sun moved steadily higher and was warm and comforting. The bright garden reflected all the life they spoke of. John sighed,"Oh, I can't tell you the power of those times, we felt such sweeping guilt, such shame, sometimes an excess- masochistic even in our humiliations of ourselves, and yet, such a deep surging, like an ocean rising in us, of hope! HOPE! Seeing our blindness made us hope that we might begin to see. It made us know we must open our eyes if we were to See."

"But Dad, it must have taken so much time. Yet it seems it was in your life time.that much of it happened."

"It was also my grandparents life times, but it didn't take so much time after all. To think there was so much change in a few generations, that's the miracle.Because we are a people maturing. He used to tell me of his time, you know. How it was gradually beginning even there. The changes began with little things, changing our diets, changing our attitudes about the natural world, becoming aware of the ecology of our world, our atmosphere, requiring changes in laws to protect life, the land. It was slow at first, and yes, there were those who exploited the rest of us and that was the cause, the energy that produced the destruction of those years. But there was the inner change making it happen. And it was not limited to any one nation, it was everywhere.We began to plant forests in one place while those who were still blind cut them down in another. We began to create programs so the poor could have homes, and jobs, even though our governments did not do anything except offer dole and use those poor. We began to learn to keep each other healthy, to create neighborhood support groups that meant people really cared about one another, and even right in the middle of a rise in burglary and rape, drug use and alcolism. Programs in small towns to help one another grew right along side increasing violence and fortunes made on drugs and other harmful materials. People were divided and didn't know it at first at all. Divided in a way that began to show a change in the way we saw life."

"The tide had turned, the old world, the old way had lost its power. Humanity was going down a different track and would not ever regress.Then after the falling apart, there was the beginning of the recreation that has resulted in this Valley Then is when we began to build the Valley. And other Valleys like it in other parts of the world." John turned his head, looking again out to the City, Santiago. Brilliant with color in the afternoon sun. He was silent, he had finished with the Telling for today.

They sat so together for a time and then went in to find a dinner from the new home processer that John had just installed. He said,"I like to cook now and then, you know, but mostly, I'm not as good at it as this fellow is." He was obviously proud of it and Ben and Rose were properly impressed."I know that you had something to do with developing them, Benjamin. I think it's a great gift your research team gave us. You know everyone will have them within three years I'd guess. My dealer told me that the manufacturers could not market them until they had the price down so that everyone could afford one. That was your team's stipulation, No?" He grunted at Ben's nod and smile.

Rose and Ben stayed for two more days and there had not been a time to talk more in this way. But they had not forgotten and they persuaded John to come to Adwin and talk at their Learning Center. And that was the beginning of a life work.

Now, shaking herself free from the long remembering, Rose sat up, then bent her head in a sudden sweep of sadness. Remembering those days, brought both joy and sorrow. She said, "Let it all come to something, all they suffered for, all we've struggled for. Oh God, let it be so!" She felt a tear slide over her cheek and rubbed it away. Old pains fade slowly, she thought. She said, "I'm a ninny worrying so. It has to be because Ben is going off. The Valley is strong. " She shook her head, got up stretching. Outside the window the day was grey, sodden with winter and a lowering sky threatened more. It didn't look like snow, but it felt like it.

CHAPTER TWO

Snow Magic

Snow came in the night. It was late for such a storm, already the narcissus were pushed up from the earth their swelled bud shafts visible. Yet it snowed, steadily and silently, until, when Steve glanced out his window just at first grey dawn , as was his habit to check the coming day's weather, the air seemed opaque, a drifting curtain. Snow swept across the northern land, from a few miles south of Jasper northward. The air was still and cold.

Ben woke, sat up beside Rose's sleeping body, and felt the sting of the cold as the blanket fell away. He reached to switch on the heating unit. Solar batteries in the basement were going to know only depletion this day, but they were state of the art and fully able to contain power for weeks. He slid back under the warm woven blankets, drew his mate close ,luxuriating in the warmth. For another hour they slept in each other's arms. Even in sleep they were never unaware of their parting.

Then early dawn light,thin and cold, filled the room. Ben felt Rose sit up, but was reluctant to wake. Vaguely he dug deeper into the warmth, wanting to put off the moment of waking. This ambivalence he felt, the first time in any of the journey's he had made, was painful to endure. He knew he would see sorrow in her eyes, no matter how she smiled. He was angry that she must be sad. Why did it seem so much harder for her this time? Rose, watching him, knew he would not wake yet. She smiled wryly, one corner of her mouth lifted but it only emphasized the sadness of her face. It must be a good leave taking. It must be! She would see to that. She should be used to these journeys, should not feel such dispair. Something was different, something she could not define.

She wished she understood more of the complexity that was human relationship. She quoted softly, gazing at the mound that was her mate, 'Relationship develops out of the trust of opening oneself to being vulnerable', as some one once told me. But it's much more -- it's an unceasing creation." The skin of her forehead puckered in a grimace of perplexity. She reached out one hand to slide fingers down Ben's bare back and gently, smoothly began to massage the firm muscles. "His skin is so soft - as soft as mine - but the muscles beneath are harder even than my own." She had always enjoyed that sense of pure physical power that Ben radiated. Always he stood out among men much taller, She liked the balance of his great body, an inch taller than her own, the way he stood, like a dancer ready to move in any direction at any moment. He stirred to her continued touch and reached out one great arm to encircle her waist and draw her down against him as he turned. For moments they enjoyed the pleasure of closeness, just being together, kissing each other lightly, carressing softly each other's bodies, but they did not rouse desire. The weight of their softly each other's bodies, but they did not rouse desire. The weight of their feelings bore down even that lightness. Last night had been a hungry expression of all the longings they knew, cried out through their clinging bodies. This morning, there was another kind of touch.

"Today you go."

He nodded briefly, watching her happily, his face content and soft with the enjoyment of looking at her. He said,"After twenty years, Love, you're still an exciting lady!"

She sat up again, curling herself to sit at his side, touching him, still letting her hand slide along his hip, down the edge of his thigh and among the blond hairs at his legs. She saw his cock stir slightly and then lie still and she pulled the sheets up over them both as she slid to the warmth of his body. The room was warming but still felt chilly.She said,"Has it been so long? We've always been so busy, we never noticed."

He laughed, "The building of our Valley, and in these last ten years, our own town, surely had to take that long, even with all five thousand people in Adwin dedicated to it."

She snuggled against him, comforted by his response. He met her lips and their kiss was long and tender. Their loving of last night had been deep and wonderful, she thought, a fit remembrance to keep. The memory of it comforted her now. But this was a time for other intimacies. She was aware of the rising tumult of his feelings, knowing he would share them with her, she said nothing. Neither did she acknowledge that awareness or wonder at its sharpness.

He rolled away so that he could look into her face."Rosy, my Love, I COULD just not go!"

She choked, the sudden rush of hope drowned by irritation and spoke carefully,"Don't say that!"

Then getting up and drawing a gold robe over herself, she stood tying the belt and looking down at him. "You know that you must. You know that not going won't help make things any better for either of us. And then --", she hesitated, a faint smile curving her lips. "Then I'd be the one feeling guilty."

He met her eyes sharply, a swift critical glance, that softened and became a smile. his gaze dropped and lost itself in distance. She went on, "Since going is what you want to do, that is what you must do. Going is what you NEED to do!" She stopped, pulling at her belt distractedly,"I'm ashamed of my attitude, my Love, ashamed of it! I know I've been acting like a baby, and that's what I've felt like. And I don't know --- yes, I do know why. But I don't want to talk about it. At least, I know I'm not as grown up as I'd like to think.," She sighed.

Ben nodded, sat up and reached for his own blue Skenna robe. He slid into it as he stood. I guess you're right. I'm trying to figure out the easy way. A way that would make you feel good about things. Would get me total approval." he laughed harshly. "Guess we're both still children,Honey!"

His defensive look fed her impatience irrationally. She managed to keep any sign of it from her voice. "Well, it's what I want too. Total approval for my effort.:

As he started to speak she held up a hand, "No, let me tell you. That's what you usually stop me from doing. You and my own guilt. It's a relief to me to SAY my resentment. That doesn't mean you have to do anything about it." She was silent, letting her eyes run over him," We've always tried to say these things but we've not done it."

He nodded, "We've usually fought until the final day and loved each other desparately and then fought some more. It was always an awful time. We've never been able to part with good feelings.. except the times when you went to the Western Station for your retreats. And that was because it wasn't so long, I think."

" Don't be modest, Benjamin, you know it was because you handle these things better than I do. You're more generous." She was still, then suddenly, "You've always been such a stubborn bastard that no matter how fierce I got you wouldn't give in the way you have this morning. NEVER! No matter how I felt!" Now that she'd said it she felt relief gush through her like a wash. She'd never got that said ever before.

He was nodding seriously,"I knew that! Did you know I knew it? I think I've known how awful it was for you, the sense of abandonment, the rage at yourself as much as at me. Your shame, and my guilt. It's been a battle Love. How have we managed to keep loving all these years?"

"Because we're Mates, you ninny. We aren't just married, we're MATES! We couldn't do otherwise." She was frowning, an atmosphere of tension was rising. She suddenly threw up her hands, stalked across the room to the small Automat unit, punched two cups of coffee. "I don't know what's got into me this time. I was so sure I was over it all. Could let you go gracefully, and I've acted worse than before, I think.I actually WANT you to go on this search this time, to find what you seek, and bring it home. I think I want to know too. But I'm afraid of something, something I can't define, as though something's going to happen here, in our Valley, something terrible." Her great wide brown eyes met his blue ones, she was realizing anew just in the shaping of words."If only you'd tell me what it is you seek, find words to name it, then maybe I could accept." Her eyes became narrow, wary and she handed him his cup.

"That's fair,Rosy, but if I knew how to name it, maybe I'd have found it. That's the pain of it. That I can't precisely name what I seek. I've tried to say what it is, you know, and all you hear is a vague fog of words. It's not concrete, you know, a thing like a pot of gold, more a thing of Spirit, I think. You remember that I told you of that time I saw -- saw what seemed to me to be pure Light like a fountain pouring through my mind, my vision." His eyes were far off, remembering, his face soft.

"It happened several times through the years and each time, I felt as though I was on the verge of realizing something, something so important that my very life depended on it.Yet, I couldn't quite understand. Even now, to remember I feel the ache of it in here." He touched his chest and was still. And it always comes back, sooner or later. It comes from the very center of my being, out of my Heart.

pulling at me, toward something I can't name but the pull is an ache of longing. I can't -- can't resist finally going out to search. When the Light pours through me, it simply blinds me to everything else. It's as though I finally have a brief glimpse of what I must find. And in these last weeks, it's been like a fire just behind my consciousness day and night!" He frowned, looking away, sipping his coffee, and shifting himself on the edge of the bed.

She frowned, held one hand to his cheek,"Why've you never even told me that much?"

"I think, because I couldn't bear to talk of it. I didn't know how. I thought you'd laugh. I think what I have told you was an attempt to joke about it."

She nodded,"I remember Ben. I've thought it was strange for you to joke. It always made me angry because I thought you were just concealing the truth." She stubbed at the thick carpet with one toe,"Oh, my darling, we ought not to be so obtuse. All our lives the Master Teachers have spoken of the Light. That it might be seen as we meditate, that Light in ourselves. They say it IS ourselves we see and that's why it frightens us at first. It hasn't been the only time you've seen that Light ?"

"He shook his head, "No! It hasn't! But in meditation, somehow it comes gently from where I've focussed attention and seems part of something special and not of ordinary life. When I realize that Light then I think I must be living in a terrible darkness for the Light to seem so brilliant. It shines through and - " he hesitated, trying to find words, "it exposes me, everything, our whole world." He shook his head. "It's that that I'm afraid of. I must keep these things separate. What you say is exactly true, it does frighten me. I hate feeling frightened. I'm a big strong man, I'm not supposed to be afraid." He grinned at his feeble joke and she shook her head, then he went on. "At the same time it's like something I can't live without, If I don't find it again, find what it means, I think I'll die inside. Or else, I've got to live it completely. I can't stand the not knowing.But if what the Teachers say is true, then maybe it'd be like losing my Self! " He had spoken so softly she nearly didn't hear. She wanted desperately to ask him to describe the experience, what it was like for him, but something refused to speak the words. She shivered, for he began to do just what she'd wanted to ask.She knew that he was more aware than he knew.

He drew a long ragged breath, determined now to speak it out. "It doesn't make sense to me, you know. And it's what's kept us from speaking, you and me, from talking about it.It was pure wonder, As though my mind filled up with Light, as though I am inside a great brilliant Light and I can't see out. It's like a wide waking up, a Seeing of things through myself almost. That wonderful Light poured through my whole body, right down through my mind. My heart ached, hurt actually, Rosy, it was so --so vast a - a consciousness. To be conscious like that - it's -- it didn't seem human at all. For moments it seemed the whole world was transformed." He looked at her embarrasedly, afraid she would think him daft. But she watched him seriously and he went on,remembering, reliving in that acute still memory."I have never known such JOY, such clear perception. Yet I don't know how to speak of what I realized, even to myself. Except to remember the Light. We've all been so busy it was easy to focus on something else afterward. Avoid thinking of it. Now -- I can't get it off my mind, It's what I must know, find out! It was as if I glimpsed a moment into the heart of -- of something infinitely Holy. The last time I felt for days lifted out of myself and the world was different, all changed, somehow. And it was as though my life had turned itself around, completely. And I couldn't understand that. Had it only happened once, I probably would have forgotten it as something aberrant, but it's been to much, there was no use trying for forgetting. I never told anyone at all.I honestly don't know why. " His eyes gazed far away, and as she watched, a great hope rose in her, drowning all her fear.

""Oh, Ben! Ben! Why haven't you, in all these years told me? You've never told me like that -- ever!" She was tremendously excited at his revelations, but also afraid.

He pulled himself from his revery, looked at her with a half smile,"I thought you'd think me mad, Sweetheart. A few days after it happened, I thought I was mad myself.And it's only happened to me three times. The first was when I was only ten. I could put it out of mind then, being a kid and all." He sighed. "You know, sometimes Paul talks of such things, not of an actual happening, but the idea, and you always seem to be impatient with him when he does "

She was startled,"I do?" Then reflecting,"Yes, maybe I do seem so. But it's only because - - because he just talks about the IDEA of it. He doesn't enter into - - doesn't --. I wonder if it's his way of trying to share his own experience with us. Does he have such experience too?" She stopped, shook her head. A hard knot tied itself in her stomach, she realized she was afraid he was going to ask her whether she too had known of such things. And why not? Why not tell him? Her mind screamed at her, but she fought away from the thought itself. She spoke rapidly, holding off any turn of the talk to herself."But why didn't you go to the Master Teachers. They NEVER laugh.?" She had come to him, leaned against him, stroking his soft golden hair.

"I should have, but I made the mistake of telling a friend and he DID laugh. In fact, he said I ought to go to the Healers.I just couldn't risk that again." He looked at her, his eyes seeking hers, "You don't think that's a coward's way?" But before she could answer, he went on,"No, you wouldn't think that. But it's what I told myself for a long time. I despised myself and was afraid of myself and so nothing happened to help." Finally he grinned," I've been pretty much of a mess, Sweetheart. You must admit that's worth a little searching!"

"Oh, My Love, I'm sure it is! It's what you must do. I've known that, even when I vowed to hate all the people you might meet while you were gone. I knew you must go, even when I tried to stop you, you know." He smiled and she laughed. "At least now, I 've grown up a little. I can bless them that they give you comfort and companionship." She tossed her head, a stern look,"I have that at least to my credit this year." Her body relaxed as the conversation turned away from this dangerous area. He stood, and circled her with his arms, kissed her from this dangerous area. He stood, and circled her with his arms, kissed her forehead and then bent his face to hers.

"I know, sweetheart, I appreciate you. Everything about you, more than you know." He set his cup aside so that he could hold her and she leaned against him with a long sigh.

"Oh, Ben, does anyone ever reach that point when they can accept gracefully what their loved ones are, feel, need, and so on? Without fighting it?" He laughed and she snuggled into him and then laughed too. They were touching each other as if that touch were the last, which it seemed to them both to be. She finally said,"Benjamin, there's a lot to do if you're ready in time."

He nodded, releasing her, and she turned to walk to the window and for the first time saw the snow. It was falling in thick, large flakes, a typical late snow, not a bitterly cold one. The world seemed far from them, distant somewhere through that endless curtain that hid everything. She cried out and he leaped to her side, both forgetting everything else in this contemplation of that beauty. For some moments they simply stared at it. Dimly they could see the branches heavy with perfectly,fitted white outlines that coated every tiny twig inches deep already. They looked at one another, mildly pleased, and they stood watching the snow fall. Such a familiar lovelyness, yet always fascinating. Their arms circled one another, they felt a deep joy of being together, safe, hidden away here, isolated from everything. Rose tugged at him,"Ben it falls so silently. So absolutely without noise." Then in a puzzled tone, coming from her own needs she added,"The snow comes and goes, in complete beauty, and it asks nothing at all."

The thought hung there, irrelevant, but Ben nodded, understanding. He said, "Would you take the belts up? Now! Ride the belts up into this and hang in the air before the sun is up? When the sun comes the deepness of it will be less. We'll wear a double belt and go as we are."

She shrugged, almost refusing out of old upsurges of spite then relaxed, ashamed of the thought. She laughed,"Not me. I'm not going with nothing but my robe on."

He laughed too and they turned to get dressed, but for a moment she held him,"Ben, I know I'm ambivalent, at best, it's part of my nature, I think. I swing from dispair to joy and then I want to accept both. And all stages in between." She drew a long breath,"I know I don't share everything with you either.And that's wrong, wrong to our Mating." Her eyes were miserable but he kissed them and laughed.

"Honey,I guressed. We've both got things to account for. But don't think I blame you for the guilty feelings I have. They're mine and I'll take care of them. I'm excited about going, but I'm also sorry. I'll miss - I've always missed - a lot - the kids, all the things you do. It can't be helped. A person can't have everything."

" We can use the video phone more."

He shook his head, "No, it's always important to me to break the connections and travel truly alone. I don't quite know why. But I'll try to contact you anyway this time. And talk to the kids."

him go and began to collect her clothes from his closet. "I could use a bit of snow in my face to wake me up." She began pulling on a long plasilk and wool body stocking, then a full loose purple shirt and tight brown trousers that fitted into knee high drago boots. His bright blue shirt and trousers were of fine wool-skenna blend, light and very warm. He pulled out his coverall for high belt flying and she grimaced. "Oh, Ben, my coveralls are in my cottage. I didn't bring them. Do you have another pair?"

He laughed, and got a green and blue suit from his closet."You usually have something of everything here, Honey, just as I do in your cottage. But maybe you can manage in these." He grinned as she pulled them on, too big over all, they made her look like a dumpling. He said,"But they'll keep you warm."

Then they were belted and outside. With some surprise they saw that others of the family had the same idea. They laughed and waved and then were swiftly, silently sliding up and through the vast atmosphere of snow flakes. The down ward movement of snow as they ascended caused them to seem to move up faster than they did. Rapidly they were far above the house and the countryside below where the town lights could be seen faintly stabbing through the white, pure, sheet of snow lying over everything. Then, they were so high they could see nothing except each other.

They were wrapped in the silence of the curtain about them. They watched it fall, holding them close in its dense softness. Ben drew Rose to him and kissed her with a gentleness to match the touching of the great drifting crystals. She reponded with a sudden hunger for his lips and they felt the snow gathering between their noses, on their eyelashes as they tasted the sweetness of each other's mouths, licked snow flakes off each other's faces. When they drew apart, the snow had built up enough on their eyes that they could not see at all for a second. They brushed each other off and set the belt to carry them through the drifting powder so they floated as though there were no world at all.

For sometime they played, rising and falling, soaring softly as though they had no attachments to Earth. They let themselves enter into a fantasy of being part of this sky world, cut off from all things. The constant white, the constant movement became slightly hypnotic and Rose felt herself responding powerfully to the solitude. She felt herself drawn outward, sensing the great mountains, then upward and outward, acutely aware of the sky, her very consciousness drifted,expanded so that it included the farthest reaches of these tiny exquisite forms,as though she held the whole broad miles of storm inside herself.Then swiftly she shrank into the details of their lacy shapes. examining each, she was caught in fascination. But deliberately she pulled herself from their attraction and Reached beyond. Beyond this storm where the sky was clear bright blue, full of morning sunlight and distance was endless. Fifty miles south, the snow did not fall. A little rain splashed over the bright leaves of Santiago. But the sky was mostly blue. Rose had never thought of telling Ben of her mind-travel. Never had she done so.But this morning, after his confession, the thought at least occurred to her and she dismissed it abruptly. This wasn't the same, he wouldn't accept it.

THE AWAKENING

Rose drew her attention back, to the tiny flakes around them, visible, one as lovely as the next. She watched enthralled as she had always been at their perfect design. Ben was lost in fascination of the streaming crystals.

Rose Reached again, her attention extended out into the great cascading cliffs and forests that fell from the peaks ranging far to the east . The foothills, rolling from those high peaks downward into the great flat center of the Valley, were broken here and there by the clean shining of small lakes or creeks. A few lights glowed upward here and there where small villages nestled among the forests and the wide open meadows. She focussed, her consciousness extending outward, part of that still and silent world. Detached from this little physical body, she felt herself range far, calm in a singleness of being and it amazed her suddenly to recognize that thought occurred separate from that body.

Her body seemed lost, unfeeling in this suspension, tiny in this storm, yet at the same time, acutely alive and conscious of itself, its enjoyment and breathing. She ceased thinking, accepting the Reach, the movement of life everywhere, the frozen absolute solitude of the high peaks, where bitter cold would continue for another month or more. She felt and saw even as her eyes were closed in this downpour of silence. The sun blazing on the peaks, the River, still sluggish and frozen at the edges in this northland, placid and dreaming in its slow winding through the Great Valley. The trees, swollen with redened branches and fat buds, the deep new grass bent and waiting beneath this heavy cover. She was conscious of creatures hidden away in their burrows, sleeping on last autumn's dry straw. Life at this moment, was waiting, quietly waiting. Spring time was just ahead.

This awareness of so much Life there, waiting, beneath the cold, so ready to burst forth, to flame out beyond all silence, drove through her consciousness. It permeated her attention as her body hung there, warm against her mate's. She knew the throat tightening joy, the wonder of it like an energy flaming forth from everything that lived. She was part of that energy. She was in fact a flaming of that Earth below, she was a living cry flung upward from Earth's depths. A tiny, living thread.

The thought floated through her mind. 'We are simply sentient Earth!' The thought seemed perfectly logical and true. 'But then, Earth herself is alive. So how can this be?' And the thought faded. She was lost again in awareness. Rose had not qualified as Earth Sensitive nor as healer when she took her testing in childhood at the Learning Center, but she had talent in both and could act as assistant to those fully qualified. She was glad that she could sense, could know of Earth in this most intimate way. Now ! Reaching outward, down then up into the farthest reaches of the empty sky, she exulted in her connection. she felt the fluidity of herself, the capacity to Reach out beyond the simple concrete matter of life and to return, to accept the familiar limits. No longer did she think of that Mind Reach as alien to herself. Shrinking back into this small personal self was painful and sad, these limits were so narrow. Only on such a return did she know that. She drew herself close, a small person hanging in this immensity. She opened

She drew herself close, a small person hanging in this immensity. She opened her eyes, looked into Ben's. He was calling her name and she knew that he worried at her stillness. She laughed, meeting his eyes, but seeing there the fear. She calmed. Why did she conceal from him?

He could see there in her eyes something he could not fathom, something that caused his throat to catch in an unutterable envy."What is it? Oh, my dear, what is it? You look as though you have just returned from paradise." He spoke without thinking and immediatly felt that his words were foolish. Surely he must be imagining.

She snuggled close, caressing him and feeling the gladness of his presence. Glad that she could find him here. She didn't want to speak but to enjoy. But he had confessed, why couldn't she? She knew his need, she longed to speak of some of her realization, she knew she must begin to trust, but she didn't yet. She said,"I was far seeing the Valley, Love, as if I am part of it. Oh, Ben, I felt the Earth Touch. I've seldom felt that. It's a Touch actually in my Mind so tender, so alive, but so powerful it would rend me apart if it lasted. It must be a little like your seeing of that Light. I don't understand it. I don't know how to describe it. " She felt her face wet with the greatness of the memory. The warm tears were instantly cold. She was shaking her head,"How CAN the Earth Sensitives bear the greatness of it?"

He didn't know nor did he press her. This talk threatened him. He had heard of Earth Sensitives but had no idea of what that meant. He held her close, wondering, wishing that he could know as she did. Trying to accept and set aside the envy, the sorrow of what he thought his lack. He thought perhaps she had found something somewhere that he had so long sought. But then, she would have told him, wouldn't she?

He was still caught up in the falling beauty, the stillness. Not wanting to talk. It was like a great ocean all around them, the white pouring, churning with sudden gusts of wind, currents in a great sea. With a painful urgency he wanted to KNOW, to know what those who saw more than he must know. The desire swept through him, upward, staining his mind like a dark shadow and then dissolved when he put attention on it.

Slowly he felt himself drawn outward, touching against something that taught him wordlessly of Itself. He felt himself swimming through currents of mind, racing with delight, testing his personal strength against that far perception. It seemed to him some choice was being made. There was a gentle limitlessness that allowed for everything, for all possibility. At that moment, he thought he knew that he would be capable of anything he might need to meet. But he fled the growing perception.

Ben straightened his body, focussing on the immediate physical world. He let himself rise further into the beating snowflakes, enjoying their steady movement like a drum, silent, yet heard in his body somewhere and erasing barriers he had not known were there. He felt his resistance, but he wanted to be willing to respond. He wondered how this silent blind world they had entered could create singleness of mind was like a current between them that frightened him. And at the same time, elated him. Then, there was a shift.

An instant pouring of sunlight into this dense universe broke his absorption. The rising sun glowed down into the dim world and made it golden. Then, for a moment, as though clouds above them parted, an intense clear light bathed them, illuminated their private ocean , startlingly bright. Then it was gone, and the snow thickened. They drew closer and holding each other, began to descend. Benjamin wondered what had happened to the others who had climbed into the sky with them. How could they have managed to avoid them? He forgot the question as they slid down, felt the beauty reverberate through them like a liquor that surged in rhythmic beats. His mind pulsed with knowledge he did not know how to name. Did not WANT to name, yet his search surely was for knowledge! Was his search so far fruitless because he avoided the reality that was there in front of his nose? This immersion in this moment-in this Earth life- had opened into the depths of his being so that he saw what he had not known. Was that inner world what he had sought and refused? He shrank from the question.

They sank slowly toward Earth until they matched the speed of the falling flakes. Suddenly everything seemed to cease, there was not even that familiar movement. Body sense faded, shifted. the stillness, the movelessness, the blindness within this white silence drew at them. They clung together, determined to realize this moment, within deprivation of senses,this focus inward to a realm of 'other' consciousness. The loss of the familiar pressed them into THAT. Rose recognized that edge as they crossed it into what she did not know - - had never realized. But she held firm. Ben, shifted, clung to her, felt his mind scream with resistance. So they turned in upon each other and entered into a union like to none other they had ever known.

Rose felt her mind on fire with a wordless awareness, soundless, colorless, so full of meaning it ached with intensity and yet, she could not make a thought to hold any of that meaning. It was -- seemed -- beyond thought. The fact was a rasp to her intelligence, ripping away security. But suddenly, it didn't matter, later it would when memory brought the experience into silhouette against the rest of life. But now, she could hold Ben,and he her;they could melt into one another and be one awareness without diminishment. They breathed in stillness of joy.

Suddenly their feet touched gently against earth and they felt a rush of sensations - thoughts, recognitions - tumbled down into the familiar. Ben activated the belts to lift them a little, to see where they were. They looked around, in the brightening morning light they could see dark out croppings, the darkness under forest trees, and knew they were on a familiar hill top half a mile from the Farm. Even covered with snow, this hill was familiar.A pair of deer, standing under a tree twenty yards away, stood surprised at their appearance but watched calmly, with unblinking eyes. Rose spoke slowly as she raised her head from Ben's chest, drew herself into this moment. "The Lion Rock. We're almost home."

They adjusted direction, moved closer to the ground so as to avoid getting

THE PEOPLE OF THE VALLEY

They adjusted direction, moved closer to the ground so as to avoid getting lost and in minutes dropped onto the walkway before the brightly lit Hall.

They turned to the Temple, bluelight poured from the roof and walls. It seemed the jewel in the snow that it had been designed to be. They moved toward it, and went inside. The warmth swept over them, wonderfully pleasant. Two of the cubicles were occupied and Rose and Ben found two empty. Ben was grateful, he didn't want to talk, didn't want to remember just now, didn't want to acknowledge the persistent question that nagged just behind recognition,'Was this another of the life long avoidances that had driven him out from his Family?'

Rose sank down into the cushions of the six by three space. She accepted it, darkening it a little. Then she touched a button and soft chimes began to make a ryhthmic pattern, their sounds holding long so that the next sound broke against the faint echo of the last. Their rhythm was so slow it drew her own excited body into calm. Her mind focussed on that even, steady beat and thought faded. She lifted into that absolute stillness that was like an infinitely slow reverberating drum, cleared her mind of thought, held attention alert, waiting. Aware then of the Wonder of Life she was utterly still, waiting, holding steady, focussed and receptive. She might know impression echoing into consciousness. She did not doubt. There was the direction.

There beyond thought, she held, aware, of drifting shadows of emotion and of thought, unattended, they faded away. It was as if she floated in the tides of a great sea, a sea of Mind itself, whose currents were calm and ageless. Printing itself on her own mind was impression of vast consciousness. She felt, knew its Touch, yet it had no name, no identity. Tendrils of it's electric presence penetrated into her consciousness leaving the trace of its path. She felt herself shrink from the power of it. It was awareness! That impression was like an opening, a way toward that vast unknown. She, aware, conscious, extended outward into that greater Consciousness -- where Mind and Spirit met. She knew purpose beyond herself, recognition of Vision. Nothing would shape into thought but she was centered in peace. After a while she receded from these depths, consciousness shriveling into the familiar. Her body trembled. Her determination reaffirmed.

She was ready to meet this day, whatever it held. She drew as if relieved, back into thought and emotion, not wanting to forget but forgetting much. She began to sing her prayers, chanting them in time with the sounds of the chimes. Then, sliding her hand across the color panels, she allowed threads of gold to weave into the blue, subtle fine threads that pulled at her heart, drew joy, grief, and longing as a harp touched, releases sound from its strings. Many doubts surged, hurt and were refused. At this moment the recognition was too clear. Doubt could not ravel away her confidence. Later, doubt would create bitter defenses. Fullness of emotion became a pouring - familiar, manageable. She felt herself subside in relief even with the new aliveness that filled her. She thought of Benjamin, knew that he found his own focus. He too had touched against that SELF. How aware of that was he?

THE AWAKENING

She left the Temple and found Benjamin waiting. They linked arms and walked silently to the Hall, eager to join the Family there, to celebrate this mornings broken fast together. Ben felt a lift of apprehension. The others might question him. He didn't want any mention of his Journey today. They all knew. Surely they would let him be.

The table was crowded, everyone was here. Surely they'd cut their visit to the Temple short, or got there early. The experience of the flight into the snow had been different for each of them. Silvia and Steve were laughing at some foolishness. They had played, rolling across the open sky and then nearly too late, realizing that their sight was too impaired to trust this kind of play. They saw they had come within inches of a huge tall tree, could have gotten skin torn, or worse.

Jerry was angry and sounded it, his arms gestured, extending his anger as he talked. "You fools, don't you realize the very use of the belts is given only when a person has enough sense to use them with discretion? D'you think THAT was discretion?"

Silvia, lost her grin, her almond eyes shining dark in her small pale face. She ducked her head, letting the long shining blue, black hair slide across half her face to hide the irrepressable delight. Then, she threw back her head, and her hair too, so that it slid down over her shoulders to her back, and glanced at Steve. They knew they had played at danger though the chance of hurt was small. She knew their behavior was only a trigger for Jerry's wrath. He was resenting being left out of it. He was resenting knowing that this woman, his beloved, might have been hurt. This man, his family brother might have been also. But more than either, he envied Steve's ability to play, to let himself loosen from the restraints of good sense even. Silvia knew, and knew that Jerry would apologize to them both later. They both knew they had been taking risks.

"He's right Steve, though I hate to admit it."

Steve nodded, a faint grin still playing about his lips. His big powerful body, only slightly taller than Benjamin, nearly six inches shorter than Jerry's six feet four, moved like one trained to dance, one skilled at the martial arts, which he was. His grey eyes searched Silvia's small face, but there was merriment in them. He was grinning what Jerry called his worst Irish grin , his natural rebelliousness still refusing to let Jerry be right -- yet. Then he turned to Jerry and sobering a little, he nodded,"Yes, Jerry, we know as well as you do about being responsible. We did take a chance, maybe, but not much. We did have the censors on, and they kept us from coming to close to anything. After that first tree," he admitted grimacing. " After all, we didn't get hurt." He grinned again,,remembering, "Don't worry, brother, we aren't the totally overgrown kids you'd like to think we are." There was open good humor in his voice.

Jerry frowned and said peevishly,"I wouldn't LIKE to think you are.!" Then his face relaxed and a faint edge of a grin tipped his mouth. "But then again, maybe I would." He bent his tall, thin body into a chair across from them and reached one long brown arm to punch his breakfast into the auto chef. His long dark hair, curling more than his sister Rose's, slid like a shining curtain across the brown curve of his cheek. Impatiently he drew it back and then, pulling a bright green ribbon from his pocket, tied it back. He was darker than Rose. Either of them would have been called mulatto in the old days. He kept his frown, but Silvia could see the sparkle already in his eyes. Jerry never stayed mad long.

Silvia laughed, "Aha, you'd really like to find us guilty."

Rose and Benjamin had stood a moment watching them before they came to the table, Ben whispered, "Honey, it does seem strange that none of them came even near to us the whole time."

Rose smiled, took his hand and said,"I Reached to them, warned them off, a repulsion Touch as soon as we got aloft. At least I got the message to Jerry."

"But how? We didn't have wrist phones. Oh, no, you didn't do that Reaching? You're not trying that again?"

"And why not? No better way to made connection. I won't honor your resentment Ben." She felt mild irritation at his stubbornness, especially after what he'd told her. "It's not telepathy, there can be no harm, no interfering with anyone's mind. It's a general awareness that reaches out. I think lot's of people do that, even though they don't admit it.One of these days, -- we'll -- ". Why did she take this perverse pleasure in needling him about this. She knew how he felt. She laughed at his look of consternation and said,"Oh, come on, let's go eat."

The others greeted them, but Rose was aware that they were more quiet as she and Ben came to the table.She appreciated the defference accorded their feelings on this special day. They dialed their food and hot cups of tea. Talk shifted to other things. Rose leaned to her son Andrew, pushing back the curling brown hair from his forehead. He and Anna were not so dark as she, but not so fair as their father.Anna's hair was like Benjamin's, blond and thick. Their skin was a golden olive, their eyes deep, penetrating blue. She said, "What're you planning Son? What'll the day be for you."

At sixteen, Andrew's body had shot up past his sister's, and now he towered over his parents. He moved restlessly as if energy pulled at the harness of his good manners. He said,"Mom, I'm still studying at the lab with Master Teacher Robin. You remember him?" She nodded and he went on,"He's given me some work, let me help in his research so I can learn. Mostly, I work in the film files, library and record data, just to keep up and understand what he's doing.I find things for him. He explains a lot, though Mom." He was suddenly eager to talk about it,"He's really great at that. It isn't as though I'm only a flunky. But I sit in on a lot of other lectures in the science department."

" But Son,have you time then for practice? For music?

He laughed," For six months I worked with Master Teacher Maria, you know that.She's a Simon Legree, she didn't let me get an hour of rest. I've worked, practicing, doing the math, writing the scores and learning generally how a symphony is created. She's one of the most -- most lucid teachers I've ever had, you know." His eyes had lit up, and Rose noticed how he looked when he talked of that young Master teacher.

aren't doing sex, Mom. She's -- she's different. She's special,I can't -- play -- not with her." He looked suddenly so serious, Rose was surprised, then he shrugged, "She told me to go ahead -- to compose the songs I wrote while I was on Vagabond Journey into a full musical. And I've begun that, so you don't need to worry about there being enough music in my life! THAT'S my relaxation, you know. "

"But what about today, Son"

"Well, I'm going to Center this morning, to Master Teacher Robin's explanation of what we did yeaterday, and then to seminar with all his students. this afternoon, I'll just take a couple of hours to get down to the river, too swim and sail,but I want to spend some time at the library. I've got some questions about my project and Robin won't answer them. he says search them out." Andrew made a face, then went on."I'm meeting my quartet this evening. We're playing at Jamie's party. D'you think that's enough?" She started to speak, smiling at his mild joke, but he interrupted,"Oh, yes, I'm getting enough exercise. We're going down river in the canoe races three days this week. Practice for the races at Festival. I'll take a flute along and play us past all the villages." He turned his body around, leaning against the table a little, to meet his Father's eyes. Then, standing, he leaned to kiss her, holding her hand a moment he said,"Mom, I know it's hard on you, Dad going and all, but we're here. We're going to miss him too."

She reached up to take his other hand from her hair and sat holding on to it. His caring comforted her and she remembered that today he would spend two hours with Benjamin, and that Ben had asked for those hours yesterday. So Andrew had a full day. "It's true Son, the day isn't long enough to do all you'd like. But you can eat at the Center to save time. Don't bother to come home to dinner." Then she let him go as she asked,"Do you have anything to do with that organ young Alice is building? "

He nodded, enthusiasm again in his voice,"I sure do. She asked for helpers and I was there second. Tommie was first, and the two of us got Agnes and Annetta and we've been working with Alice evenings. Alice does the planning and we help work out the building of it. She's studying with the cabinet makers Guild combined with physics lab for how to get the best sound from wood. Mom, she's got fascinating ideas and that organ's going to be something nobody ever heard before. We just pray the sound is good." His large blue eyes, so like his father's, seemed distant as he remembered. She saw that he was already in town. He shook himself, "Well, I've got to go. May your day live well." He gave her another brief hug and then another to his father. "I'll meet you at the Rock at lunch time, Dad." And he was off.

Anna had been quietly watching the scene but now she got up and began to brush crumbs and carry plates to the cleanser. Rose said, "Anna baby," And laughed at the grimace the young girl made at the name, "How about you? I don't want to pry,I just like to know ."

Anna smiled then but she couldn't repress a long sigh, "I know, Mama, I'm

Anna smiled then but she couldn't repress a long sigh, "I know, Mama, I'm going to be down at Alex's shop. I'm helping him get it ready. Three of us are their work crew and we're painting and designing the furniture. Russell is building it about as fast as we can design it. He's going to be good, you know. His term spent at Clandor wood working plants taught him how to do marvels with wood. And now he's using plasteel and metals to build with" She sighed, "I don't see how he does it.Some of our ideas aren't any good but we have to try them out sometimes before we find that out. Alex gets to put his stuff into the Market screens next year and he'll be selling furnitures in his little shop in Industrial Center by then. He's going to sell imports too. The most exotic he can find. Maybe he'll let me go on some of the buying trips." She studied her Mother's reaction to that intently, and tossed her head in satisfaction as she saw only interest.

"Well, you won't spend all day at that, will you?"

" No, this afternoon, Almira and I are going to work on that film we're making. We've got the cast of drama students who did the play's for last Autumn Festival to perform for us and help us build it into a movie.I'm going to head the camera crew this time, so I can work out some of my ideas. We have some younger kids learning with us so we have to take some time for them too." Again she took a deep breath,"And then, later on, I want to get to Almira's lecture on using music in Healing. I told Andy that I'd bring him the tape for that so he can watch it here. Anyway that's about it."

She had come to stand behind her parents and bent to kiss her father's neck.With one hand on each of their shoulders, she put her head between them to nuzzle against each parent in turn. Rose half turned, caressing her daughters cheek, smiling at her affection.

Ben said,"Anna, you won't forget?"

She said,"Not a chance, Dad. I'll be there."

Then with a quick movement, she caught up her jacket and left them. When Ben and Rose finished breakfast she said,"Benjamin, Love, I've planned nothing to day, except to help you get off. I'd like to spend time with you just maybe walking around the farm. Just talking,if that's all right."

He smiled, Honey, I'd enjoy a walk and a look at the whole farm once before I go. The snow's already melting enough so that we can walk easily,I think. I feel like stretching out, just saying farewell perhaps."

They left the hall, walked out over the deck, where the sun shone through clearing skys and the snow had begun to melt, leaving pools of water here and there. They stepped down from the deck into the hall garden where a few bedraggled narcissus were blooming through their burden of snow. Rose took his hand, their fingers twining together, and slid her other hand into her pocket to keep it warm. She said,"All this fuss I've made,Ben. It puzzles me too, you know. I can't help the feeling that I'm losing something, losing you,in fact. And I know better. I feel sad, and so angry at myself, and guilty for making you feel guilty, and then, I feel angry at you too." She frowned,"I'm being childish and I don't like it."

THE AWAKENING

She shook her head, making her hair swirl around her shoulders. "I don't know what's happening to me, you know. We've been taught since we were young to 'Balance" emotions. I've been doing it, and each time I have myself balanced, something comes into mind that unbalances me. I'm just almost ready to go see the Healer."

He was nodding, saying nothing, wanting her to talk. She went on."In the Temple this morning, I felt so free of all this. So accepting and so confident that our lives were good.I could stand beyond myself a little. See from a larger perspective, and now here I am, bogged down in myself again. I thought I'd got myself in balance, but I'm right back where I started last night." She bent her head, feelng shame like a hot stab in her throat , but she refused to turn that shame into blame of Benjamin.

He was silent. They crossed the gardens, where the only color, aside from the few early narcissus and a patch of bright yellow snow flowers, was clumps of small evergreens and a few tall slim spruce along one side. Acacia, already a great wall of gold, grew tall behind Ben's cottage. Starting down the wide pathway to the Farm fields, they could see the River gleaming through the shoreline forests, rolling in its dark winter fullness through the land. Heavy winter grasses made the ground beneath these deciduous trees green and somehow gave a feeling of springtime,even though the green showed through the mornings snow only in little clumps. The fields were smooth and still, birds rioted through the bare branches, disturbed by this late snow that covered their morning's food. One field of winter grain showed bright yellow green through the melting snow, some were stubble from last years harvest, and some deep rumpled meadow. They could see the sharp flash of reflected light from the force field posts at the edges of their farm fields. These carried energy in a thin stream around the field whenever some creature tried to cross from the wild meadows into the cropped fields. They worked much like the old electric fences of the past except they needed no wires at all and were more reliable.

The clouds swept back, leaving this strange day clear in the north and over the three north Valley towns, Jasper, Adwin and Denlock. The storm had moved south and turned to rain. Jasper and Denlock, to the east and west of Adwin, were dim bright glimmers in the morning distance. A little band of wild pigs was rooting along one edge of the grain fields, and Rose absently watched as they edged along making no effort to enter the grain field.The easy efficiency of those force field posts still seemed to her a miracle. Setting in the small metal posts had taken a few hours for all their fields. There would be no need to worry for the safety of whatever was inside that field. A Family in Clandor had invented the force field posts, and had given them to the Valley at the second Spring Festival during the early years of the Valley life. That gift had established a precedent, a competition that continued to this day. Amazing 'Gifts' had been offered, and the one chosen to be accepted, gave the Family much honor. The competition inspired very valuable inventions and those not chosen, were well paid for. The winning Family received, along with the honor, royalties on every unit built from its design.

Ben had entered more than one invention, one useful tool or idea but he had always been paid. He had not gained the HONOR. Rose broke her revery with a tug on Benjamin's arm. "Look, Ben through the river forest. There among the oaks". Under one massive oak just next to a sheltering cluster of pines where dark needles covered the ground, a group of children had created a tight shelter of pole and brush. Now the heavy dry grasses that thatched the roof were white with snow. The children were whipping the snow from the grass before their shelter. They were eight and nine year olds.

Ben and Rose watched them a moment, remembering their own wilderness training weeks and those of their children. They had lived on the land, built snug shelters, survived from the land itself,and had taken only a few basic supplies. They had been so proud. Andrew had enjoyed it so much he had continued long after the training time was over. Ben started to go to them,but her hand on his arm stopped him. The practice disturbed him and he had had a hard time when Anna and Andrew first went out. He knew it was worth while, Valley people could live most anywhere and make themselves fairly comfortable. They knew the land and were comfortable in it. Wherever they went, there was a familiar memory. He said,"It's so cold, Rosy, summer and autumn, that's the time they should go, not in this kind of weather. THey might get sick."

She shrugged. "Then they'd only know how to live when times are easy. Anyway, if anyone gets sick the Monitors would know, send help. You know that Ben." She spoke calmly, glad that her voice held no irritation.

He looked back at the children, his face suddenly stern, then finally he shrugged,"Well, at least here there's not apt to be any predator big enough to hurt them."

She smiled at him. He wouldn't admit what he had to know - the power of the Valley children to handle such animals .He was remembering Anna's month long stay in the mountains. She had felt such pride and joy, to be there alone, allowed to test herself. When she came home she told them that she had made a 'sister' of a female cougar with pups. Had met and earned its friendship. Anna had not known it was a thing an Earth Sensitive might have done, not an ordinary youngster. Ben had nearly gotten sick when he heard of it. Rose shuddered when she thought of it. But Anna had filmed much of her time there and they saw the proof of her tale. She had not thought it unusual at all. Now Rose watched the children beneath the oak, to see how well they had planned things, had arranged for their meals, etc. They were making a small fire to cook and gathering pine needles to refresh their sleeping places. At least ones this young would be out only two or three days.

She and Ben walked on, silently entered the 'shrubway' a double row of current,gooseberry and blue berry bushes that bordered each side of the path for a hundred yards. They sold these fruits in Adwin at the markets and stored what they needed for themselves in their processer. The snow was deeper here, shaded from the rising sun. Rose kicked at it, it was heavy, wet. It would not snow more. "You're better at this than I,Love. Even with all my years of practice and even with teaching Balancing, I haven't got my emotions in hand the way you do." She shrugged and kicked at the snow again, this time venting that anger.

He looked at her, seeing her nose red from the cold, her profile so familiar and beloved. He spoke gently,'You've always had better access to your feelings, Hon. It was easier for me because I'm just not letting my self feel much right now". He frowned at her look of consternation,"Well, I just have to wait until I get on my way, or I might not even go,you know."

She met his eyes, frowned and then nodded, "I suppose so. I guess I don't think of your side of this enough. But then, I think you've done what you needed to, and I've denied what I needed to do. " She looked at him thoughtfully,"You know Benjamin, maybe I'm just jealous. I do hate to admit this, and you must not use it to get back at me. I wonder how much my resentment is because I want to leave too,to go off myself? After all, Love, there's a lot I wish I could understand, know, about the things I question." She stopped, glanced at him.

He said, "You could tell me."

I've never been willing to admit, to make public my longing to know of that world of the Spirit, that inner quest that you don't deny, even though you won't talk about it." She spoke hesitantly and he knew that she was confiding a secret she had not admitted to herself."But that's a paradox, I haven't admitted to that longing, but I'm more willing to practice Talents that are waking in me, in lots of people. More willing than you are."

Suddenly a rush of tears silenced her.She was angry at the tears, angry at being thus unfair to Ben, making his leaving harder. She ducked her head that he might not know. Ben laughed, surprising her, he said,"If only you knew, Rose. I pretend better than you do. There've been times I wanted to sneak away, not tell anyone, and other times when I wanted to kidnap you and force you to go with me. Leave the kids behind even. I wanted you to ignore your own life for mine. And other times I wanted to strangle you because you seemed to be strangling me. When I denied my needs out of worry for you or the kids."

He stood still, feeling the sun warm on his face. It had broken through the scattering clouds and threw a network of shadows from barren current bushs across their bodies and on the snow beneath. It felt warm and comforting. Ben went on,"There are those times like now, when I feel such an over powering love for you that I wonder how I could permit myself to lose even an hour of time with you. Except that I know that you don't want to be with a half-person,which I would be if I denied these needs" He held both her hands in his, his blue eyes meeting her brown ones, serious, puzzled. She became aware of their intensity and her mouth curved up in a grin. Then, suddenly they both burst into laughter."Wow, Sweetheart, we're serious today." Then he added, serious again,"Maybe it's about time though."

Rose nodded as they resumed their walk. "We've avoided things too long, that's for sure. I hate to think of your leaving with an image of a poor pitiful mate left alone and grieving. I do think it will be all right.I'll manage my feelings, after a poor pitiful mate?" He met her eyes again, grinning,"Sometimes, I do. But are you sure you don't want me to?"

She bridled,"I don't want to admit that, but -- there might be a little truth in it."

"O.K. but don't be so hard on yourself." He wanted to take her in his arms again, but felt the futility of it. He had done that so many times. She didn't want comforting now. She didn't want him to feel sorry for her. Or did she? He said,"You want me to feel sorry for you? To see you as brave and long suffering? Well, maybe I want the same. I don't want you to remember me as a man who doesn't care, who's so obsessed with his own needs that he cannot consider his family and friends. So,you see, we both have wishes."

"Oh, yes, I suppose I do crave pity. I think it's my besetting sin. I've never wanted to admit that, but there's truth to it. I don't WANT to feel sorry for myself, Ben, I think I just like others to. Especially you!" She said it so seriously he almost didn't keep a straight face. But she sensed his humor, turned her face to him full of sudden anger, that changed to resentment, then shame and fear and then amusement. He watched the kaleidoscope of emotion run across her face, amazed that he was so aware of what lay beneath the expression. But also subtly stung at how clearly she had known his own amusement at her. Were they that sensitive to one another? She managed a little smile,"I suppose I'm being silly?"

He pressed her hand,"You're being Rose. Noticing yurself and admitting what you see. It's one of the things I love about you, you know?"

They walked in silence then, their hands clinging together. Their heads were bent and their eyes fastened on the pathway. Ben lifted his head after a while, looking with a desire to memorize again the fields where so much life even now occurred, the River through the trees, the hills across the flat land that rolled on and gradually were lost in the high mountains. He slid an arm around Rose's shoulders and they walked across to the River's edge. A steep bank dropped away into the deep water of a good fishing pool. Heavy grass and leafless berry vines held the edge intact. So many memories here, picnics, lovemaking, fights, family gatherings, all of it sweeping across Ben's mind, and he thought Rose shared in those images, so sharp were they. Again he had that odd sense that she realized what he did.

They looked at each other and smiled, "It feels so good to come to the familiar spots where so much has happened. Then I can keep the memories while I travel. But I never seem as able to visualize when I'm not with you, Dearest. Why do you suppose that is?"

She looked at him sharply, a piercing study of his face, a hope and then, a resignation."Perhaps you ought to figure that out, my Love. Maybe we're more closely attuned than you're willing to admit. "

Suddenly he seemed to have forgotten the question,"Oh, Rosy, I don't want to leave this time with the torn shreds of your feelings trailing behind me. I don't want to. This walk,this talking is so good.It will give us both peace. After all Honey, I think I want to feel sorry for MY self a little. Last time I was so angry for so long and then I discovered that I was using anger to cover all the hurt, and the so long and then I discovered that I was using anger to cover all the hurt, and the guilt." He turned to her, his eyes gentle and thoughtful,"I think that's what I learned during that time. Why I feel so furious when you resist my leaving. I can't even fight you, because I feel guilty." He shook his head sadly, I didn't really discover much about the questions that keep plaguing me, maybe because I have to discover these things first?" He felt her hand tighten. This was what he had not told her, had not admitted. He sighed, shaking his head. "The Teachers told us, but their teaching doesn't mean anything until we live it. I couldn't seem to work it out here with you.There are things happening, things I just barely notice, and can't quite catch, as though some meaning slips past attention too swiftly to catch. It happens between us, Rosy, between us so often." Then he frowned, a hope lighting his eyes," There was a woman I met once a few years ago when I traveled, she seemed more than a Master Teacher. I hardly dared talk to her. But I listened when others did." His eyes were lost in distance of memory,"And she spoke of that necessity for identifying what we begin to realize. Only, I think we refuse to admit it.I still don't know. I want to find her again, Rose. Find her and maybe find out what she meant. Learn from her, if she would teach me. But she was old then, and I'm afraid she might have died."

It was the first time she had heard him speak of there being something happening between them that he did not understand. And her heart nearly stopped in hope and fear. He went on, seemingly unaware of her attention." She told me, Rose, that my vision was not clear. And I got angry, and she -- she didn't say more,but talked of something else. I wish I had listened. What is it I'm blind to? I've practiced balancing, since I was a child, and I think I'm pretty good at it now.She had told us,(there were always others with her) that we must learn to keep our balance all the time.Once, out of the blue, she looked at me,and said that there was something right here at home, something between you and me, perhaps, that I'm not seeing. That's when I got mad."He glanced at her, seeing her intense attention, but not her hope, "I suppose that should have warned me, but it didn't then. I want to ask her now what she meant."

"She knew about me -our family?"

"He nodded, absently,"Of course," then, "but I never thought to ask how?" His surprise was real.

She nodded, the hope still there in her eyes, "Oh, Ben, you'll see it. It's more than I can say. Maybe there're some things a person can't really say, until the other one understands a little." She knew she sounded mysterious, but she didn't know how to say it otherwise. He looked at her surprised, then his qaze flickered away, uneasy.

"Perhaps there're things I don't see. I think there must be. But I'm not sure what's meant by it all either. I do want to know.I intend to find out! After all, it's reached the point now when I absolutely MUST!" His vehemence at first frightened her and then opened a dawning joy. He was intending to discover what she was herself knowing a little of and if he did - then maybe she could understand more.She might even be able to speak to him of her Vision beyond the darkness that was everyday living, beyond the stillness that had been shattered by the blinding Light.The Light that had waked her as if from dream. She might tell him of what she feared BEYOND the dawning of that Light.The Light he was saying had begun to touch his own mind. But beyond it? Beyond it she could not bear to enter.

And yet, focussing at the in-most center of herself, had she not stood beyond herself? Was that still place of perception not the Light that was Soul. Letting her mind touch the thought now, she felt it burn, felt her self shy from the idea. The IDEA was what scared her, not the reality of that centering point. Being there, was wholly alive, full of a dawning truth. Then there was no need for a name. Intellectually, she could admit the fact of it, because it was part of the teaching. But afterward she desparately needed to explain to herself. In meditation she was aware! But immediately returning to ordinary mind, she excused it as some anomaly, some strangeness that was no part of herself after all. And was that because she COULDN"T explain? The thought of deliberately seeking for that state of consciousness, that point beyond herself, was too much to risk. There had been moments when she had even questioned her sanity. So powerful was the difference of that Self. Yet, every instinct, every desire drew her toward it.

He said,"The Teachers haven't explained things enough, you know"

She said,"They only do what we ask them. Their task is to respond to questions, not to lecture us about things we don't seem to want to know." She reflected,"But then, they always do give us the Teaching."

He nodded, watching her, understanding growing,." But you said there were things you couldn't tell me, that I didn't understand enough. What did you mean?" Anger threaded through his voice, and he drew that anger away. She was glad .

She slid her hands up his arms to catch his shoulders."The necessity to 'know',which you seem to have in abundance, is what will make that clear to you. Maybe it's true, you can't find it with me. It may be as much our need to - to grow up, I think." She smiled at the phrase, it seemed too simple. He kept looking at her, his mind racing, bringing many things into focus, events, teachings, memories. Long struggling thoughts of his own began to shape. He felt a thread of hope. But he could not make the thoughts take shape, they fell away, as if blown by a wind of resistance. There must be something he would not allow himself to See. That thought itself surprised him. He held it there, wondering. He twisted his body in the mental struggle and turned to walk again.

He said, "Rose, I know there're things you know -- that I don't know. Things the Teachers have told us that I didn't understand. I remember you would ask questions and I didn't understand your questions." He gripped her hand so hard it hurt., but she made no sound, the words were precious to her. He had never spoken such an idea before. I think I must find a way to know, to ask. I must find the words to ask what I don't know how to ask." He gave a short brusk laugh, "Does that make sense, my Darling?"

"Whatever it is, it makes sense to me. I am glad that you said that." They like this side of me that gets selfish, petty, and possessive. Even dependant at times. I don't like that and I won't let it limit your life. I can't despise myself for it either, but I've got to learn how to encompass what it means. There are the outer manifestations of these changes in us, that we call the Talents.. Except we only joke about them. We don't take them seriously. Well, I think I ought to do that".

She took a huge breath as if entering fearful country. "Sometimes, when we see very great beauty, or become still, aware in the moment fully, when we feel the tide of music or the life of the Valley itself, we know a kind of wonder. I think that the Earth is naturally so very beautiful as to break a human heart. I think perhaps that's why so many people in the past, refused to really let themselves be aware of Her. I think Her beauty is part of our learning, that beauty is what will eventually wake us up. Look now, what we see from here! There the roll and heave of Earth, shaping itself, designing the grand mountains and the small hidden places, the endless varieties of growing things, of sky and clouds. and the whole combined, in barren austerity or in lush life. Seeing Earth - fully aware - the way we've been taught, that alone will bring us to a point of Recognition." She turned to him, frowning, struggling to make clear these new thoughts.

She nodded vigorously, satisfied."Yes, that's what I want to say! The Earth will wake us to wonder through Her beauty. And the wonder will lead us to what is beyond Her. That's what I mean. I know that you've known of that -- that you've felt the Touch of it."

"What's that got to do with this inner Light that you spoke of? This is all out here - - and thats -- " he waved a hand, unable to find words.

She was looking at the land before her, feeling it's aliveness, the thrust of power from it that helped her find words. Tears ran down her face unnoticed, and she added,"I think maybe it's all the same, inner and outer, actually seen from Soul point of view. It's that I'm afraid of. Yet I want to stand there, stand there always. I want to Ben, my Love, and I don't dare. There is something beyond what we know, something so Great it is -- actually frightening,and I shrink from Seeing. Shrink away and I don't know why!"

She realized she had never spoken these ideas even to herself, let alone to Benjamin. Perhaps this walk, this immanent separation pushed her beyond her self. It was a risk. The greatness of the risk was marked by the fear and pain of the telling . She was silent, amazed at her own words.

He nodded, frowning, not looking at her, feeling a strange embarrasment and said,"Are you talking now about that -- that Talent? What I've heard some one refer to as the Mind Reach?" There was a note of contempt in his voice that shook her.

Disappointed so deeply she could not speak, she shook her head. When, back there, had he ceased to hear? Then after a moment, she wiped her hands over her face, glad that he had not seen. She felt how carefully he was holding himself from her. She drew her voice to quiet,"No, Ben, that's only a result. It's just something that happens when we pay attention and are aware, I think.I don't understand it either. But then, who does?" With a strength born of need she tried again,"But don't you sometimes sense that there is - something 'OTHER '- something beyond everything else? Something that is so very, very Real?" She clenched her fist, trying to find words that might touch him,"Maybe it's what people have called Spirit, or God, because it has that quality, you know."

But he hadn't heard. Roughly, he shook his head, as if shaking away unwanted thoughts. "No, no I can't. I don't see how -- it makes no sense. It's too much like fantasy, and I worry about you, that you take it so seriously, Rose. Sometimes, when you seem so distant, so far from us, I worry." He finally glanced over at her,"But then, perhaps the woman, her name is Jessie, can explain you for me too." He smiled but his eyes were bleak.

She smiled sadly,"Well, I'll bless her many times if she does. I'd be glad of your going if you come to see what I mean."

Their eyes met, he said," Talking is amazing,isn't it. It seems as though I"ve realized a lot, just thinking out loud together. We're listening to each other. Other times, we've spent all our time arguing, yelling, or being silent. And our teachers told us then what we were doing, but we didn't hear. I didn't at least. Maybe that's what you mean by growing up?"

She walked with steady effort, the slow climb through the winding pathways up the high north hills. She gazed out over the Farm below, the fields flat below a low knoll along the river. The buildings were scattered over the top of the hill. They stood on the first of those rising forested hills that ranged between the Farm and the mountains. The hill on which their Hall was built, and the three on which Adwin was built, were surrounded by a rich flood plane where the river had left its gift of silt through long years. The broad flat topped hills of Adwin were directly across from the hill where they stood. The three town Centers, great concentric Rings, one inside another,on each of the three hills, looked from here like three walled castles. The Valley flattened rapidly beyond where the Green River curved several times, so that Jasper, only ten miles beyond Adwin, was built on flat land. Rose struggled with her thoughts.She wanted to say something more, something Benjamin could take along on this journey,could think about perhaps. She didn't know how. Finally she blurted out, "Surely Ben, you've sensed the Earth Life. The way the Earth Sensitives do, at least a little? I've noticed the way you feel about trees, for instance."

He looked up at the great trees, whose limbs hung over the pathway,."Finally he nodded,"I admit that's true. I do feel some kind of rappour,some - as if I sense their intelligence somehow. I wonder what they think of us,in fact, as though something in me knows they do.And yet I think that's foolish, you know." He looked suddenly apologetic. But I admit it fascinates me. So strong they are! So deep in Earth."

She nodded, hope again in her eyes,"You see? You sense them the Way Jane does, only she won't - doesn't - admit anything at all, except that she loves them. I think we Valley people just refuse to admit that we're aware of more than people used to be. That we're sensitive to -- to a lot that we don't admit." They were turning down now, into the fields again and across toward the Farm hill.

were turning down now, into the fields again and across toward the Farm hill.

Ben laughed, slid an arm around her shoulders and drew her closer,"I admit, Sweetheart that I've talked to the trees, that I do that. I always think it's sort of joke I have. But you're saying I ought to take it seriously?" He felt an obscure relief to tell her of that faascination he had always had. The air was colder. The wind had risen again. The day was clear but cold. The night's snow still lingered in shady places. They walked faster, going back down the twisting path much faster than they'd come up. Her arm circled his waist, and a thumb hooked in his belt. They reached the low fields below the Hall. They started the climb up.

Rose lifted one hand to touch Ben's face tenderly. He took her face gently in his two hands and softly explored each curve and rounded cheek, slid his fingers along each familiar line of chin and throat. They had received knowledge of trust and of love, love that could bear more reality. To be able to give and receive this day was a blessing.

CHAPTER THREE

The passing of a year. The Valley Council.

During the months after Ben left, Rose watched her anger and grief push its way through now and then, but mostly she was at peace. When he finally called, she was glad he had initiated the contact and glad to tell him of her love and acceptance and that he must make the Journey as he chose. She had settled into the daily pattern of living . But gradually as the months passed, she knew that she was aware of him, of where he was. At first the knowledge seemed to her imagination, wishful thinking, but she began to realize that her very awareness of the world around her was finer, surer. She COULD Reach, and she did do that. When she did, she found him, the clear impression of Benjamin, her mate, but he was not aware of contact. She, herself, trembled with the realization, the image of him, so real, the world around him, the people he was with. Then as instantly as she caught the glimpse, it was gone. She did not understand what she did. She thought to go to the Master Teachers - to inquire, to discover perhaps what this meant. If it was an actual skill, then how could she focus her Touch so that he could realize her presence. Should she ask the Master Teachers? Would they tell her this strange Reach was an abberation that was not healthy? Something she should forget? What was it exactly? A mind Talent? Or acute imagination? She didn't know and wondered why she had never asked. Perhaps she was avoiding any Master Teacher lately, since -- since --. Like a vivid scene, reoccurring - real, the uneasy memory of Master Teacher Gwen coming to speak to her of Anna. Gwen said Anna needed to be tested for training as Master Teacher. That would mean her little girl must go the the Monitor Stations. She pushed the memory away. She didn't want to think of it now.

Rose had attended the East Station for a year, studying with those Monitors there, but not to be Master Teacher. John and Margo had sent her reluctantly when she was ten because she seemed to them to absent herself, to draw into herself so deeply they thought she was sick of some disease. The Healers had insisted she go to the Station. She had learned much there, especially not to fear her visions, her inner perceptions. Sometimes it was a vivid scene, she saw, as if living on an inner plane, another reality. Sometimes, only a swift unexpected Touch of Light, the unexplainable and in-describable, a spreading of Light through her brain. It was as if consciousness opened up, allowed further perception, but into realms that had no familiar connections, not enough even to explain them. So what she remembered mostly was 'Light'. Could she call it an 'Illumination of mind?' It was clear she 'knew' something, but not clear what it was she knew. She could find no words to hold the experience. Yet, from that moment of awareness, the entire world seemed renewed, alive and intent with power.

THE AWAKENING

The widening of awareness occurred often enough in those years. Finally she had entered into meditation with the intention of seeking that experience of transcendant Light. Seek and try to understand. Though the Monitors told her not to fear, she continued to fear. It took her beyond herself, it opened her to dimensions of being transcendant and alive beyond all she had known, but it was as if part of herself attended and other parts slept refusing to acknowledge. And that reluctant brain-mind did not understand. Monitors had taught her how to focus, how to stand steady in the Light and listen, be aware.

It was through that focus that she discovered there were dimensions beyond this physical one and that they were dimensions of Mind itself. She had steadied, dealt with the fears of that magnificent strangeness. She learned how to perceive beyond ordinary sight and still remain functional in the outer world. Then she had been sent home to practice all she learned so that she could continue further training when she had mastered this much. But then, with the busy schedule of her adolescent years she had been utterly immersed in everydayness. She had begun to forget a little.

As a young child she had begun to ask the kinds of questions that Master Teachers watch for and they had gone to her parents the way they had come to her now about Anna. She cringed. She had felt herself different, afraid, when she had come back from that study, though the stay there had been wonderful, full of a love she thought she would never know again. Those who taught her understood even when she could only make awkward attempts at the question. And they never laughed at her or told her she was strange. That had been a gift. Would she deny that gift to her own daughter?

She remembered that none of her friends, as far as she knew, had gone to the Stations. And then came Benjamin, marriage and the children, the building of their town. There had been no time. During those years, the slow awakening of her mind had drawn her to that edge of new consciousness, what awareness of it she allowed herself to acknowledge had been when she was in Temple or in retreat and could meet the intensity without others knowing. Did she need to go back to the Station? To learn what was happening to her?

What, after all, was that immersion in Light, as though the universe itself had caught its breath in a stillness absolutely pregnant with possibility. Yes! That WAS the sense of it. Stillness that held all that was within itself. Did she fear the truth of it, rising from Benjamin's obvious distrust of such practices? He would not acknowledge even the possibility of Reaching. And how could that Reaching, that simple awareness of others, possibly relate to that deeper wonder? But she knew without doubt that that early sensitivity was reoccurring, becoming unavoidable. Light trembled at the edges of consciousness, meditation frequently carried her through the stages of mind stillness to a greater Stillness. To a radiance that seemed to threaten to penetrate her very being. Yes, threaten, for, though she argued with herself, that it must be harmless, so wondrous was it, she still felt afraid. She knew, without forming the fact into words, that she avoided that depth of meditation most of the time.

She shrugged away these thoughts. It was good just to be happy, enjoying her work, her life, the Family and realizing that she could live very well without her Mate. Unreasonably that fact roused feelings of guilt, a sense of betrayal and worry, until she went to talk to Elinda, Master Teacher who taught most of the Balancing for Adwin children. After a little talk, she realized that she could love Ben as much as before, without needing him. In fact, her ability to Love was greater as she acknowledged and released her need. The realization stunned her and she would sometimes not believe it at all, then she would return and find again, that it was true. After a few visits, she knew it within herself. The Teacher called it release, but she felt it as an opening so that a flow of Love moved through her the way breath moves in and out. Somehow it seemed related to that Love she had known at the Station when she was a child. But she did not ask the Teacher about that inner radiance of Light.

She wanted to tell Benjamin, but she knew she could not. Thought could not be Sent, but images could be. Wouldn't that work? Feelings could be Sent. Why not --? But she knew she would not because he didn't want to hear her speak of such things. What if she were to go to the Station and study further? Perhaps Monitors could Send actual thoughts. The idea troubled her.

Spring Festival came with all the eager joy, noise, laughter and worries. Crowds of people came from all the northern towns and villages. Adwin was the farthest north of the three little north Valley towns, and her festival was last of the Valley. Here it was that a final celebration always occurred. Awards were given, not for winners of events, but for participants. For those skilled enough in cooperative gaming, to complete the games, or run the distances, or make the River journeys in the little boats every fishing village kept. There were a few awards for winners of races, but such competitions were minor, few sought them out. Participation was the key note of Festival. People streamed along the Highways, swarmed into different Festival towns on belts. The Festivals began at the most southern point of the Valley and as the spring advanced, they moved north, so that some Valley town was in Festival during the whole first month of spring.

The crowds gathered for music, dance, exhibits of art, inventions, ideas, poems, new songs by the Vagabonds or by town musicians. Cooks out did themselves in preparing varieties of food, and drink. Theatre groups, dance troupes, all the entertainers the Valley had, could and sometimes did, move from one town to another. But every town had its own troupes too and every citizen became an entertainer. The winter's research in laboratory, field or factory was displayed and awards given. The Valley appraised itself and found itself good. Spring Festival was a time of celebration of the land and of making things.

The Family settled into the summer work, the Farm was well cared for by Jane and Steve and the others worked in Adwin. Days passed and soon they were looking forward again to the Summer Festival in June. That too was a time of abandon, of celebration and of Gathers. The Family Gathers of mid-summer were most important. It was the time Family groups came together to make their yearly committment and to take care of Family business or plan for the next year. Summer Festival was a celebration of people and relationship.

It was a time of reunion and assertions of loyalty or of problems among them. Rose wanted to talk to her Family during Gather about that problem of Reaching, of making contact through mind, but she could not bring herself to do it. The taboo against psychic skills had been strong in the early years. Too many misuses of those misunderstood Talents, and examples of malicious fraud had given the label of evil to what might have been innocent talents. She hugged to herself in fear and tremendous joy the intermittent Touchs of that all encompassing Light, that thrust of LIFE through her heart. But she never spoke of it.

She watched others, wondering whether they might have known that electric joy of a Reach. She could not tell. Either others were as wary as she, or they were ignorant of such Touch. Yet, so many times, she was aware that she looked at Jerry and he would simply nod, and they both knew of one another. She would watch her daughter and feel some tantalizing edge of contact which she recoiled from as at something fearful. She did not understand why she recoiled. She found herself closing - held separate from others in fear that there might be that strange unexplainable Touch. And again, she didn't know why, but she refused to ask or even to think much about it because then she must find our why.

So the summer passed and autumn came with the brilliant cool days, the sudden brief rains, and harvests and the Autumn Festival with its showing off of all that had been accomplished during the years work. People flew, or hiked into the mountains and hills, or traveled through the land in groups or alone. The people celebrated the land itself in Autumn. The Green River and the numerous ponds and lakes were full of every kind of floating vehicle. Air car ballets, colorful patterns in the sky, with streamers decorating the brilliantly painted cars. Then belt riders doings dances in the lower sky, above flaming trees, over the harvested fields, for the Autumn was the celebration of Earth, water and sky and of fulfillment of dreams.

Then came finally winter Festival, the time for celebration of the farthest reaches and creations of Mind and Spirit. This was the time of stillness, of winter whiteness and solitude, or of hibernation in the caverns of one's own thought and imagination. Here was the gestation period for all the other Festivals. And here too, Valley People directly addressed the living Spirit that flamed within their hearts and called upon it to inspire and point toward that path they must take. Rose thought of Ben, and knew that he was well. She wrote to him and he to her and their letters told them of their heart's longings. For in these letters Rose was finally able to speak of her own deep questions, but she did not, yet - speak of her tentative Touch.

He told her only of his joy, of the discovery finally of the where abouts of a Teacher he had been seeking. He had found her and her name was Jessie, the path that led to her was on his way home. Rose felt the joy of that promise. When in December she got a video - phone call from him, she found herself chattering aimlessly, then fell silent as he watched her, smiling. And then, looking at him, letting her eyes move over the image of his face, she found that a weight had fallen from her heart, that she had let him go. And he nodded, and they talked a little , but he said he was not sure when he would be home. She watched herself allow that old familiar pain, but now, it faded even as she watched. He was free to live his life. If he chose not to live it all with her, it was all right.

However, he seemed to have some joy in him that she had never seen. His eyes were serene, his whole manner carried a stillness that gave her pause and she felt a sudden shyness for here was in him something unfamiliar. Unfamiliar but deeply alive. It wasn't until he had closed the circuit that she felt the power of her eagerness to see him, to know what that new quality might be.

During that winter Rose did two things that were for her extraordinary. She deliberately Reached out toward that pulse of energy that was Benjamin, knowing he would not receive. And she held her first meeting with Valley Council members by Holograph imaging. She had a cold, felt too tired to fly to Santiago, and arranged the connection. And when the circuit closed, she saw the Council around her, she also knew for the first time, an astonishing Touch. A clear, powerful almost frightening response as from one whose vision was great. There was one member conscious beyond anything she had known, one who smiled at her as if in secrecy, but who carried a message to her. Before the meeting began, in an instant of acute awareness, Rose KNEW Benjamin would be home soon. She knew there was with him some one who would know what she needed to know. One full of some strength and beauty she had known only rarely even in the Station. Perhaps Benjamin would bring help to her after all. But now, she must discover that illuminating mind among the Council members.

That Holographic meeting with the Council, was new to her, exciting. When all their images were there, in the hall with her, and she knew that she herself appeared to be in the Council chambers, she was full of a great pride of accomplishment. The technology of the Valley was advancing steadily. Now, if only the depths of the heart could as clearly be seen. For that was the technology of the Spirit. And that was the Valley Dream.

Yet there was another event in that inner life that she shielded from those around herself. She did not speak of a growing awareness, of moments when she broke through the webs like veils between the visible and invisible,and stood in that Astral world only one dimension beyond this physical one. She broke through and could not explain how. She saw there the unseeable and was awed and afraid. And she saw that that dimension was as troubled in its own way as was this one. There was no solution to the human problem there.

She went to the library and checked through into the World Library and studied all that she could about such things. She reviewed films over and over, looking for understanding. She read of all those who had searched out understanding of the life of mind and Spirit, who had distinguished between the psychic and the Spiritual. She learned that standing 'out of body' she was simply in an outer corridor of this world, it was the Psychic realm, no more of Spirit than

THE AWAKENING

the physical world.

She read, or scanned miles of materials, searching for one passage that would apply to her own dilemma. She thought again of returning to the Station, remembering their utter kindness, their absolute firmness, their precise discipline. But she put the decision off. Why not? Did she have less courage than Benjamin? Finally the year passed and winter was ending. It was the anniversary of Benjamin's leaving. Surely, he would come soon!

She spent a morning in late winter grieving, angry, full of dispair, as if she must indulge herself with a little pity. Then, comforting herself that she knew he was near and coming home, she brushed off the emotions and settled to work again.

She was due to meet with the Valley Council at Santiago. She looked forward to the trip, to being again in the lovely city of the sky. She would feel that nugget of joy growing in her at the knowledge of Ben's return though she had said nothing to the Family because she could not bring herself to speak of her method of discovery. She had begun even to doubt her own knowledge. Who could have been there near Ben? With him?

Her service on the Council was a great pride to her and she deliberately reminded herself of it as a comfort to the wounded child in herself who wanted its Mate so. She served as a Junior Elder.

Valley Elders got their name because in the early years they were the old ones of the people. Now they could be of any age, but the name stuck. Rose was a junior member, but held equal vote. The Council was watch dog, governing body, and planning commission for the Valley. Every Citizen must serve on town councils but only those who chose and were voted to serve, took seats on the Valley Council. Always on any council there were students sitting in to learn the ways of government and economics and in the process, to learn of human relationship in such bodies. The Valley Council held itself responsibile for maintaining a harmony within itself, between its members that would be a teaching to the students and its junior members. To be able to solve problems, do business, make major Valley decisions and to do that with skilled mediation of differences among themselves, was their pride.

Rose arrived at Santiago on a late winter day when snow fell lightly in the north, but here, the forests were dappled with the gold green of diciduous trees leafing out. The fields spread for miles around the forests, groves of fruiting trees clustered here and there in both field or forest, were in various stages of blooming. Some like clouds of snow, some with fat buds reddening the bare trees. Early flowers already brightened the hills in wide swaths of color. Come so far south, she felt as though she had leaped ahead several weeks into the spring.

She stood a moment at the landing grid, then went down to the 'leaf' along which the Council Hall hung. She walked to the webbed 'wall' that edged all structures of Santiago and stood, looking out over the miles of Valley below. It always astonished her. People swarmed over the 'stemways' and the myriad 'leaves' that grew out from the main trunks. So many people! Where did they all live? She watched a few minutes, the color and variety of clothes, of behavior, skin color, size and shape of people, amazed her again. Santiago was variety. She felt the passing of people around her and knew that some of them were already moving to the Hall. Council meetings were open and many people attended. Some out of interest, some because they would run for office in another year.

She walked across the half acre of 'leaf' toward the Hall, climbed up a set of broad stairs to another and went on to the entrance. She felt the reverberations of energy from within the Hall where some of the Elders already sat. Fourteen months of her first term and she could not deny that the energy created by these gathered Elders was great. At first, she had attributed it to her nervousness, lack of experience sitting on this august body. More than once the idea had floated into mind, persisted, that there was Mind Touch between these quiet people. Could there be a possible 'Mind joining'among them ? What a way to look at a problem, she had thought, how much greater could be there comprehension and therefore their recognition of new possibilities! Then in a panic of denial, she had pushed aside the thought. Now, here it was again, nagging.

She pushed the whole idea away, as fantasy, and not worthy of her. The council needed her undivided attention if she were to be of any value at all. But the question would not fade, drifting in as though it shaped itself from its own substance. She wondered whether any of the others ever thought such things. The idea itself was not alien to her. Master Teachers had taught that when they began to realize more clearly the nature of reality, they would also know disciplines of Mind and Heart that would wake them to possibilities of realizing mutually. She remembered how pleasing she had thought the phrase - realizing mutually. This morning as she settled into her chair, adjusting it to her body shape, she felt such a strong sense of that energy flow that she looked around startled. Surely she must be imagining. If she weren't careful the Council might consider her unfit for such service.

Then, as if moved by a touch of impatience, she turned to Grace, the Elder from Clandor and one of the oldest members. Grace looked at her, met her eyes. Rose felt a press of insistence, a gentle nudge as though Grace were asking a small favor? Rose frowned, then her face went through several swift changes, from troubled to frightened, to pure simple astonishment. And an overpowering sense of relief. Why relief? What?

Rose clenched against that Touch, for that was surely what it was, and Rose could not believe an old woman, one of the old ones, would allow such, let alone approve. She loosened a little, reached out, looked finally again into Grace's eyes, not seeing anyone else for the moment,. She could hear movement around her, other members coming in, some of the seats for the public being filled, but it seemed a faint whisper against this slow current of energy. She felt herself touch against that energy, that AWARENESS. Yes, she was simply aware that she realized -- that Grace 'called' her. Silently, within mind, a contact for her attention. That was all it was, yet it was powerful and strange. Rose had to steel herself against flinching away again. She held steady, wanting to know. Willing!

She remembered the theory! Her teachers had taught her well and she summoned all her memory, drew herself to attention and focussed. With every ounce of her energy she Reached. And nearly bounced off that waiting receptive mind. The laughter she felt, yes, FELT, did not hear, was reflected in Grace's merry smile, her twinkling eyes. It was as though she were saying,"Ah-hah, so you are receptive after all, Rose of Adwin!"

It was as though some one Touched her delicately and guided her mentally, guided her into a rappour so deep, so warm and inclusive, tears came to her eyes. To be part of something like this! To participate in perception seemed awesome. And she looked again into Grace's eyes, wanting and a little afraid. But Grace merely nodded, and abruptly withdrew. Rose felt the sudden loss like a pain. To be so near another, to Touch in this way -- it had been , although without thought of any kind, so very real and CONSCIOUS. Then Grace Sent an image, clear and sharp. Rose thought no one knew of it but herself, until she glanced at the faces of the two members sitting between them. Rose translated the images and knew that Grace was pleased to have reached her and that she wanted Rose to know this strength of mind was special.

Then, at Rose's questioning face, she nodded, and said softly aloud, "Yes, we share in this way, it is almost necessary today for Valley Elders to be so attuned. There is so much we must be aware of not only in the Valley itself, but within one another. You can see that subterfuge is difficult, honesty is reinforced. We hope you will serve with us for years, we need your communion." She grinned and the old weathered face seemed to Rose beautiful and young.

The man beside Rose had turned and was looking down at her, his own smile friendly. Jerome, fifty five, half bald, plump and short, with a clear incisive mind that could see a problem from many angles at once. Rose met those deep,grey eyes, their candor reassuring."Yes, Rose, we need you here, you might consider becoming an Elder next term and taking a permanent place. You have a strong talent ,you know."

Grace's eyes had never left Rose's face, she said,"You must help us to teach, Rose. The people of the Valley are ready for greater things than they know."

Rose nodded, she wanted to do just that. This was too astonishing, too abrupt, to find this Talent she had feared and delighted in was accepted. She wrestled with old fears, they seemed to be shredding about her, loosening. She wanted to Touch again, enter into that vast -- was it a Joining? Was that what the Teachers had meant? She was relieved at the return to 'normal.' And then equally surprising, a new, strange sense of being alone,utterly alone, as if she had been torn from a greater part of herself.

She closed her eyes, nodding to Grace, with an effort to be polite but she needed desparately to be separate, closed off and within herself. The others realized that and turned from her. She felt almost as if a circle of calm had settled around her, enclosed her from them all. And in that, she gathered herself and drew strength. This, then, was an initiation. Nothing less. And she had passed across that threshold, had been able to perceive, to realize. This was not much different from that Reach she had made toward Ben last week, not knowing exactly how, not having strength enough. But then she had been stingingly met by that powerful Touch, last week, that Touch through which she had known that Benjamin was near at last.And she HAD known it, had accepted, had let the excitement of the fact blind her to the method of discovery.She did not think of HOW she knew,as if that were Taboo and should be set aside from thought.

Now, however, when some one like Grace encouraged her 'fantasies' how could she longer doubt? She let the thought shape itself, firmly, and then with a great sigh of profound relief, as if letting go of a dam that had held back energy beyond measure, she accepted again.This time, she looked around, others were glancing at her, the Hall was filling and the members were all there.

A bell sounded and she sighed. She looked around, always impressed with this lovely Hall. People still entered the great carved doors, but they hurried now. The main Hall was floored with tiles set into a pattern almost as intricate as the tapestries of the Vagabonds. It was a retelling of the history of their Valley and there was a section, the width of the Hall, and eight feet wide, yet untiled, covered with carpeting, because new tiles were added each five years. The record there would,in the end, depict history over more than a hundred years.Idly she wondered whether they would begin on the leaf floors outside after that, or perhaps one of the walls.

The center section where the Council sat was raised up two steps so that all could see and hear. Ingenious speakers, imbedded in tables and the arms of chairs made the conversation as clear to the farthest person back as it was to the members once it was turned on. Long narrow windows broke the high walls and brilliant sunlight poured into the room, so that the colors in the tiles seemed like a scattering of jewels, until one looked closely reading the pictorial history.

She reached to take a cup of hot tea, wanting that nourishment, the comfort of the heat of it just now. the Twelve Elders sat around the table with the juniors here and there among them.Juniors changed every year or two, so that a steady stream of Valley people experienced the work of the Council, but now and then, one was asked to continue membership and take the position of full Elder. Rose felt a surge of pride that she had been so asked. Was that ability to Mind Touch the criteria? Or at least one of the criteria?

The room grew still, a stillness that made the combined breathing of all the people audible like a soft sigh. Rose felt the intensity, the growing power of energy and then, gently again the nudge, the Touch. this time, she responded without hesitation, with eager willingness . She Reached, wildly, inexperienced, she felt the others slightly shaken by her suddenness and then their amusement.One did have to learn grace even in this strange skill, she supposed. But the meeting of minds was clear and affirming. So real she could not longer tolerate that nagging suspicion that she had imagined it all earlier . This was REAL.

THE AWAKENING

She felt a belonging that penetrated through all the lonliness that had lain beneath her life. She had not known of it's presence so clearly until now that she knew of its ending. She was profoundly grateful. She wondered whether she could learn to take this for granted.As she realized the thought, she knew the others shared it and nodded. Yes, she could! It was as if her mind itself opened, unfolded from long weary closure into a larger consciousness. Awareness enhanced many fold for all her senses. The world around,the room,the people,were revealed anew.

This Joining was a source of understanding and wisdom, each person's comprehension multiplied many times simply by being Joined so. Vision was enlarged so that her breath caught in amazement,she was conscious of more, so much more that she could not order it into ideas fast enough,could not absorb the meaning of all she knew. THAT would take time! She felt overwhelmed as though she stepped into a vast sea, a great resource available and as near as her breath. She felt their support, their subtle and swift Teaching. And with such tenderness, of Love! But then, how could people Join in rage, or fear? Could human minds Join in hatred? Truly Join, as this was?

She knew without understanding that Joining, by its nature, excluded minds that hated.She saw a wide sweep of images, her questioning mind was being answered. A mind still sunk in fear or selfishness did not find its way up high enough to Touch. It was a fulfillment, a condition of that highest point of consciousness.Once conscious, Joining MEANT that highest Touch, for together, humankind could know the pure energy of Love Itself and realizing that, Rose was so filled with Awe that she barely could imagine herself a part of this. There was no mental 'talk' here, only a deep Knowing, as though recognition simply swam into view from within herself. She had known then, all along, and now, she could realize . -----

However,this very unity, this coming into one another with conscious acceptance brought out their differences sharply. Like threads of steel, those differences stood before them, shaped through their awareness forming a conscious gridwork of separateness. That which lay within the matrix of that Joining, permeating that gridwork, was the material with which the Council must work. They were, together, aware of a mind among them that was unconscious of their Touch, a mind of one who was also an Elder. That mind held a pool of fear, a darkness that threatened to suck them into its pull.They could not, did not 'read thoughts'- they Knew.Feelings were like waves rippling through that knowing. Visible to one who watched. But perception was broad.

Rose felt the Joining ease, the heads lifted and turned to one another to begin the days business. She looked around, seeing them all again, differently now.

Jerome stood, his round,strong body easy , the silvery grey beard gleaming in the sun that lay across their table and themselves. He loved to eat, to indulge in drink and games in the gaming halls. But he was a tough, steady partner in a scrap. He could steel himself to total self denial or release that discipline to self indulgence and it was chosen. He enjoyed the play of his own nature. Now as he moved with seeming indolence and easy strength, he smiled with a casual charm that belied the bitter strength within, a strength born of hardships survived long before he had come to the Valley. He it was who insisted upon the law that every Valley child must spend time out Valley, even looking into the most backward parts of the world, even visiting the Zone where backward humanity still played war games. They must be inured, he said, to ways of life without their advantages, otherwise they could not understand them. Otherwise they might be conditioned to assume their's the only valid way.

He touched the table where a faintly glowing circle marked it. Immediately it sprang to life and two equally sharp circles on opposite walls, visible to all in the audience, formed themselves. They were maps of the great Valley. The Council watched them take form, every city, town, village, every winding of the Great Highway and the Green River. So accurate and well produced was it that the water seemed to cascade white out of the narrow neck from which it rose in the north. The Highway glittered here and there with camps of Vagabonds. Where the River broadened just beyond Adwin and Denlock, huge shipping barges, silent and swift, pushed heavy materials to various markets. They appeared as tiny points of black, but moving on their ways.

She heard Jerome's voice like a soft murmur, for her attention was turned to study the others. There, Edsil, whose eye met hers. He was a Vagabond member, slim, darkly alive, his body seemed fragile but she knew it's steel strength. He might be flexible but he was unbreakable and though he was in his eighties, his easy movement, his youthful face made him appear thirty years less. He was the old man among them, only Grace could remember what he remembered. He received Rose's tentative Mind Touch. She felt a shyness but wanted suddenly to try out this new Talent. For surely it was a Talent. Edsel responded to Rose's beauty, and she felt his attraction. She smiled, feeling as if mentally she nodded, allowed him to know she felt his beauty also. They both grinned, as if caught in foolishness of play. Edsil was one who knew how to play.

Guiltily Rose switched her attention to Jerome."It's common knowledge that we've got a lot more traffic in air cars than even two years ago. The plant at Bend is manufacturing twice as many and shipping nearly half out Valley. You can see the harbor where the ore is shipped in on the barges there. It's easy now and fast. New power units developed by the citizen from Toppletown and gifted to the Valley at Festival two years ago , have proved more than worth the Honor." He was rambling slightly and Rose wondered why. The increase of trade out Valley brings in new people, the Valley Learning Centers have had 2000 more children and 1000 more adults coming in for learning this year alone. Its a fair estimate of our increase generally. Quite an increase, since our own towns and cities have not stabilized and are growing slightly with their own citizens. You know the problems increased population bring. We must begin looking at those problems now."

Rose turned from him a little, looking at the others, hearing him with one part of her mind, she studied Grace's face. Grace,from Clandon, first city of the Valley, was a mild seeming woman, with a quick wit and laughter that enlivened every meeting. She was nearly ninety, yet moved and looked twenty years younger. Grace turned directly to meet Rose's eyes. Rose smiled with affection and gratitude. This woman had been more than her mentor during these long months of her service.

As if inner directed, Rose turned to look at Dean, the member from the Mountain Villages in the north west Valley. Isolated, they had no central town and so elected their representative from among the scattered population. Today Dean seemed held to himself with a strange tension. He had not been on Council long, but was permanent Elder because he replaced Cliff who had resigned, and because he had served other offices in Santiago for the North country. The north area was too large not to have a permanent Elder immediately. He did not meet her eyes, but watched Jerome attentively.

She looked on to Paul, their member from Altos and her Family 'brother'. Dean turned to comment to Paul, his frown deep, but Paul smiled, as if amused, caught her glance as Dean turned back and like a flicker of a snake's tongue, his Mind Touched hers.She started, shocked. Paul? Her own Family? He seemed to know that she was with them. Of course, he would have caught that interchange between herself and Grace. They all must know. She felt an embarrassment, and then a joy.

Something about Dean disturbed her, she glanced at him again, and Paul nodded. She felt a chill slide beneath the skin of her skull, a feeling of danger and she shrank. No! It could not be! She herself until so recently had been unable, or unwilling to Reach, to make that Mind contact. But this was different! She knew without doubt, sadly, irrevocably, Dean could not Touch at all. Did not have the capacity and never would. He was Mind Blind.The image she got from Paul's mind was so graphic it said more than many words could have. She realized then, for the first time, how amazingly fast communication could be with imagery, so much faster than with words,. But one needed to learn to create accurate images, like creating a painting.Dean was old, but not so old as some of the others. She would not have thought that old ones had these Talents. They were fortunate to have this many on the Council who did. She had guessed that ability might be one requirement of Eldership. Then some mistake must have included Dean.

She glanced at Edsil and Grace and then back to Dean. He was a newcomer, an outlander who had lived for years in Arabia , an engineer who had helped develop the extensive Arab Solar Power Center that had freed their countries from domination by Petroleum war bosses.The Solar Power Center delivered energy to nations surrounding itself, and establshed branch Centers to supply most of the mid East. The Valley had imitated the technology and Valley energy stations, four, so far, supplied most towns and villages. Dean was a very capable man,indeed. Now that she knew of his lack, she could sense, it. Though she would not have done so without having been shown. She had a lot ot learn.

He seemed shut off, closed in an odd way, as if he protected something. He didn't want to meet anyone's mind. Or perhaps he only seemed not to want to. Maybe that was the clue to recognize those who could not. He could not even Touch. Most people she knew could, even though they might not know it yet. She looked back to Paul and he sent out a surge of Love and assurance that startled her, brought tears to her eyes. How much she had been missing! How long had he known? Why hadn't he spoken to her of it? She hadn't seen him or Jennifer much lately, perhaps --.

She didn't know this Talent could be so versatile, so delicate as to limit itself just to two people. Then she caught herself. Of course, people had been doing this for centuries in a very simple way, lovers, parent and child, close friends, had mind-reached in a primitive but very real manner. She began to feel excited, wanting to know more, to find out who else? Her eyes were still on Paul, she let them move over his face and head. He was a man of medium build, a little taller than her own Benjamin, but Edsil, so slim beside him, made him look broad. His heavy thatch of brown hair hung neatly combed but loose now down nearly to the quiet brown eyes that suddenly laughed at her. He laid long browned hands on the table before him, clasping them peacefully. He had been an Elder for a year, served on Valley Counsel for five different terms during his life. Feeling guilty again, she turned back to Jerome. Listened with undivided attention for a few minutes, but this new knowledge was too distracting. Jerome was quoting prices and quantities of goods to be brought into the Valley. Rose found her mind wandering, her eyes roved to Dana, a short, plump woman from Jasper. Rose had known her for years. She was slow moving and quiet enough to cause some to miss that sharp inquiring mind. She had thick red hair that stood out like a halo from a small round face.

Next to Dana was Thomas, a huge giant, young as herself, in his early thirties. He was handsome and charming, a ladies man from Bannig, the grain capital of the Valley. Thomas was gazing steadily at the map and ignored her. She remembered their last meeting when he had reminded them of that limit to their grain production. He had insisted, told them in a very convincing argument, that population had to be further controlled. He said that the amount of bread needed in a land gave evidence of the population pretty accurately. And they were having to curtail some of the out Valley shipments to take care of Valley needs. Bannig grew at least ten varieties of grain, new ones from Altos Domes, as well as the familiar old ones. Valley government had not dealt with laws about population, intelligent citizens tended to limit themselves, But his argument had impressed Rose. And then, Edsil had said something that had stunned her and that she had not understood at all at the time. She still did not fully understand.

Edsil had said that people would take care of their own numbers because they had evolved to a point at which the caring for a few children expertly and fully was recognized as wise. But more because their minds were turned toward another level of life, of being human. Now the interests of the people, their long lives, made contemplation a real living art, through which a greater civilization

THE AWAKENING

would mature. She had been stunned at the time but now she knew the other members might have simply heard their own thought expressed. She felt suddenly like a junior indeed.

She remembered the humor resulting from that talk though, when Grace suggested to Thomas that some of the old ones could offer to remove themselves to make room for the young. Later Rose realized that she actually meant it. She had said,"If I am willing, then others must be. Keep the idea in mind".

But in a swift retort, Edsil had heatedly insisted that was the wrong way. "Don't you see?" He had cried out." The old are our most precious resource. The most vital. The presence of the elder ones, the ones who live long enough to know and realize, to contemplate and to find higher understanding,greater meaning, is absolutely necessary to Valley development. The Elders are the ones who can help bring the People of the Valley into this new Age. And, Grace, the very FACT that you are willing to die for the needs of the young, is an example of the kind of persons our old ones can be. And they are among us. There will be many in the future when the young ones age" He had sat down in absolute silence, Rose herself not knowing how to respond. Then there had been a swift movement, and the Council paid him the highest compliment they ever did. They had not clapped, they had stood, and bowed to him in silence.

At that moment,Jerome turned to her, and she knew he was aware of her wondering atttention, that she was not giving him full attention. She marveled at the old man's skill. Now he needed them all to pay attention. He pointed to his own city with a slim rod. They could see it there, unfinished, a grand city it would be, different again from anything in the Valley. It was designed after a plan made long years ago by Buckminster Fuller, a man who lived before his time. So far it was a vast circle, with hundreds of acres in its center, a wild land there, forest and field and stream, the park land for the people of this city. The circle was rising already, like a vast thick stadium for Games, It rose a hundred stories up,the map shifted to give them a close look at it. Rose was pleased, she had wondered how it was going. Five miles in diameter, it already housed industry enough in the foundation to pay for the rest of the building. The mile wide circle of tents and other shelters her citizen builders had lived in during the building grew every year narrower.

The great Stadium city was built from a combination of plasteel girders, but with walls of silica combined with industrial cement glues,many times stronger and more resilient than concrete. But more important, it would last for centuries.How many, no one knew yet. It could be poured, hardened into forms and placed afterward like stone blocks, or plastered or molded into every possible shape the sculptor desired. The building of this city was watched by builders all over the world. The ultimate test of that product.Now it was state of the art for modern construction material and engineering. It would be a continuous upward stepping of tiers , rings upon rings, each narrower than the one below until the top floor would be only one residence wide. The lower sections, above the industrial caverns, housed the Learning Center, the Temple, the markets, the shops and eating places, all the business of a big city. The upper levels, with hundreds of windows to front and back was mostly residence . But around each tier, both to the inside and outside, were wide gardens. Bushes and trees grew along the edges of these, and food was harvested from those carefully chosen plants. Selected for beauty as well as food production, they were ALL new products of Altos. Only the top several sections of residences was not finished,and there was to be built later the crowning glory of theatres, parks,music and dance halls, museums and playground. These were not yet begun. The naked girders stood against the skyline, slim dark webs of power waiting.

Thousands of people already walked the arched and pleasant walkways, sat on the sculptured wood benches or in the gathering places beside pools and fountains. It was already alive with people. Jerome's pride in his City was so obvious they all leaned to look closely and give him credit.   The city was set into a wide curve of the Green River, half a mile wide at that point. The miles of flat land, some swampy, spread to west and north where they became rolling low hills, was rich, deep farm land. Two thirds of that land had been taken for farm use, striped in quarter acre strips with wild meadow.. They raised rice,and three other water loving grains,then in the higher land, citrus and other dryland grains did well. These acres of the delta were the breadbasket of the Valley literally. The rest was swamp, meadow and winding groves or clusters of fruits and nuts. Some of the swamp land grew dense fields of wild Matta and it was harvested by neighboring small towns for sale to the textile mills, including Adwin's, but no one called that farming.To the north of the city, draining into the swamps along the River was Blue Lake, a favorite site for sail boat racing,it had a good though small, fish industry, enough for one small town's income.

Bend was called the Ring city by Valley folk Already twenty five thousand people lived and worked there. Jerome looked swiftly at their watching faces, his eyes moving rapidly around the table, as the city magnified and was visible in detail. "You can see, we're nearly finished. There isn't a lot left to do. We'll be the next to celebrate after Adwin. He glanced at Rose and grinned. The hardwood forests to our south are producing heavy crops of acorns and we've been harvesting them for several years now for export. We have more than the Valley will ever need even with the limits set to allow wild life consumption. We want to ask that our city be dedicated to the Valley at next fall's Festival. We'll be finished by then." He was grinning now, his heavy beard and laughing eye explained why people sometimes said he looked like Santa Claus.

Dana sighed,"I'm anxious to see Bend, Jerome, I've watched you build with some envy. She's so different and beautiful. She's like a snow white crown from the air. Is she going to succeed as a city though? Is it working, ? Movement from level to level, industry? The farm economy seems sound enough if what you say is true.Where do you get your power?"

Jerome's grin was wide,"Look, the Solor batteries are visible and the windmills are part of our design." He shook his head, "The city is working well, actually. We all worked to complete the industrial centers, and that gave us money to go on.

THE AWAKENING

New citizens c ame in, flooded for a time, in fact, living in the tent city, and then moving into each new story of the rising rings as we completed them. That made us see problems as we went and we fixed them.Actually it slowed us a little, but in the end, it saved us expensive corrections." He hesitated, glanced at the map a moment and they could see his pride again rekindled,"But we've got to set the date for dedication. We will be doing finishing touches for ever."

Grace spoke,"I move that the city of Bend be dedicated to the Valley at Autumn Festival and that we make all the necessary arrangements for celebration. We will be invited to look you over?"

He nodded emphatically,"We intend to have a real party for everyone, that day." There was silence, Rose felt the clear Touching of many minds, the quality of agreement, of pleasure in decision. She felt overwhelmed by that quiet recognition among them but was able to Join enough to participate.

Jerome nodded and turned to Edsil,"Now it's done! I think you've an important petition Edsil. Would you present it?"

Edsil smiled and stood, his slim body moving with the grace common to his people. They all knew that at the summer Festivals he danced along with the youngest, and taught during long winter months. He looked around at them,,his mind open and the subject of his petition clear to them. He made no introduction. He said,"We ask that the Silent City be given protective status. We want the Valley Monitors informed that this is so and a general broadcast at least each week for two months so that no citizen misses the fact."He glanced around, then sat down. Some faces registered puzzlement, other heads nodded slowly.

"Wait! Dean's voice was sharp."You finished the matter of the Crown City without a vote, and now you want to go onto this without one. I don't like that. What are you doing?"

Grace frowned slightly, her eyes troubled but only for a moment."You're right, Dean. We must have a hand vote on Bend." She watched and they obediently raised their hands, Dean included, agreeing .He said,"What you did is not so important as why. That was a gross error." He frowned deeply, then shrugged, "But then, Let's go on."

Dana said,"Your People worship the City don't they?"

Edsil grinned and shook his head,"No! Not at all! We would never use such a word. We have a great reverence for Her. We think of Her as a spiritual haven. A focus of spiritual life and I think that all of you will eventually agree. We worship nothing, however, but Mother Earth Herself and Sky Spirit, Himself. And who has ever seen either of THEM?" He laughed," We see the City as a place that focusses Spiritual energy. Actually, even our worship of Earth and Sky is similar. they are both more truly symbols of that Eternal Spirit that has no name or place."

Dana frowned, trying to understand."You think there is reason to set up protections for that City?" She was silent, letting the powerful recognitions that came from the knowledge that had caused this request to Touch her mind.She needed Edsil's images of those intending destruction to that City.

There was a startled look on several faces, calm recognition on others. Edsil said, "We've heard criticisms, but we've never felt such need before this year. We've given it serious thought. This is not an idle fear." Again images flashed from mind to mind, and frowns deepened.

Thomas and Paul spoke almost at once then Paul deferred to Thomas and he said in a deep baritone, warm and booming through the Hall. "All the Valley holds that City in respect. She's a special part of our lives, even for those who don't understand Her. Why have these disruptions come up?"

Paul's mind was like an octopus in its reach, Touching, testing. He finally said,"Edsil, there's a danger that you've not spoken. One that's new. What is it" His face was full of concern but not worry.

Edsil nodded, they felt his grief, and were puzzled, for it was not even tinged with anger. He looked at them, the sadness reflected in his eyes. " I grieve that it must be so. That it is so. The Valley People have always protected all life. The City is the center of that which is Life beyond even human knowledge. It is the symbol of what we Journey toward. It is the outer reflection of our own inner Reach. And we never thought we would need to protect Her. But now, our High Singers and Seers speak of danger. Forces opposed to Her, to Her power and beauty. To her very Presence. For decades she has been a signal light there on that mountain side, but there is a force gathering that would put that Light out. That dark force finds Her a resistance to its intentions. She is the energy of Light, of Love Itself. You all must know that by now. She is there at that north eastern point overlooking all the Valley because She is needed there. She guards against these dark forces, she has protected us while we grow strong enough to meet our next step into Life. That is what our people think." He stopped, stood with his head suddenly dropped, his mind closed to them.There was silence for several long moments then he looked up, "Those dark forces are within ourselves.Just as the Light is in us, but there is a power of dark that would seek to infiltrate our inner darkness and make it strong. That we must not allow."

The idea caught at Rose's mind, grated against it, like an internal rasp. Rose wanted to ask questions, but the words wouldn't form. What could she ask? Paul simply murmured,"Please go on."

"We know that the energy that rises comes from ourselves, from that past of our world, from the violence and greed that lived within humankind for millennia. We know that the City stands against that energy, and it intends to destroy Her. It is within ourselves!" He stopped, glanced around, his mind sending the anguish he felt, and they could not avoid it."If She is weakened, we will fall, we will regress, we will go back to those terrible days of dispair.That is what we fear. Our new life is so young in this world. Our Way is only beginning to develop into strength.We fear we may not be able to go on to that Light we see, that we steadily Journey toward, without the City's help." The statement was impassioned, though his voice was soft. He never had made such a long statement of any kind before. They believed him.

For moments they sat, separate, their growing ease with the desire to Touch stymied. Gradually Rose was aware that from one member of that group there

THE AWAKENING

was no calm, but rather rising tension, in a body rigid and cold. She glanced at Grace, then at Dana wondering, uneasy.

Dean was holding himself visibly in check. His mountain life had taught him stillness, had trained him in the ways of the hunter so that he could stalk a creature long without revealing himself. But he knew nothing of mind control, knew nothing of mind Touch. He did not shriek his feelings and thoughts as some did who were mind blind, never knowing that they blasted out more than they knew. The natural reserve of his nature to conceal himself not only from others but from himself, allowed only a quiet fury visible. They knew that they must encourage him to speak! The others opened their minds to Touch, knew there was trouble here, knew they must listen and keep a profound calm around them all. Dana felt a sudden surge of elation, excitement, and attending to it, she realized what it was. Contrite, she recognized her own fascination with any excitement! She held herself so that it would subside. She could not risk that now. Though the fact that the usual quiet meeting had turned into something different, something new, pleased something in herself.

Thomas' great hairy arm stretched out to lie across the smooth surface of the table, his hand supine. Was it a gesture of supplication? Rose watched his face, the fluid expression, worry, sympathy, exasperation. "Edsil, what would you have us do? Proclaim the City on protective status? Exclude people, make it off limits for people to fly over her? Do we teach people to avoid certain parts of their homeland?" His questions came without pause, the others smiled, at the familiar pattern.

"Have we taught of that City in our Learning Centers? What do people have in mind when they notice Her?" His face now was grim with some inner knowledge he hid from them. Paul smiled. Thomas' style was to speak out many options, to present many views rapidly and perhaps to move others to choice.

Edsil shrugged, "We've come up with all of those. We've thought of the Journey time for your children with us and ours with you. That seemed the time for learning. We like setting limits as little as you do, so we think instead to teach the young as they come to us, teach them our reverence and recognition. Their choice must be their own. We hope that all of us can see the City as beautiful, offering a possibiity for the highest Reach of our human nature." He frowned fiercely, his eyes darting from one face to another, and with as fierce a tone, he cried out, "Look! Our children grow from birth in genuine love. We nurture every single child in that Love, we hunt down any child showing signs of a lack of Love and we provide. We provide!" His face softened, the conviction was his deepest knowledge. "It is why we live in peace, my friends, you know. " He was still, his eyes looking far into distance. Then he said, softly, "A people raised so have great Hearts, great courage. They are not afraid to SEE." Now, his speech became hesitant. The effort to state what was so seldom put into words, made it hard for him to speak. No one of the Council had ever heard the People of the Way speak of their love for the City, or of their Teaching of Love, yet all knew of it. They did not have any dogma, but rather met the energy of that City directly from the heart.

   Grace sighed, raising her hand then letting it drop in resignation. It seemed to her that much ado was being made about nothing. She had grown up when people still feared the strong convictions that made them preach their faith, impose political, economic or religious dogma on others. She felt mild suspicion still and knowing that, watched her emotions."Edsil, exactly what is the problem you want us to vote on?"

   Edsil looked at her. He respected this old friend, knew her past and knew that she spoke often from a perspective others wouldn't have. "Grace, I've learned much of what I know of manhood from people like you. We grew out of a world that was not so different. I can see your concern, I know the danger you see. Indoctrination has destroyed more of human hope than wars. But we are a new people. I believe that! Our children, all of them, are taught to think for themselves and allowed to disagree with us when they do. We teach them to question us. That is the prime system of teaching in town Learning centers . You know that." He stopped,frowning, seemed to look at the picture of Valley thought as though questioning it. Grace watched him. He shrugged from his lapse into deep silent thought and said,"This has been in deadly earnest for us. We know that children taught to question all assumptions,to search for what is true for themselves, will think. We have faith in the Children of the Valley."

   He drew a deep breath, looking silently at the great lit map on the wall."The record of the Vagabond people speaks for itself. We have held your children and their time with us as a sacred trust. I know of no single time that that trust has been broken. We teach children of our reverence without asking them to emulate us. Our faith is in That which is the Source of all Life and we give no name to That. By the time your children come to us they have learned to think and their minds and emotions are as disciplined as our children's are. By then surely you have taught them to think, to have stability of mind, and to question." He spoke the last firmly, and Rose remembered long local debates that questioned whether the town people or the Vagabonds taught their children best. She didn't want that old argument wakened. She felt Grace's amusement and Edsil's reluctant grin at the reminder.

   Grace spoke, her voice warm, We haven't questioned your teaching of our children, Edsil. We have found no fault with it."

   He was nodding, "I think that's it. We want to be able to talk to them of the reasons for the City's presence. To at least tell them more of our perceptions."

   Before anyone could speak , Dean leaned forward, his face dark, his eyes full of anger. "That's asking a lot, isn't it? We turn our children over to you without limits? That's an impressionable age, those teen years. How can we control what they learn?"

   Grace laughed, "If we haven't done a decent job by then, no one will control them and their learning is in their own hands.Control isn't our aim, is it?" She Reached out, searching to realize their general attitude,"Surely each child knows himself necessary to our mutual well being because she has worked in the

THE AWAKENING

economic system all his or her life. But each knows that we support individual development absolutely also. So they do their own thinking." If they want to know of the City and Her purpose there, they will find that out. Each must control herself."

Edsil shook his head, pursed his lips, his easy smile was gone, his face deeply serious,"Wait Dean, first we must deal with the fact that the tension in your body and the edge in your voice conceals thought that you do not share. Will you reveal that to us?"

The suddenness of the request put Dean off. It was as though Edsil changed the subject abruptly. He opened his mouth and closed it then shook his head. It was not customary in his village for any person to account for his feelings, discuss them, be publicly responsible for them even to this degree. He knew the Valley practice of Balancing but many of his village did not honor that, and he had long grown up before it was begun. Rose saw the thick muscles of his neck tighten, his breathing shorten, a swift glimpse of anger crossed his face. He was not balancing, he was repressing his emotion and she was surprised at its strength. What was this? Surely he could not feel threat at Edsil's request. She waited patiently, letting the conflicting thought reverberate in her mind. Was she herself concealing? Would another more perceptive than she see through her own concealment? The thought humbled her, washed away any trace of smugness at her recognitions of Dean's lack of awareness. Dean clasped his hands, watching them all, then slowly he smiled.

"I am surprised that you imagine that all the people of the Valley have attitudes like yours about that City". He spoke to Edsil, a faint disapproval visible in his expression."Many people do NOT hold that acclaim should be given to that City. We have never sent any successful team to investigate it. No one has landed inside those carved rock walls. There is even a rumour that it is not a city at all but simply an illusion. Why is it that no one has investigated? Is it because we are afraid of what we might find? Or is it that some people do not want that City exposed?" At the look of surprise and puzzlement on the faces of the younger members, he relaxed more, and added."That's the real danger!"

" Danger? How? "Thomas was curt.

Dean shook his head, his face softening. He felt less threatened. Rose shook her head, refocused her attention and then knew why she too felt easier. She was aware of the steady reassurance from the older members. It would be an automatic response for them when meeting someone distressed. Their uninhibited compassion was available and focussed. Both Edsil and Grace would understand any old one's fear of revealing himself. Edsil saw the reflections in himself of the need to control, to dominate others; he had dealt with them enough to wrestle them into his own control, and he saw that Dean had not yet. Grace felt the memories of her own early fears and denials, and her heart went out to Dean. Edsil Reached lightly, Touched so faintly Edsil could not know, to offer comfort to this old man who must meet what he could not know. He must not feel criticized. He must feel acceptance rather than shame in this self revealing.

Edsil felt the strong Touch of the others, offering also acceptance, support for Dean. They saw the lightening of that heavy dis-ease in Dean's eyes. A brief hope flared. Then his fist, lying on the table before him, tightened as he tightened his mind, closed himself further. Edsil sighed, his eyes fixed on Dean's face. They all realized their mistake as Rose, Paul, Dana, Thomas, less experienced, watched in admiration the tender attention of their peers, but could not, dared not, join them. The students, watching in the seats below, and the people beyond them, watched too, most aware of the inner conflict. The older ones were aware of the tendrils of questions hesitantly extended but no one turned from the tableau to respond.

They had made a mistake. Their own capacity to receive with trust was so far different from Dean's lack that they had not adjusted the power of their Sending of Good will. Even that could be misunderstood and Dean had done just that. The energy of it had disconcerted him and caused him suspicion. Even Love could be fearful to one who had no power to recognize it.

For moments there was complete silence. Grace suppressed a smile. The young ones had learned something she thought, even as the old ones had. Rose and Thomas' disappointment did not show in their faces, but all were aware of it. Paul's realization saddened him, but he nodded, as if recognizing something. Grace nodded as she knew the gentle surge of good-will coming from dozens of focussed minds in the hall. The grey shadow of mind-blind people was small, but it was clear that Dean was not alone in his blindness. Grace watched! Only in this way could they meet distrust. Acceptance and goodwill must be steady, deep and true. The Elder members felt the reestablishment of confidence and balance first, and then the Juniors. Grace was grateful for those strong minds in that audience who lifted support to them.

In this time, Dean's eyes had swept from Edsil to each of the other members then back to Edsil. He focussed on Edsil as adversary. "There's something here that sounds false, wrong. You speak of my feelings, of your knowledge of them. that's a rude assumption. No one of my community would speak of another's emotions or unspoken thought as if he or she knew. THESE ARE PRIVATE."

"You don't practice peer counseling regularly in your Learning Center? You don't make recognition and management of emotions a prime training in primary grades?" Paul could not restrain the question.

Dean whirled to him. "Never!" Then his basic honesty flickered in anger through his expression, "There are Teachers who -- who do something of that, but we discourage it, when we see it. Surely attention to these things is an invasion of privacy. Better keep emotions under control and hidden." His faced was strained, anger obvious to these trained minds around him. But then, he made no effort to conceal, seemed instead to fling that anger out from control held too long. They were relieved to receive it. Edsil simply nodded, not taking his eyes off Dean. The old man spoke with a voice held under such control, that had they no mind-sight, they might have thought he was calm. His face was drawn

THE AWAKENING

into a blank stillness. "Let that matter go now, I cannot re-educate adults. The issue here is that City. I think your peculiar attitude about people's feelings is another problem." His anger radiated from his body and they could literally see it churn the atmosphere about him, but he knew nothing of that. "We've got to control this worship of something obviously kept as a mystery and correct that refusal to do a careful study of it." He breathed a long hard breath, "My people want to know why that City has not been investigated and even demolished."

His confidence was rebuilt, the issue was clear now. His voice grew strong again, even gentle. He had no way to know that the steady outpour of good-will had given him room to build that calm. Rose, watching, saw the faint lift to a corner of his mouth, the desire to smile, to placate those listening, to erase the memory of anger. He was a politician and saw the need, but too much tension rode in him, requiring his complete attention. Rose could see the conflict, see that he knew his control had sagged and he must lace it up tight again. Symnpathy for him claimed her. She didn't notice Grace's faint Touch. Rose allowed the racing thoughts to focus, surely mountain children were born with as many talents, but even more, with as much inner unfoldment, awakening of consciousness , as Valley children. What happened to them? To those wakening minds?

She knew that fear of the unknown could impell a mind backward, could crush an opening nature. Fear of fellows and criticism could shrink a heart opening to potential. The waking to that which was like a bright and wondrous Light beckoning the highest mind on toward Itself, was itself fearful unless carefully guided. If Dean's community refused and denied such realization, it would be still born. The Valley Learning Centers were dedicated to nourishment of such an opening of mind. How then, could villages in that Valley deny such things? The question stung at her mind,"What happens to young mountain children?"

"So now,"Grace spoke softly, bringing them back to center,,balancing them with her quiet. "You think we might correct that lack? We might send our scientists to that City to investigate Her?"

Dean's voice was hard now, his face controlled but a brief expression of fear and anger rippled through that control. Then with effort, he recomposed himself into that kindly old man, that smiling friendly man that was his public habit. "Of course. But my question now is why has nothing been done already?" He glanced around at them, carefully closed and feeling in control again.He could handle these people. They were too patient, too calm as if nothing mattered. Were they even human? The thought startled him.He felt a twist inside his body, a dread he'd grown up with and never understood, feelings of blind fear, unexplainable. He shoved them back.

Yes, it was true, these people were different, especially this bunch on this Council. Just as the teacher from the Builders group had told them.They were different enough not to be offended by his criticism of their practices. Surely he had only to persue his insistence and he would break that calm. There must be one here who was a weak link. Maybe a woman; he was still old fashioned

THE PEOPLE OF THE VALLEY

enough to think that women were weaker. He felt their waiting. He had no idea they felt embarrassment that he flamed with anger and distrust. He said,"Well, am I to receive no answer?"

Then to his surprise it was a woman who answered. Her eyes swept the circle, accepting agreement. Her face was serious,but her eyes held a faint amusement coupled with sadness and he sensed it and that fed his anger. She realized too late,but blanked her eyes and spoke without expression."Your request is reasonable, surely."

Dean felt that old nagging sense of inferiority, one he couldn't place cause for. These people were no smarter than he. He would have to show them their error. He had avoided people like these, this strange quality of restraint, of something -- something -- hidden. He didn't know his face was a kaliedescope of swift changes readable to everyone at the table. A faint amusement on Grace's face turned to shame and then there was nothing visible in her expression at all, except watching. He was puzzled, he had seen the sweep of sadness in her eyes.Had she felt pity? Then he thought. No, this old woman felt sympathy, surely she must know the danger too. She must see the wrong that was being done. He snapped into that assumption and asked her,"Is this a request that you can fulfil?"

Grace nodded immediately, acutely aware that he had not been included in that momentary linking that made known to themselves their vote.   "Yes, we'll record your petition and we will give thought to the criticism of our functioning. The petition that Edsil has presented must wait for that consideration." She turned to Edsil and he nodded to Dean. Edsil's face was quiet, full of deep grief, which Dean read as disappointment. Edsil could not place the sorrow he felt until he absorbed the wave of response from the others.They all knew that Dean could not Touch, could not make any connection mentally at all. Could not identify even the primative 'sense' of awareness that he did have. He was mind blind. How could a government work without those expanded recognitions of mind? Modern government at least?

Edsil remembered how long it had taken him to enter into the Reaching,the extending of his consciousness to another. The fear and revulsion,the fascination and attraction fighting one another until Grace herself, having struggled through these troubles earlier than he, offered him understanding. He, Edsil, had been awed at that first experience of JOINING. Further than the Reach, the Joining was a true mind connection. And she had been helped by the Master Teacher who wondered the Ways with them. One who was a Monitor come down from the Station to offer just that help wherever people had begun to wake .He knew that now. But knew that even such an one could not help Dean. He was grateful that Dean would give them time.

The Council stirred as a body, a soft rustling of people resettling themselves. Jerome asked,"Are there other petitions?"

Thomas of Bannig stood," Yes! We need more land" Quickly he waved a hand." Wait, there is more than just population involved. We have found ourselves host for conferences, even world meetings and week long workshops

THE AWAKENING

of many kinds. People want to see and enjoy our city. And it's not even finished!" He grinned,"Yes, I'll admit it makes us a little vain, but then, it is happening and we need food for all those who come. We believe the Valley in general needs more grain as our population grows. We have not nearly reached out peak and yet we must increase our food production to meet the increase in people.The delta land at Banig is the best grain land of the whole Valley, its true, but they've pretty well deeloped their alottment. The percentage left to swamp and meadow is full. But we, we've only used half the land we're entitled to as a city and the flood land in our River bend makes grain the best crop we can raise. You northern towns need trade products because you raise other crops better than we do.Our sandy hills have been planted to citrus and they'll be marketed in a year.Between the two and our young industries, we can pay our debts." He laughed and the rich booming sound lightened the atmosphere of the room.

"The quality of food is so much better. People do not need as much". Edsil spoke worriedly. He was a protector of wild lands.

"Yes, that's true. We use far less than the same number of people a hundred years ago. And it's because we aren't gluttons.. What ever any one says of our way of life we ARE interested in far more than eating." He grew serious,"But we have a new plan that makes sense to us.. The swamps are not harmed by our inclusion of new water grains. The swamp life hardly notices, I think, for we plant and harvest from the air. The Matta crops are not doing as well as they do farther north and for us to raise it is a waste. We could turn that wild matta swamp to the raising of grains, water grains, There are half a dozen new ones given us from Altos. Wild Matta can continue to grow all along the borders. And the wild life will be as always."

The native Matta was there when you began to build ?" Dana's voice was soft.

He turned to her,"It was. But it makes an inferior fabric, does not last the way the northern fibre does. Paul, have you any knowledge of the work on the new plants."

Paul nodded, "I have, Thomas. the word will be in your city by the time you are home. The Domes can't get sufficient improvement in the Matta yet, but they've got an entirely different fibre plant that needs your kind of warm weather. Couldn't take those northern winters at all. It's called Craski Silk after the Plant Wizard who developed it .We ought to have had a contest to get a better name. It's as tough and durable as Matta but much finer. It's only drawback is it doesn't take color as well, it's own color is a weed green so it'll need to be mixed with other fibers for color. It'll be in world demand by next year, be sure,because it's makes a very beautiful fabric and it's nearly indestructable."

Thomas had listened with a half smile."That takes care of one problem, but we won't want to turn our poor Matta acres over to raising grain, if a better product is coming.".

Paul took leadership,"Thomas your request is recognized. It's true the Valley is growing.We've not contained ourselves yet, but neither have we reached our limits here. We've got citizens moving out Valley now and then, some who want

THE PEOPLE OF THE VALLEY

to colonize on the other planets, and so on, but mostly we have to limit ourselves and that may mean allowing no more outlanders to become citizens here. It sounds harsh, but how can we keep the Earth Committment unless we do."

Thomas shook his head,"I just don't agree and neither do the people of Bend. We believe that the Valley can allow all who come to live with us and care for our own as well. Altos is developing improved varieties of foods so fast that we can already properly nourish, and with delicious food too, many more than we have. We don't have to spread all over the landscape , we've proved that.We've learned to build beautiful cities for upward of fifty thousand people that barely use a few miles of land. Sometimes not even that. A population like ours, or Santiago's would have used many more miles of country side in the past. We use very little and its better used.There's no land wasted in roadways, or approaches to the cities. And we still have the mountains almost untouched, There's vast space there, inside and out." He was so enthusiastic in his conviction that the others smiled.

Paul nodded,"You may be right. I hope you are. Thank God we don't have to make decisions to exclude anyone yet."

Grace said,"We are concerned,and we've always been.If we remain so, we'll find better solutions than denying parenthood to our people, or denying newcomers to our Valley. Lets leave that for when it's relevant."

The two men looked at her, grinned and nodded, having forgotten that they had wandered from Thomas's first request.Paul said,"Then we do a study to decide on the request by next Council meeting?"

Thomas nodded, "That'd be fine. We just need to be ready to go to work on the new land by autumn." He sat down.

Edsil coughed, stood swiftly,"I disagree! We DO need to think about population. I believe that we must begin thinking of it now in this Council. We need a Valley vote, because it must be a policy that everyone agrees to. My people feel there is danger of over population.Family size is down everywhere. People just don't bring children into this world without deep thought.But our Healers are keeping us alive, healthy into far greater age than our ancestors.I'd be willing to bet that Grace and Jerome haven't had a serious illness in twenty years."

Grace laughed,"It's true, we're becoming an older population and the wisdom of those who've lived long is one asset we have.No one wants to change that. But Edsil has a point and I agree. Unless we make some decisions now, when the danger is far off, we'll be creating anger and many problems later on. I move that we begin serious study and ask all town Councils to join us to make decisions about population.I want to know exactly what the present tendency to increase is, or isn't. It's even possible that we've stabilized. We don't know."

"Edsil," Rose said,"You've talked to our children enough to see they know about the purity of the Valley, about the dangers of careless reproduction, etc. Can't you teach them as you do about the Earth herself?"

He turned to her, the energy of attack in his body's movement,"Don't even

THE AWAKENING

suggest such a thing. That's the most terrible thing that can be done to children! To people generally! We don't - we never will indoctrinate. We will only present ideas and teach the children to think." He hesitated,"True, there is a risk, but the danger of indoctrination is greater. And don't ask where we draw the line. We know! You know! And anyone who thinks at all, knows the difference. We honor that above almost anything except the City."

His feeling was so strong that Rose sent a ribbon of apology out, knowing he would be receptive. He was, he blinked and then grinned,"Forgive me, I've gotten on my favorite soap box."

Dean still a little disgruntled, uneasy with the sense that more was going on around him than he could understand, said,"You speak as if the Valley is more important than the people. That's nonsense"!

Dana of Jasper, her red hair shining in the afternoon light coming in now as the sun fell below the tops of the tall windows, shot up. The force of her personality, that belied her fifty five years, cried out,"Of course he does. Of course, Dean. What else could you expect of a man of the Highways. They are our watch dogs, the Valley's eternal champion and they keep the rest of us from getting carried away in our zeal to make and build over the rest of life. They travel and they see everything that's happening. The health of this Valley is protected by their attention. And without the Valley's health, our life would be poor indeed." Her words were serious, but she spoke them in such good humor that the atmosphere lightened, Dean frowned but slowly nodded. Dana's quiet command of herself, for she felt deeply about the matter, was a relief to Rose.

There was silence, again unspoken agreement that a study would be begun. Dean looked from one to the other, again that uneasy feeling that something happened beyond him. The others seemed not to notice.

Rose spoke then, standing to request. Her voice was clear, the training of a fine singer evident in its timbre and fullness. I submit Adwin's request. We've got twenty life transfers to record and accept. They reached the age of choice this year. We've got five who've chosen the life of the Highways and four others who've chosen the life of Santiago, two to Clandor and one to Altos and three to your city, Thomas, and five to Adana, the new Mountain Town. The rest will stay home with us. I have their names and records for each of you."They nodded, receiving the papers and these new citizens would be duly recorded in the Valley computer files.

Dana said," Why didn't you just send them in with the rest of the Valley town Council reports at the end of the year?"

Rose shook her head, They weren't ready.But they will be next year. We've got a new council member who can handle the auto-computer.

Dana nodded, then said," We were questioning the training our children receive from the Vagabonds and their children from us. I'd like to know more, Edsil, of your way.

Edsil began powerfuly to Send, then stopped, Dean would be unable to receive at all and most here would not be able to comprehend the Sending of actual thought. He spoke,"I know our way of life is not 'strict' as you see it. We learn as the day goes, no child is ever in a non-learning situation and there fore we guide and are aware of what that is. Our older children are learning their responsibilities as adults by assisting in the teaching by the time they are fourteen. Your children don't know they are being taught, it is so natural and so much a part of play and discovery of the earth life."He hesitated,"However, I give you credit,most of them come to us well skilled in searching out understanding and in asking questions.They are immersed in a pleasure of learning. Every parent and adult among us teaches as naturally as we breath. And your children do love it, you know!" He was grinning.

Dana studied his face,"Then you think we are too strict with your own children when they come to us? After all, we have them involved in manufacturing, building, harvesting, planting, etc. even our government, just as our own children are." She realized that she'd never put the question to any of the people of the Way before.

Edsil laughed,"Well, I've heard a few comments, but generally we agree that your training is essential to our children,. We balance one another. We need your kind of discipline and you need our kind. After all, many of our children choose town life, and many of yours, our life.But aside from that, we need organized training that you give; you need the joy and celebration of life that we give. We need our differences, it would destroy either of us to try to be like the other, but we need each kind of strength." He leaned forward and emphasized,"We need our differences."

Grace nodded, smiling at his intensity."Yes, Yes, Edsil. I agree absolutely. The lovely times of my life have been Journeys. I didn't get to do that as a child, there were no Journeys as we know them now. So I take advantage of them now in my old age. Each time I join your people it is a joy, a refreshment. I would not threaten that for my life."

Dean growled in his throat, his voice came out harshly at first but softened as he talked, a flame of anger that they all felt, faded into acceptance as he talked "It's true, we've all got good memories of being with your people and good reports from our children who come home full of that joy you speak of. But then there's a looseness in your way that seems wasteful. There are some families who do not send their children to you." He stopped a rueful smile touching his lips. "We've had a few run away to join you though. The resistance to that holding back any young from their time of Journey was powerful and most do send them. I was a grown man the first time I Journeyed. And I have not forgotten the beauty of it. Your way of life has that -- great beauty.": He was silent,"But how do you manage to live so well, wtih no business, no work!"

There were smiles around the table, several were pleased to have this opportunity to question a Vagabond. Edsil was relaxed, leaning back in his chair, he was at ease."We do work, Dean. We gather each day's food and that is an act of reverent pleasure. We honor Earth and never harm her children. We teach our way. We tend our plants as we travel and plant new plants in the forests and we

THE AWAKENING

harvest with every town. We make music, dance, theatre, wonderful creations of fabric,and our wood carvings are proof of our skills. This is all work, but we do all that we do with the singing and dancing all around us. We build and invent also, and we take time to keep everything among us, and in our Gather centers very clean." He laughed, his eyes twinkling, "That's a result of your own people assuming that we are like the Gypsy's, who were never, according to legend, clean."

He looked thoughtfuly around at them, all listening,"Work for us must also be delight. Must be a part of play, work is a good, deeply fulfilling action for us. I fear at times it can become a rigid, enforcement of attention to something one dislikes, for you folks. "

Dean shrugged,"I suppose there's something to that. Maybe we do need each other more than my own people know. It's hard for me to see, sometimes." He stopped, then as if making up his mind, he said,"There must be those among us who are not capable, aren't developed as people enough to realize the finest of our way. Those who are better served doing the drudgery of the world." He looked around and they saw that he wanted very much a response to that strange statement.

Paul leaned to meet his eyes,"Oh, Dean, let's never let that old assumption ruin our caring of one another. Never must there be those who live less than any of us.There may be those who cannot think as well, cannot do as well, but our society has failed when we cannot teach them also to enjoy, to contribute and to work with pleasure."His eyes were sad.

Dean stared at him a moment, then said, "The Builders have said -- " he stopped and his eyes dropped as if he had revealed what he did not choose to. He was unaware of the cloud of thought that poured itself out around him. The imagery, the perceptual extension shared by all the others.The glimpse of impressions from Dean's mind of those 'Builders' that sent a wave of recognition to those watching. They turned their attention, allowing him privacy.

Grace broke the silence."I move that we record these requests and problems that need public educating and responses, to the Video Center for development. I will get the voting organized through Western Video Center, and I ask you, Paul and Dana to search out the reasons why a survey has never been done on the Silent City. We can contact the Monitor Station in South Valley for information on the City also. You said you would find out what the population trends are and what the attitude of the public is about that, Thomas. We will report all this back at the next meeting.Does that about sum up our day's work?"

Dean was the one who spoke, the others simply Sent agreement. He said, "That seems right". Grace asked for other business, Rose nodded, "We haven't decided on the new villages that are built or petitioning to build. We've got a small group from our northern towns wanting to build inside the mountains above Adwin, in the caverns there. The technology they need is available already. They'll imitate the other cities built inside Earth. Though new problems will surely come up. We might get a few good inventions and sound ideas out of it" She laughed, "Everyone is so aware of the need for industry in any new town area that they've planned to repeat an old pattern. They've got to cut into the living stone so much, they'll have piles of debris, broken rock and sand. They plan to set up a stone block factory similar to the one Altos used to have when they were first building."

Jerome said, I've seen the city of Rawlings, which was cut out of limestone mountains in the mid west. It's beautiful, spacious, full of wonderful color and light,. I don't yet know how they do that."

Paul said,"We've got the technology, I think they'd find out more. Yes, I would encourage them.They're following good examples. We need to study their video records and then make a decision. I see no reason why these new dwellings can't be built. They won't be harming any natural life area."

Edsil said, " Since they'll not be harming the land, I approve."

Thomas shook his great shaggy head,"I'm going to keep an eye on the progress there. I know of another set of caves in the western mountains that are a good possiility and we will have people needing them. All they need is cleaning and shaping a little."

Dean stood up finally irritable,"Are we to complete THIS agreement too without any vote among us? Yet the matter of that City must go to the whole population for vote? He slapped his hand on the table,"Into the hands of children even?"

Rose shook her head, patiently repeating what the rest knew."Children work as an important part of the study but adults will supervise, Dean. We need to let them learn that way. There's a lot of leg work, computer work, searching into old files, etc. They learn about so much in the process."

Dean shrugged, "Children are better off left out of adult affairs. That is one change we need to speed up."

There was a little more talk, and then Grace drew the meeting to a close. Rose talked a little to the members of the Council, most of whom she did not see between meetings, then she walked to the doorway with Paul. She looked out over the city, enjoying it. It was such a change from home.

The day was bright and the sun warm in the cool wind. Clouds were piled over the western mountains. The night would bring showers. Dean strode rapidly past them as if eager to separate himself but Paul and Rose knew from the scatter of emotional residue behind him that it was the characteristic hurry of a man who felt outside, who was shy, unsure of his place among his fellows. They were saddened by that fact, but more by the knowledge that he knew nothing of this resolvable conflict in himself.

Paul took Rose's hand,"Oh, Rosy, there's so much we've got to learn. So much. And how to relate to each other is still one of the most important. We need jacking up, to be reminded of what we've failed to do. There're people in our Valley that are still suffering.It's easy to feel comfortable when your own Family is O. K." He frowned, "And even that's not true now."They went into a cafe, wanting to make the best of this visit and ordered a dinner that would include what they never had at home. Other members of the Council came in, some went to other restaurants, but it was a tradition that they make this small ritual after meeting. Grace sat at a table next to them she leaned to them and said,"We're going to have to find out about this group called the Builders by the next meeting, I suspect. So little's been said of them, yet Dean mentioned them twice today and he feels strongly about them. See what you can find out by next month."

Paul nodded,"We need to get him to give us a briefing.They relaxed, began to talk of other things, to eat and to enjoy each other's company without problems of Valley business. Finally Paul and Rose said their goodbyes and left. Walked out on the vast surface of the Center leaf and climbed up to the grid. Paul promised to call the next day, and they each got into air cars that would take them home. Rose was tired, sank back into her seat and knew that she would sleep most of the way home.

CHAPTER FOUR

The Family at Altos

    The first real city built in the high peaks, was surrounded on this late winter day by the blinding white of snow. On four broad shelves extending from the feet of three massive up thrusts of smooth hard stone, the city stretched for two miles, wound into canyons and cut herself deeply into the high walls of the mountain. The structure of her buildings imitated the mountain itself. The first apartments had been cut into the living rock. Looking much like cliff dwellings from the outside, these extensive catacombs unlocked the entrance into caverns and two debris strewn tunnels. Cleaning these and strengthening them, began the early development of the industrial and business life of the city. People lived and worked inside the mountain. As development continued, a fine grade of iron ore was located and mining began. It was to be one of Altos primary sources of income. But as ore was extracted, tunnels and caverns left were cleaned, polished, and refitted into new industrial warehouses. Manufacture of metal products began and developed. As the city grew, more living space was needed. Gradually there was built on the broad flat shelves two massive pyramids of residences, one on top of the other, like a stair way toward the peaks. Building material was stone and Vitaplas, durable as stone but flexible and impervious to cold or wind. They were literally stacks of housing, each roof the broad deck and garden before the rooms above. The broad interior of the base, held food processors, utility cores and work spaces. The roofs surfaces were planted into gardens, so each residence had its fronting green space. Some were domed with clear bubbles of plasteel for winter protection. The entire pyramid looked like vine and shrub covered ridges among the peaks and became known by outsiders as the falling gardens of Altos. Between each roof area ran covered passageways, like alleys between homes, cool in hot weather and dry and protected from storm in winter. The pyramid form was so satisfactory that eventually the flat stone base of the city held four. They created cascades of color on the high mountains and the view from any one of them was spectacular. There were no homes in Altos without such beauty.

    To the north and beyond the city was a long steep mountainside that sloped far above the highest shelf into the upper peaks. It was the favorite ski slope for citizens of Altos. When the people realized their space for expansion was pretty much used up, they began the structures that were to make Altos famous through the world. These were cantilevered fields out over her cliffs and extending to hang above the forests below. They were domed and became the fields and gardens for food crops. But more importantly, they became the fields for experimental gardens.

    Begun modestly with the arrival of two people called Plant Wizards, they grew until three domes were built from the main city four and ten more stair-stepping down the mountains side. Thousands of people found their life work in these bright sheltered Domes. Altos attracted then the best of those with that envied Talent, the ability to intuitively communicate with plants enough to effect their growth. Plant Wizards they were, communicating with plants to the extent that new varieties and improved varieties became standard products from this city in the peaks. .In the first years, with only two known wizards, and those two doubted, not understood well,genetic scientists controlled the work. But rapidly they began to see the results of those with Talent, people who needed no tools, no microscopes even, to effect the changes they wanted. Plants hardy to nearly any climate, were produced. Vegetables and grains no one had ever tasted. Especially, trees and field plants that produced magnificence in bloom, fruit, and leaf, but each of these useful for industry or for food. Variety was endless. The world depended on Altos for its gifts to the people.

Altos was like a cheerful peasant girl among cities. She seemed capable of handling hardship and joy with equal calm. She was handsome, strong and sturdy against weather that few cities ever had to endure. From her heights was a panarama so breathtaking that people came from every nation to visit and enjoy. City planners had taken every advantage of that beauty and from every home the vista was breathtaking. People did not forget or become enured to that beauty,or to the majesty of that land of heights, of snow, stone and brilliant color of plant life. The great Valley lay spread for miles below. She was the source of life for Altos as for all Valley citizens and Altos watched the changing seasons, the movements of life there as to an unceasing pageant.But such an environment had taught Altos adults to teach her children to pay attention to all beauty, to notice and to fill themselves with that nourishment. She set that pattern also for the rest of the Valley.

Altos had set a precedent in the Valley and in the world for cities built among mountains.She wound between the peaks, kept clear the wide flat valley between the pyramids of homes and adorned it like a long narrow parkland running from the Field Domes far back into the industrial caverns preceeding the mines. And finally she had built, hanging against a high ledge of one of the great peaks,the Altos Temple that shone in that sunlight above many of the storms that raged across the Valley in winter. A light slim strand of bridge, webs that Altos used to weave together her heights and depths, her peaks and caverns, ran up to that Temple and so strong was the metals used in combination to build them, that they had born the weather and storm for thirty years without accident. Now that flight belts were commonly used for inner city travel, the bridging got less demand. But Altos people liked to walk. They needed and knew they needed exercise and the bridges carried every day thousands of people to and from their work.

On a day in late winter when the air had the smell of the coming spring and the sky belied the storms still to come, two men stood silently at the center section of a bridge linking the civic center and the great arching curve of the first Field Dome. Standing thus, hung so high above the stone floor of the city, was like being levitated in clear blue air. The iridescent colors of the Dome glistened softly in the morning sun. Steve, the shorter of the two men, and the young son of Paul and Jennifer, stretched out his arms in a sweeping gesture that included the whole city. He said,"Look Grandfather, it's always magnificent, our city." He laughed, and they continued their walk. He was a well built youngster, with a slim graceful body. His thick brown hair cut just below his ears rippled in the gust of air coming up from the warming city below. He turned to his companion, John, an old man, one of the few remaining of that generation."It's always exciting to me when I travel the walks."

John, nodded, but was silent, and than began to talk as if to himself more than to Steve. "The wonder of it is it's all happened so fast -- for me, it has. It's as though the human race jumped over a crevase that stood limiting us for centuries. We thought we didn't have anywhere to go, that we'd nearly exhausted everything but space travel. And here we are, living in what's actually a new kind of world". Steve listened, Grandpa seldom talked like this. He loved to hear the rare stories the old man told."Look at my work, I'm in my eighties and still there's plenty for me to do. I'm still needed , making tools that Altos is already famous for. The tools we make are durable, they nearly never wear out. We've licked the problem of endless repair. Then,look at your work, a young boy your age, already creating new foods, new varieties, miracles actually. And it's all commonplace to you. In my time, we had to take what a tired Earth had left after we'd ravaged Her soil and poisoned her atmosphere. We deliberately made tools to wear out. As if a human being wasn't worth more than spending his life making things not needed." He shook his head, his face filled with intense seriousness, "Here I am living in a different world."

Steve nodded,"Grandpa, for me its commmon sense. You told us that people used to waste things, that the economic system required that things be wasted. I can't imagine that."   "I'm glad you can't Son. We also wasted people's lives that way. How can a man feel he's accomplished something when what he makes isn't really needed but only distracts someone for a few hours or won't work after a year or two and must be thrown away. A sad time to remember, but it was already falling apart when I was young. People felt so -- so unnecessary, not needed -- and that's a terrible way to feel, I can tell you."He looked around, "I still can't take it all for granted, what we've done?"

"Would you want to Grandpa?" They were silent contemplating this question. Then Steve continued," There's not a day I don't feel delighted at the wonder of the new plants we grow. The failures even, they teach us something, so something comes of them. But mostly, Grandpa, it's fascinating to learn how to enter into that strange, wonderful world." He drew a long breath, to talk of his work left him always with a sense of amazement."If we want miracles, they're there in our Domes." He laughed, "It's what makes life exciting."

The old man nodded, slowly and sadly,"Every human being ought to go to work feeling that way. But don't misunderstand, Son. I'm grateful. Too many people in the old world had work that was dull, repetitive, monotonous and no

THE AWAKENING

wonder they made mistakes. People felt as though life was drained away behind dark walls of foundrys, or offices, never even seeing the sun sometimes. Weekends people flooded out to the land, as if starved. Now we have robots that do extremely routine jobs, the drudgery, the monotonous. We've been freed from a slavery we didn't recognize until we broke free of it. Just having a job was so important a man didn't question the quality of his work life. We didn't know our souls were sold to the market."

"You've not talked of the old days much, Grandpa. Why does it come back to you now?"

"I don't know, Son, it's just that lately I keep remembering more than before. Maybe that's part of being old." He chuckled."It was heart breaking to see the land dying the way it had in my father's time. He used to take us to the mountains and try to find places where the trees were healthy, the Earth alive and beautiful. Sometimes I remember he'd cry, and say that it was almost worse to climb there.It was easier to retreat into his job life." He let his eyes run out over the edges of this clean bright city, the mountains and forests beyond, the vast Valley spread below, green, luxuriant with growth and vitality. "How he'd of loved this land now."

Steve looked over at him, they had stopped and leaned a moment on the thick woven railing,"It's hard for me to believe, except I've seen Holos of it and they make it pretty real.

"If only I could make you see, Son. It must never happen again. It took us so long to just get out of the city sometimes there wasn't time or energy to enjoy when we did find a quiet spot. The sprawl of ugly, decaying, or cheap buildings where people lived in poverty on the outskirts, seemed endless. They made the land beyond seem beautiful even when it was dying. People had lost heart, just couldn't make their rotting cities better. Those who had power didn't seem to care - not enough of them. We all avoided thinking about it. So people got to entertaining themselves with more and more violent games and films because they felt so angry inside. I never believed we were a naturally violent people. " He was silent for some minutes, and then, with a shrug he said."Finally we began to realize the Earth was there, as beautiful as ever, if we'd just let her be. It was our own world that needed making over. I suppose I ought to have helped make the stories of the old days, the way Benjamin's Daddy did, but I just couldn't do it then." Then he shrugged again and said, "That's enough of my memory, Son., How's your work going?"

Steve was surprised at his feeling of relief. Maybe that reluctance to remember was as alive among young folk as among the old. It grieved him to hear of the old days, but he knew it must be remembered. "We're doing pretty well. We've got four crops a year now in all the Domes.And we've doubled the nutritional value of most of our grains. We're sending a new batch to Bend for their fields -- two new varieties. One is a totally new taste, a reddish grain and we don't know how people will take to red bread." He laughed, "It's good work, Grandpa. There're long days when we're trying to locate the problems when it can get a little dull, but mostly it's satisfying."

"How about your talent, Steve? I've not heard you say whether it's developed yet."

The Senior Wizard says my talent hasn't opened fully. He thinks it's a different Talent. Not like the other Wizards, so I know he's watching me. Makes me a little nervous soometimes but he's a generous man." He glanced at the old man,frowning, then confided. I am conscious of microscopic creatures, Grandpa, of their actions, their direction - so to speak." His voice shrank almost to a whisper. "I'm a little scared of it actually myself. I have to go slow . It's as though they're visible inside my mind, their nature, their relationship. Sometimes I push away what I realize, as if - as if I'm afraid of it." He glanced apprehensively at John, fearful that he had told too much for that old man to grasp.

John frowned,but nodded slowly,"Don't you worry, it'll come and you'll understand. After what I've seen done here, nothing seems impossible. You and I both look forward to every day, that's got to be the greatest gift of your time." After a moment he said,"Don't know whether I should mention it but I wouldn't mention that Talent to your Uncle William. He may be my son but he's not an open minded man at all. He can't seem to allow for talents. Except of course for -- Healing . He tells himself that the plant miracles are works of genetic engineering. He won't admit it's mind connection between you folks and the plant world. I don't know how I brought such a biased man up."

Steve glanced at John and said nothing. He knew his Uncle Will's bias, but he loved him and didn't worry about it. He deliberately changed the subject by pointing to a small group of children sitting together in a circle under a small garden Dome across the air space from them. They sat so still they drew the attention of the two men passing. The children sat straight and still, not the way John thought children ought to play. He frowned, looking at Steve who was smiling. That's something I can't get used to. But I won't deny it. I can't really believe those kids are really -- communicating with one another. That's it isn't it?"

Beside the children a vine of large blue flowers grew, protected in these cold months by the arching clear dome. Each child had picked one and wore it in his or her hair. They extended their hands upward solemnly, as if in a ritual, then laid down one on another in a stack. The two men felt their energy. Steve knew they'd been attracted by that energy. John said, "They're children, Steve, they can't be doing that!"

Steve nodded, still smiling, "They're not talking, Grandpa, just aware of one another more than usual. Communicating, like you said, thought, feelings, attitudes, wants, etc. It's an AWARENESS." He shrugged, feeling a great pleasure in being thus able to talk to this old man, more than he had even talked to his parents."Some ways, Grandpa, you're more aware than -- than lots of folks."

John turned to him, ignoring the last remark,"And I supoose you do things like that too?"

Steve shook his head, "Actually Grandpa, They're probably ahead of me.

THE AWAKENING

They've been doing that and they've been taught how to manage the Talent since they were two or three, I suspect. At least a few of the Master Teachers will teach that. I think kids are born with more sensitivity now days. More than people my age. Besides they have no - no fears, they take themselves for granted."

They walked on by, but they had been focussing their attention on the little group and Steve grinned, "Well, it's not polite to eavesdrop, but they're making enough mind noise that it's like shouting. Yelling, so to speak, just like any bunch of kids playing. Although I think their Master teacher sent them out to do this."

John studied him, amazement on his face. "They're yelling?

Steve nodded, "Yes, they haven't learned to control their Sending, nor their emotions either. Or else they just like to yell." He frowned ,"I have to screen pretty firmly to shut them out. So it must be noisy for most folk. But I think they're angry at us."

John stared again,"My God in heaven, Steve. You too? You talk as if it's so normal, so easy! That's all that's going on? Those kids are just playing a game? " He twisted his head to look back at them."You're sure?" As he watched, the children all turned in one motion and stuck their tongues out at him. Then they smiled sweetly. John was startled and embarrassed. Unbelieving.

Steve grinned, "It's true, Grandpa. They're busy with their own stuff. John walked on, he didn't want to talk of it anymore. He'd have to think on this. Ahead the walkway attached itself to the mountain side . They could see to the left the steep snow fields that were the favorite slopes for the most skilled skiers of the city. A small group of five moved swiftly down the upper end of the field. They were widely separated but were all moving toward a narrow pass through which they must one by one sweep toward the wide fields below. Timing would be crucial. Steve knew they were in Mind Touch. John couldn't imagine how they did it. They both stopped to watch the precision of movement, the control and the swift matchless skiing.

Steve spoke quietly, "In a few days a few of us are going to make the cross country run to Indiva, It's just for fun, unless someone has an errand for us." He turned to face the older man,"Now don't worry Grandpa, we've registered for Monitor watch at the Healing Center. We're going to detour through a string of villages along the Standish Ridge. You remember them, Grandpa? You were so angry at them when they began to build there. You said they were fools to build as high as Altos and only a village. But they got enough other people interested so that their are three villages being built along that ridge now. We want to see them. It's a community now of little walled towns and the news stories have it that they're doing really well, got their business going and are making a living. They've begun to have their families and the population is growing". He laughed. "They borrowed a lot of Altos technology to get their electrical power, but they'll depend mostly on wind generators in future. They aren't above average storm line the way Adana community is. But there's plenty of wind up there." He turned to grin cheerily at his grandfather,"Their view will be as grand as ours. They could look out over the entire Valley and over the western mountains to the sea.

THE PEOPLE OF THE VALLEY

John looked at him solemnly,"I still can't imagine why they built in such a difficult place. Lot's of better places. But they do have those alpine meadows all around them, maybe they'll make it. How do they expect to earn a living?" But before Steve could answer,they came to the divide in the bridge. He looked at his watch and said,"I've got to get on to work. It's been good to talk to you, Son. We'll meet again soon." And Steve heard the wistful tone of his voice and resolved that he would try to meet his 'Grandpa' here more often.

John went on up the narrower web span. It ran into the mountain itself and he walked soon through corridors of clean bored stone, Great 'timbers' of plasteel created a high arched roof where the stone gave way to a conglomerate of earth and rock. No tunnel was wasted, so each was constructed for future need. To each side as he passed there were large quiet rooms extending off into the foundries, to the small laboratories where metal miracles occurred no less astonishing than the plant miracles Steve would work with this day. John would have lunch at a cafe a quarter of a mile into the mountain, where courts of many gardens boasted pools reflecting strange often beautiful, though sometimes very ugly, cave fungi and mushrooms of every size and color. Some were large enough to sit on. Others had taken unusual shapes. Some were delicious to eat and were served in the lunchroom.

Steve however, went from winter to summer as he passed through the doors to the Dome in which he would spend the day. The grain was nearly ready for harvest and others were seeding. They needed careful collection if they were to have enough to begin the next phase of their development. He entered the great bright fields eagerly.

South of the Domes, deeper inside the City proper, William was preparing to walk across the City. He could hear Annette,his mate, already busy in her studio working to complete a sculpture for the City of Bend. He finished his third cup of coffee and looked out the wide windows through his small garden to the city below. Half a mile away, to the south east, Paul and Jennifer, Steve's and Rachel's parents, were finishing breakfast also. They felt an unusual reluctance to end this quiet morning hour.

There was a quality in these mountains that filled her citizens with energy. Perhaps it was the never ending beauty of vista and the clean lovelyness of the immediate city itself. Perhaps it had to do with the purity of air, of sky of the nearness of the great aloof peaks behind the city -- that lent magnificence to life. Can sensitive human beings live in unceasing grandeur, in the powerful energy of such an environment, and one where personal respect and pride have ample expression, and not be deeply affected so that their very natures partake of that grandeur?

The people of Altos were known through out the world for their beauty of heart and mind, their world consciousness, their largeness of spirit that made them first to support and offer aid to any struggling people, to take immense pride in the fact that there were no 'poor' in the Valley and especially in their city. There was work, useful and satisfying for every person, whether of great intellect or

THE AWAKENING

small. They had considered the most creative task they as a people had ever set themselves was that of discovering how to do just that. Every Valley town or city borrowed from their economic system . They saw themselves as citizens of the world, not only of the Valley. There had been more than one person speculate that perhaps that vast grandeur that they contemplated every day might have brought about such greatness of heart and mind.

Their music,(and Steve's mother Jennifer was a prime example of such composers), had a universal appeal; it touched on the highest human perception, as did their other arts and philosophy. Yet in spite of such wonderful qualities there existed among Altos people a narrowness of vision in personal affairs, a chauvinistic attitude at times and a tendency to smugness. Such negative attitudes were sometimes caught and acknowledged, often not. Master Teachers in their Learning Center, taught them to observe themselves ceaselessly and to watch with humor their own behaviors. Those who heard their Teachers saw these faults, and they had begun to speak of this flaw among them. But half a million people have endless avenues of difference. Difference was encouraged, nourished , especially in this city of the Plant Wizards.

Those who were not able to shed the narrowness in personal vision, who could not see their own flaws from that larger perception, Soul perception, did at times slip downward toward an exploitation of others. Down to that point at which they saw others as a way to get their own desires met. But the pull back toward that greater vision was inevitable sooner or later and so for them, a turbulence existed. The Time of Troubles had been past long enough that a few people could forget the teachings of those terrible times and their cause, could ignore the history holographs and the Master Teachers. They could convince themselves they desired to improve social conditions, a worthy desire and so could believe themselves better able to decide what improvement consisted of. These could adjust their vision to convince themselves that they were doing these things for the betterment of others. And so, one might detect such people partly by their conviction of what was right. They valued their fellows, honored them, but without being conscious of it, as means to an end. They would not have knowingly harmed another, but they were not self watching, they were deluded by their own intellects, by skill at rationalizing. In this way they were inheritors of their ancestors, those whose attitudes had brought about the troubled time on earth. They knew a growing passion for power, rising out of some deficient emptyness of Soul, of Heart, of which they were unconscious.

There were those who saw these things, who noticed the desires of their less aware fellows, but who themselves lived at that level of Consiousness far beyond petty hungers for power, could not, would not, desire to control those who sought to control. For that would only have brought them down to the same place. They must watch and they must educate their young in these subtle recognitions of attitude so that the numbers caught in this narrow perception of life be few. In this way, even those of narrow mind offered service. So far, it had worked. After all, even the least of Altos' people allowed no crude desire to order others around

THE PEOPLE OF THE VALLEY

nor to control the daily affairs of another's life.

But for those without strong inner vision, the power they sought was insidious in its subtlety. Their fellows, those without vision like themselves, did not acknowledge their intentions. They believed themselves to be men and women of public benevolence, doing what was best for their world. They could see no further and would never have thought themselves handicapped. Those who looked far beyond personal limits,who stood at that point of perception that gave greater vision, knew a sorrow and pity for those of small vision. Those who sought personal power over others did not see themselves as flawed but rather as realistic.

None denied the Valley Conviction that stated that the welfare of one must be uppermost to all,and that the welfare of all must be uppermost to each. But the people of inner Vision knew this absolutely, from their hearts. It was part of their way of relating to others. Those of narrow vision, thought it only as an idea, a good, important idea, one to be implimented as convenience dictated. Mutual caring was taught children from infancy at home and in the Learning Centers. Such an important matter was not left to chance. The Master Teachers were by their very nature, deeply caring, selfless individuals. Genuinely so. That is what made them Masters of teaching. Their vision was broad, and they sought the highest aims, larger joys and pleasures. The exploitation of another creature was for them, meaningless, painful, because it destroyed harmony of life.

And so the Teachers taught truly. But there was question as to how that teaching would be implimented. Was it to be decided by each individual, could individual perception be trusted? Or were there those who knew better how it must be made to come about? The shade of that judgement lay like a shadow over the Valley whose life was blessed as no human life had ever been. Here-in lay the seed of the new TROUBLES that humanity must meet in these new days.

The Valley Convictions were:

1. Every individual life is sacred and must be honored.

2. Every individual has a right to life, respect and self decision. Every person has a right to basic needs which the whole society can and will provide for everyone.

3. Valley People will not tolerate a condition in which any person is deprived of health, welfare of body, mind and heart, beauty of living conditions, comfort and stimulation of all aspects of growth in community.

4. Every person chooses his own way, his own work his own style of service. The community questions itself even as the individual questions him-herself as to justice and balance. The re-balancing between individual and community needs is constant. These choices and questions must be honored.

5. If any person or any community has neglected to question itself as to justice or balance, then arbitration must begin. In the case of individuals, other chosen individuals will arbitrate, in the case of communities, other communities will enter into mediation with the accused community to discover the flaw. A flaw in

perception will not be seen as a crime but as a need for correction.

6. It is understood that there is a higher vision, a perception beyond that we have reached. We call that higher vision, Soul Consciousness and we stand dedicated to reach that vision. Every person searches for that perception in his-her own path.

7. No person, or community, may be harmed physically, mentally or emotionally, by another of same. If such occurs, then either Valley court or World court must bring the parties to mediation.

8. A person who refused to live by the laws of the community may be asked to leave the community, for at least a year, when a re-consideration of the action may be made. If refusal continues, permanent exclusion may occur, but only when the community has made real effort to find a community where that person's ideas and ways may be acceptable.

9. Earth is sacred, her health and her welfare, her creatures and her body, is to be cared for as carefully as would be that of any loved one. Life is sacred, no living being is so small it can be thoughtlessly ignored or harmed.

Each city or town had laws special to its self, and these were honored by those who lived there. But there were none who did not at least in idea, accept the Convictions and honor them.

The Valley had spawned all stages and conditions of humanity. Generally these could be divided into four groups. There were those whose very presence radiated an energy and life quality felt by even the most unaware. Those who were aware, could see that steady delicate Light, the Light of an illuminated consciousness. Such light radiated through flesh itself. Such people never judged. They were focussing points of Love. They breathed a Love that was impersonal and pure, but profound. Such people lived mostly apart or disguised among their fellows. They were known - if known at all- as Monitors.

There were those whose capacity to know was far beyond the average, whose vision was expanded and consciousness so refined that they lived with little hunger for common things, no envy, great compassion and vision that saw far beyond ordinary life. It was to that vision that they turned their efforts. But that vision included all of humanity and so they learned trades, became Master Teachers, or Healers, and served as they worked.

There were those -- the majority of the People of the Valley-who realized something of the Light shining from these others, who knew the possibility they pointed toward, but whose own development was not yet complete and who sought for understanding, for expansion of mind itself, painful and slow as it might be, that they too might realize that Truth toward which the Master Teachers journeyed. These suffered much doubt, fear and resistance to the very truths they had begun to glimpse.

Then there were those whose natures were still caught little beyond the capacities of their ancestors. Whose lives among these wakened and wakening Souls of the Valley gave them insight, compassion and large vision, but who could not perceive in a genmuinely selfless manner, because it was not in them to do so. These were the minority.

It was as natural for Valley people to Serve as to breath. It was a way of life, so that it was not seen as service at all. Each offered him-herself as teacher when need arose. But never without being asked. Each watched that others were provided with good work, basic needs and opportunity for development. What those others did with that opportunity was not their affair and there a delicate aspect of service was realized, to refuse interference. The injunction against judging others was so deep that Paul, for instance, found himself almost unable to see evil, wrong, or selfish intention in anyone. He spent so much time searching explanation for hurtful actions, that he sometimes lost touch with the offender. His task to balance this tendency was clear to him but so far unaccomplished.

On this morning of early March, William prepared to meet several friends, among them Paul and Jennifer, both of whom knew more of him than he thought. The trust of his neighbors was as important to William as to any citizen, but he saw no incongruency in using that trust as a tool. He thought that his concern for their welfare made that acceptable. He intended no harm. He was capable of imagining that he knew what was good for others. The practice of Balance, as taught in all Learning Centers in this day, were not yet begun when he was a child and he came to it late. Not having vision of mind sufficient to grasp the obviousness of the necessity for such balance, he had not taken to it completely and so was still unbalanced in himself. He did not know this.

He had as little desire for things, possessions, wealth, comforts and pleasures,as the most aware of citizens. His one passion was in beautiful art objects, a sculpture, a painting, a tape of fine music,a tapestry, but he did not need these things to be his alone. He was content that others have as many,if there were others for them to have. He had well educated taste and as a result, few artists created perfectly enough to suit him. He wanted primarily what made him comfortable and that was easily had. His education was excellent, his keen intellect making him a formidable debating partner, and business man. Disciplined in body and mind he found enjoyment in finer and finer, more careful perceptions of life,rather than in the indulgence of gross sensibilities. Beauty was his greatest passion.

William knew himself fairly well in more or less a surface manner. He did not look too far below his own surface and scrupulously refused to look so within others. He did not know that his capacity to see was limited. He did not deny his personal capacity for depravity but he chose to turn his interests elsewhere, disgusted by any dark and narrow pleasures he might have glimpsed in himself. In this he was not unlike most of his kind. The welfare of others was so deeply seated in Valley life that William did not question it, nor could he have consciously used another person for his own pleasure or benefit. Nor exploited another's weakness. He was too intelligent to allow that indulgence. He could manage his affairs better.

He knew true status among his fellows but its loss would not have worried

THE AWAKENING

him greatly, unless it were out of his control. He desired only personal power and was astute enough to see that the continued trust of his fellows did contribute to that desire. He would have felt contempt for any public acclaim of his learning or accomplishment, but he was not aware that he subtly found a satisfaction in those approvals of his fellows. He thought any display of possessions was the attitude of a barbarian. He was modest, thoughtful, kind when it suited him and ruthless when that suited him. He could rationalize more efficiently than most but he knew this and was wise enough to judge his own rationalizations especially when it had to do with his desires. He could convince himself that ruthlessness was ultimately better for the victim though he would not physically harm any person. His ability to emotionally harm was not understood, nor was it acknowledged. Self deception was a tool he didn't know he used. From that concealment, he used his own emotions effectively.

William lived in a home similar to those of his friends and neighbors. His desires were simple apart form one over powering obsession which ,he was convinced no one knew of. Sometimes he denied it himself, sometimes he acknowledged it. William could enjoy being sympathetic and often played well and with pleasure the role of the benefactor.

William lived in an apartment within the north pyramid. He and Annette had changed the inside of the apartment until it was unique to them, different from any of their friend's. He loved the garden on the roof that extended before their door and brought plants to create a small private Eden. He loved to come home and rest there after a day of work. To all appearances William was a benevolent and caring business man, an astute politician who saw to the heart of his fellows. He could read the attitude of another from face, body movement and tone of voice. He felt supremely confident. Only those whose Vision was of a higher kind saw through these limits of his vision and sorrowed.

William could enjoy sympathy toward others, often playing the role of benefactor for he had no grudge against humanity and liked seeing others happy. But then, the average citizen of Altos had these qualities, enjoyed the satisfaction of contented neighbors.

The only force that pressed against all direction of his life toward its own ends was a gnawing need for power. William did not admit to this, because it would have negated the ideal perception of himself. William would never have belittled the grand accomplishment of the people of the Valley, their success in lifting the lives of every person to enjoyment of a'good life'. He admired the mental acquity, the inner development of Valley citizens, their genuine caring for their fellows. He had a genuine wish for the betterment of humankind and saw the explosion of curiosity, of fascination with learning, so that Learning Centers were busy day and night through out the Valley and the world, as a mark of great accomplishment. He was a philosopher by training and thought often of the fact that for the first time in history humankind had turned its eyes into itself to discover its nature and outward to take stock of the welfare of others. Any observer would have asked then what was the difference between this fine man and those genuinely enlightened ones who watched with deep joy the human condition shifting to another higher level of life?

The difference was that he knew the IDEA of such a higher life, as any philosopher would, but he had never experienced any Touch of his mind into such a state, nor had he seen the actual Vision of such a life. The unfoldment of his mind stopped at the idea and did not continue into the real, the experiencing of what was beyond the immediate known. He had no idea of what would be asked of himself were he to know of such Vision. He knew that there would be greater life ahead, but he wanted to be the one who directed, chose, or designed that greater life. That was his essential difference!

He would never had voiced that desire. A life time of philosophical thought had given him ideals that conflicted with that desire, He would also have admitted to it had it been pointed out to him. He was a mentally honest man. But he truly thought he could bring about that better time more rapidly and better than the slow process of individual awakening. That was partly because he was not at all clear abut what 'awakening' was. He knew the idea of it, but not the experience even of a Touch of it. When he thought of it at all, he assumed it had to do with thinking things out more clearly. The fact that it had to do with intuitive talents, realisations that were the source of good thinking, rather than the objects of it, he refused to accept.

He did not know how strong was his desire for control,but nevertheless it lay there behind every movement and thought of his life. It was not often that William was self deluded, but in this case the obsessive qaulity of this hidden desire was well shadowed by acknowledgement of his high principles. He could tell himself that he wished to improve his city, the Valley and the world and obscure his personal intention.

To see the city of Altos even, develop according to the ideas of William of Altos to be the master switch within the net work of the human social pattern - even a master switch that no one knew of,but that guided the lives of people toward a destiny he could imagine, was his unspoken longing. William's sharp intelligence would not allow him to brazenly offer himself as the arbiter of destiny of his people but it could rationalize every subtle effort to bring that about. He was not even concerned that he be given recognition, he was satisfied to work unknown behind the scenes. But to be the hidden power, that was the longing.To know that he was that power.

On this morning, just before the first day of spring, he stood watching the sunlight flow over the mountains to the west and the shimmering whiteness of the Silent City to the north east. In early morning it was often visible because the sun poured across those shining cliff walls turning them into milk white, with which there seemed to be a glowing light. He did not like that City. He could not explain the resentment, nor could he imagine any control at all over it. It gave him a sense of foreboding. He thought it had no USE. No purpose.

But worse, he didn't understand the attitude of too mnay people toward it. Since he couldn't define his repulsion, he refused to think about it. The refusal to think about something that irritated him had to be subtly denied because it was not his habit to avoid what was unpleasant. He told himself it was not worth his time, that it was actually a chimera, an illusion created by cliff and light. Since people did not talk of it often, he could justify that. Under ordinary circumstances these very facts would have pressd him to investigate, but in this case it was the opposite. There were other people who had been thus turned from curiousity about that City.

Now, sipping a fine cup of coffee, that his wife Annette had brought to him, he turned from the scene to Annette. She was looking over the mountains beyond Altos and he watched the sun shining on her fair, smooth hair. He felt the strength and energy of her strong full body. He knew she could physically endure more than he. She was a fine artist, creating some of the Valley's prized sculptures, and for that he was proud of her. She loved to ski on long treks through the mountains and to swim the length of the lake in the long stone park that ran through Altos at its ground level. She seemed to him to breathe in the very shape and color, the life of the mountains, to carry the magnificence of it through her eyes and then to offer it out again through her creations.He used to worry about her out there,far in the white winter forests, but he soon got over that. She could take care of herself. She always registered for Monitor watch when she went into dangerous territory and he knew that. Why did those people the Monitors, whoever they were, do what they did? He was on the verge of asking her that when she turned to him and said,"Good morning, Darling." ----

The familiar words moved him strangely this morning. He loved her and would have been loath to reveal the strange longings surging within him for she was as free from those longings as anyone he knew. Annette looked now at the Valley, then at the distant mountains, then, giving him another glance, as if reluctant to move her gaze from that distance, she asked,"Why is it Will that the morning never fails to delight me -- when I've watched it come to the world for thirty seven years.Thousands of times!"

He laughed, almost told her exactly how many thousands of times. He said instead,"You know as well as I." He felt impatient, though he knew it was her way of sharing the beauty. To share, for Annette, doubled the pleasure.

She ignored his shortness, "It's a living art, this Earth, a living art. It cannot become uninteresting because it is never the same. It's genuinely eternal. It has qualities attributed to God then, doesn't it?" She smiled at the thought."Perhaps then, those who are called Earth Sensitives are right and the Earth is alive and conscious! Perhaps she is a great Being!" He winced, she knew he hated those notions, and more to hear her speak them.

"Fools, my dear, only fools would let themselves be so deluded."

She turned then to him, her blue eyes intent,deep and with something in them that troubled him. "Well, nevertheless, I always feel proud that our city has complimented the art of Earth rather than ignoring it here in these high peaks."

He was surprised at the feelings that her words roused in him. Their lovemaking this morning had been especially sweet,a reminder of their youth and the ecstasy of those first times. Annette was an amazing woman, he reflected, for perhaps the millionth time. She desired to have no children herself, preferring to spend all her time creating the art for which she was making a name. Yet she loved and gave much time to the children of the Family. She taught young artists, taking them as young as they showed talent and working with them for years so that they were as close as her own might have been. He marveled at the lack of envy she felt when one or the other of them won recognitions that promised world renown. On the contrary, she had been absolutely delighted when one of them won a prize they both had entered pieces for. Annette had taken second place and he had sensed no jealousy in her at all. It stumped him as nothing before had done. She worked with the city planners, though where she found the time he didn't know. She was, after all these years an enigma.

Now she moved to reach out one hand to touch him lightly on the cheek. That touch was characteristic of her and he knew what was coming next. It was as if she needed some physical touch to give courage to speak of her inner life."It's the grandeur the old poets spoke of as being a 'mask on the face of God'." She sighed,"And that's how it seems to me, everything --- all of it there." She swept one arm out ,"seems to be a mask behind which there is - Something - " she hesitated and he heard the capital as clearly as he felt his own irritation rise, she finished softly,"something greater, even more beautiful than Earth herself. I would like to see beyond that mask." Her voice had fallen nearly to a whisper and he leaned to hear. Then she added as if to change the subject for him."Did you know that Rose suspects Jane to be an Earth Sensitive. But Jane won't hear of it."

Why should such a comment make him irritable? He didn't like feelings he didn't understand. He felt impatient again, and understood that. He knew she'd communicated something important to him and that she wanted him to respond in kind. She rarely extended her deepest thought to him and so he wanted to respond, but he frowned instead. He knew any response would carry his irritation, and that was why she seldom spoke so. He reached for something to blame his feeling on , then knew better and recognized his own inability to understand her this morning. He wanted to explain all this as her dreaming thoughts, but knew that was inadequate.

He almost spoke his anger but checked himself. The realization that he needed to do something about her attitudes, that he must get things under control, was a wash of surprise in his mind. To do that he would betray her trust. The challenge was intriguing. Surely he must find a way to turn her from this dangerous direction. He realized ruefully that one of the conditions of his love for her was because he thought he could influence her thinking at least. Had she been less docile he would have loved her less, how ever, had she been less strong he would have considered her not enough of a compliment to himself. He knew a steely strength in her but he thought he had plumbed it.

She watched his face, her mind working rapidly now with a conscious secretiveness that saddened her. Again, she must conceal. It had become instinct in these later years. Unlike her, William could not love what he thought he could not control. She knew that he believed that no person of intelligence wanted to be beyond the desire to dominate his world. His methods were subtle it was true, but they came through as obvious to one freed from such needs. She knew his difference from herself and loved him. Perhaps some day she might wear away his resistance to matters of Spirit, to matters of intuitive perception that had begun to live brightly in her, were in fact, the core of her life. As the energy began to wake, casting a light that shattered old ideas and infected her art with its brilliance, she wanted to talk about it. It was grief that she could not with William.

She said softly, unable to resist one more small try. "William, you know as a philosopher, that there is what humanity has called God. And you know that concept has not been successfully explained. That it is obvious that it points to a mystery. What you deny is the inner knowing, the awakening to a personal EXPERIENCE to that mystery. You seem to have no curiousity about it at all. If there is an idea, must there not be some reality behind it?"

He smiled and shook his head, now they were talking about ideas and he felt at home here. "It would be as foolish as to say that the idea of fairy people, or elves, has reality, my dear. It's fantasy, the wish for something strong and greater to lift us from our worries." But a small fear stabbed at him. Was it possible there was a part of her he did not know? Had she had some glimpse of some inner life he could not share? He dismissed the thought as swiftly as it came. He assured himself that he knew her well and she dreamed as all artists did. Yes, Annette was an open book to him and he said with only a hint of patronizing, "But such ideas give comfort and are fascinating to play with or for children."

He set his cup down and went to get his coat, a long dark tailored wool that fit perfectly over his equally tailored jacket and trousers. William enjoyed clothes that would have been familiar to his grandparents, in style if not in color and fabric. "He said, "We'd better go, Dear." He looked her over critically, "Will that dress be warm enough? You know there's snow out there. Beyond our garden dome it's cold".

She laughed then, wanting to bring herself into balance and to cease this mild feeling of threat that had risen. She went to get her own cloak that would wrap around her twice but was light as the most delicate plasilk. Indeed plasilk was woven into the mixture of yarns to make it more durable and full of its own iridiscent bright color. They went out on the path between apartments and walked toward the public dining hall for breakfast. They arrived at the far end of the residence pyramid, and stood a moment at the high webbing through and above which a transparent energy screen prevented any thing from falling. There hundreds of feet below were the foothills and the Valley. Across the clear air before them, were the distant Domes. Annette never passed this point without a faint feeling of dread. They entered the lift to the dining Hall in silence, their minds reviewing the morning in separate thought.

They stepped into the rich odors of food. They saw Jennifer and Paul signalling and they headed to their table, speaking or nodding to acquaintances along the way. Annette was glad there would be the two other minds to dilute the intensity between herself and Will. They had both known and loved these friends most of their lives. Their friendship had weathered many struggles, and all the hard work of building this city. William did not understand them, could not fit them into a familiar pattern. He had tried, thought he had succeeded and then they would act or speak in a way totally out of character for that pattern. But to his own surprise the fact did not diminish, but rather increased his pleasure in their company. They were like exciting puzzles that he must eventually solve. He didn't like unperdictablity, but was supremely confident of his ability to unravel the puzzle. For Annette, these two were simply brother and sister.

They found an empty cubicle off the main floor beside a window. The sun was spilling over the lower hills and into courts below them where fountains caught the light like prisms, some frozen cascades of water, others, leaping motion under clear domes. The splendid blue of the winter sky was reflected in the pool beneath their window. To the south, at ground level, they could see people skating on the long narrow lake of Stone Park.

William studied Jennifer as he sipped his second cup of coffee and waited for breakfast. He had always thought her less beautiful than Annette. Her long gleaming pale hair was cut less stylishly than Annette's. Both were generously proportioned women who would become round in middle age. Jennifer with round green eyes and an air of innocense, while Annette's blue eyes tilted up at the corners and were shadowed by dark brows that gave them a look of mystery. He smiled, he thought he knew them well. Jennifer's open friendly attitude impressed him as the mark of a simple nature. He could not imagine how she composed the music for which she was recognized. There must be depths that he had not touched.

He thought Jennifer must be full of surprises and would be interesting to live with. But he never doubted that he could uncover his wife's depths. He saw her as one with little hidden from him, whereas Jennifer sometimes made him question. He did not know that neither woman thought he would ever know them.

Paul finished punching in their orders and turned to them. "Have you seen the news this morning? Adana's made itself public at last!" He was grinning, anticipating their interest.

Will turned to answer but Annette spoke. "Yes, I saw the film study done earlier and they've done what I knew they could. I KNEW they could." There was a clear conscious defiance, in the quick glance she gave William as she added, "They've outdone Altos."

Paul laughed, "Oh, Annette, are we really outdone? How can an imitator even with new ideas, outdo the inventer?"

She nodded, smiling too, "That's a point, but I think they've gone us one better."

Paul nodded, their eyes meeting, "They've done pretty well." William broke in, "What is this, I haven't heard."

"Oh, Willy, if you'd come from your office now and then and notice the news,

THE AWAKENING

you'd know." She smiled, taking the slight barb from her words, but he frowned and gestured for her to continue. "Adana, you remember, the people who left Altos three years ago to build a town farther up in the peaks. We thought it a bad case of youthful enthusiasm, though there were several old ones with them. But we were mistaken. They got Harriet and Long, the firm of architects I worked with for some years. I know they're good. They'd done the work, had the best engineers and studied the site for a year before the first girders were taken up. The Duracrete was taken by floater after the deep pits were ready so it would not freeze before pouring, and the main girders set in the same day. It's worked. Their architects and engineers are going to live there, so they've given their seal of approval.They had no trouble getting credit with that kind of backing."

"But what did they build with? No metals would stand that kind of weather, even if they endured the cold. Storms are violent there." Will was angry, trying to ignore what even he knew was unreasonable.

"They knew that. They hired the Phoenix Plasteel Industry to test alloys and a new duracrete, more resilient, but excellent at bonding with native rock. They had sold testing rights to them several years before, you must have read about that. Helped with their credit actually. The product they got is resilient and resistant to both storm and cold. They built right into the rock the way we did, so the stone taken out was available for building in the flats. The two small structures built five years ago endured without any signs of wear even. They were like extensions of the mountain itself. The first builders lived in those until the town was well started." She had the look on her face they'd all seen before when she talked of a new discovery, idea. Always it excited her, pleased her beyond reason to see others creating. "I saw the work when it was going on, I told you about it once, in fact. They wanted ouside opinions but swore us to secrecy because they wanted to finish the job before it was public. What we didn't see then was the amazing beauty of their town as you approach it. It looks like a crystal cut from glass against the dark fields and the snow. It holds no gathering of snow or ice and so it sparkles even through winter. Sunlight fills the interior all year round, it's above a lot of storms, and they have plenty of light and heat. It was wonderful already when we were there and it wasn't even finished." Her eyes sparkled and she looked at each of them, as if to see that they believed her.

Wiliam recovered from his irritation, too curious not to inquire further. "So the city is NOT all built outside the high rock. How much is inside the mountain?"

Paul shook his head."The percentage is said to be about half. We saw the news this morning and the camera showed us inside and out. It's remarkable, as Annette said. The rock up there is grey mostly, some of it very dark. So the buildings look as though the mountain has blossomed with a burst of color and gleaming white. The part inside the caverns is just as surprising. I thought we'd just about exhausted technology for cavern living but they've outdone us. I suppose there's no end to human creativity."

"What's different?" William's voice held doubt.

"It's the lighting mostly, I think, the way they did it. Solar and wind power, plenty of both. The gardens and pools inside the deepest caverns never freeze, even up there. The air seems so pure, everything is so clear." Paul picked up his cup and sipped laughing,"Maybe it was my delight in something new, but I was impressed. And the view from there is absolutely unbelieveable. Makes ours seem small.What a place to live!"

He was smiling, William looked from one to the other not amused at the delight and pleasure this family took in the accomplishment of their former neighbors. He was impatient with himself for his unexplainable anger."Do you mean to tell me that this was done by those young people who originally announced these plans?"

Jennifer spoke softly ,"No William, I think Annette is up to her usual habit of calling anyone inventive 'young'. She watched Will alertly as though she could see his thoughts. "There were many older folk among them. Their leaving means we have more room here in our city."

William looked at Annette who was still smiling in empathy with those who had achieved such an accomplishment. He thought she was one of the most empathetic people he knew and it was another reason he loved her. His face softened,"Paul, how do you rate it. You've done inspections of new towns for the Council. Does it stand up to them?"

Paul smiled slowly. He was an intuitively friendly man, people invariably felt comfortable with him. He seemed to project a sense of ease and trust. Now his large, brown eyes, steady and calm, looked into William's flashing black ones. Paul did not know that one reason he was so often on an inspection team was that very characteristic of radiating goodwill, not only among those being inspected, but among the team members too. The one member of the Council who could have told him that was Grace and she never had. That goodness projected from Paul seemed to William to be a form of weakness. For others it was a clear mark of his strength. It revealed his own understanding of his faults and virtues and a refusal to deny either. He could accept himself as totally as he did all others. William could not define such a quality so he did not recognize it. Paul stood exactly, openly as he was, constantly rebalancing, constantly moving toward a greater recognition of himself and so of his reality. He knew he was capable of fooling himself and that capacity had brought him much pain. Such a position was impregnable and would have dismayed William had he understood it.

Paul's weather worn face, beneath thick brown brows and hair that grew like a mane over his head, carried in it a reserve of calm strength that was reassuring. He spoke thoughtfully,"I give them credit, Will. It's one of the best we've judged. It's passed all tests we were able to devise. After all, they weren't about to fool themselves or try any short cuts. After all the lives of themselves and their families depended on their work. It's one reason we insist that people who're going to live in a city build it. They had a fair number of really old folk, and that's a good test, that they could interest those from the past generations. They've built walls, you know, all around the little towns, joining them with high roads, for walking and riding bicycles or sleds. The walls will be done in another year and they'll have a privacy they seem to need." He grinned at William,"You know Will, we're going to be the old ones soon, and we might learn from these folks."

WIll's voice was gravely and he heard his own question as querilous, which irritated him again. He frowned, at the recognition."How do they intend to pay the Valley taxpayers. They have no industry."

Jennifer nodded, "You're right so far, but they'll be basically self sufficient by the end of the year, then they start building industry for export. Every new town gets five years of no pay before the notes start coming in, and by that time they'll be ready. They've got agricultural Domes like ours and they're building more wind and sun power generators and they can sell that energy. Their wind machines don't look like machines but like works of art and they own the patent and plan to sell them too. They plan to dam up a crevace below the city, seal it and fill it with water for stocking fish and for recreation. "

Annette was nodding,"They'll need more. Most cities have their own power sources. New industry might buy from them but it won't be a great income."

Paul shook his head, "They've already plugged into world communications network.They've got height on all of us and can relay every kind of message. Since the orbiting city was built, World Council has limited the number of satellites orbiting Earth. So we need high cities. Their's are fascinating little towns and they think their biggest income will be from tourists. They're already building hotels and entertainment centers. You can ski there all year round. Winter Sports Festival will probably be held there eventually."

He was silent for several minutes, their food had come and they were busy. After taking a few bites, nodding, satisfied, Paul looked up at William watching for reaction and said," Most amazing of all, the Monitors have asked them to help them set up a station near by. They'll be given the job of maintainance and will benefit from the Healers and Teachers."

William snorted, his irritability had subsided but this idea threatened to wake it further. "They should be grateful they've got a society that can underwrite such a massive undertaking." He didn't want to talk of Monitors. He wanted to eat in peace.

Paul nodded, "All new towns have to be grateful for that". And Annette's soft voice echoed, "I think they are grateful, Will."

Annette was swift to absorb the tension of William's feelings. She'd had lots of practice. He knew nothing of that, he only knew he felt relief when he turned to her and listened."You know Will, they took off some of our best people. For that we've got to keep an eye on them."

"And who was that?"

"They took two of our metalurgists and a new young plant Wizard just finishing training. He came to us from the People of the Way and is said to communicate with plants so easily that they don't need to shield him nor give him any frequent rests. He can shield himself as needed. He can work with a whole dome at a time, which none of our people've ever really done well. It's almost as if

THE PEOPLE OF THE VALLEY

he has a language and communicates without the mind shift most Wizards have to make." She was shaking her head, the mystery of it baffling her. "Plants will grow differently, produce what's never been produced. It's mental genetic engineering par excellence. We hated to lose him."

"Why don't I know of these things?" William sounded finally angry to their relief.

'You don't pay attention to what's going on except in your own business, my Love." Annette met his eyes tenderly, "But there, you're incomparable, so it's all right. And we can get this young man back on short trades. It was in the agreement of transfer. We may not need him after all. I'm counting on those twin girls from France. They seem to have Talents we haven't even guessed at. No one knows yet how to teach them."

For several minutes they were silent, enjoying their meal, looking out the window at the rising sun and the never ending changing of shadow and light over the town.

Paul looked thoughtfully at William wanting to bring him back to his usual good humor."Steve said he had a good talk with your Dad. How's he doing?"

Will felt his face tighten and then relax completely. "He's much the same, Paul. You know he gets very tired working, but he won't quit. Thank God we've got Robots to do the heavy work" He looked around at them, suddenly washed with unexpected pride at that old man who insisted on working daily into his late eighties. He looked at them, his face at ease, pushing his plate and utensils together to move them to the autocleaner. "Would you both like to go a little way with us -- as far as the crossing at least? We could enjoy the morning sun."

They cleared their table and got up to leave. People were everywhere, foot traffic, moving across the garden paths and out on to the webway. Dozens took off the jump stand on belts and soared in every direction like great birds. Far below, tiny figures moved about. Altos was a world class city.

They arrived at the intersection with little talk then Jennifer turned to them. "We're planning a journey to London soon. Five of us already going just for a holiday. You know them all and we'd like you two to join us. There's still plenty of room in the car we've scheduled. Think about it and let us know."

William nodded, promising to call that evening then he said with some nagging worry." About Adana. Did they build their towns near the Silent City after all?"

Then Paul knew why he had not kept up with Adana's progress. That obsession of Will's worried Paul more than Jennifer knew. "They did say they were planning that Will, but it didn't work." He stopped, studied his friend, "I think the City overwhelmed them frankly, They didn't talk much of it,you know. Just changed their plans." Will nodded,then turned away,"Well, I'll call this evening . I hope your day is good. And with that they went each their different ways.

CHAPTER FIVE

Rose woke on a late winter morning, and her mind was full of Benjamin's impending return. She held him there, in her mind, a visual image so real she could speak to him, knowing he approached, knowing he was not far, and yet, she could not reach to him. She had promised. She stretched, swallowed the mild surge of hurt and anger, smiled at its continued presence, and then, shrugging it off, swung out of bed. She went to look out the window. It would be a day of mixed weather, maybe some snow, maybe even some brief sunshine.

She moved back to the bed, straightened it, began to get into her clothes. She put on grey- green body tights made of Skenna and wool, light, warm and soft. Skenna was a product of Altos Plant wizards. Working with a common Valley 'weed' they had developed a plant whose fibers shredded into a most durable, soft yarn. Every River town had it's own fields but Adwin had built the first mills and produced the first bolts of cloth. Over her tights she drew on a pair of grey wool and plasilk trousers and a long bright green sweater and she was dressed. She stood in the doorway a moment, setting behind her the old griefs to shrivel in her absence. With a short laugh, she stepped down to walk to the temple. She thought of something she had read once, years ago. "Love if you dare - if you dare not - admit it!" She shrugged. Was she capable of Love? The kind of Love meant in that short sentence? Or was all the emotion she felt simply varieties of need and sentiment? Would she have been so miserable about a simple separation from Benjamin if she genuinely loved him? "To love is to let the loved one be free" she quoted aloud. That's another kink in my self defense. Her self disgust rose to hurt and she hurried the last few steps into the Temple to seek for a relief there.

When she left the Temple she had regained a measure of calm and acceptance. Evidently it was necessary for him to travel without calling home. He'd done that before. But it seemed different this time, though she had not been gracious about his long absences in those past years either. It was nearly a year this month, a long time, and he had called only four times. But he HAD called: on other journeys, he sometimes had not, but never had he been gone so long. She knew this Journey was different. He had roamed from one place to another, searching, practicing his own brand of disciplines. She knew and was hopeful. His last call had been from the north Monitor Station. That meant he was studying, meditating with the Teachers there. She had never understood why he'd never gone to those Teachers long ago. Searching this time with some direction, perhaps, for that elusive thing he could not name but without which his life seemed empty.

Empty, he said! And she still resented that! He had her and the children and his work and the wonderful town they had all built together and the entire Valley and all it meant. How could he feel empty? And she knew perfectly well how he could feel empty.

She felt enough of it herself, the pull from within herself for something beyond even this life they had created here. And part of her anger was that she too felt stymied. How to discover - where to find a Teacher who could help her. The Master Teachers said she would find her way if she paid attention. And she resented that too! If Benjamin was really at the Station, and she still doubted her own awareness of him, then would THEY tell him how to find that elusive direction? Would he have direct help? They'd surely sent her back home to 'practice living' when she'd finished her first training block with them years ago. Would they do the same with Ben? And would it fill him with defeat?

She looked down the path that curved along the northern edge of the knoll where the cottages were built. Each member of the family over seven had a cottage of her-his own. Two rooms with bath and a small kitchen unit that provided simple meals and hot or cold drinks. Each was sufficient for the privacy of each person. She thought of the night before his leaving, his last night with her in his cottage. They usually slept together in either one of their cottages, and the memory was sweet so that she smiled as she walked up on the deck of the Hall. Angry as she had been, she could not resist his loving. Not even the bright memory of it.   She walked down the path toward the Hall. Lights were on there. Perhaps the others were having breakfast. She moved a little faster, wanting to be with them. The Hall was not old, only twenty years of living had occurred in those thick walls. Built of native stone and plasteel, as was the whole of the town of Adwin, it would survive through generations. The ground floor included a long wide central room with fireplace and solar heating panels,a small, well stocked kitchen and a supply room for all the cottages, and a small office. Beneath were broad well lit cellars in which the food processing Unit was housed, and workrooms for various crafts practiced there in winter. The second floor housed two bedrooms, now used mostly for guests or when a member of the Family was ill. Next to these opened a wide room that was a combination film, library,computer terminal center, with a small theatre in one end for showing films or holographic enactments.These upper rooms would not have been completed yet had it not been for the credit loans from William, whose business acumen was already far ahead of the rest of the family. At the southern end of the upper story was a smaller room devoted to the grand piano and other instruments as well as a fine sound system for music. The Farm housed the comforts and needs of the Valley technology in miniature.

The Hall was full of light from the tall wide windows that gave grace and color to the, heavy grey and pink stone walls. She stepped onto the broad deck that ran around three sides of the Hall and turned a moment to look back toward the Temple she had just left. The brilliant colors of its stained glass panels seemed to wink and offer cheer. She turned ,letting her eyes move out over the fields below to the three knolls on which Adwin was built and then on, far beyond the town where the forests and fields made a pattern divided in several places by the great River and its tributaries. She looked at the scene, loving as always its beauty and expanse. Then she turned to enter the Hall.

The members of this Family had worked hard to build this Hall first, the cottages came later when they had more time. But every citizen spent much of the time building Adwin until it was complete enough that it could begin producing income for its citizens. It was with a pride and satisfaction like nothing Rose had ever known that she walked through their nearly finished town. It was with equal pride that she stood now, in the entrance of this home.

She thought of her own mother, who had never seen this farm. The tales she told during those last years of her life,were wrenched from her sometimes by a great need to record those years so that they need not repeat them. She had given the Valley what most old ones did not,something of its history recorded in film, in written books,but especially recorded as tales told by a woman who was a master story teller. Later when John picked up where she left off, he listened to her work, to guide him in creating plays, films, and reproductions that were as life like as he could design them. He too knew that history repeats itself if the people do not learn its lessons. He worked to present the tales so that children loved to listen and to watch these films, to stand in the center of the holographic reproductions of events and to realize what that world had been about. Such history was never dry.

Rose shrugged, wondering why her mother seemed suddenly so near. Was it because she had lately been remembering Margo and John? Was it because she was struggling to re- evaluate her own relationship, and her life? But nevertheless, it was true. Her mother seemed almost to speak from memory. Instantly she was there, back at the last meeting with her mother, when she was dying, trying to tell her child Rose, something of the way it was. She looked at the little girl out of eyes filled with pain, weary beyond belief, as though she must, must in some way,give her daughter this understanding before she died.

"How can I describe it, Rosy? There were so many who died in violent interchanges, small bursts of war, sabatage, guerilla warfare mostly, but there were also so many who simply refused to fight, to harm others. They were people who had wakened to something beyond what they had been." Her voice had trailed off, and she had looked far in the distance, and Rose thought she saw beyond this present life whose ending she was meeting. "They seemed to know something, to realize something that made all the fighting pointless. So many - so many, finally. At first their refusal seemed born out of a deep weary dispair. Death was better than to continue with the old ways. But then, there was a resurge of vitality, and refusal was alive, strong. They would simply refuse and even - in some countries, more brutal then ours, they were killed for their refusal. But there were so many who had reached that Vision, who were able to speak out to the world through news media and make the world hear. They had faces so full of dispair and a terrible longing. They said humankind had had enough of killing. That we did not need to do that at all any more and they would not be involved in any of it. It made the politicians angry because they couldn't convince such people to follow any party program."

"I remember once, when they were being covered by world news, on Television,"If we can't find another way, let's die here together because we don't deserve to live as a race." There were thousands there that day, millions more gathered in hundreds of city plazas, listening and joining their protest." That was terrifying to the governments because so many had begun to listen. They tried to shut up such voices,but it had gone too far. Too many in the networks were willing to refuse government policy and risked their lives, to broadcast such programs. It was a terrible time but people, like those who knew we must find another way, knew their lives were not worth living unless we did and they did not protest the risk of dying for that effort. There were so many in prisons all over the world,not just protesters, but people who had simply opted out of society through use of drugs. So many that finally," And she had smiled wanly, "we had to quit arresting people because there was no place to put them. It was increasingly difficult to find police officers who would arrest anyone simply for protesting. It was difficult to keep people in the military. Desertions were endemic. Yes, people suffered in the years before the last days, and they died, but they also gave birth to something.:"

"Why was the economy in such trouble? Were there no working people producing goods?"

"Oh, yes, industry was functioning but people were weary of buying goods they didn't need, knew wouldn't last. People seemed to have become saturated with "THINGS". Almost as if they hated the clutter and junk that piled up around their lives. You can see how that same attitude has reverberated to your own lives. You make nothing that won't last and work well for years, even generations. Your idea of a business success is when a product is so well made that only the few needed to supply new families must be manufactured each year. It was a kind of nausea, the way a person gets sick when he eats too much. The people of the world, even the poor, had consumed things until they were exhausted."

She took a drink, and they had asked her to rest now, to let everything go, but she waved a hand, "No, there's not much time. You must not let these things happen again. You must not. Or everything we've lived and died for will be in vain." She seemed so distraught that they let her continue," Yes, you see, here and there a business failed, an industry ground to a halt except for those producing true necessities . People seemed dazed sometimes, as though they didn't care whether they dressed in new clothes, drove a new car, or whether they kept up their business. People literally walked out on their work, their cluttered stinking cities and began to wander the highways, the way your Vagabonds do. They just wouldn't go home. So many had been living simple lives, eating barely what they needed, finding and raising food, and often simply starving, but they didn't seem to care anymore. Then there were the ones who began the Sharing. Sharing , we called it. People who'd left the system years earlier, who had built simple ways of life and could produce extra food for those wanderers. Who wove

THE AWAKENING

durable fabric to offer a shirt, a pair of trousers to those in need. There was a need for some kind of answer to all that life was. People filled up churches but no one there gave them an answer. They flocked around anyone who professed to offer a "WAY' until that proved false, and then they simply began to sit in quiet meditation. All of us began to realize we had to find the answer in ourselves. And you can imagine that shock to a culture, thousands of people in meditation, listening, paying attention to an inner voice. Hearing their own Hearts voice. Finally hearing, since nothing out side themselves seemed to be worth listening to."

Rose remembered, and the memories were as yesterday. The world had been in an eruption of Spirit,of human Mind expanded outward toward that emerging and awakening Spirit. She knew, for all her own life the Teachers had taught them so. She knew because she herself had felt that emerging blaze of inner Light. But the memory of her mother was like a tender touch, a gift on this day of her own need. She remembered when they had found two families coming in to the Valley from the North. They were wandering around, and had made themselves a home in the caves of the River cliffs below Adwin when people found them. They were hunting work. Very much like those that John had met living in the scrub beneath Santiago a few years before. Outsiders, from the lost lands to the north. John said the Council had thought they were a youth group practicing survival training. But then one of the women came to the city for a birthing and they were found out. Four men and three women and several children. The people of Adwin did much what Santiago did when they found their refugees. Surely these had not been the first nor last to wander into the Valley seeking hope.

Rose remembered how surprised the wanderers in Adwin had been when town people told them it was all here for them. They could have a home, furnishings, and work to do and they would all be enrolled in the Learning Center for what ever interested them. They thought 'school' was for children only.They did not know they had skills the town could use. They worked to help in the fields until they could be trained in some more essential work. But it had taken the town people only two days to provide them with the essentials for living decently. People in Valley towns would not have rested a night had that not been possible. Rose thought of that, thought that the Valley was itself perhaps an answer that she and Ben too might look into. Was the thing they sought, longed for, already there in the Valley they had all created if only they would look carefully?

She heard footsteps and turned. A tall young man, dark as his sister, but with hair that curled far and hung only to his shoulders, and a body topping her's by a foot, came from the temple. He saw her and waved, then ran to leap onto the deck and stand beside her. He leaned to kiss her head, "Morning Sis. How's the day going to be?"

"I don't know, Jerry. I hope I can manage without shaming myself." She managed a wry grin and he slid an arm around her shoulders. They stood together, looking out over the dark and dismal sky. The grey reflected in the

River,the barren trees, the cold glints of ice on the path below.

He said, "You've been standing here remembering, haven't you?"

She was startled,met his eyes,"How could you know? " She saw only his love there and added,"Yes, actually I was. I was thinking of Mama, and of John too. How they told us so much. You know, we seldom have wanderers from the north now, but in John's day there were thousands, seeking escape from that strange regressed world there. "

He nodded,"There's still a pocket of people there, Sis.A few still cling to the old ways."

She said, "You remember when Ben and I went to see John shortly after Margo died?" He nodded and she said,"I remember our long talks, and then once, when we were in the garden, he was playing with the children, he did love them so, you know, Benjamin asked him something that he has been asking ever since." She looked up at her younger brother, and saw that his face was serious. " He asked John if it was not true that his generation had realized something -- recognized something that changed their lives."

"What did John say?"

"He said the fact that they had recognized was the one carved into the walls of every learning Center in every city or town in the Valley. It is one of our Convictions. I can hear him, he said,'It's the fact that Earth is alive. And we carved the words,'Earth is alive and She is conscious Mother to all living things.' I remember his smile, as though it was his own invention. And how I suddenly knew more what that Conviction meant than I ever had."

"So what's that got to do with now, Sis?"

"We listened. I listened! I saw that we've ended our pattern of exploiting Earth. We began to realize we ARE the Earth too and because we realized it within ourselves, the idea was acceptable." She was silent, a shiver running through her body. "Maybe that's what I've got to do. Just pay attention. And listen to my own inner voice. There's Benjamin, out on a search for what he can't bear to live without. And yet, he hasn't found it. I suppose it may be something like that first Conviction. The finding of it may be a shock but so obvious he won't see it until it hits him in the face."

"Or it's there in him right now and he can't see it. It's what the Teachers say." Jerry looked down at her, his eyes glinting. "You know it's cold out here, maybe we ought to go in and have a hot breakfast."

She nodded, but didn't move. "I admired their generation, Jerry, they did so much actually. We couldn't have begun what we've done without the ground they laid for us. And they put the question in us. They left us with that question -- and maybe all of us find it stuck there in our minds, stuck in our hearts and we keep trying to discover the answers. They taught us that to live we have to work at learning how to live. First we have to admit we don't know how to live."

Jerry laughed,"We sure don't. And we don't know much about learning to live even. Not even with our best Master Teachers helping us."

"They say we have to learn it for ourselves. They are not here to tell us but to insist that we already know if we will look into ourselves." She laughed, her voice having taken on the sound of the Teacher repeating the familiar caution. "You know, I wonder whether it will take our own children to really realize that? They seem so much more sensitive, so much more aware than any of us."

He nodded,"I've noticed that. Sometimes I feel uneasy with those kids. And then I overcompensate and treat them more like kids than ever." He grimaced. "But you know, Rosy,Love, your Ben had to go again. We've managed without him, in fact, maybe we've found we don't need him after all.It's been longer this time because I think he feels he must make it happen this time, must find something to give him understanding. He must find out what is missing." He turned her slightly toward the Hall Doors and said,"It's only natural, you know, for a man like Benjamin."

She drew away, glanced at him, an irritable frown passing across her face,"You've told me that before, you know! She walked with him toward the doors."I suppose you're right.But then, why Ben? Why does he search so intently and the rest of you seem not to?"

"Maybe we're waiting for him to find it for us." She looked at him surprised, but he was not joking, his face was serious." And we have to learn that won't work either. You know John told me once that his generation had begun to See. He said they saw what generations before had refused to see. To see the lying, the falseness, the fear, the denials and the terror that made people cling to possessions and money even when they were harming other people. They could SEE all that, and it made a difference. But it scared them to death too, they couldn't bear what they realized at first. Until finally they had no choice but to accept." He frowned, his hand tightened on her shoulder."Maybe we have to see something for our time. Something we resist."

Rose nodded, She felt tired, tired of trying to understand, The thought stabbed against her wearyness. "I've searched as deeply as Ben is doing, inquiring of myself how I act, how I am." She was ashamed of her childish clinging. The terrible sense of need for him, but she didn't deny them anymore. She remembered when her mother had lay dying, her Mother would not allow the Healer to help her. She wanted to die. Rose had felt abandoned, lost before a world she did not understand, with her own deep questions unaswered, barely begun to be asked. Rose shook her head,"Mother gave up, I suppose,but then, she had fought so hard and so long, maybe it was right, her time to leave." She realized that she had never quite forgiven her mother for that leaving. And she had denied that refusal to forgive.." The recognition of it now was like ice in her heart. She turned to Jerry,"I think my clinging to Benjamin has something to do with losing Mother and Dad so early." She was silent, then added softly, "And blaming them for it." Tears had started. She shook her head, "I should be long over that."

Jerry knew without asking what she spoke of, and he numbly shook his head. He had been younger and at the time did not know that his mother had refused. He had simply grieved and he had not felt betrayal .The Healer had touched Rose with Love, knowing her heart's hurt, but Rose had refused the gift. She reflected now that Healers are people capable of focussing Love itself. Had she cut herself off? Refused the very thing that would heal? Had she learned more of Love she might have been more talented as a Healer. Her own talents were small, she could act as assistant only.

She felt tears running down her face. The memory, the recognition, the acceptance would make forgiveness finally possible. It was like a stirring of small knots in her chest. And one by one they seemed to loosen a little. She clung to Jerry, and he stopped at the doors. Waiting until she nodded and wiped her face with one hand. She felt his strong arm across her shoulders, his hand covering hers, and she said,"Oh, Jerry, I'm standing here getting cold and crying like a fool. But I suppose it's just as well. To see what I've been denying so long. Maybe it'll help. I don't know. But lets go in and have breakfast and worry later, Shall we?" Her smile was a relief and he opened the doors and they went in to warmth, noise and laughter.

PEOPLE OF THE WAY

Vagabonds

The Valley spread itself joyously under late winter sun. Clouds gathered far at the north, but would not likely bring rain, the land to the south already had begun to see buds bursting, early jonquils radiant gold on hillsides and along the winding Highways. The winter was at an ending. The Great Highway ran throughout the Valley following the intricate highway system the old ones had built. However, without constant repair they had disintegrated and the wild land reclaimed them. Now, with another kind of care, thick short grasses covered the winding ways and nothing of concrete and steel remained except for the four cloverleafs the Vagabond people had improved and maintained. Here and there along the ways were small stone huts, sometimes only stone rings for fires, but usually with solar reflector stoves, efficient and without cost. There were arbors, where vines bore fruits and gave shade, there were groves of productive bushes and trees scattered strategically here and there for easy access to their fruits. The People of the Way ate little meat and when they did, they took it with ritual and deep appreciation to the creatures whose body they ate. The patches of free growing vegetables, were prized and looked after as they traveled. With Altos help, they had replenished the fields and the by ways through generations of time. The People of the Way were a people characterized by joy.

At night the Highways could be marked by the sprinkling of lights here and there along her course. But they winked out before eleven oclock until the Valley lay quiet and dark, except for the great glow lights bobbing here and there through city or town. Here and there could be seen rumbling softly through the deep grasses, gleaming in sun or rain, the bright bubble domes of these People of the Way. Most families had access to at least one cart, but they were used by those with old or very young, someone ill or injured, or full with child. Vagabond artists, engaged in intensive weaving or carving, making of music or other creation, usually carried their tools in the carts and spent hours there completing their products. There were no finer artizans than these People of the Way. Their tapestries, their embroidered fabrics and clothing, and their fine carvings had markets anywhere they chose to send them. But they did not need to sell a lot, their needs were small, their lives lived around their endless celebrations and loving relationships. They considered one of their number ill who was unable to keep a cheerful and joyful attitude. They were fiery in nature, their feelings easy of expression, but they wore out their grief or angers easily and shared them to end them. They were far to astute to be fooled by pretense. They KNEW the love of their hearts, their Joy in life itself and they radiated that joy as a flower radiates perfume.

THE PEOPLE OF THE VALLEY

The Vagabonds were a theatre people, writing, producing and recording on film some of the best theatre and dance of the world. They rehearsed and produced them in their great roofed rooms that once were cloverleafs, or from their Low Carts at town Festivals. They gathered talent from anywhere they could, invited talented people to join them and, people sought to study with the People of the Way in the Great Valley. But Vagabonds also sent their best talent out to the great cities where theatre of the town people had much to teach their young. They performed at the seasonal Festivals, and in any town that invited them. But most especially, these were people of music. Not only folk music but symphony, concerto, sonata, dances, operas, and endless musicals were products of their musicians. The Cloverleaf centers, the Gathering places, they called them, were the hubs of those productions, and anyone could participate. They were times of noise and laughter, of singing and of dance.The People of the Way always danced and sang, whether there was reason or not.

However, if you had asked them, these people would have said their greatest gift was that of Spirit. It was the foundation of their lives and the source of their Joy. They seemed to have touched as a people that point of mystic Light, to have seen through into that dimension of possibility that humanity constantly sought but too often had not recognized even when confronted with its most potent presence. They knew that Spirit, the Source of Life, had no name and therefore no form either. But rather they thought that Spirit lived in every living thing, and partook of, or essentially shaped, all forms, both living and non- living. They knew how to speak to one another of that formless, nameless power that transcended everything known. But they had not spoken often to the town people of these sacred things. They revered their wise ones who knew how to enter into those sacred realms and discover knowledge of those possibilities glimpsed. They had begun to develop their refined Science of Spirit, of vision and contemplation.Those who traveled those rare ways beyond the ordinary world, who knew the gateways through into dimensions of vast Vision,came back to teach .

They sought out and taught any child who came to them, whose Talent was that of the mystic or of the Science of Spirit. And strangely, though this delicate, transcendant recognition of mind lifted them into far perceptions, they formed no dogma and no rules for obediance. On the contrary, each child taught must find his own way, after learning to discipline mind and body and emotions, for they had noticed that perception would clarify and expand, realization open out to vast possibility for those who knew themselves, both within and without and for those who had learned to be utterly still and listen. This was the beginning of the Teaching of the People of the Way.

Their only dogma, if it could be called that, was that all people must know and express Joy, the deep, joy intrinsic to life as they had Touched upon it. The Heart Joy, that swelled outward until it included Earth and all Her parts. Their music and their dance, their creations patiently formed by hands and eyes, were expressions of that Joy. That doesn't mean they were not well acquainted with

THE AWAKENING

grief, but all sorrow they considered human and wove it into their tapestry, dance, music as the inevitable partner of, and even sometimes the stairway, to Joy.

On one winter morning, just south of Santiago there was a family camping on the edge of a forest . A light frost tinged the grasses and the family was just waking in the grey dawn light. A bearded man, dressed in boots and a brilliant red loose jerkin with soft grey pants, slid silently down from a low cart and stood looking around, combing the dark shining hair that hung to his shoulders. The rest of the family slept here and there in bright sleeping bags on the ground. Color marked identity among Vagabond families. As far as one could see a family, their identity could be guessed by the colors of their clothes and cart. This family's colors were certain shades of red,grey and blue. All their clothes and cart or equipment were in those colors. They dominated their tapestries for all family groups made a few tapestries even when they, like this family,had no great weaving talent among their kin.

The man, whose name was Adam, stood silently for several minutes, his hands clasped before his chest, looking far off to the mountains, seeking in the early haze and the glowing nearness of the rising sun, a glimpse of the Silent City. He watched and felt its power as the light played over those high impermeable walls among the glowing peaks to the north east. In those mountains, at the edge of the tree line so high it was visible to all the valley, that 'City' seemed to grow out of the living rock. He watched and knew that he loved its secret beauty and he felt his mind and body respond to the power that streamed from it down through the Valley. He stood, his lips moving, whispering the morning song, the welcome to the day. His hand loosened and spread receptively as he extended his arms toward the sky. He bent his head in meditation, stood silent for some time, and then, as if rousing from depths, lifted his head, looked around to see the sky beginning to glow as Earth rolled over toward the light of the sun. He shifted into a meditation of action, still acutely aware, now of Earth stillness rather than his own. Sustaining that stillness beneath action and sound, he shouted,"Hey, Deborah, come look at the day!"

For answer, the entire roof of the low cart behind him slid back and the cart floor lay open. A woman lay there yawning, sat up in the wide bed that filled half the floor. She pushed back the blanket that covered her and, naked to the morning light,stretched as one who is pleased with and who enjoys her body. The light gleamed on her dark skin, made her pale blond hair shine. She laughed and flung one arm toward her mate, then stepped out. From one side a panel slid over the bed completing the floor surface for use. She drew clothes from a compartment in the side wall, a body suit, tight from neck to ankle its fabric soft as a fine silk but warm enough for the cold day. Then she took up a robe of skenna and wool, a bright blue with grey trim. She pulled it over her head and it fell to her calves. Pulling on calf high boots she was dressed. She went to stand beside Adam and feel his arms around her before he went back to make breakfast.

She stood as he had done, steadily looking into the light of the mountains,

THE PEOPLE OF THE VALLEY

where the sun now tipped the high peaks turning them scarlet. Lifting her hands high, she waited a moment, the sun broke over the mountains, spread a swift stain of light over the hills and into the valley and fell on her gleaming golden hair. She reached out, in gestures of reception and offering, spoke softly a rhythmic chant and bowed her head. She finished the morning ritual. But she did not turn, for the words drew her into that same meditative state of acute awareness that they had for her mate. For some time she stood, her face soft, her hazel eyes moving caressingly over Earth around her. Her voice was barely audible as she said, "Oh, good morning, blessed Mother and a good morning to all whose lives I meet this day."

She knelt and touched Earth with both hands and with a swift graceful movement, she extended her body down against the dew wet grass. She, among the People, a priestess of Earth Mother, Healer and carrier of the prescience of illness or health of all living things, in this way affirmed her strength and devotion and renewed the sensitivity of mind, heart and senses that made her a Healer. She could see the flaw in any living body before it had progressed enough to be consciously known by the creature or person. Deborah, daughter of Earth, felt the power of Earth pulse through her mind and body and then she chanted response.

> Mother, giver of Life,
> Keep my heart open to Life-Joy,
> Open to Life Fire, Life Song, this day.
> Mother, I accept renewal
> That I may give that Life to all in need.

She was for a brief moment silent, then she rose and as if the joy in her demanded action, she leaped up, turning in mid air to stand. It was time for breakfast. Deborah, serving for four years on the medical staff of Santiago Medical Center, knew the modern sciences of disease and treatments, but she knew more of health and she had taught there the Healing skills. It was her life work, Healing and keeping other lives healthy.

She sensed that this a change time in this Valley. She did not yet know what change was imminent, but she knew that it was so. A vibrant power stirred in Earth, ran through herself and all other people, all life in fact. She pondered often what it could mean. The joy of it trembled with the fear of it. Some renewal gestated and was already making itself known to those who could notice. She watched daily, held her self in stillness that lay beneath all her exuberant active life. She must be aware and ready to participate. She must participate even now.

Snow blazed still on the high peaks and sent down a chill breeze mornings and evenings. The People did not shield themselves from weather but they knew how to make clothes to fit what weather came. The rest of the family was waking now, rolling out of sleep bags, stumbling across the wet grass to the stone hut to stand a few minutes under the strong spray of waters in the shower stalls. The heat from solar units kept the water hot enough to feel very good in the chill mornings. They each pulled on tunic and pants, or robes, or loose shirts tucked into wide trousers, but all in the colors of their tribe. The vivid patterns and embroidery telling of their lives, made bright their darkest robe. They gathered plants to make dyes for all their fabrics, and they wove most of what they used. Stitchery of wondrous skill depicted in a shirt or robe the life of that person who wore it.

A young woman, Sandra, adopted daughter to the tribe, came from her morning prayers and whistled to a black horse who turned then came trotting to her. She fitted a light halter over his head and prepared grain in a bucket. Then, in a deep contralto, she began to sing. At first the sound was nearly inaudible, then it gained in volume and filled the air. Two other voices joined her in a blend of harmony that had often delighted audiences in many cities of the Valley. These were the songs of the Vagabonds and their singers traveled at certain times of their lives to sing through out the world. Within minutes every person had joined in the chorus. The first three voices sang the verses, standing with their faces in the sun, while the others continued getting breakfast and singing the chorus.

They sang while the bread baked,the fat tender roots wrapped in leaves, cooked gently. Then the songs ended and they gathered into a circle around the low fire and helped each other to plates of food. No one served himself,but served and was served. It was one of the symbols of their lives and the first meal of the day was always done so. Talk broke out, plans for the day, comments on the weather, a very real and important part of their lives. They were expert weather forecasters,but they included information from the weather satellites that came in on screens in the low cart. They used that knowledge to add to their own and made accurate perdictions.

Adam turned to give food to the slight young girl who had brought roots and leaves in from the forest. "Rachel, isn't it at this season that you began your journey? You've been on the Highways about a year,haven't you?"

Deborah interrupted the girl's reply. "Adam, I'm ashamed of your forgetfulness and she nearly two weeks with us already. What child would pick early march to start a Journey. It's the spring that puts the fever of travel into the young."

Rachel listened and nodded while she brought a plate a food to Deborah. "It was April tenth, my birthday. Lots of us do the Journey on our birthday. I've just a little more than a month to go before I'll be going home, that is if I stay the whole year out." She looked down, a smile widening into a grin at her thoughts and she looked up to say, "Not since I got old enough to get my 'M' card have I felt so much like I was growing up."

" You town folk give the card a year earlier than we do,"Adam said, He accepted a plate from his son and sat on a stone seat to eat.

She met his eyes,"Brad was complaining about that" She glanced at the boy and continued, "Last two years I worked at town chores enough to boost my credit up a quarter. Dad says if I keep it up I'll surely be able to make the space shuttle and Moon City by the time I'm twenty. That's only four years away." A wistful look came into her face."It seems such a long time though."

"Well," Deborah said, "You've been a joy to us, and we'll be thinking of you there in the sky one day. You plan to stay there and work, is that it?"

Rachel nodded, but said, "I don't want to live there, though I've been fascinated by their horticulture domes . I want to know how they raise their food, of course. But I think I want to live here, in the Valley, not so far away. Although, a person can never know. That's what that trip is for, to help me decide." She hesitated, met Deborah's eyes, "Just to go, actually!" She grinned and was the child she had not yet ceased being.

Deborah nodded, "Si and Angela's son went out there, I think it was to Mars though. It's hard on your parents, you know if you decide to stay. But it's your life to plan." Brad chewed slowly on his hot roll and then staring at Rachel's face asked, "What's so great about going on the Space Shuttle. It's not more than a big air car." His envy was visible and she saw it.

For a moment Rachel felt herself needled to react and then, with a deep breath, she made her choice. "I suppose Brad, But it's just something I always wanted to do. Maybe one of those ---"she smiled disarmingly, "one of those childhood dreams that never died out."

"And you've made your choice early?" He spoke seriously now, wanting to erase from their memories his resentful complaint.

Without doubting what he meant, she responded with a vigorous shake of her head, "No, I've only decided what I don't want to do. I know I'm not a Vagabond, nor a scientist, nor a musician, though I love to sing. I will always work with plants, but I don't know how yet. It's something I'll decide when I start study at the World Learning Center. But first I want to see a space station. Plants have a whole different quality when they're raised out in space, you know. It's like they miss the Earth." At their sympathetic nods, she went on, "It's not the life of the People of the Highways that I turn from, I like the life. I want to come back again. But you know, there's got to be something a person wants to do more than anything else. Something you know for sure is your work. My Mom says it may take some time to find out what that is. I've enjoyed this year and learned more about the Earth life than all the years before. There've been some bad times, sure, but mostly it's been wonderful. She nodded vigorously, smiling at them.

Adam finished a bite and said, "It's what I thought. It'll be soon that you're leaving us if you're to get home in a month. You know, child, we'll miss you."

She laughed, "And I'll miss all of you." She looked wistfully around, the many departures of this year had their sadness. But it won't be so long before I return, you know. I want to study with your Earth Teachers. They are amazing, you know. They seem to literally talk to the plants and animals too. And if I can be accepted, I'll come back to travel with your Teachers in a year or two."

"Then you haven't made your 'choice' yet at all?"

"No. Although sometimes I think it'll end with my being one of those who straddle two worlds. Living in Altos to work with the Plant wizards there and living among your folk to work with yours. I think I'll have two homes." She was silent,

THE AWAKENING

glancing up,"After I've seen the moon life."

Adam nodded,finishing his drink,and wiping up the last of the juices from his plate with the thick bread,"Plenty have a dual life. It's what makes us content, I think. The fact that we do have these choices. It's why Valley people aren't envious people. It was a sheer stroke of genius when our parents made those committments with one another, because if we'd been limited to their way of life, resentments would have grown among us, and it could have caused fueds,town against town, or town against Vagabond." He shrugged, looking more serious than she had seen him,"You know, wars were fought over something that correctable in the old days."

Deborah sighed, turning back to Rachel, "You do know the way with plants, child. I've seldom seen a Wizard with more sensitivity."

Rachel nodded, pleased,"There's plenty to do. I love Altos as a city. I like the idea of being near Paul and Jennifer, my parents. I know the way to work with plants, to listen, to communicate our different needs. They can show me how to redesign their growth and I can understand them. You increase my knowledge of all the plants we haven't studied, and in Altos, I can use the labs, the great Gardens and the technology. It makes a perfect combination, I think."

Brad spoke admiringly, wanting to reinforce his good will toward her,"It's the truth, You're a real Wizard.I've seen several you know, those who could nearly get a tree to bend its branches so a person could get its fruit. But you seem able to talk to them." Brad stood, his body too tall and narrow. He was younger than Rachel, but growing so fast his clothes hung short everywhere. He knew already he would choose the way of the Vagabonds at his time of decision.

Rachel now bent her head soberly. With this young man she had known times of pain and joy. He had been antagonistic at first, only with slow effort did they work out their mutual feelings to find there were deep attractions between them too.

"It isn't the plants that I speak to,Brad, and you know that. It's the very spirit of life that is within them to whom I speak." She bent her head, her eyes fixed on the thick dark grass, in thoughtful contemplation. " No one knows much of the Spirit as It lives in the plant world. People seem to experience this differently, according to our nature maybe. We don't know yet. I want especially to know more, but the inner life does not reveal itself easily". She looked up and grinned,"In them or in us. Trust,that kind of trust, comes slowly"

Adam nodded, bringing all of them fresh hot cups of tea, "She's right boy, she has the gift and the fact that she's a town child is no matter at all, for the gift does not come only to those of the Highways. Especially in Altos it shows up often". He finished distributing the cups and sat with his own,"I'd like to ask something of you,Rachel. You know the time for our youngest, Morgan,to spend his year in the city is on us. He wants to begin with Altos. Are you willing that he should accompany you when you make your return"?

She nodded, smiling with pleasure."Oh, yes, It would be a great thing for me and I know that my parents, will be delighted to see him. They've not seen any of

THE PEOPLE OF THE VALLEY

you for several years, I think. It's not like with the Valley towns, so easy for you to come in for a visit. Altos is not on the Way". She laughed, looking up into the far eastern mountains where Altos could just be glimpsed as a brightness against the peaks. Adam and Deborah nodded, and she went on,"I could get Morgan settled in the Youth Hostel and then show him around the city too. My folks would want him to spend some time with them though."

    She turned to Morgan, curled up at his Mother's feet, chewing on a hot roll."Would you like to travel with me, Morgan?" For answer,he grinned and nodded, continuing to chew. He was not a boy to speak much.

    Silence settled about them for some moments and then suddenly Deborah got up and went to embrace Rachel. Sandra, clan sister, born in Santiago, smiled as she watched them and Adam slowly nodded his head. They would continue their journey today and so they began to get their goods in order, close the cart and move on.

    Sandra slid easily on the horse,Agor"s back, grinning down at Rachel and nodding at Rachel's question. "You see, Rachel, just two years after I came to Deborah and Adam, at my time of choosing, I worked there with the Lance Family in the Blue Lake country. They've the best horses in the Valley . They rewarded my year there with the gift of Agar. He was a colt and still had to be trained, but I love to do that. I had asked no pay, because the learning was enough." She was silent, then as she moved off she said,"His sire still runs the mountain meadows, a wild stallion." She grinned as if that pleased her."He controls his family well and they dominate the miles east and south of the Blue Lake country. So you see, the Lance Farm finds him easily every season." Rachel nodded, a little envious as she watched her move on ahead of the cart.

    The People of the Way seldom moved fast. They drifted along their familiar Highways, and sometimes into and through the towns. Sandra rode her horse, feeling the familiar joy at the knowledge that they would be passing Santiago this day and she would visit her birth family for a week or two.

    The Great River wound slowly on, past town and village, among the forests and fields,reflecting the Valley's life in itself as it flowed. It was not until they had traveled past the edges of the winding forest land and walked out into a mile or two of open fields, both wild and cultivated that they looked across the expanse of Valley to see the great brilliant City, flashing with color and light, hanging like a dream in the sky above them. Approaching, they gazed with wonder for the thousandth time, or more. Deborah laughed, "Adam, I never tire of seeing her, she always surprises me even though I've seen her since I was a child. But I wouldn't want to live there."

    "Why wouldn't you, Mother," Sandra, twisted on her horse, curious, because if she were to live in a city, she couldn't imagine living in any other.

    "Too high up there, too far into the sky, I can manage a mountain now and then, or the high hills to the north,but that's hung out there without any land to stand on. I'm a creature of Earth, you know. Doomed to cling to rock and turf." She laughed,"Visiting your folks for a day or two is all the experience I need there." Deborah laughed again, and Sandra smiled at her, their eyes meeting in a loving touch. Then suddenly Sandra's face changed, very serious now, she said, "The Council will meet this day, you know. By nightfall we should have the results".

Sandra slid from her mount who followed along behind her placidly, now and then stopping to get good mouthfuls of the thick highway grasses. Bare winter trees, buds just uncurling, threw dark shadows over them as they walked. The clusters, groves and plantings of fruit or nut bearing shrubs and trees, a mainstay of Vagabond food, were already beginning to bloom, their leaves just turning the branches pale green. Some of the shrubs had already set early fruit. Sandra touched her foster mother, curious, eager, and Deborah suppressed a smile at that eagerness.

Deborah delighted in Sandra's enthusiasm. It seemed to exclude no part of Valley life. She wanted to know all the Valley affairs. She hoped to be a reporter for the Valley Central News Television - the V.C.N. That dream would take her to the New York Learning Center for Communications, the most prestigious in the world. And she had begun already to practice, listening, writing reports for local stations, running down special stories. She was a good investigative reporter already and her request for admission to the VCN had been approved. She must wait until she reached her twentieth birthday. One of the reasons she had chosen the life with the People of the Highways, was because she could learn, pick up information from all towns and cities, travel and see what happened everywhere. Now she said, "Grandfather went to that Council, didn't he? He wouldn't let me go with him. But I knew he was worried. Now what was that about?"

Deborah put an arm across her new daughter's shoulders and gave her a quick hug, then she withdrew to pull a little into herself, frowning. She looked over at Sandra whose face was half turned away, but she obviously wanted an answer. She saw there only an eager innocense and was suddenly reluctant to talk of that dark shadow that had begun to whisper through their lives. She knew most people were so far ignorant of its presence. She told herself that to educate her own people would not be difficult. The linking of minds among them was traditional, an abstract, flowing mind awareness, not of thought, but of awareness, presentness, the consciousness of things. People would simply partake of that general knowledge and not stop to think about how they knew. But this, so far, they had not done. At dawn or sunset, they could count on thousands of minds in meditative focus. Were it necessary, they could send images of that dark stain that Deborah knew as a thread of pain through her own heart. She did not want to give a birth to pain in this new daughter.

She felt the impatience in Sandra's movements, saw the others drawing closer to listen and knew she must respond. She glanced at Rachel, walking beside Brad, with Morgan tagging along close behind, already part of her journey. Did the town people have that mental link? Did they communicate on that subtle mind level that the Vagabonds did? She wanted to ask, but didn't know how. She doubted that they did. Then Brad broke the silence, "You do know that he was worried, Mother . And that he didn't tell us. It's not like Grandpa to avoid telling us -- anything we ask, you know. So, there must be something wrong!"

Deborah nodded, she sent a quick Touch outward to the sensitive minds of her family, aware that Adam and the boys received that Touch, and sadly aware that Sandra didn't. But to her surprise and delight, she felt awkward receptiveness from Rachel. She didn't know what she was receiving, but she WAS receiving. Deborah couldn't prevent a swift glance toward her and their eyes met, Rachel smiled. But through this gladness, Deborah felt her grief weave through her, touch the indestructable joy of her heart with its heavy rasp. She drew a long sigh and said." The Council is addressing the problem of difference." She hesitated, how could she tell this thing, so far formless, without making it more potent and capable of harm.She could not send a picture, because Sandra would be left out. Well, she'd just tell them her thoughts about it, her own understanding, and see that they knew it was just that.

" There's always been a tender problem with difference. When people are -- or feel -- different from the rest of us distance occurs." She shook her head, she didn't think she was doing very well."Oh, you all know that that problem's been the cause of wars, entire migrations from one country to another, terrible cruelty and just a lot of the world's fear. To be different! It's the thing we treasure when it's only small difference, but when someone decides it is a threat to his - his safety - then we -- we prepare to destroy the different ones. Literally, either destroy or make them into inferiors some how." She took another long breath, waved an arm out, "You all know the history of the land. The world history films show us how much such injustice has been our history. Today, there are people through out the world, and especially in our Valley who notice some basic differences among us and who see them as dangerous. " There that was enough. Let their grandfather explain when he got home. She felt Adam's sigh of relief, Brad's acceptance, and Rachel's dissatisfaction. But at least no one seemed interested in argument. In Brad's acceptance she felt a worry. Would he be one to avoid the whole matter the way some of the People were doing? Avoidance, in her opinion was the way to real trouble,. Indeed, the Council had avoided it too long.

But Sandra was not to be put off,"There are always differences, there's no problem there. Our Teachers have always taught us to seek and honor our natural differences. And to respect them in others.I remember when I was little and the kids were learning how to go out of their bodies, 'mind travel', they called it, and I couldn't. They told about the wonderfull things they saw, and I was jealous. But the Teachers said I could do other things. For instance, I can train animals. Sometimes I think they - communicate - with me almost the way you Plant Wizards communicate with plants, Rachel." She looked reflectively at Rachel, then blushed at what she thought was her assumption then grinned at herself. She shook her head and went on," They taught me how to allow differences then. Surely everyone else learned that too! I don't know why there should be concern. Especially not enough for a Council meeting." And it was then

THE AWAKENING

that Deborah felt a quick stir of hope for this young one. There was something there, not that embryonic Reach that was the beginning of mind reception, but something she didn't understand, perhaps as vital. Surely she had done wonders with the raw colt that dogged her footsteps. She squeezed Sandra's arm.

"You're right Dear. But everybody didn't learn, especially older ones. There are those who fear difference and most of us have been too busy with trying to build this Valley, and establish a life here that we've not paid any attention to - some crucial differences. It's something I hope Edsil brings us news of, and some understanding. I feel the danger, myself, you know. I feel it like a shadow touching against my bones."

Adam spoke slowly, his deep,quiet voice sending a measure of calm to them all,"It's something just needs attention. I don't think you need to worry. But it's true, it's also something we've got to do something about. Wait until Edsil comes home, He'll know what to do."

Sandra looked at him, seeing the thoughtful look and behind it the worry. She nodded,"Yes, let's wait for him. We'll meet him by the end of the week. He'll be at Spring Festival too, and we can all talk things over at the Gathering. Maybe that's what we need, a good Vagabond Gather!"

Adam looked sharply at her, and then nodded. "You're more right than you know, Daughter, I think." And then it was that Deborah began to see Sandra's special sensitivity. She was not only aware of animals but also of people, their balance and imbalance, their vision and their blindness and she was aware with a deep abiding love. It would take months for Deborah to fully realize the quality of this new daughter who could not mind-travel nor Reach. The Spirit in that heart was surely awake and growing conscious.

They walked on, caught now in the sight of Santiago hanging there before them over the dark forests. They could see the vast root works, vaguely through the trees, grey and massive they rose from Earth like small hills of stone and steel. But growing things had made those hills resemble natural terrain. The City did not seem to begin until it rose above the tops of tall forest trees. The silvery green of her vast broad leaves, numerous and usually clustered along the massive trunk and limbs, were connected by spidery tentacles of pathway running among them that gleamed in the sun. Winter rains had washed thousands of great globes that hung in clusters throughout the curving spaces of dark twisting 'vine'. Lights flickered through their many windows.

They followed with their eyes the largest branches and found the huge Gathering Hall which was a massive golden sphere . There was a great spread of Leaves around it and people walked down graceful stairs from one level to another. On these were the plazas and parks,and inside most branches were small shops, and industries. Wide tunnels ran through the great stems between the flat leaf clusters and in certain of these were hundreds of shops and cafes of the fascinating World Market that visitors loved to wonder through. Goods from all over the world came here, to be displayed and touched. People often clerked in these shops,but most of the business was done by electronic monitors that had contact with every single piece of merchandice. People were not tied to the endless task of selling and protecting their goods. Once or twice a year, this family of the Vagabonds could enjoy spending a fascinating afternoon just looking.

Adam walked, lost in thoughts he had never spoken, did not think he could speak. He tried to find shape for them, and thought that the real danger was something so much less coherent, less speakable than Deborah's warning. It was something that had begun to wake in the minds and hearts of the people,-- or had not begun to. That was the problem, perhaps! They must not just allow the stretch of mind that their Teachers taught steadily through these generations, but they must actively participate and strengthen that stretch. Must, in fact, make a choice. For he suspected the enemy, what ever that enemy was, was in themselves after all. So then, didn't that mean they were harboring their own danger? And so must begin to understand before that danger split the Valley, but worse, split the person in unbearable conflict? He sighed with a sinking of heart. He wanted to feel that old happiness, the old unquenchable joy of living that he had known since he and Deborah had Chosen together. He shook his head and asked,"Brad, haven't you a song?" He thought if they sang, they would all be comforted.

Brad grinned, tossed the long hair out of his eyes and nodded. He sensed his father's need and thought of the song he was making, a new song. But he knew the song formed around that inchoate grief that Deborah felt. A grief that lingered in all their hearts. Brad began a tentative verse, not finished, but the melody was clear. They heard and hummed at first. Adam felt, as he began to sing, that soft finger of darkness that had touched their hearts and would not leave.

After the song died away, everyone seemed so solemn that Brad shook his head, frowned. They did have to pay attention to that darkness, but right now, they needed strength. He began a new song, a new verse, old and loved. Then the familiar chorus. They all joined in the second chorus and then he began making new verses. It was a song of hope, of trust and of the power of their relentless courage to create their lives daily. Even though it carried sadness, it also carried their deep seated Joy.

They stopped for lunch just south of Santiago at a cluster of peach and cherry trees. Here in this warmer lowland, there were green and lush vines and some berry bushes, but all the berries were green. Sandra came back shaking her head, "Not yet!"

Deborah said,"Brad, will you please find some of the red Odo roots there where the peach trees end. I know there were plenty when we passed through last. They'll taste good with the tea."

Adam built a small fire for hot water and used some of it for cups of tea for everyone. Deborah opened a bag of sun dried grain and vegetables and poured some into the boiling water. Soup would be ready by the time Brad got the fresh vegetables clean. Morgan brought bread from the cart. They sat, admiring the country they would live in for several days,while Sandra visited her family and they all had a visit in Santiago. Morgan ran into the fire circle with a small basket of nuts, cracked and shelled out,to add to their meal.

Deborah wanted to walk alone a little while in the high grasses of the wild meadows. The forest began again half a mile ahead, the Highway wound through it but they would make camp here in the sun. They took bedding and a few supplies into one of the stone huts. They would make permanent camp,which for them, was at least a week. Sandra could visit the city and they would go with her the first day. Deborah walked away, lost in moments behind the tall field grasses . Her mind was full of swarming thoughts. A child of this new age, she knew that the Valley had undergone more than one crucial change during its development. She knew the people had undergone several. And those changes were responsible for what was happening now. If only she could get it all into focus. Could understand exactly what was happening.

What would this new life that was like a Light in her mind, a light so bright it almost blinded, bring to them? Surely there were many who knew how to stand in that Light, to walk into it and through it into that reality beyond. Deborah listened when the Elders talked of it.They said it was the next step. Would it bring dissention? Surely, they had learned enough to keep harmony among the people? Perhaps among her own people, but what of the people of town and city? They were a different kind. Or were they? Wasn't this very thinking a part of the problem?

She stood now, realizing, aware of a whisper of knowledge, listening and receiving without words. There was power, a Light like a wind pouring through this Valley. Ah, yes, that was the image that fit, a powerful Wind of Light that seemed to her to come down out of those mountains from which the Silent City was carved. Was that her own great desire creating its reflection? She longed for that promise -- the promise of that City to be fulfilled. And yet she did not know what that fulfillment would be. There was a knowledge coming to them, to those who listened, who were receptive.She knew the promise! A knowledge that whispered of such Love as they could not imagine, of Light that infused their hearts like an illumination, revealing them to themselves, but revealing more -- revealing something so beautiful, so utterly vast, that their minds quailed to receive even the touch of it. But didn't their minds already receive something of that Touch? And in receiving, were not those minds already stretched to hold more?

Surely the joy that whispered through the very air and caused her heart to lift with possibiity beyond imagination was that very same wonder their Elders and mystics had sung of for generations. The real difference now was that so many heard, so many felt its impact. The People of the Way were waking, not only as individuals, but as a people! She hugged herself, rocked with the enormity of that thought. She remembered the Teaching,'If enough are aware, enough minds open and awake, then a new time will have come to humankind.'

With a wrench, she forced herself to turn, to look far to the south where dimly she could see the ridges of dark mountain that rose there. That point, somewhere there, held a darkness, a painful seed of terror, and yet, it drew her, once she turned to meet it. Drew her and then, in a sudden remembrance, frightened her as she had never before known fear. And the knowledge of that fear stood dark against the brightness of her heart's joy and was not quenched completely. But now, she turned resolutely away, refusing what she thought she could not stand before without dispair.   In a moment of re-balance, Deborah, nodded, always her people had practiced mind focus, had held attention and listened. They had long practiced consistently that intensity of attention that took them across the barrier of this physical plane into the astral plane. And in so doing, they knew of the true nature of death. They knew that Way and taught it to their young because such passage was a doorway, through which further distances could be glimpsed. That astral crossing was a door that opened them to further radiance, to a whisper of knowledge. But now, coming from within their very beings, rose such knowledge, such light like none ever known. It broke through the limits of their minds, stretched them, even painfully if they sustained attention at that highest awareness. She breathed the words softly," So must we listen more acutely to our own hearts? Our own expanding, wakening minds? In absolute stillness could we know the distant, pure realization that shapes itself into understanding?" The words hung there and she had to review them in her mind to realize their meaning.

"How difficult to realize these things through the human brain. Such a clumsy instrument, in all its wonder. Yet we must, this knowledge must be here, in our daily world, our ordinary physical world in these times, not off there somewhere, just behind consciousness, like a half dream, but here, in the living moment, and real!" She sighed feeling the mystery of it. How could they know whether they heard aright, or heard only their own masked desires and needs?

Well, finally she had stumbled on it after all. The enemy that was within themselves. The ancient self interests, the needs and fears of humanity itself, there exposed, finally being seen and acknowledged. Could they do all this? Could they bear the in flow of that quenchless Love that Touched against their consciousness in as real a Touch as the Reach of her own mate?. She knew that she was only one among many, one who in this very effort to comprehend, to open and to be receptive, brought that realization, that awakening to all in whose company she walked. For they were carriers of that Love that transformed their lives, woke their minds and hearts and made them Aware. They, her people, were carriers of that vision from which Love would flow to all the world.

She acknowledged that she knew fear, lying dark and thick within herself. Fear of loss, of letting go of old security, of old patterns and especially fear of trusting to this new Light that electrifed her very consciousness. That stretched it beyond itself. Why must there be the eagerness to See and the fear of Seeing all at the same time? But she did not need to ask that. It was always the way, wasn't it? Humankind was of dual nature. Resolve filled her in a flood, she, this small self who doubted and feared, would stand aside and listen. She would enter the deep Silence this night and ask there for direction. She would stand at Soul consciousness and know from there. And remember!

She walked slowly back to the camp, the hut was arranged comfortably, with their own things. Already it seemed home to them. Adam had hung the last tapestry she had made on the wall. It would be hung in festival this year. But she would not sell this one. She would keep it for her foster daughter's time for Mating. She took her own that her mother had made for her, from the cart, and with a sense that this was a time for ritual, she hung it too on the other wall. Adam looked at her surprised. She seldom took it from its protective covering. He saw her feelings and went to her to embrace her and they stood together looking at the bright, vitality of the colors. This was their own wedding gift. It depicted the Valley, and the people like a stream of life and activity along the winding Shining River. The River seemed literally to flow in the afternoon light coming through the doorway. Her mother had been a fine artist, she thought she could never equal her.

Adam brought tea and they sat at the little carved table, on chairs made in Clandor. The furniture had been here for decades and would be here for many more. She listened to the talk of the family now drawn near the table. Half hearing it, wondering, she was sensitive to far more. She sensed the vast energy of Earth that rose through this Valley, through their very bodies. She knew of it so sharply that she ached in her bones. Its melancholy and its Joy. It was a very real energy. Could she learn to guide that energy, use it in creating their life? Wasn't that what they all already did? Then, could they do this more consciously? How could they bear all that was becoming visible to them?

She wanted to talk of these thoughts, but stopped herself. Perhaps, when they were all settled, when the young ones had gone on to visit Santiago with Sandra, she and Adam would wait, would join them later and they could talk. She felt better planning this. She heard their talk like something rustling about her, her mind was focussed elsewhere. Words formed unspoken in her mind. 'It's what the Monitors meant when they taught our grandparents, taught them their task. They said we must Watch, must be the Watchers. That we must listen for that Deep River when it began to flow'. She sighed, the thought would not rest. She had never really understood when her own teachers had told her of those times. Now, she thought she was beginning to understand. They had said that there would be a step in the process of growth for all humankind, and that step would begin here, in this Valley, and among these people, and that it would spread from the Valley to the rest of the world. Those who Watched must be alert to the beginning and to the task of keeping pure that growth, that humanity might step beyond what it had been. How could they keep that trust?

The children were finishing their lunch and preparing to go. She watched them pull out the belts from the cart, strap them on and like a cluster of large birds, dressed in their family colors, leap from the cart and soar into the air. In minutes they were only small birds flying steadily toward the great lovely City beyond. They would land on the first leaf they came to and reconnoiter. First

Sandra's parents and sister would be found, but she knew that later Sandra would not be able to resist going to stand waiting outside the Council Hall for Edsil, Adam's father. Deborah looked at Adam, he grinned,"Let's hear it, my Love. I can feel the need to talk like a knot in your chest."

She smiled, nodding,"It's true, Adam. I do need to know something about what's happening, what has happened maybe. Lately I constantly am reminded of how the Monitors taught our people that we are to be Watchers. They said that humankind is realizing something never before realized in this world." She stopped, frowning."I remember that, but I don't think I ever thought what that was."

He watched her closely,'You do realize that our own parents told us that there was a change in attitude -- in attitude,you know,because of the Mind Touch. Today we share attitudes among us like water running among sponges."

"We are aware, beloved, we are conscious of the nature of reality beyond this one narrow dimension of it. How can we prepare ourslves?"

"Maybe we are prepared! Our ancestors have created a way of life that prepares us, haven't they? We are not wrapped in the blinding bonds of that fear for survival that used to be normal for all humankind. We do not have that fear, for we do not fear death and we live as part of Earth life, not fighting Her always." He smiled, drawing her near with one great dark arm around her shoulders,"We are able, Deborah, to take the next step and we WILL take it with our fellows." His voice had such conviction that she twisted to look into his eyes, so full of frowning intention. And then he relaxed, wondering how soon she would get this straightened out so they could go for their holiday in town. He saw the dicotomy, the higher and lower intent and laughed.

She spoke harshly, grief in her voice,"Adam, do you see the place of darkness in the south? Do you sense the hollow Mountain?"

His face blanched, but instantly regained its color as he frowned and straightened his shoulders,"I do, my darling, I have known of it. But I refuse it attention. Perhaps Edsil will help us to understand that. But it'll have to be a unified stand, of us all together to meet the power there. Until we know, we must give it no energy of attention, I think."

She nodded, her face relaxing. And you do believe that our long trainings will hold, even with the troubles we sense rising now?"

He laughed,"Absolutely, I have faith in our way and in our Valley people to live through this, to realize what they are beyond this trouble."

" There is the Light that I sense, Adam. The Wonder that I Touch each morning that seems to me to grow greater. " Her voice had softened, and he saw that she was at ease."Perhaps that's what you mean too. That energy, that Love and Light that we sense, rising and rousing our minds to realize something beyond everything we've known. That's what I think is the crucial changing. the greatest opening out of the minds of the Valley people since the first, all those years ago. But even as that Light grows, a darkness is revealed -- and I am afraid that the darkness is in me!"

THE AWAKENING

He shrugged and got up, coming to her and touching her shoulders, "Yes, sometimes I'm afraid too, Love. But we've got to keep watch for one another, and as we do, maybe we'll discover something to show us how to keep harmony." He was silent, and for long moments, they stood, letting their eyes rest as they moved across the Earth's green fields. The harmony of the land healed, gave them courage. Deborah slipped to the ground, her hands touched Earth, and she was silent, for a long time, they sat, attention stilled, joined so utterly to Earth that their bodies seemed no more than tiny shells, waiting.

And then, they drew back, shrank into themselves, gently, without fear. He lifted her to her feet. "Let's go have a party in town and wait until Edsil comes to talk to our People and then we'll worry about all this some more."

She laughed and turned to him, kissing him fondly, "Yes, let's do. The kids don't know really how to enjoy that city alone anyway. We've got to show them."

CHAPTER SIX

Jessie

    The mountains that framed the great Valley came together into a narrow neck at the Valley's northern end. From that neck the Green River raced, pounded and rumbled, until it broke through just a few miles north of Adwin where it began its gradually more placid meanderings through the Valley itself.
    The country from which the river rose in the mountains to the north was like a great sloping bowl where indeed once in past history a lake lay. Now the southern edge of that lake was broken through so that only a small lake still gleamed in the sun. The waters drained down into the Great Valley. But the land had returned to forest and meadow and the people living there had refused much of the technology of the world, persisted in living as their ancestors had done. Torn and hurt by the break down of modern society in those years of the Troubles, they had retreated and never recovered. Farms and small villages had grown up along the edges of the small lake. It provided a good supply of fish for the villages, and made trade between them easy. .The forests provided other foods. The people kept to themselves.
    Just as the waters of the lake drained out into the Valley below, so the young of these folk year by year slipped away to find that life beyond their narrow land. Sometimes a whole family,finding a difference in their children and unwilling to see them leave,slipped away, walking south, seeking they knew not what. The villages kept the more placid, or the more fearful, or those without imagination, so the community survived.
    A trail climbed the high ranges between the small Valley and the Great Valley, it wound through the jagged peaks, cut across the steep cliffs at the bottom of which the narrow raging River frothed and slid. Finally the trail reached the point at which that ridge it had been following, suddenly plunged downward and flattened into rolling hills that led into the Great Valley itself.It was not a trail that was traveled much. The dangers of this high country gave serious thought to those who sought to escape from those northern villages. But for those who saw no other way, the danger was not too great.
    On a late, cold winter day, a time when no ordinary traveler ever chose to travel these trails, a lone figure could have been seen dark against the gleaming white of snow. At a point where the trail rose above forest and field and entered that narrow cleft between the surrounding peaks, stood a small, old woman. She stood a moment looking backward. Her eyes were full of a relief and sorrow of farewell, for she knew she would never travel through that land again. She had spent long months living in the communities of the Crescent Lake, finding those who could and would receive healing, whose hearts longed for a greater life, or whose Vision had begun to expand toward those dimensions their narrow world

denied. She offered and pointed a way of growth and hope.

She wore stout walking boots, thick wool pants and shirt with a water proof cloak that fell below her boot tops.The fabrics of this north country had none of the light yarns of the south and were heavy, the colors dull, but they were certainly warm and well woven. She felt no chill here on this snow field, silent in the bitter winds that wrapped around her and then spun off to return again, colder. She had done what needed to be done there among those people whose consciousness had only begun to wake; whose understandings were still new enough to do little more than unsettle those whose minds broke through the old patterns.But for the young, born with new minds, wakened consciousness, there had to be some help. And she had left that help among them in the form of Teachers of their own people.These few open minded adults, begging for learning even in secret, were grateful to her for her help and committed themselves to carry on. She had helped them to understand their own awakening minds and to trust their Vision. She had introduced them to each other, broken the terror of secrecy that each had lived in and taught them how to center their attention,to Touch consciously that point of deepest awareness. She helped them to see the Way was within themselves, together.They need only add the difficult practice of selflessness,without self abnegation, harmlessness,that kept a sharp attention to wrong around themselves, and mindfulness with no arrogance, and they would learn what must be learned.

Their Learning Centers were adequate, though she had had to send for a whole new category of films and books and had only been able to because of those two selfless souls who chose to remain there in that forsaken land to serve those of their people who would be in need.She felt, looking now back, that she had only barely given them a foundation. But that should be enough. They knew how to watch and listen now.

As she watched the sunlight gleam on the bright water and shine like a green curtain from the healthy fields and forests, she nodded and smiled. "It's enough.It is enough, after all. I taught them how to LOOK at the Earth and to listen to Her and She will teach them more than they can guess."

She turned then, setting her feet into the narrow trail., She had climbed since before sun up and now was above the forests. Small twisted trees and shrubs bent with their load of snow, making small caverns and caves beneath themselves within which she knew that creatures found small forage, or moved to safety. Before her there was only the face of the cliffs to either side and the hillsides covered with tumbled snow and bent trees. She was finished there. Now, frowning, she remembered the nagging worry, whether she had possibly trespassed across that fine line between teaching them alertness of mind and heart and that of pressing her thought upon them. She shook her head. She must talk with Daniel about that. He understood her besetting fault.

Now she must cross the mountains, something no one from either valley would have considered this time of year. But Jessie, wandering Teacher, felt the deep powerful pull of her home Retreat. It lay beyond these peaks and she longed to be there, to see one last time those loved ones who had guided her own development, to set her feet in those courtyards, to sit in that warm sun and doze for an after noon or two before going on. And to meet finally that young man who sought for her, who would accompany her into her last labor.

She felt the fierce breaking of the freezing wind against her body. Her exposed face stung with the harshness of it, and she drew her cowl over so that only her eyes were exposed. Frail, old and small, she stood like a bit of dark broken earth in the white unblemished path., No one had come this way this last two months. But she knew the ice broke in the lowest streams , that below in the Great Valley already there would be buds swelled and the early willows red with promise. Snow fell around her, the footprints she had pressed into Earth were already gone. She looked down at the utter smooth world around her,"Indeed, I am little more than a broken bit of Earth." She smiled at the thought.

She sighed, she must be on her way. She found a small pleasure in talking to herself this way. The trail cut into a shadowed steep ridge, one side plunging downward, the other pressed against her shoulder as it soared into the sky, its only advantage was that it was so steep it held little snow. She set her feet carefully, watching to be sure there was no ice to slip on."I need to say good bye to these lands, to these crags where so long ago, I first realized my Earth Task. It has been my Way for these forty three years." The thought made her smile. So long! It had not seemed so.

She remembered the day she had said goodbye to her son and his family and her daughter already established in the Science Center of a great city to the east. Her mate gone, killed in the building of the first city beneath the sea. A freak accident that had not happened until the city had been completed and lived in for years. It was being extended. Had the accident occurred before the city had been tried, it might have held up its colonizing for years. But it had been proved and the accident revealed only one more problem to be solved. The world had learned more than anyone dreamed from the building of that ocean city. Without it, colonies on other planets would not have developed nearly as soon. But her mate had died and she was no longer needed as mother. It was then she began the second span of her life work.

Not too long after that, day of decision, she had climbed this pass the first time. She had lived with the Cresent Lake people for a year then, and then had gone on across these same trails, but at that time it was summer and the snow was gone from most of the high country. She had found the North Monitor Retreat where she would submit herself to intensive training for the next five years. Training was never ending, but those five years had prepared her enough to begin the work she must do. She intended then to find and work with all those whose minds were broken from the old patterns, who had pressed through the limits of the old human boundaries. But who were afraid, or confused, unable to understand. Then, so long ago, when she was young, there had not been so many like that. Those who had begun to recognize the nature of humankind and of Life Itself were just waking into awareness.

THE AWAKENING

She smiled. How esoteric it had all seemed at first. Until she had been able to look beyond the surface of things, think beyond the obvious and spend intense hours exploring the abstract mental universe into which she stepped. She shook her head,"How did I ever do it? It was truly a new dimension, unknown."

But there it was, as always, for everyone, once the resistance had been breached, once perceived,it was so obvious, so clear. She brought her attention into focus. This path needed attention or this body might plummet hundreds of yards below. She pressed her hips against the cliff face. The wind was rising, she could hear it beyond this narrow cleft.She would feel its force increase as she rounded the bend into a straightaway.She drew her self together, focussing attention carefully. Then, the trail widened a little, she walked more easily and immediately spoke again."Well, my work is near done. It will be wonderful to be home again."

She had visited her children and their families during the year before she came west, teaching in nearby Learning Centers and working among those in villages surrounding them. She had been able to know her grandchildren and to teach them too. She smiled, remembering, it had been a dream fulfilled. Then she had told them all that she would not see them again. And she had taught them how to let her go.

Now, there was one more task to do, another familiar community to return to and complete her work. An opportunity for this communion with the Mountain heights, the stillness, did not displease her, even in winter. There were few choices, since there were no air cars in the Crescent Valley. Though the Station would have sent one, in emergency,she didn't consider this an emergency. She could walk the mountain trail. Then she would be on to the next -- the last - task of her life. But first, she would have a good visit with her own people, a time spent with those in that home Station. She pushed her booted feet through the soft new fallen snow. She walked for another hour, a slow climb, little to be seen here except cliffs and jagged ridges covered with snow and ice. The rise of gleaming peaks, and the fall of black sharp wind swept ridges that plunged down and down,was beautiful. The stillness, the vast distance, drew her thoughts deeper into focus. She was at once a' small brown bit of Earth' and extended beyond herself, merged in singleness of being with all that was before her, with mountain and bird and Earth rolling down to the glint of tumbling water of the young River. Her mind knew the singleness, the vast reach of Soul consciousness and the small multiplicity of personal consciousness and allowed both at once. She was silent, realizing,aware. Time lost meaning.

For a long time the snow fell, as silent as the rock it fell over. Soft blanket that protected trees from the bitterness of the winds. The blur of its heavy fall shut off the distance completely. She walked in a small cave of white silence. Her own body creating the faint glow that gave her direction in this thick curtain. The mountains filled her with their stillness and their slow patient life. She was buoyed up by it, and all the business of her life seemed suspended, faded. These peaks, the utter silence and the depthless Earth beneath her, gave her a Touch with the

THE PEOPLE OF THE VALLEY

business of Life itself.

She was acutely aware of every sound, every creak of snow laden branch, of snow slipping on steep cliffs above . She made her way. So sensitive had she become to the sounds of Earth around her that she knew, without looking up, the danger lurking above in an overhang of snow. Snow fell on, increasing the load on that massive dome above. She looked up finally as she passed beyond its reach. Should she bring it down? It would release itself soon,but there were no other travelers on this mountain just now. It would not harm other lives. Animals sensed it's nearness to release and stayed away. She would leave it. She went on.

The path widened, leveled a little and ran through a narrow plateau. Sheltered a little,the trees here were stronger, taller. She settled down on the branches of one and ate her lunch. It was late, the dark would come early. She must reach the cave in time.

The hours passed,and she did not cease her slow steady walk.She climbed delicately over crevaces that yawned beneath the snow cover, her vision passing through them and showing her the possible safe crossing. She teetered across the impossible edges of a cliff whose fresh surface told her that the great slab fallen far below had taken away the path. The new face had only broken edges, sharp and fresh on which to keep her balance and she must stop a moment to decide. The people must know that the path was gone, or she must cut out another. She deliberated. A message could be sent when she reached the Station and surely no one crossed the cliffs in winter. She went on.

Finally she came out upon a long meadow and passing across it without trouble, she began to climb again. She felt relief. This was the highest ridge she must traverse. She would not reach the end of its broken spine until morning light made the way easier. After that the mountains began to fall away into high hills with a view of the Great Valley spread like a tapestry below. The memory encouraged her and she walked faster. The winds increased as evening came, snow fell in such blinding rage and so thick she could not see through it at all. She was in a place of utter blindness and there was nothing but the white wind. She could not see where to put her feet and so she had to attend carefully, focussing mind-sight deeper into the earth around her to know the conditions. She kept on. She reckoned that the cavern, kept for shelter by the Station, was perhaps a mile farther.

In the meantime, must she obey the precept to travel without the use of the Power? Or could she offer herself that help? This old body was weary. She smiled. It was not a hard and fast rule that one refuse the help of the Power. It was part of the pride of traveling Teachers that their Power be used only for aid of others and even then, only when other more common means had been exhausted. Well, she did not need it yet, she could still travel. She pushed on, the wind like a living breathing body against which she leaned. It's push made her breath so cold her nostrils felt frozen, her face numb, and she wrapped her head scarf around her hood to cover everything but her eyes, then laughed at herself. I

THE AWAKENING

can't see anything anyway. I might as well protect them too. She fitted her mind into Earth life, felt down to the rock beneath her feet,followed it precisely and blind.

The snow covered her body, and with a quick shrug she would cause it to cascade from her, then stopping to listen, she could hear the whine of many winds, and in their lull, the whisper of falling snow. She focussed, Reaching, her listening mind like a search light ahead and there, only a short distance, was the responsive resonance that was the cave. The hollow depths of it extended far within the mountain beyond the small entrance way that travelers used. She pushed against the snow that made walking difficult. It was so deep it was like walking in knee deep mud. And wearily, she turned to lean against the cliff side, feeling with her fingers. She slid her body along the cliff face and suddenly she felt it disappear and her hand reached through into a crevase. With a sigh of relief, she slid into the space beyond, out of the wind and cold. She searched along the edge for the slim lever that would clear the entrance and then close it. She stepped in, and light flooded all around her. Blessed light. It was as welcome as the warmth. The shell of plasteel that covered the opening blotted out the sound of the storm. All was quiet here, with the sudden blocking out of the wind.. She reveled in that quiet, walking softly so as not to break it.

There was heat, food, a dry,firm mattress she could pull from its slot in the wall. She activated the heating unit inserted into the stone wall , watched the orange dance of pseudo flames, an anachronism in these days, but left over from times when people felt the comforting of burning fires. She placed her sleeping bag on a flat bench cut from the living rock and opened her pack to take out the small heat cube that she inserted into her food container. She left it to heat her stew while she went to the trickle of stream that dripped from a back wall and fell into an oval basin below. She washed herself, drank, and prepared herself to sleep.When she came back, the odors of the stew made her stomach tighten with hunger and she smiled. To be hungry and have the means to end it is a pleasure. She ate slowly, letting her eyes close now and then, enjoying the comfort of no longer needing to be watchful. The climb had wearied her old body and she slid her hands down across her hips, pressed small hands against the firm muscles beneath her clothes and said,"Just a little longer and you will be freed of me, little body, Just a little more that you must do."

She slid into her sleeping bag, let her body relax, her mind ease and her heart calm. The stillness wove itself around her, the light faded when she touched the control and she let it stay faintly on. She knew that power here was wind power with a generator deeper in the cavern. Silent and powerful, it would last for generations, maybe centuries. Humankind built for eternity these days. The precious labor of human hands was not wasted on ill made machines. She smiled at the fact, glad it was so. The soft light made faint shadows among the standing edges of rock. And the silence grew.

She allowed herself to respond to that silence, the depth of thoughtlessness, the recedence of her senses. Here mindfulness was steady, the power that flowed through the Earth around her was mentally visible. Her attention permeated the heart of the mountain, felt its life, slid through the shifting and stable rock of its core.The storm around the mighty ranges that thrust themselves out of this northern Earth was an expression of Earth energy, of the endless movement of the ocean of atmosphere around those thrust peaks. Jessie followed the streams of energy, then gently settling deeper into herself, she knew that bright Source from which all these energies drew their power, that inflow that came from -- whence? The power that gave Life itself to this world flowed deeply, releasing these lesser energies as it moved. And Jessie, attuned, focussed, utterly still, knew that Power pulsing through her very being, the greater Self creating through this person one of the doorways through which it poured. Now, in stillness, she reached through herself toward that Source. At once she was complete. She felt the power of the mountain,it's hard, absolute stillness,and then, the mighty groanings and shiftings that broke that stillness. She was content here. She would let this body sleep and rest, and she would listen and watch.

In the morning, she ate, turned all services off to conserve them for the next in need and left. The snow had covered the entrance so completely she activated the door shield to clear it away. When all was ready, she closed the entrance again and was on her way. She could see nothing ahead except the flat face of another cliff, but as she approached, she could see the break through which the path wound. Passing through, walking for several minutes in this utterly shadowed crevase between cliffs, she was deeply aware of the silence. Here not a trace of wind entered, but when she walked out on the other side the morning sun was blazing on the far peaks, snow was blinding in its reflection and there was a slim pie of sky through the rock above. Soon she would see the Valley, through a break ahead. She felt eager impatience. She passed a sharp bend and there, below, lay the undulating land. The mountain fell away, ridge after ridge dropped until they became hills, rounding out and covered with forest or with bright green meadow. The sun behind her had not reached even the lower hills, but the western peaks were shining and bright. She laughed. Another hour of careful travel and she would descend beyond the heavy snow.

She kept on, traveling slowly, but with her heart light, her anticipation a literal lifting. Slowly the winds grew less, their force no longer pushed against her back. She straightened up, relieved of their pressure. With a sigh, she moved on, tasting automatically the terrain under the still deep snow. Then, descending the ridges she found whole stretches cleared of snow, but a cold wind hammered at her. She had arrived at the scrub growth, and trees grew in the sheltered spots. She descended onto barren,ice splashed rock, her feet gripping that ice with pure force of mind, for they would have slipped from under her without it. She chuckled at herself, reminded of the letter of the law -- the use of the power to preserve life was acceptable.

Then she entered a stretch where the snow piled deep. New snow fell again, and to go on she must push her way through hip deep snow fields. She started on, resolute, feeling that old sense of challenge that made it possible through all the years to go and come through nearly impassable terrain through out the world. There was a joy in testing herself against the elements using nothing but her own physical strengths against a physical world. But finally she stopped, breathing hard, feeling a thin thread of pain that caught in her chest. She bowed her head,, humbled. "Well, I can not ask this old body to do that much more. I cannot insist lest I do not keep it well enough to finish what I must do."

Power must not be used for personal gain. Her mind weighed the situation and she knew the need was not simply personal. She must be there in that Valley, must do that work there. Gently she lifted her body above the snow with the sheer force of power in her. Every Monitor, trained to perception, to Vision,and to a consciousness beyond this ordinary world, could easily have followed her. That power had never been used in the sight of others unable to use it. But Jessie knew there was no one here except the birds and they would not tell. Easily and lightly she moved out across the surface of soft snow and finally arrived at the lower elevation where the snow was only a wash across the ridges and where trees already stood tall and straight. Below, as she set herself down softly against Earth, her whole weight settled into her boots, she looked upon the rumpling green of forest and field below. It was a rest to her eyes after so much white. From here she could see the falling hills, the River spreading out from its pell mell race down into that quiet. She stood a moment in contemplation of the beauty of it, the beauty that triggered again the mind lift, swept her to that point of perception from which she could KNOW something of the Life that pulsed through Earth and thus created this inexpressable balance and wonder before her. She stood,aware of so much and payed no attention to the fact that her feet barely touched the ground.

She began again to travel and the path was steadily downward. She thought of the young man who waited for her there below, whose quest had taken him far and finally returned him here. Benjamin! She must meet him and he would accompany her into that Valley where events must proceed. He had arrived at the Station some weeks ago and the Monitors there had taught him much, much that would help her in the work ahead. His mind was sharpened, focussed, with a little nudge he would soon break through old patterns himself and See what an awakened human Soul saw naturally and with understanding. He would be ready to help her with this last life task. She smiled.

She let her eyes follow the ridge below, move to the rounding hills beyond and the upthrust of rock that jutted outward in a series of pinnacles from one long high hill. There among the dark trees, above a lovely small valley where people lived quiet dedicated lives, was the Station. No one, not knowing where it was could have seen it. The pinnacles looked like nothing more than rock formations. But Jessie knew that down within and between that hard rock were graceful buildings and residences for students and teachers. There, within the tallest pinnacle, hollowed for the use, were the rooms wherein the highest Teaching was given and where the Watching Monitors listened and created their end of that network of mental energy that criss crossed the Great Valley below. She grinned, knowing they knew well of her coming. And she sent out like a flame of lightning, a sharp ring of joy. Her salute!

She began to walk on slowly, watching the spot where the Station was built. Soon it would disappear behind other outcrops,but now, shifting her sight a little, she could see the radiance of golden light shot through with blue that filled the air for half a mile around it. Here young people from every nation of the earth came to learn. To be trained. For every nation needed Monitors. She looked, savoring the sweet radiance, its nearness, and remembering that much hard work waited her there too. None, save those awake, alive to the Spirit that flowed through them, would see that golden-blue Light. Hearts once wakened, but making the choice of the dark way, found only a confusion, a sense of discomfort here. That the young man had found unerringly the Station, entered in without hesitation, demonstrated to those within that he was ready to learn. She too must learn more before she could complete her own work.

She felt her heart lift with knowledge of the gathering there at the Court of the Dawn. She could simply propel herself among them, in moments, share that ceremony so like that of the Vagabond's. Be finally home. But she would not use the Power for so selfish a desire.

Already the sun touched the trees around the buildings of the Station. She could see the pinnacles, a light in two high towers. The sun had brought their colors out, rose, grey and glitterings of green. She stood, Reaching out, leaning toward that place. The song touched her mind, was flung out as if from a light house across the dark hills. She could greet the sun with them, could cast her mind out among them, Join in their Song.

Watching she could see the light descend from the high towers down into the lower courts., Saw it slip like silver through those shining needles of pine and fir. She felt breathless with the strange sense of renewal that the ceremony always gave her and she had celebrated the sunrise many thousands of times. There was the familiar deep rush of joy rising from Earth, energy flowing through her body upward, bringing a tingling to her limbs, and surging in a wave on to her head and she lifted up her arms to throw that energy on, outward and down into the hills and valleys below. The high energy of Life chimed through her mind and heart as it poured forth. And she felt it returned like a reflection of itself from every living thing waking to this new day. Humankind, wakening, found the vision of Earth's inherent Love becoming visible, as visible as their own heart's love allowed.

There the sun saturated the Valley with Light as the Earth tilted herself over to receive. That same energy poured into those twisted bent shrubs, the straightening trees. She sang the celebration with the voices far below, soundless,they filled her mind. Then she turned back to her trail, the little trees. She thought,"I am like these shrubs, bent with life but tough." She laughed at her conceit. Gusts of wind pushed at her, but they were not freezing here. She drank in the wind, feeling the freshness fill her lungs. There, they would sing out below, all the Mothers,the Fathers and students, together, in one outpouring of Joy. This

THE AWAKENING

was the only Teaching Station and Monitors here took roles of Parent to their charges. Even though they might have heavy burdens weighing their hearts, in this moment, it would all be set aside, to welcome the Light. They knew they received the pulse of energy coming to them out of the Silent City, beaming through the very sunlight into their consciousness, they received and then sent it on. The energy of Spirit Itself given, offered as a breath is offered by the air.

They knew how to lift that joy and to fling it far, streaming through the land. The sky was bright, thin bands of clouds striped the eastern sky, but two great piling white thunderheads rose out of the west and moved in a stately slow drift across the distant hills. The air was crisp, clear. Jessie felt good.

She listened, keeping her attention cast beyond these high hills and she joined in their song.

> Earth Mother, we sing Life forth,
> We, Earth Children, living flames of Earth Life,
> Cry out Thy welcome reception to that great life
> That shapes itself as Father Sun.
>
> Let the vessels of our bodies receive light
> Join with the trees and all life
> To receive the gift of Light into Thy dark Womb.
>
> We sing the song of Joining,
> The linking of life to Life,
> The creating of the day.
> May the echo of our song carry far.
>
> May it meet those who wake to sing beyond us
> That the celebrating of the dawn
> Follow the returning Light around this world"
>
> Earth Mother, greets the Father of Life,
> That great Spirit who breathes intelligence into us,
> And all together we sing in celebration of the nameless
> One from which Life rises eternally conscious
>
> We hear Thy Sound in this physical world,
> The mirror of life, the womb of creation,
> We flame upward in song from that Great Heart
> That lifts all human minds into Touch with Eternal Life.
>
> We Join in the Solar System's Joy,
> When we send that river of Love outward to all life,
> Love, Light, and the Power of the ONE.

The familiar words, the sweet memory of that haunting melody, lifted Jessie and focussed her whole being at its highest point of awareness. The sense of power around her grew, she seemed herself to stand receptive and to Send on that power from Earth, from Sun! She was a conduit, they were all conduits through which that energy flowed. And she felt the last refrains of the song, she sensed those over the ridges in the next Valley, preparing to catch and send again the Light. Daily it would wrap itself forever around the world. The Earth and Sun sang through their creatures outward and inward, toward that vast Source!

Jessie felt eager to go on. The wearyness of the night and morning was washed away. She turned with the joyousness of renewal shining from her eyes, radiant from her face, and began the journey down. She watched with amusement as her legs could not push through a patch of deep snow, became balked in the stickyness of it. She floundered, came to a stop. Again, she lifted herself out in delight,playing like a child making soft footprints that barely pressed against the surface.Then she was on wind blown rock, nearly bare, the deep snow lay behind her. She walked carefully feeling the grainy sand stone of the lower paths. With relief she could forget this old body. Here the trees stood, shading her path, a few gnarled disciduous trees fought to live among them. The slopes were dark with the living green and with a cry of delight, she ran to a small bush that held out on its stiff twigs, small round yellow fruits of the alpine pear. Small and hard, they were very sweet, nourishing and hardy. God bless the people of Altos who sent their young ones to plant them on these high trails. She gathered a pocketful and went on.

The path ahead was winding, ever descending rapidly into warmer air. She walked south east and felt the pleasure of the sun in her face. She could see nothing of the station here,but she felt its nearness. The Earth rustled and she heard the reverberations through her feet, the trees reached out to her, subtle tendrils of welcome, nonthought, sentient. She felt herself walking in a landscape of friends. Time passed and her walking was steady. The ridge flattened, merged into the hills, narrow valleys opened wider and heavy grasses covered the path. Meadows stretched to either side pushing back the forests. Memories rose like a tide, breaking against her quiet mind.

She remembered the day, so long ago, when she had come here the first time. She remembered with sympathy the young woman she had been, finished with her task of mother and wife, ready to begin another part of life. How proud and excited she had been. She had not known this task would be one without an end. She had studied devotedly, trained her body, mind and emotions and learned to hold her mind in the stillness that made clear focus possible. Gradually, she began to glimpse that for which she sought. She learned enough to begin to Teach.

Then a great restlessness grew in her. She wanted more, wanted her teachers to reveal the hidden truths to her. They had smiled and encouraged her to listen, to watch. Then they had told her she must go out into that world and practice what she had learned. They had said something she couldn't accept -- that she must find what she sought for herself. Find that WITHIN herself, in fact. She had been angry, disbelieving, convinced they only put her off, that they did have that truth and refused it to her. They could give it to her so easily. Why were they so ruthless? How could she go back to ordinary life and leave this high place that she had worked so hard to reach? But she had been taught well. She drew her anger into shape and used it to demand quietly.

They had said, "Only those who have learned to forget themselves, to offer their lives out into humankind's need, have begun to pay enough attention to realize that Truth you seek. Only those who See with such breadth and wisdom that they know there is no separateness,learn of the true power. Humankind has a terrible tendency to distort and to forget." They had smiled when she protested that she would never forget." Perhaps not. But you do not know what you are capable of, either for good or evil, until you have learned of yourself in that world . Until you have discovered how deep is your heart and how shallow is your ego."

She had finally accepted. She had finally decided there must be something she did not know. She did not fully understand, but she would obey. And she had gone out into ordinary life again.

She remembered that long gone day of leaving while she let her eyes lift and sweep across this day's landscape, the rise and fall of meadow and hill where already the stain of spring time brought a gold and green through the brown hills. She loved this glimpse of the body of Earth. The rise and fall was like a breathing, a millinial slow breathing. Clouds of birds swept across the sky, descending in chattering noise to nearly fill a barren tree. She felt her spirit rise and race with them, then sweep again into the trees.It was as though a single mind contained with in that flock, moving in unison, utterly harmonious. Messengers the children called them, messengers between Earth and Sky. She liked the image.

Her path was flat and wider now, and she walked without needing to be so attentive. Her mind filled with images of that day long ago. She had left the Station. She had felt the power in herself, she had felt the Light illuminate her mind and reveal so much that she was more than willing to spend her life in discovery of what that might mean. She knew how to enter into that still point within herself to wait and watch. Her own Master Teacher had walked with her down the hill toward the town below.

He had said,"Power is a force that rises from the energy within,the Soul energy itself. You know that the nature of Soul is Consciousness itself. The power gives great capacity for good, but it can also be turned to evil. For power itself is directed by the mind that expresses it. When you have learned to live among all people, any people, with genuine grace and compassion, without resentment, irritation, then you will be ready to learn more. When you no longer hunger for things, desire to possess for yourself, when you have learned to meet the human condition, the struggle,the passions of life, the hungers and the needs, the endless rasp of fears, then you will have learned to recognize these in yourself. And recognizing, will know how to encompass them. To make them serve that

Truth you seek. This, Child, is the law. "

    She had left him, feeling intense sadness at the loss of that safe and wondrous place of stillness, of learning and simple constant Love. By living there for five years, she had learned something of what Love might be. And she had learned that she was yet to realize Love herself. To recognize It's flow through her own life.

    Discipline of mind and body had been constant, and that pleased her, the stability of that quality. She knew how to manage her strong emotions, her impulsive nature, her longing to save and offer from herself a better life to all who suffered. And it took five years more, of wandering and learning, suffering, making mistakes, harming others, seeing herself standing in selfish action, selfish thought, the selfishness of wanting to arrange other people's lives according to her understandings. Gradually, she had found a way. Had wept, raged, calmed herself, did pennance and started again to try anew. She thought she was getting so old. "How can I ever begin to serve that Truth when I seem only to have to learn?" She had found others who taught her, had found that people in every walk of life taught her, and she had been humbled. She no longer thought she knew much of anything.She knew the blinding and revealing Light had opened her mind and Heart and made the learning possible. She must complete that slow journey through herself into that Self she sought.

    Jessie stirred from memory. The last powerful memory of her Teacher crowded into vision as though it were happening now. She felt the meeting of their eyes, and the astonishment to know momentarily the depths of Love that shone through those eyes, through that whole being and illuminated the world around him.It had swept past her own tightened self and filled her. That memory had carried her far. It made obvious the necessity for learning.

    It was that glimpse of a capacity for Love that Jessie had never imagined possible, that had stayed with her for the rest of her life, spurring her on, giving courage when dispair threatened. At the last moment, he had slipped a small packet in her hand and closed her fingers around it. He had bent to kiss her forehead and then turned and left her there to go on her way. In it later she found a fine chain on which hung a small key, a symbol she understood.

    Now, looking back, feeling with her aged fingers the key still around her throat, the turned away from memory and studied the path ahead. She had arrived at a promontory at the end of the long narrow ridge that she had been following down. There were again a few trees growing at the summit of the ridge. They had spent a life time buffetted by winds that did not push against those lower down. She felt that wind now, pressing against her, and she turned her attention into the cluster of trees. So perfectly they fitted themselves into the pressures of their world, they grew slowly, bent to shed the wind, and persisted.

    Some were dying, she could feel their life force ebbing, leaving the gnarled forms. Yet they held a little longer. She felt their Reaching. In these too, there was a Reaching, inchoate, undirected, but nevertheless, a Reach. They too must send on their life as it was lived out. They had no grief, anymore than an acorn would grieve at being split during its growth into a seedling. As there would be no grief in herself when she left this little body down there somewhere in the Valley. It would be as simple a matter.

But memory pressed again. Insistently, she visualized the day of leaving after her second visit to this home retreat. It had been so hard then, for she had returned with her heart high, thinking she had finally learned and would be shown the greatest wisdoms. Then had begun the discipline, stern, silent, and relentless, she entered into herself, searched the places of her heart, listened to the lives of every person and creature around her. Slowly she began to realize the nature of humankind, the nature of Earth. Easier had been the intense withdrawal into solitude, and there, she had finally found a greater Vision. A vision that lanced her heart open and gave her mind breadth beyond bearing. Nothing had been given, everything had been discovered.

Yet of all that knowing, she could never have told another. She smiled, remembering. How she had asked to be given, to be told. And how they had reminded her that what she sought could not be given or told. And finally she had believed them. Out of the lives of those Monitor-Teachers came a perpetual staining of all they touched, a stain that penetrated her being. She saw that that amazing Light she had known in her youth, had been merely a gateway into incomprehensible possibility. Her mind was not one of those destined to build the mental bridge between levels of consciousness, or find the math, the theory and finally the words that would solidify something of its nature for Humanity. She was one who only pointed at the Light. So, knowing her work was elsewhere, after a little while, she had left again.

This time, as she stood at the Tower, watching the Station below, the beloved friends and parents she must leave, perhaps never to see again. She worried that she was getting old, maybe too old. She remembered how it had hurt to say the words. "Perhaps the Mother is right, and this is a true goodbye to something within myself, something I have refused to let go. I think now I see why this thing called practice is life long. Why can't I accept. I desire to accept, from the bottom of my heart, I long to accept." That second time of leaving had been different.

She had looked out on that day over the landscape of rolling hills and meadow and the small towns that had built up in them. She remembered the thought that fell into mind like a delicate Touch. "Earth is so beautiful, it is like a never hushed Teacher. It's voice is beauty itself, and that teaches without ceasing." The realization stilled her for some moments. It was unquestionably true. She wondered why she had not seen that before.

With a sigh, she had said," I see now my mistake. I can see that I assumed that I was different, that I could learn and use the power before others. Could break through to perceive the Vision more clearly. Why did I assume so much and assume it all for myself? I sought for selflessness and yet I lived resolutely in myself, for myself.To make myself Holy, perhaps?. I must go out and find out what selflessness is. How can I do that except in that world where the teaching is relationship itself."

She had suddenly cried out, a whimpering cry, that even in memory brought tears to Jessie's eyes. "I am fifty three years old," she had cried, "So old and yet I have not learned at all.I have been THINKING selflessness , not living it.To be selfless, one must -- must completely lose one's self." The thought penetrated through all the old familiar teachings, and was true. "And I don't know how to do that! I don't know how at all! And I think I am afraid. "

The memories crowded, relived themselves as real as this moment.She had fallen to her knees pressing her face against the railing, the heavy stone rough against her skin. Her cry a pain in her throat. Tears ran down her face, but she didn't notice." How will I ever live beyond my pride and my impatience? I can see myself wanting power, seeking power itself, not truth. Wanting of power, desire for it, is of the nature of evil. That very desire destroys good. Forever the Teachers have reminded me that I cannot know power until I am fully aware of Love. Until Love guides my every breath, every act, every thought. And then, the desire for power is gone. And Power is safe in those hands. I have heard them say that". She drew a long slow sigh of breath," No! I thought I heard but I did not hear at all."She felt a total sense of failure.

So much she had learned! Of living and of herself in these years of study and of lonely travel. She had learned of people, their beauty and their courage, their capacity for depravity and for nobility. Then in that other direction, the veils between the physical and astral worlds had long been frail and had faded so that she moved easily in both. She could Reach with the Senior Monitors to help draw the power net work that covered the Valley and that listened always to the pulse, to cries for help, either physical or mental help. Or even for that awakening to Spirit that came more and more often. She had felt the force of the will to Good, pulsing through those nets,reaching and healing, enlightening and wakening, when the moment for awakening had arrived. Those moments were more and more common now, in these past years, the awakening of humankind had swept far beyond any time in history.Today there were many Monitors working in the world, in the Stations. But Jessie, herself could not, at the time of her second leaving of the station, focus and know through that Mind net without someone to clear for her. It was several more of those intervening years before she had learned to do that.

She knew the nature of the Will to Good, for the Monitors poured that energy far and she had partaken of it, had learned to find that energy in thousands of people and wake it, Touch against that quality of their lives and see them bring it forth. They became Conscious! That was the gift it gave; Consciousness!

She could literally see herself standing there, more than twenty five years ago, even though she had been already grey haired, and thought herself old. She had leaned against the stone balastrade, weeping, desolate, feeling terrible dispair. She had quoted with new understanding the old precept,"None will have the power released within them until Love is the conscious nature of their Being." And finally she had realized that power came from Love itself, it was not a refusal, but a waiting until one saw this and knew something of the power of Love living through the life of Earth. How could she have mis-understood? She had felt small, ill-prepared and foolish.

She remembered how she had begun to speak softly to herself, sinking down to sit on the floor of the tower balcony. "For centuries people have sought power to control others, to gain their selfish ends. And I thought I was beyond such selfish ends. How mean and small I am, because my desire was no different from those of my ancestors." Her dispair was so great that her body hurt with it. She did not hear the approach of the person who came up from the stair well to stand beside her. Father Leon had climbed the stairs, the eight long sets of stairs with his cane and his broken body. He waited, sending to her strength and Love.

She felt him there and the gift of his energy. She turned to him."Father Leon, is there any hope for me?" Then in that cry she knew she thought only of herself again. Her own accomplishment. She sucked in her breath, projecting her self-contempt into his quiet gaze. But she couldn't sustain the lie. She looked up into that steady calm gaze and saw past the calm to those flickerings of pain that he lived with always.

He had put one finger beneath her chin and lifted her face as he might a child. She stood, and was still a child to his height. He was so serious, so wholly aware of her struggle that to look at him meant meeting her shame. He said,"There, that's better. You know self pity is also a trap." She nodded sadly. He went on,"You're seeing yourself. To do that is a beginning of wisdom."

She saw, but needed to ask again,"Is there hope for me, Father?"

He smiled, that wonderful smile that must have set the hearts of many women to sing in his youth. She had always wondered about that part of his life. His beautiful face and body, except for the twisted arm and leg with which he must always limp and twist as he walked.

"Dear Jessie, you know it isn't I who can tell you but yourself. You have just told yourself something that is very difficult to hear. You hear and accept in grief and in shame, but you do accept. So it is, when any person grows. Realize that knowledge of the self is a way to see beyond the self to the Self. Isn't that what we have taught you? Now you know something more. Can you speak it?"

She searched his eyes, so intense, so clear and stumbled, then spoke,"It is true, Father, I stand Soul conscious and realize this little self who hungers so and needs. I am that Self and I am this self. Knowing that makes it possible to see what I am. Even through the pain." She had stood a moment, absorbing that realization. Tears drying on her face,she nodded. And then a look of astonishment transformed her face,"Why, Father, I AM Soul and 'I' teach myself how to See". He laughed in delight.

He had taken her hand and she was surprised at the steel strength of his fingers. She felt a great held tension drain from her, a fury of self disgust fall away silently. She stood with him for a while. When she finally turned to him again, she asked, "Father can I ask you something personal?"

"You want to know of my deformity." He chuckled." Yes, child, it's time that you knew. I was once unwilling to acknowledge the pride that ruled me. I thought I could instantly be that Holy one, that angel of wisdom and Love among people. I thought I would be a Master of Master Teachers. I was a victim of pride as are perhaps all of us. And as you perhaps know, I had great beauty of body to contend with, to feed that pride. I could not see that. I fought for years to deny, to prove that there was no pride in me and I became a very 'humble' man. I denied ,even though the truth had begun to penetrate my heart. Then finally this, the event that broke my body and at that time,also my pride, occurred and I began to See something of myself.I give myself credit, I hurt more from that recognition than I did from the pain of the torn body. Self revelation is often very painful as you know.It's why we avoid it so carefully. I was more stubborn than any student here." He stopped and a wry smile played about his lips,"There, again, I find myself caught in another bit of pride."

He laughed then, with the wonderful sweetness that is often the laughter of the great singer. Jessie remembered the hours of singing he did with them, how he taught them to sing their thought. He had turned her toward the stairs, the day was growing late. She must ready herself, must say her goodbyes and must be ready to go. She must walk to the town below and then she would take an air car and be flown to a city beyond the Valley. Thus ended her second stay here at that Retreat just beyond those hills.

Immersed in memory, she had nevertheless continued steadily walking on, and now she stopped, stood lost in those memories,feeling nothing of the cold wind sweeping down from the snow above. Clouds had drifted across the sky, heavy and grey, but with brilliant shafts of sunlight breaking through here and there. One lay now on the hill below like a guide before her.

She remembered hearing the farewell song as she had traveled away from home on that day so long ago. It was a great surprise to her. The singing followed and persisted even when she had passed the town and was out into the wild land around it. Then she realized with amazement and gratitude that they were giving her a Sending that she might have comfort through these heavy forest trails. She knew then that some of those behind her would be gone from this physical earth when she returned for her third visit. She knew she walked into the unknown. And finally, there was anticipation as well as sorrow.

Now, in this day in her old age, she gathered her self into the moment and began to walk down the hills toward that late gleam of sunlight. She had been little more than a child on that long ago day. Yet she had thought herself old. She laughed at herself. Strange how perspective changes perception. It had been good to remember, to remind herself. She pulled her cloak around her tightly and proceeded toward the Station. She glanced at the sky, rain was close and yet it didn't matter. She thought of the young man waiting for her in the town ahead. Would he be getting impatient? Or would his restlessness be erased by the waking of knowledge in himself? So young he was, trusting and confused. He would go with her, would help her in her next task.

The ridges she climbed now were flattened. Twisted and wrenched as by the

THE AWAKENING

hand of a giant, they suddenly were smoothed on their lower slopes and spread into meadows and sloping forest groves. A lovely land, in shape and in its life. In another hour of walking, she came so far lower that slim twigs of willows and other early shrubs were cool fires of springs nearness. Instead of snow the earth was carpeted with needles of pine and fir and they gleamed where the sun fell like fine webs of silver. Before this day was done she would be there, in that clustering of lights, that artfully hidden Station. But the young man who waited now in the Inn at the edge of town, did not sense the flicker of her Reach. He still would not receive, though she knew he could have. She smiled, there was much for him to learn. He was now feeling his own wearyness of travel, longing for home, his mate, his Family. She must see him immediately after she greeted the Elders.

Like a child Jessie enjoyed surprising people. She smiled as she thought that had he more training she would not have that pleasure. She crossed the last ridge, looked down into the town and murmured a blessing upon those who had taught the citizens the way of communion with plants, for the fields and groves were more lovely than any she had seen yet. Human creativity could after all, participate in nature's with good result. The radiance of new growth and color of winter bloom brightened the dark evening. She could feel the unceasing flow of health rising from the land. It was a healing of the heart and mind just to walk here. Surely this Station was like unto a Temple among the Monitor retreats.

She climbed past the town, and began to circle the edge onto the very narrow trail up to the Station. It's nearness was like a Touch against her. Great Oaks sheltered the earth. Tall slim Walnuts, black barked and graceful, towered above. Other trees and shrubs clustered here and there but always she could see out into the fields beyond. The mist closed her in, and it was with a sense of secret joy that she approached the entrance way. She could hear only the soft whisper of rain, and a sound of running water in the creeks that ran through the rock. Some of the meadows were farmed, small farms with their neat and careful fields dotted the hill sides and valley, and rough, dark meadows intermingled with those neat fields. Jessie drew her hood up over her head and peered out at the changing world. Wind combed through a grove of pines, soft, filling her heart with a sweetness of their peace. Then, she heard a sound, a soft voice, a whisper.

For moments she stood breathing deeply, noticing the surges of feeling that rose from her body, swept through it and finally settled. She realized she was grinning like a child. She looked sharply through that mist, and knew that someone was near. She shifted vision from physical to astral and recognized the figure coming to her, floating across the heavy dark grass. With a gasp of pleasure she recognized that it was Daniel. How long had it been. Her last visit here he had been out on his own Journey, she had not seen him. Now, she knew that he had lifted from his body to come to her swiftly here. He wanted to meet her alone before she met the others. The fact pleased, delighted her.

She ran to meet him, though he moved with such swiftness that he was beside her before she had taken two steps." Daniel! Daniel! Oh, it's been so long, my dear." She wanted to wrap her arms around him, to feel his arms around herself, and the desire was strong enough she almost wept with frustration and then laughed at herself. They both felt the loving touch, the intimate Joining that had always been theirs. The embrace of mind to mind was so deep, physical touch was forgotten.

He laughed,realizing with her ,"Jessie, my Dearest, in just a few minutes we can touch from toe to finger tip. I simply had to come to met you first.I'm so glad you're home." She could feel him all around her as if he'd entered into all the physical spaces of her body and emotions.

"Daniel, would you be so bold among the students then? When we meet there we will not be alone."

Again he laughed, the sound delighting her, though it rang only in her mind. They began to walk, hurrying as if impatient,"Oh, my Dear, do you think the students do not know of our love? Surely I have not hidden my joy at your coming . We have been Reaching you for weeks now, you know."

She was nodding,"Yes, of course and it's only that I've come from that part of the world where people do hide from one another that I would ask it Daniel. Strange how only a few months living with people who are afraid rouses the old patterns even in ourselves, unless we watch carefully." She had become thoughtful, but shook her head,"But now is a time to celebrate. I am so glad to be home, Daniel. To be here, and to be with you too. To be for at least a little time where living is practiced with the skill of a fine artist, where relationship is an art form. It seems so long." She nestled against his closeness, glad suddenly that he had come as he had, for their two bodies could not have been as close. As she walked the rain ceased, the wind, sharp but not cold, blew against her hood and she slid it back, her white hair curling down around her ears, her seamed and weathered face brown with the sun's burning. He looked at her with joy, his eyes sparkling, undismayed at her old and finely wrinkled face.

"You are so beautiful, Jessie, so beautiful, did you know?"

"She laughed,shrugging and then felt his response of amusement too."Now, what have you done? What's happened since we were last together?"

He said, and the words were like a whisper that ran through her, a soft wind of sound inside her mind, it echoed the rasping tone of his physical voice, but full of the over tones of his living Spirit, conscious and present."Jessie, you know well that there are things for bodies to talk of and there are things they cannot. Here together in this way, what I long to tell you is not of thinking, of the lame shaping of words. Let's just be -- now together. Let's just share our heart's knowing" She nodded, reaching more fully, receptive and Joining deeply with him.To anyone watching, there was,on the path, winding up through rock and thick shrubs,into the Station entranceway, a small old woman, alone. She walked easily and with a smile of great joy on her face as if a secret pleasure delighted her.

They passed the arches of the gate and she saw his body sitting there, leaning against the stone wall and with a cry, she went to gather that old familiar loved body into her arms. They laughed and hugged each other with out embarrassment. They talked softly of those who would be waiting ahead. Jessie said,"I must meet with Ben soon."

Daniel laughed,"He'll be up here with us before long. Poor fellow. He's so young. He has been angry that he has gone so far, traveled so long and had to come all the way back here to find you and what else he sought." They both smiled, knowing the need for that. Ben would need to stay a little longer here, and so would she. For they each had things yet to learn. Perhaps then he might understand why his journey seemed so long.

CHAPTER SEVEN

How it was that Rose first got to this place, she could not have explained. The bits and pieces of events that culminated in her first moment of recognition that she was 'there' on that white cliff edge, that narrow shelf far in the eastern peaks had occurred only months before. Already she felt familiar, accepting. After all, it was inevitable that if it could happen it would, since so often she had gazed off to that very cliff face and the narrow ribbon of bench across it. For years she had gone to the same bench at the eastern corner of the deck, sought solitude under the thick screen of the weeping willow branches, when life seemed to overwhelm her. It was there that she had gazed far across the hills to those ragged edges of one dark mountain side. That spot had drawn her eyes, and she began to imagine being there, retreating into that distance, she imagined she might escape her troubles or even the daily efforts of life. So many times she had wished she could fly away, leave all sorrow and be there. She knew such need to escape was not healthy, not the way the Teachers taught, but she had nevertheless refused to meet the dispair in the way they taught. Then, one day, sitting so tight with the formless grief that her heart ached, she had suddenly found herself 'there'. She had literally catapulted herself out of body into the place of her longing.

She remembered well the first time, the intense longing to escape and then that strange tension rising in her body, the feeling of a 'shift' and a sudden soft expulsion. After that was the frightening recognition of being on that cliff edge. There was no way any physical body could get to the cliff other than with a lift belt. The narrow lip projected out from a smooth clean line of cliff with no approach other than this one she had found. But there she was, surely as she had ever been anywhere. She could look down into the Valley from this great height, seeing it from a perspective she had never before known. She could see the distant white speck on the hill beyond Adwin that she knew was the Farm.

For the first few minutes she wasn't aware that she was there without her physical body, she felt so 'normal. But swiftly she realized that she had experienced what her Teachers had described more than once, she had lifted from her body. So now, this is what it was then? When the first choke of fear had dissipated, and she had checked the impulse that had almost swept her back home, she had said, "Why, one CAN escape from one's troubles after all." This chosen point, so shining with sunlight, so unblemished by shrub or ragged bush, so high and clean with only a couple of gnarled bent pines growing up from the rock, seemed a place beyond mundane matters.

Later, when she found she could sit here undisturbed even when there was a storm in that physical world, that she could feel sheltered, even though the surging energies were strong, that this was not really a 'place' but a condition, she began to experiment with deliberately choosing to leave her body so. It wasn't difficult, it was more chainging an attitude, a way of seeing things, and she could break through the thin, membrane of difference. Gradually she realized she left behind not only a physical body but a physical 'attitude' - the limited perception of that physical world. She began to learn to use the greater vision of this astral world, but she found that 'escape' was relative. Here, she realized problems that were not visible to her in that physical world. Distinct learning was necessary to begin the see that there were mental glamours and illusions, attachments to a set of astral 'attitudes' that could claim her as surely as any she had suffered from in her ordinary life. Certainly there were wonderful discoveries. There was a different perspective, unlimited movement, for movement occurred with desire, but the astral world had its own kinds of limits, its own pressures.

She found here, the first couple of times she came, a calm, a serenity, which was what she had sought, what she had longed for. She learned that what one longed for was something that could be created from thought itself here, more rapidly than in the physical world. But she also saw that much that one longs for is not at all satisfying, or what one imagined it would be. She learned to look with candor at these desires. She learned that there is no state of consciousness, no state of being, that does not demand learning and growth.

Rose never spoke to anyone of this experience, of this place. It would have been too frightening to do so. She continued to think of the events there as somehow 'not normal' as herself inflicted with a strange although harmless malady. Even after she talked with her Teachers, she still could not quite feel the flight out of body was 'right'. Her Teachers pointed out that such 'escape' was no more wise that any other escape. She even let this whole part of her life, rare though the events were, fall into a place of 'dream', half denying them, half imagining that they were real. She found that she could travel to a strange otherwhere, or to other places on earth as she kenw it, could enter into conversation with other inhabitants there, but she almost never did that. She came here, to this ledge, this place of stillness and far isolation. She permitted this flight to herself now and then, knowing that she must not enter farther into this dimension because her task in life lay in the physical world. Otherwise she would not be in a physical body. But she excused her self on the grounds that being here was for her a profound rest.

On this cliff so high above the Valley she reflected on her life. On Ben and his need for that understanding he sought. On the children and the look in their eyes that left her puzzled so often now. It was as if some fleeting glimpse of knowledge stood there in their eyes and if she could just focus, just remain steady, perhaps they could share it. But when she searched for a way to speak of it, she could not. The look would disappear and she would tell herself she imagined it. But realizing the reality of this out of body time made her wonder if there might be other conditions of existence she did not know. She finally asked herself whether it was her imagination or if perhaps something was happening

THE PEOPLE OF THE VALLEY

with those two, Andrew and Anna. And she knew she avoided the answer.

The Valley itself was changing, some strong fierce power seemed to be entering the peaceful, hard working life of the people. People were settling down to enjoy their completed cities, their efficient economy, their fascination with learning. A new energy to look at those dimensions of thought originally left to philosophers or poets and mystics, swept through the land. The brief period of self satisfaction, comfort, and peace from old conflict seemed to be ending. There was a new light touching the minds of people here.

On this day, these thoughts began the shaping of questions that Rose had refused to see. The event at Valley Council, her awakening after the sharp mental nudge from Grace, the Reaching, the clear defined Touch, could not be denied.Could that be what she saw in her own children, but also in her friend's children and the students she taught. There was the energy shift that seemed stronger and undeniable, There was that 'something' immanent, near, but indefinable. And was it so because no one wanted to define it?

She remembered a talk with Martha, one of Adwin's Master Teachers and a Healer. Martha had seen something of that 'change' had wanted to talk of it, of the idea of the Mind Touch, the Reaching out of consciousness in a literal sense. Rose had felt suddenly so uneasy, so unwilling that she had hurried away to an errand that could have waited. Since the Council meeting, Rose could not deny that mental connection between people was real, though she still limited it to the Elders of the Council and assumed they had talents greater than others.

The fact that there were those who 'could not' Touch, could not perceive the essence or its Light within every living thing. The fact that Rose herself only had begun to acknowledge this Vision. There were those who did not look beyond the world of making and doing into the universe of Being. Who did not realize it, let alone feel at home there. Rose knew that these differences were real, but they were only a tiny separation. Now, standing on the outside of that first and most limited of dimensions, the physical three level world, she was conscious in this place wherein a fourth dimension was a fact. It was obvioius time and space were both as flexible as water here. She couldn't grasp all it meant, all it implied. But it was real. Couldn't all people come to this knowledge, this vision? Perhaps other people had! Her mind was pried open to thought that excited and frightened her.

The Teachings told of limitless universes, but if humankind could go no further in their development than this astral realm, it would offer vast territories to explore, clearly new definitions of reality, a new universe. The thought made her hesitate, she was not clear as to how this astral world related to those further dimensions, how this all related to what the Teachers spoke of as the realm of Spirit Itself.She ought to go request new Teaching. Why hadn't she? She pushed aside the question.

She looked around, pushing against the sense of lonliness, of mild fears that she was only one out of millions of people in the Valley and none were here with her, none that she knew! Why not! Were there others lonely, searching and discovering and telling no one? She said,"Of, course, I can't possibly be any different from anyone else. I know there are others but like me, they only tell those they trust." She contemplated that and finally with a shake of her head she admitted, "I've never told anyone. Does that mean I don't trust anyone myself? The thought was a tearing ache in her throat. She didn't want to look at the implications. Because they made implicit the obvious next thought. "I've given no one cause to trust me in these things. Long as I've known, I've not shared my knowledge."

She watched the sun rise above the mountains beyond. She smiled, remembering the way the Vagabonds saw the rising sun, the prayers came to mind and she uttered them, softly, knowing she joined in with many people in that at least. She said," Both Father Sky and Mother Earth are continuous through these further dimensions. The natural universe we've known is just 'MORE', it doesn't cease to be. This astral world is equally our Earth but seen in an utterly new manner." She was excited by those thoughts, looked around as if seeing for the first time.

The sun rising through the grey dawn spread light slowly down the great heights and filled the lowest corners of the Valley. "Like a sea of Light," she murmured, watching. She watched light break across the rock jutting above her and fill her little ledge, the growing warmth was pleasant. "Strange how the sun is the sun in all dimensions, but there is more sun than I knew. Here I affect this Astral dimension with my thoughts, thought is an active force here, change isn't limited to physical action." She laughed, "Well, that's not true, our small dimension is also affected by our minds, it just takes longer. Look what a world we've built, what miracles of our physical creation. But in this world, it's direct, I can change something by focussing my mind on that change right now."

The knowlege frightened her momentarily,"So, I've got to have some control of my thought. I've got to have control of my emotions, or I might be in trouble." She reflected, "Or cause real trouble." She let her self realize this, knowing now why the first order of development in people was - as the Teachers had long ago told them - the control of mind and the balancing of emotions. She looked around, seeing in the distance a couple, men or women, it was too far to tell, and she knew instantly that she could only effect this world for herself, not for them. So she would not be apt to harm another with careless intentions.

She turned again to watching the light increasing, it seemed to come from everywhere, not to come from that one source called the sun. She knew of the shining wall of rock behind her where the sun blazed. Without looking back, she was aware. It was as if the dimensions of her mind had expanded, as if further senses woke and probed their universe. She felt awe and fascination to know and focussing her attention, holding her own desires, imagination and thought as still as she knew how, she simply responded and reached in awareness. It was a revelation. For there, she was extended; what she knew as her 'self' merged outward, or was it inward? It was surely through the sensed universe and she , the consciousness she was, merged, becoming inseparable from that universe, that Earth and sky and all that had been created within them. There was no difference between herself and that.

From that merged state, she descended again slowly shedding the unlimited for limits in series that narrowed into an inclusive Self. Still and radiant,she knew herself Rose also, and knew the difference. That small consciousness was absorbed into this greater Self. And she, Rose, felt the laughter, the Joy of Life. That radiance of 'awareness?' that pulsed through the Light that was Self. She was not unconscious of her small identity, but felt it immersed, merged, and she - a Self, conscious of that same Selfness in all that lived. It seemed then that the very universe was laughing gently, kindly, at her.

A sudden swift shift of vision and she was aware of perceiving as if she lived witin the trees, the rock, the small bush growing beside her. That which was Life was conscious within everything. And she was merged wholly into that Life. She was not somebody thinking, she was BEING. Separating, closed into herself again, she could shape thought. She struggled to find words. How could she have been so clearly a part of all THAT? And for a second there, she had -- had BEEN. The immensity of it was a grand swelling of her heart, her mind, herself. To know that --to realize, spun her from that tiny observing point that she had thought she was and she knew that she was infinitly more.But she was nothing other than everything else, than the least of living things. Everything fitted into that whole as irrevocably as leaves fit on a tree. WHAT she was, she could not bear to know. What humankind was -- that was it, for she was inseparate from humankind, from that Self she still sensed through herself. That blink of awareness that could not cease, yet she had descended from it. The wonder of it refused to be forgotten this time, was an indelible memory. The reality was so great, so other, that she trembled with the immensity of even its memory. Humankind might begin to remember itself!

With a desparate denial, she shrank down to that point of observing, that little self Rose. She shrank and it was a physical pain, like loss, like fitting down into something far too small. How could she hold herself in herself now? But she closed her mind a little, drew away from perception, frantically began to think, to explain and to even talk. And plunged into her limited self, she was able to forget a little. Events occurred here unlike any she had ever known, she was not yet back to 'normal'. She still stood on this shining ledge, alone.

She drew herself together, resisting with a pure act of will the impulse to flee back to that waiting body. She shivered and clung to the shape of a little tree, fear shaking her mind. Then, without warning, from within herself, rising, a joyous song seemed to expand through her mind. Some fierce courage of Joy. Yes, a far point within her, expanding, embraced her, included her and she melted into it, accepting , included. She felt the stretch of being whole, self and Self.Within the stillness of that moment she rejoiced.She knew now that the thread was unbreakable, that within her now was forged that thread of consciousness that would forever link her small personal self to that vast and wondrous Self that was Soul, the true nature of humankind. People were not -- by their very nature -- separate from one another. We are Humanity! Her eyes were opened, the scales fallen away, and for that moment she could See. She did not know that she could not ever forget.

With a swing into herself, she literally felt her thinking mind spin into action. Thoughts clamored, pulling at her. What was she who was pulled? The thoughts massed against her attention as if having waited too long they were adamant for attention. Was she herself that attention? She was surprised at the steady stream of questions, thoughts like tiny thrusts of electricity in her brain, refusing to be ignored. But how could she put it all into order. She must take some time, a lot of time.

She put up a mental hand to calm these clamorous thoughts, gently setting them aside for this moment with a promise of careful attention later. This was too precious a time to spend in thinking. The intensity of being was overwhelming but included thought as if it were a delaying drag upon a perpetual flow. It was as if she looked through many windows, seeing herself from many angles, many selves? Focussing, as a bird flies higher the better to perceive the total terrain below, she Centered. She found a clear fine acceptance of all of this multifaceted self. The laughter, the Joy rose through her to know that.

Then, with a swiftness that was disconcerting, she was reduced to a small woman, standing on a cliff, bodyless. She felt a great loss, a grief of that loss. How could one become, realize and live as all that one was? That was the encouragement of the Master Teachers, yes, so many times she had heard it and yet, it had only vaguely had meaning. Now, it had full and reverberating meaning. Yes, How could one BE, dare and bear to BE.

But even as she stood wondering, she sighed, shuddering with the ponderous immensity of all that she had realized. She would again, dodge, deny, refuse with the skill of all her kind, not to threaten the status quo. She remembered earlier in her life, reaching points of awareness such as that had been, -- well, not quite so clear, so true, but a glimpse, and she had felt reluctant to lose the beauty of it, the wonder. She had felt stunned with the wonder of it for days. But now there was a difference. She KNEW without doubt and could not deny. Aware of the the risk she must take, the surrender of what she had thought she was to what she KNEW now. What every human was- what humanity itself was, seemed to have penetrated consciousness, to have defined consciousness. Yet to acknowledge what she knew meant that she must --- that she must -- literally die. Yes, and tears ran, her heart ached, to accept what she had known, meant that she, Rose, was not being all that she was. The ache of fear, the clutch of herself to herself, wiped for a moment all memory of that other Self.

The cliff thrust itself into the sky, she looked around, frantically distracting herself with the mundane things of the day, the sun gleaming on needles, the ripple of wind in the trees below, the movement far away of creatures, people, other? in the air, or down on that land. These were the people of this dimension, this Astral world. They might distract her. But to respond so to the beauty of things, only threatened to lift her back again to that place she fought to avoid. Beauty was a never closed gateway. One must not expose oneself too long to genuine beauty if one were not willing to See.

Suddenly she heard a rustling near by. Eagerly she turned, seeking, looking, and saw coming from a small hole in the rock face, a snake. With a flickering of its tongue it moved forward. It seemed to pause as if it were aware of her. She desparately did not want to frighten it and poured forth all the reassurance she knew how to extend. Would it be receptive to human reassurance? For moments they watched each other, then the snake slid with a dry faint sound over the rock to her. It's body strong and firm, brown and gold patterns completely covering it, it's eyes were steady. A thin membrane flicked back and she could see the darting shifting form of its energy body around the physical form. It really lived here, this was a creature of her physical world after all. But it extended into this one too. She saw no colors of fear.

Again the snake regarded her, then turned abruptly, curled into a position of ease and appeared to forget her. She felt pleased. This one would keep her company without intruding on her solitude. The light filtered pure and clear into the crevase from which the snake had come. She noticed the broken, sharp edged rock and the point beyond the light. Quickly she turned her mind toward that dark point, and she was there. Drawing this subtle body into focus she knew she could pass through that narrow tunnel and explore the mountain's heart.

Cool and smooth the walls of the tunnel, larger and larger it grew until it opened into a cavern, a hollow place that opened out into several tunnels. She marveled, she could see this mountain rock and she could also see through it. But so far, she saw nothing except that strange, solid transparency. Everything was very silent. There seemed not even small rodents here. It was untouched compared to the busy life of the Valley below. She thought there must be other snakes, these passageways known to these small lives, hidden, continuing through centuries all unknown to humankind. She said, "Here in the earth we live on, are lives unknown to us, worlds within our world." She felt some unexplainable need to explore, to satisfy that hunger for finding and discovering. To search out these things unknown, that she could then think about and put into order, into some design that she could then later THINK about.

Was it thinking that defined people of her physical world? Was it that which drove humankind? Was it the same energy that drove her to know of that other realm, those other dimensions about which it was so difficult to think. She questioned whether she could ever put it 'into order" and yet finding an order to put things into was the only way her ordinary mind knew how to understand.

That which she had so recently opened herself to know, did not give itself to ordinary human ordering. Then how could it be known? By a greater broader capacity of mind itself. Mind seemed so much more open, larger in even this first of the many dimensions. The intellect might not ever get everything into it's own terms then? And she sighed, caught up in that question. Abruptly she turned, she would think of it later, right now she had found something to explore. The pleasure of it entranced her, the newness, the small familiar newness.

THE AWAKENING

Everything was very silent. There had to be rodents, many kinds,in these caverns but she saw none. Perhaps other snakes still basked in the comparative warmth.These passageways,known to these small lives, unknown to humanity. Other worlds within worlds. The thought seemed to her to relate to that other world she had entered. Not only were there other lesser worlds everywhere within this Earth world, but there were also beyond it, other greater worlds, like a vast network, spiraling universes impinging upon one another but invisible or unknown to the thinking mind observing itself. Then surprising her, she said aloud,"But the Heart knows. I am aware of more when I do not think."

Curiosity grew and she wanted to know, to know more of this world. To search out its secrets,grasp its nature , especially to EXPERIENCE what was not known. To do so,here , in this smaller world within her world,was not at all threatening, was exciting, but it might give courage for exploring,accepting those worlds beyond and greater than her world. She knew the idea without thinking about it.To get busy exploring might push away that insistent question that whispered always somewhere in her.

She looked around at the small cavern, like a bubble in the rock, ancient, still.It smelled of dust, of dry animal droppings, a musty, not unpleasant smell.She could see a glint of water on which no slight breeze moved. It was clear and faintly green, a quality of glass, so still it looked solid. She moved closer and gazed down through the water to the sand bed beneath. Then out of the corner of her eye she caught a faint stirring, faint slivers of silver streamed from the rockwall and trickled soundlessly into the pool. Then how did it empty? She moved to the other side of the pool, found a strip of pale fungi growing in a narrow strip across the smooth floor, a shallow groove several inches wide, cut through centuries by this quiet steady stream. The fungi had pushed its way into the pool and grew along its edges where the water was shallow enough .

All these centuries, while humankind fought, struggled, built, created wonderful peons to that urgency to greater worlds, this lesser one had shaped itself.The thought brought a reasonless sadness. She could see now, and turned to find a pencil of light falling from a thin crack high in the side wall. In this tiny touch of light the fungus survived.

She bent to touch it, tiny hairs stood up in the barely perceptable current and they were black with a thickening at their tips. Focussing her sight, she identified blue green iridescence. At these tips were minute yellow cups whose centers held a brilliant green point. As she focussed her attention to see, she realized how wonderful was sight in this astral state. She could focus her eyes down to microscopic sight, or enlarge it to see to Earth's curving edge. But it was more than that, she 'knew' she knew as though she herself moved through these myriads of passageways, faint fissures through miles of rock and earth, familiar and home to all those creatures who inhabited this silent world. And who could also go out and live for a time in her own world. She, human, conscious, extended her perception to include that of these creatures and knew their lives. As though she encompassed them.

She shook her head, sobered and filled with wonder at the realization. The quiet beauty, waiting here through centuries, the perfection of everything, seen or unseen, bespoke a creator of the first quality. She smiled at her thought. An understatement! Her eyes wandered, touching on the walls, the fine dust that drifted down from thin ridges of stone in invisible flakes made visible when they drifted through the shaft of light. She thought of the vast loneliness of all things, the un- knowable complexities of Earth.

She extended awareness outward, and was aware of that sleeping self so far away in her rooms. She drew inward, huddled deeper into her own nature, and found the caverns of herself, the thread of awareness running through emotional landscapes she barely knew. She had searched out her own nature for most of her life, and yet, it still held hidden territories, not unlike this network of veins through Earth. As she sat, unseeing of the outer cavern absorbed in the inner one, she began to feel oppressing her spirit a sorrow and she recognized it. Try as she might to avoid now, it held itself there, directly in vision. She must admit that it seeped insidiously from some deep unlimited source of her self. What brought it into consciousness?

And paying attention, she felt a literal rending of that consciousness, and each torn place expanded and then reknit itself into a new awareness. Perception expanded like a rise and fall of tides, here in this emotional country. She, in herself, was another world yet to be known. A world that took on whatever shapes and colors wrestled themselves from her alert and attentive mind, for to think of this inner world, as she was aware of it, this emotional formless ocean, she must give it symbolic form. As she focussed attention, she could see a pin point of light glittering. Then it was extinguished as if something stepped between it and her eye. She focussed again, seeing a dark shape familar-unfamiliar. She felt fear, a stark twist of panic. Then she took that fear into thought trying to recognize. Years of Balancing, of practice at attention, gave her steady clarity. She didn't want to keep watching, she wanted to run away, deny, refuse and flee to her waiting body. She was familiar with that urgency too and ignored it.

She knew that the dark form ahead had been designed out of the fear that oozed from those endless currents of emotion. It looked now like a great impossible lizard, so tall its head touched the top of the darkness where it solidified. A dragon that was that inner shape of fear. That ocean was infinitely responsive, shapes rose from it to speak to the watching mind. The lizard drew her back. She forced herself to be still, watch.

Recognition brought a sense of amusement like a fragrance, then terror shoved all else aside. A thin edge of her mind told her that she must recognize this dragon, name it before it destroyed her. She must SEE!

Without warning she lost perspective. The dragon was there, real and menacing before her. The light glistened on scales shining, dry and brilliant green. Tiny eyes pierced hers, seemed to impale her, but she held steady. Needles of terror cut loose from that spreading blanket of fear and pierced her everywhere, She held, determined to know. The pain subsided leaving only sharp points of fire here and there.

Without sound or movement, they watched each other and she knew in that steady edge of consciousness not caught in fear, that as she composed herself, the dragon was quiet, yet, as she responded to the fear, it grew even larger. Could she then, taking thought, shrink it?

Swiftly, without reason she knew that she must mount and ride this beast. She must guide it to the point where the light shone. For now and then beyond it's great blocking form, she could still see that brilliant flash far off. She trembled at the thought that she must go near this powerful beast. She refused! Then shaped determination. She would!

The great beast tossed that long neck, that little head, and then, amazingly, the neck curved down and down until the little head rested near her feet. Hesitant, moved by forces in herself she had not known of, she stepped forward, and with one quick act of will, was there, on those broad withers. Instantly fear diminished, confidence rose. The thin edge of mind was released like a spring from the weight of fear and she could think.

The cavern seemed less dark, she could see footprints of small creatures everywhere now. Surely many lives passed this way. She pressed her hand against the long neck and the beast moved on toward the light. Startled, she looked down. Already it was smaller.

She felt her mind engage, adjust to this series of inner and outer events, question, take firm hold. The idea that there were worlds within worlds, and worlds within herself, seemed not strange nor impossible. Imagination, thought, emotions; what were thay after all? Intricacies of electricity and chemistry? Or were those two only the physical vehicles for them? What then was reality? At that moment she cut off the desire to persue this thread of thought into whatever limbo it might take her, and attend to the event playing itself out. She felt powerful now, capable, balanced. She could - would meet every dimension of mind or body or emotion. She would bring balance to that personality that lived in that sleeping body far away. She could. Surely!

A flash of excitement, of an old challenge, an old wisdom of the explorer warmed her. Then, it was extinguished. A sense of utter wearyness filled her, of satiation already reached. So many years of life, so many lives lived, known and unknown, forgotten but their essence of realization stored up within this depth of being, this Self that she had only touched. If such power remained and could be created out of that fluid sea of emotion, what infinite universes of possibliities lived there in that atmosphere, that even less controllable air that was Mind? Right now, she felt weary of experiencing more, of knowing more, of this patterned infinity of possibility. She wanted stillness, that sweet calm of being within BEING.

Then as she rode, the steadily shrinking body, remembering, realizing herself and her life before these moments, the fears, the needs and terrible lashings of emotions she had not brought to size, she felt a gentle sweetness of calm, a joyous touch that came and then, faded, but left her at peace. Light permeated the walls around her, like air, like a glistening of diamonds, palpable, yet breathable shining air. Like a wash of cold water through her mind, it refreshed her. But that wash also left her with another question. Surely there was all this, seen and known, and she, in these different states, knew, and yet -- who -- or what - - Sees? She spoke aloud then to the rapidly diminishing dragon. "What, or who experiences? Where is that eye that originates this perception? For surely it is not Rose? No because it's too much more than Rose. Well, it has to be consciousness that experiences! Surely that's it! But -- consciousness knows, sees. 'I' then, am consciousness?

Instantly she was out side the cavern, on the cliff face, comforted by that familiarity. She was not willing now to persue that question, the infinity it beckoned her toward. She clung to the familiar Earth and looked out at a cloud, laughed to see it and then, following, felt her self blown like a whisp through morning air toward that Farm house. She heard the sounds of people waking, her hyper-acute hearing attending. She saw people moving from the barn,,animals, a calf followed a cream colored cow who tossed her horns and looked up at her while she chewed a mouth full of grass. These were the Family animals, attached, they came home to bear their young and often stayed a while. A small pack of coyotes moved across the hill and disappeared behind a cluster of gooseberry bushes along the path to town. She followed the path slowly, enjoying this familiar land. She rode over the clumps of berry bushes, still laden, over the grape arbors that covered much of the down hill path to shelter it from sun, also redolant with the early crop, fruit trees, with fruit in all stages of growth, some already picked.

She saw all these things in a flash as she passed, drawn to that small cottage where her body slept.This was their land,their way of life and it served to bring her back to this physical world. With a swift urgency she was inside that cottage and felt the strangely familiar 'entering' and was inside herself. The sense of restriction, of limitedness, and yet of safety, was good. Right now she WANTED to be limited. But she remembered. She kept a part of her, that growing and extending part of herself, like a seed within her that would one day split aside the limits of herself and claim all of her into a new life. And she knew it, but she would not forget. Could not!

Now, she must soon begin to think about talking of these journeys to her Family. How could she do that? How impossible. She would wait, wait at least until Benjamin came home. Perhaps he would have found something that would help her make that telling.

As she woke, felt herself all over, seeing that she was as always when she woke, she wondered briefly if she had 'imagined all that'. Then she smiled at herself. She always asked that. And yet, try as she might, she could not 'imagine' any thing like this. The experience was so utterly new and unknown. No, it had 'happened' but there was much not understood about what happened.

She dressed quickly in a light, patterned playsilk shorts and shirt, pulled on Dredgol boots, the tough, resilient fabric that breathed like leather but wore many times better. She was ready to go out. Dredgol was harvested first as hard, tough stocky plant stems, thick, like heavy mallets in one summer's growth, The crop was raised by many small villages as their cash crop. The pseudo-leather was sold ouside the Valley , a good trade item for Valley credit. People could raise it almost anywhere and did. It had replaced the use of leather almost completely .The killing of beasts was not acceptable to this humankind. Their brand of wild life management meant only the infirm, the excess that threatened the balance, or the very old creatures were killed, and people of the Valley saw that even as a failure on their part to know more how to balance their world. Dredgol filled a need.

Rose went out, stood on her little deck, stretched and looked around. She could see Jerry coming up the slope from the barn and Jane was running to catch up with him. What would they think if they knew of her night's journey? She shivered involuntarily.She felt a rawness of emotions, a tenderness from that inner struggle and realized it had been a culmination of much. But she felt a hollow emptyness, as though fear itself had forsaken her and she knew that sooner or later she must tell her family of these events.

Jerry swung a bridle in his hand, he must have been out riding the mare Tembler. She came to give birth to foals, she stayed at the farm often for months,she would return to the mountains for weeks,then come back. Jerry had trained her and would train her colts. He thought he might set up a training station one day, far in the upper slopes behind the farm. He rode her as he did the stallian who also brought his mares home in winter.Rose saw his grin and knew he had enjoyed the ride. The sun slanted through tall old trees shading the path to the Hall. Rob and his mate, and a grown bitch pup that would not leave, ran excitedly playing with one another around the two people. Dogs were pack animals, they needed to live among their kind as well as their humans. And in this Valley, they did.

Rose turned her attention, listened to the trees,the soft sound of leaves and wind. She loved these trees, old when the people had come to the Valley, they were ancient now, and strong. She could hear their singing , a pure sound that penetrated beyond hearing into her mind like a kind of Touch. A simple sweet Joining.She started at the thought, she had not imagined such a thing before. Could it be that one could then Touch beyond human mind? She wanted to sing with them, whatever it meant, it was wonderful, the thread of consciousness between herself and the trees. She glanced at Jane. She was sure Jane was not aware of her own talents. Would never admit them, and yet, Rose knew, in a way obscure to her yet, that Jane sensed far into the lives of creatures and plants.

She went out walking briskly into the path to the Hall. The very sense of Earth power, the rising of energy that touched at each step she took, pleased and lifted her spirits. Surely this Earth in which they had built their world, was infinitely good.

She felt her hair loosening from its clasp and stopped to gather it in her fingers and draw it together.Fine, long, black silky hair that curled a little, not as much as

Benjamin's fair ringlets, but enough to create a halo of dark shining around her face. Like a caress it slid and then she caught it, her fingers smoothing along her cheek, enjoying the softness, the aliveness of her flesh. It was good,this body, this warm, healthy, round body. She always thought her hips a little too big, her breasts a little too small for beauty but she loved this strong lithe body She said aloud,"It's good to live here in this Earth. I want to enjoy this Valley, all of it, every part. I won't forget any of the other possible dimensions, but I live HERE, and I will pay attention to this dimension, this physical world, more than I ever have. " She walked on, enjoying the sun and the soft movement of air against her body,sensuous, delicate. It was so warm already she knew it would be a hot day.

A thought nagged at her attention. Yes, it was so. The family, the People of the Valley, needed to address those things they avoided. The Teachers needed to notice the avoiding. They must begin teaching anew. "We've got to break these strange taboos. Where did they come from. I haven't even noticed that we've been denying what we're aware of. I know other people must be too." The Council meeting had opened her eyes, opened her mind to the vastness of possibility and she looked with fresh eyes at other people, especially the children.What had happened this night, woke in her a vivid sense of necessity to search further,to understand." If this is a common recognition, what possibilities are there for us as a people. And it must be common or I wouldn't be knowing of it."

She scuffed her boot in the fine gravel of the path way. Walking slowly she felt inundated in fragrance from the garden all around her, she reached to absently pick a red and orange leaf, stuck it into her hair. "I've got to start talking to my own family. Maybe it's time we had a Gather. It's been some time. We've not had them as often since Ben left. It's as though we need him to Gather." She twisted the memory in her heart deliberately to find the pain, and found none. And was glad. He could come when he was ready. "I'm gonna drive myself crazy worrying this all over unless I get some other people to talk it out with. And I don't want to talk to teachers only, I want to talk to my family."

Saying the words made evident the need and she saw it was greater than she had known.She drew herself into attention, focussed and entered into herself to find that centered point where stillness was. And out of that point she saw, immediately, as if it waited for opportunity, that Question that she did not want to ask. Was she using these EXPERIENCES of the astral state, to avoid the very question that hung out there beyond them. The question that she would not entertain at all? Was it true that all these fascinating mental and emotional events could distract her from anything beyond them? Well, obviously she could and was doing just that! She felt a stirring, a trembling in her chest, as if some danger threatened.

She stopped walking, standing in the path to the temple, watching Matilda,the family cat, move in her clean, grace across a slim limb of the walnut tree. She stalked a big,saucy jay and Rose knew she would not make that kill. Any Jay that got caught by Matilda had to be old or injured. She felt , more than saw, the

THE AWAKENING

rippling muscles of the cat's body and envyed her. Feeling so intensely the movement that it was as if she herself were part of that body too. The recognition startled her into losing the connection. She looked down at her hands."My god, is it true that we can, with an act of will, a centering act, enter into other lives? That's a dangerous thing, if it's true."

The memory stung, invited her again, the cat life had seemed so precise, so full of another kind of intensity from her own --an animal intensity.She turned resolutely away with a faint shudder. This was not right. What was happening to her? She had felt the internal beingness of trees, of birds sometimes, briefly, fleetingly, but this was different. There was very much more. She was more? It had some of that quality of otherness that the glimpse of Light had.

She tried to remember when any Teacher had talked of such things and remembered once Mazina's talking of the way people can become obsessed with ideas until they refused to distinguiush between them and reality. Rose frowned, trying to remember, there had been something that fit this moment. Ah yes! She spoke aloud."People use these ideas to tie up their mental lives with what is familiar. They can then be trapped in idea, or perhaps a single powerful experience from which an idea radiates. Mazina said we keep refining and elaborating on them until we are so wound up in them that we can no longer see the original Light at all.

Rose nodded, remembering, knowing that her understanding was flawed, but the problem was clear. She nodded curtly, "Yes, she told us, and I remember feeling sceptical, that we humans spend centuries recreating, crystalizing and making a fetish of rituals around one tiny Touch of reality that we've glimpsed. Then we call that a philosophy, or a religion even."

She shook her head, wondering,"Am I doing that?"

Entering into the truly unknown, the clearly new is frightening."It was natural for me to be so afraid. Because that is human! But I don't want to let all my life from here on be a re-arranging and a re-shaping of the same single new idea.I want to finally SEE it and go on. " The need,the desire to find and accept , then release, and go on to further discovery, was wrenching her mind's usual patterns and she saw that. She shook her head." I've got to talk to my family or I'm going to go crazy. I can't figure it all out myself!" Pain was subtle but real.

She walked rapidly the few yards left to the hall,and went in to find it empty,the tables cleared and everyone already finished with breakfast. She felt deprived, but grinned ruefully at herself."After all, what can I expect when I take so long to get going."

She left the Hall and went into Adwin, using a belt, rather than walking because she was late. the clear morning air was refreshing.The delight of flying across the land of waving down at a caravan of Vagabonds and breathing the odors of ripening crops below, took her attention and she arrived at the Learning center and her students with good cheer.They were waiting for her, arguing about the assignment they were working on and about which she needed to inform them. These were students of Government sciences and some would

THE PEOPLE OF THE VALLEY

serve their first student terms on the Valley Council this next year. Some would work in Valley administrative offices; the agricultural Center, city banks, education administration, etc. or they studied the way the Valley industries and businesses were organized and controlled. Rose sighed. It had seemed so much simpler when she was their age. She thought there had been so much less to learn about.

She clarified their assignments, answered their questions arising from the previous weeks work in the field, and assigned more reading. She spent some time with each students records and journals, helping them see their work more clearly. And sent them on their way." The Council will have a handful with this bunch. Well, The council needs to learn too." She was smiling and watching them chatter with each other as they walked out into the Learning Center gardens and on to lunch. Strange, young ones DID seem more aware, so conscious of what they were about, and so intent on their ideas which were just forming. These had begun to know that excitement and literal ecstacy of mental stimulation that ideas can bring. They were realizing the multiplexity of them, the variety, the possiblity of seeing one issue in a number of different ways and the way one could be convinced completely by a set of patterns around an idea, and then, taking an opposite position, be convinced of it. How could a person include all the possibilities, and see the idea and its ramifications whole? One young boy had been near tears when he told her that he could not see how a person could come to any conclusions at all. Rose had suggested he watch the Council carefully and see whether they did, and if so how they did it.

When they had gone, she settled down in a chair by the window. Watching absently the rolling clouds of smoke from some forest fire set by lightning last night in the high hills of the distant southern Valley. It burned itself out rapidly in the dry wind, sweeping through the dense stands of big trees doing little damage. The meadows that wound in and out of the forest lands made forest fires easier to handle. Rarely were there fires in the central Valley. Fires cleaned the land of debris and scrub. She got up, went out into the court beyond the doorway. She could see people everywhere, hurrying, sitting, walking with slow thoughtful quiet, children running and yelling at one another, and people deep in conversation. Everything seemed distant from herself. She turned, grateful for that.

To her left was a gay wildness of wild garden, plants that lived well with one another creating a mozaic of color and life but with no formal order at all. Trees, shrubs and perennials grew together with narrow paths winding through everywhere. To the right, a formal neatly shaped and pruned garden grew. A marble fountain sent blue water high and it softly murmured as it fell again into the wide, shallow, white bowl under a pair of cherry trees whose fruit had long since been picked. Carved seats clustered here and there in cozy settings behind thick shrubs that gave them privacy. Today she chose the formal garden for a walk. She needed its order, its anticipated beauty. Here was an art whose medium was living things and it was a high art for Valley people.

She sat on the smooth chairs, willing her mind to be still, willing her thoughts to rest, and her senses to simply enjoy, to allow peace and calm. She sat so for some time, and then, suddenly shook her head and laughed. "I'm like a leaky faucet. The questions, the fierce pressure of thoughts seep in until they push aside my stillness. Even though I see them coming, I am inundated suddenly." She sat, aware of the myriad of impressions, sensations, thoughts and there at the bottom of it all a deep dispair. "Ah, there, now what is this?"

She had hardly identified that darkness, when she looked up to see two people coming toward her. People walked through the gardens constantly but none had apraoched her. These two were coming directly to her. Her heart felt a surge of gratitude. She watched them with rising hope. A thin, very old woman, white hair cut in a round thick thatch over her head, her eyes, even from here, sparkling and bright with humor. She walked with a slight limp, but moved easily . Beside her was Raymond, a large florid man, heavy bodied with rosy cheeks and an habitual scowl that did not hide the sparkle in his eyes, the stillness of his Joy. These were not simply Master teachers. Rose knew and wondered how she could deserve such good fortune. These were Mind Healers and they had come from West Station. How?

Then swiftly, like realization given her, she knew that they had responded to her own unconscious call. The call of the heart,they described it. Rose had never known how they could hear such. Their Reach was subtle and masterly, so that the Touch came out of it like a delicate brush against her consciousness, rousing and inviting. With her response, they melded with her own mind in a Joining that lifted her free of herself for moments. And then, like a weight settling to the end of its tether, she was separate and yet, Joined. She could realize,'feel' the generous outpour of Love and reassurance.

She breathed a long sigh of relief. Now she could talk to someone. She began at once. One did not waste the time of Healers, even children sensed that. "I cannot understand how this wonderful, beautiful day can be filled with such grief as I have in me. I can't lift up to live above that dispair that underlies even my good humor." She laughed, but there were tears in her eyes and she was astonished at how clearly she saw herself. Already her heart's pain was revealed, recognized. She felt it where before she had denied it. She shook her head, angry at the betrayal of her tears,then grinned sheepishly at herself. Who did she think she was that she could fool a monitor?

Martha spoke softly,her eyes holding Rose's,"You cannot find the beauty?" The comfort reaching through the steady calm of Martha's mind wove a cushion around the pain. Rose shook her head, unable to speak, then wanting to find words to fit what nagged at her heart's ease, she said,"No! its not that exactly. Martha, I do see the beauty, the goodness of life. It's just that -- it doesn't -- ", her voice was a whisper,"It's just that it doesn't seem to matter. And if it doesn't, then what's the point of living. All the things that have made life so great, the beauty, the building of things, the creating, the fun with the children , all of it, that makes living a joy, it all seems no longer to MATTER. I don't know what has happened!" She knew she was not saying what she needed to. There was something she couldn't get up into conscious reach yet. She felt her eyes fill and tears pour over, but she refused to be turned away from the pain in herself, to let this flood of emotion stop her. She had to speak it, to try to find, using words, what it was.

Raymond smiled, a dazzling smile that filled his whole face and lit it. Rose felt aceptance and took a long slow breath. He said,"What preceeded this dispair this time?"

She glanced sharply at him, how did he know it had happened before? She caught at the question as though a straw had been offered to her drowning self. "That's it! I dispair. But there's no reason for dispair. None! And in reaction, I'm consumed by an urgency to do things, to see, feel, experience every sensation all over again and find new ones to keep my mind busy, my heart distracted. Anything. To find what used to satisfy me!" She looked away, feeling ashamed as if her complaint was unreasonable. Then drawing a long breath, she tried again,"It's as if there's a whip lashing me to keep racing from one thing to another. If there is a moment when sensation is dulled, when I'm not busy with plans,or seeking -- something, recently, even out of body experience, then I sink toward that quiet place, that stillness that I'm afriad of. It's as though I'll drown. I panic. I do exactly that. Because -- because -- " she groped for words, none of this seemed to make sense to her, and she had not realized that the things she just said were true until she said them.

"You see, I want all that, try to bury myself in things, because - because there's danger - - I have to avoid being still for some reason. But then, when I try to keep absorbed in the ordinary things of living,what I've always enjoyed, " she took a deep breath, tears flowing like a river, refusing to be stopped by an acute sense of embarrassment, she went on, her voice rising like a child's "I just feel as though it's all for nothing, that there's not anything worth anything, nothing really interests me. It doesn't matter-- it doesn't matter any more. And if that's true, what can I do?" How could she be so foolish with such people as these? They would think she was a fool.

No! Only with these Healers whom she had known all her life, could she even begin to tell the tale that seemed to her 'foolish'. She glanced up at their eyes, so quiet, attentive and then, went on," I think - I think there is something else among us now. We of this Valley, it seems to me, have begun to change ,-- in mind and -- and in heart. We seek a finer kind of experience. We're satiated with the gross sensation that used to satisfy us. All of that, all of our old pleasures," she shook her head, tears flowing, "have lost their goodness." She stared at them, her eyes wide, full of amazement at listening to herself. She was silent for several minutes, they waited. Then she said slowly,"Why, it's exactly what is true,and yet, I've not known how to say that, or --" She let the sentence hang, shook her head slowly,"Until I put it into words, I don't think I knew it."

Martha nodded slowly, "Can you tell us what changes you've noticed?"

She nodded slowly. It seemed as though perception had widened, some block in her thinking had dissolved. She saw what were now facts to her. The effects of this integral change in herself."I guess I'd better speak for myself,but I know it must be for most people too.I think lots of us have, have just begun to seek something more -- and I think maybe we don't kow what it is we seek." She lifted her eyes, looking straight into theirs, and frowned,"There that's it! "

To her surprise they were undisturbed by her outburst."You've seen signs of change?" Raymond's deep rumble was gentle, with an insistence that prodded her.

She searched for words, for explanation,and nodded at him slowly, "You know how badly Denlock failed with their entertainment park? They had to change it. The old people had got it started, with a dangerous course for racing air cars and ground discs, etc. And the huge field they built with raised platforms around for watching games? So few people came they finally tore it down. The race track's still used but they don't have many spectators. People want to do things themselves,they aren't watchers anymore. Crowds come to listen to our finest musicians, then when the concert is over, there're a dozen small groups scattered all over the Learning center playing their own music. The boat races, and the sailing competition,plenty of entrants but little audience. Then that pornographic 'fair. Yes, 'fair' I think they called it. Even when they provided some of the old drugs and a few new ones to enhance reception of their attraction it just didn't go after the first few days. The Council was opposed to it but allowed it because they could not find a genuine reason not to.It lasted all of nine months. Just nine months for what the old folks said would have made fortunes for the city in the old days."

Martha said,"Those things've all happened,it's true.

Rose looked down at her hands, found them tightly clenched, and then loosened them. She looked up,"You see, there are more, things less obvious, but that's the idea. We just aren't interested in titilating our senses that way. There were a few people who continued to want to watch, to participate, but no one could make money on those few." Rose sighed, wiped her face with a handkerchief, and said,"But those things, aren't all of it, they never did interest me much, yet, all the things that did, once, aren't enough anymore."

Raymond stood,"I'm going inside to get some iced drinks for us. The young ones are going to buy out that ice cream shop before we get a share." He laughed.

Martha and Rose watched him move along the wide smooth walkway,half seeing,absorbed in their thoughts.Rose said, "I think actually most people of the Valley were unaware of that sex fair. At least Denlock tried to hush it up after it failed so badly.It wasn't their fault. People are just different."

Martha met Rose's eyes, serious,"You're right Rose, in this much at least. People don't hunt for pleasure, nor do they fight one another in public rings, nor do they take pleasure in seeing another person hurt. And feats of strength and balance, of grace and skill in movement that would have entertained a crowd a hundred years ago are commonplace, everyone can do those things. Our entertainments have become vastly more sophistocated, haven't they?"

Rose was intent, leaning forward, trying to state her thought."It isn't just that, it's something more. There's so much to feel,to enjoy,to SENSE all around us,there's so much - " She stopped, "Yes,you're right." And as Raymond came back and handed them all tall glasses with small balls of ice clinking among blobs of thick ice cream, she looked stricken. Martha smiled.

"You see that you're avoiding the very thing you wanted to say? It's true enough that people have --are still -- changing. That's a given in this Valley, in this time. But what about the changes in you?" She sipped her drink, stretching her legs across the footstool both of them shared.

Rose was silent such a long time a less patient companion might have interrupted. Then finally with a long, deep breath, she said,"There is something I've begun to do. I've not told anyone about it at all. Perhaps it's simply one of those more sophistocated entertainments after all."

Raymond nodded,"You've learned to leave your body at will."

She didn't question his knowing that, it didn't matter. She nodded. "And I can see how that could be exactly that, A new type of entertainment."

"What's wrong with that?"

"Well, it's -- it's avoiding the issue. Maybe a lot of enter- tainment has been to avoid something deeper that we couldn't meet."They didn't answer, simply listened, she went on,"I realize though when I do that, realize so much, that it only brings me closer to -- to what I avoid after all. That kind of --- of entertainment -- isn't keeping me unconscious at all."

"Have any entertainments ever really worked to prevent vision?"

Rose looked at her frowning,"Well, they did, for some all their lives, for others for years, but -- maybe for no one permanently. Vision persists, doesn't it?" She smiled suddenly.

"Gross uglyness of hand to hand fighting for sport,of mud fights, or certain games that were simulations of fighting, or in earlier history,of war, which was another entertainment in its time, were only fairly successful. People came to se them and in that very watching, began to ask questions which brought vision. Even the primitive fight against vicious animals, to their death, brought the sensitive face to face with life and death, the meaning of being human, the differences between animal and human. It woke questions of relationship itself, of purpose and value. But only the sensitive were stimulated to such response . The others lost themselves, drowned in the sensation itself."

"So again, it's a matter of refinement." Rose nodded, feeling somehow deflated. "I think I was wanting to believe that we were more -- more advanced - as a people I mean."

"Isn't that growth, to have refined our pleasures as well as our perceptions?"

Rose nodded absently, "But it isn't exactly what I thought. We do love to make and remake our gardens, to design and build our towns, to balance the whole Valley's life and keep it healthy.To make and create beauty. We don't find such - such primitive sensations entertaining.But then, maybe its just another turn of the spiral. There are joys less harmful to the spirit, of less weight on the heart. These we seek, I think. " She took a deep breath,"Raymond, what do you think of

THE AWAKENING

that -- my leaving my body to -- to explore further."

He set his glass down, slid his hand across the brillaint red blooms leaning beside him and picked one."Rose, it's what many people are doing. Some are afraid, some just play with the experience, some learn from it. It depends on you, just as all the 'entertainments ' of the past have done.

She was not satisfied, why didn't they Teach her-- tell her what to -- " She stopped the thought, tell her what to think? She would never get a Healer to do that. She grinned suddenly at the idea. They smiled too, and she knew they followed the sense of it. Finally she said, "I think that maybe we've kept ourselves so busy in the past and even our entire world, fascinated with traveling to and exploring the planets, and us, building and building and refining and making our world as fine as we know how, we've avoided something. We have, haven't we?"

"And what do you think that might be?" Raymond did not take his eyes from hers.

She shrugged, impatient,"Why can't you tell ME something. You must know. You must!" At their mild glance to one another, she bridled, unreasonable anger surging.

Martha nodded,"You think that the pace of business has been a way to avoid something deeper, something that's being missed by lots of us?"

Rose shook her head,"I don't know, maybe I'm just tired, but I feel trapped, somehow! Trapped!"

"You've begun to see much that makes people realize what life is, what it might be. " Raymond's baritone reverberated through her , literally felt in her flesh, relieving the anxiety, his smile, so sweet, so encouraging, caught and held her from that descent into dispair.She recognized that, listened. He said,"You spoke of activity, entertainment that kept you from something -- what is it that they keep you from?"

She was sober, relieved and grateful that he had finally asked the question for her."I think that things kept us from that stillness, that loosening in our minds that we know opens into something greater than we've ever known so far."

He persisted ,"Stillness comes even in the midst of work, in walking, playing, wherever, whenever we are. How can it have been avoided?"

She stared at him,what he said was true. Then why was she --? Then it is myself? It's me. I have used these things, this work, the enjoyments, to avoid?"

" Surely it may be just that."

She spoke hurriedly then, her mind open, not allowing any censor, any hesitation.The words came without being considered first."I've been doing that - what I said, leaving my body, realizing that! But I've been using it to keep me from what is beyond it. I can see that, it's a 'refined' method," She smiled faintly at her poor joke. Knowing that she must finally speak of that about which she could not speak."She stood up, walked restlessly around the fountain whose soft murmur comforted her. Then she came back and sat, lifting her glass, drinking a long cooling drink mostly because her mouth was dry."I don't know why it's so painful for me. So hard to say. " She bent her head, they were utterly still, waiting. Finally she looked up,"It's the silence, like now, it touches on that same kind of Silence, so profound, as though my entire nature is rising out of Silence. As though it draws me, surrounds me and -- then, I suddenly am afraid, as if I won't ever find my way back." She was trembling, and they poured reassurance to her, knowing that the telling would not be easy."There's Nothing beyond that Light. And the Teachers say that Nothing is not -- an absence, rather its a fullness. But, I can't realize how that can be. It's the Nothing that's I touch that terrifys me."

"It's nothing at all?" Martha's voice was gentle with Love.

After some time Rose said,"I suppose I should say nothing I recognize."

Raymond cleared his throat,"When you've been at that point of Nothing, is it of no thing that's familiar? That is, some other condition of reality?" They waited, their minds supporting her, their presence healing.

"I suppose it's because of the time, the first time, when my mind--filled up, was full but not of 'something'. I recoiled, actually that's the only way to put it. I recoiled as if my mind had been burned through, emptied, as though there was nothing in ME. No sensation left at all. Just THAT."

"And THAT"?

"It just seemed as though it was so alien, so other than what I know. And yet -- so full of wonder, so full of - possibiity. But as though it could not be named, could not!" She drew a long trembling breath, for the telling was drawing the memory into being .It was then that I -- Touched -- or was Touched -- I never knew which." Her voice was thin, soft,as though strained with the effort of speaking.

Martha nodded, waiting, her eyes still intent on Rose. They seemed to draw from her, make possible the telling. Rose felt the gift of it but feared."This must be what is called a mystic experience. I discover all that Joy, that wonder, down deep in me, and I'm not -- not beyond myself at all ." She laughed and it was harsh, angry.

"And you want to be?" Raymond's voice not only healed but drew her forth.

Her eyes slid far away now, distant but she shook her head,"I don't know! I think it might be more than that." They waited," One time, not long ago, there was something -- I thought afterward it might be what people called God. It's seemed alien. It was only a glimpse, yet it seemed forever. Finally I couldn't bear it. I fled. I shrank down, hid in old activities as if I couldn't dare to know what I was knowing. All my senses strained but there wasn't any way I could fit that into any of them." She looked at them each,"But it was true, no time at all had passed. The clock told me that."

Martha said softly,"Go on, Rose."

"There were other times. There it was, the impossible. The impossible! And I thought later THAT was perhaps the Real and this world was not actually real after all. But that made no sense. It's not what the Master Teachers had taught us of the Spirit. "

"Maybe they were talking of the 'idea' of Spirit. Perhaps you were knowing the Presence of Spirit Itself."

"But why am I so afraid now? It was actually not frightening at the moment, it was -- it was absolutely wonderful. So full of -- of Light! And yet I am so afraid!"She felt a flood of relief. There it was, said. And the final question asked.She would know whether it was a madness, or something else.

Raymond was thoughtful, a tiny frown rippling his smooth high forehead which receded into beginning baldness."But there was something there then? Something beyond that Nothing? And it was unfamiliar, You felt a sense of power, as though it might relate to what we call the Eternal?"

She was nodding as he spoke, rejoicing to hear the ideas so simply stated and accepted. They released her own voice,"It's so vast, so very, very still. Such stillness I could not have imagined. It is utter wonder of stillness. That stillness seemed to rise from Nothing. Only Nothing could be so still. And yet,it lit a fire in my heart. Yes, it did. A literal fire that has not quenched itself yet." Tears flowed, the memories were so vivid, the relief of talking so great. To experience again that wonder, that absolute beauty of stillness, even in memory, was overwhelming. She wondered fleetingly what they thought of her, shied from the idea and then realized it could not matter.

"Seems as though you caught a clear glimpse". Martha was smiling, the tension gone. The Joy in her face was so obvious Rose finally admitted it. She went on, "Perhaps it was simply so unfamiliar, so far beyond the ordinary, you had no place in your mind to put it?"

For several minutes there was silence, then Rose burst out,"You don't think then that I'm crazy,that I'm halucinating?" At their smiles and shaking heads, she went on,"Oh, it's a relief to talk about this. But it's strange that the first question I asked myself later was why everything seemed so different, and yet so VERY much the same. That is when I began to question ALL experience, and all sensation. It seemed as though nothing else mattered anymore. All that I'd loved, the beauty of things even, seemed just less, until -- until -- " She glanced at them, her heart hammering, and needing to tell them this. They nodded and she said, "Until the day when I began to find that I could --I did -- see right through that beauty and there beyond it, there within it - is the wonder again ." She drew a huge breath and let it out." It's as though beauty is a window. If a person responds to beauty, really responds, then it is another way to reach that place of blinding Light. That place of wonder." She shivered, remembering, 'To look through beauty Itself and find the Source of it.' That's what it seemed. " She was crying again, the thought itself hurt in her throat."But I don't understand. The Source was just Nothing at all."

Raymond nodded, "You have then glimpsed what is beyond this world life. You have glimpsed what is beyond everything that we know of reality. And since it is beyond, we have not thought enough yet about it we have no names for the events there, the conditions. We just know it is vastly greater. This reality seems dim by comparison. Perhaps that reality is the Source of this. That would 'make sense' wouldn't it?" He was laughing at her, gently.

"But that astral world I enter, when I leave this body, it's not that much different after all. It can't be a source, can it?"

He smiled again,"Isn't that astral world simply part of this one, a part we've not yet explored very much ?"

She grinned with understanding. If she could begin to reason it all out, could find 'sense' to it, she would feel better. But she shook her head again as if trying to dislodge something.There's something more!" She studied their faces, and fought to keep calm. How could they allow this, all this? But at their mind-Touch, she was reassured and went on,"I feel as though I am going to lose -- everything, lose this life even, as if EVERYTHING is threatened." The tears were flowing again, relieving her and natural to this stress she felt.

"It's a loss, a sense of the ending of all that's familiar, because you've seen what is beyond,what in fact, encompasses all that we know, everything. You see that it's possible to lose all you've known. Isn't that something to grieve for?"

"You mean then that it's true? That I am going to, am now, losing my life?" Her eyes were wide and staring at them.

"It may seem so. But you notice you still live." Raymond smiled. "When you're a baby, you lose that life, for the one of a growing child, don't you?"

She nodded, the fear draining a little,she watched Martha's face as if she needed to cling to that simple physical sense as to a safety. "It's just a terrible grief. None of the Master Teachers ever told us that."Her voice tilted up into a complaining tone, sounded childlike. It made the two monitors smile. Rose said,"I have lost something, it's almost as if I've lost my life, because nothing is the same, nothing seems to matter at all."

"Is that really true? You enjoy, you love your family, you delight in beauty still, you get great satisfaction from your work, your travel, your good conversations, all if it. You still love to eat, to play and listen to music, to sing and to dance, play a game of cards or Three Ball,visit with your friends. What has gone?"

She grinned ruefully, wiping tears from her face with one hand, like a child. "It's true. there is a part of me that just goes on living as I always did and enjoying life as it seems. But I know better now. I know and that longing, that sense of something MORE is so great that I felt that I was living a lie. I thought I was losing the old completely. I haven't understood, just felt threatened and I didn't know by what." She felt pressed to complete every part of this, to end the pain and grief, the fear, the confusion.It seemed to be happening just in the telling.

Raymond reached to take her hand,his strong fingers liftng hers. The warmth and energy she felt from him restored her. He was smiling, his face, so open,not lovely to look on, very masculine, rugged, was in that smile beautiful. She caught herself short, just looking at him. Gripping his fingers she said slowly, her eyes shifting to Martha."Is it always so? You folk, you have such beauty, it radiates."

He said,"There is something yet you haven't told us. Will you do what you need to do?"

With a soundless sob she bent into his lap. He laid his hands on her head and she let the sobs come, the pain push from her body, accept the relief that this telling gave. After some long minutes, the sobs stopped suddenly. She raised her head,"I feel so ashamed," then, with a small grin, "I feel so relieved too."

Martha nodded,"It's part of healing, you know. Now can you tell us the rest?"

Rose looked at her as though she had spoken a foriegn tongue. After a minute her face cleared.She understood,she smiled and her eyes shone. "There is more! Yes, there is. But I just haven't even shaped it into words for myself.I don't know whether I can now, but if I don't, how shall I understand?" She sat, looking off, reaching deep into her own mind,herself, searching for that elusive realization that she might give it life here where there was safety.

Finally she began, whispering at first."There was such a longing, it flooded my heart, even when I was little, now and then, then more and more as I grew older. I glimpsed several times, that wonder I've told you of. And it lifted me --" She shook her head, her eyes full of the wonder of memory. "It got so that I could not look across the Valley, watch the air move a leaf, touch the water in the fountains, so clear, so absolutely lovely, climb on the belts into the sky, but especially, when our children were born,then it was --there were days of time when I felt at an edge of possibility I couldn't name. I lived through both universes, that of person and of Spirit. I felt purified, literally and I felt embarrassed because it sounded so corny to say that. It was so wonderful I ignored the fear then." She drew a long,shaky breath,"I got so I dared not immerse myself in the beauty of things too much, because that beauty drew me into itself, through itself and there, I was, facing that unknown again."

"But later, I would wonder whether I approached some mental trouble." She shook her head, but did not bring her gaze back to them, frowned and then went on, her voice stronger. "Because that 'edge' that point where the promise was most acute, seemed to grow closer and closer, I felt myself growing beyond my own control." She glanced at them, her eyes steady,"I suppose I was very much in control because I didn't tell anyone at all. I kept secret all my fear and all my wonder too." She moved her head from side to side in sad remembering. "That was what was wrong, to repress one meant I must repress the other.

She straightened, looked at them firmly,"Lately,though, the denial hasn't been enough.It's as if I cannot hide, cannot avoid -- my Self. It is that isn't it?" They nodded and eyes wide,she continued, "Now, when I look out over the Valley, I cannot simply see its beauty, I see through that beauty and there looking through -- everything -- is -- Life? I am so delicately balanced at the edge of some revelation that I can't even look at a sunset without feeling near it!"She laughed, wanting to joke, make less profound her feelings. "I want to offer myself wholly. to consciously participate.But I don't".

Again she slowly shook her head, in disbelief at herself. "Then there is the music, I know now, finally, what Andrew must feel, and Annette.I have no talent, hardly enough even to know how to truly enjoy listening to music, and yet, when I practice in my bumbling way, to play a little, there are moments now, when we play together especially, that I feel something beyond the sound, something like what music itself must be for those others. For me it lasts perhaps a measure, maybe two, if I'm lucky, and then, I'm back to just a succession of sounds. But there it is. Within music there is another doorway. It's true for the other arts. There is that fine edge where I know the faint Touch. There is something beyond -- everything, I think." her voice dropped again to a whisper, "more grand, more elusive and yet, it's right here, in my heart, alive." She shook her head this time, with dispair. "How can I understand That?"

"I used to think it was only imagining, also that it was a dream or that it was something wrong with me, but then I studied and read and asked what questions I dared and began to know that it was a begining of Knowing. And I didn't know what that meant either. Although I knew Joy, so great at times it seemed to tear me apart, I was almost afraid to acknowledge it, for fear it wasn't real. I couldn't think of any 'thing' to feel joy for."

Martha was patient, her voice encouraging," It's not that unusual for a person going through that Awakening to feel these things, Child." She frowned,"What is sad is that you've kept all this held down in yourself, not allowing yourself to realize even half of what you Touched on."

She nodded slowly, her eyes fixed on Martha's face,"I think I know that now, but then I didn't." Raymond and Martha had given her space and safety to allow herself to see and she felt immense gratitude. Astonishingly she could bear that knowing after all. " Humanity is becoming God Conscious. I'm part of it. The vastness of what we are is what overwhelms us." She said in awe, wonderingly, looking at their encouraging smiles, not seeing much except their Love shining around them. She nodded,"I see that, even though I deny my Self, I see now. I realize! I AM Soul!"

There was silence. For a long time they sat, Rose clinging tightly to Raymond's hand, as if his strength allowed her to know her Self a little longer. She saw finally that their minds had surrounded hers and offered her a gentle Joining. Then she turned to them, her voice normal, quiet, and said,"I suppose it is the fear of loss of the familiar, the sense of loss a child feels, along with pride and joy, when she realizes she is no longer a child, but has passed on into young woman hood. It is a kind of growing up and it has to be happening to all of us, all of the people of the Valley. All of us. What I fear is growth?" The metaphor helped her poor strained brain to grasp something it could set into meaning for itself. "But there is more, isn't there? More for all the Valley?"

"There's much more, Rose." Martha's eyes met Raymond's.

How can you, your kind, manage to help all of us, people like me just beginning to realize, to be aware? And we need help so badly! There aren't enough of you."

Martha laughed, that light musical laugh that made Rose smile to hear,"Ah, Child, that's why we're here now. Because every one who wakes up, realizes, begins to recognize what she is, will be ready to teach another, to help us help others. You see? "

Rose laughed with her, it seemed suddenly to her wonderful, so easy, obvious. She said, "The amazing thing that I see now, see so irrevocably, is that we are

THE AWAKENING

so -- so -- MUCH. We human beings, we are so much more than we know! Why hasn't someone told me before?"

"Would you have listened? Only when a mind and heart is ready, can the person hear." Raymond reclaimed his hand and stood, walking slowly in a wide circle around the small court.

Rose nodded,"You're right. I wouldn't and I HAVE been told. I just refused to apply it to myself. Because experience is so utterly different from theory, I suppose." She frowned,"But there's still the question. What is that? What is it that I -- that I glimpse?"

Raymond shook his head,"You want an easy name, something to hold on to. That cannot be held on to. You must find the understanding for yourself" He was silent, then softly he added, "Some call it a reach beyond this reality. We humans find it painful to open ourselves to Reality. But whatever, you decide, you know now that what you realize shakes our minds loose from old patterns and wakes us to know there is a Journey to be made."

Martha said slowly,"A Teacher once said to me,'Sometimes looking through myself I See my Self and thus know Spirit looking out at Earth. It might be we see God looking back at us through ourselves. No?" She was smiling at the memory.

Rose nodded, feeling finally that she had finished, had spoken her heart to emptyness. There was so much to think on, to bring into balance . To perhaps, even talk about with Ben -- and the rest of the Family. The thought both frightened and excited her with hope. She sighed and looked around, seeing the blazing color of the gardens, the brilliant shaping and reshaping of the fountains, the lovelyness of their home place. The people walking through the gardens had bruised the ground cover of mints and Thyme and the fragrance was soft but sweet. This life, this beauty of simple living filled her with an incomprehensible Joy.She laughed,and stood up "I said that things had faded, that life had no excitement in it anymore, but now, I see that this life is sweeter than ever, more beautiful and more deeply full of wonder. Maybe we can learn to see though it's form to its source. What little I see now is so very Good. It's a constant reminder."

Martha looked at her, pride and joy at this woman's awakening in her shining eyes . "You will practice Seeing through now? And there is the Joining, perhaps you can enter into it with true acceptance, for you will find something there, something that opens the heart to know what humankind is after all."

Rose nodded, her own eyes shining, her face radiant with the gladness, the loss of dispair. She wondered how Joining related to that new perception of reality. She didn't want to ask, she said, "I would like to Join with you both."

Those two, Reaching, surrounded her as water surrounds a sponge, gradually penetrating and entering and offering her themselves to enter into also. For full entering cannot occur except when it is mutual. It was a kind of intercourse that transcended every experience of relationship Rose could have imagined had she known how to try. At first, she sprang mentally back, closed herslf like an eyelid that opened, is blinded by too much light. Their Touch was tender, sweetly aware and she gained courage, even desire to Join. Then tentatively, she opened herself, Reached and merged. There was entrance into a vast sea of consciousness, a lifting, transcendant awareness that offered something of the nature of MIND itself beyond what she would have termed possibility even. Yet it WAS. This Touch of wakening minds was powerful,extended on into that ocean of Mind itself. Strong, vital currents of love, of purpose, of life moved through her.And she learned such Joining does not occur in shallow mind, for there is no power except in depth. Without power, there is no true Joining.

How did she know this power would not destroy her, drown her self into some unimaginably greater Self? Terror gripped her. The loss of herself seemed to be so near. Infinite Mind, Touched her consciously offered self,impressing upon her consciousness truths, knowledges she could never have imagined, and so it shaped her as it would. But It also held sacred that awed and accepting self, sustaining its nature even as it revealed Its own. Her terror was like a shield, a barrier behind which she lost vision, lost the wonder. And she knew fear was at once a protection and a betrayor. From the others there came a floating thought,"Look, look and answer your own question."

Rose opened her mental eyes wide, opened and knew that she must understand if she were to accept at all. There around them was Light, and flowing through this Ocean, no, the very current of the ocean, its energy of movement, was Love itself. Light invaded all the darkness of her mind, Light revealed Joy nested deep in the cells of her body, the underlying current of all emotion. It had been there all the time. She held, drew steady, Saw, and focussed her own energy into a fierce determination to hold steady in that Light. She KNEW!

She felt their realization, "Where there is true Joining, there is also trust, Love and Purpose. There is no evil where there is Love". And it was as if all humankind stood there,she, immersed and extended through all people. She knew clearly that there is no separation. She and her kind were one. That which she perceived when looking through the wonder of Life, was also herself and all selves and all life in one fullness. She knew that, and understood though she could not have explained.

The Joining faded, she receded from them, she was left the small personal self that was familiar but now,,seemed so very, very limited. Must that always be so ? Raymond said, "Now,do you realize why the Joining is necessary for all of us to know, to practice so that we may be all that we are?"

Rose caught her breath, her face wet with the tears of such overwhelming realization. Finally, realigning herself, she nodded, "But how can I tell that to those who --who do not know?"

Martha laughed, "Do you think they are able to deny their own nature anymore than you could? Don't you imagine there are many who suffer in secret just as you have? The opportunity need only be offered them."

"But the fear, it holds us back so long, I have been years hiding from --from what I now know is mySelf."

"Perhaps talking openly with your family, with your people and your students, could bring about that awakening and that acknowledgement of the realization they fear."

Rose nodded,"We've begun to see that we must talk more, that we must tell each other what weighs on our hearts. So far we have only said we must do it. We haven't done it. But surely we can." The heat of the after noon weighed down on them, she felt her skin moist with sweat, her body weary. The fountain sent a light mist through the air, disappearing even as it began to descend but it cooled the air a little. They were all standing now,and they walked in mutual need toward the great Archways that gave access between the Rings and stood in their deep cool shade.

They began to walk through the Arch to the outer Ring gardens, and Rose was grateful for the chatter of people moving past them. That familiar chatter brought her world back into focus. Rose gave little attention, though she knew most of the people going by. They went into a corner cafe and sat down, ordering from the list of dishes written in light beneath the surface. As soon as the order was made, the words disappeared, the table was clean and white. She said,"I'm so glad you came today. I didn't know that I called. That still seems strange to me,that you could have heard."

Raymond shook his head,"We didn't. We can't. It was a young Monitor who heard. one just finished with her training. She has immense Talent and perception of Consciousness. She is a Watcher of the Valley."

Rose nodded, suddenly filled with thoughts of all there was to learn. How could a young girl be able to act as a Monitor? How? She had thought they were all very old. A swift jab of jealousy pierced her but she saw it. She said, "There's so much to learn."

"Surely, the science of Spirit is new. The way of the Mystic is not unknown among your Teachers. But the way of Spiritual Sciences has been neglected. Both must be taught, openly and persistently. We have instructed Master teachers to reveal to all what was once taught only to those who asked. Your mate, Benjamin, will know much of this when he comes home. He can show you the connections between your sciences and the science of Spirit."

She smiled sadly, a little ruefully as she shook her head,"You'd never get Ben to admit that the way of the mystic was science. He's pretty adamant about keeping these things separate."

"How long since you've seen him,Rose, Talked with him?"

"Well, some time, but I know Ben." She hesitated, looked seriously at them, "You do know of him then? How can you?"

You forget that the Network of the Monitors is world wide, not just Valley wide. We know of much that happens, even that is now happening. And Ben went out to find something, don't you suppose that what he searched for might have been him Self?"

Rose gasped, "My God in Heaven! Is it possible? Then, I could talk to him. I could actually talk to him." Tears came to her eyes. She nodded, silent and their food came and they began to enjoy it. Then they fell to talking of familiar things.

They talked of the farm, of town business, of their own work as Healers and finally they were ready to part. The two Healers strapped on their belts and kissed her goodbye. She felt a wrench of loss at their leaving and at the same time a relief. As she watched them go, she thought that perhaps these two were mates. Surely they must have a life of their own, one within which they talked to their families, their friends, and struggled with daily living. The thought comforted her. In all their time together she had found out nothing of their personal lives. That thought surprised her.

CHAPTER EIGHT

Silent City and Jessie at the retreat

On clear mornings the craggy peaks of the eastern mountains finally catch the rising sun and gleam as it hangs above them, filling crevasses and snow covered valleys with its warmth. At the base of the north eastern peaks, high above the hills below, there ran a series of broad flat shelves as though huge sections of the peaks had fallen away and left them. Two of these broad plateaus were ridged at their edges, high ridges, that hid the flat land inside from the world below. The rims were steep narrow walls of stone that fell away on their outside sheer as the carved walls they looked to be to those in the Valley. The shelves were similar to the high plateaus on which Altos was built. Clumps of trees and shrubs grew here and there in the stone floors. The down drift of debris and sand through ages had created wide pockets of deep soil watered by run off from snow that ran through that land in narrow cold streams.

In the two highest plateaus, surrounded by walls, a startling difference had occurred. Here life seemed to flourish as if a thermal current came from the depths of the mountains and warmed all their acres Near the center a fair sized pool sparkled in the sun. In these meadows, grew trees and flowers that were seen nowhere else in the Valley. It was from the beginning a hidden paradise, protected by the surrounding rim of rock. That rim could be seen far below and it glowed wtih a strange light even in the night. It was as if the stone itself gave off light. Down inside in the fields and meadows, the thick groves of trees, lay the Silent City, sculpted by unknown hands from the living rock. She remained a mystery. But not many knew of Her, only those who flew over with the intention of finding out.

William's question about that City and Dean's demand came not as a surprise to Paul and Rose who had heard both. Why no one explored her inner dimensions or asked about her origin, remained a mystery too. Perhaps the greater of the two. She had always been there, and as far as anyone knew, always would be. She was a symbol of the greatest mystery. The busy people of the Valley had had little time to turn from their work of building their world to look high into the hills for solutions to an esoteric puzzle. There seemed a tendency to put off plans to fly over and explore, a tendency no one had given attention to at all.

There had been a few who had gone there, flown over the rims, circled the strange land beneath but these had returned without mentioning their journey and had remained silent. If there had been one who noticed, he could have seen a shining in their eyes, the upsurge of Joy underlying all their expressions. But people were busy. It was easier to attend to other things.

How had that silent City become the star that drew the eye of every

THE PEOPLE OF THE VALLEY

Vagabond traveling the Highways? They rose from sleep to greet and to sing to her, and they turned to her, for benediction before they slept at night. She symbolized for them the supreme mystery. Just how it had happened, no one ever said.

The 'People of the Highway' as they called themselves, assumed they were unique in their awe of Her. Gradually they realized there were Towners who were drawn also to that Light. Why did She fill those who gave her attention with awe, wonder and a sense of inexplicable beauty? That single cluster of building that could be seen behind the high walls, the bright cathedral of spires flashing brilliant color over those smooth flat walls inspired the casual air car traveler enough to turn them for a 'look', but strangely they lost interest and found their way somewhere else.

There she remained, this City that seemed so fragile but was unaffected by the worst storms. Her strength hidden within the cliffs, in the quiet beauty there. The strange fragrance rising out of those gardens, sweet, full and itself nourishing to the spirit, was known to some and remained a symbol of possibility, of dream toward something not yet known.

From the beginning of the building of the Valley cities and towns, the people sought inspiration from the stillness, the faint but increasing light. They built their own Temples with those gleaming spires in mind and most did not stop to recognize their imitation. Temples of Valley towns were built where stillness could be ensured, inside, music could be waked at the touch of a button, from the soft chime of bells or the low sweet note of a gong, the steady chant of human voices, to a full symphony, for tastes were varied. The Temple centered the town, was it's focus of attention toward that highest point of consciousness. Insistence on discovering the Nature of the Spirit was a vivid desire of the Heart. Many minds still held it as lesser, as perhaps only a dream, but more cast sharp intelligence into that search. The City waited, watched and bided her time.

Not far beyond the Silent City, a little north east, was a smaller Valley within which harsh rugged hills thrust up, breaking the smooth meadows and farm land with wild forest dark pinnacles, giving it a special beauty. The North Station, built into one of those wild lovely upthrusts of ragged rock was the only Station that took in citizens for teaching and testing. The young who showed Talents and the presence of that greater consciousness that would make them Monitors, would then go on to the practice Station in the west. South and East Stations were closed to all but trained adepts. Power used and extended from these stations was dangerous to any untrained. A very few came to the North Station from their own decision, most were sent there by traveling Teachers or perhaps by a Master Teacher with acute perception. The Stations sought always for new sensitives.

The never ceasing urgency of Life and especially of human life, to grow beyond itself was most evident in these years. Every Monitor, not only of this Valley, but of the world, stood alert ready to be part of that awakening of human Spirit.

On this morning, at the ending of winter, with the days cold but sometimes

THE AWAKENING

fine and warm down in the protected courtyards of the Station, Jessie ate a light breakfast. Today would be the last in her loved home. She would meet Ben soon and they must begin their Journey. His time had been well spent here, and he had studied hard. Daniel had given him special attention and Benjamin had a new calmness about him, his eyes reflecting a peace he had never known. But even then, his heart both ached and blazed with joy. He had found, through himself, through his own nature, that center of Light and brought it into daily Touch. Never again would he fall into such profound dispair. Finally he knew what had been so long missing.

For Jessie it had been a time of happiness such as she had not known in years. To be home here with her beloved Teachers and friends, to be with Daniel for long days and nights, had been a true reward. Now she must go and she knew she would not come here again.

She smiled across the long shining table, Daniel smiled back. they did not speak of the separation so near them. Neither felt it as much of a separation, each of them must leave this world soon and they would be together in a manner even truer than this. He said,"It will be a good day, Sister. Your Journey will not be hard."

A young man sat beside Daniel, watching Jessie,,his eyes glistening in pride at being there. He was a student of Daniel's and had spoken to Jessie a few times in these weeks. He was a husky young man, dark brown hair cut into a bowl shape around his head. He insisted on a simple cut that anyone could do for him. His vows to simple living were, sometimes a little excessive. His eyes were a peircing green, the only clue that he was more than the lazy farm boy he seemed. Jessie felt his energy, his mind power reverberating, though he was being trained to direct and focus that power and he could do that very well already. He had been brought here when he was twelve , younger than usual, for good reason.

Jessie shifted her gaze to Daniel, let her eyes wander over the beauty of his body, including the deformed limbs that rested now. She noticed the fragility of his face,his age was more evident that it had ever been. She watched others rise and leave the table, Eating was a time of talk, these who worked and taught sometimes saw each other little except at meals. They enjoyed two pleasures at once. Each person came to bid Jessie farewell and she stood to embrace them in turn. There was silence, for they spoke directly, Touching,in a private expression of love. Daniel turned to her when they had gone. He spoke aloud, wanting to hear her talk, to see her face animated with thought. He asked,"What have you found, Jessie, to comfort you about this world?"

Chester, their young companion watched them both, his delight in being there with them evident. He thought them both saints from whom he could learn. Jessie said, "I think it is the growth that I see -- everywhere, here in this Valley, and everywhere throughout the land. There is also what must accompany growth, there is fear, and there may be -- perhaps must be death. For the old must give way to the new.

People have trouble shaking free of familiar attachments. Growth is painful. If only humanity could know this time as one of growth and not mistake it as one of loss, the transition would be easier. But then, fear is one impetus to growth, is it not? That and pain." She looked sad, and yet, deep in her eyes he saw the joy, the knowledge that would not let her grieve.

"There is a rising of Joy in the Valley too, Jessie. You do see that?"

She laughed, the light happy laugh of a young woman,"Oh, yes, Danny, I see that. It's my joy to see it. But fear has not abandoned me, I have not yet found it utterly faded, though I learn every day." She smiled again and held his eyes. "You know Daniel, the people reach outward, seek what we must find and what we offer, what life offers. But if I realize Love enough to dissolve fear completely from my own heart, how can I teach others to do so? I know that fear constantly acts as a goad and a barrier. But the hearts of the people must be free to know the Joy they also Touch upon." She was silent, her eyes distant,then,"But, this world comes to its ending. The new era is already well begun."

Chester knit his brows into a dark frown,"What is the fear that still clouds your heart? I was sure such as you would have no fear at all." He looked himself fearful, as if a trust had been violated..

Daniel spoke this time, "You know Chester, that the Valley has grown in balance. It's reaching toward that balance that we've taught all of you who pass through our halls. Balance of each self within its self. Balance of heart and mind, of emotions and reason,balance of compassion and justice, balance of growth and dying. All those others, the many balances of right living, as human beings. The Valley itself has reached that point where balance is possible among its people, through its people all lesser lives will participate in that balance. That is why the animal and plant worlds are so filled with vivid life just now. But you know, Son, just as people can learn balance, so can people topple that Balance. ALL are not yet conscious enough that the balance is secure. And in that the danger lies."

Jessie looked at Chester, her face serious."It's what the Journey time is for, you know. Each of us must make the Journey through herself and discover far within, the SELF. We must find the places of balance and stand firm. We discover what we are and that brings fear, at first. We fear such vastness of Spirit and we doubt our capacity to live such beauty. We discover what we have been, and that too brings fear for what we grieve to know of our smallness of spirit." She frowned, and he watched her intently.

Then she said,"Whenever balance is gained, something had to be pushed off the scales on one side or the other. That which is pushed off may seem precious to us at the time and great pain can accompany the loss. Even though we see that the gain is far, far greater."

His eyes had tightened, his gaze was far away,"I see that. I surely know the pain of it. And I suppose, without knowing the beauty beyond, a person unable to See might have great fear." He reflected a moment, they could literally see his mind setting various recognitions into order."Yes, hard as it was when I was a

THE AWAKENING

child, its lucky to be able to See so early in life after all."

For some time they sat, finishing their food, then, simply enjoying each other's company. Finally Daniel said,"What worries me is that there are those who will not make the choice, who are caught in the dilemma of fear and misunderstanding, and there are those who do not know there is a choice to make?"

Chester drew his feelings carefully into balance. He was delighted and elated that they allowed him to sit with them. . It seemed to him a great gift." Everyone talks of that, the Choice, but what exactly is meant by it?"

"You will define it for yourself better,and later. But it entails whether we choose to turn with conscious awareness into the possibility, the dance of life. Whether we are willing to enter into that Life of greater consciousness. It means a committment to lift, not only ourselves, but all lesser life toward the greater possibility eventually. It is willingness to know of Life as it rises out of the Love and Will of the Eternal Spirit.

Chester sighed,"I'm so grateful that you set it so simply into words. Never has anyone just SAID that!"

They all laughed,"They always told you to figure it out for yourself?" Jessie laughed,and he nodded, smiling. Then he sobered.

"But a person has to have knowledge of that Spirit. And you keep telling us that knowledge can't be reasoned out, but KNOWN intuitively. Most people I know resent that. It conflicts with everything they think. How can anyone comfortably accept such a thing?"

Jessie sobered too, but her eyes still laughed, how joyous was the task of the Teacher. To sit here in the sun, in the beauty of Earth and teach the young." No one said it was comfortable. It's there, hitting us in the face, obvious when we See!"

Daniel nodded," When Life Touches any person, that person is changed, is made to realize something. But we want to catch hold of it, want to set it into rigid order and test it out again and again. The life of Spirit is not like that. It does not repeat itself. It is too full of Life!"

Chester nodded, smiling faintly. They sat, watching the play of sunlight through the needles of the tall pine at the other end of the court, and the flickering color of the children's warm woolen tunics where they danced there. The children came now, younger every year and Jessie eyed them in unveiled pleasure. 'The spiritually precocious,' she thought, satisfied.

Chester stirred from his own preoccupation and asked, "Then what is our task, Father?"

"Perhaps it is to enter into the dance, to know we are part of the unceasing movement of Life and Love. To know we are part of what is beyond these. To agree, to participate, to keep perception open, not crystalized, but reaching far." He sighed, meeting the boy's eyes,"To be aware! Forever questioning."

"Then how can a science develop if no ideas are finally decided as the right ones?"

"They will be Son, they will be. It is our ever present sin to try to set ideas, reality even, into our own frame of reference. We must remind ourselves always that all 'right ideas' are only tentatively right." He laughed," But too much has changed in science, in philosophy, in social sciences too, and too rapidly, within a generation even, so that the science of the evolution of idea, of process, will keep us flexible. We are beginning to allow for unceasing change, growth and ever higher possibility. I tell you Son, humankind is waking up to that which is Eternal. It begins to know the Eternal in its Self." He was silent, his eyes moved to Jessie's and she nodded faintly. He went on, as if to himself.

"Oh, the hardest task, is to be sure we don't decide on the answers and give them to others as truth. We must always allow all things, even what seems like harm, like a wrong direction. People must make their own mistakes. Then our task is to help them see the mistake. Every person's path reveals something the rest of us don't know. So it has to be his own."

"It's not an easy way, Father."

Daniel shrugged, glanced at Jessie and suddenly his eyes were merry,"Oh, dear, we do make it sound solemn, and so difficult. So many people of the Valley begin to realize. A lot of them are in the - the - convulsions of the wakening. Yes, that's what I would call it for it seems so to them. But there are many more now who are fully awake and living every day aware of themselves." He acepted a fresh cup of coffee from a young girl who smiled into Chester's eyes, causing him to blush.

Daniel watched, and sipped his hot drink. It felt good in the cold air,for the sun was warm here, warm and hinting of spring. It's all in whether we can keep our balance before all temptations."

Chester sighed, "Surely not you? Surely there are left no temptations that trouble either of you?"

Jessie laughed, "Surely there are, my dear one. But they become less and less gross each year. Steadily we perceive what makes those old hungers like a sorry dream. But there's no one who can't forget - can't lose his way. Never let that be forgotten."

Chester looked positively crestfallen. his eyes darting from one to the other, "No! No! For if you cannot gauruntee what you have become, cannot KNOW you will not waver, how can I? "

"No one can guarantee anything. People only begin to See. Only begin to recognize fear for what it is. Do I want to live if survival is little more than a scrabbling for dominance? Not now. Not knowing what I do. And yet, can I be sure? I suspect I'd scramble with the worst of us were I threatened enough? You have to always watch, Chester. We aren't immune to need. A moment of grief , of struggle, of dispair, and we find ourselves back at the beginning again."

Daniel was nodding, his hand had stolen across the table and caught Jessie's."Life tests us constantly, Chester. Most testing is called suffering. It is necessary for we are human, not yet more than human. "He was silent, looking off to the distant mountains,"Though we don't yet know what being FULLY

THE AWAKENING

human might be."

"You could make the mistake of trusting someone too much, even a Teacher, Chester. Trust, but have mercy, don't hold anyone to that expectation of perfection. It is a good safegaurd." Jessie's voice was clear, and gentle. She was looking at Daniel, memorizing him again."We keep walking and the Journey is long and sometimes hard, but we must remember that we are ALL on that journey and none of us has yet finished."

Chester nodded, his eyes sad,"Now I understand better the work we've been doing. We're learning how to test ourselves, learning to lift into Soul conscious perception even while we live out self conscious lives. We've been practicing the process daily, it's intense, you know. How can anyone ever know whether his heart is pure? Or if he's fooling himself?" He sat silent, nodding slowly,"I can see we can't. We have to assume we're capable of everything humankind has always been capable of, the worst - and the best?" He dropped his head, chastened.

Chester, still frowning, looked worried. " But Mother. We HAVE changed, humankind has changed. We as a people care about each other. We don't limit our caring to our own relatives and friends. We CARE about every living thing. It isn't something we could FORGET! --" then with a smaller voice he asked,"Is it?"

Jessie met those bright green eyes, so beautiful, so intelligent; he would be a fit one to take Daniel's place when it was time for Daniel to go. She said,"Yes. Humankind has changed, a deep inner shift in perception that has placed our values a little more beyond ourselves, at least. Perhaps the very fact that we aren't desperate for personal survival gives us some freedom .But the danger, Chester, is whether the realization, the awakening is firm enough. Can we stand now against that primitive self?"

"Surely we-- surely it's a difference of more than economics, surely we are indeed a greater people, BETTER people!" His voice had a note of pleading. He didn't want to think otherwise.

Daniel nodded,"I think we are. I think it, Chester, but no one can know until we see what we do in adversity, what we do when we are threatened? When our world that we build out of that greater vision is threatened, what then do we do? Will we act as primitive self oriented persons, or will we act as selfless human beings?" He shook his head sadly, looking from one to the other. "I don't actually know at all, I can only hope. Because I think that Valley to which I return will face that very test soon."

" Ah, if that happens, then we've all got to be alert, to help in some way. The Valley must keep its life." He frowned, the smooth face immediately seemed older. "Some say we've become soft.That we'd not stand adversity, or real trouble! I've heard that."

"A person who would say that would not be a person who -- who KNEW or who had Touched another mind. It would not be one who has struggled and born the pain and terror of the growth within himself. " Jessie heard in her own voice sorrow and a dark question. "The test that stands now before yon Valley will tell us whether we have strength." Her voice was bleak.

Daniel met her eyes, his own flaring with a quick sudden anger."I don't want you to go to that last task out there with worry in your heart, my Love. We are not people of Mind for nothing. We aren't without defenses . After all, protecting ourselves doesn't have to take the form of violence, you know."

"Then we must be ingenious, we must do what humankind has never done. We must risk the power of Love even against an enemy."

He grinned mischievously," If only we always knew how to do that. The practice of Love takes a great Heart!"

She was impatient, "Oh, Daniel, that's true. But even long ago people were able to begin. Remember Gandhi? Remember King? Remember Alotia? And hundreds of simple people whose names were never known. They acted in the midst of distrust. Imagine what can happen now with millions of us conscious enough to risk Love." She was sad,"We are still a people with fear of our deaths not lost, we fear pain even as we meet it.And we need one another desparately.

He was serious, "Yes, but we acknowledge our fear. We will know how to meet the threats to this new way of life, my Dear. We will know how." His eyes were so still she felt their drawing her, felt the power of his calm and his strength meeting her's was such a flood of assurance that she felt ashamed of her brief surge of fear. She felt herself shift, and balance, knowing the recognition of what she must do. With a great sigh, she nodded slowly,"Here we are, caring about those who destroy or hurt some of us, as much as we do about those who are hurt. So we are at a stalemate. We must act without harm to either."

Both the men nodded, watching her face,"Humankind is capable of fierce loyalty, of very great devotion and when that loyalty and devotion includes all humanity, and all life, in fact, then we cannot harm, can we?" Chester spoke with hope.

"If we are truly standing selfless, then we will not harm. There is an old saying that 'every man has his price' and that is the price that would let him fall down to his lowest self, regress, in fact, into that more primitive nature." Daniel slid his coffee cup back and forth between long slim fingers, and then, picked it up to drain it."I can think there is nothing that would tempt me to deny that Vision, but can I be sure? I believe that we are truly an awakened people, that this is not simply an aberation or a sophistocation that has polished our surface. But how do I know after all. The testing of our hearts will come through the Valley itself. Will come before we know. We are human beings of vision, of Love and of a profound Will to Good. Now we will see whether we can act always from that knowledge. If so we will have found a new way to meet whatever we have to meet."

"I think humankind has been like a people lost in a forest, lost and confused about how to find a way. And now, there are many whose hearts are open, whose minds are awake. These have lifted up to see down from the sky on that forest. We can see so many ways to go, how to extricate ourselves from that endless forest and its traps. We can SEE, dear ones, we can SEE! Never again will we be blind enough to harm and to forget." Jessie's face was shining with the reassertion of that Joy they all knew and they breathed a sigh of gratitude that

THE AWAKENING

she reasserted it.

Chester chuckled, Only last week, when I went home for a visit, my friend asked me, because he thinks I am a holy one since I have come here , how he too could become holy. He wanted to be the best, the most Good among all people. And I found myself nonplussed. How could I advise him?"

Daniel watched the boy with sharp, intensity,"He asked you that? Your village people think you holy?"

Chester looked embarrassed, then defiant, then amused at himself,"Oh, Father, I'm only a kid to most of them, but they know I'm here. Some look at me and I see that they KNOW. Those would not ask me such a thing. But there are some who strive for personal perfection, they haven't seen , as Jessie says, from the heights."

Jessie's voice was gentle,"What was your answer."

He looked at her, no smile on his lips, his eyes serious,"I felt a lot of pride, I could just feel myself swell with it. And it frightened me. So I didn't answer right away. I was settling myself." He grinned ruefully, glancing from one to the other pairs of watching eyes, "Actually, I'm a little ashamed of myself, you can see. But finally, I did say to him that holiness wasn't what we sought, but rather we seek to find a way so that every human being can know of Love, and learn to See." He was silent, his young smooth boy's face full of a worry that Jessie knew, saw, and approved.

She quoted softly the words learned so long ago, so often repeated, " 'To bring every person into that place of awareness so that the Light is known, to lift every mind out of the clutch of what we once saw as our human nature and into what we now know as our true nature. To See clearly enough to know of Love and enter into IT's Presence.' So Chester, isn't that our task?" The familar words comforted Chester and honored him for his answer to his friend. He looked at her with gratitude.

Daniel nodded with them. "It's really a matter right now of balance, you know." Chester nodded, and said,"When I first began to realize it was always a feeling of being torn back and forth, of feeling terrible, because I saw both. I didn't think to balance the way we're taught to balance emotion. This is after all perception, realization,. It didn't seem at all the same." He looked at them speculatively, "I've always wondered whether you all knew how close to madness I felt before you brought me here." At their smiles, he grinned,"Yes, I suppose you've suffered that yourselves at some time. Learning how to consciously be Self aware, just as I'm becoming fully aware of my self, was a painful task. So everyone will find it so and there is where we must work.I'm not sure I know how."

"Mostly by simply being that greater Self yourself. By living as that Self knowing itself in this life. Others See! It's true! Whether we can exactly explain the process or not. It's true.!"Jessie moved her own cup idly, watching the little liquid left in the bottom slosh back and forth. She lifted her eyes, her hands sliding down to rest gently in her lap, her body relaxed and at ease, she reached out, Touching two minds, extending, Knowing and being received.

For moments the three sat, Joined with one another and Chester learned more of what it meant to begin this Journey toward fulfillment. He would continue his growth toward greater perception of what Life is, what Love is and what being human is. And these two old ones, so long alive teaching others, could show him something of what that might be. He was received and knew the power of their combined energies, the vision of their ability to receive and allow the flow of Love through their consciousness. The power of it, and he was aware only of a little of what they knew, seemed to Chester to be more than he could ever bear, and yet, at that moment, he bore with more than he ever had. Each time one was Touched by that stillness of Being, capacity to bear it grew. He knew that in these few minutes he had been lifted higher and he could See with greater clarity. The forest below, that was himself, was exposed to view.

Chester's eyes were wide, his breath came rapidly as if he had been running and he stared at the two of them."What we just did, what I realize with you. It's as though my mind is stretched. I've felt that before, it's actually painful, you know." Yet, it's no more painful than using a set of muscles that have been allowed to lay dormant for a while. It's simply waking that Mind of yours to its possibility, Son." Daniel was stern, then he smiled a broad, happy smile that touched the others with its joy.

Chester was nodding, understanding, accepting and grateful but he insisted,"But people in my village, for instance, some of them don't See, they don't KNOW, they aren't conscious of themselves, they don't know the Self, the Spirit. How can they accept, feel good about those who do?" His eyes moved back and forth to each of theirs, "I wanted to ask when I got back last week, and I've hesitated. What do we do with people who can't seem to know as we know?" Jessie met his troubled eyes,"You're concern is a right concern, Son. We've already said you must practice living among them, and you must keep yourself always open to that flow of Love through yourself that they may sense it from you. At the same time, you must never imagine it is yourself they admire, but rather the Love you channel. We are vehicles of Spirit, you and I. As we become also Self conscious we are aware that those others are also that Self and there is no lack. The duality is our life recognition. To understand and and practice living until we are Self primarily and self only as a vehicle." She suddenly grinned,"There, that ought to keep you busy."

"Then our help is as you help us here? It's living as conscious beings, extending Love and Power through our lives the way we exhale breath?" He was silent and so were they.

Jessie's eyes were far away, moving over the long, broad rectangle of red tile that filled space betwen three of the residences,. A covered walkway ran along the edges of the buildings and a tall pine glistened with rain at the far end. The other trees and shrubs, here and there were like dry sticks in this cold winter time. The stillness of the court held her, fed her heart. A tall graceful crepe myrtle, its bark smooth and reddish in the slanting light, cast clean shadows on the red tile. Jessie reached for that stillness, remembering so many years of walking there, of absorbing its quiet.

Suddenly a door opened at the end and a troop of young students dressed in varieties of bright colors, loose pants and shimmering blouses came quietly out. They were like a sudden blooming of the court. They began a slow walk that was so graceful it was a dance. An older student at the side beat time on a round tub drum and another blew a melody from a slim flute. Long sweet notes hung lingering in the ear. Jessie smiled, memories flooding back. The walk was smooth, but lifted into dance that held the quality of stillness, of movement rising out of stillness. She felt her heart lighten. These children had come from that Valley below, surely there was great hope there.

A bell sounded, deep and long, and Chester rose, said goodbye. He was shy as he turned to Jessie,"Mother, good traveling. May your Journey be well."She stood suddenly, unexpectedly to kiss him and he blushed with pleasure, then turned to go. When he was gone, Jessie and Daniel were silent for some time, then Daniel said, "He's learning well, Jessie. His mind leaps ahead at times, he's out distancing us, you know. We can only point the way to him. The Valley will be alright with such as these."

She nodded, "He's accepting, and he shares finally very well. The fear was deep in him when he came. He didn't trust at all. We've got to watch for that. It must be common among the people". She got up, and they stood moving to the door into the rooms beyond. "I must go Daniel. The time is here and I can't put it off any longer. It was sweet having this night with you. A memory I will treasure. You and I, lying there in your bed together, that, all that! And now, this little time of teaching together, and the Joining last night, and the wonder of it all. It is a lovely world we have here, Daniel, a lovely world." She was silent,"But it is only this. To know its true Life would be wondrous. To know all Earth harmonious will one day be possible. And ourselves living Earth in that harmony." Her voice was soft.

He nodded, "I know that Ben is waiting for you and you must go my Love. We mustn't ask too much patience of the young." He took her hand and pressed it between his own. "I'll see you again before we leave." She walked down the winding path to the entrance of the Meditation Hall. Glancing in, she saw Ben was not there and she went on along a passage and through a small garden. At one side was a small room and she could see Ben sitting there, patient,enjoying the beauty of the garden and eating a thick slice of bread with a thick spread over it. He saw her and stood, came quickly to meet her. He set his bread on a chair back and embraced her. He said,"Oh, Jessie, I'm just realizing that finally I'm really ready to turn to home. To be there, with my Family, my Mate and children. I was looking over the hills there through the cut in the rocks. I can actually see the Valley , , though I can't make anything out. But they are there, not that far at all."

"Your Journey is finished, Son? You've found what you sought?"

"I thought I was searching for you, Jessie. That that was all I sought. But I know now that there was much more, and that had I come here first, or gone directly to you, I would not have been finished now. Being here a little while has given me some sense, has shaken my brain loose of old patterns and I can See things a little better." He followed her to a bench where the sun was shining and they sat down. "Well, in the whole year, I've learned enough to go home now, I think"

"Perhaps you'll tell me something of what you learned?" He was silent, his forehead creased in a frown, his eyes dark under the thatch of bright hair. "There were so many places, people, life styles, to see and digest. All of them so different from one another, like the imagination of their people. I remember a town in the south where the people did as we do; build their towns and cities from a complete plan. They get funded by their state if they can show a workable industry, to begin. I visited in the town for several days and passed on through. Miles of forest and wild meadows, with strips of farming land laid between, began literally at the end of the streets on the east where I left the city. It was a checkerboard city like the old ones used to be, except that each square was planned to be harmonious to the rest and to provide easy access for everyone to all their main Centers. They will build up, rather than out into the land around them. Already the central squares are ten stories high. But they reserve one square in every nine for park. Residences surrounded the city proper, so no one had to walk far to work or play. The last cluster of four story apartments were nearly invisible among tall trees and the fields and forests began at the edges of their lawns. So I went on my way.

He turned from her, his eyes looking far across the hills, remembering."I'd barely gotten a quarter of a mile when I came on this camp. People drifting, no homes. And they weren't Vagabonds at all. Though I'd seen Vagabond camps this far east a week earlier. I talked to them and they seemed fearful, even of me. It took some time, just being there, offering them food and caring about them, but finally I learned that they didn't know they had rights to a home, to credit, to learning, to everything a citizen has a right to. I went back to talk to the town Council and they said they hadn't figured out a way to let stragglers know of their rights. They have Television reports for them, but many don't see television. They'd been utterly absorbed in building their town and finishing it and I know that could be true. But they sent immediately to bring the people in to their guest housing until they could decide whether they wanted to live here or in another town. They got them work to bring in credit and took them to the public Dining Halls. They had to help them get basic new clothes, theirs were pretty bad. Now, can you imagine Jessie that there could be people who still don't know the way of our life today?"

She nodded, "Yes, the land is vast, people have been hidden in a number of places, afraid to come out because they don't know how things have begun to change. Isolated groups feed on old fears, you know and make them into laws and convictions."

"Well, they were astonished, and so mistrustful. They thought there must be some catch to it. But finally I think it was going to be alright. I saw them to their rooms and settled and tried to reassure them. Then I left. But I knew how angry

THE AWAKENING

I'd been, Jessie. Then I knew how big a satisfaction I got playing the knight in shining armor. I should have realized someone would have found them sooner or later. I was glad I didn't live there, because I'd been such a -- such a - " he drew a long breath, "a self righteous prude. Actually I was." He was silent a moment, his face registering embarrassment and sorrow. "But Jessie, the Council heard my anger without reaction and then they were all totally silent and finally a couple of them nodded and they all got up and came with me to see. "

He sat turned from her, then he turned all around so he looked at her, "Jessie, I'm sure those people were in some kind of communication and yet I could see no device for it. They made their decision silently. "

She nodded, "You've not heard of any people behaving that way elsewhere?"

He grinned, drawing a long slow breath, and his grin faded into a puzzled frown, "I saw it everywhere. I must have finally been able to see it, because never on a journey before have I seen that. I see it happening here. I'm not sure what it is, but it must be what Rose talks about and I wouldn't listen to her. It must be that Touching, that Mind Touch?"

She met his eyes and held them, "It probably was Benjamin. It does a swift job of communication."

"Does that mean they talk to each other -- telepathy?"

"Not exactly. Usually people only share imagery, feelings, a general attitude about things. They know this and can make decisions faster when they do talk. It's really a form of sharper awareness extended to others."

He sat thinking, silent. "I've got to accept that somehow, seeing it, I can't deny it. Not now."

"What was it that made you so angry?

"Oh, I jumped to conclusions there too. I had to do a lot of thinking when I left that town. I was afraid our nation might get back to that the old pattern of people beginning to divide up into those who were at the top, those in the middle and those at the bottom of the social ladder. After listening to my grandparents, I wanted to see none of that. At first I thought the town people were holding themselves superior. But you know, Jessie, these people were not lost because they'd been pushed out anywhere, they were simply not -- not able to understand much. Retarded in development. Mental development. Physically they were fine. But, you know, they had two little children and they were sharp little fellows."

"Ben, it seems to me you were angry at what you thought was injustice. That's not wrong. You corrected your attitude later, you know. After all anger can be healthy in its place." She was silent. Her eye searching his face. "I think perhaps you've found your future work, Son. There are such people lost throughout the land, you know." She smiled at him. Then stood up, "Well, you're anxious to return home. I know that storms are developong in the north that will follow us so we'd best be going. We can talk as we travel."

He nodded, standing with an eagerness to please "I've got the boat down at the River, the north town loading ramp. There are no more rapids south of here. So we can cast right off when you come. I'll meet you there in half an hour?"

She nodded and went to get her own gear. Well, finally she must leave this home, this place of wonderful safety and happiness. She let her eyes move over everything, enjoying that last hour. She knew she would not see any of these friends again in this life. As she walked to Daniel's room, she could see the light from the cliffs far up the steep mountains. The Silent City seemed like a beacon, a reminder. She stopped looking at it there. She knew that there would be help in this last task of her life.

CHAPTER NINE

Paul's trip to Silent City

Paul waited to hear the chime of the doorbell from the library where he sat contemplating his life, the events of the Valley and the beauty of the early evening. He could hear Jennifer playing in the music room. Gradually thought diminished, his mind grew quiet. Valley events forgotten, he was simply aware. There was so much! The heights and depths of everything that filled his senses were like a tapestry of color, sound and fragrance. Lingering wisps of thought faded away from this height of quiet. Here, thought was unformed, and he entered into stillness where music,the beauty of sky and land outside his wide windows,drew him from those narrow confines of himself. The practice of focussing attention into Soul perception was a learned one, but he was adept. It required first, a dislodging of himself from the clutch of thinking and worry, then a Reaching outward, lifting, aware of himself joining with Earth life so deeply he was an intrinsic part of the living universe he entered. The expansion and the sense of lifting, always made him able to 'see' his small self sitting, or walking, heavy, blocky and less aware. And it included a glimpse of brilliant pure white Light, but the Light seemed always somewhere just beyond vision. He would sustain attention, seeking nothing, simply aware. Now and then, there would be more -- as if given, an impression of knowledge that always amazed him, left him more full of wonder than understanding.

He had always known that Vision, genuine perception of the new, comes when a person is not seeking something, or avoiding. He had tried to tell that to Benjamin, but thought he had not succeeded. He knew that when he, Paul, ceased to search,held attention in stillness, then Vision simply came. It was as though he stood within Vision, as if it permeated his mind like a gentle wind of realization. He had often pondered on why this was. Every artist, especially his wife and Annette knew a little of that. Those Master Teachers, fine tuned in life of Spirit, knew it. And Paul knew and practiced that way to realizing. He thought that when one is in a state of seeking, searching,as Benjamin was, then he has set a limited idea there ahead, something expected, or dreamed of. He thought expectation blocked possibility, acted as a false image. It must be released in order for the mind to See. Paul had lost any sense of expectation. But sadly he reflected his own avoidance was a more limiting habit.

But this evening, tired from a good day of work, free of worry, feeling the exhilaration of plans for a party, he thought he was willing - to meet whatever came. He emptied his mind, relaxed and allowed himself stillness, where time ceases. And the merging of himself beyond himself occurred, lifting, expanding awareness. However, just as that sense of inclusion, of being awake, alive beyond himself began, he frantically began again to think. Thought rising from longing, dispair, that he did not often admit to, blocked the stillness. He lost the connection. He felt angry at himself because he would not sustain attention clear of thinking, of the surge of feeling. He knew it was 'would not' not 'could not'. He was a coward! Life in these past few years seemed empty, devoid of any true meaning. Even though he had everything he had always dreamed he wanted. Something ought to happen! More than once through his life he had felt that strange, hesitant expectation, and yet, there was only this, the emptyness. And he had never had courage to sustain attention, too meet that emptyness head on, discover its nature, he avoided - desparately. The pain of it hurt too much, frightened him. Now again, he avoided and found himself shrunk to the daily level of attention.

    The stillness broken, the expansion of consciousness shrunk to safe levels,he grieved at his lack. Then, with relief, he heard the door chime . He was expecting guests. Sweeping down and into focus with the physical moment, he got up and went, a little bemused, to open the door. William, Annette and Alice came in and he greeted them with warm pleasure.

    Will's tall thin figure seemed thinner in the black plasilk suit with only a white scarf to break that austerity. But Annette and Alice made up for his lack. Annette dressed in blue green flowing trousers and thigh length tunic with stitchery of tiny jewels forming patterns on the sleeves and around the neck. Alice was more simply dressed in a fitted dress of gold and lavender, silk skenna. She wore flowers in her hair and was smiling with the pleasure of their gathering. Paul remembered that Will had once told him he liked to wear black because it made him stand out among all the bright colors of the Valley people. Paul thought that fit well.

    Paul kissed Alice last of those entering and their eyes met in deep affection while they laughed at the way his indigo suit did not blend well with her colors. "We must not sit together Paul or we'll distress Annette" she laughed. Paul had felt Annette's fingers cling to his seconds longer than need after their embrace. He knew instantly of her fear, but not its name. He did not attempt to Touch now, that must wait even if she would respond. He caught her eye, wondering, but there was a flicker of warning in her look and he was still. They found chairs for themselves while he went to make drinks and bring the tray of small foods.

    Will seemed in such good humor Paul was surprised. He had responded to Paul's hug with unusual warmth. Well, whatever it was, it was good. When he finished making drinks and brought them to his friends, Will said,"Paul, it's good to get together like this. I'm glad you have a birthday. I've missed two of the Gather's at the Farm and I regret that." Paul nodded and their eyes met, Will was aware of Paul's silent scrutiny but Paul was often quiet. Will went on, "I've missed because I've been out-Valley traveling, a number of times,in these past months. Markets for Altos are growing everywhere. Maybe because population is growing so fast just now." He laughed, "Right now, that's good for us, but we've got to watch the rise in population. We can't ignore such things as we once did." He went on to talk of the cities that were ordering the precision instruments for industry and medicine that Altos made. The rapidly increasing market for new plants, seed, and root stock that made the difference between feeding people well or poorly on the same few acres. And at the same time, of maintaining the health of the land. William was an effective salesman, one of the best.

They could hear Jennifer completing the last part of her Sonata, there was silence. Paul placed a drink at her chair and then sat down. He looked at Alice. Dear delightful Alice, always full of so much robust good humor. She was essential to this group, for they were roused from their tendency to too much seriousness at times only by her good cheer. She gave any party a spark and so was invited often. Now she was teasing Will about his 'wandering ways'. She asked him how he liked the ladies of foriegn nations,and Paul was surprised when Will actually blushed.

Annette watched William's discomfort with a wry smile. She said, wanting to rescue him,"Have any of you been to the Farm lately?"

Paul turned to her, wanting to talk of that too."No, I haven't, but I've talked to Rose a couple of times. It's not long until the October Gather and she seems eager for us to come. I thought she seemed a little anxious about something. She does miss us, you know. Rose, of all the Family likes getting us together most.

Jennifer came into the room and they all went through the hugs and greetings again, each genuinely pleased to be together again. Annette said,"Jennifer, that was so fine. I wish you'd do more concerts. I hear others saying the same, you know." She kissed her friend and then stood back to look into her eyes, saw there a sadness that caused her own smile to fade a little."You know,I think we all need to relax this day. Forget our worries and be at ease.Enjoy ourselves!" She laughed and felt relief to see Jennifer's smile reach into her eyes.

Then Annette went to join William at the long windows that looked out across the canyon of Altos on one side and on the great Valley on the other. They looked out at the lights coming on in the pyramid of residences and she glanced across at him, wondering again. The sun glinted on the checkerboard of windows gleaming in the cliff face above and beyond the pyramids. They brought light into the caverns there and made them a place where people could live happily. Behind those windows a warren of large and airy rooms were cut into the native rock and extended into natural caverns that ran deep in the mountains. Passages ran through one entire peak to open out again onto the forests of the western slopes. About half of Altos was hidden to the observer's eye. William was thinking of these facts, absorbed again in the thought from the meeting he had just left. He drew himself away, he must let all that go now, and enjoy this evening. And yet, there was so much he had to do.

Will turned to his wife briefly, his eyes flickered over her face but he did not meet her eyes. He turned to smile at the others and sipped the last of his wine. Paul was replenishing Annette's wine, the cherry red color seemed to Will at that moment, like a ritual of blood between them. He started at his own image. What was wrong with him tonight?

Paul felt again the curious sorrow in Annette , touched her lightly on the arm ,

THE PEOPLE OF THE VALLEY

sending his own reassurance. A look of sudden hope seemed to leap up in her, then faded again. He turned to go to his chair, dropped into it and said,"I'm bushed. I'm glad you're all here and I want to enjoy this evening.

Alice said, "You look tired, what's been wearing you out?"

He shook his head,"I don't know. Just getting old, I suppose, Alice." Annoyance at another avoiding made him frown.

Jennifer moved in her chair, set her glass of blue Argentine wine on the table beside her. She watched them, shielding her self from them by a face as motionless as a mask. Paul wondered at her, and wondered too how he could bring them to forget their obvious worries, sadness, etc. and just enjoy the evening. Jennifer said,"Life gets to be wearying after a while, you know. What's there left to do that we've not already done?" Her fingers wrapped around her glass again as if she would crush it within them.

Paul cried out, almost frightened at her prescience, " Oh, No, my Dear, surely there are so many things yet to do, to think about. Why, you haven't even begun to write all the music in you?" His body straightened in his chair,his eyes briefly defensive. Jennifer saw and wondered too.

She shook her head and met his eyes, her face softer , "Things to do, my dearest? No, only variations on a theme. On a few old themes. We've done everything,in essence. There is thinking to do, yes, thinking, but even that, seems so much of what we've thought about over and over." She shrugged and smiled a little but there was warmth in it and he relaxed his worry. Then she stretched herself into the clump of cushions around herself and curled down into them until she was nearly hidden.

Alice looked at her friend,"Jennie,how can you say that? You're music is fine. You cannot have plumbed it's depths. Every composition is new, is full of something special. You must know that! It's gifted the whole world, you're raising two fine children, and you teach our young to know music as you do. What more do you need to interest you?"

Jennifer looked at Alice, their eyes meeting and then, suddenly, Jennifer laughed."I do sound grumpy, don't I? I don't know, Alice." Paul watching them was alert, this was not like his mate. She was a private person who seldom spoke, even with the family, of her inner life. She was seldom so open, so vulnerable. She was not a devious woman, but he thought now that she played a game with them, tested them. As though she sought to press them toward something she herself feared to approach.

She said,"Yes, Music? It is a flow of life -- a source. Family? Yes, not just my children, but all of our big Family, you are all so dear, so important. Oh, no! I don't deny the richness of my life. Not at all." She laughed, and it was not a happy sound,"We're busy, we talk on the video phone, see each other, touch each other, and are together fairly often. My relationship with Paul is rich, warm, very, very loving and we do not deny one another." She said it almost defiantly, as if wanting to prove something ."And yet --." She sipped at her wine, the dark color staining her lips for a moment , her eyes were distant."Why should anyone complain. I feel foolish doing it now. But don't you all, any of you, sometimes feel as though -- as though there's a void, something missing. Actually MISSING! And I don't know what it could be. The very fact that I have so much, makes it so frustrating. Something eludes me. I think I started this with the hope that perhaps I could draw my answer out of one of you. Somehow there must be explanation."

She was silent and the others waited. She drank the rest of her wine and started to rise to refill it but Paul was there, wanting to Reach, wanting to Touch and not daring to. He could not believe her words. Never had he guessed she too might reflect his own fears. But for him it had been years, years of this hollow ache that would not fill. He refilled her glass and her frown deepened, her eyes moved from face to face,"I know I'm angry but I don't know what I'm angry about. It's just that --" she gestured with an uncharacteristic helplessness, "something seems to be missing. Just in this past month, I've felt it. And with no reason at all! Maybe if I knew what it was I'd feel better" She sat, looking at her hands,"As it is I feel like a fool, expecially here at our party. I should not talk like this."

Paul felt his heart squeeze, the pain of it brought a gasp from him. Here it was again, that sense of loss. That feeling of having come loose from direction. He had heard that from colleagues, from friends, more and more in these past months. But for them, it seemed to be a new experience. That difference rang against his own feelings, rousing out the familiar pain that he had carefully laid aside. Did she sense his pain, his denial behind his cheerfulness? He stared at her in distress, her revelation frightened him and without thought, he Reached. He felt a swift reflex of resistance, almost like a shield. Could it be? Could Jennifer possibly have consciousness of that Touch and never have said anything of it? He began to suspect that there was something he didn't know about his Mate.

He leaned forward, wanting to speak to her. But before he could William spoke and his words froze Paul. How could Will be so utterly unaware of their -- his and Jennifer's state of mind? Will asked,"Jennifer have you gone the circuits of the planets? It's very popular now. People seem to be reaching toward anything to distract them to do something different. So why not? Why don't you try that too? It'd entertain you for some years, you know. People are going out as never before, it's like an exodus, a flocking into space." He walked the length of the room to pick up a small plate and fill it with delicious appetizers. He seemed to be at ease.

Jennifer smiled at him, seeing his calm detachment, his assumption that this talk spoke of mild trouble. He could not guess at her anguish and Will was as astute a man as she knew. Didn't he WANT to guess? Was it sheer denial or did he actually not notice? She felt anger, then fear, which made the anger greater. She said,"I've been out there twice, once to the moon city, once to Mars City. You know that, Will. After the novelty wears off, unless you're working to build the planet, to create a place for human kind to work, then what is the difference? It's all modifications of the same theme again." She shrugged, her voice sounded impatient.

Will only smiled, evidently hearing no impatience. He asked,"Well, what will you do?"

Paul sat, a slow needle of recognition piercing his mind . He resisted it, denied and still it pushed on with a pain almost as real as a real physical needle would have been. Then like the bursting of a boil, long suffered and ignored, it punctured his resistance. A slim thread of recognition seeped through the painful and taut surface of his feelings. Then, as though it broke all resistance, realization flooded his mind. William, their brother, their friend, knew nothing of that grief each had given witness to. That Rose spoke of, that Benjamin spent so many months trying to assuage. That Tom had hinted at but covered with an almost obsessive devotion to his work as mayor. William could not understand this kind of pain. He was apart from them. Paul sighed, Surely they had known, surely he himself knew, and had denied. How long would it take to accept? He said, silently,"Why would I wish him to know pain? To feel this suffering the rest of us do? " And the answer was like a blow,"Because I don't want him to be unable -- that would mean he never could Reach, never could make that inner Touch"!

William was influential, a powerful figure in Altos and the Valley as a whole. He knew the ways of business and that knowledge had brought wealth to Altos. But he was Mind blind! Yes! Paul's heart lurched. How could he be sure others of the Family were not? As far as he knew, no one other than Rose had made the mind reach that resulted in the Touch. And she had resisted greatly. Probably thought it was peculiar to the Council even. He heard no more of the conversation , his mind was caught in questions. Perhaps he was mistaken, and it was only that Will had not been trained to far perception. He shook his head, he himself didn't know enough about what that meant. How could Will?

He heard the words spoken around him, talk of journeys to Mars, the moons of Jupitor, others,and knew in one compartment of his mind that the concern Jennifer had voiced had been buried beneath chatter. He felt her hurt, disappointment, but he did not go to her rescue. He need to think this matter out.

He felt that he had discovered a disease, a difference among his friends that might separate them irrevocably. Was it possible some members of his own family would never be able to Join with him,with Rose? How could they bear that difference? The fear hung like a dead weight in his heart, a fear he had not thought to suffer.

He recoiled from thoughts that had begun to probe too near some nameless fear. He attended to what was happening. After all this was a party, not a time for deep,penetrating thought. Annette was laughing at something Jennifer had said. Paul listened, bleakly as if in their conversation he might find relief. Jennifer said,"Well, there's an end to that even. So now,Will, what else can you suggest to titilate our weary emotions?" She was gently mocking but Paul knew that Will saw no irony.

Jennifer said,"To travel out there too much, can create an addiction. It's happened to people. Can't stay away after a while. Can't live a normal life! And you know that addictions grow in minds where people have avoided something they must eventually look at."

THE AWAKENING

William snorted, suddenly harsh,"Anything can be an addiction when you're using it to avoid something, of course. But then, you don't need to do that."

His words hit them all like a blow. They were silent. They had been so precise, and in each mind, unknown to the others, was that shadow that would not dissolve. Will was serenely unaware of their reaction,"After all, there seem to be things happening here in our Valley that demand full attention. It's true Jennifer that space travel has its limits unless you become a colonist."

Jennifer walked to the cabinet to refill her glass, the blue green of her clothes vivid, the fabric so light it seemed to float around her body. Annette loved to create clothes for herself and her friends. She watched Jennifer, critically examining the design, finally nod. When Jennifer turned to them, her eyes were full of a sadness, a pain that caught Paul unprepared. She said,"I admit there's only so much there, in all the planets, in all the galaxy. The exploring, the finding of new things, entertains us for a while, but lately there's still something missing. I used to feel satisfied but now, I do less and less." Her voice softened, her eyes distant,she repeated, "I thought I might find what I sought out there, somewhere." She shook her head, sadly, and sipped the bright liquor.

"Come on," Paul got up ,"Yes, we've got a party to enjoy. And I think we'll have some music and I'd like to dance a bit." He went to a low cabinet and opened it, slid his fingers across a lighted panel and the room was full of delightful music that made their feet literally dance at their chairs. Paul went to his Mate, drew her into his arms, wanting to hold her, reassure her and to heal her pain and yet, he didn't know how. All he could do was hold her and send what reassurance he could muster.

They found themselves laughing, trying out the new steps they had learned at the Summer Festival from the Vagabonds. The music shifted and the dances changed to group dances and partners changed. The evening sped on, and Jennifer went to swing back the wall to the dining room. The table stood, ready, candles, bright and gleaming on silver and cut glass. A steaming bowl of soup already sitting at each plate.

Will looked at the table and at Jennifer." It looks and smells wonderful, my dear, just as always."

She laughed and took his arm,"Let's all sit down, the soup is hot."

They talked of the food, of their work, the changing nature of their city, for some time. Then, in a lull, William looked up, his eyes finding theirs,"Why is it people seem to need something more? Why not be content with all we've got? It's the finest way of life perhaps the world has ever known, especialy since every single member of the community shares in it.We don't even have to deal with guilt. Why not be content?"

Paul met Will's eyes last, and found in them a simple question. Will was not , at least obviously, devious. "William, I think that people need something to keep working toward, something ahead, something they haven't reached yet."

"We've got so much, it's true. Our libraries have all the knowledge of earth stored in tri-D film and video tape, and computer memories are inexhaustable."

THE PEOPLE OF THE VALLEY

Annette said musingly."We ought to be satisfied."

Jennifer was nodding, her face thoughtful. " We've entertained ourselves with toys, fun things to do, with the arts, and the delving into the human psyche. Isn't it possible we've exhausted our known fields of search?" Jennifer raised her hand as William started to protest,"I know, we've got more to learn about everything,but there seems to be a visible ending ahead. A point at which we have got to find dimensions wholly unknown.I think it's literally beyond the human mind that our frontier lies. Certainly we've only barely recognized the fact of Soul, and how it relates to mind. Relationship, a complex science, has kept us busy for decades and will continue to, but there is that sense of - 'What Next?' Even when we still have much to learn. The question comes."

Annette nodded vigorously, "People need something new. Yes, they do! I really believe Will, my Love ,that there's got to be something else, something more!"

She spoke with such ferver that her husband looked at her with surprise and a faint disapproval.

He said quietly, "Well, there's something going on that I surely don't understand and no one talks about. I've heard some talk of psychic talents, 'Talent' they called it. It offends me. I see it as superstition, as imagination, as refusal to deal with reality but there are those who say with authority, that I am wrong. Sometimes I've seen children,doing that strange silent sitting, that intent focussing on one another silently as if they're trying to be telepathic. It's not meditation, which belongs in the temple anyway. It's something else. I can't tolerate the looseness, what you no doubt would call, fluid flexibility, of your concept of reality. It's meaningless, because you can't say what you 'know', yet you insist that you 'know'. That kind of undisciplined thinking is intolerable to me." He bent an angry look on them, then said, as if tired,"Those children should be brought in for examination, they are not normal."

They felt the intensity of his eyes and Paul knew that he wanted to find out without asking them, whether they knew about this 'strange behavior'.Paul's heart sank at the subterfuge, that Will would not openly ask.

Alice eyed him warily, her mind already checking out all the possibiities, "William, of course it's true that there never will be an end to new knowledge about the universe, the galaxies, even the Earth herself. We can't possible exhaust all there is to learn,though what we learn grows more and more refined and enters so deeply into the nature of life itself, that suddenly it opens out into -- into something beyond what we've always called life. That's the place of the unknown, the truly unknown that I think Jennifer's talking about. Maybe the things we call Psychic, are part of it. It certainly has to do with the nature of mind. But I think there is much, much more and I admit I don't know myself what it could be." She bent to smooth one palm across the fine wood of the table. "As for the children, I think they play a mind game. That is all!"

He turned to her, his face a study in control,it was literally blank, but readable to these very aware people he sat with. Behind that mask was some hidden fear

THE AWAKENING

and covering it a growing anger. For the anger must hide more and more fear. But William would not have said that of himself. Self aware as he was, he had to erect the most excellent defenses from himself. He said,"Alice, I can't imagine what you're talking about. The Psychic, at least is familiar as an idea, but I think it's self delusion. Perhaps what the old folks used to call it makes some sense after all. They said it was the 'habits of the Devil'."

Annette was smiling sadly, her eyes watchful,"Will,Love, we all know of the work at Grandstadt. It doesn't make sense to deny that there are undeveloped senses. Those studies have revealed enough validity to these talents so that we can't just deny them or attribute them to a notion of a 'Devil'. They've devised a way to research them that is even acceptable to traditional scientists , so I can't understand why they're not acceptable to you."

But his frown was doubled, for a moment she thought he might explode in that anger. Why? Why so much anger? He said,"Annette, my Dear, what they've done there is common knowledge, yes, but the reports aren't full enough to suit me. I still question how they can be intelligently used or allowed. We don't know where they might lead." He studied her thoughtfully, his anger pressed into control,"After all,you know, what if you yourself found that you had one of those 'Talents', I think they call them." His voice had become heavy, a tone of craftiness that harmonized with the watchfulness of his eyes. Paul groaned inwardly, Will had never been a suspicious man. Annette stifled a cry of dispair and grief. Paul wondered why William didn't just ask them about their involvement. But then, why didn't he, Paul, tell William himself?

Jennifer caught Annette's eye and saw their dumb appeal.

'Go along with him, Just pay attention to what he says', those eyes cried. Jennifer turned to Will, she felt the tension in the room, she felt her mind focus and though she did not know it, she had made a tentative awkward 'Reach'. Paul felt it and his heart soared, but she knew only the hard closed barrier that was Will and shrank back before any knowledge of her accomplishment could register. She felt embarrassed, as though she had somehow come upon another naked, and that hard barrier felt to her like refusal of herself. She shrugged off the emotion, attributing it to imagination. Paul turned to the window, his face so wreathed in joy that he thought it inappropriate just now. That native Talent that he had known in Jennifer in their most intimate moments, that ability to be with him so deeply, was greater than he dreamed. It could be trained.

Then, to his absolute surprise, he 'felt' Annette's faint Touch. He instantly turned to her and caught a faint smile through the pain there. He was aware then that her Reach was to Jennifer, and the two women shared the sympathy they both needed. Paul felt his heart lift, perhaps they could press through, Reach William after all, the three of them. And at that, he knew a poignant sense of refusal from Annette. Without words, she asked him to let Will alone. The knowledge that he could not, COULD not, share with them at all, penetrated at last.

He thought that Will hid himself more than they had realized. Paul said to himself,"He's no fool. I think he knows that we all share something, or could if we would. That someway others are conscious of something he isn't. That's it. Just a vague something and he resents mostly not knowing what it is." He saw, impressed swiftly, sharply into awareness, an image, and realized that Annette sent that image. Whether she knew it or not. It was a skill that the Master Teachers taught all children, every adult who would come to learn. That amazing skill of imagery, of focussing within their body or toward another mind, a picture with which to mentally bring about change. Most people used it in Healing,or for entertainment,or to enhance sexual experience. Healers were adepts but the patient had to be receptive to make it useful in Healing. So why hadn't William learned at least that? He said,"Will, surely, you learned how to do deep imagery inside your body, to improve health, to search out elusive emotions?"

William snorted, 'I was taught that it was possible, but I never believed it could be and so I never did it. I still think it's self delusion."

"But the Lifting process, you remember, we learned that when we were in our teens. What they teach the kids now at two and three. How to lift attitude, to make a choice about our moods."

"It's another delusion, avoiding your worry. I don't think it's healthy." William seemed actually then to be smug, as though he enjoyed belittling them."Simple logic can rearrange attitudes enough to bring balance."

His heart heavy, Paul persisted but with little energy,"But Will, you know we were taught to pay attention to negative moods, to find their source before we shift to another. Not to deny, but to know we have a choice. You know that." He had stood up, walked from the table and then stood at the back of the room looked anxiously at Will.

Will started to smile, a smile that threatened to be mocking, but it faded before he spoke. He dropped his eyes, then standing, said, "I do know, Paul and you're right. It's been one of the most valuable skills our people know. It's resulted in our being able to negotiate nearly any problem in government, industry or social life and I won't deny that. But I see it as simple logic, in the long run. That seems far off from that idea that people can use imagery to affect the body's electro-chemical functions." He looked around at them, severely like a teacher suddenly. Then without warning at all, he suddenly grinned, was softer, they felt the barriers relax a little and he was closer to them instantly.

Paul smiled, relieved, something had been said, at least. Something William would think about later, for that was the way of William. He did think about the things he argued about. Without thinking, or trying, the two women joined with Paul in the ritual of lifting. Together they felt that support and knew it would affect Will whether he attended or not. Paul said, his voice more cheerful, his face serene, "Well, we do know people are showing up with Talents we didn't know we had, William. I'll grant that. And whether you believe they're real talents or self delusion, we see a lot happening among our children. "He frowned and then, walking to stand facing Will, the three women still sitting, he said, "Why, you yourself, William, have a Talent many people don't! " At William's look of surprise, he grinned, "Yes, you are able to bring an audience to think, to realize. You hold their attention as if they were unable to reclaim it. You have what used to be known as a charismatic quality that attracts and holds people , that even persuades people if they're not on their guard." He laughed now, because William was smiling. He knew and used that Talent but had never thought of it as such. Paul said, "We need you to teach the children that." He laughed again, "But to teach them especially how to guard against it."

William seemed to relax more, still smiling, he said,"Ah, Paul you do seem to know how to lift the spirits of people around you. If I didn't know better I'd almost believe it was deliberate. But thank you anyway. We needed our spirits lifted. Now, there's a talent, I think, that's more valuable than that one you attribute to me." He was swiftly in a new and happy mood, feeling once again part with them. "There is a lot to find out. A lot to know and we've not had time to learn all we must about these things." He looked happily from one to another and in his expression was a plea that tore at their hearts. "I've felt a bit down lately, and though I know flattery isn't a firm base for building self esteem, today it worked." He grinned, so much his old self they hadn't the heart to deny him that assumption. Paul did not think he had flattered Will, but rather told him a fact.

Alice breathed a long quiet sigh, turning from watching with fascination, to looking at her hands folded together on the polished table. She thought they were skirting the edge of ideas she needed to explore. Why couldn't they break across this hurdle and genuinely explore what gleamed just beyond the edge of their attention. Why could they never catch hold and confront it? Was it Will? Surely he alone did not direct the conversation. She said, "We began by searching out why people are dissatisfied and I agree that many are. But we don't have to be bored. No, the Earth is fascinating, life is. There's unceasing change in our living Earth and we've just begun to understand it. It's something more. As though, with all we have, we've still missed something so essential to life itself that we are slowly malnourished. Perhaps starved of Spirit, might be a way of saying it."

Willaim nodded,"I always think of you as essentially one of the most realistic people in Altos. But when you say something like that, that religion is something we need --"

She broke in," William, think! I didn't say anything at all about religion. I spoke of Spirit. that is vastly different."

The others smiled,Paul thought This was another Alice who spoke up so positively to William. Paul was glad to hear her. He focussed his attention to that Lift, that mental surge of Loving attention that permeated the very air. He felt his perceptive attention shift. He could see the others in a radiance of soft light, splendid around their bodies. Will seemed almost to resist, the light about him thinner. It faded. And yet it was there. When Paul focussed his vision to See, he knew William had certainly the same core of light at his center that other people had but it was true, it only glowed, it did not blaze at all.

Alice turned to Paul, met his eyes. He smiled with the tenderness that she associated with him, how could he be so loving in all circumstances. If only she could find a mate like that. She thought Paul was not a common man. She had seen him furious, so that people moved out of his way, listened without interrupting, and yet, he could shift to this utter acceptance in an instant. He ALWAYS listened. Maybe that was it. He was always genuinely interested in whomever he talked to. His body was big, strong and his anger could be menacing, but somehow it wasn't. It seemed more to be protective. She knew she loved him.

Paul watched her, remembering that she too had spoken of dissatisfaction. Could all this have to do with the flaming of that inner light? Was it possibly related to an awakening of Spirit? And if so, what did that mean? Lately he'd noticed that people talked of a feeling that one must hurry to buy something new, an air car, a river skimmer, a trip somewhere, Yes, maybe the popularity of travel to planets was a desperate effort to cling to - to - what? Maybe rather to avoid? To escape the feeling of something missing? He nodded absently to himself. Surely it would make sense, no feeling was quite so painful.

Willaim spoke out of the silence, "Well, Paul, you've got something planned for us, I understand. Are you going to surprise us or can we know."

Paul laughed,"Yes, and we're going to forget my big surprise if we don't quit being so serious for a while." He looked at them,. and then at the windows where the city lights gleamed across the ribbons of travel webs, from thousands of windows up and down the mountains, and far down in the ground level pathways. It always seemed to him delightful, full of some whispering secret that he couldn't quite hear. "I want to take you all on a trip in our new air car."

"You've got one? "William sounded envious, then laughed,"Well, I'm not surprised. I'm so glad ,Paul."

Paul nodded,"I have. It's shared ownership, of course, with three friends, but it's mine tomorrow. It's on the grid at the top level right now. It'll be ready for us in the morning. That's why we needed to have you plan to stay the night."

"Oh, I thought it was because you didn't trust us to get home after drinking this excellent wine!" Annette picked up her glass to finish the last of hers and set it down laughing at Jennifer."I can't wait to see it, and I shall have to wait until morning because I won't go out in that dark now."

Paul said,"We ought to get a good night's sleep and it's late already. Let me show you your rooms and you can then sleep when you please. "He took them through the house to guest rooms while Jennifer and William gathered the dishes and slid them all into the auto- cleaner. The table was cleared and candle light reflected from the shining wood surface when they returned.

Paul came to sit down. Jennifer found quiet, music and they settled to talk a little before going to bed. Paul said that he wanted to fly over Santiago, maybe turn up and stop at the Farm. He'd told Rose they might come." We could have lunch at Santiago and spend a few hours later at the Farm. Rose says she wants to call Gather soon. We could decide on that. She also says she's heard from Ben and he's on his way home." He was thoughtful,"It is my birthday, you know. I thought we should celebrate. Thirty nine years is a long time." He laughed.

THE AWAKENING

William laughed too, he was one year older. he said,"I'd like a trip like that. We've not traveled much together. Most trips were for business or for learning somewhere." They talked of local things, of people and events in Altos, of what they'd recently heard of the rest of the family and so an hour later, they were ready to go to bed.

The sun poured over the mountains early the next morning and Paul was up, preparing a small breakfast. The smell of coffee and hot home baked bread toasted, of omelettes and fresh blue potatoes hashed, brought the others into the dining room. Eager and curious to see Paul's birthday gift to himself, they ate and chattered happily. Will seemed in such good spirits that Paul would not speak of anything that might possibly break that mood. It would be good to play with a new toy, to let themselves be carried away from all their thoughts and fears for a little while. Jennifer thought of that and wondered how long it would work for her. She wanted to just enjoy the hours ahead. She looked out at the morning sky, cloud streaked, it was bright and deep blue. A lovely day that had its own power to lift her spirits and interest her.

They went to the grid above, and Jennifer said,"I hope you had the car checked carefully before you brought it home." She was smiling but Paul knew the old fears behind her words. She had lost loved ones in an air car crash resulting from inadequate checking when she was just a young girl. Since then, regulations were far more strict, but the old feelings flared up every time she went to fly. They subsided when she acknowledged them.

He said,"I sure did, Dear. the best mechanic in Altos went over her from tip to tip. Flew her and set her into the auto scan, for any buried flaws. She's in top shape. Besides, you remember that we have four parachutes that would open and let us down without a bump if an emergency occurred. They climbed the steps to the grid and there it stood. Silver in the sun, it was bigger than Jennifer had thought, it's body squat, powerful. It looked as if it could take them safely. They laughed and inspected it carefully all around and finally with a lot of joking and laughter, climbed in. Paul was pleased. They liked it.

Annette stopped before she got in, looking out over the gleaming mountain city, down the descending terraces of green and red and all other colors. She was looking forward to this little trip. Maybe it would be good for her and for William. Tears filled her eyes. She was sure the others were not aware of what she knew. The secret that she could not share. She must be careful, because her feelings would be easily broadcast and known at least by Paul. She didn't want any one to know at least this day. Surely she would have to talk to Paul and Jennifer later. She needed to do that, for her own peace of mind.

Paul touched her arm, he felt her distress but respected her privacy. He heard her voice, soft at his ear,"It's a time of change Paul. I wonder whether we older ones will be able to survive it." The incongruity of her reference to themselves as old struck him forcefully. She drew a deep breath and said,"Well, it's natural, growth means change and that's what the Valley is all about, isn't it?" She smiled then, a determination to allow herself to forget her worries lighting her face.

THE PEOPLE OF THE VALLEY

They flew smoothly out over the Valley, feeling the change of altitude and the rising warmth of the day. Paul maneuvered the little ship along the mountain edge, then in a rapid sweep down to the river where he let it glide, dipping now and then, so that they could see familiar points. He wound in and out of the forest strips, cruised along the Highway for a few miles, waving at Vagabond camps. Their mood was one of play, good will and the wonderful sense of lazyness.

Gradually the ship curved west across the Valley, then north and east again, to slide swiftly over the Farm, where no movement was seen in the early hour. Then, drifting northward, they continued east. Paul thought they would cross the Valley again and climb a little into the hills and then around to head south slowly toward Santiago. But he did not make the turn he had planned, he found himself nearing that cliff face behind which was the Silent City. He had been idly drifting, until he saw the cliffs just ahead, stark and gleaming in the morning sun. As though a direction was finally clear to him, he began to climb, rapidly, taking the ship up and suddenly, they were there, circling the glowing walls and he wondered belatedly why he had come. They drifted so close, the light of the cliffs made them look as if they would be warm if touched. He frowned, the others were silent, wondering too what his plans were. Jennifer looked over at him, seeing his face, started to speak and was silent.

Then, with a long deep sigh, Paul said,"I think I'll just go on up and have a look. I've not done that for years." He smiled quickly at Jennifer, glancing back at the faces behind him, seeing their bemusement but no resistance. And then they were up, hanging for a moment at the edge of the broad stone rim, and then, over it and the impact of that City struck them like a physical blow.

The fragrance woke every other sense, surrounded them like a vital message, a promise. Each one responded or reacted differently. Each one drank that invisible communication of fragrance. Each one turned to see and felt the wonder of the garden, a visual symphony, and they let the ship idle, hanging moveless above the gardens until they became slowly aware of the sound.

It was a delicate whispering at first, as if strings being faintly plucked, a harmony that could not be caught at all, only dreamed. Then a bell rang, its tone continuing on and on, joined by a deeper bell and then a light series of tiny bells that danced their sounds through the still air. The strings were louder then, as if meeting that rising crescendo of bells, and then suddenly, silence. In that silence, a single bell finally sounded, deep, ringing as if from far distance, but continuing and carrying their attention into its depths. Paul felt utterly absorbed, he was not aware of the others, nor of the ship even. It was set to hover, it would need no attention, he was free to experience. The sensual richness of the surroundings was like a banquet that filled them. Even though William shrank from the thought of being there, above that City he distrusted, he could not deny the fascination of its beauty.

Paul was caught up in a sense of pure wonder. He was held entranced realizing a suggestion of great Joy, and he feared mightily, feeling himself inadequate to know it. Then, slowly he allowed the pure gladness. A powerful

THE AWAKENING

calm descended gradually thoughout his mind, as if informing his consciousness of Itself. All around him was a strange but omnipresent sense of amusement, pleased and loving amusement, such as a parent might have for a happy child. What -- who was amused? An idea formed. He, Paul, a child before his own greater Self? The idea was a touch of stillness. This City --- what was She? Why did the City seem so alive? What he knew here was a profound sense of LIFE, no danger lurked here. The deepest part of his being resounded to its glory, its Joy. There seemed no resistance, a willingness to respond, to sustain attention such as he had never known. He was aware now, intently focussed,loose from his body, exultant and connected to everything, himself and all those with him, the garden and the Life he felt here. In that greater consciousness, he knew also a simple thought."Surely William could see the beauty here!" But the thought flickered and drifted on, it did not distract his focus.

Here was life. Perhaps a greater life, maybe that was what was overwhelming. So much LIFE here! Maybe they could not bear all that IT was. Could it be that in this power of Life he -- they all--were hearing a whisper of something beyond themselves? Was that LIFE they were immersed in, were part of, itself God? Surely there was something beyond human limits in this City and it was in the nature of supreme GOOD, for there was no sense of evil, no sense of threat. Except for that unrelenting sense that he was stretched, had expanded his very being in order to bear even the beginning of such awareness, his emotions were held in abeyance. He was vaguely aware that his body wept. All his ordinary emotions were submerged in a pure bath of Love and Joy, They saturated all his capacity for feeling . There was no room at all for fear.

He was slowly aware that the others were also engrossed in this magnificence, meeting it in their various ways. What would this do to Jennifer. With a mental start, he was acutely aware of her and in that instant he realized himself, focussed in this greatness of consciousness. Thought shaped, seemed to flood consciousness. How could he think of what he could not imagine? The question lay like a ribbon across vision . He was more than this man Paul? He was Soul?   He watched himself, from this expanded view, a dual awareness. He looked through Paul's eyes, aware of himself doing so. Conscious of Being conscious.

He watched the city beneath them shift and change. It seemed to laugh, to sing to them of its delight. He saw Paul's fear. Observd Paul's logical mind wrenching itself into a succession of logical thoughts that were more impressions that shaped thinking. "This must be an abberation of my senses. Some illusory effect of the fragrance and the height. A result of all those feelings of weariness, longing, dispair that had plagued me these past months. The mind's attempt to fulfil those longings. Surely that would explain." And all the time, extended beyond himself, he Knew.

As truly as he knew he breathed, he knew this dual identity. Knew the Presence of that power, that astonishing quality he could not name except to imagine that it might be Love itself, was absolutely real. The transcendence of himself into that Self where Joy lived, was Real. The power of it, the power of Love was like an ocean that sustained his small self, even as it touched limitless shores. It was energy unending. And he had not avoided. He had sustained attention, held firm. He was present with that power of Light that had intimidated him.

And the Light was himSelf, everywhere, through, in and of everything, including himself, even the metals of the air car. He smiled as from a vast distance, feeling the tinyness of the stretch of muscle in his face as he smiled. Awareness rose and fell, like waves of expanding light, then shrinking into the tiny flame that was Paul. A great relief filled him, what had felt to be emptyness was now Light so demanding, so full of Love, he wept steadily, but with inexpressable Joy. The demand, yes,but now it was utterly acceptable. He was willing!

Then the reaction; he knew it was beyond ordinary life. The fact that he could not live there, at such a very conscious point, filled him with a sudden inconsolable grief. As exactly as he knew how to turn this little craft, how to identify that fragrance, he knew that the Touch was into the nature of That which was utterly alive, utterly true. It was as real as this air car. As his body. More real. He remained, aware and amazed, full of this nourishment that seemed limitless. Thought ceased again, he was!

Then, with a jolt, he was torn by ravenous need to think, to find explanation, to -- come again to himself. And he saw again that touch of fear reasserting itself. But stronger than fear was the overpowering sense that he could not be worthy of such Vision, such a gift. He breathed,"How can I be part of that?" Here he had Touched into a dimension of reality that still waited, was beckoning, as if he might -- might some time enter into it fully conscious. He knew that he could not have imagined it. Could not. It was beyond imagination and it was too very REAL. A part of him simply held itself still in utter acceptance, without doubt. Another smaller part continued the logical argument. He ignored it. He Knew. And the sense of fulfillment, of having found that which he had sought, exploded like Joy in him.

But there below, was still the City, around him were still his friends and it was a clear bright day, and through everything, the sky, the bright leaves rustling below. Then as if gazing down into that City had awakened him again, the wave lifted him out of himself, loosened into Stillness. Something? Something near? He felt the powerful sense of 'Presence'. He, Paul, was lost in that Presence, that utterly still timelessness of Being. Yet, he could also know himself, Paul, finite in this infinite Self. Instantly, as if revelation spread open consciousness, he participated in dual Being. It was as though 'everything' looked through Itself at him, and he looked through himSelf at It. A thought formed: 'It was Presence seeing Itself through Itself'. Then he was also of that nature? The thought focussed him back into Paul 's limits as it spoke itself from his mind unexpectedly and he listened to it and was filled with awe of its rightness. No doubt touched him as he shrank to 'normal'?

His logical mind doubted. Already!

THE AWAKENING

Yet, he was so filled with the strength of that knowledge, that realization that he smiled at his doubt. There was something here so alive it made ordinary ilfe seem a death. Was the City itself alive? Was it the Spirit that lived through Earth Herself? Or was it greater than either? What was that which was speaking to them in great gasps of perception that literally broke down the walls of their minds?

He fought to find words, this was a time to shape thought. How can a human being remember without thought? He wrestled in himself, to find words. It was an idea - he decided, the 'idea' of Love. Then without doubt, absolute conviction shook that thought away. No!. It was Love itself that this City poured around and through them like a water that saturated their very beings. This City was a conduit for what Humanity sought, had long eons sought and refused to acknowledge even when they felt its Touch. He thought then that perhaps human beings could not really Know such Love. He said softly, "We could only bear a faint Touch of it, only this Touch, for the fullness of Love would over whelm us. Would drive us mad."

The idea hung there, he shied away from it. How can I ever be all that that even this tiny Touch asks of me? Asks me to be? That which hums, sings in my heart now, does not separate itself but heals me within myself as though it were the very seed from which my life came. Yes, exactly that. The thought made him want to open his heart and mind, to breath deeply, to sing out. It made him aware of the surging energy in him, the vitality that filled him. Here above this City is that quality and It floods the air, we are breathing It, and the only word that fits is Love.

No love such as I have ever known, nor imagined, surely, but Love that,once known, is recognized. It is what is meant by that word. A hard strong, powerful quality that fills the mind and heart until they open and wake, until they breathe through themselves and become joined into that very quality that woke them. It was for him now a vast, joyful tenderness such as he could not imagine between people, but immersed in it, as if even each cell of his body was bathed in Love, was nourished by It. And as he realized, he Reached out, unable to know else but love for every thread of life, every living thing, every person alive. The transformation, continued, wrenched him loose from himself. Thought grew from idea, he found words to pattern into memory, for he must have something to keep, to build on. Thinking was so separate from realization, from perception itself.

His senses were drawn now to their limits, vivid with life, But he had fallen now into this familiar limited self, this life of matter reaching to discover itself as Spirit. Yes, to discover its Self. The thought seemed strange but true. He felt an aching anguish of loss, then a pervading flood of relief. This familiar self was 'safe',was intact. He had not lost himself, he was only stretched almost out of recognition. His body seemed small, tight, too confining.

There were living memories of what had happened, of realization. They were there,just behind perception, but waiting for that moment of Stillness, of utter attention when they could remind him of that which he Knew. Could they could spring loose the narrow confines of himself and release him to Self - again?

His eyes drew into focus inside the car, he saw the soft grey panel in front of him, where the controls were bright patches that he must touch. He slid a finger lightly across one and felt the motor wake further. Ah, it was with a gentler touch than that even that the City had Touched him to bring him to awakening. And now he turned, glanced at each of his companions in turn. It seemed as though he had been here above this City for endless time, and yet, it seemed seconds of time. The confusion did not worry him. Both were true. He touched the controls again and the little ship moved silently out into the sky above the Valley. So familiar and so strange.

, He guided the car absently, fortunately it was automatic. it would home easily if no other instructions were given. He let himself take stock of his body, stretched, felt himself move, touched his own cheek, felt its realness, its aliveness. He felt a strange exhilaration and an equally strange exhaustion. He thought he would like to go home and sleep. Allow everything to settle down and gain some order in his mind. He didn't speak. He looked back at the others and then a glance back at the City. He felt a sudden wash of benign warmth. He couldn't ever forget. What was there was Life Itself. He was convinced but he didn't understand what that meant.

Jennifer roused beside him, her body adjusting itself in the chair into which she had sunk. She moved slowly, trembling. She drew her hands across her face several times as if trying to reassure herself she was awake. He turned to her, met her eyes and found them full of wonder, sadness and a sharp pain. For a moment they shared the intensity of their emotions, their faces wet with tears, unnoticed. Their hands crept together to cling in reassurance.

William moved restlessly, shifting his body about and finally stood up to turn and look back. He felt irritated, no, truly angry and he didn't know why. The fact that he didn't know why bothered him. He felt also a depth of grief he could not fathom and that angered him more. He pushed the feeling beneath awareness. There was nothing for which to feel such grief. It was part of this whole crazy trip. Paul had no business bringing them here. Far in his mind lay a tender flame , like a touch of something so precious he could not bear to turn to look at it,instead, he surrounded it with that grief and hid it there. Swiftly his logical mind denied it ever was there. He looked at Annette whose head was bent down so that he could not see her face. Her body was straight, held tight against some unseen pressure. He was puzzled, uneasy. He resented both. How could such a lovely scene, a brilliant garden among those tall spires of mountain rock, create such unease. Or was it something else? He refused to acknowledge fear. He said aloud, "I do not like that place. I never did and now I like it even less."

Annette stirred then and looked at him, nodding. "I'm not surprised. There is something strange there. You don't like things you can't clearly understand. I was uncomfortable . Yes, uncomfortable! I couldn't say I didn't like it. I want even to go back, to perhaps find out what it was that I -- that I almost realized, that seemed just at the edge of my grasp, my perception, in fact. As though there was a promise, a possibility -- " her voice faded off. For moments they waited for her to go on. With a long drawn breath she began again." It's somewhat like when I have that urge to do a sculpture, something wakes in me and demands to -to take shape and I can't quite find it yet. And then, through the work, I find - - something as near as it as possible. But never what I sought. Never. But there, above that City, I felt that I had come upon what I sought all along, but I could not -- could not quite -- see!" She rubbed both hands across her face, pressed her fingers against her eyes, wiped unrecognized tears from her cheeks and said,"It all surprised me."

Alice shook her head, deeply puzzled, but did not speak. Paul sat as though dazed and Jennifer seemed lost in grief, tears continuing to pour over her face ignored. He had never seen her look so lost. William shrugged and turned frowning to take his seat."What ever it was, it's spoiled our whole trip. We might as well go home." He could not say that he wanted suddenly to be alone, to be apart from these friends at least for a while.

Paul set the controls then, but noticed that they were already on a course for Altos. He turned to them, feeling a great out pour of love for them. He Reached out gently, wtih a tender reticence. He knew of their struggle to understand the experience each had known. There was no response to his Touch. They were closed, held into themselves. It was as though they were weary of input. He respected their needs and turned to himself.

He took Jennifer's hand, it lay limply in his. He watched her face. Finally she turned to him and he saw the empty lonliness there. It was so naked, so acute his heart ached. He knew he could not relieve that lonliness, could not fill it. He had lived long with that lonliness in himself. He knew! Nothing in her former life would touch it. He knew that from this day on, there would be another dimension of life for each of them. The thought brought reflection. Did he want that? What would it mean?

He remembered his own life in these past few years. That deep ache that would not be relieved, that grew constantly closer to the surface of his mind until he no longer was able to suppress it. For those years, he had felt the loss he thought he saw now in Jennifer's eyes. With amazed astonishment, he realized that his own sense of dispair, of loss, was gone, was faded out. It had hung in his life so long, had kept sweeping over him at unexpected moments, prying into moments when he had taken pains to make himself happy, and had persisted without ceasing. Now, there was only a shadow of it, only a memory. He knew then that there, at the City, he had found something -- a sense of having 'come home' to some place of Love and acceptance such as he could not have thought possible. Was this the awakening of Spirit that Rose had spoken of? Spirit within himself transforming him. The knowledge was so strong that his throat tightened with the effort to keep from crying in joy. The resistance to that joy hurt, and yet he could not --could not -- be so alive. There was something stuck there --in his throat. Something having to do with that old grief. He couldn't swallow. Was it still there? Or was it only the shadow of what he had been?

Then like a sweep of cool sweet water, the memory of that vivid Life, that penetrating power of Love that had touched him, that Life presence, washed through him. His mind was filled with that reality, it was not a memory. It was again PRESENT. He sobbed, a great choking sob that wrenched from his body that knot of pain. He felt the tearing of it, the ache broken and the hurt dislodged until it abruptly stopped. He was amazed that no one seemed to notice his cry. He was aware of them even as he knew his own release. That old pain was fading. A weight was lifted from him and he was at peace.

Jennifer's hand pressed into his and he knew that she had heard . But she struggled within herself, maybe the pressure of her hand was a cry from her for help. He felt light, his mind clear, Joy rose and flooded through his body. Strange how natural that seemed. Joy so real he felt foolish as though he wanted to laugh, and to sing. It didn't make sense. But then did any of this make sense? After all, he had never believed such Love as he felt now even existed. He knew it was not 'his' love, but Love itself, flowing in the most natural way through his whole life. Like another kind of breathing. He just had to stay in Touch with It.

The relief and pleasure of this moment was wonderful. He enjoyed himself, flying lightly, silently there in the blue sky that seemed to him to pour its very blue into his mind and recognize itself there. He laughed, the thought was true. Was this what it was to be fully alive? To finally begin to be alive? He knew profoundly that he had only just begun and that what yet was there to enter into was beyond imagining as much as what he had found today had been. He must, he would return to that place, perhaps it was necessary to Journey to the City. The People of the Way spoke of such a Journey. Maybe they knew how to find an entrance from the Valley.

He began to plan the day. What would he do when they got home. First he must see that everyone rested, maybe take them home. He would walk in his city, look at it all, and see it again for the first time. Just as he was seeing the Valley below for the first time. The absolute beauty of this Valley woke in him the memory of that recognition of Seeing, that consciousness of a point of view, pervasive and inclusive. How had it been? Already he could not remember enough.

Sadness filled him that he would not keep the whole of this day fully conscious in his memory. Yet, perhaps he would find ways to relive it and create the rest of his life around it.

Then an old memory surfaced, something a teacher had said once, "The wakened perception, the glimpse of that greater life must not be crystalized into a pattern and ritually kept as though it were complete. But rather the mind must press on, further into that already penetrated unknown to discover what Life is."

He realized his face was drawn down into a rigid frown, his hands clutched the controls so that a slight movement could have sent the little car off in erratic plunge. He felt inexpressable desire but at the same time, a slowly spreading resistance. He shook his head, could I still want to avoid that ? The question stunned him, but he knew something in him did want just that. He relaxed, his

THE AWAKENING

body loosened all over and he smiled,"I am able.I will stand again at the point of Joy, I will find again that focus at those heights and Touch again that Life, breath again that Love." He felt a trembling in his limbs, the base of his spine felt hot. There was a soft flooding of heat pressing upward through him, past his shoulders and into his head, like a glowing golden light, it sped and burst there. He saw that perception had not dimmed.

He was again ingrossed with the familiar task of flying this craft. But he said aloud,"I am conscious of what I am becoming. My brain is stirred to life by Mind itself. I See without shadows before me and I will recognize it when I stand in the dark of old shadows from now on." The words calmed him and he settled, smiling, warm with a confidence he had never known. He could find a way.

He realized clearly that Jennifer must live through some painful years. Perhaps he could help, make them shorter.She must literally rearrange her own perception of reality to allow it conscious acceptance, relive through her body and mind the recognitions she had met. He knew her Heart was wakened, the flame burned bright within her. It stood guiding her life, and that she must adjust to that wakening. That unfolding could be turbulent. Could he help her? He knew so little, but he knew at least of the existance of Love. Perhaps he could stand conscious in that Love and allow it to pervade her life through him. He could not 'do' anything but he could be there.

Jennifer had not knowledge of what was happening to Paul. She saw his face now turned to her and knew that a radiance of love shone from it that she had never known. Could not believe, thought was her imagining. She said, "My God, am I still caught up in the power of that City?" But grief drew at her, would not let her alone.How could she deal with the loss? What had she lost? What was this pervading emtyness she felt. How could she bear it .In fact,how could she speak of it?

It had seered her mind, hurt in her heart, and yet it seemed somehow to offer something. But she had struggled away, for to stand in that Light exposed her very heart, mind and being to herself, made her naked in a way she did not want to bear. What she had glimpsed was not a dream, it seemed to be Life itself! She shrank away, frightened, as though some seam within her being had cracked opened letting in an alien light. It was intolerable to her then, even as she reached toward it with such a longing that her heart hurt with desire. How could anyone hurt in so many places at once. What she longed for she could not abide, refused, denied even. It was the cause of this pain, yet it was the only hope,the only life possible. She felt very, very weary and wanted nothing more than to sleep and forget.

Seeing Paul's concern, forgetting that she made little effort to shield the stream of thought and emotion rushing through her, she turned to him, closed herself and smiled. He pressed her hand,"It's something we must gradually understand, Love. There is something there, at that City. More than we ever thought!

Annette was silent, she must protect William from this sinking of her heart.

She could not go back there again. Maybe some day, but not now. Her heart felt so full, hot as if a fire burned there. She put one hand over her chest. yes, exactly, something has changed in me. And the thought elated, then dismayed her. She clutched at the ordinary activities of home to close her mind to all else. To push aside memory. When she was alone and quiet, she would remember. Rapidly she began to plan. Ahead they could see the cliffs of Altos gleaming in the noonday sun. They would have lunch at home, not in Santiago. She wondered whether they could still have lunch together. A fleet of lumbering frieght cars approached with a load and Paul guessed it must be lumber from Clandor. The gleaming Solar powered motors flashed a kaliedescope of lights as they passed. Far across the western mountains, much lower than the eastern peaks, they could see a glimpse of the ocean through a gap and everyone pointed to it, relieved to be distracted from the power of their memories. They began suddenly to chatter about the city ahead. Jennifer alone sat beside Paul, limp, silent, making no effort to disguise her feelings, her thought. Paul tried to think how he could find help for her, but would she admit she needed any. He had not. Denial had been his greatest defense.

The joy that throbbed beneath his thought, beneath everything, was so strong he knew it blazed in his face . He hesitated to look at others, fearing to expose himself because he felt so exposed to himself. He laughed at his reluctance. A thorn that had prodded in him for years was pulled. A new energy filled him. He would think, would remember, would go and talk to -- to whom? Perhaps he could climb into the north hills and visit the Station there, the Teaching Station where they might know, might have understanding. He was ready to search out without denial, without resistance, to surrender himself to what he had begun to know.

The new shiny car, laden with its five passengers, moved into the landing slot and they were home.

CHAPTER TEN

Rose's questions and some answers

It was the time when autumn begins to give way to winter. Winter winds already full of snow howled in the high mountains, the trees flamed with color and then lost most of their leaves in the gales that blew down from the north. The seeded stems of grasses lay dry against the earth and thin green winter grasses pushed through . On a morning in late October Rose came from her cottage late, having spent time writing in her Journal the on going conversation with herself that she would share with Benjamin when he returned. It helped to write her thoughts, make them real to herself and see what she had said with eyes as well as that silent listening mind. The subtle changes in the Valley troubled her, for in all the thirty five years she had lived here, she had not felt so sharply alert,so aware and as though constantly listening for something unknown. Was the change happening in herself? Or in the Valley? She could not decide.

She wanted to understand the forces at work and so to guess something of the direction of those changes. She stood a moment on the deck, pleased with the golden light streaming through the few remaining yellow leaves of walnut and willow. The wind blew cold, she shivered a little, watching the lazy drift of one leaf falling, then glanced out beyond the fields to Adwin. The meadows were a mottled green and brown, and the crop fields were rumpled with the plant bodies ravaged of their fruits or roots. There were, here and there like bright lawns, small fields of winter grain already up and started.

She felt the ending, the oldness, the drying up of life, the meloncholy of mortality. But at the same time, there was a feeling of joy, the sense of having labored well,the satisfaction of underground food processors well supplied, storage bins full and now they could retire into warm houses and focus on the labors of mind and Heart. There was much to set into order, to realize out of all that was happening. For a farming Family winter meant a satisfying,sad sweetness , a time of repairing, replacing, planning and long wonderful hours of study,and contemplation.

"Replete". She spoke the word softly, feeling that it fit this time of year. Next spring the excitement of new planting, of new growth, of the wakening Earth would rouse every living thing again. But this was a time of meditation, of contemplation. Town people fared little differently, because business offices,shops, the industries and mines, all held shorter hours, and the sense of retiring to that inward focus was endemic. Many people combined farm work and town work jobs. Adwin was a garden city, where Earth was a constant companion. The seasons were universal markers of their lives. Just now, before winter snows and freezing weather gave the chance for skiing and sledding down the western slopes of Adwin, long smooth races far out to the empty playing fields behind the Learning center, or skating on the frozen backwater from the River, was a time of stillness, the very air seemed to hold its breath. The Earth seemed to Rose to take a deep, long sigh of relief that the exuberance of summer was at an end and there was a time of rest.

She stood on the deck, wind swept clean of fallen leaves except for a few late ones, and leaned against the railing where a few sodden chrisanthemums still held bronze color to the sun."But we don't sleep the winter away as animals may do. We humans, who look into the universe and consciously know of one another, we must contemplate, we must listen and slowly absorb into recognition all we've realized through the time of fullness. So much has happened, always happens through summer time. We look through the golden leaves now, where the sky frames them with that heart hurting blue, and there is that glimpse of what we know is just beyond it, waiting for our vision to clear." She frowned, the ache of beauty literally hurt in her throat, the blue so intense it seemed to pull her into itself, thrust her through itself, until she See.

She stood, the silence like a shroud about her, and again like an open doorway into perception. For moments she was thus conscious, then with a shake of her head, she drew herself back into the day's moment. And as she did, she felt that she drew the universe with her, even as she was still there, aware. Earth awareness burst through every sense, a clamor of vitality and Joy, of suffering and pain, of dullness and excitement. And now of the dying of things, the decay and preparation for new life. Earth swept away what was done, what was completed.

She stood, realizing without resistance, pleased that she did not shrink away from that powerful symphony of life energy .After several moments, she went into the hall. The intensity of awareness did not decrease. The room seemed itself to thrust its shapes out into the air, every object to carry in itself some intention. She stood astonished for a moment,trembling - wondering.

"There is a sadness that hangs in the air, in the soft dampness of the wind this time of year. It must be an ancient sadness coming out of old fears of the coming time of dark and cold. But it seeps into the heart like a mist that softens joy." She went in to breakfast. The house was empty, it was late for a farm family.

As she sipped hot coffee, and ate a plate of eggs and baked fish with muffins and fruit, she let her mind begin to persue the question that had plagued her all this week.She spoke softly to herself," There is a sense of change. What is that change? And why don't I bring it up and talk it out with the Family? At least with Paul? Except for that one time at the Council, I've not talked about what we know. Maybe I'm afraid that if I bring up the question then I must discuss these strange changes in myself, the moments when I seem to live beyond myself, am utterly absorbed beyond myself, and sometimes I remember --what I can't forget.Memory has been so - so strange, and sometimes vague, like a lifting up into a brilliant light with no explanation. The pain too, that must be connected, the headaches, the aches through my body, inside, as though my very nerves are tender. "She was nodding, yes, it was right, this description. She did not understand.

"Life has seemed so good lately, except for Ben's absence and now that I know where he is I feel better about him." She smiled suddenly, enjoying her secret. Then said aloud,"But there again, I've not spoken to anyone of that, not even to Paul whom I know would understand. " She cleaned her plate, the food tasted so good, it was simple but real pleasure to eat. She sat silent, sipping the last of her coffee when she heard the Videophone chime.

She went to touch the button and Paul's face sprang into the screen. She smiled, burst out with words that surprised her, "Paul, just the person I need to talk to." She grinned, covering her outburst,"I was about to descend into the sadness of autumn."

His eyes met hers, searched her face, she seemed protective of the turmoil in herself. He frowned. This wasn't like Rose. Well, he supposed she had a right to shield. Then suddenly he felt anger and said,"Rose, quit being secretive with me. If you want privacy I'll honor that but don't just hide. We've got to talk."

She realized that she had been mentally divided, half her mind still caught in the surge of this morning's realizations. She focussed attention and was aware of his Touch. She felt his willingness but she did not extend herself. Why not? A shaft of anger rose and was swept away by resignation. Then she felt humor return and acceptance that relieved her as a gust of rain relieves dry air."Oh, Paul. I don't know what's the matter. I agree we must talk. I know that all these feelings are not because Ben's gone. I've managed that right well. It's so much else. So much I don't know."

He nodded listening, feeling the pain, the intensity of her focus, her mind like a honed and fine tuned instrument literally vibrating toward -- something? The aching effort to bring down into words ideas, awareness that drew her beyond herself, was visible to him." You're trying to carry too much alone, Rosy, too much. Just the way I've done."

She held herself shielded, still wanting to think through all her feelings before deciding how much to talk of. She said,"I know, Paul. I know. I also know that Ben is not going to be home for another month. It'll be a whole year by then, you know." Her voice sounded so forlorn he couldn't suppress a smile.

"Rose, Love, what we must do is make a great Sending. The whole Family together, and bring him home." He was joking, but she knew he wished it could be done. She hadn't thought that the others missed Ben too. He went on,"You need him, I need him. And you know there's nothing that'll bring Ben running faster than to tell him he's badly needed." She felt angry for no reason, then was as unreasonably pleased at his light heartedness.

"Paul, I wish I could be at ease about ---about that -- Reaching that we do in Council. I've not even dared extend myself in Town Council, let alone here at home. I don't know why I'm so afraid. Ben knew something of it, he wouldn't really recognize what it was but he made me promise that I'd not even try Reaching to him. Only he didn't call it that. I think his fear's worse than mine but it's infected me."

He was nodding, sending her reassurance,"We're children of our ancestors and they either feared or worshipped or both. How can we be born free to experience such things without trouble? It's common to us, more common than we admit, I think. We simply need to accept and the first step, is talking about these things. I suspect some of our Master Teachers think of these talents as theory rather than as fact.But then, they're careful not to impose on our minds, they want us to ASK. And we don't!"

She nodded,"I wonder about the children. They wouldn't have those old fears we inherited. Sometimes I think they -- they already Send, even Touch, and they don't talk of it either. If they do it." She frowned," I think right now, that it's inexcusable of me that I haven't found out. I'm a teacher, after all!" He nodded.

"I think the children've picked up some prejudices from us, and from tapes, from old films, history reports the terror associated with such Talents or the adolation that was as much a distortion. So our young ones don't get a healthy idea from history. But even more, they may know of our fears and want to protect us. We've got to be the ones, Rose. You and me, as far as our own family is concerned . We know, and we've got to talk to our friends as well as ask our Teachers. Maybe other Families have begun to do something.

She leaned back in her chair,her eyes thoughtful. "I think the Healers must know something more of this. Surely their work is related. But your Plant Wizards do amazing Reaches with their minds. It must have made Altos more responsive to these ideas than most towns. People there accept the wizard's work."

He shook his head,"No! That's just it. We ought to be but we're as reluctant as anyone else, when it comes to more than a simple Reach. The Touch is what scares people. When it's to do with plants, or even animals, we can accept it. When it's used by a Healer, we don't feel fear. But when it's just common folks like you and me, and we Reach out to Touch, that's different, for some reason." He sighed, "Maybe an old fear of having somebody tamper with your mind, you know."

"She nodded slowly,"We'll have to talk. You're right! At our next Gather." They were silent, then she shrugged, her face full of worry,"Oh, Paul, I'm avoiding what I really want to talk to you about. I've felt so many things this morning."

She drew a long breath, then plunged in," There's real change going on, in this Valley. In us! I know that my body is making some kind of adjustment. I don't know what! But I've felt - thought, imagined, " She stopped, flustered, "Paul, I think the old teaching - about an awakening - What did they say? Of mind waking to Mind, or Spirit? The next dimension of human evolution? Something like that? Well, I think that's what's been happening for years, now." She swallowed, nervous to talk of this, wondering when he would laugh. "Remember? At the station, when I was there, they told us that the time is near. I told you about that, because it bothered me." She stopped, looking at him urgently,"You remember?"

At his nod, she went on."Well, is that what's happening? And what does that mean anyway?" There, it was said, the question asked, at least the nagging prod of question that dug at her heart and would not cease its demand. She

THE AWAKENING

watched his face, almost afraid.

Paul caught the word 'awakening'and tucked it into his mind. It seemed to him to fit. "Perhaps Rosy, Perhaps you've hit on it. But we need to have a Gather,. We need to talk, our whole Family, and search out the things we've left unsaid. All of us together."

She nodded,aware of the vast relief that he took her seriously, "I'll set a date. I think we must Gather too. We've got so much to think on. At least get some hint of how it is for the others. But there's something else on your mind, I feel it, Paul."

He nodded,"It's William. I don't know what's happening to him. He's different, Rose. Somehow,different!" He focussed an image of William after the visit to the City. She saw little except the turmoil of his feelings. But she was surprised to see even that.

"Paul, you send images so clearly. It's astonishing. So much easier to understand." He shrugged but she went on "But you all went to The Silent City, and you've got a new air car! How wonderful! Was the trip good? And that was when you found something about William?"

He nodded, sad,,his eyes full of the worry she could feel from him. That's why I think we must gather. This time, we're not avoiding anything. Anything at all! Agreed?"

She nodded, "I think we must, Yes, we must! But what's William done that worrys you? "

"He's begun to develop an organization he calls the Builders. He questions whether we should send children to Journey with the Vagabonds. And his 'Builders' question our very way of life, it seems to me, Rose, they question more than just the Journeying of the children . That all seems too much like Dean's ideas and I worry about it. Our William! After all, Rose, how can he not understand."

She nodded, her expression troubled,"I don't question that system. It's one of the best things we do,the exchange of children between towns and the Vagabonds. We're a more united people because of it and we all have something vital to teach. But then, there's no harm in questioning it, shaking the process up a bit might result in improving it"

He was patient, a darkness pushing aside the quiet smiling of his eyes. The change troubled her more. She trusted Paul's judgement. He said,"If that's what happens it's fine. But he told us the Builders think the Vagabonds are too obsessed with the Silent City. It didn't seem to be just questioning things, but as though there was some anger, some resentment against the system, and the City. Too much again like Dean's anger. I didn't like it."

She nodded, "Sounds like fear thinking, to me. And that's dangerous." She didn't like to see Paul so worried, he wasn't one to worry about nothing.

He shook his head,"I don't want to wait, Rose, we've got to do something soon. I've BEEN with William. You don't know".

"Why don't I come, maybe with Jerry too, to Altos and visit and maybe see if we can't find out something that way? " She suddenly grinned at a new thought,"Criticizing the Vagabond's faith won't bother them in the least, they'll just smile at us -- or rather at the Builders. But I don't want to harm our exchange system with our children.

Paul nodded,"I agree. But you know Will's been a little obsessed already with the Silent City. and now he's found a focus in the Builders, who seem to agree with him. I worry. I don't know what their fear is coming from, but they radiate fear, Rosy, literally radiate it."He sighed, "William's so logical. When you discuss any of these ideas he seems so sure, and his logic is so careful that he convinces because he ignores anything that won't fit into the logic. Says it's imagination or superstition. But you know how he is". A smile was on his face and they both smiled thinking of that dear brother of theirs.

"I know how he is. He's more than once driven me to exasperation with his brand of logic. And then of course, I lose the debate. Well, come soon, Paul. I'll talk to Jerry and we'll call". He nodded, and she watched as his face faded from the screen. It had been good to talk to him, even about these troubling things.

She left the hall and went thoughtfully out to the deck again. She sat on a bench under the soaring black limbs of the walnut, letting the sun warm her in the cool wind. She must collect her thought. Surely they had avoided too many things too long. She watched the curve of River ripple around the bend just below Adwin, the water shimmering in the sun. The winter rains had brought it out of its banks and spread water across the flood plain. She watched lift discs and hover cars picking up some of the late crops along the banks. That would be Matta. Grown in the river swamps, it was harvested as late as possible as it floated on the water. The heavy coarse stalks, six or more feet long, were being hauled in great stacks on the broad lift discs to be deposited in Adwin at the new processing mill in the industrial Center. That largest of the Rings was already a hive of workers. Matta was only one of six industrial products. Getting the crop into the steaming baths to soften the fibre for cleaning and shredding was mostly automatic, but the spinning process required people to set it up. She idly watched, letting the quiet of the morning seep into her body. She would not go to work at the Learning Center until later . She wanted to spend a part of this day in thought, to give herself time to explore all that was happening, both in herself and in their community.

Rob trotted up tired from a run, she saw a movement in the bushes behind him and detected a female and a half grown pup. It was time. He was almost two years old. She said, stroking the broad smooth head,"I see you've already found your mate, Friend. And didn't let us know. Will you introduce me?"

He looked up at her, his eyes startling in their intelligence and she thought a hint of laughter at this surprise. He turned to the waiting family, whined softly, and the female looked at him, then at Rose, and crept slowly forward until she was standing out from the bush. The pup ran, foolishly leaping against her father, and Rose knelt to touch her. Yes, it was better that there was a single pup this first time. She spoke softly, knowing that they knew as much by body language and the sensing of thought patterns as by words. But Rob had a good vocabulary.

She would have to teach it to this young mate. She wrapped her arms suddenly around him, seeking the brief touch of comfort and felt that surge of devotion, of genuine loving awareness that dogs give freely to humans. Slowly she extended one hand to the bitch and was allowed to stroke lightly her extended head, her cool muzzle sniffing at her wrist and arm, getting her scent. Rose met the bitch's eyes, they seemed suddenly to catch at her attention, to nearly speak with the laughter she had seen in Rob. She stood back. "Ah, Rob, I've not told you how grateful I was that you went to search for Jerry's stallion last month in the storm. It was a bad storm fellow, not much rain but terrible wind and lightning. I hated to see you go." Rob's 'finding' had been a blessing, because there were young colts in the stallion's care and Jerry had cared for one torn by what must have been a mountain lion. He had only three mares, but they were extraordinary. Jerry constantly encouraged the breeding of these magnificent horses and he planned one day to set up a training center. Rose turned again to the newcomers.

"Welcome, Welcome lady. We'll have to find a name for you and the little one. Then you will be part of our family too. She saw the bitch's eyes swiftly looking up and past her and glanced behind. The look in those eyes was surely a calculating measurement, glancing from herself to the cat that ran on the top of the deck railing toward her. Matilda was unafraid, even though this was a wild dog from the hill packs. She was with Rob, and Matilda and Rob were friends. The golden bitch did not move, her eyes watching were eloquent, Rob moved to her side, touched her ear and nose quickly with his own nose and made two short sounds The cat stood taut, her body alert, and then, slowly Rob's mate came closer to touch lightly the cat's nose. She dropped to her belly, relaxed. Rose laughed and the animals seemed also to smile.

She said,"Where've you been, Matilda? I've not seen you for a week." She scratched between the cat's ears and then,"I suppose you're all hungry? Well, Rob, you know where the switch is, you can get them some food your self." They trotted on around the Hall, and she turned to the scene before her, her eyes sweeping again over the land as though in a caress. Paul's call had been a surprise to her, how could he have known she needed him? And it's not the first time, she thought. Perhaps the Reaching, the Touch of mind to mind was not as unusual as they assumed. It was becoming more conscious!

Her mind pressed back into her own early teachings, those hours of practice, of meditation , the days and weeks of training their bodies to respond instantly to danger or to need. But more, to be so superbly disciplined that they were like springs in instant response. The ancient Martial Arts taught the children of the Valley how to respond instantly. She stood, poised, remembering a set of movements and swiftly, she performed them, faltering only once. "And that falter could have been my death,had I been in conflict." The discipline was itself enough. An act of power, waking insight.

She had not kept in that high state of constant fitness in these past years, but the unceasing demands of her mind, and of the still perceptions of Heart, never relaxed their practice. But perception from stillness was not this inner conflict! What's this for? The eternal questioning? I've never discovered anything that way yet. Only out of stillness has insight come. And yet, I still am hounded by my questions. Perhaps I ought to go talk to Martha again, or Raymond perhaps." She felt suddenly tired. It was as if her whole body reached toward some far magnet of Spirit - of Life Itself - that drew her so inexorably that she was being pulled loose from herself. She grinned humorlessly, "And that's what they've taught us too, that the Self relentlessly demands attention, demands and draws us from our little noisy lives to Its stillness. And if this Reaching is associated, and it must be -- then there's no choice but to respond, to understand more! A matter, in fact, of survival." She caught a new thought, "It's not until I wear myself out with the questioning, that the silence informs me. That's true, though I don't know why."

Softly she whispered the question, "What can this thing they call the Self be? What is it actually? Not just as idea, but as fact? " And as she shaped the question, images flooded her mind, of depths, of heights, of extensions of consciousness that drew her outward and inward beyond every perception she had known. And an analogy came like a picture, "I think the Self is to me, what the whole body is to a finger. I do know It is vast, extended beyond my little personal self, and yet it is my Self." Then she laughed, "When I stand knowing, Self conscious, then the reality is so clear, there is no question. I can't realize and think at the same time. So now, when I try to think about it, questions increase."

The impossibility of translating 'knowing' into language, brought a shiver to her body, and she felt her heart race. "But I must! I must find a way! How can I understand if I don't? Because when we Reach, we extend through that larger consciousness to Touch another mind. And perhaps that is what it is after all. My self within Self and I the little self get the drift down of that Touch. Was that wonderful contact with the Council simply a reflection of a greater unity?"

"Then how can I know? Do I know at all? Martha and Raymond taught me, and I heard and somehow I do remember and yet I have denied". Confusion and dispair seeped through everything again, as if they lay in wait, barriers to understanding. Ready to drown all joy. She walked along the deck, sliding one hand, feeling reassurance at the touch of the smooth wood railing. "It's as though I stand at the edge of something that's irreversible.. I wonder whether other people are feeling these things too. I haven't asked. I didn't even ask Martha." For minutes she was silent, letting the implications of these thoughts resound. "I have to talk to Paul, to the Family." Her longing for Ben rose in a flood and she cried out, "Oh, Ben, we need you so. We need you now!"

But then, he might not have learned anything at all. He might have wasted these long months. Could that be? No, somehow she knew, knew that there would be help, that Ben would BRING help. She looked at that thought and was astonished. "I do know that and I don't know how I know. And there it is again. The knowing! I would have called it a hunch a few years ago."

"What ever else is happening, certainly it is an energy that rises and falls, that

THE AWAKENING

trembles in our minds, in our hearts and will not let us rest. It wakes us to Itself. It shimmers in the very air today, The Valley is charged with that energy that rouses through all life here. The flower of that Life is humanity and so,,surely then, we are at that point of waking too. It WILL not let us sleep in ignorance of Itself." She sighed,"Or is it more accurate to say, I, Self , will not let me, the little self, sleep any longer?"

The morning sun gleamed against the gold of a late clinging leaf. Her eyes were caught in the light, unable to shift as though the serenity of this final blaze of the old year would transfer to herself. She was conscious of a deep underlying presence of Joy, a Joy that had no knowable cause. Her breath slowed, held for seconds, she was at the edge of perception. There beneath that cloud of dispair that still pressed, was what she had always called a 'life shout'. But she would not hear! Today it was shadowed by this dark knot and she could not -- would not -- face into that darkness. To hear that shout, she must first feel her own a death cry.

With a wrench she pulled her attention away from the coelescing of perceptions. The longing and the denial fought for existence. She clutched at attention until it drew away from the interface of wakening perception and returned to the familiar. Her heart ached as with some denied splendor, some loss. Was this the tremendous birth right of the Valley? Its gift and meaning? This thing called 'awakening' and if so, awakening to what? To Life Itself? She sighed, what was that? What was any of it? Where were these thoughts coming from?

Overpowering her resistance was the dawning realization that she must allow the questions, must enter into them and stand steady as in a Light that demanded nothing less than everything she was. She must listen and allow and if she did -- then she would have to bear the Touch of that mind splintering Light. And she knew, distractedly, that there was profound Joy. More than once in her life Joy, so great it hurt, broke through her mind and nerves like a kindled fire that burned. And she had cringed away, fled from it as one Touched with Light shrinks into darkness. She thought she could not stand before It. She saw how she hid in questions.

Now, screwing up her courage, determined to find some understanding, she focussed attention and sought the memory of that Light. The thought moved her beyond itself,she was approaching again that edge as if it were irresistable. She held firm. She WOULD! That quality that trembled against her mind, drew at her attention,was Love. There was no point denying, It was so! Love inexpressably present within everything -- everything -- ! For long seconds she stood in the tension of that Love, trembling, aware, wanting to give herself, to Know. But, instead, swiftly she began to think about it.

The Master Teachers -- yes, they had said it. That the degree to which humanity might wake to that consciousness of Being, depended much on our capacity to realize Love. And here was she, unable to bear even the Touch .Yet, she did not deny that it was real.

She turned within herself, whirled from that interface that barely Touched her

THE PEOPLE OF THE VALLEY

mind, but was clearly there. Each time It Touched her she felt her mind open as if a crack was widened. And it was a strange bodyless pain. And in that breaking, she knew a raveling away of resistance, of the tightly clutched pattern of old perceptions. Vision shifted and revealed , her head was aching as though it stretched itself inside her skull, but the whole lower part of her body felt aflame. These discomforts, however, were minor compared to the demand, to that outreach of Mind that was a demand that she See. In one long cry of dispair, she reached out to Benjamin. He must help her. Only at the last minute was she able to hold back that Reach, to refuse it's Touch to Ben's mind. And yet she knew that she could have made that Touch. The knowledge shook her.

Teachers had given the people of the Valley the knowledge to understand such changes, that they might occur, that there would be inner shifts and body quakes, mind shifts and vision that would range beyond thought. Yes, but the idea could never prepare them for the reality! This immersion into a greater reality cut at her mind like a sythe laying flat old canes, revealing a vista that had been invisible.

Ben had said to her, that last morning,"Something's different. Something's happening! Like a ghost of wrongness slipping through our lives. Not just us, Dear, but the whole Valley. What makes the fear? Is it the fear that seems wrong? Or the changing in ourselves?" She stood now to remember and answered him." There must be something in us that doesn't want to change, to open out to that Light that we all glimpse now and then. It is when it blazes through us that the Light burns away the past and the meaning of things, it burns away the very structure of our assumptions. There is so little left and that is terrifying."

Something was happening to her. She could feel the breath of energy running through her nerves, through her body, like some heat. Wrestling she resisted, then as if defending her very ife, she tried to close herself to it, but it was inexorable, lifting through her, revealing vistas of possibiity, drawing her to an edge that seemed both wonderful and terrifying. She did not know how long the feeling of blazing heat within her body lasted, or the tension of resistance. But she knew when she ceased that resistance.

She lay against the deck cushions, conscious now and then, lost to herself part of the time. She was aware and then she was not in that small body that suffered, she stood apart and watched, knowing vaguely that she must be 'made ready'. And the question hung unspoken somewhere, "Ready for what?" She was aware of herself in pain, she knew a compassion, but perception extended far beyond this physical world. She knew and participated in the widening of vision. Lightnings seemed to break loose though her body and mind. She offered herself without resistance, surrendered. To resist was agonizing, to allow, made it easier. With reluctance to remember, she knew this was not the first time she had met such inner changing, but it was the most painful. Finally, beginning recovery,she felt deep weariness of flesh and of mind.

Rob pressed against her, nosing her cheek,, her hands, curled against her

THE AWAKENING

chest. His anxious whine was soft, and one paw reached out to rouse her hands. She slid an arm across his shoulders and he stood, lifting her a little. The cat walked there, along the railing, watching, meowing softly, her eyes bright and alert. The bitch and pup lay near by, their eyes on her attentively. She wondered at their closeness, their patience. Rob licked her cheek and raised one paw to touch her other arm, as if to ask that she lift herself more. She looked from one to the other, and as she spoke, she felt their relief.

She felt herself attend, Reach out a little and then, with a wrench like a rusty door opening,a crack broke open in her mind and she caught -yes - a kind of laughter from them all. Rob was full of a loving desire to help. She flung both arms around his neck and sat up straight. The cat came down and curled in her lap, pressing against her, purring mightily. Then, suddenly, she sprang away, and stood watching again on the rail.

She felt a weary relief. The powerful burning in her was gone. The world looked again the same, except it was shining in this warm sunlight. The leaves of the trees were absolutely still, no faint wind stirred. The color of sky and leaf and grasses caught at her heart and insisted and she felt her eyes full of tears.Every thing revealed itself with an unquenchable Joy the universe seemed to look out at her through each leaf, each blade of grass. The whorls in the grain of the wood of the deck were beautiful.She looked at Rob's great dark eyes, the knowledge behind them. Was this what Jane knew, or was her perception so much greater? Perhaps she would know what these animal friends thought just now. Rose shook her head, she wanted to find a place and sit a little and then, didn't she have something she had to do in town? Her body felt sore, tired.

Frowning, she saw it was getting late, the sun was high and she started up, realizing that she had responsibilities at the learning Center. How long had it been? She knew, having asked Healers earlier in her life, that it was not a sickness. She sighed, the excuse would not save her. They had told her it was a preparation and to accept it. But they had told her litle else.

She could think again so she would put all that had happened into perspective as she walked. It took thirty minutes to walk down the winding paths, cross the highway and climb the steep hill into Adwin. But Rose stretched that out to an hour, walking slowly, absorbing and thinking deeply, so that no part of the puzzle could be missed. She did feel different, as if some inner space had stretched and set her at the edge of something so immediate, so desireable, but so impossible, that she would not probe into it to even try to understand. She felt angry at herself for her refusal. But her balance seemed precarious and she did not insist.

She crossed the rose garden and walked rapidly toward the Learning Center then crossed one playing field where all manner of building materials were stacked or being used or already built into various shapes , small houses, sculptures, thin, sturdy towers, delicate rooms in the great spreading limbs of trees, or other structures. She fixed her eyes on the motions of a group of children building against a great tower. She took relief in putting her whole attention into the familiar These creations had to be dismantled several times a year so that others could be built, and so the students, young and old, put them together with pins and clamps. She passed a group of five, arguing about a decision. They looked at her as she approached and she feared they might insist that she arbitrate, but they settled their dispute and she gratefully went on to enter through the first great Arch in the outer Ring.

    Another pair of teenagers was laying a stone design into a garden walk beneath a fountain. She smiled at them, feeling the crisp winter air, the smell of wet leaves and some over ripe fruit that had not been gathered. The cool stillness of the winter satisfied her, felt good. She clutched at the simple business of living as to a savior.

    A young woman,Alicia, almost eighteen , met her as she walked through into the second ring. The library annex at the curve of this Ring, was a series of viewing rooms for film and hologram readings. Thousands of films and tapes were recorded and could be had by finding their storage number and dialing it. The cool archway was not welcoming today,seemed dark. She turned to Alicia and said, "Winter is nearly gone. Soon it'll be snowing again, but spring smells are in the wind.

    The craft shops,and industrial skills shops,were noisy with people working or laying out finished work for evaluation. The bright variety almost caught her to go browse through these displays. She shook her head, and passed by the farm labs. She could smell bread baking in the cooking labs and realized it was nearly eleven. They walked through the arch toward the four story tower of the inner Ring which held the library, the music and concert hall, and the long low cubicles of practice rooms for music and singing. They could hear the murmur of talk and busyness from the classrooms and a small cafe. Rose glanced up at a movement. Someone leaned out of the upper story window and shouted down at the children running across the gardens to the outer Ring.

    Vines covered the lower half of the rose colored sand stone buildings. The town people had decided it increased the beauty of the buildings to have vines climbing them. Choices of vines were made carefully so that most of the year bright blooms and crisp green leaves decorated it. True to the policy of the town, three of the vines bore fruit and added to the food supply. At least a third of the flowering plants in this city-garden bore food crops as well as brilliant bloom. Altos had done well by them. Most towns and villages followed their example and private homes made it a practice. There must be food enough for every single person alive and for all creatures. The committment was endemic.

    The pale rose stone of the upper stories seemed warm in the afternoon sun and the blue Tower Light, burning like a perpetual beacon from the narrow attic windows above the fourth floor, seemed cool, distant. The wide windows of the second floor theatre classrooms were open and they could hear the student production rehearsal. Alicia said,"I'm going to try for a part in the spring production. They're doing Mid Summer Night's Dream and there ought to be enough parts to at least get one as a fairy dancer.

Rose looked up, she could see little but she said,"It looks and sounds more like a rehearsal of the orchestra, not a play."

Alicia nodded,and laughed,"It's both actually. this time it's a musical. They're working on a series of plays and musicals for the Winter Festival.All of it written by students too." She laughed, "Some of those creations haven't been so great, but this one - this one's pretty special." They went into a cafe run by a small group of business students and student chefs. It was a hive of murmuring customers. The room they entered was larger than the average cafe in Adwin. Bright, airy, with one solid wall of windows, two of tapestries produced by students studying with the People of the Way, and furnitures brought home by other students studying in Clandors school of furniture design. Very durable and comfortable, some pieces had been there when Rose was a young student. Two boys came in from the cafeteria style dispensers with hot drinks and hot bread. Mouth watering odors steamed from the bowls of soup.

Rose said, "I didn't think I was really hungry until I smelled that bread. There's no better in the entire Valley, I think." She smiled at the newcomers who had brought their food and settled around a small table. Rose shook her head, "I'm sorry to be late. I've no excuse at all." They glanced at her, already beginning to eat. There was an odd grin on their faces as if watching her for something.

Jonni said, "We've been viewing films of the old ones, while we waited. Their cities were so strange. Seems as though they just let them grow willy nilly wherever anyone wanted to build something? They were really sloppy. Let old buildings decay and the poor lived in them. Imagine, rats. insects, and leaky old houses,and that's all you've got to live in." He shook his head, his face angry."Didn't they even care about their citizens?"

Rose nodded, "I never lived in such cities, but I've seen the 'Old City" on the coast that was preserved as it was. From what I understand cities started because a few people built a few houses or a business place and then others gathered around. They didn't plan in advance, nor did they care where the forests and fields fit in. You have to remember, we knew what we wanted, where we wanted to live and that we wanted the land around us to be a part of our city. They didn't. We design our whole cities the way they designed their best homes."

"But a city is a home for the whole town. I don't see why they didn't see that." His voice was thoughtful, but his eyes flashed in question, then softened,"But then, maybe some did. I remember you told us once that they couldn't escape their traditions. That's what you meant then?"

Rose laughed,"You're young to understand that, you know. They surely couldn't. After all, we have the same problem. But we're aware and watch for it. Young people with fresh eyes can point out our errors." She laughed, as they pulled faces at her. It wasn't always so easy."The fact that you all notice though, is proof that people have changed. You see, once a city is built that way, they were stuck with it. You can't tear a whole city down and start over very well, you know. We think of cities differently, we want them to fit the people who will live there."

THE PEOPLE OF THE VALLEY

Jonni said,"My Mom says that people now have a kind of love affair with their cities and towns." He was smiling, the idea amused him.

Raol, a lanky eighteen year old, darker even than Rose, black as Ned actually, with hair that stood out three inches from his head in a gleaming, grand bush, said, "I can't figure the way they governed. It's so different. Only a few citizens ever held office. How did the others know what was going on?"

Rose shook her head. " My grandparents used to tell us that they didn't. That the habit of governing by deceit was not uncommon, that organizations began to develop just to watch the officials, to test and question their actions, and report to the people but people had no real way to know whether they were honest either. It was left up to the news medea to sort it out and report facts, but who was sure what they did? There was so much secrecy and so much separation between government and the average person that all kinds of wrongs could occur." She turned to eat and then, after a few moments she added,"There had to be some honest officials, many hard working and deeply committed government and policing officials.But too much of the time these were few or they were corrupted, or even killed, by those using the office for personal gain. My folks said that tradition served them both ways, people didn't watch closely because it was assumed that an official was trustworthy,even though it was common knowledge that 'you can't trust a politician'. But then, the tradition brought some truly dedicated men and women too". She looked around at their disbelieving faces,and laughed,"I know, your history films tell of the interweaving of crime and political self serving etc. that went on, but there were honest officials in many countries that didn't get assassinated. We've enough films protraying their lives. We don't want you to see history in so biased a way. But all that economic chicanery through the world was what brought about the terrible times when things fell apart, you know." She met their eyes,"Don't you think some people were to be trusted? You're a fine lot of cynics."

Jean , a stocky boy with deep blue eyes and golden hair, a face like an angel, looked seriously at her,then drawing a long breath he said,"If people can be involved enough, if making a living isn't taking all their lives,then it's everybody's business to see things go well. But after all, we're a selfish people, you know. How can we watch ourselves and each other too?"

Rose's smile was teasing, "I thought the Teachers told you that if you are watching yourself well, then you don't need to watch others."

He nodded, still very serious,"Yes, I think that's actually true. But it's only because today you know that others ARE watching themselves too. But we know better than to trust ourselves even to keep our own Convictions or our Constitution. I think the old ones thought they could trust themselves. We have better checks and balances. The Video news broadcasts everything they can get good evidence for and that is like an eternal watch dog, ferreting out any discrepancies in public business or even private business. We have enough broadcasting companies so that if one were corrupted, another would tell us so. I think we know enough not to trust ourselves today ."

Rose stared at him, surprised at the implications of what he said and the obvious chauvinism. She smiled, but nodded thoughtfully. Then Ronal, another blond, but slim and tall, with a rugged and sharply cut face, said,"Yes, but Raol, I think it's different. I think we might trust ourselves, because we know ourselves but we can be as self seeking as our ancestors were. We've set up our checks and balances with a lot of thought. For instance, those Video News people,have a Conviction, it guarantees they will watch everything, including themselves!. It's part of their job, after all,"

Alicia burst into the talk,"But the same problem is there, isn't it? The tendency to let the tradition of selfless watching become so trusted that we don't question those very watchers ?"

The boys eyed her narrowly,nodding,"Yes, I suppose," said Jonni, then, "But we don't try to fool ourselves because we KNOW ourselves better. We don't think we are fully trustworthy, we know our weaknesses and we don't idolize our government people because we've all taken a turn there." He swung his arms in emphasis, "We're aware! We don't try to fool each other, or ourselves!" He turned to Rose, his young face was so serious, she could not smile. She nodded slowly.

" That's the crucial difference, I believe; we're much more aware as a people!" As she said the words she realized for the first time that they were true. It startled her, this morning's realization fit into that fact. She frowned, absorbing this knowledge. Then she said, "There's another check that we have , you know. We have the Monitors and that's a world wide system now. They keep us reminded of our vows. Especially that one Vow that no person will be without the needed and basic goods of life. They simply will not let us forget, though they don't ever interfere. They just remind us and we can't pretend. That Vow's become a given in our minds. Just as the fact of individual freedom is, we don't even think of it anymore. It's assumed that whatever else we do every person must have what's needed to take care of himself. You children started taking care of yourselves early,learning how to work,play, create; doing everything needed to make a good life. It's an attitude, to be responsible from childhood on. At one time, millions of people assumed that someone else ought to provide for them. After all, attitudes themselves are powerful controls in any society."

Alicia was nodding," It's the thing that's impressed me, that attitudes can be so powerful. Somehow we managed to build such a clear system out of all the destruction. It was not created on self serving, or on power over others. How did we ever surmount that as a people, Rose?"

"Yes," Jonni spoke intently, leaning toward her, "Who taught our parents and our grandparents the system, the ideas, the attitudes that made them write those Convictions on every Learning Center in this world" He hesitated, watched her closely, his eyes asking and added,"Is it possible humankind is different today?"

Rose turned to him, startled again,but she nodded,"It must be so, Jonni. It must be so." She thought she must think about this later.

Jonni stood and walked around the table, he seemed restless,"Lots of things point to it, is it Rose. After all, the Convictions were made. They are far beyond our ancesters, and yet, they made them, didn't they?"

Rose nodded, "That's true, but not just an ordinary ancestor. You do remember that it was the people we now call Monitors who gathered together and created the Convictions in the first years of recovery. They were simply called the Elders then."

There was silence, Jonni idly wrote names on the blackboard, and then rubbed them out, the others, frowned, their minds seemed to Rose to be gathering and adding and subtracting thought in a whirl and she was surprised that she sensed that.

"But what brought THEM to transcend the old patterns. Something must have happened, Rose. Something had to happen! The difference must be real." Alicia's voice was no longer gentle, but almost strident with demand and a restrained expectancy.

They looked from one to the other, she saw the tension, the brilliant shining of their eyes, the laughter hidden there. Then Jonni rejoined them, grinning, he sat down. He said, "Teacher, we're linked! You know! We're linked and we know together about those greatest of all Teachers out there in the Mountain Stations because you do!" She was startled, she had been thinking of the North Teaching Station, images of those memories filled her mind.

Alicia nodded, watching Rose carefully but with a look of concern. Would she handle this? Rose felt the concern, Reached intuitively, knew its cause and flushed. How could they? How could they worry for her ability to manage a Touch? The implications were like a flood released. She stared at them, each one alternately, and then settled on Jonni, whose grin was still full of a child's delight. She thought that they were taking for granted something she had only begun to think about, to acknowledge. She shivered, it seemed uncanny somehow, she had thought she would have to teach them and slowly, because it would frighten them. And now! What more did these children realize that no one suspected? An uneasy suspicion sifted across her mind like a whisp of grey fog. It moved through her thoughts coloring them, dimming perception. Suspicion could do that.

She watched her own internal process, startled at how clear it seemed and she drained emotion from thought so that they stood clear and sharp. Each thought now reflecting that bias that suspicion had cast over it. One idea singled itself out from the others and it seemed an absolute truth. She shuddered, how could she be so influenced by that emotion? When there was not sufficient cause for real suspicion? Or was there?

A soft laughter rustled through her mind, a gentle upsurge of feeling and perception righted itself. The mist cleared away, she watched the various possibilities come into view as though she reviewed them. There were so many variations of possibilitiy. She felt her own laughter grow, like a loosening in the throat, a lightening of her muscles, felt the necessity for bringing back emotions, seeing them play like lights over these thoughts, revealing, concealing, sifting meaning, enlarging meaning, The process, so clear, entertained and delighted her, then mistified her and she frowned. Where was all this coming from? She had not seen mental processes so clearly before. It was as though she realized the EXTENSIONS of her own mind, its variations of perception. A fact struck her so suddenly she jerked upright in her chair, and cried out.

"It's the linking, the Touch. You're showing me more. Oh, My God, and I assume I am your Teacher!" A shame of inadequacy of what must seem to them a blithe and arrogant ignorance engulfed her. She looked swiftly from one to the other of these young people. She found herself looking for contempt in their faces,and subsided from that error with a laugh, then with sadness,"You've -- we've been realizing all this together? It isn't something I came to all alone?"

They nodded gravely, their eyes serious, no amusement in them. they seemed faintly embarrassed. To have shamed a teacher would be unforgivable. To shame anyone was unforgivable, they hadn't intended that. They looked at each other, finally Jean, the oldest,twenty one, said seriously,"That's right Teacher, we're with you. We were Joined, realizing together. We follow imagery patterns the way you do. You see, without you, the thought pattern wouldn't have gone right, wouldn't have been so rich." He grinned impishly,the delight in having surprised her evident,he wanted to free himself of embarrassment, to let it go.

He glanced at the others, as if for encouragement then said,"It's true, we're feeling a little ashamed. I hope you weren't embarrassed. We wanted to surprise you. We've been practicing, and learning. We can realize more when we link, a lot more. I think we started out doing it in class debates. That was what made them so powerful. They were powerful, you know." He was unsure enough to need to explain. She shook her head.

"It's all right. I understand. So now you're aware! Aware enough to be using that mind link?"

"We've been doing that - for years, you know. We just never extend to our teachers. But just now, you were Sending so strongly, just now!" He looked at her with supplication as if apologizing and she nearly gasped aloud. Why would such a conscious child need to apologize? He continued, a little less sure of himself and she knew that she was closed to them. "I hope it wasn't wrong. It's just that we'd like to talk about this and we don't know how to make it obvious without an example." His smile was so sweet she couldn't be angry. He had seen her embarrassment from which anger might have sprung, but that was gone.

They were waiting, not able to know, and she relented. Deliberatly Reached . She saw they were reluctant to Join again in deference to her feelings and she was grateful for the kindness, the sophistocation of that refusal. Alicia nodded seriously, her round face soft with concern that Rose thought was beyond her years.

Raol sighed, his eyes serious with contrition."Teacher, it's just that we've been finding out how much better it is, how much more we can realize, know, of our feelings and how they affect our thoughts. We can watch and know ourselves this way. Emotions are like storm clouds sometimes, so many, so unmanagable, so fluid. They're hard to get hold of. You know! You've taught us that! We guessed a long time ago that you were sensitive." His eyes flashed, then dropped a moment,"We wondered why you did not mind-Touch with us." He frowned, then as if with a worried realization, he added,"You know, no one can really 'read thoughts'".

Alicia was nodding, holding Rose's gaze as if wanting to insist that she understand. Rose nodded, understanding more than she could say. She'd have to sort it all out later, she thought. She felt both relief and fear. What were these children becoming. If what they realized was common, what did she need to do?

Jonni spoke sharply, his eyes suddenly narrow and hard,"We're becoming just what your own kids are becoming, Teacher. Nothing less -- nothing more."

Rose gulped, swallowed, and accepted that."How far can you Reach? What is the range you've learned?" She didn't know why she asked the question. It seemed odd to her once said. She closed her mind tightly, knowing that the fear there was real and that the desire to protect her own inner thought from them was strong. Yet they'd said they didn't 'read thoughts'. But how very much can be known by attitude, feelings! They were, all of them, separate just now, waiting. They too could avoid another's Touch. The danger of this kind of control exploded in her mind like a red light signalling. She frowned , recognizing the exaggeration.

"Alicia spoke with an air finally of confidence,"Rose, we've been practicing as Jonni said, Touching since we were little. But really no mind-link until lately." She wanted to explain, comfort Rose. We've not paid any attention to distance, just a Touching mostly, and lately, we've been finding that Touch extends into linking that is -- is very exciting, you know. We wanted clarity, to know what it was like to lift our minds on each other's strength, because that's what seems to happen. We realize each others attitudes, feelings, the shift and change of all that. Imagery is wonderful -- and fun. We think we are like a stronger, greater mind when we link, but we can't know because we haven't been able to stabilize enough, to really do anything but just be there a little with one another. We haven't ever thought together, but we think it ought to be possible, shouldn't it?"

Raol broke in, eager, wanting to persue now that the matter was opened up," Yes, don't you see, it looks to us as though there has to be harmonizing, balancing of another kind than just emotional balancing that we've always practiced. Surely, this is Mind energy, and thought is energy, isn't it? A powerful energy, or it rides on energy if it's not. If we sustain attention, lift up, Reach beyond ordinary thinking, then wouldn't we be at a higher place of perception? A place where perception seems to be opening out to -- to everything?" His eyes were shining,, his face aglow. She felt excited by these children, their interest.

Jonni was nodding at what Raol had said,"And you see, we thought if it is a matter of sustaining attention. After all, that's what we do when we make things move with mind energy. And you know people do that! But we thought we could do that more fully together, give each other strength. We already noticed that thinking about it all drains the energy out as if through various pipelines and so we don't try to share thinking." She grinned at her, sensing her acceptance,"Actually Teacher, we've learned a lot from you. Why d'you suppose we picked you to bring this up with?"

THE AWAKENING

"From me?" Rose was incredulous,"Without my knowing?" She wanted to know how, when. To comprehend more of this. But they sighed, almost together and a small wave of tension dissipated.

" Rose, we needed to know! We couldn't just push your thought. We couldn't intrude. We did listen to the way you managed your own impressions, sometimes." At her startled look, Jean shook his head,"No, No! We didn't intrude,we couldn't even if we wanted to, but sometimes you weren't closed, sometimes your mental responses were pretty open. I think maybe because you didn't think we were aware. You create wonderful images, you know." Suddenly he was laughing, pleased, wanting her to approve.

They were suddenly a group of children who'd been caught in a mischief. Rose felt anger, fear, melting into amusement. With a brief shake of her head she said,"No wonder the Builder's are afraid!" As the words fell on her own ears she knew the statement was a fact that she hadn't been willing to speak. The young people watched her, their faces registering her softened expression. And she was suddenly again the Teacher.

"I think we've got a lot to think about. So much is happening, and among you young ones. I have known this - mind link, among a few adults, but hadn't thought -- " She shook her head and smiled a wide bright accepting smile that brought the atmosphere back to normal. We've got to end all the avoiding of what we've been realizing. You speak of my own children, and I -I've been avoiding things with them, I know. There must be --be thousands maybe in the Valley who're beginning to realize these things. If it's happening so naturally among you young ones, maybe even millions. I can't imagine that -- but it must be true! We've got to begin talking about it among our Families."

The look on their faces, their exchanged glances told her how much they hoped that would happen. Alicia leaned across the table, sliding her hands on the polished wood, enjoying the feeling of it, "I wonder if maybe you're not afraid we'll mis-use our Talents. That we'll pry , push our way into other minds. Is that true, do you think that?"

Rose nodded after a moment,admitting the fear.

"Well, we don't because we can't. I know it's wrong, we all do. We DO NOT do that! But it's true that in the beginning some of us tried because we wanted to see if we could find anyone who would respond. And what happens? If a person cannot respond, they snap themselves closed so fast it's like a reflex. People do leak feelngs, attitudes,more than we would like actually". She grinned, glancing at her friends. "Prying's no problem actually, I think it's absolutely no problem, Rose". The young girl was so intent, so anxious to convince that Rose laughed.

"I think you're right. I think those who aren't sensitive react. They feel some vague danger, the way people used to say they feel a cold wind in their hearts? But I believe that a highly adept mind could actually influence another mind just as people have through history, not only in words. We may have called them charismatic, but they influenced others profoundly. We have to be alert to that mind that insinuates itself into another. We must learn how to Reach, Touch and

Join and how to Shield. We have to learn so much. I can see that now! Our Teachers must begin to Teach more." Now, Rose was feeling a great enthusiasm, and she wanted to begin immediately. She looked at them all again,"It's true, you're aware, much more aware, but none of us understand all that we're aware of."

Jean said again, his serious, young, old face seemed full of a compassion and gentleness that touched Rose's heart. Such young people would not need to be warned of care for others. "There are some who cannot, you know, Teacher, some who don't or just won't,because they're afraid, maybe. But some who never will be able to." His face and voice were sad with that knowledge.

Rose nodded, the sadness spreading among them. She thought, that the Council should have noticed these developments, that the Master Teachers should have seen and alerted people. Surely the Monitors had to have known, but then, they'd have waited to let people discover for themselves. She felt ashamed of her own generation. But fear is a powerful restraint.

Then with a sudden desire to correct what seemed to her a grand mistake, she deliberately Reached out, opened her mind, welcoming but not intruding. Her attention lifted, Soul conscious, perhaps they could make a mind-link. What she had learned at the Council seemed astonishing then. What she did now, seemed impossible.

The four young people responded as though elastic, snapped into harmony with her, and increased the range of her Reach. They were all surprised that that happened. The gathering of minds extended their power many fold. They retreated briefly in surprise and then swept out, clear, strong and with an ease that was joyful.

They were together because it was their NATURE to be of one nature as well as individual natures. It seemed so obvious now, how could thay have not known? They were conscious of a perception of power, of visual images and the realization rang through them, 'We are of one nature - humanity. All of us! We would literally harm ourself if we harmed another.

It was clear to them then that anyone whose mind would Reach out,who could Join at all, would know immediately that Self that was beyond 'selfishness'. They thought the danger of mis-use was minimal. Rose sighed in relief and felt them comforting her. She felt an aching flood for those who knew no such Reach and felt the young ones entering to right the imbalance that was her worry. She saw that they truly had been 'practicing'. She sighed then in satisfaction and pride. She found the balance they sought, and together they entered into that rising lift of mind.

Then, extended so far, lifted from within that centering Self, they held, focussed, conscious of a bright distant point of light, beyond them. That Light she would not Reach to, not now! Old fears and pain guarded that doorway. It was closed. The others saw, felt, knew and did not inquire.

Then with a surge of Joy she acted , asked, and received permission. There were other dimensions to explore. With a joyous lift she drew them with her

THE AWAKENING

upward through themselves. They sat easily in their chairs, their bodies at rest, their minds soaring and with a twist, she drew them . They found a strong sharp streaming of energy, and knew it was the webbing of Mind flow from the Monitor Station and they drew back, repelled by the strength of it. She rebalanced, focussed, and they were high above the Valley, watching clouds passing by, watching the broad expanse of dark and light greens,the sweep of dark forest darkened by the patches of nearly barren deciduous trees.

They looked into villages,hovered over cities,They saw that the high spires of the Temples at the center of every town were focal points for the resurgance of the Web of Mind cast out by the Monitors. That was a surprise and a discovery. They knew the surge of amusement from those very watching Minds. They floated over the great River, letting the calm of its slow movement fill their hearts. She knew with a sudden startled certainty that Benjamin lived already at that Station there hidden among the rocks. Then she turned with the children and streamed back to the room where their bodies sat.

They sat starry eyed, amazed and a little shaken looking at her. Finally Jonni said,"Rose, we've never, we've never tried lifting like that, together, out beyond- beyond ourselves."

She smiled and corrected him,"Beyond part of yourself. Surely it was yourself too that was in flight!" They nodded, and were still, just remembering. Alicia said softly,"There was so much Light. Everywhere, as though we breathed Light." Their eyes were on her, full of memory, tender.

Gradually they relaxed,accepting and smiling at the memory."The Monitor stations, they're so powerful. It's as though a beam of energy protects them. How could anyone approach them were they not willing." Alicia stated the fact,it was not a question. Then she said," Did you know of those Stations.Rose?"

Rose nodded, smiling, she had known,but only of one with any familiarity."I studied at the North Station for a while. I didn't know you young folk were aware of them."

"We didn't know you were." They all laughed. The amount of misinformation must be vast. Rose nodded and said,"We've got a lot of work to do. We've got a whole Valley to discover. How many of you talk to your parents of these things?" At their head shakes, she was sad again. "It's not right, you know for such a separation to exist between us. I suggest we all go walk a while and sit in the gardens and do some thinking. Pure deep thinking."

Raol said,"First I want to eat.I'm hungry."

The others nodded and looked at Rose but she shook her head. I've got to much to think about now. I'll see you all tomorrow." She hesitated, then said softly,"I appreciate your trust!"

Rose settled down in the nearly barren court beside a cold little pool where one slim green water grass stalk penciled its shadow over the clear water. Thoughts clustered. There were Anna and Anthony, what were they doing with all this? Certainly they too were joining with their peers. What had they learned and did not share with their Family, or even their parents? She was not surprised, she and Benjamin had not been very responsive to such possible Touch. "We've created our own problems after all. We didn't have to let this condition develop." She sat silently, her mind growing still as the cold water before her. Then she wished that she had someone from the Family to talk to, Paul, perhaps, or Tom or Jerry or --. The thought was immediate,"Well, why not?"

She Reached out -- randomly, letting her mind extend open and welcoming. And there, across the court she saw a tall, brown bearded man, hair touching his shoulders, and already she could glimpse the bright grey eyes laughing at her. Tom! Coming to her cry. And it had only been a mental cry. Had anyone else heard? She glanced around,suddenly shy. She was overpowered with Joy at the discovery that he could and would Touch, respond.She leaped up to meet his embrace and leaned against him for a moment. Then they sat, he holding her hand quietly in a comforting gesture.

So absorbed was she in sorting out all that had happened, wondering where to begin, that she did not notice that he was still connected, her intention, her confusion known to him. She cried out,"Oh, Tom, there it is. That Mind Touch seemed so easy for you."

He laughed, his long, lean face fit rightly on that long, lean body. He stretched an arm along the back of the bench behind her and said, "How d'you suppose I do my job as mayor so well?"

"How long have you known?"

"Not so long, Love, I began to notice some years ago that I seemed always to sense how people felt, to know their needs or their resentments before they told me. People in general at least. I didn't always know with individuals. And gradually I began to discover that I reached into the general mental pattern of this town's people. I began to pay attention, focus attention. And from there, I kept discovering. My wife Angela, and my wife Mary, both know, but they don't know that they too could Reach if they would. They won't. They resist as though it were a poison. They just explain things by saying I'm sensitive. Well, what else is that but Mind Touching in some way? But I didn't think other people did it, until recently." He shrugged, settled himself beside her and said,"Well, tell me what's happened. Something has!"

She smiled,shook her head, then began to tell him of the morning. "They're so very aware, Tom, and so full of - of life. Why haven't we noticed all this?" Again she shook her head, sadness sweeping through her body like a cool air. "I suppose it's to be expected, we keep avoiding what's not familiar. We don't understand and we put off trying to. Why haven't the Monitors made us listen?"

He grimaced, and then abruptly laughed, his brown hair bobbing against his shoulder."It's not their business, you know, Rosy. they are there to watch, to be ready when we do Reach out, but not to be our parents. They won't even help, unless we ask. You know, the Teaching has always been that we must ASK!"

She sat letting her eyes trace the shadow pattern of a tall young tree at the edge of the paved court. "It makes sense. They can't intrude into our lives. We've got to learn enough to ask. I do know that". They sat in companionable silence for some minutes and then she said, "We need to present the questions and the facts to the Town Council next meeting. Could you do that? We've always been so sure we Valley People are special."

"D'you know, Rosy, I think it's fear. I think we've been afraid. After all, what're we going to do with these Talents. What do they mean? And there's still the old-old taboos . What is this thing? Not just to Reach and Touch, that's strange enough, but to Join!" At her glance he nodded," Yes, I find out things! I know what the Council does. I've not done it, but I've heard. They Join, Rose! And what that means seems to be that they enter into mental communion with many others,they pool mind strength. That could be an inexpressable blessing or a terrible weapon that could destroy us all. And being human beings we're convinced of the worst sooner than hoping for the best."

He was pensive and a little sad and she knew that he wanted to set things right. To be a good mayor, he should. He rubbed his face with both hands as if waking himself, he looked up again and met her eyes, "We've got to Gather. You've been telling us that. Our Family's got to talk. Already Paul told me he fears for William. Why? Can't we Gather immediately?"

She drew from him but held herself open, a tentative Reach toward him. Then suddenly she felt his energy like a hard thrust against her mind. He didn't know his skill. He was untrained. So were they all. That was the danger actually. Untrained minds waking to such power. "We do have to gather. Paul's already asked. And I'll get the word out tonight. Everyone has to plan for a whole day, you know. We've never got done in less and besides we need to just be with each other that long at least. I had hoped we could wait for Benjamin, but we may not be able to.

He nodded, Silvia and Ned are working hard with the building gang on the Industrial Ring and they want to get it done before the heavy rains. But they'll take time with us." He was quiet, his mind remembering those three. "How is it with them Rose, the three all loving each other and no one making a decision?"

Rose shook her head, "I don't know. Silvia won't decide but she must soon. Jerry's beside himself with wishing that she'd make some decision." She smiled sadly,"I can't blame her though, they're both such wonderful men. Even though Jerry's my brother, I'm not blind to his goodness. And Ned is a natural father, a wonderful joyful person who makes everybody happy around him. He's got a real gift, you know. No, I don't know who she'll choose and she won't talk about it."

Tom nodded, and they were silent,Rose shifted in her seat, stood and walked a little around the fountain, touching the cold water, warmed little by the sun , He glanced at her,frowned then said,"I don't think there's any doubt, Love. There's been some kind of change among us. People like those two, for instance, Ned and Jerry. It's common. Really wonderful, aware people. And look what we've done - together. With a minimum of fighting. We just arent' like our ancestors!" He stopped, stared at her, letting his eyes finally focus and see her face. Then he shrugged," It's so wonderful to think that we're almost finished building this town. We've been at it so long. What'll we do with ourselves?"

THE PEOPLE OF THE VALLEY

Tom looked across the Gardens, his eyes rested in the shivering drops of water falling from the highest point of the fountain. So clear they would not have been visible had they not been moving, he let his attention enter into that falling, that clarity, and for seconds was there, a part of that movement, that stillness just before the fall. After several moments, he shook himself. His voice was a whisper as though the knowledge was so obvious he need not even speak at all except for his own satisfaction." Why we'll begin to expand our lives beyond our town. We'll be Valley people!" Then, with a pensive look at the garden around them, he nodded as if realizing something. "Here it is Rosy, Life shouts at us, whispers, enters into us in stillness between the shout and the whisper. We are not separate ever." She nodded, wanting him to go on. Wanting words that would remind her, that she could keep and use in another day. But he was silent then. After a while, he turned, smiling inside that full beard, his eyes laughing again. "Rose, whatever it is, between us, we humans, whatever it is, we need to learn through our relationship with one another. We will not have peace until we learn it".

Rose was frowning, feeling the impact of his words, the depths of his feelings, I agree, Tom. But how?

Tom said,"There it is Love, there is no end to Life . That's what we'll do when we've done our building. We'll find the Tao. We'll find Life beyond our old lives through our own humanity?"

She laughed then, a bright happy laugh as though she had been offered a gift.

"So how can we know the Builders aren't asking for changes that are part of that very flow we seek ?" He was grinning, teasing.

She frowned,"It's probably true they are, but I can't see it. It's too big a pattern. Right now I only see that they're disrupting everything we've built."

He nodded,"They've already talked to me,they want the forests broken down the land available for what they call development. I told them the land was for all living things, not just us, but they appeared not to hear me." He stood up, paced the court, his head bent, his hands wrapped together behind his back. To Rose at the moment, he seemed a man of her grandfather's time, his loose woven garments, his fullbeard and long hair, the slight stoop of his shoulders from meeting shorter people's eyes. He talked softly, "They've been seeking individuals and trying to convince them to their ideas. They try to separate the Councils in the towns. I understand that backfired utterly when they approached the Valley Council. With Grace and Jerome there. I understand from people who bring me news", he grinned again, "my informers, that they want land west of Santiago,,hundreds of acres. But more to the point for us, they want the forests broken between here and Denlock. Want more crop land." He was quiet, sitting down again, thoughts flooded his mind, a cloud of thoughts that buffetted one another so nothing clarified and Rose felt cut off from him.

"What do they want land for? Every town has what it needs. We don't need any more crops." Then, a fear ran like strings of fire through her mind, burning out logic. She stopped trying to think, paying attention to that fear. Tom simply

THE AWAKENING

watched her, nodding.

"You see? It wouldn't take much to set fire to the Valley itself. To our very way of being here. They insist that the land's wasting, that it needs to be used. They say they can make a lot of money!" He shook his head, impatient suddenly, "It seems so wrong that we must protect ourselves from each other. But after hearing of your talk with the kids today, I think I see. The Builders are afraid. And it isn't just that they want to tear things down, they want to go back to a time when such things didn't happen. They're afraid of US!" His voice rose into almost a squeek, the realization astonished him."And we haven't realized that -- because they don't even know it."

"They don't know. They feel threatened and they look for the most obvious thing that might cause fear. The loss of control of the land." Her voice was heavy with dispair.

"Well, Rose, how could they know of anything else?. When you think of what we've hidden from ourselves, what we've denied. How could we expect ,more from those who -- those who --" He couldn't say it,he looked at her as though pain racked his mind, shaking his head slowly and in his eyes she saw her own dispair.

Rose stood up now, turned to look down at him,though standing she was not much taller,"They see something is different, that change is happening and they're reacting with fear,and we react with another kind of fear. They fear -- oh, Tom, listen to us. We've already done it. We've separated ourselves, we speak already of 'they and we', not anymore of 'us'.Our life has so swiftly been broken apart as cruelly as the destruction of a forest would be."

He nodded, "Maybe it was inevitable, we've got no longer the intensity and constant busyness of building. We've a balanced way of life. We can't stagnate and we've not dealt with the next step at all. We haven't defined that next step?" He looked away,"I wonder if we'd better talk with the people of the south cities. they've finished their building long ago, and must already have defined the next step for themselves."

She nodded, then she began softly repeating a Teaching she learned long ago and had not fully understood, D'you remember this old Teaching, Tom? "When the powers of the mind grow strong then the old familiar no longer interests, the old needs and desires are left behind." Her eyes followed the slim shadows of limbs outlined on the paved court. She felt their shape and the light that drew them there, seeming opposites, wholly enjoined. Standing, she walked to the slim tree and stroked the smooth, yellow brown trunk. "The shadow and the tree itself, a pattern duplicated, but not the same. Their fears are as natural as that design of shadow on the pavement. Yet it is not the tree. We've been afraid, we've all been refusing to talk, to make known to one another our growing perceptions, or our increasing fears either. That's our real danger, not the Builders. We're afraid of each other. Our own neighbors and family."

He took her hand, pulled her back down to sit and turned to hold both her elbows with his long fingers,"Rose, that's exactly it. We're afraid of each other and how better could we get into trouble than to be afraid of one another." He was nodding, his lean tanned face looking so pale Rose reached to touch her finger against his cheek. He caught her hand and held it. "Damn! When's Benjamin coming home. We need that man. Can't you call him home? We need a Gather and he must be here for it".

She shook her head, "He won't be here before the end of winter, and that's too long. We've got to Gather before then." Then she said with a fierce resolve, "I know where he is, Tom. I do know. He's not far away now, but he'll not be home before March. I had hoped by Winter Festival, but he'll not make it then. Winter Festival'll begin at South Valley five days before full moon and that's the twenty sixth of December. It'll be held here two weeks later. Actually just after the new year this winter."

He said, "Good for you Rose. You do admit that you know where he is. Maybe not exactly, but you know he's near. But I can Reach to him because unlike you I made no promise not to. Wow! Would he be surprisd, if he opened enough to receive. But he probably won't. He's a stubborn one."

She shook her head, "I think It may be better if we just give him time. He'll be here." But his eagerness and confidence reassured her. Suddenly she wanted to tell him the rest, the perception of wondrous Light, that edge of 'something' beyond herself, perhaps Soul consciousness! The desire to speak flamed in her mind and she Reached.

He said, "No-No! Not now Rose. Not like this!" Then he was at once apologetic, "Oh, My Dear, I'm sorry. What I've done is inexcuseable, but I can't abide what you suggest! I can't either, you know. It's too close to my own -- an edge of consciousness through which a strange Light burns and will not leave me alone." He was actually trembling and she clutched his hands, they stood, staring into each other's eyes, people passing a little distance away, seemed walled off from them, so closed where their minds. They gradually realized they had done that and wondered at it. Were they always in Touch with others more than they admitted. His eyes were forlorn, drawing from hers, looking around, softening himself and allowing normal closeness. He admitted his fear. "I'm amazed, Rose, I didn't think it would be so obvious. I'm afraid, it's true. But, I'll talk at the Gather. I promise." He knew how much he had frightened her.

She was silent, but finally nodded, still feeling the ice of his refusal. 'How much power we have over one another,' she thought, 'how easily we can break down what trust we have.' But she said, "Well, Tom, I'll make arrangements." At his nod, she added, "We need help, you know. From someone stronger than the Master Teachers. We've got to find help."

They said goodbye and she watched him walk on, through the barren gardens, with a few evergreens and the lush grasses or ground covers providing winter color. She sat quietly after he left looking around. She could see a circle of crepe myrtle trees, barren, their slim clean limbs forming a design that repeated itself against the side of the building. Tiny still red leaves, clung here and there. It would take heavy winter storms to dislodge them. She smelled the wet, earth, the decaying leaves, and felt again the gentle sadness of early winter, the dying time. It was all of a piece. She had a choice, she could see this as a time of dispair, gloom, the ending of things, or she could enjoy the sense of rest, quiet, closing into itself of the Earth life.The unspoken promise that this seeding time gave. A promise invisible as yet.

Sudden she longed for the clean bare emptyness, the silence and white of winter. Then the Earth and all Life drew into itself, bore the bitter cold and the relentless winds and retreated into its Center. She too must do that.

The Valley itself was alive, was seeking its own harmony. The sense of its slow focus filled her mind, expanded it beyond itself.. She was part of that which centered, an infinitismal part, but conscious. That was the rub! The jolt of that recognition coming into the beauty and the Light of the afternoon, was pain. Must harmony always include all that threatened that harmony? She sighed, so much had happened this day, could she persue such a question?

The question drew her down, shrank her consciousnesss to this tiny self who asked. She sat again, folded into the brilliant light, the color that filtered through the few dry leaves above her. She felt an acute sense of her smallness, of the vast organic consciousness of Earth. She attended the grief pulsing through her body, as though the cells themselves vibrated their dispair. Fear pierced that understanding, leaving her with a ragged sense of danger. She watched this painful twisting of her emotions, knowing they were born of blindness.

"I don't know where this fear comes from, but I know it's real.There's no reason to be afraid. Yet I am. Something seems to threaten my very being. And when I allow myself to admit it, I am aware of it." She sank into recognition, allowing herself to experience this dark tangle that subsided into the single dark pit over which she hung."I won't deny it any more. But I've got to find someone to talk to." The decision was a relief and a surrender.

She stood up, "I've got to go, to get home. I want to do some hard work, something that will use my body until it is exhausted. So tired I can't think any more." She started to walk, "Why can't I simply be? Why must I always -- ALWAYS have to question? I can't turn off my mind." She was angry with herself,and then she stopped, and felt the response, rising from some deep place, some point beyond thinking."Because there is so much more to Being than I know. Because it is my nature to want to understand. so, I am just being myself after all, as I am." She stood nonplussed and finally smiled faintly.

She wanted suddenly to run away, to escape herself! A tiny moaning cry came from her lips. She twisted her body this way and that. That which had lured her to Itself with the bright glimpse of wonder, now hounded her every minute, refused to be set aside, lashed at her heart and mind until she knew that she must either escape permanently or --- surrender into it. She could no longer stand apart and refuse. Her sanity could not bear it.

Her body started like a frightened deer. She responded wholly to it, leaped a low hedge, dashed across a yard of deep moss under trees , dodged people who looked at her in concern, irritation or amusement. She raced on. One person turned to follow the fleeing figure with eyes full of understanding. He Sent swiftly, Reaching to her and surrounding her with support the way a Healer might, but he was no Healer. She felt the warmth,,the strength, but did not know its source. She felt wound as tightly as a spring, refusing everything as fiercely as she had so recently accepted.

She ran without stopping down the long northern slope of town and crossed the Great Highway.A cluster of approaching Low Carts with several people walking and two on horseback was arriving at the junction but she didn't see. There among them, one lifted a hand, glanced at another, and together they sent a swift blessing and a healing that Rose felt, received like a breeze against her hot face. But this cooling was for her heart. She did not know of the source of this either, but felt a faint smile begin to tip up the corners of her mouth and a loosening of the tension. She was running still, up the steep slope to the Farm, she had to slow down, it was too much, this hill side was almost a stair way. Nearly to the top, she sank down among a cluster of raspberry bushes, leafless. She looked back puzzled at those fleeting gifts but refusing to think of them now. She laughed with delight at her body's vigor.

A calf, grazing along the edge of the hill, strayed from the herd that moved slowly toward the farther hill, raised its head and watched her,wide eyed, chewing slowly. Pleased with its lack of fear, she nodded and Sent a wash of safety, of reassurance. There had been cattle killed, along with horses, goats, deer, sheep and elk in the autumn wild harvest by the Hunters, carried back on great flat disc lifts and processesed in the town food banks, just as they were in every other town. But the animals killed were the ones that would not make the winter, were growing old, or they were of the over abundance of young males who would fight and maim one another during the spring months. The young were never killed. This one too had a life to live. Cooks used these meats sparingly in soups and stews, some deep cassarole dishes, but little else. The taste for the flesh of creatures was almost lost.

Rose breathed deeply, letting her body relax and her breath come easier.Then, she was tempted to practice that Reach. What if she too could Touch into the mind of an animal. She focussed, and sent out that tendril of Mind Touch, and there, she knew the placid belonging with the herd, the satisfaction with the thick grass, and then, it's sudden awareness that it had strayed. It jerked its head up in a sudden mild panic and raced back to the midst of the herd that was one of the protected milking herds for Adwin. Their dog pack protectors roamed along with them, but now, Rose could see them lolling at ease, confident there was no danger here near the human farm. There it nudged a small brown cow,making quick soft sounds until it felt itself one with them and safe again.

Rose smiled, pleased. She had entered for a moment into another life, felt its unthinking awareness. To practice so did not feel at all frightening. She began walking on up the hill,this time slowly,she felt as though she had left the internal battle behind . When she reached the top of the slope she turned west to the barn. It's huge dark silence attractive to her restless spirit.

THE AWAKENING

This was what Jane called the Hall of the little ones. She laughed at the memory. Of course, there were many who came in the worst weather. They had milk from three different cows they called their own for several months after each calving. Injured animals came too, those that escaped predators. Rob had a sense for them, and regularly went to find them, to bring them here.

She looked around, there had been a number of animals here during the last storm. No one had set the cleaner into action yet. She wanted work, hard physical labor that would use her body fully. This was exactly it. Three angora goats, heavy with young were sauntering easily through the meadow to the rear of the barn, they looked curiously at her, baaed and went back to eating. Jane had removed the long silky hair in the autumn and it had grown back enough to well cover their bodies in shining ripples. A group of small towns among the Blue Lake, miles east of Santiago, had made a thriving business with Mohair, and the training of protective dog bands for them. They sold pups to farms, or town people who wanted such skilled canines. Now there were hundreds of goats and their companions living in the vast meadows among the foothills. Their number limited by law that the land be not overgrazed, their people moved them into the higher mountains half the year. Rose stopped to watch them a moment, her mind pleasntly occupied with thought of them. One of Jerry's mares raced into the barn, nudged her, whinnied, then went to punch the trigger that released the feed into her stall. She settled down contentedly to eat. Other than the soft munching of the horse, she heard no sound. The barn was cool, but she was still warm from her run.

She studied the situation, what was to be done here? Tools were hanging in their place on one narrow wall behind a stall. There was a power vacuum beside them, and someone had begun to clean a stall and had not finished. She opened the door to the tack room, saw that it needed tidying. She picked things up, hung or replaced them on their stands. She stripped dried mud from one halter, clucking in disapproval. Jerry wouldn't leave tack like this. Must have been one of the kids. She got oil, rubbed the leather down, and found herself humming happily, suddenly content. Pleased to be ordering the dim, cool stone barn.

She finished the tack, and turned to the floors. She picked up a flat wide shovel and began scooping the debris into a pile, changed, used a broad hoe to pull it together and a heavy broom. She made several piles and then, rolled out the big vacuum, and set it to sucking up the debris. The smell of the mostly dry droppings seemed to her pleasant reminders of the long years of their work here. The big vacuum was only five years old. It had taken a family gather to decide to buy it. She felt her body relaxing, the salty sweat running down her face. She licked drops from her mouth, wiped it from her eyes. She grinned. Thought formed at the edges of attention and she ignored it. The quiet afternoon wore on. It seemed to her that time had slowed, had wrapped her in stillness.

Working, feeling the rhythmic movement of her muscles, the attending to this task, the smells and the sunlight slanting across the dust filled air, drew her from herself and immersed her in a new attention. She watched the broom moving steadily across the rough floor, a mix of earth and cement and emulsions of oils that gave the resulting product a flexibility and give that concrete never had. Her eyes seemed to magnify, to see as though minutely focussed, the stiff hairs of the broom, each following another, catching and propelling ahead the dust, the bits of straw. She was caught in the exactness of that simple function of the broom.

   Gradually the rhythmic movement became an entrance into another dimension, an opening, an instants perception of such absolute stillness her mind yawed, sagged against knowing. Identity shifted. She was aware of that shift and of being part of that drifting sun filled dust. The great space of the barn, the thick coarse hairs of the broom, the little woman, pushing, it was all one multi-event.. It was itself a timeless moment, as if breath ceased, all movement stretched into infinity, and yet, the breathing Earth filled her lungs, exhaled through every tree and branch, lived Itself magnificently. The dust of the barn, gleaming, streamed up the rays of the sun, making great pillars through which shadows moved softly. She felt her body striving also toward that Light, as if sensing there something vital to its own life. Attention followed, lifted, encompassing everything as if it had no limit. The joy of it was sweet. She was free, a joy, an amusement large as the wind itself blew through her and she never ceased the smooth movement of her body and the broom.

   She shook herself, wanting with such a longing that it throbbed through her heart like pain. Not able to understand, she shrank back down to herself. The persistent awareness of the singleness of existence persisted, even surrounding the little thought. That joyous Self breathed through her, and she knew of IT. Then, as if in reaction, unable to sustain, she shut herself away, was as small as her thinking. She was unable to allow more, unable to prevent that violent clamor of thinking. " What is this? What has happened? What was that absolute stillness? Am I in it? Or it in me? No, it was like Nothing at all." Then in a great cry she heard her own words, "I'm not really anything at all!"

   She trembled, wanting to recover that moment, wanting to sustain and keep that awareness, so wondrous had it been. And at the same time, she fought to cling to the storm of questions to conceal from the very awareness she sought. She could not find any word to fit, to speak of it. And so it would not hold steady in memory, for words seemed necessary to sustain memory. Wonder was too vague a word. But one thing she knew for sure. In that moment of stillness, there had been absolutely no fear. Now there was left only the quiet of awe.

   She worked silently for a while, feeling vulnerable, tender as if she had been offered Joy. Then, her mind, clamoring again, questioning, restless, laboring in itself, flooded with emotions that threatened to unbalance her, seemed for a moment like a great hive of bees giving her no rest from itself. For a strange distance had occurred between herself and that thinking mind. She could watch its intention. She straightened, practicing the Balancing for several minutes, she calmed. Listened to her internal questions and shook her head. "I don't know.!" She wanted to complete this job, engage herself in it.

   She drew the big nozzle of the Vacuum across the end of the main alley of

THE AWAKENING

the barn and it efficiently sucked up everything in its way. Leaving a clean floor. A satisfying job, she smiled, feeling happy with the work.

She began to clean the stalls. The mare looked at her, nuzzled her shoulder lightly and then, whirled and ran to the meadow outside. She didn't like even this quiet vacuum sound. She would drop her colt in a month and Jerry wanted her to stay close. Gradually the straw,,shit, dirt dissappeared. The vacuum raised its voice to a high pitch trying to draw in all this fresh manure. She picked up the heavy push broom and swept the rest into a pile that she could suck up easier. Her body worked like an automaton, sweating, tired, obsessed with its doing.

Finally she stood in the center of the barn, the vacuum in hand again, looking around. Vision flickered between the acute awareness of 'everything at once' and the immediate bit by bit world. She took a long breath. A little final sweeping up and it would be done.But she stopped, said aloud,"Why must all this be happening,now?" That sublime moment, so shattering and so healing as it shattered, had moved her out of herself, gave her new dimensions within herself. And yet,here again this bombardment of questions and feelings. This strange fear.

It's as if a growing anger settles over our Valley, like a fog blowing all over the land. "She nodded,"Yes, like a fog, a grey dimming of our lives, and in the midst of that dimming,is the lightning flash, the blast of clear pure Light. No! It's not that way at all.The world seems dim to us, because we've begun to see more, our vision is clearing and the world as we knew it seems dark. How can we meet all that? What does it mean?"

She felt anger rise like a fist against her heart. Must she become lost in the debate again. The fist seemed to spread, until it thrust itself up against her throat and gave sharp pain.

She spoke aloud then, guiding the fat tube ahead of her as she walked,

"Life has been so good, the promise of our Valley so great! Why must these things be happening now?" She worked again in silence. There was no sound but the steady hum of the machine,the rising to a whine when it met heavy material, and then subsidence into a grinding hum. Stopping suddenly, she yelled, screamed without words, a release of some fury she had not known was there. The echoes of the noise filled the barn.She didn't care, she liked making so much noise. It felt foolish, but it felt good. The knot in her throat was gone.

Rob, who had been dozing outside with his family, came in, looked for a moment at her then came close to touch her leg wtih his paw until she looked at him. She could see the new mate just beyond the door,watching, her eyes intent on Rose too. The puppy curled against a boulder in the sun asleep. Rob wove a strong flood of affection, compassion that leavened her anger, and softened the incessant questioning. She was grateful. Canine friends carried so much devotion to those they loved. A fierce clan loyalty. And how long since that was all humankind had?. She straightened her body, stroking his head, then she leaned against him lightly, hugging him. "It's all right Rob. Just something I have to work out."

THE PEOPLE OF THE VALLEY

The barn smelled clean, the air blew through it cold and fresh. And Rose felt the passing of the air like a touch. Her tool hit a broken edge of the concrete and her body lurched forward, stumbled and recovered itself so automatically and gracefully that she smiled, "Well, there's that! At least my body seems to be together with itself,."

The great barn hung cool and shadowed above her, She had helped in lifting these massive beams, and in placing them tightly into the fitted stone. The sense of belonging, of having a home place, of unquestioned relationship with land and family and the town beyond them, filled and reassured her. The day blazed beyond the wide doors. Her muscles tightened and relaxed, her body gave itself easily to the work, and with satisfaction she looked around. The floor was clean, the job was done.

She stood a moment breathing deeply the cool clean air, enjoying the cold in her lungs, but she felt the sweat drying cold on her skin and knew she should move or go in the Hall before she was chilled.

Something nagged at her attention, something she was avoiding. She said aloud, "Yes, that again. We've talked enough about how we are avoiding something. All of us. Our family. And now, it seems so acute, as if there's a thorn at the back of my mind and it won't withdraw, won't stop its sharp demand." She stood still, willing herself to meet that prodding insistence. But with a rare swift swing, her mind began a clamor of thinking again. But this time, it was attention to the way she used thinking to avoid. "I DO need to pay attention. Find out, be aware of - everything I'm realizing.. I do think too much. I convince myself that I AM what thinks. That's why there's so much arguing,. And there it is again. Thinking about thinking. There's no way out. The battle that goes on in me is endless and I feel lost to everything when it is going on". She drew a long breath, she WOULD look at herself. "Exactly what is the argument?" Attending, watching her mental battle, she nodded. On one hand something in me is afraid, another part of me refuses to even honor that fear. It tells me 'There's nothing to be afraid of.'" She was still then," But I know there is. That part of me who realized, knew the Light, the wonder, knows there is something to be afraid of. But also to -- to seek for." Then an astonishment struck her to still the debate entirely.

"Who is this who sees both sides? Who can see the battle for what it is?"

Tears were in her eyes. The quiet of the afternoon nourished the quiet within herself. She felt atunement, a balancing . She asked, "Why have I denied so much? Why do I fear so much? When there is such pure and Joyful wonder?" An uprising of old resentments blew past her attention the way dust blows from an opened attic. "Is it the wonder itself that I'm afraid of? I will have to accept that I'm more than I ever thought I could be. And yet, that's a paradox. I cannot be more than I am. I just don't know what I am. What every human person is."

The sheer fact of this recognition numbed her for a moment, then she said, clearly, "Well, that's it. I'm done with denial, whatever the cost." She felt the turbulence in her mind, her heart, and she knew with surprise that she was watching that conflict. She was not the conflict. In that moment, will held firm,

THE AWAKENING

emotion yielded, kept its distance, settled, visible among thoughts that whirled still. Thoughts that whirled in an attempt to shape, but mostly they drifted, shapes forming and dissolving in a repetitious redundancy as they had for so long. Then the drifting slowed, silence grew all around what seemed to be a dream of herself, and in that silence was no judgement or censor. There was only an inexorable command,"Be Still!"

Slowly everything came to a halt. All the struggle drained of energy, and the divided thinking ceased. She was in a place between, she could see herself there, two twins of herself, reflections of that quarrel. They looked exhausted as if the battle of years had worn them down. Then precisely the thought of Jonah came, his desparate fear of that Voice that called from within him and that he fled. She surrendered to that truth as consciousness flickered from those tiny weary selves, and expanded to this single pure awareness, watching, surrounding and including. Was she then fleeing that same Voice? This was the eye that integrated, this was AMUSED. And here there was no separation from the images of those two arguing selves below. The perspective was simply multiple like light through a prism.

She knew this! Accepting, she reached, where thinking could not follow, she was, and Knew. Residing at that point of stillness, she simply was and she waited . Thoughts flickered, faded, that same strange sense of being outside her universe, in unutterable stillness and yet, part of everything that was. She was Conscious, conscious of Life itself pulsing through as if she herself was one of the pulses of that beat. She realized 'who' was aware! She had entered the realm of Spirit, consciousness extended into Spirit. She knew how she had used her own self to avoid this greater Self. There was no time, everything was still, and in no place at all. Thinking was irrelevant. Knowing occurred.

Eventually time reasserted itself, she was limited again. Thought crashed through her attention. After all, thinking was part of it too. She must remember that it was only part. There was -- Life also. One dipped consciousness into Life and retreated. A taste was enough at first. Up and down, in and out, the rhythm of waking awareness had become more gentle. Consciousness shrank, but she was aware of that shrinking. Accepting. She could return.

Slowly, again, she returned to the limited dimension within which her body lived. Slowly thought regained itself and strove to shape idea of what was. But she had not lost contact, had not denied Consciousness. There was rhythm, its beat subtle, lightedness, radiant Joy. She could not understand or put it into words to think. Everywhere was Life. Instantly she was Life realizing Itself through - herself? - an aspect of Itself? And she Knew!

The rhythm slowed, she was immersed desparately in thinking as if clinging to it as a lifeline. It was the identity of Rose, that thinking. That vast Self, was 'other'. She was small, parted from that 'other,' but she knew she could never again think she was separate. She felt sore of mind, watching, tender as one who has been stretched to breaking.

She felt a shy wonder, as if she could not be part of That. Yet, at the corner of her mind a great Light persisted, refused to be hidden, promised and threatened her with immersion in Itself. The memory was a throbbing emptiness, she would drown in it. But the memory also soared, lifted, expanded and was a peon of Joy. What matter that she drown?

How could this all be so. She feared she could not realize all she knew. She was a mirror in which everything was reflected. Her mind trembled, her body shivered, but she held firm. She would sustain perception. She knew finally what humankind was. For she could not any more think of herself as other than humankind. A relief spread through her, established a core of quiet, calm that she could depend on. The argument was ended!

Then, from a distance, penetrating through everything, a clear voice called. It was as if she stood naked, stripped and raw, exposed and unable to shield herself. She swiftly drew herself into familiar memory and shaped herself within it. And looked around. The world seemed lit with wonder, the air gleamed as if it were full of diamonds, the barn was solid, still and as she let her eyes move across the rough stone, she thought she could enter into it and lose herself again within that stillness of stone. To lose myself, yes, to lose myself in my Self and in everything is no loss at all. After all the years I was afraid of losing myself, there is no loss at all!

An unceasing flow of Love for everything, for each pebble, each torn leaf, for the great alive dog watching her with strangely bright eyes filled her and spread out over everything around as if the day were full of a Light that was Love. She wanted to shout, to sing, to dance, to embrace all Earth.

She heard the sweetness of that human voice calling again, and surrendered to herself, sinking into her personhood to walk there, coming from that barn, out to the shimmering air.

Steve said,"Hey Rose, you've been working here like a house afire. What's got into you?"

Rose looked at him, tears coming at the sheer beauty of him. Steve watched her intently, his usual grin fading, but he said nothing more. She spoke softly,"I don't know, Steve. I don't know what's got into me, but I'm beginning to guess!"

Steve nodded slowly, still watching her intently as though not sure that it was really all right. She sobered before his look, and realized steadily that vast pervasive Love that surrounded them, included them, extended through Earth into everything that was alive. Because everything was alive. So intensely ALIVE. Did he know? She spoke softly to relieve him of her strangeness,"You called. What was it you wanted?"

He answered automatically, his attention absorbed by the beauty and radiance he felt around her, the recognition made his voice a bit hushed as he said,"I came to ask if you could help us. If you're finished here."

Rose looked around, drawing her attention out. There was pain in her legs, they seemd to vibrate slightly, she thought every nerve in her body was aflame. Her head felt literally sore inside, as if a terrible headache had nearly passed. Her love for Steve seemed to her boundless, yet she felt weary with a delicate frailty of being. As if she were too small, too inadequate for this containment. She felt like crying and at the same time like singing. Her wearyness prevented either, yet a surging energy seemed to be rising through her, as if the wearyness was of a body not yet acquainted with the boundless power of her Heart. She seemed to Steve to be so deeply quiet, that he hesitated to speak. He wondered if she had heard him.

She looked at him, seeing that he was slightly taller than herself, this man who she saw for the first time today, his face sharply fresh, a little dirty and beloved. His body breathed vitality, strength and energy rose from him in a fountain. He stood now, looking down,drawing the toe of his boot across the ground to make a rough design in the dust. He had no idea all that he had to offer. All that he WAS! She wanted to tell him, and knew that there were no words.

Rose said, her voice suddenly loud, "Yes, I'm finished here. I'm glad you came and that you need help. I need to do something worth while."

He hesitated, glanced at her face,,looked down, "Rose, something important has happened to you.I don't understand,but I do know that you might need to be alone. If you do, we want you to."

Rose was quick to notice the 'we'. She smiled at the promise of that. Perhaps the loneliness she had seen in his eyes for years was fading? But even more - he knew, without knowing he knew, what Jane intended. She felt a gratitude that brought tears to her eyes. She was acutely aware of the great caring of this man, of his persistent generosity. She reached out a hand to touch him and he took it in both his own, cradling it in that warmth. It seemed that time stretched, slowed between them. She thought it was always good to be with Steve. 'Even when we're mad at each other.'

She remembered that she had thought he was almost too giving of himself, as if he had little solid ground of personal opinion to keep his feet firmly placed. He seemed almost too flexible, yet at this moment, he was exactly what she needed. He offered a comfort he would have under valued, the comfort of acceptance. She was grateful that they needed her help. She wanted to go with him and be busy with them.

She said, "Right now I want to be with you and Jane". The world seemmed to finally shift, time righted itself, things were happening in normal speed. She grinned ruefully, relieved to say that. She could feel her mind stirring again, thoughts rousing one another, not even clearly set into words. They would over take her will and begin another endless spiral of demand for explanation. It was better if she had company now.

Swiftly in response to his troubled look,she went on,"I don't understand everything either Steve, but I just seem to torture myself sometimes,thinking too much, maybe. I'm like an addict, I can't let events alone. I have to take them apart and make them fit into something. See, I'm doing it now. Let's go!"

He shook his head,"I don't know Rose. Couldn't the - the Teachers at the Station help?" He felt awkward, not knowing exactly what she needed.

She nodded, turning into the path,"Yes, they probably could and I ought to go talk to them. I thought I could work things out myself. And maybe I have, a little. Maybe I have discovered something after all." She shrugged. "Well, I feel good now, I want to get down there and finish up with what you and Jane have to do so we can go home and have a good supper." She spoke in a breathless rush, as if wanting him to get on with it.

He said softly , "The work will bring you back. Make you feel better."

"Yes, it will. My body saves me from myself sometimes. " Steve saw her face change, her eyes distant, knew she was remembering. But he could not have known the unrelenting power of it, the heartbreaking beauty. Then she felt his arm on hers.

"If we're going, we better get there. It'll be dark soon and Jane says there's more rain on the way."

Rose nodded, drew herself to focus on him, then walked swiftly to the tool shed. "What's to be done then? You must be pulling the power stakes from the field corners and getting the floater discs into the sheds." He nodded, We've got the discs in, but there's a warning of a break in one of the shields of the winter grain field and the grain's just barely up. We have to be sure it can't be breached or the little critters will ruin the spring crop. The old grain field is full of mice and rabbits cleaning up the droppings and they're welcome. We've turned those off."He was talking to relax himself. Then he said, a look of pensive sadness coming over his face,"It's really winter, Rose."

He walked beside her until they reached the equipment room behind the barn, they got the testing gage and the repair pack."We don't know what's wrong, but if you carry the extra pole and the gage, I can manage the kit.He lifted it to strap it on his back. She was enjoying the evening light, the intense color of the sky. They turned into the path down hill.

CHAPTER ELEVEN

Winter Gather

    The long awaited Gather was finally set. Everyone belonging to the Farm Family agreed to make time for a full day or two together and the date was set for December.

    The desheveled look of early winter comes out of the death of things. The swift falling out of tons of leaves from the trees, the dropping of twigs and branchs, and even whole trees in the strong winter winds that sweep in at the solstice, left a changed world. Leaves half rotted don't blow easily but they sog down into Earth, mixed and rumpled with heavy weedstalks and create a look of decay, of uglyness. That decay contributed to the sadness that whispered through the early evening air, that rose unbidden out of hearts attuned to Earth. The land looked disheveled and grey, even the gardens of Adwin where the fall cleanup had not kept pace with the degeneration, though teams of young people worked weekly to ready the town for Winter Festival.

    Yet to the observing eye, the alert mind found the threads of color, subdued, the delicate, melancholy colors of death and the revealed patterns of barren limbs against the sky. Observed dispassionately, they gave interest and a quiet beauty to the land. The distinctive, vigorous odors of decay, the wet, mush of shapelessness, that gathered in the corners of garden beds, humped around the trunks of barren trees and the rare bright drifting leaf that fell in dry brilliance over top everything, filled many hearts with a sweet satisfaction and a sense of completion. Perhaps there is as much a nostalgia of lovely autumns remembered when creatures of Earth can lay down their wearying labor of summer and rest. Can go into their warm dens, hollow trees, or houses and gather their family around and tell the tales of the old days, or the adventures of the heros of yesterday. It was in these times of retreat that Gathers were held.

    Walking through the land, over sodden debris that hushed the sound of footsteps as well as the steady drone of the rain, people knew again the ancient feelings of melancholy that were part of the dying of a year. Then came the snow. By late December, before Festival had reached Adwin, the world was white through out the north land. No ground vehicles turned that snow to slush, or marked the pure unblemished white and so the town, except for the narrow paths, kept that look of clean smooth sparkling white.

    Festival time at Altos in mid December brought crowds of participants for winter sports, the most advanced ski runs, as well as cross country ski trails and bob sled slides were busy. Hill sides in the lower country were alive with amateur skiers and sleds, packing down the snow on those hills and enjoying the new winter. When Festival reached the lake country near Blue Lake there were skating exhibitions, races and ice games. But winter was also a time of creating things, finishing a building project, continuing research in the several laboratories, writing a play or a poem or a symphony, it was a time for finishing a large complex tapestry, or fine needlework that would be given to a loved one or sold at the Spring Festival. Millions of people created books, plays, and films and out of many came the few great ones. But such involvement meant that those artists whose talents stood out were appreciated and had a large knowledgeable audience. When many are heard or read, debate and discussion of their fellows works can become heated and exciting to those would be critics of the land.

On the chosen winter morning, the sun not yet up, half the Family was still in the temple at morning meditation and prayer, when Paul ,Jennifer, Rachel, Annette and William arrived in Paul's air car.The bells of Adwin were still ringing, faint and clear across the fields and as they climbed down from the roof landing grid, and the Family came to welcome them eagerly. This Gather must accomplish so much.

By the time they'd hugged and greeted one another, they could see three forms riding the wind currents in from Adwin. It would be Tom and Ned and one of Tom's wives. No one could be sure which had been home at the time. But Angela had been expected and so it was likely she. Tom spoke before he had his belt off, ripping the woolen face mask from his head."Hey, Paul, I saw your car fly over, it's looks like a fine one. When can we try it?"

Paul laughed as everyone climbed into and around his shining small car."I've had it for several months. I'm ashamed that I've not been here more. Before we go home all of you must take a ride in it. It'll hold five with a little squeezing." He watched them as they admired the upholstery,opened the motor covers and inspected the small, power pack, the gears and control mechanisms. They laughed and chattered in the ritual of delight that a new car always received. Andrew and Anna came running from the Temple, Rose and Steve followed a little more soberly. Rose sighed, pleased that this Gather was beginning with pleasure in being with one another.

Inside the house the warmth surrounded them like a benediction, everyone took off their robes and coats to hang them on hooks and piled gloves and hats in a bin at the door. Silvia had already settled, curled up in a deep chair with a hot drink and a hot sweet roll to eat. She nibbled happily, greeting everyone as they came by pulling them down to her kiss. There was talk, laughter, hugs and foolishness such as any family indulges in after a time apart. Hot drinks and hot foods was gathered on plates and soon everyone settled, eating and drinking and feeling the sense of celebration.

The low, deep chairs were drawn close together, great soft cushions filled the circle they made and for a moment there was a hush, as serious eating began. Rose glanced around, "This is like a picnic rather than a Gather." She was smiling, her face felt almost stretched with the excitement and delight and she couldn't stop smiling. "This is the place where we all started. Every time we come together, we always say we must Gather more frequently, but we never do."

Tom was nodding, eating happily, "It is good to get together, I've been looking forward to this time. I for one make a committment to at least eight Gathers next year". Others echoed agreement, but Paul shook his head, "I'd make it six minimum for us, and figure we'd be more apt to honor that. We managed five last year, after all."

It was Paul who set the tone of the Gather, His daughter Rachel slid into the space between him and Ned on the long couch and he slid an arm across the back behind her shoulders. All the children loved to be near Ned, his great tall body seemed, even sitting, to tower over the others but his grin , white in his black face, seemed to express the general mood. Rachel would one day be a handsome woman, not a pretty one. She was now the gangly adolescent who had the looks of her father and the temperament of her musician mother. Paul said,"Steve will be here, he had to finish a ski run this morning and will be late but he wants to be here." Then he took a final bite of his buttered roll, "We've got some serious things to talk about and I don't want to delay. I want to talk about what we've avoided talking about." He watched their faces, unease, hope, fear, confusion, and frank puzzlement, confronted him. "We might as well make things clear at once. We've avoided talking about some things for years, literally. That's no way for a family to be." He hesitated, surprised that he himself was hesitant. Then he grinned ruefully,"What we've got to do is talk about the changes that are occurring among us. We can begin with the talents that are developing among people, young as well as old ones." He sobered, hesitated. "Even more important to me, we must talk about the awakenings, the fact that people are seeing what they call the Light. It's time we talked about the fact that we don't talk about these things."

Will frowned, sitting across the room alone, his arms stretched along the arms of the chair, he clenched the carved wood ends. "You don't mean that! Surely a reasonable man like yourself cannot take those things seriously. Those are notions, they are more simple hysteria than anything else. People don't have enough to do now and they're imagining things to keep them occupied."

Paul sighed deeply,"Notions or not, we still don't even discuss them and we must. They are happening!" Then he laughed,his eyes suddenly warm, "You don't allow us even common sense, Will. I think we have got to take these talents seriously. Whether you want to attribute them to hysteria or not, they are very real in the Valley." He sighed, then looked seriously at Will. "After all, you've got to admit that even hysteria can effect people."

Will looked around at them all, felt himself suddenly separate from them. He was surprised, turned, frowned again, sober, serious. "Well, then,let's look at it. After all, these things have been imagined for centuries and people have attempted to prove that they exist. These psychic Talents, I mean. We all know that no one's proved that there is anything but imagination involved. So why would Valley people indulge in such a dangerous game?" He shook his head, a look nearer to pleading came over his face . "Surely, Tom, Rose, Jerry, none of you imagine these are serious matters!"

They looked at each other. Paul had not expected the question to be whether Talents existed, but what Talents they were living with. He frowned, then sighed.

They'd have to deal with things as they came up. Rose said,"Will, we've been taught all our lives that there is the possibility of -- what we now call Talents - that develop as our inner life is more conscious to us. We know perfectly well that we're aware of more when we practice meditations and enter into that Stillness that is at the heart of our lives. Master Teachers have taught us all these ideas since childhood. Modern children have so much more of those teachings, so much earlier. Our consciousness has been wakened to a greater -- greater Universe. Its no longer hundreds of people aware of transformations. Its in the millions." She stopped, frowned, unsure whether she could prove that, if William insisted. Then shrugged and went on. "We can't deny what we're realizing, William!"She was leaning toward him, her face intent, and that look of pleading there in her eyes."We've learned these things in theory,and now they're becoming fact. We've been refusing what we already know, and what we might be discovering were we not so stubborn. We haven't even been willing to THINK about it. That has to stop before we all go crazy." She stopped surprised at the last sentence, yet she decided it was true.

Will persisted, a small knot of panic like a sharp needle in his chest. "Rose, I read too,you know. I know people write of literal transformation, of inner Light, of what I call mental gymnastics. I think at best they're talking about improvements in their ability to think, maybe greater sensitivity to life in general. But I thought we all knew that ideas of Talents, or especially of awakening, or enlightenments, are theory, they may have some symbolic value, but to take them literally can lead to -- to insanity." His face was full of his distress.

Tom nodded, "I'm having trouble with it too, Will, and some of the rest of this family are as puzzled as you are." Rose blessed him for bringing a 'we' for William to rest in. His intuitive sensitivity to other people would be invaluable today. He went on,"But too many of us are realizing what we've never even been aware of before. I can't insist it's imagination any more. There's a lot we don't understand. You've seen some of the younger children sitting in silence together, and it seems unlike children to you. They don't seem normal, do they? That strange silence among a gang of KIDS? Man that's not imagination, whatever they're doing, its surely something! We can't go on denying !"

Will stared at him, relieved and yet unsure whether Tom was with him or against. "You really mean it. You're going to take it all seriously! You don't think those kids really talk to one another do you?" He looked from Tom to Paul, then to Rose, and finally glanced slowly around the room. They were serious, though many looked confused.

Tom said," Absolutely,I know they communicate, though I doubt they actually'talk'. But they are Touching each other, mentally." He was intensely serious, then he relaxed, leaned back and said, "I can feel them myself because they have no finess." Then he grinned and was absorbed in an image of the children so absorbed they were mentally 'noisy'. Paul wached the image, musing thoughtfully on that power in this brother.

There was silence for several minutes. Every one absorbing and trying to

THE AWAKENING

keep calm. Then Rose said, "We don't have to completely accept everything that we see, nor even what we experience. We do have to talk. Maybe Will's right, there may be some imagining going on too. But the fear of these things is so great, I think we're more apt to err in that direction. Maybe if we can just talk today, and let some time pass, while we think it all through and watch what's happening around us, we could come together when Benjamin comes home and work it out more fully." She knew suddenly that she was delaying again, and wanting Ben there to help. "We're familiar with the IDEA that humankind can and is developing, that we are changing as a people. That's something we've talking of before. But we didn't know how we would change. I suppose everyone had his own pet theory and believed it would be like he or she dreamed it. But the changes seem to be deeper, more fundamental to our very consciousness. It isn't something we can take lightly."

Tom said, "Maybe we need to watch other people, talk to them, find out whether we're experiencing what others are? We ought to ask our own children." He turned to them,"We've not bothered to find out what you folks know, or do!" He grinned at the five children present and saw their solemn faces, unsmiling even at his grin. Then he looked with sorrow at Angela, "Sweatheart, we've not really talked at all to our two boys about this." She shook her head, worried, uneasy.

Tom, nodded curtly,he'd see that was done as soon as the boys came home.Then he said, "It's a big job you know." The room was so quiet that he almost held his breath. He could feel a gentle seeping in of stillness like an atmosphere, that emerged from no where and enveloped them. He sat with held breath, feeling the power of that quiet. He glanced at the children. They seemed to know, to have perhaps even drawn it to them. He sat feeling the comfort of it for moments and then he said so softly it was more a whisper.

"Are we agreed then? I want to know what each of you experiences. We can and will begin to watch, to talk, ask people about their experience? Can we agree to share those experiences with each other when they occur? We won't keep up our denial and silence?" He looked at them all, watching their faces, knowing their agreement even in the midst of their puzzlement.

He cleared his throat,"All right, I'll begin. I've heard that the Valley Council itself recognizes some kind of 'Mind Touch,' they call it. I see people standing sometimes as if in conversation and they are silent, not just kids, but adults too. Then there's the way I know how people feel when they come to see me about city problems. Sometimes I even know what they've come for before they speak. Or the people who commit crimes in our north Valley. I've known before a crime occurred, at least half the time and been on my way before anyone called me. Once I got there in time to prevent it". He stopped, the looks on several faces worried him. "Then there's what can't be seen very well, that goes on inside us. The awakening, its been called, awakening to - what we've not yet named. From all the teachers have taught us, I think it's Spirit. Just as humankind woke mentally, millions of years ago, we now begin to wake spiritually. Have been, in fact for a couple of millinia. But we've only just begun to be fully conscious of it. That's my conclusion. The way I explain it all to myself. Although to be honest, I could never define what Spirit means." He was silent,, letting them absorb that.

Rose nodded, "That's a lot to hear all at once, Tom. It's exciting to me, it's putting into words what I've imagined too. Maybe if we all just say what we've thought these past years, we might come to something." He was surprised that she was uneasy.

He nodded vaguely at her and went on. "Then there's the reaction. That's what I've got to pay attention to. How're people going to see all this? I've got to keep order, keep the town together somehow. It might not be easy. If we ARE changing, we have to remember some will change at a different rate than others, some may not change at all. Some may imagine that there is evil in that difference. Some may imagine evil in the changing itself! Just the way William does." He looked bleakly, but directly at Will." We have to watch assumptions. Assumptions have caused wars, rebellions, horrors our world does not want to ever see again." His voice had risen, and was full, deep and full of urgency. His eyes flashed at them as with command.

The warning at first seemed vastly overdrawn and then, as they remembered the Builders and the unrest regarding them, it seemed appropriate after all. They sat, each one remembering their own brief contacts with that problem, vague as they were, they were real.

Then, Tom broke the silence, He asked,"Just consider this. Have any of you an idea where Benjamin is?" Since everyone knew that Ben had not called home for over two months,and that he never told them where he was, they all looked at him puzzled. He nodded,"Yes, you all know he hasn't contacted us, yet several people here know where he is."

Abashed looks crossed the faces of several and the others watching,caught that look. Surprise brought silence again. Then Ned said, "Well, I'll be damned. So you have kept up with him? I thought you would. And Rose too." He laughed,"Oh, come on, don't tell me all of you are ignorant of Rose's sending. Don't tell me you don't already know that she Reachs mentally, and then that she actually Touchs. You must know that! Or else you've been denying even worse than I have. And I'll admit that I push such thoughts aside without a bit of guilt. " His face was black as a thunder cloud but his eyes were bright and laughing."I'm an adept at avoidance and I practice it diligently." Then his face cleared with his laugh.

Rose felt the old fear flush through her body. How could he have known? It couldn't be! Who else?" She looked around apprehensively. She felt a disappointment at that fear. She had thought it was gone. They were all looking at her. William cool, his face held in tight blankness. He would reveal nothing. She nodded."I know. It's true we've all been denying. But I didn't know -- I didn't dream that anyone -- knew about -- about me" Suddenly she wondered who else. But she went on, wanting the familiar relief of explaining. Explaining would certainly make it alright.

THE AWAKENING

"After all, the Teachers have taught us to be aware and ready. They have told us to watch. It's supposed to be one of the normal skills for those who are -- are beginning to do what the Teachers call 'wake up. We were always confused as to just what they meant, remember? But the disciplines they taught us, made us practice and that we've continued -- body, emotion and mind, all these disciplines, years of them, how could we not discover something more." Suddenly she knew that she was talking beyond any need. They knew all this! She was caught up in the explaining of it, she couldn't help herself and for the first time she saw how effectively this habit of explaining served her to avoid what she wanted to avoid.

She shrugged, just reviewing the ideas helped her, maybe it'd help the others. " We know meditation continues through action, talking, ordinary living lifted to its highest perspective. We've practiced that when we work, play, walk, whatever and the years of that, -- well, it's had its effect, you know. We HAVE touched on centers in ourselves through which we - - we -- see beyond ourselves." She hadn't meant to say that. Maybe they would not notice. Suddenly she felt anxiety, a shivering and a recognition of her own denials more acutely than she wanted. Desparately she continued, the Teacher in herself defending her own fears.

"It's not new actually, it's been going on through eons just as Tom said, only in the past people put realizations into the form of myth, fairy tales, multiple Gods who talked to them, then finally formal religious with one God. We've just refined all that today, become more conscious of it, I think." She stopped, surprised to hear herself. She didn't realize she thought all that

She looked to Paul for help but he only nodded, smiling and finally she continued. "For the first time in history a whole people practice the reach toward higher consciousness. that's the crucial difference. We all learned how to focus, how to sustain attention at the highest point of consciousness. Everyone knows that, although everyone does not continue practice. People get busy at other things. But we, our Family, we've all continued, I think." Everyone nodded, bemused, watching her. Will was the only one to speak.

He said,"Well, it's true, Rose, that the teachers, at least the Master Teachers were always putting us through these rituals, insisting that we learn meditation practices, because they are valuable for relaxation, for business matters, for speed learning, for calming ourselves before a trial. It does refine our thinking, I grant you that we think better, actually. But I've never imagined that it was meant to be used to expand consciousness. I think that's just talk. It isn't real, Rosy. You must know that!" He looked at her with such heavy disapproval that she thought he would think her to blame for everything. She couldn't suppress a smile at the thought though her heart ached.

He drew his body straighter in his chair, even as Ned, lanky and too long for his chair, slid down to stretch his legs out half way across the floor, and Jerry, stretched there with his head on a cushion, rolled over to give him room. William looked around and everyone felt the sudden presence of that quality every citizen of Altos knew, that charismatic attraction, that pull of personal vitality."Let's assume that the Teachings have been actually practiced as you say, for the expansion of consciousness. Now I think all that means is that we've done two things. One, the average person thinks better, abstract thinking is immensely better among ordinary people. Two, we may have touched on some form of organic consciousness, that sense of being open to all life, to all other people. That might have occurred. I suppose if a person focussed carefully, it is possible. I don't know, but I'll accept that it could. However, I cannot believe that it has any practical use at all, except to plant Wizards. And we don't understand what they do. But surely it would not be a way to communicate!"

Tom was curious, now that he had these two born teachers going, "That kind of consciousness you speak of,it's consciousness opposed to what other kind of consciousness?" He was aware that he wanted to push William into a philosophical corner, just to see him work his way out.

But William smoothly went on, as if grateful for the opportunity, his face and manner seemed now to be one of control, command, and he radiated his own power, "Why, of course, the ego consciousness. The greater mind and the lesser. But no one demonstrates that greater consciousness except in the realm of ideas. People use it in philosophy, the sciences, and the arts, of course, to discover, to create even, but there it is. That's pretty much its limit, I think. That whole matter of there being many dimensions of consciousness is one of idea only." He had relaxed, he was on familiar ground."There are hundreds of ideas as to what consciousness is. Who knows?"

"What about our experiences of changing states of consciousness? Surely you acknowledge they're real" Paul shivered, something about this discussion dismayed him. What made Will so stubborn? How were the children faring in all this. He glance at them and to his surprise, not a glazed expression among them, it was as if they hung on his words, were literally willing him to speak more. They were INTERESTED!

Tom turned to him, his eyes clouded, a heavy frown darkening his face."Paul, you're one of the most honorable men I know and as versed in philosophy as Will is. You accept the possibility that there might be a dimension of reality beyond our limited one? William knows the theoretical idea of such a thing. But Will, you insist it's simply idea." The accusation and the request both were critical and William flushed, then as swiftly recovered, and laughed. He preferred to take this as a good debate which he loved and with no holds barred.

Will answered the question himself,"Oh, Tom, of course it's an idea. We've no concrete evidence of other dimensions of reality. We have serious questions about the behavior of atomic particles, about energy fields, but they'll all be proved to be quite sensible, I'm sure. It's like a fourth dimension. We know of it, theoretically, but we don't experience because we are incapable of it. It probably doesn't really EXIST." He crossed his legs, sitting straight and attentive obviously enjoying himself.

"That's where I draw the line here. For you to do what Rose says she does, to Reach out her mind, to extend her consciousness beyond herself, her senses, and to Touch another mind, literally, -- well it's just not possible. You all feel close to each other and you imagine the rest." He almost laughed, but he had too much respect for Rose's mentality to do that. He drew his face into a serious frown."At any rate it is so subjective no one could prove it and there fore how can we know? I agree she may experience some kind of contact, with Benjamin, her true mate. She's lonely for him, she is carried on wings of love and her desire is strong. Desire can create many very real imaginings." He looked all around, his good humor restored.

Rose spoke out of frowning,"So you think that I cannot distinguish between experience and imagining? What do you think that experience brought about by intense desire is after all. It is REAL. It's what we do when we 'focus'. The desire provides the energy." She stopped, astonished at her own words. She had not thought this before. For several long seconds she sat absorbing what she'd said.

Then blinking to realign her sight, she persisted. "If it can happen between me and Benjamin, then it can be extended to others. When a mind is lifted to its highest point - touching as it were, on that level beyond ordinary experience, standing at that interface between finer degrees of consciousness, then there is EXPERIENCE of a point of perception. It's as though we've stepped across the edge of the unknown. It's been called the 'Void'. Philosophers have called it the point at which they must make a leap of faith. The point beyond which nothing we know can take us. But it is also the point at which a glimpse of what is unknown can penetrate our minds. " She stopped, surprised at her own eloquence, her own intensity. She hadn't known that she knew that. "There is no doubt it is EXPERIENCE." She was angry, she blinked realizing that and drew her anger down into view. She sighed, she would not fight with Will.

She looked at Tom and was sad to see a strange look of defeat on his face. Will saw that look too and assumed that Tom had given up the debate, had admitted defeat. Will felt exhilaration. Rose felt a throb of grief, she knew William had not heard her after all. Paul was silent, watching, then Tom felt the soft Touch of Paul's mind at the edge of consciousness. He started, Paul withdrew leaving only a strong impression that they must let this go. They had argued this with Will before and he would go on for hours without every getting anywhere. He had always won, in his opinion. He believed clearly that if he could not know a thing with his senses, with observation and if it could not be proved by repeated experiment than it was not so. Paul had no way to tell Tom he wanted to explore these new thoughts of Rose's.

Here they were, Tom knew he had received a clear image from Paul and was unable to make that known to Will. Rose felt their dilemma, yet she was silent. Jerry watched and listened, fascinated. The children, watched with a puzzled hope in their eyes that worried Rose. Together they knew that Will would not Reach, nor could he Touch even a little. If only they could tell him. If only he would at least believe that they did experience what they reported. How could he imagine them all to be deluded? There were other ways to experience besides the familiar ones, but for anyone unaware, they didn't exist. It was like trying to describe the magic wonder of early spring time to a blind person.

Rose's mind raced, she wanted so much to explain, to tell William that to the mind, Light designated a point of perception beyond thought. At that point knowledge formed as out of an atmosphere of MIND, formed the way a sculpture formed in Annette's hands. Literally it was Mind stuff, unknown to ordinary thinking. That Light, that unknown energy, could and did impress upon ordinary mind what that ordinary mind could not have known through thinking. And that knowing was instant, all perception complete. It was an intuitive process, beyond common intuition even. Out of that Knowing the greatest revelations of art and science had come. Yet she didn't know how to tell that to William. He would have such logical denials.

She had just drawn a deep breath to try when a loud thump was heard from outside and they saw Steve arrive, his body laced with snow, he shook himself,snow cascading all over the deck, then came in and began to unbuckle the belt. His face and hands were well covered. He had ridden through this snow storm on a belt all the way from --then Paul knew that he had taken an air car as far as Adwin. He sighed in relief,not surprised that he knew. Steve removed his outer clothing and came to join them. After he was greeted and provided with a plate and food,he sat down near Anna and Andrew. Anna leaned toward him, her eyes meeting his and a tiny shake of her head was her only visible comment. But he reached out a hand and enclosed her's, his face full of encouragement. Paul watching, knew that understanding flowed between them. He felt a sudden fierce jealousy. Then he felt it subside. Greater even than that jealousy was the profound grief he sensed from Anna. She needed that support.

Rose felt impatience, Paul sorrow, and they both knew that the debate must end. Thoughts fled past Tom's attention, he watched them, selecting and rejecting, wondering whether anyone would find a way. He too wanted to let it all go, to end argument. He finally felt himself accept defeat and that was the sadness Rose felt.

Paul drew himself together carefully and ideas shaped themselves, hurried through his mind, possible images they could Send, and knew that nothing would work. Will would not receive. They could only speak to him through an intellectual process . They could not convince that brilliant mind of what it could not itself experience. Could he be said to be intuitively handicapped?

Thoughts fled past Tom's attention, he watched them, selecting and rejecting. He had already made a choice between several emotions, letting resentments drain away, choosing compassion because both had risen. He said quietly,"Looks like the burden of proof is on us. We'll have to bring you better evidence, Will." He too wanted to end the debate. The futile hopeless argument about something that could not be proved to Will's satisfaction because he could not See. He watched emotions of anger, hopelessness, futility , pity and contempt flood past his attention and he let them all fall away into acceptance.But they had registered and he knew of them.

THE AWAKENING

Paul drew himself together carefully and ideas shaped themselves, hurried through his mind, possible images, ways to present the idea but he rejected that, it was always only an idea to Will. An idea would not make a difference now. He knew of Rose's tolerance, she had known long ago that they would not convince Will of something he had never experienced. Could they convince anyone else so? Paul felt a yawning realization break through his sense of insistence. It was possible there was no way to teach those without inner recognition. At least some trace of that recognition. After all, they couldn't find words to shape what happened into clear thought, how could they convince anyone.

The sun had broken through the clouds, shining now so bright that the world seemed blazing. They looked out, then went to get fresh cups of hot drinks and soup with fresh bread. The smooth cover of snow had not a blemish, not a footstep, it was as though they were silently, softly isolated from all other life.

Rose said, "We need a break, we need to go out and breathe that fresh air. Clear our heads of so much talk. Beauty will heal us, it will inform us. The Earth has a teaching if we listen!" Memories of that last morning with Ben, almost a year ago, filled her mind. The way the snow had seemed so totally to surround them, hold them together. She got up and walked to the windows and as she looked out, she found her eyes blurred with tears. Paul came beside her, holding Jennifer's hand, they stood silently with her. She felt their support and love, and then Paul delicately Touched and she shrank at first from that comfort. Then she turned to them both, receptive. At least these two could make some contact, two at least of this family could consciously choose to Touch. But they Touched and withdrew as though the act was completed.

Jerry turned to her, his face beaming, ""We've missed our chance for a snow walk today, but that smooth purity must not be blemished. Let's stay in here and pretend that it cannot be. Just then, a bird landed on the soft snow on the deck. Its footprints pressing down and making a pattern. Then it flew up away, leaving that momentary record of its passing. He laughed. It does not disturb the beauty at all. Not the way we would!"

Rose turned back to the room, she was smiling faintly at Jerry's comments. But her heart dealt with both a yielding sorrow and a bitter helplessness. She could not allow either to claim her but she could not deny either.

Paul met her eyes, his own clouded, willing, asking and she needed no mind Link to know that. Wasn't this knowledge of one another something that had always been, only now was stronger, more acute and accurate? The others seemed to her relieved that talk had moved to other matters. But how did she know that, if not --? She looked around, saw Anna and Andrew, huddled in close conversation with Rachel and Steve. She told herself they were catching up on events in their lives, they hadn't seen each other for some time, except on videophone and there would be lots to talk of. But suddenly she knew better. How did she know? Their manner, the faintest movement of their heads - their hands? With one accord they turned together to meet her eyes. She was so startled she almost turned away. She knew it would be an inexcusable denial. After all, what had they gathered for? She responded to the clear request and went to them.

Anna spoke as immediately as if there was no question between them, "Mom, we just skirted the edge of it . We could tell Uncle Will that we do Touch one another mentally whether he thinks its real or not". Her voice was so decisive that Rose didn't recognize her . She studied this new daughter.

"Why is it so important that he accept it? " She was surprised at her own question.

Anna was nearly in tears, another surprise for Rose, "But Mom, YOU'VE never admitted and it's something you DO. All you adults are alike, you don't want to realize what's happening even when you experience it yourselves. It's as if you're half conscious! You're all hiding from things, from the very life around you! We're so tired of it, we want to be free of all this hiding, we want to be able to communicate openly and we should be able to. To be fully conscious! That's what our Valley is supposed to stand for -- freedom to live. And also the courage to Know!" Her voice was trembling, to speak so vehemently to an adult, her own Mother. She was aware others heard, and glanced around abashed.

Rose frowned, never had she seen Anna so distressed, seldom had she seen her when so much pain filled her voice. "Anna, can't you see? It's just something we have begun to recognize. We have to have time. Even those of us who know, have to have time to adjust. "

Andrew took up the talk,"But you've had so much time Mother. We love Uncle Will too, you know. We want him to accept us. You've had time to do so much more than you have and we don't want to wait forever!" His voice cracked in a high pitched break,and he swallowed, embarrassed."We've waited, we keep thinking that you'll all open up and talk to us and you don't. We'd hoped for so much from this Gather. The kids told us about your teaching at the Center the other day. And we had such hope. Now, you'll let Uncle William's blindness stop you again. You use him as an excuse." He drew a long breath, all their eyes on her, and she felt the intensity of their need. "It's not just us, Mom, most of our friends are counting on this Gather time. Lots of Families are Gathering this week. We want you to admit what's happening."

Anna turned away, with a sudden burst of grief, and slid her arms around her brother's waist, leaning against his shoulder, one hand still gripping Steve's. Andy turned to hold her, saying nothing else. No one needed to, the depths of their desire was evident.

Steve nodded, touching Rose lightly on the arm,"Aunt Rose,it's true. She's been wanting this so much, counting on it. This talking, to have you all talk about all this."

"Everything?"

"You know , Aunt Rose, You do know!" Rachel moved closer to them, but turned a little away to seek her father's eye. She met his, and heaved a sigh, then turned to them, "Aunt Rose, you must know there're lots of people not just in our Family, but all over the Valley who can Touch. Who know they can. There're more than you know. Not so many who Join, of course. But some who begin to.

THE AWAKENING

Even my Father will try. He's begun to recognize us."

Rose stood, mind racing, her thoughts stumbling through the images and questions, memories, teachings of her life and she had to begin putting things together again. Had to begin paying attention to the intense perceptiveness that her people were discovering, recognizing. She frowned, wanting to be given time, knowing there was no time.

Steve, older than the other three, a little more practical, said, "Why don't we just sit down and try. See what happens? It can't possibly hurt anyone. We'd only Touch and then release, not even try to Join."

Rose turned to him, Anna's tears were gone, she stood now in her Mother's arms, finding comfort and what she felt was forgiveness. She leaned against her mother's shoulder and listened. Her mention of Joining startled Rose, but she refused to pay attention to the question. The incongruity of the whole thing struck Rose so forceably that she suddenly laughed, "Oh, my dears, look at us. We act as if we're facing a firing squad. It's only ourselves after all! Yes, let's try just that. A genuine Touch. We'll tell William if he doesn't want to try he can watch."

She turned to the others, seated now, sipping their hot food, eating the thick slices of bread, or sandwiches made from it. . There was a quiet among them all, they realized the seriousness of the concerns of the children. Rose stood at the edge of the circle, the four young ones taking their places silently among them. She said, "There's one thing we must do today. whether we like it or not, we've got to admit that we can -- that people of this Valley can, Reach out to one another, can Touch mind to mind. At least that much we can admit to?" No one denied it, and there were nods here and there, but she saw the look of bewilderment on Jane's and Steve's faces. Silvia was frowning and bent away from her look, as did Angela. She went on," So let's take some time after everyone has eaten and try to make that mind Touch together here in this room. We could just try, see what we find." Paul nodded and said, "Yes, I agree. We've got to at least find out."

Rose turned to Anna and saw she had filled a bowl and gotten a sandwich. All of them were cheerfully beginning to eat. She felt glad that their spirits were lifted, surprised at Anna's swift recovery. Anna said, "Mother I miss Dad so much. I wish he were here. Right now!" Her voice, so young and demanding, contrasted with her eyes which were serene and Rose thought they held a wisdom beyond her years. She felt disconcerted by that look and bent to her own food.

When everyone had cleared away the dishes and wiped clean the table they found their seats in the big circle of comfortable chairs. Will was grumbling, but good naturedly, preferring to act as if it were all a joke. Paul asked Rose to sit across from him and then, frowning looked at the youngsters. "I suppose you four might as well arrange yourselves one at each corner. Energy flows steadily into a pool if we focus well."

Anna, feeling intense hope, cried out, "Oh, Daddy, it won't matter will it. Energy flows anywhere, everywhere. It does flow but I don't think we can direct it. Not yet." Then her eyes widened, "Or could we?" Her confidence, her tone of assurance surprised him. What had these children become? What were they becoming?

He nodded, disconcerted but agreeable. "Well, suit yourselves then." He sat down and Rachel promptly edged in close to him. He said, "Let's just focus our attention now. Just focus the way we all do in meditation. Just lift, balance, and sustain attention at that highest point of consciousness. When we are centered, entered in that Stillness, then focus your thought toward Rose there. Let's see if we can make a mental Touch. Or whether we are aware of Touching at all."

The room became silent, a stillness like a draining away of time itself seemed to grow around them. Outside the snow had begun falling again, deeper and deeper grew the white cover of flakes, one by one, they fell, but endlessly, deepening the stillness around the farm. The fire burned in the fireplace, an anachronizm in this time, but something Benjamin had demanded to have in his home and now it was enjoyed on special occasions. The flames licked upward, red, bright and comforting.

Rose felt the rising strength in the room, the light Touch of it against her mind. She sat, receptive, drawing that energy to herself, surprised, aware, focussed. There was a gathering power, a light Touch, a withdrawal as if frightened at the Touch, and then the inquiring, return. There was the familiar Touch of Paul, then others, firming the contact, Tom, Jennifer, delicate and hesitant, then Jerry, and Ned though she felt Ned's Touch as a question. For moments the tension held, the contact was firm. Then a strong current entered the mental web, grew with it. They were aware that Rachel, Anna, Steve and Andrew had Joined together and were Reaching as one. The fact shocked and almost broke her balance. Then they Touched so softly, so delicately as if to be very careful, yet that sophistocation evidenced much practice somewhere. These children were far beyond their parents. She knew that both Steve and Rachel worked in mind focussing jobs with plants daily, they were skilled. Why had she not realized they would be. Why had she not put two and two together before.

She stopped thinking, opening her attention, completely focussed. Amazingly Rose realized her body's participation, a current ran through her limbs, streamed through chest and throat and into her head. Then, gently, an unfoldment, as of petals of a flower, her mind extended and Reached. And it was as if she entered into a reverberating circle of mind substance. So unexpected it was, as if electric currents sought, and then in one fiery instant, found one another. The Touch was an implosion, reverberating deep into their mind-bodies and loosening last resistances. Rose realized how much more she was able to experience this, to sense what was happening than she had been at the Council. There her only entrance had been through Grace, protected, guided. Here, they all Reached together. Then, settling, finding balance, they were aware of minds that had missed the initial Touch.

There was Jane, her mind flexible, powerful and alight with some brilliant energy, yet she held away, she would not enter into their singleness. There was Silvia, awkwardly focussing,, but with no focussed Reach. Angela fumbled, began

THE AWAKENING

to focus just as the rest were withdrawing. Steve, Cassandra's father, sat stunned, watching, frowning. And of course, William, unaware.But the others! Their Touch was true, an immensity of awareness, a fulfillment and Rose's heart sang. Then, suddenly it was done and she was alone. The loss like a brief swift pain.

She sat in silence, the others recollecting, Rose opened her eyes, looked around, and said softly,"Well, there's no doubt that we -- most of us, Touched one another. There were some unwillling, some hesitant to even try, and yet,I believe we all COULD. I felt you there, everyone of you."

Paul said, "We've made that contact before, that mind Touch, in the Valley Council and we know that others do. We also know that some who could, will not. And perhaps there are some who cannot -- yet." He let his eyes move slowly around the room, meeting curious eyes, and finally looking at the five young people whose faces were aglow with delight, hope.

William looked confused for a moment, then belligerant,"I suppose you thought you were making some kind of a mental contact? Well, there was none. I assure you there was nothing at all. It is as I have said, all imagination."

Paul said,"Will, you might wait until you hear the experience of the rest of us. You said you experienced nothing, and so let's see what others realized."

The others spoke, Anna, Andrew, Rachel, Steve, Jerry, Tom,Cassandra, Ned and Jennifer. Each said they made that Touch, a powerful mental touch of mind to mind and they did not doubt it. Jane was nodding, her eyes pensive, her face sad,"I knew that there was a flow of energy, a uniting of consciousness, and I wanted to -- to Reach out and I would not let myself.I don't know why.It's so strange compared to the Touch of animals or of plants. But Steve, you've worked with the Wizards a longtime, perhaps you could tell me."

Silvia had been so surprised to feel anything at all that she had been frightened. Mental Touch! Electrifying! It was not intrusive and very brief but it had unnerved her and she would not talk. The elder Steve, shook his head, nodded, and then shook his head again, moved and determined to find out more of this, but speechless now. Cassandra laughed, went to sit on her father's lap."I think it's time you folks knew that all this is what we do. We do it a lot of times at School. Angela was also speechless, shaking her head, her eyes filled with tears for the tenderness and the delicacy of that Touch. She nodded, clutched Tom's hand.She wondered,if these children had this power, what of the two that were hers and Tom's and Mary's. She had never guessed or thought to ask.

Will said,"Well, I'd like to have some kind of statement from all of you. Just tell me."

Silvia shook her head,"Will, I can't. I won't talk of it. There was surely something - as though some one was coming near me. Strange, a mental Touch? I don't know how to speak of it."

Paul said, "You have, very well, Silvia Love. That's a beginning surely.

Annette was silent, but Jennifer put both hands on Andrew's shoulders, so that he sat down on the floor in front of her. She gripped his shoulders, not thinking she could hurt him. She felt invaded, her most private and secret self exposed. She was not sure she liked this. She saw her children watching and knew they wanted her to speak."I know that between me and Paul there's been -- a Touching but it has been very private and now, I feel as though my private self is exposed. Threatened, perhaps".But these were her Family, she loved them all . Why not? Why not make that Touch? Why not share intimately with them?

    One by one they spoke as they could. Rose saw where they were , what development they had reached. She reassured Jennifer that there was such a thing as shielding and that she could teach her, or anyone else. She had had to learn that herself. Maybe one day, they would even be able to do that wonderful thing that Grace had called, Joining.She did not know how to initiate a Joining.

    They spent the next hour talking and comparing, allowing their feeling to subside, their excitements and fears to quench a little. William was exasperated and convinced that they were imagining. He said he hoped his Family was not degenerating into a witch's coven and everybody laughed, but he went out to take a walk in the snow and they knew he had not meant it as a joke. He seemed to take a perverse pleasure in kicking out against the smooth white perfection, in rumpling and disturbing the blanket of silence.

    Ned and Silvia offered to cook everyone a fine dinner and the children were so elated and relieved that they organized a dance for the evening. They went off to arrange for the music and insisted that Andrew and Jennifer must play for them later. Tom and Paul and Jerry with three of the children went out to take a short ride in Paul's new car. Silvia took young Steve to the kitchen computer and they began setting up a special dinner that everyone would remember. The evening began with a return to that quiet joy that a Gather had traditionally held.

CHAPTER TWELVE

Silvia and Ned, Stone Masons

On a clear bright morning in early February, Silvia left the Hall, heard Jerry shout at her and waited for him. She could see the heavy roll of clouds coming down from the north. She hoped they wouldn't disturb this morning's work. A storm today would mean they wouldn't finish the final work on the Industrial Ring this week and she was so anxious that it be ready for the Spring Festival, when Adwin, the town, would be presented to the Valley. The last of the great Rings of Adwin, the Industrial Center was also the largest, covering half a mile of land in its three concentric Rings of barns, warehouses, workrooms, and laboratories Only the facing of the Industrial Hall was left to be done. The working areas, the barns, mills, the winery, the warehouse for manufacturing small farm machinery parts, and business offices were already occupied. Most of these bringing in a growing income. Adwin already was making significant yearly payments on her building loan from the Valley Council .

The two story carved stone facade of the main Hall was nearly finished, just enough yet to be done to make the workers anxious not to lose a day. The town would be ready for the Festival. The thought of that was exhilarating. So many years they had been working on the town, it had become a way of life. What would they do with themselves when it was all finished? She reached up to touch a smooth branch of a young almond tree, one of several along the path to town. It was white with lovely snowy blooms. And yet, there could still be snow. These trees and the very early berry vines, could handle a lot of cold after blooming. Only once in all the years she had lived here had they failed to bear fruit.

Jerry caught up with her and took her arm."Oh, what a morning, Sweetheart. February always seems to me to make the promise that it will be spring one day." He laughed,"Then March comes along and makes me doubt again." He walked easily with her and she found his warm touch especially comforting this morning, she glanced up at his profile above her head. He went on, "For me it's down into Earth again and a fine loss that is on such a day. We've got to finish work on the main food processor or we won't have dinner at the public dining hall this day."

She shrugged,"There're enough cafe's in business now that it'd not be a tragedy. A lot of people are still eating at home yet from winter habit, too. It's during the rest of the year that it'd be a catastrophe."

"Sil, you know the cafes have to have the processor working too. They won't have any fresh frozen vegetables or fruit until we do. And a lot of other things too. But we'll have her done." His cocky air irritated her for no reason.

"She asked,"What's wrong with the processor, I thought they were nearly foolproof. They're gauranteed for a life time and we've only used this one for ten years."

"True, and they are foolproof. We're just adding on another unit. You'll be surprised. You'll be able to dial for gourmet foods that you've never known we could have. It'll put all the hobby cooks in Adwin into a frenzy trying to out do it." He grinned down at her. He was one of those 'hobby cooks'.

They walked in companionable silence for several minutes, then Silvia said,"Look at that storm building to the north. I thought it'd be all day getting here but it's not going to wait that long. It's already blowing a chill down the back of my neck." Berry vines edged the path and they walked on beneath a long arbor where grape vines made a shadow pattern below. Leafless still, they wound through the big beams of the arbor like a net. The grass below grew soft and thick and their passing made no sound. They both remembered when it had been their adolescent task to prune these vines,and to harvest the fruit. They had both resented and been proud of that work.

Silvia smiled, remembering," Look, Jerry, it'll only be a matter of days until that little grove of almonds bloom and the whole path will be lovely. After that there will be something blooming here constantly for at least two months." She smiled up at him and he squeezed her arm, feeling a happy pleasure in this morning walk.

"True, my Love, we've planned well. We've done the best of any town in the Valley, I think." He grinned again, and she laughed at him.

"Every town says the same, you know. And it's good that they do." Her mood had lifted and she seemed so happy that Jerry felt a rush of joy and slid his hand down to find her fingers.

"Honey, it's going to be a special year. Ben will be home soon, spring is nearly here and we'll celebrate the dedication of our town. What more can a man want?" He stopped, a slight frown touching his forehead, but his eyes still danced,he could not tell her what else he knew would make this year special. He looked down at her face, so serious now,and his love for her flooded through him. How much he wished to speak again, to convince her that he must be her chosen mate. To tell her he knew of her pregnancy, to tell her so much more. But he could not. It must wait. She must choose without pressure. But he said soberly, "It's going to be the best year ever."

She kept on walking, wondering briefly whether he could possibly know her secret, and shook her head. He could not! She said,"How do you know?"

He grinned sweetly, his eyes tender and as she met his look, she felt, as she often did, the wonderful charm of this big brown man she loved. His voice was full of joy,"I feel it in my bones. It'll be just as I say. You wait and see."

She laughed softly,"Let's walk a little faster, even this little shade chills me. I want to get to work. We've got to do as much as we can today." They moved out from the first run of arbors and walked toward the second. But their steps were faster, nearly an easy jog. They both ran for sport, and for body health and could easily run all the way to town had they chosen, but Silvia hesitated. She wanted to prolong this walk with Jerry, to feel his presence just this way.

A neighbor rode above them on a belt and waved and they hurried on,

THE AWAKENING

walking single file when the path narrowed through current bushes that should be cut back a little. Silvia touched her belly, secretly full of a joy at the life she knew was there. She knew that Jerry was father to this child, but she did not know that he was her true Mate and she wanted to know true Mating before she made her choice. The brilliant gleam of sunlight from the domes of Altos caught her eye, she asked,"Have you heard anything of the Family in Altos since the Gather?"

"No," He spoke softly wondering why she would not speak of her child, but he drew her closer and they walked again together across the broad width of the Great Highway. No travelers were in sight. "It was the finest Gather we ever had, I think. Makes me glad just to remember it. But I miss eveyone more now. And Rose's worried about Will."

"Will? Old poker face? Nothing could bother him. What's she worried about?"

Paul says that his resentment of the Silent City's blossomed into a mild paranoia and Annette is not at all amused by it. It's hardest on her,I think. Will's petitioned to make the City off limits to flights. He wants to keep people away from Her and to discourage any one from talking about Her. He wants us to forget the City except for that investigating team he's trying to get up there." He shrugged,"Surely he's bright enough to know that'd only make people more curious to fly up there.And that's what worries Rose, he IS bright enough and he's not paying attention to what he'd know any other time. It's not like him."

"I don't know what drives him. He's a puzzle to me, always has been, though I've gotten to love him anyway. He's got a lot of good qualities. I respect him too, for the work he's done. Impeccable precision marks any thing he does and excellence can't be denied. He does seem to be blind to certain things though, and he surely doesn't understand Annette. It's hard on her, you know."

"You think he just doesn't notice things, isn't aware?"

"Jerry, you saw how unaware, how completely unwilling he was to even try to make that - - that Touch, that we all tried. Now, I was afraid, I admit, it seemed strange and unnatural, but at least I tried, and I'm not nearly the scholar he is. I would have thought his normal curiosity would have made him try. But he's got blind spots, he doesn't understand Annette but he thinks he does." She was frowning, her voice full of irritation. "There's something wrong, something missing!"

Jerry nodded. They were climbing the hill and the steepness slowed them considerably,"I agree with you.I don't know what's really happening up there." They walked on, climbing now as fast as they could take the narrow twisting trail, stopping only momentarily to look around. The view as they climbed was always a pleasure, and they liked to look back at the Farm buildings and see it from this point of view. Jerry felt a worry nag at his happy frame of mind. The senior members of the family had always seemed to him sure and solid in their knowledge. He resented that they were unsure suddenly. He shrugged, noticing the feeling and knew that he was plenty old enough to be among those older ones. Rose and Ben were only seven years older but the habits of years as the child of the family were still there.

Silvia walked on, they were nearing the top of the slope and he watched her anxiously. She was not far enough along to show yet, but he wanted her to be careful. He wondered how many of their Family already knew. He was surprised at his own question. Of course others would know.

They could see belt riders circling to land ahead on one grid, and a few air cars drawing close to another. Most of the air traffic was over the industrial center now, incoming supplies and outgoing freight. The busyness roused a swell of pride in his heart.

As they crested the rise into the center Ring knoll, he asked,"Ever taken the time to hover over town and look down from there?"

She nodded, "I've looked when I've been coming in on a belt, but I never actually hovered there to see it. Why?"

"Well, Love, you know Valley towns are designed to be beautiful from the air as well as from the ground, and it's worth a real look. It's as though we've got sculptures arranged in a floral park"

"What did you like best?" A curious envy dulled her tone.

"It's the whole thing, Sil. We've a right to be proud. When we picked the three great knolls to build on in the first place and then planned the three Rings, one on top of each knoll, with living places between , we got something that reminds me of a medieval city, the loveliest kind. You really ought to go and stand there a while, see what we've done. The green forest motes surrounding each Center, the flame of the temple - " he laughed. "I'm bragging, but it's worth it."

She smiled, looking ahead where they could already see the spires of the Temple."Remember the argument about the Temple? We wanted it exactly in the center of town, and people sent up scouts to hang over and make the decision because no one would believe the engineers when they told us. Look, now, it's blazing like a fire through the trees. I still don't know how we managed to do it so well." She turned to him."How'd we ever get it all done, Jerimiah. Looking at it now, it seems impossible that we could have. And I was so young I hardly realized the start of it at all. It was just a way of life."

Jerry started at her use of his full name then, grinned,"There were two thousands people in the beginning, Sweetheart, all ready to work, to live in barracks, eat camp style, until we got the Learning Center started enough to live inside part of the rooms. And more people kept joining us. I think it was the organizing, Tom and Benjamin were part of that, but Elders like Jonothan and Gladys really held us together in the first years. They taught the rest of us what real organization meant" He laughed, "Don't you remember some of it Silvia. Everybody was organized into work crews, even us kids, doing little else but building our town for ten years, aside from raising enough food so we could all eat. It's no wonder, actually. It was inevitable that it would be a great town. We had a lot of people with talent, and you're one of them. The Learning Center looks like an old established town already. We borrowed some useful precedents from Clandor and Santiago, like public dining halls, so we all could keep working, and the idea of including food plants and fruit trees everywhere in our gardens. But we gave another good idea to the Valley, that of bringing our children into the building program and teaching them that way. Then we turned over a lot of the work of caring for the gardens, harvesting, hauling food to the processors -- all that. It made it work." He was talking to himself, adding up the memories, and smiling. Silvia looked at his face, he turned to her,"I love this town, Love. I really do!"

She nodded her own eyes wet, and was surprised at her feelings."It's a great place to bring up our children." She started when she heard what she'd said and hurried to conceal the suggestion. "But what'll we use to set them to enjoying work, to learning how to do things."

He grinned, "Just exactly what we're doing now. There's always maintainence, or improvements on old structures or even building a new residence now and then, adding a third story on to our Ring Centers. Oh, there'll be more to do, my Love, always there'll be more to do." They were silent for some distance, beginning to breath fast with the exertion.

Then Silvia said, It's the ponds and the fountains that make our gardens special, I think."

He nodded absently,"Remember Marguerita? She came to design them and never went home. She's already earning a good credit line with other cities." He was letting his hand brush over the tops of goose berry bushes that lined that walkway. Stiff and prickly, they were alive with fat buds.

Silvia frowned, "You always want things to be the way you dream, don't you Jerry?"

He grinned at her, "Doesn't everyone? I must seem to you sometimes like a demanding kid. But then, how would we have built our town if we hadn't dreamed?

Silvia laughed, relenting,"You're right, Tom and Benjamin fought even then to keep all the plans intact. Some people were afraid we'd tackled too much. Those two were never much for compromise. I'm glad, Jerry. It's a wonderful town."

The path met the circular court from which several paths branched out toward the other Centers. They must separate. He turned to her and she reached up to kiss him lightly, he felt her warmth and a sudden brief hope, then watched her as she went her way.

He ran immediately into a group of youngsters arguing about an idea they wanted to present to the Master Teacher. A girl named Gail thought it would be silly, "He'll think we're nuts." She shouted. Earnest, a short, slim boy walking backwards while they all talked, shouted, "No, he'll like it. At least he'll like the fact that we've got an idea at last. And it's sure not a copy. He says a mistake is better than a copy."

Jerry wanted to ask what their idea was but knew better. He had to get to work. He remembered his own Master Teacher and how hard it was to realize they weren't going to tell him what to do. He looked critically at two small cafes that he was passing, built into the space between offices in the inner Ring of the civic Center. They had been built and rebuilt by generations of students, then run by them, over the years. Some had been more successful than others, but they had all learned about business. He could smell the hot food and decided to sample this group's wares at noon.

Turning around a small fountain court, he descended the steep stairs to the underground rooms. He thought of Silvia and her last words. She'd said,"Have a good day, Love, I've got a lot to think about. But don't forget to meet me when it's time to go home." Surely she saw him as a companion, a special companion after all. But she would be spending this day with Ned. He breathed a great sigh, frowns and then sorrow flickering over his face. She was going to have to talk about that baby soon,because soon there would be no way to pretend she did not have it.

Silvia had crossed the saddle and walked up to the farthest eastern knoll where the Industrial Center was built. The vast outer Ring, nearly half a mile in diameter, was busy with people coming and going, mostly going in for their morning of work. The few small shops and cafes here were already open. The sound of machinery humming, or rumbling in some cases, could be heard as she passed by entire walls open to the morning air. The steady rhythmic beat of the looms, working steadily, day and night, computer controlled, created the hum that seemed to her to be the voice of the Industrial center. Since it's first completed Outer Ring, the mills had begun work and were now established businesses. Air cars hovered in to settle on the roof grids above the third floor ,delivering supplies or picking up orders to be taken out Valley. The mills produced their best income so far. The people who created the new designs and programmed them into the computer, were busily talking and going about their morning work. She felt, as always, confident of the economic welfare of Adwin. She always got a lift from the activity in the Big Ring.

She passed through the dark Archways of the Outer Ring into the center gardens, nearly finished. Already good sized trees brushed against the bottoms of second story windows. Pathways wound through planted beds or curved small lawns. She passed a public dining Hall and smelled the hot food. People just finishing breakfast, came out to join in the busy stream of workers. The Archway through the center Ring was full of the light from the rising sun.

When she came out, she was standing before the Industrial Hall itself, the heart of this inner Ring. The crew who would place the stones she and her fellow stone workers carved,were already at work. Already the facing was more than half done, and going well. It looked good. One unbroken design that seemed to have no joints covered two thirds of the front of this three story building.She grinned in appreciation and pride. She went to her locker and got her tools and a roll cart and went to get the first piece of fine,smooth rose colored stone.

The sky was still clear, though the air had a feel of rain in it, and the breeze had begun, light and cool but not threatening. She looked for Ned. He was not there. Her fellows were pulling their equipment into a spot they liked and getting to work, the steady hum of their tools and the intermittent talk, lulled her gently and she immersed herself into work. Ned arrived, got his tools,a cart and stone

THE AWAKENING

and rolled them toward her. The gardeners were bringing in huge tubs with trees, shrubs and flats of other plants. They were like a small hive of people, their sound a soft murmur. There were many children helping. The Center must be finished and beautiful everywhere by Spring Festival. The paths were being laid,and a court between the twin fountains that decorated the front of the Hall. The fountains were finished and she idly watched people adjusting the pumps that would get the water moving thorough them. She and Ned had made a bid to do the one large sculpture fountain that would decorate this plaza when all the finish work on the Hall was done. They'd worked hard on the design and she hoped they could do it. She shook the thoughts from her head and got to work again.

Selecting a new blade, she studied the carving tool that cut so cleanly into the smooth stone. She'd had it for years, a product of Altos. She nodded to Ned. He seemed absorbed as though something was on his mind, but he grinned and then they both settled in silence. The soft sound of tools, the sigh of a worker straightening to stretch cramped muscles was all they heard, except for the hum of machinery off in the middle Ring.. The sun rose higher into the sky. They worked in silence mostly, steadily the hours passed. The planting crew transformed the bare earth around their paved court into a living garden as they worked.

Finally, she stood up to stretch, went to stand at the Archway through which she could see the hills beyond Adwin and the forests and River running like a silver snake through it.The sun was still bright but the air was colder and the clouds were darkening the northwestern half of the sky. She turned at the sound of footsteps and smiled at Ned, towering above her, his black face shining with a fine sheen of sweat. He was laughing softly, as usual. When did Ned not laugh, as though life were one great amusement? His hair covered his head in a black gleaming hat of tight curls. They stood together there, beneath the roofs of the covered walkways that ran around every Ring. The sun threw variegated colors down through that patterned glass roof of the walkway and they were both splashed with those colors. Ned's face changed, his look suddenly deeply serious and a little sad.

She said,"Jasper - look at it through the trees there in the bend of the River. It's at its prettiest, now, from a distance." They both laughed at the neighborly prejudice and looked out at the changing distance.

Jasper, one of the elder cities of the Valley, had made the people realize again the absolute necessity of learning to live together. There after much struggle and near fighting, the people had called a historic meeting and chosen that Conviction that had been adopted by every city in the Valley. It was carved into most Learning Center walls . "Either we learn how to trust and live in support of each one of us and every nation of us, or we will not survive to live at all."

It had been serious, the memories of the past were fresh enough that people knew the truth of that conviction, were willing to teach it and to live it. A friendly rivalry continued at games during Festivals, even as the cooperative games increased in popularity. Such teaching had become a major practice in every

THE PEOPLE OF THE VALLEY

learning center from toddlers on to the adults. Teachers did not quiz children, testing their memories only and risking humiliating one before his peers, but rather taught by insisting each child persue his own project.

In the early years Jasper had flooded, in a terrible and unexpected cloudburst . Even before the people of Jasper had fully realized their plight, both Adwin and Denlock had crews there. Valley Monitors, already watching from their quiet towers, had sent word. Little had been lost, work crews moved in efficiently and swiftly to carry out what was precious to the people. Within an hour a deep drain had been cut into the hillside so the waters poured out into the River fast enough to leave most homes undamaged. The earth cutters, a type of laser tool from Altos that had never been tried before, had cut that ditch with speed and ease. Afterward, Jasper had built a long, thick wall. Beautiful, broad on top and overlooking the land for miles, that it was a favorite walk way, it curved around the town and butted up against the hills to the north. The people wanted ramps up to the wall from three parts of the town so that there was easy access to Jasper Creek for sports and fishing. Gradually people built on the wall, small cafe's, and even one cluster of residences. The town had the look of a medieval village and was unique in the Valley although it had originally been built as a traditioinal grid of streets and avenues.

Ned shook his head. "You know, Silvia, this is going to be some storm. You and I had better get ready to go home or we won't get there before it gets here."

She nodded absently, lost in the power and beauty of the raging clouds overhead. The full force of the wind was not yet low enough to pound the town, but they could see its effect in the clouds above. The sudden gusts pushed them nearly off balance. Silvia knew well how powerful the northern storms could be especially at this ending of winter. "Don't you think we'd better sound our bells? Let the others know we're going?"

"Yes, I'd love another excuse to ring my bell anyway and even more to cause them all to ring." He grinned and his foolishness made Silvia smile. 'The most infectious grin in town' she'd once told him--then she found he'd heard that from others and didn't like it.

She felt his presence here beside her - the pure physical power of him. A magnetic sexual vigor radiating from his lean, hard body roused in her a response that was simply accepted as part of her enjoyment of Ned. He was friend, lover, brother and work partner. Their lives had been joined for several years. She was not ready to choose, to recognize her Mate. She did not doubt that she would find that Mate, that she would not simply decide on a partner, but would know that she was Mated. She had decided to have a child, because that was important to her, but who its father would be, she did not know. A biological father did have some rights but not full fathering rights. So she waited. She looked up at Ned, their eyes met and his smile was one sided, rueful. "Baby, you always turn me on, you know. Matter of fact, it's one reason I like working here because you and I have the same job and I like being turned on all day." He laughed aloud like a child at her reaction and grabbing the bell, danced a jig as he rang it. Putting his other arm

THE AWAKENING

around her, he swept her into his dance. She was smiling, enjoying the intimacy and the play and glad that he was so able to play with these feelings.

Their feelings, she had decided, could afford them both enjoyment if they were kept on that level, Weighted with expectation, they could cause them to avoid each other. She decided to confront him further now. It would have to be soon any way. Others had begun ringing their bells, clear toned, sweet, they made a chorus of sound. Silvia and Ned were silent, listening. Some who lived near, would go on working for a little time. She turned to pick up her tools and waited for him before they began the walk to the tool shed. She caught his arm, moving close to him. They opened their lockers and she set her tools inside then turned to him.

"Ned, Have you ever wondered how you'd know your mate if you met her? No one's ever told me, maybe no one knows'"

"Well, if you don't, it's because you didn't pay attention to the Master Teachers. They did tell us. They said we'd not doubt it once it happened. The knowing is so strong you KNOW. And then there are tests too. You'll see."

"Oh, dear, I can't believe I didn't even hear that. Are you sure?"

He nodded,then putting his tools into his locker carefully, he turned completely around and faced her. He took her shoulders cradling them in his palms, then tightening his fingers until he held her firmly . In his fierce,intent look, she saw a pain that surprised her.

He said, and his face was dark,"Silvia, you know damn well what you and I feel is too strong to play with. If we responded to it --if we became lovers again, it would get out of hand and I don't want to make a decision that involves our lives and the lives of children on emotion alone. I can make love with women who are my friends, but not you, my dear. Not you.I want to know where I am before I loose all that's between us." He hesitated, looking seriously into her eyes, tender now. Softly he added, "And you do too."

She felt the excitement of his nearness. The intensity of feeling brought a tightness in her chest so her breath came hard. Then she took a long breath, relaxed herself consciously and without words leaned forward to put her arms around him. For a moment they embraced in silence. His long arms reached nearly twice around her. She drew back then, studying his face- its wide mouth, unable to conceal the faint smile even now, the narrow thick beard curling around his jaws and the jet black of his tight cap of hair. Their eyes met again,held. His were steady, deeply serious, filled with humor and with pain. Deep in the grey and gold depths she thought she saw a fear,as though he had met something in himself that he would like to run from. She smiled and nodded,recognizing that in herself too. They stood thus, appreciating the great energy between them and their ability to control and direct that energy. She was glad there was this understanding between them. They could talk, or be quiet, and there would be understanding. She thought of the talk in the family, at the Gather, about the Reaching--the Touch, that the others had said they practiced. Was this in any way related? That they knew so deeply of one another? She let the thought fade and said carefully, choosing her words ." How would you feel about being the father of my child?" The question seemed terrible to her but she had to know for sure. There could be no room for doubt.

For a moment he seemed not to have heard, except for a quick movement of his eyes, then he grinned and said,"Sil, I'm the kind of man who is going to be a father if I have to HIRE someone to bear a child or two for me. You know how I feel about children, about watching their growth, guiding their development, loving them , earning and keeping their trust. Everybody else in town knows so you must too. Therefore... I would be delighted to be the father of your child, whether I created it with you or not. To love and to help bring him or her to adulthood. It is a great profession, being a parent. It is a great art. I think it might be my most pure talent."

Silvia nodded and smiled, "I think that's true.I envy the children you will raise. I've seen you working in the children's classes, in their fields study and labs, and there's always something happening between you. I hope whatever happens that you always have a lot to do with my children.

"No way I won't" he said.

They moved out of the way of others coming with tools. Jerry called from the other side of the Archway, impatience in his voice. "Hey, you two, we won't make it home unless you get a move on."

She took Ned's hand then, holding it gently and protectively. It was a hard strong hand of a craftsman, much like her own. She felt a great tenderness toward this wonderful alive part of him. He pressed her fingers briefly, waved to Jerry then turned to walk toward the gateway. He called to others who would be going his way and joined them.

Moments later, Silvia and Jerry were walking thoughtfully along the path that led to home. It was only a mile walk, which they usually enjoyed. Now there was a feeling of urgency as the damp wind and lowering sky warned them.

"We should have ridden belts in today." fretted Silvia trying to keep up with Jerry's long strides,."Or we should have borrowed some to go home."

"Jerry shook his head and walked faster, taking her hand to keep her with him. "We sure didn't read the weather well this morning. We all knew it was coming but not so soon." He spoke almost angrily, irritated at the mistake.

"Neither did a lot of other people. After all, there's no such thing as a totally reliable weather prophet, thank God." She spent the next few minutes keeping up. Then she said, "Anyway, it gives us time to talk."

Jerry glanced down at her, exasperated."What a time to pick for talk. How're we going to breath at this pace. " They were both used to vigorous work, but the hurry of their walk was taking their breath. It would have been easier to run."Maybe we should run, to keep warm."

Silvia shook her head," Wait a bit." She needed to think how to say what she wanted to say. She was afraid of his response.She frowned, it was always that fear she used to keep from asking hard questions. This was going pretty well so far, she had to get it done. She said abruptly, the easiest way "Jerry, I have a

THE AWAKENING

child growing in me."The blunt statement seemed awkward to her. She searched the face turned toward her, but he smiled a sweet, tender smile and bent his head, pressing her hand. She said,exasperated,"You knew".

He nodded. The smile broad, smug. It pleased him to surprise her.

She didn't feel pleased,"How, Jerry, How can you know?"

"Honey, I'm...I... Oh, Sil. I just know.I'm so pleased we can talk about it now."

She studied him, skipping a few steps to keep pace. Then in near gasps she asked,"Does it have anything to do with what we talked about at the last Gather. That-- 'Reach' that we all tried to do?" He stopped, turned to her, his eyes searching her face,and he nodded. She went on,"Then you must know too that this baby is your own?" Again he nodded and she frowned,"You must feel something about -- about it. I need to know."

He turned to continue their walk but he held it down to her stride. "Hon, you know how I feel about you and that more than anything I want to be our child's father. But mostly that I want to Mate with you,not just marry you. I KNOW my committment to you but I don't know yours to me. You're younger, and we're -- different too. But I know what's right for me." He turned to search her face again, his smile faded. He was uneasy. Had he sounded patronizing, like an older brother?

Silvia was thoughtful."That sounds pretty clear. It makes me feel good, Jerry. But I also feel worry. What do you mean when you say you want to be father to our child?

"Isn't it obvious? A father is - wait - are you asking me whether I want to be a Mate to you, rather than a father to our child?"

She spoke softly then, gently, knowing that what she was saying might cause him pain . "Yes, Jerry, I think that's what I'm asking. I know nothing could prevent you from being a father to your child. And your relation to our child will be between the two of you. Whether you and I decide we're Mates is another matter.Do you see?"

He nodded but said nothing, He pulled her into a slow run as the gust of wind grew harder and the rain slapped against their faces.

Silvia finally slowed and spoke again, "You see Jerry, I honestly don't know what my feelings are now. There's so much to think about. Just now, with Ned, I couldn't speak positively and I know that's mean of me.It's not fair to either of you. But I can't decide just because I feel I'm being mean." Her face twisted in pain at these thoughts and he stopped.

The wind blew his long dark hair down across his face. He caught her shoulders much as Ned had done, his eyes narrow as he looked at her searchingly. Then a strange smile played across his face, moving the muscles of his jaw slightly as if some inner joy pushed itself through, nearly breaking the surface of his feelings. He was puzzled by the conflict of this joy underlying the tight pain of his fear and anger. Strange things emotions, they never seemed to order themselves very well.

Silvia discerned more of this than he meant her to. She knew Jerry's feelings

THE PEOPLE OF THE VALLEY

were more complex than Ned's. She had been longer with Jerry, their intimacy was shared in real affection and love that had grown over years. She knew that her own confusion must be resolved and soon. For this baby there must be a clearly welcoming world, a father and mother ready and able to be committed. She must handle her own feelings so that nothing endangered this necessity of her child.

Jerry spoke then again with that flickering half smile that confused her."Honey, there is one thing you have got to know. You have got to realize that both Ned and I are able to handle our end of things. We can take care of ourselves. You don't need to take on the worry of three adults! We both enjoy your mothering, but that's going too far. Don't worry, especially about our child. I am a father and will enjoy being one. Ned is a father to every child he ever saw already. He has it in his bones. You have only to think of yourself now." His smile now was for her like sunshine breaking through clouds. It relieved and heartened her so much that tears suddenly came.

'Jerry, Jerry, she thought.How great you are.' Then, remembering, she added, 'How great they both are.' He looked at her with a quick frown and then said quietly, a special gravity in his voice, as he turned and caught her arm again to hurry on. "No, No, sweetheart,I'm not. Maybe Ned is. Rather, I'm learning how to live just as everybody is. "

They resumed the smooth light run that would bring them to their door in minutes. They were climbing the hill below the farm and the steep path seemed less so now that they had their second wind. For moments her mind seemed blank, then she realized what he had said.She was amazed and uneasy, what he had said had been - been impossible. She cried out, just as they stepped into the paved roadway below the Hall."Jerry, You answered what I was thinking, You answered what I was thinking!".She withdrew her hand, stopped dead in the path and stared at him, the rain soaking through her hair and pasteing it to her face.

"I'm sorry, but the images were directed at me whether you intended it or not and you must know by now what that means. You have to, after the Gather anyway. I could SEE the images you had made, of me and Ned. I am Rose's brother, you know,. What she does is not far from me.I don't want to have to go on being so careful about what I respond to. When people shout mental pictures at me, I have a right to answer. " He glanced toward the sky, the spits of rain had stopped, but the grey wall of cloud was descending and ready for real business. There would be a down pour in minutes. He was suddenly impatient.

"Oh, come on Silvia, we all know that this is a natural talent and that it's pretty common too. We just haven't admitted it. Just when it happens to surface in our own family it can't be ignored anymore. Your own best friend has that talent more than you know. Even more than she knows,in fact. and she didn't feel right about telling you, But you do know." With a frown he went on, "After all, the father of our child should have certain privileges." He spoke with such innocent resentment that she smiled,then laughed aloud.

"At least it made you offer me a little ordinary human resentment. I think I'm

THE AWAKENING

more afraid of your generous tolerance of other people - of my meanness and resentments, than I am of your 'talents."

They began to walk, she held his hand tightly as if somehow she might lose him. They wound around the Hall and then out into the garden that let them onto the path to the deck. Neither wanted to go to their own cottages. They had passed Jerry's hut, sunken into the hillside, and he had not thought of going in. A thin curl of smoke came from the chimney of the Hall. They thought no one was home. They had seen three in the fields below as they passed around their knoll. The children were in town? Or where? It wouldn't matter, they knew how to get home. They would go in and turn the heat up, begin dinner and a hot meal would be ready for everyone.

They stepped under the covered part of the deck and stood a moment watching the world darken and the sleeting sheets of rain make everything grey. Silvia said,"Someday Jerry, you and I must talk about these things, these Talents. But right now, I want to confess what I just realize,. I do resent goodness in people., I don't know why. I don't admire you when you're petty like me, but I feel better. Maybe because it give me a little excuse. I feel less hopeless about myself." Her voice was serious, her face frowning and sad.

He nodded, pulling his jacket close. "Believe it or not, Sweetie, I know exactly what you mean. It must be a common feeling. But you can't think that I'm 'good' because I'm different. Whatever little goodness is in me has been learned and struggled for because I want to learn how to be so. That's a fact. A struggle it always is, I think. Maybe there are some people born good but I've not known them " He looked at her, thinking they ought to go in the house but he was reluctant to end this talk, it had not been easy for Silvia to begin it. Maybe the storm gave her courage."As far as the talents are concerned, you know that you've been at least aware of Rose's linking, her Reach out to us. She hasn't been too secretive, thank heavens. But then, we do have similar characteristics. At first it scared me to sense her Reach, then finally one day, I knew that she had Touched my mind. A conscious mental Touch, you realize. It was a strange sensation. Like something unreal that was also too real. It isn't something a person takes for granted. I just closed up, held her off and -- actually, she wasn't sure of herself. She didn't insist.

He stood, silent, remembering,"I'm not sure she had any idea she had actually Reached me. We have been so slow, so much denial. It's amazing we learned anything at all. If it weren't for the constant deep attention, the meditation and the Light Itself -" He stopped, at her puzzled look. He held her hand tightly, wanting the talk to finish, wanting to get it all said. "You know that she does that other thing. She leaves her body, actually, Silvia. It's not just a notion, she actually does it and she spends time somewhere that's not in this physical world. She feels afraid to tell us. I know only because I tried to follow her once until I got scared and withdrew." He felt her hand wriggle in his own and tightened his grip.

"Don't worry Jerry, I'm not going to run this time. I know we've got to talk more, got to talk about all these things. But I'm not going to accept that. I don't mean I don't believe you, but I can't accept what I can't see, you know. Maybe some day, I'll understand.

He let her hand go, touched her cheek gently with one finger and said,"It's true, it's hard to believe, maybe a person actually can't believe it until it happens to them. I remember when we were in our teens and I fell in love for the first time. Well, my friends had been telling me what it was like, and yet, well--I sure wasn't prepared at all. It's not something you can tell anyone". He was silent, watching her,"There's something else. I think you need to know." He grinned, his eyes dancing with a laughter she wondered at. " I feel a sense of your own amazing 'goodness'at times., Something in you that is so balanced, so truly loving.:" He laughed at her expression of astonishment and disbelief. "You see, it isn't easy to hear what's good about us."

She didn't answer, she opened the door, shivering finally, She really didn't believe him but she didn't want to talk about that at all. She said,'You spoke of - a Light? What was that?"

He shrugged,"Something else, something - " he shook his head, his face tight,"It's beyond my understanding, but maybe we can talk about it. Maybe the next Gather!" She wanted to insist, but his eyes were so far, so full of longing. They turned in the Hall entrance, to go to work.

She switched her mind to the tasks ahead, getting everything ready for the others when they came home. However, she was aware of a glow of warmth that he had spoken his admiration for her.

As they moved about the house closing windows and bringing in anything left out,unnecessarily checking the auto-heat which was as dependable as any equipment on the farm,they each found their thoughts wandering. Silvia gathered an armload of broken pieces of dropped branches they had brought in from the woodland and as she ripped a resinous pine oil over the top to start the blaze, she began to think of the journey home. A journey that neither would ever forget. She stood waiting for Jerry at the door way to the main Hall ,the fire behind her sendng bright color onto the stone walls. So many feelings stirred in her. She didn't want to explore them just now. She wanted just to withdraw into the comfort of quiet warmth.

Jerry went about the methodical work of checking the house he thought of the emotions turbulent in him. He knew his desire, the power of it, the demand to possess, to be secure in the absolute committment of another to him, to enforce that commmittment. Anachronistic - and yet - it was still awake in him. He went to the kitchen and found that someone - probably Steve - had started a pot of stew in the slow cooker. It smelled wonderful when he lifted the lid to stir it. He turned up the heat and tasted it.

Silvia went up to swiftly check the second floor, ran lightly up the stairs to the attic rooms, encouraged by the violence of the storm outside.. She wondered how they would resolve all the rising differences, confusions. What could Jerry do with the flames of anger that she saw now and then break through the warm patience of his eyes. What of those moments when he seemed on the verge of telling her

THE AWAKENING

something, and never doing it. She thought there must be more than one person living in Jerry's skin. She felt a sudden eagerness to know the parts of him and allow him to know her as deeply. She thought, unless I can balance all my own confusions, I can never link, never make the Touch. And then, there's still the Joining. What can that be? What is this all doing to us? She shook her head, to even think of that strange experience troubled her. Five years ago she and Jerry, finding themselves all alone like this after a hard day's work, would have sought a room upstairs and made love, lost themselves in the joy of it. But now, that pleasure seemed pale, empty, before everything else. She remembered that time, only a month ago now, a special time with Jerry, but fringed with loss even in its pleasure.

She went to the window to the north east from which she could see the fields where Steve and Jane would be. They'd surely be coming now. She opened the window, felt the sting of wind and fine rain, liking the hurt of it. Slowly she brought stillness into herself. Felt the steady loosening of her body and mind. And then she knew a focussing, extending her attention until it encompassed a visual image of Jerry, then of the Family, spaces opened in her heart, there was room. She could- did Love more than one. There was room for the loving of many people.

She remembered when her Teachers, not so long ago it was, had taught them all that loving was not desire, was not need, and that if they were to learn to Love they must also learn to love without desire. Or at least to know that desires were a small part of that Love. They had said that, and the children had listened and believed and known that what they said was true. even though, then, in that youth, they could not understand the complexity of it. The difficulty.

She stood still, letting her mind range backward to a time when she had been shaken by a Touch from Something beyond herself. Yes, beyond, for it was not familiar but when Rose talked of what she knew, it so reflected that moment. A Touch of the Love Rose described. "Beyond myself", she whispered, "beyond my ability to realize". Forlornly she shrugged. "I could never be part of that! If it exists, it's for those who are greater people than I am." But the longing to know such Love persisted, swept from her heart like a breath of intense desire. That old brief memory caught her up in a tenderness of hope.

She knew that she had not 'learned'(if one ever could) that kind of Love. She thought she was not large enough to stand beyond all the needs, desires, hungers that clamored. Maybe Jerry could show her how to encompass these needs in such a transcendent Love. But then, someone had said that Love itself transcended all such need. That would be another matter, surely. Then would she be able to Reach? To Touch and maybe even finally Join? The thought excited her, but was also frightening. How could she sustain, keep herself safe in such a giving?

She shook her head, wanting to let it all go, to do no more thinking. How does a person stop thinking? She laughed. That in itself was a practice. She wanted the evening to be one of peace. She looked out over the fields and recognized three small figures moving up the hill toward the Hall. Surely she loved them, her heart reached out to them, wanting them here, safe out of the storm. And yet, she knew that she also felt resentments, jealousy, toward each one of them . There it was. She refused to believe that Love and jealousy could exist in the same heart. She was convinced that it was because her heart was not empty enough for Love to enter. In the darkness that was the absence of Love, angers bred.

Jerry took a spoonful of stew,then another and drew back. With careful resolution he put the lid back. "Wow, I'm hungry, but it'll not be right for another half hour."

His mind gnawed on the conflict that gathered in a twist in his chest. Tight and burning, it would not cease. If he could not have Silvia as Mate, then he wanted no one else to. If he could not make his life with her, he thought he could make it with no one. And as the angry thoughts formed, he grinned. "So, you think those old attitudes will work in a modern man. I also want her to have what is her choice. What else would be worth it?" He sighed and then the flickering smile of his heart, that softened the edge of conflict and gave him vision as from a higher point, won out. He felt the conflict fade, the anger settle like a heavy weight that shrank as it lost his attention. He loosened, straightened and the inner smile extended to illuminate his whole face and body. It would be all right.

Silvia noticed the change in his appearance immediately when she entered the room. Her love for him surged then was darkened by a swift rush of anger that his beauty was another demand upon her to comply and to fulfil his longings. She laughed when she realized that. He heard the bitterness in her laugh. She knew the truth that he demanded nothing. Nevertheless, his refusal to demand seemed perversely to anger her.

Jerry said,"You know, Honey,sometimes I want to snatch you up and carry you off to my castle in the woods and say,'Now, you do what I say .' Is that awful?"

She had bent her head, he could not see her eyes and doubted that she shared his humor."No, because sometimes I want you to do that too. It's so much simpler,Love," She dared not meet his eyes. The fantasy lived itself briefly and faded. She was struck forcefully with the knowledge of what she wanted in a Mate. What a Mate had to be. She shook her head, resolutely refused to think more and went to get glasses and some wine.

They sat feeling the warmth, the resting after hard labor, and the secure pleasure of a safe place in the storm howling outside . It was their own wine, home made and a quality red. They could hear rain against the windows. The wind was still gusting and strong,but it had dropped its high whine and was only a drumming around the chimneys and the trees. Silvia sank comfortably into the pillows beside the hearth . Jerry stretched on the couch,slid off his shoes and put his feet up. They were silent, not thinking, feeling the pleasure of the moments.

Finally Jerry set his wine aside "You know,Silvia, we live in a wonderful time. We were born in a world where people still saw Love as an ideal, something to strive for. But we're now grown up in one in which people know it is a fact. That

THE AWAKENING

Love is something people are capable of sharing. We seriously believe that we are able to Love each other and we know the difference. That's why you and I and Ned all have such a problem deciding and coming to terms with each other. We don't say that we 'should' love, but that we are able to love. That is the difference."

"I think we've realized that Love is a Presence we can be a part of. I think it enters us through the heart."

He was surprised, Silvia didn't usually speak so clearly of old Teachings. The change in her set him off a little. Perversely he grinned, deciding to joke, "Well, it does include our bodies my dear, it does indeed. I think my body knows of Love through that power of it that pours into me from the heart. It fires up every nerve and cell and especially when I look at you, sweetheart!" He turned to her and this time she met his eyes.

But she only nodded, grimacing, and then she smiled, "You're a clown." They were silent again. Then he began to speak and she knew he spoke as much to himself as to her. She did not interrupt.

"To Love another person-- what does that mean? We've lifted up our capacity to Love, so that it comes through the whole being, Mind, Heart, and body, surely, that is so. And there is such a pull from the body, that old hungry pull that can get us off balance. To overpower us in favor of itself. I've had to deal with that a lot lately. And so I've thought a lot about it. I decided Silvia, that what this means to me is allowing the other to be wholly what she is, no false expectations, no demands that she fulfil my needs. Yet my needs are there and I wonder if I can take care of them alone. I do need help with that. I do need you, my dear. But I can take care of them too. I have found that out. No one and nothing can fill that bottomless pit that I fall into now and then, that terrible need. But then, that's something I must heal in myself. Maybe even see a Healer. There it is, if I can't take care of myself, what good would I be to you?"

"Oh, Jerry, when I make a choice, I want that man to be taking care of me and I of him. I want a mutual loving and caring, not a separate self sufficiency."

He laughed, "Ah, don't worry, Dear Heart. It's not being separate, just not being so dependant. Oh, there're so many ways we need each other that make life delightful. I don't minimize that."

She nodded, seeing that he meant it, seeing that he wanted to give her unlimited choice, and seeing that she didn't know whether she wanted that much choice.

"I think, we need each other to help us heal ourselves. To help us to learn to be complete". He heard no self pity in her voice, no sadness, only a simple acceptance.

"You've already done that so many times for me, Love, you must know that". Jerry turned now more directly to her, his face tender, "Our loving has always been so happy, so full. The healing is happening. We know enough now so that our children will not need so much, will not have that empty hunger in them. Always, when you and I are together, it's as though we - fit- and are right.

Perhaps that's only my wishful thinking. But I think it's true."

Silvia heard herself reply, "What can be done to relieve the ache of it, Jerry? He nodded absently,"It's the Mating that ends it. If there is a Mating for us."

"The Teachers say that when we are capable of knowing Love Itself, it is not less for one than for another. Yet, there is the Mating, that is something else isn't it?" The problem seemed to much for her now.

Jerry was solemn, looking off into the space in front of them, not even focussing on the fire that was bright orange ,warm and comforting and a perfect place for this kind of talk. The heat wrapped around their bodies, creating a drowsiness lovely to slip down into. "See, the little pleasure of this heat and comfort? Here is healing, this little thing. How simply our bodies can be nourished. And that greater need, that stands like an unceasing reminder in our minds is not so easy to fulfil".

"Then there is -- until that time of Mating at least, the learning how to comfort and wait. To see the pain, the longing, and to recognize it without pity. Then to seek comfort, from whatever source, a warm fire, good food, loving friends, and all the good things of life even. I think it's the not knowing that makes it hard, not the losing." He had spoken without criticism and she heard that but she felt a twinge of guilt.

"I know that, Jerry. I think I must make a choice and be clear in it sooner than I had thought. It's not fair to either of you this way." She sighed and nodded. "Right now I'd like to just relax, forget the problems of our lives and soak up the heat and quiet before all the others get here. There's nothing demanded,nothing needed, just being here content and at ease is so good."

He smiled, closed his eyes, knowing that her promise was serious and he would not have too much longer to wait. She curled up in her cushions and listened to the crackle of the fire and the rain on the windows. They heard a door opening, and it seemed far away, voices, soft, distant, and then they did not hear.

CHAPTER THIRTEEN

New revelations, new beginning .

While Jerry and Silvia hurried home from their day's work, others on the farm also looked anxiously at the sky, moving as fast as they could to complete their work. Below the hall, in the fields near the Green river, Rose and Steve waited for Jane.

Jane ran with the peculiar grace tall women often have. Her fair hair, bound behind, bounced against her shoulders and her face reflected all the satisfactions of a job accomplished. A job she loved. All her life she had heard, applied to herself, the phrase,'run like a deer'. The wildness in her responded to that image, the shy, light, soundless flight of deer through shadowed woodland.

This winter afternoon that running was not light. She ran across a broad field from the three cornered shell in which she had left the day's tools, the autotiller and the boxes of seeds. She'd got the tools in before the first drops fell but now she thought she would be soaked before she got across the field and home. At least, the field's deep loam would absorb enough water so that she would not have to cross in mud.

Rob barked and danced beside her. His voice full of the delight he always felt when anyone ran with him. She reached to touch his head and laughed at his joy. But though there were drops, big and cold, the rain seemed reluctant to begin in earnest. It was early afternoon but the clouds were low, and early darkness descended with the throb and weight of atmosphere characteristic of storm. She was aware that the wild creatures had already dived to shelter, hidden in deep dry burrows. The break from threat into actual rain would be a relief, a lift of the heart even though this storm would be one to continue into the night.

As she ran, she could see the mist beginning already to rise from the Great River , spreading in over the low fields. The world shrank, her clothes felt damp and the two figures across the field stood still watching. Her feet sank slightly in the soft earth. Earlier in the autumn, pulverized stalks and leaves had been spread roughly through the field and on top of it, a thin layer of fruit pulps from the processors at the Main hall. Town vegetable and fruit pulps went on town fields first and then the farm people could bring their share to their own fields. She knew this field was well mulched, she felt the sponginess against her feet.. She glanced up at the heavy clouds, feeling a joy and eagerness for this storm. Last summer had been hard work, wonderful work and the harvest was good. By the time it was winter, she felt ready to leave the land to itself and withdraw into her warm cottage and into good family life at the hall. Winter was a good time to rest and think and do some study at the Center. But there were always a few repairs that brought them out on sunny days, and this morning had been bright She stopped, waved to Steve and Rose, bent to touch Rob, caught her breath and then continued slowly. She could feel the moist softness about her and the sense of power, the immense gathering going on through the air, the tremendous energy of movement as molecules drew into themselves more and more, like a vast streaming from everywhere to form droplets.

Ten years ago, Jane would not have imagined that she would end up here in the community of a Farm family. She who had been raised in more than a dozen cities, learned from the most fully equipped learning centers in the world, and was familiar with people of world renown from her childhood. Her parents had been of that small percentage of citizens who never settled in any city, or country. But rather spent their lives living first in one and then another. They felt at home and had friends in several cities and these usually the major cities of the world. They thought of the country as some place to visit for the day, but not as a place to live. Jane had followed them peacefully until she was old enough to develop her own strong interests. Then she had protested. She had settled into a Learning Center in one city and demanded that she be allowed to stay there until she finished the training. In those years she chose three of the cities her parents frequented and made them home. Her brother had happily followed her parent's style of life. They were called 'city gypsys'. Jane had met Rose while Rose visited the city where Jane studied. A short time later, she had come to visit Adwin as it was being planned and built. Had left, then returned and had watched, become interested as the Farm was found and planned and then, after a year of indecision, had returned to ask if she might be part of that life. She felt herself fully and irrevocably 'at home'. Her family had come to visit, she had visited them, but she had never left her new Family for long.

Steve's people had been more ordinary. They lived and worked hard to help create their eastern city, to build it and to plan it's life according to the world Constitution that provided for the creation of environments within which people could recreate their lives. His family had lived at the edge of the city they helped to build. The forests and fields surrounding the city were wild and undisturbed, they grew against the back walls of the great circle towers that were the apartment complexes for this city. The young boy had enjoyed the paved pools and playgrounds of the parks surrounded by the circle of towers where all city business was done. Towers that reached a hundred stories, with bridges vaulting from roof to roof. It had been a good world, where children and adults found what they needed to entertain themselves. But Steve, like many of the citizens, loved the wild lands that surrounded their city. Steve loved to roam through the forests, to know the creatures that lived there. He was acquainted with the people of the small villages near his city and grew to envy them their feeling of belonging to one another. Most of his study in the city's Learning Center had been of that forest land.

When he was sixteen, he left home and traveled, went to live for a time in Africa in a high bowl shaped city called Eichano. There he had met Elana, the woman who became his mate and the mother of Cassandra. All had gone well in this city that sat like an immense white bowl in the green ocean of forest. Built

THE AWAKENING

much as Bend was later, it fascinated Steve and he felt ready to commit himself to it as permanent citizen. For seven years they had lived there. Cassandra, born in their second year together, grew to love the place of her birth. Then during a camping trip into the Jungle, an accident, a violent storm, and Elana had been killed by a falling tree. Steve could not forgive himself nor the forest. He had not been able to return to their home except to arrange for their things to be packed and stored. He took Cassandra and returned to his parents home for weeks and then set out to search for another place to live. He had never returned to Eichano except for a short visit just a year ago, to find out whether he could begin the healing of that wound.

He had met Jerry when he was younger, during a period of Vagabond travel near that eastern city of his childhood. They had become friends and in his grief he had sought out that friend and come to the family. In a few weeks he knew this was a place he could live. Jane loved him almost from the beginning . But Steve had remained aloof, reluctant to even allow close friendships. Gradually their affection had grown and he could pour all his love into Earth and the fields and the raising of food for their community. Slowly the healing of his pain occurred. Rose took Cassandra into her own life with her children and loved her as her own. They watched Jane coming across the field, they smiled at her wonderful energy, her grace and delight of life.

Jane felt the growing weight of air, the change from light, airborn particles to that heavy globe of rain that surged and lowered, eager toward its reunion with Earth. She felt the breathing of energy, the gathering of electrical charges through the entire sky. She felt herself there, high above, one with that energy, powerful and brilliant.

Suddenly as she reached her friends, the stillness ended. Great gusts of wind pushed at the trees, made her catch her breath and flung debris,straw and leaves all over them as they began the climb up the slope to the Hall. They stopped, turning their backs to the wind, shielding their eyes with their arms and waiting until the gusts had passed for the moment. Rose seemed preoccupied, defending herself from the onslaught mechanically,without real concern, but Steve frowned and brushed the damp broken leaves from his clothes. Jane laughed,exhilarated, while she combed her tangled hair down with her fingers. Something about the storm was exciting, promising, waking in her something she could not name. Rob sat now, watching, alert and hoping for more action.

Steve looked at Jane as she laughed and said, "You like that attack Huh? Well not me. It isn't a comfortable feeling,the roar of that wind rasps against my bones. I think it's going to be a bad storm. It makes me uneasy."

Jane was puzzled. "I do like it. I like the wind and the dark lowering clouds. I feel good out here against it and in it." She was watching the swift,scudding edges of dark cloud. Steve shrugged and ducked his head as they continued the climb. He had never talked much of his Mate's death. No one knew about the circumstances.

Rose glanced over at him, her heart ached for him. She knew the memory only as a shadow in his mind, but it stood there so powerfully for moments that she could not but notice. She shook her head, startled at the intensity of that flung image. He did not know he revealed anything at all. She mentally shielded herself, stood looking off at the mist tangled trees , walked with dragging steps, feeling the power around her, Earth's reach to draw down sky gift. Then a faint smile touched her face,she seemed to listen, to see something far off. Jane touched her arm, puzzled at her expression. But Jane went on talking to Steve.

"You feel uneasy Steve? What brings that?"

"I'm not sure. I - it's probably just not knowing what might happen. The winds are almost enough to blow us off the hill." He tried to laugh but it came out a grunt. He thought of all those times when he had wanted to talk about the fears, the terror of storms, the dread that sat at the pit of his stomach when the winter storms began and especially when, as now the violence of late winter storms erupted unexpectedly down on them. The quiet steady monotony of winter rains were no problem. But he knew he ought to speak, after all, he'd decided to begin his healing hadn't he? "It's just - just that I've lost so much in storms." He drew a long breath and said it,"There was that storm my wife died in!" The words seemed to rasp from his throat.He went on hurriedly as if to push away from those words, "But then, even earlier, when we lived on an island in the hurricane Zone, there were frightening storms. I was a very young child that year that my mother was hurt. All of us had been caught out because my father wouldn't believe they could be so bad. He loved storms -- until that happened! Oh, there are all the memories."

His voice faltered, he knew he was not touching at the truth. "I suppose the fear of it started then". And then a knot stopped his voice, he choked, felt the pain of that knot in his chest. "Oh, it isn't the hurricanes that gave me dread, though they lay the foundation perhaps. It's the storm that-- that killed my Elana, the storm that killed her, and the way the winds sounded." He was crying, his voice ragged, angry, determined to say this, knowing that he had needed to long ago."Oh, it was then, then when we were just getting ready to wait out the storm. We'd been in storms in the jungle before, we were well covered, and I thought the place was more than safe. We should have been all right. It shouldn't have happened, it shouldn't have and if I'd only - only realized," Then he shook himself, became aware that he was clutching Jane's hand so hard it must hurt, and said,"Oh, no. I won't get into that blaming again. It was no one's fault. I had done the best I could. And I know that. The tree just fell,there was no way to know it might. It was a strange freak of an accident because never had I known of such a thing. Trees there, in that part of the forest, did not fall like that." He spoke now, steadily, angry, and strong, the hurt leaking out, releasing him, dissolving the knot." I can understand how you enjoy these storms. I did once, but now, after that. I just endure." He turned to them, drawing himself a little apart and letting go of Jane's hand. "I think watching you enjoy them so much actually helps me. I've got to clean out that old pain."

Jane nodded, "Living in a city might have been easier for you. Especially

THE AWAKENING

domed cities."

"Oh, yes, I know, but the country is too much in my blood. I've tried living in cities, but I can't. After all, there aren't that many bad storms in this land. And I feel fine when we're all inside, in that great thick walled house up there. Let's hurry and get there. The fact that I helped build those walls reassures me that they are safe." And he actually grinned a little, so soon after speaking of that memory. He had not yet been able to do that before this day.

They walked silently, watching the movements of a deer across the hillside. Suddenly a young fox appeared atop a small rise looked at them and without startling at all, continued briskly across the path ahead of them and on to its lair. Steve was aware that Jane spoke softly to the fox. He'd seen her do things like that before and thought nothing of it because it was a form of talking to herself, he thought. But now, it seemed different, maybe because he was paying attention. It seemed to him that the animal responded, gave a backward glance at her and a short bark before it went on. The quick memory of the children talking about the cow, or of Jerry, mentioning his friend the horse, and in these occasions there had been the same feeling, as though there was communication. He frowned, pushing the thought aside.

A streak of lightning reclaimed his attention and he waited for the thunder. He thought again of the large, squat stone farm buildings that he felt willing now to run to. He recollected the early days, the endless hours of work, the planning, the arguments and the agreements until finally it was done. Every member of the family had been actively building and could feel that security of their hand's work. He smiled. The storm quieted somewhat, rain fell steadily but less heavily and the wind and furor seemed limited to the upper strata of the sky. Steve said, "I'm glad I put that stew on to cook. It'll be ready."

For a while they walked in silence, each feeling the world around them, responding to it, reaching out into it. Steve said, "I wish sometimes that I could live in a city. My favorite was the new San Francisco. That's my idea of a beautiful city, the way it's built out over the bay, with the shoreline incorporated into the streets, so that narrow lagoons of water poke into the city edges. The Temple, built in the middle of the bay, standing up on that great island of rock, is like a centering Light and the two bridges out to her are like golden wings. But all the lights of the city at night, surround that whole bay like an endless wealth of jewels. It's a city a person can get lost in. Maybe because it's so big, maybe that's why I liked it."

"It's sure an angular city, all cubes and oblongs, pyramids, and towers shooting up hundreds of stories high. But then, they'd not have any parks if they hadn't built up and left land free among the high rises. Now the parks alternate with living and working space so there's plenty of green life." Jane looked at him, glad that he was relaxing. She smiled, remembering, "They took some cues from Altos and built gardens on top of their buildings too. The winds up there get pretty high sometimes," she laughed, "but there's usually sunshine."

Rose nodded, getting involved in this memory game, "It's different from our

Adwin, for sure. It's another kind of world there. I like it but it's not a place I would live. Then you know, how different Standler is. The one built over the Clear Lake. It hangs there like a castle in the air, and the water rolls under it and all around. I love that city. The shores of the lake are natural wilderness and that's where their gardens and paths wind up and down.The people planned to have their land wild.They won't need to ever change it .From the air the city is like a vast comvoluted gathering of castles. It looks as if it floats, though it's well anchored to Earth."

Jane nodded,"Standler does have a fantasy quality, like something in a fairy tale. It's so snowy white with colors splashed in here and there like signals of something. It's almost like someone's dream. That's one I love to visit. I'd not want to live there but the people who built her wouldn't live anywhere else, I think."The others sensed her excitement, her delight in these memories and Rose thought that she had enjoyed her childhood years more than she had believed. "

There are so many lovely cities, so many different ways of life. I sometimes think I'd like to live in different places after all." Jane laughed," I think maybe my childhood is catching up with me, finally. Next time I phone my parents they'll laugh."

Steve nodded, not altogether hearing her. "You know, the old part of San Francisco, that they left as it was and rebuilt as it had been. It's fascinating to see how cities were once built so sprawled and mixed up. It's more than history, it's a whole way of life we can see. I'm glad they did that. They rebuilt the sprawl and the ugly dark tenements as well as the beautiful old houses."

Rose turned to search Steve's face a little anxiously, then a slight smile nudged the seriousness from her own face. Steve answered with his wonderful good natured smile. It never failed, she thought, it never failed to appear, no matter what was happening. Everyone knew it was a smile 'habit' but still they enjoyed it and were grateful.

Rose turned to Jane,"That's not the first time that I've heard you speak of an old wish to live in more than one place. To live in a city even. Why haven't you done that?"

Jane laughed, relieved and pleased that Rose had remembered and asked."Oh, I ask myself that. But when I try to leave the land, when I've gone to my folks, and visited friends, then something happens like a terrible loss. I miss the stretching mountains, the long distance of simple natural growing life and the wide sky, when I can't feel the touch of Earth at any moment, and when I can't grow things as I choose, then it's as though my life is lost somewhere. But there's so much in the great cities. So much of art, of business, of creation of all sorts of neighborhoods, each one working out a way of living and - then not denying the other either.The Learning Centers in some cities are literal towns within the city. Wonderful places to learn. Well,you both know the advantages." She laughed apologetically at her own excitment."I guess, I wish for a way of life that would include everything at once. And I know that's unreasonable."

"No, it's not." Steve nearly shouted in a sudden desire to help Jane find what she wanted. His heart had gone out to her as she talked, her soft, almost breaking voice, telling them of a dream seldom spoken of.

Rose interrupted,"I can't believe the problem is so difficult. Her voice was almost irritable,"After all, what's to prevent you from living in one of the cities you like, in an outer ring, where Earth life comes to the city edge,only a moments walk and you are there, in forest or field. You could even be part of the city farm and work outside the city every day you chose. There're all these choices, so there must be some other reason,"

Jane grinned, nodding. "Yes, you've got me there.It is more than just the earth. It's all of you, you're my Family, you must know that!" She met Rose's eyes and saw the relief sweep away the hurt." Then also it's our Adwin, that we built and that we keep building. It's the Great River here beside us and it's the Great Valley itself. I think I love you all, all of this more than anything I know. It's our whole life, and now, it's this new life we keep touching on in the Gathers, that we keep --pointing at and that I don't understand but --" She stopped, then went on, nearly whispering, " But I know it is so very important! Do you see,Rose? And I wish I could have it all, even if it's impossible."

Steve had waited impatiently,"No, it's not impossible. Just listen to me." He stepped in front of both of them, stopping their walk. Both his arms flew up, he looked up,the rain running over his face, down his neck and plastering his hair against his forehead."What about an air car? One of our own that we can use as we choose. No limits on time, always available. Several of us could buy together, like the group that Paul bought his with!" He took her hands lightly, then let go and returned to walk beside them. His excitement obvious.

Jane watched him,moved by his excitement. A great power seemed to emanate from him now, an energy of pure childlike desire and release which was very good to see. They grinned at each other with shared longing. Then he began to tell her how this could be done.

Rose listened, faded into her own thoughts and then drew her attention from thinking to centering. She felt the stillness grow, surround them all.Every sense was acute, realizing the Earth, the steady drum of rain over their shoulders ,the odors, lights going on up the hill in the Hall, and then,she looked into the clouds toward that cliff face where she had so often hidden. Instantly she was there. This time only a small part of her consciousness stretched beyond the place of her body. She could watch the brilliant sunlight play over the solid sea of clouds below. Watch the turbulence, the lightning, the serenity of that great, grey mass floating so gently below. Great thunderclouds piled above the dark cumulus below and were like shining mountains, majestic in their slow,ponderous movement. A new dimension , a higher point of view, to see weather this way, from above.

As suddenly, she was wholy present beside Steve and Jane, her thinking reducing consciousness to itself. She marveled that she could literally experience being there WITHOUT leaving her body. Her eyes fell to the path before her and the rain. Wholly present now, aware of the surroundings acutely, she frowned, then again reduced her attention to thinking. 'What is the fact of it?

Consciousness is not what it always seemed. Is it possible consciousness is fluid?' But there had been such Vision. She reflected that were she able to see everything in her life from that vast and inclusive point, much grief might be avoided. How could she manage it?

Rose stumbled slightly, Jane caught at her and looked with concern into her face but Rose just laughed."I was daydreaming again, I suppose." She felt guilt. Again the refusal to tell them what she actually did. Hadn't they decided at the last Gather? Wasn't it what they wanted- to share all these new experiences? She ducked her head, chagrined. But she wasn't sure what she did herself!

Jane looked searchingly at Rose but didn't intrude. She was engrossed with the ideas Steve was so effectively giving her. She would talk to Rose though,,later. There was something about her, she knew there was something concealed and they HAD said they would not conceal. Rose listened as they continued, glad and relieved, amused at them and herself. She could sense Jane's struggle. Her bouts with the conflicting emotions that swung her from one decision to another in seconds. Rose sympathized. She felt their presence with her, she opened her mind to accept them, to 'be with' them. The quality of intimacy was sweet. She felt herself expanded in that recognition.

She would pay attention, 'see' them in these new dimensions that were so strange but inviting. She let her attention, her vision shift, she focussed and the queer tilt of her mind surprised her. She was able to see them, these two, the trees, Earth, the rain, the misty distance, all, from that larger vision. There was a fluidity of the atmosphere, there was a kind of glowing radiance emanating from the near barren trees and the bushes, but when she focussed on Steve and Jane, there was a shimmering, an energy pattern that surrounded them. She could watch, the changing colors, the dark replaced by light, the sudden shaft of muddy red and then the clear, lovely, clean orange rose, the pure blue. She lost attention to what they were saying, watching in awe. These two people were incredibly beautiful seen from this point of view. The recognition that this 'point of view' was a different condition of reality flooded her mind. Of course, from wherever one stood, then truth might be different. The thought fascinated her and she lost the focus she had held. "Well, there it is, best to get as large a point of view as possible if one were to find any truth at all".

The enclosure of the steady rain, the fluid quality of her perception, the allowing of herself to extend and to be so open, brought her to that point in which she felt loss of separateness. She was aware through her body, aware into the Earth and the world around her. She was not afraid, though she saw how consciousness straddled this interface of identity. She could see fear in the pattern of this small self. But it was just that, a part of the pattern. Then, turning in this endless convolution of perception, she saw the building blocks of thinking, words shaped themselves but this time they did not claim her attention, rather they formed at an edge of it. 'There is fear in our Valley, and we who pride ourselves on not being afraid, are afraid of that fear'. The thought stood there, part of that conscious whole. She let it fall, released from its attachment, her awareness inclusive.

Walking now, safe within this place, inside the cocoon of rain and cloud, with friends she trusted completely, she could include those fears as though they were part of something greater. She shifted attention back to Jane and Steve, their talk, their projecting emotions. Jane spun from sadness, disbelief, guilt, to a rising vibrant hope that Rose wanted suddenly to encourage.

Steve's suggestion, so obvious now it was said, roused a blossoming of ideas, possibilities, images in Jane's mind. She felt exultant. She felt such relief, greater than it should be, that Steve didn't see her wish as selfish,or foolish, or disloyal She watched Steve, his grin, his delight in their mutual plans. He said, eager,boyish, "I heard some people talking of the 'Vagabonds of the sky'.The idea seems so lovely. There're all sorts of things we could do, you know, that we've not done yet. I heard that some people in the Soviet Union were building a whole town that will float a few hundred feet from the ground. So it would travel always". He was laughing with delight at the thought of it. "A whole city, like a vast ship,moving across the land, able to descend at will and visit, enjoy, experience, and yet remain always free." Jane had stopped walking to turn and clasp Steve's hand listening. Rose felt their mutual eagerness to weave the possibilities into all sorts of fantasy. But the rain and the growing darkness pressed them back to climbing.

Steve put his arm around Jane's shoulders, sensing her need for approval of this desire. Why had she so long refused herself these things she so wanted? What old patterns still shaped this young woman's life? "You know, having a private car has been an old dream of mine,but we were always so busy that I let it go. Then the town needed all we could manage to buy . But now. We've got time and credit to begin to think of some of these things we wish for. And we could do it together, half a dozen of us. It would work!" He felt her warmth pressed against his side, and his own body's reaction to that closeness. He stopped talking, lost in the intensity of feelings. He loosened his hold, surprised. He had not felt such things for any woman since Elana's death. Almost frantic, he stopped the thought there. Spoke too loud,"Well, then, we're going to do that. We're going to begin planning it."

Rose was nodding. "It's other things besides being busy. I think we had a notion that living here, creating our lives with Earth Mother, that we'd be better to keep machinery at a minimum. At least in our private lives. But that's not happened, you know. Look at our homes, our kitchens, our cleaning robots, our field floaters, machines help us to live and to create."

Steve frowned, "We've never wanted to take time for all those little jobs while there was so much to do. Now we have the time. But we want to spend that time in other ways. So we'll keep our machines , I'm sure."

Rose laughed,"There'd be no way we'd forget them. Anyway,I've got too much to do, too much that I must find out about, to understand. I need even more time."

Jane was still thinking of the possibilities she could imagine. "Well, I think it could really work. We could live here and still spend time as we chose out there.

Oh, it will be so exciting."She raised her arms in a gleeful gesture, "After all, Angela and Mary do that, they're gone so much yet they're still part of our family."

Steve said, " Then we'll get Tom's vote and if Rose approves, then the others will, I think. We'll have to save a while longer, but we can do it. Would be a surprise if no one here at home objected at all. After all the worry I've done. Even if someone doesn't like the idea of it, it'll still be all right I think. Give people enough time and they get used to the idea and then think it was their own." He laughed, pleased at his cleverness.

Rose's answer was so thoughtful that he felt irritation . It made him feel young. She said,"Steve, you know, you've got us figured wrong. Ben and I are in our mid thirties and we've done a lot of thinking. We don't think because something isn't right for our life style it'd be wrong for yours. I doubt most people would want to belong to a car owner's group anyway.The public ones are too convenient. I don't certainly. I can't think of anything I want, matter of fact, right now. Anyway, the sky might become too crowded." She grinned,knowing they hadn't worried about that. She had.

They walked in silence for minutes. Jane turned to meet Steve's eyes, feeling grateful to him for this talk, for being able to ask for what she wanted and know of his own wishes shared with her. They looked toward Rose, grateful for her tolerance, her willingness to listen always. They noticed her face, smiling faintly, with a vague tautness and intensity,as though she were listening to something far off. They exchanged glances and wondered. Then with abrupt suddenness Rose turned to them.

"Hey, we'd better move faster. We're all going to catch the flu. We're pushing against the wind now and it's stronger. I'm getting cold.". She was smiling with such a deep pleasure that neither of the others could resist asking, "Hey, Rose, what got into you. You look as if you'd heard a secret." Steve was surprised at his own words, but was glad they were said.

Rose hesitated, then, still smiling, remembered their agreement at the Gather. Well, they had asked."Would you accept it if I told you that Ben's coming right now? He'll be here the day after tomorrow! Imagine it! Would you believe I know he has a friend with him. He's coming down River and he'll eat with us tomorrow dinner." She danced around in a circle, running up before them and turning to watch their faces, her own wreathed in smiles.

She received no reply, the other two were staring at each other and then at her. They were sure she wasn't joking, yet they couldn't see how she could know. Jane finally asked,"How can you know? You aren't a clairvoyant.Or is that what happens sometimes when you seem to withdraw from us. You're listening-- or watching something else?"

Rose was surprised that Jane could-- would-- speak so bluntly. "I didn't think you ever noticed. Maybe. Yes, I suppose I must seem to be far away. I feel that way. But it's just what we've talked of, you know, the "Reach', the Reaching out to try to Touch another mind. And somehow I managed to find him. He wasn't astonished, actually. I thought he would be. But he didn't much like it. Makes him

THE AWAKENING

so uneasy. As uneasy as you two." She grinned at them and they smile sheepishly. On the other hand, it seemed more believeable now. She shook he head."We agreed we would talk, remember." She sounded almost pleading an(Steve felt ashamed that she must. They were walking faster now, it was harde to talk and climb this fast.

"Rose, we do have to get used to the things that are happening. We can't be afraid of ourselves."

Rose said,"Yes, it does happen, so we might as well accept. No, I don't understand, any more than you do."

Steve searched Rose's face, puzzled, and curious. What was this? Then as his eyes met hers, he looked startled, then a great smile spread over his face and he said,"Why, you did know what I was asking you. You can do that, you - we 'Touched".

Rose turned to look now at the lights of the Hall, just ahead. "Well, your feelings - puzzled, uneasy, I sensed them. Your wanting me to help. It's like that Steve. It works just that way, so simply. When I focus, Reach with total attention, I'm very much with you. We human being aren't really as separate as we think."

The wind blew in sharp gusts sending fine sprays of rain that felt like needles. each face lifted to receive it like a baptism, enjoying the cold of it. A great grey cat leaped from a low tree branch where she had been huddled down in a hollow out of the rain. She looked at them, mewed softly in greeting and question, then streaked toward the Hall where she waited for them to let her in. Steve laughed,"Oh, It's beautiful, look, the rain's washed everything clean and the house is full of light. We're like the wondering heros come home after long voyages. We'll be welcomed there. And I'm so glad I set my thermostat this morning so my cottage will be warm and ready for me later. Let's never criticize the wonders of technology."

A voice calling broke into their last few minutes walking up the steps onto the deck. Jane looked up then waved. They walked carefully over the electronic door mat so that their feet would be cleaned of mud or leaves and went in. Jane pulled off her wet jacket and said wearily. "This is the kind of day when I'm deeply grateful for all inventions that make automatic dinners for us. I don't want to lift a finger and I want to be served." Her lack of interest in cooking was well known .

Steve hung his jacket in the dryer by the door with hers and said, "No, we won't have to cook. My stew should be just about ready, expecially if someone turned up the heat. I can smell it cooking now so someone has. Let's get a hot drink and sit." He stuck a head through the doorway and peered at the fire, saw Jerry and Silvia, dozing there."Let's join them, we need a little heat right now too."

CHAPTER FOURTEEN

The Family - admission and acceptance

When Rose woke in the morning, she felt a settling of purpose, and a vague dis-ease. The doubts of the past months were faded, the confusion less. But a clear question prodded at her mind and she turned to it. Why did she shy away practicing the Reach with her own Family? After all, she accepted it when she was in Valley Council, even accepted the Joining. Was it because she feared there might be others who could not? What would that do to the Family? William's lack had hurt enough.

During the night she had dreamed of Ben, that he spoke to her and that he was nearly home, would be there soon. How could it be so real. His voice, his face, and especially the Touch of mind. The memory was so real it was a pain without the physical reality. And she had not told him, even in the dream, that she knew he would arrive tomorrow. The thought startled her. Tomorrow! She leaped from bed. "Oh, Oh, Oh", her joy spilled over inundating her worry, it made the questions academic. Yet they persisted and she pulled on her clothes, found the colors, the fabrics that Ben liked best, that she would wear to meet him, a green tunic and pants, simple, except for elaborate embroidery done by Marian that told of their honeymoon journey with the Vagabonds. The green was so pale-golden it was like young spring leaves. He would remember. She smiled, her whole body seemed to smile. And as she did, the question pushed itself through her delight to insist. Why did she still refuse to Reach out there, Touch Ben truly and Join with him?

There were other questions. The easy communication between the children. Was it a simple form of Joining, or maybe a more complex form? Why had she been blind to that all these years? How constantly one sees what he thinks is real, rather than what is real! She sighed, well, surely it was time that they learn to talk easily of the Talents at least. Even though they might need more time to be able to speak freely of the Light, of Spirit.

She frowned as she stood to stretch and tie the belt of her tunic. Joining -- it seemed so much more than simply another Talent. She spoke slowly, sliding her hand down the lovely soft fabric, enjoying the feeling of it. "After all, it's transcending ordinary mind, it's focussing upward-inward toward Soul Consciousness. Surely it must be a talent of Spiritual nature." She sighed, "Well, for sure, we've got to learn more. I want to know more about what Seeing Far is. Can you become adept at it, so you're able to See into other dimensions? Or just across the country in this one? And what is really happening when a person leaves his body, enters into another state? I don't know at all. We're going to have to admit to and study the way children are moving things with mind energy". The thought troubled her, made her think sharply of William. Could he be right?

THE AWAKENING

Standing motionless, lost in thought, she suddenly shrugged and turned to her mirror. These Talents were strange, but they were at least somewhat related to ordinary living. If they talked of them, then maybe later they could talk of that utterly different state of Being which was the Spiritual state. It was in that state that there was the sense of 'too much ' to bear. Only there. The decision gave her an obscure comfort.

She combed her long hair and tied it loosely behind her neck. Got a pair of boots so soft, each could be mashed into one hand, from her closet and pulled them on, found small pearl ear rings that Ben had given her and put them on with a small happy smile. She could talk to the Master Teachers. After all if people felt so much reluctance, and fear, wasn't it the Teacher's fault? She took one last look at herself and turned to go, "I think I'll begin talking about it all right at breakfast and just find out what happens. I think I"ll break that taboo, if that's what it is."

She laughed at herself, her anger, impatience. "Wait a minute, Girl", she told herself,"You'll have everybody freaked out if you rush into this". She walked down the steps of her cottage, out into the pathway. No one was in sight. Was she late? Her eyes fell on a cluster of bright yellow daffodils, nodding in the light gusts of wind, and she stopped to touch one. Their beauty caught at her heart a little.

She began walking again, stopped at the Temple and said aloud,"I am the one who is afraid. I am the one. And the worst of it is I can't find a single reason for it". A feeling of suffocation grew, the sound of her voice hung hard within her as if in a hollow drum. She stood, washed over with denial and stiff with the necessity of accepting this fact. Slowly her body relaxed and she heaved a sigh. She let her eyes fasten on the colors radiating from the small Temple and breathing slowly, keeping her attention focussed, she drew her self into that centering that was her practice in the Temple. She would not go in now,the few moments of focussed attention sufficed. She turned toward the Hall with calm strength.

The morning was a clean washed morning,rain would surely lash them by afternoon, but the air was sweet, cold and clean. She heard Jerry's voice, he called her from the doorway of the Hall. "Rose, we're ready to eat and we want you to join us."

She thought the request strange. When did anyone wait for another for breakfast? She waved and hurried her steps. Why couldn't she be uncomplicated and confident the way Jerry was? She smoothed her short tunic, let her fingers play over the raised embroidery, feeling its richness. Then she was there, opened the carved doors and was inside.

The small tables had been pushed to the wall, the great long table pulled out and everyone sat around it. She was surprised. She picked up a glass of juice and nodded to Jane, Silvia, the others. She felt acutely conscious of them. Her senses seemed sharp and absorbing of everything. Jerry was looking at her, his expression one of amusement. She frowned. He said,"Well, Ben's due back. We want to know when."

She turned to the autoserver, dialed her breakfast and waited until it slid from the machine. She turned to look at him as she walked back to the table. "Jerry, I-don't -. How would I know?" she finished lamely then slapped with her denial, she was angry with herself. He didn't speak but his eyes held hers. She looked away. With a wrench of decision, she said, "All right, Yes, he is coming. He'll be here tomorrow ." It was as if she had broken a thin veil in her consciousness.

Jane caught her breath, studying her friend's face. " Tomorrow Rose? Tomorrow!" Her smile was like a light to Rose. Clearly delighted, and obviously not thinking of the implications of what Rose had said, she went on. "It seems so long this time, longer than usual that he's been gone." With a new awareness Rose saw how Jane deflected the meaning of her words, how she simply let them slide from her attention. She thought, 'It's what I've been doing. Why does it make me angry when she does?'

She took her thick slice of bread, smiled as she glanced over at Jane, "It's been more than a year. I don't like it at all and I want him home. But I'll not hurry him one bit, I promised and I'll keep that promise. And I won't Reach to him because I promised that too. Not even if I thought he was Reaching to me." Deliberately she used the term, accepting the fact that they must begin. No one spoke for several minutes. She felt angry but refused to give it expression.

Then Jerry looked up sharply, met her eyes and nodded. His face very serious now. The usual humor gone. Jane made a pushing gesture with one hand as if defending herself. Then she turned her face away like one who sees a thing and does not want to. Rose's eyes widened in surprise, she turned to Jerry. He nodded again, sadly. Silvia glanced back and forth from brother to sister, her oriental face not at all inscrutable, the emotions playing vividly across her fair skin. She said softly, "I'll be damned." She frowned, "Then you could have, even as far away as he's gone?"

The bright sun broke through the clouds, it's sudden light flamed in the room around them, and then was gone. Outside the weeping willow branches, green leaves opening already, rattled against one another in a rising wind. The air was warm here, Rose felt the cozy, safety. Why was she so aware of feeling 'safe' lately? The closed dark of winter, the inevitable opening up of spring, that awakening that was already visible in the swelling red of buds along the River, the early bloom of daffodil and crocus in the garden outside. It was a wonderul time, this ending and beginning. She suddenly felt a longing to have everything as it was during the last decade. Such clear undoubted direction. The work, the hard ceaseless work of building and creating. The Gods held themselves off at the edges of things then. But now something touched the edges of their minds. A flaming, secret Touch deep inside still moments. It could not longer be ignored.

Jane was staring into her cup of coffee, her tall slim body sitting in its usual loose jointed way, dressed in a brilliant blue wool-plasilk coverall, with strips of gold at color and sleeve. Her fair hair hung loose across her temples and drifted in to nearly conceal her eyes. The freckles already visible across her nose, made her skin seem pale in the morning light. Rose, watching, wanted to touch

THE AWAKENING

her, gently, not to frighten, but to comfort. She felt the contrast sharply of that long, fair body beside her own small, dark one. They were so different.

Jerry came to a decision, he knew his sister's troubled thought just enough to know he needed to help. He was excited, wanting to bring the whole matter out, to speak finally in this very ordinary moment of breakfast. What happened at the Gather must be continued in normal life. He felt odd fear but did not want to honor it. He sat next to Jane, only a few inches taller than she, but so dark, so hard and 'male'. His hair, curlier than Rose's hung to his shoulders, and was tied back for this mornings work. He finished his plate of eggs, mopping up the last with a bit of hot bread. He said, "Sis, you're right. We've got to talk. We've been taught to be honest and we said that we would and then we don't. Ever since you and Ben and I came here, ever since we started our Farm, we've promised that we would talk about everything important and now here's a whole area of our lives that we've concealed. Even with all our teaching, we've concealed, and the worst of it is you're scared of us and we're scared of each other. That's inexcusable". He shook his head but Rose was grateful for that forthright courage. He would not dissemble.

Silvia was silent still, thoughtfully sipping coffee, her pale grey shirt was decorated with the insignia of her home town, and her black smooth hair was held up by small silver combs. She was impeccable, as always. Her small delicate face would have looked almost childlike had it not been for the strong set of her jaw and the steady quiet of her eyes. Rose loved her dearly, and that love was stirred into concern by the pained frown that passed briefly over Silvia's face. Their eyes met with an intimacy neither shied from. Finally she said with a burst of exasperation. "Now, look here. If there're things you've not told us its a mystery to me. I don't know what this is all about."

Jerry broke in, pleased, his love for her naked in his eyes. "Honey, we should've depended on you. You'd never have let it get to this." He leaned to kiss her cheek, "Rose's finally talking about 'Reaching' about the new Talents showing up among us. What we agreed to do at the Gather but still haven't done." He waved his huge hands commically outward, "Simple, isn't it?"

Silvia looked at him, turned to study Rose, her mind absorbing remembering, connecting, "So that's it? I've been wondering if there wasn't something I didn't know. You, Rose, what about you? When you just disappear on us sometimes, when you're just not with us and we can't get your attention. Is that part of this?" Her no-nonsense persistence, so devoid of any visible fear or unease, shook Rose's carefully drawn calm.

She was surprised at the hard knot of reaction, a clear sense of fear. Why, for God's sake, why in this safest of all places among her family? She let her eyes sweep across all their faces, all intent on her now. They wanted to know. Were willing.

"Well, I'll try to talk about it, tell you." she said lamely. She lowered her eyes. "I don't know why this is so hard for me. I suppose my assumption that you wouldn't accept me, was my refusal to accept myself". She swallowed, glanced around at them. "That's hard to admit, damn it". She was silent. Their quiet was reassuring. "I suppose that you'd say I 'go someplace' but it's not so different from just losing oneself in thought". She shrugged, "Oh, No, it's a lot different. I do leave, I am not with you at those moments. It's like an inner vision. I see it as clearly as I see you now. And there it is, I can't do both, be here and there at the same time." She shook her head, knowing her words were confusing. "Consciousness is - is expanded, I think I would say, perception is so much larger, extends so far." She thought she was not saying what she meant. She hesitated, frowned, then tried again, It could be said,'I' am larger, I think."She looked worried, scanned their faces again and asked,"Is that clear?"

Silvia smiled ,"Well, not very. Are you saying that you see with what the old ones called 'second sight'? That ancient idea of the 'inner eye?"

Jane broke in,"I don't understand this at all, Rose. Sometimes you talk of things I don't understand, or maybe I don't want to." Her smile was shy,"I think that I must understand though, so please tell us."

" Rose swallowed, grateful and surprised at that. Their reaction was not as she had thought. She felt the sweet relaxation of relief. "Yes, I suppose it is the same, maybe, something like that, at least. Though I think they meant to inply something far more deep into reality than this simple distancing of myself mentally. They were concerned with that true 'far Reaching' toward what they probably called God. But that's not the same as this."

Jerry set his cup down, slid his plates into the auto washer, and said, "Sis, I've wondered why you didn't go back again to the Teaching Retreat. Wouldn't they have helped you?"

Rose felt impatient with him,they must not talk of ideas now. They must stay with these facts. "Oh, No Jerry. When I studied there, I was very young. It did help me so much. But they sent me away and said I must live and work among our people for a long time before I would be ready to learn more. There is the practice of living that we must do here. You all know of it,whether you took the Master teachers seriously or not. We must practice living, with each other, before we can learn more."

Silvia watching Rose intently, nodded and said, "I want to go back to where we were. You think that there is more to see, more to reality than we ordinarily notice?"

Rose almost cried out,"Oh, Silvia,yes! You know that! It's time we stopped insisting that human realization is limited to five senses and a thinking mind. We do at least admit,in theory, that we don't know the limits of reality.It takes courage to really look at that,but we do look at it. However, to practice LIVING from that expanded point of view is another matter."

She shook her head, impatient, angry, puzzled, "Damn it, you all know, you've not lived so consciously in this world without knowing we've broken old limits." She looked at Jane, and her face was full of worry." Surely, you all know that!"

Silvia looked at Jerry. She did not know of what Rose spoke but she thought these were the things Jerry had sometimes hinted at and did not explain.

Jerry was silent, letting these thoughts settle in his mind. He wanted Rose to go on. When she didn't, he said, "You're right. All of us in this Valley know what is meant by the IDEA, at least, of waking up. We are trained to know of the subconscious, as were our ancestors, but where it was a few of them, its ALL of us that gets that training." He looked thoughtfully at them, realizing as he talked, seeing that some new focus was at work here among them. He felt the power of it, a sense of quiet awe. But he went on as if nothing had changed for him." We aren't the same, you know. All of us are also trained to the supraconscious. It's a big difference. We do know - even though we deny, we know there's more to - to know. We learn of it through what we call our subconscious mind, through dreams, through trance states. But, it's obvious we're willing to study them without really accepting them . Only the monitors have taken them seriously enough to do more, they ACCEPT them. Now, we 're faced with the reality they reveal and it's intimidating, at least for some folks. We're a stubborn people, we like to keep our little world intact and not have it stretching out of shape. We like familiarity. There's a little Zenophobia in us. We know and we deny. Please don't feel betrayed". He smiled gently, tenderly at her and she felt the strength of his support. "You've just been a little ahead of most of us, Sis, and being ahead can hurt sometimes."

Rose met his eyes then, and she saw there much that spoke . "You too Jerry? You know too?" Her voice broke, she wanted to cry with sorrow and joy.

He nodded silently, "Isn't it a matter of taking mental life seriously. Accepting that Mind is as real as a rock? We're a different people, Sis, I think we are. There's been a change in us, in humanity itself, people CAN know more, realize more than our ancestors. I believe that!" His face was so serious, so intense with his desire to tell her of this, that she smiled. "I've thought no one else realized it. I've been lonely too."

With sudden decision she Reached, gently, tentatively, Touching. Responding to her was a mind, a strength that had great power. With a final hunger and need, she plunged on, Touching into this mind. He met her mental Touch. It was brief, but very real. She sat gazing at him, her little brother, one she still thought of as a child. "Why?" was all she said.

He shrugged, glancing at Silvia, who watched them in confusion."It's an old habit, Sis. Just like it is for you. You think you're the only one who thought she was going crazy ?"

Rose nodded, deeply frowning, the smooth brown skin of her forehead creased above her nose and around her great dark eyes. She thought with her whole face, "I know my fear is exaggerated, but it's very real fear. It's time now though that we end the resistance, we stop using shadows to scare ourselves. Obviously we are not going to be hurt. You're right, Jerry, we're a different people, but we're afraid of ourselves. If we don't accept what's happening we deny these new Talents and, worse, the glimpse into that Far Country. "She was silent and then softly, to herself she said,"We don't know yet what we are becoming."

She suddenly wanted to go on, to tell it all, to talk out the whole bound up lot of it. But she thought perhaps she had said enough, Let them carry the ball now. Her excitement brought a chill to her body, she felt herself trembling.

Silvia frowning, cried out,"Wait! What're you talking about? Let me in on it too!"

Rose turned to her, reached out an arm and slid it around her shoulders,"Excuse us, Sil, You're right, we're rude. We --" Then she met Jerry's eyes and they both focussed mentally, Reached and Touched until they felt Silvia there too. Silvia, resistant , then, firmly responding. She came into their tentative connection as though she had not feared. She gasped with surprise. "It's even more than at the Gather. What else?"

Jerry shook his head,"It might be dangerous." He seemed uneasy. "But it's good to include you, Love!"

Rose nodded,"We've always imagined mind Reach, and we've historically associated it with some kind of danger. People have even said that it's courting at the gates of madness. I've felt that. Surely everyone must. I wonder if what we have called madness is when human minds break through into that Reality that is so unfamiliar that we don't know how to think about it. Have no words that will carry the thoughts into useful shapes. No wonder the Monitors tell me to go home and practice, practice learning how to bring our whole nature into balance. They showed me how to Reach. But I haven't practiced that part." She shook her head, remembering, impatient with herself. "I've denied so much. They insisted we must practice. Learn to sense something beyond ourselves and grow a little accustomed to that vast endless universe that waits us as we open our minds to it." She sat looking at one then the other,for several minutes.

"It may be that Valley people are doing what a certain few rare people have done through all history, we're recognizing what is simply the potential of human beings. I think many of us are awake, aware that there is such a potential." She shook her head, her eyes wide, surprised, "There it is, I didn't know that I could say that, or that I knew it. There is in me much that I have not listened to." She nodded then, gently, "It's true that we have to learn slowly, but we don't have to block ourselves off entirely. And that's what I've done. I can't forgive myself for that. It's wasted so much time."She shook her head, "Just listening to my Self, that deep inner voice, would have saved so much pain. But I was afraid of it."

"Maybe that's part of the learning itself. To see how frightened we are of real, significant change, especially when it comes from within our own minds, our own hearts." Jerry was smiling,but his face was full of surprise.

Silvia,amazed eyes on the faces of her friends, said,"It's as though you're talking about something - - alien.:" She swallowed at the word,then repeated it,"Alien!"

Well, it is. Surely it is. If we start from our ordinary thinking. It's not easy to think beyond experience, you know. Maybe its impossible. That's why we have to have little glimpses, the small Touchs, the Reach, into whatever we can be aware of. We are having to extend experience so we CAN think about it. We've become very conscious of how limited we are - and it's hard to extend beyond our littleness. Yet, I think we are all straining at the bit to do just that, as though we can't bear not to." Rose sighed,sad with the difficulty. "It's not an easy thing to talk of. You know in the past, only people already enflamed with inner knowledge they couldn't deny went to seek out a Teacher. And some were put into mental hospitals before they found one. They already had the start of it. But they hid away in such teaching places until they were able to balance themselves, their minds, hearts and bodies to all that they were learning. So it's not surprising that we're having trouble is it?"

Jerry shook his head,"If we'd been willing to admit that we've had small glimpses, small Touchs, at different times in our lives. If we'd talked of that, explored it, we'd 've saved ourselves a lot of grief. Surely, today nearly everyone has known such glimpses."

"But we've all denied because we couldn't talk, think even in sensible sentences about it. It's still too easy to make a kind of mumbo-jumbo, to fool searching people, to do the terrible crime of leading such people into traps. There've always been false teachers who pretend to fulfil that longing, the desire to know, to See more of that unknown. People are vulnerable when they first begin to wake. Our Teachers have told us that."

Silvia, listening, suddenly nodded,"Yes, I've heard that. I didn't know what they meant. But they also said that people waking can deny it all,or begin to make a dogma out of one new perception." She gazed at them in silence, then softly,"So that's what's been happening. that's what you're talking about?" She slid a hand on Rose's arm.

Jane slowly moved her head in a bemused denial, she had been so silent they had nearly forgotten her. "Oh, Rose, it's all so strange, it's touching on something I don't understand but it makes me hopeful. I don't know why!"

Rose laughed, easier now, though her body was still tight with the tension of this talking. So intense, so dangerous, her instincts said, But she shook her head and went on," Jane, I wish that I had been as open to at least think and to consider when I was your age."

They were quiet for a long moment, then Jerry softly recited familiar words. " 'The human race is asleep. When we glimpse that greater reality, we are just starting to wake, so we see, through our half closed eyes, like glimpsing the sunlight just before we wake from ordinary sleep. Its brightness makes us shut our eyes and return to that dark comfort. But then, once we have glimpsed that there is a 'sun'out there, a 'day' and new life, then we can never truly ever sleep again'." He looked around at them, his eyes full of a sharp sorrow."Oh, I wish we could understand. We need Teachers who realize more!"

Rose nodded, "We do,Brother, and maybe we'll find one soon."

They were silent for sometime. Then Jerry said, "We ought to talk of this with our own Master Teachers. Ask that they help."

"Well, at least in our own Family, we have got to promise that we will not just give lip service to the decision we made at the Gather. We will not just SAY we will talk to one another, but that we will DO it. The way we have this morning." Rose caught each of their eyes, and they each nodded solemnly. She smiled and they were quiet.

They turned at the sound of running feet, three people came dashing in. Their hair was damp, wind blown and they pulled off their rain coats and hung them quickly on the door hooks before they sat down. The twins, Andrew and Anna, and Steve, brought with them the vitality of the stormy day. Steve was barely taller than Anna but her twin brother, at sixteen, was a head taller already. There was laughter in their faces, their manner, and they jostled each other in fun as they settled down.

Rose watched them, wanting to reach out a calming hand but, knowing better, was silent. They were full of life and she delighted in both Anna and Andrew even as she saw them growing so fast away from her. They had the blond hair of their father but the dark brown skin and eyes of their mother. They seemed always to Rose to have a look of wonder, innocence and of great alertness.

Steve, was great, large bodied, with a beard that gave his face even more of a look of bearishness. He radiated a good natured easiness with himself as he settled between Silvia and Jerry, creating an atmosphere of cheerfulness for them all. It was one of Steve's endearing traits that he always seemed to be lighthearted, but one that exasperated his friends sometimes when they wanted to be serious. His powerful body seemed to burst the silver shirt that fell down to his hips, and his eyes, so blue they seemed purple, rested briefly on each face, a knowledge lighting them that surprised Rose, alert as she was now to others.

"What's all the excitement?" She asked.

The three of them laughed and glanced at one another, a secet was fun. Then Steve said,"Anna beat Andrew at milking and Andy has accused her of having some secret commmunication with Maggie. Andy insists Anna persuades her to stay here with us, though her calf is five months old. He settled himself more comfortably in his chair after dialing his breakfast. There was something in this argument between the kids that he didn't want to think about,he must treat it as a foolish joke. But he had the feeling that they tested him and that made him question. He was not a man who appeared to pay attention to all that was said, and so the family sometimes underestimated his perceptiveness. He often found out more than anyone knew. He turned to Anna."You did pour the milk into the refrigeration processor, didn't you." She nodded and he looked around smiling, he felt good this cool, dark day at the end of winter.

Anna laughed, drawing her hot plate to her and picking up a slice of bread. "He doesn't realize that what he's accusing me of is a fact. That I do have a secret communication system."

Andy took his own plate and sat again beside her. "I already know. You have no secrets from me, my Sister. You just think you have."

Anna glanced at him frowning, then attended to eating. Rose had the

THE AWAKENING

distinct sensation that her daughter reprimanded her brother. She sat watching them unable to restrain a smile of pleasure at the joy and beauty of these two. She knew that her maternal pride caused her difficulty in seeing any fault in them. But she told herself that everyone needed one person in their life who thought they were wonderful. There were plenty who would pay attention to their faults. She insisted that she always listened when she was told of her children's faults. She took that role for other parents and felt justified.

"Where's Cassandra?"

Steve finished chewing a bite and answered,"She's finishing with her chores. She called down some ducks who were going north, fed them our grain too. I told her they didn't need it."

"There! You see! She talks to them all. All of them. So don't be surprised if I talk to a few." For a moment Anna's eyes met her Mother's and Rose caught in them the trace of appeal. Rose's mind swiftly reviewed a number of possibilities and she felt a cold tingle in the muscles of her spine. What was happening here? She glanced at Jane in time to catch a dawning question, a great surprise on her face.

Rose thought of Cassandra, how much was she conscious of her own Talents. Was she -- could she actively - Reach? Rose wondered why she had not found that out. She was only ten, Steve's daughter, obviously, in looks, build and temperament, a feminine counterpart of that strong man. She inherited his infectious cheerfulness and delight in life as well as his ability to plunge into a labyrinth of gloom. But her natural cheerfulness always rescued her before she had spent much time there. Andrew and Anna were more even tempered, they didn't have her explosions of Joy but neither did they have periods of dark dispair. Jane studied them, these three, already they seemed to be her own children. She resolved to find out more about that Talent of Cassandra's, so much like her own.

Silvia said, "Rose, before we forget, I want to have a talk with you. I want to talk about -- all that we've been discussing. It's still a mystery to me, and I want to -- to know about you, Love."

Rose nodded and Jerry reached out a long arm to touch her hand,"Me too Sis." Rose looked at them both, surprised and pleased."Yes, We'll talk soon."

They listened to Steve and Jane planning the day's farm work, The ritual of spring planting would be coming up in a month and they must be ready with every field prepared. Jane had ordered seeds from Altos, had plants already up in her greenhouse and the two of them had repaired all the corner posts so the force fields were working well. Steve said,"The new Rye from Altos gave a third greater yield last year and its nutrition level is higher. That's mighty good. We reported the results and they've given us some new bunch corn."

Jane nodded,"The rye seed we planted in the wild meadows did nearly as well and it's coming again from its own seeding. It'll improve those meadows a lot., If we ever need it it'll make a good combination of grains for harvest."

Jerry asked,"Will we need to increase our acreage in Adwin? We keep getting more people, you know."

THE PEOPLE OF THE VALLEY

"No! Master Farmer Nelson said the fields in use could even be decreased. The production and quality is high. People just don't seem to need so much to eat. I think we've got other things to do, maybe?" He grinned. Then he added, "There're some new varieties of vegetables he's going to try on us so we won't cut out any acres yet, though." He turned to Andrew,"Has your field crew tested the wild meadows for their condition yet this spring?"

Andrew nodded, "We've been assigned the swamp rice and acorns north of town. The rice is growing every where through the wild swamp. Matta's worked its way into some of it so if we need to harvst any, it'll be harder, but the fields are fine. We can't tell about acorn crops until May." He glanced around, "We've been busy enough! We had to check out all the floater discs this month, took all our work time to get them in shape. After all, Uncle Jerry, I've got to have some time for music and study, you know." His frown faded and he turned to his sister, "Tom, told me you won't work with our team this year."

She nodded."I'm working with White team. We're doing the wild Skenna and raspberries along the River. They told us to begin watch on the young fruit groves that are in Denlock forest. They begin fruiting this year. We've been studying diseases and problems of fruit trees this winter and I think I know TOO much about them. But I wish I could communicate the way young Steve does. It'd help a lot." She said it as matter-of factly as she might ask for a glass of water.

Steve laughed, "Master Farmer Nelson says that the new plant varieties are coming too fast for him. I never thought I'd hear that complaint. We begged Altos for new stuff for so long. He likes the idea of getting more crops growing through the wild fields. We can harvest if we need them, but we'll not have any labor at raising them. Like, the 'Paper Vine'. It's growing like a weed through the north hills on rocky slopes that won't raise anything else . No much to do but harvest it for our little paper mill. Most towns planted it on their poorest land so there'll not be much trade in it. But everybody'll have paper. It was the melons that it fruits that really pleased Nelson. It's just what he likes, a double crop plant that'll grow wild."

Steve grinned, "We'll end up with no need for farmers one of these days. The new legumes make the hill sides look like a planted garden all summer and produce a heavy crop of beans by late summer. Then there's Oca,it grows right in the midst of grass meadows and yet the tubers are huge, as big as when we've set them in special fields. That's what planting with legumes will do."

Jane was nodding, they both loved to talk about their work and the others seemed interested. "Have any of you seen the acorns that came from the forest beyond Denlock where we planted young trees just three years ago? They were sweet as hazel nuts and nearly as big as a baseball. We've never had such fruiting. The animals like them too,though so we have to shield them to get our share." She laughed. For her the animal's rights were just.

Jerry stopped eating to look at them,"You kids are lucky you know. When we worked on the harvest and watching crews, we had a lot more to do. There wasn't all the equipment."

Andrew shook his head, "I think there's just as much work now. We've got more crops in and we've got it more organized, more efficient. You old folks had to work out the system."

Jerry laughed,"I remember you told me once that it was like mobilizing an army, getting all the crews together, assigning positions, fields to work out, and the skimmer floats . D'you still think it's a waste of the time for you budding scientists and musicians to take time for that work?" He was enjoying this teasing of his nephew.

"No, not anymore, Uncle Jerry. We did complain a lot. But I think it's part of the ritual." He grinned, "The Council says we learn how the town is run and we know we're needed to make it run right. Well, Uncle Jerry, that's true. We do. You couldn't do without us." He smiled at them, a radiant cockyness that they smiled at. Then he sobered. "The more I get into it, the less I complain. It's not easy running this town, you know. But it took me until I was fourteen to begin to suspect that. It's a good system, I think. And so's the one of serving on Council. We don't get too separated from each other or from town life." He was speaking in earnest and Jerry remembered he'd been doing a lot of study of history tapes this winter. They ate in silence for a few minutes and then Andrew looked at Steve. "When's the shearing begin? Rob and Sally will have to train their pup to herd this year."

Steve said,"They will,, but they don't need to do it for bringing in sheep. Edelwine Animal Center finally gave Adwin our guard pack. They've already brought in our flock for lambing. They'll be out again soon's the lambs are born. Then shearing's not until May, unless we get a very hot spell."

Jerry had been listening attentively, and he said," Don't know why they still call it shearing, no one shears sheep anymore".

Steve nodded. "You're right, it's instant wool drop, two hours after they drink the white water in the tanks of the catch pens. We'll have to cull out some too. The meat eaters of the Valley will have their quota of lamb this year. Numbers are up and the predators don't keep them in check fast enough. Hunters say they'd balance them out in a few years but by then the wild pastures would be damaged."

Steve shook his head, "It's good we're able to shield them during lambing. It looks as though there'll be a really good crop of young this year. It wasn't too hard a winter, I think. Tom's working on the system all the time to keep it balanced, the predators have to be weeded too, you know. The Master Hunter's job is not easy, balancing and keeping the wild world healthy. He has to make hard choices, but I think it's a better one after all. Starving is harder than being shot clean by arrow or bullet of a trained Hunter."

Jerry nodded, Well, no one can complain about our wool crop. The weavers've made new blends with plant fibers. We've got a good fabric industry but half the towns of the Valley are doing the same. We'll not get rich, but we'll do all right with out Valley trade." He looked around thoughtfully," We've almost done what we set out to do. Most towns're basically self sufficient, enough to eat and clothe and house every citizen, and a brisk enough business to get what we need. If this Valley keeps improving things the way we have been, we'll all begin to be bored."

Rose laughed, "There's a whole universe to learn about, planets of this Solar system to explore and develop right now. And if you want trouble, there're those two billionaires, seeing who can get richer fastest, mining the asteroids and the moons."

"There ought to be enough for them all. The possibiities for expansion are unlimited out there. Already they're supplying the colonies and the satalite cities. They are half finished with a new space city that'll manufacture space ships. It's good they've got it all off Earth"

"Steve, They're master manipulators, like old fashioned politicians. They tried to get control of our politicians until the public reaction forced World Government to make it clear exactly what help we'd give and what we won't give. For people like that to find officials who won't be used is frustrating to the extreme. They don't know any other way to operate." he laughed, shaking his head sadly at the same time."That is one fact that began to convince me you were right when you said this world is changed."

" Steve fiddled with his coffee cup, looking off in the distance. He had gone to the one completed satalite city, during his wandering and had found no home there. Strange how the people of the old ways are leaving our world. So many of them.And they are building new ships that will take colonists to other planets one day. They make money trading with each other. And they operate pretty much the way the old folks did, fighting, manipulating each other,with power shifting from one to another. Little more than promises and bloodshed for the poor fools that get caught up in the game. They don't keep Earth's covenants. They're still greedy as ever and thoughtless people are controlled by the powerful. It's as though the past keeps reproducing itself out there." He was shaking his head, a sadness flooding his face. With a frown he added, "We'll have to deal with them one day. They say Earth's dead but it's our Plant Wizards who've staffed their hydroponics and created a food supply there."

Rose nodded,"It's the same with the colonies on Mars and on Triton. From what I've heard, dis- satisfied people go out there to look for what we don't have." She was silent, they waited, a pall settled over them, and finally with a long sigh, she said,"But that's not fair. Every good space scientist is eager to research his or her specialty out in those colonies. And they're doing fascinating, and hard, work." Then with a brighter tone she said, "Well, we've got to get on with our world. We can help them, but we aren't a market for what they want to create." Then, with a lighter tone, she smiled, "No, Jerry, I don't think we'll have time to be bored."

They all laughed, Cassandra bent a peircing look toward Rose and then finished her toast in thoughtful silence. Rose added,"There's something very important taking place in this Valley, you know, we've got to be ready to take part in it. We're going to need time. I think what's happening here will provide us with a whole new direction, more to do than we ever imagined."

As if all the talk had burdened them, they sat in silence, finishing their meal. And finally Rose stood to carry all her dishes to the cleaner.

Steve finished, pushed an empty plate aside,"Cassandra, you're up for final tests this spring. Are you ready?" He looked at her trying to see in the little girl face that wisdom and maturity needed for these tests. He had no idea what they were, having never taken them. His early education was not yet so different from the old ways. One that had only begun to free itself from the pattern of memorized information. His generation had barely begun what these kids took for granted. Hers was a series of trials in whether or not she was practicing in daily living the knowledge and the understandings she had learned, whether she had polished skills in careful reasoning, problem solving, and inter- relationships. He shook his head, these trials had seemed so esoteric to him, so unrelated to earning a living, but she always laughed and kissed him and ran off.

He had never demanded any Teacher tell him their value. He knew there was something called 'emotional balance' and that seemed to have some sense to it, but when she had told him she would be tried in intuitive perceptions, focussing of attention, imaging, and worse- that she must demonstrate ability to enter into at least one other state of consciousness, besides sleep,at will. He had protested - she was only ten years old, for heavens sake, how could she know what that was about. What about math, history,composition, science, all the tried and true skills of school? And she said she learned as she worked out the solutions for the endless series of projects every kid had to do. Finally he had to admit that it was he who didn't know. He met the eyes of these young ones with an odd sense of embarrassment at times. They lived in a world unknown to him. They seemed to know what he could not imagine. And yet he was never jealous. Cassandra had watched his face. She knew he asked now with everyone present because he wanted support.

"Dad, I keep up with my friends,I think, but how can anyone ever know until they enter the testing? I think that's what it's for, you know. Not to test us, but to bring us- closer- focussing, so that we recognize what we know." When she said that, her gaze had passed through Steve, was on some perception far beyond him. He heard a faint gasp of surprise from Rose and felt grateful. Even Rose found his daughter's understandings unusual? He turned away, drank coffee, wanted to talk of something else and yet, wanted to demand explanation.

Rose dropped her eyes, not seeing her plate, pushing it aside mechanically and picking up her nearly empty cup to drink. Surely she had known that it was not only her own children who were 'different'. She used the word distrustfully. Was that it? Little Cassandra was out distancing her own father. And if they were 'different' what did that mean. Different from what? From what her own friends had been when they were little. Well, times were vastly changed, things were so very different even in those short twenty years. She thought of Dean, and the strange vacancy in him. Surely there was another side to all this. The Valley was a place of extremes, children like this, and people like Dean, and maybe William.

Their own William. What he must feel! She tore her thoughts away from this painful direction they had taken. She just didn't know. The knowledge that she had better well find out, saddened her and she felt the burden of it. She said,"Well, I've got work to do too. I've got some students waiting for me and some meetings with the Council members." She glanced around at them, heaved a long sigh and said, And I'm going to have a talk with Master Teacher Harris. We need to look at the way we've been doing our Teaching."

Silvia and Jerry pushed back their chairs, the silence in the room was full of questions. They wanted to get on with their days work too. Jerry said,"Well, we've got something to be mighty proud of. We've got the whole town done. There's only some final polishing and a few gardens to design and plant and we'll present ourselves to the Valley as a town." He laughed, the idea always amused him. Yet it was tradition already in a Valley so recently creating tradition. He stood there looking at them, his long hair flopping against his shoulders and his long frame moving , stretching as if a spring released itself within him. Energy he had to spare, and he used it with flowing precision.

He stood towering over the table, his body almost too thin, his green shirt hanging limp below his narrow hips, he drew his arms up , pressed his elbows out to loosen the muscles. The breadth of his chest tightened the shirt. Rose could see in his eyes the glimpse of that half hidden pain, a pain she saw there often and that he thought concealed. She had asked him of it and he had not admitted knowing it's source.

Silvia said,"I think it's about time. We've not gotten this town done in a hurry. " She waved a hand at his move to protest,"Yes, I know, we've built to last,and it took time.I'm not complaining, after all   I was as insistant as you were. But we are a little late getting done. It's taken all of us, working all the time,nearly, ten years or more. I'm glad , after all - - it's a wonderful place to live. But what'll we do now?" Her voice was joking, but they knew her words were not.

Rose shook her head slowly," To do it we had to learn a lot about organizing ourselves, and how to work together. We did that! We'll not forget. Now, Silvia, we can get down to the real business of living. What its all been for." She glanced around, unsure of their response even now. "The development of our lives into what is possible. Even when I was young the Teachers made us learn that mixim, 'The awakening of Mind and Heart into full consciousness.' I think we're just beginning to know what that means."

Silvia turned to get her jacket "Yeah, but we thought it was just something to carve on buildings" She grinned."I'm still not sure it isn't."

Rose frowned, nodding, "Yes, somehow we've got to know more what that means. Know and talk about it, so it gets shaped into action."

Cassandra looked at them, puzzled and troubled,"But Aunt Silvia, it is already, isn't it? It's what the testing is about. It's the - -. It's what my friend calls it. - We say the Teachers shake us over the edge. They zap us into attention and see whether we notice. It's the testing"!

Silvia looked at her with a growing look of amazement and

THE AWAKENING

consternation."My Good God! Out of the mouths of babes". She shrugged on her jacket. "I'm going where things make sense to me." She stopped as she reached the door. "I did want to ask you Rose. I wish I knew that you do things you really want to do now and then. I get the feeling that whatever we suggest to you that needs doing, you're willing. You fit into what people want of you. I can't tolerate that. I know that I want to do what I want to do. But I want you to do what you want to do too." She grinned quickly, and added. "Maybe so I don't have to feel guilty!" She watched Rose in silence. "You any where near to being a martyr?"

Rose nodded slowly, her eyes meeting Silvia's seriously, "Maybe! But I don't think it'll go that far. I'm also selfish enough to hold my edge. Keep a watch on me, little Sister, Let me know if you see the signs of martyrdom." Silvia looked searchingly at her but she was not joking.

Silvia nodded, watching her friend, something seemed to her to be not right. Rose was too edgy. Rose thought Silvia looked prettier with pregnancy. It was good that pregnancy made some women happy and beautiful. She suspected her perception was effected by her own longing to have a new baby in the family. She had not spoken of her knowledge of that pregnancy to Silvia and she smiled now, Silvia would be surprisd to know how many people knew. Jerry stood by the door, waiting and they turned to leave. The cold air hit them like a bath of ice. They laughed and clutched their coats tightly.

For several minutes there was silence then Anna pushed back her chair,"Jane, shall I go with you and Steve this morning? I've got to be at the Center this after noon but I can help now."

Jane nodded, putting one hand on the fingers on her shoulder "Good, we can use help this morning. The weather's not going to hold long at all."

Steve got up and picked up his jacket and hat,"Rose did they get the Market Computer screen repaired? I want to start getting supplies for the planting. By the way, you're sure Ben'll be here soon."

She nodded,"Soon, Steve? I've told you! He'll be here TODAY! This very night! It's too good to be true." her eyes sparkled, "And yes, you can use the computer. I told you, test me out. Ben'll be here, He'll sleep among us tomorrow". The exultation in her voice was obvious to them all. The children laughed, their eyes shining looking at her with a joy that surprised her. Of course, they must know too. And they would never have told her. She realized that last with sadness.

Steve nodded, frowning, wanting to ask and then deciding to let it go. He shrugged and left. Anna and Jane followed, and Andrew came to kiss his mother and dashed whistling from the Hall. She finished her coffee silently then pulling on a coverall of wool-Skenna mix, water repellant and warm enough for what she had to do, she went to stand a moment on the deck, looking over the Valley as she always did. The air was full of mist and rain, but none of it really serious yet. She hurried into the Temple, and settled herself into the corner booth.She listened to her own growing quiet.The distant ringing of a bell, the washing sound, the fading of these into the great growing extension of Silence so profound it itself rang. She focussed her attention to that distant pure sound. Lost herself in that point of focus. Her whole body relaxed, she was aware of it, of the sensation of the cushion, of fragrance, of the hard smooth wood of the walls, the extending light and glassteel frames of the temple walls. Acutely sharply aware. She was aware of herself here in this point of the Valley, silent and utterly conscious of each life, each form and at the same time of the stillness, the distant slow ring of that bell somewhere beyond everything. She was at peace. The Valley was at peace. Was peace a genuine possibility for humankind? The great fascination of power games, war, shiftings of power and using of people as though they were pawns in a game, industry and science as simply other dimensions of that game, had absorbed strong people through centuries. Could humankind turn its restless, living mind toward something greater? More alive? The questions gathered, stung at her attention. But steadily she drew herself into stillness again. the possibilities were mute. Life was.

Then without warning,like a flood, thoughts and feelings surged up again, inundated that stillness. She held, sustained her attention and watched as they subsided, slowly sank away. She was absorbed, bringing her attention as close to that soundless sound as she was able. Reaching attention in the stillness and acceptance. Holding there in that Light that was there, that was always there, beyond the edges of consciousness, she waited, patient, receptive. If there was to be anything realized, any understanding, it would come through stillness. Questions only laid a pattern for the stillness to create through.

Silent, waiting, listening and attentive to nothing except itself she knew no sense of time. But finally, her body drew a long free breath, and she sent out into that still place one thought."I am in dire need of understanding. Let there be one who will give me help." The prayer was clear, and it spoke her need fully.

As she left the Temple, she was grateful for the respite. The old weight of dispair was lighter. A new found touch of Joy lay beneath it, beneath everything, like a promise. She didn't understand that - neither the joy nor the dispair. This was a time of waiting and of patience. She sighed. She was not a patient person.

CHAPTER FIFTEEN

The River Journey Home - Ben and Jessie

Ben let the boat ride on the current. It was a swift, hard winter current, willful and powerful. The heavy rains of the season had brought the River level high and water continued to pour in from every tiny stream. But Ben felt at home on this broad Green River. On its quiet flow he had traveled through the entire length of the Valley more than once. This northern section, narrower and just below the long dangerous rapids that roared between the high cliffs from which the Valley began, was not as familiar. He relaxed, attending to the small boat, his mind full of the events of the past weeks.

Ben's body adroitly managed the 'Barb', keeping it steady, watching its progress through various bits of debris that had drifted out from the flooded banks. He was skilled and his movements were easy, his thoughts on other things. He sat at the center of the wide seat and periodically, rhythmically, pulled the oars with powerful strokes, smooth, unhurried. He was riding a current and needed only to use his strokes to guide the swiftly moving craft. His body enjoyed the work, his mind was free from it. His feet encased in sturdy grey boots, were planted firmly apart. He felt a joy in his own power.

For most of his life he had lived through his senses and he reached out to life as Rose reached in. In this frail shell of wood, small and wonderfully crafted, carved with the images of his exploits through years, he could feel every nuance of the immense energy on which he floated. This little craft was the one physical creation of these months of deep self searching while he was at the Station. Building it had been his relief and pleasure. Now, feeling the power of the River beneath him, borne utterly upon that energy, he was in joined companionship with that power. The River was a personal friend, he knew its ways. He did not underestimate the River, he recognized his strength and his dependence. Out of years of fierce independence, of separation and isolation, he had begun to build an awareness that enabled him to see the world as an extension of himself, a vast, intricate, interwoven extension, a multiple identity. He knew that Rose saw it as an inclusion of herself. A giving, permeation of self into Self. He knew the difference, and as he guided the craft through the debris, he reflected on that fact. He did not know, however, how much he and Rose had absorbed of the other's tendency, during their years - or how much they had resisted and denied.

He stopped rowing, glancing at the sky, and the wide spread of water ahead, sat for a moment resting, then stood up, looking far ahead, balanced the way a dancer might be, ready to move instantly. His body seemed over sized for the boat as he stood, bracing his feet to either side to keep the craft steady before settling down again into the little seat.

He sighed, the year had been long, the learning had been intense and not until these last days had he realized how much he had begun to accept. The teachings of his childhood, had been only a foundation and the teaching that the Monitors had offered him, seemed to him to build so rapidly on that foundation he could hardly absorb all that he knew.

He said softly to himself,"If I were to remember what I've learned how would I act, or think? And what've I learned?" He frowned, remembering,and muttered as if reciting, "That every hour, this mind, body, and emotions are at the service of that Divine spark within me." He sighed,"And that's what my Teacher called the Soul, living and real" He shook his head, puzzled and wanting to realize now, at this minute, Soul contact. But the recognition would not come. He said, "When I focus attention at that highest point of consciousness, I am aware. Soul Conscious? At any rate I know the teachings are true! In such moments I am more alive, but I am detached from myself." He frowned, pulled a slow, hard pull on the oars, bringing the boat out away from the banks a little,"But then, I can see myself more clearly."

He was silent, letting the thought shape."Yes, detached, such a strange idea,but In that transcendant state it seems so natural. In this state, it seems queer. I am one or the other, never able to keep vision at both points at once." The failure disappointed him. He frowned again. He spoke again so softly the water tapping at the sides of the boat, drowned the sound." Even when I stand Soul Conscious the weight of the familiar pulls awareness back down into itself. A life time of habit thinking is hard to rise out of. Can I remember? They said that as I know my Self, then Right action will be natural to me. Then, Right thought too is natural?"

He sat in deep attention turned inward, seeking that inner light as he had done each day there at the Station. As his thinking stilled, and focus refined itself, recognition gradually strengthened." That is what I am.'I'am Soul.'I' am not simply a man called Ben. However,I live through this person Benjamin in this world." He murmured the words to a chant that the teachers had taught him.

> I am Soul, Love also I am.
> I will to lift this little self into the Light Divine.
>   That which desires to lift
>   And that which cries out for lifting Are one!

He sat for some time with his head bent slightly, oblivious for long moments of the craft, other moments his hands moved to guide without thought. He became aware of being and doing simultaniously. It lasted only a moment. Then thoughts rushed in. How could that be? How could his body act without his personal attention? No! There was attention, that which was Life permeated his body utterly and moved with a current as persistent as this River current. He felt amused at himself, seeing the two edged consciousness. Awed at the realization, he muttered,"I am more than myself".

"I'm not always Conscious. Even now I avoid my Self. I've lived most of my life

THE AWAKENING

so. But if now, I remembered, each morning when I wake, to live from that greater life, then would my life be worth while?" He shook his head, "But what then of me? Of Benjamin?" The puzzle seemed to him unsolvable, yet he knew of the duality that he was and he could not ever forget again.

His words had been murmured and barely audible, but the figure behind him in the boat, huddled into itself, heard. His companion was wrapped in a long dark cloak, woven of the tight rain resistant blend that came from the people of the northern lake country. She had forgotten how long ago she got it, but it fit around her comfortably. Between the man and woman was a quality of being together that needed no words, The sky hung heavy, clouds ragged and low nearly grazed the hill tops and scattered bits of mist through the higher glens and rocky peaks. The wet coolness around them seemed as saturated with an incoherent longing of living things for that ending of the cold, of winter and for the waking of spring. Ben felt the urgency of it, the promise like a touch.

"What is it? he mused, his eyes drawn into the soft movement of the grey, low fragments which, as if lost, tangled in treetops and settled like torn fabric around the great rock outcroppings. Old sodden leaves piled around the trunks of trees and caught like great, heavy, deformed bodies in the brush thickets. The acrid smell of vegetation rotted by drowning, the water smells of fish and thick muds settling against the bottom, mingled with the sweet freshness of the air blowing down from the high mountains. All together it delighted him. It smelled like River country.

He responded to the beauty, feeling it soften the underlying sense of unease that had persisted with him all day. He wanted to greet this world before him, to send out some word that would enter into it and make him more fully belonging. He smiled, spread both his great arms, and breathed deeply of the mist. Late February, he thought, a time of constant change. It was a year since he had been in these lands and it seemed like many more. He thought he had lived a life time during that year.

The boat moved suddenly into a bank of low fog and he felt the entrance like an embrace of the sky itself to include him and his companion in the drama of the coming storm. With utter stillness now, he watched, feeling the gathering of energies, the rising power above and all around. Objects about him faded, letting his thoughts fade, he held himself taut with attention. He felt the streaming of communications between all things, all life. He lived and was part of this flow. He let his whole being reach forth and become involved in the living event of this morning.

Ben could see beyond the great trees along the banks into the open spaces beyond as the fog thinned and parted. There was the movement of people - families already completing the preparing of fields. Some would be sowing winter grain or tubers, some repairing and clearing out old debris. Ghostlike through the drifting fog, they appeared then faded. At times he saw someone lift on a disc float and move smoothly across the fields. Everything seemed to be seen through a veil. He could faintly hear the chants of those who planted, the cry of a disc rider. For some family here it was the right time, the Earth was ready to receive the seed and the people sang of their intentions. The travelers could hear the voices, rising then fading as they passed. He bowed mentally with them as they offered their seeds into Earth. He felt a needle of worry. He so wanted the Family's spring planting to wait until he was there to help. He must be part of it this year. He felt a faint odd touch, a nearness in his mind, and wondered, but felt obscurely his own closing away from that touch. Was it that? Were there people there who knew of their passing? There again, he was refusing him Self. He had drawn in again, a small solid body within this endless Earth life.

He turned himself to the River, attending again to the guiding of his boat. The detachment of the River seemed to him profound, yet it meant nothing, neither good or evil. It allowed all things, allowing his boat as simply as it allowed the half rotted logs that bumped against his watchful oar. He thought he would like to communicate with this River, this powerful energy. but it was too vast a life, Godlike in its length and detachment. It was no wonder the primitive peoples of Earth gave a name to the God of their Rivers. He thought they could have done better to have seen the River itself as that God. But they had had to separate the two, to make the God of the River in the likeness of a man. He felt a reverence in being allowed to sit, floating on that great power.

The River had risen out of its banks several times during the winter, but it receded gently down again, leaving little harm. Along the banks were forests and heavy grasses with thick clumps of shrub or berry vines clustered here and there. The river swamp plants that were harvested for Matta, grew for a mile at a time along some banks but for many more miles they held on only in narrow clumps here and there, behind the forested edges. The River would return to her banks cleanly, with little trace of silt.

Ben thought of his power to control the 'Barb,' of the pleasure of this journey, even though now, his heart was beginning to cry out for its ending. He was nearly home. The thought was a constant joy. Should he activate the tiny power unit that hung in the bow, connected to the propellor folded beneath the boat? Should he race on, swift through the water to the Farm? He liked using his own power. Was that a careless conceit? He hesitated, reminding himself that he had a passenger whose welfare he must consider.

He glanced back briefly at her, then turned fully to look at her, letting the Barb make her own way. He enjoyed the anticipation of this part of the journey, and he needed to think, to try to prepare himself for that homecoming. He was aware that his companion agreed, but he did not think about how he realized that. When he turned he could see that her cloak was thrown back and he was startled by the expression on her face.

Jessie's body was old and she looked old. For eighty eight years she had gathered to herself the experiences of this life She sat now with that strong face open to the air, her hood dampened by the mist. Her eyes seemed to draw into themselves the beauty of the gathering storm. It was as if she drew energy from life itself and returned to it a profound love that radiated from her body openly. It

THE AWAKENING

shone almost nakedly from her eyes. Ben felt that he had invaded a deep privacy by his advertant glance and then this searching study of her expression. He turned back with a quick movement to the world surrounding them.

"It's almost as if I've caught two lovers in a moment of most intimate exchange." he whispered. He could feel the rising wind, the storm closer, the trees bending against that wind and it seemed that he was partaking of a great event in which the River figured and the Earth orchestrated. Yes, of course, all storms were such, all droughts, all natural events were Her doing. Was he then a natural event? Surely he had not felt so involved before. Awareness was acute enough to drown the surges of thinking. He felt power, a straining of Earth toward Something. The question was flung into his mind as a stone is flung into a pond. "To what does it reach". Then from that stone, he felt reverberations rippling through his whole consciousness He felt that upward surge pulling against all the weight of his body and mind. He knew himself here, included in that Earth Reach,something conscious and yet, so much an integral part. He wanted to know - to understand that. The desire was so great he felt his body tremble and he wrapped his arms about himself,letting the oars once again lie quietly in their locks.

His attention moved along the surface of the green-grey water, along the backs of great winding roots of trees clutching at their soil and heavy rooted grasses. Slowly, he Reached out, unwlling to recognize that this was one facet of that same Reach he feared in Rose. This time, the familiar Reach into depths of the life of Earth. Without any reluctance, he sank into that tangle of root and grasses. His consciousness mingled into that which he found, that strange wordless awareness. Acutely aware, he sank into the deep soil where drove the great roots, thicker than his own body, their power and strength bounding the bed of the River. Thick grasses, wiry rooted shrubs and berries bound the soil between their spreading roots and together they held the River's shape. He was surprised at this interchange between River and Forest. Another different consciousness.

The River and the great trees respected each other profoundly. They both responded to the myriad forms of life-lesser forms, insect,rodent, lizard, silent cradles of cocoons , snakes,somnolent among the rocks and all those others who lived parts of their lives beneath the surface of Earth. The trees communicated to one another the approach of imbalance that would cause harm from insect or rodent, and activated chemical protection. Ben felt their touch, the touch cool or warm,,here in this still cool surge that was so close to spring. He knew himself then in a way that gave some definition to that power he had felt earlier. He knew himself as part of this life and as alien. That alien quality was the unease in him. It could create or destroy. He felt watched . Then he knew that he had often felt watched by Earth life and with a seeping in of understanding, he knew it was mankind that Earth life watched. With doubt and sorrow and hope, and a vast patience.

Leaning here against the massive roots momentarily, he felt the power of endurance, consciously he partook of that strength, and then he let himself loosen and extend. The unceasing surge of energy through trunk and branch was alive for him, as vividly pouring up as the down pour that flowed in from the sunlight. He felt and rode on the upward flow. He could feel the slow give as the great limbs met against the wind. Leafless, they felt the wind race through them, unobstructed except for their rough thick bark. The whole tree hummed, stirring with a low rhythmic sound as though murmuring chants that fitted their lives. Ben knew that they were aware of him, as he of them. He thought his presence an intrusion of a privacy to which he had not been granted welcome. But the actual mental intimacy of this strange unhuman consciousness, was thoughtless, aware, present, so alive, intense and true. He felt he had been given a gift more valuable than any before in his life, yet he could not have named it. He shrank back into that uneasy personal self. Drew himself to where thought could shape and make concepts of this experience.

The little boat bobbed quietly on the surface , moving swiftly now and Ben must attend to moving debris. Time seemed to stretch and contract for it had been only moments since he had drawn the oar steadily against the current. He remembered, letting thought take shape, images find words in his mind. The touch of other lives, other consciousness, filled him with an unexplainable joy. He wondered whether he had given anything at all to those lives.

It was time to eat. Hunger gnawed at him and he knew that Jessie must be hungry too. He turned to touch her lightly, "Jessie, we've come a long way since we ate last. Let's eat. We'll be home before we need more and we might as well eat what we have." The thought of home, spoken aloud like this, swept joy to his heart.

He watched the hood she had replaced earlier fall back again. The gleaming silver hair was touched with fine droplets of mist that took the pale light from the dim day to shine softly. He had an impulse to take her hand in affection ,but restrained himself with a deeper sense that it might be disrespectful. He smiled at himself. She would have room for his touch.

At that moment she looked at him , her face quiet with the distant composure that results when one looks out at the world from a deeper place. Her eyes were bright and full of a curiosity that penetrated his reserve. Then she smiled and he felt briefly that radiance that seemed to shine from her at times.

"Yes, food, Benjamin, that would be good. I'll help get it ready. and we might need to hurry if we finish eating before the storm pours water into our bread." She laughed aloud as if the idea pleased her.

Ben took out the brown packages of sandwiches. He found his mind caught up in that image, the two of them sitting in the down pour and their sandwiches soaking up the rain. He smiled, knowing it would not happen. He sat across from her now, their knees nearly touching and he looked at her. She was again gazing into the distance. The air had grown colder but he was not uncomfortable. Small gusts of wind had begun to sweep past their faces, blowing his hair into his eyes , brushing his cheeks and nose like touches of ice. As she began to talk, he listened attentively . What she said seemed very important and yet he didn't know why. Perhaps something in her tone.

"I think of it often now - it is there, just beyond, like a soft mist that nevertheless is heavy around me. It softens everything and remains always just a little ahead, though it is invisibly present. I am filled with Wonder that has no definition."

She laughed shortly and continued, in a very different precise tone,"It's a great wonder isn't it? And I enjoy wonder!" Ben listened, his eyes repeatedly flickering over the water ahead, watching for logs, for debris that might block their movement. He chewed his sandwich hungrily. He felt the distance in her eyes,drawing him as they gazed beyond into the far curve of the River and he envied the tenderness of her smile at what she saw in the mist. Her hands were still in her lap, one holding her sandwich and the other folded close into a small fist. He thought that it was not important to her whether she ate or not. He marveled at her stamina. His curiousity grew as he watched her.

He swallowed the mouthful of food and asked,"Jessie, what is it? This thing you speak of? Is it that same thing that you said hung like a dim glow over the dry fields of the mountains? If this which lies in the mist is the same, it seems something of great beauty, but a great sadness fills me to hear you." He fell silent, letting the words repeat themselves in his mind,then he asked,"Do you understand?"

The old woman nodded silently, her eyes still in the distance and the conversation seemed suddenly as strange as the world around them yet equally as natural. Ben had become accustomed to such talk with Jessie. Now in the curtain of the coming storm, shutting out the sky that held them close in the dim grey green world of water and trees, it seemed to both of them an intimate aloneness with no other world out there at all.

She answered firmly, as though most of her mind was still involved with vast spaces beyond the distant hills. "That which I refer to is Death."

Turning to him now, looking directly into his eyes, she smiled with the bright warmth he loved. Immediately the sorrow increased, becoming a thin stream of pain through his heart. He stopped eating and touched his chest, where he felt the sharpness. It faded, he smiled and they sat thus, smiling at one another. At peace.

Then she lifted her sandwich slowly and bit into it. He felt a nameless relief such as he might feel at seeing a feverish child eat. He dismissed the thought but found her eyes on his, grinning as if she knew his thought. She was nodding, munching slowly, enjoying herself.

After a while, she began again to talk and Ben forgot everything else, except the absorbed pleasure of listening and eating.

"I can tell you Benjamin, what I've not told many people. I see the hills rolling curved and plunging into the deep shadowed hollows, both hard and infinitly soft,but also enduringly tough.Oh, yes, tough those hills. There is in the gentle flow of them a vibrant life that is a presence around us, especially through this wet atmosphere, you can feel it. Then it is as if I look and respond to my Self. I am extended throughout Earth. My mind is attuned to Her, not any moment am I separate. Leaves of trees fall in their time to Earth and roots take nourishment from their decay. It is natural that this body of mine must fall and give itself back to that Earth life."

She spoke so thoughtfully and slowly that Ben was puzzled. This seemed to him something she might have found easy to have said to others. She began again with a soft intake of breath."It's important to know Ben, that the time is drawing near. It won't be long now. It won't be long before my time of dying."

For several minutes there was no sound except the soft slap of water against the boat and the rising breath of the wind. Ben said, finally, "I'm glad you told me. I'm not willing for you to die, but I know that's my own selfishness. I hope there's still time left for us to be together -- won't there be?"

She nodded, seeing the wet brightness of his eyes, but said nothing.

Abruptly anxious, Benjamin frowned,"Jessie, it isn't soon, not so soon that you must - - " he stopped.

She shook her head,"Not so soon we won't reach where we have to go and do what we have to do, Son." She smiled,"There is work in the Valley that I must do, not only with your Family, you know. Your search was not for yourself alone. You know that." He wanted suddenly to be able to offer something, to help, and yet, what did he have that she needed? His strength? Maybe, but she seemed tough as a hickory sapling.

They sat in silence, feeling the smooth riding of their craft through the swift water. Ben idly directed its movements, his eyes flickering constantly over the water to spot debris or half sunken logs. The River was wider now, wider and more smooth. He could see the water flooded over the banks stirring the tall grasses and lapping against the trunks of trees. The coming storm had driven the farmers away to their homes, and there were no shadows moving through the mist beyond. Lights flickered here and there from those homes, and Benjamin felt comfort from that human nearness through the mist and water. He leaned forward, his arms resting on his knees and the oars resting in their locks.

His mind stuck on that phrase that Jessie had used, that she was 'an extension of Earth'. Then he heard her talking softly "It's as though I finally live more consciously between two worlds. Maybe, as though I've seen the distinction between the two and corrected the distortions of vision in each. It's a matter of perception, because there is only one reality and I've divided them for so long. We humans do that, you know, divide reality into dimensions according to our perceptions. According to how much we can bear to See and Know."

He saw that these thoughts were those gathered through long struggles to understand, but that she told them now for his benefit, and for her own reminiscence. She went on, "The distinction between worlds, or the dimensions that we devise, was not clear to me early in my life. But gradually I have learned to understand the interface, the point of extension beyond one into another .When I ceased to experience the dimensions as separate it was a great relief. Things became clear. I saw that humankind is the connector of all conscious movement of life through these dimensions. To do my part I must be aware of difference and unity, of the flow of life through the stages of reality."

She looked at him and in her eyes he saw the gladness of this teaching."All that is becomes clear as if saturated with a pure - - shining - through which one can see , then it is that a true Joy exists. There is sometimes a glimpse of the Way of Things, the Way of existence. And each glimpse is a revelation into understanding." She shook her head, a slight frown penciling lines through the network of wrinkles, "This world we know, our lives, it is so terribly, terribly limited,Benjamin."

Then, suddenly she smiled a broad amused smile, laughing at herself,"Even when perception has broken out of those limits,and I stand aware, without warning sometimes, I am reminded of myself and that small consciousness draws me down into its limits, familiar duality obscures the simplicity, clutters the wholeness. It is then that I know again the points of separation and realize the nature of appearances. I know that appearance separates me from all that is. But to see beyond appearances, I must lift up out of myself!" She shook her head.

She was smiling that bright cheerful smile that made the dim, grey afternoon seem brighter."We cannot truly be separate, because we are all of one nature. At the same time, there isn't anything that can end the ceaseless changing of existence. Nor would one want there to be. For change is the nature of existence, I think." She laughed aloud, as if pleased, "There is no way one human mind can know more than a little of all that IS. Even the Farthest Elders among the Monitors speak of that at times. And their lives are nearly wholly of the Mind-Spirit."

"They don't live as ordinary people, Jessie, those Old Ones?"

Jessie shook her head, "They live so much beyond us, that they come to function through their bodies only now and then, for these bodies are so terribly limiting they use them almost as one might use a hand. It must be painful to them to find it necessary to live in a body. Yet, only part of what they are ever does.It is strange to know those Old Ones. To be among them is to be buffetted by powerful energy. But if one can bear to be receptive, then there is a little gift of the knowledge of what LIFE is, just a little. Whatever one can bear to know."

He watched her face with a growing awe in these revelations,"But Jessie, they are human, persons, just as you and I."He felt a deep grief, a sorrow he couldn't understand, and a profound hope at its depths.

She nodded, eyeing him thoughtfully, "Perhaps during your life, Benjamin, you will have the opportunity to know of them. They are the most precious of our people and the Stations where they live are well planned to care for them their bodies. For just to be in the same Station with them is to be gifted with perception. Sometimes I have felt they seemed amused at us, the rest of us. But among them one feels so lifted into a vast tenderness of Being that makes all things possible and all wonder real. That tenderness rises out of LOVE itself and is not ordinary."

" How does one ever know such?" Benjamin felt his voice tremble.

"It is a gradual thing. Such knowing takes adjustment of the body and emotions and the mind too. It must be gradual. Our very brains cannot bear the -- the vastness of it. We are learning to be closer to one another, to meet in a new relationship that might make our capacity greater. Actually, we are beginning to create a finer kind of body, your children are born in these bodies and living in them will be easier." She stopped and he was astonished at her words, but said nothing.

After a little she went on," When the coming together occurs, then it will be time. We are impatient, because there is so much yet to know,but we will learn. I know well that I must learn to detach myself from what I've been, what I still am,enough to be aware of my Self wholly. That is what the Elders lead us to. They are wholly Soul conscious" She was silent,"It is what frightens, I think, the immenence of that knowledge when we are in their company. It is not they who frighten but what they are - in comparison, and therefore what they lead us toward." She frowned, studying her clasped hands thoughtfuly for some minutes. He waited for he dare not interrupt."They fairly radiate with that energy we can only know as LOVE. So powerful is it, it seems to burn into our hearts and Minds and expose every atom of our being to itself. It is the self naked before the SELF and us conscious of that, that frightens us, my Benjamin."She smiled then,aware that he understood only a part of what she spoke, but she knew the speaking was for herself as well.

For some minutes she was silent, her face so still it seemed she had gone from her body. Then, suddenly she said, "Oh, Benjamin, my Son, it's so necessary for us to strive for that Vision that you sense in Rose and in others too. In yourself especially, though you have denied much. It's important to reach that place where perception begins to stabilize into knowledge. After a while a rhythmic flow between the self and Self begins -- a movement in and out of the eternal and daily life so that both are known. There is a rising and falling of the water of consciousness, fluid and natural. New realization comes drifting in on that flow leaving us with treasures brought on that tide. Treasures we could not imagine or have sought." Then with a brief flashing smile, she said, her eyes dancing,"My words may confound your confusion, rather than clear it? "

He slowly shook his head, then stopped, for he was indeed confused, but he was also much informed."Jessie, somehow something in me hears what you speak, even though I cannot grasp hold of it all just now."

There was stillness then, the soft rushing of the widening River, for they were not far above Adwin now, and the rising wind, brushing through the trees, pushing up waves on the water, surrounded them like a blanket, concealing that world beyond them as though they were lost to it. Then, in a voice so full of memory, of poignance, that he knew she spoke again as much to herself as to him,"When I was young, before all the wonders that humankind has brought to our world were commonly available to us, I lived for a time at the first Monitor Retreat. At that time it was one of three in the entire world It was establisherd by three of the wise ones and it had become quite a large community when I arrived.

It was there that my Teacher told me that when the separation ended and we did not cling to ourselves, when we could see that we were actually more -- were the SELF in truth, then, at that time we would begin to know of freedom. We would have broken through the illusion that we are ordinary animal people and know ourselves Mind-Spirit." She laughed, and her voice softened,"Friend Curtis was my first Teacher there - that was what they called themselves then. The Teachers each seemed to radiate their teaching, as though it came through their very bodies and minds at once. For there seemed no separation between body and mind with those folk. It was then I realized what true Teaching was. It was where we got our Convictions for training Master Teachers."She was silent, remembering, and his unexpected glimpse of the vivid images, startled him.

"Listening to ideas, my mind grasped them as ideas only, they had no life. But watching those Teachers, being among them, I began to absorb the life of these recognitions. They were not just idea, but living consciousness. I 'Knew' for the first time. And Knowledge became a reality for me. You see, these were living truths expressed through the lives of those Monitors. We saw them demonstrated in every smallest act or word. Now, after many years of practice, daily practice, and waking realization, I am sometimes able to live and breath these recognitions also." She smiled apologetically, as if in amusement at herself.

His elbows propped on his knees, Ben held the last bit of sandwich forgotten in front of his mouth. Now he let his eye rest on it and seeing it, moved it into his mouth. He moved his body slightly as if waking, he said,"Jessie, some of what you say seems to have meaning just beyond my grasp, as if there is another part of me, a separate self. Is that what you mean by the Self? Is there then some deep level at which we learn first, one that gradually surfaces as we listen to ourselves? Because what you tell me seems to be only a reminder of what is already known somewhere behind my thoughts. Perhaps there is knowledge in us that we do not bring to speech."

She nodded soberly,"Yes, Benjamin, it's so. That knowledge lies deep in you and it is available if you seek for it. In your thinking mind the words seem to lack life, unless you are listening with your whole heart. But deep within they grow in meaning, for they have found your own knowledge stirred to waking by their truth. So tell me, how do you understand these things?"

Ben shook his head, his voice carried a quality of wonder that rose from his deep attention."Some of these things you say relate to the ideas my own Family has talked about, some of us at least. Paul, Jennifer, Tom, sometimes others and of course, always Rose. She seems to realize farther than I. Sometimes I want to hush them because I feel fear, and other times such talk makes me tremble with a hope that I cannot name. But the ideas seem to sprout seeds, as if they grow in me long after the talk. Seeds that have lain dry in my mind, that carry that image of what is beyond life-- what used to be called God perhaps. Or at least of the nature of the Eternal. That which is so alive it breaths through us, through everything about us. Those seed-thoughts sprout, and slowly, I think they grow. "

He was silent, finishing the bite, wiping his hands together, looking out at the lashing fine drizzle of rain that had begun finally, ignoring its stinging at his face."Sometimes I feel very angry, Jessie, angry and afraid, and the anger is because I don't want to be afraid. There are so many old notions standing in the way of accepting what I realize. There are old ideas, old traditions, and attitudes. I have been trained as a scientist and so there is the whole heritage of science that denies, or at least doubts, what it cannot test with the senses, or controlled experiment. Even though for a hundred years we have been thinking beyond what we can test with the senses. Our atomic microscopes, and our photographic plates, and our amplified hearing, are simply extensions of senses. But they are also more." He shook his head, a frown still creasing his forehead and mouth," There is knowledge that is found in these instants of awareness, knowledge that transcends our extension of senses. I think there is a very great reluctance to let the old order go. To accept this new universe as it makes itself known."

"You mean as you create its knowing?"

He grinned then and nodded, "I think our children will not have all this trouble."

Jessie laughed, That's what your parents said. And you have no idea how much more free you are than we were. The very acceptance of those glimpses of what LIFE is, were almost impossible for us at first. We truly denied, with total blindness at times. We didn't want to conquer the possible, only the probable. And it was not only fear of what awed us, but the fear that we could make fools of ourselves in each other eyes. We feared what we called superstitions, not knowing that we might find something of worth in a close study even of those. But today, you of the Valley, most of you, know that there is more than you can sense, there is that which is beyond the senses to be known.It has been officially reached so far by only the very highest thought, Math, contemplation and deep listening.But it has been known to some through trained intuition."

Ben nodded and smiled, "We aren't so wise, Jessie, we're stuck in our old patterns too." He looked far beyond their craft, through the mist that blew and revealed now and then a stretch of turbulent water ahead. Fog drifted and broke, then gathered again cutting off all vision. Infrequent spatters of rain, large drops and then the fine thin curtain of needle sharp drops, came and went. He straightened and said, his voice strong and clear again,"We don't deny what we are beginning to know, Jessie, but we doubt and we are often afraid. It threatens our very selves, I think, but I don't know how. I've heard Rose say that, it troubled me very much."

She drew her hood closer and nodded, her eyes shining with a look of intent watching,"You do see that Light that is the mark of the beginning of sight? You have told me of that!"

He nodded,"We do. Rose too, and now some of the others, though they seldom speak of it. I have -- I'm afraid I have refused to talk of such things.I don't know why, unless it was my fear."

She frowned, looked a moment down at the thin sheet of rain water that had fallen into the bottom of the boat,"I'm afraid I trouble you Ben, perhaps I have spoken too much of my own thoughts. They are of my own Journey."

But he broke in, his voice stoutly impatient,"No! Never think that! We do want to know, to learn. We are willing! Even when we are reluctant. I feel my mind open in this talk, feel something wake inside my Heart that is like a bird opening its wings. The strength of it lifts my very consciousness. It's like a tiny crack of light shining at the end of a dark cavern. It doesn't matter that the talk exposes also the darkness of that cavern. It's what I'm willing to know in order to see more clearly that Light.It is a light that comforts me even when I'm most afraid. It's growing so obvious to me that we live in a universe of many dimensions. We've only faintly dreamed of them, or glimpsed a little of them in our most far reaching sciences. I know that." He was silent, and she waited,"It's been a thought that brought me fear, but more terribly a harsh dispair that I could not shake, and so I came to this Journey. Unless I could begin to understand something of what I perceive beyond myself, I could not live." He was again silent, bringing thought into balance. "I was caught in an absolute absence of Light for a long time. Now, I would rather know fear than dispair."

He looked up at her bleakly, his eyes asking."There's no more awful terror than to feel that there's nothing, no meaning to anything. Or to think that I am all there is, small, so alone and so incomplete. Though I don't know where I go, what lies ahead, I see that Light, guiding through this waste land that is myself. It is as though in my mind I wind about on narrow threads of pathway between yawning pits so dark and deep that if something drops there is no sound.I think I create those pits with my fear. I know that I do. What torturous urge leads me to suffer so?" He sighed, shaking his head wonderingly,"After all, I do see that Light ahead." His voice became a whisper, "I know from whence it comes!" For some time he was silent.

"That which leads to Life has frightened me more than that which leads to death. It is as simple as that. I fear the Light, and the endless possibility it offers." His voice broke and he shuddered, the sound of the words was like a rasp through his throat as if he fought to still himself and yet fought also to speak."Yet, there it is, Jessie. It is LIFE ahead, offered to us. And we have feared, raged in anger against Life Itself." He shook himself, surprised at what he had said,"Why yes, that's it exactly."

The old woman smiled gravely, nodding and so deeply pleased with this young man. She said, "Listen, there is a rhythm growing, the rhythm of wind and water, the pulse sound of the arteries of Earth. Listen, it reverberates and makes conscious to us the sound of a great Life. Like a beating heart,it is" She glanced at him, questioning, but found his attention sharp on her words.

I've thought of our evolving out from the waters of Earth, from single atoms into cells and then into changing life forms. Using the energy of Sun and Earth to begin becoming form, quality, mind and Heart. We contain in our bodies that element that gave us birth. That deep and beating rhythm of the oceans. "

He frowned, not knowing where she led, but she went on,"But now, billions of years later, we turn again from Earth stuff, we open our consciousness outward, through mind itself, into Spirit nature as though through another ocean. From that first emergence out of oceans into the light of the Sun, animal life suffered and was afraid. Now, we emerge from this deep ocean of flesh wrapped about us, and we emerge again outward toward another Light. It is no less alien than that ancient sun ocean life saw through the waters. Or that other time when humankind broke through into Light and we knew first that we were a self, a person, separate from all else. Now, we return a little higher on the spiral, we find ourselves again including all that we separated from. And again we see the Light. Through that Light we will find another universe to explore and to know. Through ourselves, we enter into what is beyond ourselves. Even as our ancestors did. This sea of Light has nourished us so long, it's time we went on beyond it and carried it within ourselves as we did before." Her eyes were full of a kind of Joy that made him turn his eyes away, as if he came to close to bear it.

Then suddenly she was grinning so infectiously that Ben had to join her. She seemed to be playing with images, with thought itself, and he liked it.

"Well, Jessie, the symbols give us something to think with. It isn't easy to think of what we realize through our Reaching minds. And that's the same Reach we use to Touch one another, isn't it?"

"It is one of the practices of the beginning Reach." She put her hand out to touch his, letting her fingers slide lightly across his folded fist before drawing back to her lap. "It's as though one has lived all one's life inside a shell and for reasons unknown that shell cracks. Through that tiny rupture Light shines and there is no explanation for where it comes from. Shell life seems precious, desparately confining, yet comfortably safe, then painfully limiting and yet, again, suffocating. All reality has been within the shell, and now, how can anyone speak of what is beyond it?"

"There it was, what was seen through that crack in the shell that had limited life, could not be - could not, because it was not the nature of the shell and the shell was all that had ever been . That which was unknown, of another nature even, COULD not be. Yet it was more, it was a glimpse of a frightening beyond. Imagine a bird just hatching, looking with conscious intelligence out into our vast sky, the unknown forms there. Wouldn't it be full of fear? Would it accept, allow, even let itself continue hatching? How could it define anything - even its own mother whom it has never known or seen at all.? This is what we face. The recognition of that which is beyond what we know as reality. It takes a courage not common."

She paused, bringing her gaze back from the distance and looking at him ruefully for a moment. "Oh, Ben, my Son, there is such a difficulty in talking about something we have not yet got language for. For me the symbol that fits best is that great beating heart in which I live. It is again symbolized by this River, its grand power and calm rhythm. I feel my own small heart respond, its tiny sound seeks to join in the sound of the beating of the mighty Heart of the Universe." She sighed and smiled, shaking her head, "But talk! Words don't say it at all. There are many symbols of That which we only know as 'What Is'. This symbol of the River and the Heart only comforts me in part."

They were silent, the wind tore now through the pine trees, humming, rising and falling like a dim song.

Softly she said, "I think the human race forgot that it was born out of Spirit into matter, that its nature is two fold. That we are creatures of Earth, but also of air, which is a symbol for Mind, we seem willing to accept, and now we accept that we are creatures of Light also, creatures of Spirit as well as of Earth, water and air. Thus do the Vagabonds understand. They see that we are what Earth Herself is, matter and Spirit within one another." She was smiling now, as if the thought brought memories of her years traveling among those happy people. She shrugged, "But it is no wonder that we fear, right now, with our minds so polished and fiercely protective of thinking as the foundation of life. It took us so long to learn to think." She laughed. Now, that ancient knowledge that we call Heart knowledge, nudges us to remember it's right." She laughed again.

Ben pulled steadily at the oars, so silent in the water, his skill was obvious. She smiled at the smooth movements of his body and the boat. He thought how easy it seemed for her to talk like this. Yet she had often been silent in their travel earlier. After a while she said, "I always seem to need to explain things. Always have. To find words that will express what I've realized. To sit in silent realization has never been my way, I cannot rest until I find words. I think your Mate Rose has this habit too." She smiled at him and he was surprised and confused. How could she know of Rose? But he was drawn from the thought by her words, "Simple knowing comes as a light into darkness. Simple knowing. But we cannot rest without concrete proof. Maybe it is as well. We fool ourselves less that way. Often I know clearly what I cannot put into words. In this way, striving to shape language to hold the idea, the concept seems to stretch my mind, to wake it to further awareness. All the effort seems to be worth while, Ben."

Ben nodded and they sat silent, letting the River once again carry them on its swift current. After a bit Ben let the oars bite deep and he rowed hard against the water. The exercise felt good, the control he could exert on their movement reassuring. The day was half done, the air colder, and he thought that this would be a winter storm, though spring was showing signs everywhere. He hoped there would be no snow, the small leaves on buckeye trees, and blossoms of the early almonds were already unrolling themselves and would be burned by too much cold. He thought it would be warmer farther south at Adwin. The farmer in him evaluated the land as he passed it by. His eyes found and held, as if nourished, by a pale, gold-green thicket of elderberry. They would not mind the cold. He drew his eyes away reluctantly as the boat slid past.

Then he said, "Well, Jessie,, I can see that I've been blind. It's our task to understand that extended perception of reality that we know of now. It's what we've begun in our Valley life! And when I state it that way, it doesn't seem such a big deal. Why haven't I seen it?" His tone was so matter of fact, that Jessie grinned and watched him until he raised his eyes and met hers. There was no fear in his eyes, but a puzzled embarrassment that changed to amusement. "It seems so obvious now. I feel like a fool."

"Well you can't very well say it's 'nothing big' when you realize what it all means. The ideas, they aren't exactly new, if that's what you mean. But Ben, what have you allowed, what have you known of all this"?

He slowed his movements, but continued rowing,"I've mostly known fear, of ideas and of myself when I did realize." He seemed weary as if a hard task had been completed , relieved and weary. He nodded abruptly as if coming to a decision. I think now that fear blinded me to everything else. And it blinded me to Rose. That's what's so painful to acknowledge. " He drew the oars into the boat and settled to look at her, "The only thing I've allowed myself has been what I call the Earth Touch-- a little while ago on this River, I was there,Reaching down into the River and into the life of the trees, their roots, all of their great still lives. I was touching all that. When I do that,it's a widening out, an enlarging of myself . But I never thought of it as the same as the Touch she speaks of." He stopped, "You know,Jessie. You must know."

She nodded, serious, then, "The Touch is the same." Then she frowned, watching him, "What of Rose? You've never accepted her Reach?

He shook his head,"I've felt drawn - felt her Touch - I won't deny that. But it scared the hell out of me and I'd tell myself that my Mate was weird, was not normal. I'd refuse to think about it until that got to be a habit. She knew. It must have pained her, now I think of it."

She nodded again, watching him, her hands folded in one another. He pushed one oar out to fend off a floating log and tightened his mouth. They sat, he rowed a little more now and then,and Jessie dozed off, letting her hood nearly cover her head again. Then he turned to her, "There is something that worries me, now that we've mentioned Rose. It's something different and I don't know what but I know she's afraid. It's something I can't protect her from because I don't know what it is. I don't think she knows what it is."

"Have you asked her?"

He shook his head, his eyes miserable, "No, I suppose I was more afraid than she."

"Benjamin, she's seen possibility. The Light that opens the Heart. But these other things, the Psychic senses that seem to be cropping up, accompany such awakening. With discipline of mind, continued over time, there is a natural unfoldment and these new senses begin to develop too. It accompanies all greater awareness, the Touch with that which is Spirit. She has begun to realize that and it is disturbing to her very organized and trained mind. Rose isn't afraid of these new Talents that she has discovered, she enjoys them. She is afraid of how she might be received if she uses them. She is only beginning to know of the extent to which they are common in the Valley. But this other, this Touch with Spirit. THAT she does not understand. She senses that it asks something much more profound of her" She saw that he wanted to understand but did not. She said,"Tell me, how do you know of her fear?"

He searched her eyes, their depths seemed to swallow his own vision and give him courage to look at the sources of his knowledge. He looked away and then with resolution that heartened her greatly, he turned back, and meeting her eyes steadily said,"I do link. I do link with her. even when I won't admit it."

She nodded, waiting. He was silent then with a sigh he went on."What is it I'm afraid of? I suppose I'm afraid I'm not normal, just what I accused her of. But she closes herself off from me and that's when I know I refused to link with her." Then he stopped , pushed the oars aside and leaned forward, his face full of intense worry."That's what's wrong Jessie. It IS wrong. It's too dangerous, you know. We've been taught, all our lives that to desire control over another person is ultimate degradation for both. We cannot allow such power, for in that linking, that Touch with other minds, I could exert power. I could do that!"

She laughed, even though he seemed so distressed,"Don't worry Ben, that's part of the whole, the   recognition. You have been taught you know, through deep trust, the sanctity of individual autonomy. After all it has been a supposition for millinia that even the Gods had to honor free will, individual choice. And you see how horrified you are at the possibility that that be threatened ?"

"Then you think we can trust ourselves?"

"No, we may not always trust ourselves, but if we know that then we will stand guard over ourselves. You do know of Love, you of the Valley. You know of the waking of consciousness. You vow to care for all life as if it were your own. Which it is. You of the Valley have accepted a trust. Love is active among you, it drives your intentions and protects you from yourselves. "

Ben was silent a long time, "As long as we can keep our committment we made when we graduated from our elementary Learning - that committment to practice selflessness - as long as that is observed, we might be safe."

" Remember this new mind power to Reach and to Touch, is not the same power to manipulate people that people feared in the past. That was blind use of what we did not define. Today we know the difference. We do know. and it is why we must consciously acknowledge our knowing and our Talent. You have been disciplining yourselves for years to live by those committments that you seriously vow to. These are not empty ideals.They are real." She hesitated, then,"You already make contact with your own Soul nature. You are Soul Conscious, and such consciousness is beyond petty misuse of Talents, is it not?"

He nodded sadly,then spoke out of an aching grief,"But I fall back, I forget and am lost again in myself." He drew a long breath, "If we are able to sustain Soul Consciousness, to practice it, in everyday life. Can we do that? Can we test ourselves and know?"

"We are always being tested." She sighed and he thought he heard wearyness in her sigh. "But new Talents are not dangerous even in a loving disciplined human being. Which you are even when you are separate from your Self."

Yet, Rose is afraid. So afraid that she closes herself off from me and won't let me know.?" As he accepted himself in these minutes, accepted his denials, he found realizations swimming into his mind, realizations that he had denied successfully for years. He knew precisely that Rose was afraid of something she could not speak of. He had insisted to himself that it was herself she feared. He had thought she feared him too.

Jessie waited until he had absorbed these things. Then she said softly, looking away over the water, the roiling swirls that swept constantly beside them, "She is afraid of what is revealed by that Light. What might be called possibility and that brings changes, brings perceptions that cannot be explained. Just as we spoke of before. The struggles of my life were similar, Benjamin, and even though you said you did not understand, you at least accept that they can be real. She is also afraid because you won't share with her and that makes her feel more alien." He nodded after minutes of thoughts, and she said,"

Then, as to that wakening of the Spirit in her, she is afraid of the demand. She senses it's demand, though she does not attend enough to know the nature of the demand. She does not trust herself."

"And what is that demand, Jessie. Why should there be such?" His voice was almost a whisper. He feared something intangible was threatening this Love of his, something he could not fight.

"It is the demand for one's entire being, one's whole self, one's very identity. To put it simply, though not accurately, it is the demand to give oneself up into that which is greater - and which is a shift of identity, so that the self is known as not self and the Self, is recognized as identity. " She shook her head, fearing she had only confused him more.

He nodded slowly, "I think I understand something of it. After all, philosophers have talked about that as an idea for many decades. The Self and not self. The IDEA was interesting, but it wasn't supposed to be something you lived with.. Oh, Jessie, I want to join Rose now and learn what it is all like for her. I want to help her and ask her to let me help. I want to ask her to help me."

She shook her head, "Benjamin, you're avoiding again. You've searched all your life for something. Isn't what you search for exactly the same as that which she fears? The Divine? The Spirit? That which is revealing Itself to our hearts and minds? People of our western world have called it Christ Consciousness? It has been called by many names, but it moves within us so strongly that we feel it's power and fear it. You are familiar with the dispair, the depressions that are common among people when they are not busy. That depression is a denial - a denial of what lies just ahead. Fear of what is awakening in us!"

His body jerked slightly, so shaken was he by the recognition. After some time, tears in his eyes, he said."My very search has been my way of avoiding, hasn't it? Of keeping busy so I would not have to be aware!"

She did not answer. They sat again in silence, absorbing all that they had said and felt. The air was changing, growing heavier, the sky was dark now, They seemed lost in a world of water. Then a piercing shaft of lightning broke the sky, lit up cloud and forest and in seconds it was followed by the roar of thunder. Rain fell, turning the air into water too. Ben suddenly wanted to shout. He felt released somehow, his longing for home rose until it was all he felt. There was understanding, there was no reason to hesitate. He wanted to be home, to seek safety in the warmth of the Hall, to be among his family, to hold his two children in his arms and to hug every other member of the family. He wanted to feel their presence. Of a sudden his relief and joy could barely be contained. His hand reached for the switch to turn on the little power pack. They could race this storm to home. But he withdrew his hand. He looked up at the water heavy sky and felt the surge of his emotions whipping over him even as the waves whipped upon the water.Yes, he wanted again to escape that which he had begun to See! But he would not, he would meet it!

Jessie looked far to the south, through barren trees and the wall of water. "Benjamn, you will ask Rose to talk of her fear?"

He nodded, serious, "Yes, I will ask."

She nodded, satisfied. Then she said,"Well, the Valley is changing, it's not only yourselves who are changing, you know."

He nodded in his turn, "I have heard of these same things all through the country. Sometimes spoken outright, but usually whispered. There are Builders organized there. And a pervasive fear seems to surround the changing. I didn't ask much about them. Do you know? It's said they want to bring the Valley back to what it once was before the devastations. How could anyone want that?"

" You think it's great evil. That these who would regress are evil ones?"

"It's what I've heard people say. But No! I think it is a mistake. Not evil."

" What is evil? This darkness that comes like a cloud sliding silently into our lives. We've all been so pleased with ourselves during these years of creating, so convinced we were beyond all the evils of humankind." She looked at him sharply and was surprised to see fear again in his eyes."Isn't that so?"

"Yes, but my God, Jessie, You aren't afraid are you?"

She laughed then relieving him a little. "So I'm supposed to be beyond fear eh?" Her smile was pensive." There is one end of fear, that which Rose is afraid of - that life of Spirit, that would lift us out of ourselves and reveal us to ourselves at the same time. That Self, that Soul, that Consciousness, is overwhelming at first. It is the opposite of Evil. But there is another end of fear. That exposure of our littleness, our cruelty, rage, duplicity, greed, lusts of every kind, and especially our self delusion. To suddenly have them revealed, here in our own hearts, substance of our very nature, that is frightening also. How can we bear to know ourselves, either the meanest, or the greatest?"

His face was a mask of sorrow and puzzlement,"At least out meanest self is familiar. It does not overwhelm me the way the - the glimpsing of the wondrous Light does." They were silent, the wind making a soft drumming around them, sending fine spray against their faces. Then he asked,"Isn't evil part of us too?"

"The satisfying of selfish desire is. It is constant. Until we See! But real evil, Ben, as you remember your Teachers taught you, is beyond most of us. Just as truly great Good is. This shadow that threatens us, is as you say, litle more than the incompleteness of understanding? Won't we have to complete that understanding somehow, for all people? Can we stop here, being Valley people, thinking we are complete because we have built our towns and cities, created sound economic supports? Made laws that give every person and every living thing a right to live a decent life. Do we think we have gone to our limits, that all is done? That life is complete?" She shook her head,"Have we forgottten that we are entering and must acknowledge the other half of life. We have built well to create a humane and wise way of life, but we are yet unfinished. We have taken the first step toward Spirit. We must know both Spirit and Matter." She let her voice drop into a softness he had to lean to hear,"For me, Ben, all that I've practiced, learned, and taught others, is not enough. I see glimpses now and then, glimpses that have slowly led me to perceptions of infinite beauty and possibility. Then I know that we've just begun. So you see, the first matter is meeting fear."

He sat for a moment absorbing, trying to realize her meaning, then he said,"I think I understand. It's what we've been doing at home isn't it? We've been meeting fear in a lot of forms. Our Family as well as the Builders."

"You are preparing for the meeting of greater things."

"But there it is. Don't you see? " His voice carried the anguish that filled his heart, he could see what he had not seen."We're so afraid, all of us, that we might even regress into the old way, the way of war and destruction just to avoid meeting our fears. That's what it amounts to, isn't it? Oh, no Jessie, Oh no." He felt as if his heart would break, as if he had finally said the terrible thing that had hidden for so long. The thing that had closed his mind so forcefully he could not even open himself to the simple joy of Mind-Touch. He shrank from this evidence of his cowardice.

She watched him and nodded,"Then it looks as though we are afraid of ourselves."

He nodded, miserable,"Given the history of our race, we have a right to be." Bitterness hardened his voice, his eyes were bleak.

"Maybe this time we'll have to transcend our history, We have looked closely at it. We do know it. We can choose whether to repeat it." She was silent, then, "After all, knowing one is ignorant is a help. All your people practice the balancing, the recognition of their behaviours. You persist in peer groups, sharing in love your self revelations. And those are never demanded, but offered freely. The division among us, actually, is one of whether we can sustain that perception of possibility. What you've just said that Rose is meeting."

He grimaced,"We're fraid of evil but what we call evil seems to mean anything that goes against our idea of the way things ought to be. It's the evil in ourselves, Jessie, that's what we've got to deal with." His eyes were full of the pain he felt, the fear he would not deny. "I'd translate that as fear and anger and hurt pride, as pure self interest. I have marks of evil in me and I can't deny them. I know my own nature. I'd like to gather up all the Builders, the people who deny our way and run them out of our Valley. I don't want them to destroy us. Jessie, I feel like - " his hands clenched and he knew the word he sought was 'killing'but he could not utter it. Tears filled his eyes, "like hurting them and excluding them ."

"And what does that mean Benjamin?"

"Well, it obviously means that I'm going to bring back the same old violence and terrors. It means we haven't learned a thing. Not really learned. Here I am full of hate and anger, capable of denying other lives because they are different from me, because they don't think the same as I do." His voice broke and he sobbed, the pain in his chest cut like a knife embedded there. He was surprised to discover so much emotion wrenched from him. How much more had he hidden? "It means I'm no better than the most rigid of those people who differ with me.I don't like this. I've always thought of myself as kind,fair and not bigoted. To have anything make me feel so helpless, so furious, is itself frightening. No wonder I've avoided looking at it!" He took a deep breath, " Everything's wrong. We never used to be like this. I wasn't like this." He pounded his fist against the side of the boat, making it rock, water splashed in and he said,"I want to make things safe again."

She nodded, her face revealed her tiredness. Was there no end to the task? So many years, so many thousands of miles of travel,and still so much to do. She lifted her attention, half smiling at herself. There it was again, her impatience. Would she never learn? Quietly she spoke,"You can see the problem"

After a long painful sigh and a wipe at his eyes, he nodded,"I suppose so. It's what you said. We could destroy ourselves unless we meet this . It's really ourselves we're meeting,isn't it Jessie? We have always been like this!"

"And all your teaching, all your Convictions, so proudly carved into the great buildings of your cities, have taught you that you know better. So now you have the question - must you continue or is the possibility for true Vision awake in you?" She was immensely relieved. the weight of her heart lifted a little. Perhaps it would be possible. Ben was speaking of the problem. Surely knowing it was the first step. "It's ourselves always, Ben. We just didn't know it before,.You know,your Teachers have always told you that evil is ignorance. Maybe they're right".

"The Builders are not evil" He said it with a sad dispair. For to have thought the evil was in the enemy would have been so easy. "They only want to protect themselves and their values."

"The Builders are human." Her answer angered him, and yet, there it was. He found the understanding growing in his heart. "The darkness in our Valley is a darkness that is in ourselves." He was silent, watching the darkness around them , the sleeting silver of dashes of rain. Oh, Jessie, how can we sustain ourselves, how can we keep on the right way." He spoke with a wistful hope that she could give him an answer. And knew that she would not if she could. His eyes sought the land, the Earth life, for rest from thought. The River was whipped all over with sharp small white waves, breaking and causing the surface to shiver. The rain had slacked off, but now it started to fall again in earnest. The lightning and thunder had ceased, sometimes they heard a rumble but what lightning there was was hidden beyond the clouds. Out of his reverie he softly muttered a childhood poem.

> "I will know myself and knowing that
> Will know all life,
> Through knowing the farthest reaches of one Life."

Then he said to her,"It seemed a lovely poem then,but I did not know what it meant truly. Though I thought I did. We used to have fiery debates about these ideas. How little we knew. We could all lose direction. We are human after all. How can we become more?"

"What do you know of the possiblities of being human? Have we become as human as we might be?"

Irritably he nodded then shook his head, "Oh, it's too much. Is there never an end to it all?" This Journey had been taken to discover something; understanding? meaning?

She said,"We can be trapped again into our past and into our terrible fears. Yes, we could be. But you see, Ben, there is something amazing, something we have not had before to guide us." At his look of hope, she half smiled,"You do realize these things. You and I are understanding our nature and seeing its weakness as well as its possibility. That is different. If we can do that, so can all the others. Isn't it the task not just of individuals, but of all humanity to know ourselves? Don't we have to acknowledge that those we call Builders simply express another part of our human nature? Can we also acknowledge that those like your own Mate Rose and other members of your Family, perceive possibities of being human that we have not admitted? There is much to be accepted. Both the limits of our old nature and the possibility of this unfolding consciousness. That is perhaps even harder for us, No?"

He grinned,nodding,"Never thought of that."

"You see, we do have our eyes half open. When the Light flashes through the mind, when our perception clears a little, it lets that Light into our small darkness. And we see ourselves. Steadily, as we allow. there is no other way."

He said,"My God, Jessie. I don't trust myself now. How can I trust anyone else to act with - with Love instead of fear." When he said the words,he stopped to hear himself. "Why that's it isn't it? That's what we must find a way to do. We must learn how to act with Love instead of fear."

She smiled in encouragement."Knowing we are not perfect is a big help. And knowing that there is such a talent as Joining, being willing to Reach in Love to others, wouldn't that perhaps reveal the possibility? What might happen if human kind Joined in Love with one another? I don't think you've yet experienced a true Joining". At his look of incredulity, she said,"There's more to learn now than we've ever learned but perhaps we are ready now to learn it."

They both sat silent watching the shore line,the trees swaying, and drew their cloaks over their heads, closer around their bodies. Ben maneuvered the boat into a swift current and it leaped to faster movement. Jessie's voice was

THE AWAKENING

gentle,"Ben, we must recognize another fact. One we've denied, perhaps." He looked at her, expecting a blow."The children are not afraid ."

He shuddered, absorbing it. The children were different. He hadn't wanted to talk of them. He had thought more than once that there was a difference that made either them or their parents monsters. Unnatural! He always denied and told himself this was a kind of insanity. "They! They're fools, Jessie. I think that we must teach them how to be afraid, to know what they could be if they do not watch themselves. That they too have the heritage of our ancesters and can act out of selfishness, out of fear."

She shook her head. "They must be taught, yes, Benjamin, but taught to continue to trust the deep and abiding Love they know and accept. After all, Benjamin, don't you think they know of fear and that they have chosen Love? Maybe we need to help them see that the choice was conscious, choice coming from that Life that fills them, that Light that lives and enlightens their wakened minds. They are of a different breed from us, Son. We have to think of that, perhaps."

"To act from Love one would have to know of it." His voice was thin, bitter.

"And that they do, though they must be taught to understand. And taught to be on guard from that ancient human nature functioning out of fear. But then, Love Itself will guide us, Benjamin, if we can allow that. If we can actually act with Love. The children may know the way. We must learn to trust enough to find out."

He swallowed,"What our parents gave us was fear, doubt, an abiding refusal to trust themselves or each other. They could not risk trust. It was too dangerous. And they brought our world into disaster." He nodded, slowly understanding. "Surely anything would be better.If we cannot trust one another, then we might as well die. Life is not worth living otherwise." His voice was tired, full of a terrible sadness of recognition.

"Do you realize the absolutely wonderful feeling of knowing that every person of your town has what they need, has opportunity and knows how to take advantage of it? Never before in the history of the world have we had the luxury of that ease of mind."She spoke with great seriousness, her face sad.

He turned his head, frowning, and then nodded slowly."I guess I've not known it as the comfort it is. It seemed normal to me." He moved the tiller and guided the little boat through a great cluster of debris. Jessie bent her head and closed her eyes. Ben was startled at the sudden increase in floating debris, the heavyness of the breaking waves, the rocking of the boat. He glanced back,"Jessie, you've been guiding, you've been keeping us on course and out of the path of this stuff."His tone was accusative,"Mind power isn't that?"

She laughed," Yes,Benjamin, We would not have been able to talk so well and we needed to talk before we arrive home. You must remember that Mind power, of one kind or another, is what we will use to meet everything we have to meet in these months ahead. The whole Mind includes an open heart able to respond to that natural flow of Love among us."

He looked at her curiously, puzzled, but then went back to work, attending the

Journey. He brought the boat into deep water where the currents were swift but less rough. He wanted to think but he needed to pay attention to this craft and their safety. He settled into a careful watching, but his mind raced on. He thought of the pull of the old ways, the drag upon his spirit, his mind, of old patterns and then he knew that there was also in him that longing for flight, the freeing and the release into new dimensions."There is a sluggishness to the human spirit, as though some weight dragged at us. And the freeing of ourselves is at once wonderful and frightening. I think that's it."He sighed, "We've got to learn to fly, and yet keep touch with Earth and balance it all."

The rain was slanting now against them, driven by a cold and steady wind. Jessie had packed up the small remainder of their lunch and huddled now in her great cloak. It would be waterproof enough, he thought,because they were not far from home. . He thought their decision to travel on the River might have been a mistake. There were all the other easier faster ways. But Jessie had preferred to travel 'at the body's pace', as she put it. He knew she had wanted to talk and to meditate in these last few hours.

The rain fell steadily, clouds were no higher than the trees. The drumming of water against water filled their minds with drowsiness, and thinking ceased. They rode in a quiet that grew and filled them. Jessie closed her eyes and sank deep into the seat, content. Ben immersed himself in the unceasing movement of water beneath him,around him and slowly lost himself to it. A single thought kept rising and breaking through the quiet.'Tonight he would sleep again in his own home and with his Mate. With Rose.'The thought was joy.

They passed by the rain dimmed lights of a River town,built at the shore line rather than above flood level as were most towns. He could hear a faint shout now and then from the water front,where a few fishing boats were still moving in to disappear into the wharves underneath the town itself. The massive pontoons on which the town floated were attached to tall slim towers grounded in the rock of the River banks. In these towers were business offices and communication centers. Two others would undoubtedly house the Learning Center and their Temple. Between each of the three broad floating sections of the town were trees and water plants. These tiny River towns supplied the Valley with fish . More than enough could be taken from the swarming waters. On the water front, was the cannery, fish stalls, restaurants and open markets. Those farther inland, held other buildings, residences. Two slim canals cut into the bank made a safe winter dock for the fishing fleet. In summer the fleet parked itself under the edge of the town, settled then on its solid foundations. Ben could see the lights of the Learning Center far behind,,highest on the land. Wide windows glowed yellow in the dark. People were there, doing things and he smiled. Through the mist,the town seemed dreamlike as they drifted by.

Benjamin, knew that Rose would be Reaching out to him. She could Reach, could seek for some Touch, except that she had promised and he felt now how foolish that promise had been. He wished he had the courage to try himself, try to Reach. Could he? He felt surprise at how rigid was his reluctance. Even now with his mind willing to consider the normality of such things, his old resistance was intact. He shrugged, resolved that he could break such old taboos. He focussed, then Reached through into unfamiliar territory, felt the energy of it. Surprised at how easily his mind moved out. Yes, moved out. And he did not know how, it just did that. He gave himself up to the Reach, unsure but willing,wanting with intense desire to Reach Rose.

Immediately the shock of Rose's Touch startled him- he recoiled, unable to sustain his timid Reach- then there was reaction-- a flood of Joy, guilt, fear, feeling sweeping to a peak and as suddenly subsiding. He was left with pure delight. He wanted to Reach without limit,to be unafraid.

Struggling uneasily with his dilemma, he heard the old woman behind him chuckling. Turning he caught her laughing face, lifted now to the falling rain, wet and shining in the dim light. He knew she was laughing at him. He felt annoyance and as quickly dismissed it. He grinned sheepishly,"I suppose she talks to you without any trouble?"

Jessie laughed out loud then and he knew she was glad for the end of the Journey too."Yes, she waits for us and so do the others for she has told them. There are those among your family that know , have known, and there are those who do not. Most of you underestimate your power. Even those who are very strong" She watched his face, saw his puzzlement. Surely no one was stronger than his Rose. "How can it harm to allow a small greeting and the joy of it shared?" She curled up again and closed her eyes, beginning to doze .

He turned back to the rain and the River. Slowly the water was creating a puddle in the bottom of the boat and he began slowly ,steadily to dip it up and out. Now and then, he allowed himself the tenuous Reach, tentative but real. He felt her there, somewhere at the end of that Reach.

After a little while he was aware that Rose was gone, no contact, no sense of her at all. He looked around, and he knew that there was something different about their little closed world. Jessie sat in a strange attention. He had seen it before,in their journey, at the Retreat, but he had never spoken to her of it. Now he thought she seemed to be communicating with someone there just beyond them as if another boat rode there. He had pushed such thoughts from his mind before, assuming that old people did strange things. Now, he thought,'Why not ask?' the simplicity of the idea made him smile.

"Jessie, what's happening? I feel as though someone is here. How can that be?"

She started slightly, then looked long and searchingly at him."Yes,Benjamin, you're right. There are several people here and we have been talking. But I didn't want to disturb you or hurry you." She gestured to her left, then patiently said," "These are people who do not live in physical bodies,people like the ones who die and leave their bodies, except these will not re-enter bodies at all. Seeing through from the physical plane to their astral plane would not seem normal to you,I'm afraid."

She turned from him, spoke aloud, but he couldn't follow her words.It seemed a kind of shortened talk. He watched the spot at which she looked trying to see some form there, but there was nothing. He felt angry and then frustrated. Then without warning, something in his mind shifted, something he couldn't think about, but that nevertheless was very real. A shift in focus, it was, just as he quit trying to see. He could see. He could hear. There was a group of people, four, either sitting or standing there above the water. As if they had no weight. Of course, they would have no weight. Perhaps the River did not exist there where they were. They seemed to be friendly, ordinary people. They talked to Jessie but seemed to consider him irrelevant. He listened, let his mind empty of thought, his feelings subside and with effort he brought himself to quiet attention. Open, unjudging. The strange sentences began to make sense, a rapid and simple way to communicate. Only key words were needed. Images flashed through the conversation, illuminating it. he was surprised and pleased. He could not hold contact. His thinking about it, trying to explain it all as he heard, brought him back to old familiar limits. The world lay around him as before, dark and full of rain.

Jessie turned to him with a bright, joyful smile. "Benjamin, I'm not sure what you saw or heard, but there is someone here who may be able to help, someone special in fact."

Ben looked at her startled, wondering at her joy. Somehow things had gotten out of hand, but he was determined to see it through. He felt a sense of expectancy, of hope, then a tremor of fear shook him . The fear was like a blinding screen before his mind. Never before had he seen a blocking by fear so sharp. Then it was as if a hand touched him, the fear thinned, he could see through it. He took a deep breath, calmed himself, let fear dribble away. Gently there was clarity until only curiousity and a little unease was left.

Joy poured from Jessie, she was radiant with a beauty he had not seen in her. There was a shining of some inner light, it poured from her whole body. He realized that he was simply seeing Jessie, as he had never done before. This was the woman, fully recognized. He turned to look at the stranger. At first there was only a radiance, a lightedness in the rain. Then Jessie reached to put a hand on his arm. In that instant he saw standing there, beyond them, a tall radiant figure. It was a little beyond where he had seen the four. The glow of light took shape and was a distinct form. It moved through water, reached into trees, it was not standing within this dimension at all. He could see that, it was obviously extended through these physical forms as though they were not there. It was perhaps between these two dimensions, in a spacelessness he did not understand. He accepted.

The figure radiated a power that silenced Ben's gasp and intent to speak. It was a body, resembling that of a human, but of living, flowing, moving Light. It was surely alive, it was Life, it was more than alive. It seemed to Ben that this one could Itself give life. He felt the wonder of it, the beauty. In this radiance he felt his own nature expand, his consciousness lifted to reveal a power in himself, weak, wavering, but of the same nature as that of this radiant life. There was in himself, he could see, a tiny Light shining, a tiny flame from which came that

THE AWAKENING

same Joy and living sense of Love. In himself? Surely there must be some mistake.

It was a magnetic energy that flowed between them as though two streams merged and the greater gave of itself to the weaker. The small flame shivered and then grew stronger. He could not make out a face, it did not seem to matter,. There was, present for him, a poignant sense of affirmation, of infinite caring, a caring that was beyond Ben's understanding .At the same time there was a sense of gentle amusement, as a loving parent might look at a child.

He did not understand but he knew. He could realize this wonder. It filled and overflowed his whole being. Feeling swelled through him. The extensions of mind and heart were great, he felt stretched and open. He thought he could not endure this wonder. The beauty pulsed through him. Tears streamed from his eyes and he wanted to shrink away and yet longed for it to never end. The longing ,the fear, tore at his attention. His hands did not know what to do, alternately reaching out,imploring and wanting and then withdrawing to clutch at his chest in defense. He finally bent his head, so full he could not look longer. Jessie drew back her hands, and the vision faded. He had not spoken a word. The light seemed utterly gone. But he knew that the Presence was not gone. The whole world was filled with it. He would never forget. The Light of greater consciousness illuminated his mind, wakened his heart's attention. His life was changed, his being was ripped lose from itself. He was broken like a seed cracked into the Light. And his heart rejoiced even as his mind quailed. He looked at Jessie, seeing that for her the deep communion continued.

After a bit, he knew that the Being had withdrawn and Jessie was quietly gathering herself. He thought he must explain the vision. Was it a shaft of light through the rain? A sudden reaction of an over tired body and mind? Was it delusion? Was it real? He knew that he would have explained these things away swiftly in the past. But he knew that he did not even consider such explanation now. This was a true happening. There had been ONE there who was unlike any life he knew. This then was what Jessie and Rose meant by 'possibility.'One who was fully conscious had touched him and he was forever changed, more alive to himself, to life!

When Jessie spoke again it was as if she had roused herself from a deep reverie. Her voice, however, was brisk and firm. "It isn't often one touches so consciously with such as That." She smiled at him,"The Vagabonds know of them. You've heard the People of the Way sing of them but you might have thought them dreams.It was good for us."

"Then are these the ones of the Valley myths? The ones said to have led the people back into this land and to have helped them begin the first building? "

She shook her head, "The Elders who came into the Valley to reclaim it were our first Monitors. They might have been Touched by such as these. It is said that they were. These great ones don't do things for us, they bring us energy and they open our eyes when we are ready to wake. Just as this one has done for you, my Benjamin. It is a most unusual gift."

"It's an energy that lifts my mind, my heart! I feel stretched beyond belief. I feel as though Light has come into my mind. It's a strange sensation but that's what it's like."

She nodded, her face full of her pleasure in him. "They bring to us all the time that energy called the Will to Good. It is their very nature to bring that and it reinforcs our own small energy toward good. It is that which stimulates our children to know, to see and to trust and to Love."

You think our life here is based on that energy, that Will to Good?"

"I know it is. If you were as old as I you would see the difference. Humankind is capable of more, able to see and realize more, much more, than ever before."

For some moments they sat, and her attention was so acute that he was astonished. "What is this thing, Jessie that we mean by possibility?"

It's only that which is before us, the next step in anyone's life. It's what lies beyond fear." She said the last sadly, as if talking to herself. He tightened, he did not want to think of Jessie afraid. Finally with effort he asked,"What is it that you are afraid of, Jessie?"

She turned her great dark eyes on him but they seemed not to see him. He could see pain lurk there, and a deep pool of knowing that would have drowned his consciousness had he persisted in meeting it. She said. "The power to misuse what one has discovered. The power to misuse and cause harm. To harm life. that is what I fear, because I know my longing, my own nature. Ben there is not one of us beyond the power to destroy, and the greater our knowledge the greater our ability to destroy. We spoke of evil as ignorance. Ignorance of what is Life and true. It is so, evil is fed by self service. To wish to make things as I would like them to be, rather than as they must develop in their own way. To have such power, even the little I have, the temptation lies always there. I suppose you could say Ben, that I have had to learn. I know now that I do sometimes desire what is not born out of Love . But I can know of my desires and keep them in check. To long to 'do good' on MY terms, is a great temptation. That is a power that is seductive and dangerous."

He sat appalled,"How then, Jessie, can one dare to do any good at all?"

She smiled sadly, "Fortunately, most of us are not capable of very great good or evil either. We know more as we wake and realize our powers. Humankind has done great harm, great harm to Earth. To life. And we know that we can. We watch ourselves doing harm and we begin to see, to admit that we do. We of the Valley must meet ourselves again and again. We can learn how to stand in Soul consciousness,for Soul nature is of that which is strong enough to turn from all evil. Or rather it is free from the hungers of the little self. Selflessness and harmlessness are its very nature. It can act in no other way. But there are still those old patterns, I must meet them and I fear I do not always stand above them."

A chill of icy fear knifed through his chest. He drew his eyes from her and shrank from what she had said. He did not want her to have any fear. He did not want her to know doubts. She was his guide and she must stand apart from all harm. She saw his thoughts as clearly as if they were lights strung on a chain and smiled with a sad loneliness."Benjamin, my greatest safety and yours too, lies in that I have told you that. It's not to frighten you but to disarm me. You must remember that I am human and capable of harm."

He nodded, not understanding but accepting. She went on, "You know Ben, most people don't want to be evil, they want happiness. we just do not know how to find it. Because we look for it in satisfaction we imagine will come from feeding our hungers. But then, we just don't know. We thought we could find it using tools to remake our world and so we might have done well there, except that we misunderstood and were lost in the very obsession with making things and owning things. That did not bring happiness either and we felt betrayed. The universal desire for happiness was the tool the Great Souls used to open our eyes so that we could understand that only through one another's happiness could our own be assured. Only through feeling loved and loving could we know safety." She shook her head,"Humankind has had thought of those ideas for centuries, even taught them, but we could not live them."

Ben nodded, "I'm very glad Jessie, that I live now and not two hundred years ago. It must have been a terrible time to live."The rain increased to a torrent, pounding down on them so steadily they could not see through it. Ben began dipping out the boat, then switched on the motor,it began a nearly silent pumping out of the rapidly falling water. The hard drops stung their faces and hands and they both ducked beneath their cloaks. After a few minutes the rain let up, fell more softly with a steady droning sound. Ben felt warmth and quiet. He listened,heard the sounds of his body beneath the skin, his heartbeat, sounds of organs and of breathing, and he felt entombed here in this drumming of low sound.

They floated on, silently enjoying this time of peace, of expanded realization, of the nearness of home. His heart sang, filled with so much, so much that needed thinking about, he rejoiced.

COUNCIL

The Builders! Ben arrives.

Rose hurriedly got into her coat, pulling on gloves and glancing at the weather outside. She would have to hurry, if she made it to the Council meeting on time. The morning talk had been worth it, it had been long needed. But now, she frowned, disliking being late. She turned to the door and the Video gong sounded. Impatiently, she ran back, flicked on the screen and there was Paul. He grinned,"Just wanted to check in. And find out what you know about Ben."

Her impatience faded like water in a sieve. She laughed, "I'll see you in half an hour, Paul. But yes, he's traveling through this storm and he'll keep coming." She hesitated, then reaffirmed her decision and added, " He'll be here tonight. Tonight Paul, can you believe it! By the time Council meeting is over, he'll be coming in. I know it! Then we can have the Gather."

Paul was beaming, she saw his delight and was reminded how much the rest of the family loved Benjamin. Jennifer had come to the screen too, smiling she said, "Won't he want to rest a day of two before plunging into all we've got to tell him."

Rose laughed, "I don't think so. You know Ben. And he knows a lot is happening. He's going to want to see everyone right away and a Gather's the best way to do it." She hesitated, then said it, "He's bringing someone who'll help us, I think. We'll call as soon as he gets here." Neither of them asked her how she knew but in Paul's face she saw no surprise.

Rose arrived on time in Santiago for the afternoon meeting of the Council. She was excited and impatient. She wanted the meeting to be done so she could go home and be there for Benjamin's arrival. Never had she been so sure of anything. He would be there. She stood watching the bright flow of Santiago people moving about on the high hanging limbs of the amazing city. Her mind ran over the issues the Council must debate this day. Behind her the vast Council Hall, a Golden Globe big enough to seat two thousand people, hung shining in the sun. The great broad 'leaf' fronting it and extending out to the roadways that branched in every direction, had the standard webbed railing that not even a kitten could get through, and just beyond that,visible only as a shimmer in the air, the never ceasing force field that prevented any possible fall over its edge. She looked beyond that field, not seeing it, watching the new green in the forests below, the fields planted already beyond them and into the distance to the low hills and the little lakes dotted among them. It was a lovely view, but her thoughts were on the task before her.

People were gathering now at the door of the Hall and moving in. It was time. Surprising how quiet they were, a murmuring as of whispers. With a sigh, she stilled her own mind, emptied it of thought, letting the stillness of this high clear

THE AWAKENING

morning aid her focus. She closed her eyes a moment, enjoying the fragrance of the forest and newly planted fields below. She was held in a sphere of clear calm, lifted above the circling confusion of thought that had claimed her this morning. Deliberately, knowing she must, she held her attention at that point and felt her whole body, her feelings and finally her mind too, relax and loosen. Perception expanded. The Valley had room for differences, the people were flexible. She established a decision of trust. Yes, alert trust! She sighed, she was ready now to enter.

She turned back to walk to the Hall, The brilliant colors of the residential globes far behind the Great Hall gleamed in the sunlight. There was a touch on her arm and a felt presence, unobtrusive but clear. A middle aged man, barely taller than she, greying and round bodied, stood beside her. He watched her, smiling but her mind held itself apart. He spoke and his voice seemed loud out of the silence. His name was Ted, she had known him for many years.

"Rose, how are you." He stood a moment, refilling his pipe and tamping it while she watched, wondering about that habit. It made for useful action when conversation was just getting started she knew. She smiled. That should be no problem here.

He grinned at her, turning again to walk, she said, "I'm very well, thank you. I've missed Ben, of course, but he'll be home soon .Suddenly she wanted to know whether he could - or would - Join. The desire to know surprised her. She thought that she must find out as much as possible, as if time had wasted, time when she should have known these things. She focussed and knew his concern for her was genuine. She felt ashamed of her doubts of him, and then realized he knew. Their Touch was brief, but he knew. He smiled warmly, meeting her eyes. He nodded, the whole experience of Touching was something he too was just adjusting to. He had not yet decided what he felt about such public intimacy. He said, "Ben's been gone nearly a year now. He ought to be back, we need him."

Rose nodded, accepting that. She said aloud, "It's lonely at times, But then, though he's gone physically, he's with me. Being Mated has its advantages, you know." Her eyes were serious, wondering how much she might share.

He was nodding, "I know that. It's been a grief in my life, never to find that person who is a Mate. But then, my wife is a wonderful person and our life is good." He stopped, looked toward her, their walk nearly stopped, then he blurted it out, "Is Ben, willing to make contact, does he Reach to you? There's such a fear of it, you know. You surprised me just now. I never know if anyone will." He shook his head in irritation, "We don't talk, you know, and that's a shame in this Valley. We pride ourselves on our skills of listening and talking to each other. Yet in this most important part of life, we don't. We've set a precedent in Council at least. That's why I'm -- taking the liberty now." He seemed a little embarrassed.

She nodded, her eyes never leaving his. She wanted to talk, to this friend who was not part of her Family. There were advantages. It was strange that simply talking about something should be hard. She remembered when Ted and his wife had been visitors to the Farm, and when the four of them had traveled.

So little contact lately. "How's it been for you, old friend?" Her voice was soft with the love she had felt through many years.

"It's been fine actually. Our two kids are doing well, ready to make their choices, in fact." He chuckled,"I doubt that'll be much of a surprise. Sometimes I wish we were all young again, playing the old games, dreaming of our Valley and the way it would be. But here we are instead, standing grey and tired in the middle of a Valley that's so well begun, a success." He shrugged again, laughed shortly and turned to continue walking toward the door."Well, maybe we'll all get together more now. Maybe we'll have more time for old friends. I'd like to see Ben again. And I haven't seen Tom or Ned, or that lovely girl Silvia, for a long time.

" He smiled wistfully,"You ever miss those old days, Rose?"

She shook her head,relieved and warmed by his words."No, Ted, I don't think I do. Mostly I remember these past years as a time of almost unceasing labor. I'm glad for time now to think and search out the meaning of what we're doing.Don't you want time to reflect, Ted. Reflect on all that's been?"

Well, maybe, sometimes. But mostly, I'm just glad to enjoy my life a little. Look around and gloat over all we've done here." He laughed. His face suddenly was serious,"We've got a lot to do today. Looks like something on the agenda is drawing a crowd. Never have this many people come to our Council meetings."

"Must be someone's petition. I don't know of anything on our agenda that'd rouse much interest .The only thing that'd even get a debate is the issue of public air cars. Most cities need more now. Surely Santiago does. Even Adwin's been running short. What d'you think of it?

She touched his arm lightly, then slid one hand into his elbow a gesture he remembered from their earlier years and he felt glad for the acceptance. Rose and Ben were important to Ted. He had begun to value his old friends now, in these approaching middle years. A life of somewhat casual relationships had preceeded his marriage, a lot of fun, he'd always told himself, and they were. Jeana had been good for him. Their life brought him a stability he'd never had. Then lately, for no reason he could name, something seemed to change. He felt a lack in his life, a loss,vague and troubling. Jeana insisted he was being foolish. He thought she didn't try to understand.

Now, here with Rose, he felt as though that loss might be at least named. He trembled, wondering how this could have happened. There was something in his relationship with these friends he'd missed and yet, he couldn't have said what it was.He looked at her now, promising himself that he would rebuild that old friendship.

I'm fully in favor. We have enough credit, You know our tax base was designed to cover transportation costs. We'll get them."

She nodded,"Well, we agree on one thing so far. What about the Computer Link Up? How do you vote there?"

"I'm in favor. Valley libraries and communication centers ought to have been linked together long ago. We need that. It may squeeze our finances for a while, but it's worth it. Rural people especially need that connection. As long as people

THE AWAKENING

don't get the habit of staying home instead of coming out to the Center."

She laughed and he chuckled as they climbed the steps to the great open doors."I think the ceremony for the Harvesters will be no problem. We've needed to improve that for some time. After all, when we graduated from our teens and became adults, it was pretty important to have everyone notice that. So these young people need to have a ceremony that fits for them." He was nodding and they moved slowly into the hall. Rose thought aloud about the agenda, "Our contract with Banig for winter wheat only needs to be renewed and the new citrus, the M12 trees, from Altos will be easy to agree on. We've never had really productive citrus this far north."

"Yes, we've got the fields ready even. There." He pointed through the wall of windows, and she could see in the middle of a forest a great open field. Santiago will have another trade crop, no one will refuse that."

Rose nodded, "Paul brought some to us. They're sweet and very juicy, although they're smaller than the ones near Brand and Afton. These trees produce close against the limbs and can carry better crops without breaking branches. I wish Adwin could raise some. But we're too cold."

"It was a job getting people to agree. Most citizens love those forests as if they were their own gardens. Which I suppose they are. But we did finally agree and there's no fuss about it. But nothing we've named could have drawn this crowd." He looked around frowning.

They were both silent for a moment.Then Rose said,"I think I know what's bringing the crowd, - what Paul said we had to talk about. The question about the Builders."

He was nodding,"You're right,I'm sure. And when I heard of it I thought it should not be brought into Government attention. It should just die of itself. I thought it would. But it looks as if I was wrong. "He bent his head, drawing slowly on his pipe, frowning."How'd I miss that. Have I been fooling myself?"

If you have we all have. I wasn't prepared for this either. The idea that the Valley ought to return to the old days, to times of town fighting town, of unceasing competition between towns, or citizens,between countries even. No, look what that all brought to us. If we've learned nothing it's that survival means cooperation. We don't have to dominate anyone else. We just don't need to go back to those old days."Rose was surprised to hear her own emotion suddenly so strong.She had thought the Builders would simply be nostalgic people, longing for old memories that had been romanticized, perhaps still trapped in those old wishes for 'having things'. She thought that in itself defined their maturity, then caught herself for being spiteful.

She looked around, seeing the great hall more than half full."My God, Ted, looks like we've got a major problem here." There'd been meetings when a group of people came to ask for change that satisfied some private need or fantasy, the Valley Charter allowed room for such. A lot of compromises had been made, but none that changed the basic Valley Convenant. Council had worked out solutions so people found some outlet for their needs. There was the 'old world' a place where people who wanted to live in the past, could go and find their own kind. They had contributed to establishment of the "War Strip' between Arizona and New Mexico, where people fascinated with intrigue and violence, with the fierce excitement of dominance and submission, even of battle, skirmishes that might wound many, or even kill. People could play out their fantasy and not hurt anyone else. There were other places, that to Rose were even less understandable, but if people wanted to indulge old hungers, they could not be denied completely, otherwise, Valley Convenants would be betrayed.. Such arrangements were part of modern living. But now, this. These folk didn't want to live a private fantasy. They wanted every one to live it.

Ted was shaking his head,"Rose, I feel it. I can sense what's happening finally. Why didn't I see it long ago? I can only assume that I didn't want to know. Because there it is like a great flag in front of me now. I should have known. I should have been willing to pay attention and get my head out of the sand. We've come too far for that. We know better, and yet, here we are unprepared because we wouldn't even admit such a thing could happen."

She nodded,"We didn't want to think it,Ted. We have struggled so hard to build what we thought would make things safe for a new approaach to living. We just didn't want to see what was right before our eyes." She turned to him, her eyes both sad and angry,"How long did it take you to admit that you knew what that Reach was ?"

He sighed,nodding,his pipe in his mouth. "It took nearly a year, actually from the time when I had to admit there was a Reach to the time I consciously started using and accepting it. It took even longer to make a choice and to Touch . Even now, it's only very surface Touch I've been willing to do. At least,its all I've done. I don't actually know what I'm capable of. I feel ashamed, Rose, simply ashamed." He turned his pipe and began to empty and prepare it for a refill, then thought better of it and tucked it into a small special bag which he put into his pocket. "Hadn't been for Grace's persistence in Council, I'd probably be farther behind."

Rose looked around. The time was near. The Council was beginning to sit and she must go.She squeezed his hand briefly,"We'd better take our seats, Ted. Maybe we can make sense of it today. There's just so many people. I feel afraid. And that's the last thing we need. Of all people, we of the Council must remain calm, must keep balance. " She knew she spoke as much for him as for herself. He already seemed too angry.

Ted was angry, his voice strained as he spoke. His self criticism lending strength to that anger. "Hell,Rose, they could have a place, there 's room, if they want that. They could go clear back to the middle ages if they want and build themselves a castle. Lord it over each other in fine style. Why do they want to involve the whole Valley in this?" She saw his fear, he resented the disturbance of his own order, his own way of life. She didn't trust that fear,and yet was it so different from her own? How could they acknowledge that? Wasn't that another denial?

The great bell sounded, people moved swiftly and silently with a grace that would have surprised people of an earlier age. They seated themselves almost silently. She and Ted took their places and Rose snuggled into the soft contours of her chair.There was a soft rustle of talk through the room and then the final bell sounded and there was total silence. Each person held still, balancing mind and emotion into a personal harmony that could be literally felt .The focus of attention to this balancing brought a mild linking among them, one that had become famiiar but it was assumed to be simply heightened awareness It was not generally recognized as a genuine Touch. Each Council member turned attention to the Conviction that stood carved in light four times around the ceiling of that grand hall." There is no problem that cannot be resolved through a 'Will to Good'."

How many times had she looked at those words? She let the thought settle into her mind, found the meaning of it reverberating through her, exposing her fears. She smiled. They just had to remember and stand outside their own emotions. But first they must admit those emotions. She sighed. Testing was not limited to the children.

A few minutes of silence was followed by a flute note. It held in the air, fine and high, sounding in their brains like an echo. It marked the beginning of the day's work.The speaker, Abel, a delegate from Bend who had served many a term on the Valley Council, walked swiftly, briskly to the center platform,placed himself under the Ring that would bring his voice clearly to the farthest corner and then began, in his usual brisk manner to put the routine matters to the Council. An hour later, after a very peaceful session, he stood in the silence of the room. Rose enjoyed,the absolute stillness around her after the noisy discussions and debate. Even with Grace to lend her strength, they could not share images silently, but must make their decisions aloud for the benefit of the crowd. Then Abel said, "Well, we've taken care of the daily business, and we did it like professionals. We've gained a lot of skill here in our Valley. I wonder if you all realize how much? Our system, with all citizens taking a term of service in their towns, brings us a constant supply of experienced Council members. Perhaps you all know that two small nations in the mid-east, have chosen our system to imitate. Most western nations already follow one very similar to ours. I think we can be proud of our record." Rose felt reassurance. He was stating what might give a lie to future criticisms of their way of life.

He took a glass of water, sipping slowly and then said,"You all know the background of our Valley, it's history. But I want to make a short summary of some special points before introducing the matter up for debate." He let his eyes sweep the house. Word had surely gone out. This was the biggest crowd he'd seen in years. He knew that video screens were on in most homes too. This business of the Builders was creating a polarity that could be healthy or it could tear their land apart. He felt a tightening of his resolve. He must himself hold steady. "We are several generations past those times of devastation. We are a people who have always been builders. We have created the Valley out of a deep committment to a belief that people can and have learned to work out problems through negotiation, we do attend to every citizen's welfare and we take seriously the special needs among us. We do what we say we'll do. Ours is not a 'promise and forget' kind of government. You all know that!"

"We've been living proof that we can govern ourselves this way. But we are more. We are a people who have felt a tide of new Life surge through us, through us all. We cannot deny the visions, realizations of a greater life that come into clear perception in these days. The old ways brought a terrible destruction to humankind. Destruction to Earth and to civilization. Those ways were not life giving. We vowed to change our way of life so that such destruction would never occur again. We will not forget!"

His voice had been strong, he spoke from deep conviction that carried and held his audience. He looked around, knowing that he had to make them remember and to pause. He looked intently down at the Council members seated in a circle around him.

"That is the miracle of this Valley and that is why people from around this world have begun to imitate us. They see our way of life as one that will bring new life. It is our gift, our pride. May that pride not be false - may it never overwelm our good sense. " Again he was silent.

Then, his voice soft, "Our old folks, our parents watched us. What they had struggled with in pain we have managed with comparative ease. Our technology grows swiftly. Now we watch our own young standing free of much that we struggled with, ready to approach new dimensions of thought and even of consciousness. There is a genuine growth, an unfolding of consciousness itself among us. What our parents called ideals of life, we accept as normal living. What they dreamed of, we practice. We call these facts of life. These changes have been fundamental .But I insist that they rose from that burst of Life itself that is now surging through us as a people. Through all of us in some way.. It crosses all lives, races, creeds, and political differences. That tide has made us know that those old differences were illusions. It broke our old habits. Stripped us naked to be reborn to a new life.

At first, I think we stood torn as a people, remembering the devastation brought about by the tantrums of a race still in infancy. We destroyed our world so many times. I want to believe that we've grown up a little, that as a race we've begun to take on the behaviors, at least of young adults. We begin to think of someone besides ourselves!" He laughed, a faint murmur of chuckling swept through the Hall. "We aren't a wise people yet, but we're beginning to know that wisdom is what we want. We live in the beginning of a new time. We have possibility and we intend to fulfil that possibity. There is an acceptance of new attitudes among us, We know that we are capable of Love, of attending to the welfare of all life. We know that. That has been a revelation of our Valley life. We have not ever known that in the history of humankind before. It is our birthright now."

As Rose listened to this discourse reminding them of what they had done, she wondered why he must make this reminder so strong. He must fear something she did not know of."

"We must watch ourselves, we must not take too much for granted. We must be able to see always the difference betweeen ideals and reality. And yet hold both precious. We've begun to trust our way of life and we may not always know whether there are those who don't. We might have become inattentive, in our sense of safety, or of 'rightness'. We must be always vigilant. Perhaps we have let that vigilance slip. Rightness must not become 'self righteousness. We know we of Earth are one people."

"We people of the Valley have learned to listen. To listen to one another and to hear. We know that unless we persist in practicing that skill we will not survive. We nearly did not survive because we refused to listen, even to know how to hear each other through the world. When we finally learned to listen, we found that it worked. It worked! People could listen. Governments could listen. Governments could hear, not only the great and mighty, but the small and helpless. We discovered that what had made us deaf, was greed. We admitted that."

He leaned forward now, his eyes flashing, his voice commanding attention, "We learned another great truth that makes for harmony among us. We learned that when the basic needs of human beings are filled, people don't run berserk, don't harm others to satisfy them. Powerful people may strive for more power, more goods, more riches, but they won't have an army to follow them unless those basic needs are threatened." He sighed, stood relaxed, quietly, "Or unless they are convinced that threat is being made by some one called 'enemy'. But it's not so easy to threaten us today. We've learned how to talk to each other, to find out whether a threat is real or not. We don't wait for our government to tell us. Or that powerful person who would use us."

Rose smiled, he had the audience, his voice and intensity charging his words."We've learned that when people listen, they relate as human, rather than as stereotypes. We have little crime, little insanity among us, because we begin at every child's birth to attend to his or her needs. We see that every citizen feels safe, has shelter, food, clothing, education, honor and responsibility." He paused, looking around, assessing the effects of his words. Then he spoke in a new voice, a tone that woke any drowsy mind," Do we realize how revolutionary this is? What a miracle? We've done it! Our generation has begun a new civilization! We believe that every human being must have a place among his fellows. A place where each person from birth feels that he belongs and knows he can contribute. That is what we have offered the world. A system that does that. A system that does not promise, but actually brings about that condition. We don't just talk, we do it! It is Valley Conviction by which we live. And those Conviction aren't just ideals, but facts! we found a way, when nations had said it couldn't be done, to give every child the chance for health, learning and love. We found that way, because we were forced by that destruction to change, in our hearts. Then we knew that a person is more important than power, riches, or anything else we had."

THE PEOPLE OF THE VALLEY

He stopped again, sipped a little water and continued, his eyes surveying the room as carefully as an artist his pallet. "People don't get into crime when they feel self respect, and when they feel and know of Love around them. They just don't need to. Our police force is small, always has been. Oh, we still have our wars, yes, but these are inner wars. The war we fight every day within ourselves, and that we teach our children how to understand, is one of learning how to create harmony within ourselves and between ourselves and all other lives. We blame no one for our failures, not even ourselves. We take responsibility instead. In this way we have learned. Yes, we've changed, and we still are changing. Some force moves in our Valley, an energy that promotes growth. We don't yet know what that is, but we know it, feel it. Live with it!

He looked down at the faces around him, the council members waiting and listening. He knew he was summing up enough truisms, he knew they needed to remember. They made this new idea possible. The waking of the people! He looked around and saw their support, felt their energy offered him. He drew a long breath and said the words he found difficult." That energy is what we seek to know. Humankind seems to be waking up. Becoming alive with spirit, an energy, that promises us new life. That wakes a new life that is within us already and has not been noticed before." He watched the acceptance of this thought, then went on,"The changes are fundamental in us. That simple will to life has shifted and has become that Will to Good for all life and all life has become so obviously precious that we as a people, take it for granted."

How much furthewr dared he go? Could he be sure they would understand? he must retreat to old teachings a bit."We grew up convinced that our personal welfare was the welfare of all life. that we could not have a good life unless all life had a good life. That is an axiom of this Valley. It was an ideal to our parents, but it is not an ideal to us. It is a fact, a reality. There is an assumption of the sacredness of life and of individual choice. " He stopped because an unusual wave of applause drowned out his words. It was unusual because in this council chamber applause was seldom heard. A deep standing silence was usually offered instead.

He nodded, smiled, obviously pleased that they accepted his thoughts."We see our young ones, sometimes some of our old ones, leaving to make new towns, to do things their own way, to live differently, within that basic Conviction that is a Valley creed. We encourage those differences, those experiments even when we are convinced they'll fail." Again his voice rose, strong and filling the room. "Even when it costs us!"

He grinned, remembering some recent such attitudes."Fortunately we are often wrong about that. We all make choices, and choices are encouraged. We lose our children to the Vagabonds and the Vagabonds lose their's to us. We lose people to other cities and we have those who come to share life with us. We learn to encourage all kinds of differences. That is our creed. You all know that. We have seen our own children able to meet and accept differences among themselves, able to honor those who want to live differently. And we see they

THE AWAKENING

teach us in their acceptance. We have a Conviction that humankind must learn whatever is needed to live in harmony and we persist in that Conviction." He stopped, drank again, held the clear glass loosely for a moment and then set it down. His voice was firm and confident.

"It is one of the most important teaching of our Learning Centers. Children taking for granted that they can solve the problems between themselves and others, that they can contribute to community living, not because they are forced to do so but because they choose to do so. They know that it is a good part of life. We know our Convictions as the way a normal man or woman thinks and acts.So that is what we are".

"Our young people will make changes, their minds already lift up to new heights. They will go on to what we haven't even thought of. They will stand on our accomplishment and wake their hearts and minds to new dimensions we have only glimpsed and that's as it should be. But they will only do this if we continue to keep the trust, to act as if we too took for granted the truths that we have found." Slowly he spoke the words,"And if we persist in seeking further into our highest consciousness as they do!" He stopped, looking at the faces below, holding his breath. Would they hear? Accept? Their calm attention gave him confidence. "So today, we are to debate matters that have begun to polarize the people of our land. We must pay attention, and stand apart from ourselves in that point of recognition we call 'Love'. We must act with Love."

He moved about, walking to the edge of the small space around him. He looked at the Council below his stand, Rose saw his eyes meet Grace's then Jerome's and finally Edsil's. She felt their Touch , a powerful rhythm. Then he returned to his place where sound systems could pick up each word clearly. "We have learned to Trust. We do trust ourselves and each other. And we have found ourselves sometimes awed with the beauty of people in this Valley. The beauty of mind and heart. We cannot actually be surprised at the movement that is called the Builders. Because we have fostered difference. There are many members of that group here now. We want to listen carefully to what they say. But we must ask that they listen as carefully to what we say."

The room was utterly hushed, not even a movement occurred to bring small echoes up. He was silent for several minutes, then went on,"An old teacher of mine used to tell us,'We're on to ourselves,children, we're on to ourselves. We can't fool ourselves the way we used to. We've opened too many closed doors.' And I believe that he was right. We can't fool ourselves and we can't fool each other the way we used to long ago. For that reason I believe in us. People of the Valley, we will practice the Will to Good for all Life. All life is precious and nothing we decide here must minimize the value of a single life."

A sudden faint whisper grew, and from the left of the speaker there was the sound of people rising. The movement swept through the Hall until,in this act of appreciation, the people stood silently offering the highest honor. Then with the same sweeping whisper of sound, they sat down. He nodded, and those close to him could see the tears that shone in his eyes. They knew that those tears were in response to the knowledge that he had been heard. These were his people and their hearts were great. They understood. They could meet this thing he saw as threat and meet it as people who loved their fellow men. He sent that message with every fiber of his consciousness and silently poured out to them through that Touch of mind to mind. The silence rang within them. Then he said,"I am finished. We have a few minutes of rest and then we will hear the delegate from the Builders."

People visibly relaxed, turned to one another, murmurs made a sweep of soft sound around the room and then there was stillness. A slim figure rose from the right of the raised circle. He walked carefully to stand beneath the ring that hung above his head and not only made his words clear to everyone but gave his image directly to each side of the room. His back was to no one. Rose recognized the young man as Ansel, a young friend of the family who lived in Adwin. William had sponsored him today. She had known him all his life, and yet a strange uneasiness grew. She shook herself. Told herself Ansel always spoke well, that she must attend to this fear, otherwise she would not hear without prejudice. And she spent the first moments of his talk in practices of balance. Ansel looked around, his poise evident. Rose thought that much had been happening during the winter that she had not been paying enough attention to. She knew little of the Builders, knew what Dean had told the Council, had heard a few rumours, but little else. Why? She was grateful for that moment of Touch from Abel. Now they would hear Ansel more clearly.

Rose frowned, suddenly aware that William had brought this young man. The strong focus of his mind on Ansel located him to her and she felt her body tighten. She must protect him, he was of her Family. And then, deeply clear, she knew that was no reason. Every person in this room was her family and she could not single one out for special favor. But she could not help but feel a personal grief. She saw this and accepted it.

She wondered whether when the time for choice came would she be true to all the people or would she favor William. She knew that every person in that Hall had to make that choice. It seemed unfair, but then, lots of things were unfair. She returned her attention to the speaker. She knew that tomorrow Spring Festival would begin in Santiago. Three weeks earlier than their own, it would draw people from Adwin looking for the play and entertainment after the winter. Festival time always brought a good mood among people.

Ansel stood quietly during those moments, testing the crowd, looking about slowly, sipping from his glass of water. William would be proud of him, thought Rose. He's handling himself well.

Ansel straightened into briskness,"Friends, people of the Valley, we are here because we think. We care! As Abel has said, we want to build this Valley into that great land she can become. We, the Builders, want the same thing.. It is through us that a series of ideas have begun to grow into a plan that will transform this Valley to world wide admiration. I am grateful for this time to speak to you as a representative of the Builders. I want to put to rest all the rumblings of rumour that have circulated through our towns. We want you to know the facts. We trust your respect for facts and especially the fact that knowledge must be concrete and useable."

There was a faint murmur of amusement. The people here were already in festival mood, they'd be easy to talk to. "I've listened to our Historian Abel and I wonder whether we've not forgotten too much. Too much that was good about our ancestor's way of life."

"It's true that they were unable to protect their world. They were unable to see how fear ruled their lives,political, religious and economic. They were unable to separate emotions from reason especially in their public and military works, yet they were convinced that they were doing just that." He had spoken with the careful diction of a school child repeating a lesson. Now he smiled and his voice grew strong,a power of conviction carrying his word out to the farthest corners of the Hall. "We are an older people. We have learned that human Beings must not be separate from each other. That we are not separate! I cannot, and you cannot, rest today knowing another - a neighbor, is in need. We have learned! Yes, we have! Greed has fallen victim to simple humanity and the fact that we are a people more mature that our ancesters. Abel spoke the truth, a truth so obvious that we seldom think of it."

"Abel reminded us of one powerful fact, human kind has learned, too late to prevent world wide pain and destruction, but learned nevertheless. We learned to talk! To negotiate our differences! To talk until we found a resolution, a way to proceed other than war. And that way, as Abel said, is the capacity to listen. We may forever feel pride for that. We learned that self discipline is manly." He grinned and people chuckled in response. "That reverence for all life, human, animal and plant is to be admired, taught,and we make laws to inforce that conviction. We reverence the Earth's ecological balance enough to protect it. All this is a reverence for the greater Life itself. It is in our primers, our first teachings in our Learning Centers. Our children grow with this reverence as part of their knowledge of living. For many of us, that is the true miracle of this Valley, the reverence that is deep from our hearts. And so Historian Abel has reminded us also of these things. We have listened! We Builders do not in any way suggest these things are less than important." As Rose heard, she caught her breath. How could one question the excellence of these ideas? But she feared they were still IDEAS for Ansel, not a living reality. And she was afraid he did not know the difference.

"But our concern is that we do not turn from our heritage without careful thought. We must not lose what does not need to be lost. We ask that you give thought to all that our Valley stands for as you hear us." He sighed, seemed relieved that this part of his talk was done. Then, looking around, glancing over at the group of people around William, he began again.""My greatest concern today is that we are confronted by an influence that is not healthy. Yes, I will say it is unhealthy and only partly because it remains a mystery, has not been explained. I refer to that mountain side that we call the Silent City. Is there any evidence that it actually is a City? Is it a City when no one can enter, or travel to and from?"

"That City hovers over us, seems ever present in our lives, visible from almost any point in the Valley; it is a mystery and a malevalence. It disturbs good minds that have flown above it and looked down into what seems to be strange solitary gardens. What then is this? We begin to wonder that it is an influence for evil! It has to be for it is, yes, it's very nature somehow has prevented us from studying it and knowing its nature. Why? Why have we not , in all these years, examined this thing we call the Silent City?"

He waited, letting these words do their work. Then, in a softer, gentler tone, he went on,"Our ancestors paid a price for not examining places of malevolence in their world. We cannot allow that to happen. Superstition must not again take root among us and ruin our world. We the Valley Builders, ask you to think."

Rose knew sharply with a heightened sense of awareness, that the mention of the Silent City had loosened something deeply angry in this young man. She leaned forward as if to meet and thus be prepared for a blow. Ansel sipped again, his eyes searching out his friends and resting finally on William's face. The contact was a reinforcement, he tossed his head slightly, his voice was louder, the rich baritone, over which he had precise control. A hundred years ago he would have been called charismatic; he would have mesmerized those who longed for someone to show them the way. But Valley people were more sophistocated and would recognize such intentions. Then as Rose looked around,she wondered just how much Valley people had learned on that score.

"It is necessary for us to do something specific about that City. We, the Builders, ask you, the Council and the people of the Valley, to complete those studies and if we cannot enter, to force entry into that place and destroy it."Rose's heart ached,how could they want another 'study'.

William's smile faded. The pride he felt in this young man to whom he had given guidance was real. But now, these words worried him. This was not the plan. The job today was to introduce the Builders and to state their concerns, but not to develop those concerns beyond that. William knew his peers. He knew their formidable minds and knew they were perceptive beyond even his power to decipher. He wished there were some way he could warn Ansel now. Could Send a mental warning. He frowned at the thought. With sudden unreasonable resentment, he knew neither he nor Ansel had a trace of that ability that his own Family said was real. If it did exist, how he could use it now! A bitterness settled out of that resentment leaving its taste in his mouth. There was no way he could warn him. Maybe the boy would end it here. If so, not much harm would occur. He sat back, listening with unease.

"These dangers only blind us to those other very evident dangers as our world moves out into interstellar travel. We will soon leave this solar system, unmanned vehicles have done so for some years and people will follow. We are a people traveling out into the GALAXY. But this home world is our source of strength. We must be more than ever practical. We must protect ourselves from superstition, from self delusion." Rose relaxed, smiling. Well, that was pretty obvious and harmless. Those were statements any politician might make. She grimaced at the idea that this boy was a politician. But she could see that William had relaxed. Ansel continued.

"Yet knowing these things, and I know that you all do, we waste our strength. We live in our Valley as though it were a little world, developed to its fullest. We seem to be satisfied, now that we have built enough cities and towns to house our people, have got our industries going and have an obviously successful business community. We are satisfied! I ask you why."

Rose allowed herself to mindlessly listen. to respond to the sound, the rhythm, the music of his lovely voice. She thought how easy it would be to rationalize whatever she wanted to persuade herself to. And then with a start, she wondered if that was what she, herself, was doing. Why could she assume that her own position was the right one? She must listen without prejudice. Could she do that? She certainly hadn't been. How could she expect it of the others here? She felt a sadness, a weary dispair touch her mind and steadied herself carefully.

"We use so little of our resources, our wealth. We waste the values of our wonderful Valley. If we become self satisfied and willing to allow ourselves to settle for less than is possible for us, we have made a grave mistake. " His voice took on a quality of intensity and persuasiveness that Rose found invasive. She did not know how Paul heard this, but Paul sat enthralled, listening, attentive, admiring the skill of this youngster. But he was also unmoved.

"We waste! Waste materials, labor, time, and we do not seem to know it". His voice slid up and down, his arms rose in a gesture too dramatic for Rose's taste, but it seemed to effect his friends because they were nodding. He clearly believed what he said."We waste the land itself. It is lying there, useful only to animals."

It was then that Rose saw William's face pale slightly. She sensed his worry and wondered why. But Will was aware that Ansel spoke of what he must not speak of yet. He must stop this idiot. He must end this mistake. He felt his hand grasping the arm of his neighbor, crushing the flesh to the bone. His tension of fear, and the feeling of that thin old arm in his grasp, gave him an idea. He whispered intensely into Harvey's ear, even as Harvey was trying to pry loose William's fingers. Will hissed angrily at Harvey, "Stop him! Pretend a heart attack, anything, we've got to stop him. He's gone too far.don't you see?"

After a moment, Harvey nodded, then his eyes widened as he realized fully but he nodded again. He clutched his chest, his body weaving from side to side, his head bent and a strange inarticulte cry erupting in tiny intervals from his clenched teeth. The people around immediately responded. Around them was a small disturbance and Ansel seeing it there below him, stopped. He reached out one hand in a gesture to help. Worried, caring. He stepped forward,"We've got an emmergency. Is there a Healer here?"

William had caught Harvey as he leaned forward, then adjusted the seat so Harvey could lie back and rest. Strangely a long moment passed when no one in the huge Hall moved. No Healer would have waited so long and there were several Healers here. They looked at one another sadly, shaking their heads slightly with a faint, sad amusement. Then a woman, a few seats from William stood and moved toward him. At Ansel's first cry, a call had gone to the Medical Center and help was already on its way. Neither Ansel, Will or any of their friends knew that. They were deaf to the inner calls.

Abel leaped to the stand and conferred with Ansel, then Ansel stepped into the circle and announced,"Let this meeting be adjourned. We have stated our concerns. Our ideas have been given you. Please think, then we will contact the Council for further discussion."He went down to help the old man who was his friend.

The Healer sat beside Harvey, holding his hands together,her eyes full of a strange sorrow. She watched him, then slid one hand slowly along his arm, touched his chest, then his forehead. Her face took on some concern. There was nothing wrong with this man physically but anyone who would pretend there was a heart attach when there was not,needed a Healer for that reason. The emergency unit arrived and the floater was brought to carry Harvey out. William looked on with amazement. His thoughts were racing. How could they get here so fast. How could they know? At any rate he would have thought the Healers could take care of him here. Why all this? He answered himself by deciding the Council would have a unit near by for emergencies when there was such a crowd. The explanation was pure rationalizing,surely in clearer moments he would not have accepted it.

Both Ansel and William followed the carriers out with Harvey. Will keeping Ansel in front of him to ensure his going.

Rose sat unmoving, even as others began to move. Her thoughts were racing, her feelings rising and falling and she needed to bring them into calm. The astonishing fact was not that they had witnessed a small charade,but that those participating did not know that they were unable to fool the people around them. She glanced at the people moving out of the Hall. They were the people who wore the bright buttons of the Builders. A few others got up and quietly left. Now those left here must accept the enormity of the differences. The fact of their self imposed ignorance amazed her and she knew immediately that it amazed the others. Those realizing felt a deep grief. The silence around her was a silence of sorrow. They did not want to move, but to contemplate these unavoidable realizations.

Gradually there was another pattern, another significant number of people felt little grief, were not shamed by ignorance or denial. These were mostly young ones,who sat now,watching, wondering how their elders would handle what they had known, had been aware of for years.

With a shiver, Rose turned her eyes to look over the audience. People were beginning to move about, to stand and talk. They knew finally what their young ones had not been able to tell them, to even speak of. Here today, something had been revealed that must end this unnatural denial, this blind refusal to see what was in front of them. Rose finally stood and left too, wanting to meet friends, to talk a little with those she knew before going home. Outside, the storm to the north, which she knew was beating down on Adwin, had begun to drop a light drizzle here on this high city of the sky. She thought of the Family there, watching on Videos the results of this days meeting. Then she realized, and her face opened out in a joyous grin that pushed all other worries away. This was the day, it had to be now, that Ben would come, he would be there and they could talk. Ben! Ben! He would be home tonight surely.! She could think of nothing else but finding an air car and speeding on her way home.

When she arrived home, the Family was there together in the Hall, a thoughtful quiet among them as they talked over the events of the Santiago Council. "Wow, Mom, there it is, no one can pretend there's no difference now." Andrew was excited but not sad.

Rose shook her head, "It's a tragedy, Son. It's something we didn't think would happen, that some - any of our people, would be mind-blind."

Jerry nodded, half hearing, "Rose, how'd it feel, to see that. To see the Healers go to him. Surely they knew, they knew it was a sham. Yet they never said a word."

"Well, of course not. They're mind healers as well as body healers, you know." Anna was angry.

Rose said, meeting Jerry's eyes, "It felt sad. It felt like I'd been found out in some awful betrayal. Fooling myself, refusing to listen even. When I've been teaching right Listening for years. I fail! It's humiliating. So many of you young ones already know, have known."

Anna nodded, "It's true, Mama, we've known. But we never could talk to any of you." Then suddenly, going rigid, her attention distant, she cried out. "Dad! Daddy's here. Let's go. Let's go. To the River," She was gone, Andrew following and Cassie racing after them. The adults got up without more talk and got on rain gear, catching some up for the kids who had gone without it. They ran down the wide pathways to the River below.

The River steamed with fog and rain. Rose stood at the end of the pier, looking into the distance up stream and they saw movement, shaping into a dark small boat. She marveled that Ben would insist on coming this way. And the companion! Why would that one agree? There was a shout and then as they gathered near, the boat came silently drifting in, touching the massive timbers and before it had been stopped and been caught by the ready hands, Benjamin had leaped from it onto the planking and caught Rose's hands in his own. They stood silently looking at each other, their eyes hungry, searching out the lines and messages of each others faces.

Then swiftly he crushed her to him, her arms gripping his shoulders so fiercely they seemed to claw. Then with a laugh they released each other and turned to help with the boat. Ben handed up bundles, Ben always brought gifts, wonderful strange and special gifts from far places. They could see the quiet figure in the dark cloak handing up these packages. Now and then a flashing eye inside that hood drew Rose's curious attention. The rain droned down. The sound of it hushed their voices. Finally Ben, leaned to take Jessie's hand and with a gesture as courtly and protective as Rose had ever seen from him, handed her up to the pier. A faint jealousy touched her and she smiled, but wondered. Ben was busy hugging everyone else, openly crying with joy.

The darkness had grown, they could not see one another well, but Jessie swept her eyes rapidly over them, identifying them as she did, knowing and greeting them as she could. The smile she turned to Rose as she took her hand was full of a sweetness that brought Rose's heart to her throat. Not for long and long had she felt such an all consuming Love, such absolute welcoming into a belonging that was sure. The realization of what that meant was like a flame in her body. She took Jessie's hand and led her protectively toward the hill path.

Ben and the others followed with the bundles, luggage and a few pieces of gear from the boat. Jerry and Andrew and Anna drew the boat into the entrance of the boat house. Jerry said, "Wow, look at that carving and the lovely shape of it. Ben's built this craft with all the love in his heart." They turned then, running to catch up with the others. The whole Family walked with swift little gusts of laughter and bursts of talk up the trail to the Hall.

Jessie could see the hall crowning the hill top and rejoiced. It would be so good to stretch her old bones in a bed this night., She smiled at these thoughts and continued Reaching out to Touch faintly with those who would allow Touch. By the time she reached the hall she felt she knew them, knew more of them that they realized. Those with whom she linked firmly, for a few seconds, grinned in delight at such an one among them.

Dinner was full of joy of homecoming. There was an abandonment, an ease of laughter. Everyone got up now and then to touch Ben, to hug him, make sure he was physically there. He looked at them, his gaze roaming the room, tears flowing unheeded. He shook his head, "It's hard to believe I'm really here! If it's so wonderful, why do I ever leave?"

When the gifts had been given and Jessie taken to her temporary rooms on the second floor, Ben and Rose finally went to Ben's cottage. He felt that a great weight had fallen from him, a clear knowledge that he would not have to leave again to search for something he could not name. They closed their doors, surrendering to the moment, to each other, feeling again the shape of their familiar bodies, finding again the completeness they had so long known. They allowed time to fulfil that desire for touching, loving, and the promise of this night. To taste and look at one another, the way young lovers do, lost in seeing again the beloved face, feeling the beloved touch. But before they had taken off each others clothes, to slide into bed, Rose Reached with a delicate flickering Touch and to her relief and delight, found Benjamin there, not afraid, not disappearing. She felt his shy faint Reach toward her and rejoiced. The new closeness made their lovemaking deeper than it had ever been.

THE AWAKENING

STROM

North west of Adwin, eighty miles of rolling field and forest, groves and towns ended in the rapidly rising high hills that formed the edges of the Coastal range. These forest covered mountains, hid hundreds of little villages, some large towns, and a few cities. Each planned to be little visible , not out of fear but out of a deep protection for the land itself and its life. Among the highest villages, built into the tall evergreen forests was the village called Strom. It had begun as a natural meadow where a few farmers chose to build and to raise their food in the rich soil of that meadow. During the years it had grown to the status of village. The forest cut into it in two wide curving lanes. The people had built frugally, stair step buildings, a rising series of half circles that ran up slope and left all the flat land free. The trees cut had provided building material and the slate found beneath the thin hill side soil, had roofed the town. Then that slate had become a trade product. In front of the curving town, spreading far to left and right was fifty acres of meadow,fields and orchards. The orchards were planted in rypical Valley style, small groves,each one with several varieties of fruit and nuts .The open land below the village allowed a view of the Valley far to the east and north. Adwin's lights could be seen and the setting sun often blazed like burning stars from her highest story of her Learning Center. The people of Strom looked out over a northern land that might have been uninhabited . On a morning at the ending of winter, when spring had already greened the River banks and brightened the forests with the early leaves of deciduous trees, the early sun reached long shadows across the courts and the streets of Strom.

These were forest people who nourished the wild plants and many bloomed here and there along the edges of pathways. They delighted in the beauty of their forests. Their craftsmanship was as fine as any in the Valley and so their town was shaped and carved of the finest hard woods, combined with the common grey stone of their hills. Small fields of grain and vegetables, alternated with the groves of fruits,nuts, berries, grapes grew in the great meadows and were planted so as to appear to be naturally growing there.Here to, the people prepared for Spring Festival, though their own Festival would be a one day affair and they would take their products off to the fairs of the larger northern towns to trade.

This was the village from which Councilman Dean came. He had served as Elder in the village for many years but had only recently gone to serve on Valley Council. On this morning, dancers and singers were practicing and the sound of music that greeted the dawn would continue much of the day. Craftspeople were putting the final touches to their carvings, cooks baking their special breads of acorn flours to be sold in Adwin. The children swarmed through the cobbled courts of the Learning Center. Strom citizens ignored the general Valley

THE PEOPLE OF THE VALLEY

conviction about population growth. But she built her buildings up and not out over the land.

The writing of the chants and prayers for the planting ritual was the task of the children here and they worked to perfect them. The poets and musicians guided and advised. Then these were added to the Strom library. Today, however, another important meeting was being held, one for which children were not needed.

The three story building, far at the southern end of town built of small grey stone blocks, was unusually busy for a winter morning. People gathered on the smooth court around the doorway, and slowly talking and visiting, entered the Hall. The would hear the report of the last Valley Council from their Elder, Dean. People were dressed for work in forest and field and in the slate diggings. A freight cars sat on a hill above the plant, waiting the first days load. The meeting would not be long. They entered and sat in the carved oak seats that ran in long rows twenty deep. The walls were paneled with the polished wood of several colors, words of the Convictions were carved in the walls and the people read them, even though they knew them well. These were a serious people, committed to their chosen way.

Elder Dean stood ready waiting for the crowd to settle. He raised one hand finally and there was quiet. He let his gaze move along the rows, evaluating the faces, listening for the signs of their attitudes this morning. There was no one here he did not know well. With that thought, he smiled. It was as it should be. Dean's life had begun in the great city of San Francisco, and the impersonal busyness of that city in the early days, before it was rebuilt, had left a bitter scar. Now, he would not live in any city for longer than a few days. He loved this town, its size and its familiar friendly people. He began to speak, his voice full and strong, belying the small wiry body from which it came.

"Friends, I want to report to you the information from the Valley Council." He was not a man to be formal nor to waste words. "We have to vote within the week. I will present to you the plan given to us by the Builders and then I will tell you of the Council response to that plan and to our intentions. We can vote when you have heard both sides of this issue." He wanted the voting done. He would send William of Altos word this day perhaps. He had talked to everyone in the town, this formal and final discussion was only to bring it all into focus. Surely they had already decided. "Simply put, We request that we citizens have the right to use the lands of the Valley and to develop it the way our forefathers did. We've built our cities and towns, we've created our power sources for every town and we've all pledged to the Valley Convictions by which we live. Now it's time to see this Valley as our ancestors did. There is land to open up. We can protect our forests, and we can protect all the animal life of the valley and still do much more than we now do. The Valley should be used for HUMAN use, it's main function if for human development, not for the protection of its wild life. We ask that we be free to build as many villages as we need or want. We want greater choice in offering our young ones their space to build. Surely the population restrictions only crush initiative. We must have greater choice in extending our lives out to new and fuller life here." He stopped, took a slow sip of water and studied the crowd.

"However, the real issue before us is another matter. We are in danger here, in our own land and we do not know from whence that danger comes. We only know that it is here. We have seen a little of it even among our own people and you are aware of those who have needed healing to rid them of the strange ideas they have revealed to us."

He paused, utterly quiet for a moment, then, lifting one hand to gesture through the hall, and raising his voice, he cried,"There are witches and wizards among our people in the Valley. There are towns where these dangers are not found, the persons are not taken to the Healers. These are evil practices, that influence our lives. We must get back to the ways of God, to the ways of our ancestors. They knew well that such things must be stopped. Probably most of these poor misguided people do not intend to hurt others. We can see that they often do not know what is happening to them and so are unprepared to ask help. But we believe that there are those who do. We believe that these are the results of minds and bodies damaged through our own genes by those forces and the poisoned atmosphere during the times of destruction before our Valley was even entered.

We who came here were as healthy as any living on earth, yet we brought the strain that still effects our children in our blood and we must watch, listen and be prepared to separate such from our healthy young. We have had children born even among us who show signs of that devil. Some who think they know the attitudes of others, who think that they can speak the future, who might even now be listening in to our own private thoughts. But worse," his voice hardened, his eyes were hard,"there have been a few in our north villages who fell into unconsciousness, who imagined themselves seeing visions, who rose from that terrible spell and pronounced a vision of angels, of heaven itself!" His voice trembled now with the intensity of emotion, the awfulness of what he spoke." This verges on madness, my friends, on madness! But the Healers do not define it so and if our Healers turn against us, we are in danger."

He stopped, took the glass of water and drank , his eyes full of real pain,then with a wearyness that his audience could see, he said sadly,"The people of the Valley now talk secretly of some kind of a 'union' - a practice that knows no limits, that can include people of any age. I do not understand it because they cannot explain, and what can't be explained cannot be right.It sounds diabolical and will wrest people from their own selves even."His voice rose, a faint note of hysteria touched it and he knew, heard, and stopped.

He took a deep breath. " It is my conviction that we must insist on watching, on keeping sanity in our Valley. We must weed out those who say they hear or know what no normal person does.We must find Healers who will listen to our fears and take them seriously. If we cannot find healers, then we must find other medically trained people who will . We must cleanse the soul of our humanity and seek out those who would destroy the life of our future.And we must do this with

THE PEOPLE OF THE VALLEY

civilized restraint."

A voice cried out,"How have we been harmed by such people. I've known no harm from them."

Elder Dean was grateful for the question. "Of course not. We have protected our people. We have taught our children the evil of this practice and we teach them to come to us to be cleansed of it. Our community has been favored and I think it is because we pray that that will be so. But when we see such signs in any child, we have taught the child to rid himself of these things before he is five. We have been successful in that. The seven villages of our forest land here have joined in this effort, but the rest of the Valley is not so fortunate. Out there, the number grows. There are many and they increase. Even the Council of the Elders has some such within it. Worst of all, it has been told me, though I haven't seen it, that there are those who insist that they enter into the land of the dead, that they leave this world and speak to those who have gone beyond waiting for the time of judgement. What else but satanic practices or serious mental disease could cause a person to say such a thing? What can be done? My friends, we must think seriously and we must think what is best for all of us." He thought he had understated the facts, he thought he ought to have spoken more of the practices and their evil results. But he could not think how he could tell these things.

He stood with bent head, and then with a gesture of finality, he said, "You have all heard of the Builders. Some of you are members of that organization. They are the ones who want to make of the Valley a place where human need stands first before the needs of other life.They are people who insist that we cleanse ourselves of the rites and practices of Satan and they wait to welcome any of you who wish to join them." He stopped, looked around, breathed slowly, to calm his own feelings, and then said,"Well,we said this meeting would not be long. I have said what's needed. We've talked and met together these past weeks, We know what we must do. I present my case for the vote."

He left the stand and a younger man, a huge, bearded, powerful looking man, a woodsman, who walked with the balanced refinement of a forest creature, came up the steps to the dais. The low conversation faded, he stood waiting.Then, in a voice that rang in deep mellow tones of a trained tenor, reminding every ear that this was the best singer in these mountains, he began. "What Elder says is surely one side of a very important matter." A gentle lessening of tension began at the very sound of his voice. He worked a magic they could feel,though they didn't know it occurred. His mouth, generous and wide, held the smile that seldom left it.

It is so important that we consider it carefully, There are two issues here, not one. The Builders would change the Valley forever, it is not an experiment they are asking for.Do we want that? We have built into our way of life room for all life - for animals, plants and humans to live in harmony, We have built our cities, farms and our machinery so that they are harmonious to life." He heard faint murmurs but he raised his hand and there was silence."The old ones ruined their world, our world.You know that! We have read and watched the films of our history.We know! We have a healthy world, a world where the potential of humanity can be allowed to develop its own pace". He stopped to drink and to look slowly from face to face for a long second or two.

"We cannot know what is possible for us, for the race. We only know that great and highly Talented people have occurred here and there through history and have turned the world into new directions. All of these have not been positive. But now,,we may be on the threshold of a time when the majority of people will be people of great Talent, of great insight and truly enlightened. Most of us! And those of us who are not so talented can offer help and refuse to be envious. Doesn't that strike you as right? The development of the race must be toward greater understanding and a vast expansion of mind. Expansion of Mind but only as a true and loving Heart guides. That is our belief. Valley Teachers have taught us and our children these Convictions. We have talked about these things, we have argued and listened to one another, we have tried to see through our fears and private lusts. Surely, we recognize that when here-to-fore unknown Talents appear among us we must be ready to test and train them.We must not, as our esteemed Elder suggests and tries to practice, erase that Talent.He forgot to mention that many of those whose Talents begin to surface simply leave our town.We don't erase them.

However, every talent is as all talents are, they can be used for good or evil. Think how much evil has come from the brilliant scientific mind - the Talent of our ancestors - because those minds were not taught the talent of the Loving Heart.Those people had not vision enough to see the futility of personal greed and personal lust.The emptyness of a life lived so.I believe that we know the difference now, that we KNOW that such lives are empty, miserable even."

"Surely any God given Talent cannot be used until it is trained in the way of the Loving Heart. I insist that those Talents we discover among us must be from our natural growth,gifts of God. Not disruptions of Satan, as the Builders suggest.Let us watch for fear. It can destroy our Reach toward Love. And that Reach toward Genuine Love is what this Valley is about!" He stopped, looking around again, his face stern, the persuasiveness of his very tone moved them to careful listening."

" But Love itself can melt away all fear. If we are able - capable of Love.We are capable of thinking, of all the skills of focussed senses, of creating, of building, all the arts, all the penetrating into the secrets of the plants, the healing remedies, and other valuable products we've found in them. Was this all the Devil's work? Was it Devil's work that we discovered atomic science, the Solar drive that lets us travel between planets almost instantly? Or the focussed and powerful minds that discovered how to use the sun and the wind to provide our World with endless plentiful energy? All the medical and biological discoveries that make disease almost uncommon, that make genetic practice in Healing what would have been miracles a century ago. These were not Devil born, they were born of human Talent! And though harmful things were done with these discoveries,that was because we had not yet discovered the Teaching of the

Heart! Of the Intuitive Mind!"

He paused again, this time his audience seemed utterly attentive, even the dissenters, restless when he began were still."Surely we must look carefully now at these new Talents that we say are cropping up. First we must make sure they are not our imagination. Then we must make sure that we understand their best use. And we must be sure they do not harm the person they gift. People use their minds for good and evil. It is our task to see that we train and teach our children so that these Talents are used for good, are developed with the foundation of Loving Hearts. If these are Talents developing in humanity naturally because we have evolved to that state at which it is time for them, won't we simply end up having to destroy all people eventually, if we insist they must be denied. Can we deny our true nature? We must be sure. We must ourselves act with Love. And to act with love we must find out more about the very talents we now fear. We must use our own minds to understand what we don't now understand. Is it this lack of understanding that makes us attribute these strange events to the Devil? I ask that you consider that possibility seriously. " He stood looking out at them, his gaze roaming here and there, picking out faces, trying to see their response. He felt a restlessness in certain groups, a look of anger pinching many faces there. He knew there were those who would not hear.He had asked for reason and there were some whose emotions already drowned reason.These, mostly old ones, who had not learned the practices of 'balancing'.

Then, Charles extended his hands in a gesture of offering,of asking." People must explore, must discover, must search out this new territory of Mind and Heart. It is the new land, pioneers of our day enter into this land of the Mind, for it is that greater expanded Mind that opens into the regions of the Heart.The emotions are not the Heart. Love is not an emotion. It is a Quality of Spirit!"

"And Spirit is our new dimension! It is the rightful place for search of modern Minds. It is more truly the territory of discovery than the planets that we have so recently begun to live on. For without these new Talents, there is possibility that we cannot ever fully develop those planets, or visit the stars.Our future of discovery must come out of a meeting of our fears. If we fear these Talents, then we must meet them and learn their nature, not suppress them, not deny them. I understand that denial has been common among us . The denial blinds us and the people suffer from that. We must not let our lives be determined by fear." He stopped, sipped water from a glass near him and then, even though his voice was suddenly soft,gentle, it carried out through that small crowd of his fellows.

"We have discovered Love, let that Wonderful quality determine our lives. There is no fear that will not fall before genuine Love." He stopped, let a long second pass, steadily looking at the sea of faces,"There is no one here, I trust , who does not know what that means, that kind of Love!" He stopped again, then with a quick nod of his head, he said,"Well. I think we can decide. The issues have been stated."

He walked down the few steps, wondering, feeling a deep nagging worry. Were there enough private, selfish interests that the exploitation of the Valley for those interests might occur? Surely humankind had come farther than that. But on the other hand, humankind was not so far away from that old base of separativeness, of selfish lusts for power, the fascination with an endless collecting of 'things'. Some might fall back into that old trap. Charles knew that it was a trap. He had himself nearly succumbed, nearly been persuaded against his better judgement.He could not condemn anyone else. He could only sustain his courage and his faith in enlightened human minds. He dismissed the talk of Talents- he thought they were only red herrings. People could not be truly afraid of such new skills. and yet, he remembered years ago, when he had been quite young and his oldest brother had been brought before the town council because he had done something Charles could never quite understand or get explained. His big, kind gentle brother whom he loved. And that brother had secretly in the night, left the town,gone away and Charles had missed him terribly. Later, he had known that his brother was well, was studying at the Training Retreat for Monitors. Even then he had feared. What were those people, those Monitors? Town people had reluctantly accepted that saying that 'they would surely straighten him out'.But they didn't know who they were either. they thought of them as a kind of police.

Charles family talked with him often by video phone and he was well, and seemed always happy. His reverie was broken by the rising hum of talk, of people moving steadily into the entrance way where the voting boxes were set. Small villages did not have electronic voting systems but there were plenty of boxes and voting would not take long. Charles heaved a long sigh. He wanted to go out into that Valley, find his brother and know something of his world!

CHAPTER SIXTEEN

William and the Temple

    The day after Benjamin and Jessie arrived, the family gathered in welcome. It took most of the day to listen to their stories, get re-acquainted and tell each other all that had transpired. Explaining their worries to Jessie and Ben, required they be clearly stated. What had been half spoken, or even avoided, had to be talked of openly. And had to be faced more intimately than they had ever been. Benjamin asked many questions, Jessie listened with a manner that encouraged introspection as the story was told. She did not ask questions. Rose thought she wanted mostly for them to tell it all clearly. She frowned, watching the quiet woman. What was this one? This one who could Send so easily, could touch so gently? Surely what Ben had told her before they came from their rooms had suggested she was more than ordinary.

    The Gather ended with a good dinner that began a celebration and party. Friends came from town to welcome Benjamin, meet Jessie, and just catch up with one another. The Hall was a busy place of laughter and dancing, of music and repeated tales of the past year. Everybody stayed late and most ended up sleeping at the Hall rather than take belts through the cold sky back to town. So Ben and Jessie were welcomed home. Before they separated for the night, Rose said,"We've only given you a picture of what's happening here. We must soon take time to talk seriously, but this party has been just what we all needed. We'll plan another Gather when you've had time to visit the town, talk to people and feel a litle settled."

    Paul and Jennifer would use Rose's cottage this night and as they started off Paul said,"There's no way to tell you how glad we are you're home or that you've brought Jessie with you. We need you both more than either of you know. But we'll get to all that soon enough." He drew Jennifer to him and they went out to their rooms. By morning the normal busyness of life began again and everyone was off to work or to learning. Ben and Jessie wandered about, he showed her the farm, talked to Steve and Jane who were preparing for the Spring Planting, and stood finally looking over the Valley from the deck. Jessie said,"Benjamin, we must talk to them all again, and go into town and talk to the people there,so we understand what these problems are that your family worries about. I have people to see in Adwin and Jasper and Denlock. Other families to greet. Then we must have a proper Gather here, not more than a week from now."

    He looked at her, wondering, and nodding." Not more than a week,huh? I'll get it arranged". They walked in silence, both thinking of all they'd been told yesterday. So much! Then he said,"Well, for now, lets go back to the hall and have lunch and then I'll get belts and we'll go to Adwin this afternoon. You've not seen the town finished. He grinned, proud and eager. Then maybe, later this

THE AWAKENING

week, we'll take a trip to Altos and Santiago." He grinned, enjoying being host.

Altos was immersed in many changes, not least of which was the ending of storms and the beginning of spring. The weather had the blithe, sweetness of early spring, and it brought a lift to the hearts of the people. Like the Seasonal Festivals, spring time traveled from the far south at Clandor to finally arrive at these northern towns. It transformed Valley towns at least two weeks before that change occurred in the mountains. Finally, even Altos was bursting into life. The end of cold released the frozen fountains and melted the ice on the Stone Park lake. The transparent domes over roof gardens were slid back and down so that the fresh breezes washed clear the winter's closeness. Fountains shattered the frozen stillness of so many months with their leap and play of light. The sunlight poured like an oil over the pale green of opening leaves. The mountains above Altos would be white for another month, but the dark forests surrounding and below the city were rich green and rustling with life. Skis and sleds still carried people down the slopes above the city and into the prongs of white that penetrated the forests.

William stood upon the edge of the circular balcony that surrounded the great Temple. The Temple hung high above the highest roof or carved cave housing. The winds that sang around its roofs were cold and yet the sun gleamed from it with a warmth that beckoned the people below. He watched the city waking, the movement of people everywhere beginning to fill the long swaying suspenson bridges that frightened visitors but that the citizens loved enough to keep up the cost of maintenance. People on Belts flocked like birds through the sky above the city, going to work in the industrial centers inside the mountains, to the great agriculture Domes and through the tunnels to the mines. Everywhere there was movement and he thought a case could be made for its resemblance to a hive. The thought irritated him.

He watched the lights flicker off in the great field Domes where the magic of plant sciences had made his city famous. From this city, he thought in a pride that warmed his heart, the human race had been literally freed from threat of hunger. Food crops high in nutritional value, self resistant to insect attack and disease, especially when planted with companion plants. That combination planting resulted in self fertilizing and longer life. All this Altos had given to the world. The plant wizards of Altos had done much to change the focus of humankind from a need to survive to one of freedom from want and it had done it without overwelming the rest of Earth life in fact. It not only did not destroy forest or meadow, but rather enhanced, enriched both. Human kind could turn its energies to a fulfilment of human possibility, to creating a world that enriched and empowered human life. William's pride in his city's accomplishments were deep, as if he himself had brought it about. It never occurred to him to think of these plant wizards, so well known now around the world, as a people with strange and questioned 'Talents'. Had someone persisted in forcing him to recognise that blindness, he would have been horrified. For William,'Plant Wizard' was simply an affectionate title for Plant Scientists. He did not know how they worked.

THE PEOPLE OF THE VALLEY

Walking at the edge of the balcony he estimated the number of people walking or running on the hanging walkways, as equal to the number riding belts. He smiled, it was as it should be; his people were not lazy. He watched the flash of bright belted people swiftly moving from one place to another. He had worried when the belts became used so commonly. He thought it would result in a people weakened from lack of exercise. But he reckoned without the Learning Centers and the yearly Games and Festivals. Children learned to love and care for their bodies as consciously as they learned to train their minds and to balance their emotions. The people of the Valley found great pleasure in physical activity. He knew it was one reason the webs of bridges got the money they need to keep them up. Metalurgists, constantly testing new metal combinations with polymers,for materials resistent to extreme stress of high mountain building,kept these spans at the state of the art. William's first real success as a politician had been in insisting on the maintenance of these delicate lovely webs of transportation. He had wanted to limit the use of belts too, worried that this city of athletes would become a city of effetes. He needn't worry, friends tried to tell him, because Altos people liked to walk, but William had persisted until everyone in the city knew of his worry. At least he had given them thought.

He looked down, running his gaze across the smooth stone floor of the Stone Parkway. The heaps of sand and rubble that had nearly covered the lovely stone of this water carved park way between the two ridges into which much of the city was cut, had all been removed years ago and a new industry came of it. The people, desparate for building materials then, had found a way to cart off the rock rubble, crush it to a uniform fineness and then bind it into light weight, stronger blocks. Adwin had used the same process to build blocks from the debris from her stone quarry.. Other cities through the world now used the method and improved on the product. One advantage was the flexibility of the material, poured into molds, or shaped by hand, it found endless uses. That process had been Altos's first major income producer.

The Plant Domes were only foundations then. He smiled,remembering those early days. Removing the debris that filled Stone Park uncovered a deep hole two hundred feet long and sixty wide. It filled with water from the thin clear stream that ran the length of the Parkway. It had served as a favorite swimming and ice skating lake ever since. There were irregular gardens in crevases where soil had collected and clumps of trees and shrubs brightened the long narrow park. It had become the show place for student sculpture and even for a few fine works of professional artists. But mostly the people loved the quiet, stark, barrenness of stone and water where they could come and sit beneath lone evergreens and meditate or talk with friends. It contrasted happily with the hanging gardens of blooming plants cascading over the honeycombed ridges, and over the stair steps of homes with roof gardens.

William drew his eyes from the city below and shook himself mentally. He turned to look at the temple, a great golden dome catching this morning light. The lovely curve of the massive building seemed to him to float, to sway slightly in the vigorous morning breeze. But he knew it was solid as the mountain itself. The temple was like a finely crafted jewel, simply and exquisitely formed where light seemed to flow, to shift and blend into new colors. The people of Altos had built it after their city was fairly complete. They had taken time and money because they wanted it to express their highest aspirations. William was irritated with himself. He had not come here to look at the city or the temple. He had spent his usual half hour in the Temple, in the thoughtful quiet that brought his ideas into focus and calmed him for the day. He lingered now for something he thought more important.

Always these few minutes in the Temple gave his day a good start. He felt distinct nourishment from the sheer magnificence of the Temple itself but he liked being there alone. Seldom could he arrive before others, but now and then it happened. Sometimes he thought the Temple had a strange power over people. It made him uneasy to think of that now. A power beyond its right. Any beautiful work of art would have power, yes, he could testify to that, but this seemed something else.

He watched now as the people came from the Temple. The sun was coming up and its light flashed brilliant color from the radiant walls and roofs. The people moved slowly down the hanging webway and he wondered what they thought. What had happened to them in there? Some had been there for an hour, much too long, in William's view. So many came out with that look he had come to notice, a look he could not decipher. He felt an old anger, impatience, rise and clutch at his chest. He wanted to know. There was something -- something he knew of from unguarded comments, from the way people looked, their smiles even. He could not understand that. He wanted to know because he could not tolerate not knowing. He could no longer deny there was something he did not know among his people.

What was going on with people in this city? He prided himself on being able to figure out anything, given enough facts. He intended to get the facts. People didn't give him facts about this Temple when he discretely questioned them. He remembered so many times he had asked, carefully not to be exposing his worry. They had finally turned to him with such a quiet silence, a silence that seemed suddenly to become a sharp, prickling one that left him feeling a terrible sense of separation. He waited for an answer, wondering at that silence. There was an awkward moment and they would murmur some inanity. He could not see what the problem was and it would not leave him alone. He had to know. He thought some people behaved as though they hid something and were reluctant to reveal that fact.

As a result of all this, William had for some time felt a mystery, dark and shadowy around him, something that stung his pride and questioned the proper order of things. He hated these feelings, they fed that terrible sense of helplessness he had known as a very young man, just come from the narrow village of his parents and knowing so little. He told himself he was simply curious, never admitting the fear that fed a growing resentment. Something was being concealed from him. Since it was reasonable to be curious, and William was an infinitely reasonable man, he knew he must discover the mystery. The Gather with the family in December had given him fresh questions, but answered few of the old ones.

Now what he wanted most was to have done with it all, to prove to himself that there was nothing to worry about, there was no mystery. Then he could end this foolish vigil. But William could not resist this watching, though he made up his mind each time he came that he would not waste such time again. Nevertheless, each time, that demand to know was hard upon him. He came.

At first he told himself it was simply the nature of a people who lived in the grand world of these high mountains, simply a result of that quality that seemed to emmanate from these peaks, radiate from rock and the stone of her buildings, from the cascade of gardens. He tried to convince himself it was the wonderful creative energy, the joyful inventiveness that marked the people of Altos,but the relief was denied him. It was something more. He could not fully accept those explanations. He knew he was not creative in the way other citizens were but that shouldn't make a difference. Why didn't anyone talk of this strange attitude relating to the temple? Sometimes when he watched people coming from the Temple, he felt mostly envy and that worried him more than his anger. He thought the creative mind slightly inferior to the supremely rational one. He thought of himself as supremely rational.

He watched the people and thought they imagined themselves privy to some lovely dream or fantasy that brought that strange far off smile, that pensive look as if expecting something - even something from him. Yes, as if they waited for something when their eyes touched his. It was as if he had been touched by an infinitely tender touch something that he could never have named and didn't consider to be real. Yet when they would finally turn from him, there was that great quality of sadness in their eyes and calm stillness in them- that he could not find for himself. How could he bend himself to ask? This was where much of that helplessness was triggered. It infuriated him. He thought that since the Gather, he had noticed more. As though he had been alerted to something by that meeting.

Slowly a suspicion had been building that he COULD not grasp something that appeared to be going on all around him. Not only with the adults but even with the children. Perhaps especially them. He noticed their strange silences, their looks of impudent surprise after they had met his eyes, and turned away. Sometimes he thought they laughed at him. Even Paul and Jennifer's children, Rachel, and Steve, both of whom he'd known since birth. These two loved him as an uncle and yet- there was a guardedness, an evasiveness that he could not understand. Then, in these past months, he had noticed among his colleagues, even the Council, that look of distance that he had at first been contemptuous of because it seemed to him a flagrant removal of attention from the business at hand.

After the Family Gather too, he had to wonder at himself, with a subtle hint of panic, something William did not recognize because it was not something he ever intended to feel. He began to see that these differences were more common than he had thought. Could this be what they talked of at the Gather, that Reach they said was possible? Mind Reach? Rubbish.It could not be!

The nagging suspicion grew. He could usually talk himself out of it, could avoid acknowledging it completely, but lately, he had not been able to . What was wrong, why couldn't he just ask people?

He bent his head, a slim tendril of fear pushing its way into his heart, prodding his mind with the signals of danger. He refused it again, as he had so many times, but this time it would not fade. With a relief, he heard his name called. He turned. A heavy bodied, dark man dressed in a loose woolen tunic, approached. He had time to judge his appearance and thought,if he'd lose some weight he would look better. However, Will saw that the colors were beautifully blended and that his friend made a handsome figure, big or not. He came rapidly toward William smiling as with a genuine pleasure in seeing him. Suddenly Will felt a wave of gratitude that this man had turned to him to talk, to relieve him in this silent vigil. Immediately he felt ashamed of his judgement and then uneasy at his relief. He smiled warmly, wanting to talk.

Gerald reached out one hand, as though to touch but not touching. It was a gesture of welcome. "Will, I'm pleased to find you here. I've talked with your father recently and I've wanted to know your thoughts about his ideas. I've heard his suggestions for the mine crews,he's got good ideas, you know. But I'm worried. Not about the mines, of course, he knows more of them than most of us, but about him. Isn't it time he took some vacation? He's late into his eighties ,it would seem to me he needs rest." His eyes were friendly , but William recognized the glint behind them, the intention that was not spoken. He relaxed, he could deal with this kind of man. A man whose own feelings were not evident to himself. Who did not know that others could read his behavior well enough to know his deceit.

"My father will die at his work. He would be devastated were he to turn his life to other things now." He spoke severely, forgetting his gratitude."But this is a matter I would rather discuss only with him." Gerald blanched, his face quickly turned down into a frown. But he simply shook his head as if denying all that William had thought. His eyes were on the people coming along the wide pathway. "There's something wrong here. Look at them, Will. They're nearly asleep, in my opinion. There's something wrong in this whole city. Something that grows worse day by day. It's all you can do to get their attention when they come from the Temple this way." And now, Will saw the cause of his duplicity and felt a tired contempt that the man thought it necesssary. But as he spoke the thoughts he himself had worried with, thought coming from another rich and responsible citizen, swept away any criticism. He suddenly admired the man's courage. Or was it foolishness? Or fear?

He glanced at the people passing, and nodded,"Yes, indeed, it seems they are filled with some religious ferver, yet I can't really think that would be true in our time." As he spoke, Will realized he had found one answer to his own question. But he didn't like that answer. He looked at Gerald thoughtfully, his mind racing with new questions.

Gerald was encouraged, " I think they've either drugged themselves or they have a traffic with the Devil. It's something I've thought for some time."He said it with conviction and then, as swiftly glanced at William with unease shading his eyes. He laughed to relieve the tension. Will nodded to himself, this man was not so sure of himself after all. Gerald muttered something then said, "That's no explanation, not a serious one at least, I suppose. I've heard people speaking of such things lately though. It made me wonder. At any rate, they don't act as they ought". His eyes were sharp now, he watched the others in unrestrained curiousity,nodding to himself.

William found himself nodding too."They seem to me engrossed, as if - as if they know of something so absorbing they want to dwell on it. As if they 'know' something,I've thought." He felt he'd hit on the exact word."Yes, something they might have discovered- there in the Temple,in fact. It's a look of pleased recognition that I see in their faces and I keep wanting to know-- for what?" He had forgotten Gerald, but seeing him there, was surprised at his ease at talking of this whole matter with him. "It's like good students sometimes will look when a difficult problem suddenly begins to unknot and become clear. Surely, you've seen it when you have students learning your trade with you?" His own words brought him a sweep of recognition, but were followed by such fear that he caught his breath and closed himself in cold anger.

Gerald shook his head."It's not something they know. It's something lost, in my opinion. I have never liked the Temple, or any of the ones in the Valley. I couldn't understand why our parents, or our own people built them anyway. Wasted money when we didn't have much" He frowned, "I've seen this look before. Far off. Half asleep. I think it's something wrong, very wrong."

His voice dropped to a conspiratorial whisper,"In fact, William, I think we ought to investigate this matter. He gave Will a glance ,his frown deepened and he nodded as if he accepted his friend's agreement without it having been given. Will was suddenly repulsed. This quality of gossip, of secretive distrust of his fellows, smacked to him of an old past that he did not want to see return. He was so surprised he said nothing for several minutes. Gerald turned ,met Will's eyes and said,"Well, I must go. I'll call and arrange a time when we can talk more fully." He bent his head, nodded curtly and walked swiftly out into the flow of traffic. Will watched him go with deeper misgivings than before,. He resented the new worry that had begun to prick at his mind. But he resented Gerald's connection to these worries more.

Whatever might be said of William, his short comings, his blind spots, which he himself would admit to in some cases, it could not be said that he was in any way a fool nor a dissembler. What ever he thought he would speak of and when he questioned, it had been his habit to go directly to the person he questioned. Why he didn't do that now, both puzzled and angered him. He was as astute a business man as the city could boast and had been completely supportive of the architects of Altos when all the world said their plan to build in these peaks was insanity. His greatest strength was his ability to organize and get things done. He was especially appreciated for his restraint in dealing with the most creative people. Often they were not people who could organize well and some business people became exasperated with them. He could work with them to realize the dreams they so well imagined.

But William was not flexible nor was he able to leave reason and take flight on wonderful imagined ideas that such artists loved to explore. He could not free himself so totally of the old ways of thinking and experiment mentally with any possibility imaginable. And so he had begun to realize he served as the stable point from which so many creative people sprang and to which they returned for the completion of their dreams. He knew enough to restrain the somewhat condescending smile with which he heard their joyous, eager tumult of ideas and plans. He knew he could do nothing without them, that they had to work their own magic in their own way and that his ideas fed on their imagination. He sometimes resented this fact, but would not deny it was true. He also knew the value of his own contribution.

Now and then, Will would remember (as one might remember some small foolishness that he had indulged in during adolescence) That there were two times in his life when he had come close to a realization, to perception that frightened him. He remembered something that flickered into mind, into vision, perhaps, and that he had dismissed immediately as some aberration of his brain. Perhaps the resulting surge of fear had helped in his dismissal of it. He had heard the Teachers speak of meditations that led to heightened awareness, not just to better thinking for the day, but to something esoteric,and it did not seem at all reasonable. It seemed closer to madness, a disorganization of the patterns of things as he knew them to be, a loss in stability. So he simply didn't believe them. Teachers were, after all, often given to flights of fancy.

Therefore when any suggestion that might become inner revelation rose into awareness, he feared it as if it were close to madness, a step that might lead him to an edge from which he could not return and that he surely did not understand or trust. He knew how to circumvent that dangerous point of inquiry, of wondering. He could turn his mind swiftly to other paths.To think of other ideas. He never simply opened himself to experience so that for a period, thinking ceased. William based his meaning of life on his power to think. Why then could he not simply ignore the people who disturbed him, reject them as fools,dupes to their own neurotic needs.

He always answered himself without delay. His was an honest mind. No thinking person could insist that such people were simply fools. For one thing, there were too many of them now. He had done business with them, knew them as scientists, teachers, skilled technicians and business people. He had begun to notice more and more people who could combine his own skills for organizing, for careful rational explanations for things,and the ability to put dreams into practice, with the associative thinking, creative genious and utterly brilliant insights of those he had once thought of as creative children. .A wild creative visionary who had learned to use creative skills and organisational ability together , was a formidable being to reckon with. William knew the facts. This culture, growing as it did out of dreams and 'impossible'ideas, was too dependant on these new and vigorous 'double minds'. The thought sometimes made him feel near to being an anachronism,,but he comforted himself with the fact that he had much still to do. But here was a mystery more delicate than any he had every found. And he studied the people coming from the Temple searching for an answer.

The flow from the Temple was nearly gone. Most people had walked to the Belt stand and taken off to their day's work. Some still walked or ran across the narrow bridges. He debated whether to walk or fly and decided he needed the exercise and would enjoy a brisk walk. He gazed down into the jewel like city below. So very, very beautiful it is, he thought. He always a felt a surge of pride that the city he had helped build was his favorite in this world.

Master Teachers talked of a flowering of human creativity, an extension of consciousness that expanded perception and had brought about the world's great modern cities. The whole idea had always seemed to him somewhat vague. He began to think of a slowly forming plan that had clung at the back of his mind. It was a secret even from Annette and he did not let himself think of it often.

Seeing the city below had triggered that plan. The idea that he might have the power of the whole of it. Already he took steps toward that aim. He could be the power that would direct its flow of life. He would sit behind the scenes, would not allow any gross personal acclaim to seduce him to its whim, rather he would be known to very few and yet,-- he would wield true power. His influence would decide and choose the city's government. The city was larger now, it would grow still. It needed a different Council, a different charter even. He thought there were some new Convictions that could be designed.

He had begun recently to allow his 'idea' (he would not have called it a dream) to develop, to take form. He must build it into a clear rational picture, must be ready to begin each step that would lead to this end. Now and then, as he demonstrated that he had at his fingertips solutions for immediate needs, he had seen a nod of a head, a glance between two or three, and he thought they saw him as a true leader. He must continue to build their trust, their respect and their admiration even.

William drifted so far into his fantasy that he was at peace. He had forgotten for the moment his morning's concern. He longed to bring this most beautiful of cities to the highest status of the Valley cities. He saw himself a humanist of the finest quality, one who thought of the welfare of humankind and of all that the Valley stood for. He had spoken of these ideas tentatively once to Paul. Paul was a man who had learned steadily through the years to integrate the dreaming and the practical minds. He did not doubt nor underestimate either. He had practiced integration and had sought to persuade Will to join him in this effort. He called it the art of self realization. Will had thought that was a practice too esoteric for him, too much inward focussed. Yet, when Will had brought his ideas of change in Altos, of creating a plan for Altos to stand as the hub of Valley politics, it had seemed to him that Paul had simply not grasped the ideas at all. He had said that he did not understand the value of it.

Will had been at first angry, then contemptuous. He had felt angry too that this contempt had made him so sad. He did not want to feel so about his own Family. And yet, what else did he feel for Benjamin when he went off on those strange pointless 'journeys' that he could not explain. Paul had said, "It's interesting in itself to consider. It's out of the blunders of humanity, out of the past that the longing to control other people comes. What kind of people can be dominated today? Do you really see our people as accepting any kind of hidden government agencies? William, I think we've passed far from such possibiity. We are simply too aware, Will. Too aware. We don't trust secrecy."

William had been astonished. He thought Paul misunderstood him completely. Paul was, after all, too gentle and too passive a man to reallize his own power. William had ended up feeling a nearly smug superiority and noticing it, pushed the thought away. He knew people generally distrusted any group or person who might gain any real power over the lives of others. Too much pain had occurred in the world because of such dominance. People were wary, attentively wary and too aware of themselves and their world to allow a reoccurance of controlling groups. But then, William knew that his own interests were for the welfare of the citizens, of Valley life. He could not see that his ability to improve things would be misunderstood. Besides, he was himself a student of history and knew that most rulers had used fear or rage to control. Or they had manipulated people by threatening the basic sources of survival. He was far above such primitive tactics. Fear of a common enemy had made humankind gather together and then they could be manipulated. He intended so such ruse. Nor would he admire a people on whom it could be perpetrated. No one had to spend all his or her time at basic needs for survival today. People DID pay attention. All people were aware enough and free enough to want to learn. He knew these things, but he had plenty of time. His plan was a life task. He would study carefully the way people thought as he served on the Council in these years. He would be ready, as his own work and the dependence of others on him, grew. The long walk and the thoughts of these plans restored his good humour.

He felt good as he descended the last ramp down to the great cluster of buildings that were the Civic Center. Set a little apart from the rest of the city, they served to emphasize their purpose as special. It had been his own suggestion and influence that had convinced the Council years ago to build here in this small forest at the edge of a finger lake that prodded into the northernmost canyon behind the City proper. There was a refreshing quiet here, a peacefulness, so that many times they held meetings out on the curving stone courts against which the water lapped gently. He walked steadily, greeting people he met.

With relief, he saw Jennifer approaching from the air. She settled down gently on the path beside him, laughing and waving. She walked to him and

THE PEOPLE OF THE VALLEY

impulsively hugged him. He submitted a little stiffly, it was not comfortable for Will to receive affection in a public place and she knew that well. She said,"Will, I'm so glad to see you. Paul and I wanted to ask you if you would be able to come with us on a cross country ski trip next week. We thought we could leave early and travel through the back country behind Altos Range. The snow is better there. It may be the last time for the year for us."

He smiled to look at her, genuinely delighted. He had known Jennifer long before she and Paul were mated and he had loved her most of her life. He nodded, thinking of his schedule. "I think I could do that. I think there's nothing that would stand in the way. I'd enjoy one last long trip into that snow country. He turned to wave at other people near by, and thought that Jennifer looked especially pretty today. He remembered the sadness he had felt when she had made her committment to Paul -- and the relief. He smiled to remember. He had wanted no committments then. He had preferred to live in loose relationships with those he loved and needed. Annette had been willing to accept that on condition that she be the central figure of his life. But that was later. He had wanted no children. Now, when he was with Paul and Jennifer, or the other family members, he sometimes wondered about that decision.

He had met Annette not long after Paul and Jennifer had committed themselves to Mating and she had loved him with an open,good humor, accepting him so utterly that he had been almost ashamed at her capacity. It eclipsed his own. He had never been sorry. Annette had changed his plans somewhat, but he had begun to turn to her almost exclusively and it was not long until she was truly the primary figure of his life. She seemed all he needed. He had been surprised at that. She had made no effort to deny his power, his control of his life and hers in some ways. That this was a measure of her own great power, he did not fathom.

Jennifer turned to him,bringing his attention to her."I'm pleased that you can do it,. We've not had much time to talk these past few months and we all need that. We surely didn't get much time to talk together at the Gather for Benjamin."She laughed, remembering that joyous occasion.

"I'll go for sure."He was nodding, pleased at her wanting him "Even if I have to rearrange some things to do it."

She took his arm with a squeeze of affection. William's reticence had never intimidated Jennifer. They walked into the great doors swung wide to allow the crowd to enter. Weather screens activated as the doors opened, blew their hair slightly and then they were across its influence. She took off her cloak but William only loosened his outer coat. A long line of pegs in the wall already held many coats and rainwear. She hung hers on a low peg and turned silently toward the central circle where the members of the Council would sit. She knew that she and William were on opposite sides on several issues. He was a formidable adversary and would be hard to convince. But then, he probably thought the same of her, She smiled ruefully. Well, her own convictions needed counter conviction. How could she be absolutely sure her's was the wise course. But she knew she would need to offer her most convincing arguments and do it with careful thought. She had prepared well.

For a woman whose whole life had been centered on music, a woman whose talent was acclaimed through much of the world both as composer and performer, this role as politician seemed wrong. Yet, Jennifer had also spent her life learning the kind of integration of body, mind and emotion that made Valley people versatile and so flexible. She had become proud of her ability to manage affairs that in her early years she would have ignored. She never left off trying to persuade William to develop his own recessive abilities in creative directions, but he laughed at her. He thought he was as much a self realizing person as anyone, and he was, except that whole sections of his nature were not yet recognized and so were not realized at all. He rejected the idea that there was a Self to realize beyond himself.

Today they must make decisions about the future population of Altos. Could it grow larger? Jennifer had spent long hours this past month with engineers who were studying the effects of further cavern cuts into the mountain. The depth of solid rock was estimated and ready for report. She had worked with the City planners in estimating resources, business growth, new industry possible and the environment, and had what she thought were good reasons to hold the size of the city to its slow and limited growth. They couldn't make the final decision, but her report would be followed by a public vote. Then there was the satelite village being built ten miles east and nearly a thousand feet higher in altitude. They wanted technical help from Altos; decision on that would be routine. She shrugged, the trade agreements were going to be the most time consuming, she thought. They must increase their income if they were to have any growth at all.

She felt a touch on her arm and turned, drawing William to a stop too. "Mary Anne, you've returned! I'm so glad. We've missed you. How was the journey? The Soviet States any different?"

Mary Anne laughed. She was a short woman, small boned with uneven features and a little too heavy for that light frame ,but with such a smile of affection that she was beautiful. Jennifer hugged her and turned to William. "You know Mary Anne?" He nodded and touched her hand lightly.

Mary Anne said, " When I remember how it was when I visited with my grandparents,I am astonished. I think things haven't changed as fast as they have here, but it's changing,Jennifer, changing as much as this country is. There is the same - difference - among the people that we see here." Her blue eyes met Jennifers and then briefly swept to Will's. "I think we're doing a better job here though."

They walked on to find their seats and Will went to get cups of tea for them all. Jennifer turned to Mary,"What's it going to be? Can we settle this thing? I really believe in the Valley Conviction for basic self sufficiency. That's not much of a problem. It's earning enough to go on, further than those basics, that gives us trouble. We like our city, we don't want too much change."

Mary Anne frowned, her small body bristled with indignation. She studied her

THE PEOPLE OF THE VALLEY

friend a moment," We're the lucky ones. We're here. What of those of the next generation? Where'll they live if we don't make room? We've got to come up with something!" She shrugged and looked away, "Or we old ones will have to die sooner."

Jennifer laughed,"Mary Anne,I see why you've convinced so many people in this city. You have such an energy and such a conviction that it shines out of you."She turned, looking around,"What is that wonderful fragrance? It's everywhere."

Mary pointed,and they both looked toward a corner of the Hall where great hanging vines of evergreen clematis were a water fall of snowy bloom. They were delighted. "They just planted that wall shelf last year too. We've got the best here, Jen. I especially appreciate such blooms in these cold and rainy seasons." Then she saw Will returning and said, "I wonder what William has decided about the city size."

Jennifer laughed, "I can tell you. He thinks we must raise our limits by at least ten thousand." Just then he arrived with their steaming tea and both women took them gratefully. She looked at him as he settled himself and asked, "What do you think, Will, of keeping our conviction to be self sufficient?"

He looked around, assessing rapidly who was here, who in the watching crowd had come to hear the decisions rather than watching the meeting on Video news? His eyes roved as he answered. "I think that's necessary. It prevents a town from becoming dependant on one main industry or business. They have to use imagination and create diversity. It stimulates people to create new ways to solve their town problems. It keeps us on our toes. I'm in favor." He smiled and radiated a gentle benevolence as though he permitted all this in fatherly kindness. Jennifer frowned, it was his way. Well, she loved him, even though he irritated her often enough. She was glad they could agree on many things. His sharp mind was a valuable ally.

William called them all to order, silencing the hum of talk. He had talent as chairman, the meeting did not drag, and he held them to the issues gracefully. They worked through old business and then tackled the new without great debate. Jennifer accepted defeat as they chose to allow the expansion of the city. She agreed that they had shown her how it could be done without damage to the land. There were new caverns left empty in the mines that would make excellent residences. There were open cliffs a quarter mile from the main part of town that could be cut into and a whole new series of homes opened to use. Her own reports from engineers made it clear this would be safe. They could use the crushed stone taken from the new building to make a new thick wall along the edge of the cliff shelf. It would curve around the extended city, cutting off the north winds that blew hard against those cliffs. The decision was a relief, now there must be a public vote. Jennifer sat down, glad her part in this meeting was over.

William talked about the new industry. He seemed confident. They would trade their polymer glues for Arizona copper but he'd already made four other contracts out Valley for the glue. Arizona had requested permission to send young people for training in the making of their pseudo stone and it was agreed upon. A teaching industry wasn't a bad idea here. Students liked to come to Altos. Arizona would manufacture building materials for desert towns using the excess slag from their mines. It would double the income. It would take years to use up all the slag from the century of mining that country. Then they moved on. The two small towns being built in the mountains east of Altos asked for the rights to ski resorts since that would be the main source of their income. The request was granted only if each town developed two other sources of income. Four hours after they began, they were finished.

William closed the meeting and was amazed when the entire council rose to applaud him. He felt a wonderful lightness, a sense of satisfaction. He said only,"Thank you." but his beaming face told them of his pleasure. Jennifer knew more, and she frowned again. How was it she felt such a penetration into the feelings of other people today? Was her impression accurate? She had surely felt more of this since the last Gather. That Gather when they had deliberately Reached for the first time. The people were moving about, talking, planning lunch, meetings with friends they otherwise seldom saw. She listened, focussed her attention and was startled to feel that same sense of acute sensitivity to emotion - - to thought? She stopped, drew into herself, listened. An image of the hovering visit over the Silent City swept into mind, and she swiftly dismissed it. She turned to Mary Ann, saw her look and knew she too was aware of Will's unease, his pride and elation and a hope that trembled in his eyes. She stopped walking, listened. William's voice seemed over loud to her.

"I'll admit I love to be in charge of things around me. But then, who doesn't?" He was smiling. "Surely modern people do not want any crude control of others. We've outgrown that. To lead and influence, however, that's another thing and can be valuable." And she knew the excitement he felt at the thought. She frowned. It was as though he confessed to something, so that later he might be forgiven. Jennifer stood, noticing how much she realized of attitudes, feelings around her. She wanted to deny them. But she knew that Will was surprised at his own words, at his naked speaking of his feelings to others. He felt his own lurking fear at this self disclosure. Why had he done that? Was his pride and pleasure at their obvious approval of him tipping his usual restraint off balance? He turned, frowning and started to go out. Then he was stopped by another group of people. Jennifer turned from him, dealing with astonishment at her consciousness of his dilemma. One she felt she had no right to know.

She was troubled, watching herself, Will, the others, acutely aware, as though she stood apart from them but was tuned precisely to the dynamics of this moment. Others, their responses, reactions in a few cases, his disturbance, it all seemed so 'loud. If so, why? She did not dare to think of her own growing perception just now. She thought Will had seemed obsessed with the desire to speak, to reach them. Now, she saw Eric, Mayor of Altos, listening, and she knew that he was aware of the influence William could be to his career. Eric said,"You're saying there's a different kind of influence a man can make in a community? Perhaps more subtle, more natural among a more conscious people." He nodded his head, his eyes full of that admiration that was a fire to William's pride.

"Absolutely! The control that results from the stimulation of vigorous minds is really an excitement that stimulates everyone, you'll see that." He smiled now, his former unease gone and she felt a sinking of her heart. That great expansive smile was empty, the smile of the politician and she had seen it only twice from Will. She didn't want to think that he was false even to himself this way. There was too much she loved in him.

She felt her friend Winslow beside her, watching Will too. She sensed his worry, and knew it was the same as hers. How did she know? The two of them turned to Mary Anne and without speaking they felt her calm, reassuring as a summer lake. The image flashed in Jennifer's mind. The three of them mind Touched, aware of each other's flow of attitude and feelings, aware of Will's. How could it be? Jennifer wanted to turn from the knowledge and yet, she knew it was vital that she remain. Mary Anne held her. Memory of the December Gather pushed aside all else for long seconds. She caught her breath. Yes! this was what they had promised to practice. The reflection that they had done too little of that pulsed like a thought among them. The knowledge that neither Will nor Eric could or did Reach, and surely did not know of their own interchange made Jennifer feel a vague guilt. They looked at one another with slight embarrasssment that became conscious and then shared and they shook their heads and grinned. "Well, that's a strange, strange experience."It was Winslow who put it into words.

Mary Anne shook her head."Why is it? You both need to acknowledge things, get your heads up out of the sand." Jennifer had never heard her so sharp. She seemed almost angry."You can't call others incomplete when you yourselves are so blind, blind mostly to your own selves. It's time you woke up."

She had spoken softly, but with restrained fury, as though they were guilty of what could not be endured. Then they heard William again,he was talking as from some aching need to find words for the thought that shaped itself. "There is great energy in this Valley. Energy among us. Something I don't know how to name. But I know it is part of our lives. We must understand it and use it."

With a sudden conviction that surprised her, Jennifer laughed and said,"The word that comes to mind - the energy is Love." She laughed again, unsure,"As simple as that. The energy of Love Itself."

He was silent, as were the others around them. The three stood not looking at one another. Jennifer felt the loss of their Touch. William did not take his eyes from her. Then she felt him, felt the strange aborted focus of attention that should have matured into a true Reach. His didn't. He could not sustain it to consciousness. He's helpless, falling there, just at the edge of Touch. She wanted to cry out with chagrin and pain. Yet her own knowledge and acceptance was so incomplete that she shrank even from knowing. Then William nodded slowly.

"A strange thought. A strange definition of Love perhaps. One difficult to be part of, I suspect. Can that be? Love as energy? Available energy? The idea intrigued him, fascinated him. She could sense his mind stumbling, baffled by that near Touch. The desire for it present yet the pain of unreachability and of not knowing what was unreached. Something missing. Something missing!. His hand went out as if to touch her. Then fell. He turned. "Well, this is all interesting, but I must go. I've an appointment."He turned from them hurriedly and Jennifer thought she saw tears fill his eyes. Something was troubling him very deeply.

Mary Anne bluntly said,"He's also very angry. Very angry. And the worst of it is he doesn't know why."Jennifer nodded, though she was having to adjust to the fact that Mary Anne had just responded to her own unspoken thoughts.

William walked swiftly, blindly bringing his feelings into order. he felt distress, compounding things, that his emotions were out of order in the first place. there was something he had not known of. Something that he felt just at the edge of consciousness and it was so elusive he could not catch it at all. It was Jennifer. She had drawn it from him, or she had imposed it on him. He did not like that. He resented her unreasonably. He thought of a man he had talked to recently at a meeting at Black Mountain. Edward was his name. He had told them that there was an inherent weakness within people of the Valley. Some inborn weakness that was infecting their schools, their business, their very lives. Will frowned, could he have meant this, these things he felt now? He had thought the man over reacting, creating demons out of air. But now, he thought he must talk to him. Edward had addressed several Builder meetings, he was acting as an advisor, evidently. Will frowned. Should he go to Black Mountain? He'd never been there since it had opened as a vacation resort. He must think about this. No, it would be better to forget it. He was just tired with the day's effort to make various kinds of contact with Council members and then with the audience. It had been enough. He shook the whole matter from him, settled his feelings into a quiet calm and went to meet Annette. He would tell her of their standing in applause today. The memory comforted him and reaffirmed his confidence.

Jennifer sat for several minutes after the others had left. She went out to the balcony of the Hall, looked across the wind wrinkled water of the lake. She spoke into her wrist communicator and heard immediately Paul's voice. "I can meet you in ten minutes. What do you say to the Cliff Cafe. I haven't seen it yet and everyone tells me they have wonderful soups. It's a good day for soup."

She smiled, amused at his delight in anything new. "Great,I'd like that too." She turned,took bloom from the vine dropping across the balcony and tucked it into her hair.

Chapter Seventeen

Paul and Jennifer

After the flight over the Silent City, Paul immersed himself so deeply in work that he was able to push aside the memories, the persistent questions of that journey. He spent much time preparing reports documenting research in the Domes. He found out and recorded what had been done and what needed to be done.After Altos Council approved it, it would be sent to Valley Council. He helped draw up trade agreements with refineries in Arizona, sent agents to San Francisco to contract for new products coming in from Asia and Africa and to trade those new and improved varieties of food plants Altos had developed. New products needed to be marketed. He could count on the big market screens in the Civic Center to do the major work of educating people. Like animated catalogs they listed everything available. But his staff kept them up to date, traveling the world to learn about new products. By the time of the Gathering to welcome Benjamin, he had integrated the realizations of that day. But he still found himself keeping busy, avoiding himself. However in meditation, he practiced stillness of mind,and what discovery occurred there, he slowly began to draw into focus. He would not avoid! He had made a decision and he would keep it.

He walked on a sunny morning through the ground level Market that was built on one edge of the long Stone Park and looked across the lake. Paul liked the sprawling colorful Market Mall. Only a month ago they had installed the first reality simulator. Sitting in the booth, a customer could literally try out a new product, smell it, taste it, USE it. The possibilities of these for teaching devices made Master Teachers demand one for the Learning Center. Students could familiarize themselves with foriegn cities before going there, test their own dreams out, relive old memories, or experience early Valley life .Could sit at the ocean, stand atop a mountain, before they were able to do it in actuality. It stimulated an eagerness for the real, though Paul had feared it would do the opposite. They could find flaws in their ideas or inventions by putting them in action before they were finished.

At the Spring Festival people would try out new products before a vote was taken. Already they prepared for the event.

The whole length of Stone Park would be filled with games, bicycle riding, gymnastics and floater jumps, every variety of food,circus acts, performers of every art. Whatever was needed to entertain guests and citizens. The Council kept order and that order was an easy one. As he watched work going on, he breathed a sigh of relief that he had no responsibility for the Festival this year.

He had spent yesterday with Monitors from South Station whose engineers would tell them how many years the mines would be workable. Altos engineers had estimated half a century but when the two Monitors, a slim,middle aged woman and a beefy, medium tall man with mild grey eyes,that seemed to always

THE AWAKENING

laugh, met him after their survey, they shook their heads. He had felt a little impatient, they hadn't done anything but walk through the caverns, back to the deepest work area. He thought his reaction to them was like that of a child, intimidated by his teachers. There was the same strange stillness about these two that he always felt with Monitors, any room they entered always seemed full of well being, a presence of radiant energy. He wondered how they did that.

Remembering now, he was unable to explain. He had asked John, William's father, what he thought and the old man had laughed. Then, he had said," It's their presence, just that! There's power in them, I think. Not them as people, not that, but something deeper." He frowned, searching for words. It wasn't often someone like Paul asked him for advice. Finally, with a shrug, the old man had said,"I always watch them when they're around. I don't know how they do it, but they've never been wrong yet."

"But John, they've said the mines won't hold as long as we thought. Our engineers don't agree."

John had nodded,serious." Disappointing, but I'd bet on them if I were doing it."

Paul had finally gone to question them. "How? How can you know with such confidence? Our engineers are the best, you know that. They've given us at least twice as long."

Dwight, nodded as if the question was reasonable, though Paul felt an impudence in questioning such Teachers. "You are familiar with the work of those you call plant 'wizards'who know of the inner life of plants, so have we found in ourselves a Talent that enables us to see into Earth, to know Her inner conditions. Barbara and I literally see into Earth beneath the mountains and behind your city. We understand how your engineers made the judgement they did. But if you will look at our charts carefully, you will see that it is not accurate. I think, in fact, that they already are agreeing with us."

The woman,Barbara nodded,"We have for a long time trained your Wizards, along with the training of the People of the Way, and so perhaps you have a geologist who would come to us for training. One who has learned the basic knowledge of your technology but who seems to learn too fast, perhaps?" She was smiling, and he suspected that she knew of such an one. He stood for a moment astonished. Of course, he did know that Altos trained botanists spent time at the Retreats, but he had not thought about it. Did he want to deny the influence of Monitors on the Wizards? Why did he ignore what was common knowledge and why did he not apply that same knowledge to these other sciences? Was this one of those blind spots in Valley perception?

He turned to the local geologists who stood listening to this report. Three were older, a woman and two men, they looked surprised and a little disapproving, but he turned to the young man behind them, his face was full of longing and hope. He had stepped forward at Barbara's words and then stopped, hesitant, seeing his colleagues reaction. Paul saw his eyes meet those of the Monitors and the almost invisible nod from Dwight. Paul shook himself, affirmed his own knowledge and Reached out. The boy, he remembered his name was Everet, grinned, and with what seemed to Paul a vigorous response, Touched his mind. Paul withdrew so abruptly he saw the look of surprise and distress on Everet's face. But he felt also the shift in focus that was so kind, so perceptive of Paul's feelings that Paul was left feeling himself the younger.

Here again was another example of the Valley refusal to acknowledge the Talents that were growing among them. And what a foolishness. With a swift decision he knew he would NOT conceal his Knowledge this time. His head lifted, his eyes met Dwight's and then Barbara's and with clear understanding he had felt their acknowledgement, their delight in his Touch, his communication. He, at least, would see that the young geologist was sent to them. He drew his emotions into balance easily and felt the resulting quiet. He nodded to them.

Then, with an uneasy glance at the other city geologists, Paul had said, "That would be generous of you. Perhaps young Joseph here would be interested in such training." The sense of awe he had always known around such people faded a little. The Monitors were grinning too, like a couple of friends. He relaxed.

Paul smiled, remembering how Everet's face lit up, "I would very much Sir, I'd like to go with them as soon as it's possible." And so it was arranged, though two of the geologists who had turned to study the maps and charts of the Monitor engineers, had frowned,they had not disagreed.

The next morning he woke thinking of that meeting. Like a splinter that had stabbed through his peace of mind, it refused to ease out. He heard the pound of thunder outside,and lying quietly, wondering about the event, he listened to the rain steadily washing down the stone city. After a few minutes, lightning tore all the darkness away and he turned to Jennifer . But she was not there beside him. He opened his eyes, looked around and found her beside the bed in robe and slippers, holding a tray with cups of hot coffee and small, hard, hot rolls.

She was smiling secretly,"Why don't you talk about it, my dear one."

He grimaced, sat up to take his cup,"Is it that bad,Sweetheart?"

She slid into the bed beside him and sipping slowly, nodded,"Yes, you are that bad. You toss and talk out loud, and I think you have not slept well at all!" Their eyes met briefly over the steaming drinks and they smiled, letting their minds Touch softly. He shook his head. Closing himself suddenly from that tenderness of Touch. That was part of his problem, even this, intimate, acceptable and so much a part of their loving.

He shook his head,"I've been telling myself to settle down, be realistic , attend to business here and get on with work and relax, but it does no good, not really. So many things remind me, and so many things seems to be different, things I would not have noticed before." He drank, grateful for the heat in his stomach, the comfort of her presence. He sighed and felt his sadness as palpable as a living thing. Swiftly, mobilizing a talent she did not fully acknowledge, she radiated the tenderness she felt for him,,gave support and swept it around him. He turned to her, his face drained of worry, soft and full of awe."My Darling, it had to be your doing., This sudden difference. It had to be and I would never have noticed before. How did you do that? You must tell the secret to the Healers."

She was embarrassed,"Oh, Paul, any Healer worth her salt offers more than that before they begin to heal." Then, seriously,"I'm not sure how I do it. I'm not sure that I do anything at all. I guess I've always told myself I didn't." She stopped, wondering and seeing that all these years she had denied what seemed now so obvious. "I have always denied it. It's true. And now it seems impossible to do that."

"I want to talk more. I need this. It's been a difficult month."

"Perhaps we could try consciously Reaching. You know we promised at the Gather that we'd practice. I think we've never thought to Touch except when we make love, and then, it seems a part of it, Paul. I had not called it that, but now I know that is what we do." She set her cup down, leaned against him,"I thought it was part of loving, not something that could occur any time." She slid her hand into his big warm one."But wait, we've avoided your orginal problem, what's causing all this sleeplessness." The thunder nearly drowned out her words but he heard.

He nodded."Oh, Jennifer, I've been working like a person running from demons. And I think I was avoiding as hard as I could and yet everything I got into brought the whole matter before me in a new way. One I couldn't deny." He laughed,"Funny, isn't it. Things seem to happen that way. I think I want to go back home to Adwin . The Gather in December was so very good for us, so important. Then the party to celebrate Ben and Jessie, was fun. I enjoyed that. But we need a real Gather! Like a kid running home, maybe. But I think there's something for all of us to consider. It's not a good time, we've so much to do here, but I want to be there, work out all these things together!"

"There's ALWAYS lots to do here. We just have to leave it now and then. No reason we can't call a Gather. In times like this we need to get together more often". She picked up her cup again, steadied it on her bent knees and leaned to kiss his cheek. "What's to prevent our calling today? Ben's had time to adjust, to show Jessie around. It's time! We've got to talk. All of us." She was silent a moment,"I've missed Ben. Maybe I just need to see him again. And Jessie makes me curious. Something special in that old lady."

He was nodding, his face serious,"It's true. We've all got things to admit to, to look at. To question. We saw that clearly at the last Gather, and maybe that's why we haven't already called another." A violent flash of lightning was followed almost immediately by thunder so loud it seemed to crack against the walls and tremble in their room. "The storm's right on us. We'll have power enough to sell, from that lightning draw. There'll be no problem of power for the Domes, at least.

The drone of rain on the courts and roofs outside gave them a feeling of being inside a safe, secure cave. He sat thoughtful,"You know, Jen, there's another example of Monitors gifts that we accept but don't think about. They are the ones who devised the system that drinks the power out of lightning. They taught our engineers." Paul got up to open a window slightly, enjoying the sudden thin shaft of cold air. He snuggled up close to her, "Honey, it's good to take time, just to be with you here. We don't do it often enough, you know."

"It's as much my fault as yours, Love. We get too busy. The cardinal sin of all Mated people, I think. Will you call and arrange another Gather"?

He was silent. "I will. That I'll do. And as soon as possible. Will you persuade Will and Annette? It should be a full Gather."

After a moment, nuzzling his neck, sliding her hands along his leg and ruffling the long dark hair that covered it, she said, "I must, surely, I do want William to be there. I know Annette will come. She thinks much as I do. I suppose it's natural to avoid these new experiences, these --- " and she quoted softly, "These conditions accompany an awakening mind." She turned to him surprised, "That's it, isn't it. That old teaching, there in my memory."

He studied her, the light silk robe molded itself to her body and revealed the sweet curves that he loved,. He felt his eyes moving over that barely concealed form, feeling its power to draw him, to rouse his desire still after all these years. He wanted to hold her, to comfort and to be comforted. At the same time, he felt an abiding union with her, deeper than comfort. He wanted to understand it and didn't. That closeness had shifted, had deepened since they had hung above the City, He realized that and frowned. "It's since that trip we took, the trip over the City. It's since then, Jennifer, that it's all been different."

"How, different, Dear." She nearly held her breath.

Well, there are different feelings, not just things happening. You know you're as dear to me as you ever were, and yet there's something now that seems larger than anything else in my life. It includes, you though Love, the kids, everything, I think"! His voice firmed, "Something I Touched upon there. I can't name it. Can't quite realize even. I don't know how to speak of it, but maybe I need to try". He nearly crushed the hand he held between his own". It's something that we are. Together we're so much more than we've ever been. Sometimes when I kiss you, feel the Touching of Mind, of Heart when we make love, I don't just feel the SENSE of transcendance, the way I used to. I feel as though we have transcended all we know of ourselves. Everything!" He shook his head. "How can anyone speak of it?" He set his cup down and raised her hand against his chest, holding it gently closed.

"I think I know. The feeling of it. It's not the Touch, that's something we've always had though we didn't call it that. There's a difference now. I don't even allow the little listening that I used to do and thought was simply sensitivity to body language. Which may be part of it. It's as though something is waking in me, but I'm resisting so that I deny even what I know. If we allow ourselves to respond, allow our minds, to 'wake up' to that, then, the Touch -- would be, might be, beyond what I could bear. It might be more than just a Touch". Tears had filled her eyes, and she was surprised at what she had said. She did not understand that she could have said these things. But Paul had listened without surprise.

"Yes, that's it, exactly. Jennifer, Love, as always you've intuitively known what I come to after much effort. I think we've begun to realize something that we ARE, distinguished from what we do. Something that we've denied. Weren't capable of understanding. But we might if we accept ourselves. I've felt like a stranger to myself since - since then. And there's something in you that seems unfamiliar to me, something I can't claim, can't hold on to." Sadness swept through him with such a powerful surge that tears filled his eyes. The sensation surprised him."But now, there's something different between us. Sometimes you seem so far away, as though you've gone where I can't find you.

She nodded, a tightness about her mouth,"I know, I need to draw into myself, to retreat." For a moment she was silent and then as if in decision, she asked,"Have you heard my new music? The Tolspeak?"

"The Sonata? No, my Dear,but I read it."He hesitated, realizing."It seemed,seemed different from anything you've ever done. Yes,you're right, music; your voice speaks clearly there. Maybe we'll understand in the hearing of it. Perhaps it will tell us something when the orchestra plays it this spring."

"Well, I don't know. I think besides acknowledging something through that music, I'm also trying to confront myself. I keep going to the rehearsals and I feel disturbed. Somehow I think maybe I refused to really let the music complete itself. Say what must be said. There is that lack in it, as if it is not complete. The last movement is - is a let down. I know that." He watched her. "How do the musicians feel about it?"

She laughed shortly,"That's it, some of them keep coming to me wanting some kind of - completion. They aren't clear. Technically it's complete. The director says it's just fine. He likes it as it is. But some of the musicians: they are special, I think and so I take their suggestions seriously. It's as though the whole work suggests something but doesn't resolve it, won't bring it to completion". She was silent, then softly she added, "Because I won't?" After a few moment she shook her head. "I don't even want to think about it. I just can't see any thing more." They were silent, letting the thoughts clarify.

"There is a difference in our lives and though Teachers've told us, I never imagined it would be like this. Not at all like this!"

He had spoken so softly she could barely hear his words.The sound of the storm was fading. It was moving on out over the Valley. They would be feeling it in Santiago soon. These same rains would fall all around their Family Farm. The thought pleased her. Finally she said, "What can I do, my Dear. What can I do to help?" And she set aside the cry for help she herself heard from within her heart.

He shook his head, "I don't know. I think your being here for me at times like this is the greatest gift I could ever be given. I know you are here, my darling, I know it and that gives me courage always. He unfolded the fingers of her hand and fitted his own into them. It was a simple gesture, but it was a physical Joining. "What I see when I look out over our land, or into the eyes of other people, is not familiar. There is a Light as though Spirit Itself is shining through - everything." he tightened his fingers, surprised at his own words. "My heart is sometimes so full of - of wonder that breathing slows to stillness." He was shaking his head. "I can hardly believe my own words." For long minutes they were quiet. She frowned, fearing, hoping, wanting, and then she nodded slightly.

After several minutes, he gave a quick shake to his head, as if returning from dream and said, "As for the Talents we notice, the Teachers told us that too. That we'd not at first understand. I think we didn't pay attention because it was - it seemed so unlikely to us. With all the work of building our Valley we didn't take that seriously. But I wonder if our children are not having to." He stood up to dress, drew on skenna-wool sports clothes, loose and soft. He sat beside her a moment, pulling on long socks and boots, then watched as she slid from the bed and went to her closets. He said softly,I'm not saying the most important part. Do you remember that the Teaching also said we're an unfolding people, that our minds and our entire inner nature is unfolding as though we are making ready for another dimension of human consciousness. Something like that. I wish I could go ask again, maybe that's what we should do. Go ask again, now that we are ready to hear."

She nodded,"Yes, I remember. I thought it was like philosophy. A theory about what life was. I didn't expect to have to live it. My God, in Heaven, Paul, we're dealing with recognitions that could turn our world upside down. In fact they're doing that". She clutched his arm, relieved to ask the question that had been knotted in her mind for days. "What are we becoming Paul, What are we becoming?" And then, relaxing, leaning back she said, "I need time. I need time alone. I have to work this out in solitude. Please don't worry when I seem so distant.

He nodded, "I can accept that, Jen. I 'll wait. But you must talk to me now and then, let me know that you are all right,that these things are not worrying you too much. Or I will imagine that they are."

She nodded,"I worry about the children. I think I've been neglecting them. I've been so busy with the music, because that's my way of thinking things out. But there are times when I imagine that they know. That they know how I'm worried and they don't want to interfere. Isn't that a strange foolish notion, Paul."

"I don't think so. It's probably true!" He shrugged, "I think there's a lot about our children we don't know. But there is one thing I do know and that is gratitude that our children were born out of our deepest love. That they were conceived during a pure and deep Touching. I know that now, though I didn't then. They are the gifts of our youth,the joy of that time. And they are so beautiful because of it. I know that." They were both silent, she snuggled into his arms and kissed him on the lips, hungering for the sweetness of his mouth but after one kiss, she drew away as if she had had enough of this pleasure just now. She said, "We've got to call the second Gather Paul. We need to be together more in these times. Now that Benjamin's home we can open up all our secrets. I'll talk to Annette and we'll try to convince William, but you know how he is lately."

He nodded,"I'll get some changes in my schedule. We could go right away, in fact. Now that we've talked, I don't want to delay."

Jennifer was thoughtfully searching his face,"I really appreciate the fact that you can understand me. That I can talk to you,you know. It's hard to talk about these things." She wondered whether she had been as able to listen to him. Whether she had been sensitive to his suffering in the past years or even aware of it. She knew suddenly that she had not, and was sad to realize it.

Paul nodded, following more clearly than she knew the wondering movement of her feelings. She was open to his Touch. He wondered whether she knew that. Whether she might need to learn how not to be. The thought sobered him. There was more to learn than he had thought. His arms were loose around her so that she could move away, and she did, turning again to the window, looking out at the mountains due west of Altos. Her face changed and with a long sigh, she gestured toward the white peaks. "There is something solid, Paul. So unchanging. I appreciate that."

The breaking clouds let shafts of clear morning sunlight turn the white snow to rose. Dark shadow lay yet over the city but the far peaks were full of light. She smiled, "Look, Paul. The storm swept down from the northeast and now its going to the west so fast you can see it move. Down there, its like a grey broom sweeping along through the River flats. The River'll swell again."

For some time they stood and watched, letting their minds rest in simple absorption of the scene, the smell of rain and sounds of the waking city below. Then Paul said, "Well, it seems good to me. I'll call Rose again today and we'll plan to leave tomorrow."

She nodded, "What about Will. D'you think he'll come with us?"

He shook his head, It's hard to say. He's been jolted, he's felt something that's bothering him. But what it is or how he's handling it, I don't know. He won't talk, not even to Annette. Alice and Annette talk about our trip to the City. They were deeply moved, and they want to understand what happened too. Just like we do. But after the last Gather, and all that happened, William seems withdrawn." He shook his head, "Will can be so stubborn sometimes."

She did not turn to him, "D'you know he's been badgering the Council members to vote the Silent City off limits again."

He nodded, "I know that. Will's almost got a vendetta going inside himself too. It's as if he wants some kind of punishment for Her". He laughed shortly, "The City can handle any investigation he brings. It'll never reveal Itself, you know, unless the person is prepared. It couldn't, you know".

She turned, worried, "How d'you know that?"

He started to speak and then stopped, surprised himself, "Why, I don't know. It just seems true". He looked at her and they stood wondering. Then he turned, "Well, Dear, we've both got things to do. I need to get on my way. So I can't spend the day worrying about Will. He's also been busy talking to the people he calls the Builders and that I can't understand. I think they're a bunch of reactionarys who won't get anywhere with their complaints." He was so brusk in dismissing them, Jennifer was surprised. That wasn't like Paul. He must be angry with them, she thought.

She said, "What's the project you're working on today. You said it would be finished this week."

"It will be. It's the new design for the full Kitchen unit, food processer, everything, all built into a single package that will take less room than the old units but they're primarily for new families setting up homes. All our old ones are still operating fine. We don't need to change. These also will last for more than a lifetime so that means we need to make only enough to supply each new family. We've got other things to do with our metals and our time than to make equipment that will wear out". He stood looking toward her but he wasn't seeing her. "Jen, the engineers say that these units will continue working for - indefinitely, maybe generations. That they're efficient enough that we don't need to improve them. They've even got a gourmet food program if you want to store the ingredients. And it has built in additional space in case anyone comes up with something in the next hundred years.You know, sweetheart, we can take care of our daily life, we can take time now to explore these new -- these dimensions we've just touched on." He shrugged,was silent while she dressed.

"It's still so amazing to me. We're making some very real changes in this Valley that'll -- no, that are NOW effecting the whole world. People have so much more time for themselves. More time to think and to realize what their life is". He looked at her seriously. We DO that, we think seriously about living. It's one of our - habits?"

She laughed,and went to get her jacket,"Paul, we need time, surely we do when we have these imponderable questions, these events that shake our very minds awake and force us to search our hearts as never before. I'm glad for time to think, to plan our Family Gather, for time to study at the Learning Center and talk to the Master Teachers there. I need that ,don't you?"

He nodded, and was preparing to leave when they heard Steve's voice calling them. He appeared in the doorway to his room, still in his night clothes. His face was wet and tears still over flowed his eyes. He was unashamed, but he hesitated to come to them. His eighteen year old pride stiffened and denied his need. He scowled, refusing the tears, and his voice was angry,"It's the dream again. It's painful, wakes me up" He looked from one to the other."You don't both have to leave right now do you?" His voice broke slightly - enough that they saw his need.

His parents exchanged glances, then Paul went to Steve and drew him nearer."No, Son. We don't have to leave right away. We've got time to talk."Jennifer stroked his hair and felt the perspiratioin wet on her hand. "Perhaps you were too warm Son."

"Is it possible that you need to go back into that dream, Son. Go back from choice and see whether you can meet it's condition"? He saw his son shudder and hurriedly went on."I know, it's not easy. But we'll be here. We'll wait at home until you wake again. We can begin today's work on our own computer hook up".

Steve shook his head,"Not right now, Dad. Maybe you're right about doing that. Maybe, I have to. But I'll try again tonight. It's been coming, that dream nearly every night lately, so it's not likely I'll have trouble getting into it. But to do it by choice, that's asking a lot." He was dispondant. "Ever since the last Family

Gather, you know, it's been coming."

"Have you asked the Healer?"

"Yes", he said, a little sheepishly, "They said the same thing. That I must go back into it and meet it. But Dad, Mom, I don't know. It's pretty awful". He sat down, bent to hold his head so they had to pay attention to hear. "Won't I ever reach that place where I can just look at it? I'm tired of running away. I hate the dream and try to forget it because once, I tried to stay there, hang in and just look at it, at what was happening. I can't tell you how the terror increased. I don't know whether I could stand through that." His face was pale and drawn, now, he looked up at them and he no longer seemed the young man he was, but a young boy afraid.

Without thinking, Paul Reached, and though he had not attempted, nor thought of doing so, with his son, he held the Reach until he felt hesitant response. But Steve was somewhere else, invading a dream world where some terror lived. He turned hastily and stiffened his body. "It's got to change". he shook his head, "Being afraid's what's so awful. I can handle the loneliness. I don't like being afraid." He tipped his head, paying attention to the thought. "But there're the headaches too, the aches down my spine, like some kind of fire running through me. I don't know which is worse."

"Being afraid is painful, Son." Paul frowned, these other symptoms sounded serious. "You will see a Healer again?"

Steve heard his words as a murmur, He was engrossed,"Maybe the only thing to do is to talk about it. To try to tell you exactly what it feels like as near as I can and describe the whole thing so at least it's not so mysterious. I suppose I might as well go see the Healer. He'll know how to enter it with me, maybe. Maybe it would make it possible to talk to you then. I can't go on just refusing to do anything. But promise you'll be here tonight, I don't want to sleep again unless I know there'll be someone here in case - in case - " He took a long deep sigh that trembled a little, then with a tightening of his jaw, "Well, I've got to do it, see the Healer today. I don't want to go on like this." He stood up, put his arms around his mother and said,"I'll go back today, I'll go to the Center. But you'll promise to be here tonight"? At their nods, he turned to his father, bent his head on his father's shoulder for a moment,"I've got to find out,Dad. I've got to."

They watched him return to his room and felt both pride and sorrow. Why must people suffer. This very bright and especially conscious boy. Was there no easy way to learn?

CHAPTER EIGHTEEN

William at the Black Lodge

Leaning from the arm chair in his study, William punched the button on the flashing video-phone. The insistent flashes had tugged him from an hour's contemplation and he felt impatient. Ordinarily this solitude left him quiet, patient and balanced. Today, his feelings seemed incongruent. The face that popped into view on the screen was for a moment, unfamiliar, then he recognized the man; Dean, a Valley Council member from the northern mountains. He studied the image before him, a tired face but strength in those steady eyes, a firm but sensitive mouth, a face lined with wrinkles. Premature? How old was Dean anyway? He looked ancient. People's bodies didn't age this way in these times. Sorrow had carved its share of those lines, and even through the instrument he saw the tension. His ears caught Dean's words and his attention caught up belatedly. He responded from memory. Dean had said, "William! Good you are there. Please excuse my haste. We need to know whether you will meet with us at the Black Mountain Lodge this Wednesday." Dean's narrow look, obviously assessing this William of Altos, in turn, said that he questioned whether they needed this Altos leader. William felt his irritation rise. His voice showed no sign of any emotion.

"Black Mountain Lodge? That's about an hour south west of Clandor, isn't it. On the very southern edge of the Valley? It's been a long time since I've been there, but I'll make arrangements to be at the meeting."

Dean nodded, surprisingly, looked relieved," Good! We want to begin early. About ten A.M. It'll likely take the day though. I plan to bring Denner and Rice, the two young hot heads who've been stirring up the young. We'll hear their story. Maybe they've got a point. If not, they must be disciplined."

William nodded, not remembering who these two men were. Dean turned away, a brief hand signal and he was gone. The crisp, almost unfriendly manner of dealing with people satisfied something in William. He had not expected it in a mountain man. Why waste time with familiarity? They both had work to do. He eased back in his chair, a little tired after the morning's rapid walk over the bridges of Altos to attend to business and meetings. He could arrange his schedule to allow time for walking and in that way accomplish body fitness as well as business. Gave him time to think between. He felt satisfied with a good morning's work. He ran his fingers over the autoSec. Watched the page of appointments slide past and changed three, keying it to call in changes, until he had cleared Wednesday. He leaned back and closed his eyes. This evening should be relaxing, a good evening. Annette was taking care of the planning and he only needed show up in time to greet their guests.

The Lodge was built into the mountain, cantilevered in a manner similar to the

THE AWAKENING

Domes of Altos. The main building jutted out from a nearly flat plateau on top of a forest covered ridge. The land around the Lodge itself had been cleared in wide lovely meadows and planted with shrubs and blooming gardens. The visible building looked small for a world famous lodge but William knew that most of the entertainment, the dining halls, baths, courts for games, small shops and recreation areas catering to nearly every kind of taste were underground. People walked among the gardens, a few belts landed and an air car hummed above the roof-grids. I wondered that there weren't more people. Business not picked much yet? Puzzled, he thought of the Blue Lake resorts, so busy he and Annette had to get reservations in advance already this year. Well, maybe this meeting was part of their publicity campaign.

He stood surveying the entrance and a panel of lights that directed the newcomer to whatever he sought. Bars, saunas, fountains, swimming, gambling, gaming tables, and many variations of these. William touched a series of lighted squares in the wall, and a list of those variations told him enough to make him frown. Those variations were many that provided for pleasures of the body enjoyed alone or in company. As Will read the list he found himself tightening. He had known of the Lodge vaguely, tried to remember what he'd heard. Now, he wondered who would find it interesting. Were his own views of entertainment so narrow they didn't fit here? It seemed to him an old decadence had taken root here, the old desire for any kind of titilation, of emotional and physical excitement. He thought them anachronisms. Where else were such activities practiced? He realized he didn't know. His own life did not include them. He had thought people beyond such peurile pleasures, or wanted to think that. But then, why not? Didn't people need to indulge in certain kinds of pleasures to relax from the work of the day? The difference was the choice of those pleasures. These kinds of enjoyment couldn't be common after all, otherwise this place would not be so unique in the Valley. He wondered at his own curiousity and then shrugged and left it at that.

The Servo-desk registered him and offered him his key. He went to the elevator and in moments was whisked silently up. The door opened and he passed three people ready to enter. He looked around, the long hallway wound around the curving building, no windows, no sound. He found his room and left his small bag. He was not yet decided whether to stay the night, but thought suddenly, it might be interesting to look over the offerings of this strange resort. In his room, wide windows gave him a view over the forests. Far beyond them, the Valley stretched. This farthest south end of the Valley was so different from the north. There were dense old forests growing over rocky hillsides that gradually climbed into the low southern mountains. To the north, these hills leveled out until they became gently rolling meadow and farm land. To the west the broad Green River moved slowly down a small valley into the sea. The air was clear, he could see for miles. He stood a moment in thought and then abruptly turned and left. He wanted to look over the rest of the place.

He found the elevator again and this time, punched the button for the lower levels. He entered a curving entry way from which many doors opened . He chose an open doorway leading into a large room where a cluster of comfortable seats were arranged around an eight foot screened wall. A man and woman were just leaving, otherwise it was empty. He took a seat and felt the panel on the arm of his chair. Touching one button,he activated the screen. At first it was a simulated window, over looking a lake and gardens, a lovely finger of forest narrowed and broke the center of this garden, touching the edge of the lake. He knew it could not be a window, so he pushed the key a little to the side. The scene changed slightly, instead of summer, it was autumn, leaves moved in a soft breeze, he could smell the fragrance of drying leaves and feel the faint coolness of the air. He was amazed at how real it seemed.

A simulated environment? No, it was only one wall. He wasn't inside it. He tried pushing the button up. Winter, white snow over everything, ice in the lake, a few animals moving through the snow, a fox darted suddenly through dry grasses projecting out of the snow to persue a frightened mouse. He watched the scuffle and the catch. The Fox gulped the mouse and started on, sniffing at the bases of the trees. Will was fascinated. He knew such screens were used in Altos, but they were expensive and only a few, mostly for the Learning Center and the World Market Hall, had been purchased. Although at least one evening gathering place claimed such entertainment. He switched the button again and it was spring, rain fell in a light shower, but soon it stopped and the pale gold -green of new leaves and early bloom delighted him. Flowers swayed, the air had the feel and smell of springtime. It was wonderful.

He studied the panel. A different set of keys lined the opposite edge. He touched one. Now the scene surrounded him, all four walls were alive. He was in London, walked in the streets, looked into some buildings, entered a cafe,a great world famous restaurant, then another and he felt himself relax. He could enjoy travel rooms at the Learning Center of Altos,though he seldom had. It was the way world geography, history and social sciences were taught. He thought he ought to try the rooms there again.

He decided to look further through the resort, went down a corridor and entered a restaurant. Good there weren't many people, it would be quiet here. He had just settled himself to enjoy some fine food when a short, very fair man touched him on the shoulder."William of Altos?" At Will's nod, he went on." I thought I had you right. May I join you?" Will nodded again and he went on, "Our meeting will begin in less than an hour and I would like to talk to you. It's important to the cause." He reached out a hand which Will took, then he sat down and leaned forward,his manner tense,impatient. William felt as though his peace had been exploded, lost. He frowned, applied himself to the menu. A human waiter came for his order. William looked at the smiling young man, puzzled to see him instead of automats. Why would a man do this kind of work when there was so much else? He shrugged. He finally gave his order to the man and turned his attention to his companion.

"I'm puzzled as to how you could know me?"

THE AWAKENING

"We know of your work in Altos and other cities. We admire the dedication you've given to economic policy and it's been your ideas that have stimulated me and others to think of making changes in this Valley." He held up a hand at Will's attempt to speak, "Let me explain a little, then perhaps it will be clear. We sense a lack, a laziness in people, a tendency to turn their attention inward maybe. We can't pinpoint the problem yet, but we are studying it. Your writing has helped. You wrote that there's a dangerous dilitantism, an idealistic spending of time and money on non- essentials and on unproductive concerns. Perhaps in the early years, we needed that, but now, cities have paid off their building debts and will have real money. Well, William of Altos, we agree. People don't seem to know what to do with it. It's our turn to show them." He was smiling, but William's eyes were still on the waiter. Impatiently he said, "Oh, don't worry about our food, these young people are almost as fast as auto-servers, and a trifle more pleasant, don't you think?

"I'm just not sure it's something people ought to be spending time on". William was uncomfortable, but he drew his attention back to his guest."I believe there is a problem about how to use money in this Valley, yes. I don't think I would offer a solution yet. But you say you have one?"

"We do! We must make people see that we need to build more industries first. Maybe if they want bigger Learning Centers, that can come later. We liked your questioning of the Temples too. It's true Learning Centers are equipped to start the young on job skills, but there's too much that's not practical. For example instead of so many rooms for the arts, whole fields left for kids to build things, when they ought to be in the class room studying, they ought to develop great sports teams for entertainment of the people. That's good business."

Will clasped his hands before him, resigned to hear this man out. "But the arts today have tremendous participation and good audiences."

"But that won't last, it's just a relief from all the years of hard work. However, a true waste is the way Valley money is spent for all this wild planting, creating of new gardens, of planting whole hillsides and mountains even. Let them take care of themselves. The new legumes and trees produce better,yes, even naturally fertilize the soil, but for what purpose, to feed wild animals? We see the wasted land, the forests no longer used fully. Good farm land gone to wild meadow. It's been going on long enough. We can begin to exploit that land again for the use of humankind". He turned to look directly at William. The waiter brought drinks and he picked up his cup to sip thoughtfully, Will met his eyes briefly and nodded, bent to his own hot coffee.

The man frowned and went on,"And it's simply not good business to allow this waste. When I think how little land we actually farm today, I am appalled. Our ancestors would have been contemptuous of us." He smiled, meeting William's eyes but looking immediately away. "And so, we agree with your ideas, William of Altos and we want your help." He had spoken candidly, little attempt to flatter, he obviously expected acceptance. Will found himself acknowledging these reports of his own writing and speaking. His eyes slid across the bland unrevealing expression of his companions face. What did he conceal? One hand absently caressed his nose and chin, smoothing - a sensuous gesture. Obscurely, William felt irritation. Wasn't that part of what was wrong? Wrong? Yes, something seemed to Will to be wrong. He realized the man waited for response.

"I don't know whether my ideas fit into the thinking of the Builders but I'm surely glad to consider the possibiity."

The other nodded, then "I must apologize. I've not introduced myself. I'm afraid my enthusiasm for our cause makes me forgetful of my manners." He grinned and for the first time William felt a pang of disquiet. "My name is Jennel. I'm from a village just twenty miles from here. In fact we helped build the Lodge in the early days. My ancestors did, that is. When there was still fear, when people had not yet gotten over the worry that they might again be attached, hurt. They wanted to build down in to the ground and so the rooms and halls that eventually became this resort, were once the living quarters for people not yet trusting enough to live above ground. They never intended such a place as this, I'm sure." He laughed. He suddenly seemed to Will to be condescending. Was he devious? Or just self serving? Any Valley Master teacher could have seen the difference. He must be the product of different teaching. Will nodded and Jennel went on, "You'll hear from Councilman Dean from Mountain West, and he'll make it all clear, Sir." He added the honorific diffidently and Will felt the jolt of it. It had been a Valley custom to leave off titles. Suggestions of superiority seemed out of place. But then, perhaps it was only a mark of respect. William wondered at the ebb and tide of his feelings. He liked the sound of that 'Sir'.

The young waiter brought their food, served it silently and left. Jennel said, "You'll enjoy our food. We've the best cooks, all done by hand, no processors. His smile moved his mouth but left the rest of his face unaffected. His eyes seemed to William bleak - a lack of something there. He searched to find what it was. Surely something familiar among people of Altos. Was it friendliness? No, Altos people were not always friendly. Finally he found it, glancing up to find Jennel's expression all of a piece, the smile gone. He was enjoying the food, a sensous, whole immersion of himself in the pleasure of it. The realization startled Will. There was nothing else in his face, only that. But why not? Surely, focus, applying a singleness of attention was taught Valley children. But this did not seem the same. It was as though - as though - Will gave up, it was only that he felt something lacking. He said, "Surely you do use processors for the general cleaning and preparation. Those are not jobs to interest people."

"Oh, there are many of our people who prefer the simple work of preparing." He raised a hand with a broad smile, "Oh, I know other cities teach the mentally slow to do such operation, but we haven't time for such people. We can't let everyone take responsible work, those who are superior must be recognized by their work." His gaze bored into Wills, "And given due compensation." He grinned and abruptly looked down to eat again, "After all, you must acknowledge that there are differences among us." And then Will thought he knew what was different about this man. He had no Joy. The recognition surprised him. But he acknowledged what he never had before. Among his own people, Joy seemed to be a sustaining energy underlying every other emotion. Even the deepest grief. He felt shaken by that thought. For he knew that he had not - would not - have thought it if he were at home with it. It was just the way people were.

They talked as they ate. Will found that Jennel had lived in the small towns around the Black Lodge all his life but that he traveled constantly being actually at home now only half his time. "I find it everywhere, this lack of attention to getting things into production again. Too much time lost already. People seem to be lost in thought, lost in some kind of a dream and I wonder whether many of them have not been damaged by these years of such incessant labor and building. There seems so little desire to - to get ahead!" He shook his head, absorbed again in his enjoyment of eating, then after a while, "I've studied the old films. People used to use intensive advertizing to sway people, or to even create a market, to get things done. We've almost lost the art , you know. It's the subtle art of persuasion, and we've got to redevelop it." He grinned again, his white teeth flashing. Immediately, he seemed more simply real, a huckster without a back-up. William didn't think he agreed with him but he thought he liked him better this way. He was eating a prodigious amount, as though the pleasure of tasting food could not be satisfied.

Will said, "The food is absolutely delicious, don't know that I've had better. But you ought to know that there are some programers in Altos who can make a processer put out food as fine." He glanced up and saw the look of disbelief and even irritation on his companions face. It surprised him. After a moment he went on, "Advertising. I think I remember reading of that system. It doesn't seem to be worth the effort today. "

Jennel laughed a short bark, "Wait 'til you see." He had ordered a second helping and ate easily, relishing the food. Then, finally finishing his breakfast and drinking the last of his coffee, he turned abruptly to William who had set his cup down. "Shall we go? I've got something to show you that might change your mind." William had never seen anyone eat so much, far more than he needed. Was it merely another kind of indulgence that this place seemed to encourage? It troubled him vaguely.

William followed Jennel down a narrow corridor shimmering with its silver light and finally out into a large room provided with rows of chairs and walls that shimmered. People were gathering and they found seats near the front. The room was full of light though he could see no source. It seemed to him to literally 'rain' light. He was surprised to find men and women leaning to welcome him. He felt a surge of pride, of gratification. He was evidently better known than he had realized.

He recognized Councilman Dean at the speaker's seat. Three younger people, two men and a woman sat in seats behind Dean. There was a hush of expectancy. The room seemed to have that same utter silence he had felt earlier. Life seemed to have hushed itself in here. He was surprised at the thought. When Dean began to speak his voice filled the room, coming from everywhere, sourceless as though the very air carried it in its molecules. William was again impressed. Dean spoke softly at first, conversationally, no hint of the public speaker.

"We won't take time for anything but the matter at hand.We've got a lot to think about today. We are pleased to see so many of us here." He hesitated, looking at them, "I'll outline our objectives to freshen our memories and inform those new to us and then we will get on. First,the Builders speak for all those whose lives in the Valley seem incomplete. Those who want more than the Valley as it is now can offer. Or is offering. Second, we speak for those who recognize that there are wasted opportunities, that land, resources,people are being wasted by the system of life here. We blame no one. We think it is lack of foresight and understandable during the years of trying to get the Valley functioning so that we could all live in comfort. Yet we know that we are not satisfied. Opportunity for real wealth is nearly ignored. We've not invested enough. We've been obsessed by self sufficiency. And it leaves no place for a man to - to climb above the rabble." He spoke the last words defensively, as if some personal need was touched by them. Then, looking around, speaking more softly, he frowned,"Third, there are forces that appear dangerous to us,dangerous to all of Valley life., We don't have complete understanding of these dangers. We only know some of them. There is a conspiracy of silence around us among some of our people The learning Centers are dominated by the Master Teachers and we think they have too much power. Then perhaps you've become aware of that growing cult of the Silent City that the Vagabonds encourage. We believe that it is spreading to the towns.The Vagabonds are a good people, surely, but certainly somewhat irresponsibile and we must not let them influence our people too much. That cult is based on some kind of strange worship that includes the Temples themselves. The worship seems to rise out of the attraction to the Silent City". He stopped, letting them absorb these thoughts, his voice, rising now, emotion giving it strength, suggested personal fear.He looked all around, watching their faces. William felt his eyes moving down the rows and finally he knew Dean was searching for someone. Those eyes fell on William and he felt the intensity of that gaze, met it, felt the power of it. He was drawn to respond and the impulse surprised him. He settled deep into his seat. This man had a personal power that would move others. But he was old. Would he last? Would he keep that power?

Dean went on, "Fourth and last, our greatest worry, at least for many of us, is that reappearance among us of the so-called Psychic powers that we thought we left behind before the devastations. There are children,children, mind you , who seem unnatural in their behavior. At first we thought it was simply another form of that distant dreaminess we notice among our people and that we fear is a loss of energy. But this is different. They seem to sit together in silence, their hands touching, and then, after a while,they will all jump to their feet and go off together or in separate directions as if a decision has been made. Is it possible that these children believe that they know of one another's thought? Is it possible that anyone could? If so, or even if they simply imagine this, it is a dangerous - a very

THE AWAKENING

dangerous matter. So many of our citizens do not seem to notice or if they do, are indifferent. Perhaps that has always been humanities greatest sin - indifference. Has anyone asked the Teachers to investigate?"

He raised a fist, Will saw the depth of his anger. "Why haven't the Teachers done so on their own? I have had people look at me as if I am daft when I have mentioned to them this phenomonon. I have asked for explanations and there seem to be none. None except those I have just given you". He stopped and the murmur of voices rose, they were surprised and baffled. Most of them had not noticed the children doing these things. But now they were remembering and a few began nodding their heads. How much had they ignored? A blue light flashed and Dean turned to the woman behind it.

She spoke in a worried tone, "What can we do? I have seen my own children infected with this obsession. They call it a game and I cannot imagine how it can be a game. I feel - closed off from my own children. No one talks of it. It is a conspiracy of silence. Yes, you are right, that is what it is."

"That is the inward turning that I have mentioned. A refusal to turn out and to again conquer our world. A turning inward toward those dark things that we cannot understand." Dean was pleased to have reinforcement to his fears. His voice was loud, with one hand raised and closing into a fist, "We've got a whole country to reclaim, to use, get back the way it was."

The woman cried out, "But these strange ways, they're built on superstition; they can destroy what we've done."

Dean raised his hand, "It's surely the focus of our anger. These strange activities among the people. These are the superstitions that we thought were buried with the past. They even include the ancient evils of necromancy, for do not some speak of conversing with the dead? These are the devils of our past and they must remain buried.," His voice rose now, the natural persuasive tone increased.

William knew much of this skill, he practiced it himself. He could charm his listeners with his voice alone as did Dean but Dean's words were also full of a meaning they wanted to hear. William thought that any child trained in Valley Centers would know how to meet that 'Persuasive Voice', that intimate and tender tone, without succumbing. He himself was not as skilled as the children in his Family group, because he had not been so taught. But regardless, this man had charm. He focussed his attention, listened to the words and noticed the effects of his Voice use at the same time. Dean said, "There are great goods that our ancestors have taught us through our films and libraries. They knew how to use the land, to take advantage of resources to the fullest. We can learn that again. We will remember their ways. They were as adamant in their refusal of these psychic dangers as we must be." The audience burst into spontanious applause. He had voiced their thoughts exactly. He had made public their private convictions . He dared to speak their hidden fears.

An old man, grey haired with the tough weather beaten look of a small farmer, stood. He was recognizd and said "Councilman, the Master Teachers have taught our children that the powers of the mind will emerge as humankind grows into purity of attitude. When we hold enough Love in our hearts. Is this not true?"

Another Citizen rose quickly , "It is!." Then apologizing for interrupting, he waited to be recognized. Dean nodded and he went on, "It is true, and we have been taught well. But who has 'purity of attitude' today? There are none wise enough to hold that kind of power yet. We have not done that growth that will make us so aware. It is too soon,.Humankind is still too full of lusts and of greeds and of hungers that are not of the Soul. We are not ready. And surely you know that children cannot be trusted with such power." He drew a deep breath,"Human kind is not ready for what the Teachers have called the Power of Mind. The Master teachers are to blame for this inward turning, I think!"

Another leaped up, waited briefly to be accepted by Dean and then cried out,"What are you saying? I've not heard such teaching. But then, I was not educated in the learning Centers, they did not exist when I was young." There were murmurs of assent,"But this, it sounds too much like another superstition to me." He turned to the crowd. A young woman rose and spoke but no one heard her, another and then Dean knew that he must bring order to this room or he would lose them all. He spoke then, his voice clear and loud with that peculiar force that the trained in 'Voice' could use. "Wait! Silence!" And immediately there was silence. People sat down and turned again to him."We are all aware of the complexity of the problems. We all have questions. We will have time to talk and make everything clear. My job was to state our situation. We have another who will answer questions"

At that moment, Jennel came to him,,spoke a moment and Dean, with a sigh of relief, turned to his chair. He was tired. He could not understand this depth of his weariness. People waiting behind him turned to look at a figure approaching. Jennel extended a hand toward the new comer and spoke to the crowd. "Friends, we would like to present to you the man we have all heard about, that we came here to meet. Emmanuel Greyson has agreed to speak to us this day. He was the builder and architect of this lodge when it ceased to be a town. He is the leader of the organization to which most of us belong, the Builders."

The tall,thin man, balding,middle aged, but with the vigorous step of a much younger man, stepped into the center of the stage . His face was long and oval, handsome if it were not for the pallor of his skin. His long, thick lipped mouth slit the lower half of his face into a near smile and he took the slim wand of the speaker easily as if it belonged to him. His voice was low,strong with the resonance of a good speaker, singer perhaps. William watching, felt the jolt of power, of pure energy, as though he shot electric impulse into that crowd. Here was one who surpassed Dean completely. William leaned forward to hear.

"Friends, your concerns are real. You are right that there is much to understand,to question. Yes, there is power in the land,and yes, there is a question as to whether human kind is ready to wield such power, How can we trust ourselves? How can we trust others? This is what the Builders is organised to find out. Who controls this Valley, who wields power now? Perhaps it is the people? Or perhaps the Monitors? Those strange ones who listen - -- or are said to listen - through all our lives. People who live among us but remain nearly invisible to us so that we don't know who they are". He paused, riveting their attention, "It is the Builders job to find the answers."

William's precise mind balked at his statement about Monitors. They were clearly known to those who wanted to know them, even to talk to them. If one did not choose to talk to them, he could go through a life time without knowing or ever meeting such an one. But as Will thought these thoughts, he wondered. He himself had never met nor talked to a Monitor, nor had he thought of doing so. Why not? Greyson went on, "Is it perhaps that control comes through some unknown energy rising from the wandering Vagabonds traveling constantly to keep us all in view? Or even from that City that they worship and that no one has ever entered? What -- where is the power? We the Builders intend to find out. We, the Builders, intend to know who made the decision to allow the Valley to revert to the wild. Can a people grow to greatness, develop their own power, when they live in limited opportunity? What limits us? We want to know." His voice played them easily, moving them, imperious, tender, fierce and then gentle again. He did not hesitate, but stood with his confidence acting as a weapon quieting them.

"Friends, your concerns are real. There is much to question. There is a power in our land , a power that we do not understand. You question whether humankind is capable of wielding such power without harm. You ask whether we trust ourselves? Or whether we can trust others? We ask questions now that we have inwardly pondered for years. Finally we ask them aloud. And that is our strength too. Know that!" Greyson stopped and looked quietly from one face to another. His poise was perfect.

William envied him. But more than that, he felt a reaction that puzzled him. He had known of this man, known for years of him, but Greyson had lived behind the scenes, acted through others, had not been seen or known to many. Yet his power had grown and William felt it. That power, that amazing attractive quality that made him want to offer his loyalty in a manner he had never thought possible. He felt that, watched it in himself and was skeptical of those feelings. Yet, there it was. This man exemplified that plan of his own to be a power in Altos, but an unknown power, to act behind the scenes and to move things, to bring about changes through those few who knew his strength. Could that plan that had grown in his mind for months now, be based on the career of this man? He frowned, he did not like the thought. He wanted to have come to that on his own, yet, as he watched, felt the presence of the speaker before them now, he began to feel himself succumb to the attraction of his personality.

Then, with an unexpected sense of consternation, he felt Greyson's eyes on him, steadied his own gaze to meet them. And for an instant he was pulled totally off balance. He could not deny the energy of that attraction. He felt himself touched, drawn as he had never been before by any single person.

Greyson was talking again, speaking of the importance of their questions. That they must now take charge of the new direction the Valley must take. His voice again was deep, full of that intensity that caught them all. Will was not listening to the words, but to the play of voice, persuasive and powerful. There was a pause and a group of young men and women, seated just behind William, began to applaud, standing, they waved to the audience to join them in honor of this man,Greyson. He had swayed them in a way William had to admire. He felt a twinge of fear, of anger, then those feelings were swept away by a desire, a longing to be part of Greyson's world. He was on his feet with all the others. People raised their arms in a Valley salute to Greyson. He responded, by returning the salute and then with a smooth movement of one arm, his hand turned down he literally waved them to their seats, as if his reach touched and pressed them all .

"Look, among us here are young leaders from every part of our great Valley. It's time we listened to them. Its time they spoke of their intentions. Some of us have called them hotheads. Yet, isn't that just the kind of energy that we need in this quiet Valley life? Don't we need life, movement, progress and achievement in our lives? " His words were simple, but the tone,the carefully used emotions In his voice, served to reach to their roused emotions. William thought,'He is a mesmerizing speaker and it is primarily through voice he influences,not words. He asks the questions we are either only beginning to ask or afraid to ask, but that reverberate in our own hearts. He reflects us and we are fascinated. He could be dangerous were he espousing a false cause. I am glad he is on the side of the Builders.'

The young men were approaching the speakers circle. Their faces were lit, their excitement was obvious."We haven't done enough",one young man said,"We must bring changes. The Valley is ready for growth, new growth and we want to begin now." Another pushed forward,"It's true that people are lax, few want to create new business, new industry. we've got to change that attitude. The People of this Valley are lost in dream and I don't know what it is they dream". They spoke eagerly, their strong young voices had little guile, but much of passionate intensity. A young man, that William recognized as Curt, from Clandor,a powerfully built giant, fair with long braided hair and a thick beard,stepped forward toward the audience and his voice rang out."It's time we moved and there may be some who will not be willing. These we must leave behind. Let the sleepers dream on. Those who are ready to create a world empire born here in our Valley,will know, will see, as we teach them the way. The Valley must be a world leader. It is our task as Builders to press on, to be first and to win that power for the Valley. It is our right".

A young woman, nearly as tall as Curt, but with a round,soft figure, long, dark brown hair and a tight composure that William found himself envying, moved into the circle and raised her arms in a gesture of appeal. She too had use of that strange talent , unrecognized as such, called the Voice. a nearly hypnotic quality that carried far more conviction than the words it spoke." When we say that the

Valley has become a place of dreamers, what do we mean? There are people who talk of exploring dimensions of mind and heart that humankind has long set aside as impractical or worse, as destructive. We must know that and avoid their persuasions. The reports we have heard are not false. There are those who dabble in the Psychic, who sit lost in trances together, so absorbed in silence that they can't speak to us and later, they cannot tell us what they were doing. I say they experience nothing, that they are lost in their imaginings, in escapism and we must save them. The temples have influenced too many, both sitting and active meditations have become a habit, encouraging this dream state. What they do is surely detroying those minds. It's a kind of addiction. If we cannot give our people a cause, an action toward a goal that will lift them from this lethargy, then our Valley will fall and all our hope will be lost". She drew a long breath, and nodded as if acknowledging herself.

William caught his breath, It was as he himself thought. She was convincing. He could see people nodding, leaning toward her. The power these people demonstrated was greater than he had known. And he was himself thought a leader in his own city. But here, there were these. And they mentioned again the Psychic. Was it then actually so prevalent? Was it true that such superstitions were emerging again to haunt their lives? He felt the familiar stirring of fear and anger that always followed the fear. The image of the flight over the City came to mind and yet he did not want to think that was the same. The last Gather! Was there something of that there?

There were more coming forward to speak. Leaders from towns and cities everywhere. He listened , but his thoughts were racing. The Builders would begin to grow after this meeting. Surely there would be a surging of their power and they could teach the people of the Valley. He no longer heard their words, he watched their faces, saw the eager vitality and the intense desire. But something moved through the room, he felt it like an undercurrent pressing against his thoughts. Focussing his attention, he realized what disturbed him.

A powerful energy drew its current against him, pulled against his very thoughts. The entire hall seemed to vibrate with it, as though the mountain ridge in which this vast Lodge was built, had come alive with some dark power. He thought swiftly that it was energy focussed among them, that it gathered and focussed the energy of the crowd. Yes, that was it. Using their very minds and bodies, - the thought disturbed him, but there it was, Yes, it seemed as though they were being used, were providing a channel for that energy coming among them. How could that occur. Surely he had to be imagining, was so moved by all that was happening that he himself was being effected. He must control these feelings. All that was happening drew him. He felt a desire to be part of that, even as he held himself firmly against it. He could not succumb. He saw people around him drawn into the flow of it, eager, laughing with enthusiasm. He knew that he might not resist. Was it only that old resistance to being convinced of any idea beyond his own control? Or was this something stronger? He wanted to get up and go and was furious at himself at the thought. Surely these people were right.

Surely the economy and the Valley must be plugged back into the traditional values, more work, more trade, more new products, a re-educating of people to wake up and use their resources. A people without enough to do, without a genuine direction of growth might surely become a people turning to the forbidden, the mysterious, the terrible lost fascination with evil powers. Yes, the Builders were right.

He stood up, pulled from his doubts, giving himself into that energy and exultant that he was part of that crowd. He raised his arms with them and shouted, "Let the Builders save the Valley". Over and over they shouted, a sound of conviction. Even as he yelled, a part of his mind shrank away, obscurely repelled.

He left the room, hustled happily in the crowd, people spoke to him warmly, as if they knew of him. He actually did not mind the press of people today, the jubulance and the talk. He found himself standing at the entrance when Greyson came out. He was alone. The people were interested in further talk with the young speakers and William saw how that had been Greyson's aim after all. How expertly he had turned the focus of attention from himself. He walked toward William with a smile of satisfaction on his long face. "Ah, William of Altos, I have not had time to talk to you. Would you have time for a moment with me? I'm just going to my rooms".

William nodded,,"I have some time yet before I must leave. It would be a pleasure to talk. I was impressed with the meeting. I'd no idea there was so much energy in this movement."

"Movement, you call it? Yes, I suppose it is, an uprising of the people who are seeing themselves excluded from something in this Valley. And when you have people feeling left out -- you have energy for action. It's a strong emotion, that sense of being left out." He smiled a strange and distant smile. "All we have to do is fan it." Will felt a jolt of surprise. Left Out? How did he see that? Greyson was looking sharply at William who surprised himself by nodding. They turned then and went to the lifts, spoke little on the way up and it wasn't until they were turning into Greyson's rooms that William asked, "You have worked long to create this organisation ?"

Greyson nodded. He glanced again, searchingly at Will, then went into the room and rapidly walked to a finely carved cabinet to take out glasses and bottles. He began to make them a drink. "I trust you've seen the art of our wall screens. The ones in the rooms and also those down below in the halls. I think you must have seen the seasons change?" He held out the glass smiling with an air of secret knowledge and Will felt an anger that he might have been watched earlier. But he let the feeling fade. He took the drink and nodded. Greyson went on.

"Altos needs to increase its credit, doesn't it?" At Will's surprised nod, he went on."I want to show you something that could be a multi-million credit business for the Valley. Something only a few pleasure lodges in this world have at all and none as fine as ours. Our technology surpasses anything they've got.

But it isn't hard to duplicate, once you've access to the technology". He turned and went to the blank wall at the end of the wide room. William looked around, amazed at the opulence, the sheer luxury of this apartment. He started to speak when his eye was caught by the flicker of the wall and he turned to it. First there were the usual changing seasons. Greyson moved them rapidly through their phases, as if shuffling through a selection. Then he touched a different button.

The room was no longer the luxurious apartment of a rich man. He was outdoors, in a city street and in a crowd of people. William caught his breath. He felt the jostle of people, the smells of bodies and of market products for sale. The crowd extended down side streets, everywhere, coming and going, talking, fighting, buying, selling. There were poor in rags, the well to do and here and there, a cluster of magnificantly dressed men and women being given right of way through the pressing crowd. The noise was a rise and fall of talk and yelling, of laughter and fierce angry retorts. People were going and coming like a vast parade. William felt stifled by the crowd, looked around hurriedly as if to see a way out.

There was a shift, and into the crowd rode men on horse back. Then there were more and the crowd began fleeing, running in all directions and he saw the men on horse back were armed, he felt himself pushed to one side. A clatter of hooves and another group of horsemen rode in and immediately clashed with the first. With astonishment William realized he stood on the sidelines of a genuine battle. Horses, men in uniform, town people caught in the fighting. There were women and children, ordinary citizens, small houses, suddenly caught in a cross fire. Flaming arrows lodged in the wooden buildings, that began to erupt in flames and people ran from them screaming, caught on fire themselves or hurt, bleeding and crying out with anguish on their faces. William knew that this scene was real, these peoole were being terriby hurt. It was so real he was stunned with horror. Surely these people were actually dying, torn apart, burned. He could smell the blood, the burned flesh, could feel the terror. Surely this was no clever 'effect'. He caught at someone's coat, looked and it was Greyson, standing calm and slightly smiling.

William felt shame, stiffened, turned again to the struggle. Just in front of him two men fought with knives, but a horseman pushed through, knocking people over, trampling them and cut one man down with a long sword, then chopped at his fallen body again and again, blood streamed across the ground, against Will's feet. He heard a scream, a woman was being dragged against a building, her clothes tearing, her terrified face, turning every which way for help. She fought, fought well, but three men held her, laughing. So! William shuddered, surely not - not rape! Obviously! He started forward to help, to stop the horror, and felt his face pale. Before he could take more than a step, he stumbled on a burly man who had just thrown a young girl to the street, and the man turned to hit him. William felt a blazing rage fill him and picked up the man and threw him bodily across the street into a crowd coming out of a house. He was horrified at himself

THE PEOPLE OF THE VALLEY

then. How could he do that? He thought he would vomit. But he turned to help the girl. She had fled. He raised a hand, stiff before him and shook his head. What happened to the woman the three men were dragging off. He turned to get help. Greyson?

Greyson had been watching him. He nodded. "Too graphic for you? Too close? Or maybe violence is not your interest." He nodded, "Try this".

The scene changed to a quiet woodland where men and women were gathering to enjoy a picnic. Music came from some distant place, flowers grew among the grasses, the smell of hot summer, hay, trees and earth filled the air. William felt relief, pushing aside an almost uncontrollable rage that he had been subjected to that. That Greyson could be so casual about it. Then he felt embarrassed that Greyson had seen his reaction. He stood a moment adjusting himelf to this quiet scene.

But now there was something else, something tantalizing, unnamable, yet bringing him swiftly to a state of excitement he could not resist. For moments he could not identify, and then he did. The raw smells of sex. He felt his own body respond, excitement stirred him, a stream of fire ran from his crotch to his throat. Women were removing their clothes, slowly, sensuously, as if it were a slow dance. A high soft music wove a seductive atmosphere around them. There were children there, they too laughed and moved toward the women. Men who had been lying half asleep, their upper torso already naked, watched, laughing, joking, commenting on what they saw.

Again the scene seemed to surround William, he felt himself in the middle of it. He wanted to participate and yet he felt a sense of revulsion. He cried out at the presence of children. But clothes were tossed here and there, women began moving their naked bodies about, their positions changing, more and more lascivious, more brutally sexual. And the men stroked, touched, then were pushed aside with laughter . But the children carried drinks and served the adults, the men and women both leaning to kiss and fondle them. Some adults began to remove the clothes of children and suddenly William wanted this to stop but for some reason he could not say it. He felt timid to ask for that. Greyson had found him unable to stomach that last. Now this. Was he unable to deal with, enjoy the sensual. He tried to remind himself that this was a created scene, not real. But his mind insisted it had once been real to exist at all. Try as he would to keep distance, he felt himself growing more excited, but as adults in the background blatantly coupled, those nearest him, were still involved only in that slow, erotic play. The children were brought among them, being drawn into their arms, laid on the ground among them. Some men and women alike were beginning sex play with these tiny ones. William felt his body react so violently he cried out. Greyson, seeming to misunderstand the cry, touched buttons again and two young children were caught up, dispite their cries, they were stripped naked and tied, tied to saplings in the othewise lovely grove. Whips were brought, two women came and they too were tied, their cries were no less real, their tears as wet. A man began a fine light whipping over their bodies, leaving thin red marks, marks that faintly

THE AWAKENING

bled. William stood, stunned in horror and the terrible shock of his own reacting and betraying body, he did not move or speak.

Then, as through an act of will, he broke some restraint, he gathered himself, appalled by his own fascination and revulsion, shamed by his own sexual urgencies, he cried out,"Stop!"

Greyson was calm."Perhaps it is too much all at once. His face betrayed nothing, but his eyes seemed to William to hold in them some secret satisfaction.He said," Perhaps something simpler, maybe only a few at a time. One or two women, or a few children. There is a hanging, also, and - well, there is no end to possibilities. We have much available." Greysons's eyes trapped William's. He saw the sardonic amusement at his discomfort, the contempt, the subtle torture of a man fastidious in his habits as William was. A man whose writing and teachings had stood for decades as an expression of the ideals of Valley culture. He turned off the wall,the room was as before with only a slight shimmer left. He said,"You cannot deny the fascination. You know that we will make a fortune for the person who markets these."

William said,"Those are decadent, they are monstrous. How can any man enjoy such things?"

Greyson smiled quietly,"That sense of decadence will keep them in your mind, you will find yourself returning to the memory and the desires. They don't fade, you know, and in retrospect, they are more attractive." He frowned suddenly, "After a few days, men and women cannot wait to try again. The desires burn in their bodies, wanting satisfaction. And they can tell themselves, it is only a simulation,after all! They can justify their desires. Then they can find themselves a partner to help them enjoy." He was grinning then, his eyes shining in a naked pleasure at William;s discomfiture."That too, we will supply."

William fought to control himself. He would not give the other the satisfaction of his shock. Feelings rose and fell, he monitored them, amazed. He would not admit the extent of his own roused desire. He wanted to escape from these memories. He said, trusting his practical intellect, when he could not trust anything else."Who makes these. Where?"

Greyson looked at him thoughtfully. Perhaps this man was not such a fool after all. His capacity for pleasure seemed flawed but he might after all be the man he sought. Then, narrowing his regard, he realised that William attempted to hide himself. He enjoyed the fact that he could not. He said,"It's a secret that I cannot divulge just now. Only those committed to build the market will know. Only through me can these be distributed. But you must admit that they are good. Very good. It is not play acting. These were real scenes and that is why they are that good.There are places where people still live as the old ones did. Where they do not -- resist our persuasions. There, we are able to enter in and make these films."

"You mean against their will? They did not choose, surely they did not choose that." Will's horror was loose in his voice at last. He refused any longer to dissemble. The fact might be there now between them. Only in that way could he regain self respect before this man who had so attracted him earlier. He took caution however. He felt a clear sense of danger here. He knew he must tread carefully. He said, regretting the exposed emotion, that made him have to clear his throat before he spoke,"How? Where could you find such people? Unable to defend themselves?"

Greyson's smile was thin,exultant,'You must realize that there are people living as little more than animals in the far rural areas. Places where they've been separate from the vigorous creativity such as created this Valley."

"More than that! The power behind modern civilization is more than creativity, it's clear thinking, its - "He stopped, lamely, not knowing what more it was. Then shrugged and asked,"But how could they agree?" As the light dawned and he knew, he shuddered."You took advantage of them?"

"Why not? They wanted out of their misery, their lives had no hope."

But they could have - could have become citizens in any civilized community, where people've joined together to build lives."

The extent of evil in Greyson seemed more than Will could have imagined. He was smiling, watching Will as though he were an interesting puzzle."And they will, my friend, they will. When we have finished our work with them. We'll give them credit enough to build their own village. That is why they work for us". And William knew then that he was a man who took pleasure in pain and degradation.

Will spoke again, out of a constricted throat, his eyes turned away. He did not want to give Greyson the pleaure of his own pain. "Where? Are these people working in this Valley?" A fine rage trembled just at the pit of his stomach. He thought it dangerous to allow that rage full expression.

Greyson, shook his head," No. They work in the Wyoming mountains. But the people come from pockets all over the country. We were careful in our choices, certain drugs helped to stimulate the proper responses." The smile never faded. "I think that when they build their village, they will live by working for us."

With a long, deep breath to re-establish his balance, and with a sense of betrayal of the people of the Valley, Will said,"I've never seen anything like it, like nothing I could have imagined. I'll have to think . How could this be done. It's more than a man can adjust to immediately." He preferred to allow Greyson to think he was still overwhelmed and in his power.

Greyson shifted, became the orator, "Yes, it's powerful. It'll effect people even though they don't know it. There are so many more, much more subtle. These are admittedly crude. I thought to jolt your attention. Even though you may want to right now, you will not forget. As foolish as those young men in your meeting were, they spoke one truth. The Valley has become lax . These are the strong basic emotions of normal people. These will wake those apathetic people we worry about. Their own bodies will betray those mesmerized minds, rouse humanity from the passive dreams they have sunk into. These pleasures will expose the falseness of the seekers of Spirit. They will see they are of this physical world after all, just as are all the rest of humankind. The world will turn -- ." He stopped, as if having said more than he intended. But William knew that

THE AWAKENING

Greyson never said more than he intended. A memory of the faces of people leaving the Temple came swiftly across his mind and faded.

Greyson picked up two more cold drinks and handed one to William, and Will was grateful not to have to talk. They turned to sit down, Greyson seemed absorbed in a piece of sculpture, turning it in his hands, and the gleam of jewels set into the golden form, caught Will's eye. He started, his heart constricting with a cold fear. The sculpture was identical to that one Felix had given him. He had seen nothing like it since. He dropped his head, unable to think. How could there be connection between these two men?

For minutes he gazed at the floor, his eyes lost in the blended colors of the thick rug. He was intensely aware of a need to run, to escape from here and at the same time of the desire to turn on that Wall again, to see more, to participate. He wanted to ask about that sculpture, but dared not and worse, he couldn't imagine why. He was ashamed, shocked, afraid, for the first time in his life of himself. Did he truly want to enter into that depravity? What then was he after all? He sipped his drink, and like a man barely able to contain himself, clung to it as to a straw in a flood.

Finally Greyson began to speak in a flat, monotone, meant to be hypnotic. William was roused to attention and to anger at that assumption that he was vulnerable. Then to a pleasure that he had after all fooled this man. He had been caught off guard, but he was warned now, not only to Greyson's intention but to his own unadmitted nature. He heard the words and felt the pull into persuasion but now he did not respond. He felt a numbness, a surprising sense of loss. Greysons's words were simple, "You may even think to report these panels as depraved. Certain people would see them so. They could credit you with saving their morality. That would be the Valley way, among those who do not act, who have lost their manhood. Who fool themselves that they are not attracted, who deny their own desires! But there is no possibility that anyone would believe you. It is your word against mine. That chimera your people pretend to search for, what they call Spirit, is false, does not exist and people will know that. Real men and real women know that." He studied William's face and for a moment a flicker of doubt crossed his face. Then with a slight shake of his head, he smiled," Do not try to make public what you have seen, unless you decide to join us. I could ruin you". His face hardened, cold and unrelenting, "Absolutely! In ways you cannot imagine."

Knowing that he could, William said, "I have no intention". It was true. He could not mention these things to anyone. Surely not Annette. Although he thought with a wistful wonder, Annette might handle it better than he did. With surprise he knew she would have felt no horror, only profound pity. Except for the children, for that she might be in an absolute fury, worse than his own. He could imagine that. Greyson would not have fared so well. He almost smiled. He thought of Ben, then of Rose. He had thought of them more than once during this strange disturbing day. The thought of his family served to balance his emotions, bring him strength. He felt them near, offering their -- health. Yes, that was it. His family offered Health and this man, Greyson offered - sickness. He knew his face was flat finally, emotionless. His years of discipline, of restraining his feelings, so exposed and torn asunder this day, came now to his aid. Greyson saw only the nod and read it as further assent.

"Well, just as a marketable item, what do you think". His voice was normal again, the friendly tone, his eyes watching. Behind everything, the sardonic, touch of superiority. He felt himself in command here.

William nodded. "It is surely amazing. As clear as a simulation would be, I'm sure. Though I'm not sure the Valley is the place where they would sell." Just beneath conscious thought, he was vaguely aware of a desire to protect the Valley from this obscenity. Then he was aware that he feared to know whether the Valley would succumb even as much as he himself had. Could this Valley, this experiment in living, be corrupted? Was humanity still victim to its worst urges? He did not shape the thought into words. He could not have spoken it. But Greyson was attentive to that subsurface web of surging emotion, conflict and was content. He did not know the deep fury William felt. His talent to Touch was small, he had never Touched into the depths of any person. He could not have born that interchange, for in those depths burned the spark of Light that would have Reached out to his own deep hidden Self and exposed him more harshly than he could tolerate. He avoided without knowing why. It was the chief difference between himself and Felix. Felix had looked into his depths, the worst he could be, and consciously chosen to embrace that.Had seen the possibility of his best, and rejected it. He hid nothing from himself. Greyson, still divided, would not let himself know of either the best or the worst. He hid everything. But he was an excellent tool to that worst.

Greyson stood,"Well then, you will think on this and let me know. I'm sure that your work with the Builders will be valuable to us all. We will meet again. Just remember that with enough credit we can bring this Valley into a new age, a time of growth unimagined in the world. Remember that, William of Altos. because there is going to be that growth and you can be part of that. If you enter in and become one of us here, you can see your own hand in something the world will envy." He had touched on that point of William's vulnerablity and William did not notice. "You are in the central Valley. It is vital to our work. We will reach all the people who want things to begin to happen for us again,who are tired of the apathy. The time has come. You will agree. The time for change has come".

William nodded. He was a student of history, he knew well how people of the past made fortunes pushing the debauchery and rousing the lusts of lesser people. He knew that often there had been little effort in that rousing,mostly, simply offering satisfaction,had been enough. Could it happen in this Valley? In this time? His heart sank. He feared it could, humankind was not, after all, any more than they had always been. He stood, consciously bringing his own emotions into balance, drawing that familiar screen over any hint of these in his expression. He was not aware that the other watched that inner effort with amusement and a little admiration. William was surely well taught. The Learning

THE AWAKENING

Centers had done their best with him. But Greyson saw it as repression rather than Balance.

William looked at Greyson's face, but avoided his eyes. "You believe that these are marketable in the Valley then." At the other's nod, he frowned and went on,"I think it might take some doing. You are aware of the training of our young people? There are few sexual inhibiitons among them, what with their training and the work of our healers in their development? But they are a healthy lot, they would gain no pleasure from degrading another. Or -- " He was at a loss for words.

"I think that's an asset. But they don't know the possibilities of their own lusts. No one can convince me that humankind is not still as devoted to physical need and pleasures as it ever was. In this day, that need can be exploited as it never was before."

"William met Greyson's eyes, saw in them a glimpse of that amusement. Then it was gone, and Will believed he had imagined that. Surely Greyson was serious. But he felt a slow distrust building beneath his wish to do business. He must watch this man, more carefully than he had ever needed to watch any business partner before. That fact sobered, but did not discourage him. Again he felt a twist of revulsion at the kind of business offered. But then who was he to make judgements for others? Feelings rose again and warred within him. He stood, his face showing little of this, but Greyson needed no visual revelations. He looked at that innocent exposure of mind and emotion and without hesitation Reached. His Touch was light, not at all deep, but neither would have recognized that. Greyson could watch William's inner struggle without shame. He thought it was just as well. A man whose ethics were polished and well placed, made a better partner in the work Greyson planned to do. He thought he could use him more effectively, and even trust him accordingly.

"I want to think about these possibiities. I would like to talk of them with another businessman who I think would be interested."

Immediately Greyson shook his head,"You must not. This is to be known only to the two of us. Perhaps there will be room for partners later, but right now, no one is to be told. Is that clear." He fixed his eyes sternly on William's, they seemed to bore beyond that gaze into Will's mind and he felt a strange sense of weight there. He did not know why he felt the compulsion to hastily agree,but he did and he said,"Of Course, I can understand. But I think there are complications and I want to think about the manner in which these products could be presented to Valley people. Can I call you, make contact within the week?"

Greyson nodded,"You can reach me here. Here, take my card and call perhaps at this hour in one week?"

William found himself mildly nodding and a sense of satisfaction made him smile. He picked up his hat, and walked to the door. He turned suddenly, saw a trace of that strange smile, but it disappeared even as he turned and so he simply nodded, and went out. He went rapidly down into the lobby, out the huge doors into the sunshine of this South Valley evening. No freezing weather had left trees barren, or Earth frozen. Growth was rampant. He stood a moment at the edge of the broad paved circle, watching the play of light in the fountains, letting his eyes run in relief over the colors of the banks of bloom , out over the prong of tall trees and up into the hills. He wanted to move about, to think. He must get farther away from this lodge. How could he stay the night, and yet aleady evening approached. Then he felt his mind quiet, felt the firm practice of years bring him to understanding for what he must do. He must know more. He must stay and learn all he could of these plans, of this place, of these people.

He looked around, walked out over the pathway that wound around the ridge. The view was spectacular. He let himself   become lost in the beauty of it for several moments. There was some kind of strange compelling power here, in the very buildings, the ridge; he felt it and since he could not understand it, it left him with distrust. He thought he was imagining something that was malevolent and that resulted in   distrust of himself. How could he imagine such things? Nevertheless, he must take care. He felt his heart heavy,but he knew he would at least honor that distrust, whether of himself or of the place. He must keep his thoughts hidden.

In that moment William came as near to realizing a recognition of mind power as he ever would. He did not know that. He knew only that he felt something he had never dared to think. The man Greyson -- was he part of that malevolence? Surely it could not be! He was tired, there had been too much stimulation here. Greyson's attentive regard had an invasive quality,as though he reached into his mind. He shook away a sense of darkness that penetrated and made fear tighten his heart. Why was he imagining such things? He decided then that he would steel himself to inner calm and he would stay here this night and watch, and talk and learn. He turned and went to his room.

He came down to dinner,wanting to meet and talk to some of the members of that organization that had begun to complicate his life: the Builders. He grew to realize they were serious and intelligent, that they thought a danger threatened their great land. They thought of this as their homeland and they were roused to a fighting stance, though they were convinced that all could be settled through peaceful means. Hadn't they been learning the finest skills of negotiations for years? They talked and laughed as their reminders to each other of those skills allayed their worries.

But among these were those who found peaceful means too slow, who's words roused fears,even to push the others toward a mild paranoia. He watched as they built questions upon questions. Questions created out of the stuff of fear. "If there were those who dealt in the evils of the dark ones, how could they possibly meet such? If they allowed these things to develop, wouldn't they be helpless against them? . They must act swiftly to nip any such behaviors in the bud. He watched those who fell into those fears and those who remained firm, trusting their fellows and able to think their own thoughts. He felt proud that the Valley had such strong citizens. He knew that there was much to think on and that he would not be alone in that thinking.

Obviously Greyson was not one of these. Where did he come from, how did he develop such ideas, such interests? Were there others who wanted to entertain themselves in the ways Greyson had in mind and if so - then why not make money on that desire? How could it hurt any innocent person? Simulations did not involve other people. Greyson had committed a terrible error (crime?) when he used those vulnerable people to make the scenes he did. That never need happen again. Simulation only required the imagination of the person involved. He would demand no persons participate unless they chose. With a self righteous mental shrug he told himself that there were people of many different interests in the Valley and he could not stand as censor. He felt confident,the business interests Greyson had roused, began humming into high gear. What they could do!

As he sat alone at last, the people he had met gradually leaving the dining room, he relaxed a little, the euphoria of his talk faded. And he was face to face with the nagging questions that would not rest. He ordered a small bottle of Cabernet Sauvignon. It was a good solid wine with body, he sipped it, he could enjoy this. He watched the waiter pour and thought there was an odd pleasure in being waited on by another human being. Then his fair mind questioned, Did the man have choice? Or believe he didn't?

Greyson had admitted that real people had been pressured to play those parts, had been forced, perhaps? No normal human being could use children or even adults so. He shook his head,So what did that make Greyson? Surely he might be confronted with an evil humankind could only dread. Here might be a man deliberately using human beings to make money. The awful implications of that sickened him. He knew that all that the Valley stood for would be threatened by this distortion of primitive urges. Surely humankind had developed enough to feel contempt for such indulgences. He wondered. If so, then why did they continue to exist here? He thought again of the little sculpture, the twin to that precious one he owned, and had hidden in his office so that Annette would not touch it. He finished his wine and, grateful for its help, was ready to go to bed. He could forget it all at least in sleep.

But in the morning, he knew without doubt that he must act with care. A dark weight was heavy in his heart,twin feelings, one of fear and the other of elation, which itself troubled him, were left from the meetings with Greyson. He knew it was not simply the question of whether to involve himself in this questionable "business" or not. There was something else. And it made no sense. perhaps the fact that it made no sense to him was most of the worry, most of the fear. He felt an actual menace in that man, in these mountains even, and that was wholly unreasonable. He was not an unreasonable man. Then he was reinforced in his worry during a talk with a couple from Bend.

Roger and Elena joined him at his table for breakfast. Roger was a stocky man, a little shorter than Will, but powerful. His keen watchful eyes missed little. His mate, Elena, had a head of rather coarse but beautiful red hair bundled into a graceful knot at the back of her head, a round face with pale and lightly freckled skin that was also was smooth and youthful. She smiled often and William thought she seemed without guile. He liked them both and they talked quite freely about yesterday's meeting. Roger said,"This place gets to me though. I've never been in a place like it. There's a sense of - - well, the only word is foreboding. And I can't explain that. It's utterly beautiful."

Elena laughed,"Oh, Roger, it's just so different. I think we're not used to living so much underground. Perhaps people from Altos even, might feel differently"

William had shaken his head, "No, I'm from Altos and I'd agree with your Mate. There's just such a feeling. I wouldn't have used the word, foreboding, but when you did I thought it fit. At any rate, we don't have to come here any more. Let those who enjoy it, come." He smiled, relieved, himself, at his own words.

Roger had persisted,"Well, perhaps you're right. I'm sure I must be simply tired and ready to go home. But there is in the mountains here something that isn't common to the Valley. The Valley seems always to me such a place of - - well being. I think those words are accurate. Yes,a place of well being". Then he leaned forward and said softly, "There is none of that here"! He too smiled,now that the thing had been talked about. William exchanged cards with them and told them he would stay in touch.

He caught the outgoing Air Car and got home in the early after noon. Annette saw his wearyness, sensed his distress and brought him hot bitter tea. A flashing memory of that human waiter swept through his mind. the difference struck him hard. He tasted the tea and frowned up at her, "What's this. It tastes awful."

She smiled, patient, "It's what will make you feel better. Trust me, my dear." With a frown, he drank it but was pleased to begin to feel it's lift to his spirits. He reached up to take her hand, then suddenly, impulsively, unlike his usual quiet reserve, he stood to embrace her, holding her close and whispering that he loved her. Her simple love and acceptance of him, her trust and care, seemed to him that moment to be so precious. She laughed,"Well, surely I hadn't known that tea could rouse such gentleness and sweetness. I'll have to recommend it again." But he saw that her eyes were moist.

They had eaten and he told her about the journey, the description of that amazing Lodge, the meeting and his fascination with the speakers. He told her he had met the man Greyson, who was a founder of that Organizatioin in which he had become so active. She questioned him but he told her little of that man. He felt an odd betrayal in that silence. He realized he would never bring Greyson into their home. But Annette knew her man, and she felt the questions lying behind that account, the troubled heart of this man she loved.

He woke the next day hearing voices in the rooms beyond. Annette came into the bedroom with coffee and he asked her who had come.She smiled, a pleased look on her face."You'll be surprised. It's Andrew. He's come to visit Altos for a few days and I know that he wants to talk. He's grown Will. He's not been up here for two years, and we last saw him months ago. We ought to see the children more". Will nodded absently wondering what the boy could want. He felt a pure pleasure in being home again. the familiar, safety, the warm comfort of it.

THE AWAKENING

He was in a good mood.

"I suppose he wants to see all the changes in the City. The new Dome fields, the residences inside the Cliffs, the additions in the business Center, all that. Well, I'll arrange to take some some time. Would you like to go along?"

"I wonder that he didn't let us know"? She knew it was not like the Farm children to forget their manners.

He shook his head, "Don't fault him. I'm to blame. He did call me and I forgot to tell you". He realized her disappointment and said, "I'm really sorry. I suppose you've got appointments you can't break?"

She frowned, "Yes, I can't change them now, but I can have lunch with you and I'll try to free up some time tomorrow. But Dear, I know he wants especially to talk to you". He glanced at her in surprise. She went to the door and beckoned Andrew to come in. They talked a few minutes, then she and Andrew went to make breakfast and left Will to dress. Andrew wanted to see the Temple first. He hadn't been up there in years he said and Will smiled, that would be two years ago. But now, Andrew knew of the method used here to create the music for the Temple. He wanted to study their equipment.

"You've got the best, you know. Everybody concedes that. And we're planning another system for Adwin and we want to know what the improvements have to be." They went out into the bright sky, under the great high clouds. They stood a moment on the balcony, overlooking the city and Andrew turned to them, a big grin on his face. "I'm supposed to tell you the news, too. Dad's friend, that he brought with him. She's so old, even older than Grandpa John. And she seems so ordinary. But, I think she's actually a Monitor from the Northern retreat. She's going to stay a while. She's something - really she is."

Annette looked quickly at him, met his eyes and felt the faint Touch of his mind. She was startled, wanted to extend her own Touch, but drew away. His excitement and the desire to tell them more, came through to her.

She said, "Can you wait 'til lunch, Andy to tell us about Ben and this - Monitor. Is she truly a Monitor?"

Andy grinned again, "I think she is, though no one's said. Yes, I'll wait. But first I promised I'd say right away that the Family will hold true Gather in a week and I'm to tell you that we all want you both to come with Uncle Paul and Aunt Jennifer. And this time, Steve and Rachel too. Dad says please try to plan for that."

Annette looked up quickly, wondering if that was a faint criticism of her unpreparedness for his visit now. But his clear, friendly gaze held no trace of that. She wanted to make that Reach, but somehow, dared not, just now. He seemed to be inviting her. And she thought she might have responded had not Will interrupted.

"Well, we'd better be getting on our way, Son."

Andrew was leaning over the railing looking down into the cascading gardens descending to the broad stone floor of the River Park below. "Wow! I forget how impressive your city is. You've outdone us, I think, Uncle Will. But why not?

You're where all the new plants and ideas come from aren't you?"

"Well, we can't make use of much of our own creation. Our little gardens are designed to give us fresh food most of the year and to look beautiful all year. But there's so much we can't raise in this climate. Except in the Domes of course. But Andy, we don't need to talk of Altos. How's Ben? Did he accomplish what he set out to do? Was he glad to get home this time?"

Andrew turned to his Uncle, "Oh, He's fine, he seems really happy, more than I remember seeing him ever before. I'll tell you all about him at lunch. But look, yonder at that view. I forget what it's like. I've been doing some exploring on the mountain trails north east of Adwin and we've found some old caves there, in the cliffs below the Silent City. It's something there, Uncle Will. Something! You can FEEL it's energy. It's like something given to us. We felt Her power, but we just didn't want to go any nearer."

Will was appalled, he controlled the impulse to shout. He said, "Andy, not that place. It's not a place for young people like you. It's a dangerous cliff, in the first place. Surely you aren't going there." He watched Andy's face, watching for the look of betraying fascination. There was none. The boy seemed to feel no interest in the City at all, even though he had been so excited to tell them. He said, "No, Uncle, We made our journey. We were interested in caverns. Uncle Tom said there are some people inquiring about liveable caverns, big enough for a small town, and we were to let him know if there were any there. We didn't find any big enough." His voice as matter of fact now, and William was relieved.

They went down the walks between gardens to a bridge entrance and stepped out onto one of the slim web strands. The gleaming metal gave slightly with the weight of the people walking. It was like walking on a softness unfamiliar to Andy. He stepped out and laughed, "It's like walking in air, the bridges are so narrow, and the height is so great. He glanced back, his gaze running back up along the hanging gardens until he saw Annette still watching them. He waved and shouted knowing she could not hear, but that she would feel his Touch. He grinned impishly at the knowledge that it would surprise her. She was beautiful and he loved her. Will watched the waves they exchanged and smiled at their exuberance. A flicker of wistful envy crossed his face, but he turned away. They walked on climbing up until they were approaching the Temple and Will found himself again watching the faces of the people coming out. Then he saw that Andy watched too, met their eyes. The boy was ecstatic. Will saw his face light up even as his eyes became distant, as were those of the people he met. The recognition troubled William. Something he couldn't explain seemed normal to this boy.

Andrew Reached to a grey haired couple - though they did not look at one another - and they offered him a support he had not recognized he needed. His Uncle Will seemed to him so - exposed - and Andy felt a little embarrassed. How could he tell his Uncle that his envy and anger were obvious to them? On the other hand, why had he come if not to talk to his uncle? He and Anna had decided that one of them must come and visit. Must find out what was happening to their

THE AWAKENING

Uncle Will, to see what made him unreachable. Now Willaim's neighbors made it simple. They knew and had known and were accepting. Andy frowned, saddened, then broke his Touch and turned to the Temple."Even before you get inside, it's so beautiful, Uncle. It's worth everything Altos had to spend to build it. Have you paid for it yet?"

The questions surprised Will. He didn't think young boys thought of such things."We have Son. This last month, we sent a thousand new crop fruit trees, four varieties, to Italy and that was our last payment for our debt to them. Those trees were worth more than any new trees we've bred in years,. Italy will have the first world trade with them because part of the payment was the agreement that we wouldn't sell any others to any country. Of course we can raise them in Valley. They will sell young stock as well as the fruit, you know."

They were entering and Andy went to a cubicle while Will sat on a low bench in the center of the Hall. The stillness was profound. The wind up here was a soft murmur, constantly rising and falling, always heard unless the great doors were closed, which was seldom. He thought that he would rather take the boy anywhere else. What could he be doing there alone. Surely a boy so young was not practicing meditations on a holiday.

Andrew returned in only half an hour, touched his Uncle on the shoulder and turned to leave. Will followed surprised."I thought you wanted to study the mechanism."

"Oh, no, I don't have to. I just wanted to hear how it is used, and to see the process inside the cubicles. We have clear diagrams of the mechanism and I already know how it works. I had never remembered hearing it". To Will's surprise, he began to plan his visit to the mines. He stopped at the lift belt rack and took down two. "Can we fly down, Uncle. We don't do this as often as you folks do either, you know." They strapped on the belts and tested them in the required manner before stepping off. William watched, amused as Andy played in the air,before turning to travel. Slowly they lifted a little then fell gently toward the wide Stone Parkway. They landed together, and Andrew laughed, "That's the best! We have to climb the mountains or do a spin straight up to get a fall like that. You do it just coming to town."

Will smiled, enjoying the young boy's excitement. Then he said, "Andy, I've known you all your life. I'd like to ask you something that might seem personal."

Andy smiled, inwardly glad,he nodded, met his Uncle's eyes. William felt a shock of connection and then it passed. He frowned,hesitated, ,then said,"Back there, before we went into the Temple. That couple seemed to effect you strangely, And you seemed different after you looked at each other. I don't understand because it seems to me I've seen that happen before."

Andrew smiled, cheerful and willing,"How was I different, Uncle?"

"You must know, Son. You seemed to have gone away, to have that look of great distance in your eyes. Maybe as if you were all three lost in thought. But you were looking at each other. It was not normal at all. And none of you spoke."

"You're right there. I was - thinking of things. They reminded me of what I

THE PEOPLE OF THE VALLEY

must do. It's just something that --, well, it's something I can't explain". The tone of his voice was almost that of a parent soothing a child. Will felt it and frowned. Andy turned, pointing,he knew he had avoided the question, was ashamed. Hadn't they agreed at the Gather they wouldn't do that. But Uncle William was -- was not easy to talk to always and old habits were hard to break. "Look there's the latest Video news coming off the band on the corner. Let's look at it. We don't have them in Adwin." They went to the Kiosk from which the news vended itself hourly. There had been some disturbance in Clandor. A group of people gathered in the great wild meadow east of the city. The report showed them walking, running,and doing a lot of gesticulating. A brown haired, powerful man, who reminded Will of Ben, stood before the cameras. His face was stiff with anger. He threw his arms out, gestured widely and spoke in a deep rumbling voice. "We've come to claim what is not being used,. We insist on the use of the land. We Builders have waited long enough for action, we've been too patient. We are taking this stand so that you can know that we are in earnest" The man moved closer to the screen,"You must realize that three fourths of the Valley, not including any mountain land, is wild. Humankind only uses one fourth of this rich country. That is not enough. But worse, Master Farmers keep planning to REDUCE the farming land!" He looked defiantly into the cameras and the photographer panned the area so that people saw others gathered behind him, also angry.

Andrew shivered,"Why did they get so angry, arguing? The Council will hear them." He looked at Will, "There's something about them that I can't understand. It's an excitement, maybe, or maybe something - foolish, maybe. I don't quite know." He seemed surprised at his own choice of words. "But I want to go see. I want to know what's happening. You remember my friend Steel. Uncle?" At Will's nod, he continued, "He says we've got to go up against the Builders. He says what they're doing is a lot of foolishness but it could be dangerous. He's really excited about them, Uncle Will." He was watching his Uncle's face, waiting to see how these words would effect him."I want to go there too. To see what's happening for myself."

"Andy! No! You could be hurt. There's no way to know how people are going to react to demands like these. Let the Healers take care of it. Or someone like Tom. You stay away."

"Oh, Uncle. Surely no one is going to do anything that would hurt anyone. Not really hurt them. We've not gotten that far off track."

"I don't know Son. I can't say what's happening in the Valley now. There're things I can't explain myself. Surely things aren't the same anymore. "

"But people don't solve problems with violence, so I can't get hurt. It would be a good way to learn about negotiations in the political world." He Reached before he thought, wanting so much to tell his Uncle what he felt. He felt the Reach go flat. Nothing received. He sighed and said, "Anyway, it wouldn't matter that much anyway, would it, Uncle, even if there were trouble?"

" What wouldn't matter?" Will's voice was strident, apprehensive.

"Well, it doesn't seem that important after all, you know."

"Right, it's not important enough to risk injury, possibly even death, No, it's not that important."

Andy, chose his words carefully,"No, Uncle, I meant, that my death is not that important."

"Andrew"! The horror in William's voice brought the boy to a stop. They had begun walking again along the Parkway on smooth paths winding through a grove of trees in which were set stone sculptures. William turned to face his nephew. Something in the boy's quiet complacency infuriated him. He knew that that anger rose from his own fear. Andy meant what he said, he really felt that way. "You are as insane as those hot heads who keep yelling for 'action' as they call it. They seem to think the way to act is to take what they want by force! Yes, Son, there're people who think that!." He knew he had revealed a secret, knew Andy was surprised to hear that, But he could not stop. "Surely you can't be willing to die at your age? Your whole life ahead?"

"Uncle, I don't wish to, no, not now. But it's only the loss of a body. Not such a big deal." He reflected, seemingly oblivious of his Uncle's horror," Right now I do want to get on with this life and see what I can do with it."

William was finally speechless,something he had experienced few times in his life. Finally he sputtered,"Life is all you have, Son."

Andrew looked at this Uncle, met his eyes, knew surely that he must make himself clear."Yes, of course, Uncle. But one cannot 'lose' life. One can only lose a body. I don't mean I WANT to do that. I think I don't have the right to endanger this body. I've got a life to live in it and I'm responsible for it. So I'm not going to do something rash and stupid." He nodded to himself as if that settled the matter. William looked at him with out having an answer. Another first for him in a long time. Finally he turned and said, "Well, let's get onto the mines, Son. Annette will be waiting for us.

Andy spoke softly as if he was lost in thought,"But then, you know, I might not have the choice to keep this life after all."

Will started to speak, his face was pale, his eyes brighter than Andy had ever seen them. Was the boy teasing him? Surely he would not tease about so serious a matter. His voice would not come. He looked at this sixteen year old, lanky, beautiful young man. His body so dark, like polished golden walnut, his brown hair swept back and shining. He had promise. More than most people. Will knew that it was true that Andy did not feel any fear of death. Neither did he court it. Will had to give him credit for that. But he saw that Andy would not see giving his life for something he thought truly right as a sacrifice, but rather as a fulfilment of that life.

Suddenly Will was more afraid than he had ever been. He shook his head, walking now slowly beside the fierce, healthy body beside him. There were things stirring in this Valley that were darker and more confusing than he had any idea of. Or was it they were brighter and more wonderful and he was ignorant of them? Or both? He had to learn more. This was part of that changing that was happening around them. Will thought that he himself saw more than most people. His mind was adept at seeing relationships where others saw nothing. Yet if Andrew was an example, these young ones out distanced him. He felt as if the world were tilting. He shook himself pushed the thoughts from his mind.

He took Andy's arm,"Come on, Andrew. You wanted to visit Grandpa John, you know. He'll enjoy a visit. Then we'll meet Steve. He's eager to show off the domes and the new work he's doing. We're all going over to Paul's and Jennifer for Dinner and you can have a talk with Rachel. You remember you told me you wanted to see everyone?

Andy kept stride with William, his legs nearly as long. He accepted the decision Will had implicitly made. They would not talk of those things anymore. Andrew felt a deep sadness start, and it was one that he found familiar. Then, without expecting it, he felt a Touch. Steve, calling,inquiring and then they made contact. Gladness wove itself through the grief and made it acceptable.

CHAPTER NINETEEN

Spring Planting and Gather

By everybody's agreement the Family would gather in a week's time. Andrew brought news of folks in Altos and assured them all would be there.

Spring woke the Great Valley in a long slow sweep that ran from the far south slowly upward to that northern most neck within which the Green River was born. Along that River the sweep of green moved northward until in Adwin everything seemed to break forth all at once, leaves, blossoms and all the sweet scents of springtime. The need for a Gather was clear and spring was a wonderful time to get together. It was also time for the planting ritual so they decided to combine them. Within another week, everyone would be preparing for Spring Festival. Always it seemed after the quiet of winter, everything came at once.

This year there was something new, urgent, calling from some point that eluded definition. It kept attention focussed in a hope to catch the source of that call. No one spoke of it, nor thought that others felt it. That old habit, that tendency to hesitate when these elusive feelings occurred served to create silence about them. But the Joy of spring seemed this year to emanate from every living thing. The dark forests were lit with the bright new leaves of disciduous fruit or nut bearing groves, growing among the great old oaks and walnuts, madrone and ash. Cherries, almonds, wisterias, wild roses, and the brilliant blue of plasilk bushes, and wild flowers splashed their colors along highways, paths and in open meadows that extended like broad fingers into the deep woodlands. Over the rounded hills the legumes, planted by children under direction from the Master Forester, splashed acres red, yellow, blue and bronze. Animals came out of their dens and tree hollows, shook themselves and began the eternal ritual of mating. The Valley was alive again.

Every village and town began preparations for the Spring Festival. The People of the Way unrolled their precious tapestries, carpets, fabrics, all sorts of intricate stitchery in cloth and leather, hung ready for display. As the season moved north, so did the festivals, and the Vagabonds followed. People practiced songs, dances, music in all forms, from solo instruments or singers, to full orchestras and choirs. Actors, dancers, singers, gymnasts and Game players, in each town, practiced long hours to perfect their arts. Boat and sailing teams had to juggle practice time because the same people were on several teams and the Learning Center was full of light and activity late into the night. Prize bottles of wine, new fabrics, inventions of child and adult, were finished to be ready for the full moon days of late March. Finally the Vagabond fires could be seen clustered near Adwin and Jasper. On some mornings ground fogs and rain dimmed the highways, but the sound of singing persisted for they were a hardy people who laughed at the need for comforts of the Town people.

There was the sense of new life invading the northern world that could not be denied. The Earth fairly glowed with a radiant vitality that took hold of people and cured them of all their doldrums. Jane loved this time. All her years labor would be brought to a finish. The Planting season was a supreme celebration for her, even more delightful than harvest. Silvia watched her, wondering, elated herself at Jane's joy. Rose saw that effervescence of energy and knew the immediate source. She knew that this year, added to all the rest of her happiness, was the maturing of the love between Steve and Jane. Everyone except the two involved, knew that soon it would be openly admitted.

Rose knew too, that Jane did not understand how deeply she lived in a rappour with Earth life. That communication she knew with the vast, deep energy of Earth Herself was holy for Jane. Yet with each footstep she took through root and leaf, rock and soil, she felt connection. She knew a connection in nameless joining with basaltic rock so old it knew the Earth's birth. She was drawn even to that molten center where fires raged such as none could imagine. She knew a pulling down, a rootedness, from this outer shell of light and rich green growth, of birth and sudden death that new births must demand, to that soundless fiery power. Jane was dimly conscious of these thrusting energies that ran through her own nature as though she were simply part of the whole stretch of it. But she could not have told herself or anyone else of it. She was dimly aware of that downward Reach of consciousness just as she was of the power of the upward thrust that swept through the green crust into blue air and out to the blazing sun. She could not have named it but that power was alive in her.

On a fine morning, warmed with a blazing sun but tempered by chill breezes still blowing down from snow peaks to the east, only a week after Ben's return, Jane went out to look down into the fields they must plant today. She felt she could have planted it all alone, could have sown the grain, skimmed the dark soil on a floater to carved the designs for the fields of vegetables and set the seed into those curving grooves. Her energy seemed boundless and she was eager to begin. She knew that all over the north country families were doing the same. The People of the Way were entering the forests, planting wild roots in new places where they would grow, scattering seeds in the fields or under dark, dense trees where ever they would grow and provide natural foods for human or wild creature. This year, the Vagabonds would buy a hundred new young oaks, to plant on four hillsides twenty miles apart. These would produce a sweeter acorn, large as small apples that they could harvest as they traveled. Their children, gathered in teams, had set into wild hillside meadows young new legumes whose stiff vines would produce flowers so brilliant blue the color could be seen for miles and then, late in fall, long thick pods holding fat seeds that tasted like chocolate and would be gathered by town people and Vagabond alike. The People were proud of these gifts they gave to the Valley.

On the farm the time arrived none too soon. Tools were gathered, baskets of seeds and plants ready. It was the favorite of the year's Gathers. They watched in pleased delight as Tom, his son Nathan and Ned rode the wind in from Adwin on belts, and then only minutes later, the soft hum of the air car from Altos

THE AWAKENING

bringing the family from there. After greetings were made, they began the trek down the hill to the fields. Jane trailed behind. she carried two flats of plants from straps that ran through a cradle on her shoulders. She carried them with care and the attention one might give a small child. She enjoyed the clean swing of her body walking smoothly down the hillside. She looked up at the great fat white clouds floating here and there above, and felt a kinship, her own ability to change as the air did, as light increased. These great ships of moisture would dissolve as the day heated the air. The sunlight seemed to her this morning to be so sharply present around her, to transform everything. She said aloud,"There must be intelligence there, there in that great vast outpour of energy. There must be knowing going on between that fire and this Earth." She didn't smile at her thoughts,she took them seriously. It seemed to her that there was truly a vast cosmic consciousness radiant from these great bodies on which all this little life depended. She said,"After all, if this tiny body can be conscious, how can I assume a great cosmic body wouldn't be?" That settled it for her.

Ahead of her, the family reached the fields and gathered under the great walnuts and oaks that stood between the fields and the water maples and willows that edged the River. Among these two kinds of forest, was a broad stretch of deep grasses. At the side nearest the fields were the rounded humps of grass covered earth in which the equipment was kept. The land seemed untroubled by its users. The woods were green, but the leaves were small and little shade broke the sun shining warm under trees. This ritual of the Planting was an occasion for solemnity and delight.Jane was choreographer and every year these rites brought the people close again to their source.

As Jane approached the fields, she could see that Paul and Jennifer were there among them, but neither of their children had come. Well, she expected that, both would be involved in Altos Dome planting. She searched among them for William and Annette and didn't find them there. She felt a shadowing of the day at their absence. She approached the field. She said,"Find a place in the pattern I've grooved into the soil and stand at the edge of it with your basket of seed." Everyone moved into places along the pattern. Cassie stood half way across the field,one of the inside circles, her small body alert, full of eagerness to play this game. Jane watched her face, so intent, impressed with the ritual. She was pleased. the ritual did not grow stale. Each year they created it all over again using basic foundations set by the Earth,,the seed and the season. There were traditional songs, but there were also always the new creations given each year by their planting.

Jerry began spontaniously. He lifted his slim seeding wand, flinging his other arm higher and laughing aloud. His joy was infectious. Every one smiled. He sang out:

> With my bare feet,I feel your life, Oh, Mother!
>   With my joy I bring you seed to cradle,
>   I give them to your life, your care!

THE PEOPLE OF THE VALLEY

Let all our seeds enter through their deaths into life.!

He didn't have the fine sense of melody others might but the strength of his voice reached everyone and they felt his play,his joy. Jane went to him and flung out a handful of water, the silvery drops arching into his furrows. She sang softly,"Let the waters of the sky join Earth and create new lives that we may have food."

Jane always thought that her part in this ritual was minor, the words inadequate, foolish even. But then, as she threw that clear water out, they seemed right. She heard another voice making a melody with no pretense at words and she turned to Andrew. He sang his melody through three times, a lovely lilting sound, then he let a few seeds drop into the tight spiral beside him. Each person stood barefoot feeling Earth beneath their winter thin skin. Andrew looked around, then Silvia moved, spread her arms to include them all and nodded to Andrew and Jerry. They grinned and she went on.

Her light sweet voice took Jerry's words and Andrew's melody and made them into a song. The two men joined her,their voices a harmony rich and full. They rearranged Jerry's words and then repeated them. They modified Andrew's melody. They heard the others joining in, making a harmony that carried over the field. Then to their surprise, Silvia began to offer new words and they fit into the music so well everyone took them up to sing.

> Let our feet and hands re-unite with Thee, Mother.
> Let the power of our Father Sun warm our heads
> And anoint us with Light and purity,
> That we may wake into the Love
> That courses through between Earth and Sky.
> Let the seeds we give know the Earth power,
> Burst forth in life, unfold in magic ,
> That we,Earth children have added to them
> Through our Mother's knowledge within us.

As the song ended there was a moment of Silence, Jessie moved, extending her arms to the gesture of wide embrace and sang in a clear contralto, it's strength and beauty surprised them all.

> "May the Spirit that is Eternal join with the Sunlight,
> Pour out from every life of our Valley
> And bless us with every breath.

The others took up the new words, made a refrain of them and sang them over several times. Then Andrew created a new melody, fitting it around the old, encompassing it, the song was growing. Steve called out from where he stood, flinging large seeds into the design at his feet then singing over the old verse, he added a new one.

"My joy is awakening through these my fellows.
Mother, let us know the beauty of Thy dark power.

The whole group repeated this too, then added to it. Then Ben's turn came. His deep voice bellowed out, carried far enough to be heard by neighbors. His verses were repeated in turn and the whole of it sung again. Jennifer laughed, delighted by the weaving of melody and words. She brought a flute from her pocket and began to play a contrapuntal variation that lay beneath that melody and to improvise as she went so that suddenly the whole music was a dancing shifting play of shadow and light.

Now Jerry's first verse had become a chorus with Jessie's added, and the other verse became the body. Each one added a line or two and the whole was sung over that it be not forgotten. These Valley people whose memories were trained since they were not yet walking, had no trouble keeping the song in mind. They sang each new addition and added more. Then they began moving across the field, singing and either walking or gliding on discs, the slim planting wands reaching to the furrows from bags on their backs. They finally had planted all the seed, still singing, still carrying the sound of it. When they had planted the first field, they moved across the force field 'fence' and began the next. Finally, all the seeds were planted and with stained feet and empty hands, they gathered one by one at the clearing between the trees. The last and slowest planters ended their work and turned to the carpet spread out on the grass. Food baskets sat around the edges of the wide carpet and everyone tossed on to it a cushion or two. They threw themselves down to stretch and rest. Acres of wild meadow laced with the gold green of young grain glistened over the low hills to the north.

In silence they began to eat. They listened to the River, the birds, the creatures that ran here and there among the trees. Above them now and then a faint hum of an air car passed. A feeling of satisfaction and contentment grew and each one wanted the moment to go on, the silence and the feeling of well being.

Rose stretched out, feeling the shape of Earth beneath her. There was a languor, a dream like quality to everything today, she thought. Then, speaking to break the capsule of silence around them, "Tell me Jessie, how is it for you here?"

Jessie laughed, then was serious, "Everything keeps waking old memories. Especially the smells, the harmony of our singing, the flickers of color when birds fly. It's as though our lives sing in harmony with Earth,. Earth herself sings with us! How can I feel other than as though I've come home-- again. The Earth has no place that is not home but I must be aware enough to recognize it." She stopped, looked around, something secretly radiant in her face. "Can you hear the Earth Sing? Pay attention, you will hear!" She watched them, her eyes intent, seeing them, and far into them, "Yes, you do, you do. Then can you notice the light that is more than sunlight, flooding all round us here?" Her eyes laughed, "Yes, you can see that too."

Jerry said abruptly, "Well, yes, Jessie. Just as you speak of it, my ears notice, my eyes see. We seem to be within a _ _ almost as if we're in a great globe of Light. I couldn't have thought that - if you hadn't spoken. I mightened even have noticed. But look, it's so wonderful." He laughed with pure delight," A wonder, that's what it is -- it's so intense. It's delightful. Is that right?"

She seemed a little surprised at the question. "Right? Jerry to be full of joy is always right, you know." She grinned at them, looking all around, "We live our lives consciously shared with one another. Lives that are lived consciously are lives that teach. You all know that. It's a Valley promise, isn't it?" The reminder sobered them. "It's that kind of day for me."

Rose said thoughtfully," This is our second Gather since winter, Jessie. We said we would talk with one another of the changes we feel. But we have not done very well at that. We still resist! I'm as bad as anyone. I'm still pretending. Afraid to talk about that inner wonder, fear and confusion that has made life a tender, painful, joyful changing in these last years. We have to learn to talk to each other!" There was a long sigh, finally it was said.

Ben slid to draw Rose's hand into his, "It's true, my Love. We've denied, even now, knowing better, we still deny. At least let's acknowledge that. What we deny is that we Reach, and then Touch mentally. That meditative awareness has become a constant state of mind."

Jerry laughed, "And, we said we'd acknowledge what we do and end the secretiveness. I'll repeat it, we mind-Reach and then we Touch mentally. I think it is the intuitive mind in action. I think it is perfectly normal. But we've never accepted it as such."

He was looking at Jessie and she saw his hope. All the others turned to her in expectation. She smiled, but an old pattern of self depreciation, that perhaps she would not be adequate to their needs, grated against her heart. She thrust that obsolete assumption aside. They themselves would lead the way. She asked, "What does this Reach and Touch feel like.?

Jerry nodded, frowned to bring memory back, "There is an electric tension for me, a sense of extending myself, from within, so that another person is more real. Then, just as I suddenly saw this Light around us, when you pointed it out, a farther dimension of my mind seems to function. I am together with her or him intuitively. I am aware beyond myself where personal body- mind seems to - just flow through its own edges. If I sustain the Reach, then there is that magnetic Touch. It feels powerful. I've never been able to hold it."

Rose nodded, "Yes, that's well said, Jerry. It's what it's like. But it also brings a deep seated fear. Because to Touch another, I think a person has Reached deep within and Touched her Self." She shook her head. I don't know whether I'm afraid of myself or of that Self I meet during this stretching." She was silent, thoughtful and then, "Yes, it is a stretch and often it hurts. It makes me afraid because it is - not normal." She had fastened her eyes far over the River among the trees but now she brought her gaze back to meet Jessie's eyes. I worry that all of us may not know this extension of consciousness. I want to know how many

THE AWAKENING

of us do."

She looked around. There was confusion in some eyes, eager joy in others and a faint uneasiness in a few. Tom nodded emphatically, "It's time. We've got to speak more about it. I will. I do know what this is. I do Reach and I know that I Touch other minds. Sometimes I can continue, keep steady, and then I -realize more."

"You think this is telepathy?

She shook her head,"No, Jessie, I don't read other people's thoughts. It is as though the matrix of their general attitudes, emotions, way of being at that moment, is known,shared. There is a profound closeness."

Paul nodded. "It's true, I've avoided admitting it too. I've known more with the Valley Council than with any of my own family. Grace brings us something called Joining. I have never done this without that group. Mostly I think Grace and Jerome guide. But it is like a lifting, then an extension, the way Rose said. There is a sensation of light and clarity of some inner atmosphere, then the Touch merges into a Joining. It is electric,powerful. I felt at first that I was losing myself. But then, I knew I was enhanced." His eyes searched hers, pleading that she understand this strange talk. "I can't fully enter into it yet, but I intend to. It's like being hooked into an immense consciousness, a group's consciousness." His eyes were distant, thinking of that experience and how it had surprised and troubled him at first. "I've only known a little of it, but it is --" he shook his head, not looking at them,"awesome." He drew a deep breath,"We are so very much WITH one another."

"I'm glad you said that, Paul." Tom leaned across the pillow he had moved into his lap,"I thought I was the only one struggling to Reach out beyond that first Touch. The Council calls it Joining? Well, that's a right name. And what little I've known., yes, it's overwhelming at first".

Ben was frowning, "You all know that I've fought even the idea of that Reach for years. I knew that Rose Reached and even that she Touched. What I called that 'strange stuff'. I think I caused her to lose skill. I was so adamant that she stop trying to Reach out that way. I'm sure she didn't stop though. Did you, my Darling?"

Rose smiled, tucking her head into his shoulder and said,"No, not completely, though it's true that your fear of it made my fear greater and also made me feel as though there was something really wrong with me. I didn't actually begin to accept that Talent until I felt Grace's clear Touch that day at Council. That's how Council makes such clear decisions. We truly know each other's attitudes and feelings. We are -- more conscious together. We can see a larger picture of things."

"But you can lie even there, can't you. Can't you conceal and pretend even in that closeness?" Ned, didn't want to commit himself yet.

" Not if you are truly present, and it's obvious to the others if you aren't. Besides, I think we make this contact through that Soul consciousness, we Reach through that level of being, and so, pretense is impossible. People who are that aware, conscious enough to Touch,are people who also think and care. They are people whose basic sense of humanity is very great. Touching is a sign of development of both Heart and Mind, I think." She turned to Jessie."Is that so?"

Jessie smiled, turned to Tom, "What would you say, Tom. You've practiced enough already haven't you"?

Tom stared at her a moment, then slowly nodded, "It is absolutely so. You all remember as well as I do. The Master Teachers have told us enough times that Mind is omnipresent. So I think there is an interface, we hit up against, between mind and Mind. Reaching is the beginning of breaking through that interface." He shrugged, looked surprised at himself, then said seriously. But I think a reach only comes when a person's been trained to deep mental focus. Attention has to be placed and held. All of us practice contemplation, we've learned to listen and receive impressions out of silence. It's using intuitive mind skills, I think, isn't it?" He looked around at them,listening so attentively. "He nodded to himself. So it seems to me thai Reaching is focussing, but with a mind that contemplates abstract thought. It encompasses all thought and extends beyond it. So we're not apt to lie or deny much. D'you think I've got the right of it"? He looked around and saw some understanding, but much perplexity. He frowned, looked down at his strong slim hands folded together, then glanced up at them and said,"I don't think I ever explained that to myself before."

"I'm just glad you said it,Tom. This is like a Healing for me." Paul was solemn, absorbing his own thoughts." And have you thought how the Talents relate to that"?

Tom laughed, "Go for a dime, I might's as well go for a dollar. I'll give it a stab. I think Talents are normal senses, or abilities coming from a newly fired up brain. We're using brain cells that's been dormant." He grinned, looked around and settled on Paul's face.

"You may be right. You think maybe whole new parts of our brains shift and begin to function in response to that Light we have begun to be aware of." Paul looked slowly around, wondering. How had this woman managed without even talking, to open this kind of talk. They had failed to share like this for years.

He looked at Jessie, decided to continue."Right now, I know the Touch is most important to us. But I'm especially worried that some Valley people fear the Talents that we see developing. That there are some who think they are Evil". Then with a sharp shake of his head, Paul said,"Oh, it's just more personal than that. That's what William thinks. He won't try to Reach. I don't want to say he can't. It grieves me more than I would have imagined. I can imagine how painful it is for Annette."

" Oh, Jessie, do you know why these things are happening? Are we all changing, all the Valley?" Rose's voice was sad.

Andrew spoke suddenly. So far it had been talk between adults. His voice seemed deep at first, then suddenly and to his embarrassment, was the high voice of a child. It was the first time it had done that in weeks and he was angry. He swallowed hard and shook his head."I went to see Uncle Will". His eyes met

Anna's. At her nod, he went on," Anna and I, thought something was wrong. It is! He doesn't Reach out at all. And he seems angry. Whether he can or not, I don't know. I think someone ought to do something. We can't let him lose- lose - all that." He looked around at them, a look of resentment for their carelessness on his face. "We can't really help him Son, unless he's willing to let us. But we'll promise to look into it, we'll find out exactly what's true. After all. Lots of people are afraid. Look at what we've done, we've denied everything we knew! It may be no more than that." Ben spoke comfortingly, wanting to reassure these children he had so recently returned to, but a note of worry haunted his voice that his son was not deaf to.

There was silence, the breeze blew through the young leaves, rustling them faintly. The River sounds became audible and the odor of deep water filled the air. They ate in silence, enjoying the sensations of their bodies, the spring day, the sounds of birds, two squirrels who ran in t he brqanches of the trees above them, barking, scolding at their presence. The three dogs, lying stretched on the carpet in the sun, raised their heads, glanced up and then, sighed and dropped again to sleep.

Rose said,"It's so still. All of Earth is so full of Light. It's the Light you brought to us, Jessie. This stillness of Light IS like a globe all round us." Her sense of awe was so strong it carried to the others.

"And perhaps you'll talk of that other matter you avoid. The Touch is a beginning, but most of you have seen further, much further."

For moments more,everyone was quiet. Then Anna said,"How can I speak of Earth separate from myself? Through this Light I am extended, I am of Her nature and not apart." It was so soft it was almost a prayer.

Cassie, sitting next to her father, looked around curiously,the Light seemed to her more a pulsing glow through the air, a moving light as though it blew into and among them. Never before had she been so aware of simple sunlight,or of this greater Light that was a radiance glowing outward from living things, literally shining up from Earth. She delighted in it, laughed and spread her arms out wanting to feel it with her fingers. Rose impatiently rolled over on the carpet, leaned on one elbow to look at Jessie, whose eyes were unfocussed, though her attention included them all.

When Jessie spoke, her voice had the tension of power. "Here there is utter tenderness of Life Itself. Here Life perceives Itself through Itself. Notice, how from within you looks forth that very Life that shapes you. Shapes each living thing."

Rose focussed her attention, aware, sustained, She was aware of Life,a Stillness that included all the Earth sounds around them. How could stillness include sound? But everything seemed different today. Yes, a great Joy expanded in her Heart, so great it threatened. It was true! Life looked through this form it had created.Self looking through Its self to see Its works. Then as though thinking about it cut her off, awareness was gone. The power of it,the reflection remained. The thought was a shadow of the real. She sat stunned, the memory filling her with tremendous sorrow at its loss. She thought,'Oh,dear, here is my family that I see. Here is Earth life! And we are not separate from it'. She felt that quality Jessie had spoken of, that strange sense of an infinite Tenderness.

Jessie nodded, "Life wakes within us, opens our consciousness to Itself, and thus perceives Itself there in us. Perhaps only a spark. We are like fireflies lit in flickering seconds with that Eternal Life that shapes our being. Perhaps it's all that our conscious minds can know in one time, but it is enough. We cannot ever forget once we have been Touched alive in that Light, that Life." She was silent, they were enthralled by her words but as much by the timber,the power of her voice."You do see that? You were aware of that instant perception, you were conscious that it rises from within yourself?"

Ben finally spoke,"Jessie, you aren't speaking symbolically. You mean that literally. Here! Now!" He seemed to hold his breath,waiting for her answer.

She nodded and he blinked, thinking his eyes were fooling him, for all about her there was a silvery glow. Different from the Light in the air, different and part of herself. He shook his head, looked away a moment. Defensively he began to think rapidly, to keep that farther reality at bay."Then there it is. There is a kind of memory, isn't there? There is an - opening - like memory, that I see through." He chose his words slowly, stumbling because they were not easy to find. He too found his eyes reaching out, fastening, as to a lifeline, on a tiny golden leaf above him."Sometimes, like now, there's a dream quality in everything, the world around me, myself, as though I am looking at myself, my world, from some place else. Out of that opening."

He was still. Everyone listened, the sound of birds,the River, came into them in a tumult. His voice was a whisper, " That's true now,Jessie, as though life itself is a wonderful, terrible, dream. And we are waking up!" He stopped, his eyes moving from one face to another. What was happening to him? He had never talked of such things to any of his family. What would they think of him?

Rose nodded, murmuring,she was lost in his meaning, oblivious of the difference in him."Yes! Yes! It's the glimpse - maybe a reflection of - of something more! But there IS the glimpse and I am overwhelmed. That's what I resist, I recoil from. If the glimpse is so -- so mind shaking, so terrible and beautiful, then what might the whole of it be? "

She too was amazed at herself speaking so. Being able to find words, so little afraid. "I've never been able to speak of the Vision when I am realizing. I have such overwhelming pain of loss, a grief that is nameless. But now with you here, it is -- at least bearable, that sense of loss. My old fears seems to be pointless because they dissolve into -- into perception. I am conscious of the Light - even as we talk! That is remarkable." She stopped, old fears pressing against her heart, demanding she stop. But identity was extending, including. She saw her body small, sitting in the shade.

Jessie did not answer, but asked instead," The perception beyond yourself, the instant's glimpse of Light? of Wonder? That frightens you?"

"I suppose that's it. Yes, it does frighten me. So much, I've tried to hold onto my attention and then to shift away. To NOT see. But then, Jessie, it's so much.

So MUCH. If I allow myself to be conscious of that, it seems to have no end. I would drown !" She gulped, but looked at no one except Jessie, holding to her as to an anchor. "When you sang with us, you added something new. We have been satisfied with the power of our knowledge, the Earth power, the Sun power, but you added that other POWER. Which is more than all of these. It must be true, as you said, that what we glimpse is a tiny spark of That, and That must be Spirit Itself." She spoke for herself but was aware that somehow she was speaking for them all. "That is what frightens. It is not understood. It's so very vast - unending. It feels alien to me, and yet, I KNOW that it is - what we are. What humanity is. There is something vast and deep and full of what has seemed to be Light, but Light is only its shadow."

She was amazed at her own words. Never had she been able to find words. She looked around, saw that the others watched her, attentive, but there was confusion on some faces. Then she turned to her children, and saw in their eyes a radiance of great Joy. How beautiful they were. She was taken aback, she felt uncomfortable and turned from them. Their eyes met, and exchanged a secret joy, but their mother did not see.

Jessie said gently,"It's a lot to bear ,at first. There is a stretch- a literal Mind stretch. One cannot avoid that necessity and so there is Wonder. A wonder of Knowledge that is so beautiful it wounds the little mind, causes pain and breaks when it stretches it into greatness. But it cannot perceive much, only small shards of greatness pierce and leave the mind forever roused from sleep. We know at least that reality IS, whether we can bear it or not. That's natural, you know. Part of the process." She smiled.   Rose was silent, her eyes fixed on Jessie's, "

If there is a process, it must mean that one can finally bear it. Is it that the Mind grows larger, my consciousness expands to allow such knowledge?" At Jessie's nod, she went on."It's like the way the body grows when we exercise our muscles. It can do more, be more." Jessie nodded, and watched them all, saw the differences in comprehension. The moment seemed to her crucial. She held herself in a tension of waiting.

Jerry burst out,"Now, please be specific. I know - there's something - I feel- something of what you 're saying, but I'm so confused. I want to know! What IS this knowledge you speak of. What is it! SAY IT!" His voice was both angry and pleading.

Rose looked at Jessie, at Jerry and then she saw all their eyes on herself. She hesitated at the hope, the need there. Then her gaze moved to Jane, Steve, sitting together, puzzled,uneasy. To Silvia, who looked angry. "I don't know, Jerry. When I try to say it, then it's so much less, it's so much less. But I'll try. We humans are so much more than the personalities that we think of as ourselves. I think we absorb very little at a time, but we're so much more!. It's the only way I can say it. Because what we are that's 'more' is not the self we are familiar with, but that inner Self that we are just beginning to - to realize." She grimaced."You see, it doesn't make much sense at all to talk of it. After all, I never really knew the meaning of that word 'Soul'. But now I realize, I am Soul." The words were like a prayer. The awareness of that extended Self drew her far from them, at the same time, deeply with them. She could not speak.

Helplessly she turned to them, frustrated, and then with a suddenness that startled her, she lost the vision. She resorted to childhood teaching. In a hasty effort to keep that mystery, to understand, she said, "The Master Teachers always told us that we are both personality and Soul. You remember. It was never more than an idea to me. But now I see that it's a way of speaking of something that doesn't fit into words very well. That word 'Soul'. It's just a word, until you SEE. Then you understand what it means when someone says we are 'more' than we know.." She sighed."If you haven't glimpsed that -- other consciousness -- then maybe if you pay attention, very deep attention, you'll see too!" Jessie was nodding, pleased, but the others were silent, trying to absorb what she had said.

Rose took a deep breath, looked at Jessie for help, and then said, "It's strange, that glimpse, we speak of. The spark of Light, or the deep sense of extension or inclusion- or whatever way one experiences it, because what is reflected even appears to be nothing at all." She frowned, trying to find words, thoughts that would fit. But I think that's because I don't have language for what has never been part of our common conscious experience." She mused, letting the memory work its meaning.

"It's as though I have become transparant, like water, and on the tension of my surface there is a reflection of That which I cannot grasp. The Self doesn't hold still, cannot be got hold of like a 'thing'. The reflection of It comes from within the very depths of my mind. Is it that I can only know THAT which is beyond Light by its reflection? As a River cannot know land except in that same way? Even though it flows constantly through the land." Again she grimaced, shaking her head, "You see, I seem to be only able to make metaphors, images that might reflect but never are the Real. Our Earth, our lives here, must themselves be metaphors for that Real!"

Andrew sighed, his heart beat rapidly. He was excited and elated by this talk. So seldom in his life had the adults talked so, and almost never his own family. Here was what he had longed to have them speak of. This Jessie, she was the catalyst. He thought she would be a help to them. He said, "Maybe it's more. Sometimes what I call 'me', seems to be transparent. In that instant I can begin to see -- everything I've ever been, what I seem to be. Then, everything that I experience as myself, as world, or as feeling, thought, fear, joy, -- all of it has become a transparency. In this state of being, then 'I' see through and am MYSELF".

"And then you see?" Jessie's tone was eager.

He met her eyes and searched for words, "That there is absolutely no real difference between me and --- anything. We are - - everything is -- one Life. All of this" He waved his hand, indicating the people, Earth, the fields and all they saw, "All of this is 'I'. Life is what we ARE."

"Then what is the difference?" Jessie did not let her eyes leave his.

His own eyes narrowed, "There is a difference. Of course, isn't there?" He let his mind search, range, include deeply and limit itself again to the thought."Why,I suppose the difference must be consciousness. Then maybe I am - consciousness within Life Itself?" He was surprised, pleased with the way his words shaped the idea. "I don't know whether that means anything to anyone else, but it does for me. I can't imagine any more."

Ben leaned to his son, "Why do you say 'imagine'?"

Jessie nodded,"He's right though. It's possible isn't it, to at least imagine something of consciousness? We've tried so hard to define it. But think of the other qualities, Love, for instance. We cannot imagine Love. We only imagine those faint stains of it which are relationship for us. We even attribute Love to what we call God, because we know, intuitively that it is far beyond us. Yet, by imagining it, we can begin to experience a faint bit more of it. Stretching ourselves into imagining, we can perceive what we have not known. This place Andrew speaks of, the 'transparancy', it's at that point perhaps that we might experience something of Love. The glimpse seems to be necessary, for most people, to awaken imagination."

"What then would you call that Glimpse?" Paul's voice was a whisper.

Jessie nodded,"Is it a shaft of prescience, a break in ordinary consciousness that allows us to see a greater Consciousness, beyond our knowledge? Allows us to see through a crack in the shell of our existence?" She looked around at them." But we were speaking of Love, perhaps at some moment of great awareness, even of lovemaking, or of birthing a baby, or such, you have known a glimpse of Love?"

Jerry's voice was full of grief,"Aren't we capable of Love more often, Jessie?"

"It seems to me that it isn't that we're not capable, but that we're too small to sustain, to consciously realize it. Try to remember those moments,and you may find they're usually only MOMENTS, when you've known some touch of that wonder of Love. It lifts us utterly out of ourselves, does it not? For Love isn't something we 'do' but rather something we realize, like the wind, everywhere, but not seen. We become aware! And for most of us, the faintest Touch is more than we can bear." -----

Rose nodded, her face rapt. listening and hearing with her whole mind. A faint frown played at her eyes, drew a darkness upon her brows and finally she blurted," But Jessie, I still don't know why I've always been so afraid? Afraid of the very Wonder that exults my heart? Afraid to acknowledge even the small degree to which I am aware of Love."

Jessie turned to her, letting her eyes settle on Rose's fce, deliberately sending comfort,making no attempt to conceal her Sending."It isn't uncommon. That Fear. It's a fear of being different,I think, and the fear of that overwhelming recognition that that which we begin to know, is absolutely changing our life. Any perception of THAT which IS, even a fragmentary glimpse, changes us forever. Is that not true, Rose?"

Rose nodded slowly," I think it is so. but there is something else, something I have been ashamed to admit to myself. In some way,I don't WANT to know what it is I glimpse. I don't want to realize what I am becoming conscious of." She shivered, "It disturbs my - my sense of reality."

Jessie laughed,"Disturbs? Rose you are restrained. Most students say it drives them crazy. To realize what we are, at first. What humankind is. To just faintly begin to realize that." She shook her head."To realize that at all, is the first task. To allow perception and be willing to acknowledge what we know. That is the task. And for that, our mind must be stretched. Becoming aware in Soul Consciousness stretches everything we - we are. It stretches mind, heart, self, until it hurts. Literally hurts, Rose, and for that we know fear too. Knowing that we are also Soul consciousness, accepting it even as an idea, tears apart old assumptions and old identities. It turns our universe upside down. How can we do that and not have periods of fear?. But also periods of utter Joy?" She let her eyes move from face to face, noting the varied responses. And then,her gaze turning inward, she said softly as if to herself. How many decades was the scientific world clinging to a mechanistic theory of the cosmos, afraid, refusing to recognise any other, even though evidence mounted." She shook her head. "Thought - thought itself was denied a part. Yet today, we know that thought is an energy as premordial and universal as what they called the Big Bang. Consciousness is a quality of the universe." For some minutes they were silent again, the idea bringing a shift in attitudes, pushing old assumptions aside as they registered its implications.

Anna stretched out on the thick carpet, rested her head on her brother's waist, and looked up into the scattering of small green leaves brightening the dark limbs above them. For her there was no question. Of course thought was an energy. She shook her head faintly, amazed at the struggle of adults.

Andrew's face bore evidence of the conflict he felt, the unasked questions, the joy of this talk. He felt the stab of his own guilt at conclusions his own age group had already reached. Now, there was question, and he feared they may have been wrong, hasty. He looked at Anna, resenting her open trust - her obviously single minded delight. For the first time in his life he consciously wanted to hurt her, shake her from that trust. He recoiled from the thought as soon as it surfaced. Andrew did not fool himself too often. For moments though, he drew himself apart, held his mind closed, looking closely at himself .He finally turned again to Jessie and Rose.

There was not a sleepy eye among them, they watched these two, listened as if the words were food to starving minds. Rose persisted,"Those students - do they go crazy ever? Can they finally bear the reality of this they learn?"

"Slowly the capacity to know, to bear knowledge, grows. Jessie smiled, glancing from face to face, reading them, touching their minds gently she revealed to them a faint glimpse of that tenderness that was a harbinger of Love Itself. She said softly, but with that Voice that drew their attention like a magnet,"Pay attention. Be aware of Love Present - now!"

For long moments there was silence. Jessie's mind held them, Touched, focussed, her mind open to them, that they might know something of what was

Present. She was like a window through which they could see. Trusting in her they opened themselves, their minds - realized without assumptions. With steady strength she held. And they accepted the gift of her strength to sustain attention. The silence enveloped their world, nothing stirred around them, for time was not a part of where they were. Jane's face was washed with silent tears. She clutched Steve's fingers. Other faces registered attention, listening, their eyes distant, they saw through and met the powerful knowledge of Love present. The touch of It they could bear. The fact of It? All they had ever known of Love had been less than a shadow of what was Present in that moment of consciousness. So obvious, so absolutely PRESENT, there, so unceasingly there. And IT HAD ALWAYS BEEN THERE! Would always be. They had only to become aware! The recognition filled them and they wept, turned and avoided out of the fullness of more than they could bear. In ordinary time a short moment passed, yet that moment had been outside of time, timeless! Every mind registered that fact. How blind they had been. How blind they still were. For a long time they sat absorbing.

Rose nodded finally, accepting, feeling the raw tenderness of that wonder. "To imagine this in our lives. To imagine human life with consciousness of THIS - even this brief awareness of Love would tranform us. It seems clear to me that to know of Love at all, one must be Conscious - Soul Conscious. Is that not so?"

"You see that?" Jessie murmured.

Rose frowned, puzzled, "That was like a Joining! But it was - was so unlimited!"

Jessie laughed softly, "Joining is not only communing with one another, it's recognizing the inseparable quality of Life!"

Benjamin spoke, hurriedly as if to fend off awareness with words, to break that overwhelming attention. "But what does that mean? That one must be already conscious? Is it that unless I am already Soul Conscious I cannot recognize that I have not been before?" He subsided into thought, wanting no answer.

Jerry shook his head ruefully, "All that Teachers taught are words. They are like opaque walls with a sign written on them that says,'See through me'. But this! This is Seeing! I can see that there are degrees of awareness, degrees of Soul consciousness even. It has to be a gradual process."

Jessie nodded to his questioning eyes,"You've learned well, Son. And its time to apply all you've learned."

He looked blank. Rose spoke, "It's the battle we've all had Jessie, the battle in ourselves. We are dual beings and we don't know how to balance all that we realize. We don't give up ego identity easily, I think. That Soul Self, it is so alien, yet so familiar. It is 'I', and yet it is so 'other'. When I stand there, at that point of Consciousness, then realize the universe from there, I know no conflict. There is no fear, no separation, no grief of loss. I feel so utterly alive. I, Soul am full of Life. It is so." Her voice rang and they looked at her with amazement for it seemed she spoke then from that high point. But then, settling, letting herself descend, feeling the difference, she smiled, tears filled her eyes. "I think I am willing to accept everything I am. I, Soul, live this life through a person called Rose. But Rose does not see far, Soul has far seeing. And there it is."

Paul was nodding, his eyes on her face. Rose glanced at Jennifer, wondering how it all seemed to her. Paul said, "And that's what we've known. What we now know. We do stand there, at that high point. We are beginning to be Soul Conscious. And awkwardly trying to speak of it in ordinary language. It doesn't work well." He felt the statement as a declaration of recognition never before acknowledged. It was as though he had passed through a painful narrow gate and found himself beyond that pain.

Jennifer, so long silent, said,"I feel torn apart- as though this-this- me, that is familiar, is also of little value. Is not really very conscious. I faintly suspect that there is more - that I've begun to experience being more. Then, I turn from thinking and remember the creating of music, and then I know that finding the new, the creation of anything, comes from that Soul state,by way of the intuitive mind. In those moments, I don't think at all. I record what I realize." She was silent, absorbing her own meaning. "But I couldn't have shared that with you - until now." She looked around as if only half seeing them,"Except for that - making of music - I hear what you say, and it still seems only words. I cannot grasp the ideas as real."

"Your self honesty is more valuable than you know now, Jennifer." Jessie reached out a hand, then let it fall. But Jennifer felt that she had been touched. "We must nourish all these parts of ourselves, none are of little value. It is the personal self, this familiar personal self that must finally know of Love and be able to bear IT." The Touch she had extended reached out to them all and they felt the encompassing closeness of it. Just as the Light had seemed to encompass them earlier, this quality of Love seemed now to unite them and to bring them such a sense of belonging that they could not have named it had they been asked. Such they had never known.

Ben watched Andrew, wondering about him for the hundredth time since he returned, and uncomfortably aware of a nagging guilt for being gone from him so long. He wanted to hear more from him, more of the ideas his son had developed during this year. At sixteen a year is long, much change occurs.Ben said,"Andy, do you understand these ideas? Are they different from those your Master Teachers give you?" He thought his question was lame, but anything to get Andrew to talk, to tell him something of his attitudes."

Andrew shook his head, frowning, wanting to reassure his father but refusing to. He felt ashamed, but anger overrode the shame and he answered bruskly,"Oh, Dad, the ideas aren't important. I don't think they are. It IS what the Master Teacher's tell us, of course. They've been doing it for years, but it's not the idea here, it's experiencing, it's doing exactly what Jessie's said. Knowing because it's real." He met his father's eyes and was startled by the look of fear that flashed before Ben hid it in a smile. Andrew shrank from that glimpse of fear, he resented it.

Jerry spoke suddenly, too loud, as if suddenly roused from reverie. "Oh Damn it. I feel just furious. There it is, just what you've said, Jessie, the whole thing - it's real. And it sets every familiar habit on edge. Questions everything I've thought. How can I believe what I can't explain? And yet, there it is, how can I deny what I experience, what I know?"

The mood among them had shifted, and Paul laughed."Don't feel alone there, Jerry. I've been listening too. Just notice the amazing quality of Light here. It isn't something I see, but rather something I'm -- Conscious of. As though it penetrates my mind. Vision isn't only through the eyes, perception of Light is direct mental seeing. From inside I see. I realize that to follow that light further, is all possibility, and yet, to do so loses me from myself. I feel myself disappearing and entering into what I cannot name." He sobered,"True, there is a fear -- but more,I feel an unreasonable hope. And I can't name what it is I hope for." Now his voice was sad, and when he met Jerry's eyes, he held himself distant. Softly he murmured so they could barely hear,"What humankind might become."

Jennifer came to sit on the grass beyond the carpet in front of Jerry, she used his bent legs as a back rest and leaned her head on his knees. She said,"There's bound to be problems. After all, remember , 'Old identities fear to be left behind'." She quoted the Learning Center maxim of their school years and for the first time in her life it made sense.

Silvia had been sitting up against a tree trunk , her hands playing with a small yellow daisy. When she spoke into the silence it was with the slow intensity of one who reaches far back in her mind and fears to lose the fragile hold on an idea lying at the fringe of awareness. "I'm trying to tie it all together. I keep being reminded of Martha Dresden's research in psychoneurology nearly fifty years ago. She established reasonably that consciousness is a condition of life itself. That there is no life without consciousness, regardless of how microscopic or how different from ourselves. Humankind had always erred in thinking only animal life had consciousness. Now Valley citizens've proved that plants are conscious too. And now, you say - Earth Herself." She stopped, frowning, fumbling for what she wanted to say. They waited.

Finally, with a long indrawn breath, she went on,"So now, you're suggesting that there's consciousness and Life at a higher level, beyond human, beyond everything we know? I'm willing to accept that possibility, it helps me to explain these experiences of my own." She looked around, her mind so absorbed on her effort to complete the thought that she was wholly unselfconscious. "You've said ideas come down from that point of highest attention. I think they sweep over me like a tide, breaking up mental patterns, impressing themselves on my mind. As long as I'm willing, receptive." She smiled, then frowned again, suddenly unsure of her own thesis."Do I make sense?"

Paul spoke softly, as if to protect her intensity of attention,"What do you think it does to you?"

She looked at him gratefully and nodded," I think that automatically, once that possibility is allowed, it creates a shift in our entire perception of reality". She waved her arm vaguely, letting her fingers spread and push against the air,"It's like what happens in a computer when you insert a new phrase in the middle of something. Everything, in the flash of a second, readjusts to let it fit in". She turned then to look at the others,"I don't think we can expect to find that without pain."

Jerry was suddenly eager to pick up her thought."It's still a jump. It's as though we have to leap over - to project our minds over - empty space. to bridge a gulf." He was nodding now. "Yes, that's what it's like, a feeling of leaping from this dimension to another and not being able to live in both at once. One has to be either here, grounded, concrete, thinking in words, or one has to be there, mind conscious, dealing with some kind of 'mental substance' which must be mind stuff. It feels like going from something to nothing. But nothing is much, much more than something. But then, when I limit myself again, to this physical substance world, its like having to leave great roomy beauty and realness, to squeeze myself down to fit into this little universe." He shook his head, wanting her to continue.

She wanted to travel on this thread of thought that was her bridge from that greater world down to this lesser one. "But Jerry, I can't believe you just because you tell me about it. I can only know what I, myself, realize. Yet, when you tell me, since I do value your ideas, I make room for them a little and so a shadow shapes itself beyond me, beckoning, shaping out there, a shadow through which I might make the same leap you did."

Anna was nodding, and she surprised them by saying,"Yes, that's what Master Teacher, Nora, said last week. That we have to use imagination and focussed attention to lay a mental brick down on which we can step in order to lay the next. Then when we have a certain beginning, we can stand up and suddenly we see something of our direction. She says people do realize in a sudden perception once they've pushed through the thicket of assumptions. It seems very clear to me now." She stopped, her face deeply serious and the adults listened in surprise at her obvious understanding of what they found confusing."But then it's also obvious, Aunt Silvia, that we can use each other's imaginations and step out on another persons bricks of perception too. Make them our own in a way. Especially during the times we Touch mentally."

"Maybe you can, but I can't. I have to See it for myself. To realize, experience. Or it seems like I'm lost in clouds. Then I don't accept. " Ned frowned. wishing that he could realize everything at once, could perceive as easily a these young ones seemed to.

Silvia was looking at Anna, puzzled, shaking her head. "It's what they taught us too, Anna. Maybe we've been taught all these things and not until now did we really take them in. But still, I'm not sure what it means - - to use the imagination. Just what is that any way. I can understand something of what intellect does, how it works. I see it, use it, and it is effective. But imagination, seems so out of my control, so- - it seems actually to work better when I am not in control."

Anna laughed,"You know what Gerald would say to that? He says and it's his constant reminder, "Just what then is 'you' here? In this case, it looks as though 'you' Aunt Silvia, are your intellect who wants to be in control always. There is intuition too, you know. I wish Aunt Jennifer would tell us what she does, because she is not 'out of control' when she creates music. Yet it isn't done with her intellect. That's imagination, isn't it?" She was smiling but at Silvia's startled frown, she looked contrite."Oh, I didn't mean to - - "

Silvia shook her head, "No, don't apologize, Baby, if you can enter into this conversation at all you have a right to speak clearly. No, I think that's right and I hadn't thought of it at all. Imagination must be when the intuitive and intellectual minds bring realization down into concrete form?" She suddenly brutally tore the daisy to bits, scattering the broken petals over the ground. " Damn it , you all talk as though you have known of that sense of emptyness and that you've figured out how to leap across it. You are saying that you stand then in a place of clear perception that transcends what I get mired in." She was frowning, her face full of anger. "How am I supposed to do it? I can't bear the awful sense of dispair that is at the edge of - emptyness. If it's true, that you've met it, and been able to go beyond it, then for you the first bricks are set, you can go on. But for me, the IDEA of emptyness, the thought of it is so terrifying,I feel cold. I shrink away from every glimpse,from whatever perceptions I've had. I don't let myself think about them, I'm afraid thinking might just increase the hopelessness." Her face was suddenly bleak,with fear and hope interchanging in her eyes. She leaned forward, spreading her hands in the air toward them.

Instantly she felt the Touch of Jessie's Reach. She flinched, unaware from whence it came, but feeling the reassurance and then the acceptance. Energy flowed between them and Silvia relaxed.

Steve had been watching her closely. He said,"I don't blame you Silvia. But I just feel completely confused. How on Earth do you get to that place at all? To feeling real fear, or awe either?" He stood up, walked to the edge of the thick carpet, leaned against a young water maple tree. He lifted his hands in gesture of appeal, dropped them in resignation and said, "It's not just the creative process. It can't be. That doesn't cause either fear or awe, does it? Every research scientist does it, the very abstract glimpse, or vague 'idea' and then the imagining, the free play of imagination, and then the bringing into focus, etc. just as you've said. Artists do the same, a song, or dance goes through much the same process? But in this - this metaphysical research, how can one ever IMAGINE that Light you speak of, the wonder, the insights that seem to make you experience reality differently.

You don't! You realize them! That's very different. You say no one can imagine until he has realized in some degree?" He frowned, shook his head. That's new, the idea that intellect and intuition working together are imagination." He looked puzzled, wondering.

Benjamin, who had looked as though he was asleep, sat up,turned to face Steve with excitement in his eyes. "I think you're right, Steve. No one just imagines a new mathmatical concept, a song,or a poem. The truth of it's always given, the given seed, we call it perception,that comes through the intuitive mind, doesn't it" He stopped, his gaze off among the hills, wanting to catch hold of logical understanding. "There is a process, you know, that creators use. They focus and sustain attention at as high a point as they are able, through deep thought,or intense desire. It seems to press against an interface, the separation between the known and unknown. The attention held there, seems to tire the thinking mind and finally released, consciousness moves out, receptive to the unknown. It happens in intensely focussed meditation or prayer. That was the way of the mystics. Long term pain, grief, joy, or unrelenting thought can result in that breaking through. The flicker of perception, the seed, is presented to consciousness complete. It may overwhelm, true. Then we try to form what was realized into thought or numbers or sound. I think sound or numbers holds a perception even more accurately than words, maybe.But we can't talk about it without words". He looked around at them. "This is what I believe has been happening with us."

Benjamin held his hands poised before his face in a tent, he was completely absorbed in thought. He frowned, persuing the elusive edge," Yes, yes,Steve,I think you've got it. I really believe we don't imagine until the new is perceived. We translate perception into language so we can think about it." He stopped, looked around as if surprised to see them all there.

Rose asked, "Benjamin, at the North Station you saw people do this deliberately, through intense attention of some kind. So it means we can bring ourselves to the edge of perception by choice?"

He looked toward her, his eyes unseeing," After all,it's our own mind into which the perception comes, I think the old austerities, humiliations of the flesh, intense meditations, were ways to leave the mind nothing but itself to look through. And to turn the attention from flesh to mind. But that's like burning the barn to get roast pig. We learn to focus attention as children and focus,emptying the mind, brings us to that point of perception." He was silent a moment then,"Did you know that people once used drugs to fling themselves across the point of perception? And it worked, but they had not the mental equipment to make use of it. It only resulted in mental fireworks that couldn't be translated".

Tom broke in,"But we're finding ourselves realizing whether we've chosen to or not. We see that Light for instance, the Touch of Love, of Life around us. We realized so much just a bit ago. That was spontanious."

Ben nodded," Yes, but I think it's because something's changed in people. We've taught ourselves, we focus, but there's a new quality in us that sees more clearly. It has to be. It's true,it takes great discipline of mind to Reach, and to Touch to one another's minds. But to Reach further, into that ultimate point long enough to perceive beyond it, requires all our being. To know the Touch of Vision" .

Rose spoke softly,"Ah,Love, you've learned so much. Your understanding is clear to me. I know you've seen that Vision, even though you might have denied it. You are able to Reach to us, and beyond us! Isn't that so?" She wanted him to speak the words she had so long wished for.Their eyes met, he drew himself out of that profound contemplation of idea and then he slowly, reluctantly nodded.

THE AWAKENING

"There is no doubt of it, my Dear."

Silvia watched them, sighing. Jessie said softly, "Silvia, if you haven't experienced something beyond the ordinary, then how can you know anything at all of what you call 'emptyness'? The very fact that you speak of it suggests that you have come to the edge of it."

Silvia shrugged, She was silent. Her mind raced, catching at the stream of awakened thought, shying away, returning. "Oh, I get so angry."

"Angry, Angry at what?"

She dared to meet Jessie's eyes in a brief look, then stared off across the River. The quiet flow of water, so natural and so 'real' gave her peace. She watched a bird speed to the water surface and skim then rise swiftly with fish in its beak. Finally she said, "I think because I'm afraid."

"Is it a sense of what Rose called "too much?" Jessie spoke from a stillness that surrounded her. Her body unmoving, relaxed and her whole person radiating a quiet that extended among them.

Paul reached over to take Silvia's hand, "Sil, you know you aren't alone on that. It does seem to be 'too much'."

Silvia nodded, bit into an apple, resettled herself, looked around at the Earth, the trees, reattaching herself to this everyday experience. She said, "Yes, it is TOO MUCH". She leaned back again, silent, wanting to ponder what had been said and wanting to run away and forget it all. It was as though her mind reached out of her. She wanted to bring attention back to this crisp, sweet-tart apple. She focussed her attention on it, on the sensation of this moment and felt a comforting. Then with surprise, a wash of amusement that poured through her stretched and receptive mind. She was aware! Here was everything, here just in this instant of tasting. Present! The reality of it swept away thought. She was aware, shaken, full. She caught her breath and then closed her self with a mental snap. The idea came, 'then that is the glimpse?'

There grew a great silence among them then, so dense it seemed palpable. No one wanted to press through it, to injure its perfection. They sat under the young green leaves, the sparkle of the full River. The world seemed to merge, to separate, to encompass them and to reject them. They swung back and forth from forgetting themselves in awareness of everything else, into an acute self consciousness that exposed them to their own recognition mercilessly. Then as if in reflex, they swung again out to notice themselves as from a distance, their bodies unseparate from Earth. Each point of view seemed incomplete, yet, they would not come together. They could not see all the facets of perception at once. Jessie watched the process, seeing their recognitions, seeing their knowledges penetrate each other, and seeing their mutual support and their rising power.

Steve felt himself propelled from one state to another, wanting to resist, wanting to be a part of this. He could not speak. Everything seemed unfamiliar and yet so deeply preciously familiar.

Jane listened thoughtfully, aware of the energy among them, conscious that she kept wanting to run away. She wanted to know, and she didn't want to know.

Tom broke the silence finally, speaking his rambling thought."I thought that this Touch, this thing we know now as the beginning of Joining, was the ultimate, that that was the greatest Reach human beings would take. I thought it was the big thing. The Healers do something similar all the time: we've always known that but never added it up. We thought they did 'magic'. When Cassandra told us about doing that 'lifting',I thought it was the strangest possible experience. But these are like all Talents, focussed uses of the mind. What we're trying to find words for now -- is vastly more!"

Ned had sat up, small leaves caught in the tight curls of his hair, gave him a rakish look, but he spoke with intense seriousness. Abruptly he said," It's this - this! That we've just - - just Touched against, you'd call it glimpsed, wouldn't you? That HAS happened to me. Long ago. I - I tried to ignore it. Too much, just as you say." His face broke into a vast look of surprise." What is beginning to happen, what we're trying to name - to understand - is REAL. It's what we see first as Light. The consciousness of Spirit. That's it isn't it?" He sat utterly absorbed in that revelation.

Jessie watched him, wanting more, wanting him to make it clear for himself and so for the others. Rose met her eyes, their minds met and Jessie saw images of that secret cliff, the long vigils there, the bodyless state that Rose had kept secret.

She nodded,"There is confusion about the way our minds change as we wake and realize. Soul realization is an evolutionary process that includes many changes, of mind, heart and body."

Paul nodded slowly, his eyes never leaving Jessie's face. "Now we must deal with that, because it is the Builders who have noticed some of these things and they do not know that they are simply psychic Talents, that they accompany growth and that they can be misused as easily as any other trait we have. They are afraid of them and they have a right to be. They hate what they see and don't understand,but as you've mentioned, one can't explain what one has not at all experienced. They do not, will not, hate us for the depths of our Love, the heights of our mind. Largeness is never hated, only smallness. They may not know that, but they will respond to it. We'd better watch that in ourselves because we see our personal smallness acting for us every day." He was intent that they see these differences.

"Then what do we do?" Tom's gaze was troubled. "I think much of the time, I AM small."

"Of course, and you know it." Paul smiled, " We've got to talk to them. We've never done that because we weren't talking to each other. If they can't hear us, then, we get help."

" Everyone has been taught by the Master Teachers. We didn't understand enough to prevent our mistakes, how can they?" Jerry sounded angry.

Jessie was silent,then slowly she said," They may not. But we can begin to listen."

Rose nodded, her eyes moving from one face to another,"We've been afraid ourselves. And fear against fear will result in trouble. We, ourselves, fear the Builders." She watched them, letting the thought register. "Isn't that enough evidence that we react in fear rather than respond in Love?"

Ned nodded slowly, "Yes, I can see why they're afraid. After all. If I didn't know why, I think I'd be afraid when I see people, and yes, especially children sitting silently looking at one another, in some kind of 'trance'. Yes, I'd worry about them."

Jerry said, "Well, you can find a lot of people beginning to Reach and to Touch and yet we've denied it. If we who are only in our thirties can refuse the facts, then surely those older ones, with less experience and knowledge, would have trouble." He glanced at Silvia and found her face full of consternation, even shame. He wanted to comfort her, reassure her, but aborted the impulse. She didn't need it.

He hastened to go on, "Look at us. I've denied. We've all denied. We've all pretended that we were the only ones afraid, or aware. Our kids didn't talk to us because they thought we were not willing. Which was true! We stll refuse the Joining. Even the surface Joining." He turned to Steve and Reached with a cruel sharp insistence and as Steve's resistance broke, Jerry saw a dawning knowledge there. He saw the startled amazement on Steve's face. But Jerry felt the shock of those in the group who watched the mental action. He withdrew instantly, shaking his head. "Oh, No. I had no right to do that."

"You're right. You know enough to know why." Paul was stern.

Jerry held his head, shaking it still, "It was not an act of Love, it was one of anger. Oh, My God. How can I expect more from anyone else, when I let myself react that easily? I'm sorry Steve. It wasn't fair of me to pry. It's that one permanent Taboo of our learning and I had no right!" He was so abjectly sorry that Steve couldn't resist a grin, even though his own mind was absorbed in trying to grasp what had happened. Fear and longing wrestled in him, but astonishment wiped them both away. He bent his head, wanting to accept that glimpse.

Jessie, watching, nodded, her face quiet and sad. "It is something that needs correcting. These hidden talents, these denials, these fears of acknowledging even the facts. But what we've reached today is another matter. What our earlier talk touched upon is crucial to our development as human beings. Do we consciously see that? Everyone here realized that Light that surrounded us earlier. We were aware of the Touch of Spirit, the wakening in our hearts. Are we ready to agree that Reaching toward that Light extends our minds? And in that extension is Vision of what has been unknown?"

Silvia said, "I will admit that, Jessie. I think I realize something now. Something beyond myself, about Earth, and about that Light, that I see now literally shining around Paul." She looked wonderingly around, "It's there around -- all of you. It's hard to believe that that is the nature of each one of us. It's such a wonder that I ache with its possibility. I want to find words to say what I know right now."

Jerry longed to Reach to Silvia, to Touch in that true way. He had wanted that

Touch for so long. When she is ready, he must be aware.

Ben was silent, then spoke in a whisper."Even though I fought the knowledge, I know now it's what I've looked for all my life. What we've all been looking for. And all these years it was right here. Right here in ME. I didn't even have to move out of my room".He looked aound at them, as if seeing them for the first time. Cassandra got up and went to him, wrapped her arms around his neck and leaned against his shoulder. His arm went round her waist and he pulled her to his side.

Again silence held. Then finally Jerry said as out of an explosion of thought,"Yes, yes! Knowing together! Knowing together! What an old phrase." He sat up, reached for another sandwich and sat eating thoughtfully staring at the grass beneath his legs.

Jessie shook her head,"You will see. There are not limits to this gift that is given us, the limits are our own awareness. Talent may or may not be present in those who perceive the inner Light."

They were silent for some time. The sunlight slanted now, spreading long pencils of shadow across the fields. The late afternoon air was growing chill. But no one noticed. Rose broke this silence with a long sigh." Even such little experience as I've had with the Joining, mostly during Valley Council with those wonderful people there,has made me know it is like nothing we can do alone. We create something with our minds together,something that isn't there when we are alone."

"The whole is greater than the parts? " Silvia spoke absently. Her voice was light as a child's, not the strong alto her woman hood had given her. Then she cleared her throat,"This is a special day, we've been together doing the planting. Everybody has finally talked about all their secrets. I feel more tuned to all of you, to Life itself. I think I actually see now that there is life and there is Life. So - maybe if we tried to listen, listen with our entire minds, to intuitively sense what we know, maybe we might be able to share it." She found her eyes seeking Jerry's and his were there, on her face, finding her and with a joy such as she had not seen in his eyes. He thought,'she will be willing'!

Jessie was nodding,"It's true. If there is to be anything come of it then it must be daily practice, daily focus of attention and daily Reaching out without fear."

Anna moved, a sudden impatient gesture, her face tight with a frown." I think you all - " She stopped,then determined, she went on, " You talk too much. You don't need to. Just DO it. Join! Know that way! It's all right in front of us!"

Paul snorted, frowning , then his face relaxed and he smiled at her,"I'm sorry. I didn't mean that . I- it's just that -, he stumbled lamely, a wry smile softening his face, "It's not so simple for us old folks". She leaned against him, sad, and he stroked her hair, "We just have to do it this way, Honey. We haven't talked until now, and talking will lead us to that Joining that seems to natural to you children".

Jennifer stood up, walked slowly out into the field and then came back. Her hands tightly clasped,"I'm only barely willing to listen to the talk. Oh dear, Anna, please don't ask more, Sweetheart. I cannot yet bear to understand all I am

THE AWAKENING

realizing.I keep myself intact with an effort."

Anna went to her, tears in her eyes that she had brought pain to this loved Aunt. Together they sat down near to Paul.

Rose heard but her gaze was far off into the mountains beyond the Great River, letting her mind drown in that far mistiness where no thought formed, then with a long sigh, she said. "Finally we admit that we are aware of that Other. That Presence of Spirit.I am sure all humankind is and perhaps all animal kind also. In some deep place in us we have always felt that 'Other'. Whether we can name it or not,is irrelevant."

Jessie asked,"What is that like for you, to sense that Presence. What does it mean for you."

Rose did not bring her gaze back to them. She spoke out of that distance. "Sometimes I feel as though I'm like an eagle,soaring everywhere, seeing everything. Sometimes in dreams I can live out that experience very realistically and it is as though every fragment of existance, every possible thought or thing of Earth and of human creation is glimpsed somehow by my sharp eyes. There I go, to grasp one thread of each thing of Earth, one thread which I bring back and carry to the heights to build my nest. I know I will not cease to do this. But then on that other hand, I know that I steel myself to fly just as steadily into that 'unknown' to bring back one thread of Vision of what is beyond this. I struggle to make that fit somehow into some acceptable form so that it will be a part of the nest I've built here in this world. This mental nest of what is known and safe. But then, it's only a nest. Does any bird know at the moment for what the nest is being made. How can it know of the egg, until the egg is there,how know of that life unseen within that egg? The Eagle builds on an inner trust, unknown to it. Must what is to be born wait for a complete and perfect nest? Must I wait until everything understood, is completely safe? Why can't I just embrace what is unknown? The Eagle does, by not thinking of tomorrow but accepting what is now. Consciousness is the receptive nest which will receive new life. How can I know of the egg? Do I prevent the very coming of that Life, by my insistence on understanding everything first? Understanding before I will allow?" She turned her head then, moving her gaze from one to the other as if hoping to find an answer. Finally she met Jessie's eyes and saw the quiet nod.

"But the nest, Rose, whatever it is, it does create a place from which to see. Perhaps seeing the flaw of the nest is an important matter too."Jessie looked at the others. "Well, the blind men who sought to understand the elephant were no less struggling than we to understand, in our own blindness, this unknown that we glimpse. Maybe the rest of you would offer your own images."

Rose sat up straight, "Oh yes,that would help. I never thought of asking anyone."

Paul nodded to her, willing. "I've never tried to speak of it at all. It's too strange. But, I see how it could help. What YOU said, helped me Rose." He was silent, gathering his memories, "I think that sometimes I sense a far vison, as if all Earth is before me, as if I must be far out in space. Only I seem to be aware of the whole of humanity and the streaming energy of our Reach toward what we might become. Then, I know of that resistence, clinging to us, darkening the brightness of the energy stream, weighing it down so it cannot flow. Energy flows freely through all creation, all lives. We animals who are self conscious,have been burdened with a terrible gift and with it came a loss".

He bent his head, letting his fingers smooth the fiber of the carpet, slide off it and break off grass blades which he drew to his mouth. "It's learning how to stand in my fear and pay attention to that Light.I desire to enter into that Light with all my heart, yet, I deny its existence with all my thought.I deny and yet I long for that next step. I feel as though my life depends on it."As Rose watched him she could see the radiance that trembled about them all.

There was a long silence, everyone absorbing what Paul had said, feeling the great depth of energy that rose all around them, formed a sphere within which they sat. Finally Ben cleared his throat, he sat up, leaned back then sat straight again. He wrestled with his old desire to surpass Paul and he knew disgust with himself for the desire. Immediately aware of the trap that hovered in that disgust, he shrugged and a surge of mild amusement dissolved it. No, he would not go down that by way. He turned to them, acknowledging his dilemma and shook his head."I don't know whether I can say what that Touch of Spirit is like for me. I've not acknowledged that that is what it is. Now, though I understand the times when I feel lost to myself, as though I don't know who I am. I've lost track of myself.I can't quite settle for my identity as this 'Ben'. Somewhere in me is a knowledge - clear knowledge - that I'm, no, WE are something more. Yet, I've never known how to understand that."

Steve's voice was harsh,on the edge of dispair,"Well, you're not saying what you do. What do you DO, Man, when you don't understand?"

Ben shook his head,he didn't want to talk about himself.He didn't want to try to think so deeply of things that he had avoided so long." I don't know. Maybe what I did this morning is something of it. I was just watching the Valley from the Deck, things waking, the cool air,so grey,before the sun rose, the wonder of the whole waking life. I lost myself in it. It was as though I was seeing beyond myself,beyond the Valley, including it but also far beyond. Right! I - I actually felt as though 'I'was included in the whole Valley. It was like watching a pond, the surface of it, and suddenly, the eye drops through, to what is beneath and there is something called 'Pond' that is a whole life, complete and wonderful. And I, a reflection, in its surface."

Everybody smiled except Steve, who was watching Ben with a keen intent gaze. Finally into the silence he said, his voice very low, filled with astonishment, "Ben,you too! Even you?"

Ben glanced at him but remained silent. Jerry stood up, walked around the group once, came back to his place and stood struggling with his thoughts. The day was drawing to a close, the sun hung near to the horizon and when it went down it would be colder. No one noticed, the Magic of this moment held them. The vitality of this communication offered from depths seldom shared was so

THE AWAKENING

intense, their attention so close, they had actually joined with one another in a light strong Joining. Only Jessie noticed.

Finally Jerry said, "Sometimes I feel as though I am in the center of a sphere that is all hurricane. When I am fully aware, then I seem to stand in the center and watch the racing universe go by,. All that we are,do, seem to be, is racing past me and I see. Then the power and grandeur of the great winds of our world business, our world creations, forming and unforming, becoming and ceasing to be, seem immeasurable. Humankind seems so hungry! Yet in this center, this place of stillness, I stand alone." He hesitated and added softly,"Conscious!" The admission was llike a blow. "And suddenly, in the midst of this vast perception, I feel dispair. How can I ever pass through this whirling ocean of everything that is our world, that constant storm of energy. It will tear me apart,absorb me, blind me. It does!" He stopped, his eyes distant, reliving the experience, his voice trembled. He passed his hands over his face as if wiping away a veil from his eyes. He blurted suddenly, " I've never even tried to describe all that to myself. Never put it into words. It changes things. Makes it a little less terrifying. "

After a few minutes of silence, he went on. His voice steady, his eyes soft now, His hands rose and fell suddenly as if in wearyness. "The Presence that comes through and pierces into our minds, opens us, breaks all the patterns that restrict our thought, our lives comes from the point of silence where I can see. Then I'm whirled into the current of events, of daily assumptions and habits, and sometimes I forget that. I lose perspective. I'm lost in the whirl." He was quiet. After several minutes, he said, his voice slow, as if finding each word carefully.

"Sometimes with great attention and balance, I can carry the stillness within me, I can enter into that whirl and remain conscious. If it were not for daily meditation, I could not find myself again each day. It's obvious to me that we, humankind, are so much more than we imagine. And it's equally obvious that we are beginning to know that and it scares us". He was silent, and no one spoke. The moment seemed so very full.

Jane spoke hesitantly, but her voice was clear and strong."I don't think about these things. I haven't -- been willing, I think. But now, listening to you all, I realize what I know. Sometimes when I stand alone, somewhere in the land, the beauty of living things, the pure wonder of Earth,saturates me, takes me far out of myself into itself so that I am lost." Her eyes were sad, then they widened in surprise."No, rather, I find my Self there! Yes, that's true. I have never put these thoughts into words before." She sat silent, her eyes narrowed and gazing across the freshly planted fields. Her voice softened,"But at that moment I'm at the edge of a sense of knowing that I've always feared. It is a feeling that I dare not enter, take one more step, one more breath of that wonder. If I do I might break! I don't want to move, speak, and surely I never think. I simply am."

She laughed shortly, and the spell of her memory was broken by that humour. She looked around, drew a long sigh, shook her head,"When I remember like this,I know again the Earth's breathing, the movement of Earth through me,as though the very colors of the spring paint me into themselves and I know no place where I end and Earth begins". She trembled slightly and her eyes were seeing far." There is the danger that I might See through -- everything -- especially myself!" Then she was silent again, for several minutes, and they waited. Finally she said, "Something there is that peers at me through beauty itself, something I cannot name." Tears ran down her face, and they knew she had never before penetrated so consciously to the depths of these experiences. "

The sun nearly touched the distant peak, it's light would soon be gone. They looked around now, seeing the wild life, feeling their interconnectedness intensely. A troop of wild pigs, all sizes, stood beyond a hedge, staring at them, drawn to their energy and their strangeness. The people and the pigs regarded one another silently for several minutes. Then a great boar grunted and stepped lightly forward, then stopped, the coarse bristles on his nose moved as he sniffed and tested their odors. Jessie smiled, pleased at their trust. Jane made a soft sound, the Boar turned to her, then dropped his head, began rooting in the grass. Ben stood suddenly, stretched, releasing the tension of his body with a yell. The pigs scattered disappearing among the trees. He smiled at them. Then he turned,"Jessie, would you add your own impressions to ours, then we'd better get home. It's nearly sundown and it'll be cold."

Jessie looked at the great red sun broken by the limbs of the trees and nodded,"I'll tell you of an image. I feel as though I am a seed, that there is a hard shell all round me, but within somewhere there is a tiny germ, just as all seeds have, that is their Life. That germ, in the human seed, is an eternal spark. And it is the germ that has waked me, pressed against my substance to cause growth, stretching and the shell that is my ego has cracked. There are thin roots that probe now deeper into that outer Life, that darkness that is unknown, and there are tiny thin shafts that pierce upward into that blinding light that is also unknown and fearful. How can I bear this? This breaking apart of what I think I am? Yet, now, after much refusal, I know that it is I who is to be consumed by that sprouting root and leaf." She smiled absently, as if she saw what she described.

Never have I known other than the inside of this shell. But somehow, without reason, the germ that is Spirit, Knows, insists and persists. I feel myself at times slowly dissolving, becoming nothing at all, And yet, I choose to permit this, because there is that which I also am , the growing plant, and as yet I do not know 'my' name." She was silent, they listened and what she said, seemed exactly true.

After a moment she said," The shell of this personal self has become so thin. The Light shines through, absorbing what I have been, and saturating me with Itself. I could not close myself away again, even were I to wish to. I am not separate any longer from that Light. I am giving myself to become root and leaf. You can see why death has no meaning for me, life is unceasing, penetrating everything, including everything, even death. And Life beckons." She bent her head then stood up in one supple movement. "There is no end, no end at all to Life." She laughed and stretched herself up, reaching her hands toward the tiny uncurled leaves above.

THE AWAKENING

Rose wanted something more, "But doesn't it ache within your mind,when you are conscious of it?"

Jessie laughed softly," Isn't the ache the desire to live at the height of consciousness, the desire to break apart and expand into Life opposed to the fear, the refusal to respond to Life?"

Rose nodded slowly, accepting, "What can I do"?

"Several of you spoke of fear, the denying and resisting the growth, the change. It's part of the process, it is natural that the familiar self will resist the journey outward into that Self. Just as the seed envelop resists rotting away to allow the inner heart to send forth new life. For there is an unfamiliar universe. Allow that Light to soften and wear away the old shell and know that that Light is Life. Accept as you gradually See.And the fear will fade. Observe, speak of it, share with one another the experience so that you can see that it is universal and that it is natural. After all, soon you will find what has seemed strange, to be not strange at all, but normal."

" She waved one hand, "Now, look and see how our children take our seriousness?" She laughed again and they looked to see Anna and Andrew curled asleep in the deep grass."They listen to us in their dreams perhaps. They listen to their own hearts without fear" But the children woke, turned to her, meeting her eyes. She nodded.

Anna said,"Look! We've come together, Mother, we've come so close. Can we continue. At Jessie's nod, she glanced at her brother and together they Reached, encompassd and felt Jessie's presence with them. Slowly, they drew each of the others into that Reach, so that the Joining deepened. Light, delicate, tentative, but true. The family had Touched against one another in a Joining. It lasted only a moment, but was an intimacy, an expansion of being, such as none had known alone. Then, it fell, faded, and Anna and Andrew tears in their eyes, looked at Jessie and laughed.

They began gathering their baskets and tools, rolled up the carpet and went slowly through the fading light to the Hall. There was no talk during that walk home.

The next day was the first day of Spring Festival. The time for Adwin to be presented to the Valley as a finished town. The honors and the speeches, the music created for the occasion, the dances, would make the celebration memorable. The whole town seemed to burst forth in color and action. There were Gaily decorated bicycles, air cars, floats, Vagabond Lowcarts, horses, boats of every size and belted travelers coming in from every direction to celebrate.The Vagabonds came in off the Highways, swarming into town, people descended from the skies in every kind of vehicle that would fly. The town was so full it was itself a fair. Every restaurant, public dining hall, cafe, or bar, was full. People met to talk in the paved courts all over town, children plunged into the fountains and there was laughter, talk, noise.

The Vagabonds gathered in Learning Center Halls and in open courts and

THE PEOPLE OF THE VALLEY

taught the town people their dances, their songs and many came with instruments to join the music. Singing was endemic. No citizen of the Great Valley was without training and knew enough to enjoy the best when it was performed for them . The products of cities and towns all over the Valley were displayed in stalls for trading and the Vagabonds brought not only their songs and dance, but their wonderful creations of woven, embroidered and knitted clothes, rugs, and tapestrys.

The games were played on fields of the Learning Center and the great five acre field north west of Adwin, where three games could run at once with enough seats for the comparatively few spectators. People wanted to do things; they were not as eager to watch. The last day and night of Festival was reserved for the final performances of Games, theatre, music and dance . Then the Hall or stadium was filled.

After four days of Festival in Adwin, Jasper's began and after that Denlock's,and there were crowds for each one. But life got back to normal by April. Silvia and Jerry brought the Family together to talk of their idea of opening a restaurant in Adwin. There was only one in the town. Most people ate at Public Dining halls, because they were cheaper and because during the long years of building the town, everyone got into the habit. There were cafes sponsored by the Learning Center for teaching, but only two were owned and operated by adults.

Silvia talked with the eager animated manner that characterized her when she was excited."We want to find cooks who know how to cook food from at least four nations. Especially those not well known. We want something different every day of the week. And we want to decorate to fit with ethnic themes. She brought out a sheaf of large posters on which were beautifully painted the interiors of such a restaurant. You see, we've got ideas here. We'll go over them with the cooks and see whether they're accurate enough. But that's the idea"

Jerry brought the posters to an easle at the front of the room and everyone could see the bright designs. He said,"We've got credit built up from our years of work and now that Adwin's been paying us, we've saved enough to get started. We want to begin this spring. Anyone have any objection?"

Everyone looked at everyone else, no one could think of any reason not to do it. Rose laughed, pleased that they were finding a new adventure for themselves. It would not strain Silvia's strength during the months carrying her baby, and it would be an asset to the town.She nodded her head briskly,"Well, Silvia and Jerry, if it's what you want to do, then I say, go ahead. Silvia's skilled enough with business methods that she ought to be able to attend to that. You can see that everything else goes right. You'll both have to learn a lot."

Jerry said, "We've already registered at the Learning Center to take the 'Fast Training'on Restaurant management using those Learning Hoods that the town bought two years ago. It'll be the first time we've tried them. Do they really work well?"

Tom said, "They do. If you're really willing to learn and what you need to know is basic information, facts, etc. I understand they don't do so well on an

THE AWAKENING

unwilling subject or to teach people to think." He laughed as at a private joke. Jerry looked at him puzzled but didn't want to persue the question. But Tom said,"You've heard of 'brain washing? Well, it seems when the inventers first demonstrated these they were received with horror that they could be used by an unethical government to force train workers for particular jobs. So they went back to work and fixed them so they won't work for that. I suppose that someone will come up with the way to by pass the barriers,if there was someone unscrupulous enough to want to. But then the World Council saw the possible danger and passed a law that this could not be done. No equipment that will work with an unwilling subject can be manufactured, So it's safe." He sobered, looking at their smiling faces,"It seems funny to you, but there is still that possibility among us. We aren't so much more wise than our ancesters were sometimes. We still have greed among us. It's just that we recognize it."

And so within a week, the two were happily in town creating their new business. The rest of the family was back at the routine work of life, trying to absorb the profound changes they knew from the Spring Gather. Jessie went about, remaining away for two or three days at a time, sometimes a week. She seemed always to be there when she was needed, but the work she chose kept her busy.

CHAPTER TWENTY

Jane and Roderick, Silvia and Justine

The Gather at Spring Planting made a very real difference for family members. Each one needed and found time for solitude to explore what had been discovered. Each one looked at the others with a new vision. Benjamin went back to work at the designing of small machine parts, to the laboratory at the Learning Center and to his hours of teaching. He felt renewed, ready to take a new place in his community. The world seemed to him unfamiliar, as though he had been blind all his life. He walked often with a sense of wonder, and a searching eye.

Jane wanted time to herself. Time and quiet. She said to Steve, when he sought her out,"Just give me time,Love, it'll all work out. I have to think. And maybe you need to as well."

Her avoidance of him hurt. He examined his feelings and realized how much he depended on her company, her presence. And finally it made him fully aware of his need for her. Out of that, he acknowledged how far beyond need was his love for her. Had she intended it, she could not have chosen a better way to wake him up. But she seemed unaware of him. He watched her, wondering. Finally, after three lonely days, she seemed to gather together her thought, to accept something she had doubted and as if she wanted to make up for refusing him,she went that evening to his cottage and found there a reception deeper than any she had known. He was relieved, full of a joy he had thought would never be his again. Her abstraction, her habit of meeting his eyes with a puzzled wistfulness, only increased his desire to protect and care for her.

Jane worked hard in the fields, she was so absorbed in work and thought she seldom spoke and so it was with relief that Silvia got a message that she must bring Jane with her to next Town Council. Why, Silvia didn't know, but she was convinced that involvement in town concerns would bring Jane back to them.

On a bright day in late April Silvia reminded Jane at breakfast that it was today the Council met. Jane said,"I'm going in immediately, because I've a couple of things at the drama department that I promised to help with. I'll meet you there." Silvia nodded, idly eating and letting herself enter this day slowly. Her increasing belly was visible enough now that she felt a shy pride in it. Feeling the rounded contours she thought she should indulge herself a little in consideration of this immense project. She said, grinning up at Jane, who was pulling on a soft brown jacket,"Ah-hah, so someone else is worried that you aren't going to get back to us!" Their eyes met and Jane smiled, nodding. A few minutes later, Jane left abruptly, still deep in the thought that had occupied her for days.

She met Steve just coming from his cottage. And suddenly, surprisingly she went to him and sought his arms, there on the deck as if seeking comfort. He happily gathered her into his arms and buried his face in her hair. And she drew

THE AWAKENING

away slowly, meeting his eyes and seeing them seeking understanding from hers. She nodded,"These few nights we've been together have been wonderful, my Love. Even when I seem to ignore you. You are more important to me than my life right now. You don't know how I look forward to our being together. It's like finally coming home." He nodded,and let her go on down the walkway toward town.

Walking toward town, she thought of those wonderful nights, the surprise of them. Steve's long grieving had caused her to expect little response from him and in these days of trying to bring to balance all she realized at the Gather, she had let her longing for him drop beneath notice. And then to her surprise he had changed, seemed different. The talk about how everyone had been denying because they didn't want to see the facts, had made him think. He began to recognize what he had been denying and in his case, it was not the Builders. It was not of the new Talents. It was his genuine growing love for her. Jane smiled, enjoying the memory, the way he had so swiftly acknowledged his denials. And she had refused to play the games of resentment for that denial though a little resentment had surfaced in a kind of petulance of retaliation. She had so long wanted him to know of her love. She had simply accepted and been glad for the change in him.

Her long strides carried her rapidly toward town. What could the Council want with her? She knew what the drama department wanted, she'd already been working with the stage crew for a couple of days,this morning they would look at the results.They had needed help with a set,and she had experience back stage from the years with her parents and their constant interest in theatre work. She reached tenderly to touch a vine as she passed. The tiny bunches of grapes were green and abundant. It would be a good crop.The older vines already traveling over the arbors above the pathway, were barely leafed out but their fruit had formed as soon as the leaves opened. As always, she felt that she walked among friends, and smiled at that. She thought of this special Council meeting,it had been called to decide about the Healing Center Building. The rooms that had been used in one end of the Learning Center, were no longer adequate, if they ever had been. Now the town could take time to build a proper Hospital and Healing Center. She thought she had very little to suggest. How could she help? She went to the theatre in the great Hall of the Center and they were waiting for her. Their sets were done and she looked at them, surprised as she entered. They were better than she'd hoped but something was wrong. After an hour of talk and adjusting,they found a solution and the crew went back to work. She left.

She saw Silvia coming across a field from the Learning Center and then watched her disappear down the slopes where the clusters of residences were built. Jane waited at the plaza that opened into the Civic Center gardens. The great outer ring of the Civic Center seen across this wide swail in which the residences were built, seemed to her to be like the walls of a city. Long wide windows made a checkerboard of the heavy stone walls, but from where she stood, the walls looked solid. Down the slope in front of her, two and three story

445

cluster houses dotted the land between trees and gardens. One long curving set of apartments, for uncommitted young or bachelors made a wall at the bottom of the saddle near the River edges. Wide courts with deep fountain pools filled the flat area between them the first cluster houses. In the early years of building, everyone had lived either in these or in the Learning Center, first built of all the Ring Centers.

She was remembering how it had seemed to her then when Silvia appeared, popping out from behind a long row of blue berries that edged that path. Jane's practiced eye scanned the bushes, thirty of them, set here to curve around a sudden bend and to give more privacy to the cluster of homes whose roofs she could see just beyond. She nodded, pleased at their obvious health and at the buds ready to break into bloom. She slid her fingers into the dropping branch of a dark purple lilac, drawing it to her to inhale the fragrance. Daffodils and narcisus bobbed and bent in the breeze over the hill side. Then Silvia was there. They walked up the slope and into the Civic Center path.

She said,"I've been thinking I'm probably the poorest selection the Council could have chosen. What do I know of building a Healing Center?"

Silvia smiled at her absently, her mind still on the decorating of her restaurant. Then she realized she had not answered and said,"Because you know about plants, and how they grow and what they're useful for. We can't be asking for help from Altos every time something like this comes up. We need to plant the gardens for the Healing Center, all the herbs, the trees, everything that can be grown for their use. And it needs to be done soon, so it'll be ready by the time the building is done. In fact, we need more herbs now, in the old center. You have to tell us how. And besides, it's your turn."She grinned impishly.

Jane nodded, looking down at the small woman who was her sister-friend and slowly nodded."I suppose so." They walked swiftly through the outer ring and crossed the inner gardens. The deep shade of the center ring archway seemed to Jane uninviting on this cool morning. They stopped to read the big sheet of duraglass that held a map of the Center, and announcements of meetings. It was chily standing reading there. She was glad to find the morning sun slanting into the large circle court and garden around the three storied plasteel and stone building where town business and government was done. They walked past Tom's offices but didn't stop to visit. He would be busy . They went into a small room. People were drifting in, some seated already in chairs or on great cushions on the floor. Jane and Silvia got hot drinks from the dispenser and went to sit down. It would be a very informal meeting. Jane was glad for that.

They settled into cushions and sipped their drink, responding to friendly nods and smiles from various people around them. Then someone initiated the beginning by taking his neighbors hands and as everyone followed suit, they became a large circle connected. Some bent their heads in deep focus, others fixed their gaze across the room and out the windows, and some simply watched the baby who crawled around in the circle they made. He was grunting with every move and had obviously only learned to crawl.

THE AWAKENING

For some moments there was a settling and bringing together of their energy. Then a woman softly began to sing. Her voice was light and sweet, the song a spontanious expression of what she was thinking.

> We are gathered together,
> Gathered together, all of us coming here
> To learn how, to learn how,
> To create our Healing center.
> A place of healing, of body, heart and mind,
> A place of healing where the soul wakes,
> Where the Soul wakes and expresses Itself in health.

She stopped then, paused and began again with another melody.

> Where the heart sings,
> where the mind bursts into fire,
> Where the ocean of consciousness wells up,
> And overflows into joy, realization and wonder,
> There is the heart of the Healing Center,

Others joined her, singing her words as if they too knew them. Then as suddenly as it started, it stopped. Jane was startled. Obviously other people were thinking and talking of that waking of Spirit too. Abruptly a small, thin man said,"What do we have to remember in planning this center? What must a Healing Center be? What needs to be included? For a time again there was silence. Then an older woman began chanting a prayer. She called the Eternal Presence to bless their efforts and give them knowledge to create a center where true healing could occur. Her voice rang out like a bell, then faded into a whisper. Her chant filled the room with calm. The pain of some sorrow darkened her eyes, but pressing through it, radiated a still joy that touched Jane and erased the sympathy she had felt. There was silence again.

Then a man that Jane knew as Oscar, lifted his head, looked around, reached his hand to touch another man sitting near. The other had been turned away, but now, after hesitation, he lifted his eyes and finally met Oscar's. There was a taut second before he let his own arm move, reach and meet Oscar's extended hand. They slid hands up to clasp around wrists and exchanged a faint smile. There was a long sigh of relief around the circle as this long standing resentment began resolution. A low hum rose from the other side of the circle and then the simple sound of the OM filled the room, rising and falling like gentle waves. The baby turned to find the source of the sound and then eyes wide, watched the adults, all the while making small sounds of his own. Suddenly, he curled up and tipped over on his side, his eyes closed, then opened to watch, then closed in sleep.

The sounds ceased, they dropped hands, settled back, and a woman named

THE PEOPLE OF THE VALLEY

Natalie,, an architect, said,"I'm very glad we're finally getting this done. I've always thought it was wrong to wait so long. But then, maybe it's true, we'll do a better job now that we have time to give to it. We not only need the building, but our Healing staff is too small. Adwin's grown, we've got a lot more people now and people depend on that staff for a lot of things. We need at least one chemical and three medical specialists, three more Healers, and ten more nursing staff. We don't need much stock because we've ordered recently with the new facilities in mind, but we have no place to adequately store all the supplies when they get here."

"Do we have any Healers living here that aren't already part of the staff?" A short stout woman with a cheery face questioned.

" We have only one. We'll have to find Healers from other cities. There are two Adwin children in training at North Station, but they've got years ahead of them. We do have two students finishing training as medical specialists in New York and they'll both be home soon and the new center'll give them space to work". She frowned, "As far as nursing staff is concerned, we'll have to count on student help until we can find qualified professionals enough."

A woman big with child adjusted her body more comfortably in her low chair and said,"I'm here to represent the Healers now working in Adwin. I've got their requests. I volunteered to represent them, since I'm soon to deliver and am not much use in the Center." She looked around,"We've made contact with North Station. they'll send two Healers in a month, but those only are willing to work here until our children finish."

Natalie nodded, " Well, that'll help. As for the building,we've got the construction site. It'll be at the far end of the playing field south of the Learning Center. It overlooks the River on that bluff there and is a wonderful spot". She cleared her throat and went on,"We've also got the basic plans, but Jennifer and Arthur, will you please get the architects to finish the details". The two referred to, looked at one another and nodded. Natalie turned to a big bearded man next to her, "Billie, when will the stone masons be free from other building to begin.?"

He laughed,"We've been waiting. We're finished with the work of this town, except for a few small jobs. You just give us the plans and the word and we'll begin work."

Natalie, nodded,"We'll have the plans in your hands in two days. I've never known a Healer who didn't know exactly what she or he wanted". She turned again to the pregnant Healer.

But it was a man across the circle who answered. "Just as you say, we don't waste time. As Clara told you, we've given her the job, so we'll settle for what she decides."

Billie,laughed, "Then there it is. You meet today, and if the architects can finish the plans tomorrow, I'll call the crews in by Wednesday." He look over at Silvia,"Will you be working with us this time, Silvia?"

Silvia shook her head."I'm too busy working on our restaurant. And I'm also pregnant enough to want a little less heavy work. Jerry and I've finally decided and we're already starting the decorating. She hesitated, frowning,"Do you think you'll need me?"

He shook his big head, frowning, but with a friendly look in his eyes, "We've got plenty of help, now the town Centers are built. We've even sent some of our crews to work at Adderson. But then, a restaurant? That's a risky business you know".

She grinned ruefully."That's what I'm finding out now that we're taking the Fast Learn training. One more session and we'll know whether it's going to work for us."

Natalie began handing out white sheets with drawings on them, Here are what we've got so far of the plans. Look them over and when you meet this afternoon you can make the changes. Now, we've got the gardens to consider. You're our herbalist, aren't you,Jane?"

Jane shrank away from the sudden question. Then straightened and smiled, "I suppose I am. I didn't know that I was until today."

They smiled at her, "It's about time you did."said Natalie." We'd like to put the gardens into your hands. The Master Healer will give whatever help you ask for. He knows the plants he needs most."

A fair, very young man, sitting with one arm around a young woman with long dark hair and blue eyes, who held on to his hand as if uneasy here,spoke hesitantly,"You speak of the Healing, and the - the Reaching too as if it's all normal." He glanced around, then down at his mate,"We've just come from the north and it's such a relief to hear you so accepting." She was nodding, her face seriously intent."We want to help with the gardens, if -- if the lady will have us. We've done a great deal of plant search in the forests and are good Finders." He looked hopefully at Jane and she smiled."My name is Gregory and my mate's name is Mae. and we -- we " He heaved a deep sigh, "we've the Healing touch. We weren't allowed to practice there, and so we never were trained. We want -- we thought maybe here, we could be trained." His face was worried.

Jane smiled with warmth and the two visibly relaxed. "I'd welcome the help with the gardens. I've so much to do at the farm that it'd be impossible for me to do it all. And as for training, well, we've got pretty good Teachers, there's no problem there. We can start you here and if you prove adept enough, we'll send you on to the Station. We'll not lose a Healer for lack of training in this Valley. In the meantime you can earn your living gathering herbs,"

The young woman spoke then, a voice so soft the others had to strain to hear,"Thank you. We do need credit if we're to live here. And we'd like to stay here in Adwin. You can't know how glad we are." She still clutched her mate's hand but they smiled and those near by, reached over to touch lightly their arms, or shoulders.

Natalie spoke then in that silence." The First Healer has asked that we petition the Main Council for credit to buy a Scanner. The Healers do a faster and deeper job with their own mind-scanning but when they're busy they need other medical personel to do them in the emergency rooms. Then they want an Auto chem. We just don't have time for all the lab work and that will take care of everything and do it faster. People get careless when there is monotonous work like that and machines don't. The Healers always double check any way."

Silvia said, "It's going to cost some credit. Can we get that much? Wouldn't it be cheaper to just find a couple of extra healers?"

Natalie frowned,"Oh course, if we could. But they're just not that common." She glanced at the two young new comers."You really are going to be mighty welcome here, you know." She watched their obvious relief. "We'll have a formal Council next week. Those of us who are regular members can support the petition. We really need those tools." She looked steadily at each of the members who were present and then gave a curt nod."Well, Jane, that's a bit of a detour. Are you set?"

Jane said,"I'll plan the gardens and start collecting herbs. What we can't find or order from Altos, we can get from other Healing centers. It'll take a little time, but we can get it done by the time you have the building done. Can I count on the Gatherer crew to help with planting?" At their nods, she went on. We need a processing plant too , you know. These herbs have to be dried and stored carefully."

Natalie and Beryl were writing as they listened and they both looked up at her. Beryl said,"Can you explain that to the architect?" They had not thought of that at all. Jane nodded, glad she had something to add. Then Beryl said,"I'd like a card assessment,and names and addresses and useful skills. Can we do that before we close this gathering?"

Cards were passed out and everyone was busy for minutes, then the circle closed again, people drew together, there was silence. A woman reached out to gather up the baby and settle him in her lap so that he would be part of this. They began to sing, peeling their separations away, bringing them into a gentle Joining. Every Healer present focussed and sent a flood of Healing energy flowing through them all. There was a sweep of gratitude as small scratches and bruises healed and faded from their skins. Aches and strains of the weeks work eased. Gregory and Mae felt that flood, their eyes filling with tears that such power was possible and that they could join in it. They wanted, knew, that now they could be properly trained. Jane felt the power of this giving. She could not withhold her own response, though at first a fear tugged at her mind to resist. Then, with a new and unfamiliar willingness, she Reached out to them, allowed them, Joined and felt that intensity of belonging. Oh, if only she could learn to make that first Touch, she thought.

After ward Jane went out alone to stand beside a small fountain that gathered blue into a pool. How such clear water, ascending, could become so blue on settling in the pool, puzzled her. It fell from a high spray into silver discs and filled them then brimmed over into others below. Silvia found her there and caught hold of her arm to get her attention,"It's time to go home, huh?"

Jane turned to her, glad of her company. "Yes, let's go home. They turned to start on the path that led out of the Ring of buildings and finally to the trail home.

Then someone waved, and Silvia ran, calling out, "Oh, Justine, we missed you. But you can still catch Beryl or Natalie and get the summation." She knew that Justine had been asked to come, she knew something of why she had not come. Jane wondered whether Silvia saw the hurt and anger in Justine's eyes. Her manner betrayed no evidence that she did. Then when Silvia turned away from Justine to Jane, she saw that Silvia knew, was well aware .

"Hey", said Silvia,taking Justine's hands,"It's good to see you." Justine relaxed,smiled a little,accepting the love in Silvia's eyes and touch. She said,"Well, did you settle everything, is the Center planned?"

Silvia shook her head,,"Not quite, but it's going now. We've got things moving. Beryl's got the cards and you can just give yours to him for the next meeting."

Justine caught her lip in her teeth , turned away and Jane watching, felt her pain. She was surprised that she could so well know those feelings. Then she saw Justine take command of herself, refuse the pain and meet Silvia's eyes, seeing there a friendship she did not want to risk. "Yes, I'll see him. I'll talk to him."

Silvia nodded, satisfied, "Then,could you meet me in ten minutes for lunch at the Star Bound Bar? It's a new place, and I think you and I both could use a cold beer and a talk."

Justine looked startled then a quiet settled over her face and she nodded. "Yes, I'd like to. I do need to talk, Silvia. Thank you."

Silvia squeezed her hands and then turned to Jane. They began to walk again."Justine and I haven't seen each other for so long, Jane, we really do need to visit. Will you tell Jerry when you get home?"

Jane said,"No trouble. I think I need to think a little about all this anyway. But don't trouble yourself about me, I'm fine."

Silvia made a mock face at her, shaking her head,"Oh, now, Jane, You know it would be no trouble, but a pleasure to go with you!"

Jane looked blank and then flushed. "Oh, My God, there I am again. I thought I'd got over that. Well, anyway, you did want to talk, No?"

Silvia nodded, "That's why I asked her for these few minutes, I wanted to tell you about Justine. She 's a real friend, I've known her all my life and I'd trust her with my very life. Even Jerry's life." She laughed," She's a fine medic, a surgeon and nurse. There's no one with better reputation. She seems to have no Talent for Healing at all. Can't imagine how they work. But she resents it. Not that I'm much better. But I do know that a Reach is happening whether I can respond or not. She doesn't even know that. For a long time she didn't really trust Healers. You can imagine THAT in a Valley where Healers have been the main stay of medicine for two generations. She felt so awful when she found out that their closed silence with a patient was FOR something. Something she couldn't understand. So she didn't believe them. Now, she's forced to accept them because she sees their results."

Silvia sighed, She's a Vagabond, you know. And she knows of their faith, their talents, even though she does not ever talk of them. She has as much love for the Silent City as anyone, but when she grew older, she was absorbed with her body, sexuality and a very demanding mind. They served to get her through medical school with all the worries of that. She was one of the Singers, when she was an adolescent. She has a sweet, small voice but it's perfect for the guitar or harp. Oh, Jane, she's such a fine person, we've got to work it all out." She walked nearly to the point at which the path started down hill before she spoke again. "It's hard enough for me, and I don't understand much, but I CAN sense the Touch and if I hold to it, I can Reach a little. I know it, whether I want to admit it or not. I can. I'm not - not mind blind, the way she is. And it doesn't bother me that other people have strong Talents. Maybe I would be able to Join too some day. But I want to talk, to help her see that she's pretty important as she is. I've got to try."

Jane suddenly leaned down to kiss her friend, she shook her head, smiling at her, "You know that you're one of the best people I know, Silvia. One of the best."

Silvia looked puzzled at her, "I don't see how that - . Oh, well, I've got to get back. See you later." And she was gone, running down the path back to town. Jane watched her go and then still smiling, feeling suddenly very fortunate, she went on home.

She climbed down the steep, winding pathway toward the Highway. She stopped once, looking across learning Center fields, and she could see a pale yellow Lowcart softly humming its way toward the point where she would cross the Highway. She felt attracted to it, as though there was someone there she knew. Yet she did not know many Vagabonds. She had taken only two Journey times in her life and they had been fairly short. Now, she stopped and watched when she reached the edge of the grass covered Highway. The domed top of the LowCart had been slid back and down and a man sat reading in a low chair beside a small table where on were two cups and a plate of small sandwiches. He rose and smiled, "Will you come in? My name is Roderick of North Glen and I have a message for you, Jane of Riverbend Farm."

She studied him, her mind racing. The name was right, but almost no one called the Farm by all its name, and how did he know her name? She studied his face, quiet, a look of calm that pleased her and green eyes that laughed above a wide mouth. His head was nearly bald but a fringe of white hair gleamed in the sunlight. She decided abruptly and went to the cart. As she moved she heard a soft sound, a murmur from Roderick. Swiftly her eyes swept through the cart now visible as she came close. She almost gasped, then instantly relaxed and a great joy pushed up from beneath all other feelings. In the bottom of the cart lay with slowly twitching tales, two great cats. They were puma. To one side an English Setter stood wagging his tale slowly in welcome. He was laughing at her and she felt her own joy grow. Squirrels scampered from hiding places to look at her, a kit fox with four young, half grown, stuck her head through the man's legs and peered at her curiously. There was no sign of unease among them. It was not until the two jays, mocking and loud, landed on the edge of the cart and she heard the irritable hoot of an owl, disturbed by all the racket, that Jane finally let all her resistance fade and turned with eager interest to the man who was Roderick of North Glen.

Rapidly she began to talk, a nervous energy making her sum up all she knew of him."I've heard of you Roderick. You're the man who speaks with all the creatures, who calls the wild swans from the sky and brings the little ones from their burrows. I am more than pleased to meet you, Sir". She reached out both hands and he took them, nodding and grinning as if completely pleased with her.

"Jane of Riverbend," he said formally,"I've not come just by accident as you might have guessed, I've come because I need to talk with you. I -"

She interrupted him,"How could you possibly know I'd be here - now?"

His eyes sparkled, holding his smile like a whisper of joy and she knew he lived from that Joy. His face was otherwise serious,"You do know. Your Family has told you. We human kind, are not separate in our consciousness of one another." He watched the surprise in her face and the acceptance and shrug, then went on, "You have already begun to work - to do this work that I do. The joining of the animal world, the conversation with these younger ones. It's time you accepted the responsibility, consciously admitted that it is your work." He frowned,"There aren't many of us yet."

She stammered, her eyes moved back and forth from one animal to another. There seemed to be others, sleeping beneath a narrow bed and chairs. She avoided his eyes, their sharp gentle gaze seemed to draw her into themselves so that she felt that to meet them directly would be her undoing. Then, finally with a sigh, she turned to do exactly that. The clear bright green seemed to descend far beneath the surface, down into some quiet serenity that she had never thought possible. She felt their power, the gathering of thought behind them and suddenly, she was aware of those clear images. Through the mental pictures he informed and she stood enthralled, aware in minutes of what would have taken long in talk. He showed her the lives of the forest creatures and their responses to certain people who moved among them, not excluding the Hunters. For those who hunt are also fitting the emerging patterns of Life. She saw that a Forest Singer, such as he was, could be of any age or sex. She saw briefly one memory of Roderick's in which he realized his Talent as a young boy.

He had been in a secluded woodland and idly he imitated some whistling calls. He waited, grew increasingly restless as if an expectancy grew in him. Then, experimentally, he began to hum and then to sing. The singing grew more sure, he felt a direction and sang with stronger intention, and the song was a variety of sounds, without words. She was aware that his singing was a message sent out to forest creatures. The images came rapidly, her atttention was complete. Slowly at first, then with more confidence, birds wheeled in the air, squirrels and rabbits stirred in their warrens and crept near to the surface to see this calling. A fox, nestled in her den, pricked her ears and came out to listen. Deer in two different meadows and sheep among them, raised their heads and turned toward the Singer. Soon the little meadow was filled with those who came to the call. Then the young boy Roderick sat on a tall rock and sang to them, finding new shapes of song, finding new ways to speak and discovering as he did, the meaning of his songs. It was his body that shaped the sound, but his Soul that sang. The animals listening, watched him with shining eyes, absorbed, attentive. In a few there grew a faint sense of recognition, so that their eyes were lost to sight and they knew something greater touching their locked minds. Then it was gone, but its bright reflection would never fade completely.

There was quiet among them all, a peacefulness increasing. They settled into the grass with no fear of each other. Then, as suddenly as it began, the Singing ended. The creatures were still for minutes, then began to look around, to be aware of their surroundings, and began to disperse. But most of them did not flee in terror, rather they moved slowly and resolutely away. The meadow seemed to stir with something exciting but unknown. The Singer waited, and when they had all returned to their ways, he found that there was one still there. With that one he traveled out of the forest and the great cat accompanied him.

Jane watched, listened, felt the wonder of it and smiled because she recognized that delicate Touch against minds locked into instinct, the edges that over flowed that instinct and were aware, just faintly aware. She felt a knowing tremble in her own memory. Had she not called down the Geese, and the Eagle, the Raven and the Vulture, among others? Had she not swept into that flock mind of Starlings and felt them take her into their swirl? Had she not brought to walk beside her more than once, the passing Wolf, the pair of Foxes in the spring? She saw that she knew the language Roderick spoke and she knew that she had denied herself its full import. And he taught her swiftly of herself.

Jane drew her eyes away, looking into those of the great cats, quiet in the cart. She met those large yellow eyes, they purred loudly. They seemed to her to laugh. They were conscious of her. She felt awe, amazement and joy that wouldn't contain itself in her body. She leaped up, laughing and whirled away dancing. She leaped from the cart to the heavy highway grasses and danced there with her shoes flung off. The birds came from the neighboring trees to fly about her. The great cats came leaping from the cart, playing at a fight, and the Fox threw her head back and called out in a long wailing that was full of a peculiar clear longing. For minutes they were all so noisy that Jane didn't hear the notes of the flute that Roderick had put to his lips. Music that sang of life and joy and gave her feet even greater energy. She danced with abandon and finally, she stopped, standing still and renewed before them all. The creatures went back to their places.

Roderick stood looking up at the Farm Hall. There on the deck was a tiny figure waving, and he raised one hand in salute. Jane looked and saw Jessie and felt from this distance the power from that friend. He said, "What we must know is whether you will become one with us and join in the teaching of the little creatures. It is not only humankind who must learn. A significant part of our learning is found in teaching those fellows. Maybe you will teach through dance?"

Jane was silent. Then she said, "I suppose that without admitting it, I've been

THE AWAKENING

one of you for years. I've neglected it, because I've denied. My Family is beginning to accept their awakening minds. They tell me of wonders I have never guessed. And I think I must accept my own realizations." She glanced at him. His eyes were calm, waiting. "I do want to learn. I haven't been willing. Afraid, I think. Would you accept me as student, Sir?

Her formality amused him and he smiled. "By asking you are already student to me. The first thing you must notice is just how you do your own speaking, just how you call, and who responds. You seem just now to have a way with birds. But I don't know yet all you hold in you. If you begin to pay attention, pay attention to your own style, you will learn what it is and how to use it. Then we can talk again. Remember that -- pay attention from this hour on for one month. Then call for me and we will talk."

He offered her food and drink and they sat for a few minutes happily munching in the afternoon sun. After a while he said,"You've known the ways of plants for some time. You are a rare one, you know. Not many hear the pulse of both plant and animal. You're truly a daughter of Earth Mother, Jane of River bend Farm. If you watch,listen, and attend, She will teach you Herself!"

She nodded, numb with recognition, her eyes shining and eagerness rising up enough to choke her. Someone knew what she was. She wanted to shout for joy. Something that had lodged like a dam in her had broken and Joy was a fountain flooding her whole body and mind with its light. She had acknowledged her Self. She nodded again, speechless, He smiled and took her hands for a moment.

Then she went down from the cart and stood in the cool grass, retrieved her shoes, and watched him turn the switch that activated his low cart. He grinned, taking up his book again, "If you have questions you might ask that one up there."He waved toward the Hall. Jane nodded and turned toward the path. He said, "But you and I will meet again, Jane. We will meet when it is time." She watched as the little cart hummed its way slowly down the Highway. She thought her life had tilted into a new light. Her heart felt the upsurge of emotions - so many, both painful and Joyous. The presence of the man who had invited her was gone. She felt all the past darkening her Joy. But she could not forget nor deny that very real sense of new Life that throbbed in her heart. Paying attention, as he had advised her, she saw that she was letting old shadows come down around her. She threw up both arms as if to press them away. To free herself. She felt them shed away as one might shed an unwanted coat and the lightness of it thrilled her. She stood at that point of Self discovery, stood watching the inner turmoil subside in this new realization. Then she knew they both, Jessie and Roderick, Reached to her in one final Song. Her heart felt a profound blessing.

Back in Adwin, hurrying to her meeting, Silvia saw Justine waiting at a corner table. Yes, that was good. It would be quiet here. Silvia was smiling in pleasure at the thought of their lunch together. Justine watched her and waved and her own seriousness fled before a grin. "Sil, it's been too long since you and I met for one of these little lunches. Let's promise that it won't be so long again."

Silvia nodded, drawing out her chair and settling down at the table. "I agree. I do promise. Let's order, I'm starved." They took up the menu and Jean came to take it bringing steaming cups of tea and a beautifully arranged plate of appetizers. Silvia said, "Justine, I've always thought that I could trust our friendship. What we've talked of needn't harm us. But there's something else I want to tell you because I want our friendship to continue. To lose you would be terrible for me."

Justine looked at her thoughtfuly, a faint tinge of fear passed in her eyes and was gone. She said, "Don't be bothered by my bad temper. I do want you to talk. I want to listen."

Silvia shook her head,"I've managed your temper just as you've managed mine. It's not that! It's something important." Then in her usual blunt way she said, "I think you've begun to notice that there are differences among us, in Adwin, in the Valley. Difference that you can't always understand." At Justine's nod she went on. "Our family has been talking a lot lately. We've just begun to talk about things we ought to have talked of long ago." She felt that she was evading the issue.

Justine did too. She said,"Silvia, I think you'd better just out with it. Don't try to make it easy. Whatever it is, I'm half consciousness of it anyway and that only makes it worse."

Silvia grinned in relief. Then the food arrived and smelled so good both women found themselves utterly absorbed in it for several minutes. "Wow", Justine murmured, "It's still true. Really FINE food has to be prepared by human hands.Every time I eat here I'm impressed all over again." She took a sip of the icy beer and smiled, "And Adwin has the best brewery in the north country, I think!

Silvia nodded with her mouth full. "The processors are getting better though, you know. I did a recipe program for ours and its really fine. But, you're right, not as good as this. And that's reassuring, you know." She ate a bite more and then said, "Justine, what's begun to happen with us, is happening all over the Valley. We're beginning to recognize that we have a Talent called Reaching. It's a Reach of one mind to another. And a Touch of mind to mind. Then there's a linking or an exchange. I don't think anyone is doing what used to be called telepathy, but rather we're aware of one another, our feelings, our experiences, our attitudes, and images. Even I have had glimpses of what it's like. It is true." She took another bite, watching Justine's face, but Justine was eating quietly.

Silvia swallowed and then went on a little hurriedly," You remember our Teachers used to tell us of such things. We thought of it all as a theory, not practical. But now we know it's real. It's come out of that training in attention, to pay attention so we are aware of everything, remember? Three hundred and sixty degree awareness! The awareness of the Samurai warrior." She stopped, then warily she asked,"Do you remember their telling us that humankind is changing, mentally and emotionally, that we're capable of more than people have ever been, mentally, spiritually aware and capable?"

Justine looked up then, rememberng and frowning. "I don't know. It seems to me I do remember though, something of that.I never knew what to make of it." She ate thoughtfully for a moment then said,"My people taught us differently, you know. But I've heard all these things, all my life, I've heard. I thought I was a late bloomer." She made an impatient gesture.

"Well, people are beginning to mentally reach, and then to Touch. I've not been able to do it, but when my family did at last Gather, I felt - included- at least. Jerry says that when mind touches mind and we are together so, then we are stepping up consciousness and that we're aware as though in further dimensions. Then, if we're able to, we See, we realize what we can't realize alone."

Justine eyes tightened, her gaze became hard in self protection,"Then it's like the Healers I've seen. They get silent, they seem to draw together, and I always had the immpression they expected the same of me. Yet there I was -- just watching -- left out! Completely left out!" She stopped, her voice small and sad. "Oh, ,Silvia, is that it? Is it true that you can do those things too, and I can't. Surely if I were ever to be able, I would be now."

Suddenly tears ran down her face, a terrible upwelling of grief and dispair from the hidden pain of years of denial. She felt safe here with Silvia, safe with this good friend. She sobbed aloud, her face in her hands, as if a dam had broken and Silvia knew it had. Justine reached out one hand, while she mopped her face with the other, her eyes still brimming over . Silvia took her hand and held it in both her own. Justine said softly,"I thought it might be something like that. Something I could not do and could not ever learn to do. It made me study harder, to learn how to do what I could, better than anyone. I can choose the exact amount and kind of drug needed. I know the herbs totally, how they effect each kind of person. I'm good at surgery, and every other medical skill a person can learn, but I can't -- can't do what they do. They seem to do it so easily. They just look into the person, mind or body, they See instantly what I must figure out slowly and with all the mechanical help I can get. And even then, I can't be sure. They are!. They --" she took a long breath, broken a little with stifled sobs, "There's no hope for me is there?"

"Justine you're one of the finest medics in this valley now. At your young age, you already know that. You have a reputation already as a surgeon. You're a Healer of one kind, they of another."

Justine was gazing off into the air, tears still washing down her face, but her thoughts raced."I suppose you'd expect me to deny that they can do what they do. But I've seen too much of the work of the Healers. I've watched them work together, sometimes two at once literally work inside a person's body without once opening it. I've seen that, Silvia. It's -- it seems miraculous, but they've explained, the best they can, what they do. It's actually seeing and knowing of the inner cell life." She was shaking her head in remembering. "I think that it IS a kind of mental capacity, a mind awakening to greater consciousness, just as they say it is. I think there's no other explanation." Already her own mind was searching for understanding. She was beyond her own emotions, using her trained intelligence.

"Instead of denying, I ought to learn how that can be a normal human skill." Her face lifted, her eyes met Silvia's in anguish, "But, oh,Silvia, to be able to see like that!"

Silvia felt her grief, but smiled, rejoicing. Justine would manage."I think you might be one of those few people who could help us figure it all out on scientific terms. "

Justine stared at her, puzzled and then her face began to clear, slowly she began to nod. "Perhaps I could. How would I go about testing, setting up research. And for what purpose? Those who Heal aren't interested in that kind of testing. They already know. Those who can't --" She stopped again, her eyes on Silvia,were dry now, bright with a new interest." But it would be fascinating to find out." She finally smiled ruefully,"But still, it leaves me out of so much. Why can't I do that thing you call Reach. At least why can't I do that? What is it? Is it a matter of learning how to focus mentally?"

Silvia gulped,"Oh, no, it can't be. You have far more capacity for that than I do. Than most people, in fact". She stopped, "But, maybe - I think it's a different kind of focus. I wish I knew what brings it into functioning in us." She shook her head, sadly,"But it's not going to change our friendship, is it?"

Justine was silent, studying her,"Silvia, you don't think I'm going to fall into that kind of foolishness the Builders are getting into, do you? I'm certainly not going to regress to the past. I've studied enough history that I don't have romantic ideas about how our ancestors lived. I surely am not going to hate those with talent. Oh, my friend, you must know me better than that!" She nodded to herself, as if finally deciding something, and at Silvia's movement to protest, she held one hand out, "No, that's what I think they are, emotionally damaged people. Even some could be healed by -- by some of our best Heart Healers. But I don't think our psychologists could touch them.You see, I do know there's a difference. I think especially that Builders lack imagination." She brightened, already beginning to think of this new study, "That may be one of the traits of those who have that inner Knowledge! A highly developed intuitive mind able to work effectively with the intellectual mind and create a fertile imagination? Have I begun to find a direction to study?"

"Then, for you it isn't witchcraft, or an evil desire to dominate the world?" Silvia asked without thinking, her own worries uppermost .

"Good God, No! Surely, we've come farther than that. After all, I did go to some of the Healer's training sessions. I couldn't get much out of it but I understood they were doing something very profound. No way I could be intellectually honest and still deny that. Even though I might have wanted to.But then, I thought I'd develop the skills later on and now it looks as if I won't." She looked sad again.

Silvia felt a great wash of relief sweep through her,"But Justine, you'll be able to work with the Healers, you'll be able to really use their help and they yours"

Justine nodded, resigned, picking up her fork to finish her lunch. She wiped tears from her face unashamedly , then grinned at Silvia."Well, I suppose I had to accept it all some time. It would have been easier to simply deny it. I'm glad it was with you, Silvia."

Silvia was silent, stunned with a new thought. Surely there must be other people like Justine in this Valley, people who would not be able to Reach, might not know of that vast far Light, who would not be jealous, angry or afraid of those who did. Surely they would need people like Justine to teach them. She said, "I value your friendship more than you know, Justine. I do want us to see more of each other. Especially now that you're going to be here at the new Healing Center. Perhaps you would be willing to be with me when my child is born." She laughed as a good idea struck her, "You've a free dinner waiting as soon as our restaurant opens too."

Justine nodded, smiling," 'If' it opens -- you mean! I'd like to see you succeed though, Sil. It sounds like a good addition to this town. And there's no question that I'd like to be there when your child is born. I've noticed that you were carrying it and wondered if you'd tell me. In fact, at first, I thought it was what you wanted to talk about" They were silent, finishing and sipping at a last of the amber beer. "Well, Sil, let me think all this over a while. And I'll call you and we can talk again. Maybe I could talk to that old lady who's living at your Farm. I've heard of her, you know. She's getting well known around. Maybe I've got a place in all this that's happening after all"! Her eyes brimmed but she laughed at herself. " Now, let's just visit, catch up on all the gossip and you can tell me about Jerry and Ned. By the way, who's the father?"And they went on to talk of every day affairs.

CHAPTER TWENTY ONE

Jessie at work.

    In May every shade of green painted the Valley, from the mountain forests through the lower hills where the colors brightened and changed to pale golden greens of lowland and meadow. The hills were purple or yellow with blooming legumes that piled their thick growth over the land, drawing the grazing herds up from winter grazing in the low meadows. Scattered herds of cattle, sheep, buffalo, deer and elk grazed as they moved through the land, sometimes mingling a bit before they passed on in their routes through the hills. Horses sometimes scattered them, or came face to face with herd bulls or bucks and were routed. The best of the wild horses were gleaned by horse breeders who raised them for racing and for pleasure riding and for training in the circus rings. Intelligence was the criteria for selection, rather than specific conformation. Horses were companions to their human partners, they needed intelligence and that deep loyalty that fine horses can give. The dog teams or a trained stallion brought in the herds in spring, when mares and colts could be looked over and given opportunity to display both intelligence and heart. It was not a broken horse that Valley breeders wanted, but one who could be won with care and slow building of trust. Most breeders freed many of their animals for free running in the hills with the wild herds during parts of the year. They thought it gave them strength and resistance. Animals competing with the difficulties of that life developed intelligence and mares came back bred by the magnificant wild stallions of those herds. Dog teams tracing them sometimes acted only as messengers to the lead mare or stallion.

    Predators stalked through hills and mountain meadow. They took their toll of young or very old animals . Human Hunters stalked with almost as much skill, with no weapons other than a single shot gun, powerful enough to kill a buffalo at a hundred yards, or a bow and arrow, tool of the ancestors of the race. But these were beautifully designed tools, superior to any known before. Young Hunters, learning the trade, were taken by their elders to their first 'kill'. The elders insured that the kill was for good reason, done with very little pain and according to the Master Forester rites. Then the accomplishment was celebrated during the Spring Festival though there were those who deplored that rite as barbaric.

    At this time of year too, town Councils might need to decide the fate of a young one whose learning had not succeeded in the Center and who took some borrowed weapon, a serious breaking of law itself, and shot at living things. They never succeeded in deluding the Master Forester, because any wounded animal testified to the presence of such a miscreant. Such incidents, few as they might be, worried the Councils, because it was clear evidence that the teaching missed here and there. Such children were brought to the Healing Center and their

THE AWAKENING

teaching begun all over again.

Spring is always full of excitement, but in May of this year, a thrust of new energy invaded the Valley. The Family felt its presence, knew of its stimulation. The clear blue air was full of a fragrance of blossoms, of new green fields sprouting with new crops. It was a heady time, though the nights were still cold .The new Planting Songs were sung in town and country and the best of them recorded and kept for the next season. Earth was restless with birth and sprouting, and with the deaths necessary to nourish those births. Life woke, and sang of renewal. Underlying the pain and sorrow, a keen sense of joy spread like morning sunlight into everything.

When Jessie was at home, Rose contrived to spend a little time each evening talking. It was in those talks that she began to realize that Ben had slipped back into his old patterns. She wanted to know whether he realized that.

Ben spent his first few week at home, just walking everywhere, often in Rose's company, she didn't want him out of her sight. Sometimes he roamed in company of his children, or others of the Family, but he had to see and touch everything again. Often they invited Jessie to accompany them, but she had turned away, saying she would explore later at her leisure. On one bright morning Ben and Rose had just finished a last walk up to the rolling hills behind the Farm, they had looked out over the farm and the town beyond it. Standing silent, lost in the wonder of the beauty of this land, they watched birds wheeling in a closely knit flock, rising and falling as one being, and finally settling into trees to shout out their sounds. Rose had not asked him to tell her much of his Search beyond what he told her in the first few days, wanting him to bring it up, to tell her of the deepest discovery. She met her own impatience with the explanation that she must let him make himself at home, look over everything and then they could talk of those things.

Ben watched them and thought how important each seemed in the whole. He frowned, realizing his own strange feeling of being superfluous. He didn't seem to belong. Everyone went about their chores, their work in town, their journeys, travels, whatever they elected to do and seemed to need no help or word from him. Had they all grown past him in one short year? He looked at her, standing beside him, rapt in her immersion in sound and color around them, drew a long slow breath and said, "Rose, I feel cut off, redundant.No one seems to need me. Jerry never asks me questions about - his work. I'm not sure what it is now. The kids - at least I would have thought they'd need some advice now and then. They seem so grown up. And it's only one short year". He looked at her with worry in his eyes. She saw that and sympathized."What's happened, Rosy?"

She laughed then, "Ben,dearest, you've not always been as aware of them as you thought. The twins've been growing up for several years, and for several years too, Jerry's asked less and less of you. Lately I think it was habit. He's grown a lot this past year, you know." She was smiling at him and he relaxed, nodding slowly,"It's just that this year they could finalize their independence."

He frowned then,"But Sweetheart, the children need advice. They're children after all."

She shook her head,"Ben, Jerry's a man now and probably a father. Of course Silvia thinks we don't know that. And our kids are beyond us already. You just talk to them seriously and find out where they are. You'll see!" She looked sadly at him."So much has happened in this year to all of us." She looked into his eyes, wanting to Reach, to Touch without hesitation but she wouldn't. He'd always been so angry if she tried that. Would he now? Surely it was time they talked seriously about the things both of them needed to know of one another.

Ben searched her face, seeing there something he didn't understand, but he chose to focus on the one sentence he could easily talk of. "You say Jerry's a father? How d'you know? Did he tell you? Or doesn't he know himself?" The questions raced one after the other, covering his reluctance to talk of that one thing he wanted so to talk of. Why didn't she ask? Was she not interested?

She smiled again, "No, he didn't tell me, I am sure he knows the same way I do but he'll not talk about it."

Ben was nodding,"And I suppose you know who the father is too just in this same mysterious way. And yet, you could be wrong" She saw that he wanted her to be wrong. He wanted to wrest from her some return to the old life, the old patterns. He felt angry with himself. Even as he tried to pretend things were as they had been, a huge balloon of urgency filled his chest as though to burst forth in speech, in the talk he feared and longed for, but before he spoke, she did.

"Ben, I shouldn't have said that Silvia will have Jerry's child. She hasn't told anyone at all. And she has that right to keep it a secret if she wants to. So don't mention anything about it" She was thoughtful,"After all, she just might not want to mate with Jerry at all, you know. She just might choose- another."

He stared at her for a long moment, his mind digesting all she had said and all he knew that she hadn't said. He shook his head, impatient with himself. He said,"I've been pretty busy getting back to jobs, getting in touch with my old students, setting up new work in the labs. It's been a pretty busy time and I've just let it absorb me. I haven't noticed much else." She started to speak, but he hurried on,"I want to travel to Maryland to talk to the people developing intersteller drive. What they're doing's incredible. I think they'll have it in just a few years. And I want to talk about it to our students and Teachers. You just can't get the same understanding by video hook up. Not nearly the same". He was eager again, his mind racing and his face smiling and she knew he had leaped into his old work, his old habits of distancing himself from something he didn't want to think about. She felt torn, should she insist that they talk of things they had met squarely together in the last Gather.

She felt a sharp needle of disappointment, an abrasive hurt of it. She couldn't just let it go. "Ben, look, you're off again, away from us. You can't do that any more. We agreed, at the Gather that we wouldn't deny, we WOULD talk. Now let's do it!"

He frowned,memories crowded, old pain, and he pressed them away, let them fall before his new found urgency. The pressure in his chest was real. He

THE AWAKENING

knew he had to talk! But he was silent, looking down at his sandals.

With a long breath she gained courage,"Well, Ben, there's no way you can deny what happened at the Spring Planting. Too much is happening all over the Valley. You have to have heard of it. How can you teach any more with those young people outdistancing us the way they are? You'll never have their respect unless you at least accept what they know, what they do!" Her intensity gave fire to her eyes, anger pushed away all fear.

His frown darkened, he searched her face and their eyes met.Then, with a long trembling sigh, he nodded. The pressure in his chest began to release, so that his shoulders dropped and relaxed. She thought for a moment he would cry, but instead, like a sunlight to her,a smile smoothed his face. "Sweetheart, yes, I do recognize that. I've never admitted it. It's true. The kids are different, they look at me sometimes as though they wonder what I'm doing. It's disconcerting. They already know what I'm just discovering. Maybe that's why I want to go east, so I can know something they don't!" He laughed harshly."I think I've completely refused to admit to the change in the twins, or little Cassandra."

She trembled with relief. "Why am I so - scared - of you of all people. We've accepted where we are, Benjamin, my Love. You have too, in fact. Yet you avoid Jessie, since you've got home, as though you're regressing, as though you've lost all you gained!" The accusation angered him, but her voice was so desparate with her plea that he reached his arms out and drew her close to him.

"I know that what you say is true. I know it. And yet it makes me so angry to admit it. I've got to turn completely around and look at you all again. The Reaching and the Touch are only part of it, but I know now that's what's made our love making so wonderful all these years, even when we wouldn't admit it. I think it was the beginning of it, of that closeness that was beyond ordinary intimacy." He smiled at her, "I know that now. I know it clearly." He hesitated, kissing the tears from her face,"It's hard even now for me to admit, but Jessie showed me. She proved to me that I COULD receive you and just wouldn't. She made me see that I had been simply denying. So there it is. Just as you said. It's what we've all done, then?"

She was crying soundlessly, in relief, and old memories of hurt, "We've all done that. But why are you denying again, Ben, Why now?"

He started to speak, "It's different now I'm home, I " then he stopped, turned from her to look away, drawing a long breath, he finally said," I don't know why. I WILL test myself though.Reach to me and let me see whether I can meet that Touch." She almost smiled he looked so resolute.

She let her mind Reach out, like mental arms that reached out to embrace him. She surrounded his mind and then with wonderful recognition, she felt his mind Touch hers. The experience, voluntary, and open to her, allowed a flood of Joy to rise up from depths where it had waited for so long. Because that Touch met Touch and they knew one another in a way that caused differences to fade. Here in this hillside, in ordinary daylight, she was finally WITH her Mate, Ben and all the questions and explanations were redundant . In a few breathless moments there was the fulfilllment of a promise.

Ben leaned over to touch her lips with his. "It's time, my dear one, in fact it's long past time. I see what I've denied, and I make a pledge to you that every morning and evening we will make this deliberate Touch until I lose my resistance to it. After all, we have Jessie here. She has a lot to tell us."

"I'm so glad that she taught you. That you could learn with her. But I'm jealous that you could not learn from me." She grinned, then "What else did she teach you?"

He was serious now, holding her close to him, feeling the warmth and belonging they needed from one another. "Mostly she simply broke my resistance. You see, sweetheart, she had no personal stake in it, she didn't feel bad at all when I refused. So there wasn't the resentment and guilt, the pain, for me to climb over. Then, she is so - so - powerful. She is that." He drew a long breath remembering. "I think it was just her being there with me, being there in her strength and her - there is a strange beauty in Jessie, Rose. She has such beauty that I never could have seen a year ago at all." He was silent, thinking of that revelation.

"But then, I think it was not just these things, You see, with her I caught a glimpse of something, - of something I can only call 'Divine'." He did not notice Rose's sharp intake of breath, "It's like something I'd gotten to the edge of and then lost, or refused or been terrified of maybe. The beauty of it. The feeling of something 'outside' but encompassing all our ordinary experience, something that is - just IS, you know, this quality,,this -- Presence. It is a sense of wholeness, of belonging to - everything!" He was still, remembering. Then he said, "When we learned about the idea of Soul, of that spark of the Divine in us, we thought it just an idea. Something to comfort us. But now, I know its REAL. I have been aware of - that part of me, a greater Self. She taught me that. I want to be able to make that contact through my own recognition!" He shook his head, "I can't really speak of it very well. It was so - mind shaking. I was shaken for hours just realizing a little Touch of - of that singleness of Being. Yes, that's what it is!"

"Why didn't you tell me -- as soon as you got here?"

He shook his head, a little shame faced, "I didn't think it could be the same. That Reaching, you used to talk of, it seemed so foolish. Then, when I saw the way Jessie helped me to see, I was afraid to - to be aware of so much - without her support. After the Light, the wonder of it, that Reaching seemed so irrelevant. So I thought you wouldn't understand!" His eyes were pleading that she understand now.

"And now?"

"Now, I know they aren't the same and that doesn't deny the existence of both. That Reaching is the ability of a Mind that has perceived the Light. That is aware of the singleness of Life. It's a natural ability then." He looked at her anxiously, "Doesn't that seem right?"

Rose nodded, her eyes dry now, listening intently, her heart so full of gratitude to Jessie, It was finally true. He had consciously wakened, was aware of his true nature and they could finally talk of it. They sat thus for some time, absorbing and being together. She said,"Let's remember, and each morning and evening we will return to one another. To practice!" He nodded. She felt such a peace that she had never known. A gusty wind had spring up, pushing at the branches of the trees, tugging her hair loose and she moved closer into the circle of his arms for warmth.

    After a while, she turned to him, "And you've got new ideas for your research at the lab? From all this stimulation new ideas emerge?"

    He nodded, "She says they do." He was suddenly eager again, wanting to go and to put some of these ideas into words for his colleages and students, wanting to look again in their eyes and see what he had refused to see. Maybe even to talk of it a little. He turned to her, Reached, deliberately, accepting enough to initiate the Reach and the result was electrifying. That mental Touch evoked powerful memories that flooded his mind, filling him again with that energy that seemed to shake his very brain. Thoughts shaped themselves, seemed to touch against possibility that revealed breathtaking insight. Wordless and as stimulating as an electric current. He must find a way to shape them into thoughts that could be spoken. They refocussed and looked at each other,Benjamin laughing softly,"Rosy, I feel as though I've been relieved of a heavy burden, as though my brain is just now turned on. I want to go to town and begin to work, to talk to my friends there." He laughed at himself, stroking her hair from her eyes,"I want to spend a lot of evenings in my cottage just talking.And trying ourselves with this new possibility! Shall we?" He kissed her and standing, drew her to her feet. The slope before them was purple with plentiful bloom of oga, its oblong fruit already forming on the lower stems in clumps like peanuts. Rose caught up a handful to smell the fragrance.

    She nodded,"I'd like that Love. Right now, let's run down the hill and climb to the Hall and take belts. We've not done it for so long together.It's faster and more fun today and it's a long time since we did it together." With a wild abandon , holding out their arms like children to keep their balance, they ran, leaping over stones, small shrubs and twisting here and there for the best footing,,they raced to the bottom of the northern hill. The climb to the Hall was slower, but their bodies were relaxed now with the exercise. They strapped on their belts and were swiftly air born, like rapidly shrinking dots they flew toward the town.

---- ---- -----

    Jessie watched them go. She sat in a small depression below the main Hall. A huge spreading Digger pine grew to one side among boulders that were clustered together so that a peaceful hidden little grotto was formed.It was cool,shady, and large enough for three or four to sit and talk. Shrubs grew down the hillside below the grotto, and their tops, green and blooming above its edge, formed a low hedge but allowed an unobstructed view.

    Jessie had been thinking of Adwin and of the two sister towns, Denlock and Jasper. Each so different yet settled by people little different from one another. Already she had been visiting in each of these towns, walking to small villages in the woodland between. It was an intense work, but it was her work. She walked to the eastern edge of the little garden under the Pine and from that vantage point she could see the mountains in the north. There where the whole second half of her life had been spent. The odd part was that she had not known of it until after she had raised a family and lost a husband. She was forever grateful for the support of her children and their mental growth that meant they understood her work and encouraged her. But these were no longer her only children. Now there were thousands, equally dear. The thought was reassuring. The work here would not be easy.

She started out on her day's journey. She followed the little pathway that wound down the hill side to the Great Highway. She walked briskly, eager to begin. When she reached the bottom of the Farm knoll about twenty yards from the thick turf that covered the old Highway bed, she stopped, looked down the rumpled deep growth and saw in the distance a caravan moving in its slow way toward her. She estimated they would both arrive at the crossing ahead about the same time.

"Good, I would like to talk to those folk." She spoke aloud, watching the gaily painted lowcart Two people walked beside the cart and she could see that there were at least two inside. She focussed and with delicate control, Reached. For seconds there was hesitance, surprise? And then, a joyous, boisterous contact, a mental bear hug. The contact of Touch was swift and deep.It was like a shout of joy. Adam and Deborah one after the other then together, made contact. The old woman, Adam's aunt, remained silent,separate. She, recovering from illness, rejoiced that they had got here so soon. She smiled with anticipation. The Reach from Jessie had been so strong, so confident and without hesitation. They all knew at once that here was a Conscious One. One with whom they could share much. The Vagabonds turned to look with physical eyes at that woman they had already greeted in Mind.

As they approached their inevitable meeting on the Highway,they continued conversation. Jessie received in images some of the excitement of the spring festival, swift scenes of the dances and songs. She met the children of Adam and Deborah and their adopted ones. She felt the Touch of that whole tribe and she laughed. Then, gently, she was drawn into that greater sphere of consciousness, for these people went beyond the simple Mind Touch. They Reached far, farther than the familiar daily life, into farther dimensions of being alive. They KNEW as Joined Minds can know what no single mind could bear.

She rejoiced! These were the right ones, they practiced daily and they stepped each morning out of that half life of their physical inheritance and entered knowingly into that greater life of Soul consciousness. The Earth blazed with color, the air was a shining of Light, all things radiated that Life they knew in themselves and the world was entrancing. To live was an adventure.

How beautiful it was to walk with such people. Her desire that all the people of the Valley know such simple Vision and Joy of Life, grew stronger and her determination stronger. She felt the deep undertones of that old one who was

THE AWAKENING

there with them but who held herself in profound stillness. Then, nearing the center of the road and the softly humming cart, she saw a rainbow of brilliant color, shape itself, lift from the Earth around them and create a great tent over herself and the people who came smiling all around. The old one had teased them with her play. But it was delightful.

Then, as they remained in Touch, Jessie knew their worries. She saw the images of the lower Valley where destructions had occurred. A field ripped up, a small wild meadow torn to be used for personal crops without community agreement. It was a small matter, perhaps, but the Vagabonds knew the energy of distruction was invasive and they grieved. True, it was only a couple of acres, but no concern for the wild life of that meadow had been shown. No request to any council had been made, no consideration of community law. Valley Law was set by public vote, and the agreement had been more than unanamous when that law was made. Clandor people had hastened to protest this illegal use of land. The Builders finally agreed to wait for further action until a council meeting could be held. But they had made their point, and they waited now for that Valley Council.

Jessie saw the sorrow in the minds of the Vagabonds. They had felt the pain of the Earth at being so violated. They had traveled past the devastated land and stopped to listen to the debate. They told Jessie of their preparation to offer stability, if that were needed. The anger among some Valley people equaled the determination of the Builders. They were sorrowed to see that conflict growing. There in the Highway, silent, attentive, as statues, they waited, their communication completing itself. For an outsider the scene would have appeared strange indeed. A group of people, just met, standing in utter silence, their attention intently on one another. But the time it took to complete the exchange of images was only minutes and then they broke the tie. Moving across the grass leaping from the cart, coming to embrace and to laugh with pleasure at the meeting, the Family prepared to share tea and coffee there in the shade of cherry trees. When they stood again, ,just looking at one another, Jessie said, "Then it's starting there, in the south. The people here don't know."

"They should, it was surely sent out Valley wide on the Video News." Adam searched Jessie's eyes, and finding there no fear, he smiled and nodded, "It's true it has begun and yet it's time. The people of the Valley must discover and acknowledge what they've refused to know. They haven't been willing to see, even when we tried to tell them". Then he grinned, "Except for the children, most of them can see and are aware of the denials of their parents. They will be surprised when they discover all their children know".

Jessie nodded, "It's the wonder of these times, the children. I can not get used to them."

Deborah moved to touch Jessie's hand lightly,"What would you have us do, Teacher? We have hidden knowledge in our songs for long years and the people have heard even though they have not acknowledged their hearing. We know because the children know.But now, we must do more.We have known of your coming - and the coming of the others. We wait for your advise."

Jessie nodded, "Yes, you would know of my companions. And would you also know of the - the ones who seek to destroy?"

Adam and Deborah looked at one another. The young people stood a little behind and were listening only. The old aunt, Maggie, sat up in her bed and Reached. Their minds Touched, but then she spoke, her voice thin and sweet, "We know of them Sister. They are not as aware of us! But among Valley people there are many who are unable to perceive. Most of the builders are such. Out of an ignorance they cannot be freed from, they fear and are angry. We have no anger toward them but we must find a way to teach them." She frowned, "But there are those who do have anger, you know. There is danger that some may lose their balance, may let anger direct them to violence."

Adam went to help her sit straight, her body was frail but healthy. She nodded abruptly and said, " As for the dark ones, Sister, they are those who know well the implications, who Reach and who Join, even as we do. Who are CONSCIOUS, yet have chosen another way. Consciously chosen, that is the dispair of it. For these we feel anger, but even greater sorrow." She spoke with a deep seriousness, her face full of grief.

"Their Hearts have not absorbed that streaming Love that flows to us out of the City. It's not that they're ignorant of love, every one who wakes at all, knows at least a glimpse of Love. They have, at least briefly, known what Love is, but have fallen victim to their own lusts, to their dark dimensions, and have turned from Love. They have CHOSEN to destroy, to take the power into their own hands and use it for selfish purpose. They have Chosen! Chosen to reject Love in favor of personal ambitions. That can be destructive beyond our imagination". The old woman's voice had grown strong.

"But it's incomprehensible to me. To choose separation in a universe where separation is illusion." Adam's face was dark with sorrow.

"It's not an average citizen who falls so far. Those are of another kind!" Jessie's face was somber.

The old one nodded, smiling gently, "But Adam, someday even they will realize. And they who 'Know' and have chosen the dark way, are few in number, but they feed the petty human lusts of humankind and use us, to their ends. They have begun among those who are called Builders. Those who do not know they have choice nor what the choice entails." Then suddenly, her eyes met Jessie's and their contact was deep. Jessie saw images of that Black Mountain Lodge, where there lived a man who knew fully the extent of his desire to bring destruction, knew of the depravity he hoped to introduce into Valley life. Counting on the survival of old ways. After a few seconds of contact Maggie said aloud, "He prays on our darkest fears and hungers because they match his own. But his pleasure is in using his powers to control others. He does that by reducing them to the least they are capable of." The old woman was sad, "It is subtle, Sister, subtle and can draw even those of us who know better. He knows our secret fears and the old human lusts that none of us have quite outgrown. We must constantly be on guard within ourselves even as we See and Know that Wonder that has become our life."She sank back into her cushions and Jessie nodded sadly.

"It's true, our direction is toward greater human possibility, and it takes constant effort and focus of mind. The direction of those like Greyson, is down and backward toward that old animal nature, the least that humankind can be.It is easier, it is familiar, it requires no effort nor focus of mind. Many who do not see the greater Vision will be seduced. We must be on our guard. Until one's heart is steady in that Light, the choice can go either way."

Deborah and Adam stared at their Aunt, "You've known all this, and have not shared it all with us, Aunt Maggie?"

The old woman smiled wanly, "It is this that has brought me this weakness, this wasting. I try to contain in myself something of that Evil that pours as resolutely through this Valley as the Good pours from the City.It must be caught and caused to feed in on itself so it will destroy itself in its own limitedness. And so as we travel north, near to the Silent City, I will carry my burden and there it will be drained from me. There I will regain health, or I will die. One can draw Evil into oneself and render it harmless through Love."

Adam frowned,"You didn't think we could help?"

With a sigh Maggie looked at Jessie, then back to Adam. "You wouldn't ask that if you knew the extent of the danger. You were in the midst of your dawning realization." Then turning again to Jessie, "It's true, that they must know and so be prepared to protect themselves. I may have made a mistake. But I was working alone here. Perhaps - together- we could show them". At Jessie's nod, the two old women Mind Touched, establishing a strong connection. They invited the others and felt their Joining awareness. Then they extended beyond that Touch, wove into the electrical blaze of Consciousness that created Joining.The others felt that mental power reveal to them images as clear as through a window. They saw the deep caves, the dark caverns beneath the beautiful buildings that was the Lodge, and the two old Teachers showed them something of the technology that created wonders of invention. Not unfamiliar were the Holographic creations, or the simulated realities that made an entire room into whatever world you wanted to imagine, to create,but which Greyson had made into worlds of excess, of depravity, of misuse of physical senses and lusts. Or they were dream realities, romantic, self indulgent dreams of self satisfactions, where a shadow of love was a fantasy of mother-child or an all powerful master or mistress lover, or even the fantasy of adventure where the ultimate seeking was drowned in passionate battles and struggle to find a physical treasure. Each lived out, could dissipate a life time in blind wrong direction. The playing with power, control over others, fed that fading desire in any young heart, and fought the rising consciousness that saw the Light. Such practice drew the consciousness downward to less and less awareness of Life and Joy ceased to exist for them. Their lives thickened the darkness that hid their own Soul light.

The power Greyson used to seduce mind and heart was very great. But

Deborah and Adam were puzzled that Maggie had considered them not strong enough to meet such temptation. At their exclamation she said,"You cannot know how strong he is.And you have not completely separated from the grip of your own lower desires. Conviction and intention are not enough against him. Once the desire is flamed to life in simulated experience, he provides opportunity in this Valley life for real experience that seals the hunger so that it blinds the Heart. The loss of such desires must be total, or he can draw them out. His power is to manipulate,charm, delight, and convince with subtle rational processes, using your own emotions against you, your very trust and loving hearts against you."

She was silent, searching for understanding in their eyes,"His power is great because he has no hesitation, and will gladly betray trust, since that is a useful weapon. But worse, he is expert at bringing your own fine trained minds to doubt and question and finally to submit to his convictions. He is a master at bringing to the surface your own weakened, but still present, lusts, desires and resentments, then he can manipulate them and finally yourself. It is not something trusting people are armed against." She sighed and showed them scenes in which was something of her own struggle with such temptations, before the loss of desire freed her enough to be at peace. Then with a shrug, she gave a curt nod, " But I know too that you will never be able to meet such power if we do not teach you to be".

Adam realized, appalled. "Then, the Builders are as nothing?"

" Only as they can be used by that one. And he surely is using them, and will use them more, to turn the rest of us against each other. Builders have fewer defenses against their own inner lusts than do we. True they have been educated to our Convictions, justice and individual rights are part of their habits, but for them these are still ideas, convictions, not yet realities, as they are with us." She looked for a long minute at Jessie and then nodding said, "But it is ourselves he seeks to find and pervert, we are those he aims his greatest arts toward, for he must stop the rising expanding Reach of Mind and heart toward Spirit. He knows of course of the presence in the Valley of such people as Jessie. He is desparate and will do anything at this point".

Jessie was silent, her face serious, and then she looked beyond them across the mountains to the west. Could she show them more? Could these People of the Way meet the whole of the truth? Her attention, held like a steel rod, Reached across the eastern Valley and south to that Retreat far above Bend where,like a beam, it was caught by the Monitors there, drawn into their greater power and swiftly she was Joined with them. Instantly she knew what she must do. And she felt Maggie following, aware there beside her. Good, she would need her help!

She glanced at Maggie's radiant face, smiled, acknowledging this small gift of perception. Together they knew that again the task was only to plant seeds. The people must grow them or not, as they chose. But they must know all the facts she could bring them. She asked,"What do you know of that dark force, we call the Dark One? Do you know where it Nests?"

Deborah and Adam shook their heads,"We have known of it, as all of us know,whether we admit it or not. It nests within ourselves. It is our own separative, selfish, natures saturated with Fear. We all know of our capacity for harm, for selfish intention and those rise out of one kind of fear or another. Subtle fears masquerading as benevolence, or love, or need, and a hundred other emotions. But as for a specific point, from which such a focussed power 'nests' I do not know." Adam looked at Maggie,"Do you,Aunt? Do you know?"

THe old woman raised herself slightly, "I do not. It has been necessary for me to rest from such focus. I hold my mind silent as much as I can. For there are mind powers willing to bend and use any mind strong enough to identify It. It is only when I Join with those who are strong of mind, such as yourself Sister, that I dare think of It."

Jessie, nodded, "But Adam's already spoken it. It nests within ourselves. It draws us down through its own magnitism to a kind of death that is true death,the prevention of the life toward consciousness of Soul." She watched their eyes, their troubled frowns and smiled, "Perhaps we can come together there where you camp beneath the City, perhaps there, near to the Northern retreat, we can create a Joining that will call on help from all the Stations, from the City Itself! There, protected from our very selves, by those transcended beyond the attraction to that lower self, can we Join and make some plans. We must teach the people, we must educate the Valley to truth that is not yet revealed to them. And that task is ours, is it not?"

When Maggie nodded, Jessie went on,"You see that all people must understand that what they begin to KNOW is natural and that it is good. That it is to be nourished and developed. They have felt fear,both for their realization of beauty and Wonder, and of the Presence of Love and Joy just because it is so wonderful. One fears such wonder because it sweeps us from our small familiarity. Yet, these must not be feared. We must learn to recognize all that we are, that in us is not only a nest where fear and littleness lives,but a vast ocean wherein there is the endless bright flow of greatness and Joy. It is Love that will finally give us mental freedom. And Love alone can meet that threat of our lower selves. Those lusts, or self centered desires can become exaggerated and expanded because once the capacity to Join is learned, it is possible to Join in our depravity as well as our greatness."

Maggie eased back, smiling now,"If only we can admit to those urges within ourselves,recognize that we have capacity for both and make our choice. If we can acknowledge our limits, our lowest lusts,which are simply the shadows formed out of blindness of that which is possible for us. When we know the truth, when we experience Love, that is to say,acknowledge Love, the Light floods all parts of our being and that which is called Evil is illuminated, that is, it is understood as false. And so it is dissolved. It's very simple, after all. We SEE beyond the darkness." She looked around,"Yes, Friend, we must meet there, beneath the Silent City and find our direction."

So it was arranged ,Jessie would meet them when it was time, at their northern camp beyond the Farm where the Highway narrowed where three branches ended in one single road, and the hills climbed rapidly into the peaks. There they could plan and communicate freely.

Jessie took her leave, the cart and its people rolled on. The day was as bright and golden with life as before, and she stood silently, taking a long breath, bringing her attention back to full consciousness of this wonder of life around her. But now, she was more acutely aware of that dark shadow that thrust a fine thread of fear within her. She stopped, considered that fact. Looking without emotion at this fear. She would not either reject or embrace it. She would simply be aware of it. Surely she must consider it. There was a danger and so fear was a correct response. But she could stand far above that fear, and she stood at that point of perception that was Soul consciousness. Here the Light penetrated even flesh. She stood, knowing that fear was part of a pattern,desires of many kinds were also in that pattern, but underlying it, sending forth bright new threads that tranformed as they wove among them, was knowledge and love. She knew she need not fear any fear. Here she would take her stand.

She said aloud, finding the words carefully as they came from that depth that was true,speaking them as she stood in that early morning slanting sun light,"I know you,Fear. I know your subtle burrowings into consciousness. You would create a wall between Love and this little self so that I will fall from Vision. You would have this mind forget Soul Knowledge, for Soul is also Love. I am Soul,and I include this person who fears. No harm can come. I will to sustain Vision,and Vision is the point of perception where Love is the very breath we breathe." She stood, let her eyes run freely through all the land knowing it as her own body and she knew strength. With that recognition, she shook herself, feeling again free of the heavyness of worry, and proceeded into Adwin. She had not had time to see and enjoy this garden town in years, and she looked forward to wandering slowly wherever her feet took her.

Her path wound through the Rings of the Civic Center past the World Market screens. She glanced up at the rotating three dimensional displays. She discarded a flickering curiosity to go into the building where she could view specific things in detail. She passed by small shops lining the inner ring where all sorts of strange and fascinating goods from everywhere in the world could be touched, handled, tried out and bought if desired. The display was colorful, fragrant, and exciting for an afternoons idleness. She had not spent idle time in a world market Center for years. Adwin's was small compared to Santiago's but it was fascinating nevertheless. She thought it would be fun to look these things over. But then, she decided that she must plan that for another day. She must go on to the Civic Center in the center Ring. The gardens were sheltered enough inside here that they were blooming ahead of the open fields and she delighted in each new discovery.

She could see people gathering at the entrance to the Council Hall. A group of children turned to her as she approached, looked at her curiously. For moments they watched her attentively, focussed. Jessie was Reaching lightly through the crowd toward another person, but she felt that insistence from the children. She turned attention to them. They were demanding almost to the point of rudeness. She felt something anxious in their minds and focussed to them. The Touch was light but its impact surprised her. She always Reached to strangers very gently, giving them time to refuse. But these children rushed, surrounded her mental attention like a shouting and a crying out. She stopped walking, stood before them, meeting their eyes and minds without restraint. Such power they had, but their control was fragmented. She was pleased and curious. Images that were introductions occurred, question ran over question so that she could not untangle them and she laughed. They relaxed.

Then with a little more order they took turns, focussing images clearly. They were unaware of how great their anxiety was, of how strongly it projected. They were unaware of the skill with which she tempered her own Reach. They seemed unable or untaught. They wanted to know who she was and where she came from. In one clear series of images, she informed them. She sought their anxiety and found it. She felt the darkness troubling their minds, the confusion. THey were troubled by currents of energy they did not fully understand. But there was a brightness , a Joy that ran through their minds, their attitudes, that heartened her. Swiftly in image and Touch, she showed them that they must learn to control and use the energy of their minds. That they must learn to Join. Must Reach as a single Mind, rather than, as was now the case, shouting in loud mental cries and a confused jumble of emotion charged idea.

Then she knew she too could learn here. Did they know of the Builders and what did they think of them? She asked them briefly, projecting an image of a Builders Meeting.

One boy was instantly belligerent, a girl began to cry but with anger. Another boy cringed away from the fact, withdrew. Two others bowed their heads but their minds held steady observing the image as if willing to think about it. Jessie said aloud, to relieve them. "There are many things happening, many things that trouble us but there are many who are prepared to meet these happenings. Can you see that?" She felt their mental nods , the focus of attention,their practice of that learned skill of Balancing. They stabilized from the strength of her steady attention. She added,"Notice, pay attention, remember how to do that?" At their shy smiles and nods, she went on,"Your fear and angers create an atmosphere around you that dampens your very Reach. Did you know that?"

At their immediate surprise, puzzled attention, she nodded,"Please think about that. Your fear or anger can be harmful to you, to all of us and you have been trained in the method to release both. Practice that release. Establish it before you Reach. Then rebalance as you just did, until your skill grows and comes so swiftly that it hardly allows imbalance. In that way you transcend the burden of your fears and have clear sight."

A young boy, not yet twelve, nodded, turned to his friends and they looked at him, then at Jessie. He said, "We've been getting information that we don't want to believe. We couldn't actually talk to any adults because we don't know whether any could or even would talk of it.Some of our parents won't, or can't. We don't know which. Some of our friends, some our age, won't either."

Jaell, ten, with abundant auburn hair almost concealing her face, said softly, "It's so sad to think maybe they can't. It's as if they can't see. Can't Mind Touch at all, and that IS seeing. How can we bear that kind of sorrow?" Her voice was soft but Jessie felt her strength.

"You must learn to bear the suffering of others as well as your own, you know. Because we have not taught ourselves to end suffering."

Jessie met the little girls eyes, her mind, Reaching, she touched that eager child mind, felt the hesitation of surprise, and then reception. Totally untrained, awkward, only partly able to separate emotion from thought, unable to focus clearly, she was nevertheless amazingly strong. Jessie held steady, helping the child bring her mind into calm. In instants she showed her how to focus and then how to direct the mental probe that made choice for her as to what she wanted to Send. These children seemed to Send everything, without discrimination. It was almost embarrassing. No wonder they had not found receptive response in other untrained minds. It might even be frightening to another. The child Reached out to her with a strong emotional current that Jessie caught and redirected, focussing the energy deftly in order to steady both their minds. She thought that she had found another of her tasks in this Valley. There must be many such children.

When she had brought Jaell carefully into balance, demonstrating clearly how to hold firm mental Balance,she sought out the others. They were responsive, Jaell's delighted cooperation convincing them. They came like children come for comforting and help. Jessie felt a swift flame of anger that they had been left untaught. They knew how to Balance emotionally, though they were not particularly adept at that, but they had little or no skill at mental Balancing. Anger faded in understanding. Their Teachers undoubtedly did all they could. They too needed further training. Before Teachers could teach mental balance and Joining, they must acknowledge that the people could do these things. They might not know how soon to start training in mental Balancing, or perhaps they thought complete emotional Balance had to be learned first.

As she met these child minds she realized their range, separately, then especially together. She felt a pleasant excitement at the realization. A group of such children could build enough power to Reach others and create the network that was 'World Sight'if only they were fully trained.Even now they had the power, if they Joined, to Reach groups across a continent and with maturity, to half the world. But they didn't know it! Her heart sang, the joy of it was great. But the worry was also great. Such a Reach could frighten them so they would shrink from any Reach at all. They would not know how to interpret what they met. Their potential was exciting, true, but also dangerous. She thought what that one who strove to destroy could do with these young ones, not yet free of their own lower desires.

This day she would call a Gather of all the Master Teachers and teach them how to train the children of the Valley properly. Would they respond? Or was their

THE AWAKENING

hesitation due to concealed doubt? Surely no Master Teacher would conceal emotion or question from her or himself.There must be another problem. She wanted to begin their training now, this minute. She smiled faintly as she also quenched impatience. Her nemesis .

The children had no idea that she carried on a conversation with herself separate from her attention to them. She stood with them, silently, locked in total attention to one another, they did not see curious glances directed their way. Jessie was aware and knew they must break this contact soon. But first,she must know. So she opened her own mind momentarily ,focussed at that highest point of Soul consciousness at which she daily re-established her own expanded point of view, and was overjoyed to feel them follow, know their own Soul consciousness. They could stand ouside the lowest human denominator, they could feel and know the pull and persuasion of their lower lusts and desires but refuse or satisfy them. At least they knew what they were! They were not helpless before those lower natures.

These were Aware! They KNEW the inseparable nature of humanity, that there was no stranger, no one not 'related' to another. And knowing that, they could not harm another without personal pain. These were the new people of the Valley, the ones who would create this new world if they could meet their own selfish intents and prevent harmful actions. Her heart sang. Together, for long seconds, they knew of the steady flow of that Love with which she was so familiar.Then, one by one they flinched at its power and descended into their separate selves.

She spoke then, within this tight connection she felt the words like slow drumbeats that penetrated their communication."Ah, there's so much to learn!" They laughed with pleasure at that, the sudden shock of it after the stillness of the Touch. Then they too began to talk, and chattered so that she had again to ask for one voice at a time. People passing only smiled at their exuberance. Their minds still touched lightly, still were open to one another, but the children could not shield out the mental impact of others around them. She noted that .

She listened to their talk, smiling and enjoying them. There was time here for Jessie to show them their beauty, to take two minutes to make visible to them, the Light that shone around them all, around herself too, for that could not be separated. They tended to focus on the Light that was herself. She had to turn their attention to each that they might see the Light that blazed from every person, from every living thing. They looked around at each other, awed at the radiance of their inner natures.

"But you're so much brighter, you're like a fountain, a blazing damned fountain,Ma'am. When I look at you my mind wants to laugh." Aden, a twelve year old was grinning. She felt their strength fading and the link weakened. Like closing a door,Jessie closed out the Link. They stared in amazement. "Why can't we continue to see? What has happened to the light?"

She shook her head, "First it is impolite to direct the attention of others to your perceptions so -- loudly. Second, you would have trouble living your daily life if you stood in that place of perception constantly. You must learn how to shift perception, shift from the place you mentally stand. Choose either this personal state, or that Soul state."

"Why can't we do both at once? Why must we choose," Jaell's need to know overcame her shyness.

"You will one day. It takes daily practice, daily learning how to live so. Training of the abstract Mind which you do daily, the ability to be aware of the divided mind so you recognize that you think on two levels, will come to you with practice, just as consciousness on both levels at once, will come. Jessie smiled at them. Now they looked only like any group of children with their Teacher and no one looked at them at all. You see, you all have been taught that the true nature of a human being is the Soul nature. It is not this personal and temporary nature which of course one day will do what we call die, or cease to function. You do know that?"

They nodded slowly,"But it never seemed to mean the same as it does now." Mark said, another twelve year old, with black skin and hair and bright grey eyes that gleamed just now with an inner excitement.

Jessie walked with them silently for a few minutes, their communion strong, then she said,"You do also remember that it is false pity to allow the anguish you have all felt for those who cannot Reach or Touch. That one is moving in his own way and the sorrow for him or her is akin to being sorry for a sapling that is not yet a tree.Do you see that".

Since she had spoken directly to the grief they had been struggling with on her arrival in the ring earlier, they looked at one another in surprise and then in grateful relief. "Why that makes good sense. And I do know your name. May we call you Jessie?"

She laughed and nodded."There's another kind of childhood, that of Mind-Spirit, not so different from that childhood of the body. We must give each one time to discover, to develop."

"Then there's no reason to feel pity or guilt. To be sad?"

"Absolutely not! Simply attend to your own focussing within that Love you already know. Project that Love through your lives and it'll do more than any grief or pity could". She felt the wonderful sharpness of even this faint Mind link. Without it they could not have fully understood. She looked at them, keeping her attention beyond their notice, she studied them.

Surely they were developing rapidly. She asked softly,"What do you do with your fears? Or with the anger you feel?"

Jaell said, "We recognize them most of the time and when we don't, we remind each other. Should we do more?"

Jessie laughed,"Good, you'll do, dear one. Just remember to be on guard, to do just that. Know when it is fear or anger and watch yourself rather than react to the other. These emotions can be turned against the very task that Love attempts to do through you. Subtly ,your own fears can smother your knowledge in waves of emotion. Watch for that, catch it before it overcomes your Vison. Remember

THE AWAKENING

that taking time to stand in that state wherein the Light fills your mind and heart is the first safe guard."

One of the younger ones who had not yet spoken, a very solemn child, with blazing gold hair and green eyes, startling in his physical beauty, nodded and met her eyes, "Then is when there is a shift - a changing. Then is when a person can see the utter beauty of, of --" he gently kicked a short twig in the path with a bare toe, "of everything, like that twig lying there, shaped over its own shadow in the smooth stone, and the living foot beside it." He raised his eyes again, met hers and she knew that here would be one interpreter of the new way.

Jessie nodded, moved with gratitude at his perception. "Yes, take time for that. Take time every morning, to See, like a meditation. Such practice, each day, brings with it power to perceive and live within Love itself."

" Ask for help if need be. Never hesitate to ask. We are all still only human." Their eyes met and she nodded, "Go now and find your own Master Teacher. Tell him or her that you have realized you need training. That one will know what to do. With anyone who comes to ask, there is no denial. Remember I will always respond if you call."

They nodded, smiling now. They looked more like children now than the worried, suspicious youngsters she had met. They felt the confidence of protection . Their energy could be dealt with. Jessie watched them, she said, "You've given me a great gift. I thank you."

Aden smiled back, "Nothing to the gift you've given us, Mother, Thank God you're among us." They nodded again and turned away. The whole interchange had taken less than fifteen minutes, but when Jessie turned to the huge polished stone building, the crowd had gone in. The council would be meeting.

She found a place a little apart from the crowd, wanting to see and hear and be unnoticed. She softly allowed her Reach to extend, attentively aware. Instantly she felt response. There were minds here who had accepted the Reach at least.

Then she felt a strong Touch, she responded swiftly. One man, sitting far to the other side of the room. A swift image, and she turned to meet his eyes. Pleased to know his appearance, for he looked different to himself than to her own eyes. She withdrew, waited and Reached again, this time in a different tone. She felt response, felt a soft brush of several Touchs, and was pleased. They sent greeting as one might to a friend but did not seek to send more. She knew their shy surprise at her unhesitant strength.

She nodded then, focussing attention to the Council. She had made light Touch with all but one council member and she knew that that one was simply unable. She was a young woman,,physically lovely, full of a gentle, loving attitude for those around her. However, as Jessie watched, she knew a conflict raged within her. She was totally unable to hide these feelings, since she knew of no reason to do so and was not fully aware of them herself. She strove to bring herself into balance, her training obvious. She wanted to be loving, and yet, anger she could not accept, built in her.

What was her desire? Was it harmful? Jessie read the attitudes, emotions and naked needs. The young woman wanted to have some degree of power here, on this Council. She had served several years as apprentice,hoping to finally be given permanent status. She wanted to sway their purpose, move them to her desires and in these years she had been able only to convince them rarely, and she had moved them not at all. She was perplexed at that fact, but in this last year, she determined to find out why. She was brilliant in intelligence, her mind able and with a piercing wit that sometimes was resented. The trouble was she could find no fault that she could blame anyone for.

She realized that no one had usurped her power, they had not refused her any right to speak and had met her ideas with courtesy, even accepting some of them. She had never admitted to herself that she wanted to gain power here. For to do so was against her avowed ethics. She was less than half aware of the entire situation.She knew only a vague anxiety and had begun to feel subtle resentments.

Jessie felt a sadness as she realizd these things. The young woman had no idea how obvious was her body language. She didn't know that emotion poured from her without control, sometimes through the very words she chose to offer her ideas. Jessie was aware that only two others in the Hall were even faintly aware of the young woman's dilemma.None saw the whole picture. It was at such times that she must acknowledge her own powers, must notice her refined perceptions.

The Council was dealing with the usual problems of the town. The Master Farmer reported that three of the field discs had been in service for thirty years and that they were not functioning at their best. The new models would last at least fifty years with proper care and with no major repairs. In fact, he mentioned in a sort of pride, that the company that manufactured this equipment had ended their construction in three of its factories, setting up to manufacture other equipment. He said,"We've begun to learn how to make things that last. We don't need to repeat ourselves. The technology was about as fine as it could get.

The young woman, whose name Jessie realized was Edith, asked whether that wasn't a loss, when such work was no longer needed what would people do. There was a general laugh, The Master Farmer answered sincerely, that same pride evident, "We've got our whole selves to attend to. There's so much to learn and to create on this world and other worlds, in our minds and in our society,that we're grateful that industry has learned to put itself out of business. We can make machines that will last indefinitely, now, and we are beginning to do just that.People don't need to serve as laborers only. You notice our Learning Center is busy night and day?"

Everyone laughed, even the audience.This was a special concern of the man who spoke. He looked as if he'd accomplished it all himself. But there was warmth in the laughter and appreciation. The Council granted the Master Farmer's request and went on.

Some parents wanted to buy more belts. They said children could meet them for lunch even when they worked in the Industrial Center at the farthest Knoll of

THE AWAKENING

the town. But this request was not granted. Too many thought that walking was important to all citizens, old and young. The public dining Hall in the Civic center was half way between the Learning Center and the Industrial. "Good Heavens, it's only a ten minute walk, or less they way children run. You remember we voted to limit the number of belts available for all of us because we want to keep our bodies in shape."

The Chairperson broke the following silence with a raised hand and said,"We can vote on the matter, but we've got something more immediate for our money to be used for. There are a half dozen new citizens just sworn in. They're living in the exchange student residences. They have no homes yet. We've got to help them build their homes,which means a new residence section on the eastern slopes above the River. That leaves us only the south western field for future residences. That'll be probably another fifteen hundred families. When these two are full, we will have to close our town or vote on a change of our constitution. "

"Do the new citizens have work? Are they trained?"

The Council leader shook his head, "No,not yet. But they know something of building, thank God. They've come down from the north and have not had good teaching there. We've got them enrolled in the introductory program for newcomers and out of that the teachers will find their possibilities and train them for useful work with us. However, before we spend money on anything else, we have to get all citizens with homes and jobs."

There was general aggreement.

The Summer Festival plans were beginning to take shape. Tom, their mayor reported that the fields were being prepared for the new games that required dense very short grass. He said that teams were already practicing for the marathon runs and the boat races. This year,there would be many more boats involved , the marina would have to be enlarged. The local news casts repeated daily that they needed more people for the orchestra. Two bands were practicing, as everyone had noticed who passed the music Center, and there were four trios and five quintets of string and woodwinds. There would be no lack of music. The Vagabonds had agreed to set up their booths on the Highway to the north this year. There would be a video-phone applications for cafes and market stalls, people were already applying. Jessie smiled as she listened, it was not so different from any other Town meeting. Then a pause that was broken by a mention of the Builders.

She listened carefully then, for the name itself had created a faint stir in the Hall. The petition was read aloud. It was a request for use of forest land to be cleared for new crops. The crops desired were to be wine grapes. The Builders insisted they could persuade people to buy and use more wine thus creating a vastly greater market than presently existed. The suppressed mirth in the faces of some of the Council surprised Jessie, but they maintained their sobriety and the petition was tabled pending more study. Most thought this a decision for the Valley Council not a town Council. But Jessie realized others of the Council were disturbed, not amused. Who would want to persuade more people to drink more wine. Did they not have what they wanted already?

Jessie left the Hall with a sense of having touched into Adwin life fairly well. She must do the same with Jasper and Denlock. Find the nerve center of community life. The eager Reaching of minds had been brief and obviously unskilled, after the meeting, for there were many who barely knew of it, and there were an unknown number who did not know at all. Yet, the affirmation of Good Will, with which the Council always ended its meetings, was strong and, for Jessie, reassuring.

There were some who were utterly unaware of the sending but who basked in the flow of that Love, that Good Will, who received, as a birth right that affirmation. How different were human beings, Jessie reflected as she listened and watched. Those who received the energy with unease, felt a trace of fear which engendered anger.

Jessie reflected on these things as she walked with awe and delight through the lovely garden town. She marveled at the beauty of it. It was only begun when she was last here, but now, she watched the small fountains in paved courts while she rested for moments in little nooks designed for solitude and pleasure. She passed formal beds so precise they seemed made with a ruler, and just around a corner came upon a stretch so wild that only a wondering path broke the cacaphony of blooming plants.

After two hours of walking she settled in a small cafe, across from the entrance to the Learning Center. Above the great Arch that admitted all to its busy Rings, were carved one of the Valley Convictions. She read the words thoughtfully. 'Not one life is more important than another, Not one mind that cannot be lit from within'. People came and went constantly through the Arch attesting to the constant use that Learning Center got from citizens of every age. Someone ws giving a rare lecture, and the room was nearly full of people, children and adults. There was no period when children were 'attractive nuisances'. Their self esteem as important partners in the life of their community never was lost.

Jessie reflected that that had been a success, the involvement of people in mutual welfare was high. But more was needed. Now, there were certain teachings that must be enhanced, made more specific and primary. Ideas about the inner life, the life of Spirit, had been for too many only ideas, and now that they were beginning to know from experience, they needed further help.

It was time to go home, to rest, to think. She sipped her hot coffee and enjoyed the few moments, the quiet and the fragrance of the air.

Jessie sat in the silence of her own sphere , the town noises were shielded away, the odors and visual cacaphony were not. But for several minutes she closed her eyes and dropped into a deep rest state. Then, opening her eyes, she sat feasting on the world of color and life around her. People came and went, the paths were not crowded as would be the case with Santiago or Altos this time of day, but they were constantly full of movement. Birds were busy among the trees and house tops, other animals came and went. Dogs usually in groups of two or three, pacing their watch rounds, or simply traveling, sometimes as companions to groups of young children. A noisy troop of small monkeys were busily picking small weeds out of a bed of flourishing plants. She smiled, that was new.

Children clustered in small groups among the gardens, studying, observing, working on some project or simply preparing for a test. Adults moved through the Rings, intent on business,or pleasure. She watched, unthinking, enjoying and taking a measure, sensing the atmosphere of this town.

She opened that sphere of silence, allowed the soft hum of conversation, an occasional shout, the sound of air cars lifting, the faint starting hum of belts, the backgrond noise of birds, insects, and a strain of music from somewhere in the distance.

She smiled, it was so safe, so right, and yet, there was the feeling growing, as she projected her sensitive attention to hover out, lift and merge into that town fabric, that something was not right. Sensitive to atmospheric nuances, to that aura of design, of a people's signature in mass, she held her self listening. And slowly there was a definition. She realized that people were not acknowledging disturbance.

The peacefulness so long dreamed of, pervaded the town and no one wanted to break it. This was the first year that there were not building crews working everywhere, finishing, beginning, laying walkways and courts and planting gardens. This was the first year that everywhere in town there was a sense of completion. And it was a heady, joyous, calm. No one wanted to question it.It was easy to deny any flaw in the pattern of their life. She began to see the flaw, the strain in that fabric that could grow into separation.

She knew that most people felt something about those who were unable to Reach, unable to communicate mentally at all. What they felt ranged from pity, acceptance, to anger and resentment and even contempt. What the Builders felt, she knew was primarily anger, resentment and a sense of deprivation. There it was, a sense of being excluded, of difference that they could not understand and so feared.

She drew her thought into fine focus, striving to know the precise nature of that danger she felt. She held a point of attention firmly , distanced from emotions, aware of the hard, rough stone of the carved chair in which she sat, aware of the sky, the buildings behind her,the movement of millions of living beings, the smells. Aware! Aware -- three hundred and sixty degrees -- all around herself and far beyond she was alert to every tiny shift of sound , movement or smell. Her mind moved out to enter into that state of Joining with the mental world of the town. She knew thoughts, feelings, emotions running out and uncontrolled, thoughts random and incomplete like bits of mental straw, broken and drifting. The debris and undefined mental clutter that would be typical of any town of people only beginning their awakening.

She listened! She found small spots where thoughts rotated like buzzing bees, where people gathered in an obsession with those thoughts for minutes at a time. There were angers, settling in grey pockets, or stirred and flung about by the sudden shaking of fear. But there was, underlying everything, that bright, silvery Light that she could see clearly, that held life safely in its Presence. As yet, the energy flowing from the Light was firm. And focussing, she turned attention toward that southern, dark mountain.

Even as the dark shadows streaked into the Valley from those points far south, the Light simply shed them away, filling the dark with itself. She recognized points where shadows penetrated into places of Light. Pencils of dark that pushed deep into a tiny village or a pocket lurking in a corner of a city and holding the Light itself at bay. Jessie's task was not to record or map these places, others did that. She must take the assessment and begin her work there where the shadows penetrated in each small town and village of this north country.

Now, she prepared herself, holding her mental Reach steady, she shielded that delicate Touch from any mind straying near, from anyone able to feel the power around her and stray into it. She must build a bridge of consciousness that could extend from another deeper stronger sphere of Silence, one that would be opaque to any mind simply curious , and then she could Far Reach. As she built the shield, she accepted that any mind strong enough to penetrate her shield would be strong enough to deal with what it found.

------   -----   -----

Justina stood at the balcony that ran around the lookout rooms at the top of one of the three, twenty story stone and plasteel towers rising from the eastern mountains. They faced directly west, but the curve of the Valley gave those high rooms visual access to the Monitors Stations of south and west Valley when their flashing lights signalled one another. They had easier mental access to all three of the Stations. She could look far south to Clandor, invisible in its forest and massive granite boulders, She could see with the naked eye the triangle created by the Great River and the two tributaries flowing into it from western peaks. At that triangle was the city of Bend, her golden grain fields rippling across the flat deltas on land never plowed, each new crop seeded into the stubble of the previous one. The wild grain meadows were darker and stretched miles on into the delta. They were harvested but never otherwise disturbed.

Far across the land, like a toy sparkling in the sun, she could see the great gold, red, yellow and green Vine City that was Santiago climbing far above the forests below. But sharp as her eyes were, they were limited. She shifted to mental sight. She stood alone and patient. Sending relentlessly and steadily, her mental Reach like the sweep of a powerful beam of light. She did not need to lock into the web, not unless she found something needing special attention. She let her mind roam, alert, attentive.

She was young, but she had lived at the Monitor Station since she was four. Found by just such an one as herself sweeping through the Valley and watching for such Minds. She was now a senior Monitor, thirty seven years old and she was skilled and sensitive to any cry, any call, mental or emotional that told of need. Or told of a living mind awakened sufficiently to be able to undergo training here in this Tower.

THE AWAKENING

She thought of those whose Mental powers far surpassed her own. Even now, Drune's and Azelda's bodies lay quietly in their rooms. There were only three such beings in all the Valley. They were precious beyond imagining. Drune was often gone - living and working between worlds, or between dimensions of this universe. He worked always on a world scale, with other World Monitors. Zelda was gone more and more. Each usually returned to activate their bodies and exercize them a short time every day or so. Sometimes they were there to talk to at meals. Justina had at first been awed by them, found it difficult to talk, but soon, their easy, friendliness had won her trust.

These people had seemed ordinary human beings until their mental powers had been revealed. They had simply developed faster and earlier than their fellows. Azelda, still comparatively new to the work, was only sixty, had broken through to world level consciousness ten years ago. They needed her, there were not enough at that level yet. Now, she mentally Reached out from this tower, engaged in that strange wonderful work of those World Monitors. Justina wondered often what it might be like. How they lived, there, so extended out of the physical limits of life. But Azelda could only bear to be Far Reaching a fourth of the time that Drune could be. She feared that Drune would discard his body soon. The burden of taking care of it was more a nuisance than a value. Justina marveled that they took their tasks so seriously. They felt no burden in their unceasing labor. They seemed to need no personal life. She winced at the thought of not being mated to Lester. His face swam briefly before her, and winked out. Or their child, bright, fair, sweet Jerome. What would life beyond such personal attachments be like? Would Love Itself fill them so they loved all life the same? Could it be so?

Of course, she told herself, these two had felt themselves destined, had sought this work, from early childhood, had never sought ordinary satisfactions. They had both lived many thousands of human lives and exhausted their needs of them. What unknown extensions of life they entered now she had no idea. For both Justina and her mate, this new life of the mind, the Teaching of humankind of those farther dimensions that were its birthright, was more satisfactory than any other 'ordinary' life. Then with a sudden recognition, she smiled at herself. She herself would be thought by her own family to be sacrificing her life here at this Tower. Yet this was the most fulfilling work, life, relationship she could imagine.

She could sense Azelda there from time to time, swinging back and touching the workers of her own Tower. When she was not bound into the World network, Azelda's time was focussed on this Valley and the Teaching of the Monitors who ran the Stations. Justina allowed the thought of them to flicker through awareness, comfortingly, for only a moment. Then she refocussed all her attention into her task. What she glimpsed there, on contact with those far ranging minds, was overwhelming. She could not hold attention for long.

She leaned against the rough edge of the low wall, her mind cleared of thought,,empty, focussed again, receptive. She was trained to Reach, she could receive as accuratly as any person anywhere. Justine felt a gentle nudge like a sudden burst of energy, pushing at her mind and then swiftly gone. It had to be the new youngster, the young girl, brought in just a few months ago. She had been found in the northern swamp land, a backward community of non-conscious people, living as the old ones did, denying any talents, or mental powers that showed up and repressing any bright Visions of that greater consciousness. Azelda had seen her, like a bright mental light, flickering, because in her fear and pain, she had tried to close herself completely. Raymond and Martha had gone to find her, two of the Travelers. Her parents had not interfered, thinking the child insane they thought that these Travelers were Healers who would hospitalize her. Ezelda was awed by the power the child's mind promised, but she must be carefully trained and taught. Everyone had been so excited at her coming.

This little girl,whose name was Pauline, spoke of the Visions of the Virgin,the Vision of the Christ, and of the Buddha, though how she had heard of Buddha puzzled everyone. Her parents worshiped in their church as the 'old ones' had. And so they were not so disturbed when their daughter said she spoke to the Mother of God. It was when she refused to stop, and when she told her folks that through these visions she learned it was not wrong to sing, to dance, and to laugh. They decided she was insane when she began to enter those strange silences, sometimes lasting a day. She would watch for and try to talk to outsiders. Something the leader in their church forbade.

At first she had talked of her visions, then she had ceased, afraid of the whippings, the anger among her people. Her parents silenced her, hid her, afraid that their neighbors would destroy her or them selves. But the child had continued in secret, and had Reached out her great wakened conscious mind, awkwardly, fragmented, and sometimes blasting with power in a confusion of images and distortions of realizations. Sometimes her call was so faint it could barely be caught. Justina had been on duty the night that mental cry had Reached to her Tower. She caught it almost as a blow against her own mind. Full of pain and rage, of fear and longing. She had called to Selda, and found her, so desparate her own cry. Selda had caught,absorbed,and identified the source of the anguished calling.

But now, when Justine felt the slight shock of the child practicing focus, learning how to send and to listen, she felt a pang of jealousy, and smiled sadly. That very pang, that there was in herself still the capacity for jealousy told her her own consciousness was not yet pure enough, great enough, to be one of the Elders. That child would surely be, and soon. She must have been born with purity of nature, with a great heart open to the flow of Love already. Though Justina was a little jealous, she would be glad, would rejoice that another would begin to help in this work. She turned back, to clear her mind, focus and send again through the great Web of energy from Tower to Tower.

The Tower needed no instruments for this basic work, but their computers systems connected all parts of the Valley and made contact with every government,Temple, learning Center, Business office in the Valley instantanious.

THE AWAKENING

Justina knew that a separate group of elders were experimenting with direct brain-computer interaction. Nothing near it was known yet in the ordinary world. The real work of the Monitors was mental, a network that laced the Valley and that net could be shifted the way a lace curtain could be moved or shaken. For ten years now, the Monitor Stations all over the world had begun sponsoring world voting forums and slowly the idea was becoming acceptable to most nations.

Now as she listened her fingers played on a keyboard, recording what she received. When necessary she sent messages to rescue units. Now a distress call from an air car stranded in rough terrain, a mountain crevase. They did not know that anyone heard, they only felt a terror at their helplessness. Thinking to test their own skills they had set the car down into this ravine and misjudged its depth and narrowness. Now the air car was wedged in and they couldn't get it to release itself. They had refused to call for help, ashamed of their mistake until the motor was smoking with their aborted attempts to extricate themselves. Justina heard and alerted the rescue squad at Greenton, the nearest town.

Justina's attention swept on as soon as the report was sent. There were the usual low key turbulences, bursts of fury within a gathered crowd in a town in the mountains but they had their own policing crews. There were sudden waves of pain from one of the Healing Centers, but these were only background. She heard, knew and went on.

Suddenly her body tautened, she smiled, and the long brown hair curling slightly across her shoulders switched suddenly as she turned her head. She wanted to face physically this call. This was something different, something Monitors did not receive often enough and that they delighted in. Here was a Mind-Call from a citizen. She trembled with excitement that someone had called from there below in that vast Valley where millions of people went about their lives, mostly oblivious of their constant watch. Eagerly she set about locating the source.

Justina was not a beautiful woman, as most standards go, her body was short and round, her face round too with a mouth a little too wide, sensual and inclined to facile expression. Now that mouth curved into the sweet smile that won people's trust and revealed the inner Joy and warmth that people yearned to know. She felt the alerting of her body, her pleasure then swept them aside to focus wholly in that habitual discipline of a life time. She caught the flow of energy, the incoming call and Joined.

Swiftly, preliminaries done, identity known, permission received -- they exchanged personal comments, pleasure and interest in each other. Justina, so much younger, felt the undercurrent of lonliness in Jessie, her isolation and knew sympathy for that. Jessie's message was simple, yet her delight in reaching Justina of whom she had known, and Justina's pleasure in meeting thus one of the 'developing Elders' who traveled as a field worker, was clear. Then there was a mind shift, images began to play through from mind to mind and Justina saw as Jessie did. The task of the field worker was to report, and such a report Justine had not often received.

Here was Adwin, the Gardens, sculptured buildings, the Great shining River curving around the town, and then a swift picture of the members of twenty different Families. Jessie sent the thought,"It is my dying year and these are the people who will be entering the City soon. Their Journeys are imminent. There are others, who will be ready in a few more months. I must wait for them." Justine saw through this great Mind that sent images so clearly. It was as though she stood there in that place with Jessie. It was her only way to travel about the Valley. She enjoyed it.

Justina could not help her glad response."There are so many now, so many Journeys. It is an exciting time. People emerging and merging within themselves. They realize Spirit as the dimension into which they step, they wake into Consciousness. Their eyes are opening and they can See, they breathe the brilliant Light of Life." Her exuberance was characteristic of her, Jessie smiled.

She had waited long for the day when these increasing Journeys would signal the awakening Consciousness of humankind. She was sure that's what this was. She had wondered so many times in dispair whether that day would come at all. She had met her dispair, knowing it as one of the attachments she had not yet shed. She learned how to look at the dispair as a paradox of her own nature. For the Joy she had entered into on her own awakening was indestructible. She KNEW and the knowledge rested in clear Joy.

But now, it was a fact.That time had surely come.She asked,"How do they manage it all? Do they understand enough?"

Jessie answered,"They fear, they are not able to shake off the old coat of habits. Emotions still drown their vision much of the time. They struggle up out of the miasma of pattern and old fears. They do See, they perceive the Vision and the possibility as that experience of a great Light flooding their minds. They do not know yet all that it is, but they are awake to it. They break free, they do emerge, and they are so beautiful, Justina, So beautiful." She thrust out images that showed these things for Justina so that the young woman could share a little of the life of the field worker. Justina was grateful. She recorded the facts Jessie gave her, automatically, Sending into the Computer memory down in the lower floors of the Tower.

Jessie sent visual images, scenes that were examples, to show her meaning clearly. She Sent impressions that woke ideas in the young woman's attentive mind, and Justine understood. She showed her the differences, those who fear, those who accept,and those who resent and plan to demand regressions to old patterns. Then happily the ones who joyously accept their more developed fellows and look forward to their own future growth. Others feel fury at these differences and are suspicious. Jessie drew a deep, long breath,"There are, however, a very few who have wakened to that revealing Light. Who have become conscious, but who turn back into themselves. These choose to turn from that Light, the revelations of the Touch of Spirit. They cling to patterns of selfish greed, caught in the lure of the Dark One. And because they are so conscious, they are truly dangerous to themselves and everyone else. They will not be able to truly awake to the Vision because their underdeveloped egos hamper them. But they think they have fully developed beyond all others."

Justine sighed, receiving and recording in the same mental movement. "Oh, Jessie, we are aware of them. It is a grief!"

Jessie paused, went on. There was another part to record. "There are those who have no capacity to See at all, are as though retarded, but they will be developed in another life time. Such people sometimes are fine and beautiful individuals, sensitive and loving, of a high human quality, but they have not yet the capacity of mind needed for Conscious Soul perception. What they perceive is unconscious and so they translate it as myth or symbol. And that is as it has always been. However, right now they are easy prey for those who know the Vision and can Touch, who know the difference and yet have chosen to cling to the self life. Those find satisfaction in exploiting the situation. They can harm deeply those who do not yet consciously See."

"Then the number of people beginning to awaken is nearly eighty percent. That is unprecedented. It will make possible the difference. Your report is wonderful, Mother. The changes encompass the world. Now that your report is in we have only two more to wait for. As you guide those whose minds are aware, you will know their readiness for further realization. If the other reports prove the same, we will set many energies in motion, we will re-establish new webs of communication to be available as soon as anyone is able to sense them. The Elders will meet the threads of dark that come from those who choose the downward way. We can work openly and together to reveal the world of Spirit through these extraordinarily awake and trained minds.

" And those who fail? Those unable to See further than their bodies and physical minds? Or those who faintly See but are unable to drain off the old lusts and greeds that normally dissolve as consciousness expands beyond them. They have no strength and so, turn to their awakening as to another obsession for self service? What of those who do not choose, because they don't know there is a choice?" She hesitated, and sadly added, "Even more, what of those who choose to descend into darkness. What of them?" Jessie felt the power of the exchange flowing through herself. The strengthening of her own awareness.

"Those we must watch and pray for. When they are willing we can help them. But mostly, we must wait while they watch the lives of those of you who radiate Light itself, and wonder how they can live so. Spirit lives in them too, though it is hidden. It is only the Light in themselves that can help them. We can only strive to nourish that Light with our own shining. There may be suffering before that happens."

"But won't they not harm the others? Those freeing themselves, readying themselves for full Awakening?"

Justina hesitated, she Reached to the quiet rooms at the bottom of the Towers, and Ezelda heard, Justina gratefully tied her into the connection.

Jessie was aware of the change, the clear, strong, pulse of mind, of thought, as though a speaking occurred in her mind, not only the visual imagery, and indistinct 'idea' of the younger Monitor. The words shaped carefully,"My Sister, you know well, those who have begun to awaken cannot be damaged seriously. They have met their own darkness, awakening itself expands consciousness beyond that dark nature, and the Light dissolves all dark. They will turn away from the undercurrent of regressive needs of those choosing the way of dark. But, yes, there is danger. But we cannot interfere, except to continue our own offering of streaming Joy and Love into the Valley. Love is a powerful strength!"

" Yes, of course! I needed to hear that reminder, Mother. I am well aware that the people are approaching a major test and that we must allow them to meet it themselves." She felt her own longings, her impatience, present there in that exchange and made no attempt to conceal them from the young Monitor or the old Elder who was Joined with her. She felt a rumble of chuckling and Ezelda's mental smile at Jessie's weakness. Every human being had their own natures to deal with, the fact that one was a Monitor did not change that fact.

Then Jessie thought sadly, "Perhaps my own inadequacy has something to do with this. Perhaps I am so little beyond them in development that I cannot see well enough their waking Light, their loving Hearts."

Justina listened, holding her breath. She knew the smile of the Elder also. Jessie's admission was crucial. And to hear it coming from one like Jessie was reassurance for herself. Even the wise ones must persistently discipline their personal natures.

Few among them could identify the shades of wisdom and folly. She herself saw easily those colors and shapes called auras that were the astral bodies of all people, She could see also that bright flame of Light within the Heart of any person, however dim it might be, that was Spirit Itself. But she was not yet adept enough to know how to identify direction for another. She thought no one ever could. Each must choose his own way!

The Elder Sent a familiar image this time. Jessie must help, must guide, must encourage and must act from the guidance of Spirit within herself, always. She must constantly strive to know the difference between self and Self that she not fool herself and choose to listen to the wrong voice.. In doing so, she might be able to avoid harming any living being. But the way was narrow. "Your LIFE is the teaching, you know, my Dear."

Jessie was there among the people, watching from her own personal frame, needing to deal with her own private encumbrances of personality, with her own inherent needs and lusts, and she must recognize these even to know when she was enticed by those masters of persuasion who could and would seek to draw her from her task. Justina thought she, herself, had a less difficult task, for she was seldom confronted with temptation or with conflict in herself. With supreme sympathy she sent,"Oh, Mother, how tenuous, how delicate must be your hand, your mind,, in this matter. I don't envy you.I long to realize how this might be done. I am not yet able." The Elder,Ezelda,faded from their Joining. Justina said, "Please let me call for our own Elders. I'm afraid I'm not conscious enough to help. I need to learn with you."

Jessie smiled mentally, sending acceptance and gratitude. Tuning their Reach, they focussed attention, held, listened. After a held breath, there was a wave of such power that Jessie felt a new light had been turned on in her mind. Her heart was blazing with life. The focussed minds of the two, Jessie and Justine were met and held. They relaxed utterly. They need do nothing but attend. The great Minds the two women had contacted were like fresh air in a stale room. Like sunlight after long years of moonlight. They surrounded the two with energy and shaped that energy into mental images. Two were Senior Mothers,and one a Senior Father. They had joined one another with a small part of their consciousness, because the larger part of each mind must continue with the work they were engaged in when they were called.

The great overpowering energy that filled them, in which they felt themselves swimming mentally,,was the energy of Love. Jessie knew, without question, not even asking how or why, that Love as expressed through these Elders was beyond any idea of Love that even she had known. Was there no end to it? The knowledge of it broke through fine reserves, thin walls of herself and quickened her receptive power. Tears ran unchecked down her face into her neck. Her body reacted to such wonder and that was right.

Then she became aware of three bodies, three bodies of Light itself, pear shaped, flowing within themselves, but clear to her mind's eye. Faintly she imagined faces, and searched them to see. Then within the center of each she could see a point of such pure white Light that her mind was blinded for a moment. She sought again the 'face'. Knowing it was her own conceit that she sought it.

The three Old Ones waited, letting Jessie and Justina adjust to their presence. Jessie stood receptive, familiar enough that she was swept with profound relief at their coming. Now she would understand. The voice that spoke was gentle, infinitely calm, and the calm transferred itself to the listeners. The voice echoed in their minds, as if ears were bipassed.

"Your task, beloved ones, is to watch, to guide and to watch. Your task is to give direction and how can you do that? You can see that there is no force,no advice, no using of another's way to find your own. So it must be. Each must find the way that is his\her own. However, you will be always ready to give guidance and do that best when you are clear in mind, pure in heart, focussed and not doubting your own path. If this balance is not "true, keep to yourself until you have re-established it. They will see how it is with you. Any person will sense that quality in you that is Soul consciousness, even when they don't know its name. People of this Valley know a lot they aren't conscious of.

They sense your power. They will be inspired by your firm stand, your calm knowing. You, standing within your own love for them, aware of Love itself,will open to them a door to the Presence of Love." There was a silence like a soft rustle of cool air. Then another voice, deep and tender, spoke.

"Not one can pour out Love. Love is Present, it can only be recognized! We can't manipulate people to see what we do, we have to allow them to find their way, and their way may lie through what seems a wrong direction to you. You can help most by living a life utterly conscious. By being aware of the Presence of Love and acting from that." He was still, with a stillness that seemed to pervade everything for those few minutes.

Then he said,"Here you must learn to distinguish. Selfishness is so endemic in your world that it is not always easy to recognize when it has dominated an action. The action of selflessness rises out of Love. Those you work with will feel the Love that springs through your life, and will respond even when the pull of need, or hungers for old satisfactions, rise up in them. You MUST stand firm!" Again the stillness, like a refreshment.

"The dark one prepares a storm to push you off center, to conceal the flow of Love among people, and to masquerade within that storm in a bitter parady of Love, a twisted, dispondancy that is lust, and need, not Love, a defilement. Some who are ignorant will not distinguish. Some who do distinguish but are caught in that dark trap, will choose that dark parady. But most people of the Valley will know,their hearts are full of Light and the Vision has opened their eyes. Have courage!

Always your own focus must be strong. You must stand as the pivot point. The possibiity for choice. Call on us if need rises, but if you stand firm, at your highest point of consciousness, other people will drift upward to join you . Do you understand?"

Jessie nodded, physically numb,but the message she sent was fine and clear. Mind responded to Mind. "I understand." She must keep her own balance,because if she could not sustain,the ones she taught would have no centering point to reach to. She stood aware of the gift of energy that flowed from these great ones. She held herself still, receiving and gathering her strength.

After several moments, the figures in the Light faded, and dissappeared. She watched until the last trace of that Touch left her. She nodded slowly, breathed a deep long breath, trembling with the recognition of the task ahead. Was she able? She turned her attention and Touched in farewell to Justina, and gently drew away, until she realized herself sitting in the small Jessie body there in the gardens of Adwin. Everything was the same, though all existence seemed to have shifted itself.

And life went on, air cars spun overhead, busy with business and pleasure, children brought their projects to and from the Learning Center or the industrial center .They came with the adults from labratories where they learned as they did small jobs to help. Festivals held four times a year, made a public so familiar with the process of preparing and showing their work, their creations, and artistic performances that it had become part of the years approach to all work and play. Runners ran along the Highways, cheered on by the Vagabonds camped along the way. Singers sang in Hall and field, or in secluded gardens. Field discs floated, moved easily from field to town, from Farm to city. The world was full of color, Life flaunted its own creations. Business was brisk bringing air freight cars

THE AWAKENING

full of goods to be sold, and leaving with those cars again full.

But Jessie was aware anew. There was beneath all the gaity and anticipation a note of somberness. Children looked at the adults with a new recognition, and unspoken questions. Adults watched, with wonder and apprehension, their own children. Knowledge of the difference in the people was no longer an idea, but a fact. However, as spring had passed and days went by into summer a people busy and happy, had found it possible to put aside what loomed ahead. Clouds hung quiet in a blue sky, only a grey ribbon against the mountains hinted that a storm might come. Jessie got up and walked back to the farm. She would continue her work among the people tomorrow.

Since Adwin's gift of its self to the Valley at the Spring Festival, every reminder of their accomplishment still filled the people with pride. The feeling of celebration continued through the beginning weeks of summer. The offices of the Civic center hummed with communications systems linked with the every city of the world. The Learning Center Library tied town scholars into conversations across the world. There was a sense of completion, of vacation.

The relief from the endless labors was itself a renewal of energy. Shouts, singing, choruses,laughter, foolishness and serious conversations all filled the air with sound. Music, dances, games, wonderful foods and drink (and there were a few who drank too much) made the evenings joyful. But a deep stillness of a people sharing the meditations of their heart in conversation,study,realization,had begun to underlie all of social life.

The daily work was good. Adwin began finally settling into the ordinary work of running a city, building their business and industry to compete with those of other cities. They had plenty to do. The air traffic increased as business did,and the skies were flickering with the bright flash of air car and freight car.

Vagabonds rolled along all the Highways, eagerly visiting through the new summer all their familiar land. Life was quiet, with an undercurrent of expectation.

CHAPTER TWENTY TWO

Andrew and the children

One morning only a few days later, Andrew sat reading in his cottage. He needed to study and to find information for a paper he must submit in a week. The access panel to the Valley library, and from it to the world libraries, flashed intermittently doing a job he had just given it. He was deep in thought for this study, had stayed home just for this opportunity for greater privacy. He looked up and out the window at the ending of the showers that had fallen through the night. Good, it would be clear by the time he must go to town. His eyes narrowed, feeling that familiar disturbing restlessness that plagued him in these past weeks . He knew how to avoid it, to set it aside, but it demanded more frequently now, he could not put it off much longer, and yet, he did not want to turn and meet it. Why not? Usually he had no hesitation to meet emotions that surfaced. Identifying then dispelling or satisfying. He saw his friends struggling too. None of them talked about it. Yet they used always to talk - about everything! Strange, now that adults finally were talking, his peers had fallen silent. Things were not the same, but how to put a finger on just what was different?

The way he felt about people, the way he responded, or, especially, the way he reacted, all different. Jemmie had said it was sex, they had to find a serious girl friend. But Andrew shook his head at the memory. Jemmie had to know better. Their girl friends were as interested in experimenting as they. They were all finding out about their bodies, and sex was one good way to learn. No, whatever was different was -- deeper, even than their feelings. At least the feelings they knew.

He put down his book, what he read didn't register. He was obviously NOT ignoring his problem now. He wanted to know everything about what made people act, their emotions, from the most depraved to the most sublime. Men had indulged emotional appetites,history tapes told them that, but what did it FEEL like? He thought he could put aside any dark desires, surges of impulsive emotion, because he watched dispassionately, and recognized them. On the other hand, people had always sought with unceasing intensity for that highest desire. The desire for whatever they knew as GOD. He wanted to know that too. What had it been like to know in these ways? But he thought he always kept the choice. He didn't choose to indulge himself in ancient lusts, he just wanted to know what they were like. He thought he had amused himself with a small taste of them. How could a person detach himself from what he could not name or show himself was undesireable? But on the other hand, could he avoid the trap, could he stand observing and not be sucked into them? Lost to himSelf?

THE AWAKENING

His friend Steel had insisted that he knew nothing of the real possibility of human lusts. He had spoken loftily, as from long experience, and Andrew doubted him. "Lusts of the flesh, Andrew, there are a lot of them, you know. You don't even know how to name them, let alone meet them. And those of having things, grand deluxe air cars, a palace on a mountain all your own, beautiful furnishings, the very best. Or think of art works, all the music of the world in your studio, you could have it all, you know. But you have to WANT it enough. Oh, you don't know the sweetness of that, little Andy," Steel had said, his eyes glinting. He thought Andrew hated it when he called him by that child name,'little Andy', but Andrew knew he had shrugged off any attachments to it. But those words rang in memory still. He asked himself aloud,"Is there so much I haven't any idea of?"

Well! Was that it? He knew that to play with such feeling, could be dangerous. He thought he was grown up enough, strong enough to quell them when he chose.. But then, something wrestled within him, something he did not understand, and that he would not name! Would there come a time when he could not resist -- even himself? And what part of himself could that be?

After all,there were safeguards, that's what the Monitors were for wasn't it? To keep an eye on things? He thought he was on shaky ground here. He remembered asking Jessie about the work of the Monitors, partly hoping she knew, partly to test her. He had asked her what that web of energy was that they kept intact through time.?" She answered with a question, which she often did."If it is energy, can you imagine the nature of such a web?"

Without thinking he answered, "Why, it must be of the nature of Love and Good Will. Yet, I don't understand that at all, even though I've said it." He grinned sheepishly, He was not unfamiliar with that dilemma.She had smiled and nodded. "Just so.Andrew. Just so." He had frowned and wanted to ask more but she had left him, seemed to think he had enough to figure it out for himself and he had felt frustrated and a little resentful of her. Master Teachers were always doing that. He still didn't know whether Monitors could be depended on to protect him. From what? From himself? Surely not!

He pulled himelf back to the present. He could hear the songs of Planting. Jane and Steve were finishing some late planting in wild meadows. He looked up, listening, remembering the Adwin Planting Festival when the whole town, thousands of people joined in putting in their crops. He watched a mental image shape, of the floaters gaily decorated skimming over fields with stubble broken enough to receive the seed. He had sung a new melody and the town had kept it to enter into permanent Planting songs. He felt good remembering.

He shook his head, returned to the book and the Screen where he could see the working out of his problem going on. He checked it. So, THAT material was in the library in Budapest, he made a mental note of it. He lifted a book to read further. But a movement caught the corner of his eye. He turned. A small boy stood silently watching him. He turned back, made a note from his text to the screen .Then, realizing what he'd seen, he stopped, turned again. The child was still there.

THE PEOPLE OF THE VALLEY

It was Tim, Rodney's and Alice's son, aged eight years. Rodney had been Jerry's friend as long as Andrew remembered. He had hiked with Jerry and Andrew and Anna on many an expedition into the mountains, or fishing in the Green River on flatboats where they camped for days. Alice had come down from the north land and had joined them. Then she and Rodney were betrothed. Now, their little boy leaned gently against Andrew's knee and asked,"What are you doing?"

Andrew felt irritation, couldn't he see? But he'd dealt with Tim before. He shrugged, intending to refuse talk, then succumbed."Can't you see?"

Tim nodded,"You're reading. But you've been sending out some messages too,huh?"

Andrew nodded, glanced around at the books lying on the tables, His impatience battled with his love for the little boy. Tim sighed and said,"Will you teach me to read?"

Andrew was both elated and chagrined. He shook his head, "No, I want to read myself, and to finish this problem on my screen." But as he spoke, he knew he could not hold to that before such a request. He glanced down at the child,leaning now firmly at his crossed knees and studied the wide serious eyes. Andrew had known Tim since his birth, he was like a nephew to him but he smiled, then continued reading, ignoring those eyes,. For minutes there was silence. Then the Reach he felt touched his mind delicately, with a shyness of the very young. He felt the tentative hesitance and then like a snapped rubber band, it was jerked away. He held his breath, realizing and noticing his first impulse to deny it. It was impossible! Neither Rodney or Alice Reached, never had he found them able to Touch. His heart raced as he realized.

He rallied. Tim HAD Reached! Little eight year old Tim, whose parents had never made that connection .But then, why not. He himself had Reached at that age, had tested his Mind Touch. And had received mostly rebuff too. He would not do that to this one.

With a long sigh, Andy closed his book, turned to Tim and met his eyes. Any request to learn anything was a mandate no one could refuse. The fact of that Reach gave him no choice. He said,"Just a minute, Tim". He turned, touching switches to complete then save material he'd gathered. After a few minutes,he shut off the computer. Then, turning, he made a gentle and tentative Reach to Touch the child's mind. Tim gave a start, his eyes widened, and then narrowed and then he laughed with a wild joy. His face shining he said,"I knew ! I felt you with me, Uncle Andrew. I knew you were there." And Andrew thought he had not been so complimented in his life.

He set his book aside and touched the little boys' hair. He smiled at him and was rewarded with a bright happy grin. The child accepted that comforting smile. Deliberately Andy Reached once more. Then he Touched gently the questioning mind and gave full approval. Tim looked up, his own swift smile equal to Andy's now and a wonderful look of relief and joy poured out from that Touch. The emotion was pure pleasure but it flooded everywhere, and Andy saw he had no

THE AWAKENING

control at all. He must talk to the Master Teachers about Tim. And he, himself, must be willing to teach. It was a mandate laid on every person. He had been benefited more times than he could tell. Even this new person Jessie, even she held that trust. She too must teach when asked.

A memory flooded his mind, of walking just a few days ago, with his friends in the Fields beyond the Learning Center. They could see Jessie walking toward the Farm across the field and suddenly, impulsively, in Joined agreement, they Reached to her. Their combined minds greatly stronger than any one mind could have been. He hadn't expected much, the usual blank refusal. To their pleased surprise she stopped instantly, turned and came to them. They looked at each other, each one wanting the other to explain. It was such an absolute response from the young to an adult. They had not thought it would apply to her too. Mary Lou had been pouring out her grief about her troubled relationship with a lover, Kevin. She cried out to Jessie, finally willing to ask for help."I can't go on feeling like this. It hurts. But I can't make him feel what he doesn't feel either. How can anyone solve such a problem?"

Andrew had sympathy, he knew how that felt too. Jessie smiled, nodding. "Yes, how indeed." Mary Lou's eyes widened at Jessie's knowledge. How could she know? But Jessie's eyes had met Kevin's and woke there a willingness.

Kevin turned to Mary Lou. Andrew watched, knowing that something terribly important was happening. If he wanted to know about people, here was one time he might learn. He held his breath. Kevin drew a long breath of his own and said,"Mary Lou, you know that the Teachers say we have to constantly practice. To practice ! We keep telling them that we do practice, that we remember and so - now - maybe we should practice ourselves, you and I". The two young people held each other's eyes, undisturbed that Mary Lou's question had been deflected to Kevin. It was a habit of Master Teachers, so it would be for Jessie who was something more. She was grateful that Kevin did not dodge. His guilt troubled him and he was willing to help.

She turned away, angry and weeping. He caught her arm but she pulled free. "I can't understand how. Oh, yes, they tell us that such problems can't be solved when one is 'drowned'in emotion and obviously I am," her voice was sarcastic and thin with pain. "I know as well as you do that we are supposed to 'Balance'ourselves first. Oh, yes, Kevin, I've listened, I've learned. I think I'm better at Balancing than you are, in fact. But how does one do it right in the middle of all the hurt and pain? If I can't work it out in the midst of the pain and I'm hurting all the time, then when?" Her tears flooded her cheeks and she ignored them, looking at him angrily.

Kevin swallowed,obviously in pain to see her so hurt."I don't know Mary Lou. I don't know why it's like this. I wanted to tell you a month ago, because I saw that what you felt was more than,-- more than I could respond to.I should have told you I didn't want to be your lover anymore. That, I wanted to be your friend, instead. I couldn't tell you, because I know how it feels, to be told that.I think maybe it hurts me as much, to be the one has to say it." He sighed, reached one hand toward her and then drew it back. His eyes were as full of pain as her's now. She met those eyes, saw that pain, found some comfort in that fact." He said lamely, "I do love you, you know."

Finally she nodded slowly, "I think I know. I can see a little. It helps when I see that it hurts you too. That you don't want to hurt me.In some way you do care." She wiped her face with both hands, and frowned, the pain lifted a little. "That makes me wonder whether I need too much. Why would I need so much? My friends, all of you, get involved, then break up and relate to someone else and you don't fall apart. I wish I could know." She looked at Kevin but he only sighed, relieved to hear her voice more normal but unable to answer.

Jessie reached, Touched so gently that the children were unaware . She felt the surging anger, fear - hurt, that clotted and blinded Mary's thinking, that would eventually push her completely off balance. Jessie gently held, focussed the perspective the young people were gaining, that they usually had. Her steady strength helped them right themselves, bring themselves into control without denying the feelings. Mary Ann was looking steadily into Jessie's eyes - aware, clinging to that help.

Mary Lou said,and it was obvious that she was quoting, a note of bitterness in her voice, "To do what we must, to Reach into our own inner selves,to lift consciousness, to stand beyond the turbulence of emotion and see." She grimaced,"That's what they teach us and it's what I've practiced. But now! now!" They felt the tremendous effort, the swimming flow of her mind drawing through that liquid drag of emotion. Then the focus, wobbly at first, gaining stability. Then - suddenly, the change.

Her face cleared , she looked from wide surprised eyes at them all, "Why it's already different. I've done that, just that. I see that being lost in the feeling makes me blind. So it does. I ALLOWED it to drown me. I allowed it myself." She dropped her eyes,"I wanted to hurt you. To - to make you see how much you hurt me too. But even more, I actually felt as though I ought to sit there in that pain, because it was all I was worth. That I deserved that pain,because if Kevin didn't love me, then I'm not worth loving. I did that. I - " She was frowning now, looking at Jessie but seeing none of them.

"I couldn't even see that Kevin didn't want to hurt me.I couldn't begin to see that people do love me.I didn't even want to see that." She sighed,"You know, it's true, it's like a self fulfilling prophecy, I had to make it true.I got some kind of perverse satisfaction out of being so miserable and that makes no sense at all to me. I hate that. I hate to admit it too." She looked bewildered at Jessie."But I've known this, all of it. I've told myself these things, before and they just didn't stick. I seem to forget and pull the misery over myself".She was shaking her head. Seeing herself as she never had and without self contempt. The emotions of a few moments ago, faded in this new astonishment.

She looked across the gardens,her face already dry in the sun."Then, to lift clear out of it like this. To See! It was because you were there with me.I could stand it! But to realize finally, to let go of the need,so there's no pain. Well, that's

THE AWAKENING

another thing. It'll take time to learn to do that. It would be better if I didn't see you at all, Kevin. Not at all for a while." She looked at him. Her eyes clear now, unafraid.

Kevin nodded, a sadness filling his eyes, but relief flooding him."I know. It's what I had to do too once. But then she didn't agree and I had to go away for a while." He reached out a hand,then dropped it,"I will make a promise to avoid you if I can be sure you know it's not because I don't care."

She smiled wanly, holding his eyes." O.K. I believe you. The Teachers say, 'to lift above and See.' That's what I'll practice. But I don't want to see you for a while. I'll let you know." She turned to Jessie,"I'm sorry Mother, that when we meet you it always seems to be with a problem."

Jessie nodded,"What else are adults for?" She laughed and Mary Lou smiled. Then still keeping her attention on the young girl's fear, Jessie continued to offer strength. Watched the mental- emotional struggle , waiting.

Mary Lou said," I suppose it's in what you said, that I'm afraid to talk about, to even think about what - what - must be the cause of all this." She sighed and looked down.

"How old are you, Mary Lou?"Jessie's voice carried a comforting warmth.

I'm seventeen. I should be better balanced oughtn't I, at my age? She frowned, her voice harsh.

Jessie shook her head. "Emotional balancing for human beings is endless. There's no ought involved. What is this you refuse to talk about?"

"I don't know, because I've never talked about it. But it's what's the cause of - of neediness, the thing that makes my clinging. I know it is! Whatever it is, it's the cause."

She dried her eyes, shrugged with an angry gesture and went on," It's what makes me afraid when I can't keep someone involved longer than just playing at sex.. Teachers tell us that we must know our bodies, how they function, what is right for us, and their needs. But I get so dependant. I just need one person, the one I'm in love with, and being in love seems so overwhelming. I can't think of anything else and I have to keep that one person as my own, my possession, in fact." She was crying again , speaking this much of the trouble released the old pain.

"What are you afraid will happen?"

She swallowed, shook her head, to get control. Met Jessie's eyes, hesitated and then, resolutely, she Reached. She longed to get this problem met, she caught at the mental strength that Jessie offered. She felt the stabilizing of her emotions, felt the pain loosen, and suddenly she said,"I'm afraid that if this lover leaves me then there won't be any other and that I'll be left all alone." She burst into sudden tearing sobs,"I'll be all alone."

She stared at Jessie with surprise, even through the sobs. "I've never said that, I've never known that." She reached out a hand, and Jessie took it in both her own. Kevin caught the other and she clung to them, her eyes seeing only Jessie."Oh, Mother, I remember! I remember!" The pain she felt was harsh, like vomiting up a vile food, she wanted to fling it away. The images racing up into her mind now were sharp agony. She made no effort to shield, Jessie thought she didn't know how to shield selectively. They saw the image of a very small Mary Lou and the terrible pain of abandonment. She leaned her head against Jessie's shoulder, because she felt unable to support herself for a moment. The sobs were like a ripping out of inner substance. Jessie poured through and all around her the Healing Energy that would help, would replace this pain with relief, perhaps with acceptance. In one quick movement of dispair, Mary Lou drew her hands free and plunged into Jessie's arms.

Jessie held her, whispering softly, stroking her hair. She let Mary Lou cry, heaving, racking sobs that came from her whole body. Finally after ten minutes, aching long minutes, Mary Lou drew her emotions into balance. Then as suddenly as it had begun, the storm of crying was done. She stood looking at the three friends who stood silently around her, their eyes clearly loving. And she consciously willed away the shame that made her want to refuse them.

Jessie kept the outflow of Healing entering into the deep places in that body mind, clearing that tightness of muscle, dissolving that knot of repetitious hurt that had been hidden so long it had begun to crystalize. The tensions drained away, the muscles loosened and Mary Lou yielded to that Healing. She felt sore, raw as though with a new wound, but it was clean now, ready to heal. Turning to the two boys, she Reached. She was there more definitely than either of them had ever known her to be. She met willingly their Touch, a growing sense of trust shaped itself as she gave herself up to this gift. Now the tears that poured across her face were tears of relief, of acceptance.

With wide clear eyes, she looked from one to the other. Then they were separate and she stood alone again, realizing. "Oh, my God, all this time I've pushed you all away, allowing only one I could cling to. The Teachers always told us we could not know love unless we are willing to give ourselves" Her eyes were bleak, "They told us that we can't be Healed unless we're willing to trust. It was all words to me, until now!" She reached her hands to Jessie, moved close and kissed her. Then, still clinging a little to Jessie, she reached to the boys, for reassurance, affirmation, risking refusal. She had to know, to be able to ask and accept either refusal or acceptance.

Kevin flinched, but Andy responded wholly, then slid an arm around her shoulders and hugged her. Kevin righted himself, extended a hand to take her hand. Jessie watched the mental embrace of these three children, giving a little balance where it was needed. Then Mary Lou withdrew, nodded, and bent her head. "It's all right, I'm not finished with this. I know, but it's at least begun. Perhaps now, I can talk about it in my Peer group. I never could before, never even could begin." She looked sad but gave herself a brisk shake and said, "Well, I'm not the only one's got troubles in this valley today."

They continued with their walk, Mary Lou deep in thought. She glanced at Jessie, whose hand she still held. She turned wearily into herself. The startling brilliance of everything, the sweetness of the bird song, the absolute beauty of the sky, seemed to her to be greater than ever in her life. She knew that she was simply paying attention finally. She was, at least for this moment, free of her obsession. Now she knew what it was, she would finally win permanently free. The world had always been as beautiful. She just hadn't been able to See. She laughed, a clear, joyous ringing laugh that had lightened Andrew's heart to finally hear it. But at the end of the laugh, came a sudden sob. There was much yet to be done here.

Andrew had watched her, his eyes full of relief, they moved from Kevin to Mary Lou. Jessie's eyes caught his and she smiled. He knew suddenly that this kind of happening could occur for anyone, maybe not so painfully always.

Now, immersed in the memory, he remembered how relieved he had been as they walked on to their study rooms. And now, he reflected, he knew more clearly what he had learned that day. All rejection, even to the confident, was painful. Some just learned to cover up better than others. People NEED people. We are inseparable!

Then a thought came that struck his mind with the force of a blow. All those people not able to Reach, to Touch, must feel this rejection. Powerfully then, the Teacher's warning that no real growth could occur without pain, came burning against his mind. He had entered so wholly into the memory he was startled at Tim's voice, calling to him.

"Andy! Andy! Can't you hear me?"

He jerked himself back to the present, a little embarrassed, still feeling irritation at being disturbed, he turned to look at Tim's waiting face. So patient he was. He thought, turbulent as this Valley life might be, here is something very stable, here is a normal happy thread, keeping something of our good life intact. And this little boy absolutely trusts me. What an obligation. And I want his trust. I CAN support it. Andy loved to teach, he loved Timothy, He could feel the sharp clarity of the little boy's mind, feel it's tentative Touch. Finally he grinned, and Tim smiled his wonderful radiant smile that would be just like his mother's when his teeth finished filling in. He said, "Tim, that's a right request, and I'll teach you to read."

Tim said, "Right now?"

Andrew shook his head, "No, it'll soon be lunch time. You go play until after lunch and then I'll take you in to town and we'll begin. O.K?"

Timmy spoke excitedly, "Then I'll bring Eddie and Edith. They want to learn too - with me."

Andrew visualized the other children, Eddie, nine, and Edith eight. They would be as was Tim. Yet there was something about that little Edith, something elusive and fascinating. Maybe he could find out what it was. Did she Reach and was unaware of it? Or was it something more? Could it be he had spent so much time trying to keep his family from knowing of his own Reach that he had not noticed others? He felt suddenly excited at the possibilities. He could show them how to work together and learn from each other. He agreed they could all come and Tim went on his way.

Andrew was left alone, but his concentration was gone. He thought suddenly of Stella. The girl who was his lover, her face a visual picture in his mind, and remembered the ways that these friends of his had learned from one another through their young years. Then Steel, his long serious face, his strange separativeness. Something about Steel had always tugged at his heart. A boy whose parents were strangely elusive, distant, who had come down from the North land when Steel was already six. As a little boy Andrew had felt a burning fury in Steel and at that time he hadn't understood. It had taken time to earn his trust. Yet in the early years, it was Steel who had met his own mind more powerfully than any other friend. But the Reach was incoherent, fragmented. Something was there in Steel, some anger, some resentment, and he would not bring it to his Peer group anymore than had Mary Lou. He thought the wall in Steel was more rigid than it had been in her. He felt a strange dread rising through him, stopped to notice it and wondered at it's source. Then, seeing that he would not study more now, he put his work away, turned off the machines and went to hunt for Steve. Steve could help him sort things out.

Steve was, as Andy assumed he would be, in the fields with Jane. He stood beside a parked hover planter, he'd just completed his design and seeded it into the unplowed field. Jane was still working on another, Andy could hear her singing the planting chants and the soft purr of the hover disc. Steve turned to him and asked,"What's on your mind, Son?"

Andy said, "Something I need to know, but it can wait a minute. I was watching as I walked down. I could see the design where the blade cut into the stubble and broke the dark of Earth. They look fascinating even without the plants to show them off. D'you think you'll win the design award this year?"

Steve shook his head,"It's not going to be me this time. If it's won for this Family, it'll be Jane. She's done something wonderful but you'll not be able to get the measure of it 'til the plants are well up. She knows things about how plants go together that I'll never know. I think she talks to them. We're about done for the day and it's only noon. Matter of fact, this little job will finish all the planting. So we're going to town and meet some friends for a bottle of beer and good talk. Want to come?"

Andy shook his head,"No, I've made another appointment. I hope her design is chosen. But then, Jane never seems to care whether it is or not."

" Oh, ,she's pleased, but it's not important to her. It's just fun to do it as far as she's concerned. But what's on your mind, Andy. You didn't come down here to talk about planting design.

Andy looked absently through the grove that grew between the fields and the River. Water shining in the sun flashed bright through the young green leaves and the day seemed dreamy, full of peace. Already warm. "It's Tim. You know, Rodney's boy and a couple of his friends. He asked me to teach them to read. I decided I'd like to teach them, but how does a person teach reading?"

Steve laughed," I see you have't been in the chidren's section of the Learning Center for a long time. In the first place when the kids ask, they're really ready.

THE AWAKENING

Cassie didn't ask 'til she was eight, and by that time she already knew more than I did at twelve. But she was ready! They've got all kinds of equipment and the Teachers are patient. You just point the kids at it. Show them where the rooms are, take them in and the rest is easy. You haven't seen the new machines yet?" At Andy's head shake, he went on,"Well, they're amazing, science fiction kind of things."He grinned, "You remember when I took you? It's a different world, Son, a different world."

Andy made a face,"It seems like a long time."

"It isn't. And you know how many things the little ones do at the Center as soon as they can walk? Well, by now, Tim'll've learned a lot of things. He's READY! When they're ready, they just seem to soak it up, they're reading by the next day."He nudged Andy with one elbow,"Look at that lady out there. Think she'll ever be surpassed?" Then grinning still, he added," You watch those kids, You'll learn something your self."

His face sobered, then he gazed away across the fields,"I remember what the Teacher said the day I took Cassie in. He said kids were changing,they just seemed to learn without help. And now, it's even more so, Andy. The children are different from kids when I was a boy.The quality of people, of the children anyway,seems to be - better. I wondered when we talked at the Planting Gather, whether it had to do with this -- this Reaching? I don't see how that could make a difference. It must be what Jessie said, that Spirit wakes in us." He shook his head, was silent, looking across the fields, the sun slanting across his face made the sprinkling of premature grey hair in his beard turn silver. He went on softly, "I watched Cassandra that day at the Center, she was so absorbed, I just went out and sat in the garden and thought."

Andrew shrugged, "Well, then, it's mostly a matter of getting them there, isn't it? I can do that.I wonder what machines they use. I've heard of Reading machines, but never thought much about them, thought they were experimental." He was silent then, remembering his own early years there, the long hours he had studied with film and tapes in the library, the hours and even days in the gardens, the hills, when he had learned how to see, to hear, and to smell accurately.

The Teachers had sent the children out to find one object that they must look at, or listen to. Only one, fasten attention on it and attend so closely that the thing became totally sensed.They called it the Watching! He had loved those days. The Teachers had said they must watch long enough to discover something, something they never knew about that thing, Or maybe a question they could not answer about it. Either of these would get them back to the Teacher to tell what was discovered. Andrew remembered that it had always seemed to him like a treasure hunt. It was a watching that had trained the children to see as much as it was possible to see. Had trained their minds to see clearly before making any kind of decision.

It had worked, he thought, had become so natural to him that he did this now as a normal way of responding to things. He turned now, focussing his senses, hearing, seeing and smelling with that sharp acuteness that brought him identifiable knowledges of every part of that scene before, behind and around him. Strange how easy it was to shut off and look but not see, not hear or smell. He remembered that he had often as a child become so fascinated in whatever it was that he went to 'watch' that he had forgotten to come back to the Teacher until long after the others had gone. The Teacher had come to find him more than once. He smiled, remembering the flood of his questions.

Steve was talking,Andy shifted the focus of attention to include his words." You know Andy, what I said was true. The people are changing. Children ask to be taught. All of them do that, sooner or later. But this other thing, the Reach, not all the people do that." His eyes were sad, he glanced inquiringly at Andy. Intent on his thought but wondering how these facts would strike this youngster, so soon out of his own childhood.

Andrew was nodding, wondering what had caused this uncle to bring that up."I guess that's true, Uncle Steve."

Steve glanced at Andy, the 'Uncle' odd just now,but he wanted to go on,his eyes were angry, and he gestured suddenly with downward chopping movement, " You remember, at the gather we talked of it. There're other people like me who can't seem to Reach. Who don't know what a Mind-Touch is." His eyes held grief, the admission was painful and somehow only possible now with this child who would not judge. He said,"I don't know how to do that, you know. To consciously choose to Touch another -- another Mind.I'm barely able to admit that anyone does. But, at least, I know I can't -- or won't." He frowned.

Then his anger faded as swiftly as it had come. The slow smile that transformed and made the rough ,square, face beautiful, came to soften the worry that rose in Anthony's breast. Watching Steve, Andrew felt a surge of that great love he felt for this 'Uncle'. Surely it must be a terrible grief not to be able to Reach and to Touch.

Andrew cried out, wanting to change the facts."But Uncle Steve,,you do know. You did make that Touch with all of us, that day. I felt you there." He wanted it to be true.

Steve shook his head, "Not really, But I'm willing to accept that if you do. What you feel as 'me' there with you is from yourself I'm sure." He was pensive, looking away, watching Jane in the far field. "But, you know, there was something -- something that might have been -- I don't know. It may mean that I might learn how,if someone taught me." He laughed abruptly, "Maybe It's I who needs teaching here too." He was silent, then softly,"You know sometimes, Andy, I feel something, as if, - as if - there's some kind of a barrier that I could step over, if I would. That if I would,, then, I'd be there. If I could reach out, I might just Touch something. But then, I refuse, something in me just refuses, and I never do. Something closes, just closes. But the point is, I know about the rest of you, and I'm not resentful. I see the difference and it's all right with me. I don't see a problem of accepting it. People will do that I think, accept each other. I've tried to decide how my attitude is different from that of the Builders,they feel so fearful and then they get angry. I don't mind at all."

Andrew studied his Uncle's face, "Maybe that's it. Maybe they could if they'd try, or get someone to teach them. After all, everyone learns differently. How do they know they can't?"

Steve was emphatic,"No! The thing that infuriated them was not the Reaching itself. They don't seem to know about it. Wouldn't admit it if they did, I think. It's too mysterious" He shook his head, frowning. "Although that might be because they haven't been taught. They resent the fact that they see things happening for which they have no explanation except superstition. And they are angry. It's more dangerous than you realise, Son. We've got to start realizing that."

Andrew nodded, his mind racing,,"I suppose so, But if it's fear, then we could teach, if they'd be willing. No one can learn to actually Touch though unless his brain is ready. And there's something more that we didn't talk about. What's called a Joining. Jessie drew us together a little at the Gather but we've never done it with each other at all. And I don't know how that can be taught either."

Steve looked at him, shaking his head, not seeing, just fastening his eyes on Andy's shirt and rubbing his bare toe in the dirt at their feet. Andy said, "If it's the fear, and some are stopped by fear, the Healers could change that. Healers do know about how to treat fear, you know." He hoped Steve might consider that for himself.

Steve kept rubbing at the spot, digging a little hole, and his eyes were turned down,"Well, maybe that's for me too. Maybe if it's fear in me, then maybe I'm afraid of that fear and don't want to face it. After all, Son, it's not hidden for nothing. But then, maybe I'll think on that." He shook his head, looked at Andy and grinned again, "We've really digressed, Son. You were going to take kids in to the Learning Center. I think you've got no worries. They don't have Master Teachers in there in the reading rooms,but they have good teachers." He was silent for minutes, and Andrew knew he had something else to say before they parted,"I look at my little girl, Cassandra and sometimes I don't think I know her at all." Steve's voice was almost a whisper, "My own daughter, Think of it. She's doing those things I can't explain. She's aware of so much! I don't understand it. I've completely avoided thinking about it. And you all act as if there's nothing to worry about." He turned to face Andy and there was accusation in his eyes, accusation and an appeal.

Andrew nodded, felt a painful ache grow in his throat, a sympathy, a longing to help. He knew that long time hurt in himself that his parents had not known or could not know, of the experiences he and Anna were dealing with in their childhood. He had not talked to them either. He had avoided. Now the revelation from Steve wrestled the hurt from its hiding place, He had hidden his growing abilities and also his anger. Just as Cassandra was doing and Anna.

Andrew reached out one hand and grasped Steve's arm lightly, he wanted to reassure, to comfort, and felt awkward in trying. Steve's voice was brusk, rough, "Well, I'll not get any work done this way, you better go on and take those kids in, and just don't worry about all this." With an abrupt shift his face broke into a gentle, half apologetic smile, but it served its purpose ,Andrew felt comforted. Steve added lightly as he turned away, "Pay attention and you'll learn something too."

The children were excited and full of questions. "What would they do? Were they going to the rooms in the children's section where they had seen all the colored pictures, and the screens and the pretty helmets? Would they go on a space trip? Would there be wall screens and the world where the screen people lived?

Andy finally got that straightened out. They meant the room of simulated realities. They created foriegn cultures as life like as standing in the street in a foriegn city, or living in an ancient village."He shook his head,"No, you already know what that is. You've been there lots of times,this is different. You'll learn how to read. Soon you'll see." He noticed that most questions came from Tim and Edith. Eddie seemed absorbed with things around him. He daudled now and then, falling behind as he watched something going on in the fields or the clumps of forest. He stopped twice when he heard sounds on the river that grew louder as they neared the town. Maybe a boat race. He stopped to call the little boy,"Try to keep up with us, Eddie. We will be very late if we stop so much, and I called the Teacher there so she's expecting us. He took Eddie's hand and continued walking, deciding to ask them a question they could answer as they walked to keep them together."Tell me what you've done at the Center,"

"Oh,we play and we dance and listen to music and we go and watch in the places where other people are learning and sometimes we go to the rooms where we visit the other worlds.."Edith answered.

Tim was nodding vigorously and broke in,"We paint things too, and we make music with each other and we sing."

Eddie spoke then, "We do. We do,Andy, we dance to the music, we just dance and dance."

Edith caught Tim's wrist and tugged him forward. Then with a grin the two of them,their eyes shining with remembrance, whirled and leaped along the path ahead, dancing with such a grace and delight that Andrew stopped to watch. He understood why they had been so pleased in telling of it. As they danced, laughing and playing within their dance, absorbed already into it, Eddie said,calmly,"We make things too, Andrew. We make all kinds of things."

Andrew continued watching the two ahead, enjoying their movements more than he would have expected to and asked, "What do you make Eddie?"

"Oh, lots of stuff." He became thoughtful, wanting to remember. "I made a bowl out of clay and I eat out of it. It's yellow and I made some for my Mom and Dad and my sister. I made some other things,some animals.I made them too.Then we all made some little bells, and I made one out of plastic stuff but it wouldn't ring. Some kids made their's out of clay and they rang a little. Then Elaine, our teacher told us she'd take us to the metal labs and we could make some that would ring fine.

The other two had fallen in a noisy heap, half angry, half laughing, arguing about who had caused the wrong step. Andrew got them up and started on again, Then as if she had heard all that had been said, Edith said, "Yes, and I'm going to make a real bell too, , because I want to. To learn how to make them, but Eddie isn't going to. He isn't going to make a bell."She shook her head as if to emphasize that fact and took Eddie's hand in a gesture of condolence. Andrew felt a puzzle there, but said nothing. Eddie was nodding vigorously as if to agree fully with her, "I don't want to." And that seemed to end the conversation.

Their talk roused memories of his own early years,for Andrew. He had dabbled too in all sorts of things, watching older students making things, listened to whatever he chose, watched films, and played games. But most memorably, he had made things, all sorts of things. He remembered his pride and excitement. He smiled as he remembered, They had invented things, he and his friends, things that worked sometimes and sometimes didn't. Some were interesting, older students had looked them over and talked a lot about them and sometimes one was picked up and taken away be to used in another idea. He remembered how pleased he had been when his own invention had been displayed in the Winter Festival. The next year, he had heard his own song sung by the choir.Then finally, he had played a piano concerto during the Summer Festival with all the people listening. That had been a highlight of his childhood. He smiled, remembering, but asked,"I remember building houses and caves in the practice field south of the Center. Do you do that?

They nodded their heads, and began telling of their successes and failures, of helping in building with the older students a tree house, and one cave in the steep banks of the river on the south side of town. "The Teacher wouldn't let us make a cave until the big kids helped, then we learned how to make it strong." Eddie was so delighted telling all these things he stopped in front of the others, blocking their travel. He frowned then, and spoke in a whisper,"But Andy, we found the big caves, the ones already there in the north bank. But the Teacher didn't let us go in them much." Andrew turned him around gently and they went on.

The children continued to tell him tales of their exploits but memories flooded his mind. He thought of those years when he had begun to swing to fewer and fewer interests, until he finally realized that he had chosen the fields he would work in. Music and physics. It had been a time of sadness and excitement. The ending of childhood, the loss of those free exploring years. He felt now the two hands in his own, warm and small. One began to tug lightly on his .He turned, "What is it Tim?"

" I want to tell you what I really like to do."

Andrew looked down into his face, surprised at his need to insist."Yeah, what's that?"

"What I really like to do is go in those little narrow rooms where the magic is. Where the walls all go away and then you're in that place where people used to live. Sometimes it's way off in some other country. And I can see how they did things,and how they made their cities, and how they - - did things in the old days. There're so many places where people live, so many countries. There are so many different ways to live."

Andrew nodded, he knew the fascination of the culture rooms. A good imagination resulted in a deep feeling for peoples of the world. His own fascination had been satisfied with simply visiting, but maybe Tim's wouldn't be. It could hold his life's work.

They arrived at the Learning Center and Andrew felt somehow reinforced when he saw that several people were there busily engaged in working with young children. Most of the children were between eight and ten. He felt pleased when the three charges he had committed himself to began immediately examining various activities and equipment without his help. All of them seemed so at home in the Learning Center.

He saw children in head phones sitting at a long table watching and listening to tapes. Others had on helmets, that covered most of their heads. He had never seen such equipment so he went to the Teacher. She was a several years older than he but he recognized her. He had seldom spoken to her.

"Just a minute Andrew", she said,"Let me get these fixed and we can talk." She completed the task of getting an eight year old settled into his helmet and chair and gave him the control device then turned to Andrew.

He looked utterly puzzled and she laughed, "I can see you haven't been here since you were a kid. Right?" He nodded, and she went on,"Well, these are new anyway, they just arrived a few months ago and they're amazing. We've known the principle by which they work for a long time but it took a bright young woman in North Dakota to get it working. She's been working in your field since she was twelve and with a Master Teacher these last two years, I understand. But she got the final relationships, brain tolerances and receptiveness, precisely enough that these work."

"But what is it? It looks as though you're playing space games. These children are about the age for the space travel simulators aren't they?"

"Oh, I imagine they've all done that. In fact you ought to try them again, those helmets and simulators are vastly improved since you were a kid. No, these are Teaching machines. Just exactly that. We only use the ones that teach how to read English. We have other languages for later.. When those kids come out of that in about a half hour, they'll be able to read the simplest of our little books. And after a few more sessions, they'll be reading fast. They're really READY though. We can't keep them satisfied here, once they learn they go on to the library.It's nothing short of miraculous, and I've been helping for a year now and I still am amazed." She was silent, watching the room of busy children, They literally teach themselves, you know, Andy. But I wonder whether they ought to be reading even at this age. There's so much to learn, to explore, to dream about, that we don't want them to tie themselves down too early to standard rational systems of thought. Up to now, as you know, they've thought as freely as a firefly. And some ideas are as flashing and brief." She laughed. "But that's exciting because they do come up with astonishing ideas."

Andrew moved closer to the children. He glanced around to see what the

THE AWAKENING

children he had brought were doing. Seeing that they were fully occupied he bent to see the face of the child in a helmet nearest him. She seemed relaxed, thoughtful but strangely, for him, she was smiling. Then suddenly she laughed. Well, then, at least it must not be uncomfortable. He was intensely curious. He turned to Marie. "What would be the chance of my trying one? Is that possible?"

She laughed at him nodding, "You don't suppose we bought a pig in a poke do you? Oh yes, the Center Elders tried them out and then several of the Teachers did. Funny none of the Master Teachers did though. I suppose they already knew." She grimaced, then went on,"Sure, you can try. There, on that shelf are the adult helmets. Other languages use a more complex system. It has to teach them to speak as well as read. Most children learn at least two besides their native tongue."

Andrew told her about the three children he had brought and she turned to watch them busily using some of the preliminary reading games. "Yes, I can see they must have asked. We don't put the helmet on any child who isn't ready. Who doesn't ask. Sometimes kids who are ready, don't ask. If your friends have asked, your troubles are over. We'll put a helmet on as soon as one is free and you'll see. In the meantime, why don't you look around and try one out yourself. We have other new teaching equipment that works too."

Andrew nodded, thinking that she might be politely suggesting that he take care of himself. So he thanked her and began to walk around the room. He was curious about it now, all the devises, all the equipment and shelves full of colored chalks, paints, blocks, balls, boxes of many shaped, wooden forms. So much. He walked here and there, studying everything. He went happily about, working as interestedly as if he were himself eight years old. He saw his three charges being strapped into helmets, waved at them with a smile and went on.

Marie watched him, knowing that he was doing work in the field that produced these things. She wanted to ask him if he might be interested in devising an improved way to teach music. Surely a perfect coupling of his interests. She watched him approach a small group who were dancing and when one asked him to dance, he joined in with no apparent embarrassment at all. She liked that in him, liked the gentleness, the grace of his young, strong, lean body. Maybe he'd have time for lunch.

Andrew felt happy. No one disturbed him. Few asked him anything at all. The children took care of themselves or hunted up a teacher. He felt free. Gazing nostalgically at a collection of children's paintings hanging on a wall, he became aware of a conversation that gradually intruded itself into his attention. Marie was talking with someone on the phone. her voice was animated and excited, a little loud. He didn't intend to eavesdrop, but she seemed not to care if anyone overheard. She spoke frequently of someone called William. Andy's ears flushed hot, wondering. Then she said, William of Altos, and he was sure. Marie nodded her head vigorously in agreement with the other.

Then she said clearly, "I think he's one of the most exciting men I've ever met. There's power simply radiating from him. I'd like to go to hear him. Please count me in." There was an answer, then she nodded,"Yes, why not? It sounds like a good idea. People don't always know what's good for them,you know. " She was smiling broadly now, eager about something and Andrew felt a strange unrest. Those words stuck in his mind and he heard little more. She closed the circuit and left the machine. "People don't always know what's good for them" That was opposite to the Teaching he knew she had been taught.'People must and will find their own 'good' for themselves,but they must know it is their task.' He thought, 'If people understand all the options, then they will know what's best for them. Why doesn't she see that.'

He shook his head, he had studied avidly in the history film rooms, and he knew too many times humanity had been led astray by benevolent despots who thought people did not know what was good for them. And saw to it they didn't know their options. He wondered at his own worry. Marie was a good person, concerned and loving. William about whom they were talking, was very much so. Yet it might be from such 'goodness' that people who were unsure,or lazy thinkers,might be persuaded that what was William's 'good' was also their own. Well, maybe it was. He argued with himself, wanting to justify. He thought he should not feel so chilled by those words he had overheard. He stopped, his eyes no longer seeing the paintings. It had to be Uncle William about whom they talked. He felt anger, grief, confusion, and then he said,"Well, so it is. Uncle William supports the Builders and he thinks that's best for him. I have to accept that" But he didn't want to accept that, and he saw with a wry smile, that he too thought that he might 'know better' what was good for someone else. Of all the people he knew, Uncle Will would know all options. It was a puzzle.

He mused, his eyes idly roaming the busy room,"Is it because I think they're selfish? Well, that's a part of growth too. After all, and the words rose from memory precisely - 'Until a person establishes clear 'selfness', a strong confident ego, he will not be ready to give - to reach beyond himself either to others or to the Self.' He quoted the familiar Teaching and found its meaning clearer than ever in his life.

He thought of Marie, a Teacher. She'll influence a lot of lives. He felt his mind whirling. Where does concern and ethical convictions end and interference with the rights of another begin? He had to allow people to differ from himself. Whether or not it seemed dangerous to him. He had to let them establish their own self identity, be persons to themselves and others even if it took their whole lives.

He knew! He knew these things and yet -- a rage brought tears to his eyes, tears of frustration. It seemed so obvious to him that they were going down a wrong path, a wrong way. Images of Will came to mind, so immaculate, always a little apart, always so precise, and so contained as though none could touch against him, against his mind? His heart? It was as though he didn't notice much at all, Andy thought. With a sigh, Andrew finished the thought,saying it softly aloud, "It's as though he's never noticed his Self,that inner Self. For him it's only an idea, I think,not a reality. And yet,he's not like young girls, like Marie. I'd say

THE AWAKENING

Uncle William is really sure of himself, of that self he always must keep complete. He has established himself, strengthened himself, why doesn't he look beyond himself?" And the thought spoken in a whisper, making it more real, seemed full of grief. He was silent, tightness filled his throat.

He watched the activity in the room , seeing it as a pattern, aware that he had lifted out of his previous narrow focus, had extended his attention. He was perceiving relationships and intentions among all those here, seeing the room as a design, a moving pattern. He stood absorbing the implications of that pattern, it puzzled him. He could let himself become absorbed in persuing that puzzle and forget these worries.

But other thoughts intruded, his own secrets, loomed larger, shaped like shadows over his mind. They too more visible from this point of perception. He had not talked to his own parents, never told them all that he realized, all that he could Reach to. Even after the Gather and the recognition among them, he had not talked much to them. Really talked. As if he was afraid! He had not told them of this constant daily practice of 'lifting consciousness'. Master Teachers taught all children to do that,but he did not know whether many did. He wondered again at that. Why wouldn't the others if he did? Why didn't he know. He talked only with his close friends, He knew that other kids didn't talk of the practice, the Reach,except to close friends, though they did sometimes talk of psychic perceptions. Why not? There were too many secrets. Surely he saw his own little cluster of secrets! He was startled at that thought. But he had to admit it was true. One thing was clear. He must talk to his parents to begin.

He turned from the class room. Walked slowly down the hall . Someone had once told him he seemed arrogant. Was that true? What was this self searching now? Was he feeling sorry for himself, or lost in a bath of self contempt. He couldn't tell. He felt very uneasy. Then he realized he had not reminded Marie to tell the children to meet him in the outside gardens when they were through. He could just Send her an image. It would be so easy,. But he didn't know that she would accept, receive, He thought perhaps not and dared not try. He walked back in and gave Marie the message. Then went on out again.

His mind seemed stuck on that memory, the accusation of arrogance had hurt, had made him want to defend himself, to prove them wrong. But, he had done nothing except listen. He felt better about himself for that. Well, maybe there was truth in it. After all, why had he not told his folks about all that he realized? Why had he been slow even to talk to his friends? He had not even told the Master Teachers that when he practiced the 'lifting' he also realized something beyond his ability to find words. Something that filled his heart with awe and made him long to understand. Neither had he told them that when he focussed, and Reached, he Touched others and also Reached beyond what was familiar. Reached to what was -- was frightening and wonderful! So why didn't he tell his folks?

He talked to a few friends, only a few. And he was sure they only talked to each other too. Why? Wasn't that why the Family was together? Couldn't he trust his own family? He frowned. Maybe he WAS arrogant.

He settled his mind into that deep attention to this flow of thought, and knew that he persued something acutely important to himself. Perhaps to his Family. What would happen if all of them, no longer concealing, were to to JOIN. Jessie had brought them at least to the edge of it at the Spring Gather! The thought excited and frightened him and he didn't know why. What was it anyway, that Joining. He had never experienced it. They'd reached to an interface, what he thought was the edge of Joining, and were daring each other to Reach further. His closest friends talked about it. He wanted to know more.

He spoke aloud,"I've just avoided a lot of it. Could I be denying more?" He walked slowly, vaguely through the fragrance and breathed deeply, enjoying, touching soft brilliant petals with his fingers absently. "Oh, there's an end to what a person can conceal from himself, there has to be. Maybe this -- this sensitivity to others, what we call Touching, is what a person has to develop before Joining would be possible."

Now he wandered through the gardens, aiming for a secluded corner where he could think alone. Where no one would come to talk, or to learn of his worry, his fear. He smiled at himself, seeing his usual response."Why do I do that? But then, there's no use despising myself either. After all. It's important to think things out and that's my way." He knew he was explaining to himself, justifying his actions again and he breathed a great long sigh. "How long must I do that too? I could at least take this whole thing to my peer group. At least I'd know how other kids handled things. But then, none of us talk of it. What's wrong. The very thing we ought to talk about."

He found a bench among bright green leafed plants, their blossoms ready to break into bloom. He settled himself, listening inattentively to a fountain just out of sight beyond the shrubs. "Well, no use worrying about it. No one can expect me to ENJOY seeing my faults." He laughed suddenly at himself.

Then, quieting himself , focussing his attention, lifting it so that he was centered beyond these narrow fears, he settled. Emptied his mind. The draining away of emotions released energy. Stillness grew. Then, later,a thought flickered -- his friends, why didn't they have this out? They HAD at least talked of these things. How secretive we are!

But the depths of stillness drew him. His mind, opening beyond thinking, received his attention like a small boat in a sea. He was still, listening, watching the surge of emotion that troubled that sea, dispair, resentment, all the attempts to defend himself,and the reason for that need. He watched himself without comment, or judgement as though he stood apart from himself, impartial. He felt gradually a quiet amusement at himself. He saw that this was the way he was and that was his nature at this moment. It would have to do. For some time, he sat, accepting and accepted in that garden. Then, finally, he shifted. He frowned, felt himself leave the endlessness of realizing and shrink into the narrow focus of thinking. Choice had been made.

"Well,I suppose it's a matter of caring about people but not taking on their troubles. I've gone too far when I imagine that I'm responsibile for whatever's happened." He stopped, frowned,"That's obvious. Then why do I do it?" And the answer came as swiftly,"Because I FEEL responsible." Nodding his head, he thought of it."After all, how can I be so important to things?" Then after further reflection, he added,"Maybe that's why she said I was arrogant."Wearily he sighed, a smile playing on one side of his lips, as if half amused at his perdicament.

His thoughts roamed over somewhat familiar territory. He had met this in himself before."Now,do I have to go though it again? All the way from self contempt to dispair, then finally to just agreeing to watch myself again? Well, this time I'm going to let myself be. I see what I do. I can practice catching myself before I start wanting to take responsibiity for somebody else again. Like now, for instance, I've done that now." He smiled, feeling better."It's all because of Marie I've learned all this. My wanting to correct her, to convince her that she's wrong. As though its my job. As if I could be sure I'm right! Still, there was a nagging worry about Marie, that she could not or did not Reach. Surely, if she's a Teacher - then - but he knew that all Teachers were not Master Teachers. Perhaps that was one difference. Surely she knew her own job; she was good at that.

He started to walk again, through the inner Arch out to the third Ring and rapidly through the winding paths, absently seeing the trees, fountains, greening plants around him. He knew he had always been sought out by people needing sympathy, that he often left them feeling better and himself feeling worse. He had taken responsibility for making things right for them. He stood very still, lost in the question as to where this fitted.Surely no human quality was entirely wrong. And he said aloud, recommencing walking,"It's important to care about other people, that's not the problem, maybe, I just go too far". And then, with surprise, he realized that his peer group had told him that too. He laughed then,"Well,I guess I never heard it well enough."

He had arrived back at the opposite Arch in that Ring from the one he had entered and walking through it, was again on the path to the room where the children worked. He walked a short distance, glancing into the tall wide windows to see the activity there, then found himself crossing a curve of deep moss. Back from the path, half hidden, a few carved wood chairs set inside a curve of gooseberry bushes invited him. Outside that curve, taller blue rose bushes already reached fat buds into the sunlight. He studied them thoughtfully, they were blooming well this year.

He settled into a chair,relaxing, realizing how tense he had been. He enjoyed the play of sun and shadow on the stone and moss courtyard. A light wind moved branches over head, the sun was warm against his skin. He could see people walking, hear a voice now and then, sometimes a shout. He Reached lightly, as though brushing those passing minds, and though he felt light response, none made any deep Touch. A few turned to where he sat and waved. They sensed his desire for privacy. Then he was more aware that several passed without notice. Then he noticed a young woman, named Nellie, a friend, approaching,and he shrank into himself,feeling a little guilty. He didn't want to talk and she would insist on that. He grinned,"My friends will be pleased that I didn't react to her need this time."

The thought stopped him, and then he knew that it was not need on her part but habit. He had closed himself from any Touch. It was strange how that dimmed things around him. The very colors were less deep. He said aloud,"Then Reaching is part of being more aware generally! I suppose that 's it.If we're open to others, we're also more open to every sense. Then those who do not Reach, who cannot, that is, must be deprived of - - of so much,so much of beauty. But then, they couldn't know that,the way a person born blind does not know what he has never seen.

A sadness at that thought settled over him. How could such grief be. Then he caught himself and grinned,"There I go again, and this time, I'm wanting to deny the sorrow of others so I won't have to make them better. Either deny them, or take them on, it's what I've done. And neither works." The thought sobered him.

He looked around, deliberately turning from his thoughts. The carefully chosen stones, paving tiles, mosses, plantings had been arranged to form a whole, a balanced small garden. Surely one of the Gardeners had designed this one, or at least a student with that help. It was the work of an artist. The mood and composition of space and color was more formal than most in these Learning center Rings. He shifted attention,saw before him the wide distance of mind, still and aware. He lifted his attention to extend consciousness within it. It was a small matter to shield himself for privacy. He could do it! He could and he had to practice that more often.

He put all his attention into experiencing the garden. He wanted to know this garden the way the artist might have. As he did so, he was aware that everything increased in sharpness, color, sound, smells, and emotions too. He held steady, aware. He felt deeply relaxed and alive.

After a little time,he heard singing, turned his head, to see through the branches a group of children sitting at the other edge of the court, their backs to him. At first it seemed an intrusion, then he loosened himself a little gave it room, let it become part of the harmony of the garden, and like a picture coming into focus it was. Their harmony was exquisite, so perfect he felt it draw like a string at mind and nerves. He wanted to join in, then to simply enjoy. He remained silent. Listening, being here, more deeply aware. His thoughts drifted and faded. He felt as though an opaqueness had been shattered around him, a dim veil gone. He was no longer focussed in his own body, but literally extended, inclusive, and the garden, the children, the singing, breathed through himself also. Or was it that he breathed through it all. The thought faded, he attended.

Then conditions shifted, movement caught his attention and brought it down into his body.Clearly a thought formed, 'Why couldn't he think and 'be' in this way, at the same time?' He didn't know. Thinking always brought him back to this narrow dimension.

THE AWAKENING

Four children moved from a doorway out to the gardens. They stood near him. He thought they didn't notice him. Watching the other children, they began their own melody, a new combination of sounds, one that demanded something of the other but did not interfere. Their tone was off a little. He wanted to help them, but resisted the impulse in time. Like a conversation, it was. The first group did not look up, but simply responded to this new condition. They picked out from their combined sound, a new melody, and Andy was astounded at their skill. He was used to people, groups, singing in the town gardens, everyone did, but this - this was unusual. Children were taught to sing before they could talk usually, and to dance, and he wondered whether he had ever been aware of how fine they were. He settled into a quiet enjoyment of the morning and the singing.

Then, the children were silent, broken a moment later with sudden shouts and laughter,the groups joined and chattering noisily,they went off. Andrew felt their absence like a hole in the fabric of the day, until it stitched itself together and he was caught into thought again. An image of Anna rose in his mind, he thought how different she was, Her response to people so different. She seemed to know intuitively the need of another but never to get lost in it. She was like an offering of great space, quiet space where he could relax and rest himself without thought for her welfare. Yes, it was true. She did not catch him into HER troubles and that was a strange fact. Though she surely talked of them with him. There was an unspoken understanding betweeen them, one he could not define. Each knew the other was absolutely present for the other.

He smiled, thinking of how angry she had been last week, and then was suddenly sad at that memory. Slowly his thoughts dissolvd into a quiet peace. He was half asleep in the sun.

A scatter of rapid footsteps woke him to attention, a laugh and shouts, then his name called. A barotone voice speaking his name was so close he stood to see. A black head bodded on the other side of the roses. Then a young man, a boy he knew well, stood smiling at him. laughed suddenly then reached out, hit him lightly on the upper arm."Hi,Andy, Come on with us. You wanta have some fun this evening?"

Andrew felt the power of the boy 's personality, felt it like warm wave, a live ember ready to flare. He was drawn to the excitement of him."What're you planning, Dave."He said, looking rapidly around. Other boys ran through the Ring gardens, vaulting the low shrubs and catching low limbs of trees and swinging across pathways. It was their gathering place. He knew them all, had grown up with them. Two boys,slim, young, beardless, sat in chairs near him. One leaned against a tree, his hair as dark as Dave's but curling and long enough to tie in back.His great soft brown eyes studied Andy with a direct,calculating look. Andrew knew, in sudden sharp recognition that this boy did not trust him. He recoiled, his pride slapped.

But then, as if in explanation, atonement, a tall heavier boy, grinned at him. He had a light down of beard, his thick long brown hair swept into a tight braid down the back of his head., A wide genial smile broke the slight tension that had

THE PEOPLE OF THE VALLEY

risen. He clapped Andy on the shoulder and said,"Hi",in such a sweet and friendly voice that Andrew was startled into memories of childhood days when this boy had played with him along the River bank gathering all the creatures they could find to make a great aquarium for their class room. It had been a lovely summer.They had had to learn how to feed and name everything they caught,then to care for the whole. He said,"Russell! Say it's good to see you again."They stood, meeting each other's eyes, measuring, and then they embraced.

"Yeah, it's good."Russell said,"I've been down at Clandor for a year." Then he stepped back, looked at Dave, wanting him to do the talking.

It was then that Andrew knew that they had planned to see him, knew with a blinding flash what they wanted, he was aware of the excitement and the unexpected cringing within him. He listened to Dave saying it. "Andrew, we're planning some watches. We've got a watch there, behind the Center. Where the steep part of the Running slope drops off beyond the playing fields to the west. Well, you know Jeff ? He wants to take charge of things, make it all come out his way. He's got a gang, you know. They say they can stop us. What do you say?"

" Wait, stop what? Make what come out his way? " He fumbled for words. He felt their feelings flung wildly at him, jamming up on themselves so he couldn't make sense of them. They were recklessly pouring out their angers, but mostly some other energy, he could not name it. But his attention was dual. That calm attention, lifted, outside this narrow one that was closed in eagerness. At that level he knew. It was surely a lust for action, for any kind of action and preferably for battle. Andy could feel it, the challenge of it, the excitement, an emotional excess washed around them all. It's power moved him, attracted him.

He wanted to respond, to lose himself in it! But he wanted to pull away, to refuse. For most of the boys it was all simple excitement, fun. Something in which to lose their boundless energy. Something different. Andy realized they saw it as another game. He'd had little to do with this group of boys for a couple of years, gradually they had seemed to drift apart but they had all been childhood friends and maybe he ought to keep up that friendship. He felt himself being drawn in, assumed he could extricate himself when he chose. He grinned, put one hand on Dave's shoulder.

"I don't know exactly what you've been deciding on, but if it's good fun, then I'm in. Even as he said it he knew the seduction of it, the pull into what might be hard to withdraw from. He knew the difference, stood listening as he leaned against the stone wall of the building behind them, listening with all his alerted senses. But he felt pleased at their shift from distrust to a partial trust. He thought that was not wise, but they didn't seem to notice. How could they know to trust him? He felt powerfully their eagerness to be off, to be doing something. With surprise, an image of Michael and Richard, two of his best friends, rose in his mind. How would they respond to this? He shrugged them away, it was his business.

Dave shrugged,"Well, that's good, Andy. We wanted to know." There was a sardonic smile and behind it a question, but he went on,"Meet us tonight, seven oclock, down where the cliffs end in the caves by the River. We'll let you know then. " His eyes bored into Andy's, jolting him with their ferocity. "It's good you're with us. You've been off with the others these last few years. We thought you'd forgotten us." Andy heard the question and threat behind the words. He felt the surge of emotion, a dull anger, not acknowledged, lending the words vigor. It all puzzled him. The tension in their minds was strange, why was he noticing things in them he had never noticed before. Had they all changed so much? His own thoughts and emotions he must organize later, but something in him wanted to smile.

As suddenly as they had come they were gone. Leaping the bushes, racing up the paths, shouting in a high unrestrained glee. Andy sat down slowly, a wearyness flooded through him. Here was something else to sort out. How to do it? the excitement of their animal spirits excited his own. He saw that. Yet a steady warning washed across the impulse until he gave it attention. The fact that he'd not spent much time with Dave and these others for so long, made them strange to him now. His present group of friends were as deep into their practice, their study and their life work as he. What was their difference?

He felt diminished and tired. Burdened. He would NOT sort it out now. He leaned his head back against the stone wall, rubbed the roughness, felt it hurt with satisfaction. Then he stilled his thought, drew himself from that welter of tangled thought and emotion, was aware with a growing sense of well being. He smiled, surely, he must unknot it all and sort it out. He stood up, stretched, and said aloud,"But first I'd better go pick up the kids and take them home."

CHAPTER TWENTY THREE

Andrew -

  If the trip with the children immersed Andrew in a final reminder of childhood, the meeting at the River Cave that night, began an ending of those years for Andrew and two days later, rambling through the foothills behind the Farm, he completed it. Together they broke him away from clinging to old dreams and woke him up. He came home from his trip with the children feeling a light hearted sense of accomplishment, and telling his parents that he would be meeting his friends, he left home just after dinner. The evenings were long and much could happen in those cool, quiet hours.
  He descended the narrow trail down the cliffs, preferring that danger to the long route along the shore line. The winds gusting around the cliffs were cold and pushed at him unexpectedly. He enjoyed the danger, the necessity for constant alert care, at times feeling his way between narrow rocky outcrops. When he arrived at the cave the other boys were there. He knew they'd come directly from their jobs or from Learning Center training. Why hadn't they told him it would be a picnic? A small fire still burned in a circle of rock. They offered him a choice of hot Ander Tea or a cold beer. He was still a little chilled so he took a steaming cup gratefully and settled on a long piece of driftwood. Then he looked around. He felt the excitement of the adventure, and at the same time, an odd sense of chagrin, but he shook that off and entered into the game.
  The other boys were either sitting or standing with a studied ease, as if planned. He was puzzled. Dave sat across the fire, his dark body like a shadow in the twilight. Andrew waited. He Reached again, half heartedly, expecting little. Nothing. He was surprised to find his heart heavy, the excitement of adventure dulled by a sense of loss.
  There was some rowdy laughter, foolishness from Tomas, and three of the boys Andy knew only by sight. Then they began to talk of their suspicion that Jeff's gang was meeting this night too and they knew where. They'd spied on them. They laughed like children planning mischief. They wanted to plan a raid. Dave glanced at them, his eyes constantly returning to watch Andy, and Andy listened with a sinking sense of disappointment. They sounded like kids to him, but they were at least sixteen, several eighteen. Yet, as they talked, their intricate plan, their laughter, the simple foolishness rising from their high spirits, began to interest him. For these three, it was a game. He relaxed a little. "
  When d'you plan to go". He asked.
  " Tonight, right after we finish here." Tomas grinned at him, friendly and entirely trusting. Andy felt better until he caught Dave's eye and knew that there was still suspicion in their leader's mind. This was more than a game for him, he was forming a strong bonding with these boys, a bonding he could use. Andrew knew that and was surprised that he knew. But he became increasingly aware

that the others were more innocent, more playing the old games of childhood, than he had thought possible. He determined to be forthright,"Dave, you've not said what your plans are."

Thus challenged, Dave must make his position clear, He looked at Andy, their eyes met, a shaded hostility against open questioning."Before we go a step further, we make sure we're all together. Tom,you're a fool. How do we know Andy's not a spy?" He was unashamed to use that word, far-fetched as it seemed to Andy. It was true that this was more serious to Dave than to the others, that for Dave it was not just a final game before they left adolescence.

Andy nodded,"Good idea, after all, if we're going to depend on each other, we've got to be sure we can trust each other. He looked around at the sudden silence. He had not reacted to Dave's accusation. Puzzlement flickered through Dave's eyes. He said,"Let's get the fire built up. It's cold." With a shout,as if to break tension, the others began bringing firewood, bits of branches that had drifted down during the winter in the high water. When the flames were higher, the heat comforted and the light pushed back the gathering dusk. They gathered close together, their loudness calmed. They could hear the steady beat of river current against the rocky bank and the mild breeze was full of dampness and river odors. They brought sweet and sad memories to Andrew. Dave waited a moment until each boy was silent, serious. His eyes met Andrew's again and Andy thought he could see a glint of friendliness there.

Dave said, "Then it's to be the blood committment?" At the gang's obvious approval and eagerness to perform the rite, he nodded. Took a slim,beautifully crafted knife from his pocket, it's blade gleaming with a fine edge. Andy watched him calmly. He knew that the rite was not dangerous. He thought the regression to childish theatrics was strange but obviously, with this gang, effective. He had decided to go along with the game itself. After all, it had once been fun to play at danger. But a nagging disappointment weighed at him.

The rite was simple. Performed millions of times by boys and girls all over the world, it was the simple letting of a little blood through a prick in the wrist, then a joining of arms, so that the blood dripped down over their arms, exchanging and rearranging so that it could be thought every boy had shared the blood of each. Then the ritual washing in the River and holding their arms over the fire to dry and seal the covenant. It was not the ritual that concerned Andrew finally, but the covenant. Dave spoke it as the bright red blood of their pierced wrists ran down and dripped into Earth below.

"I do vow that I, (name) will forever stand firm as friend and partner, defender and protector, of each of you, for as long as I shall live. I do hereby vow that all those who seek to harm any one of us, or to deviate from the committment to each other or our Valley life, shall be my enemy." The boys repeated the covenant and Andy spoke it slowly, wondering. Surely there was no harm in it. He felt such a committment to Adwin people already. But why that reference to anyone harming or 'deviating from Valley life'? He decided to confront the issue.

" Dave, I'm not sure what that means, how would anyone deviate from Valley life in a way that would be threatening?"

He looked with frank question at the older boy. And Dave's gaze flickered a little before he solidly met his. He seemed to think he was meeting a confrontation of leadership. Andy saw that suddenly with absolute clarity, and sighed, even as he tightened himself to meet what was to him a strange assumption.

Dave said,"You have to know, Andy, that there are people who want to tear out our forests, want to destroy our way of life. You have to have seen it starting, even if you don't know the whole of it."He looked slowly around at the watching boys, their earnest, serious faces, already smudged with soot, so young, so wide eyed, that Andy almost smiled. His original worry subsided, this gang was not going to do anything dangerous. But Dave went on,"Are you honestly not aware of that danger?" His voice had become harsh, brusk and angry. Andy sobered swiftly and nodded.

"I'm not unaware of it, Dave, I just hadn't thought it was a serious threat. Maybe I was wrong. I suppose I thought they were just complainers."

Dave nodded, his mouth drawn down in a sudden frown, a sullen resentment darkened his eyes. Andy watched carefully, resolved not to use that Reach to know more than they wanted to tell him. "Then maybe you'd better think about it. We've seen it becoming a threat. Have you been down near Clandor?"

"I heard about the leveling of a few trees and ripping up of some meadow, but it wasn't much and I assumed the Council would stop it." He was silent, thinking. Perhaps he had been remiss. After all, even his own family had been avoiding and not facing up to some of the real facts of life. Maybe he needed to pay more attention."I think maybe you're right. I guess I need to find out what's really happening." That seemed to satisfy Dave, he relaxed a little and they began their plans in earnest, faces darkly serious, but sharp bright bursts of laughter and the broken voices of adolescent boys, took away any sense of danger among them. Dave went along with their planned 'raid' taking little leadership this time.

Andrew had gone home after the 'raid' exhilarated and laughing with the fun of it. It HAD been fun, the stealthy sneaking out of their cave, round the narrow trail and then up the dangerous cliff trail. They had insisted on that to add to the danger, Andy was sure, and he refused to withold his Reach because he must know swiftly if anyone was in trouble. He had monitored that dark journey up the cliff steadily and had touched the minds of three different boys, during that climb when they were near to panic. He was confident they had not suspected but thought it their own self control that steadied them. He glanced up at the ascending moon. Had they waited only another half hour,its light bright over the fields would have made the climb easy. He thought he had done something his father would not approve. It was not the having of the Talent that was dangerous, but the misuse of it. Hadn't the Master Teachers warned them enough, long before any of them knew what they meant.

They had gone on from the top of the cliff, restrained with difficulty from shouting and yelling so relieved were they, to cross the saddle in which residence clusters already were lit with warm light.Then, cutting directly down to the south of

THE AWAKENING

town, into the fields, and passing through two force field fences, they had skirted the edge of a grove of hazelnut trees to hide in its shadows and finally after some waiting to watch,continued on in further stealthy maneuvers. They worked their way through field and woodland until they came to an abandoned underground equipment shed. There they saw one lookout sitting on a rock ahead, but before they were seen, Dave signalled a retreat.

Andy thought his decision not to make themselves known was wise. For their game plan at least. If the enemy knew they were discovered, they would almost surely think of the caves as a new hideout. Then Dave's gang would find themselves discovered. Dave had convinced the boys that they would plan a more exciting exposure of their 'enemy' later on. He smiled sadly to himself. He admitted he had enjoyed all the intrigue, the stealth, finding out whether they could approach without being seen, all that. The signals, the bird whistles and owl hoots, ets. to send messages of position. He had abandoned himself to the play, returning for these hours to childhood. But now there was a subtle nagging disease.'All that' was no longer what a man would be doing. It was surely part of his past. The loss of it brought sorrow tempered with amusement; he also longed for his years of manhood.

For two days he could not let his mind rest. He struggled with the questions, the problems that seemed to increase even when he was busiest at the Learning Center. He began going to the music building to immerse himself in music in hard practice for the coming Adwin concert in which he would play a concerto . He went into the practice rooms and worked for hours, wanting to drown the thinking. At first he was successful, was lost in that intricate music, mastering the fingering and then the dynamics and then finally, just playing with such whole absorption that he forgot everything else. As he began work on a second piece, the questions persisted,and finally interfered, even between notes. Finally as evening drew down, he gave it up and went home and entered into a Holo-Video about a young prince of the middle ages. It lulled him to sleep.

The next morning, he woke, restless. Rubbing his eyes,he flung himself from bed,then sat waiting, letting the flow of feeling and thought identify themselves. What was today? What was he going to do? He drew himself away from the clamoring of questions. He wanted escape from all the nagging worry he had done in the past few days. He wanted to find solutude where he could be still, alone. He wanted to forget everything that was going on and just - he realized that he wanted to play again, the way he had as a child. The way Dave's gang did the other night. And the way he himself had last night, living in that Holovideo as if it were real. He felt the sluggish sense of danger, the knowledge that to escape in fantasy was no way out. But he refused to listen to himself.

He pulled on shorts and a light shirt,opened the door of his octagonal cottage, a modified replica of the Temple. This cottage was his own world. He was safe here. He flooded the two rooms with a soft rose light,then let it drift down to shadow. He turned to survey the rooms that were his private world. The harmony of color, the easy disorder, comforted him. And in that moment, he decided. He didn't want to hide, nor to be 'safe' today. He had to get out, to run, to do something else, to be alone!

He ran down the back trail away from the Hall. Went to the deep cleft behind the knoll on which the Farm buildings were built and crossed it rapidly. He began to climb. In half an hour he had passed through the wide meadows and farmed land and approached the foothills. He began to run. Like a fleeing deer he raced without stopping,up one hill, down its other side, and up a higher one, until he had fled far into the high wooded grassland. He looked around, drew long breaths, then he went on, feeling his body respond, his breath grow hot in his throat and his legs ached with the labour. But he continued, pushing himself hard.

Finally topping the third hill north of the Farm, he ran down the rocky broken far side, into a high saddle, he crossed that,leaped the stream that threaded it's way through these hills, and began slowly to climb to the top of the meadow. Then he looked back. He stopped, breathing hard, tired but relieved, relaxed and feeling infinitely better, He could see the hills he had crossed and the Farm far down on it's little hill. Then beyond that were the three hills,each at least a quarter of a mile wide, on which the town of Adwin sat. He could see only the thick growth of the garden town. Above them,at the center of each triple Ring Center, projected the stone walls of the third and fourth stories of the inner buildings. Here and there the gleaming white of some cluster residences in the broad saddles between the hills, suggested there was a town there. The rest was hidden in the garden growth, except for the Temple which flamed crimson and gold towers and one splintering shaft of bright green. It was like a fire in the midst of the gardens of living green.

He let his eyes rove, moving through the trees, catching on a great dark vulture floating, riding its waves of air, it seemed utterly at peace, but he knew it watched the ground for the first sign of a fallen creature. It's grace pleased him and he deliberately practiced the Lift, drew his consciousness out of the narrow confines of worry, soared from himself, rode the great bird's back,then descended into the tops of great old oaks. Still descending, he felt the dark solidity of the wood. His mind fused into the tree, moving through molecules, finding the steady flow of liquid moving steadily upward, saw the scattering sparkle of energy climbing through interstices, cells, the liquid of the living veins. He had flown past thought, but the looseness of everything in what had seemed a dense wood of the tree startled him, making thoughts flicker ,but come to nothing.

He followed himself, followed the energy dividing and dividing through trunk to branch to twig, riding the gradually lessening flow of it. Then, dividing into hundreds of small green leaves. It spread like a thin vapor through green light manufacturing energy again. Sun energy blended there, blended in a furious dance that created free energy. There it was,,the flow, unstoppable. Andy withdrew himself and floated down into the whispering grasses and he knew their sensing of his presence. He was aware of the tree and it of him, he realized it's - what? The quality he felt from it, was not translatable, but the nearest he could

THE AWAKENING

come was 'amusement?'. Yes, it was that. So had it tolerated his invasion.

He felt delight at the extending of himself through the grasses,over stones and broken bits of rock, like simple listening. The hours of attention to seeing and listening, during his childhood, had taught him precision. He listened and nearly disappeared in the softness and whisper of the deep grasses. Such a quietness within living things resulted in a surge of joy in himself. What did it matter what humankind did? The power and the endless variety of life, of lives, the myriad tiny sparks of consciousness, like scintillating bright rains of light through out everything, could not be destroyed by the heavy,burdened, struggle of humankind.

Why then? Why must humanity struggle so. Nothing else alive did. And as he felt this slim long thought shape itself through his exploring consciousness, he knew the answer."We seek for That beyond ourselves, we seek to KNOW, to perceive Spirit. We are not content to simply be." Then he was silent, realizing an astonishing idea. "Maybe, we're the growing edge of Life itself." The idea burned into his consciousness like a truth. But he questioned. "What proof do I have that the lesser lives of Earth don't seek also? Some primitive Reaching of their own?" He looked through that thought to all that was around him and saw them anew.

Reaching out, knowing of awareness, unceasing, through all life, through Earth Herself, he exulted, and then, without warning ,he knew fear. Could he, Andrew, dissipate, Join with the Earth Life until he could not return? He wanted to cry out, to thrust himself through air, crying out in challenge to all the trees, but in one tightening grip, he saw he had, at that moment of the thought of fear, drawn into the limits of his small ordinary mind. He focussed attention out from himself again, and was still. Gradually aware of ducks rising and dropping down again among the reeds. He looked up, the sky was pure blue. Space called to him. The endless distance between planets where light again wove itself through everything and lifted, lifted always. Invisible until it met the dust and planets of solar systems.

His body flat on the ground, his arms and legs stretched and spread out, he rested. Conscious again of how that body lived, and he lived in it. He felt a pride of himself, and then,laughed gently, with a lightness of heart, a happiness that brought the day into brightness of childhood joy. It was a pool of peace, but his restless spirit wanted more! Briefly, swiftly, he reached,in one vast sweep, extended himself, aware of this five mile radius, aware of Altos, the edges of Denlock and Jasper. Their waking life was just discernable. His mind-vision was acute.

Life was an ebb and flow, moving in streams of living consciousness. Yes, Life was aware. Being aware was being alive!! The thought held him. He shrank his own awareness to the limits of his personal self, overwhelmed, barely able to sustain identity in that flood of consciousness. Where was it that he ended and the OTHER began, a great pulse of Joy flooded everything and he knew it made no difference. There was no ending nor beginning, but a single whole that had no end or beginning. In that second of insight, his mind and heart felt stabbed with something beyond them both, like a Light that penetrated them. His heart absorbed in acceptance, but his mind rallied into thinking. "Is that what humankind has arrived at? The edge of knowing of That which the language has given the name Spirit? Or the interface? Or the fourth dimension?" No word seemed right. He extended, aware, sensing.

Everywhere he knew of billions of tiny flickers of consciousness, from insect, rodent, bird, plant, even that dull glow of stone and deep hard earth shapes. There was a surface, where consciousness formed itself and shaped into thought, simple thought of larger beasts, of intelligent birds, that too was like a tidal wave that threatened to inundate him. He focussed again, sustaining identity now within that vast Vision. He reached out to touch against a tower of consciousness, massive, powerful pooling of life. It was a human town, Adwin. Like a mental mountain it soared above the green undulating landscape. He stiffened. It shook him, the power of it. What then was Santiago like? He shrank, drew together now to this tiny dark form where centered the focus of Life in himself. He shook with relief.

He had gone almost too far, risked nearly his own sanity. There was just too much --too much. As the knowledge sledge hammered itself into his small private brain, terror, shock, set him falling backward, like a light extinguishing. He felt the coolness, heard the thin whispering of sentient grasses, the shadow of the tall trees across him. He groaned, wept fearfully. One thought threaded and throbbed through all his senses exultantly. "After all, I've Touched far beyond myself".

What kind of Mind would be needed just to endure the whole of Life Itself? He lay now, limited to the brain that could form separate thought, could limit him so utterly. This wonderful delicate safety of his limiting brain. He lay resting. Never had he risked so much without Anna to support and bear it with him. He must be careful. Was it that youthful arrogance that allowed him to take those chances? He sighed. Then began to reconsider, the wonder of it -- that was worth the risk. He felt a loosening in his mind and Joy streaming through , a strange new knowledge, a memory of possibility. The wonder of it would never fade. yet he was reluctant to probe memory too deeply just now.

He wanted suddenly to forget, to be only a human boy, limited and presuming himself to be nothing more. But given his probing mind, the thought immediately surfaced, 'What was - is - human? Is it possible that humankind only touches upon humanness? Am I not more human when I Reach out so?'

He got up, feeling his way, letting his feet discover their way through the rocky meadow without help of his eyes. He touched the great boulders, wanting to communicate his kinship. Great trees leaning against and away from one another, grew about the meadow, bushes, already stippled with their tiny bloom that would produce berries and nuts. He felt the power of energy rising. He said, "The Earth creates Herself constantly, even in a casual gesture,, she out does what humankind has done. She is so - so - absolute. Yes, that's it. Absolute. Nothing can touch her actually.' He laughed, "I am a casual gesture of Earth." Then with delight, he added, "And I am conscious of it." He was exultant and

THE AWAKENING

frightened!

He laughed, ran across the thick meadow grasses, lifting his feet high as though they were in water. He let his mind play. He climbed to the top of a small rocky outcrop and stood looking at the saddle between himself and another hill top. That one smooth, nearly covered with trees, it had small meadows here and there between the prongs of forest. Below, the saddle was clear, heavy grasses, a few great ancient trees standing apart, a few shrubs that had pushed their way through the grasses. A thin stream trickled down the center, wound down and settled into a small low pond, nearly hidden by tall Tule grasses, then fell over a flat stone outcrop and splashed white into another smaller pond. He watched, the beauty of it, the sheer loveliness of this natural garden delighted him. He wanted to take it all into himself, to 'feel' it all, but it was itself too much and he could only delight in a little of that beauty at a time. The air seemed to shine, to be radiant, the trees and grasses pulsed with the Life in them. He wanted to dance.

He turned, waterfowl chattered and nested in the small ponds. They swam across its pale green water and lifted now and then to wheel and scream. Then there would be silence again. He could see the towns below. Farms, small glimpses of holdings among the forests.

A great log lay split and half rotting, a huge dark green fern grew in the split end, smaller ones starting along the shaded crevase against the ground. The log lay in a small glen created by a dark rocky outcrop under two huge old trees, a pine and an oak. Andrew felt along the rotting trunk with his eyes, seeing its sharp spiny snags, the great empty sockets, where limbs had rotted away and where now small creatures made homes. He could hear a busy scuttling within. He stood silently watching, feeling with his eyes the damp softness of dark mosses that grew over one side and the top. He went and sat in a hollow of the log where moss grew thick, crossed his legs and was quiet.

His thoughts drifted, faded and he ignored them. Like a lazily inquiring insect they interfered now and then with his attention, but he brushed them away. He watched the movements of a caterpillar hunching itself across the slim, pale green, twig of a blackberry vine toward a great snowy blossom. He slid his eyes to the blooms along the twigs, some not yet open. The crop should be good this year. He visually entered one opened blossom, sank his eyes into the yellow center, saw-felt its stiff softness. It seemed to hold stillness itself. The whole day seemed now to be immersed in stillness. The memory of childhood, practicing the 'watching, came and was gone. This was deeper. There was a great ocean of stillness that encompassed the sounds of birds, the splash of ducks, the slight sounds of insects and creatures in the log. It poured into his body, his mind.

He felt the growing warmth of the sunlight and felt it enter into his body. It seemed to rouse his attention, brighten it. He felt a sudden chill when the wind blew a cloud across before the sun and a sweet sadness sprang up in him. He absorbed that as the sun once again brightened everything.

He heard a sound from inside the great log, or rather from beneath it. A movement, a tiny head, alert eyes, a tip of a tail held high and then his eyes met and held those of a great grey squirrel. For seconds they gazed at one another, then the squirrel turned to scrabble in the bark, attending to its own affairs. He felt companionship of the little creature. He was pleased it did not fear him. The trust touched him so that tears came to his eyes, suddenly unexpectedly.

Why should he feel so? He remembered the trust of the children yesterday. He looked away, looked out over the high eastern Mountains, toward Altos. He could see only a flash of light there now and then when the sun caught the Domes just right. He thought of William there, the question in his heart about William. Sadness again weighed down his thought.

He let his hands trail slowly over the rough cool moss, taking comfort in its presence. A large blue jay dropped onto the branch of the pine tree before his eyes. It cocked its head, watching him, spoke harshly, then shrieked and hopped closer. He watched it, feeling the presence intensely, the gift of its trust. He felt the power in the strong ready wings, the smooth exquisite over lay of blue feathers. How perfectly created you are, he thought. The bird raised its head again, regarding him brightly. He met those eyes, and they stared at one another intently for a moment. He was filled suddenly with a reasonless grief, of something nameless lost, an ancient loss. The Jay moved, effortlessly, it spread its wings and lifted up, swift flight beyond the meadow. He envied that flight.

For the second time that morning, Andrew forgot himself in remembering him Self. He was here in the world around him and his breath seemed no longer to be separate from the sky. He was silent, utterly aware. He sensed life, movement from behind the great log, and waited. A family of racoons emerged from a great hole behind the log. He did not see them at first, they made little sound. The great mother moved slowly, alert, watchful, but the young ones, very small, maybe their first time out, bounded and played with one another and the tall grasses, twigs, bits of bark, and anything that came into sight.

Andrew did not move, he held himself, his very presence still and projected the calm that he felt. He sat in his own quiet, joining that of the Earth and felt stillness include him. He watched with delight that one might have in a theatre when one has great knowledge of theatre art. He watched the play, the response of the young to their mother, she grunted as she lay down much as a dog does when getting comfortable. Yet the alertness of her eyes, her nose, never ceased. He felt himself present at a great secret ceremony and rejoiced. He listened, saw the birds building nests, diving for an insect, the riffling of leaves in moving air, the floating buzzard above, saw with the heightened vision, hearing, of one who has practiced Watching since early childhood. He saw.

"Why isn't this enough?" The thought caught against attention. He considered it. He focussed and answered, "Because there is more!"

"To sustain awareness of all this is life fulfilling. Why must I make a town? Write books? Make music?" He was immersed in stillness. Then whispered, "Maybe we refuse to sustain such awareness, to make our human world relieves us of the power of this. It distracts attention so we need not KNOW!" Again silent. then, "Or is the world a result of humankind's bitter struggle to find that very Life

THE AWAKENING

Earth is? To remake it for ourselves? Refusing to see?"

Sunlight glowed through the air, shadows were thin and firm, soft springtime air carried within itself whispers and fragrances that threatened a revelation. He waited, breathless at the promise of the revelation. Tremendous power of Earth surged upward through his body and inundated his mind, freeing him from assumptions and he saw steadily through everything. It seemed to him he saw the nature of Life itself! He gave himself up to that knowing. Experiencing himself fully through this vast and ceaseless day. He caught the knowledge as it impressed itself on his mind, "I must complete myself, before I can offer myself. Must cling to myself in order to complete myself." The words he shaped from the knowledge seemed inadequate.

Jays flew suddenly from their perch on a tall bare snag. They quarreled and jostled one another in air. One settled on the log near Andrew. Blue feathers shimmered, ruffled in a gust of wind, then it turned began pecking industriously at the lose bark. The racoons lay sprawled, still near their hole, but some ventured farther. The mother's eyes watchful, moving, alert. Two nuzzled deep into her body for milk. The buzzard's great dark body floated high, watching, floating in a widening circle, waiting for whatever fell. A flock of tiny birds swept down, across their space, circled and away.

Andy felt tension near by. A red fox, its coat shining and thick, leaped to a boulder across from the great log. Too late, the racoon saw, swept herself up, a gutteral cry, warning her young. In one motion of eye and brain the fox dropped to snatch a wandering baby racoon, then wheeled away. The mother had barely gotten the rest behind her as she leaped after it. The fox swiftly shook the youngster, broke its neck and loped away, ignored the intention of the mother. She made one leap to intercept but he had gone. She made a sound, a strange plaintive sound, a helpless cry at the loss of her young. She stood a second, shook herself and dashed into the hole with her brood.

The day grew, only in the event was time present. Yet the petal that turned in the air, dislodged from a bloom, falling, falling, catching and emptying itself of sun as it fluttered, seemed to hold in itself all existence. Andy loosened himself, Reached, felt the extension of mountains far off, all around the Great Valley they rose, so far away some were only dim blue in the sky. Then he returned, sensing another life near.

A great shadow fell across the grass and he did not turn, he wanted to test his senses. Cows! Yes, he turned to look and two wild cows and a calf moved toward him, grazing as they came. They raised their heads, expecting perhaps to rest and chew their cud in this quiet place. Then they saw him. The lead cow stopped, her ears forward, her large eyes wide and watching, curious, unmoving. She looked at him for several minutes, then moving nearer, she sniffed at his body, satisfied herself and folded her legs under herself to sink to the ground against the side of the log. The others came close then, found places and dropped. The calf sniffed about a bit, curious, restless, then joined his elders. Andrew felt their great bodies near, their trust, like a gift. He cherished it.

THE PEOPLE OF THE VALLEY

He stretched his bare legs, slid from the log, startling the near cow who made as though to rise, then sank down as he moved away. Jays flew upward suddenly shouting at him, they lit on a branch above. He moved silently from his moss nest, walked from the protection of the little glen. With a sudden burst of gladness and joy of movement, he leaped straight up and then began to run wildly toward the pond. His feet seemed barely to touch the ground, he was careless and paid no attention to where he stepped, so full of the joy of himself, his body. Then he felt his foot touch something alive. He shrieked, hurled himself sideways , twisting so that he instantly knew he must roll to prevent injury. He fell into tall grasses along the bank of the pond. The pale green water beyond him was shaken by the swift movement of ducks,mud hens and heron moving away from his disturbance. He looked back, crying brokenly with pain of recognition,"Oh,Oh, what've I done?"

Then Reaching, finding, seeing in mind sense, he knew that he had stepped on a duckling. He had felt the small life beneath his bare foot, only a second,but it was so small, so tender. He knew he had hurt it.He turned to look. THe mother had turned also, the little one lay with its neck stretched, it's body still. One leg moved, then jerked, and began a repetitious jerking. The mother ignored Andy, she ran with a raucous broken cry , such as he had never heard from a creature, though it seemed so much like that of the Racoon earlier. She bent to the duckling, her actions were suddenly frantic, she struck it gently with her bill. She ignored him and he realized she didn't connect him with the hurt to her young. He exuded no quality of danger. That is why she had not taken her remaining young and fled. He was awed.

She stood over it, bending again and again striking it lightly as if wanting to get its attention, yet with the recurrent cry, full of a dim, dumb pain. Andrew felt a sickness of repentance and speechless shame. Then he knew that helplessness, that emotion that drew the mother to cry for her young. For at that moment, she pushed at it, once more, turned and fled to where the rest of her brood was paddling in a circle in the shallow water. She made the same motions, touching her bill against them, against the water. They drew close, crept behind her as she returned. He felt in himself the pain of creatures. Like a thin wire cutting into him her pain reverberated in his body.

Anthony pulled himself close together, held his arms along his bent legs and hugged his knees to his chest. The soil was damp and the grass hid him from all except the buzzard soaring above. The boy huddled watching the frantic urgent mother, the inchoate grief creating a dome of realization between them. Andy saw that dome, he saw it shimmer,weaken then reassert. She stopped her ritual movements, scrambled back up the bank to her lost one, caught the duckling with her bill and drew it slowly backward into the deep grasses. When they had dissappeared, Andrew whispered,"Oh,I'm sorry. I'm sorry." He heard his own words as an excuse. They distressed him more.

But he did not move. He sat for some time now, deep beneath this astonishment of relationship. The mother duck knew - and did not fear. The

THE AWAKENING

power within her body, the fierce resistance, the ignoring of him, left him with sorrow that he could not quench. Here was something alive, deeper life than he could fathom. Could understand. A yawning realization of another truth stabbed his mind. Trust demanded responsibility.

Finally he stood among the grasses that grew above his waist and looked out over the pond. The water was quiet now, creatures silent again, except for neighborly chatting and muttering of active bills probing the mud beneath for food. He watched them for a time, letting himself release a little of the shame. Then moving with a care that left hardly a ripple in the sea of grass, he walked across this low part of the saddle up into the hills that would lead to home. His heart felt on fire, his mind shaken, his body filled with emptyness. He was again fallen from that throne of humanity, the superior being. He stopped walking. He must release this pain.He remembered something Anna had taught him.

He stretched down into the grass, he could hear the water fowl faintly behind, the sudden cry of other birds, the faint whisper of tall stalks in moving air. His dispair was a wedge within him. The death of the tiny racoon,,the duckling, the endless deaths that life might continue, all created their rasping in his mind.

He let the grief build, felt it rise from it's darkness , like a wave it rose, inundating his joy, his eagerness. He spread his arms wide, pressing his body into the Earth, He acknowledged that grief. Senseless or not, it was real. He let the grief pour into Earth, A thin sobbing sound racked his chest and pain drained away along with tears that the fine new grass brushed from his face. The anger and pain loosened its darkness. He felt relief. He pressed close, all his consciousness focussed into that soft darkness. No thought intruded, release grew.

His mind surged out, Reached gradually to a widening awareness. Earth beneath him, all around him, Earth was life! Life is never ending, death being a shifting about, from one form to another, of Life. He was included. Painful,joyous thrusts of himself outward through the barriers of emotion that clouded things. Pain, grief, guilt, slowly spun downward, losing themselves into Earth like water absorbed. Calming, he realized steadily. And body and mind were immersed in realisation. Stillness surrounded him, through which the sounds of Earth and air came clear and sweet.

Finally, thought reinstated itself, rushing in as though denied too long. Words formed,"Here it is,Earth Mother. Here I am again. Life does not ease us, does not comfort. Yet, these grasses, trees, creatures rocks, all of this - comforts more than any human thing. This kind of grief is for humankind alone, for we know what we do. The two mothers knew a grief that was simple loss. By now they have forgotten."

"We are separate after all, even as we are part of this life. Are we, perhaps,the Mind of Earth life, all of us, humankind, like cells of the brain-mind of Earth?" He lifted his head, shook himself a little, he was dreaming. He said aloud, "What an idea, but it isn't so fantastic. I can see what the fox cannot see and so I grieve. I can know what the duck cannot know and I grieve. Surely we humans are the best and worst of you, Mother Earth. And I am guilty just as my kind is guilty of world evil. It is that darkness within ourselves that is the thing called evil. The darkness is what we refuse to see, or won't admit about ourselves. Our unacknowledged capacity for harm. It's not something outside us. We want to bend Life to our own small ends."

He lay, letting these thoughts absorb him, letting them penetrate through the cells of his body into memory , holding the meaning. Then he spoke again," If that's so, then Good, is also within. In every single human being, - - even in those we fear or despise. Then we must need to acknowledge our goodness, admit to it, our capacity for Good. No wonder we are in conflict!" The knowledge, the whole of the thought, replaced all emptyness. Filled him.

He rolled over, dry eyed, feeling the bonding of this Earth energy. the laughter, the unassuageable sorrow, and the silent pulse - like a deep resounding Earth smile. He lay still for some time, soaking in these things. He thought of his twin, they two talked of such things. She would be surprised when he told her of his realization. He spoke slowly, as if trying to reshape what he knew. "Being conscious, we are the voice and right hand of Earth. Life cannot come from that which is not alive. Earth Herself has to be alive." Again realization filled his mind like a cool water.

He sat up astonished, feeling that he had received a gift in exchange for his grief and pain. Evil is done when we forget that we are of Earth Life as utterly as are all creatures. Jessie said that evil is a forgetting. Is it a dark denial of what we are? Is it fear? Or does it generate fear? And all the qualities that bring us down to dispair, greed, lust, blind hunger. Hunger for what?" The answer was there, just behind the question, but he shook his head. Surely there was something here he need talk of with a Teacher. He nodded satisfied,"He will know!" He shook his head, a sense of discovery filling him. " Is it possible that everything we need is here, already given? Just demanding to be discovered?" He stood and looked around at a new world, a brilliantly shining Earth. He stood for long minutes amazed.

After a while, walking along, settling into more ordinary thought, he said aloud,"Now I can understand a little the problem of the Builders. I can see what makes them so angry. They sense something is awake among us all. They sense a lack in themselves and don't know what it is, deny it exists! We humans are great at denying." He frowned, let the thought hold. "Is it that they cannot, truly cannot know the way we see the Earth Life, are not able? Then they do not know all the Joy - or the pain. Pain because we CAN see but deny instead."

He walked rapidly now, climbing rock and winding through narrow animal paths, he climbed to the tops of hills and down again to the widening valleys between. "But that spark, that inner Good, that I see, like flickers of light, in every ---" he stood still a moment in surprise,"Why in everything, not just in people. Yes, when I truly look, truly See, there it is. And the Builders too, they too bear that inner light. Why then, are they not awake?"

"If their only evil is that they are ignorant, and cannot push past the old

THE AWAKENING

patterns of humankind to See, then we cannot place any blame at all. None at all. We must carry that ourselves, for we can--- we can See."

The grief of these facts was like a thin wave through his body. He shivered. Drew himself into silence. It was true that some people could see what others could not. That for some there was a light blazing, illuminating their minds."There it is," he said exultantly, as if he had found something of infinite value at last. "There it is,. One must consciously lift ones self out into that Light, in order even to see the Light in everyone else. And that doesn't seem fair". He remembered long days of study, of talking to his Master Teacher, and of half understanding and now so much fell into place.

He said aloud, cresting a third hill, from which he could see the Farm again, see people moving about, "How can it be said that we human's can know of Love when we keep on hurting living things? When we are so obsessed with ourselves we don't see how it is with others? Does self love comes first, to make it possible to love anyone at all?" He stopped in his rambling walk, to lean against the dark trunk of an oak. He drew a long sigh,"I suppose we ought to be grateful we're finally able to know that Love is more! Even to know that. Maybe we - are not able - to know Love." Other questions came, a flood the new insight had broken loose. He wanted desparately to talk to Anna, to Neal, his best friend. He stood looking out over the hills, their sculptural beauty rousing his heart's alertness. Then, the vibration of a thought, trembling through his mind, coming to him, out of air it seemed, grew until it could not be ignored. "You, Andrew, have only to ask and the Monitors will teach. We wait for your asking."

He sat down, on a grey mossy boulder. Trembling, with the power of that speaking within him. He had known that one had to ask. He had known. And he never had. Why not? Even now, in the moment of a tremendous desire to know, he still did not ask? Why not? The power of the Sending throbbed through him. Was he afraid? Was he stubborn? Must he do it all himself? Attentively he watched a stray bee moving its barbed legs delicately and precisely as it walked across the golden field of a daisy. The simple wonder of that little life , so perfectly designed, moved him.

Softly he breathed words,"How could I kill such a creation?" He saw that he had adroitly avoided the Sending once again.He knew he could not keep avoiding that necessity. He must find a way to Ask.

He walked on home. Ready now to be with his family. The day had worn to lateness. He thought briefly of that avoiding and resolved that he would at least talk to his Master Teacher to find the source of his reluctance. He shook his head. There in his own home he had one who was of the Monitor people. He knew that, had refused to acknowledge all it meant. Jessie!

He knew that Jessie would know. He could talk just to her, perhaps. Would it be a waste of her time? Then he saw one cause of his resistance. How could such as she, be bothered with his worries? He saw and was surprised. He was unwilling to appear foolish before such wise ones.

He could see ahead to the left, a farm house, clean,white in the heavy field

THE PEOPLE OF THE VALLEY

grass. Great oaks grew below the house. He remembered a visit there, two years ago. A visit when he held that arrogance in his heart and did not know it for what it was. He stood looking at the house remembering.

He had passed that way on a short travel through the land. he had found a woman in the garden. She had said she didn't know the trails ahead, maybe her men folk would. She sent Andrew to the barn where men were putting up great bales of hay, It was then that Andy suspected these must be a family of the 'olders'. Valley people did not pen animals up, nor farm in this way. Here were fences, fields of grass,kept green even in dry spells with irrigation. Valley farmers never needed to . Cattle, sheep, horses, even, were penned near the barns. Andrew remembered how he had felt anger, and a strange subtle fear that he would not admit.

The men had come out to shake hands in the old way. He pointed out his own Farm, they wondered why there were no fences there, no 'stock'. Anthony asked them what they did with the animals,and the old man said,with a sudden questioning frown,"Son, you are like all the Valley people. Asking strange questions. There's only one thing to do with farm animals. We sell them for meat." He pointed to a small stone building, narrow but long, and when he opened the door, Andy saw carcasses of animals strung on hooks, the room icy cold around them. Andrew stared, how could they find enough people who would eat so many"

The son interrupted when they had closed the slaughter house door. "We saw bear up there, on that second hill, looking over our cows, I think. We'll have to kill them, they come down, you know. People might get together and have a real hunt, kill them out so we don't have the trouble of it. They way the old ones used to do." Then,turning, Andrew saw the vivid picture in the grandfather's mind, a picture of his young man hood, never forgotten. Images so intense Andrew felt them. A hunt, where animals were carefully herded into a cull de sac, where they could not escape and then simply slaughtered, their carcasses falling one on top the other. He could feel in that single flash image the glee with which the men killed. They took aim but did not bother or were not skilled as were the Valley Hunters to make clean kills. He saw hurt and pain- riddled animals, their bodies jerking, a low moaning, or sudden sharp cry. The image was one of men caught in some wild frenzy, a passion to kill, but even worse, to hurt, and he shuddered as the image faded. The old man had held it in mind with satisfaction.

Andrew had turned away very soon. They knew the trail and told him how to find it. He had walked half a mile before he was aware that he was not on the path.

He had known then that they did not know. That they could not sense what he sensed. He remembered the rest of the day, like a nightmare. He had cried, raging that his father must do something, must stop this terrible thing. He had told them and Valley people had acted. They had persuaded the farm men not to carry out such a wild slaughter, showed them how to protect their cattle without random killing by using force fields instead of fences. They discovered that the

THE AWAKENING

father did not want to kill so flagrantly, only the grandfather and one son felt no remorse, wanted the killing. Angrily they called the others cowards because they shrank from it. But the hunt had been stopped. One boy began coming to Adwin to the Learning Center.

Yet, all the talk and the force poles did not change their way of life much. They stuck to that, except the son did see a Healer for a while. Andrew finally realized that understanding did not heal the pain, it made it worse. During the next year, Andy saw that these farmers lives had changed a little. It had taken time because they would not believe that Valley people would not buy their meat in enough quantity to make it pay. Not enough people still ate the flesh of creatures. They had to ship it out Valley and that was too costly. Ben helped them set up force field poles so that no fences were needed. They saw it work against bear. Now, Andrew knew they killed few cattle, they were raising milk cows and sold milk. Began to raise a few horses that they sold to the trainers down in the central Valley. A Master Teacher went to talk, a Healer visited, slowly a different way of life was built. They learned to grow crops that could be sold in the Valley. It was a better living.

Andrew drew his eyes away from the farm house, children could be seen, tiny dots, playing, working and adults leading horses to work. The Grandfather had never accepted the use of disc lifts and float seeders. But the young ones would, one day when they were free to do so. Andrew turned his eyes toward home, his feet moving with new eagerness, a longing to be there where things were 'right'. He wondered if that were true.

CIRCUS

On a grey rainy morning in May, Jessie announced to the Family that she would expect a visitor during the day. She would like to invite him to visit for a day or two if it were not inconvenient. Hardly had the Family agreed with eagerness to see what kind of guest Jessie might invite, than they heard in the distance, the merry sound of bells and a flute . Steve looked up from his breakfast porridge, a mixture of several grains and chopped dried fruits. Hey, d'you hear that? Sounds like music",he grinned, "And a fine kind too. My feet are already dancing to it." They could hear his heavy boots tapping away beneath the table. Then he turned in disbelief toward Jessie,"Couldn't be your visitor, could it?"

Jessie was up and moving toward the door. "It could be. He's apt to such silly sounds." She was smiling in eager anticipation, though they could not see her face.The music grew louder until the air was full of it, a lilting joyous tune that would start the feet to dancing and the heart to lifting even for one in grief. Anna and Andrew and Cassie did not leave the table. They looked at one another with questions in their eyes. Then silently they Reached and the question was answered with a blast of melody within their minds. No detail, only that seductive tune.But they leaped from their half eaten breakfasts and ran past the adults to stand on the deck outside just as a fantastic person rode through the air on a belt, flowing ribbons of every color trailing behind in the wind, a bright green pair of breeches and deep red, calf high boots,a flowing, brilliant blue tunic with long pointed sleeves that hid his hands. He carried a grey pack so covered with Vagabond embroidery one could hardly see the grey. His hat, tied for the journey under his chin, carried a row of brilliant feathery plumes. But the surprise of his clothes was second to that of his face, which was painted with the bright colors of the traditional clown. He came in, his feet raised to miss the deck railing and landed with a graceful lightness on the deck before them. He swept off his hat, bowed and performed a quick complex dance step to his own music and then, folding the flute up into his sleeve, he said,"I am pleased to meet the Family who shelters my very dear sister." He shook himself lightly as he laughed and the little bells that hung here and there on his clothes, rang surprisingly loud for their size.

Jessie, grinning like a young girl, ran to him and threw her arms about his neck. They kissed and he whirled her around two times and then, stood beside her, looking down at her face. "And it's too long, my dear. Too long that we've been apart."

Jessie nodded."Surely it is,can you come in and have breakfast with us. Surely you hadn't time to eat before you left West Station."

He eyed her quizzically, and their eyes met in a keen interchange, then he nodded,"Well, now, I'd like that. But do I need to be introduced?"

THE AWAKENING

She laughed,"It's certain that no one needs to be introduced to you, but they might need to know of you." Again that strange look between them and the grin. She turned to the waiting Family members. This is Carroll, my friend since we were only children. He's come to us from the West Station."

"Then he's of the Monitors?" Anna spoke, a note of surprise in her voice but a nod of understanding followed it."It was that then that I felt."

Carroll turned to her and laughed,"Ah ha, a young one whose eyes are too bright for her own good, eh?"

Rose broke in,"Please come in, Sir. We've just begun breakfast and we'd be honored to have your company."

He turned with a fierce frown toward Jessie, "Now see there, what you've done? You've got them to calling me 'Sir' even before I've begun acting like it." He turned back to Rose and in the most graceful way, he bowed again, danced a quick step toward her and said,"I'd sure be pleased to join with you and a bit of breakfast would go well."

They went back to the Hall and found their chairs. Carroll dialed himself a breakfast, fruits and nuts, seemed all he needed, though he eyed the porridge with a thoughtful glance before settling on his choice. He accepted his plate and picked up a red- yellow plum, his cheery smile radiating from his whole face."Ah, now its good to be here among you. I suppose that foolish old woman there has told you nothing at all about me and so I'm a complete stranger,No?"

Benjamin said,"It's true, she's told us nothing. Then who are you Carroll. Are you - could you be - is it possible that Anna is right? That you're one of those called Monitors?"

Carrolll laughed with such infectious good humor that everyone felt the air itself lighten. "Oh, now, I'm no more one of those staid, fussy folk than Jessie herself is. And she's a wonderer who seldom sets her feet into one place longer than a few days. How is it that she's here so long?"

Rose watched this happy, colorful guest warily. After all,he'd just parried the question adroitly and hadn't answered at all. She thought she'd let it go just now. At any rate, it supported her own suspicion that Jessie was one of Wise Ones after all. She met his watching eyes and felt the warmth of his grin Reach right into her own feelings. She grinned back at him. But what an easy manner - he had literally Touched her emotions as if they were tangible. She felt no trace of fear or surprise, somehow it seemed so natural, so right. She said, "We've brought her here to help us. We need her help in this Valley and you must know that well,if you're acquainted with it at all."

 He finished off an apple and accepted a large cup of hot tea. "Ah, such wonderful tea. Who ever programmed this processer has the hand of genius. I'd like to meet that one. And as for the Valley needing help, well I come to tell you of the best help possible and it's coming your way within days."

 " And what would that be, Old friend,"Jessie was smiling at him, her pleasure at seeing him obvious to the Family."What magical powers have you conjured up for us?" Her own bantering tone seemed unlike her, a new playful part of her that they had not seen so much of .

"How'd you like to go to a circus? "He glanced about at them, his keen watchful attention masked by the foolish good humor of his smile and his voice. But he saw that these things were not lost on this company.

Jerry leaned toward him,"You mean it? A Circus? We've not had one this far north in three years. It'd be grand.!"

Steve nodded, soberly, because he was too puzzled by this strange man to allow himself to enjoy even his own good humor fully. Such clownishness in a man, such clothes, the ribbons still lifted and swayed about his body, attached to his clothes in such an odd manner that Steve could not guess how. He said,"I don't suppose you'll tell us you're part of that circus?"

Carroll turned to him the broad grin seemed to lengthen as he nodded,"I am that. I'm part of it and it's true that it'll be here within the week. For it's played to Santiago and the crowds were so great we thought the main Branch Plaza would be permanently bent down. But they seemed to all leave safely. And no one fell over the edges." His eyes twinkled with some inner merriment that it was all they could do to keep from asking him what was so funny. That merriment was infectious; they found the tensions and worries of the past weeks fade and a happy light heartedness lifting their spirits.

Ben nodded, "Yes, it's true about the crowds. The last time I went to Santiago and to Altos too, I thought they were crowded. Thousands coming and going through the air lifts, you can hardly drop down through them without bumping into someone. And the trains inside the trunks of Santiago are full now even in the middle ofthe day. It's perhaps a crowded Valley we've got in these days."

The clown laughed again, a merry sound that seemed to have the music of his flute in it."Well, the more the merrier, isn't it? "

Steve shook his head, "No, I'll not agree with that. We've got to watch this crowding of our land."

Then suddenly Carroll was serious, he turned to Steve, met his eyes and as if not aware of the sudden consternation he brought to that serious worried face, he said,"I agree that we must. Though surely the crowds at Santiago were there from out of town,so many visitors! The city itself hasn't passed her limit." And instantly his joyous grin came back and Steve seemed to lose his solemnity as it did.

"Well then, if there's to be the Circus here we'd better plan to take a day away from the farm for it." Jerry finished his breakfast and set his plates into the cleaner. He stood up," For me that means getting a lot of work done these next few days.Can we pass the word along? Or is this a secret."

"Oh no, tell everyone. It'll be on the Videos all day and for several days that we're coming and just which days your town will act as hostess to all the northern towns. That'll put you to some doing now, won't it." Carroll leaped to his feet, lithe, balanced, he seemed a young man, and yet, there was a look of great age about his eyes.

"Then that's what we'll do. We'll get word to Tom, if he hasn't already heard and we'll begin to prepare. But mostly, we've all got work to do in town and here on the Farm. I think, we'd better be at it. Perhaps you'll want to have time for a good talk with Jessie anyway, Sir." Ben got up too, the others began leaving the table, and Jessie nodded, "Yes, it would be good to show you our new fields, and our land and to show you my new, fine cottage that this Family built so swiftly for me."

The holo-video had brought the Circus at Santiago into the northern towns and villages. The people gathered in small villages in the town plaza where the screens cast images into the plaza itself and though people could not talk to or touch the performers, it was as nearly real as anything could be. The Circus seemed to be there ,in their own Market plaza. The voices, the colors, the smell and feel of excitement, all reproduced in three dinensions .But everyone was more than excited that that same circus would be performing in Adwin in a few days.

The morning of the fifth day after the Clown's visit,they heard the circus arriving. Miles before it reached even Jasper, it could be heard. The music, the brilliant lights, scattering designs on the clouds, on the mnountains beyond; the long train of riders and carts that drew slowly toward them on the Highway;the dancers preceeded the caravan leaping and dancing a complex pattern among the the unbelieveable variety of animals that ran free and even participated in the dance . Wild creatures within the forests they passed through were drawn to watch as if their own kind there in the parade called to them somehow. Several varieties of deer gathered in fields here and there, sheep, wild cattle and carabou, antelope and others of their family,came down from the hills to see.The wolves, foxes, wild cats and the small burrowing creatures of field or forest, were represented along that route. Not in great numbers, only those whose territory this was. But they felt the attraction coming somehow from their counterparts who traveled as participants of this circus. No one asked they knew. It was enough that they did.

Interest grew. Always the performances were astonishing. Each circus of past years had always been different in each town. Something utterly new was part of its delight. Now, the animals who needed no restraint nor bridles even, drew these human animals to see, to find out what this curious , foolish group of traveling players had done.

Along the Highway the Singers led the way, followed by the musicians, many of these rode on the larger animals, whose willingness and head tossing interest in the sounds, seemed itself a performance. There were animals from every corner of the world, elephants carried the drums and their drummers, camels carried baggage, a small pride of lions gamboled into the fields or forests, then returned and slept in the carts or ran along beside the Slow Carts. Other huge cats, leopards and tigers among them, peered sleepily over the edges of open carts where they rode with the children of the troop.

As Andrew and Anna watched from where they had raced with other youngsters down the hills and highway to accompany the procession to town, they thought that a curious energy played about the circus. Anna turned to her brother,"It's as though a light that we cannot see radiates out from them. It's not my imagination."

He nodded, fascinated, his attention intent on the circus, trying to discover the source of this strange power."You're right Sis, it's not imagination. I see it too, we're seeing that Light with our mind's eye. If we pay attention, maybe we'll know more about it. Surely, it's not like the circus we saw last."

Someone else said, "Let's don't worry about it. Let's just enjoy the show. I don't want to try to find out about it. I just want to have a good time." He was frowning at Andrew so fiercely that Andy laughed.

"Suits me, Joe, Suits me, too. I'd like to know how they handle all these creatures though. Surely must have at least one animal Talent among them."

Joe nodded, "Didn't you see them last night on Video-Holo. they were wonderful." He turned to the passing circus, the long streamers of shining ribbon, the great, fat, bright balloons dancing along like a loose cloud above them, the seemingly tireless dancers, and no one talked as they followed along.

The Great Field,along the Green River below town was nearly twenty acres wide and three miles long. It held the main playing fields for the Adwin Learning Center and always held the Games during Festivals. Today this north eastern end under the bluffs of the town was a sea of people, great colorful tents, bobbing balloons, ribbon streamers, carts where wonderful smells of exotic foods were being prepared, sweets, drinks, a low ring of tables in which bartenders served nearly any drink anyone could name. After ward, few would remember there were no drinks containing alcohol, such healing, stimulating, or calming qualities they had. Andrew and Anna roamed everywhere, watching, helping when they could, exploring and noticing everything. The Circus had been set up in a brief two hours. The crowd watched in amazement. Animals took their places to pull or push. A group of eight dogs, collies, german shepherds and retrievers, large powerful animals, joined together to chase down, pick up at its edges and drag back a huge canvas sun shelter that had been caught in the wind. An elephant went where three men labored to move a cart that had been drawn up out of place.She trumpeted a signal, and another older elephant came lumbering to her, the men stood back at the sound and the two elephants, one on each side, lifted the cart easily, waited to hear the human instructions and set it down just right. Then they wandered off as if this were just another day's work. Horses cropped the lush grass, now and then looking up and around as if assessing the amazing activities for themselves. No one seemed to think these behaviors were amazing at all. That was what caught Andrew's attention.

Anna said," Tomorrow's going to be wonderful. I love these folk. All of them." He saw her eyes roving over the field, taking in the laughter, the gymnasts literally walking across thin nearly invisible lines high above Earth, fastened to slim poles that seemed only to be stuck into Earth loosely. People were already absorbed in never ending dancing, music, eating, drinking, enjoying af all the physical senses. Already before the circus began everyone was having fun. Anna turned to her brother, a wry smile playing on her young face,"Andy, don't you think we ought to just join in. We're trying to figure everything out, to understand it all, and we ought to be just enjoying, the way they are." She waved her arm to take in the huge field.

At that instant they saw the dancers who belonged to the circus, obvious by their brilliant costumes and bright streaming ribbons, turn from the crowd that had come from town to dance with them and, in one fluid movement, run up the guy lines of the high wires. They formed a solid line that slid as though on oiled wheels up that steep guy wire, then onto the horizontal wires above the field. The children were amazed to see by their placement of themselves on these invisible wires how much of a grid they formed. Then the dancers danced, there, high above, perfectly in rhythm, without missing a step, they laughed down at their former companions from the adjoining towns and encouraged them to continue. The Circus was nearly ready. And suddenly Anna and Andrew and their friends looked at one another and knew that the circus had already begun. How could so many people up there, dancing, on those wires so thin they could not be seen from below, manage the balance, the perfect symmetry necessary? They watched in awe, and a slight tremble of fear. And that fear, they knew, was part of the excitement of it all.

By the next morning, most people were all ready full of the mood for celebration. this was a high spring day. A light rain falling in the night had cleared the air, dampened the grasses and the new blossoms of the fruit trees glowing white or pink here and there among woods or along the Highways. A few huge fruit trees dropped their petals down on the tents and carts of the circus. The air was full of fragrance. A feeling of sweet joy seemed to increase as they approached the Fields. It was even more beautiful than Festival, Tom thought, as he approached. He could see people gathered along one farthest field, the little soccer field. In it was the strangest collection of animals he had ever seen. He stopped to watch, standing on a little rise he could see without obstruction. There, dogs, horses, lions, cats,big and little, A great strutting ostrich, a small flock of bright green birds, three hawks that circled above the whole of it, and Tom could see there were other animals too small to identify from his place. But they were playing a game. A 'GAME'. he stood speachless, it was impossible. They were obviously divided into teams and they had a great soft ball with prongs that stuck out on all sides, but were soft enough that the ball could roll easily.Only two humans played with them, one on each team. And As Tom watched, he felt a strange unease, a growing sense that there was more to this circus than he could have ever imagined.

He saw Jessie and Rose walking in from the Highway and went to meet them.

Rose laughed, nodded toward the huge tent erected beyond them and said, "We're late too, Tom, let's go find the others or at least get into that impossible tent. It must be where the main events are being held. They walked toward the field to that bright, many colored tent. It's sides were lifted in long loops six feet above the ground. Inside they could see tiers of benches. The tent itself was made up of eight vast gleaming fabric cones. At the top of each cone was a cluster of floating streamers and balloons that reached on in the wind. The highest of those cones must have been sixty feet high. The whole thing covered at least two acres. Rose turned to Jessie,"It's impossible! Impossible!"

Jessie laughed, "You don't trust your own eyes,eh?"

Tom shook his head,"I don't. I've got to get inside and see whether this is an illusion." He stopped to look at her, "Do you know anything about these circus people, Jessie? We've never been able to find out much about them. Their answer to questions have always seemed perfectly logical until you get home and try to remember what they said and then they seem so vague they don't tell you anything at all. Just where do they come from?"

Jessie laughed,"Well, Tom, we'll have to try again to find out. But does it really matter,they give us such a good time. I've never eaten better food, and even the wines and beer are extraordinary. If you drink too much, you don't have a hang over." She laughed."Do you know why?"

Tom was interested,"I've noticed it before and never knew. Why?"

"Because there's no alcohol. Yet the taste is fine and the lift it give is real. A true lift, not a false one that alcohol gives."

"We need to find out how it's made. Adwin bars would better serve that and would attract more of us if they did."

They went inside,there huge rings filled every tent and one could actually watch what was happening in more than one at a time. Highwire walkers and trapeze artists wove about among the distant upper limits like small bright dolls performing lovely leaps, somersaults, double, triple, quadruple and more, as they rolled and leaped across seemingly empty space to catch the hands of partners who had already launched themselves into that space. Then there were two, three and sometimes four, coming together, catching one another and forming pyramids of spinning color, then leaping away to light on some point of wire distant but still continuing a design.

They looked out into the rings, and found that there were acts going on everywhere. Gymnasts with pure white horses all in one ring, doing complex rhythmic patterns of movement with the gymnasts while small brightly dressed monkeys leaped from one to the other. A troop of dogs and cats, performing an intricate dance whose very pattern seen from the tiers of seats above them, was facinating as it changed with the dance. The big cats came in,their gleaming coats sliding over powerful muscles, they moved wtih ease and control. They entered the ring, eight lions and tigers together. A leapard sat yawning at the side, and then, a ring of chimpanzees, dressed in brilliant color, carrying small shining wands trooped in to begin the performance of the cats. The Chimps stood, lifting their wands, directing, putting the cats through rings, over hurdles, and finally in an intricate weaving pattern through and across each other. Never had the people seen such acts, and never with Chimpanzees as trainers. The whole troop, sat sprawled along the edge of the great ring when the elephants came in. And they seemed to enjoy watching the performance of those great intelligent animals, whose courtesy between one another, gentleness with their young and their riders, was lovely to see.

These acts went on for an more than two hours. There was a change, then, small groups of musicians came into the rings and suddenly the watchers realized that only that ring on which they turned their attention could be heard, so, though all were playing , they did not interfere with one other. There was an intermission time for refreshments, while the music played.

Then, while people walked about, listening and getting food to eat, talking to one another, or just resting from the sitting,the Rings changed. In each Ring, and one each of the center points of the wires high above, there stood one person,dressed in bright tights with multicolored tunics that were cut at the hem and sleeves in jagged diamond shapes. Around their heads were radiant halos of light. The animals were gone, or were themselves watching from the sidelines.Each person waited silently in place until the crowd was again seated and watching. Then slowly the new show began. First there were the traditional performances of the clown. Their leaps, their foolish antics with barrel,umbrella, mime, and gymnastics gone awry. Then, across the open space, rolling like a ragged ball, came another clown who joined the first and the second series of foolishness began. They had the crowd laughing, the unexpected, the ridiculous, caught their sense of humor and they felt the wonderful healing delight of genuine laughter doubling them up in amusement. As Rose watched, she thought she had never seen such perfect skill at Mime. The invisible ball seemd so obviously there, the precise, delicate movements that made the rest of the scene shape in the empty air, was magical. These were artists in fact.

Finally these clowns were suddenly still. One standing, the other sitting. They seemd to wait for something. Jerry, sitting beside Silvia, his face still loose with the laughter of the past hour, said,"I haven't laughed so much in years, I think. How they manage to make such simple actions so funny, I'll never know."

She turned to him,her own face still smiling, soft,"It's the juxtapostion of action, event, idea, ect, that creates a ridiculous relationship or lack of one. It's the catching of our minds into that play of foolishness with them. That's how I think it works."

He nodded, looking happily down at her small, face so near his shoulder."Perhaps. But there's one thing I know for sure, Sweetheart, and it's that I've seldom seen you so happy, so relaxed."

She smiled up at him, nodding."It's true. I feel as if everything is all right. Better than for weeks."

The scene around the clowns on each of the stages of the vast tent, began to change. First a slim pole of some gleaming silver material began sliding down from the highest shadows above. It descended until it touched the floor at the feet of the clowns. The people watched the shimmer of the pole, as though it were not solid, yet it seemed solid enough,for the standing clown slouched heavily against it. The seated clown, suddenly leaped to his friend's shoulders, did a somersault there and landed ,light as a leaf, on his companion's shoulders.He caught his hands around the shimmering shaft and proceeded to climb. He had gone only a few feet up, when a projection shaped itself on which he could stand and himself slouch lazily against the pole. A hush had fallen on the thousands of people in the great tent. The strange light of the pole, the stillness of the Clowns, and the sense of expectancy combined to hold their attention at full focus. Now, another rod of silver appeared, coming from the first, it extended horizontally out from half way up the length of it. Then, rapidly, others, like a growing forest of slim, shining silver rods, until there was from this first pole, a forest of arms in every direction each one attached to new vertical poles coming down again from the invisible place above It was an intricate three dimensional grid. The two clowns had not moved. Each pole was glowing as if with its own light, and the audience only began then to notice that there were no other lights in the tent. With a sudden clap, sound issued from these poles, or seemed to come from them. A lilting melody with a strong beat. It shattered the stillness and startled the people, watching, but the surprise only made them laugh again. Then as startlingly, sudden, each of these slim, fragile looking poles, held other human figures. Some were clowns, some dancers in flowing white, nearly transparant short gowns. Tight body stockings of many pure clear colors covered their bodies. And these began a slow multidimensional dance in these many spaces in the air. The exquisite beauty of movement, of their falling, catching themselves and leaping into the air to touch lightly another pole and be flung to bars high above or out into those to every side. They interchanged places, passing one another in midair, they caught one another to fling each other up or across to another pole. Every move seemed an impossible feat of gymnastics while suspended far above the floor and hung betweeen poles they must reach in order to save themselves. What they did was beyond expectation. It seemed similar to a lovely ballet of birds, or butterflys, all singing with their bodies in perfect harmony.

  Rose felt the power of this compelling performance, the sheer balance, the energy of minds linked to minds knowing and responding to one another in split second reaction. The movement became faster, a joyous quality growing to build in those watching that equal sense of delight. And then, the movement slowed, became the easy, languid and unbelievable control of bodies falling slowly, lifting slowly and still reaching their goal; of the shining pattern that was creating itself in this rhythmic slow motion. She was stunned, and absolutely transfixed. The crowd was completely silent, as if holding its collective breath to give the performers the greatest support. Then, as suddenly as it had begun, the dance ended. Every dancer and clown stood again as at the beginning. So utterly focussed upon them had the crowd been that there was not a sound. No applause for several long minutes and then, without hesitation, every person stood spontaniously and began the singing accolade. It rose like a wave of sweet, harmonious sound, over the fields. Then it ended and there was again stillness, the performers there, quietly on their gleaming rods. Then, with a sudden wink, the rods were no longer there. The performers motionless in the air for an instant before they floated slowly down to stand as a troop of players there, together on Earth. And with a shock that shook the spectators so that they gasped, the people knew that there had been no metal rods, no strong supports for these lovely ones who danced, but that these 'rods' had been nothing more solid than Light itself.

The questions that would come later,that would nag at the minds of the people of Adwin and these northern towns, did not interfere with the sheer enjoyment and delight at this amazement. In this magic day, all things could be accepted.

And now, to emphasize, as if such might be needed, the fact of that power among them, the rods of Light reformed themselves in rings, loops, half moons, rings within rings,and curving rods that ran into and out of one another. The clowns inhabited the shining world of slim lines. The Dancers hung as if tantalizing them from just off the edges of things. And they played at this new game like children loosed from school, a merriment and laughter rang down from the changing lines of Light.The game was to see how many times one could leap through a hoop before it shifted to a line, or to stand on, run the length of a line before it changed to a curving half moon and slid the runner off into the empty air below. The clowns were forever getting caught inside the change and being slid off, or walking upside down into a circle. Now, the audience watched in awed wonder. And now they began to know of the mind power that held this performance in balance.

Tom shook his head, sitting next to Jessie, who was beside Ben and Rose, he leaned forward to see Ben's face and then Rose's. He said, "My God, that's impossible. Can you feel the pattern they're building there? It's as though they're talking to us, talking to us through the creation itself." He sounded puzzled, searching toward the dancers and the clowns. Then there was a flock of children, who appeared as if from nowhere, to settle in a thick cluster of the shining rods. They stood for a moment, getting their balance, peering at the sea of faces rising in tiers below and around them. Each of the patterning stages had this flock of little ones. Tom muttered fearfully. "Good God, they can't assume those little --" then he stopped again, shaking his head.

Jessie laughed, she seemed pleased completely with the joyousness of these people of the air. "Tom, if they got there the way they did, we've no cause to worry."

He shrugged but said, "Well, maybe so, but how the devil did they get there?"

Rose turned to him. Her eyes seeing, but also far distant so that she looked through her mind's eye beyond him." Tom,you know, yourself. You know. Pay attention and you do know.Look beyond your eyes."

He look at her, meeting those depthless eyes. His own face drew into a troubled frown, then as he felt the energy all around him, he allowed himself to respond. The frown eased away and his face was quiet with clear listening. Jessie watched them, an alertness about her that, had they noticed, would have set them to wondering. She held her mind steady in that scintillating harmony, that beat of rhythm that pierced her body like a current,her mind like a streaming invitation. But for the other two it had not yet reached that pitch through which it would enter as simply as it did into Jessie. She thought, that it might take a little more power, a little more intensity. She focussed her own attention with that Reaching Group Mind sustaining and joined with it.

And slowly, as they watched, their senses caught by this wondrous sound and movement, enriched by an echoing fragrance that had built from nowhere and filled the entire vast tent, they began to know another event. Senses alert, enjoying, delighted in fact, and held at their highest point of attention, they waited. An aspiration swelled in them, to know that beauty that they responded to in its entirety. They found their minds drawn, fine tuned, attracted as to a magnet. This focus, this entering into something that KNEW, was their combined Reach, began to have its effect on the people of the North Country. And they began to be aware of that effect. They began to enter in, to seek and to respond with conscious desire to Know .

Thus, in conscious choice and focussed mental energy, they found their own talents to Reach strengthened, drawn beyond their imaginations, lifted up into a purity and beauty that astounded them. They paid attention to that refined vision, that ability to SEE and to be aware as they had not been without conscious effort. Now it seemed natural and simple to be so aware. They began to realize that mind itself wakened here, that every aspect of each person's nature was at highest peak, tuned as near to perfection as that human person could be tuned. They felt the tuning, the lifting and knew that they were being given - offered - opportunity and vision.

And there were few whose eyes did not fill with tears of Joy, whose hearts did not overflow with that profound and utterly Tender Love of which they were growing steadily more conscious. And there were few whose minds did not strive toward their ultimate possibility. Here was the sharpening, the honing that would make awakening possible. Here was an energy that seemed to extend beyond everything they had known and to offer Itself, but to include them as they were willing to receive. They began to know of the Land, the Valley, the People and Earth Herself as they never had. They began to listen to the consciousness of plant and animal and mineral and to know of each what they had only begun to guess before. The world and their own natures were visible, why and what they were, was clear, and the perception of these three dimensions of the human nature was so expanded, that they were amazed.

Now, the children seemed suddenly to explode through the air and the radiating lines of Light, the Rings and bars shifted and changed as they approached them so that they must shift and change their own directions as rapidly. It was a Game, a game such as the watchers had never imagined. The dancers and the Clowns were off at the tip ends of these bars of Light, as if waiting for the new performance. The children whirled and leaped, laughed and caught at one another to join in flight across the empty,then suddenly full spaces. They shrieked as children do in play, they tumbled and caught themselves or each other. None fell, none missed a slithering rod that was suddenly becoming a

Ring. And then, as the audience began to feel the inner tension, the bright charging of that play of energy in their minds, they suddenly flickered out. The flocks of children were gone.

Tom sat stunned, feeling as if he had just learned a whole library in a few minutes, feeling as if his mind was stretched beyond it's capacity to contain. He felt exhilaration, even as he felt weary. He wanted to shout and sing and he wanted to turn and bury his face into Jessie's shoulder to hide himself. He finally opened his eyes and, cautiously he bent forward to look around her to Ben."What d'you think of that." he said softly.

Ben grinned at the apparition peering at him over Jessie's shoulder. Then he nodded,"I feel as if I've been chiselled out and opened up and made so much bigger I'm afraid of myself."

Rose turned to him, thoughtful and crying silently,"It's a good discription, my Love. It's about like that."

Ben turned to Jessie,"Who are they?" He nodded toward the stages where nothing remained of the intricate pattern of Light in the air, but the two clowns were completing a mild series of stunts .Jessie shook her head, "Wait, we'll talk later. Look around you right now. Look around you.Do you see that there are those who have not known the inner flooding of Light at all?"

Tom turned, and found his neighbors with that look of bemusement, of having perceived more than they could explain.There were here and there, a few, still intent on the clowns antics, laughing, seemingly unaware of anything other than that foolishness and pleasure of it. "He nodded, Oh, Dear, I think that they did not even see much of it.Is that right?"

Jessie said, "They saw what they could allow themselves to see. They saw what their natures were ready to see. Some were not ready to see it all."

"Then, perhaps there was in that whole wonderful pattern and dance, in that song and fragrance, more that we ourselves did not see?" Rose wanted to hold her breath for the answer.

Jessie nodded, smiling," But if you know of all four of the modes, you must have been aware of most of what was there."

" Then, it's just that. We've been invited? We've been shown? We can respond as we're able and none but ourselves knows of our vision.?" Ben looked from one to the other, his eyes finally meeting Jessie's.

"Perhaps. It'll take some absorbing. It'll take a little time to bring it all into meaning. Give yourselves time. Don't try to explain everything, to figure everything out with only your poor over whelmed intellect to do the job." She laughed. The Clowns had laughed and began to move to the exits, they waved and fipped themselves into every direction and yet their path led to the exits. And then, as the people stood again, beginning again the Singing applause, the many rings under this great multiple Tent, began filling with all the actors, all the animals, and people who had entertained them this day. They could see already the sun was nearly down outside, but none wanted to go. The performers bowed and smiled, and then as swiftly as they had come, they left. And the people began to move toward the exits. The people began slowly to stand and walk with very little talk toward their own exits. Since the walls of the tent were raised at least six feet from the ground, everyone left whereever they reached the earth level. Rapidly the Tent was empty. And as it was, the great poles that held it slid into one another, and the tent folded itself into rolls and by the time the crowd had moved away and turned to look back, there was only a neat pile of wrapped poles, stacked now in six small pyramids and ready for the elephants, gorillas, baboons,and chimpanzees to pick them up and load them on the carts. The people watched with the same absorption they had watched the early setting up and as if they had seen no greater wonders at all. Their minds were saturated and ready to rest. In a strange silence the great mass of these thousands of people began to walk toward the Highway. Hundreds strapped on belts and lifted like a swarming of great bees. The Circus was over, the color seemed not a bit faded, the sound of the music being played to help the workers not a bit less bright. So many left the field absorbed, silent, smiling with a soft, reflective smile, as if remembering. There were other people, lingering, talking, chattering, happily watching and enjoying these strange events unaware that more than the usual circus had occurred. These were the people whose minds were not receptive, and as Jessie looked back at them, she was relieved to see how few there were.

CHAPTER TWENTY FOUR

Revelations

Jessie woke, lay still beneath the blankets, enjoying the comfort of softness and warmth. Years of travel, of sleeping in every kind of condition, had taught her to value the times of comfort. She thought that humankind valued comfort, sometimes above most other things. Surely that desire for comfort could cut a seeker off from his quest, a student from her deepest study. But hadn't that desire also been stimulus for growth down through ages. That had been worth much.

She remembered being submerged in the need to comfort herself. With food, lovers, acquiring of things, even work, whatever worked at the time. And though she looked back on it now as a time of being trapped, she smiled. Out of it she had learned, those comforts were so temporary, had to be protected with one's very life, time, energy. So life became constant alertness to defense, rather than genuine awareness. It was relief to realize, that though she still enjoyed them now and then, finally she had no need of them. Like a leaf falling from a tree, the need had released itself.

Surely, every human experience, even one of depravity, was a learning eventually. She remembered how she had been afraid to risk standing free. "Why did I need to literally sicken myself before I could turn away?" I know others who avoided that trap. Why couldn't I? So many wasted years." But the necessity of it was obvious. She shrugged. "Well, maybe those who avoided it, were caught in some other kind of trap that I avoided. No one walks without struggle."

She listened to the wind bending the trees. Branches brushed her roof with a soft sighing sound. The great pine, landmark of the Farm knoll just outside her cottage, sang in the wind. Gusts drummed rain then nearly ceased, then came again. Such a storm would not last long. It would blow itself out.

She stretched, snuggled deeper and looked around the room. Six narrow tall windows broke one wall. Another wall hung with a bright tapestry picture of a small lake in a high hidden valley. Buried into a huge outcropping of dark rock, were the towers and sloping roofs of a Retreat. Trees, growing from paved courts between buildings, softened the hard edges of the rock. She let her eyes rest on it. There she had been taught, and had taught others. There had been her only home for decades. She felt the nearness through the tapestry, as though her eyes could pierce its fibers and see the people within those stone towers. She knew that woven into that tapestry were the threads that would bring those loved Teachers near. Was that not a comfort? Those threads bore within them computer chips that tied into the main heart of the Station, but more, they carried power most Valley people knew nothing of. She felt no need for help today, but she could bring them fibrantly alive in her minds eye.

Her eyes moved on, to a desk standing in one corner on whose top shelf, a

THE PEOPLE OF THE VALLEY

carved candle holder wound three feet tall, nearly to the ceiling. Carved by Adwin craftsmen, it held twenty one candles. Each could be lit in one movement from a touch on a carved rose bud at its base. The desk had a small body-adjusting chair, a deep, soft, chair filled a corner opposite the bed. Through a door was the sitting room, two cushioned chairs, a low table, book shelves, a four foot wall screen for video and the small cabinet in which was a communication hook up with Valley centers.. She smiled to see it, remembering so many yeas ago, sitting by one much less refined, wanting to call the retreat, wanting to call home, and not wanting to need that comfort.

She frowned,then smiled again, remembering. She had been convinced she needed such a machine to call home. And it wasn't until her very longing to reach them there resulted in sudden, clear contact, that she finally accepted the fact that she did not. She was aware of the quick desire to call, to Reach and make contract again. She shook her head even as it was cradled in the pillow. She would manage alone!

Even as she set her mind in its disciplined attitude, quieted her longing, she caught her breath. Beside her stood the old Teacher who had received the unheeded heart's call. He was smiling, pleased at her surprise. It was a Holograph image, so real she took seconds to realize it was not he in the flesh. But he spoke and she felt the comfort of home again. He said,"No one works alone, Sister. No one assumes such arrogance." His twinkling eyes belied the riprimand and he nodded, "So when the Heart calls, don't deny it."

She sat up, looking at him, only faintly ashamed, and nodded. The image faded backward through the tapestry across the room.

She felt hungry and thought of the little kitchen unit at the far end of the living room. But decided to wait, so often in the years past she had had to eat alone. She enjoyed eating with the Family. There was much to do here. She felt eager to be up. But she lay still, soaking in the small pleasure of the moment.

Jessie was not a Seer. She had friends who were, one of her Teachers had been so talented. She had another Talent, so valuable the retreat had found and brought her into service. She could sense the Reach in another when it was barely awakening. The first faint tendrils of mind Reach, from minds just opening, just aware. So her task had been one of travel to seek out such minds and help them over the first fearful steps. It was not to teach or train a new talent, Master teachers could do that if reminded, but it was to be aware of their waking to an emerging Self. The Valley for Jessie, was a living entity, a consciousness encompassing all its life and glowing with the light from the minds of its people. She saw such beauty here that caused her to catch her breath, that held her constantly in wonder. Could this Valley truly be that birth place for this new world's future?

She smiled at herself, burrowed deep into her comfort and sense of safety now, while she listened to the winds that blew away last night's storm. Human beings could be tempted to maintain the status quo especially when it was so pleasant. But even now, she already felt a restlessness to leap out from it and

THE AWAKENING

begin anew.

She sat up and slid her legs out onto the floor, the day was grey light, the sun not yet up outside. Her thoughts built on one another and she needed this time to contemplate them. She sighed and said aloud, "Is it possible for me, and for my brothers and sisters to offer strength and direction? We can do only that, and will that be enough?" She felt the chill in the early morning air and shivered lightly.

Her voice was soft, musing, saying the words deliberately, slowing her thinking."It's true a lot of people are afraid.A lot are reluctant to acknowledge what they begin to know! It was indeed very much like a physical birth. The hour of birth was the crucial moment in any unfoldment. That was the time when greatest care must be taken. Surely, a baby, in the womb, did not know what it approached either, and yet - yet - there seemed to Jessie danger now for this evolving humanity. Was it only her own fear? She must think. Must be sure her own nature did not add to the problem.

The wind howled suddenly in one long thin wail. She could see through the windows the sky breaking into blue, then covered as swiftly with grey cloud. Ragged clouds,though, the day would clear and be bright, cool and lovely. It would be windy. There was a basic good-will here, permeating the farm, just as in Adwin and the other small towns. In fact it was part of their life, firmly fixed into the Convictions, the very attitudes toward Life. It was not just a friendly, vague, half conscious attitude, easily dismissed when personal desires conflicted with it, but a true, conscious Conviction of Good Will toward all life so that it must be cared for, nourished at all cost. One of the signs that the Valley was ready.

She stood, drew a robe around her round old body and went to the window. There she could see far across at least fifty miles of Valley. She adjusted her sight, focussed and instantly began to see the energy flow through out the Valley. Light,streaming in currents of color, silvery, rosy flame, golden currents, a pure blue that radiated through the air. Here and there she could see flickers of other colors, reaching into the whole, withdrawing and receding, flowing again and changing as the life of the Valley changed. It was in essence the very aura of the Valley life. She saw.

She caught her breath, for within this streaming that was the trace marks of Love Itself, of Spirit present, there were thin muddy flickers. A grey-green-yellow finger of darkness protruded, then receeded, then broke into minor forks and extended again,thinner but multiplied. It gained strength, was washed and obliterated by the lighted streams, then reasserted iself and wove in again from another direction. It rose from tiny points of dark, of holdings of fear that scattered like gnats over the Valley and spotted the inflow of Light.

How could this be? Surely the monitors must know of this, surely they must be watching. Or had their attention been focussed elsewhere and they were lax? As she had been? Not that. No people could be more attentive..She shivered again,reached out one hand to flick on the heating unit.Then she turned to go to the small bath and stepped inside.

The water was hot and strong, its pounding against her body was a luxurious pleasure. She delighted in the hot steam, and took her time, lathering herself with scented soaps. Laughing at her self, enjoying like a child. Then the swift roughness of towels for drying. She had never accepted happily the waterless cleansing stalls that were universally used. She grew up in a time when baths were more than just places to get clean. She had never overcome a desire for hot baths on long journeys, though she happily accepted life without them. And Benjamin, found that out and had this installed. She came out, her grey-white hair damp, and pulled on light, warm underwear, then a long blue robe that hung to her midcalf. Long bright colored socks that were hidden in soft calf- high Matta boots shaped to her feet, finished her dress.

She stood hesitant,looking out the window again,seeing Ben opening the door of his cottage, only barely visible through the trees and shrubs.. He looked so sturdy,so powerful and sure. She knew both the fragility and the strength of his mind and smiled sadly. There was much to do.

Then her eyes were drawn to the tapestry.She could see a glow, beginning faintly, strengthening at the lake where sunlight seemed now to shimmer. She felt the power of Presence from those who watched and thrilled with anticipation. She had seen this use of the Way before, but she had never gotten used to the magic of it. The Wonder. Slowly, a vague darkness, then rather suddenly the shapes formed there upon the wall, as though coming through the tapestry itself. The focussing devise was woven among its threads.The Monitors themselves did the rest. She felt a deep gratitude, that they came just this morning.

Estella and Jedro were the names of those two who stood in her room smiling at her. She went to them, reaching out her hands, wanting to touch, aching to embrace the forms even as her mind already did. The delicate forms lightly embraced her, smiling almost as one might at a child's eagerness and she smiled at herself with them. She noticed their legs and feet were only faintly formed. She breathed out words,"Oh, I'm so glad you came. there is so much. I did not intend to call but I see now the darkness through the Valley, where the draining of the brightness occurs. I fear I've not recognized the threat clearly." She looked thoughtfully at their quiet faces.

Jedro nodded,glanced at the tapestry,"You have never truly recognized the depths of the tapestry's tuning to us,dear Sister. Surely you have lived with it long enough now to know it's power? You did very clearly call."

Jessie frowned, her mind receptive, realizing as she focussed, then she turned slightly, to indicate welcome to her quarters. "It's so good to talk to you. Thoughts hold in my mind so much better with words. Especially if it is a perplexing matter. Can we talk?"

They nodded." We have time. It's good for us to talk, to use language this way. Yes, let's talk. We spend so much time Listening, Sending, keeping the webs firm. Mind life lifts us out of ordinary perception a little."Estella smiled.

Jessie felt, knew, an inflow of warmth, of loving extension of affirmation,like a gift of Love. She looked at their youthful faces and suddenly, surprising herself, cried out,"Look at my body. I am getting old and perhaps my service suffers."

"Your body will last and the spirit in you is greater than it has ever been. Know that, Sister. The temptation to feel sorrow and dispair has not yet quite left you." They grinned, seemed suddenly very human.

Jessie sighed, grinning also ruefully. "You're right! Forgive me. It's my worry about the Valley,the people and the dark threads that I see weaving through the Light. This is what brought you?"

Estella shook her head. the robe forming itself more fully about her body was blue with a white trim. Jessie watched the small face inside the hood, glowing with light through flesh that seemed flimsy before it. "Jessie, there are many gathered in this Valley in this time. Many Sisters and Brothers, you know that?" Jessie nodded, watching, listening, and realizing more than the words spoken."You know that we must pay close attention, must Reach for strength to meet this time. We cannot but know your needs. We are attentive."

"You know then, much as I wish it were not true, I must constantly watch to refuse in myself the same fears and doubts that I work to resolve among our people. Those old fears cling to them, still make demands for fulfillment of old emotional needs. And I - I am not completely free!" Nodding to herself, she had finally spoken her worry. "There are so many people who know,,they See, they are capable of Love and yet, they shrink from what they know. Even the best of them. Even as I have done."

Jedro nodded, "As long as we are human we will need to monitor our human qualities. The great difference is that you are fully aware of these attachments. Your stage of unfoldment is just far enough ahead of them so that you can most easily understand their problems. Human qualities don't cease, they simply become more balanced,each of them has its value. Fear, even, is necessary in certain times. Greed, which has done so much harm, is simply a distortion of the desire to have and to keep. Isn't the harm rising because we don't pay attention? You are aware of these qualities in yourself, you know how to meet and end them. That's what you must teach of course, but mostly, we rely on you to make open the path for Love as it grows greater among us. Vision must grow now that Minds are waking. Yours is to prepare the way. And also to sustain and balance that process of awakening."

"How can I sustain, keep always awake enough to know of Love in our lives?" Jessie knew she spoke out of her own doubt.

Estella looked at her with eyes gentle and accepting,"You do sustain, because you are awake. You can't stop that steady awakening of humankind. It can only be delayed. But you can nourish it, speed it. Those who are awake to the energy of Love,who consciously receive, have chosen the Light. But remember Love is not always tender, it has also to be harsh, stern and relentless." She stopped, looking about the room, letting her own senses register the world Jessie lived in. Then, with a faint smile, she went on. "People don't doubt the Light they realize, their doubt is mostly of themselves, just as with you. That is also your task to teach them to know and trust themselves, and in doing so, you will learn. You must remember that to have chosen to Love, even when Love is not yet fully understood at all, is vital to Life and to possibility. There are many who stand at the edge, just waking, and not yet sure what their half open hearts and minds perceive,"

"All of us must hold firm." Jedro added.

"My work is to watch and guide when understanding begins and to blow into flame that burning coal of spirit ?"

"As it has always been your work, my dear, so it is now, but with greater intent. And central to your taask is that one of holding focussed the Love that flows through this Valley, that it may be realized by each person." Jedro smiled and his voice was stern. She bent her head, they held out their hands, she raised her own, palms up and theirs were set firmly against her own. The quiet in the room was intense. She lifted her eyes and met those above her. For a second, she felt a desire to flee, to close her eyes and with an act of will, she chose to meet that double gaze. As though enfolded in Light, she felt herself received, drawn deeper. It was Light she had stepped into before, now it blaze up when new understanding grew.

This time she was drawn to a limit she had not endured before. For a moment she trembled in resolve, so powerful was the current, depth and power. It filled her, raged through her body, setting its bones to humming, the flesh to murmur. It poured down upon the sea of emotions and settled them as oil calms troubled water. It pressed against her resistance, found the places of welcome, like breaks within that resistance, and leaked through in steady nourishment. To one who did not know she was starving, the discovery of such nourishment was a revelation, and she felt resistance dissolve in willingness, so that she lifted through it and rose without hesitation to the highest point she had ever found.

There, at that transcendant place, the Light poured in a radiance that was intelligent, nearly she could grasp the Knowledge of it, but not quite. Or could it be called Knowledge? Surely like no knowledge she had ever known. It was awareness! Something that beckoned and promised if only she could Lift, perceive beyond herself, could Reach, could bear to go on further through that doorway that was Light.

She did not notice that her body shuddered, nor that tears rained across her face, and down her neck. Joy released every possibility of power within her. She felt the yearning of a life time fulfilled and reasserted, made new, into a greater life. Her mind steadied itself, stood firm, with the support of those who guided her, and then they gently withdrew and she was there, alone.

Alone! And she did not falter! She stood beyond that blinding Light, the threshold crossed once more. She could again See and what she realized there would have to slowly come down to her brain-mind, else it stagger. All her life the Light had been her friend, her Teacher, her enemy, her destroyer. It had always drawn her to Itself. And now she entered into it and knew its nature. That knowing WAS! No time passed, yet it was an eternity, and an instant at once. Slowly she shaped realization. Her brain was on fire, impressions shaped themselves into

THE AWAKENING

meaning it could absorb and the quality and quantity threatened to overwhelm that receptive brain. Thus, in that Light she taught herself again, she accepted that living Self that taught. She realized understanding such as she had never imagined. She held herself firm with all the strength she possessed, stood and received, sought and accepted. That which she had known as Presence was beyond name. And yet It was.So much that she had striven toward was abruptly Present to her. She knew that the journey had been slow, but steady. A stage of it culminated in this moment.

A thought formed itself and she knew of it,"I cannot bear this." Yet, even as it formed, she felt herself smile. She could begin faintly to know what she had formerly only glimpsed. "I will bear this and more."

Gradually she drifted down from this new intensity of being, into that familiar limited nature that was Jessie and she knew she was no longer limited to this. Her body had lost consciousness for moments, her bones ached. Her head felt sore. The human form cannot be stretched too far to fast. She knew that her whole being was stretched beyond itself, that she would never be as she was, and yet, she knew too that she had just begun the next step, the continuation of Journey. She was more than she had been. The wonder of it kept tears flowing, her body thrummed with energy, her face stretched with smiling she could not cease. A radiant Joy filled her, glowed from her eyes. Oddly, a clutter of old needs, desires,that were tattered but still clinging in her, loosened and fell away.

Estella and Jedro were still visible, waiting. Jessie bent a little her hands clasped in her lap. "I have stood, I have made the choice. I understand. And the knowledge is like a fire in me. I want to spread that fire into every human heart. And yet it is not for me to do that". She looked up at them, wiping her face with both hands, smiling still, trembling with the raw emergence of herself, the birthing. The small body stood, but they could see the very subtle bodies of a greater nature encompassing it. Fluid forms were radiantly alive all around that little body, and they smiled to observe their brilliance.

Then they greeted her again, Touched mind to mind, a gentle healing touch against that raw small brain that must absorb and use all this. Then swiftly, they were gone. Morning was barely beginning, the sun just beginning to sweep across the northern hills.

For some time Jessie sat, unable to move. So full of vibrant energy and yet so weary, so drawn to some inner limit she had not known was there. She tried to think of what she knew, find words, thoughts that would fit and could be shaped into explanation for her finally patient intellect. Slowly she found short sentences that satisfied a little, made her able to recognize herself anew. She felt a new confidence, a knowledge about the work she must do. That knowledge opened like a flower within her mind. She could find it by paying attention to it. It was simply there. Patiently she began to form sentences.

She knew a dimming of the personal Jessie, submerged into the brilliance of a Self radiantly alive. She stood, vast, Reaching, Touching, in communication without separation and she was at peace. She could focus at either point of identity.

　　Long ago, Jessie had stepped consciously into the point of perception that brought her into this Presence for the first time. Then, the knowledge, the reality had been too great to bear, and she had receded from it. Had remembered only a shadow,but the Light had penetrated all darkness in her enough that it broke all resistance forever. Now she was stronger, she could will to hold and to Know. To bear that which had been too great to bear. To realize without fear. She knew what the people of the Valley must endure, must realize. With both Pain and unutterable Joy they could step by step approach what she knew. They could find that eternal sweet Light that would not dim. It nourished and strengthened her. She could not yet define that which had Touched her. She had no words to speak of the reality she now knew.

　　Slowly, she moved, made the bed, cleaned the small disorder in the room,quieted her body with stillness for a few moments and then looked all around. The tapestry was glowing with color as the sunlight streamed across it. The light seemed clear, pure carrying the lustre of diamonds. All her senses were as though polished and honed. Outside, the sunlight warmed the air,made her small grotto a place of comfort. So early it was. Would the others be up and about? There was the faint whisper of pine needles brushing against one another, intermittent shouts of birds. Everything was intensely clear and bright. She Reached, felt the presence of the family there above in the Hall. She felt the fierce energy of Earth in spring time, hurtling life through every seed, billions on billions that thrust that life upward. For a moment, in a tiny dance of delight, she leaped, lifted and hung two feet off the floor, playing. The foolishness of it pleased her and as she settled down to walk to the door, she smiled .

　　 There was an electric quality about the early morning. The storm had passed, the sky was clear, winds had swept clean everything. Rains had washed dust from all surfaces, Far to the south,she could see streams of grey rain falling among the distant hills. She tied a belt around her waist to draw the robe closer and went up the slope to the temple.

　　Jane met her at the Temple path,Jessie felt the joy of this young woman and like a shadow upon that joy, she saw that troubled awakening of perception. For Jessie there was mainly delight in her beauty. Jane was a pleasure to be with.

　　Jane bent to embrace Jessie, kissed her lightly and said, "It's going to be a grand day for everything but farming. The storm did our work for us.It'll be too windy for me outside today, and I'm going to enjoy watching the wind blow from inside my cottage with Steve. We've finally a little time for each other. We need that!" Her smile told of the joy between them, their discovery of each other.

　　Jessie laughed up at the tall woman and nodded,then left her to go into the Temple. She watched a moment the seven golden balls that danced so slowly and lightly above a table at the far end. She settled into a cubicle, slid the door closed and began to enter into that stillness within which all that had happened would sort itself out.

THE AWAKENING

Ben and Rose came into the Temple after Jessie was settled in her cubicle. They found their places and for a time silence prevailed. Then Rose came out into the center arch, where all three points of the temple came together. She saw a figure at the far table of the seven Lights and stood watching.

Anna sat utterly still before the table, her body seemed to radiate light and Rose gasped in surprise. She watched, wondering, uneasy. Had Anna changed or was this her own growing abilty to See? Her little girl! To see her so! Swift shafts of awe, anger,then fear, cut across that underlying brilliance of calm. Rose saw that, frowned at the fact of it. There was a bright but pulsing,changing energy around her daughter.

Rose folded onto a bench, emptied her mind of thought, judgement, and sat aware of her daughter. Gradually she realized a flowing radiance around the young girl. A quality so pure Rose caught her breath to realize it. It was a reflection of that Presence of Love that filled the Temple. She stood rooted, aware and without thought, for some time. Then, slowly her mind pressed thought upon her, her questions demanded attention.

How could this be? Anna was so young. How could she reflect such Love? Rose thought Anna's experience with love was the body love she knew her young daughter delighted in, emotions of needful affection and sometimes stray fragments of the dependency of childhood. Rose acknowledged those were fast disappearing. She herself grieved now and then at their loss. Anna seemed to need her so little now. Though Rose had known, had seen Anna's deep compassion, unusual in one so young, it was not unheard of. Seeing her here, she could not doubt that mature capacity for Love that dwarfed her own. Contemplating the fact of this revelation, she was gradually more and more aware of that Presence of Love that was the basis for all relationship.It held her, swept away thought of Anna, and held her lifted like a release of doubt. The hard, demanding, yeast of Love that permeated every living thing, relentless in its urge toward growth. Or the tender spontaniety of Love yeilding from within everything.

Then she snapped back to herself. Her mind yawed, full of that glimpse of what relationship was. Anna! Anna had revealed that to her. Yes, that was it. Every living thing was drawn, through some small thread of that wondrous power, a flicker of that Love, drawn to relationship. Relationship, the need for that, wasn't that the first stirrings of Love within life forms? The desire for others, for that which was not oneself? Then, perhaps, it was Anna's true gift? The thought held her,she had discovered something.

She withdrew then, went to join Ben who had stepped out of the Temple and waited for her there. Her joy and grief rose and fell in waves and she stood beside Ben as though she stood alone for a moment. Then he touched her and said, "Rose tell me. What is it?"

She smiled softly, tenderly, and secretly, gestured with her hand back toward the Temple. " It's Anna, there. I feel deprived of my baby. She's out grown us, you know." She shook her head, her fingers finding his. "Oh, Ben, she knows beyond us. We don't need to try to teach her. She's realizing what we just begin to suspect."

He was startled and turned to look back. But she caught his hand."It's best to leave her alone. I'm sure she was aware we were there. Maybe she'll come immediately, if not then it's a statement to us, I think."

Almost as she spoke Anna was there, her hair held back with a bit of blue yarn. She wore a single garment that covered her from shoulders to knee. Her arms and legs were bare and both her parents found themselves wanting to send her for a sweater. The sun was not yet high enough to warm the air.

She touched them both, coming between them. Her eyes were very soft and filled still with quiet. She spoke softly , more to herself than to them,"Mother, I was so glad that you came. Of our being present with one another. I want to tell you something of that place where I was." They stood speechless, listening, wondering and so intent on her radiant face, they scarecely heard her words."It was an ocean, mind you, and I was within that ocean. It was Joy. Mother, Dad. Joy itself! Can you imagine? Yet there I was also and even at the same time, in an ocean of grief, such unending grief that my heart broke with it." And her voice trembled as if barely able to contain that pain. She drew a long trembling sigh. "But then, no more than it broke for Joy. But then, there was that ocean and I was of it, moving as though myself liquid, Mom, formless, and yet, so very present. Me, Mom, feeling the motion of everything. I was conscious beyond myself, lost in Self. And I saw these things. Then the oceans broke their barriers, and one flowed into the other and the Joy and Grief were merged, and I saw that they were a continuation of one another and that there is no real difference at all."

The thought seemed to astonish her. She looked off across the distant hills, frowning, trying to absorb what she realized. "I'm not saying it well, it was much more than that, and yet - Well, the Master Teacher says that true perception imprints a reflection on our minds . They tell us to shape it into words we can speak. And so I have." Her voice became so soft they leaned to hear,"But the words don't hold half what it was." She seemed to have forgotten them, they were the excuse for speaking, perhaps, but her mind had taken hold of that perception and would not let it fade. "The most near idea of it is that there is no separation between anything or anyone at all. The reality of that singleness!" She shook her head in wonderment of realization. "No separation whatsoever.Now the idea puzzles me. But it's a grand thought! And all the rest -" she shook her head, "is too much to make into words."

Her eyes came back to them, and she started as if surprised to find them there. Then with a shy smile, as if to plead with them to accept, she nodded. All the time, there was this look in her eyes, of conviction, of strength that needed no help from them. Rose, seeing that, cringed with loss. Anna slid her arms quickly around her parent's shoulders, pressing her face into their two necks and then was gone.

Rose and Benjamin, watched her move away. the slim, child-woman body obviously was changing, but the mind that accompanied that body, seemed to

THE AWAKENING

have changed even more. Her strength and her innocence contrasted with fear and uncertainty. And her clear certainty and Joy put a lie to all else. What indeed was she?

Rose turned to Benjamin, took his arm in some wish for comfort, " There, our own child, and she speaks of things we haven't known. refused to acknowledge. There is no excuse for us, Ben. For you and me. Why have we deliberately blinded ourselves?" She searched his eyes,wanting an answer and knowing there was none.He met her gaze and brought her only a sadness and acceptance.

"It's true, Sweetheart, it's true. We've got a lot to make up for." Then he took a long breath, smiled and said more confidently,"She's finding her own way. We've found our own, even though it's taking us confoundedly longer than it seems to be taking these young ones.But where we had fear of all that we were realizing, they have acceptance and recognition ." The stating of that thought staggered him because he had not known he thought it. He looked at her with surprise, distress.

She was nodding,as they walked,"You know, Benjamin, my Darling, that even our own Master Teachers taught us that we must wake up. Remembering it now, I thought of that as a romantic, a poetic expression. Yet, it is exactly what occurs." He shook his head," And even so, Rosy, what is it, why 'wake up'?"

She wanted to say it, for herself as well as for him,"Wake up because we've been asleep - asleep to everything beyond physical senses, beyond mental response to what we physically knew. We begin to actually experience what is of subtler nature. We've begun to live through the farthest dimensions of Mind itself, I think. I heard that thought once, and it seemed -- seemed to fit. We, our generation, has that unbelievable opportunity to know beyond our physical nature, beyond any astral nature, and into -" She was lost now in the Reach for the idea, "In the nature of Mind- Spirit. And that's surely waking up -- to something! A big step."

He was looking at her, clutching her arm with almost painful intensity, "It's what is real in a different -- a further dimension, isn't it. Perhaps it's what would be called fourth dimension? It's not an easy thing for me to say. People in sciences still shy clear of that word Spirit. But it's because no one really knows what it means. Yet, when we found, particles we couldn't see, sub-atomic particles, existing particles that were also waves,particles that moved with no time required, we had begun to step into another way of seeing reality. We searched for smaller and smaller states of matter." His face darkened, "Then came the destruction and the ending of so much of our work, we were set back, we should have been far ahead. Yet,now,today, I think we are at the verge of finding what Anna already knows. All these years we kept avoiding implications. But it was our job to avoid implications and seek fact." He grinned, studying her solemn face. "I'm afraid we know more than we can prove already.And it's like a jump across a chasm. We so long to perceive the reality we're glimpsing somewhere in our minds, far more than we can replicate. I want to deny what our children take for granted, their vision, their perceptions. They aren't imagining, they really KNOW what they experience." He turned a truly distressed face away, watching the path again as they stepped upon the deck."But now, there's so much I, myself, have seen. I think, Rosy, our children do more than glimpse that further realm." He stopped, then in a changed, soft voice he added,"I think they live in it."

"Well, Dear, we've had no business denying what we have begun to know. To KNOW, Ben, we've just denied because we couldn't explain things in traditional terms. Now, we've got it to meet. We have language trouble for one thing. But the young ones, they must have made up words, made up ways to explain to themselves, or maybe they don't need to.I believe that they 'think' in a different way." She stopped, turning to him, seeing movement inside the hall, she wanted to finish her thought before going in. "Perhaps they know that their minds are receptive to more, to -- " she stopped again, her eyes distant, frowning,"Oh, they must see THROUGH that Light that we are so overwhelmed with. Yes, Ben, they must see through and see what we -- what we're afraid to See."

He nodded, his arm tightening around her shoulders, and she took his other hand, They were unaware of the picture they made there, standing in the morning sunlight, holding to each other so desparately. Jessie saw them there but the others at the table were so engrossed they did not see. He said,"It's actually a kind of revolution, for them. And they're not hesitant at all."

She sighed, "Oh, no, Ben, not revolution.!"

"Yes! Revolution! Just that. Violent overthrow of things as they've always been. Revolution of the mind, perhaps. Revolution can be very great change, you know, a turn of the wheel, a shift into another paradym, another perspective. It can shift what we think of as reality if enough people share it."

She was silent, shivering a little, the air seemed cold. The sun was hidden. Two great clouds that had drifted above them, suddenly sent a spattering of rain down, startling them to look up."Oh, dear, right from that lovely blue sky, we have rain." She laughed."Anything can happen, I suppose."

He nodded, watching as the clouds raced by, and the sun swept over them with renewed warmth again, "We've not begun to talk to them, and we said we would. I think I'm afraid to find out they're -- different, not just kids the way we were. They know so much, I think. Whether they can express it, I don't know. Strange how Anna talked to us this morning; she hasn't done that before, and --" His hands still held to hers, they felt like two children themselves standing at a great gap in the path of their life. His voice was suddenly a whisper, " I suspect that their very consciousness is refined beyond ours. Their capacity to know, to See, even to BE, is greater. And such capacity can bring power. Have we taught them how to use, how to meet power rightly? We haven't known, so how could we have prepared them ?"

"Surely the Master Teachers would notice, would have taught them? Surely, Ben?" But he shook his head and they both knew,many Master Teachers were only a little more than highly talented teachers. They might not have noticed any more than they themselves had done."You know, the most Perceptive Teachers tend to work in the great cities, where they touch the most people. Maybe we could send our children out."

"What of Jessie? She's come here?"

"She's surely much more than a Master Teacher. Surely she could help, could tell us what to expect. What to do. We'll ask."

He smiled into her eyes, turned them both toward the Hall doors,"Dear, we've been good parents, We love our children, and have given them much love. We've taught them that Love has always to guide thought and especially action. And that's a concession for me to make. Our children are good people, they will understand how to meet what power they find in themselves. In fact, I think maybe they're better people than we are. Surely, the Monitors must be noticing all these things! Isn't that what they're supposed to do? Surely they would!" A touch of doubt entered his voice which had sunk until it was so soft she almost did not hear the last.

Rose said as softly,"We talk of teaching our children. Perhaps they will need to teach us."

"They already do, sweet Love, I see them passing me by and I haven't wanted to admit it. They understand intuitively what I labor to figure out."

She pressed her hands to her face, "Don't say that, how can we know. Every path is different, not necessarily one ahead of the other. After all, look at all the people who do not, will not, even acknowledge what we begin to perceive? There is just great difference!"

His eyes held hers, saw the plea in them, and he smiled."We'll have to watch, be more aware of things I think, my Dear." He stopped her just inside the doors, stood looking at her, "There it is, the differences that we'll have to meet.Ourselves lagging behind the young ones, and the others lagging behind us. Can we manage so that that revolution isn't actually a bloody one?" His face had turned grim a hard fear in his eyes.

" So many different levels of awareness. There's Herb and Greta. They're fine engineers, gifted in fact, You know that. Yet, they seem never to See, even what to me has become obvious. Is it that they don't know? Or that they too avoid and refuse to speak?" She was silent, letting her eyes wander through the hills, seeing there, registering without out disturbance to her thought,the condition of the forest, the meadows,the flowering and the setting on of fruits." Surely, that's not strange though. None of us talk of it.It's as though we don't know how. Maybe if we had churches like in the old days, where people came and talked to us of Spiritual matters, then -- but we don't." She frowned, "But we have the Learning Center and the Teachers do come there! We just don't hear them. We've not even asked about the Joining,another mystery. We don't know what that is."

She drew him to the big solid doors and into the Hall and toward the dining room, "Oh,,my Love,it's so good to have you home again, To talk to, just to talk to if for nothing more." She glanced back at him,"And there is much more too." They reached the tables where the others were talking and eating and eagerly sought their own food. Hungry now, after the relief of talk.

Family breakfast was one of laughter and talk of the day's work. Everyone seemed in good Spirits. Jessie watched and smiled, pleased with the eagerness but intent to see where it denied problems. Later, she left with Rose and Ben, walking slowly out into a sudden spatter of rain. The day was as suddenly changing as any late spring day could be, clouds and sun alternated in claiming the sky. Jessie stopped at the edge of the deck to caress gently with the tips of her fingers the young buds of Rose bushes. Some already bright with color. She seemed so immersed in those delicate movements that Rose stopped, hesitant to speak. She searched the face before her, the old worn face, stippled with fine and deep lines of long living.

Jessie glanced up, meeting Rose's eyes with a smile,"What's worrying you, my Dear?"

Rose started, grinned with relief."I think I've wanted to talk, Jessie. We've been missing time to talk lately." At Jessie's nod of enouragement, she went on,"There're so many things happening. I suppose they've always been happening, and we're simply more aware today. The children certainly,I'm sure you've noticed,but adults too." She stopped, frowning.

"And it worries you?" Jessie nodded, she was silent, gathering her thoughts, listening to the morning, drawing herself in from that morning to focus on this situation ."Well, you both know that everybody sees differently. Everyone. That's one of the joys of being human. You can always find variety. It is perhaps, as your daughter says, that there is no separation, but there is endless difference." She laughed at their surprise." Yes, you're right, the children are aware of much. Most of them. How do we traditionally perceive the universe ? Isn't our view limited? Even the far Seeing, reveals only THAT THERE IS MORE, isn't that true? Hasn't vision been very narrow then? Now, perception expands, and we are forced to adjust. Some just don't want to,are afraid, and there are some who cannot."

Rose was nodding, her face full of the sadness she felt," We've been open to endless speculation about the universe. We've probed and taken apart and -- ". Then she shook her head,"But we've actually seen only from our ordinary three dimensions, our ordinary familiar material world. That means one way? Yes, it's true. Even particle physics and astro physics relies only on mechanical extensions of our ordinary senses. But there is math and through math some of our skeptics may See."

"But those who do See already, know that old systems won't work anymore. We cannot remain so separate, nor can we deny the intuitive mind, the Heart's knowledge and the perceptions rising from those. We see from an inner eye that far exceeds our thinking mind. We see that things are not at all what they seemed when we accepted only a material reality. The possibilities are -- well, to say the least, they're terrifying to many of us."

Ben was nodding,"And there's no way we can deny anymore" His face was so mournful that Jessie could not repress a faint edge of a smile."And this morning we've realized something that we've never noticed. Things that shook me hard, Jessie. Not only the children, somehow I can absorb that more easily than I can what's happening to William. He's my brother, Jessie. I've known him

THE AWAKENING

and trusted him. He's is part of our Family and now, I can't find him - - unless, I go backward." He stopped, surprised at the thought.

She said,seriously,"You're right Benjamin, even though you didn't intend to say that.You know more than you thought you knew. I think that if you pay attention, you'll know what it means. If you are aware!" The wind had begun to rise, a cool wind that made them pull hats from their pockets and put them on, and they turned into the sheltered side of the deck to sit where the sun could warm them.

Jessie went on, " In the Temple you practice simply being aware. Isn't that true?" At their nods, she went on. Such practice enlarges consciousness. So, being conscious, of everything around you, everything, insight occurs. It's the way of learning that the Master Teachers use constantly and build on. People your age have learned these things after you were grown,but the practice has resulted in gradual understanding. You're doing what you call Touching? Reaching finally to one another's Heart energy!" She was smiling with such Joy in her eyes that Rose felt great hope.The tight muscles of her body smoothed and relaxed.

She said,"You! You've been doing just that. Helping us! You focus, you are AWARE, of us, of what we are becoming. Your focus draws our attention so we See. You're doing what you are telling us we must do. Showing us how. And there it is, Ben, a perfectly clear example of how it works. She didn't say a word this morning about it, yet I felt myself stir, wake up, listen and -and desire to live , to listen! And more, I want to be aware of the center where Love is!"

Ben looked from one to the other,"It does work then, I felt that too, that - like a light turned on in my mind, like a loosening, and - - it IS like a waking, an opening up, a NUDGING. How strange the sensation of this. And you think we could do it with other people?"

Jessie grinned, "I'm sure you can and in fact already do. Pay attention! That's all that's needed to focus that stream of Love that already is present. Your mind simply uses attention to focus vision of the heart! There it is!

"Rose was exultant in finally understanding,"The Good will in one is roused through recognition of Good will in another. We don't DO anything to each other. We allow Love to effect us both. It's as though you fanned a flame already there in us.That's it, isn't it?"

Ben was nodding slowly,"But it might not happen had we not already been taught. And almost every Valley person has been taught. So it can work". She frowned , then hesitantly nodded, Ben went on," So now, we must practice, constantly, with everyone what we've been taught. What you just did."

Jessie's face was serious but the smile still blazed in her eyes. "Yes, you've all been taught, but look to our William,he was taught, but is not willing to be receptive. Taught but perhaps unable to stretch mentally enough to perceive what is not explainable to the rational mind? You both know that what you realize is beyond idea, it is perception beyond thinking. A mind has to be willingly elastic enough to stretch out of its familiar pattern completely. To train itself in abstract thinking until it can acknowledge the subtle Mind beyond itself. Will's mind is not willing. He refuses to pay enough attention to his own process, his own inner awareness."

"But why not? Jessie? Surely, we can find explanation?"

She sighed, "Have you? Ever?" She met each of their eyes, There may be some things beyond explanation by our traditional logic. But explained clearly from another larger,perception.These are things one will directly know and then, explanation seems pointless because understanding is inherent in the knowing."

"And William is closed to that knowing?" Rose's voice was small, and sad.Then she turned to Jessie, "We know Will can't Reach. But he might be able to perceive the Light anyway. If he were willing to - to lose control? Is that it? To be open to paying attention in stillness without thinking, long enough to See?" So then - " With a shudder of new realization she turned stricken eyes to the others, "But still,even his beloved brand of logic would teach him. He would know that to control others is to be controlled by the necessity to keep control. He knows that creativity is lost in people controlled. He knows! He knows! Surely he will not forget? Surely his needs would not blind him."

Jessie nodded, "Yes, he knows how to THINK about intuitive perception, but not how to perceive from there. It's a kind of maturation of the intuitive mind, Heart, that he lacks, simply incompleteness. In some people it is undeveloped, cannot seem to make itself known into consciousness. It will come to him. We mustn't be so dispairing. You can't demand someone else be like yourself. His awareness must unfold in a natural manner."

Rose caught all her grief up in one cry, and then turned, to Reach as one who longs for the comfort of Touch, and there it was, that triple Mind Touch, there, like a flame , an electrical brilliance that woke her. Woke the three of them to each other. The joy of it blew away the old fears, and she could see the fears as debris of old habits, still clouding things a little. She saw as did Ben, the difference, the power and courage to break through old thought patterns. Her fear was made up of old patterns. They were aware that Jessie's presence was catalyst to contact.

They knew that this was more than Touch. That here was what Jessie knew and practiced. Like a flower the knowledge opened in their minds, this was a beginning of JOINING. Never had either Ben or Rose known such a contact, such possibility .

Rose drew apart and cried out,"Jessie, that -- that is what you spoke of once then. That is what is meant by Joining. When we're beyond Touch, when we are wholly together! Jessie, it's like my mind is on fire."She felt the tug of their Joined minds and responded again,willing. "It's so much more than that kind of Joining we do in Council."

"Grace cannot bring such a group to true Joining without full awareness. And that hasn't occurred among you yet."

Ben drew apart," It's as if William is retarded! No! It can't be, Will is brilliant!"

Jessie was silent, Rose answered,"You DO see Ben. It's not a retardation of

THE AWAKENING

lineal mind but of that intuitive mind that makes him unable to See. You DO know!"

Ben shook his head, unbelief on his face, his eyes wet with tears. "I do know. I do, and I don't want to." Just then a spatter of rain caught them. Rose shook the drops from her face and hair and ran to the chairs at the side of the deck that was roofed. They laughed, the wet air was not so chill now. The sun succeeded in warming the day. But they settled again, sunlight again all around.

Rose said, "I've heard Will talk about the necessity for the well being of every person of the Valley. He does believe that, his last campaign for Elder on the Council, made that clear. But he doesn't see that what he calls 'well being of others'has to be according to his own terms. He cannot see that he can actually trust the wisdom of other people to find the nature of their own well being. To ask for it even." She turned back to Jessie, her sadness lighter, a look of patient amusement on her face briefly, then she was sad again."He simply doesn't see that! I suppose I must accept William as he is. It's easier to accept those not of our Family who cannot See. I suppose in some way I imagine that HIS lack reflects on ME And my selfish intention is exposed." She dropped her eyes at the charge against herself."If I see that he wants people to realize on his terms, then I see I'm doing the same thing." Her expression was dispondant.

Ben laughed,"You can bet pride stays with us,nothing to do but watch it. Whatever more we've learned it's there still and it exposes as well as seduces. Probably adjusts itself to fit into every new situation." He stood watching the shimmering drops of rain, like clear round beads of glass that slowly slid along the surface of leaves. The gleam of sunlight fractured into color in them,they held a pure stillness that was beautiful. His thought intruded and as if wresting himself from sight, he sighed,"I can appreciate where Will is. I know that longing to put things right for people, the conviction that I know more than they how to do it."

"How did you meet that?" Jessie whispered.

"One day, I saw how the longing 'to put things right' in itself, in which I always felt such pride, was the trap." He looked around, as if feeling exposed in his shame.

"You wanted to control too?" Rose was searching.

"Yes, to control things.It makes a person feel better, feel powerful. After all, who doesn't want to. The only person without that desire that I know of is Paul." He nodded his head, surprised to realize that."

"Then that's it. That's it. There's nothing we can do to reach him." She looked at Jessie, a hint of accusation in her expression.

Jessie shook her head," You can continue to love him, and demonstrate with your very lives a different way." She smiled ruefully, "After all, he's a grown man. We aren't the parents of the people." Then with a short sigh, "And if we are to practice what we preach, we will rely on Will's own fine mind to see something of the error involved in the Builder's plans."

They were silent, Rose broke a small leaf and put it into her mouth to chew. The sky was finally clear again, rain fell several miles away, but the sun's warmth felt good against their bodies. Rose looked up, letting her eyes draw the deep blue of the sky into her mind like a calming flood. After a minute she said, "As perception increases one would presume that problems decrease. But they don't, they're just different."

They turned silently, letting the fresh gusts of damp air blow against their faces, feeling the sweet energy of it. Rose wanted to just talk of daily matters, to rest from such acute attention. She listened and slowly their talk dwindled into silence, aware of the light and the day.

Back inside the sunlit room, tables were empty except for Jerry and Anna who sat talking. Their faces were full of troubled intensity. Rose caught the movement of their hands, as they talked, and stood to look inside. She turned briefly toward Benjamin and Jessie, then went inside.

Anna looked toward her mother, absorbed her mother's attitude, sensed it's nature. Rose was willing to listen. Anna rejoiced that she need not conceal her knowledge. She said, including her mother in the conversation as if she'd been there through it all. "Mama, it's more than you think. You know what's happening in the Valley, maybe more than most people, but do you know that your own son's been trapped into it? Do you know what's happened to Andy?" Her voice cracked with a squeek of anxiety, tears wet her eyes.

Rose studied her face, feeling her heart leap into her throat. Shocked at the suddenness of this personal fear.After all, had she looked far out and neglected her own family? And why was trouble for her own more wrenching than trouble for others in the Valley? If her private need eclipsed the Heart's inclusiveness? Then how could she demonstrate any true vision? She was aware of Ben and Jessie coming into the room with them, settling as she stood, trying to absorb what was before her.

Was her's any different from William's response? She was bitterly honest, every one in the room saw the convolutions of her thought. And were themselves dealing with their own. Then she thought,'Well, I do know what I'm doing at least. I can watch myself.' She said aloud,"What is it I don't know, Dear?"

Anna studied her mother's face, saw the fact of her fear. She nodded, "Yes, Mama, you do know. You just don't admit it." She waved away Rose's start of protest, "No one could blame you, Mom. I don't. It's not like Andy, not like him at all. Something,'s wrong. Like maybe he's hiding something, won't look at himself at all."

Rose nodded, her heart sinking. Wanting to deny still, to excuse and find justification. But she shook her head at that wish,"Tell me, Honey, what you know."

Ben broke in,"It's not surprising that he'd not know what to do. He's only a boy. After all! How can he deal with -- with all that's happening?" He knew as he said the words that he chased excuses.

Anna was angry,she turned impatiently to her father."Oh, no Daddy, not now. Don't try to excuse him. I'm not blaming him. I'm just reporting. He's old enough to know, to -- his friends, our friends, they have -- most of them --."

"Have what?" Ben spoke numbly, shocked by Anna's harshness. It was not like her.

Anna looked around, seeking help from the two women, her eyes tight in a frown that drew lines across her forehead. Jessie met the young girl's eyes swiftly and with an almost imperceptible nod.

"Ben stared at her, then his gaze moved back to Anna, and then Jessie. His mind raced, remembering moments of succumbing to certain urges, to basic lusts of an undisciplined nature. But his nature was no longer undisciplined,and Andrew's never had been.He frowned, shook his head, started to get up then sank down again,"My God, he's only a boy, and boys always have some pressure from those old urges, those old -- like lust for fighting, for adventure, for -" He stopped, dodging Anna's accusing gaze, and then he nodded,"You're right, Anna, no more than a girl's pressure." His head sank to his chest. He sat so for minutes, "I'm aware of such feelings, but you -- you children are of another kind."

Jessie was patient, half smilng," The whole body keeps its ancient defenses and needs. They do still push against their new perceptions. But Andrew is a modern boy, he's developed far beyond those primitive urges. He doesn't need to honor them at all. He can command himself, Unless there's something that's pried him off balance."

Anna took a long deep breath, nodding with relief. Finally they recognized something she wanted them to see. Rose turned away to fill a bowl with hot porridge and took a glass of juice. She was hungry, breakfast time was long since past. Jessie and Ben went to do the same and when they were all seated, Anna said, "Maybe I ought to tell you all of it . Uncle Jerry said that'd be best."

The others nodded, beginning to eat. The odors of the hot porridge was comforting and good. The threat that seemed to spread like a darkness through their family could be held a little away through such a simple comfort. Anna met Jessie's eyes, felt herself quiet under that friendly gaze, and they decided between them. Anna said,"Wait, until you've eaten, it's better." The quiet seemed so very welcome to Rose and to Ben. They ate, attending to the moment, to taste, smell and the quiet. Nothing intruded to spoil the pleasure of it, not even their thoughts.

After they'd gotten their cups of coffee or tea and sat back, Anna Touched with Jessie and Jessie responded to her unspoken request. She said, "I want to do this through Mind Touch images. I want to SHOW you." The others were startled, but after a moment, they all nodded. Together they Reached, made that Joined Touch and woke the minds of the others to their intention. The tingling power of it, startled Jerry, surprised Rose and Ben. Anna wanted to tell them in her own way. She would show them the pictures of the event, of what happened, so they could judge for themselves.

Then the images began, clear and sharp, as they leaned back and closed their eyes to focus attention. Swiftly, the scene developed. They were in a garden in the second Ring of the Learning Center. An old man, whose white hair shone silver among the thick blond, brown and black thatches clustered around him, was talking. The students had clustered around Teacher Edmond demanding explanation . One youngster cried out, "It's tearing the Valley apart, Sir, can't you folks see that?" His eyes were shining, a hint of excitement burned there. Anna saw and winced and the joined minds saw what she saw.

Anna stood a little apart, more watching than part of the demand. Surely some trouble was tearing these boys apart, she reflected. They were so full of righteous anger. Andrew stood just to the left of the Teacher , his eyes on the boy who shouted. Anna Reached, wanting to contact her twin. To her pain and astonishment he refused her, blocked her Touch.

She looked around, suddenly afraid. The teacher said,:"There is dissention and it could unbalance things. We've worked hard to bring the Valley harmony. Let's keep that among ourselves."

The boys were impatient,"Well, then how? They're ready to tear it all apart. I don't see how you can just let that happen. WE don't intend to!" Anna could hear such emotion in the young voice she wanted to define it. Was it anger, or fear? -- no it was excitement, and some quality of desire, some wanting that she couldn't name. She shrank from it almost as much as from her twin's refusal.

She opened her mind, allowed the tension , the emotional bulge of energy to touch her, she wanted to see it,to define. And there it was, they had blocked themselves from seeing through the cloud of their emotions. These boys, refusing as if deliberately, their own good perceptions and disciplines, refusing what they knew. They denied that the Builders COULD not Reach, that they had never known the Touch of mind to mind. These, boys she'd known all her life,were behaving like strangers to her. They were insisting that the Builders CHOSE to tear apart the Valley way, to deny the Convictions even. They said what the Builders did was unconstitutional, so they were putting themselves outside the protection of the law.

The enormity of the accusations were like a physical blow to Anna, watching, and to those who saw this scene from her mind. These boys were insisting that the Builder's refusal to stop their development of that small field east of Santiago was cause to force them to stop. One boy cried out as if in pain,"We've got to stand up and fight. Are we wimps that we don't even do that?" The over all feeling was that they must defend their homes;they must defend the Valley. For a moment she felt a surge of agreement , and she didn't hide that from her watching family. They needed to know all of it.

There was a rising crescendo of emotion and it had bloomed out like a fog that permeated all their better knowledges,blinded them to their greater vision. It was like a weight that drew them downward, into darkness of raw desire.The excitement of it was magnetic in its pull. It was almost a holy rage, a self righteous conviction. She watched as it built.Knowing its attraction. She was aware of their fury to act, to do something.

The old Teacher shook his head, he could not see very well what was happening. But he knew fighting was not the way. That fact saddened her. Where were the Master Teachers? They were gone today, gone to a meeting called

THE AWAKENING

Valley wide of all Master Teachers at the North Station. They should be here!

Anna caught at Andrew's jacket. Maybe simple physical pull would attract his attention. He had never before denied her. This time he jerked free, turned an angry face to her. She looked then at Andrew's drawn face, seeing there a tiredness, strain of the past weeks. She caught also a brief flicker of Andrew's conflict that gave her hope. But it was gone as suddenly as it had come. He was refusing with amazing skill. She sent her own love and support, felt his familiar response but only a touch of it. He flung her away, closed himself and the anger she saw was dark. His face pulled down in a heavy frown, she trembled. "Andrew, do you know what you're doing? Do you realize these others don't know?"

He was angry, angrier than she had ever seen him. Out of balance and doing nothing to correct it. How could he let emotions dominate him? He knew better, had trained himself to more than that. He had told her of his experience at the pond, the quaking fear that humankind could not protect all that the Valley meant. That very fear was blinding him. His guilt still nagged at him. She watched and grieved at his fury. It could not be Andrew, her own brother who had lost himself. He was a stranger. She grieved as if at the loss of him. He shook her off, saying roughly, "Anna, leave me alone. You don't know".

In a moment of anger of her own, flashing out before her like a blinding shriek, she shouted, "Andrew, we are caretakers of Earth. Of ALL life! Those who See must stand as protecters. Those who don't must not be harmed." As she spoke her anger bled away, and finally she said softly, "To meet fury with fury is to meet nothing but ourselves." She trembled, feeling the balance return, the quiet awareness of her deep knowledge fill her. "To act otherwise would prove we have been unable to act with Love, and so we deserve nothing."

The others had turned at her cry, their eyes changing, shifting from hope to anger, then back to that strange absorbed excitement.

But the sharp thrust of her words penetrated Andrew's mind, he could not deny them even though his eyes were bleak and hooded. At the last word, his mind closed viciously, clamped as if in desperate attempt to shield himself. She felt it and a dark dispair chilled her heart. Never had her brother refused her, closed himself from her.

She turned toward the Teacher but he was unaware of their interchange. She went to the edge of the garden, across an oval court to the slim fountain that filled the cool air with a light fog. To her surprise Andrew had followed, he stood meeting her eyes. His pain so stark she felt it in herself. "You know Anna, we have learned. We See. See what people have sought to See for ages. We can Reach and we Touch with one another and some of us, you and I even, know something of Joining. But we know more, we have seen that Light that beckons to us to go on beyond our ordinary world. We've seen what we can't name. We've seen the edge of the life of Spirit. Yet how has the town met that knowledge, met those talents, that growing realization, the AWAKENING?" He stumbled to the fountain edge, sat and his face was miserable. "Even the Master Teachers haven't acknowledged what we know."

"Now those Builders have spoken hate toward those who See beyond the everyday, those whose eyes are clear toward that highest place of Mind, whose minds have reached across the chasm that is between dimensions of reality. We SEE Sister, we SEE across that emptyness into what is beyond. What we can't name, can't even rightly see but we can See that it's there. We can know that humankind can stand there if we would acknowledge ourselves, acknowledge the Heart, the Vision, the awakened Mind. And the people of this Valley prefer to cling to a past so narrow it's ugly." She saw that his eyes stung with unshed tears, his face was taut with strain, but he went on.

"They don't insist upon the Conviction of protection, of Love, or of Lifting to that highest point of mind. They want to regress to the past, to use violence to get what they want, to lose what humanity we've gained." He turned, shook himself as if in exasperation. "I can't see why you object to us, to our effort to stop them. They want to deny the powers of Good, of reverence for Life itself. Our parents say they begin to understand us, but they deny too, they all deny everything we Know! I'm so tired of that."

She nodded, "And you want to use violence to stop them!" She brought herself with intense effort into control, he must see her dispair and make the choice she hoped he'd make. Then, with the greatest effort to focus she had ever made in her life, she deliberately focussed attention and lifted out of emotion. She stood free, very aware of the pain around her. Aware of the deep quiet through her mind and Heart. "I see the power of your feelings. I see the thoughts they shape. Those thoughts have truth only from that lowest place of perception. They have no truth here at this Soul conscious place. They are the thoughts of the half blind. Old emotions try to control your mind, brother, they try because they've succeeeded for ages with us, with humanity. Emotions have done our thinking. Well, Andrew, you know that does not work. It does not work! You do exactly what the builders do!"

Andrew was nodding, his eyes torn with conflict, "I know, I have seen that, I know, Anna, and it tortures me to see. But I won't let all we've realized be lost, let us be flung back into that old narrow world again. No!" His cry was like an animal in pain. and she feared she had lost him. He held his head in both hands, his body slightly bent. He was shaking his head so that his long hair flew back and forth, dark and gleaming, his dark face seemed darker than she'd ever known it. Then with a sudden jerk he stopped, "No, No, Anna. It's a manly thing. As Steel says, it's a manly thing to protect our Valley from those who would destroy it."

"But your very way of protecting it is destroying it. Is there no other way?" Her voice had a note of pleading that at first caught him and then angered him. "After all, there are others, not of the Builders, loyal and convinced of our Convictions who do not See either and they don't seek to regress." She saw he heard little of what she said now, the flood in him sweeping away his attention. But that last had caught his attention again.

"What do you mean?"

THE AWAKENING

"There are those who do not struggle as we do, who shout for battle with no doubt that they are right. I can see the conflict in you like a roaring fire. They cannot See. Don't you realize that, Andrew, most of those boys there behind you cannot See? These aren't our close friends. They are unconscious! They don't know the difference. They want to chase the Builders from fields legally given them by Valley Council. They are acting with out Love. They break the Convictions in attempts to save them. You and I are only beginning to be aware, and we aren't strong enough alone to deal with such emotional demands. We aren't strong enough Andrew unless we stand together absolutely in Love. We know it , we KNOW. If we betray our knowledge, what are we? We will be even less than these! Because we KNOW better." Now her own eyes were filled, were stinging and she would not let those tears fall.

Andrew stared at her, he had never heard this sister talk for so long at one time in his life. She was one of few words. She was one who could be counted on always to be there in Love.He hadn't realized how much he counted on her, and the thought infuriated him perversely. A great longing to deny swept through him, even as she saw that he knew her words were true. He wavered, but there was a force stronger than he could meet, as if coming from outside himself, a force feeding some longing in himself, some longing that gave it entrance into his very self. He was his own betrayer, and he vaguely realized that in that instant before he drew away from her.

She spoke swiftly, "Andrew, are we to lose all we've gained, all we've known? Are we to deny our very consciousness of Love? We have that Knowledge. We are AWARE of Love. We cannot deny that can we?"

She felt his trembling,,his leaning toward her, his fumbling Reach and she Touched him gently, almost receiving his Touch. But at that moment, a great cry rang out. The teacher had told the students that they must find the answers, must discover for themselves. A common teaching technique, but misused by ordinary teachers when they were unsure of themselves. Now, the students took it as permission and cried in delight. They would go to the fields were the Builders were building a Winery, the industry that they thought would make the heart of their new empire. That would bring them unheard of riches. There they would make their stand! Their energy moved Andrew, caught him at his point of imbalance and drew him to it. The lure of adventure overpowered reason.

He said,"There, that's the right task. We'll see what the Builders are. We'll learn what we need to know. We'll harm nothing. We'll just find out! I'll let you know." She felt the release of his body like a spring suddenly loosed. He leaped the low bench and ran to join his friends. She glimpsed his face, still drawn, but full of some strange excitement that she quailed to see. She saw too that there were two young people still there, who,like herself, had tried to reach their friends. The images ceased.

When Anna turned back to her family, she was weary. She didn't see their astonishment that she could Send imagery so clearly. The mental interchange had been a focus such as she had never held so long. They were silent, tears streamed from Rose's eyes, Ben's face was strained and wet with tears also. Jerry shuddered, wiping his face and blowing his nose. A mixture of anger ,, dismay and hopelessness moved across his face. He said,"There it is. And it's our own fault. They've gone to set themselves up as heros. To prove themselves before the whole Valley. It's the oldest story of the human race. Is there any chance they'll use discretion?"

Anna heard but she looked at Jessie, who sat in complete silence, her eyes gentle, watching. Anna frowned faintly, wondering, but felt a peace from Jessie that comforted her.

Rose's voice was strained, she clutched Ben's hand, "Surely there's still the knowledge within them, surely within Andrew. He does know. He can't fully forget." She knew she was trying to convince herself.

"That's another old mind set, my dear. That the young will come to their senses on their own." Ben was gruff, wiping his face briskly with a large handkerchief. His own old sense of failure and anger at his long denials tore at his heart like a knife.

"Well, we've some thinking to do, that's for sure." Jerry sighed, he reached out to draw Anna into the circle of his arms."Anna, little niece, we're going to get ourselves busy, we're not going to deny that there's trouble in this Valley anymore. We've got to correct our errors". He looked at her face, calm now, "Maybe we need your help, sweetheart, that talk with Andrew was better than I could have done."

She turned a sad face toward him, smiled faintly, and then finally said,"No,Uncle Jerry, I want to go now,.I want you all to decide what you'll do and then, when you know, tell me." She got up and left the room.

There was silence for some time, then Rose said,"I feel such a fool that our daughter must bring to us what we should have seen". She drew a long, long breath. "We must begin - we've got to get ourselves alert to the problems that we've been avoiding. I'm ashamed! We avoided one another for so long, avoided what was happening among us, and so it's no surprise that we've avoided what's been happening in the Valley too."

Ben sighed, frowning, his face set in bitter lines."We need the Master Teachers. What've they been doing. Why didn't they see all this? Now, the first week they're gone, all this happens." He made a dismissing gesture with one hand,"That's not fair, I can't blame things on them. We HAVE been remiss. We've not been paying attention." He looked around, his eyes found Jessie,"D'you know when they'll be back?"

Jessie nodded,"They'll return in two more days." Her face was calm, at peace and Rose felt angry at that calm. Didn't it mean anything to her? She couldn't know that Jessie had heard the whole event with great Joy, great pride even. Jessie thought that with young people like Anna and her friends, even like Andrew, the Valley could not fail in its growth.

Ben stood. "First thing then Wednesday, I'm going in and have some talks with the Master Teachers. Surely its true we can't expect them to run our lives, but they must be more alert, mustn't they?" He stopped, a thought lighting his face,"I'll bet that conference they're having is dealing with this very kind of thing. Surely, it must be." He looked relieved.

Rose nodded, a look of relief softening her own face,"I think that must be so, Benjamin, but then, we've not asked the Master Teachers to pay attention to what our young ones are up to away from the Center. After all, even if they knew, wouldn't they have waited for us to ask for their help. They can't interfere , You know, anymore than a Monitor can." Suddenly she laughed,"To think that when I was Anna's age I wanted to enter training as a Monitor. I couldn't hold a match to my daughter at all.I thought entering a retreat was separating oneself from the troubles of living. And she already knows that it is the opposite. I had a dream of becoming a Holy Teacher, and now, I know that I don't even have any idea what holiness is. Though I think I know something of what it isn't."

Ben said, "The only way I know to live with all this is to keep one eye on that Light, that point of perception that we know, all of us know, even if we don't understand. And the other eye on everything that's happening here. To learn how to live with the knowledge of Light, that farther dimension, what's beyond - that we Reach for.To learn how to live with what we know. But I can see I'm going to have to pay attention to -- to everything. To the patterns of my thought, to the sweep of emotions and the way they change the color of perception,the way I see other people, how they relate to me, or I to them. I must be aware of everything I'm conscious of."

Rose turned to him, her face alight."I've wanted to hear that from you for so long, Love. We can pay attention and we can continue to Reach through everything we are to find what we are becoming.We can be still until we are aware of ourselves in relationship. Then we may be able to understand!"

He turned to her, lifted her from her chair and gathered her in his arms,"We've got a problem, my darling, but Andrew has got to work himself out of what he's in, doesn't he? We've got to make known to him that we want to talk, to help, to discuss these things we've not talked of.But he has to deal with his own lower nature." He stopped, feeling unsure, looking suddenly at Jessie who only smiled at him. They were carrying plates and cups to the cleaner, and tidying up around him and Rose drew away, to help. Ben was aware then that he still wanted to simplify things, wanted to have things work out with no pain. He said,"We've got to get that boy in here and talk!"

Suddenly, there was a deep thrust of attention, a Reach so powerful and so intense that they stopped in their tracks. It intensified, as they responded, strong as plasteel, like a rod that would bend but would not break. And that rod brought them together, drew them into mental rappour that wiped away all distractions. Emotions were quiet beneath that mental Touch. Thinking stopped, a clarity grew, and in that stillness of mind, that gradually growing Light of perception, they began to Know of a Joining. They responded.

Jessie Reached out and drew them to one another with a power they had never suspected. Like a blast of Light she enveloped them and they found themselves responding with their own power, amazed at their own capacity to focus, to merge and to be together. They knew finally a true Joining, only the four of them, but it was as if their minds multiplied many times in realization. They leaned on that strength that was Jessie, conscious of her gift but so immersed in the event that they had no thought of it and would not until much later.

Here was true Balance, an awareness that suspended questions. They stood at that point of consciousness that had been termed Light, realizing that it was simply the place where ordinary perception broke free of habit and patterns. They saw beyond those limits. Learning instantly that they were beyond them. And they could not imagine, nor shape even into idea what they knew there. That was of another dimension inexpressable in terms of this narrow one.

They felt the power of Jessie's sustained presence slacken, and the Joining fade, and were separate. Ben let out his breath, Rose said,"I feel naked, naked and suddenly so alone!" Her own words puzzled her.

Jerry set down the dish that he still held,"Finally I can see that we must Join in Love. But our whole Family must Join. All of us. The power of it is so wonderful. We can understand what has confused us. Perhaps some day, we may Join with the whole Valley, and we will be able to know what we only glimpse and wonder at now. It takes Joined Minds to step across that limitlessness we call the Light, to create a path there. But it takes Minds conscious of Love to Join. The bridge of mind we've built in our own Reaching, is strong enough to let us glimpse, but to See, to truly know, we must JOIN. I believe that must be so." He shook his head too, having listened to himself and learned.

They were silent for some time, settling emotions that were flooding into attention. Clumsy thought begin to shape wanting to speak the realizations. Finally Benjamin said,"Well, we've got work to do. Thank you Jessie. We'll begin this very day .

CHAPTER TWENTY FIVE

Jerry and Rodney go fishing

As the weeks passed, Benjamin was more aware of how different were his relationships to the other members of his Family. He realized gradually that Jerry was no longer the 'young brother' of his Mate. He was a grown man. Andrew and Anna were young adults, their eyes seemed to hold some watchful, alertness he had never noticed before. They no longer accepted without question his dominance,they were pulling away. He felt thrown off base, feeling both sadness and pride.

Some days he thought he wasn't needed, problems seemed to solve themselves without him. He felt brief rushes of anger, relief, deep unease, confusion and then he resorted to watching again. Surely, he had not been - what they had all called him,the 'Big Boss'. He had heard the name as a term of affection. Now, he wondered. Had he been a tyrant? Had he assumed he must have final say? He thought that kind of blindness was well gone, but why had no one told him?

He spent some time brooding about these things. and finally came to the conclusion that he would have to find his place again in the Family and it wouldn't be as it had been. During the time he spent planning and building Jessie's little cottage he watched his own behavior when others worked with him and learned with some chagrin that he had been just that; a Tyrant. He finally talked to Rose and she simply kissed him and laughed,"It's about time, Love, that you saw that."

Jessie had been so delighted with her little cottage that he had felt somewhat mollified, and Jerry had seemed to enjoy working with him, so he decided he was learning. On a bright spring morning, Ben sat in the Main Hall, sipping a third cup of coffee and watching the birds sweeping across the new early blooms of the gardens beyond the windows. He was unaware of Silvia, so silently she had sat, hunched over in a big deep chair. Turning at a slight sound, he saw her and reflected how small she looked in its huge space.

Silvia untangled her small self, stood to stretch and glanced at him. She dialed herself a fresh cup of tea, got one for Ben and returned to him. She waited a moment, setting the cups on a small table between them and then spoke his name.

He started out of his absorption, then said, "Oh, yes, Silvia, what was it you wanted?"

She smiled, then frowned, took a long deep breath and said,"Benjamin, this baby is going to need a father who is a real father."

He grinned,amused at her characteristic way of plunging into things."So you've finally decided to admit to us that you're pregnant"

She looked surprised, "Of course, you all must know,it's obvious enough now. I just didn't talk about it because I - I couldn't decide what to do."

He nodded, watching her, wanting to pay attention to how she met this situation. He was determined not to tell her what to do. He said,"So?" She glanced at him, with a frown, but went on,"Well, I'm certain that Jerry or Ned qualify. Both of them are true fathers in their very nature. Ned especially, he's almost got a talent for it. That's not the problem."

"Then there's no problem. The baby will have good parents and be happy." He was teasing her but she refused to notice."By the way, who is the physical father?"

She looked at him half seeing him, "Jerry, of course." He nodded, frowning a little, "Well, which ever man you choose will be right. And Jerry will go right on loving his child whatever you decide."

" Ben, that's absolutely cruel" Her face radiated rage, she stood up and walked back and forth, anger pouring from every movement. He started back, surprised."You're not even trying to see the situation. Don't you realize this is important? I need to make a decision that'll effect my whole life." She stopped, stared at him, "And more importantly, my child's life, and Jerry's and Ned's lives. It's important!"

Ben nodded, sipped again, and reached out a conciliatory hand, which touched her as she passed. "Honestly Sil, I didn't mean to imply it wasn't important. I guess I don't understand the problem."

She shrugged and calmed down,settled into her chair, tucking both legs under her until she was barely visible over the broad high arms,"Well, then, Ben, I'll tell you. I don't know which to choose. I don't know for sure whether Jerry is my true Mate. You know, like it should be." She was silent, staring at him, I'm not sure how to tell, but for me, Jerry - I think Jerry is -- is my Mate. But how can I be sure?"

Ben grunted, "Two of the best prospects for fatherhood I know of. Either of them. But you don't know how to be sure who's a Mate?" She was silent, her face a struggle reflecting the feeling trying to emerge. He looked searchingly at her, "That's not all that's bothering you, is it?"

She succumbed to some inner release and relaxed visibly. "No,Ben,that isn't. It IS worrying me. But it isn't what's making me so anxious. I think I just wanted to talk to you about it. But mostly I feel so uneasy about Ned."

Ben didn't show surprise,he well knew that feelings are illogical. So now that's clear. What's wrong with Ned?"

She looked at him solemnly, drawing her thoughts together and absently she began, "Well, you know Ned, and what kind of person he is. He's a powerful man, not just physically, he's got certain qualities - he's perceptive, imaginative, absolutely kind, thoughtful, clear headed, and he's got an absolutely inextinguishable sense of humor. But then, he's petty at times,he can be sulky, even narrow minded, and then he bursts out of that and he's so large and generous, so strong in his tenderness to other people he's like a - a mountain. He's almost like some one whose more than human sometimes. He's really fine."

She said the last in a rush as if not sure she ought to say it. She shrugged,"I could go on describing him, but you know him. I've thought there couldn't be a better person to live with, for my child to have as father. But then, there's something wrong with that, there's something lacking between us maybe. It's not just Ned, but me too." With an impatient gesture, she got up and commenced walking again. "Oh, I don't know"

She thought for some minutes and Benjamin waited, suppressing his immediate desire to advise her. He realized with chagrin that he'd always done that in the past."You see, Ben, I'm not in love with either of them. I've already been in love and got over that. But I can't get Jerry out of my mind, I can't budge him. He just seems to sit there, as if he belonged. It's almost as if Jerry is nearly a part of myself, an extension, a compliment, maybe. Could that be? Or I of him." She stopped and looked at him with dispair.

He laughed, took her hand that hung limply over the dark rust pile of the chair arm. It seemed so white and small there that he wanted to hold it in protection. "Honey, you've heard of being in love and you've heard of being responsible, and now I'm going to tell you something more, that your own Master Teachers have talked about,I know, even if you weren't listening that day. There is a skill to being able to recognize something that's right in front of your nose." He smiled, feeling happy that he could help finally. "You're a very fortunate pair, you waited, experienced more than one lover, tried out the extent of your feelings and got to know them. Now, since you can't loosen Jerry from your mind, it might be that you have found your true Mate." He waved a hand at her,as she started to speak, "Now wait a minute, It isn't like people think, a blinding flash. It's just what you say, we can't get that person out of our mind. We can't spend a day without wanting to know what they think, how they feel about something. It's that sense of something missing in other people, other lovers, and not in this one. And so, there is strong evidence, that you, might have to pay attention to that. But, if it's a true Mate syndrome, then Jerry would be feeling the same way. Have you asked him?"

She had stopped in front of him, searching his face as he spoke. Now she shook her head, looking steadily at the floor with a strange embarrassment.

He said triumphantly,"That's what I thought. You haven't checked the obvious."

She flashed him a glance of resentment and then stared off out the window. Then slowly she went to sit down again and sipped absent mindedly at her tea. "But then, Ben, what of Ned, I know he loves me. I think maybe he wants to be my Mate."

Ben nodded, He does, that's obvious,but he's not stupid. He knows what Mating is. He'll know himself whether it's for him. But even if it is, Dear, and it does happen, he is a grown man and able to manage his own feelings and he will be glad for you and Jerry, if you two decide that you are Mates. Don't worry about him. He has to be freed from his hope so he can find the woman who WILL be his true mate.

THE PEOPLE OF THE VALLEY

She was silent, her mind filled with memories, scenes, voices and thoughts that came, floated out of view and allowed more. Nothing caught, things flowed by as smoothly as a river. She felt cut off from herself, from that reasoning, worrying small self, as though the recognitions just accepted had broken some thread that had tied her. The state of mind she was entering deepened, and she deliberately tore loose and was free of herself. Thinking seemed a separate function, going on at one side, while she stood apart, waching the flow of impressions, images and thoughts. Her mind seemed opened, fresh with large perception, the world out the window seemed to live, each object sharply alive to her. She turned to Ben, her eyes shining with a renewed energy. She smiled, standing up, with a movement of dignity and pride that made Ben smile. She said,"Ben, I think I understand. It's clear to me now, what I must do." She went to him and kissed the top of his head. Then went to stand at the window.

Ben sat quietly for several minutes, then went to stand beside Silvia. From this south western side of the Hall, one window looked over the barns and the land beyond. The rolling hills rose rapidly, dotted thickly with walnut, ash, various oaks, elm and other hardwoods. Not until the hills reached the lower mountains did conifers darken and thicken their growth into forest. Through out this grassy spread of rolling hills late blooming prune trees splashed white in small clumps. Patches of color painted the hillsides here and there, and below them, clusters of wild blue Matta flower on their tall thick stalks brightened and revealed the curving creek that ran into the Green River to the east. He sighed, relishing the scene, the feeling of being truly at home filled him. Then, with a start he saw, far to the south west, a spot between low hills that drew his attention. It seemed to recede into itself, away from the greening forests, to shrivel and exude a grey darkness that repelled him. He spotted the place, determined that he must investigate sometime today and know its cause. Could it be a diseased forest. He frowned, uneasy.

He was jolted back to the moment by Silvia's arm slipping through his, drawing herself against him. They stood watching the day.

After some minutes, she pointed, smiling and following her finger he saw a small figure far to the edge of the western fields, down the wide path that led from the farm up into the foothills. The figure moved at the end of that pathway and up into the trees. Ben nodded,"Yes, it's Jerry. Looks as if he's carrying his axe and the cutting rod and wearing that old green hat. Look at Rob dance, he loves a work trip. We ought to all walk with him more. Looks as if Jerry's got something on his mind, that's when he goes out to chop things."

She nodded, It's Jerry all right, I'd recognize that walk as far as it can be seen. But now, yes, I agree, he's got something on his mind that's bothering him a lot". She sounded worried and he smiled. Their eyes met briefly. She didn't need him, he wanted to get on to his day's work in town. He kissed her lightly and told her he'd see her this evening. Silvia knew what she must do.

She stood for some time after Ben had gone, letting her eyes wander over the world beyond. A small herd of cattle and deer, grazing together, moved slowly over the hills just beyond the Farm. An Opossom, heavy with young, her body

THE AWAKENING

swaying, moved a short distance along the river bank into the cover of heavy brush. Silvia wondered about their lives, how did they live, how meet the inevitable death of part of their young each year. She wished she was able to reach to them the way Jane was. A gentle sadness rose through her body and she felt it, watched it's coming, wondered and knew it had to do with her own lack of Reach. "Lack," that's it, she said softly." I just seem to lack the Reach the others have and so I don't even realize as much life." The shaped thought, saddened her. Finally she resolutely accepted it. She must meet that fact."I am not as alive as the others. And maybe its because I haven't practiced." Anger mixed with her sadness and she turned. How could Jerry know her as his Mate? He was so - so very much alive."

She half turned to go and then her eye was caught by a movement at the edge of the Highway south of Adwin. A band of dogs? Or coyotes? She couldn't be sure. They ran, playing or intending to hunt? She watched their movements, finally smiling a little at their antics. Wild things could play as well as kill. It was a hopeful thought. She drew back into those thoughts, realizing she had moved far from her worries about Jerry and Ned. Now, she must get into town to work, and let the ideas stew in her mind during the morning, then perhaps she could talk to Jerry later. Though she longed to do so,,she felt a strange reluctance.

------   ------

Jerry swung his axe like a pendulum between his legs as he stood looking at the downed old tree. It still had two limbs with opened leaves, must have come down in the last storm. Most of the limbs were bare, no longer alive. He focussed his attention, listened to the forest, he could hear, sense, the vibrations, the sounds echoing softly in his mind, from healthy trees, but from this one, there seemed no cry at all. Only a dull hum, a very slow tremble, he decided, as though it were ceasing, ending its life. He went to it, placed a hand on the thick dark bark, felt an absence, wished Jane were here, she would know. And then, suddenly, without warning, the dull hum stopped and there was nothing at all. The tree's life was withdrawn, not there, It was without life. He shook his head, having been there at the moment he felt some small sorrow, as though witnessing loss, yet relief. He nodded, it was the same when the Master Forester's students cut diseased limbs from a healthy tree. That sense of something ended within it. He had served a short term with that crew and it was then that he had become aware of such tree 'sounds'. The Master Forester had waited, known just when to cut, and had tried to show the students. Jerry knew the ones who did not sense as their teacher did, would not be taken as apprentices into Forestry. They would find another niche in town work.

Now, he leaned his axe against the trunk, and considered. Then, picking it up again, he began to cut into the hard oak body. He lost himself in the pure pleasure of the work, the movement of his body, the rhythm of arms, hips, legs all fitting into that task. He let his mind trail, his emotions jumble among themselves, his attention lifted beyond them all, he held himself at that peak of stillness that gave him clear awareness of physical joy. Finally, weary, breathing deeply, mopping sweat from his face, he stopped. He looked around, bits of white flesh lay all around the thick limb he had severed. The great trunk, three feet thick, had fallen so hard it had pushed a young tree, probably it's own get, so that it leaned a little. It would grow around its parent's body.

He looked at his work, several pieces, firewood size, lay against the limb, but he would not get it all cut this way. Later, when he didn't need to hit something, he'd use the power unit he'd brought to finish the job. The branches, would have to be stacked. He surveyed the great long trunk. It should be left here, to rot away and provide living room for all the creatures needing dead trees to nest in. Well, the foresters would come and settle that, decide whether that was needed, or whether it should all be taken, sliced with the hair thin beam that would leave no trace of cutting at all, and carry it to the mills for pressing into sheets for building. He turned from the thought of it finally let his mind take up the nagging worry that had projected him here. He looked around, the sky was intensely blue, as it sometimes was in spring or autumn. He swam in that blue, felt as though he were at the bottom of a sea of sky. The sun had grown warm around him and he pulled off his jacket. He looked over the land and felt familiar pride. Life was still good after all. He murmured,"I understand why Vagabonds speak to the Earth and honor Her as truly awake to them. At this moment, it makes absolute sense." He grinned at the thought.

Then, memory jolted up into focus. He did not want to avoid it, he had to think it out. The frustration, the rise and fall of anger and hurt, tore through his calm and ended it. All that was serene disappeared under the onslaught of this worry. Then he shifted mentally, as though released, the work had loosened the pain of it, he felt the hurt in him shift and slide away. With an act of will he deliberately drew himself out from under all the feelings, stood watching himself. After all, what was all this work for if not to loosen him from this obsession? He grinned, and then suddenly laughed. He could handle it. Whatever she decided to do. But damn it, he wished she'd make some decision. Even that would help. "But I've got to settle my own feelings, or I can't talk to her at all!" He pulled his thoughts swiftly away from that endless pit of conjecture and looked around again.

He was ready to stop, but he didn't want to leave. He looked into the forest a few feet beyond the great old tree. Perhaps had it been among the others, the wind would not have shoved it down. He saw two other tiny trees, sprouted from acorns. They'd have died under this old one, Now they'd live. And the bigger one that leaned from the dead trunk, they'd compete for this space. He shrugged. There was a wonderful sense of privacy here. He drew a long breath. Something hurt in him, something that wouldn't let go. He began again the rhythmic swing and cut against the hard, white wood. For some time there was no sound except that sharp sound of axe against wood. No movement except the rhythmic shifting of his body into each stroke and swing. The clear ring of the axe defined something for him, white chips flew out and finally the whole limb was cut into eighteen inch logs. He began to stack the branches left from it. They would provide cover too, for small creatures. The Forester might send Teen Gatherers with a chipper and use some of them for making paper. They didn't do that often anymore, not with so much Paper Vine growing on the rocky slopes below Adwin. But that was not Jerry's worry. He wiped his face again, knowing that the breeze was cool enough to chill him if he stood too long without his jacket.

He picked up the logs and threw them too hard into a small pile. The bitter energy pleased him. He would get them later, but thoughts jumbled again. He said, aloud, "I love you Silvia. I want to live with you. You are my true Mate. I want to make you see it, make you agree, to do what I want! But I can't put my desires on you. You're your own person, and even if I could, I'd not respect you for letting me. I want it to be your own decision. To know you made the choice." He swung the axe hard against the great trunk once, let the sharp edge sink into it, "No, I don't want to have to wait, I would like to demand, demand your love, your loyalty. But then what value would it be?"

He spun around shifting his feet in the heavy deep grass, "No, that's not true. I want to just make her do what I want. I want to make her BELONG TO ME. There it is. I do." He shouted, "Belong to me. Belong to me." His rage and helplessness, the conflicting desires tipping that calm he had achieved back into rage, he cried out, "She should not ever belong to any one else."

Then wearily, feeling the wash of emotions recede, letting it fall away as water down his body, he shook his head." There it is, I want that, but I don't want it. Never can anyone belong to another. I don't want that. But why doesn't she speak? She's too sensitive not to know how I feel. And if she doesn't, then she's not the Silvia I know. So I must wait, must allow her the time it takes. I haven't been living with a fantasy, but a real woman. She will know when it's time."

He did not see the man who had come down through the forest, moving as silently as any wild creature. But as he drew near, Jerry caught sight of him from the corner of his eye. He didn't stop talking, but finished his sentence and then stood watching the newcomer. They stood a moment sizing each other up, then the man came closer and leaned against the far end of the trunk where the roots had torn loose and stuck many yards up into the air.

They both grinned, Jerry waved one hand toward him in greeting, then the man said, "Well, looks as if you've got a lot done here." He readjusted his gun in his hand, and said, "I couldn't help but hear you, Jerry. You were shoutin' a bit. I'm sorry if it was private. Sounds like the same old trouble." he searched Jerry's face for signs of displeasure and finding instead a quiet smile, continued, "You finally decided what you want to do about it? That would be a lot in itself".

Jerry nodded and said softly, "Yes, I know now that I want to live with Silvia. I want her as my Mate,, not just my wife. That's clear to me."

"I'd a thought she'd be tired of waiting around for you by now. Seems like it was near eight months ago you was trying to make up YOUR mind. Course there was more than that you was tryin' to decide then." He watched Jerry with a shrewd and kindly expression, a trace of amusement glinted in his eyes. Jerry smiled then and nodded, seeing that affectionate amusement and knowing it came from Rodney's love.

Rodney was a man only a year older than Jerry, though he looked older. His body was lanky, tanned and dressed in loose grey-blue over alls of tightly woven skenna-cotten. Jerry knew the fabric would outwear Skenna. Most Foresters amd some farmers wore it. Rodney had chosen early and he and his wife Alice lived in a small holding just north of the Farm. They and their two children worked hard, wanted self sufficiency, which they had, and yet, came in to help out with the building of the town when there was work they could do. He was known as an honest, serious man, but one whose frank comment on any situation could be counted on. Rodney's was not an easy life, but it satisfied him. It was in his eyes that his youth was noticed, eyes that were large, green and full of a strange innocence that Jerry had never been able to understand. It was his eagerness to life, his joy in it, that had always drawn Jerry. He seemed completely tolerant of the ideas, the life style and attitudes of other people. He only insisted that they make no effort to change his own.

Jerry, assessing his friend thoughtfully asked,"How'd you know I was here?"

"Why, I, just kind of knew that I ought to come this way this morning. I'm out to get a rabbit or two. I think my family should have meat now and then, even if Alice doesn't." He grinned again, his good nature comforted Jerry but his explanation puzzled him.

Rodney came to town regularly but not often. He sent his children to the Learning Center and never objected to their spending time there on weekends or even evenings. But he insisted on knowing exactly what they were doing there. He had been known to come in himself to see. The family only had two belts, ones the children used,because he did not want them traveling late nights home alone. So when he came to see what they were doing he must walk. Jerry, and Rose too, had more than once told him that he needn't worry, they'd keep as close eyes on his kids as on Rose's, and so he and Alice had accepted that but Rodney, still must see for himself now and then. He had not been convinced of the town point of view, but though he didn't realise it,his opinion was valued. Jerry thought that Rodney's mind was being teased into a new curiousity. He asked about things he never had before. Seemed puzzled where he had used to seem so sure. Rodney might be affected with the changes in the Valley too. The idea surprised Jerry,but why not?

Jerry enjoyed his friend, though there was a shyness about both Rodney and Alice that caused him to treat them gently. He knew that their children puzzled both parents. They did not understand their penetrating minds, their gentleness with their parents, the fact that they were not demanding as many children might be. Rodney and Alice knew their children were different but deeply respected that. Jerry thought that any parent who could keep respect of a young one even while being as different, as out of 'style' as their parents were, must have some special secret of child rearing.

Rodney squatted down beside Jerry, picking up a pebble to toss in his hand,he said,"You want a woman that might be carrying another man's child and that man one of your best friends and both of you knowing it. You think that's right? That's what's so hard for me to figure. Man, what's it like? Why I'd be ready to kill him" He reflected a moment, knowing he could never kill. "At least ready to run him off my place. But it don't seem to bother you none at all."

Jerry looked at him, his own feelings drawn and thin with exhaustion, he would as soon not talk of it. But then his mind seemed clear now, he heard the questions inside his head, without registering them, then he repeated,"Bother me none? Why I suppose not. It doesn't bother me."

Rodney was thoughtful, "It don't figure. But they say, every man to his way. But you and me been friends for years and I'd like to see you settled and happy. Like me and my Alice. Our kids are half grown now and you without one even. I know you could get Silvia to tie up with you. I know a way. It works with women, Man. It works. I think." He added the last in the first tone of doubt.

Jerry shook his head gently and spoke with sureness that he had lacked before. "Silvia's not just any woman, Rod. Even if I could 'get her to' I wouldn't. I wouldn't use persuasion on her. She's too sharp for that. She knows, Rod, she knows. She has to make up her mind on her own. It wouldn't be much of a marriage or Mating if she didn't, now would it?"

Rodney laughed shortly,"Maybe. Maybe she would if you insisted."

"But she'd despise any man who sought her pity and she'd never marry a man she pitied. She's too much a person for that and that's one reason why I love her, just because she's a strong person. So you see Rod, I want her to decide all herself. After all, Rodney, it's what I've done. She didn't push me, when she was wanting to know my feelings last year."

Rodney nodded, silently, he took out a pen knife and opening it to the longest blade, he began idly tossing it in the movements of mumblety-peg, the old game of their boyhood. Striking it into the soft earth, pulling it and changing position, he was thoughtful. Jerry watching him, smiled, remembering the long afternoons beside the river after swims. "Damn, you're still as good at it as you used to be."

"Comes from havin' kids to teach the game to." He glanced up and continued. The sun was warm, the sweet smell of woods and field surrounded them. For several minutes there was only the sound of the creatures of the forests, scuffles, bird songs and a plaintive soft call far in the distance.

Jerry Reached, held steady, listening mentally to the sounds, to farther Touches. He thought he could sense the general state of things around Adwin. If there were someone calling there he could have heard, but that was his limit, from here. Why was that? Why could he Reach no further? Was that limit for everyone? Rodney looked up, "Something goin' on in this Valley that ain't for the good."

Jerry grinned,,swiftly realizing that Rod's senses were acute but Rodney didn't know how acute. He knew Rodney couldn't Reach, or at least didn't Touch. Many times in their lives he had tried, and knew Rodney would not hide from himself. So if he didn't, he couldn't. He said,"I think so too, Rod. Something we don't want to see, even." At the statement of the words, Jerry knew that it was true. He hadn't recognized that."What is it we're not seeing?" He was silent then, his mind stretched swiftly, Reaching to its limits, held, focussed in a wide openness of awareness. Like an antenna, he thought, we can use our minds like antenna's, just listening. There seemed to him then to be a faint staining of the very air, somewhere to the south west, somewhere that he couldn't find. A stain, a cloud, a concealment, that oughtn't be there in this Valley. He drew attention away, not wanting to offer himself as possible focus for that dark energy.

"How many of us are blinding ourselves out of fear? Or maybe just habit?" He muttered the thought but Rod nodded.

"It's exactly what I told Alice. We're like a bunch of ostrichs. We're just gonna wait too long." He stopped playing and stood up.

Turning he pulled at Jerry's arm . Jerry stood beside him and Rod pointed,"Look over there, look at them forests above Strom. Can't you see the logging? There's trees missing but they ain't enough to catch most people's eye. Unless you're looking. The Master Forester'll be noticing, unless he's thinking it's all right and doesn't want to mention it." He looked darkly at Jerry. But Jerry shook his head,"No, Rod, Master Forester King, is devoted to the forests, You know that."

Rod nodded, "I do think that's true, but I'm wondering." His eyes were mere slits beneath a furrowed brow,the sun making him squint," Alice says I'm imagining but she's the same as most people. She don't want to believe anything's goin' on."

Jerry stiffened, focussing all his attention at the far hills,the edges of those mountains, above the town of Strom. He had no power to Reach that far, but with no Reaching at all, Rodney had simply noticed. The keen eyes of a woodsman and hunter and farmer, he had noticed what 'Reaching' had not found. Jerry felt a deep shame and sudden anger. All Valley children were taught to See, to notice, to really see what they looked at, and he was lax, letting his Sight slip into lazyness. He said angrily,"My God, Rodney, we've become so complacent we're not paying attention to anything around us. Rodney, we need to appoint you as official watcher for this end of the Valley. We need you to prod us, let us know when we aren't paying attention."

"What about that - thing you do - Reaching? Can't you find out things that way?"

Andy shook his head,"Oh, Rod, we've all been so scared of it, although we've at least named it. They're new ways to perceive, actually, to See!" He looked at his friend as if he'd just discovered something." We're just now admitting we can do that, that Reaching. And the kids, already knew!"   He frowned a sudden suspicion sweeping past his assumptions,"Rose's admitting to some things she never did before. You're right, things're changing." He spoke angrily then suddenly was sad, so that Rodney gave his upper arm a tap and said,"Hey, now, I didn't want to get you feeling bad."

Jerry grinned at him, gripped the powerful hairy wrist a moment and said,,"Don't worry, I'm really glad you woke me up." He grimaced and added softly,"And I thought it was me that was to wake YOU up." Without explanation, he turned to look across the land."You know, we ought to go off into those hills for a hike, the way we used to do. Look things over."

"Yeah, we ought to. D'you think you can still track. Ain't no body heard me in my rounds yet, after all these years, and I can find a trail as well as ever."

Andrew sighed, "Well, I keep in practice, but I don't improve, not doing it enough. I'd be like a beginner with you though." He laughed, knowing it wasn't altogether true. Then realizing the insult, he had no excuse for placating Rodney, he ducked his head and, "But you might not find my trail if I really tried." He smiled lamely, the apology had been transparant. He couldn't understand himself just now."I'll do a bit of practice this week and then we'll go see what we can do. Eh? I want to look at that place over there that you pointed out."

Rodney nodded a gentle look of tolerance and acceptance on his rugged face. "How about next Wednesday at noon right here. We can get there from here."

Jerry nodded, "Sounds good. We've got to know what's goin' on in the forests. It's not so much the loss of a few trees, you know, Rod. But the attitude of mind that'd make people destroy wild land life without concern for those lives, or for agreement of their fellows. We've got a commitment to Earth, and we have to remember that." He looked at his friend for agreement, but he knew he argued with himself. He studied Rod's serious face, accepting his nodding agreement and said, "After what our ancestors did to the land, we've got to be careful."

For minutes they were silent, then Jerry looked up with a grin that tranformed his features into sunny cheerfulness."Hey Rod, why don't we go fishing right now. It's been a long time. It'd do us both good and we might catch dinner, since you didn't have much luck with Rabbits."

They gathered Jerry's tools, set them on the log together and went to Rod's house to get supplies. The day felt better to Jerry. He wanted the good companionship of Rodney and the River for a while, to bring his mind to rest before he next saw Silvia.

The Great River was still running full, with a swift whirl of currents down the center in the narrows. By late summer it would be quiet and low,but now,it was dark green and clear enough to see a couple of feet down. The depths grew dimmer, as they should, with green microscopic life. The two men settled down in the tall grasses along the shore, the tall trees hung over the banks, formed a woodland a hundred feet back from the water's edge. That woodland strip along the Great River varied in width, and sometimes gave way to marsh with only willows, water maples and the thick dense cover of improved Matta plants, tall and stiff and already beginning to show a few deep blue blooms.

Rodney picked off a bloom from a stray plant, and laughed,"You know, if we didn't know from any other way, we'd be able to tell Altos plants just by their bloom. They can't seem to let a plant just grow and produce the fruit,or the nut, or the fiber, they've got to make them bloom pretty too. And smell like a garden everywhere." He shook his head,smiling with the pride that his comment concealed.

THE PEOPLE OF THE VALLEY

The afternoon was sunny, and the River was silvery where the water broke and swept before the wind. Looking down into its depths was like looking into clear, turbulent, greenish red glass. Currents of movement threaded within this deep rich color like a pattern of vibrations reflecting, repeating and intensifying each other. The shadows of the limbs above them, lay repeated on the ground and on their own bodies. So clearly they fell, they gave the afternoon a quality of great fragility as though the very world around them could break.

Jerry felt immersed in the beauty of this day, the clarity of light, of color and fragrance. He slouched against a tree trunk holding his rod, drawing the bait slowly through the deep water. Big mouth bass was what he was after and he knew their tastes. He wanted just to lose himself in this day.

Rodney whipped the stream a little distance away. His rod and bait moving with grace and rhythm , his skill wonderful to watch. Both men felt themselves drawn into that simple world of water and air. Jerry was content, knowing the effects of the River and the rhythm of things around him on himself. He eased into that, letting himself surrender to its benign influence. Aware of the process, he focussed into the stirring of wonder that roused his mind's attention. The clarifying of his senses, his awareness heightened at every level. Slowly the familiar lift of Joy that always accompanied the first moment of attention, claimed his mind, emptied it of thinking. Briefly he registered the thought, "Why do I ever let myself get to worrying so." And then he lived in the silence of his centered Self.

Attention widened, extended. He was aware of the movements and odors of fishing, of the water, trees, sky, everything. He was aware of being conscious beyond all that he sensed. But he made no effort, he was simply there. Thought could come later. Then, he focussed, realized a triple level of awareness, each acute - body, emotions and mind - all three lit to their depths by that pervasive radiance that Earth flooded through Her life forms. In his youth such intensity and vision had occurred spontaniously but unexpectedly. Now, he knew how to bring it into focus, how to still himself from that point deep within so that his consciousness included everything around him. Then slowly, reaching on, he extended and was included in some natural kind of Joining. It had to be a time of deep inner focus, however, a time of the dissolving of separatness of mind and heart. Today he felt that dissolution. He was inseparable from the Earth life in which he lived, he breathed through that very breathing Earth.

He sighed, attention centered enough to be aware of himself realizing. It never failed, like an out pouring from a spring, pure Joy saturated his being. He let himself be, there , one edge of his mind watching and noticing all that was. With flickering bits of thought, he recorded the power of it, the exactness, smiling at the impossibility of thinking about it, but knowing he knew that. After all, he was a thinking animal and that was his nature, included with all the rest. He was, touching through Life, even as Life poured through him.

A few thoughts, half formed, drifted through, as though they created themselves. Then, again, thought faded, disappeared in the intensity of just being, movement, response and attention vastly inclusive. And then a flicker that was so acute with Life, it stabbed, first, with pain of tearing away whole structures of thought, then in an unlimited attraction of pure wonder. Why of course, there it was, the edge, beyond which he could only long to See. His attention focussed, pressed against that interface, nudged it farther, passed its old limit. And he was acutely conscious of having Joined into Life Itself somehow, of being over that edge into someplace- or non-place, so utterly different, transcendant. It was unbearable beauty, and longing so acute it hurt. He hung conscious, unaware of time or self.

Then, in one instant, like a defense mechanism automatically going into action, his quick thinking mind cut like a knife through everything that was and drew him down into explanation. Saved him from immersion in Light. In that instant all was lost, yet the memory was an epiphany of joy in grief. His eyes were flowing with tears, his body thrummed with loss and a memory that stretched his heart as though it would burst. It had been as if every blade of grass was known separately and yet, that there was no separation between himself and the knowing and the grass.

He shook his head, held clear for minutes, not wanting to think, not wanting to close himself from that Knowledge. Then he was abruptly down into the narrow confines of his thinking mind, trying to find words. Why did he lose contact? Why did perception fade? Was he afraid, actually afraid of what he longed for? Was he simply incapable of sustaining consciousness at that point?

There had been a glimpse - of something - unnameable and the glimpse was not an illusion, for it had the intensity and precision of LIFE. The thoughts clustered and beat against his calm. His automatic assumption that such experience was secret, yielded to a second thought. No! Now, of all times in his life, he must talk of these things to his family, his friends.

He heard a tremulous sigh and knew that Rod had moved closer. He turned from himself to pay attention to his friend. Rod looked as if filled with something of that same Light, that Wonder, yet how could that be? Jerry impulsively Reached, unhesitatingly as if it were right. And suddenly he did not ask what was happening; he Knew.

Rodney slipped down to sit against the tree trunk beside him. He felt the rough bark against his skin, the sun staining everything with Light, and knew that Light as alive. He was roused loose from himself, aware of the trees, of the endless growing of the sodden earth. This Life stirred everything into consciousness. Rodney had never known such wonder. His mind had barely touched at the edge of a knowing he had no preparation for. Unlike Jerry, he was not familiar, could not bear the power of it. He knew only the brief awakening glimpse of Light and Life.

Most any child of the learning Center could have told Rod what was happening. His own children could have, but for him it was unique. Jerry knew that he must simply be still and allow. He felt envy and sympathy - it was overwhelming at first, and yet so beautiful. That first time!

He wondered whether Rodney would refuse what he realized this first time.

People often did, explained it all away and forgot. After all, Rodney's parents had clung to the old ways, refusing to send their children to the Learning Center except for a very limited set of 'classes'. Rodney had missed so much, yet the forests and fields had been his teachers all his life. He was absorbed by them and they by him.

Jerry waited, experimenting with his own training in paying attention. Of seeing and sensing. As he did, memory poured back, he was almost immersed again, consciousness shifting as if it were no longer so absolute in its limits. He trembled, wondering whether he could hold steady, or had he lost some essential ingredient of perception. His gaze fell on Rodney again, feeling the blaze of Rodney's attention, his absorption. And then, Jerry remembered his own ' first time'and was protected by that screen of memory. It had been when he was three. He had not thought it was unusual at all. He had talked to the Master Teacher and she had taught him that this was important to remember, to seek again.

The two men sat, their poles drooped, yet held still in their hands. There was a soft stillness all about them, Jerry was conscious of the hesitation of time, as though each particle of air even was simply radiant with Life. As though Love breathed through his flesh, his mind, through the Earth life. He knew then, watching Rodney, that it was true, what the Teachers said, that the nature of life was Love. Tears filled his eyes, the sadness of not having known that. But at the same time, Joy. He smiled, knowing his friend was knowing that.

Slowly Rodney reached out and took hold of Jerry's hand. He seemed unaware of the motion, or that he was gripping so hard it hurt. Then, he moved slowly, as if moving were just discovered. Finally he bent his head, sat drawn into himself, shook his head, and turned to Jerry, releasing Jerry's hand. His eyes were wet, his face soft, open.

"I tell you Jerry, I never saw anything like that. It's about the strangest thing ever happened to me." He screwed up his face, looked away, trying to find words, "It's like , like, everything is all shining, like it's different, so soft, so - - " He shook his head again,, "Like I can see everything without hardly looking. What do you suppose happened? Maybe the sun has burned my eyes from looking at the water too long.": He sighed, staring at Jerry without seeing him.

Jerry said, wanting to be sure the memory was clear for him, "Tell me about it, Rod."

Rodney's eyes did not shift, they seemed to be unseeing. He spoke out of that abstraction, "Well, you remember when we took that acid? When we were kids. At first I thought it was like that. So sharp, everything like it was brand new. But then, I realized, right there in the middle of it, it wasn't nothing like that. My mind, Jerry, it's clear, it's full of - I don't know what. But I can think better." He grinned now, his eyes focussing on Jerry's "But that'll not convince you. You could probably think it was drugs . People on drugs say things like that, don't they?" He was silent, his eyes turning again inward, "I want to tell you, Jerry, boy, to tell you. So it'll make sense to me too . It's like I know - for sure - that I'm

THE AWAKENING

somebody good. Good, Jerry! Me! Like something so good is here, all around us, inside us Jerry. Inside us!. Good! Think of that!." His eyes were full of an urgency to have Jerry share his knowledge.

Jerry wanted to be sure he understood, that he would not minimize it all later."You're sure you're not imagining it all?"

Rodney met his eyes, a faint smile playing now,"No Jerry, I couldn't imagine anything at all like that. It was real, it was more real than we are now. It was so 'alive', man." He let the tears overflow and run down his leathery face without notice.

Jerry murmured,"Maybe the world is more, Rod. Maybe what you've just experienced is the way it really is and we just haven't noticed. Maybe it's really a lot more." He reeled in his forgotten line and absently adjusted it for casting." Once you remember, when we were fishing, we talked about that. That it might be."

Rodney nodded mutely. Then after several minutes he nodded again."Yeah, it's like you said, I remember. Only now it's me seeing it and it can't be believed, if it wasn't so real. Why I think Alice wouldn't even believe me. It is a wonder, a pure wonder."

Jerry nodded, again, he said softly,"It's a wonder to see things so clearly, to be able to See like that. It's what the Teachers call Seeing, Rod. Did you know that? It's a wonder but it does happen."

"How come I never seen it before, Jerry? You said it'd happened to you. I guess a lot of times, hasn't it." His voice sounded more firm, normal, he watched Jerry now with acute attention, "You're no older'n I am. How come I never did notice? Is it because I didn't go to the Center?"

Jerry was silent, while Rod sat, looking around, just nodding and smiling at things, as if recognizing something he never had noticed. Jerry heard him whisper a word or two. The sun glinted on the tears that coursed his face, and Jerry thought Rodney would have been the last person to have allowed them to stay without wiping them away. Then, he stood up, walked to the edge again and began silently throwing his line, a kind of joyous quiet in his straight thin body, he moved with wonderful rhythm and grace. Jerry smiled, he was glad Rodney was finally awake, finally knew what the world opened up into if one paid enough attention and allowed themselves to See.

Rodney turned to him suddenly, an anguish on his face,"Oh, now it seems like I'm goin' to lose it. What was so fine. I can't hold on - I don't want to lose it. I want to see it again, Jerry." Jerry saw real pain in his eyes.

"You will, Rodney. Now you know of it. You'll learn how to bring yourself to the edge of Seeing. It's a kind of focus, and then, like a leap out of yourself, there you'll be, Seeing. It will happen. But you could go talk to the Master Teachers too. They'll teach you how to focus attention to that point where you can See! But you have to ask them. "

Rodney slowly shook his head, a rueful smile softening that pain, "Funny, I thought I couldn't bear it, so fine it was, but now, I think I can't bear not Seeing it again. Not knowing." He was silent for some time, then he said, "Maybe I'll just go in to the Center with my kids in a day or two. I'd like to see just what they're doing in there anyway."

They fished in companionable silence for some time. Rodney drew in a fine trout, playing it, lost in the skill of it, utterly absorbed and finally he stood taking it off the hook, proud and delighted with himself. He said, "It's something, isn't it,Jerry. And this here is too. This fish. It's a gift, that's what it is, a gift. Everytime I fish I think that. Alice always tells me that it's God. She says God is around us, right here now. She says that she can see that. She won't ever tell me how. I don't know what she sees but she says it's God, like a light . Do you see that Jerry? Now, I wonder if it isn't the same thing I saw." He asked the question so simply, like a child inquiring that Jerry's smiled.

He nodded, for he thought the two were the same; what Alice sensed and called God, and what Rodney had known this day. Rodney had turned again to the River. "God!." he said softly, "I don't know many prayers but my Alice does. She'll tell me how. I won't make fun of her ever again either. She'll be glad of that". The brief admission cost him a lot. The wonder was fading and he felt the sudden sense of loss. But Jerry had said he would be able to 'See' again, and he trusted his friend. He had to trust.

Jerry said goodbye to Rodney,after a little time, and buttoning his shirt against the cold air now blowing off the water, put his fishing gear into his box and prepared to leave. He must get home. He wanted to see Silvia, for one thing. Though he didn't know whether she would be there.

As he left the river woods, a flash of movement caught his eye,down the path. There, through a copse of hazelnut bushes, he thought he saw some one. But the path turned just beyond it and was hidden behind a bend of the hillside. He grinned,looking at the hazelnut trees where they had gathered their winter supply of nuts when they first came to the Farm and food was not so plentiful as now. People had chosen to work, without pay, to build their town, as long as there was enough for everyone to eat, and eating together had made the whole town a family. They had kept planting until now there was a supply of nuts, of fruits and many vegetables, everywhere. People could survive without much trouble, even if the towns fell apart, or someone was lost in the forests. The practice of developing food crops with high concentration of nourishment and planting them everywhere, for people and all other creatures, was in his opinion, one of the best things Valley people had done. He smiled, people were learning to care.

His thoughts were cut off suddenly when he saw Silvia coming from around the bend. She was walking slowly, glancing here and there, as if looking for something. Then she saw him. For a moment he thought she was going to run away. Then as if catapulted by some inner fear, she suddenly ran the short distance to him, her face full of anxiety. He caught her in his arms, his grin of welcome gone, concern wrinkled his forehead.He held her close, feeling a trembling in her that slowly relaxed. She drew away.

She lifted her head, shaking it in a characteristic gesture to reestablish her

THE AWAKENING

dignity, and then said,"Jerry there's something I've got to ask you."

He nodded, puzzled again,,knowing that something here was very important, wanting to Reach, to Touch but knowing he must not. She kept her gaze on his face, then suddenly looked at the ground, rubbing one foot there, like a child searching for words. It was so unlike her that he worried. "Jerry,I need to know - do you know - have you ever _ ?" she glanced up almost defiantly, and then with a gesture of dispair, she said,"Do you know what a 'true Mate' is? Do you know how to tell when one is found?"

He wanted to laugh, to cheer, to shout for joy, but he held himself still. "Yes, I have. I know that it's a person you cannot get out of your mind, even after that feeling of being in love is gone, they stay there, just solid. As though they are part of your very self." He said it softly "So the person just seems to sit there waiting for you to notice. And my heart is so full of love for her it surrounds her whenever she is near." He added the last with deep seriousness, then smiled broadly, his eyes tender.

She looked surprised, but she took his arm and leaned faintly toward him,"Is there such a person, someone there who waits for you?"

"There sure is. Been there a mightly long time too. I've been impatient for her to notice." He was suddenly enjoying himself.

She spoke sharply, a hesitance of anger and of fear in her voice,"Who then? Who?"

"Why, my sweet Silvia, of course. You, my darling! You!" At her droop of relief,then return of anger at the teasing, he went on hurriedly, realizing that teasing at a time like this was a mistake, "Only you, Sweetheart, ever settled in my heart, my mind, so immoveably. You've been there for at least two years without another even touching me. You are the one I cannot forget, the one who is my true Mate." He grinned now, forgiving himself for her anger, his delight apparent in his whole body,"The only woman I will ever be committed to is you, Silvia." Suddenly his face was serious, his eyes soft and so loving, she forgave him herself. He took the hand that lay on his arm into his own and drew her slightly closer, then stopped. She must come herself.

She asked, her eyes holding his,"Why didn't you tell me?"

"I didn't know it myself, you know, until last year. Or rather, I wouldn't believe it was real, because, I suppose, I wasn't finished exploring other - other partners." He flushed and was surprised that he was embarrassed.

She studied his face, then with a faint sound she rushed into his arms, wrapped her arms around his neck in an embrace that did not intend release. Neither of them could remember such feeling, such tender pain of hunger for one another, as if they had been lost.

"Oh, Jerry, it's so. It is so. I cannot make any other choice, and for that I grieve for Ned, for I know he loves me. And yet, it was there before me all the time. I just didn't think that you - you - " She drew back, looked at him with a frown, " But you should have told me, helped me choose?"

He shook his head, "Maybe I should have at least let you know, more than I did. You know that I've told you more than once that I love you, Sweetheart. You know that. But I had to let you choose. It wouldn't have been right if I influenced your jugdement, now would it?" He felt a sudden apprehension, seeing that it might have turned out differently.

"She was exasperated, "Oh,Jerry, Oh, my Dear Love, you over did it. I thought you were not feeling the same feelings. If Ben hadn't encouraged me, I might have, might not have," she didn't finish,"Oh, don't ever let things go like that again, not something this important. You should have told me that you knew we were Mated. Ned did."

Jerry was astonished,"He did? How can it be? There can't be two true Mates!"

She shook her head, "No, no, he told me WE were mated, you and I".She leaned again into his arms, they stood,kissing one another's neck, arms, and faces, and their talk was a series of murmurs."He knew, even though he didn't want to admit it."

He shuddered, "Wow, Ned is something, isn't he? He's our friend the way few could be. But then, Ned would have asked you, wouldn't he? He didn't wait for you to try to figure it out, did he?"

She shrugged,"Let's not worry about it now, it's all right. Just remember in future don't be careless with our lives." She nestled in his arms, her small body finding curves that fit it in his long lean frame. "You're a part of me, Love, you belong with me, and I with you. It's true." She sighed now with a relief, vast wonderful relief .They felt again something of that earlier feeling of being in love, yet this was deeper, richer, full of something that seemed to touch to their very centers. The joy of it, released doubts, was profound. Their lips began searching now for lips and their talk ceased. She finally drew back, turned a little to his side, and looking up at his face, she laughed,"Then you've known? You've known all along? About our child, everything?"

"Yes, I kept telling myself it would all work out. I kept trying to reinforce my faith that things would work out for the best. And if a person has to do that, there's something wrong, I should've known better. I heard a month ago that it can happen that the Mating sense if not returned can bring terrible reactions, but that may be superstition. At any rate I nearly panicked. It's what brought me out today to do some hard work and think. Rodney helped. He thought I ought to tell you right away. He thought I was insane to wait."

She grinned, as they began to walk on toward home."Rod is sensible, if nothing else. He's right. I'll tell him so. He isn't handicapped by too much thinking." She glanced up at him, herself teasing now. He stopped, smiling down at her, tears in his eyes, he lifted her chin gently, their eyes met, their lips met again, a long sweet kiss, and he forgot everything for that long moment, except that it was all right finally. Then, turning back, he collected his fishing gear and they began walking home.

THE AWAKENING

It was two days later that Jerry met Rodney again. His friend had been waiting for him near the barn, knowing Jerry would come to groom and ride General. The stallion had been gone for some time, roaming the mountain pastures, he'd obviously been in a fight, perhaps trying to take a harum from another stallion, but Jerry heard him call the night before and had gone to talk to him, dress his wounds and feed him good mash. The four mares with him shied a little at Jerry's presence, but accepted the feeding with a tolerance and intelligent assessment of this strange man their Stallion loved. Jerry whistled as he came to the barn, and General nickered. Rodney stood as Jerry approached and went diffidently to meet him. "Jerry, you got a little time to talk?"

Jerry stopped in mid stride, surprised, "Rodney! Yes, sure thing, we can talk while I groom General. And if they'll let me, the mares. What's on your mind."

Rodney twisted his jacket in his hands. He'd taken it off in the rising heat of the morning and his face was eloquent with worry. "It's what happened, the other day! Remember?" He waited for Jerry's nod and then looking away over the hills past Adwin, he went on, "I just can't get used to it. I haven't even told Alice. Thought she'd think I was bonkers." He frowned heavily and then went on, "You see, Jerry, it was so - so - strange for a plain man like me. I can't think it was meant for me. You see, it was probably you, being there, that did it, don't you suppose?" He looked with hope at Jerry.

"No, Rodney, it wasn't me. It was you. Whatever happened happened for you and within youself. You know, you have to realize that what the teachers say is real. Is right."

"I don't know much about that. I never did get finished with schooling, don't go to the Center much. Though now - . Well, anyway, it was just something -- it was too --there was too much Goodness in it. That's it, Jerry, strange as it sounds, Just plain Goodness, and I'm not the one for that. It was so _ so very fine, so full of something - something - I think is only for better people than me." He shook his head, as if trying to dislodge thoughts he couldn't make right. "I'm not fit, not fit for that kind of thing."

Jerry nodded, "Well, there you are, Rod. That's what the Master Teacher's told us. You should come to the Center more often and talk to them. They're real fine people, you know. They'd be glad to talk to you now too."

"No, you tell me, Jerry, that's what I came for. Thought maybe you could tell me what they said. Anyway, I don't know how they could know. They're not even my friends."

Jerry sighed, caught Rodney's arm and drew him into the barn where General was quietly eating in a sunny stall. The mares, moved restlessly, pushing at the stall doors, unsure of this confinement. But Jerry's morning feeding settled them. They began work on General which included changing a couple of bandages on the most serious wounds.. "Let's talk while I get General ready. Then we could go for that long walk through the far west mountains. We'll do some tracking practice too." He grinned at Rodney over the horse's back. "I'd ride if General weren't hurt. I need to get away from home for a time." He got brushes and began work , brushing out the loosening winter coat, feeling the warm strength of him, General turned to look curiously at the two of them, and nudged Jerry's hand, huffling at him.

Jerry frowned, searching, he wanted to say the right thing. "Rod, they tell us that it's only natural that most of us will feel that way. Like we don't deserve such a wonder, such a 'Goodness" as you put it. And yet, what you saw is just the beginning. There's so much more. You'll see, next time." He had almost become lost in his own thoughts, remembering and feeling again the beauty of them.

"You mean it'll happen again? The same wonder?" Rodney's voice was full of both hope and fear. At Jerry's nod, he frowned, then asked, "Your teachers taught you those things? Talked about it?"

" Sure, Rod. That's what they're for,the Master Teachers especially. But they don't talk much unless you ask, you know." He turned to study Rod's face, "I'm not sure why they want us to ask. In fact I hadn't thought about that until now. But it's true. You have to ask. But I've heard them say that when a person first perceives that Touch of the Light he often does feel unworthy, like he wasn't fit for it."

"Well, that may be, though it's hard to think on. But I know I'm a pretty sorry piece and there's no way to think I'm the one meant for it. You know what I mean."

"Rodney, listen to me. You have to know too. All of us do. It's not something has to do with learning, or being a town man, it's something has to do with - with - well,your heart, maybe, your being something inside youself. I guess if you asked Alice about that, she'd tell you you're worth it." He grinned and at Rodney's hopeful face, he went on. "You know Rod, what they said is that a person's mind begins to break through old patterns,to open up to what's really out there all the time, only we don't see it, we're too blind with our own - our own stuff, our thoughts, and our assumptions of things. You know we keep assuming things are a certain way, the way we like them to be, or the way they make sense to us, and it's not necessarily so. Then, a time comes when you're not thinking, just aware, being there, like when you were so quiet fishing. I think then you were completely present and the Light broke through!" he stopped, "Wasn't it like that?"

Rodney nodded, "I guess that would say how it was. I wasn't thinking about anything at all, just feelin' the air and the water, there, the way the sun was making the water shine and the strength in the water. You know, Jerry the way the water seems to be curving all around inside, like it's alive, nearly?" He frowned again,,the memory rousing itself. "It was as if I was gone and everything was there instead!" He shrugged, "That make any sense?"

"That's it exactly, Rod, you were so open, ready, aware. You don't know how willing you were, but there it was, you were able to See. You could See beyond all the - the habits." He finished lamely, not able to find better words.

Rodney was watching him,but he wasn't comfortable watching some one else work while he stood idle. He took another brush and began brushing the

THE AWAKENING

General's other side. Their hands rhythmically stroking, they found comfort in the familiar task. Jerry stopped a moment, met Rodney's eyes, General turned again, their start and stop brushing was puzzling him."Rod, just remember that the rest of us get scared too. It's always like that. Touching that - that goodness, makes a person feel like punk, because we can't imagine it's for us. It did open your eyes, didn't it?"

Rodney's eyes narrowed, searching his friend's face for signs of a joke. Then he nodded, "Yeah, I suppose you'd say just that. That was it."

"Well, then - seeing that - must make you realize that you wouldn't have seen or known, if you weren't good enough. You must see that there's something in you, right inside you, that is that Goodness. It's really what you saw, your own self, looking then, at the world."

"Aw, Jerry, you're kiddin'. Ain't nobody gonna believe that." He started stroking again, is face softened, a strange longing filling his eyes, "But maybe Alice would."

"Seeing what you are, that there's that very Goodness in you! In you, Rod! It's all part of what's there, the wonder of things, that's what it is. You're part of it, all of it."

Rodney shook his head, "Well, it's still a puzzle. Maybe I'll get to that place again, and then I'll pay attention. So far, I keep thinking about it so strong I can't stop thinking, and then, I can't feel quiet inside, the way I always used to. It's tore me up, you know!" He looked sadly over to Jerry, then back to his work. "Strange, I never had that trouble before. But I'd like it - I'd like to See that again, to feel that." He shook his head again in solemn hope."It's seeing what I am inside myself then ? You think that's it ?"

Jerry nearly gasped, the insight was so unexpected,"That's it exactly, Jerry old friend."

For a long time Rodney went on with his work, leaning to clean the dust from the horses belly and legs, and then, setting both hands on the broad red back, so high these tall men could see little more than each other's eyes, he sighed and said,"Well, there it is then, isn't it? I guess I've got to do it, to look at myself a little? Notice how I am. Maybe I'd better come to the Center with my kids sometime." He chuckled,"They go there often enough,,seem to be always there for something."

Jerry nodded, pleased and nearly holding his breath, wanting so much for this friend to grasp that a real difference had come into his life. "You mean pay attention more?"

"Yes, I guess that's it. Isn't that what your Teacher's taught you? " At Jerry's nod, he nodded too."I think my kids're learning that way. Sometimes they look at me kind of strange, sometimes when I'm showing them the fields, or maybe taking them into the hills."

Jerry grinned, "I know about that, Rod. I've watched you too, listened to you. You've got a deep rapport, a kinship to this Earth like few others, except maybe Jane. You're amazing when you show us the forests. It's like you feel them in you. That's what you watch for now. Be conscious of it!"

Rodney grinned finally, set his brush down and stood aside, "Well, I suppose I could do that. I noticed my kids was learning things I didn't know, but I never thought it was things like this." He wiped his hand across his cheeks and for the first time Jerry realized he had been crying. "Well, then, I'd better get home, "This time, I really will tell my Alice." He turned, then stopped, "About that tracking practice, I'll meet you at the tree where we were theother day, in two hours. That about right?"

Jerry nodded,"Suits me fine, It'll take me that long to get these mares to let me clean them up and check for hoof problems. One of them seemed to me to be limping a little." He saw Rodney's nod and watched as he walked out of the barn and disappeared into the sunlight.

CHAPTER TWENTY SIX

New understanding for Ben and Jessie

Anna moved with alternating silence and effervesant joyousness through family life. She seemed born with a wonderful tolerance and gentle acceptance of others. All griefs, joys, successes and failures were to her interesting and she could accept them with equanimity. She could give such total attention to others that the need for approval was satisfied for them without ever having been noticed, and even when she didn't agree with them. She did not have to learn, as Andy did, that feelings came and went, and that assumptions based on them were not necessarily valid. She knew intuitively that many people needed to talk out their feelings in order to understand themselves, they might need to search about in those feelings for what was real and permanent. She was willing to listen because people interested her. She could hear someone berating himself for short-comings and never assume those short comings were real, as Andrew would have done. But she did not assume they weren't either. She stood in observance not in judgement. She was aware that she often found herself mirrored in others, and thought they might notice themselves in her. She knew that most people struggled to define themselves through talk.

Listening to people, Anna usually found herself thoughtful afterward, contemplating, trying to fit all she realized into some understanding of humankind. She did not know it then, but she had begun to understand people the way one trained as a Monitor would, though her perceptions were not yet clear. When she took her testing in her sixteenth year, she was marked for watching. She would be trained soon. She had a strong Reach, and her Joining was already acute without training. Those with the qualifications to be trained as Monitors must live in a Station during intensive training. Growth changes in the brain and other parts of the body, could cause untold anguish if not properly managed and guided. Such people needed solitude and care until they were fully developed. So Anna was carefully watched.

Her peer group was seen by those watching minds to effect real growth among its members . They had created a harmony that managed to absorb and bring into balance every disruption that occurred. Anna knew intuitively how to enter into relationship so that communication seldom failed. It was the nature of all Valley peer groups to be especially alert to building self esteem. As a result there were few people who lacked a healthy sense of self value. Anna sensed those wounded by poor self esteem instantly and somehow they ended up in her groups. She was seldom leader, but her position did not matter. She knew that the basic problem solving skills, and inter-relationship skills that were taught in the Center, must be honed and polished in the interaction of the group, and in daily life, and she had grown acutely conscious of these processes. Now, when

THE PEOPLE OF THE VALLEY

she found an adult whose self esteem was genuinely poor, who must resort to devious devices to insist on his position among others, (a position she saw as his right) she was deeply troubled.

In this summer of her sixteenth year she met Henry. He had wondered into the Valley from points north from whence he had been encouraged to leave. Anna felt some lack in him, some distress that clung to him and flung itself out toward anyone he was with. As if he sought constantly to relieve himself, to justify himself. It made her uncomfortable, but more, it demanded her attention. She must try to help. It was as if some committment toward others lived in her and she could not deny any true need. Neither would she be fooled by false need. It was especially this ability to distinguish that pleased those who watched.

Her natural good manners prevented any Reaching into his mind, emotions, to find the cause of the distress, but since he did not respond to her tentative Reach, she must wait and watch. He saw all others as more capable, more of value. But worse, he didn't know that and so tried to prove himself constantly, or to criticize others. He did not revert to normal good self esteem with a little help. She was pained by the obvious discomfort he lived with. He was forever searching for what he believed was a lack in himself, yet perversely denying that very lack. Unlike most Valley people, he didn't know the cause of his distress. It was, for Anna, as if she had met someone 'self blind'.

On one afternoon when she was on her way home from Learning Center, she met him and they talked a while. When she left him, worried again, she hurried home, she must talk to her parents. Surely one or the other must be home. Anna had learned long since that there were people who 'would' not Reach as distinguished from those who 'could' not. She accepted that difference as she did all others, with calm . People could be different and she did not tax herself with worry about that, as Andrew did.

When she entered the Hall she found Benjamin with Jessie talking. Jessie was drinking iced tea, Ben an iced beer. The weather had become warm enough to warn of a hot summer ahead. She kissed them both, wanting that comfort. Then she sat down and took the tall glass of tea Ben handed her. He looked at her, thoughtfuly, "What's on your mind, Sweetheart?" Jessie met Anna's eyes and nodded.

"Daddy, Mother, I'm worried about a man in town. He hasn't been here long and there's something wrong --- either with him or with me." She felt frustration , a hint of anger and a growing sadness. Something at the edge of her mind told her the cause but she could not grasp it.

Ben nodded, "Well, Anna, what's his name. Would it be Henry?"

She was startled, almost Reached, but her family taboos restrained her as much as good manners. "How could you know, Daddy?

"Because a lot of us have been worried about him and because we know something of your sensitivity to people. What's he done now?"

"Oh, it's all the things he says. For weeks, he's been talking about how hopeless life is, how hopeless --HE is. He thinks people don't like him, people he works with. Says he fails at everything he tries. He took a job helping the Master Farmer, said he thought it would be simple enough for him and then he couldn't do it. Farming is an exacting science you know, but more than that it is an art and he - well, he didn't expect that. He said it hurt his feet, and it was shit work. You know he has few usable skills and he hates to take time to learn. Then he started helping in the film rooms, and within three weeks he quit because there were too many kids coming in there. He found a cubicle and went on a film binge. Did nothing but watch films all day and half the night for -- must have been six months at least. That's where I first knew him. I'd see him there so much. He said -" she stopped, sipped a long drink of iced tea, wiped the beads of perspiration from her forehead, "for us to stay out of his way. We didn't bother him but we worried about him. Why hadn't the Healers done something?" She stopped again, anger in her eyes, then she said," Finally he made himself sick of films I think, but it's always the same, no matter what he starts, he's soon wondering around with nothing to do so we run into him a lot and his dispair worries us. There he is, sitting looking miserable, then today I overheard him telling some one that he was planning suicide. Not as though it was a choice, but as though he just didn't have a choice." She struggled to keep tears from her eyes, but failed.

"So you think it's your problem, eh?" Ben asked.

She shook her head,"I don't know, but I end up feeling guilty somehow. My peer group says I'm trying to rescue him from himself but how can I live with a person so miserable and not feel some guilt? We're responsible for each other, you know. I have to do something."

Ben nodded, met Jessie's eyes. Jessie to his surprise was smiling faintly, her eyes watchful. Ben said, "You can't feel otherwise. Any Valley citizen would, so don't feel wrong about it. But you see, Henry's been around long enough that we know of him and the community is doing what can be done, Sweetheart. You've done what you can, you've told the adults responsible. It's just that you need to leave it up to us. We'll deal with it. " He sighed,"I'm sorry we've been so slow, so that you kids had to worry, but you see, he won't go to the healers. He won't look at himself to see what's wrong. It's as though he really wants to be miserable."

He drew a long breath,"At one time I thought I'd just let him be miserable. " Ben grinned at her disbelief, "Well, it's true there are such people. Until they come to some choice to help themselves there's not much we can do. We can't force them to the Healers unless they're dangerous. Although now that you heard him talking of suicide we could maybe. Can you leave him to us, Anna dear. We'll attend to it, now that you've prodded our attention again. " He was smiling now and she came to sit for a moment on the arm of his chair. Leaning to kiss his cheek she felt his strong hairy arm surround her and draw her to him.

She smiled, nodding. "I'd appreciate that, Dad. I don't know what to do with him." She went to kiss Jessie good bye, taking her hand for a second as if seeking her comfort.

When she had gone, Jessie shook her head." There's one more sign, Benjamin, that she's ready for her training. We'll have to send her out in a year at

THE PEOPLE OF THE VALLEY

least. The Monitor training is intensive but she'll do well. She must learn to live beyond her emotions even more than she already has." At his look, she waved a hand, "Don't think she'll lose that wonderful tenderness and sensitivity; she won't. She'll just not suffer from her own or other people's emotions."

Ben looked at her with consternation, "But she'll be gone from us then, won't she Jessie? Monitors don't live any more with their people, do they?"

She smiled, "They can and do visit often. Remember they have skills that allow them to arrive home when you least expect them. She'll not forget her family, although eventually you'll be only one more part of her true family, which will be all humanity."

He looked at her then, sympathy stirring his heart, "Then it's been so with you too? You left your own children and your Mate, didn't you?"

She nodded, "My Mate had died by then." A shadow passed across her eyes, then cleared into a radiant smile. "My children were grown though, you know. It's why I went for training so late. And of course, I've seen them more often than many Monitors see their blood family." She was silent, "But let's think of Henry, there's something to be done. What do you plan?"

He got up. "I'm going to talk it over with Tom, since we have already discussed Henry he knows and he'll settle it. He's mayor after all. It's his job, No?" He grinned and she smiled at his sly look.

" Most sensitive people in Adwin know of Henry, and the few others like him. They'll support Tom's decision. But who besides Tom?"

"Well, maybe Rose, but she's pretty busy right now. There're a lot of good people in Town. You've found that out?" She nodded and he said, "I'm surprised Anna was worrying about him so much."

Jessie shook her head, "You shouldn't be, if you watched your children closely. You've let yourself be blind to what's happening to them, Ben?"

Ben frowned, annoyance in his voice, "What do you mean?"

"What do you know about those two?"

"Why, I know --" He stopped, flustered seeing she meant more than the usual school activity and social life, etc. He took a deep breath and started again, "She's a very sensitive young lady, and strong, and aware, aware of more than most people." He stopped, "I realized that at the Gathers. Though I'd never admitted it before. And now --" he frowned, aware he still avoided all the facts. But when you say Anna's to enter Monitor training." He frowned, looked away. "I wouldn't have guessed that."

Jessie nodded, "That's true, but you don't know, or won't speak of the important things about them. Remember when she showed us the images of Andrew? She knew and knew something's wrong. Did you know? And what've we done even yet?"

Ben squirmed, unwilling to listen and knowing he must. He sat down, then got up and refilled their glasses, stalked about a moment, "All right, what're you getting at. I just feel my mind going blank."

She was silent and finally he shrugged, "All right, maybe I don't - haven't, wanted to know. Anna's always puzzled me, more than Andrew has. But both of them - puzzle me." He glanced at her angrily, composed his face and then allowed himself to frown again, "Damn it Jessie,, it's why I shied clear of you the first two times I ran into you. The times friends sent me to you. You won't let things rest, will you? You scared me and I told myself you were a meddler." He heaved a sigh, watching her face, only a trace of a smile visible in her eyes. "Well, all right, I know things are different now, we've got to look at things and I - I do want to. I know I've got to pay attention to what I've avoided seeing in my own children. So help me to see it."

"I see that you avoid knowing about your children and that seems very dangerous." She had met his eyes and he did not twist away.

"Dangerous? I wouldn't have thought that. Careless maybe, foolish even, but not dangerous." He was frowning.

"Wouldn't you consider it dangerous for any person not to know all his assets when he is in danger? Or to know the strengths and weaknesses of his friends?"

"You mean my kids might effect what's happening now? Might effect the changes in this Valley? The eruptions the Builders are causing, the rest of it?" He paused, thoughtful, troubled.

"And the "rest of it' is what is the greatest danger. Unless you know, how can you protect, or guide anyone?" She deliberately used words that she knew would catch at his attention.

"Protect? Jessie, you think we are really in danger here then? Our very Valley life is being threatened?" When she simply met his gaze, he nodded finally, and said, "All right, I don't know enough about it. I need to learn." Then settling down again in his chair, he waited. Her eyes moved off across the room to the windows from which she could look across to Adwin. As he watched the small lined face, serious and relaxed, a great fear rose, swept like a pain through him, and was itself swept away by a growing confidence in Jessie. He felt the strength in her, felt it and realized it was reaching around him, touching, available to him. Now he knew he had been depending on that strength without acknowledgement. He thought, "With such strength available to us, we don't need to fear." The thought jolted him, he had not thought that he had feared, but more, he did not want to rely on another so. He had always thought of himself as offering strength to others, not needing it. If HE feared, and hadn't admitted it, what of other people? How much were they all dependent on such people as Jessie, on the trust in Monitors rather than on themselves? Wasn't THAT a danger?

He brought his thoughts back to Jessie and found her looking at him quietly, a slight smile straightened her lips, her eyes were gentle, shining upon him. At that look he was flooded with a sharp clear light that swiftly illuminated his mind and his heart. Just for one instant, but it was enough. Was it Light? Or did it seem so only because he could not else identify the unfamiliar? Nevertheless, he knew what she meant, saw the shadow that was his own fear slip aside, saw his children before him. He recognized what he had denied. And the effect was overwhelming. He slumped down numbly into his chair, looked with unseeing eyes across the room and tried to assimilate the realizations about himself along with everything else.

After a while he said, "Jessie, I'm flooded with questions, but first of all ,how did you do that? You literally opened my mind as though a door was turned into a window. But wait, that isn't even so important. It's WHAT I just realized, not how, What happened just now?"

She smiled and said softly,"Put it into words."

He nodded, as if she reinforced his own thought."I believe I just looked into myself, looked through a window that's been there all along.

Yes, through that I see how I've refused to see the 'greatness' in our children.I can't find another word. That's it.'Greatness'! They've been giving me evidence, and I've been refusing to admit it. I kept telling myself they're just kids and they're our children and they can't be more than that." I didn't want them to be." He took a deep breath and said reluctantly,"They far surpass me, surpass Rose even. What can we do? All these years, they've been protecting me - us, and I'm their father". The words ripped from him in searing pain. "Ben the protector, the one who is supposed to care for them. Whose strength they could count on. I have been carefully protecting myself from the facts." He shivered through himself, contempt and tears flooded his voice. '

She shook her head,"You have,Benjamin, you've known, but you've refused to admit it. You've also denied yourself the enjoyment of their beauty." She frowned, then looked sharply at him,"Your worry that you might become dependant on Teachers, or on Monitors, that is a genuine worry. It's why we won't teach unless we are asked. You're right. You must be dependant on yourself."

He looked at her bleakly, his heart sore. "Oh,Jessie, don't think I can't see, the way I've been the blustering boss man, the one who would see that every thing was taken care of, would look after the family. It's been my image, for myself at least. It's false, as false as a lie. Being dependant on yourself doesn't mean refusing to ask for help, but I've refused." He shook his head, brought his feelings into balance and said, quietly, "You know more of my own children than I do. Their own father. They see, hear, know in ways I only begin to imagine. In that one instant you wiped away a blinder and I do see, more than I want to admit. Their consciousness includes what I quail to even glimpse and it is as natural to them as drinking water. That makes them seem unnatural to me. Or has, until now." He drew a long trembling sigh,shaking his head as if he had to force the words."They have minds developed into levels of Spirit that I fear to acknowledge and it is radiant within them and when I really look I can see that and it frightens me and it -- makes me envious. There, that's a fact and I'm ashamed."

She said, "Ben, be at ease,Son, You have forever been too prone to blame yourself.It's an indulgence you've got to forsake."

" Not now, when that blame is right. It's true, it's what they do. They drink of Spirit. It is in them, and visible through their lives. And I have denied."

She spoke more sternly than he had ever heard her, "Ben, you could not even see that, or see their radiance this moment, if you were not of the same nature ."

He spoke as if he had not heard, yet her words worked in his mind,"Oh, it's that, that quality of Love in them. They breathe the Love you constantly walk in. I HAVE known, I have, and would not speak it. I feel the terrible energy of that Love and am afraid." He shook his head again , his face a mask of pain. Besides, how can I treat my children like -- children, when they're -- they're so -" He shook his head in dispair.

"Benjamin, one fault you do not have is self pity. And one virtue you do have is self honesty, almost until it is itself a fault. But it's not as bad as it seems to you just now. You are so far on your own way to self knowledge, and even more, to SELF knowledge. Already that Light burns through you like a beacon, visible to more people than you know. And visible to your children." She let the statement soak in, sitting silent for several minutes.

Then, when he glanced up, accepting a little, she went on, " Consciousness of Soul-Self, grows in you, and you know that. Acknowledge your Self. You are included in that Self, you know." Her eyes still smiled, but her face was serious, not yet ready to show her joy at his revelation. "Perhaps now we must only consider those of the family who have denied themselves in order not to disrupt your --"

He broke in ,"Not to hurt my blown up ego, you mean? Yes,I can see that."His tone was still full of fury at himself,."We've done that to a lot of our young ones in this Valley. And has that denial prevented them from maturing properly? Well, I don't know, Jessie. Has it?" grief pushed his voice louder.

"You forget the Master Teachers, but even more, the Monitors who watch and who will not allow the destruction of these developments among our people." She spoke more positively than usual.

"Well, I'm going to change it. I'm going to be one who recognizes these things publicly! I have work to do, I see that." He stood up again,"How could I have been such a fool?"

"Self criticism won't help much now, you know. You see what you have been blind to. That's a new start, a growth. Let's let it be." He saw her face, the radiance of joy in it, the delight she felt was obvious, no longer hidden.

"Oh, Jessie, you work so steadily among us, sometimes I wonder how you can see so much and not dispair, and here you are overjoyed." He turned glumly toward the windows. "Look, there is weather coming to fit my mood. Clouds gathering up from the west. Dark and heavy, they're inexorable, hovering down and making dark the land. That kind of weather can sit over us for days and finally end in gentle steady rain. That one looks like such a one" Then for a time they were silent, watching the gathering roll of clouds. "I've sought all my life for what was already here in my own home, right in the place I lived. I could not see."

He longed to accept this truth about himself. He thought of the long journeys, the leaving of his family and their grief at that, their loss of him. The years of false teachers, and his dispair, the dead end paths and the coming home again thinking he had failed. And all because he could not, no, would not, See." What he realized hurt like fury but it also released and healed. He was silent for several long minutes, then he drew a long deep breath,absorbing, accepting.

Finally,he turned to her and relief was obvious in his face. Joy stirred in him. He wanted to run to her, to catch her up in his arms, to hug her as a son might his mother, but he did not. Something in her quiet self possession, her stillness, held him motionless. To act so just now seemed foolish.

He leaned forward in his chair, reached out both hands and held them there, palms up, waiting. She looked at him, smiled as she entered into the game. She laid one hand on each of his. For several seconds they remained thus, touching, warmth of skin to skin, he felt the intimacy of that moment. Then he wrapped his large hands around her small ones, giving the promise of his strength, his protection, for what it was. He vowed silently that he would be to her as a son, as perhaps he had been to some degree already. He became aware that a radiance filled the room. He could feel strong currents of energy flowing through his hands from hers, like a steady pulse of electricity, it traveled up his arms and down through his body. He felt fear - then swiftly renewed joy. He checked the impulse to pull away, instead, tightened his hold.

Sustaining contact, he began to notice a grid of resistance that lodged in his mind, acted like a barrier so that the flow of energy was balked. Gradually he could see it literally as though an eye had been opened. He looked into himself, feeling a swaying astonishment, but too much fascination not to continue. These were his own barriers, a tangle of emotions, of habits, of fear and pride, laced and jumbled so that they were difficult to sort out. He shrank, fought to avoid the sight of this. But she was so calm, so utterly steady and he began to settle into acceptance, to watch and to see himself there, a tangle of misunderstandings, a shadowy confusion.

With the energy flowing into him came radiance, it brought a faint, then growing lightedness into the shadowy tangle. He began to relax, to recognize himself, to realize he stood before a point of Light from which energy ran like a clear cool water into his mind. He could observe himself without shame, or dispair, a cool detached interest. And what he saw he could accept. Such as that, he was. The recognition was pain but the pain drained away in that gathering Light. He loosened from the obsession of himself, felt his awareness lift, was there, beyond himself.

He stood, lifted in renewed identity out of the tangle, he knew himself a part of his Self. He was Self conscious. The tangle of his life was illuminated from within, as though light bloomed through all of him. He was alive, AWARE as he had never been. A dual identity, the greater smiling in loving amusement at the lesser.

The image of a great window opening, flickered before his eyes. From that window he could see beyond himself, beyond his life even. Fresh new vistas beckoned, possibility such as he could not have imagined, was there, simply

THE AWAKENING

there and he was part of it. Understanding flooded his mind, Yes, there was so much more to this world, to this universe - to himself - than he had dreamed possible, because he had locked possibility out at that point of denial. He had not called it denial, but rather objectivity. And he saw now that he had not been objective after all. His vision seemed to him to be finally cleared and he could see what had always been there. Had always been HERE.

Jessie Reached. Benjamin's old mental-emotional patterns faded, but he felt them briefly resist before he reasserted his own strength and responded. He, Benjamin, so resistant, so many years demanding absolute 'scientific ' proof, stood now within the proof itself, part of it. He could not duplicate it at all nor demonstrate its reality to anyone at all. Neither could he deny. He not only Reached in return to her Touch, but held firm, full now of an awe of the dimensions of his own nature that he had denied. Of the nature of humankind itself. Yes, that was it,Soul is the nature of humanity! Jessie extended her Touch and Benjamin knew a little more of what it was to Join.

The delight of the Joining, the intimacy of it, amazed him. The sense of 'withness' drew his full confidence, but he knew his body was crying, was overwhelmed by emotion at this wonder. He wanted Rose to be here, didn't realize that he Reached for her until he felt Jessie's help. He felt the jolt of her Touch. Rose! Where was she? How could she know? He felt her with the two of them. It startled him. So strong, so sure. She was practiced. And he had denied himself this through years. Realization of that loss was like a blow. But her surprise and delight was reward. He felt her withdraw. But now, she knew!

Jessie left him abruptly,her eyes were laughing."Don't shout like that, unless you warn others first. You nearly shook me away."

His mouth fell open,"Of course, it would be like that. And of course you were with us". She was shaking her head, pleased - the Teacher whose pupil understands the Teaching. Gently she withdrew, They were clearly separate and it seemed so poor to him, so inadequate. The lesson in Joining had ended.

Her eyes were tender and sad when in a soft voice , revealing her own questioning, she said,"Benjamin, it's all to be learned. I too constantly learn. For all of us it is a beginning. You have taught me much, Son. I must grope my way sometimes too, not knowing the next step."

He studied her face, serious, a flicker of unsureness in her eyes that was quickly replaced by a curious amusement as if reprimanding herself. He felt astonishment at his prescience, that he could see so much. Sense it. He said,"It's a mystery to me how I could help you?"

She laughed. Oh, but you do see something of that. Just pay attention and notice how difficult it is to Reach to one who resists. Then there is the Law. We must not interfere unless we are invited. It was your invitation and your responsiveness that taught me. It is that way we learn together."

Slowly he withdrew his hands. "And to think, I wanted to offer YOU strength -- and protection."

For moments there was silence. He watched, listening within. The unbelieveable sense of responsibility accompanying this greater Self awareness frightened the old small Ben. How could he live up to this? He stared out across the fields and in a shift of vision saw the Valley as if for the first time. There was so much more there, so much more life, so much he had not imagined beyond the simple physical world his eyes saw. His mind saw and knew and marveled.

He turned to Jessie,"This thing that is happening to us,this disturbance in the Valley, among the people, it's what we've got to learn. We are creating it ourselves, all of us! There's no difference really between one group of us and another, we're simply growing at different rates. How amazing, the way seeing that fact clears my thinking,and changes my feelings. Just -- it's like magic, actually. We've got the past to put aside and the future to enter.I remember you told me that once." He liked talking out the thoughts this way. The 'wonder' faded a little. To experience wonder was without doubt, was just right. But to remember, as it faded, was uncomfortable. All the old assumptions re-erected themselves and brought vigorous doubt. But the knowledge was too firm, the doubt did not threaten it!

Her voice was quiet, "It's there for us, you know. It's in ourselves that the doing has to start, not out there. The Valley is an expression of ourselves, of ourselves exactly. We can look at it and see ourselves. As clear as the morning light. We must look at ourselves to know what we've been and then we can see what we are and what we are becoming. But we must look together, perhaps we cannot bear it alone. But we could not See alone either. It's a perception of Joined minds. Humankind seeing its true nature!"

Ben was nodding, wanting to understand."The Teachers told us about shadows, how the shadows block out the light. Now I know what they meant. I think I am my own shadow. I choose to recognize that Light that reveals me to myself. I feel fear, and I see my personal greed, lust, needs, and they show up big and terrible. No wonder I avoided it. The shame, the dispair of seeing myself is hard to bear." He wiped his hands over the tight mask of his face, then said in a whisper,"But to See, the way it was, the Light erased all the shadows, the Vision was clear and then, I did not fear. I do remember! I must remember! It's what we humans can be - if we help each other become."

She nodded, waiting,and he went on,"It's just that, Jessie. For us, we've been thinking we are invincible and now we see that we can easily be defeated by our own greeds, our own fears. Or we can literally transcend them! We really can!" He stopped, a raw tenderness ached within him, as though things had torn loose and been exposed to that Light that he could not forget. They sat silent again, then as if drawing himself out of depths he nodded.

"Whether the difference is only one of degree, it still exists and for us, living our daily lives, not always Self conscious, difference can become exaggerated. The Builders believe their difference is very real. They haven't the vision,the ability to See beyond themselves, they lack something and so what we See does not exist for them. Therefore we can't talk to them of it. What has just happened to me would be only insanity to them." He sighed, letting these familiar thoughts ease the strangeness he felt, sad that that was so."And yet, they too are ourselves."

For several moments there was silence, they let the realizations settle through their minds. Benjamin drew a long slow breath, his eyes sad, but beneath that sadness Jessie could see the underlying Joy. "Ah, The Builders, we've got to do something there, Jessie."

She nodded,"You have begun! The Council has permitted the use of some land. Has given them permission to use those acres east of Santiago that they took, and began to clear. They are already planting vines and fabric plants." She grinned then,"Did you hear what happened when one of their people went to the Vagabonds to 'make a deal' as he put it, to use Vagabond labor to do the designs and make dyes for this new fabric? They plan to make it in vast quantity so they need expert help." Ben shook his head,and she went on."They talked to the Vagabond Elders, and there must have been hundreds of their people there, listening. That's their way and the Salesman was discomfited. He'd wanted privacy. Couldn't imagine doing business without it. But finally he made his offer to pay steady credit for a few hundred workers. He said they'd build buildings along the Highways for them to do the work in, the Council was very serious. They told him that it was a deal if he could find the workers they needed. He was so tickled, thought he'd made a fine deal because the Elders didn't question the low credit he offered.

The Vagabonds hadn't even bothered to dicker with him. He thought they were pretty dumb, at that point. So he asked them to pass his sign up sheets out and all who wanted jobs could sign." She laughed softly. "The Council sent the sign up sheet to him a week later and there were five names listed. He thought they were holding out for more credit and offered it, but the Council took pity on him and told him that no Vagabond ever could design or create anything according to such a schedule, and that Vagabonds did not want their work on fabric that would not last a minimum of ten years and preferably much longer. And that they wouldn't stay indoors to work. That stopped him cold. Their fabric is MADE to wear out within two years of wear. We have finally learned how to make things to last, so people can be free for more important uses of their time. They want to go back to the old exploitation of human lives. I was sorry for them, actually, they were so disappointed, didn't understand. But then, I could not help but laugh. It was so typical of the Vagabonds. You can see how blind the Builder's are. So now, how do we teach them?"

Ben was smiling, imagining the Council of Elders dealing with that. Then he said,"It would be funny if it weren't so sad. But there are people who don't fit either us or the Builders. People who are blind to what we see, but who choose to live according to the Convictions regardless. Such people are great Souls, surely, Jessie, whether they have Talent or not. Whether they See or not!" His voice was full of sadness and a hint of anger. She heard it and trembled. Even here the anger lived.

"Ben,you may need to learn to bear grief. To meet and deal with anger more than ever in your life. Surely it would be better than to bear guilt. For no truly conscious person can harm another for his own benefit. If there is violence toward us, do you think we will meet it with like?" She watched him, seeing his mind pull one way then another, the conflict in him visible to her.

"He said, "Why, I don't know. People have always met violence with violence? Except for very special people. But the precedent was set with Ghandi in the twentieth century." He hesitated, then frowned. "I remember Andrew's reactions to his friends, and THEY see this as an adventure! See themselves as knights in shining armor come to the rescue! Jessie, that's dangerous!"

She nodded, "Finally, you see that. Have we learned enough? Are we CONSCIOUS enough? It remains to be seen, Ben, my Son. What we will do tests us. Just as the Vagabonds were tested." She was silent. "And what of another fourth group, those who cannot bear the test? Who know of the vision, who See, even Reach, but who choose the narrow way, the 'self' centered way to live?"

He looked at her, puzzled and then as he realized her question he was filled with a tremendous fear.

"But Jessie, you said those who See cannot harm others! How then can they choose the selfish way?"

"We always have choice. And so we choose according to the degree of our Vision and to the strength of Heart and of Mind!"

"My God in Heaven, Jessie, there it is. The shadow of the old way, the Shadow of the people together. The refusal of the Light, of the Vision. Can human beings stand beyond our own ego needs? We never have." He shuddered, "Can we See what we begin to See and still choose to live as separate animals, people of the past. How could that be? For such people would also have much power, much strength of their new knowledge. Even enhanced mind powers. If they chose ego over the Self, they could - could -turn that power to selfish ends. It would be, could be, pure hell."

She laughed at his terror, for he could see the most terrible possibilities. "Oh, wait Ben, there is yet hope. Those who are Master Teachers, have already passed that test. For them, the ego is a shell, a tool of that greater Self. It must be so before we can develop into full power of Self Consciousness. Then, what we know makes it very clear that selfishness is, literally, self defeating. The Self contains the self and functions in this physical world, through it. The very nature of Life sustains this dual life. Once the heart speaks those truths in our mind, we cannot deny Life." She spoke so quietly that Ben leaned forward to hear. He felt better, but the danger seemed great still.

He said, "Are you saying, Jessie, that there is some kind of limit, some control over our growth and awakening?" He recoiled at the thought and she felt it.

"No Benjamin, Not control. Ah, that word has become pejorative in our time and maybe just as well. But you saw how I could help you meet and pass beyond the barriers of your own habits and fears. I could not do that unless you were ready, unless you asked for help, which you did. Had I not done so, could you in this life time have thrown off those restrictions?"

"He shook his head, "Surely I HAD not, and I've been trying all my life. I could not!"

"You understand that when we are ready, when perception is clear, we see that all life is sacred, that we're not separate at all, but one life called Humanity. And we also know that all humankind is Joined in a great undertaking too much for us to comprehend. If you have experienced your own inner turmoil, seen yourself split into many conflicting parts which you must learn to integrate if you are to be healthy, then you see it is exactly so for humanity. We have to integrate ourselves as one consciousness. But first we have to see that we're NOT integrated. We have to know the reality of our nature. That's what scares and overwhelms us. It's what you said, when you see your own fear and lusts, your needs - you dispair. Imagine the same on a larger scale when as humanity together, we see that same depravity. It could sink us into an anguish of self disgust. In fact it did, a hundred or so years ago. We began to see what we were as a people, began to look at ourselves. We saw humankind killing and torturing, riddled with greed so that some died of hunger and others lived in opulence. We saw ourselves exploiting and being exploited. We saw ourselves! We began to fight among ourselves until wars exploded all over this Earth. We were so appalled we refused to remember our greatness. You experience the same process as a person."   " Oh, Jessie, is there hope for us? Surely,we aren't good enough."

"That sounds like some of that self contempt I mentioned." She was smiling.

He frowned and shook his head."But we do have to deal with Evil. It does exist, doesn't it?"

"Is it perhaps true that evil is what we create when we are blind to Love? Does evil occur when we use what vision we gain for personal ego ends? Surely that creates harm, disharmony, and suffering. Are those evil? Aren't they rather the markers that force us away from the wrong path. Suffering serves also, else we might never turn from our selfishness."

Benjamin frowned,"I've always thought we create our own evil. It's our own invention. After all, the events and behavior that seem evil to us are our own doing!"

"So you see they are of our own natures. Then you'd say that evil rises from within us, just the way that Good does? If that's so,then we can refuse it. Just as we can choose or refuse Good. Once Love has begun to fill our minds and hearts, then what we've called evil simply seems a 'wrongness' even a foolishness, doesn't it?"

He shook his head,"I hope so. Jessie,I don't know whether I'll ever be capable of living a life of Love. I think I've only begun to learn what Love is"

She stood up, stood looking down at him thoughtfully, then touching his shoulder lightly, she said," You can see Son, how very important it is that we develop the capacity for Joining. We have to do this together. Well, I've got some things to attend to, and you have a task to do for your daughter. She turned and went out.

Everything was quiet around the house. The morning chatter of birds had subsided as the day warmed. She could see below someone - probably Jane, setting up floaters in a field. It was time to hang above the crops, loosen the soil and clear weeds. Idly she wondered how that experiment to train monkeys to do these repetitious jobs was going. One way to bring monkeys into the total scheme of things and insure their survival in a busy world? She knew the trained ones already in the Valley lived free among southern forests, except when they were needed. She must remember to ask about it.

Jessie walked down into the wide path toward town. The sky was still open, the sun hot and bright in a great patch of blue, the clouds riding slowly toward the town, sent gusts of cool air through the trees. She walked easily, lightly, She could feel the rising energy of Earth, its power enough to restore her own. She looked at the doubts that rose in her mind, doubts roused by Ben's own. At familiar edges of old patterns of thought, of fear. She knew them well. Her own capacity for getting off balance was a knowledge she had learned carefully. She must watch, must constantly be alert, she must not get off balance. Too much depended on her to allow a moment's lack of attention.

The color, sound, fragrance, of Earth life soaked like a sponge through her attention. The stillness of it, the beauty comforted her. It was like coming home.

The Valley was changing, but was it so great a change? Was it much more than the race had done eons ago when it threw off its rough skins and put on fine cotton or bright silks? Was there a different quality in this, than that change from the beating of a drum to that full orchestra that she had heard in Adwin last evening. The movement of Life was steady. The spiral of consciousness extending beyond matter through Spirit, was inevitable. She walked now with peace. Half way down the hill, she stopped,gazing down the Highway, a wide stream of green grass, with islands of fruiting trees and bushes, here and there. She let her eye follow for miles until she passed several bright gatherings of the Folk.

She stepped off the path, into a shady spot among fruit trees. It was just a little below her own cottage. The air was cool here, the breeze almost steady. She knew that Rob had followed her, she felt his head against her fingers and when she sat, he dropped against her foot. She looked down at him, marveling at the intelligence that had waked behind those large dark eyes. The Valley was giving birth to more than human wakening. "Yes, Rob, even you and Matilda, who watches us there above in the tree, you grow too. In a week or two it will be a time for another round up. Isn't that so?

He nodded his head, his mouth open a little as if he smiled. The round up would send town dogs out to contact flock gaurdian dogs and help them bring their charges in. Another variety of sheep and angora goats must be sheared before the wool bagan to break. He was a pack leader,,and would lead his pack far into the hills and mountains. Other packs would work from many places in the Valley. Jessie saw the picture in his mind. What Altos was to plant life, Denlock was becoming to animal life. The discovery and the training was nothing to the

THE AWAKENING

evolvement that occurred among creatures of the Valley. People did set up some breeding programs but dogs were not limited to it. Many roamed the mountains, chose their own mates. Their own intelligence led them to strong mating. People had not created the change,but they had seen it and learned to monitor and guide the training.

Jessie shifted into a place against the rough boulder that was more comfortable. She waited, the day was warming. She smoothed her embroidered trousers and tunic absently, loosened the bright green belt a little and relaxed. Her eyes swept the sky then reached far into south west. They would come on Belts, and she thought from the Station beyond Bend.

She focussed her mind, listened carefully and in the silence she heard the fine sweet call of a bell. How far away it seemed even when she knew it was in her own mind. It rang intermittently, as if catching her flagging attention. She waited.

The odors of bruised warming grasses,of the blue and yellow lupine splashed across one slope, rode the light breezes blowing up from the River, fed her, entertained her senses. She felt settled into this small cradle of Earth, a place to retreat and observe, for the world beyond seemed sharp and clear, the town almost as though at arms length away. The coming weather front was like a dark curtain already casting a sweep of far western lands into shadow. It was raining in those high mountains and across the foothills. But she sat in warmth and sun. She spoke softly the Earth blessing with which she usually greeted morning.

> Blessed is the air, the sky and the Earth,
> Blessed are the trees, the creatures and the plants,
> Blessed are all those who sing to the day
> And who cry out for Joy at Life!
> Blessed also are those who are in pain or sorrow,
> May the new Light lift their Hearts into Knowledge
> Where pain and pleasure fade.

She felt a peace and calm greater than any she had known for days. This was enjoyment.

After a little while, she Reached out with powerful focus, drawn from the depths of her deepest energies. She shielded the Reach and felt the tingling Touch of her Sisters. They would come! There was laughter in their Touch that relieved her unease. But as she shrank back into herself, limited, she felt a trace of that strange cold, that sharp splinter of 'call' and she knew it was danger. Her very Reach had exposed her presence. Was she herself immune to that 'call'. Like a seductive promise, a sweet dream, it Reached into her mind, suggesting a tenderness, a plethora of pleasure. A wry smile tipped up her lips,how little such a one must know of the Monitor trained, their feeling of the hollowness of so many pleasures. She sat still attending, she needed to analyse it in memory. Paying stark attention to it, rendered it no longer seductive, but obvious. Those who were coming, were adept at mind shielding. She must learn, she must learn from them how to keep herself unknown even when she extended her mind far.

She leaned back, turned a little to the side, to slide her fingers along the deep fissures in the thick bark of a young pine growing out of this cluster of boulders. This kind of consciousness still fascinated it. She longed to know it more fully. She sensed its knowing, knowing of her presence even. She smiled, no possibility there of betrayal. Trees did not betray life, only humankind did that. The thought brought sadness for a moment. That grief she had long ago accepted. It was her task to do something to wake people to these losses.

She entertained herself then by naming aloud, calling out in greeting, all the plants she could see from her vantage point. She enjoyed their company and their awareness of her call. Jane had showed her the pleasure of that greeting, and had laughed in her shy way, but Jessie knew she meant it. The world was a surrounding of friends for one who knew their names. Then, was it also true that plant Wizards could depend on plants to protect them, to hide them by scent or shadow, by confusing the eye of the hunter? She had heard it said. She thought it was true.

And did they help some one lost, by revealing in subtle ways, their nourishments for the hungry? That too, she knew was true. She herself had sensed the gifts of plants while traveling and had not thought how they gave their gifts to her. Surely the plants themselves had had something to do with her knowledge of them. And she had not offered gratitude enough, thinking it was her own acute senses. She sighed. How one found out about oneself at unexpected times!

Suddenly two tiny forms appeared in the sky far to the south, coming rapidly, then she saw there were three. Good, they too thought the matter important. Now they could form a triangle with one person as center point and they could Listen further.

They drew close as she watched, She could see the bright color of their trousers tucked securely in high soft boots and the long flowing tunics that were belted at the waist. The fabric literally gleamed in the early sunlight, blues and greens, one in dark purple. There must be more than a little plasilk in the fine wool to give it that gleam. They would not be cold, even at that height, they knew how to keep their bodies warm. She felt a surge of eagerness. Her own people, her own kind here to Join with her! These would be fellow workers though they might be longer in service than she. It was an indulgence, but also a joy, this meeting. She stood and lifted her arms up in a gesture of welcome.

They landed silently around her. slid from their belts which they piled on top of the boulder. Their hair loosed from hoods, fell long to their shoulders. Two women, one blond, slight and smaller than Jessie, the other well built, tall, with raven hair. The third was a man whose braided hair was dark brown around a long irregular face. His body was thin but well muscled. He was laughing at her delight. They nodded to her in greeting and she did not conceal her surprise that they were strangers. They each embraced her warmly and she felt utterly

THE AWAKENING

belonging among them.

The taller of the two women said, her voice sweet and clear "We need names and we need to talk. It's for that reason so many of us have come, to form into hard words in this level of life the knowledge needed." She looked at Jessie, seriously then smiled with such warmth that Jessie drew a deep sigh of gladness. Such people were not common, she had forgotten how much she missed the company of such as these. The woman said, "Jessie, I am Mundra, and this," turning to the other woman, "is Marina". She reached out to set a gentle hand on the man's arm, and their eyes met and Jessie knew these two were Mated, "This is our brother, Jedro."

Jessie nodded to them. "You know our need. You know there's trouble in this Valley. I'm not sure how we proceed."

" You know well that disruption is always the beginning process of change, and often feels like danger. Sometimes it is the opposite, and not danger at all, but invitation, although it usually brings pain." Jedro looked at her hopefully.

The lack of worry puzzled and slightly angered Jessie. She observed her anger with a quiet surprise. Was her own fear greater than she thought? She spoke again, wanting them to do the talking, "But it can destroy so much".

Marina glanced at Jedro, nodding, then said," To plant a new garden the old one must be cleared away. Let's sit down, and form a triangle, and will you, Jessie, be the center point." At Jessie's look of surprise, she nodded. "You have that strength, young friend, you sustain it and we see it clearly." Her voice seemed to deep, too strong for such a little woman.

Jessie, felt a slight jolt at anyone calling her 'young' but she knew that compared to these, she was. Quietly she took her place and they sat out in the full sunlight, yet it did not seem to warm her. They might have appeared to be a small group of children playing at a game there in the grass under the great trees. Then Marina began the prayer with which they usually began their Joining.

> All people are one and we are one with them
> We seek to Love not Hate,
> We seek to Serve and not exact due Service
> We seek to Heal not Hurt.
> Let pain bring due reward of Light and Love
> Let the Soul control the life and all events
> Let light reveal the Love that underlies the happenings of our time.
> Let insight come and wisdom
> Let the future be revealed
> Let inner unity demonstrate and outer cleavages be gone
> Let Love prevail
> Let all people Love.

They had all spoken the words silently, and when it was done, they were silent for moments. Then Mundro spoke again. "This Valley is ready for the new perceptions of Life. Here the people are receptive to Love, to the incoming Light. Their Hearts are open and willing to Know. No where in the world are people so ready. It is the time for awakening among humankind, Jessie. You know that as well as we."

"You're concerned that we manage to save the Valley through all the disruption? That the Valley manage to save itself, is better put, you know." Jedro smiled with gentle amusement, as though sharing a delicate joke and Jessie was not offended. In fact she felt suddenly younger, suddenly less conscious, and at that, the three were swiftly contrite."Dear one, you would not be here if you were not wise, were not yourself ready,. We know well your power. You have yourself to acknowledge fully. The reluctance of the people to acknowledge their recognitions among one another is causing a kind of death among them,a kind of stagnation, You were chosen as their Teacher because you reflect that very reluctance on another level. Listen! Listen to your Self!" Then with a bright smile, said,"But let's begin the Listening!"

They settled, silence surrounded them so deeply the birds near by stopped their singing, watched, with bright eyes, then flew away. At first Jessie felt the simple vortex of mind energy,like three rivers meeting and circling in full spate, reaching deeper,drawing every fiber of her attention until she knew their intention as her own. Then, out of the well of her own knowledge she realized her part, and caught back her attention, like a powerful fish on a line. She must stabilize, must limit the depths, the range. But an awe-ful desire pulled at her to know more of the unlimited living sea that surged in powerful currents around them. It lifted and carried consciousness to transcend thought itself. She wanted to give herself into it, allow its possibility, but she was aware! She must stand firm. Must forego desire. She drew her own mind energy like a riveting force, held, stood unshakeable, firm, surprising herself. From whence came this strength? The question was a drift of shape that blew off as lightly as mist.

To sustain this point that was their stability, seemed at first too much, but she set herself to it. Held attention until the energy that was her own mind curved back into itself and stabilized at that point within herself where Light gleamed. Light that was like a hole in the fabric of time and space. She was a stake set firmly deep into substance that was interfaced between the physical world and the nonphysical. Her strength grew, drawing sustainance from that point between.

The three minds linked into that strength, then, as in the spokes of a wheel, turned outward, free. And so the circle began to widen,expanding, it searched the depths of Earth, of space, of Being itself. Sustained thus, listening, the ear held. They listened, through hearts and minds reached to their limits. And as they steadied, they heard. The sounds of life, of unceasing evolving of Life, time-space blurring and becoming transparent, so that all that was seemed to be motion itself. Motion, wave and particle of substance, still and unceasing, the sound of Life in essence, omnipresent, inclusive. And in this ceaselessness was a kind of rhythm, like a vast, infinite sea, drawn and released into ebb and flow.

They fought for their own point of being, within that vast flow, and knew they were part of the resistance that created the ebb. Like a great knowing, offered, unlimited, consciousness shaped itself, drew down limits that shrank them into focus. They were conduits of energy but that energy had receeded now to the Great Valley. The power of their Joined sea of mind curved back into itself and ceased to expand. They wondered at the existence of limits, and offered gratitude for their own. Too much, mind extended too far, would lose them consciousness. Their actual safeguard in this experience was that throughout existence there was resistance. And thought formed as if of itself. What was the reluctance? Matter resisting Spirit? Or Spirit itself, in sweet persuasion, that it penetrate and infuse matter willingly with Itself? Was Mind the field of this cosmic marriage?

The unknown was a dense blindness around their farthest vision. But the Light out of which Jessie held them stable, flared into revelation.

Suddenly, they could realize the stifling of sound, the resistance of motion, the strands of obstruction that reached through everything they could grasp as real. It descended into the Being-aliveness of Valley. This small point of the universe, this tiny focus point of Being that was the Valley, separated itself from unlimitedness and was all they knew. They turned to look at their world, their own land and saw that the stifling came from shafts of dark that pierced the Light and drained possibility.

Those shafts came from a point nearly at the end of South Valley. A cold that sucked back into itself the evolving Reach of Life, had a point of effectiveness there on a white, frozen mountain. It seemed unaware of them, though it was certainly conscious. They held, aware, knowing and no time passed. Finally, the ranging minds drew back, separated, and Jessie felt their release. She was amazed in one tiny corner of her awareness that there was no dispair. That which they had realized, was the unceasing surge of the sea of Being. They, motes of participation, knew it's ebb and flow was ultimately irresistable. No matter the resistance, the direction was relentless. Yet they had work to do, that relentlessness was living also in themselves.

They were silent, allowing themselves thought. Mundra frowned, sat squatting on a low flat stone, her knees up in front of her chest, hugging them, her face resting against her knees thoughtfully." You see, Jessie, Life, through the universe, through existence, has its own rhythm, its own inexorable direction. But we, who live as Mind-Spirit, who stand forth, can sometimes know, consciously participate. But we have to translate such essential nature into this physical life. And so we have here your task."

For several minutes they were silent, thinking, balancing. Then she began again. "Your problem is how to turn the attention of the people to a recognition of their own resistance but also to their very great strengths. You worry, because you find yourself touched by the fears that blind them. Is that it?" Then she added, slowly, watching Jessie's face. "You also feel the intrusion of that resistant force, the stifler of Life, the Dark One, the creater of havoc. You see that as the destroyer. That sense of bitter cold you noticed earlier, that was its touch, Jessie.

It is surely not insensitive to your presence, but you surround yourself well with stillness." She smiled encouragingly and Jessie felt renewed strength. You work with a delicacy that is remarkable in one so young. That one who exemplifies that destroyer there in our Valley,cannot keep track of your intent." The compliment surprised her. Then she realized it was simply a statement of fact. Jedro said,"You are deeply grounded, your consciousness is rooted in Spirit, it will not waver."

Jessie nodded,relieved, grateful at this summing up. "That dark one. He is powerful. His mind threads our network with darkness. He is drawn to those who are angry, or afraid and their fears make them vulnerable to him." Now she allowed her fear to rise, to be laid naked there between them and she saw that it was greater than she had known."How can I have allowed such fear in me to go unattended? I am ashamed. Because though I knew that my own fear would draw his Touch, I also knew that to refuse to acknowledge my fear would give it room to grow." Her eyes were bleak.

Jedro nodded , meeting her eyes, giving her that Light that flamed in them. He lay down to ease his body against Earth, smiling at the familiar contact, the drawing of power and giving of himself into it, enjoying himself. For a moment she thought he did not take her weakness seriously. He said, " Just a few moments ago you stood firm, attending the danger, meeting it, so that it no longer had power. Now,with us the fear can be fully brought forth, now you can safely share it and explore it's nethermost parts". His face was serious but his eyes were full of laughter. He said,"Some destruction is necessary,you know. Death makes room for Life."

She sighed, a trembling sound,"So it may be. And he who calls out from that sodden darkness of Soul is not more nor less than another human person! I had given him greater power, I had thought him to be like that Devil who brought temptation so long ago to that one called Jesus."

"Was even that one more than human?" He shrugged, "Well, no matter, such divine definitions are not for us. What ever this dark one is,he lives to bring the lowest in us to power, to foster the seduction of material life,to slow the growth of Life, of Spirit in humankind. His voice is the voice of our own self serving, our own lusts. His hope is that he can turn humankind from serving of Love to regression to that narrow darkness of ignorance and blindness from which humankind has so recently wakened and which is the true grave. But in his way, he also serves, he forces us to SEE. We must recognize our whole nature, the least as well as the greatest." Mundro was quiet, her voice so soft, Jessie likened it to the air that rustled in the pine. "When we KNOW our true Self, we desire nothing except that Light we seek. Our hearts are then beyond the dark. Thus, little Teacher, he has not touched your own!" Her eyes were blazing with the truth of that and Jessie felt her heart surge with new strength.

Jessie studied them, shaking her head slowly,"I think that its true, we're afraid to risk. Even with what we've begun to know, its too hard to believe that there is a new life ahead."

The three laughed, their merriment disconcerting to Jessie at first and then suddenly she saw. She smiled sheepishly. "Of course. It is so obvious once you think of it. All that we've spent so many years building, all we've dreamed into existence. We're clinging, just as our ancestors did. It's all we've known, the best we could do -- in our past." She was silent, the fact filling her mind. Once there, it shifted the meaning of everything else. The hurt of it made her face grimace. Musingly, she added,"It's often that we who work here in the field of this daily life, find ourselves stained with the fears and desires, the longings and attitudes of our people. It is probably the most difficult task I have, to enter among people and yet remain free of the staining so I can keep a clear vision."

Mundra nodded, smiling in a friendly manner that puzzled Jessie,"That's why you were sent,you know. None of us are completely immune to those old attachments until we meet them and choose to be. It's why each of us must go home at intervals to give us time to clear and purify mind and Heart again. You sustain resistance to that staining remarkably well, Jessie. We learn from you,though you don't seem to know that."

Jessie frowned to find she felt astonished at all they knew of her. Then, shook her head. Of course they would,. She said,"We have finally caught the butterfly, we gaze at its beauty, but we want to hold it to the limits of our own hands -- we fear its flight. Our desire for its beauty endangers its life."

They nodded, their faces holding only a kind of gentle amusement. Jessie moved her body, sitting now cross legged, tucking her discarded jacket under her for ease. Then memory prodded,the cold shard of Touch just before they came. Her fear must be brought to view, met. She looked at it quietly now, bringing balance back into her body. She said,"There was that Touch! The Cold. The bitterness of Cold." She nodded at her surprise in the fear roused, then at the strength she felt in herself to meet that fear.

Mundra nodded,"We know Jessie, We could not have been unaware. We could shield you a little, but we knew that you must know exactly what the opposition is. That is the opposing force, it is also necessary if change occurs. It is a matter more of balance between energies that are very great. You know it's a risk to call us! Because you're identified then, that man who serves the opposing force,knows you. But your call was swift. I have said that your power to be unnoticed by such as he is finer than anyone I have known still in living body. And now, we have identified Fear, and you have acknowledged its nature. You are well prepared. So don't worry. We will keep watch you know. You are the key marker in this end of the Valley. You must know that." She hesitated then added, "You know, of course, that I work in the east of central Valley, Jedro west central and Marina is south Valley.

Jessie had blanched, but did not shake her head. She had not wanted so much responsibility but she knew it was hers." You're right. I do pretend, in my way, just as the people here do in theirs. We deny and hide ourselves from the very Light we love and long for. We do that and it has not been spoken so fairly until now. Each of us has to see the dark of ourselves that works for the Dark

THE PEOPLE OF THE VALLEY

One. Many people have begun to shrug off the heavy weight of self-service. Begun to see it is a blindness. Yes! So narrow, so dark, so without possibility. That's the grave in which we have lived as a people. And repeatedly we go back to cling to ancient fears that justify our lusts and hungers, as though we could not see the beauty beyond us. Sometimes we don't, that's sure."

Jedro was sitting now, watching intently as Jessie realized and spoke. He said, "You see that it's through those old needs people can be found and used by that Dark power. It is the way of the little self. We have to choose!"

Jessie drew her mouth tight, holding her thoughts clear, "I recognize that dark power in myself, I foster in myself that which can deny me the Light. I must CHOOSE the Light while the Dark sits persistently familiar using pleasure and pain alternately to entice me into its prison. And it is myself who has the choice. I see you're right, it's exactly that. I have my own way of doing what the people of north Valley do. I feel the shame of it draining out of me with the recognition." She paused in thought. "Must we destroy ourselves to know ourselves?"

"Do you think so?"

"No, it's not that. We shed the shell of ourselves in order to expand into Self! But it feels like self destruction at first." Marina's low voice interceded.

Jessie felt her mind stretched again, filling and remembering, "Of course, of course, it would be so. The conflict is part of the growth itself. It cannot be avoided."

"Inevitably, "That's why it is so crucial a stage for our people."

Marina had risen, stood now,, tall above them, stretching her body, "Jessie, Here we are, knowing one another and living together in the world of Mind. It's then that we realize the true tragedy, the terrible lonliness of humankind, the separation of life from life. I wonder sometimes how we have kept our sanity,, unable to know one another, unable to know those who call to us."

Jedro met her eyes and nodded. Jessie spoke slowly, "I've thought of that. We've always been so cut off, half conscious. No wonder we are so tortured by that first glimpse of what it is to be Conscious. No wonder we fear when we begin to See!"

Jedro nodded, "It is not the Builders you need worry about but their fear, and your reaction to that fear. Their anger can trigger old fears and resentments in those who have begun to See. Their fear creates a sink into which anyone of those just waking might be sucked down again. The first Vision of the people is delicate and still not stable." At Jessie's nod, he went on. "Have good cheer, Jessie, we see such Light in the Valley now, its power is lifting life above the sink of fear. We believe that the Light there has grown greater than the dark. Pay attention to the Light, let the dark alone, it will fade of itself if given no attention. That is the secret. Fighting the darkness, the old greeds and lusts of humankind only serves to reinforce them. Fear is like a whirlpool, once caught in its force, whether to fight it or to embrace it, a person can be drawn down. Light however, pours Itself into darkness. simply ending it with its inclusion."

Jessie, said softly, "Don't fight the dark ones, ignore them! Or include them!

THE AWAKENING

What a command. And I know it's true. The task is not easy."

"It never has been, Dear One. But it is Life itself, is it not?" Mundra was smiling and her face seemed calm, unworried.

Jessie nodded, slowly, knowing all this, but reminded and remembering. Her heart was somehow lighter even though she felt the burden placed upon her. It must be done. Somehow it must occur. "The Valley must know its own nature and that nature is full Consciousness."

For some time they were silent together, enjoying, experiencing Earth life. Finally Mundra stood, reaching for her belt,"Jessie do not dispair. We'll always be near. Each of us is aware of each other. That's our strength. Together we send Light through this Valley in a network that leaves few places untouched. We've had fifty new students entering the Monitor training every months for three months this year. You will know how great is the rejoicing for that? There are at least twenty among those you teach who will come to us within another year. That means that children are being born in bodies far more sensitive and aware and can soon take their places sending that energy forth to all of you. And fortunately we have found better ways to teach them." She laughed and the joy in her face was clear. It gave courage to Jessie.

The three of them stood thus around her, and she stood up with them, and then she felt that in flow of energy, that swift, steady increase that pulsed through her, lifted her Heart, blazed in her mind, opening regions not fully illuminated, revealing and exposing but making way for Itself. She felt the jolt of that exposure, and the blended healing of that perception. The compassion they radiated, the Joy they lived, nourished her as she had not been nourished for months.

She watched them, pulling their belts on with wry grins. The use of them was so unnecesary, yet they had to appear to Valley eyes as normal as possible. "Remember, there are the others. The six of you working in the north land must Join often, must Gather and remind one another. For it is also easy to let that pride of accomplishment darken your vision and tempt you to work alone. They depend on you Jessie, it's true, and now you know your own strength." Marina spoke softly, sending the thoughts clearly, implanting them so Jessie would not forget, would accept the hint of warning. They knew the need of Jessie's personality, the reluctance to call for help.

Jessie nodded, "I will rememember." they came to her each in turn, and embraced her, and she felt the greater embrace of their subtle natures, the power surrounding her and giving of itself to her. She must keep their faith,their wisdom sure in her thought. For it was the thought that must reach the minds of the people. She watched them go with misgiving, but then, determination swept the misgiving from her heart and replaced it with firm conviction. She sat silently in the summer sun, watching the tiny figures fade into the distant mountain mists. Then she settled down to plan the afternoon.

CHAPTER TWENTY SEVEN

Marian and Joseph

Long rose colored rays of late sun lay spread over the great Valley. The fields and forests were heavy with their summer leaves and tall growth. Poppies, Yarrow, Penstamin, wild sweet peas, bush lupin and mimosa trees with blooms gold,or blue, splashed color through field and hill side. Many other scattered flowers bloomed half hidden among the tall thick grasses. The dark forests wound among the fields and pressed against the rivers edge here and there. Among them were speading miles of wild meadows, thick grass seas with here and there islands of trees and shrubs. And through it all, wound the dense short dark grass of the Great Highway.   Above on this summer evening,thin clusters of clouds bunching at the horizon reflected light in streaming bands of rose and red. The day was nearly ended.

As the setting sun drew shadows down across the Valley, towns, cities, and outlying farms began to sparkle with bright lights. The Great Highway, threading its way through the length and breadth of the Valley, branching into the hills and between narrow hollows between ridges was already dotted with tiny flickers of evening camp fires. At one of those fires, half way down the Valley, just east of Santiago, the family of Joseph and Marian, drew in to a stone circle to prepare supper.A one room stone hut, holding toilet and bathing facilities, and emergency supplies, stood half hidden among bushes and trees, half a mile from their site, several other sites surrounding the solar heated hut, would use that facility.

Just before the low western mountains blotted the sun from view, a wonder of magic seemed to fall across the Earth. People who had lit their night fires, hesitated from their preparations in reverent attention. The tender sadness of twilight touched the minds of each individual, most of whom separated a little from one another to offer the prayer of evening and to keep a private stillness after the day's busy activity. It was then that the Earth energy seemed most to ascend and envelop their minds. They dedicated themselves and their lives once more before the night fell.

On such evenings in early summer,Marian often felt that combination of deep joy mixed with some inexpressable sorrow. She never knew the cause, and never sought one. It was the way of summer evenings for her. Of the seven people moving about, busy with evening chores, five were of Joseph's and Marian's tribe, two were visiting towners. Any Vagabond could have told whose tribe it was by their colors. Now, Joseph, a tall, lean man, middle aged, with very black hair, dark skin bent to adjust the fire and feed it small twigs. The Solar heat available at every Vagabond rest site,would heat their food. A large pan of water steamed over a very small fire of twigs that flickered flames at the sky. It was ready for cooking the roots they had gathered along their evening way. The tiny evening

THE AWAKENING

fire was a Temple for the People of the Way. Always there must be a bit of living fire. The main meal would be cooked on the solar heater.

Marian, nearly as tall as her Mate, but fair as he was dark, gathered supplies from the cart for making supper. Two young men brought sleeping bags out, spread them ready at the far end of the camp. A young woman, dark as her father, gathered a few more roots from the fields beside the road, and brought them to clean for supper.

The two from the towns were doing a summer Journey. Anna, and her friend Mathew. Anna had journeyed more than once with the Distan Family,and she had met them this day little past noon. She felt at home helping prepare the evening meal. Mathew watched and found tasks for himself helping to prepare the nights beds. Marian had set pots on the ring of stones where the Solar unit was growing red.

Now the hiss of water boiling drew Marian to the big pot to add the ingredients that would be a thick and delicious stew. Anna, hungry after the steady traveling of the day, thought she could already smell it. Circles of flat stones arranged around the fire box, held brilliant scarves, robes and shawls, embroidered with the colors and patterns of this Distan tribe. Anna had helped Dora gather parsnips, dark purple potatoes and vivid golden beets from the fields off the roadway as they traveled. Dora had picked small delicious beans from the vines that climbed the bowed snag that leaned over the shelter.

Joseph tore apart a pile of small dark green leaves, dripped them into boiling water slowly. A basket of red, blue and golden fruits was ready on the slab of stone that would act as table. Slanted light gleamed on the smooth stones of the circle, and Anna drew the edge of one scarf under her self because the stone was rough and hard.

Dora said,"These beans are the first for the season. Not too many yet, but they'll be good. There were enough for us and the folks at the two other sites yonder." She gestured at the flickering flames of camp fires in the distance.

She watched Joseph, stir and replenish the fire, coaxing it into a bright hot flame. His shaggy long hair held by a band about his temples flopped against the collar of his red shirt. Loosely buttoned, the shirt exposed the heavy black hair of his chest. Idly she watched as she worked while her father rearranged the smaller pot where a peeled and chopped lemon yellow sweet-squash already sat bubbling faintly. . A baking oven, molded of fields clays a generation ago, glowed inside ready for the long sticks of bread that Marian molded. Built to be heated by wood fires, it was refitted for solar heat. Vagabonds did not intend that their multiple fires would ever dim the clear Valley air with smoke.

Dora left Anna to finish cleaning the last of the roots and went to stir the contents of the pot. She spoke softly to her father, and he stood, towering tall over them all in the evening light, silhoueted against the fading rose of the sky. He looked up the long curving road, past the other fires, and then turned abruptly so he faced Anna but looked piercingly out into the forest behind their clearing. They had chosen this place, open fields between two strips of forest, because they wanted to enjoy the full moon of this night.

Now the sun set left them in the soft warm dusk but already the moon was faintly glowing beyond the eastern peaks. Joseph's face was set grimly, he looked worried, thoughtful and at the same time sad. Anna wondered about his thoughts, knowing that they were his own and sacred from her penetrating attention, but the temptation rose, and she shook her head angry at that wish. She could not avoid noticing the quandary, the rapid succession of half finished thoughts, the apprehension, the eagerness and the sorrow. She nodded, smiling as his eyes fell on her face. He looked at her searchingly a moment and then nodded curtly, knowing of her recognition of his feelings.

Then as abruptly, he smiled a radiant, winning smile, sweeping away the former concerns, letting them fall, spilling from him as though he had given them sufficient energy. He relaxed, his eyes twinkled and with friendliness he said, "It's good to have you join our family this night. Will you Journey with us long? The latter was as much a request as a question and Anna met his eyes silently for a moment. Then she said softly,,"We would be grateful to join you for a while. Mathew and I have traveled alone for long enough since we left home and the privilege of being with such good friends, would be great. Thank you." Their light formality pleased them both.

Joseph laughed a short abrupt laugh. She was startled, the slight bitterness of it surprised her. He said,"My Mate lived for a short time in Adwin, as you know. We've never passed there that we do not Send to see whether friends there can receive us". He turned toward her a penetrating glance that was a question as well as a warning and she frowned. He deliberately talked of Sending. As if he tested her. There was a defiance that puzzled her. He was not a defiant man.

She started to ask,but he turned to the fair haired woman, who came now with an arm around a huge crock, and she waved one hand with a cheery comment Anna could not hear. Anna was immediately light hearted again, attentive to that swift shift of emotion. These two, he so heavy,intense, serious, was balanced well by the woman, so cheery and lighthearted. Her ability to meet his weight with her lightness was their gifts to one another. She needed his depths to extend her own nature and he hers.

The young woman, Dora, so like her father, was quiet as she stood beside him watching their new friends. Mathew had come into the circle, He had been busy setting their bicycles with their wide field tires,out of the way and taking their packs to where he had placed their sleeping equipment. Now,he came to stand just behind Anna. Barely seventeen years of life had he lived, yet his very young face seemed to Anna weary with age and she laughed. He had not done as much traveling by bicycle as she had. He'd get used to it after a few Journey's.

He slid suddenly onto the bench beside her and said,"Wow, it's a long climb from Adwin. I never realized how steady the climb is, until I tried riding it. Even walking it doesn't seem so steep".He laughed then, just sitting down was a relief to him."It'll be great to crest the ridge yonder beyond the forest and then we'll have a long slow downhill trip all the way to Benedict."

THE AWAKENING

Dora watched him. He was almost as old as her elder brother but seemed to her much younger. She thought of her betrothed, who traveled now near Bend, but would meet them within another day. Memory of his alert, thoughtful face seemed somehow to make Mathew look like a boy, and yet their ages were nearly the same. She wondered why and looked at Anna with the question in her mind. Anna felt the Touch and without hesitation grinned, responding. Here it was again, young people had an open willingness to Touch. She opened her mind projecting an image of Mathew so intent on his study, his family life, his fascination with learning of the thoughts of humankind, and so showing Dora how he had neglected some of the practical things of living. Neglected knowing of people more. And Dora, receiving the picture, understood and nodded. Anna glanced at Joseph, wondering whether she dared Send such a picture to him.

Mathew bent to open a case at his feet, and took out a violin and bow. Anna nodded and fumbled in the bag at her feet to retrieve her flute. The Distan family turned to glance at one another with smiles and evident pleasure at this surprise. Marian, stirred something in the big crock and grinned over at Anna,"Well, so you remembered to bring it this time?"

Joseph laughed, "Give us a little tune to make supper by." He waved one arm at the forest to the west,"The boys aren't back yet with their offering, but they'll be here in a few minutes." Anna and Mathew looked at one another and then played a light, airy tune, simple and familiar. The others laughed and began to sing the words easily as they worked. Then, Joseph, got instruments from the cart, brought them and began tuning them. By now the sons, were returning from the forest, carrying two bags of little twigs, enough to keep the little fire going all evening. They knew how to select twigs that would make a nearly smokeless fire and leave them just the light and comfort of it. They must leave enough that those coming in tomorrow would have the beginnings for their own Temple fire. Young Joseph, already in the camp circle, called out, "Hey Dad, Uncle Tony and Grandpa are settled in up ahead. They said to join them in the morning if we like."

Joseph nodded and spoke with his mate briefly and she nodded. then as Joe and Tony dumped their loads at the edge of the fire circle, she added aloud,"You've brought enough twigs for four fires, but then, just as well, someone will need it." She swung one arm toward Anna and Mathew," Well, Anna brought her flute, and Mathew seems to have a bit of music too. Surely we'll have a rare evening."

Tony turned to them, his thin fair body strong and lithe, already stretching out into the awkwardness of adolescence, but he made that single move one of grace and ease. Anna watched with admiration. He said,"Well, are either of you song makers? We can use a new song." He knew the training of city bred children and though the Vagabonds were renowned for their endless supply of music, songs and dances, they were always delighted to find a true musician among town people. Anna could see the eagerness and a touch of envy in his eyes, for he wanted to get the formal training towns provided. He went to get a clarinet from the instruments his father had brought. He came back to sit beside them and Anna was very aware of his trembling eagerness. He was nearly old enough to leave the family for a year or two. He longed for that day. He was younger than either of his siblings, a late child and yet he had grown rapidly and would soon out strip his older brother in size.

Anna said,"You did study with us last time you were north, didn't you Tony?"

He nodded, his eyes shining in to hers,"Oh, yes, but only for two months. Father says this year though, I can stay. I can learn until I get full of it." He laughed at the expression as if he could ever get full. Wistfully he went on,"I want to be able to have time to play the grand pianos, to learn in the Music Hall. I've had so little time with pianos.

"But you have pianos in your family Festival Centers here on the Highway, don't you?"

He nodded, frowning, "We do, yes," he admitted," but they're just not what yours are, and all the travel pianos are electronic. I want to work on the ones Andrew showed me there in Adwin.

Anna knew that Tony had learned more than the average town child ever did already from the great Vagabond musicians and from his frequent short stops at the towns they passed. His hunger for music was as pervasive as her twin's was. She sympathized at his longing to put all his energy into learning. She knew that his talent was remarkable and so did everyone who heard him. Already he had composed music that was being played througout the Valley, and though he did not yet know it, in other parts of the nation.

She Reached tentatively toward him, focussed so only he would receive, and he did. To her surprise and delight, he knew her anger that he had not been fully educated, then her acceptance that his own people thought his original talent would flower more fully without such intense training at first. She asked,"When will you study in the world Music Center in Milan."

He answered, "When I'm fourteen and have spent my year at Adwin or Santiago my parents will let me go. Has Andrew been there?

She shook her head,"Only for six months when he was fourteen. He's still got more training to do there. Perhaps when you go he'll be there to."

"I'd like that. I don't mind too much the wait, There's so much to learn along the way, you know. I've not learned all I can from Uncle Anthony, I suppose. But I heard Andrew's Sonata in A flat for the piano last Festival and it was wonderful. Yes, I would like to study with him"

She looked at the lanky, tall body, and the young child face atop it." She thought he didn't even look his twelve years. "You know I think I agree with your parents."

Mathew leaned forward, "You're talking about Anthony Distan then?"

Tony nodded, "Too bad I'm named after him. How'll I ever have my own name." He grimaced without anger, "But then, will I ever make songs as well as he. Will I ever know as much?"

Joe, watching the three of them, with dark, quiet eyes, said,"Tony, he says you already surpass him. He says his name will fade before yours." He had a heavier body, broad, powerful shoulders and narrow hips. Not as beautifully built as his younger brother, he was nevertheless handsome. And the sweetness of his disposition left not a trace of jealousy of this younger talented brother. He had his own strengths which he knew well. Anna let her eyes move over his body, appreciating it. Joe said,"How'll you get your audiences to come hear you on the Highway, brother? Can you see it? A whole international fan club descending on us to hear our little brother!" He was not making fun and Tony knew it. But Tony's face grimaced.

Mathew laughed at the comment, and at Joe's comical gestures as he talked, deliberately playing the clown as he so often did. Then Anna joined in the fun, which became a game between them with Tony and Mathew joining in. Finally they were all laughing foolishly at Joe's antics and their own responses.

Preparations for dinner were proceeding. Joseph made room for a frying pan and began slicing rabbit meat into thin pieces absently watching the young people as he worked. Marian slid her big pot off the heated area, and took out a fragrant heavy loaf of bread. She handed it to Dora to slice and nodded to Joe to stack plates on the cleared part of the smooth stone circle.

Anna began to sing, She looked at Marian, who nodded, pleased, and then began to create a song about these brothers. Her eyes were dancing and happiness was in her voice. Tony listened, and she could see he felt the shape of each turn of phrase, each shift of notes. He watched intently then, suddenly, he lifted his clarinet and joined her. Improvising on her melody, he provided harmony and counterpoint. The weaving of the music created a magic of sound as the moon slid above the ridge of mountain and flooded down into the great open fields and lit the trees tops. Joseph came with his guitar then but he waited, not able to enter into the complex patterning of these two. By now dinner was simmering, waiting for them. Mathew fumbled with his violin, played a little, bringing a bit of melody in to join the flowing harmony, but giving up after a few minutes for they were beyond his skill.

Then Marian came to sit beside Anna and putting an arm around her shoulders, she began to sing with her, already able to repeat the chorus without faltering. She sang a clear Alto to Anna's pure soprano and their voices made another dimension to the song. For some time there was nothing but the music and the spell of that unity and intimacy that wove about them all. Friendship was being created and cemented here. Anna found words to speak of that, of the brothers and of their family and their people so that the song grew and became one of humankind. Her songs had a way of doing that. But now, the music was also expanding and it was no longer a simple folk song, but a complex wonderful weaving and interweaving of phrases .

When the music ended, they sat in the electric silence for some time and then Joseph came and kissed Anna. Marian leaned to her and drew her into her arms for a quick warm embrace. Then reaching out she took young Tony's hand and placed it into Anna's."You are brother and sister," she said, "because together you have created a true song."

"But I'll never remember, you all added so much, it was so - so big by the time we ended. I'll not be able to keep it"

Marian laughed,"Tony will. He never forgets. He'll make it into something even more lovely. Won't you son?"

Tony shook his head,"No. It's her song. I will remember and I'll write it all for you, Anna. But I won't change it."

Marian left them then to go to the pot and begin serving dinner. Tony turned to Anna,"It's the way of my people. We are one family. All of us, even those who don't -- who don't reach and receive." He met her eyes and she nodded, both of them feeling the sadness of that division.

Anna looked at Tony seriously, wanting him to believe her,"I'd be honored to be sister to you, Tony. And then, that makes me sister to Dora and Joe, and daughter to Joseph and Marian, doesn't it?"

Joseph and Marian looked at each other, an amused look in their eyes, usually a new sister for one was not so for all the family. Then Joseph nodded to Marian curtly and said,"Anna, we've known you through the years, traveling the Highway with us. Remember when you and Andrew left the Valley with us and we traveled across the Prairie country? Ah, such adventure. Then when your parents joined us and we climbed the canyons and went into the north country ? And that strange, young woman Silvia was with us. "It's always been a Journey full of Light when you join us, and so you're surely daughter to us. May we travel many times on the Ways."

Dora turned to meet Anna's eyes, wondering whether she had accidentally or deliberately forced this choice. Surely, Anna was too conscious not to know the rituals. "Give us another song tonight, Anna, and I may ask to be sister to you too. I've not had that, it might be good,"

Anna laughed then, a sigh of relief escaping her and they all laughed with her. Marian stood suddenly silent, holding a huge ladle and in the other hand a stack of light permaglass bowls with handles. She started as if just returning from depths of thought that took her whole attention."Welcome then. She turned swiftly catching up a three foot square scarf, embroidered and dyed with the tribe colors."Here, daughter, your sign for us." She came and kissed Anna, and said,"Now then, before we do anymore singing we need to try this soup. It's just right. Any more cooking and it will not be good."

They ate and Mathew watched Anna as they talked and told tales of earlier years, of other members of their families, He thought he had not noticed how lovely she was. Here with the moonlight gleaming in her hair,so animated, laughing, she seemed full of an energy he had never noticed before in any girl. He remembered the Teachers explaining to them the various feelings people had for one another, friendship, and courting and then finally Mating. They surely didn't describe those he felt now very well, but he recognized what they had meant. He knew that he was 'in love' with Anna. Had been for some time, but this Journey had made it undeniable. Such a powerful light headed feeling! One that struck into the pit of his stomach, and spread fire in his groin. When she touched his hand he felt literally an electric impulse. But the beauty of it amazed him, the beauty of being here with her. No one could explain this, no wonder they had failed. He wondered whether he should tell Anna. What if she refused his love?

He sat in quandary, unable to simply enjoy the evening, and yet, wrapt in a delirium of joy at being here so close. He laughed at himself, and at the same time, suffered. He must tell her, must relieve this tension. He waited through the dinner. Finally Tony collected the bowls and set them into a pot of water. A large bowl of mixed vegetable and leafy greens was served along with hot bread. Joseph had gone for the moment, and Mathew leaned forward, his head barely touching Anna's and said,"Anna, I'm in love with you. " then embarrassed at the suddenness of his statement, he added,"I just had to tell you." He felt his heart race and his body flush."

Anna turned immediately, slid her hands into his and her face was serious. She met his eyes, troubled a little,then said," Thank you,Mathew." She felt his thoughts, tumbling all around them, his feelings tumultuous and unrestrained. She leaned closer and kissed him on the cheek," That isn't an easy thing to say to anyone. I don't feel the same for you, and for that I'm sad. It's what you'd like, isn't it?"

He held her hands tightly, enjoying the touch, "I'd like that if it were true, but enjoying loving you, being with you, is enough." And he actually thought that was true at that moment. She nodded, and he knew she understood, because she had been 'in love' herself.

She said,"Yes, well, we'll be together for a while. I think it'll be all right." She sat a moment ,musing, remembering all the old flims when the struggle to say that simple statement had taken a whole series of events, sometimes lasting years. Such a plot wouldn't work well today.

They helped themselves to salad and everyone gathered again around the small bright flames. In their silence there was room for the vivid sounds of night , the frogs, insects scampering among leaves, the lone ragged scream of a screech owl. The rhythmic music of the Earth thrust itself into their attention and they felt its pulse. The nearby forest reached on beyond them, its mystery always just ahead. It wound among the open fields, disappeared completely for some miles, appeared again over the summits of the foothills, grew wide, then narrow and finally joined the great mountain forest covering the slopes to the high peaks. It was a stream of darkness in the fields of open moonlight, but the gleam of light on that sea of leaves made ripples in the dark.

After a little time, talk began again. Joseph told a short tale of his youth when he had first begun to dance. The others listened, full of the comfort and pleasure of the lovely evening. As he finished his tale they cleared away and brushed the space before the fire. "Well, what'll it be then?" He asked smiling around at them?

Marian settled herself expectantly, a woven cloak wrapped around her shoulders. "You're story made me nostalgic, let's have the songs of the building of the cities." She saw the quick glance from Anna to Mathew, noting, nodding slightly to herself.

THE PEOPLE OF THE VALLEY

Joseph was full of renewed energy, he laughed, "The building songs began before we even got started building Santiago. Early ones are songs of the forest cities. Let's do the Clandor version." Then suddenly he turned to Tony,"Now there Son, is a need. We've no songs for the newest cities yet."

Tony nodded, tuning his clarinet then stopped and said, "Well, they came so fast after the first ones, that we didn't keep up But it was your time, Dad! They were all built, or nearly so,by the time I was old enough to notice".

Joseph nodded, and caught up a bright striped wide band from the cart, tied it about his waist, letting two ends hang to his knees, he rolled down his flowing sleeves and hooked them at his wrists, another colored band wound about his head and he was in costume. The others began humming the melody, trying themselves out. Then they burst out, singing the words. This time Mathew played along, confident in the old ballad. Then Joseph began his dance. Tony stopped playing to sing the chorus but his brother Joe, a rich fine tenor, sang the verses high and true and Tony played again. Dora joined Mathew with her six stringed guitar. Joseph danced, improvising, then reverting to old familiar choreography. He seemed tireless as they felt more than heard or saw the dance and sound weave together. It was a night of the People of the Way.

The air seemed to Anna to be magic now. The sound and movement joined to create a world within which they lived both part of and separate from the Earth life. She felt herself drawn in, joined through the music to this family. Along the road, others had begun their own songs and their music faintly carried on the evening air. Like beads on an endless string that wound its way about the Valley, the sounds of each group united the Vagabonds in another one of their powerful Joinings.

The night was clear, the soft air felt sweet to the skin and Anna thought she had never been so happy. Yet even this must end and when the time came for sleep, they reluctantly put down their instruments.

Joseph turned from putting the fire out, setting the supplies in their place for the night. He glanced upward toward the great moon,now riding high amid a cloudless sky. He laughed and said, "She has dimmed the stars to disappear, with her brightness. As many nights as I've slept under the full moon, she never loses her magic."

Marian nodded, and her eyes traveled on from the moon to the mountains beyond. As she did, the others turned to follow her gaze. They stood silently watching the moon light as it fell across the peaks, snow still gleamed at their tops. She started slightly as her eyes slid over to the shining peaks of the Silent City. She shook her head sadly, "There, always the City looks upon us,always she seems to see no matter where we are in the great Valley. How I long to climb those cliffs and enter that wonderful place."

Her voice had fallen to nearly a whisper and the others wondered at the vehemence of her words. A sadness gripped Joseph's throat. To 'climb the cliffs' was sometimes used as a synonym for death. He shook his head, reached to her and laid an arm across her shoulders. It was a gesture of protection and comfort, but he didn't speak, though his mouth moved as if he would. Joe came back to them from a trip to the shelter. He was drying his head briskly and stopped to look at his mother thoughtfully, then said,"Ma, you've talked of the Journey so many times. Is it Pa, or is it the rest of us that keeps you from that journey?"

She turned to him and her face was soft and her eyes distant. She answered again softly,"Neither Son, neither. Though I know you'd miss me for the trip.I don't plan to wait 'til time for dying either." She heard Joseph's soft release of breath in relief. She reached and took his hand." I've not hesitated to go on journeys that were longer than that would be. It's something in myself, something that stays me each time I think perhaps it's time now. What it is, I don't know. I just don't think it's time yet." She was silent, still staring off at the sky."But one day, Son, it will be time and then I will go."

Anna listened, heard the longing and understood even though she would not have known how to put that understanding into words. She nodded murmuring softly, "I wonder if I will be ready when it's time for me to go there? All this, this meeting and entering the lives of Valley people, seems to be part of the preparation somehow."

The thought held her attention and she did not see Dora moving, shifting her body to move closer to them,uneasily,searching their faces in the moon's light. "Ma, you know what you're saying? I've heard things in Santiago when we passed through and Joe heard it back a month ago before we left the South. About that City. Are you sure you know what it is?"

Her mother made an impatient gesture, bent to straighten her sleeping mat and then stood again and reached with one hand to touch her daughter in reassurance,"What are you talking about, Sweetheart? What've you been hearing."

Dora glanced at her mother,then Anna and they both realized she wanted their support. "It's the Valley Builders,that's what they call themselves. They say the City is not a right thing, that it's a waste and it should either be used by our people, or that we should destroy it. Some think it's evil itself. Some say that we must get inside, make an investigation of it."

Anna murmured,"She - the City is She, not It." Dora shook her head, impatient, afraid they were not understanding."I know that, but they call Her 'it'."

Marian shook her head as if waking from confusion,,"Oh,dear, I have heard something of that talk, but it's so outlandish,so foolish. I just ignored it."

Joseph spoke suddenly, staring at her,anger shaking his voice. "No Marian, No. I don't like your putting it aside like that. It's the way people let a dangerous disease gain strength to ravage the people by ignoring the symptoms. We must not be afraid, or if we are then we must stand before our fear.There are symptoms. We see them everywhere, in every town." His face lost its fierceness, became so suddenly full of grief, that Marian started toward him. "Even among the People, Even among us"!

Marian stopped,her hands rose, gestured in front of her body and face as if warding off danger, she felt her face flush,"No more. No more! It is bad fortune to speak of them."

Joseph looked at her, the anger flared then died, sadness won. "You're hiding, beloved. You've never been superstitious. We can NOT HIDE. Never again." He shook his head slightly and she lifted her own to see his face. So full of sorrow, anger and (she realized with renewed fear) with dispair. Their eyes met, she moved closer to him and then she nodded.

"All right, husband, I'll not hide, though it grieves me. But what is this thing, this fear that emanates from the Builders so palpably that any one of the People of the Way can feel it before they even tell us they are Builders. What is that fear?"

With a quick nod, he took her hand, turned to them all then back to touch her face,"Listen my darling, just pay attention. I know that just down the Way, just two miles, Wanda has gathered with her family for the night. She listens when we Reach. Right now she is there! Thank God it is not in our family, this sickness, this danger. Yet in some families there are those who cannot - cannot know. Who have never felt the Light pierce their hearts. Have never opened their eyes." He knew tears ran from his eyes. He didn't care and felt the power of their attention. "Listen! Attend, and I'll show you what I mean."

Then he Reached out. The power of his Touch was the power of a virtuoso, an artist, energy poured like a stream between them. The tenderness of his approach dissolved all fear, all hesitation. Marian was startled, she had not felt the power of his mind in full function for some time. It seemed stronger than she remembered. But as she experienced, delight filled her eyes. She met with practiced ease the power of this man tuned to Earth. Then she began to breathe softly an evening prayer, "Oh Mother, be with us. Let us know Thy Life this night. May we act with Love not fear. And may the One Life hold us with Thee into Itself"! and then she was with him so totally it was like a melding of their beings.

Anna felt that, knowing it was something she could not share, but knowing the power of it. But the two of them swept their attention out, gathering in their children and then, swiftly Anna too. She was part of this family Joining , a Joining that brought their minds together like lights gathering and entering into one broad beam. Even Mathew focussed and found them. Joseph, reinforced with multiple mind power, Reached further. There were answering Touches, brief acknowledgements, and then there was the strange sense of stumbling. Anna felt it as that, a stumbling against something that resisted the Joined consciousness they pressed outward. Joseph held steady in that stumbling. He recognized it as a pool of fear. It sucked at the mind like an icy draining..

Joseph saw that pool as real as the grass beneath his feet. Fear was a shape that he knew. He felt great grief at its presence and with drew, that he avoid enlarging it with his own grief. They all knew the dark pool, felt it prod and cling at the edges of their Joined Mind. There was a snapping sound and it was gone, then, a gentle calm that seemed to enwrap and protect. Another Mind had reached and without preamble Joined them. They were aware of a name, Wanda, and then it faded. She was there like a pair of wings to lift them high above the dark. She was there streaming through them with a Joy that could not be sucked into those pockets of fear. That entered into the fear to fill it with her Light, her warmth of acceptance. But it moved away, receeded unwilling. Joseph leading, they moved, and passed through the listening and non- listening groups of people along their Roadway. There were here and there, the sudden blocks of darkness, of resistance, even of no response. They found the source of Fear.

Then, with one swift gathering of energy, other focussed minds Joined with them, Wanda led them into Santiago. Anna knew that City, had Reached into it before to meet certain constant minds, receptive and known. But now, she felt Mathew lag behind, felt other Vagabonds join the wondrous lifting. She realized she was one of those who drew them on. Glad, released, soaring on that swift flight of this Joined Reach they were conscious within that sky City. They could support one another easily, she thought.

It was literally flight, mind flight, a song, shaping itself from their hearts in Joy. She thought, "Why has my Family avoided learning, avoided Reaching like this to find our own Soul Song? Why have we never practiced Joining?" And the thought was a brief sadness.

She drew her own power together, she could Reach without restriction here. The Joy of it delighted her. She was there, wound close into the whole, Joseph felt her power and lifted with her. Wanda Touched and encouraged her. Never had she known such permission to Reach to her limit! She felt the exultation of stretching her mind as one held cramped into a small container might feel relief and joy at stretching his body.

They felt a drawing of darkness, of a sinking down. There was a blue residence Globe that was meeting place for a group of citizens and from it came that cool sink of fear. They Touched lightly, held attention, and were repulsed by that stark block of Fear. Swiftly, they withdrew home again. Then separated, falling like small sparks of light from one great flame. They drew back into themselves and separated, silent and thoughtful.

Their bodies sank down on their sleeping mats, resting, the moments of that mind Journey seemed to hold time stilled. Joseph looked weary, having seen and known together, they could not deny ever again. Marian turned to him and set both hands on his shoulders and slowly raised her own eyes to his. "Well, there it is. Deny it no longer. The fear gathers."

"And that is the danger we have felt. The NAME of that danger." Anna was astonished to see that. To admit it.

Joseph smiled wanly, looking at her."You, young lady, I'm surprised. And I was worried that you denied your gifts. You won't be part of that danger. The name of that danger is fear." he repeated. "What greater power is there? What else has done the terrible harm among human beings through ages?"

Tony spoke with awe in his voice,"But Father, Why? I could see greed bringing pain to everyday life, but fear is a result isn't it?" His voice broke, he shook his head,"A result, not a cause?"

Joseph shook his head,"Son, greed, grew from old neediness that we have learned to recognize and resolve. At least many people have. Yes, it caused boundless pain, even for those whose greed bought them wealth. But I think fear is the very cause of greed. The desparate need to survive - then the need to be secure and to surround oneself with things that would ensure that security. Or to force oneself into a position of power for the same reason. Even when humankind was well to do as nations, the ancient fear still lived in us and we didn't recognize it was a source of our greed. You see that,don't you?"

At the boy's slow nod, he went on,speaking now slowly, thoughtfully,"There're other fears - of loss of love, of being helpless, of being outcast, probably the most terrible fear. Only by having control of the good things of life did one feel safe from such pain. To have enough wealth so that we would be included surely in the chosen group, to be always safe in our belongings, could we feel comfort. It became a distorted unhealthy state that was ingrained into our society, that is,the society of our ancestors. Fear of pain, if you will, pain of loss or of exclusion, or even of being hurt. So you can see that fear lies at the heart of all our suffering."

"But Father, we do know that we can survive. We know as long as we take care of Earth, she'll take care of us. I could survive having nothing at all from the towns. But then, I couldn't - no wouldn't want to, without our people". He was trying to make the ideas fit, see how this worked in his own life.

Joseph was almost impatient,"Of, course you could survive, and live well, Son. We've made it a priority to prepare every person in this Valley to take care of themselves." She stopped, a sudden realization struck her. "Why, do you know, it was our very insistence on finding ways to help crippled people become independant, take care of themelves, that led to the development of the Belt. Then, of course, everyone began to use them. But initially, we wanted those hurt ones to be as free as the rest of us." They were silent, considering this, the children had not known that bit of history, Marian had forgotten. Then she said, frowning fiercely, "You are 'able'.But you already can see how terrible it would be to be excluded from the group, for ANY reason." He turned, frowning, to Marian, wanting her to go on.

"Being excluded is terrible because human beings cannot live without one another and live fully. Even hermits have chosen to be separate from something. If a person thinks he is different, he is afraid he will be excluded. So people were afraid of difference, afraid they wouldn't be safe in the familiar circle. Change makes people fear, you know. When people notice that other people act or live in ways that they don't understand, then they fear them. Not belonging, a terrible fate. " Then she smiled brightly,"Today, we've only got to be human and we belong to any group." For moments they were silent, then she went on, "That old fear of the unknown is at the base of it." She was nodding to herself, setting it out in her mind so it made sense to her too."Fear of the strange, fear of the unknown. How does one educate to relieve that?"

Anna wanted to speak, but refrained. She thought this was a Teaching by the adults and she was shy to interfere. Joseph said,"The way we have always taught it, by sending children out into the wild and letting them learn that they can meet the strange and unknown and learn of it, absorb it, become safe along with it. And that they are self sufficient. Our children learn that when they love that creature who is threatening, it ceases to be an enemy. They learn it first hand. But only because they learned it here with us first. Such confidence destroys fear."

"But, my Love, town children do not get such training as often as ours. Many never have. You must realize that."

"But most of them, ours and theirs, have to also go to strange cities and live, try themselves, learn that they are safe with strangers. But everyone doesn't. And I say that's why we're suddenly surrounded by frightened people. Because all the people haven't learned that they are simply safe in this world. No, in this Earth." He was nodding his shaggy head as he spoke, his face frowning with the vehemence of his conviction.

She nodded, as the children watched, fascinated by this conversation,"Well, we'll see whether our Teaching helps. After all, you just said there are those among us who do not See, do not sense the Reach even. And now, can we trust that these will not be overwhelmed with Fear? They can't help but feel different. Will they let fear lead them to harming?"

His face blanched,"Yes, You're right. It's the test for our Way, actually, my Dear. But we have constantly taught our people what Love is, to know that the fact that we are conscious of the Presence of Love is our greatest strength. We - the People of the Way - teach that daily." The two of them were silent .

Then after a bit, Marian nodded, bowing her head, her voice half muffled, but heard,"That is because we take that Love into our own hearts and unceasingly send it out as we receive it." And they could feel her Sending. In the sudden silence they all waited, letting these strong, words and their gift settle in their hearts. Grateful.

Dora came and slid her hand into her Father's in a gesture of seeking comfort,"Then, there's danger, real danger, isn't there. People afraid can do what they would never do otherwise." She sighed, pressing her head against his shoulder, then standing suddenly straight as if with resolution,"You know, we've been taught always to aware of the Presence of Love, to always act with Love. That's what you have insisted we learn. And now, is it enough?" She turned to her Mother, her face reflecting something that made Marian start.

"Dora, child, don't ever be afraid of your fellowmen, don't allow yourself to consider that. We block our consciousness of Love with fear. But Love is ever present, Love is the very breath of our Lives. Only by forgetting It, can we be drawn down into fear. When such a fear intrudes into your life, you are lost to Love, lost to yourself even. You know the kind of self defense that requires no hurting of others, you know Aikido-Chan, our version that makes you safe even from one who has lost control. So do not fear your fellows" She turned to Anna and Mathew,"Have you had the training? Is it common, as I thought it to be, in the Learning Centers?"

Anna nodded, "I don't know of any Learning Center in the Valley where it is not common. We practice the skills as a game all during childhood. We do not need to fear harm from another to our personal selves, and most of us also learn to live with the wild ones. But I didn't know you folks invented it." At Marian's nod and look of relief, she went on,"What you're telling us then, is that we must hold love steady and we must keep faith with the wild ones. Because if we begin to fear, it means we have lost connection with Love!"

Joseph searched the young face sharply, Here was not an ordinary child,he thought."If all the young ones of the towns think as you do, my child,then we are safe." He laughed, "It's well we chose you for daughter."

They all smied at that, feeling somehow better immediately, but Marian said, "We've got to remember that the Builder's anger is against the City. They don't know what we are, or what She is, they cannot See, nor Reach so as to have even a faint sense of the Joining. And so they fear. They cannot See and so we cannot teach them. Our care and our forbearance won't help such.If we explain, it would make things worse."

Dora cried out,"Oh, No, Mother. Surely to teach them, to explain and allow them to see that these knowledges,the talent of Seeing and of Joining , are not evil.Surely that would help."

"It might harm more. Children are taught the nature of Love. They're taught to care about living things. Most adults under forty were carefully TAUGHT these things. Just as they were taught that the task of humanity is to learn to Love. But when it is not EXPERIENCED, it's only an idea, and the question become,'What is Love?'." Marian sighed, then said, "Now, close your eyes," When Dora had complied, she said,"Now imagine that you have never seen a butterfly, and I am trying to tell you of one here, dancing in the air, irridiscent in the sunlight, shining and lifting and falling, lighting on a bright flower. Yet you have known of things only by touch or smell, and have not watched those delicacies of color, movement, and such dancing lightness. Would you believe me when I describe a butterfly to you? Or might you think I was imagining, and trying to fool you. Or even that I was delving in witchcraft?"

Dora felt tears gather in her eyes,"Oh, Mother. For you to be telling me such stories would be a game, fun, unless, I thought that you really believed them. If I'd never seen a butterfly, I would want to believe you. I wouldn't think you insane, because I trust you, but I don't think I could - grasp it's real beauty, only a vague image." She was so sad her mother touched her hand gently,"But then, because I love you, trust you, and am intelligent enough to know there might be something that did exist even if it was outside my personal knowledge, I could also believe you simply on faith." She was firm now, her voice strong and insistent. "But your telling me would make me so aware of what I couldn't see and I would be so sad."

"Exactly! All of that is true. And there are those who do accept because they trust us. Simply accepting on faith. Already I know of such among us. But partly that's because we've never denied, we've always told our children there are

THE AWAKENING

Visions, there are greater perceptions, beyond physical sight. We experience the literal flow of Love through our lives, through ourselves, and we know that Love can be entered into consciously. We ourselves EXPERIENCE that Love. We KNOW. And all those who do not feel it in our lives, see our lives as examples of Love. Then, they can imagine something of what it is." She stopped, thoughtful, wanting to find the right words. "It's in the Joining that we share something of the glory of it. Those who cannot Reach even, miss that. We cannot show them our evidence. That is our grief. That is our pain." She leaned against Joseph and he gently stroked her hair, his own eyes wet.

Finally Joseph continued the Teaching "We have taught our own children that we Reach, that we mentally Touch and Join, and we have not denied. So they have grown up knowing and expecting that it is a natural thing. Just as we know that one has talent to dance, and another might not, though he can learn something of it." He took his daughter's hand and drew her nearer, then he turned to Marian, "My Dear, I think we have prepared our own people. I truly do. But I don't think the town people have prepared their's." He looked sadly at Anna and Matt. They met his gaze with a growing sorrow. But they did not flinch.

There was silence,long and fragile with grief. After some minutes Marian said."This is the time the songs told of. The times when Teachers of Light would come from the North,the East the West and the South, from each corner of Earth, to help us. We must search for such, for surely they must be among us now."

Anna started then, her mind swept clean by swift recognition, "Of course, they are. It must be. There is a Teacher come from the north to us. One who came with my Father, Benjamin. There is Jessie. She has to be one of these the songs tell of.Don't the old songs say the People of the Ways would be the ones who would recognise the True Teachers ?" They nodded slowly, wondering at her excitement. "Then your people must know!"

Joseph was on his feet again, "You know of such an one?" His face cleared, filled with dawning realization.

"Why, yes, she is one I've heard of from some of our own Elders.

Yes, and there is talk of others, but I've not met them." He sighed, then turned again to Anna."Tell us something of the one you know."

Yes, she came with my father when he returned from his long Journey. I know she works with all the northern towns. But she lives with our family. She's never worn Teacher's robes, though." Their eyes met and he nodded. She felt her heart heavy. There must be a way to meet the problems , to unravel the danger that threatened the Valley. She said,"Will you come, meet her, tell us if she is one who comes to help? Perhaps Edsil, your Council member would know. He is prescient. Or Adam and Deborah, they are too!"

Joseph heaved a great sigh, nodding, he opened his mind, focussing into a Sending as powerfully as he could to Wanda, that one who might know. But Dora broke in.

"So there are a lot of people who're afraid. There is danger. What'll we do!"

Marian laughed then, "Good, you're not defeated, but ready to take some action. Well, my sweet, it's not the action of attack but of deep knowing. We must surround, fill the Valley, with that conscious Sending of Love. We must be ourselves open to that energy that flows now through our Valley and project it steadily. I know of no other way to end fear, except through Love." They watched her, listening as if they'd never heard such words. She frowned, shook her head abruptly, "We must learn even more how to Love."

Tony said angrily, "But those who fear us do not love us. How can they know of our love?"

Unable to restrain herself now, knowing she must also offer, Anna cried out,"Oh, no, Tony, - look! See! Love is not something we do, or have. You know that. I know you do. Love just IS. We know of IT. We only have to allow Love to flow through ourselves, so that it might wake the spark in someone else. Love is PRESENT among us all the time. Our Teacher Jessie says that Love is SPIRIT itself and cannot be separate from us. We only have to acknowledge and -- and tune in to IT. It's all we can do!" She looked so anxious, so longing to have him remember that knowledge, that he dropped his eyes in a brief but fading shame, nodding.

Marian raised one hand, her fingers seemed to caress him even as he stood yards from her. "Son, whether we always know or not, it is our way. That's what is meant by the name of our people, the 'People of the Way'. It's our task to sustain consciousness of Love, regardless. Else we are no different from those who fear. Will you then allow fear to fill your own heart? You know there's no end to fear present, we have constant access to that emotion and it is no more than that! It's really a matter of making a choice!"

Tony looked up at her, his eyes shadowed,"I'm afraid I've been making a choice without realizing. I feel so afraid now." He straightened, "But you're right. I can make a choice!" His voice took strength. With a deep breath, he smiled,"I know of Love. I know and I won't forget again."

Dora was openly weaping,"The City, they must not harm the City."

Marian put an arm around Dora's shoulders and drew her close."You are full of sentiment, and though sentiment is fine, at times, it doesn't have anything to do with that great City. Ah, as for the City, my dears, I do not fear for Her. No one can harm Her. I am sure. She has her own life. She will care for Herself. I know that. She will be there when it is time for me to make the Journey." She took Anna's hand too, and said softly,"She'll be there with her wonderful Light" At those words a calm fell over them, a relief. It was as though her trust, an inner knowledge lit for them the very darkness that had begun to invade their hearts. She added softly,"Stand steadily in the Light of that Love and It will extend Itself through us."

Joseph stood, drawing his mate to stand with him, his hands pressed upon her shoulders. Bending his head a little, he touched her cheek with his lips, "Dearest one, when you make that Journey, I want to be with you. I want to be ready!"

She reached up a hand to cover his and said ," Perhaps that is one of the

THE AWAKENING

things I wait for!" Their eyes met, and Anna, watching, finally turned away, so naked was the intimacy. Then with a light laugh, Marian, said," I've known few people of the Way who do not want to make the Journey. But then, Joseph, there have always been some who don't know what the Journey is."

Anna nodded slowly, She had known all her life the reverence the Vagabond People felt for the City. But never had she seen it so clearly. She said,"Maybe that'll give some knowledge of the Teacher, Jessie, for she talks of the Journey, that we must all take that Journey. Our Family, and - and others." She looked surprised at her own recognition. Joseph and Marian looked at each other.

Marian said, "Perhaps we must meet this Jessie you speak of. Perhaps she will know of any others who Teach through the Valley. I trust the old songs."

But Anna was still caught in her thought,"There is a secret there then? A secret that we've denied in that City?"

Joseph watched her closely,"Little one, your Family has the Sight, they know of the City. Surely they have spoken of Her, of her Presence?"

She shook her head,"Not much, We do, some of my friends, feel - something, as though we're being drawn to her, to see the beauty of the light there. But no one told me what that was. I thought it was just myself. My family hasn't TALKED at all", her face lit up in surprise,"That is, not until lately, after Jessie came."

"I can see we'll have to meet this lady, surely. I think she must be the same one Adam told us of. And none of us realized she might be, might be one of the Coming Ones.I'm not sure even Adam did." A soft smile played at his lips. His eyes were distant, as if looking for some speck in the bright moonlit sky. "Such people rouse us to Life."

They sat, again, leaning into their bedding rolls, looking at the sweep of moonlight over the land, feeling the benediction of that light. A light breeze carried scents of blooming fields, of forests and of the crushed grasses around them. The night seemed infinitely lovely so that their hearts were ready to break with it. After some time Marian began again to speak.

"And so, there is an energy moving among us, an energy that everyone feels.Those who do not understand at all, begin to feel fear because the energy is great". Marian summed up her understanding."She nodded, bringing the palms of her hands together she touched her chin with the tips of the fingers, "Our people have always thought that the City pours the energy of Love out among us, and depending on our capacity and our intention, we receive." Her voice was almost a whisper, and Anna accepted the gift, for it was not often the Vagabonds spoke of their deep knowledge.She felt the light of the moon radiant all around them. Then, in this open land, she realized that the light of the City too seemed to pour like a streaming down among them. Never had she seen it so bright, so radiant. As though their very talk had opened a pathway for that light.

Dora spoke softly, "When I was younger I used to think the City was a gateway into another world. I thought if one stepped through, one could never return. That's why I was fascinated and fearful. But She shines so bright tonight.

The other peaks do not have that Light."

They all turned then to watch the City. The Light did seem stronger, it shimmered, gleaming in the dark water of the River, It could not be explained by saying it was the brilliant moonlight. For the moon lay upon everything the same. Anna felt the Light on her face, and started to speak but she saw that they were sitting in Silence. She felt nourished by the purity of that Light, and then as they sat for some time,she lost her desire to speak. The others slowly, one by one, turned to their bed rolls. She still sat though, caught in wonder, for the first time she knew the longing to go there. To make a Journey. It had meaning now, that idea of a Journey. The words seemed to be exactly what she meant. She gave a curt nod. "Yes, I will. One day I will go there."

She drew herself away, slid into her blankets and settled against the soft pad beneath. Then she looked around,, all the others were sitting up, in their beds, silently meditating, softly singing or chanting. She felt somehow left out, cut off from the depth of life the others must know. Mathew seemed not to notice, he was buried beneath his blankets. She felt deprived of some beauty, some conviction that these people gave to their children without stint.

They were so calm, their faces so relaxed, and at peace. She wished impulsively to be one of them. Then she shook her head,"No, I have my own family, to whom I belong as deeply. After all, Anna girl, you can't have everything." But she smiled at the thought and realized that she had much to learn from the Vagabonds. She reached one hand out to touch Mathew. One by one the People slid down into their bedding and slept.

In the night, Anna woke. She got up. went to relieve herself in the privy within the stone shelter. When she came back she slipped into bed silently still feeling the magic of the moonlight. She didn't want to sleep. She heard a sound and saw Joseph walking naked from his bed. He pulled a light robe over his head, it fell to his knees. She knew then that his thoughts were troubled, and that troubling would not let him sleep. He seemed to reach out in a delicate Touching so as not to waken anyone. She felt that Touch as a call and slid from her bed, pulled on pants and shirt and went barefoot to follow him. She took his arm.

He turned at her touch, surprise and then pleasure, then amusement broke through the sorrow of his face. "Anna, you've come. I ought to be surprisd but I'm not. I don't know why. But then I'm glad. It's a long night when one can't sleep. He sat down on a stone seat and smiled at her.

She said, "Oh Joseph, I know, I'm a child and you have little need of me, but I heard your call and I wanted to come.I hope you don't mind."

He turned fully to meet her eyes, a sardonic smile playing about his mouth below the steady sorrow of his eyes,"Mind? I welcome your company, child. But how can I call you a child? No one is a child who knows as you do. You have lived and understood many lives, little daughter. We ignore age among us when the heart tells us there is wisdom." He turned away.

She nodded unsmiling and then said seriously, so that he would understand."Tell me then. talk to me about those things that are troubling your mind."

He nodded seriously, looked to the mountains and after a bit began to talk as if to himself. "During these years, teaching people, walking in the careful manner of one seeking the Way to the true Self, speaking understandings I have been taught,and what I learned from my own heart, I have followed with deep devotion and singlemindedness. It seemed right. I've known great joy and a sense of direction. But now it's all changed."

Anna asked,"There were things that gave you confidence once?"

He was silent, then,slowly nodding, he went on,"There've been wonderful visions of what I have decided are the truly real. Wonderful times of seeing the Divine nature of Earth Herself,and the Divine nature of every man and woman I met. There've been times of being sure. The path under my feet was right and I was confident. But now, there seems to be something that is changing all that was."

"There is a slow dissolution. Even the great Silent City, once a terror and eventually a Joy is sometimes for me an empty futile relic. I look with pain on what seems an empty shell when I look at my beloved Mate. It's as though she's - gone, otherwhere. She about whom all meaning has woven.I feel as though all has slipped from me, has dissolved, has faded from that time of splendor of my youth, when all was my own." He choked back the pain, his grief being thus spoken,grew full."Oh, child,how can I burden you with this?" He turned to look at her,their eyes met and their minds Touched , then Joined. She moved into his knowing. His eyes lost a little of their pain."You are not a child at all." He spoke softly, as matter of factly as if he had known this all along."Or else you are a child of a new race of humanity."

She sighed."I am a child. But I am also aware, just as you are. We can support each other. I know of this loss you speak of."

He drew then a little away as if to protect her, his mind shielding her from his roiling emotions. He spoke with a choking cry,"Loss! Loss of my very life it is!" Then, quieted, he spoke softly. "Why, after all these years of confidence, of knowing, does everything seem only an empty shell. Everything I thought was so important? His voice was full of strain and grief. His hands clutched at the air and then fell helplessly at his side. "I can't speak of it to Marian, I can't cause her such sorrow."

" The worst perhaps is in the daily life of our family. What was so long the joy and delight of life for me,has -- changed. My love is no less clear, not less great. No, you must realize that. It is as great as always. To see them grow, to watch them become people with joy in their hearts. That is a wonder, yes, it still is. But -- -."

He had been speaking with a desparate insistence as if these truths had never before been wrenched from him and he must finish the job now. He knew he spoke the thoughts he had not admitted before, had steadily denied. Why did he speak them now? He didn't know, but refused to consider. "Over everything,there is a sense of pointlessness, of loss --" He spoke the last softly, wearily, as if he had just realized it. Just acknowledged what he had fiercely denied. He stood now, nodding his head, tears steaming, his face bleak with a nameless pain that Anna felt in her own body as she Touched."Yes, even all that, all I have of life, it is nothing, it is lost, as if, what I lived for all my life, has no meaning, yet, I know, intellectually it does.

"All of this," he waved his arms, took in the land,the sky, the family, the Earth life, "all that I've lived for. Even my Marian! It's not enough, it's not enough. Something is missing. Something I do not even know how to name."His voice rose to a thin cry, "Why not? Why not? All that I've lived for, all that life meant for me. The absolute beauty of Earth, of my people,why is it not enough." He pounded his fists against the air, then caught his face in his palms and rubbed away all the tears fiercely. "Always my people, the daily journey, the music, dance, the Land itself, filled me, gave life rich meaning, and now" he shook his head, bewildered by his own words ,"Now they just don't, there is some crucial ingredient missing and how can I discover it if I don't know what it is? Something inside me has broken free, has begun to insist, to seek what I do not have, do not know. I don't understand."His voice had fallen to a whisper. "I understand your father now, my dear, I understand why he kept running away, searching so desparately."

Anna had no idea what words could help, she said, "It's a terrible time for you, Father Joseph."

He heard only the Love in her voice, and nodded,"I see them all, I see all that our Valley is, with such Love it reverberates through each minute of living and yet, it's -- it's just not ENOUGH. I don't know what is in store for us in our future,because I cannot break free of myself , of this dispair ." He was clenching his hands at his chest. His voice flattening into emotionlessness that was more frightening to her than his tears had been. He stood silently rubbing his hands over the rough side of a four foot boulder extending up from the grass as though comforted by the physical reality of the Earth.

Anna nodded, struggling to understand. She refused to Reach again, to Join with him for she was sure it would wake Marian and he evidently did not want that. She wondered whether Marian did not already know, how could a true mate not know when her mate was in such anguish. If so, she chose to allow him this respite from herself.

Anna thought her own life was at that place when all that happened seemed to fit, to be part of a meaning. She was full of Joy and love of life. What must it be like to have lived so long, to have seen friends, events, come and go. He was not that much older than her parents, yet just now, he seemed ancient. She visualized, as if it were real, a glimpse of having lived to a hundred long years, the power and the vision of it,then the glimpse was gone. The memory hung there in her mind. Where had it come from? Some far memory? It had been so real. He noticed her sudden detachment, her inner drawing and smiled.

"You're wise beyond your years young one. You've lived many lives and those years speak themselves through your eyes". He shrugged, his face falling again into dispair."It's unfortunate that you came to me. For now you are burdened with my pain."

She shook her head." No, I know it is your pain.It teaches me and I want to understand, to support you if I can."

As if he could not wrench himself away from that inner outpouring which he had dammed from sight for so long, he blurted out,"It's all a natural thing after all. It must be. The very nature of dispair is that one feels no hope left at all.There is no point at which one can say, 'Yes, of course, there is a way, there is direction.' It's gone, Not there. There's nothing I can see except the slow drift of grey and repetitive days. I see no where to go from here. I've lived long enough, perhaps." He drew his hands over his face, pressed against his eyes, Yet, underneath the pain there's that strange sense that something is missing, that if I could find it, then purpose, meaning would right itself again." He looked unseeing at her face, "What a strange thought that is. For what can be missing, I have everything a man could want."He screwed his face into a grimace."To be truthful, I think I'm afraid to turn around."

She was puzzled,"Turn around?"

He turned to look at her then,"Yes, the thought keeps pressing at my attention and I want to deny it. It is that I ought to turn away, turn deliberately, with choice, from everything I've known, loved, lived for, to turn around, and ---there would be --- " his voice had dropped to a whisper and she leaned close to hear.He went on,"Then there IT would be, whatever it is, and I don't think I want to know." With a shuddering sigh, his body relaxed, as if this final confession released him. He had not known that that confession was there to be made. He sat then in wonder at the fact of it.

Then he murmured, his eyes lost in distance,"It's there, that which I refuse to See. That I did not know I refused, and yet, now -- I see it's alive, a fierce life in me, with a burning demand to go on, beyond everything I know, everything I live for, everything I am." He stopped, and she felt his body shiver slightly."To tell it that way, to speak it aloud, seems to make sense, irrevocable sense, as if I've passed a point of no return." His eyes were lost among the mountains, forgetting her. And after some silence, he said,"As if I've actually turned around somehow."

For a long time they were both silent. Their eyes and hearts filling with the moonlight, the Light of the City and the upward thrust of Earth power. Finally Anna sighed, and he looked at her. She met his eyes and held them."I appreciate your confidence. I value what you've told me. I want to ask you something, Joseph, because you are more than friend to me. I ask that you talk of this with Marian. She is one who would know, would not be afraid. Trust her." She ducked her head, sighed and then met his eyes to add,"As a matter of fact, I think she knows now of our talk."

He shook his head, tightened his lips, then slowly, he began to nod. "Oh, My God, it may be she does, that she knew -- knew that I could not speak to her. She is -- she is after all, my Mate." His voice was a little stronger, a faint smile began to play along his lips," Everything seems so different now. It is as though a twist in the path has been turned, that I have chosen. I still don't understand, but I think I can talk to her, she does know my heart. Perhaps she has known my pain and suffered that I could not ask her for help." They sat in silence then, the sky grew light slowly. The moon had set, and now, a faint glow brightened the edges of the eastern peaks beyond which lay the rest of their country.

Anna finally spoke, watching the thin, grey, color of dawn seep through the air,"There seems to me to be a kind of rotting of oneself, a dying away, maybe, that's what it feels like. It's like a fruit that's matured and has produced its seed and now must rot away so that seed might begin its life. That seems to me to be the happening that changes living. Perhaps it is like that?"

He nodded, fascinated,"What an image, but it fits. It sticks into my mind , and I know we use it to talk of death of the body to our children, to teach them the way of death, and life continuing. We have not used it, or rather I have not used it to speak of the death of -- of " He looked at her in surprise,"Why, it's a death of 'world attachment', just as our Teachers tell us. Is it not? That's why it feels as though nothing matters anymore." He was suddenly caught up in the help of her image, "Yes, it's the rotting away of world desires, of personal intentions and beliefs. Yes, it is then, another kind of death and that's why it hurt so, was so full of grief and loss. There is surely death in me. Only now, it is loss of myself for which I grieve." His voice had become so mournful that Anna reached to take his hand, to draw it to her and cling to it for comfort for herself as much as for him.

She said, watching the place where the sun stained the sky with orange,"It's what they taught us, our Master Teachers. It was a puzzle to me once. I see now, as you explain," intuitively she turned him into the teacher to save his dignity later."That's what they meant,this dying of the self, this ego." Her face radiated surprise and delight,"That's what they meant. They didn't tell us it hurt so much, nor that one wouldn't know what it was as it occurred. They missed something there."

"How could they have told us? We wouldn't have heard. After all, I too remember having heard the words. But I didn't remember when it came to me." He frowned. "I think I didn't want to remember. It's almost as if I wanted to suffer."

She nodded, "That may be. I know I didn't understand. You've taught me so much this night."

They sat thus for some time, his hand closed around her small one, warm and strong, it gave her courage. He straightened his shoulders, sat up, "If it's true then, that rotting you spoke of, then I'm the fruit itself, the rotting fruit. How can I know myself except in pain of dying. How does one leap over, realign, and know oneself the Seed? To seek so far within, to find the center where the new life is! How? The identity shift, the change?" He sat for another moment, his hand pressing hers to pain. Then suddenly he leaped to his feet, laughing, as the sun rose above the peaks and spread like a flood across the land."But there it is! I do know my Self after all.I do recognize that inner Life. Of course, and it's done by wondering how, by knowing the leap is there. That it must be made. It's part of the recognition. Remember. The Teachers did tell us. 'I am not the fruit'. I am and

THE AWAKENING

always will be the Seed. This person Joseph is the fruit of this life, and as Joseph, I have added nourishment to this inner Life, this seed of Self. All that Joseph has learned." Then he ran across the grass, glowing like a torch of the sunlight.

After a moment he came back, one part of his mind already aware that Marian was up, ready to greet the Sun." But how can I know how to realize that yet. To realize all that I am ." He was smiling through the pain that lay still in his eyes. I do not know how to realize , to fully KNOW myself Seed. Or from what vast tree this seed has sprung! It is like a fire within the fruit. Within me." He spoke the words as though trying out the ideas," I am a fire within myself." Then he laughed again, almost his old self, finding words to speak to himself. "Ah, Anna, you must not tell anyone that this old man has lost his balance" His face was illuminated, the sunlight stirring new life into him.

Anna laughed then too,"I will talk of this with Jessie, when I am home. "

He nodded, "We pass that way. I'll ask her, perhaps she can show me how to realize what I know, to fully consciously grasp, or at least live what I am discovering."

They sat quietly while the dawn grew from grey to rosy light, flooding the forests, the fields wet with dew that sparkled where the sun was caught. It lay silently and impersonally on all things, yet it transformed all it touched. They heard Marian then, walking from her sleeping place to make her morning prayer. For the first time in days he wanted to join her, to repeat the familiar words, to greet the new life that had broken the resistance in him.

A flair of hope like a bright flame cut through his preoccupation. Then he knew that the familiar prayer,the old ritual was also that which had lost meaning. How could he return to it. He must find a new way to Reach to that City that she honored as she did the dawn. What had once had meaning was only a shadow now but he did not dispair at that. The sunrise, the City, they were as beautiful as ever, their promise could be seen now with new perception. There had dawned in himself the edge of another, a greater Knowledge that told him life itself was meaning, if it unfolded in steady unresisted discovery.

There were loud yawns and a sudden burst of movement from the boys. Joe jumped from his bed and smiled at them, a great smile of pleasure to have a new day ready for him. Anna and Joseph nodded, pleased at his joy. Joseph stood and stretched, feeling the stirrings of hunger and he murmured softly,"For these small things, that give pleasure, I give thanks." He watched the climb from their sleeping bags, walk across the wet grasses to raise their arms, lift their faces to the sunlight and the City far away. He turned to face his mate who came now, her face wreathed in smiles, her eyes spilling tears of joy.

Anna went then to join Joe as he turned on the Solar power unit of the stone stove. It would not take much. Breakfast was partly eaten on the road. At this early season, only berries would be ripe along the way so they would take dried fruit from the cart and some good bread with their hot coffee. Anna enjoyed being in Joe's company, he seemed so exuberant, to so enjoy his body. They leaped over the great round boulders that marked the Highway in this field, and laughed at each other. The journey would be good this day.

CHAPTER TWENTY EIGHT

William speaks of the Builders

Rose called William in the early morning on a day in late May. When his face appeared on the screen she studied it with attention and could not see unease or hostility. She was surprised at herself for expecting that. He seemed as he always had. He looked at her with curiosity, a searching swift study of her face, as though he were seeing it anew, or as though he had not really seen her at all before. He let the first few seconds pass wherein they each studied the other,"Well, it's good to see you Will." She finally said."How are you?" He knew she really wanted to know. Her voice carried the love she felt.

He nodded as if accepting the affection," I have been very well, Rose, and Annette has too. We've been busy, of course. I'm sorry I've seen so little of you all in the last months. So much is beginning in this Valley. But surely you know that. There's so much to do." His smile was only partly genuine and she winced. But then he frowned as if realizing that himself."You're still planning to make the Journey to that City. I can't abide that. I think you're wrong."

Rose shook her head, impatient. "Oh, now, Will, you know that no one expects any one do that journey unless they want to. It's not that kind of thing. It's very personal, in fact. We'd just like to see you here with us. You're part of our Family after all. We miss you." He didn't deny that, but his eyes shifted suddenly, and she realized that he felt pleasure at the reminder of his belonging. "But we're coming to you, since you won't come to us. Ben and I are coming up with Paul and Jennifer. They've been here for a visit this week. Can we see you?" She didn't realize how much she feared his answer.

But he seemed genuinely pleased, nodded and then laughed as if with some relief."Yes, Yes, of course. We'll get together as soon as you're here. When will you come?"

Rose was relieved at the genuine pleasure in his voice, her heart lifted and she smiled happily ,"I'm glad, Will. We'll be there by noon."

She closed the connection, turning to Ben and Paul who had been listening. She looked from face to face, surprised at their seriousness,"Well, you sour pusses, what's the matter. He wants to see us."Paul nodded abstractedly, his eyes met hers and she nodded sadly,"I know Paul, I'm ignoring my own apprehension whenever I can. I've got to be hopeful about Will. Something about him worries me a lot."She looked so sad then that the men were a little repentant. But she Reached impulsively to them and felt their combined Touch as an affirmation. The trip to Altos would not be with out sorrow.

Rose said with resignation, "Well, we're lucky, actually. Only one of our whole family and we've known William was not able to respond for years. We've simply ignored what we knew. Just as we've denied so much else." She turned to

THE PEOPLE OF THE VALLEY

the window, looked out toward Adwin in the early morning light. The grey softness of rain seemed to enclose them, to separate them from the world, and at the same time to make all the world one vast wet sea. She could barely make out the flaming color of the Temple across the fields. "After all, some Families have had to count two among them who are -- limited. " She used the word quickly as if not wanting to let it be heard."

They nodded, and she turned back to them. Paul said, "I was surprised when Jessie said that though they can't Reach or Touch, can't sense what we do, they are still aware -- aware that they can't. A good many of those mind-blind people know there is something going on they can't realize, can't understand. They sense that there is a change happening in this Valley. They just don't know what it is. We'll have to see how many can see the difference and at the same time accept it without resentment. Such are truly great Souls, I think."

He shook his head, "I think I'd be angry. Fearful. If I saw some thing was happening and didn't understand."

"But the Master Teachers are correcting that, aren't they? They're begun special training for children, and adults, to show them although differences are beginning to be obvious they don't set one above the other." Rose spoke as if testing the idea. "But then, it doesn't mean everyone will accept."

Ben said softly, "No, some people are reacting with fear. Some simply don't understand and want to go back to the old days, to the past. As if that would save us ."

"Well, we can convince Will that we love him, at least that. We can stand with him. Surely he will know that." Rose was full of a grief that she could not name, a grief having little to do with William.

Ben shook his head,, "We might NOT convince him. I don't know enough about the Builders. We've let so much time pass. We've been ostrichs with our heads in the sand. I ought to know more." He was angry, his hands plunged deep into his pockets , fists bulging against his thigh.

Paul leaned back in the chair he had dropped into as if weary. He stretched his legs, sliding his arms down the wide chair arms, making himself comfortable. "Well, do we have enough Love. Are we going to be able to love a man who seems to have betrayed us? Brother, he may be, but it's happened before that people've denied their brother for turning against them. I don't know whether I have that kind of Love. That kind of selfless Love."

Ben nodded, "I don't know whether I have. But we'll find out! Anyway, Will might resent our love. Might see it as patronizing. He's proud."

Suddenly Jennifer, who had been sitting silently watching, said, "Oh, now, every one of you know that what people resent is not Love at all. There is no other kind of Love except selfless Love. What you are turning on Will sounds more like your own sentiments than like Love."

Paul visibly flinched, then held out a hand, "You've spoken it, my darling. It's exactly true. It's up to us to see that, to remember. To keep constantly in mind that we do not HAVE LOVE. We'll do well if we can stand in Love while we meet and talk. But we do have affection, and caring, and perhaps the need for our family to be intact. Those are at least the reflections of Love."

Rose was watching, nodding sadly, She drew a finger idly along the fine enbroidery of her green plasilk dress. "How easy it is for us to return to old patterns. How can we learn. We've nothing to crow about. We've begun to think ourselves superior without even realizing it. That's a danger we can't afford."

Ben nodded, got up to walk about. He was dressed for their trip to Altos in a soft, flowing, deep blue, shirt,with pearl grey trousers tucked into blue boots. Rose measuring him, thought he looked fine, with his blond hair grown long enough now to touch his collar. He went to stand beside the window, watching the forests to the north, seeing the dense sea of leaves underneath which little grew except ferns and lichens and clumps of shade loving plants. The sun blazed in the wide fields of grass that flowed like a living sea through the forests even there in the hills. His eyes followed through the flowing of that sea, were caught now and then by clumps of shrubs that created islands of dark green. The land was healthy and looking at it comforted him. A sudden image of the torn and devastated acres east of Santiago that the Builders had taken, swept before his mind's eye. He flinched. Still, the land itself was healthy, even though there were places of destruction. He said, "Well, we'll find out, I'm afraid, before this day is much older.But I'd like to talk to Tom a little. I'd like to know more about the Builders before we go. It's true, we've denied so much that now, we aren't prepared at all. Well, no more." He moved resolutely toward the video-phone.

Two hours later they arrived at the Altos landing grid. There was a message for them at the reception computer stand. Will wanted them to come immediately to his home. Minutes later they were entering the apartment in the pyramid of homes. Rose ran into the room, caught Annette in her arms, seeing her shy glance, and then the strangely closed look. A look that held for them also an entreaty. Her manner was more of a blow to them than anything William said,though he greeted them with the usual affection and hugs. Dear sweet, Annette,always she had responded to them with such an abandon of love; cheerful and full of trust. Rose's heart sank. Even the wide grin on William's face couldn't relieve her fear. William spoke rapidly, cheerful, "It's about time we got together here. We've been careless and haven't done much Gathering in these past two years." He seemed astonishingly oblivious of the fact that he had not attended what Gathers had been held in this spring.

Ben met William with a handshake first then he moved forward and wrapped him in a bear hug. He felt William's initial resistance fade to participation in that gesture of affection and was comforted. He couldn't decide how he felt toward William. He seemed so much the same, glad, eager, full of welcome. Benjamin shrugged, determined to believe that he was mistaken and that all was truly as it always had been.

Annette had prepared a lunch for them, wanting them to know her welcome. William helped her set the table, then brought the plates. They began to eat and Paul shook his head,"I didn't think anything could get better than your auto-kichen programing, William, but your mate has surely proven me wrong."

Will shook his head, gesturing toward Annette and she smiled. "Believe it or not this is an auto chef lunch.I take credit, I've worked with this unit for several years to get it to reproduce my own recipes just as I do. It's getting nearly as good too. I could set the program into your unit next time I come to the farm if you like. It's not difficult now that I've got it working right." She frowned in thought,"It seems so long since I was last home with you all."

Then at the memory that William had chosen not to come to that Gather, they were drawn back to the question in hand. For moments no one spoke, they ate, enjoyed,smiled at the wonderful scents and flavors. They talked of ordinary events of their lives, asked about their various children and laughed at some of the answers. Finally they leaned back into their chairs to drink their small cups of liquor. The drink was at once stimulating and an aid to digestion, it felt like a sweet fire in the stomach at first and then it brought a calm. But it was also a signal, and every person there, availed him-herself of years of training in Balancing, to stabilize that calm and keep it.Rose said,"It's always so good to be here, in Altos, with you and Annette, William." She met his eyes and he knew she meant what she said."

The others nodded, William shifted uncomfortably in his chair, He caught at the edge of that unease and drew himself sternly together, reminding himself of his convictions. The others felt and acknowledged the change in him.

Rose said abruptly, "Annette, we've missed seeing you. I know you're preparing a show and that takes a lot of time, but we do miss you!"

Annette had not prepared herself for questions, and she felt the question in Rose's statement. She was caught off guard,opened her mouth to speak,but was surprised to find tears flooding her eyes. She blinked to stop their falling. She felt helpless, defeated, and those feelings were terrifying to her. "I was busy it's true. I don't know whether I could say I could NOT have taken time." She would not dissemble, she met Rose's eyes and there was a steady strength now in their gaze. She went on," There was so much William had to manage these last months too.He just felt that my being here --- my being with him,--". She stopped,,knowing full well that the others were aware of her avoidance. And helplessly she saw that she was dissembling after all. She stopped, looked from one to the others, then shook her head, and spoke gently, all pretense gone, tears ignored, "I don't know, I don't know."   William was visibly angry. He stood. With a fierce control he brought himself into balance but to do so he had to cut himself off from them all and they felt as though a cold draft had entered the room. Rose felt her heart sink, she knew she could not refuse to acknowledge her own recognitions anymore. Ben's face had settled into a mask of grief he made no effort to hide. Paul sighed, unable to hope now that they had been mistaken.

Rose asked, "William did you know that Annette has often stayed home for your sake? Did you want that?"

William glanced at Annette,whose face was expressionless. The thought flickered through his mind that that was strange. Annette did not conceal. He said, "Why no, I think she didn't go because she had too much to do to get ready for her show. Wasn't that so dear?"He had drawn himself back until he was only a reflection of that affable friendly brother they knew. There was falseness here.

Annette's smile was faint and stained with contempt, but it only lasted a moment. Rose was cold with that recognition. What was happening to them all. There was hidden meaning, falseness, refusal here. They had not succumbed to such before. Annette said,"You said you needed me" She would not cover for him and Rose felt relief.

"Well, yes, I did say that. I thought we ought to try to take care of things here. Things have not been easy for us."

"Us? For you and Annette? I don't understand. There are problems we don't know of then."

Will was visibly uneasy,"No, No, not anymore. We've worked out the trouble left from that birthday Journey". He glanced at Paul with a gleam of resentment, though his lips smiled. "It's a hard time for Builders. You must all know how hard it is for a young organization just beginning to grow rapidly. We've got so much to do and there are misunderstandings that must be ironed out. You realize I'm chairman for the central Valley Builder's League? He spoke with uncharacteristic pride and smugness that startled Paul. Of all qualities that was one least expected from William. He had always had too much sense to strut. Rose nodded, her understanding growing sadly. She and Ben exchanged glances and she noticed that Annette saw their exchange with a new flush of color to her cheeks.

Ben said, quietly,"You are working with the Builders then!" For a long moment he absorbed that fact. Then, visibly shaking himself, he asked,"What is it they're trying to do?"

William drew a long breath, glad to have the question finally spoken.. "There are changes that need to be made in this Valley. it is a growing time of change, surely you all must see that. You've all seen the reports on News Video. You must have seen the interviews with the Valley Council. You've heard our requests.But the organizing of our people takes time." He stood to walk nervously from window to door and back again.He was puzzled at his nervousness. Then, drawing another deep breath, he let himself relax. You see the Valley is at a point of change. We've got our cities built. We're pretty well established as a society, but now, we must get into business with the rest of the world. Plan for the future." He saw Ben move to speak and stopped.

"What do you think needs changing here?" There was an edge of hostility in Ben's voice. He heard it and the sentence ended in a faint note of apology.

Will was too intent to notice,"We want to open up wasteland, build pastures where wild fields are wasting away. We've got wonderful grass land, we could raise cattle enough to feed everyone in this Valley, if not more for export. Finally, people can have meat again, all they want! " He grinned, his body taking on a new animation. He was sure of himself. "We can open up new markets in foriegn countries. People have fallen away from eating meat but that can be corrected with a few steak houses. He took a breath, glancing out into the rainy day,"We need entertainment, places where we can go evenings for a drink and talk. We've so few even here in Altos and it's time we built them. There we could sell wines, beer and especially hard liquor if we start making it. Two new businesses just waiting for us to develop them.There are others - the simulated reality halls down in the Black Lodge are astonishing. We could have them here."

His voice took on the note of a politician business man, they listened in shocked silence. This was a strange unfamiliar William. Annette saw their astonishment and bowed her head, finally they would know."We could do much more. The soil here is rich. We plan to plant thousands of acres of wine grapes, build that market too, people have forgotten how to have the kinds of parties people used to have in the old days. People used to flock into the local pub, for evening drinks and talk. We can change all that I think. We can build wineries, good business for new young towns. New businesses built out of new products. Magazines for advertizing - only three or four in the whole Valley and they have only announcements, no real advertizements. You can't imagine what power skilled advertizing can have in making people want things. And paper mills to supply paper for that. Advertizing worked. It persuaded people. It'll provide a huge market for paper. The big mill in Trencher is small, we've got forests that need cutting. And that new vine our Wizards gave the Valley, they call it the Paper Vine, I think. Makes fine quality paper. So there's no end of supply. We could expand, give other towns new industry. We have hundreds of acres of Matta plant growing wild in the river swamps and yet, we harvest only enough for our own Valley. We can increase the market for carpets and draperies, persuade people they need a change of the old ones."

He took a long breath, his eyes shining now, immersed in his convictions. "Don't you see? We've got to end this attitude that things must last. You'll never keep sales up if products don't wear out fairly soon, or at least styles change. We've got to persuade people that they want to wear a new style. The way the old folks did. All of us choose what styles we personally like today, but that doesn't have to be so. If we have a style setter, everyone would go along, want to be a part of it. Then the next year, we change and whole new wardrobes would have to be bought. A vast market, you see?" He waved his arm as though encompassing the Valley.

"It's a simple matter to direct the market as we need it to be. Fabrics can be woven that are beautiful but won't wear well, but mostly we have to get people to throw away used things. Our fabrics now are almost indestructable. We'll never build business on that. We've got to get back to the way it used to be!" He looked from one to the other, insisting that they absorb his enthusiasm and they felt the attraction of his persuasion. Then, there's the petroleum industry, only a few wells re-opened, people turned to Solar and Fusion power. But petroleum has its uses too and we've got old wells in this Valley that can be redeveloped if we cut the forest to get at them. The possibilities are endless if you look at it."

THE AWAKENING

Jennifer couldn't restrain her dispair, "But Will, every able person is already busy, working, learning, all that we've always done. We CHOOSE our own styles, can vary them as we like for ourselves. We don't need someone to tell us what to do. People aren't herd animals! As for expanding the liquor industry, I don't see how -" She was shaking her head, hard put to speak.

Benjamin took it up,"Ah, yes, Will. There's some mistake. Every town has a Pub and no one's felt a need for more! You know that. And as for cattle, we are not a meat eating people. The few the hunters bring in are enough for our needs." He stopped, reflected, then added,"We ARE starting new businesses but they're providing goods and services for a new consciousness, not an old one."

William looked at them in astonishment, as if they had lost her senses. Jennifer, demure, quiet, seldom argued with his ideas. And that statement of Ben's about new consciousness was one of the things the Builders did not trust. He swallowed, perhaps they were only presenting argument in order to understand better. He plunged on with that assumption, saving himself."Surely you must know that people want to get back to the old days. We've had to wait all this time, it's long enough. Surely you must know that people are no different than they've always been. There're still the same old pleasures, we just have to remind people. It's just as I said, all we have to do is to remind them that they're missing something." He sighed, turned to them all, letting his eyes move over their faces, only half seeing them. He was relaxing, explaining, the familiar patterns of inspiring others to his view took away his anxiety.

"Don't you see? We've over reacted to the last century when everyone was so deep in dispair, so hopeless. We'll change all that. We need to enter the Learning Centers, teaching children the normal way of life, letting them see that a whole new business world is opening and how to manage it." Then with a smile of simple pride, he added,"The Builders can get us started into that new life."

Ben said, "But you must realize what it would do to our wild life, it would destroy much of what we've built."

"Oh,Benjamin, we've not built this. It's just happened, you know this peculiar reverence for animal life is not natural. It's almost obscene. People have become dull, too serious. I see children sitting silent, just silent. Teenagers even, who should be having fun, enjoying life. We need those old partners, fine wines,good liquors and good food to give life zest again. We've all been keeping our noses to the grindstone too long. It'll wake people up."He looked around, searching their faces.

Ben was shaking his head like one who cannot understand. He said,"But William, you do sense that there are other kinds of energies in this Valley now, energies that can --" He didn't finish, Will stood interrupting.

"No, No! You don't understand. You must realize the possibility! First, something to get the young people going again, to show them how to have fun. Wines, fine dinners with entertainment in great little Inns along the Highway. There is an entire people out there wasted. The Vagabond people could be transformed, could make money entertaining. Can't you see it? The old Highways lined with entertainment centers, and that's where the simulation halls might be built first, to make a focus for the pleasure centers. They are the natural ones to start this. they love to entertain. They could sell their crafts at the same places. Better than spending their lives wondering about." He laughed."Everyone could prosper. The Builders have already laid out plans for these." He laughed now, his pride evident,"You don't realize how excited the builders are. We have a great gift to give this Valley!" His pleasure in having finally explained it all, was evident.

"But Will, we have restaurants where exactly that is available. The best food, imported liquors, wine, beer,as people want them and I've never thought we needed more. People just don't want more. Nor do they want more meat than we have to offer. We are not a people who keep millions of beasts just to slaughter them. They have a right to a life of their own. What we kill from our wild herds is enough. We do have chicken and water fowl farms and even fish farms along the river. Some people don't even want that. We've got enough food businesses. We need businesses that provide for the Spirit, the heart's growth. Those are the businesses of our time, not the old ways!" His voice had hardened, he leaned forward, intent himself on getting William to see his thought. "We're a different people today, Will, don't you see that?"

William laughed then, they thought he was too excited, something threatened his usual acute sense of reality. Surely William could not believe all this.But with calm conviction he went on."You see? It's only because we've never advertized, never told people. That word,'advertize', no one even uses it today. It's as if it's some insult to the intelligence. I've heard it described in history holograms, and that's the attitude our people have. Now you know that's nonsense." He stopped, looked around with pride and confidence. He knew he was convincing.

"It's not. We inform people adequately of every new product, or of improved old ones. The central thrust of our Learning Centers is to tech people to THINK. Whether we teach them anything else, they learn that. They're not as tractable, but they're not easily convinced either. People know what's available and are intelligent enough to locate what they need. The World Market's Three Demensional Screens are more than enough. Everything gets shown there, from all over the world. Advertizing as it was known in our past did insult intelligence. Used whatever manipulations it could to influence people past their better judgement, rouse them to desires they did not have. Make them want, need, where no true need existed. Identical products vying to get public approval one over the other.It was a waste of human creativity. Talented young people sold their lives to process products people could very well choose for themselves. Or to sell people junk that had to be replaced or thrown away. It was wrong." Ben spoke now with intense conviction and William stood silenced.

But he only shook his head, as though a fly had momentarily disturbed him,"Ben, we intend to exploit the world markets, we intend to make markets where they didn't exist. Just wait and see. You ought to invest credit in this venture.You could be a wealthy man."He was suddenly silent, his face changing,

THE AWAKENING

frowning hard in the bright lights of the room. Outside the rain was falling, a hard pounding of huge drops, a good summer storm. He looked past the windows, watched the steady streams dim the glass. "There's work to be done, you know. Among the people. Some people seem -- seem so disinterested in any kind of progress!" His voice was softer as if he spoke to himself. Then shaking his head again, he said vigorously," But you'll see, you'll see, Paul, Ben," Rose and Jennifer were sharply aware of their exclusion. "This will be a man's world, you'll find it a better one. I'll get our business office to send you research we've done."

Softly Benjamin murmurred,"But Will, I'm already richer than I ever thought I could be." Will seemed not to hear at all.

There was silence,Rose looked at Annette. Her face was empty, sad, Rose said,"What else, William?"

He turned to look at her, shifting his attention visibly,"Well, of course those are the things most exciting to me. But then, we've some real problems. We've got to end this strange attraction to these 'psychic doings'that some people experiment with. You remember, Paul, that it's always been true in times of upheaval , people got involved in psychism. A decadent pattern we don't want to repeat. Some of our people even suspect Devil worship in the Valley. We've got to look into that. I told them that was superstition, but they believe it and even the idea can cause trouble. I think providing new business and entertainment will take their minds off such things."

"Do you believe that about Devil worship, William?"

"I don't think that evil is something most people are capable of, but everyone's capable of depravity. And Devil worship leads to that, you know. It starts with people playing with their own minds, trying to probe into what they call other dimensions, astral etc. Such people must be hunted out and -and-" They waited with baited breath "Well, we must teach them or -- the Builder's say, 'get rid of them'." With a glance at their faces, he hastily added."By that I'm sure they mean to put them in a special healing center until they're cured."

But the fire had gone out of his eyes, a curious lassitude seeemed to touch his body, as if something fierce in him had been denied.

Ben's lips tightened. Rose had to suppress a gasp of disbelief. "Will, you have never been - one to deny people their ideas.You think too well to deny a reality to what another person experiences. You cannot label all people who perceive beyond their noses 'misled'. That's not even intelligent. You must know that psychics are not evil" They perceive something the -- the rest of us don't, but that's not wrong, nor to be denied.She caught herself, drew her own horror down into view,saw she herself was entranced and allowed it to wither. This would not help. She deliberately lifted her attention, stood at the highest place her mind could reach, and focussed attention there. And then she was able to stand receptive of Love, focussing that flow of energy toward William.

After a moment, she felt the others join her, Jennifer, Paul and Annette too. Ben hesitated, needing to draw his own emotions into balance. His own anger blocked his participation. The fact made him heart sick, until he righted himself.

THE PEOPLE OF THE VALLEY

He lifted attention, and finally joined their intention.

Rose continued, "To think otherwise is pure prejudice." Her voice was almost a whisper. The fear of their own limitations dragged against their desire to open their hearts to the Presence of Love and focus that Love toward their brother. If only Jessie were here. Their ability to Reach, to Touch was still new to them, still had its own fearfulness. That fear, small as it was, left them weakened. They saw this, in the light of their focus, their Mind Touch, they saw the power they might know. With a gasp of recognition they felt a sweep of self disgust. As one mind, they felt it. They were unworthy. Before they could meet this thing in their beloved William, they must meet their own problems. Rose longed for courage to try that thing Jessie had called a JOINING. Perhaps there would be help. But she didn't know how to bring the others with her.

Will looked at Rose, his eyes shifted for he had felt their Reach, felt a change in the energy around him. His eyes became hard, a whisper of fear swept through them. He had felt that flow of new energy, unrecognized as Love, he felt and FEARED it. Would that -could it - be a danger to his plans? What was this attitude they seemed now to have? He was tremendously attracted to it, to them, and he distrusted that attraction. Had not Greyson warned him of such attractions?

Rose could see the quandary going on in William, in seconds of time, she read the distaste, the attraction and the fear. She worried! Had their own fears threaded into his consciousness drawn by his fear and torn their effort assunder?

They wondered and their minds raced, trying to find the cause. But William was speaking, "No, Rosy." the use of the affectionate name seemed brutal to her. "No. To call it prejudice would be only for those themselves guilty of evil. Look around you. Surely you see the effects. It must be stopped." Then he said something that swept like an icy breeze over their hearts.

"It's the children. I see them showing monstrous actions. I can almost believe that my people are right. That they have been defiled by the worship of that City." His use of the phrase, 'my people' was accidental and they knew he had not intended to be so revealing, it grieved them that he was already so distant. "That unnatural silence I see among them at times, is nothing to -- the other things, And surely you must know that. But we will see to an end to that City. That is a priority of our people." His voice seemed strange to them now, hard, verging on the ring of a fanatic, and that was hard to believe. William had always been the finest of the rational. He seemed obsessed with a self righteousness that stifled his own good mind.

Ben was leaning forward, and at the last statement he dropped back. Rose Reached instinctively to the others, uneasy about Annette, but feeling her grief filled heart respond. Now they sat in silence. Ben, astonished and unable to believe that this was his brother of so many years. This man who seemed so different. His eyes met William's and saw there a stranger. Had he always been so and they had not seen? Or was this something grown in Will that had never been there before?"

Annette Reached then, to their surprise, initiated a Touch. She must make this decision, and they felt her with them with out reservation. It was the only choice she could make. She had lived in between too long. Now, she was safely among them, relieved but sad, full of the pain that was the cost of her decision.

Will glanced around at them all, "What's wrong here? Can't you see the sense of what I've told you? Surely you grown men and women haven't been convinced of that Vagabond foolishness! We need to get those people to work, regular hours, contributing something. That'll shake this foolishness out of them. Town folk are almost as bad. Do you realize Adwin could have been built in half the years, had you tightened discipline?" He looked at them, his eyes moving from one to the other. "Why are you so silent?" There was a note of fear in a voice that had risen to the edge of shrillness that was not natural to William. "You Annette, surely you don't grieve at this evil we must root out?" He plunged most harshly against the one who could be most hurt, intuitively as one who fights and is not conscious of all the damage he might do. He felt something among them and it left him with only anger. But they didn't answer. Tears ran down Annette's face, he frowned and turned away, both guilty and angered at her. With a wrench, she drew herself into balance, wiped her eyes swiftly, and smiled. He was unseeing, "Oh, but we're here for a party. And all this - is business, to be settled later. There's been too much talk, at any rate. We must ACT." His eyes blazed with exhileration. He repeated, "We must act!"

He looked at each of them separately. They did not challenge nor did they argue or deny. They did nothing and he was not prepared for that. Didn't they understand? It had to be that they had only waited for his explanation and they must think about it. His suspicions faded with this thought. He must convince them. Surely if he could not convince these, his own Family, then he could not hope to convince others. A twist of pain touched his heart. He had missed them. Perhaps they would join him after all.

"Maybe you've not gotten the right information about our work. Maybe you've heard rumours. At first, I too thought the Builders were malcontents, just trouble makers. But then, I listened and began to see they made sense. That's what you must do, listen. They didn't seem to be able to organize themselves so they could be effective, just drifting around complaining at first. And so, the sociological aspects of this event interested me." A peculiar look came over his face as he smiled, then it smoothed away instantly. Ben caught his breath. A part of Will still thought that. He was after all a man divided, but his strength had swung to that smaller, angry part of himself. He went on, his voice soft, remembering sadly.

"They were unreasonable at first, so like children actually. They wanted to overthrow everything, to go and make unbelieveable demands on the Council. Organize a revolution." He laughed, and did not see their shrinking at that phrase, "Yes, literally. They talked of that! They needed someone to help them organize ! They hadn't been able to organize anything so far. That was what I brought them. And a few of my friends who have their minds working. Now we agree the Builders only want to make the Valley a better place. They are no more prone to violence than the rest of us." He stopped, looked at them with new confidence and humor.

"And what do they think will make it better?" Rose asked.   William smiled, his face calm now.

"To bring back the old ways, all the things I've just told you. Some of the old traditions, the little pleasures of life. A little more discipline too. The Valley has become so undisciplined, you know." He stopped, his eyes full of the memories, and he smiled,"They were exactly like children, they had such fantasies. The idea of building great estates, great mansions, and Lording it over those who were not able to see the right way. To ride in gilded carriages, actually decorated lift discs. They were playing out old fairy tales, I think. Old historical romances must have inspired them." He laughed again,,wanting them to share his humor. Of course they didn't say they would Lord it over others, but that was what it amounted to. They wanted to bring what they called 'the common man' out of his blindness. To make all of the people of the Valley see their mistakes."

All of them were aware that had people like William stayed out of this matter,those harmless dreams of power misused, would have faded away of their own weakness.

Will went to draw himself another cup of coffee. Outside, the rain had swept into a minor storm and beat against the large panes of glass so heavily they could not see through them. The room was a closed, safe haven, a place of well being. Paul looked out, looked across the city, blurred white shapes rising high into the summer sky. In that moment he knew that that safety, that peace was real, not just an image created by the beauty of the city but something deeper, built into her very walls and mountains and their people had found it and would not let it be lost. He breathed a long sigh and was still.

Rose settled deeper in her chair, signaling Ben to bring her a cup when he went to get his own. Ben turned to the others and refreshed all their cups. Again, that lack of attention was not like Will. He was always the most gracious host. He said now, when they were settled again,"We had to work with them some time, to teach them that the old separations between rich and poor were gone forever. The absolute equality of every person, is one of our first Convictions and cannot be ignored. None of us would allow division to be brought back." His eyes were twinkling now, he was more his old self,"We reminded them that there was not a place in the world where people would tolerate any limiting of their rights as human beings. Not one citizen would tolerate it and every government would support that citizen. They were a fascinating sociological problem for me, in those early days. They really believed in those old fairy tales they'd dreamed up. And they did not seem to realize that the old awful phrase,'the masses' has no real meaning today". He shrugged, accepted his cup absently from Benjamin and frowned. " And yet, I began to listen a little more. Here was a group with a grievance, and we had always agreed that we will listen to all grievances, have we not? We will not only listen but we will act. That is our Valley Law. His eyes had suddenly grown stern, narrowed and his voice harder. "Then was when I began to notice something they said was true, people WERE drifting off, sitting in

THE AWAKENING

silence. I think it was the children that got to everyone the most. The CHILDREN! Paul asked, "You've been working with them then for several years?"

Will nodded, sipping his drink, stretching his legs out and obviously enjoying this audience, "Yes, but only for the last year have I begun to organize them into a group that can speak for itself. We are trying to find those with natural power and bring them in to lead, to help. There is something wrong in our Valley. That I am convinced of." He soberly looked into their eyes, wanting to enlist their support. I think our system of insisting that every citizen over eighteen serve some time on the Councils in the towns, is foolish. All councils should be elected, some one who wants the office should hold it. It should not be simply normal citizen work."

"But how can our citizens know what is happening and learn our government system if they do not participate?" Jennifer asked.

"They don't need to. Surely you must see that choosing a few to run things is better. Too many involved makes a clumsy confusion." He stopped Paul's attempt to speak with one raised hand. "No, don't tell me of Altos, or Adwin even. I know they've been exceptions, but it isn't a good plan in the long run. It worked while we were so busy building. But not now! Most people are not that interested in government."

Rose broke in, "But Will, it was our intention that the Council be both a governing and educating body. We knew that citizens in the past lost any real voice due to disinterest. We cannot allow that!"

"Oh, that must be changed. You see we need people who have strong minds to serve. Not just anyone. Men, Men who know what the real world is like. With such control, the Valley could begin to take on the beauty it deserves. It's place in world power. Business could quadruple, We have resources we aren't using." He sat back now, convinced that his argument must be successful. He drank his coffee and smiled at them.

Annette was watching the faces of her guests, her own thoughts set aside. She seemed waiting some signal, not trusting that she would recognize that signal or that it would lift her from dispair. Rose glanced at her briefly, sensing her grief, wanting to turn to her, to heal, to Touch. She wanted Annette to be angry, not so dispairing. She thought that William had fallen ill with a disease so subtle she could not name it at all. Dis- ease, surely it fit. But then, were the rest of them also infected? Vaguely she heard Ben asking a question.

"William what is our chief problem, in your mind?"

"Inefficiency. That is what we must correct. We can be efficient. More, much more, efficient. We have the computer systems that give us instant communications, that tie us into world market and library services. We can read the stock market and invest from our homes. At least half the business of the land is done from home centers. So we're ready. But our Valley is behind. We get updated information on needs and products hourly in the World Market screens downtown. We can eliminate nearly all of the human error. Don't you see, this Valley is ready for World Economic Conquest." A frown touched his forehead,"And yet, people refuse to develop new industry."He let himself drop back, his face alert, waiting for the response that he confidently expected. And when that response did not come, when not even another question was voiced he looked puzzled, wondering whether these old friends of his had somehow become dulled by age and over work.

Finally Ben, glancing swiftly at the others, spoke, his voice was soft, gentle with a kind of tenderness as though he were speaking to one who was in fact ill."William,the problem with these plans, with the foundation of your plan, is that it won't work."

Of all the responses Will had expected that was the last. His face fell. Annette saw the hurt, the disbelief, behind the mask. The others glimpsed it. Astonishment of disappointment came like shadow over his eyes and then vanished, replaced by that cool control he usually allowed to mask his interior life. They felt that change as though it were a thorn within their hearts . William spoke, his voice quiet, faintly impatient,"If it's not clear, if it doesn;'t seem obvious to you, then maybe I've mistaken your ability to use your mind, to vision even. I thought my old friends would immediately see, once I had time to tell you.To explain. But it looks as though maybe you've been back on that farm too long." He laughed lightly.

Ben was shaking his head. "No, William,it's not that we don't see. We've been seeing for some months now. We've been worried because we thought that you were beyond such dreams. You see whatever the value or harm of such ideas, they simply wouldn't work."

"And why not? I'll listen. Of course, it's your turn." He drew a long trembing sigh and finally smiled," Of course, you would question things more carefully than most people I've taught. The Builders agree right away. They see the situation and agree. They seem to want someone to state the things they've been feeling. But you must explore it further. That's your way, so let's hear it." He was smiling again,his confidence restored by his own explanation.

Rose said, "The reasons we think it won't work Will, aren't connected to any emotional response. It's different." She spoke slowly,wanting to reach him. Out of the corner of her eyes she saw Annette's sudden swift movement, immediately aborted. Annette would stop her, but she also would not. Dear Annette,her affection for William wanted still to spare him,but her Love knew she could not."You see William, you of all people know the terrible tyranny of letting people do our thinking for us. We simply aren't built that way anymore. People aren't, none of us. We've grown out of it. Literally grown. People insist on being on Government bodies, people insist on choosing what is produced in their land and in deciding for themselves what they want or need. To coerse us, even subtly, you would only get strong resistance. People want to LIVE their lives, enjoy their Earth, their arts, each other, create their world together. Work is pleasure to them when it is part of that and when it is not regimented. People of this Valley will not agree with the Builder's plan." She sat back wanting Ben to continue, Will might listen better to a man right now. She felt the pain of knowledge that William would surely not be taking the Journey with them. He couldn't see what was for her so obvious.

"You speak with the emotions, just like a woman." The statement was such an anachronism, Rose shuddered. Not William. No! He did not label people. Her heart sank.

Ben said, "You want to change the City. That is part of this?"

"Of course," Will settled back again, relieved that Ben would speak with reason." We want to open it up. Make it availiable, useful. Prove it's just a construction in the stone peaks and not some - some superstition. It's one of the wastes of this Valley. We want to end the wastefulness.That seems a good intention to me."

Ben went on, "Have you been there lately?"

"Yes, several times. It's been called a ghost city but we know it has to be something absolutely natural and I intend to find the cause and get rid of what makes it seems so strange." His eyes took on a sudden shine of excitement,"We would not bomb it unless there was no other way. we want to use it if possible."

"Bomb? You couldn't," Rose's voice was almost a squeek,"It's illegal", she finished lamely. Suddenly she was struck with the whole enormity of the plan, the sheer impossibility, and her grief faded in a vast relief. It couldn't work, Ben was right.

Will suddenly pounded his fist on the chair arm,"I'm disappointed in all of you. Even you Annette" He met her eyes, but her face did not flinch. "All of you, must know, that City is a danger. It's so obvious,. I begin to think it has already influenced you like a thing of evil." He stood up, walked back and forth, aggitated. Rose had never seen Will like this before. It shocked her more than the words he had used, which revealed more than he was aware at that moment, how torn his own attitudes were. He thought one thing, but he felt another. He had not meant to reveal those feelings. She was sure he didn't realise that. Certainly William had never been torn between thought and feeling before, he had always known exactly what he thought and brought his feelings to fit. Sometimes almost brutally.

She said, "William, you can't really believe that City is evil."

"I could, almost,were I to set aside reason. The Builders do believe that, and that's what's important. That so many people do. And so I've researched everything I can about it. No one understands what is going on there. The Council promised to send a team to study it and I found that they did do that, but the team that went, biologists, geologists and the Master Forester, simply returned with a very unsatisfactory report. They were explicit about the amazing abundance of animal and plant life around the cliffs and beneath them, they said only those with good mountain climbing skills and equipment could get up there and that there was no way, absolutely no way, to get into the City itself. I read the report and was apalled. None of them seemed to be the right people to have gone. I thought two members of the team seemed to have some mental disturbance afterward. They haven't been the same. The others just delay writing up any report except strict records of the wild life and mineral resources there.

Nothing about the City itself. It's not reasonable, I wanted another group to go and we plan to send a group of our own people. I don't know how so many things could happen to delay them. I think they are reluctant. People avoid the place. That's suspicious enough." He was suddenly shouting. Will, who never shouted." Well, we will go! We will find out for ourselves!"

Rose watched him with growing apprehension, He had to have a personal vendetta against the City. He was too brilliant a man to let the reactionary Builders sway his reason that much. What had happened to cause it?

Will stood looking rapidly from one to the other, what was the matter with them all, couldn't they see the obvious? Had someone been persuading them? Yes, that must be it. He had heard of the plan to make a Journey to the City. Some religious pilgrimage, it seemed. It would make matters worse. Surely that could only come from people swayed against their reason. His voice became quiet, controlled and reasonable but his body, as it moved across the room and back, betrayed his anger. "It's that woman, isn't it? Her talks and ideas! She's trapped you all, brainwashed you, literally. I never thought it could be done to people like you. She's going to get you there and then it'll be too late. And you insist that Valley People think for themselves.!" Now anger surfaced again, but he calmed himself, quieting his voice. "You'll be damaged at the best, if you go."

"I suppose you mean Jessie? " Ben nodded, "Yes, we intend to go on a Journey. When we're ready for it." Then he frowned, stood and walked across the room got another glass of iced tea. He stood looking at them all, wanting to carefully assess what was being said. To their relief, Will had finally sat down. Ben waited by his chair,quiet, "Well, you think we've been convinced against our better judgement. That's a serious statement, Will. If there's any possibility of that we've got to recognize it." He searched all that had happened, all that Jessie had done and said, he knew the others were doing the same. After several minutes, he went on,"Well, I won't deny absolutely, but I think that whatever we've been convinced of, it wasn't Jessie who convinced us. It was our own questions, our own need to KNOW and to respond to that deep questioning that keeps rising in our minds. The City itself seems to draw us, to cause us to seek her out. At dawn when the sun makes her glow so brilliantly, she begins to fill our hearts, our minds, and we find ourselves thinking of Her often. Jessie seems only to impliment something we already know."

"But it's the same with those who listen to William, isn't it? Doesn't he impliment something? Or is there a difference?" Rose was puzzling through these accusations. Surely there must be a clue to the truth. "How does a person ever know when he has acted from choice and not from some powerful influence?" She frowned, "How can one be sure she has been convinced of right rather than wrong."

Paul smiled at her, "The very fact that you so carefully search out that question is one clue. It is a good question. Does the Heart know it's rightness? Or is it an emotional choice? Do thoughts of that choice include harm to anyone or anything. Is there a strong emotion involved with the choice? If so, what emotion, one a person can honor? A right choice does not bring harm. Although it might possibly bring death in certain circumstances. A right choice will respond to reason. It will speak for what is best for the Valley, for her growth, for her life. It will keep a harmony and vitality present, and will not try to control others, but will leave them free choice also." He stopped, his smile faded. He had recited another Teaching. All of them remembered as he spoke."I think we have not been persuaded against our choice, or judgement, but I am afraid, and that fear is what puzzles me"

"We must not allow another to control our lives, but we must not control any other life either. All life must be free to choose its way. We teach our children early to make their own choices and live or suffer by them." He looked at William, his eyes intent and stern, the love he felt for his old friend lay behind that sternness, almost hidden.

Will stood up, went again to fill his cup, then returned to sit deep into his chair, he seemed aggitated, suddenly not sure. "I don't think you would find anyone among the Builders who would not say the same. It's a feeling of 'right Heart' as our Teachers say." He looked searchingly from one to another, then with a curt nod, he said,"You say you checked your actions by the Teachings for Right Action, and I say that we have too. We feel that we have finally come home to something we can understand. Feel comfortable with. We want the old ways,the sureness of them. To build an empire and have it respected is not a bad dream for a man." His voice was gentle with these thoughts,. He turned suddenly to fix his eyes on Ben's "Don't you understand, Ben? We've got to control this thing that's happening. These strange things, the unnatural behavior, is even gotten into our own Family. THAT is what I call harm!" He stopped, a furtive look of guilt crossed his face, he glanced at Rose, then looked away. "Don't you see? It's permeated our own family,I think." He let his body sink down, sipping tiredly, he seemed exhausted.

As Ben watched his face, he noticed the tiny lines of tension deepen. He felt a growing pity for this brother. That surprised him. He didn't want to feel pity for this strong friend."You said you've used the Test for Right Action. But then, if harmlessnes is one of them, then how do you explain the ruthless ripping out of trees and creatures from the fields that you have taken?"

Will studied Benjamin over the rim of his cup, sipping as if to gain time. " I didn't say all of our people have taken that test seriously. I do insist that I do. But I question whether harmlessness includes the unconscious plants and lower animals."

Ben nodded, swallowed at the last statement, but decided to ignore it just now. "So, it's true for you Will. The City is a genuine danger to the welfare of our Valley.It is harmful?" At Will's nod, he went on. "Do all the Builder's hold this worry."

He saw the light of hope kindle in Will's eyes. Then suddenly extinguish into an angry amusement."Good God, No. I can't get any kind of committment from any of them about that monstrosity. There are a few, though,a few who do know what I mean. The rest,-- they're just interested in getting the Valley back into control and the way it was. But then, even though only a few of us know the danger, we still must act. It's always that way with society. Only a few really know what's right."He thought of the fear and anger among the Builders, that could be used to impliment what he saw as a more serious plan and his honest mind questioned whether that was Right Thinking but he deliberately shrugged it away. Those old Teachings themselves had to be restudied.

Paul was nodding and caught the others in a quick Reach. Touched their mind's with his conclusions."It looks as though we've found our main point of difference, Will.It's not that there's less concern for others in you, you are the same good man we've always known." At Will's startled glance, he smiled but went on." Yes, we worried about that. The difference is in the vision we each have. We think that the entire race grows and refuses its childhood, it's time of dependance is over. We as a people no longer want a benevolent or tyranical father -- or mother for that matter. We want to learn to rule ourselves, each of us separately so that we can rule ourselves collectively. Each able to hear the needs of the other and honor them." Will started to speak, but he held a hand , "Please let me finish. Whereas, for the Builders there is that conviction that they cannot allow human beings to govern themselves; allow each person to make his mistakes and suffer and learn from them. They don't trust that each one knows what's best for himself. They think we need some one to tell us what to do. But never have people of the past chosen the wisest and best to lead them. They chose the strongest and those who knew how to manipulate people. The wisest and best would advise but did not choose to control. People do - actually do have the ability to govern themselves today! And yet the Builders think we should go backward to find the good life.Isn't that about it?" He sighed, his face serious, but no longer full of grief. A quiet acceptance began to flow from him and the others felt it.

With a wrench Rose stood up, her body expressing the pull she had felt at Paul's words. To recognize and accept demanded discipline,She had held herself quiet while he spoke,,knowing the knowledge that bloomed within his mind,. But she felt anger,.She did not want to'give in' but she knew that she must. This must be no contest. She sighed deeply,knowing the nearness of the others, feeling William's separateness acutely. Finally she swallowed her anger, sadly watching it go,"William, I see the difference now. I agree with Paul that we must honor your choice. It seems to me that if there are those who want to return to the old days then we must let them do so. If we did not, then we would give the lie to what we stand for. Every voice, every heart must be safe to speak, and act. We lose all possibility when one mind or life controls others."

William sat forward,,his cup cradled in his hands between his knees."But you don't understand. You aren't thinking clearly." He felt them slipping away. He had not convinced them at all. He had thought they were so close to agreement.

Ben spoke matter of factly. "Perhaps. But right now, we must advise you that we must let people choose their way. We must continue with our plans to Journey

THE AWAKENING

to the City. You must continue with your plans to destroy Her."

Paul spoke softly,"We wanted you to join us, William , to think as we do. But remember ,if you don't, our love for you will not change. You are still our brother always."

Williams eyes blazed,"But you can't believe all this. Why, if we let everyone choose, speak, if we honored all the different opinions, we'd have anarchy. Nothing would ever be done.It's some madness. Another kind of madness." He looked from one to the other, a strange pleading in his voice.

Jennifer interrupted ,"Will, you're a student of history. Is that madness of letting people choose their own way anymore arrogant and cruel than our history of letting some self styled leader choose for us, and choose war, murder, rape, torture? Shall we choose that millions have no food while others feast, millions whose homes are hovels while others live in luxury? Is that what you return to?" Her voice was as soft as if she suggested a walk in the garden. He frowned harshly.

"But Jennifer, those are not our intentions. We don't have to turn from all our progress to bring back the best of our past. I don't even think we can wait for people to choose otherwise. Too many people don't deserve to live free, won't take responsibility for themselves. I see it already among our Builders. Some just want to be told. And that's the way it is. We must persuade them. If we wait for people to come to see things right, the City will destroy us. It must be cleaned out and USED. People aren't wise, they are generally stupid. They want to be led. They don't want to think for themselves."

Paul was patient,his very patience irritated Will. Paul sensed that and frowned, it was true, Perhaps he had sounded like a parent to William. He shrugged," I wonder if you've been working with Builders too long. We've been teaching our children for three generations to think for themselves and to honor the opinions of others whether we agree or not. We haven't taught them to try to convince others beyond their usual debates. You know that. It's where you got your fine training. And it's what you yourself have taught. And taught well."

Will burst out, "But it's not the same." He stood up, walked again to the window,his neck red, flushed with his in-held anger, frustration. The storm seemed to be passing, the rain was fine and soft now,drizzling down like a veil that made the afternoon softly grey .

Rose said, "Will, if you think the City needs to be attacked, that it needs to be destroyed, I disagree but I can't say you're wrong. I wish you would not harm Her, but if you must go there and search out her secrets then do so. Do that first, then if you still think she is Evil, make another decision." She was silent, watching him, and then added thoughtfully, "Maybe if you CAN destroy Her,then it would indicate you might be right. Maybe she's false. Maybe we must know that if we are to grow ourselves."

Annette cried out,"Oh no, Rose. You mustn't say that. They will destroy her. I know that. They intend that. " Tears washed her faced and she ignored William's amazed stare. He thought she was betraying him. Before he could speak, Rose went to Annette and took her hands, held them tightly in her own. "I understand your fear, Dear, but listen, maybe it will come clear."

Ben said,"Just what you've said, Annette. Your voice is important too. What YOU think will be honored. But it won't be unless we can honor their thoughts too. Each must have his voice. The Valley Builders must have theirs. We must trust that the choices will discover the truth. We will find the right way out of it all. Because you see, if we are a people grown far enough from our ancestors, then we will see clearly and the Earth will make Herself known to us also. The City will speak, as we insist She does. The truth is here, we must watch, think, observe and listen carefully."He got up, flexing his legs to loosen the tightness of the long sitting.Then with a long sigh, he went on.

We have access to communication systems that make every person of this Valley able to speak and be heard.The computers can easily sort all opinions, and give us a true voice. They can also show us the probable results of various courses of action. The people can be shown those and they will make their choices more true. Will thinks this is impossible and would create chaos; humankind has always assumed that, but we think it is not true. Now we will find out." He stopped, his face composed, but sad.

Rose nodded,"You see, the City can take care of Herself. Maybe,so can the Valley. The life in them both is very great now. And if they do not. That in itself tells us much."

Annette looked from one to the other. Slowly she nodded, her mind Reaching, listening, knowing their vision which complimented her own and erased her fear,. With a small smile she said,"I think I see, But I must think on this. She twisted in her chair to look at her Mate, still standing, amazement and hurt still visible in his eyes. Visibly she wanted to reach out to him,to protect him, and she knew that was wrong. "I think it's my own weakness, I stand tortured at the point of difference. I cannot always hear the voice of my Heart. I cannot always trust, trust that others know their own hearts. I doubt too much. I doubt the wisdom that comes to me. I am pulled one way and another. I must learn to listen and at least be sure what I do know, what I think and what I feel."She looked up again to meet William's eyes and there was no wavering in that gaze.

He said,"That's right my Dear. Listen to yourself and as you do, I am sure you will join with us wholeheartedly. We will welcome you."

She sighed, "And if I choose the other way?"

He was unwavering,"There is nothing more I can say. You are with us or against us. I must go on with my work."

She nodded slightly the tears still running over her face unnoticed.But suddenly she slid her hands across her face and realized how much she cried. It embarrassed her,she said,"I must go now, I want to be silent, to rest." She got up and went to the door to her room,then turned,"I'll let you all know. I must decide alone, but I want you to know surely that I love each of you dearly. You are my family, whatever happens."

The others sat, when she had gone, feeling a great tiredness. Will said,"I'm sorry she had to do that. But she's right."

Paul laughed, his face filled again with the good humor that was his nature. "That's a relief,William. One thing I've always appreciated in you is what I call your finest trait. You are absolutely fair as you know how to be. Fair and intelligent. I count on both."

William looked at him in surprise."Of course, what else?"

Rose moved slowly, curling up in the chair "Then it's settled, we must allow each of us to make up her own mind and we will accept that? Our family need not be threatened?"

"Oh, I'm confident she'll come round, see the right way. After all, I think you will too, when you see what we find out about that City." He grinned, the old look that endeared him to them. "Once you think, once you see what we discover, you're also intelligent and fair, you know. I hope you wait until after our search before you take any Journey. It could harm you,all of you, you know. Especially, I hope you won't let the children go." He drained his cup,"It just doesn't make sense any other way. When you start noticing the strange things going on, you will have to change your attitudes. Just watch and see that I'm right. I think you haven't been noticing."

Seriously they all nodded, looking at him with the love they had always felt, but now it was leavened with sorrow. He felt their love and did not notice their grief at the knowledge of what they knew he must suffer in the years ahead. He could not Reach, nor even know that Reaching was real. He was cut off from them in ways none of them could heal. He would not be able to learn the Joining that Jessie had promised to Teach. He would never realize the wonderful intimacy of that Mind deep Touch. He was deprived and the fact that he didn't know it did not change the fact that it was true. They could only reassure themselves by reminding themselves that he would one day, perhaps not until another life time, but one day, would Reach and know as they did.

Rose sat thinking of the days ahead, the work to be done, the practice she must keep to discipline herself and to harmonize her own nature. She must keep Watch. Could it be that there were enough Builders that they might desparately harm the Valley? Could that be possible in this time when human minds knew and Reached into that Vision beyond ordinary sight that those same human beings could still destroy their possibilities?

Ben was frowning, sitting in a pool of his own indecision. He wanted to explain to Will again. Surely if one could explain enough then another could see? Then he knew that was the foundation of manipulation, to insist until another was worn down and doubting his own thought. No! Explanation would not help, Will must find out for himself. Should they have told him they could Mind-Touch, and what that meant? Would that have helped? He thought not, not yet. Not until William began to doubt his own convictions a little after making those searches he spoke of.

Rose stood, turned to Ben and said,"It's late and we must be getting home. I want you all to come soon, don't wait until another Gather. Annette, please come spend an afternoon with me. I miss you."

They all began to move about, saying their goodbyes and Annette went to hug Rose, whispering softly as she did,"I will come. I need to spend time with all of you."

THE AWAKENING

CHAPTER TWENTY NINE

Summer Gather

Silvia paced the living room, her small face drawn into a frown, her long black hair swinging about in expression of her anger. What was the use, no matter how much she thought,it was going no where. She sighed.Her anger pressed against her chest and all her thoughts had a knot of anger that tangled them. She thought they broke against it the way water breaks against a barrier and so created an eddy that made clear thought impossible. She decided she wasn't accomplishing any thing.

"I'm just going to have to talk it out. Saying something out loud makes it more real. Damn, I should have had it out yesterday with my peer group." She grimaced,adding anger at herself to the rest. Who could she call? Rose and Ben had gone to Altos, it was raining, and she felt awful. She felt ashamed. She stood in a quandary when suddenly Steve came through from the kitchen. She turned suddenly to him, giving herself no time to justify waiting. "Steve, I've got to talk."

He laughed,"It's a great morning for talk,Honey. Look at that weather out there, no time for field work. So shoot." He settled happily into a big chair, stretched his legs and sipped at his big cup of hot coffee.

She turned to face him, her words tumbling out rapidly, "I feel so helpless, and so mad at Irene -- and myself too, I suppose." The final admission calmed her a little. The worst was over. She plunged into explanation. "I've been working in the City clerks office, alternate to serving on Council this time. It's my town service and until the restaurant is running full time, Jerry and I need all the credit we can manage. And I like this. I've done it before and I'm good at it. So I want to continue. But then, Irene runs that office, you know. I get so pissed off at her I'm ready to leave. And there's no real reason. It's all little things. I can't even really blame her. It's been going on for two months but I wouldn't admit it. I let it pile up. You know?" She saw his nod, "Same thing I've done here at home,huh?" Her eyes filled with sudden tears as she thought of her struggle with that habit. She impatiently wiped them away and said, "I know it, it's the same old problem and I thought I had that licked."

She took a deep breath "Here I am trying to help and Irene wants everything done just so. According to her way. She is good. She does do things well, I don't mind doing it her way generally, because she has been doing it for years and she knows how. Setting up for a job means more to her than the job itself.But she's gotten -- so trapped in her own system. Even when it's such a little thing that it doesn't need setting up. I have to stand and wait 'til all these preliminaries get done and I could have had the whole thing finished. I'm as busy as she is. Maybe more so. She seems to me to waste time. I know I don't like to do things slowly, but she does waste my time. I don't need to stand and wait." Her voice had risen as she told the story, anger biting the words out."The restaurant is taking more

663

THE PEOPLE OF THE VALLEY

and more of my time and I do want to give town service as long as I can. "But the problem is I don't tell her! I don't tell her! She doesn't seem to see that my time is valuable. Yesterday was the worst of it. The straw that broke what little patience I had. I was sitting at my desk working on the reports, completing them to be filed. I wanted to get the job done so I could help Jerry with plans for a big party that's scheduled with us. Irene and a couple of friends came in, chattering and drinking coffee. Enjoying themselves. Where was the harm of it? Oh, yes, they could've talked in the lounge, not in my office but that's not the problem. It was what I didn't do that got to me. I was so irritated I could spit and yet I couldn't tell them to get out. I needed Irene's help with one paper and I was so mad I couldn't ask her." She was silent, her eyes wide, digesting that fact.

Steve asked, "What would have happened if you had?"

Her eyes were on the floor, her head nodding faintly, "Yes, that's it, isn't it. I realize now I couldn't risk her anger if I told them they were disturbing me." She was shaking her head as if amazed as the facts stood there before her.

Steve nodded, "O.K. I get that much. You didn't want to risk offending her. She does take offense easily. But then, what's the worst that could've happened if you did?"

Her eyes were unseeing, turning toward Rob, who lay on the floor watching them. When she met his eyes his tail wagged gently, she felt comforted by his attention. She turned back to Steve and sat down, leaning foward, "Oh, Steve, it's both of us. Not just her. I know I'm afraid to tell any one when something irritates me - except you folks at home here. And I don't even do that well. I admit that --" she smiled briefly, wanting to say it all before he spoke. "My peer group's let me know that it wouldn't bother me so much if it weren't my problem as well as hers. We compliment each other negatively. And that makes me even more mad. To think that's true." She grimaced.

"But you asked what would happen. Well, I think if I'd told them, then they'd've - Irene would've heard it as a personal criticism right there in public . She strikes back when she feels questioned, reacts before she thinks. At least in my opinion she does. Then the first thing you know, if you answer back - react, I suppose it is, which I can't seem to stop doing - there's the whole history of your relationship, every little thing, laid out before the world. And garbled too, exaggerated, until it's awful. It happens so fast when she feels attacked. I never can get in an apology, I just feel put down and then I react!" Her voice had risen and she lifted her hands in a gesture of defeat, her face a mask of dispair. "And the worst of that is, I cry! What the hell can I do?"

He watched her, glad that she was talking it out, confident she'd find her own solution. "Well, Honey,, you feel a little afraid of her, actually, that's it, isn't it?"

"I do. And I don't like it. What's wrong with me?" Rob stretched himself, tired of waiting for their notice and came to sit against Steve's knee, pressing his big head against the hand that hung there. His mate was sprawled asleep on the cool tile near the door. She flicked one eye open, and didn't move. Steve let his fingers move in the great dog's hair, caressing ears and nose.

THE AWAKENING

Silvia shook her head, and dropped heavily into the chair. I suppose she has to work out her problem. It isn't mine. But mine is one end of her problem. I'm not the only one who has this problem with her, but I don't want to have it. I can't meet her the way Rose does, or Molly - and Ted too. They seem to slide right over the irritations. I've watched them. They seem to know just how to say things and so gently,,without threatening her at all. They do it right when it happens, and it doesn't build up. Why can't I?"

Steve smiled at her, reaching out to touch her hand a moment,"It looks to me like you've got a lot done already. You recognize the problem. You aren't blaming her. You see how other people handle the same thing. You're already aware of the dynamics and you want to change it." She looked up then to meet his eyes, he went on,"You've been in family peer groups enough to know it's half solved. What's next"?

Her eyes narrowed,she was relaxed and felt easy.With a self deprecating laugh she gave her head a quick shake and said,"Well, yes, it is isn't it? I hadn't realized it. Your seeing that helps. After all, I do know that Irene is also a sweet and helping person. Too helping sometimes. She demands a lot of herself and that's why she can't abide that she's done something to irritate someone. She sees that as wrong, not just normal human behavior. So if I tell her I'm angry, it's not just a fact, it's a judgement. I see other people letting her initial caustic comment slide off, ignoring it. And she seems to accept that. Then there's no build up. I have to learn to speak t the beginning, or bite my tongue when I've got riled up, I guess." She nodded to herself , her eyes staring at Rob's tail. Steve drew Rob between his knees to stroke his back and Rob slid his head into the curve of Steve's hip, enjoying.

"It's the same old thing, isn't it Steve. What we've talked about in Family Gathers. I'm afraid of someone disapproving of me too. I hear it as criticism too, as a rejection. Her fear is my fear. Afraid of not pleasing people - I guess it's another example. I have to go on with it. I have to remember how tell myself that I'm not bad because she is irritated. The very same thing I wish she'd do!" She brooded,"I think I'd better ask that all of you folks here at home help me do it. That you tell me immediately when you see me doing that. I think I could learn to see it then, before I react. But then, with Irene - Well, d'you suppose I could ask her to help me too? She's the other half of my problem and it happens so often between us. It'd be working things out for her too wouldn't it?"

"Exactly." He breathed, relieved that she was clarifying the solutions for herself. "If she'd do it, it'd give you both a lot of learning. After all, sweetie, isn't that what the whole point of our peer groups is?:"

She was nodding now, smiling wryly,"Well,you know, she might be at her home in town, talking to some one in HER family about me. Could that be?"

"If she's bothered, and if she's lived in this Valley all her life, which she has , then she's bound to bring it up to her peer group as well. She'll be ready for your suggestion, I imagine.

"I have to ask. If she won't then I'll have to learn how to speak as soon as I feel irritated or bite my tongue. Learn how to reduce the pressure at least. Maybe learn how to say things the way Rose does."

"Rose is a politician, always has been. You aren't. Just do it your own way. Find your own way whatever it is,. It'll be enough." He stood and came to her chair."Well, whatever. You don't have to do anything right now. Let's put on some music and I'll give you a back rub and we'll just relax a while. I've got some reading I want to do. What better use of a rainy day. Jane's in her cottage writing, and she'll join us later."

She reached out one hand to smooth the fine hair over Missy's face. Silvia always called the beautiful red and white bitch, Missy, and she responded as if Silvia were her pack leader. Silvia took the long finely chiseled head in her hands and looked closely into Missy's eyes."I wish I had your calm, Missy." Then she came back to Steve's words,"That does sound good. I am tense. It would help." Her eyes met his and she stood swiftly to hug him hard. She drew back, looked at him laughing, half shy suddenly,"Such a comfort you are Steve. Such a comfort to damsels in distress."

He laughed,"O.K. Lady, down there for the best back rub in the Valley. You get set while I get some music on. I'm wanting the Harp sonata by that fellow Gerald K. the Vagabond itinerant Teacher. He's some musician." He came back in a few minutes, rubbing his hands together to warm them, the music already filling the room. After a while Silvia said, "It's never ending, isn't it Steve? This learning how to live together?"

He nodded, softly answered,"Well, Honey, you weren't born here so you didn't start as young as most Valley people. Neither did I and I can tell the difference. Kindergarden they begin now,and earlier. It's just part of being alive to them. But all of us have got some training through our years in the Learning Center. Thank God for that!"

"She nodded,"When did you start?"

"My parents were of the old ways. Couldn't adjust to things. resented the new way of thinking. Then while I was married, living in Africa, we followed the new thought pretty well, my mate and I. When I first came to live here I resented the way people just accepted the Valley Convictions as a way of life. Then I began to see how right they were, how much better life was. I learned. But I'd missed a lot of the training. I started right in meeting with the Master teachers, going to the training for the kids even. I learned! But I've had to ask a lot of questions and watch pretty closely the way people behave. The Peer groups've helped me most."

"I had to do some of that too. But I've been working out problems with people all my life and I suppose it'll go on the rest of my life. At least it's considered the natural thing to do in our Valley. Jessie says we all know how to climb mountains now,it's the mole hills that catch our feet up." She laughed, and moved a little under Steve's hands.. "That feels so good." Steve found tight knots in the muscles of her shoulders. The music moved into a series of subtle harmonies, one playing against the other, then replying to one another. Each one

THE AWAKENING

was simple, but together they created a complex pattern. She let herself flow into the sound, becoming the shape of it. Thoughts swept aside, Steve moved in silence.

--------   --------   --------

A week later on a Thursday after noon in late June, Paul and Jennifer rode belts all the way down from Altos, enjoying the wonder of silent flight, of hanging undisturbed as free as a bird over the land. They came early for the Gather, wanting to be there, to talk with Jessie. The Valley had settled into the natural summer subsidence of energy. The fever of growth and birth had given way almost completely to the quiet langour that was different from the meditative time of winter. This was the time of steady, quiet growth and blooming. Fruit swelled on tree and vine and fields were lush. In the cool of evening the acres around the Learning center and in the flat land below the round hills of the town were noisy with sounds, of people preparing for the Summer Festival.

Young people and some elders, practiced Aikedo-chan in the pathways. There would be an initiation ceremony this Festival. In the gymnasium and on the gymnastic equipment in the High Field outside the Outer Ring of the Learning Center, people gathered to practice. Music, theatre, dance, always part of every Festival, occupied people of all ages whenever they were free from other study or work. The ring of metal being shaped, the buzz of wood being sawed or shaped, added to the low background of sound. Jennifer floated above the town for some minutes, requiring Paul come back to her. She watched and listened and asked with a smile,"How can a town put out so much energy in mid-summer?"

Paul grinned, took her hand and drew her on to the Farm."It's the same at home, you know. Festival creates its own energy, I think. And there isn't a single person, old or young, who isn't involved. I think it's what keeps our few old folks so healthy."

The three days of Summer Festival, at the full moon closest to the twenty first of June, would be preceeded by a day of meditation and prayer so the temples were already polished and all sound and color systems checked. The regular business, industrial and farm work had to get done, so people got up early and worked late to keep production up. Festival was all absorbing and the fun of getting ready was as exciting as the performances. Practice in the fields lasted until dark with glow balls bobbing like giant fireflys over the acres. On this day, the TriDor teams were on the fields across the Highway between Adwin and the Farm. The Game was a flexible team game, taking from twelve to thirty players. There were three goals and it required at least three teams to play. There were two balls, one large, one small. Since it was complex, and since it relied on intricate and precise teamwork, it was usually a game bystanders got into playing rather than watching. As with most Valley games, it required much skill in cooperating to bring any team to goal. The difficult part came in the requirement that each team bring another team to goal. Each could lose points if they interfered with the teamwork between other members of a team. But at the same

THE PEOPLE OF THE VALLEY

time they must strive to bring that team to goal and yet complete their own strategy to avoid making a goal.

Besides TriDor, there was Tennis, Volley Ball, badminton, out door and indoor games, gymnasts, dances, a modified version of basketball. Baseball, played by twelve players, with innovations that changed it from the old game, was popular. Runners ran the highways, hundreds on some cool evenings, and dancers filled some of the smaller fields near the Center. Musicians practiced both inside and out, singers spent these last days practicing in the music rooms on the third floor of the sprawling second ring. Vagabonds came in flocks, creating camps in favorite spots along the Highway, and boats filled the River to the vexation of fishermen. The fish farms south of town were off limits and boats gave them a wide birth not to be disqualified . Swimmers and rowing crews worked out. Several little keys, which were actually widened small creeks deepened to let the River water in, made excellent practice space for swimming and provided spectator seats on each side. The smell of fish, river mud, and the soft sound of boat power packs, created the familiar summer atmosphere.

How did the Valley work get done the weeks before Festival? The energy of the people seemed endless, but the crops were in, the factorys amd mills cut to three quarter time this last week and the evenings were long. Everyone was involved, every one had some part in the drama that was Summer Festival.

But for the farm Family, and more than one other Family of the north towns, the week before Festival was also Summer Gather time. They looked forward to the event as much as to Festival. This time would be special. Jessie would surely teach them of that advanced kind of Joining,the further step into a communion they had not yet known. An eagerness filled their hearts that evening as they began to gather.

When Paul and Jennifer arrived,the sun had just begun to spread over the tops of distant hills. The family had been up before the dawn when the light was grey,faintly glimmering with the coming sun. Everybody, except Will, would finally be home together. Annette would come in an hour in Paul's air car. She had simply made the choice to leave Will at home. Paul smiled sadly. He was quiet, watching each one arrive. Ben would be late, Tom was arriving, surely he must be bringing the whole family. Paul saw five small dots racing the clouds toward the farm. Ned was already here. Now and then a bright splash of sun brightened the fields through clouds blown apart. It seemed to Paul that there was no end to this soft still morning. He felt a power in the air, a strengthening of energy and he marveled at how clearly he felt it.

Ned, his huge lithe dancers body curled about in a nest of cushions , seemed half asleep as he waited. Tom entered in a splash of sound and with him were both his wives and their children. Angy looked tired, but seeing, hearing everything as acutely as she always did. Mary came in slowly, her bright intense gaze recognizing and cataloging everything that happened. The big room was brightened with the color of cushions and low couchs. A long narrow table crossed the far end, gleaming in the light of the broad windows. A thick rug

THE AWAKENING

covered the tile floor and five young ones sprawled there, chattering quietly, laughing, enjoying one another. Small windows, built into the stone of the walls near the ceiling, shaped like diamonds and circles or triangles, threw color like a flash of brilliance whenever the sun came out. The great wide wall windows were half shielded by thick drapery, the other half open to the breeze. Jerry got up to open two large windows but he pulled all the drapes back from the rest so the day was with them.

Jennifer smiled, her eyes soft, enjoying the sounds of people entering, the settling, the quiet peacefulness of this great Hall. It was good to be here, a feeling of safety enveloped her. She wondered that it should be so. She had not thought herself unsafe. She wished Steve and Rachel had come. They were practicing for Altos' Festival. She looked around, everyone was here, except Ben, even Tom's two boys, catching up with the Farm children on their past month's doings. She watched them with pleasure, she didn't know them as well as she wished. Angy took them off so often on her many journey's and they were studying in the Undersea City at least six months of the year, with Mary. Then, Ben came running in. He threw himself on a cushion at Silvia's feet. There was a moment of expectancy, of celebration. Paul felt their attention, met their eyes, he knew he was to begin this Gather.

He spoke slowly, without bothering to identify the reasons for the meeting. "I'm glad we're here, all of us. I'm grieved that William is not. But we've all needed to talk. You all know that. There is something beginning in this Valley. Something new coming awake in us. I know it, even when I can't name it. It is good, that I know, it has a grandeur and it rises from our deepest selves so that I want to call it Spirit. But then, I don't know what Spirit is. Only that it's related to what we know as awakening and that it is the source of the Light most of us have seen through mind focus." He spread his hands out pressed down against his thighs. His eyes were full of awe as though he already saw beyond them.

After a little he went on, "We've got two things to discuss. One - that very Light we've all begun to see. The light in the mind," his voice dropped into a whisper, "the fire that blazes in our hearts." He glanced around at them, his eyes resting longest on the children. "We can't - I think we don't deny that." He waited, and no sound interrupted the silence. Two - the fact of those who are NOT aware of that Light, and who do not feel that fire. Since they don't, they fear those of us who do." He drew a long breath. "There, I think that's about it!"

Ned lifted himself to lean on one elbow, "And that's more than enough. It's bigotry we've got in this world again!"

Paul sighed, nodding slowly, "If it's true of those who cannot See, that's one thing. But if its true of those who do See, then it marks a terrible flaw somewhere. We have to search our own hearts, find our blind places. But maybe we're wrong. It's possible to see the Builders as simply blind, not wrong or bad. I know that the rest of you See as well as I. Surely that means we look beyond our own limits." He looked at Ned with a pleading look, but Ned shook his head and slapped his hand down hard against his thigh.

THE PEOPLE OF THE VALLEY

"Maybe we do See,and maybe we KNOW better, but if we don't balance, we'll let our feelings overpower what we know. Then we'll be exposed to ourselves. Real change is not superficial, its a deep shift of attitude and perspective." In his turn, he frowned and looked so morose Paul almost smiled. Then suddenly, like light after darkness, he grinned, wiping away all sense of worry. "But Paul,love,there's not a one of us that doesn't want to balance. I believe the change is deep!"

Paul relaxed in spite of himself, who could avoid it before that radiant smile. It's part of being a Valley citizen, Ned, it's part of us now." Then he frowned, We have to talk of the dicotomy, the conflict that may tear our Valley apart.But we've got to understand ourselves, before we can even begin." He steepled his fingers, drew them to his chin, then opened and slid his hands over his face in a gesture of weariness."So before we discuss that, I'd like us to talk about where we are. Each of us. And I'll start!" He heaved a sigh as if unburdening his heart. His words came in a rush, as if they'd pushed hard behind his control and demanded expression."There's so much I don't understand, Something is seeping through my whole life, my being, it's like a river that erodes the old structures of my identity so that I'm not familiar to myself. It's insidious and until I began to pay attention I didn't notice how constant it was.It's as though I'm changing every single day!" He looked at them, amazement written on his face. He'd just realized that as he said the words.

When he began again it was with quiet acceptance of a new fact." Maybe you're right Ned, maybe the changing in us is deep, but I want to UNDERSTAND! And lately we agreed that we'd enter into a Joining, with Jessie's help. We know that informs us, enlightens us, wakes us up inside as if a light is turned on in our minds. That's what it is, for me. And when we began the joining, it was as if that change was acknowledged. I'm hoping that we'll learn how to make that kind of contact, so that it isn't just something we do when Jessie shows us how, but with ourselves, any time!" he stopped, looked around noting how many faces showed surprise. "You remember the Spring Gather, at the Planting?" At their nods, he went on,"Well, the sharing we did, it -- it opened my mind, woke something, I think I stepped up onto a threshold. Up to a doorway that I never even knew was there. A door that may be closed, but now I know it's there."

He was silent, remembering, putting his feelings into balance."That Gather broke some barriers, opened my mind to new perception. And believe it or not, it HURT! Hurt as though my very consciousness was tearing open." He stopped, considered that and then curtly nodded,"Yes, strange as that sounds, it WAS like that. It was a good pain.I would like that to happen again. I want to stand again at that threshold, to find out whether the door can actually be opened. We see a powerful Light through that small crack. I KNOW the door does exist and there has to be more beyond it. So I wish that each of you would talk the way we did that day. Tell us what you see, know, and what is happening to you. Let's research what change means with each other." He stopped, as if he had asked more than he could expect to be given."I suppose I ought to begin since I asked it."

    He was silent for several minutes, closing his eyes, breathing deeply and letting his attention focus."The sense of something entering my life is so gentle, but the implications are frightening to me when I THINK about it. I'm aware of more than I've ever been. Aware! As if my eyes see beyond what I look at, or more accurately, through what I look at. I just had to stop everything and ask myself,'what is happening?' " He looked around from face to face, attentive, listening, concerned but not puzzled. He saw a nod or two, as if these who were his brothers and sisters, knew exactly what he meant, "I feel as though -- as though I'm torn -- torn into wakefulness. Yes, jolted awake. Some clock has struck in me and finally sounded an hour that will not be denied. It is insistent, demanding, and unless I pay attention, there is pain."

    His voice was low, his eyes down, He was silent. Then, slowly he continued."We've talked of 'waking', we've used that word, but what I mean by that is hard to describe.I think Rose used the analogy once that it was as though we've been asleep and can't quite get our eyes open. But when we do, we are so slammed by sunlight in them, we can't see anything at all. You've had that happen on a sunny day. And so this is the same,after the dark of ordinary life, our vision is blinded by the very Light that reveals what I think are new dimension of reality. We dream, and are in an inner metaphoric universe, we live daily life, and are in a physical universe, we create and are in a mental universe, and now, we find we wake further, into a greater, more complex universe that includes all these others and more. And the reality has no name." He stopped, nodding as he found words to fit his thought.

    When we wake up then all our previous universes are intensified, Earth is a new place.It's as though everything, absolutely everything, the great as well as the minute,-- people's voices, the color of a leaf, the sound of a tree frog, or the entire Valley industrial Council,all those interactions among humans -- EVERYTHING -- is brand new. That's not quite right, more as though I never really noticed them before."

    He shook his head, "The light, the sunlight on the garden, sifts through my body. My mind sweeps with the sunlight, into every crevase, down every lizards back, spinning over water. The leaves seem to literally speak a language that I can understand.It is I who am finally aware of things because I am not separate from them!" He was still for a moment, "Every where I turn, among people as well, it is the same. At that Council, I realized we weren't separate entities. I was aware of dynamics and the play of ideas as if -- I were part of it. I was aware of thought patterns as an immense, intricate design that shifted as people prodded their different ideas into it. And when there was selfish intent warping the pattern,it showed so darkly I knew, if everyone were really seeing, they wouldn't miss it." The memory itself puzzled him. "But, you know, we INCLUDED selfish intent, as though that was part of it too."

    "Do you know what woke you, Paul? And can you remain awake, or do you - fall asleep again?" Rose was leaning toward him,insistent wanting him to reveal

what would explain to her herself.
He shook his head,"I don't know. I am beginning to suspect it's not just me, its all of us, we're waking up from some deep, ages long sleep. Humankind becoming Soul conscious! Not just one of us, but all of us. Can you imagine what that would mean? SOUL conscious! That word fits, because it is a consciousness beyond and greater than any I have ever known or imagined. And the teachers have always said that there is no separate 'I'. It's clear that 'I' is the whole of life on this Earth." He shook his head,"As far as explaining -- how can we? Eons ago, we were only physically and emotionally conscious, then came mental consciousness, and now, building on and maybe out of Mind, comes this spiritual consciousness. I don't know whether that's the way you'd describe it, nor do I know how to define spiritual, but it's what I've figured out. I know what I mean."
"Why've you never talked of this?" Ned sounded almost angry.
"I think I couldn't understand, or believe what was happening. It was so alien to ordinary life. Until the Spring Gather and that changed things." He was silent. They could see he realized another cause and was surprised. With a quick nod, he added,"But then, it was after I'd experienced the City that all this began to become clear."
He accepted a cup of hot coffee from Tom, who was serving, sipped it and sighed. "And the changes -- they're numerous. It seems as if everything I've always thought were important, joys, pleasures, griefs, pains, needs of my life, have lost almost all their --- their energy. I've lost interest in them, they have no place any more,except as they are part of the human dynamic of living. Or as they are a kind of play." No one spoke, all their eyes were on him,but he felt their insistence, as if he must make sense of this strangeness for them all."But you know, I've heard others speak of this phenomonon -- so many familiar things no longer have central interest for me. All the things I've built my life on, accomplishments, success, failure, griefs and joys, all of them just seem -- seem to have little meaning . Like something left over from childhood actually. Yes,like something left over. And at first I felt a terrible depression I couldn't shake. Some of you know about that."
His voice broke."I continued to do all the usual things, because that was my life. But the energy was elsewhere. For a long time, I felt empty, so empty. I had nothing left that was important, except Reaching farther into that Light. Had it not been for that glimpse, I think I might not have lived,except for my family. The sense that life was without purpose was so acute. Nothing else mattered." He turned to Jennifer,"You remember, my darling. It was hard for you." She nodded.
But now,a greater perception like a Light in my mind shows me there is something beyond my ordinary awareness that I must -- must Reach to. Must keep my attention on long enough to begin to - understand. How can I explain?" They could see the tears in his eyes, see his reluctance to speak so that he spoke against that reluctance, like pushing against a tremendous weight."At the same time, I was refusing to believe myself, buried myself in work and play, anything to prove that life was not changed. Gradually I could not deny. It's like

some terrible loss, a death even, inside me. Like something of my life is gone, forever lost. And then there is the grief of that. Strangely I denied the memories of that Light, refused it as an illusion." He was silent for some minutes. Then he said slowly. "When we were at the City, I UNDERSTOOD those memories were the only reality worth attending. I saw that change was occurring, a healthy change, I wanted to accept, to allow it. Then when we got home, I doubted again, felt fear. But what amazed me was that there was another side of myself who felt a vast relief. As though a burden was finally gone." He spoke wonderingly, as if just realizing it,"A vast relief. And that feeling of gratitude has grown through these weeks." He turned to look at Jessie, smiling finally a crooked little smile. "And then, Jessie showed us a little glimpse of the Joining. The door opened a little then. Yes, it did open just enough for me to know it could. And for an instant, I knew that here was the richness of LIFE, that this was the Way. But then, I could refuse it again. There was only memory. Blessed memory! And still -- I don't understand."

Tom's voice was a whisper, He could not suppress the sense of awe he felt at these thoughts, he heard it in his own voice. "But, Paul, that's the way it's supposed to be, isn't it?" His questioning look took in the others.

"What's supposed to be? Like what?"Paul's voice carried a note of dispair.

Tom looked to Jessie but she only smiled, "Well, isn't that what our Teachers have taught. Isn't that how the waking up effects people, to feel that terrible sense of loss, of being no longer able to connect with the world we've known." At Paul's continued look of question, his voice became strong, emphatic,"I know you must remember what they said,that when people wake up to the nature of things, to the reality of what is real beyond our everyday world, that it feels like a loss at first."

"But Tom, it isn't at all what I imagined. It's not comfortable at all." Paul's voice was strained, anger filtering through the pain. "I didn't do anything to make it happen,. I just flew over the City. We all did. It didn't happen to the others!" He sounded now almost furious with his disbelief. "What the Teachers taught us must be a different thing."

Tom turned then to Jessie, who sat with her head bent, a faint smile on her lips, her eyes hidden. "Jessie, is that what's meant after all?"

She looked up then, her face sober. Nodding slowly she met their eyes,"The experience is always different for each person. It is never what we thought it would be. That is one of its marks of authenticity. It is after all an awakening, you know, so you are aware of what was unknown, and what seems now to be utterly new to you. You cannot imagine it. Nor be prepared. Neither can anyone give that vision to you. It must be your own!"

There was silence, while everyone turned to look at Jessie.She bent her head slightly, touching Anna's head,which was against her knee. Paul spoke with hesitation,"You mean it's natural? This thing I've worried about so long. This changing is natural? My God, Jessie, I didn't know how to make sense of my life anymore. That's not natural?"

She nodded, smiling at him with a tenderness that surprised him."Tell us

THE PEOPLE OF THE VALLEY

more. When did this begin?"

He lowered his eyes, frowning as if to remember, his long thin fingers smoothed one cheek as if finding the very real touch of flesh reassuring. "It was when I started having to re-balance every day, every morning especially because if I didn't I'd slip down into a genuine depression. I thought then that had I not had training for so many years I could not have found that balance.

He stopped, looked at them with a dawning recognition bringing light to his eyes, recognition of his own past change."Why, Yes, it was that, I began to question things and kept wanting to turn to - to what I called 'matters of the Soul'. I didn't have any other name and I'd heard that once." But now, I see, yes, it was a changing, wasn't it? At first it was very slow and I could ignore it much of the time. But then when I felt the City - the power of it, it was as though a point had been reached in me, a point of - change? I wanted to stay, to realize, but then, I also wanted to get away from there fast. And then, there was that - that strange , unforgetable Touch of Joy." The last was whispered so some of those listening did not hear. " Who went?" Ben's deep voice seemed so very solid and sane just then.

"It was my birthday. Annette and William and Alice were having dinner that day and we decided to have it in Santiago and try out our new Car. Well, we ended up at the City. I don't know quite how. We never did get to Santiago." He smiled ruefully, remembering. "I think William's never forgiven me."

Suddenly Andrew burst out, as if he'd been restraining himself, "Sounds to me like you shorted out your batteries , Uncle Paul." He caught himself with a foolish grin and then said,"I didn't mean-- I didn't --"

Paul laughed, "No offense Son, It's exactly what it felt like. But how do you know?"

Andrew shifted in his chair, embarrassed, glanced at his sister and Jessie and muttered ,"Oh, I'm probably wrong."

Jessie and Anna both smiled, but Rose frowned darkly, studying his face. Paul watched him closely. Ben interrupted ,"Paul you said Will was there. And he's been different lately too."

Annette spoke then, her soft voice barely audible,"It's true. It really shook him. But he won't talk about it. He's taken on nearly a vendetta against the City since, but then you know of that, " She raised her hands , reached them forward palms up, "William is - William. He's denying everything until he can find a way to define everything, to explain."

Angy spoke then, her soft drawl contrasting sharply with Annette's clipped speech. "Which means until he can control the situation. Finding explanations let's him have some control." Her voice was resigned. Silvia watching all this, was puzzled, as were Jane and Steve sitting together in one big chair.

Paul nodded, "Annette, you've kept pretty close to William since that happened, but I thought that that City effected you too." He looked at her questioningly.

She nodded, "I've tried to ignore most of it. Partly because Will was so,- so

THE AWAKENING

distressed at first. But lately, I've insisted on paying attention to my own responses,- there's a difference in me, something seems to want to - to erupt. That's the only word that fits. It's as though my heart is opened a little and there's something that hasn't yet come forth. I haven't felt that sense of loss you describe, and that I've heard Rose speak of. But I cannot feel at ease, comfortable anymore. It IS as though something's missing" She was still, her gaze turned within."My sculpture once filled all need for speaking my inner life, but now, I'm balked. I cannot shape what seems to be hidden there just behind perception. I keep starting and putting aside what I've done. Inadequate! And I don't know why!" Her voice nearly broke at the last word.

Silvia sat curled in cushions, her eyes fixed first on Paul, then Annette. An astonishment ran through her. A great excitement and joy that she could not define, but it was good.It would not hurt her child. She moved, adjusting her body to accomodate her large belly. As she did she thought that the baby stirred, and she imagined that Joy rose from the child itself. Not from herself. The sensation and idea was so strange that she felt fear in it. Memories of things happening lately, of noticing things she never had before, of thinking thoughts that were different and so intense, rose into her mind. She had thought it was aberations of pregnancy. Now she wondered.

Rose felt a great relief. But she also felt irritation."Listen, all of you. What we're finally talking about is exactly what we need to talk about. I notice that you, Jessie, seem to turn our talk back to us, that you deflect our questions and say very little to us. Maybe we need you to say more.But whatever that may be, we still have a lot to talk about. And Paul's given us the beginning."

Silvia straightened her small body, combed her fingers through the long,shining, blue-black hair that fell like a dark veil over her shoulders and breasts and looked very serious. "That's what I want you to do. I've never thought of the things you're saying, but what you say reminds me of events in my life that I've ignored."

Rose almost interrupted,"There's a new energy present among us, there IS change. We're not the same, none of us is the same. We MUST notice, we must acknowledge that the changes have upset, disturbed and in some cases, terrifed us. And we've got to agree that we can, and will, talk about these things from now on. Not just Paul, or me, it's got to be all of us!" She looked around with anger, supplication,in her face,"Don't you see, we suffer when we don't talk, don't find some kind of mutual understanding, even if we aren't sure what it all means."

Paul nodded vigorously, "I agree. We've got to do that.I for one am willing to talk and to listen, and to search out the meanings of these things. If anyone wants to talk about what's happening,call me." He was surprised at the relief in several faces.

Ben and Rose, Tom and Ned, nodded, murmuring agreement, and Rose looked at Anna, sitting so still, her mouth slightly open in amazement. Anna realized more than they knew. She wished that her daughter would speak of it. She said,"Anna, and you too, Andrew, we've not been fair to either of you. We've avoided a lot during these last years. I know it now. But I didn't then. I wish we had been more willing to hear you. Won't you please talk of your knowledge, your own experience."

Anna turned her large dark eyes to her mother, drew herself back from the distance of her thought. Rose studying her, thought she had grown so tall lately, her hands lay quietly in her lap, brown fingers woven together as if seeking comfort. She met her mother's eyes and nodded seriously. "I'd appreciate that, Mother, I'd appreciate being able to talk". Her dark face was suddenly shining, the solemnity swept away in smiles. She seemed inordinately pleased. Rose thought it must have been lonely for her. She wanted to ask more, but knew that Anna would find her own times to tell her.

Unexpectedly, Anna began to talk softly," You're talking about losing interest in things. I don't know much about that. It's a wonder to me how things are, how the Earth lives, how living things relate and -- just how they are. It's a wonder and I never am tired of noticing. I've noticed change though, even in that. Lately I've had the sense of being more alive. Something is there, just beyond awareness that I can barely Reach to, yet I know it is there. Something that I know is - not at all ordinary. You called it a door, I can see that might describe it. But the door is open, the Light blazes through everywhere all the time. At first it blinded me, made me full of awe. But now, I see a little through the Light. There isn't a name for what is beyond, within, that Light. But I see what I don't see anywhere here." She spoke so matter of factly that even Jessie turned to look at her.

For minutes everyone was silent, then she went on. So when you say you lose interest, Daddy, I don't know what held your interest before. There is so much to just Earth herself, the wonder of -- of life. And then of people." She stopped, embarrassed, not sure she said what she meant. She tried again, determined to keep these adults talking finally. "Sometimes I can spend an entire day just walking through a garden, paying attention. Or talking to people! There is so much. So much." She sighed, looked around, her body sitting straighter, her hands coming apart and gesturing lightly toward them, as if to touch them. "It's as though I know something I can't find words to tell anyone. I am AWARE," She shook her head. Her eyes shining and far away. Softly she added, "And when I am AWARE, then the very Earth is fascinating, everything is. And we are not separate at all!"   No one spoke, their eyes were intent upon her. "Sometimes I lose connection, as if I've broken off from my Self. Then I see that Anna is just a little piece of what I am. A little narrow piece. That's when I slide down and am afraid I will forget what I am. I've learned something though!" She swallowed, glanced around as if reluctant to say more, then frowning, she seemed to decide, "I think I know the difference between life and Life -- because that's what I think we are entering. LIFE! And I've learned how to refocus -- instantly refocus. I have to do that a lot.

"She was silent so long they thought she had done, but something held them and finally she said softly, "Life thrusts forth within all things and I know now It has thrust forth through all of us together. There it is."

676

THE AWAKENING

Softly Jessie spoke, nodding gently, her face alight."It's been said that consciousness is a field within which our lives function, shape, and through which our consciousness extends itself. People have become aware of being conscious, other living things haven't, but that doesn't make them unconscious. That Reaching, far seeing human mind, CAN glimpse, can be aware of intelligence operating as a quality of that field of consciousness that extends beyond the aware mind. We quail before such intelligence. We fear what is beyond us." They waited, Anna was smiling softly now, her eyes on Jessie, they seemed to have entered into a communion. Then Jessie said,"To experience, extend consciousness into, Life - or Love - is shattering. Perhaps Anna experiences these a little. One can only bear a little Touch of either -- though I think they are the same."

Again there was silence. Everyone taking in these thoughts, realizing. Rose didn't want to speak,but her mind was full, thought came in a cloud, refusing to settle into words, but intense, demanding. There was a sharp, clear sense of their being together that no image defined.There was a mutual Reaching among them. It seemed a miracle, an unprecedented closeness.. She became aware of the power among them, a consciousness being shared through their minds and hearts and through the very cells of their bodies. Yes, it was as though it strummed through flesh even. They were bathed in it, a Light that permeated everything. She held firm and could see the Light flaming through each member of her family, young and old alike. It was surely stronger, and as bright as it had been at Spring planting.It was akin to that other moment they had shared.

Rose looked at Jessie, desire firm in her mind, and Jessie laughed, and said,"Then you would learn to Join?" She looked around and their faces were expectant."What you've done so far is a beginning of Joining, just beyond the simple Touch. So first let's Reach altogether, then Touch. Come, I'll show you. Focus, attend, and REACH". Her powerful energy drew them and they were there. They could feel the Reach of many individual minds. One by one, they entered that flaming strength that was Jessie's consciousness. One by one they loosened from their narrow limits and braved the larger consciousness. Then they seemed for a moment to hold, as if willing those who hesitated to Join their efforts. Gradually even Jane and Steve, focussed and turned their minds to her. As they did, they too felt the surge, the expansion and the electric tingle of mind Reaching mind. Jessie held them there, her own mind like a great light to theirs, illuminating the narrow way, until they all together burst forth, Reached out of their limited universe and exploded into hers. They swept toward her, caught up in the flow of energy, and Jessie, joyously, laughing within the center of it, drew them and welcomed them. They felt the electric Touch, the strange country of many minds together. Only in memory of it would each be astonished at the way consciousness extended, as if riding on the flow of itself. As the event occurred, it was utterly natural.

They felt a sensation like the deep chime of a bell that reverberated in their flesh and lifted their hearts to its Joy. The Joining began the process that would erase the sense of separation. For whole seconds they were lifted and still, while the effort drained away and the naturalness of such awareness established itself. They were Joined. There they knew what they had not known and could not have spoken, a vastness of vision, a depth of awareness into life around them. Their individual minds quivered with wonder, but held steady in this Ring of Being. What they saw and knew eliminated questions as fast as they broke into thought. Thought itself was seen as a shifting and knitting together of perceptions, then a shift again, and a new pattern, much like a kaliedescope rearranges elements to make new designs insistently. Here, thought rose out of the limitless field that was consciousness, a lattice work of possibility, it molded itself into language, always leaving most of possibility excluded by its limited nature. But there were many thought structures that could be chosen, or even, perhaps, with time, combined.

Then, leaving that, unthinking, aware, extending into consciousness without thought, mind realized within MIND as naturally as breathing. Nuances, colors, fragrances, possibilities, were not eliminated, but visible even as a particular chosen thought-design was selected out. Perception was flexible there was no congealing of ideas but a participation and fluid extension of possibility. When one idea was selected, the others were also known and valued and their reflections continued to influence the chosen one. They could be aware of that play of mind when language did not hinder. The intense focussing made conscious the unceasing flow of Love that healed and renewed. Life around them was so obviously knowable. They saw the radiant doorway for jessie had opened that door and they stood at its threshold. No time passed, they could not think, could only realize as if that Joined mind was a mirror in which Mind left impressions of Itself. The state of their Joining held, steady.

Then, the wonderful, fluid, mental landscape shrank, one by one they withdrew, fell away. For some of these the return to that limited consciousness of one personal mind was painful, for others escape.

Rose pulled her attention into this room, these loved people. Her very mind ached, her thought stunned. In awful stillness she turned to look at Jane and Steve, holding on to each other's hands as if for courage. They watched with wondering eyes, yet without resistance. They had been part of that, participating. Andrew watched his mother,, aware of her actions and realizations. He was smiling, his eyes shining, his hands clasped around his knees. She thought, "I would like to touch against his mind, to listen. But he is not open to me, just now. My Son, My Son, how far away you can be." She felt sadness. Then her eyes moved on, it was as though within her mind still lingered that thread of sight, that moved from one to another, drawing them all into a woven connection. She let her gaze touch Cassandra, lying with her head on Jerry's back, her hair a bright fan over his green shirt. The little girls hands were flung to each side, one under Jerry's brown one. She seemed not to notice, but Rose felt her attention.

She looked to the side, Tom sat with his head bent, eyes closed, listening, attentive. She thought, and the thoughts were simple individual little constructs, surrounded by possibility. What a game thinking could be. Fascinating to see how many of the possibilities could be drawn into one construct. But she shuddered, the game seemed too complex for her at this moment.

Ned, sat stiffly, his hands crossed on his belly, his eyes wide, questions filled his eyes. Tears still rolled down his black cheeks, but he seemed unaware of them, his heart felt expanded to include so much it hurt. Painfully he drew himself into the moment. He was watching Paul with the alert wonder with which he might watch a wild creature he was stalking. Seeing him for the first time.

Angy was quiet, a deep inner quiet that pleased Rose. She had moved to sit near Steve and Jane, her lower lip caught between her teeth. And there, Annette, hesitant, almost holding her breath as Rose's eyes moved to hers. Then with a great sigh she relaxed, and accepted. Rose knew that decision has been made. There, Mary, her long fingers wrapped over her drawn up knees, watching Rose as one might watch a snake charmer, her eyes wide, waiting, and when their gaze met, a great wide grin brightened her face. She was not sure how to understand all she had realized and she was utterly willing. Then Rose finally met Paul, Reaching, as he offered. She met his mind and felt the harsh confusion, the conflict and its battle lines drawn up. What he had realized in that time of Joining was doing destruction to some of his long held assumptions. He felt relief and fear, and she felt pity. It was hard to live through such an upheaval of recognition. Her pity touched him and he grinned suddenly. Then he ended the long silence.

"Well, there we are. I ache and tears fill me. We've extended farther beyond ourselves. We've been together as we've never known people could be. We have done what we all feared. What we've denied. It is so, isn't it? So now we know how the Self is conscious. Soul consciousness is not fractured it is inclusive." He frowned, sighed and then looked around, a bright, wry, sad smile changed his face."I want to remember, to keep awareness of that. At the same time - I want to turn away as if it never happened. I am amazed! I feel a wonder that floats my mind beyond itself. Now Anna, just as you said, the wonder of life is everywhere present?" His face was tender now, soft and without guile.

Again silence surrounded them. Could they? Would they be willing to enter again into that vastness of Mind? Rose felt that thread, connecting her to them all, a living mental thread that united them and would allow the sudden bloom of a Joining to occur. Suddenly they had been together in that mental universe, so vast that it might have overwhelmed, torn their sanity had they not supported one another. But there they had known the brilliant edge of a dimension called Spirit as far removed from the mental world as the physical world was and at the same time, as fully included within it. Physical, emotional, mental, born from and faintly expressing already that limitless Mind-Spirit that was possibility. But now, the reflection of It glowed through their very hearts, unforgetable. They knew that now. Knew and wondered. It was a glimpse of a totality they could not have dreamed of, for its very dimensions would not fit thought.Even now, they had trouble remembering all that they knew, for it must be shaped into language for them to speak of, to think of. But blessed relief, memory was not dependant on language. There, extended beyond any consciously imagined possibility, had been an immensely different perception of reality. Yet they had only touched upon its nature. There were further dimensions of Being to be eventually perceived through those knit, Joined, Minds.

They felt the slide down into that ordinary familiar state, and were grateful because they did not know how to bear all they realized. Jessie knew it was enough this time. Then Paul shook his head as if shaking out the vision. And the silence continued for some time.

"That! What we did. Were! Jessie! It was unbelievable. I feel - - I feel as though I want to just be still, to meditate on what I realized for a long time." He was silent. They all had retreated into themselves, as if comforting those small amazed selves. They went from time to time to fill a cup, or to just walk a bit, along the window looking out, but no one had words to speak. Now and then some one walked out into the air, across the deck to touch the rain laden leaves of the willow tree, whose green screen of branches glistened in the erratic sunlight. Or to weave slowly through the gardens, leaning to catch the fragrance of a rose, or the cascades of petunias along the border with the careful attention of one just realizing the magical beauty of these living things. Then, finally, the ordinary world reestablished itself. They began to talk. Paul was first, as if something troubled him too much to remain silent.

"We've got a lot to talk about. We won't be able to deny anything anymore. We've experienced it together. We're beginning to See,to realize what is beyond our ordinary senses. I think eventually we'll know it as clearly as we know this world. Right now we can't hold our minds at the point of attention long enough to realize much. But we can't stop now, we've got to keep on, learning, realizing." He stopped, nodding, his eyes unseeing, "Yes,until we realize what humankind actually is -- but more - what we are becoming."

He was silent again, and no one else spoke, so after a bit he went on." On my birthday trip,when we hung there over the City, there was that sense of Presence, that sense that there is energy that we actually live in,an energy as constant, as omnipresent as air itself. And we breath that energy with our minds, as our bodies breath air. There it is.I have finally found words and it seems so simple after all. That was clear to me then, but I could not have said it. Now I can say it. I know the energy now, but I don't know what it is. Though I suspect. But I've worried, worried about that trip, whatever it opened up for me, I may have been wrong in taking the others.Was it unfair to the others to take them when they might not have been ready."

"Did you know you were prepared? Were ready?" Jessie asked.

He eyed her thoughtfully." Actually,I didn't. I suppose maybe a person doesn't know."

"A Teacher does." She smiled."Knows when a student is ready."

"But we didn't have you there, Jessie, nor anyone else, and we've not had a habit as you know of talking of these things. But you see, there it is, I might have taken the others when they should not have gone."

"A person who is sighted cannot make a blind person see autumn colors. That is obvious. And a person who is unaware that he is ready cannot know of any other who is or isn't. Your Teachers pointed out the way to you. Some of you saw it,and began and others were still deciding. But how can anyone be hurt by someone offering an opportunity for knowing? You can only know what you can bear to know."

Paul stared at her anxiously,"But they were not ready, and there is what happened to William. He has been hurt."

"If they were not ready, truly not ready at all, then they would have experienced nothing, except perhaps a mild sense of energy. Will is just not ready to break old patterns. He has to deal with what he sees in the rest of you, the difference. That he is doing. He has a mind that reasons sharply, thinks perceptively, but he cannot see beyond his traditional system of thought. He has trouble observing more than one structure of thought at a time. Just as a person born blind cannot See. He will though, one day. As for the others, each of them was able to wake a little in her own way."

Paul was nodding, relieved, comforted. He drew a long sigh and then said. "I finally am ready myself to ask - to ask you for some answers, if there are any. What is the reason for the fear and the pain, Jessie? The perception is so utterly wonderful and yet afterward there is fear."

Jessie was still so long they thought she would not answer, or as if she sought in herself for answer.And then finally she began to speak softly,"We have chosen to speak openly and so I too must tell what it is for me. Each person knows the passage differently. Remember this is my experience, not yours. But it might give a reflection that is helpful." She sighed, her eyes wistful as if remembering a great far distance. "To stand there, at that threshold, that point of clear, cool fleshlessness, that absence of the familiar warmth, the body comfort of physical life consciousness, is rightfully frightening to the person just on the verge of awakening. To know there is are further dimensions of reality, that this isn't all,and to know it forcefully as experience so that it is no longer an idea but a reality, shakes up our entire concept of what is real. It's bound to be frightening. All humanity finally known as one Self? How much more drastic an idea could one realize?"

Again she was quiet,letting them absorb that. Then she went on, "To KNOW that! It reveals us to ourselves. We've all harmed our fellows. And now we know we live the pain of humankind. We suffer if any person, yes, even a creature suffers. Finally we see how we immerse our lives in suffering. All of us together creating our world's pain." The sadness of her eyes shifted, gladness filling them." But we live also the Joy and the grandeur of humankind rising from its torpor and brutality." Her hands unclasped themselves from her lap and she held them out, palms up, as if offering. Then they dropped like brown leaves against her knees and she went on.

"In the moment of realization, I left everything I had been behind. At first it seemed an entrance into the heart of loneliness so deep it is known without color or temperature or familiarity, without name or sound. It was through a silence that never knew sound or movement, through the null! The NOT. What is, ceased into what is not. At that place, nullity, there was the glimpse that fired awake my mind. Because I was dis-illusioned with the world, thought, all I had known, I was willing to reach toward something beyond those. I was becoming conscious, Self conscious, but I did not know it then. I knew my head hurt, my brain on fire. But more, my psyche stripped of all its defenses and its hiding places, was exposed and raw with recognition that I am what my brother is!" She was still again, then recited softly, "When we learn to obliterate and efface out of our consciousness ourselves as the central figure in our life drama, then only can we measure up to our true potential." With a wry smile, she added,"It became so obvious."

Again she was still, her body moveless like a rock, a bit of mountain side, Then she said, "When the return occurs, and one is closed into sound and motion again, then the mind cannot process that 'unknown' so it builds fear to protect itself. There is nothing to shape thought. And without being able to think, the ordinary mind quails. But you have been taught how to still thought. To stop the chattering mind and to Be. And you are aware of Being! Yes, that part cannot be hard for you. And the wonder of that silence is remembered, for memory is not limited. It fills the body and the heart as well as the mind. That place was where desires ceased and happiness was not. Where sorrow ended and tears are unknown. But there is Joy. Never have we known true Joy! There is something completely 'other' that includes but also stretches far beyond any of these." Her words drifted to an end,like flakes of sound that had filled the air.Then she gave an abrupt nod, frowned and said," Through dispair, through dreams and being alive, through knowing into unknowing, we must pass in order to awaken. Once awakening, whether we can find words or not, we are never the same."

She laughed softly,"Here am I, a person familiar to you, sitting among you,talking as if I knew. This little self, trying to make itself large." Again she laughed as at a happy joke."The self is made large in this world, you know by holding on to things, by attaching, adding until the self drags endless tons of debris, of needs, possessions, pains, pleasures and names. Names that define a longing to be but are never anything but that, names of longing. And this must be, for the self must grow large to finally be large enough to encounter the Self.It must reflect its self in numerous forms before it recognizes what is beyond form.Therefore, we make ourselves large by attaching ourselves to a business, a school, an industry, an organization anything that will convince us we are greater than our individual selves. And all the while, we have forgotten that we are one Soul, who is larger than all our devises, is large as humanity itself, is large as Life and Consciousness. It is the unconscious longing for Soul Joining, that causes our eternal attaching of ourselves to things. We cannot understand that greatness of being is never found in things.It is found in singleness of mind and being,the singleness of Humanity. The greater singleness of Life itself. It is the natural state of human kind."

They did not talk, their hearts blazed with these reminders, these words that

THE AWAKENING

seemed finally to carry what they themselves had perceived and could not shape to words. Slowly they began to move about, to find food and drink. They brought bowls from the kitchen until the table was filled with hot steaming foods. Plates and cups were filled and each person found a quiet spot where he could eat and be still. And so for this time they lived in that transcendance.

Finally, as the rain ceased, and the afternoon began, the sun poured its heat down into the land, the went out to stand looking at the freshly washed Earth. They turned again to one another.They began to look at one another, ready to ask and to speak.

Seldom had they heard Jessie discourse in so steady a manner, she was taking her role as Teacher and she did it well. Jennifer asked, "Then Jessie, the feelings Paul speaks of, those of losing interest in the things of his world, the fear of finding nothing in its place, and the loss,the terrible sense of loss, are part of that changing?"

Jessie nodded, her eyes clear and bright, her voice firm,"Yes, it is a natural process."

Paul nodded, Rose bent her head, filled with an understanding she wanted to absorb. The others waited, and finally, they began to talk of the familiar world again.

Rose murmured," The City has caused so much excitement among so many people. We need to understand why. It is a strange City." She was feeling great excitement of a new hope that Jessie's words had given her. Yet she could not say why.Nor could she say why the City filled her mind at this moment, why she wanted to know more of Her. "I think the strangest part is the way we've treated Her. We love the thought of Her, the fact of Her there. The People of the Way seem to know more, they seem to include Her in their lives in a manner that is wonderful.But the rest of us Valley people don't talk much about Her."

Silence fell around them again, as if her words had lodged securely in their minds and were expanding there, to include their meanings. After a while,Ben shook himself, as if waking from a trance. There was something he wanted to ask Jessie, but he could not yet find the shape of the thought. He said," What you say reminds me of that day I hung conscious over the Silent City. You wake those memories as if they were this morning.I've never flown over the City that I did not feel that - power. An energy that moved me to run away at first, but to long to return. I always have known She is more than a 'place in a cliff face'.

Others nodded, Steve started to speak, then sank back, clutching Jane's hand as if holding on to life. Silvia's face shifted from anger, to curiosity, to fear, and she too started to speak and did not. Paul was nodding, "It's been true all my life and I've denied it. What a strange reluctance we all have. Through the years, I've flown over, and breathed the amazing fragrance, that life enhancing fragrance, that alone should have told me it was good. And the sound,the sound of some music I could never quite identify, yet it lifted my heart. Even as it frightened me, with its power."

"You've realized a blessing Paul. You know that beauty." Jessie nodded.

683

Anna was leaning toward him, "Uncle Paul, have you spoken of this to Steve or Rachel?"

He turned to her curiously, surprised,"Why no, Anna, I think I haven't. I thought they'd think me foolish".

With a swift gesture of impatience that made Jessie smile, Anna frowned,"Oh,no Uncle Paul. Oh, no. Pleae don't forget to tell them, to talk to them. You don't realize -- you mustn't think because we are young that we don't know ---" Her voice faltered, she glanced at Andrew, the other children, and they nodded to her. " That we don't know more than you think."She sank back somewhat embarrassed at finding all eyes on her.

Andrew said, with an erupting anger."You've also refused to see us, you know, sometimes. Your own children, Adwin children. You're our own folks but you've refused to see us." He was obviously angry, but he also radiated a request, a plea.

Paul looked as if someone had dashed cold water into his face. He frowned with pain."I'm afraid you're right. I think we've done just that." He looked at the other adults in the group. The fact of their ignorance weighed down on him at that moment.An ignorance they had fed by refusing to discuss these things. He heaved a sigh and determined now to change that,"Well, you know, at one time, I thought if I were to talk of this, how would I describe it. And then I knew that in our Learning Centers the Teachers taught us the Idea. The Ideas! Remember? That there is a Source of Life, that some call that God, and that that Source is One Life. That we are beings of Spirit. That we are SPIRIT. But then, how was I to understand, for that had no literal meaning for me. What was Spirit? All ideas, nothing more. It didn't seems to be something I could see, nor could I imagine it even. Spirit was something etherial and not even imaginable therefore it was not real." He sat contemplating them. Finally he went on. "So I assumed that if I talked of my own experience, it would make no more sense than those ideas had." And now, Jessie speaks of Spirit. And the meaning is clear, because I Know, have realized. I understand that to know is not to think. But to KNOW." He met Andrew's eyes, and finally the boy gave a curt nod, and relaxed into his chair. Paul felt odd relief.

He began again with a wry grin."Thinking comes later! What you say Jessie is alive, wakes memory in me now.The old Teaching, was an idea, not real. And when our own experiences began -- experiences that we did not fully understand at all,we did not connect them at first. The real is so vastly beyond words, so vastly beyond theory and so we didn't connect them at all. Neither did we ask the Master Teachers. I think they might have helped. But we did not ask."

Rose, listening carefully, began nodding as if coming to a realization, she grimaced at her own thought and then said, " Giving something a name doesn't help much. But maybe it does prepare us after all." She was still, then her face cleared, she added,"When we are 'there', during the experiencing, the being there, no questions arise as to authenticity. No doubt troubles me.That's why the remembering makes me know without doubt, even when I can't tell of it at all."

THE AWAKENING

Annette said,"There's been one result, we all have to acknowledge. Lifting to that point of awareness has introduced us to what Love is. To that eternal energy that we can't define at all. But we do begin to know of it." She smiled, "There has to be some reason for all of this though!"

Jennifer was nodding, "Absolutely, "We can't really understand, we can't really - walk through that door you spoke of even though we know now that it's there, so what do we do?" She looked to Jessie, the question a throbbing pain in the room.

Jessie waited, and then said,"You learn how to live! You realize already that we are becoming more than animal human, we must persist in standing at Soul conscious levels of awareness until our unfoldment increases enough that we See. That we can walk through that doorway and Know with full awareness."

"And it is done by learning how to live as -- as Human Beings, rather than as animal human?"

"That's the first step!"

Ned roused himself, as from a deep trance,"Does anyone here think we've begun? Have we learned anything at all?"

Tom stood, stretched, and walked around the room. "We are learning Ned, can't you see? We're not the same people as our ancestors. We absolutely will not battle against one another as animal human's always have. We don't want to overpower our fellows. Or control them. We want to live together,respecting one another, even, maybe beginning to love one another? Isn't this our new and blessed birthright.The birthright of this Valley." He stopped, turning suddenly to look at them, his little speech had been as much a revelation to him as to them. "Isn't that what you mean?" He turned to Jessie, a serious frown on his face.

Steve spoke, surprising them, out of his profound silence,"Well, there it is! Haven't we known? All these years, we've been learning how to balance, to be aware of what's around us, to pay attention, to realize the Earth as our Mother, even that's been growth." He looked at Jane, their fingers twined comfortably together,"That's part of what you mean,isn't it Jessie?"

She nodded,"It's exactly that. You as a people are unfolding within mind and Heart. You know already much that humankind has never known. We had 'ideas' about it, but we have never KNOWN!   Now we begin to recognize a new relationship with all Life."

"And those new perceptions upset our familiar way of seeing things, of seeing ourselves even?"

"Absolutely! You've all experienced that. It's part of the fear." She laughed. "We do have to repeat that fact. It seems at first so hard to believe."

Jennifer shook her head, " When we all went to the City, with Paul on his birthday, I recognized something I could barely tolerate to realize. And that's a strange phrase to use but it fits.I think it was that Touch with - the energy we've been talking about.As though I was open to something I'd never known before.It was unmistakable. I didn't speak of it to anyone,, because I was afraid. Anna asked if we'd ever talked with Rachel and Steve. I couldn't. I thought they'd think

685

their Mama had lost her balance entirely. You see, at the time, it was so profoundly wonderful,so deeply stirring that my mind woke to knowing something utterly new. Just what you're talking about now.It WAS as if I COULD know something I hadn't been able to. But I couldn't make a thought out of it. Later, I felt foolish, felt lost and yet with a longing I can't describe. I cried, I think, for days. Tried to keep anyone from knowing." She swallowed, the telling was not easy for her even now.

"I tried to tell myself I was imagining, then I would be angry with myself for thinking that. No imagination could have imagined such as that. But underneath everything, even the fear, was an underlying Joy." She sighed, I didn't know, what to do. I couldn't believe that anything real had happened within me,and yet, I knew absolutely that it had. I was afraid of that piercing Joy, afraid of it. As though I didn't deserve such wonder and therefore was playing false. Somehow I couldn't think about what I realized. I denied." she took a long deep breath , her face pale with a look almost of apology.

Gently as if words could not be stopped now they'd started, she went on. " It must be what you're describing, Jessie, an unfolding. It was as though my mind opened, literally opened. My head ached for days. Perceptions defied shaping into thought. Then gradually fragments of perception began to be selected by my frantically searching mind, and they congealed into ideas. Ideas that were only bits and pieces of the real. But they gave me some ease.I could not think of explanation so I feared. And maybe that's part of why I cried, because I couldn't allow myself to just accept and know the Joy of it." She stopped, letting the memory float through all awareness,"How can there be such Joy?" her voice was a whisper."I remember it, even through the fear.What Paul's said, the sense of having lost everything, has not happened to me. It may begin sooner or later, just now, I am simply trying to get the world to fit into all I realize."

After several minutes, she shrugged and said, "So when you say that we've got to learn how to live with one another, that the path to full consciousness is learning how to live as Human Beings, I think I understand. I felt - so different about people. about living things.I look at the trees, when I go to walk, at a single leaf, or a worm crawling and am amazed by the beauty, the exquisite perfection. I cannot take living things for granted at all, and that brings much hurt, you know. As well as -- much delight." This time she smiled, as if remembering again. "But most of all, there is the sense of - of losing myself in just Being." Her eyes were far off, her smile faint, but sweet.

As if to bring herself back, she shook her head, met several eyes. "I've never been able to talk this sensibly about it. Why now? Was it the Joining that -- that gave me understanding?" She reflected now, her eyes distant and remembering. Her face warm with memory."Is that what you mean by the unfolding?"

No one spoke, sensing that she was not finished and she went on."Someone said, that there would be a sense of being stretched, as though one's entire being is somehow larger, deeper, greater in it's nature. And that's how it was. I felt almost sore from the stretching of my Mind and Heart. But since I had no

explanation, I just didn't speak of it."
"Why not Jennifer?"
"To speak of it was to remember and to know that I couldn't explain. To speak was to admit what I couldn't admit. To speak was to feel, to know again and I was afraid. Even for my sanity. I did not seem to be sane. Just as now, as I speak,the memories are roused, and they have no compunction. They ARE. First, I feared I could not bear such power again.Then I feared that I would find it all a dream, or a figment of imagination."

She looked at Paul, then slowly to Rose, and finally to Jessie." Is this what is meant by Spirit? The heart awakening to being alive? Do we learn to live by realizing more and more?" With those questions she fell silent. Jessie watched her intently, her eyes shining.

After several minutes, she wiped her face with one hand, slowly shaking her head in wonderment."I surely understand now why we have feared so much. Why all of us have, and refused to talk together!" Then startled at her own words, she gasped,"Why of course, it's part of this learning, you speak of."

Paul nodded,he looked at the others. Ned grunted, his black face furrowed with frowns, he rolled over and sat up, turned to look intently at Jennifer. Then he too turned to Jessie,"Well, there it is, Ma'am. We're talking of something called Spirit and no one knows what that is. I get an impression it's some kind of higher more sensitive mind, or as Jennifer said, the Heart of humankind itself. We're becoming spiritually Conscious whether we will or no! But we're talking about learning, about growing into Human Beings, whatever that might be. Obviously we don't know what it's all about. I don't even understand except that what they say strikes at a few memories of my own, and that I've pushed down out of sight too. Things that happened especially after that Spring gather. So I ask, can you help us?"

Jessie nodded,let her hands fit again over Anna's shoulders as if leaning a little, her face seemed then full of her eighty some years, weary and yet alert with fresh life. Then she smiled, and her face shone with the light of that smile." Yes, you must ask. Could we say that Spirit is all that is before us? The nature of what we're beginning to realize, and also more - more than we possibly can ever know? That Life that is the source of life? No one can tell another the truth of it. No One! Think of the most wonderful, wise, compassionate person the world has known.Think of the saints, the Buddha, the Christ. And think that all humanity might be as they were.That each of us might live lives as pure, as aware! Then perhaps you will imagine something of what humanity is becoming."

"I don't see why the Monitors don't explain all this. Teach us more?" Steve blurted out in sudden resentment.

Jessie looked at him and said,"Monitors cannot. You do know that. They cannot ever interfere. They cannot even help if asked when it comes to your own realizing. You must open your mind and heart to know yourSelf. It is your own Self that you must encounter, not another's.The unfolding of one person must be from his own nature. It cannot be imitated, nor planned. It is spontanious as he or she develops into that Spiritual nature we speak of. But remember, Monitors are Monitors and nothing else. We do have Master Teachers, they could have at least listened as you talked to yourself." She was smiling."The Monitors are also citizens, their job is not to pull our chestnuts out of the fire. That is our own job."

Steve, nodded, it was obvious to him now. He knew he would resent interference from anyone who sought to give him answers.

Jessie gave a curt nod, then went on,"You've all been taught by your Teachers, the Master Teachers, that is. But no teaching has meaning until you reach a certain point of readiness. There must be experience. And for that, the City is there. She is a catalyst. She is like a magnifying glass, perhaps. She reflects whatever is within the person. When you come to Her, and there is that spark of beauty, of Love, of Trust within yourself, then the City rouses it, makes you conscious of that in yourself. But it is in you all the time. She wakens you to that Spirit that is in you. She doesn't make you different from what you are. And that Spirit is the power you feel. It is your own, the power of Being Human!" She stood up, walked to the tables and gathered up a new cup of iced tea, and an apple. "And the Joining can sometimes waken also."

When she came back, she looked at them thoughtfully, and suddenly seemed to them to be their grandmother after all. She said," It isn't a strange power from outside at all. But it is your own Life power, your Heart consciousness that is in every human being." She nodded to Jennifer,"It is a stretching, as you felt. But it cannot harm. But one can be uncomfortable, certainly. Growth means change and most change is uncomfortable. Now that you have begun to speak, to share this recogniton of Spirit within each of you, you may not fear so."

" But Jessie, it's a cliche, the idea of Spirit within us. And it never has had meaning for me at all." Angy spoke thoughtfully, and held out her hand wanting to go on,"And yet, when I listen to you all, when I realize, then I remember too, those moments, those times when this sense of recognition, of Knowing something beyond my self, as if I, myself, were more. Today, this Joining, brought me into that same state of consciousness. I resisted at first. But if by Spirit within, you mean that which extends through me like a -- like a living yeast, another dimension of my own nature, mostly unfamiliar and unknown, one that stretches to all that we can be, then I can see. I understand finally, perhaps, what is meant by Spirit within. That which makes us finally See, Hear, Know, without pretense or fear."

Steve shook his head, his eyes fixed now on Jessie, wide and trusting. She saw the responsive child in this man and honored that child trust and wisdom. "Jessie, I'm baffled, you speak of energy and I feel energy here, among us. What is that?"

"It's actually a reflection of the power within yourself. The Soul, or Self. To most of us it's a surprise to discover. When we acknowledge that Self, we acknowledge the power and the responsibility for that power. Energy is the movement of Life through all living things. Power comes from yielding to and learning to impliment the movement of that energy." She met his eyes, and held them for a moment. His face changed, registering surprise and then delight. He shook his head, turned to Jane who gazed at him in wonder.

Jessie smiled at them both,"There is great power in each of you two. Do you know that? There is that power that you have not acknowledged, but that you participate in." She was smiling that playful delighted smile that made her seem so young.

Jane spoke in a whisper, "Why have we, Steve and I, never felt that pull the others speak of, that attraction?"

Jessie watched them, flicked a glance at Angy, who was watching her with amazement,"For some of you there is a different way. For some there is -- yet a little time. But there is such Love present in you, all three of you, a love that surpasses most of us,though you would never have thought that. The flame burns high within you, and you are not aware consciously of that.You already realize that Love in it's simplest expression, is attraction. And you, all three of you attract all life around you. And Life attracts you. You respond without resistance to it.But you did not know that it is the precondition of Love."

" Remember, when you fly above that City you will know,you will See and meet that Love that lives in you now." She laughed, her eyes sparkling with that laughter, "No, there's never harm in going there. One only meets oneself and discovers what one is. One discovers only as much of oneself as one can bear too. For there is that problem, you know. But then, there is the need for reflection and solitude. They are necesssary in order to absorb all that is known there."

Tom looked around, sighed deeply and then said reluctantly,"Well,there you are. For some of us it's not much to see, especially when what we feel is fear. That means we are seeing something in ourselves that we fear?"

"Yes, it may be. What you fear may be the recognition of yourself. When the spark flames up, it reveals what has been hidden. But it is also rouses deep unquenchable longing for that which you sense is beyond you. The flaming up of Spirit brings great change for your very nature must stretch to hold that greatness of Life blazing up." She frowned briefly, then said,"You were taught as much as possible in school to prepare you, and now the actual reality of it must be met." There was a hush in the room as they all thought of that.

Steve finally broke the quiet, speaking from a heart ache he could not end. "Jessie, the Builders speak often of 'Devil practices' among the Valley people. I've heard that often, and it must have something to do with the City, since they always combine the two. There are so many people who -- who seem to have these Psychic Talents, and other strange ability.Even my own little Cassie.I cannot believe that she had truck with any 'devil'."

"The City has no influence on the emergence of these Talents, except that the City raises the energy level of all people. Her energy surges through all of us and so whatever we are grows stronger. It is what we already are, however.If we have a Talent,it is also enhanced and we are conscious of it.. We have trouble because we don't want to acknowledge all that we begin to see. We must learn to see all that we are, negative and positive. Whatever we are grows stronger in the flow of energy from that City."

"And what if that which we are is selfish, cruel, and lusting for power?" Tom spoke his voice trembling.

" Then we see that. Do you think there are any of us who do not have those qualities? That's why it's so frightening to realize -- to see ourselves! It's only if there is genuine Goodwill within our hearts, that we can grow out of our self contempt when we first encounter them." She was sad,"Some of you have said your first Touch with Spirit has resulted in terrible grief and self disgust. It is the seeing of ourselves that can bring that. It is seeing that we are more than that, that brings joy. Good Will grows in us, good will toward all life, including ourselves."

"Good Will? I've heard that. The Teachers told us of that too." Anna spoke softly, for this was something she needed to know of. " What happens then, if we have not sufficient Love?"

Jessie nodded," Yes, there it is, Good Will is wakened within us by that energy that flows from the City, and meets the small flame of Love that is already in us. The City is a point of focus and Love can flow into our world because the spark has waked into flame,the entrance to our hearts is open. When we are ready, emptied of constant self needs, Love begins to fill us, just as water flows best into an empty pond." She laughed, "But there I am, myself forgetting. We are not empty enough for the unimpeded flow of Love until we have lost selfishness in knowledge of the singleness of Being.Then Good Will is as normal as breathing.

" As for the Psychic Talents, Steve,they are simply natural extensions of our senses that are being stimulated by this influx of energy.They are not evil.But they can be used for evil if there is not sufficient Good Will. They are not the waking of Soul Consciousness but they may accompany that waking."

Cassandra sat up, "Why yes, that's what the Teachers told us. We all know that. Why're you worrying about the Talents, Daddy. No one's been hurt by them have they?"

Rose nodded,"It's true. I explain those facts to the children and they seem to understand. But there's so much happening among the children. It's a blessing that Cassandra was tied by the children, even though it frightened her.It made us pay attention."

Tom spoke slowly,forming his thoughts into words with care."Well, I think the Builders are also waking a little.I think that energy inflow fills their minds too, and they are afraid. So they cannot grasp the whole of the wonder, they resist with fear, pinning it on the most likely suspect, the way a young officer might judge too soon in a crime. "

Jennifer said,"Jessie,you're saying we must look to what we fear in ourselves, or don't want to see. To meet that, and learn of it?" She drew herself up, seriously shook her head,"That would be hard. I shudder when I think that I must return and visit that City, that I must respond to that energy. Yet I know I will.What I saw of myself was not comfortable at all."

She was silent for some moments, then, "But,you know, I want to go,

THE AWAKENING

something in me longs to be there. To touch again that very energy I fear." She smiled thoughtfully,shaking her head.

Angy watched Jennifer's face intently as if seeing there something that informed her,"I don't want to look at myself either Jen. I've even managed to avoid my peer group a lot of times, in the past. But lately,I can't do it. I have to look at myself, painful as it is. I get a lot of comfort out of remembering that I have all of you. As often as I'm gone from here, you may forget how important you are to me." She looked around at them, this confession a relief. "We've already tried each other out, we don't have to fear rejection because of - of what we see in ourselves, what we want to deny."

Tom shook his head, "Sweetheart, that may be true,but there're things -- things I'd rather not - I don't want to admit to MYSELF." He sat quietly looking from one to the other, "With all of you to support me, maybe I could. But would you? After all, I probably hide a lot from you." He was studying their faces and saw the amusement grow in their eyes."All right! All right! I haven't hid myself, but then - that means you aren't going to reject me for what I despise in myself. I haven't thought of that." He was faintly smiling as if just discovering something. "Actually, its a comfort to remember that.It may be the Builders don't have such friends."

Angy searched for words,"The Builders are -- unaware -- I think that's the best word. They're dissatisfied . They want something they can't name. Just as people always have.I suppose they have reason to fear us. We're unexplainably different.They project their fear rather than see it as their own. No wonder they so desparately want to build empires "

Rose said, "We've got to meet that somehow. That fear of us. And I don't know how." She sighed, then with a cheerful voice said, "This Gather is going to last a while, I can see that. The weather outside is fine now, and we can move out onto the deck." She looked at them and without words, they began to get up and move about, go out into the sunlight, the heat of the day hit them forcefully as they walked to the deck, into the gardens, and Rob came with his family, bounding up from the barns, leaping in exultant delight around them to call them to play.The children responded and ran off with him through the upper fields. The adults watched, ruefully, and Jerry and Ned joined the shouting children. Silvia slid her hands around the rounding burden she carried and watched pensively. But Rose came out, after setting the autochef for dinner later and said, "Let's run down to the River, the kids can follow, if they're not there already. A good swim would be just what we need. And without discussion they went. The young ones had got there first and were splashing about in the cool green water.Rose thought nothing had felt so good -- since the last time. She laughed then slid beneath the water to catch Ben's feet and pull him under. Play and shouting in the cool undercurrents, revived their spirits.

They climbed back to the Hall Benjamin brought fruit and hot tea. They talked of everything. They talked happily of the amazing success Rob was having training his young pup in the round ups. He'd had him out to practice and Jerry

THE PEOPLE OF THE VALLEY

watched them work.

"He's a natural. He just knows how to work a young one, but that pup's smart. Intelligence is high in Rob's line, you know." He was beaming as if the success were his own. After an hour, they began to return to thoughts of the Gather, the talk and the sharing. . Annette abruptly took them back.

"It's as though we're entering into a new dimension, literally, not just in imagination. I've been thinking that the old limits of artistic vision have been passed. Artists touched and drew echos from that far Vision that you tell us of Jessie.But they didn't stand there, walk in that country. That far place that you - - seem to have come from or maybe that you live in ." She looked then at Jessie curiously,"Yes, Jessie, you seem to have come from another place." The others nodded and Jessie felt herself inspected. She grinned and waved their eyes away.

"I've come from exactly where you come from. And we will travel together. But then, we still have the problem of how to meet the Builders."

Rose nodded, set her fork down and turned to Jessie,"Isn't the answer in what we've done today? Isn't this what we must do? I remember the Teachers telling us about a state of combined minds, called Group Consciousness, in which people could realize what they can't ordinarily. If group consciousness is a very heightened awareness, then maybe with intent focus, we might be able to experience it, to BE group conscious. Wouldn't that enable us to see what we can't see alone. To see the larger pattern and understand how to live through all this. If we were to Join - with enough trust and Love, could we - ? Could we - perhaps Touch on that level of Consciousness?" She was looking at Jessie, wanting it to be so. Isn't that what the Joining will become?"

Jane moved, cleared her throat a little self consciously and said, "Are we the only ones of the Valley who would be trying this?" She frowned, her fingers weaving through one another.Then, as if pushing on to another worry, she asked,"What about - our being together after Spring Planting. Wasn't that very much like this Joining that we've tried today? " She looked at Jessie. As if in apology, she added, "You said we must ask."

Jessie laughed, they could hear the Joy in her,"Oh, my Jane, you've touched on two most important facts. This Joining is simply focussed and deeper, but yes, it's similar. We've been more conscious today." Then she grinned happily,"And of course there are others, this very day. You all know we aren't the only Family who will meet these problems this very week. And of course, the People of the Way have had more than one Gathering, and they've had two interfamily Gathers with nearly all their people there. They don't usually have those. There are divisions, between their clans,there are those who don't Reach, don't See.To bring harmony out of such diversity requires great compassion. Genuine wisdom. I believe the People of the Way have those. They must deal with this in their own way. Everyone has to meet the problem, whether people of the Cities, towns, villages, or farms. People of this Valley are becoming aware of the tension."

"Then, since there are others, why can't we come out with a solution, after all,

THE AWAKENING

if all of us Reach, all of us Call out, ASK, won't the Monitors respond?"

Jessie nodded, "It's surely worth a try." She was smiling so broadly now that they felt her Joy at watching their recognitions grow."All the Master Teachers are alert now. Then also, those who are - are like me, Traveling Teachers, are also alert." A wry smile touched away the slight embarrassment that crossed her face. Rose watching, was suddenly acutely aware of how great was her love for this woman who had come to teach them.

Ben said, hurriedly,"Well, we can't be concerned about them just now, can we?" He didn't want them to move too far from Rose's request."If we're to focus, to find that Joining that will lift us, then we have to attend to ourselves,don't we?"

Silvia said,"Wait, I don't know whether that kind of intensity would be good for our baby. After all, what we're talking about unsettles me and I'm full grown."

Jessie shook her head,"He's all right.He needs it, needs this Touch and the flow of energy that accompanies it. No, Silvia, the very opposite of your fear.It's good for him." Silvia met Jerry's eyes, and he nodded. She looked to Rose and then Jessie again and finally nodded herself."You mean that we will make the Journey together? "

Jessie grinned in delight,"Silvia, you must acknowledge that you are making that Touch, that you were with us in the Joining this morning, you realize more than you admit. We all understood that, and now you see, though no one said it, you also know it."

Steve shook his head,"Not I! I didn't know it." He looked at Jane,"Did you know it Sweetheart?"

Jane first shook her head, then frowned,"Maybe I did know,.It doesn't at all surprise me."She thought a moment, "It IS as if I knew."

Silvia said,"Wait, There's something I need to know. You said 'he' when you spoke of our child. I've had no sex check. How can you know?" Not waiting for answer she added,"And you said he needed experience. How can that be?"

Ned broke in, shaking his own head in puzzlement, his booming voice dominating the room," I'm not sure I know these things either. Yet, there seems to be no question in my mind when you speak of them. So maybe I know and haven't thought about it. But as to making that Journey, well, I don't know."

Jessie laughed aloud then, "Everything you say needs attention. There isn't any rule about all this though. You will go or not go. it will be up to you. It isn't really my idea that you go, you know. It's already lying there in your minds. Some of you -- ."Someone started to speak but, uncharacteristically,she raised her hand."Consider this. Paul did not bring us the question of a journey, but a deep dilemma, a demand in himself. The rest of you have found the same demand stirred by his report and recognition. It's true that there's something to be done. There is a bridge that must be built-- a bridge between several ways of experiencing reality and it's only through the effort of human beings entering into a mutual process that this can be built.It is a shift of perception, a step beyond what we are now.It is an unfolding of your very nature as living beings.A nature you're only just becoming conscious of. Some of you know what I mean already,

THE PEOPLE OF THE VALLEY

some of you are confused, but all of you are able. Otherwise I would not be here." She smiled lovingly at them all, the gladness in her eyes was clear and they were warmed by it. She asked,"Isn't that true?"

Slowly there were nods among them."So, in answer to you, Paul, we must begin to practice the Touch and enter into small Joinings until we realize the process. For the Valley, we must begin to engage with the Builders in very profound ways.That problem is for Valley citizens to solve.." They were listening attentively, and she turned to Silvia," So you see, Silvia, how I know this is a boy child is not important. But this Family has already seven children and each has waking Talents. We need this one you bear to be as he is. But it is surely true the Journey will not harm him." She smiled down at Anna who's head was bent forward on her own knees,and touched the shining hair,"Isn't that so Anna?"

Anna looked up then, her eyes clear and steady as they met Jessie's, solemnly she answered,"Yes, I think that's so."

Rose watched her daughter and felt a stab of sadness,"The little girl suddenly was not a little girl. And Rose thought she had not noticed. This was a young woman. What she would be when she matured, Rose could not imagine. Anna seemed for a moment to be a stranger to her own mother and Rose felt a jealousy and a brief stab of guilt. Then those emotions dissolved as she saw them and a rising pride and joy replaced them. In this reverie she heard Tom speak'

"When? When should we go?"He was an organizer, he needed to plan.

Jessie shook her head."That's not for me to say. When you're all ready we'll begin the Journey. We must go on foot, the mountain is steep and it'll take several days. There's dense forest between here and there and a lot of rock climbing. We must prepare."

"Why walk?"Ned wondered.

"You know yourself. There's no way to get there otherwise, for all of us at least. No one's ever been known to have landed inside from an air car.Some of you have tried and it didn't work. But then, people don't talk much about having been there,as you know."Tom was standing, stretching his arms high and loosening his body after long sitting.

Ben said sadly,"Then the Family will go without William." It was not a question.

Paul nodded,"And it's up to you Annette to make up your own mind.It's a grief for all of us."

Annette met his eyes and nodded, "I already know that I must go." She said softly."After a moment, she added, "I don't know whether I can go with you." There was silence. Then Ben stood, looking around at them all.

His face looked angry, "I don't like, it. I've heard he's brought more people into the Valley from outside and they're people who think the way the Builders think. That's dangerous, isn't it?"

Jessie shook her head, "You don't think this problem is limited to this Valley do you? The WORLD is involved. If it is solved it must be solved everywhere among humankind."

THE AWAKENING

"But if he keeps that up, we could have a revolution building out there. It's not fair, you know that they bring outsiders in." In anger and frustration a pleading note entered his voice, "Why can't we do something? We haven't even admitted that the problem is really serious yet. Not all of us. We haven't said in so many words that William, our brother, is one who doesn't see, that he is blind. That his handicap cuts him off from us. He's a throw back." Brutally he spoke without softening the thoughts. He was crying then, "There, it's said, what we wouldn't admit, and there are lots of people like that in our Valley."

There was silence, nods, slow movement. Jerry unrolled from the floor cushions and stood, bringing Cassandra up with him. Others moved from their chairs.

Then Tom said, "I'm just too full of too much. I don't want to think anymore right now. I want to just be with all of you. Maybe Andrew and Jennifer will make us some music, maybe Anna and Ned and Angy will sing. Maybe we can sleep a little. I want to digest, and just be here this afternoon." He looked around, saw the tired nods. "O.K. then, let's take time to think about all we've realized. Everyone will be here in the morning and we'll be fresh. We can even make decisions, O.K.?" There were nods and silence. Sadness filled them, William was their brother and he would not be here.

Slowly the gathering melted. Paul and Jennifer were going to visit friends in Adwin and Jasper and Annette would spend time with Angy and Mary whom she had not seen for a while. Finally, only Cassandra and Jessie were left in the room. Jessie looked at the little girl and Cassandra came over to her, leaned against her chair and slid a warm arm around her shoulder.

"Cassandra, there's a new Transmitter being opened in New York City today. It's a new design and it'll be on the wall screen Holovision. Why don't we watch? I've seen so little of that new technology, it fascinates me. It was Science fiction when I was a girl." She laughed.

Cassandra nodded, snuggled down then into the wide chair with the old woman and sighed, "Do we have to move?"

Jessie chuckled, "No, I've got a manual control here on the table -- there, it's on. Let me tune it to New York." She slid her fingers over the controls and the large wallscreen shifted and then settled on a busy street scene. She marveled at the reproduction. Surely it was as though they stood in those city streets themselves. People swarmed around them as though the camera was their own eyes. Then the crowd thinned and an orderly movement of people was seen coming and going on steadily moving ramps. The color and light changed, reception was excellent. They sat at first fascinated by this very urban scene. The truly big city, where no building was under ten floors, and most were in the hundreds. The necessity for connections between buildings had resulted in the building of Skyways, long winding pathways that ran across from building to building like another street system on three different heights, twenty, forty and eighty stories high. The ground streets would have been constantly shadowed if it were not for the thousands of float globes of light bobbing gently everywhere.

THE PEOPLE OF THE VALLEY

They never went out, so the streets were lit day and night with a light like soft sunlight. Then they felt the scene shift upward, past the endless floors of tall buildings, it moved them out onto a flat roof. Here was another world. The sunlight streamed down over roof gardens, and flat courts that gave onto the Skyways. Spires, domes, towers, and blocky squares rose on above them at every side. Buildings of such different heights each with roof sized gardens, most the size of city blocks, but some much larger made the top of the city into a green and flourishing world of growing things beneath a wide sky.

They moved across a short section of Skyway to another roof top, a paved court with carefully selected trees growing along one side. Among them were very formal beds of bright bloom. But the rest of the Court was empty except for a great square raised by four steps into a plaza forty or fifty yards square. On the plaza shimmered four shining cones that stood at equal distances around a large circle on a higher platform. A ramp ran from the circle down to the roof where people gathered in a great semicircle. Men and women in bright harlican suits, or imaginative combinations of color and design, sold cold drinks and food to the crowd. Jessie studied them carefully, curious, and it was as she thought; one of the rites of passage for young teen aged people, just as harvesting was for Valley children.

Some young people danced or played musical instruments. They appeared to enjoy their roles, laughing and playing as much with each other as paying attention to the crowd,. Jessie studied the cones, they were broad based, tapering upward for twenty feet or so with intricate murals covering their entire surface. The air was cool with a light breeze ruffling the hair of the spectators. There were several huge frieght air cars lined up along the far end of the vast roof surface. Jessie and Cassandra felt themselves part of the crowd with people to either side.

Then two men moved into vision, the camera scanned the crowd again and then homed in on the circle where the men took their places between the cones. They signaled to one another and turned to smile at the camera as they slid their hands over an invisible series of buttons. The circle between the pillars glowed slightly, a radiance that grew until it was almost too bright to watch. Then, as if a great opening had appeared in the air itself, a cascade of blue containers filled the space between the cones. A wide section of floor moved carrying them toward the freight cars. As they moved off, another collection of boxes and crates began to fill the space. People loading the freight cars went into action, guiding them off the moving ramp onto the car lifts. They were swiftly stowed inside until the car was filled. Then it lifted off and another took it's place.

The crowd cheered and drank, lifted bottles and glasses high. Every one seemed to be laughing. This was not an event unknown to these City dwellers, but this Transmitter was the biggest and most precise ever placed in the country, and it was hooked into transmitters in eighteen other countries. The announcer who had explained the whole event was talking and Cassie yawned. Jessie laughed, "Well, I guess that's that. It's an improvement for sure. These cones are lovely and the process is working so efficiently it out classes anything we have in our whole Valley."

Cassie snuggled down again, the day was warm and the talks had been long. "It's just too big, that city,. I wouldn't like to live there."

"That's good, their population is a trouble to them already. But those wonderful transmitters have cleared our sky of an awful lot of traffic you know, Dear. It's one of the inventions that keeps our Valley beautiful."

" And lets us travel when we please." Cassandra spoke in the pedantic voice of a teacher reciting a ritual. She flushed slightly, suddenly thinking she might have crossed the line to rudeness."Grandmother,it's true. But the city, is too much."

"It's one of the biggest in the world still, you know.It always has been. There's an atmosphere there. New York City will always attract people. At least to visit. There aren't so many cities of that size any more, you know. But I remember when, so many years ago, my Mate and I went there we thought it was fascinating. So many, many things going on. So much happening all the time! It's no longer the way the history films show you,full of sprawling, dirty little neighborhoods where people struggle just to survive. It's -- its changed as much as the Valley has, you know. It's a solid city now, and its becoming more beautiful. They have credit for wonderful buildings, museums, entertainment centers, museums that are like vast Learning centers themselves and --" She was shaking her head, lost in the memories that had overwhelmed her as a young girl."D'you know their Healing Centers are like small towns? We studied there for some months and we loved it."

They sat in silence, half dozing for several minutes then Cassandra said,"The lower bridges and the ground streets are so dark, it must be like living in tunnels."

"Yes, that's so, but the Glow bulbs make it pleasant. Like some of our underground cavern towns here, you know. At least they did clean and develop little streams to run through the city so they could make parks large enough to allow some sunlight down to ground level for part of the day. For them to do that, to use such valuable land for green forest and meadow is a mark of their wisdom. It's a lovely city now, in its own way. My mate and I had to work on the building of it while we were there along with everyone else, if we were to share in the housing when it was done. But we did not live there many years."

"What on earth happens to all that sewage, all the waste and garbage." Cassandra asked what Jessie thought an unchildlike question. But she answered seriously.

"In the first place there's very, very little in comparison to the old city, but you wouldn't know of that. Now every neighborhood has its own processing plant, and everything wasted is used, or made into another product. Pretty sophisticated system even when we were first there."

Cassandra had not heard Jessie speak of her youth often and she glanced up curiously."What has happened to your family Jessie?"

Jessie sighed, "My son is now a Teaching Father in the Eastern Seaboard retreat. He has three children who are already grown and with babies of their own. His mate runs a printing office near the retreat. My daughter is a mother and grandmother too, but she studies now with her mate at a Monitor station in Utah. They live so far away that I shall not see them again." At the matter of fact quality of her voice, Cassandra started and looked up at her. She laughed, "Oh, I saw them all just last year before I began the journey here." She got up, spilling Cassandra and catching her as she did so. She laughed at the little girl's surprise."Mind power isn't always foolish, sometimes it can be useful." She took Cassie's hand and said,"Shall we go for a walk?"

In mutual agreement, they walked toward the River, Jessie watched as Cassandra created mind pictures of them both playing in the cool bright water. Then she laughed and countered with less strenuous pictures of herself floating quietly. They arrived at the River and saw a small transparant submarine floating at the dock. And they looked at one another. This was another excitement. They would come down later and give it a try. But for now, the water would give them a pleasant place to cool off, and to rest, to contemplate all that had happened this day. They stripped off their clothes and plunged noisily in.

The next morning the air was clear, cool and the sound of birds was clamorous. The family met in the Hall. Now Paul, having walked for hours the afternoon before, was ready to come to terms with their situation. They would gather on the deck. Already two big pitchers of iced tea and juices stood on a small wooden cart waiting,glasses of chipped ice beside them. Slowly everyone came from their morning chores to gather there.

No one spoke for several minutes, they looked at one another. Slowly Jessie created a way, opening,Reaching, like a fresh breeze that brought breath and refreshment to the minds of the others. Inviting, offering, risking herself in perfect acceptance of them,,she waited. Slowly, one by one, they responded. With a surge, Anna reached out to Touch,lifting awareness, focussing, the power of this old Soul in her young body like a new fragrance, tripling the possibility. With no resistance she Reached out and Joined with Jessie's mind. For seconds it was a question as to whether anyone would be able to bear the energy felt among them. Then Andrew laughed with a Joy that abolished resistance, delight that was also a sob of relief. He turned mentally to the two Joined minds and was completely with them. Such a different power, such bright, clear Vision. He marveled and centered himself into this triple consciousness.

The others were aware, though not yet Joined. They felt the waiting union of minds drawing them into its power. It was clearly different from anything they had experienced. A fragrance filled their minds, and they knew Jessie, Healer and Teaching Monitor, surprising most of the Family. Anna, not knowing her own scent, her full nature, nevertheless sang of herself Creator, unlimited possibility awakened and present, and accepted herself. Andrew melded a consciousness of direction and Will, one whose strength of mind could be invincible against doubt. And in this matrix, like a nourishment, he would learn to balance. Whether he would be able to balance when he was alone, he could not know yet. But he saw for these moments his own truth. He also saw his lack but did not grieve. As they began to settle into a tenuous stability, held in focus by Jessie's practiced ability to Center and sustain, they knew the flaws that could break or, worse, twist, their Center.

Andrew knew that he must depend on the others to help balance, and that his power of Will was necessary to the whole. It would be a formidable danger if not balanced. He was young, still untried. He sensed currents of emotion, thought, that led into evolving patterns and they were not explored yet. The merging of Soul and self was incomplete, he did not know how to bring into full focus his own power. He feared his own intentions. Jessie watched, saw his tentative Reach into himself, into that center where the wisdom of thousands of lives lived, breathed and was available. He must bring himself into full Consciousness. But it would take time. Just now, he must simply help with this Joining.

Then, Rose caught fire from that expanding center that was their Joining. She Reached - merged with them, Joined, her own strength far more than she consciously knew. Jessie saw that she too had much to practice and realize from within herself. Rose's will to stand firm in adversity, to bring harmony and balance, was what the growing Center needed. Rose knew how to bring harmony in the midst of differences, and she was only dimly aware of how great was that Soul gift. The Center pulsed with growing power.

Then Ben was there, the intensity of his deep devotion filtering like a sweet indestructable oil through all the spaces between them, his mind tolerant to a fault and knowing that fault, guarding. In moments of his Joining, they felt Tom enter among them. Tom the organizer, could widen and deepen the Vision of perception out of Love. His power opened further the channel through which Love Itself poured. Thus, was absolute acceptance made known to every other member of the Family.

Paul tuning his attention, focussing his mind to know the event taking place here, suddenly understood. He decided without doubt, his fear dissolved. He saw the growing current of their combined strength and knew it needed his, the still courage of his own vision. His vision would lead as he learned to direct his strength. Then there was Ned, so eager, his great selfless heart full with the inpour from his own Source, his own willingness to offer. Through him they could feel the far Reach touch their joined Mind. The hundreds of other families in the Valley making this same decision. And he was there, a giant of brotherhood, he would be a receptive well in that powerful black body he lived in.

Now, Joined, these knew the streams of energy pouring in to them, the flow of energy through them, and knew they were not separate from all those others. And in this heightened awareness, this standing mentally at that height of Soul consciousness, they knew what they had never imagined, the unceasing Touch of the Monitors. There, the high sweet tone that rang constantly over the Valley sounded in their hearts and released doubt. Like a web of fragrance and sound,

THE PEOPLE OF THE VALLEY

the Joining grew.

With swift surrender, Silvia, Jennifer, Jerry, Angy, Mary, and Annette came to them, realizing their own strengths in the act. They knew finally that they had something to give. Silvia created a design, a visual creation of their being. Mary saw her creation and strengthened it, Jennifer filled that growing identity with Joy, with a laughter of delight a fine perception of shaping. Here was Life such as none of them had known.

The ceremony of inclusion, of Mind Vision, filled the room and extended far beyond, for stone walls were no barrier to that power. They felt themselves linking into that network that sustained in its highest form, human Will-to-Good. The Monitors welcomed them, even though their joining was still tentative. Finally they knew that there is only one 'I' and that 'I' is humanity itself!

Jerry felt the powerful devotion and faith of his nature linking as though it fit into natural grooves of this Mind building. His power increased the natural beauty of Rose's balancing, deepened Ben's devotion. Cassandra, diving in, in characteristic enthusiasm once she realized and accepted, literally lifted them all physically from the floor, then swiftly settled to increase the power of Jessie's Teaching. As she opened her self to the flow of power, she knew of her own wisdom, her Talent to teach must be made manifest also.

Then there was only Jane and Steve, both feeling the power of these currents of energy, the lift of that Loving encouragement, the dignity of that restraint. They must make their own choice.

Jane closed her eyes, knowing that the shutting out of physical sensation would open her to greater awareness of Mental consciousness. Steve, listened, heard the Song being sung, the Mind power that called to him, this unbelieveable fragrance that literally saturated the air and their breathing. They breathed that energy. Steve knew then that this was what the Teachers had meant by the phrase 'those who live in the Mind'? He thought of that, looked in Jane's quiet face and wrestled with his own fears. Then he decided! Focussing, sensing the grand Joining taking place, he met his doubts and chose to Join. As he did, he felt himself entering the gradually whirling vortex of energy with an ease that astonished him. He had not known his powerful good nature, his innate good will, would be so valuable.

Jane was there swiftly, like a rock, like the foundation of Earth Herself and her heart was singing with relief as she felt them include her wholly. Her mind melded and joined and her personal self was nearly overwhelmed with Joy. She did not yet understand, nor did Steve, but she knew clearly that this was right. This Joining was the healthy self realizing its full nature.

Then they listened as one, listened and heard the winds of greater Minds surrounding them, speaking in a purity of consciousness, vision of Heart, that they only faintly realized. They knew, together, that the Valley could find its way, that the Families were there, focussed, alert, ready to make that Reality they had begun to realize, a living expression.

But then, sustaining, they questioned. Why could they not realize more from

THE AWAKENING

those great Minds they sensed to be near? Why could they not Reach to create a Valley Joining- a total Valley Joining? What resistance Touched and stung against their mental edges? What needles of doubt pierced like an old remembered pain, only to be turned aside in this moment by the rising power of their joining. But it was there.

Then, slowly, they reaffirmed themselves, this new, whole Joined Self. They focussed, creating of themselves one Being and the needles of doubt vanished. Joy, a quality of Love unimaginable, and a new strength literally wrote new dimensions of awareness into their waiting and accepting minds. The fine precise Song that was Mind Itself seemed to reverberate forever, through time and space, beyond consciousness. Mind, extended beyond human capacity to follow, was the path called Spirit! The promise, the possibility haunted them. They could begin now to develop this singleness of Life lifted to its highest point of consciousness. Humankind could develop as fully on the mental level as they had developed on a physical level. And what that meant, they only glimpsed so far.

Slowly each person drew away. Some appeared to be asleep, resting, gathering all that he or she had experienced into personal consciousness. Remembering as the precious memories were still fresh. Those just waking felt primarily a great alertness, a wide awake sense of heightened awareness, as though life presented itself anew. They sat together silently for some time, none the same, all stretched beyond measure, and they needed rest. But after a while, they thought of the daily work, the chores, jobs waiting, projects unfinished,and prepared to begin the day's work. But they knew now that they were together as they had never been.

Anna sat silently with Jessie when the others had gone,gone in silent bemused tenderness to commune with themselves, to think and search their hearts. She too was silent for a long time. Jessie seemed far away, drawn into a place of recognitions such that Anna only sensed as one might sense the fragrance of a wonderful garden through a key hole. She waited. And finally she asked,"Jessie, Where are you? What is it like there, where you are?"

Jessie wiped the tears that trembled on her lashes and smiled faintly. Her own heart so full she wanted to offer herself. But she shook her head,"Dear, dear Anna, all you want to know will be clear to you one day. But how can anyone know what its like until she is here, until she has opened the eyes of her Heart. When the mind has fine tuned itself, when it hones itself to its greatest perfection and is stretched beyond thought into That of which any idea is only a reflection then you no longer ask, you know. And THAT cannot be shaped into words, not thought of.It is beyond thought!"

They sat, communing, Anna content, just to be with Jessie. Then Jessie finally said,"There fore don't ask anyone to tell you of Being here when you are only half conscious that 'here' is. At present, you know that where I am exists, is real. You know that it is POSSIBLE for human consciousness to stand aware. You stand in the doorway itself. I stand only a little beyond. To know that is the beginning. And that, my dear one, you do know.

Anna nodded, and they remained together, silent.